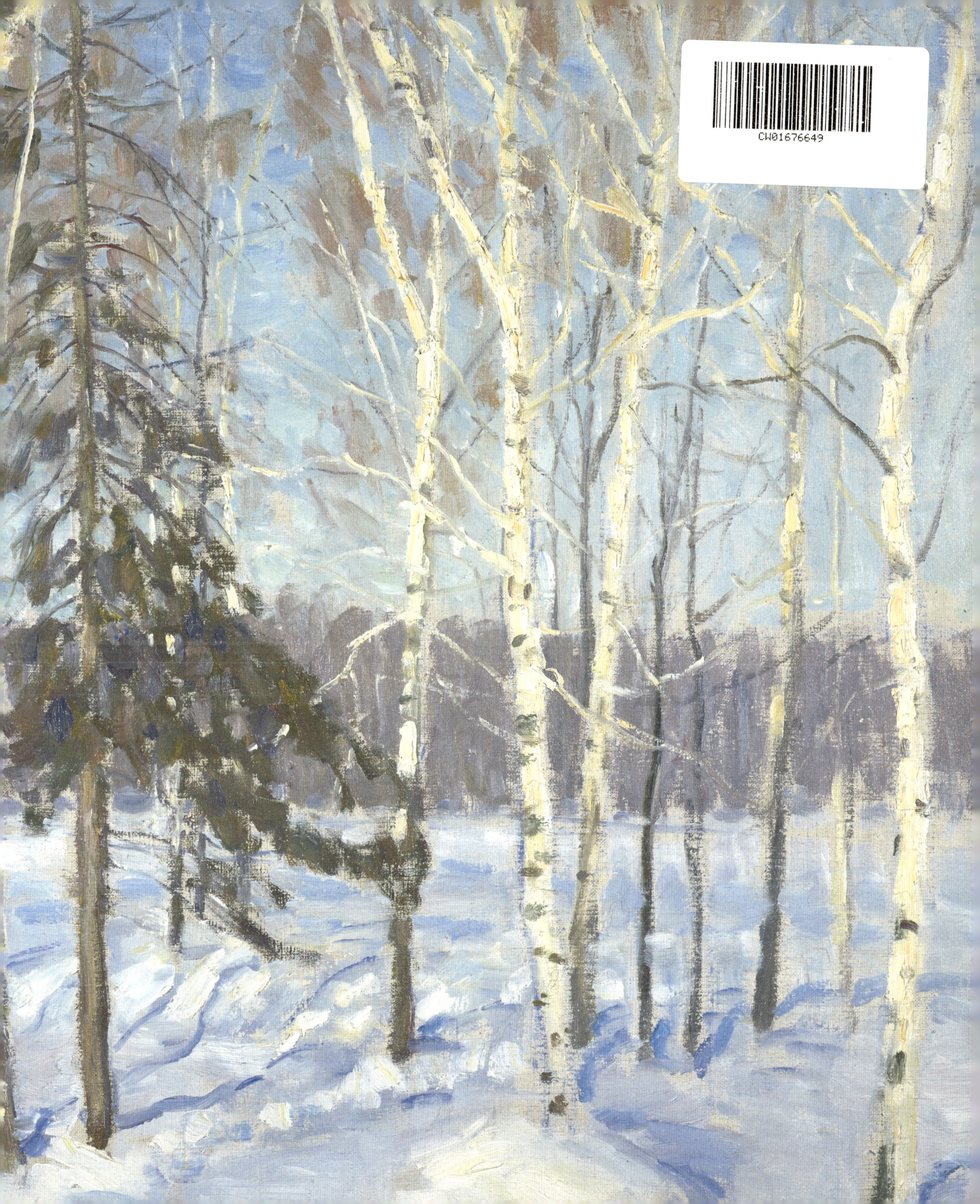

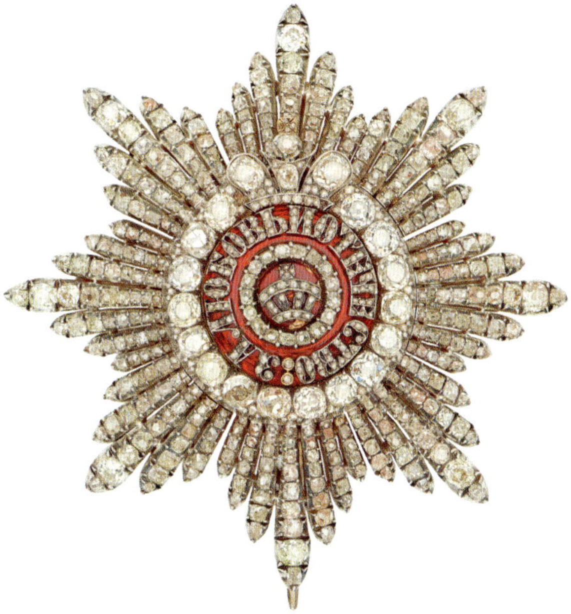

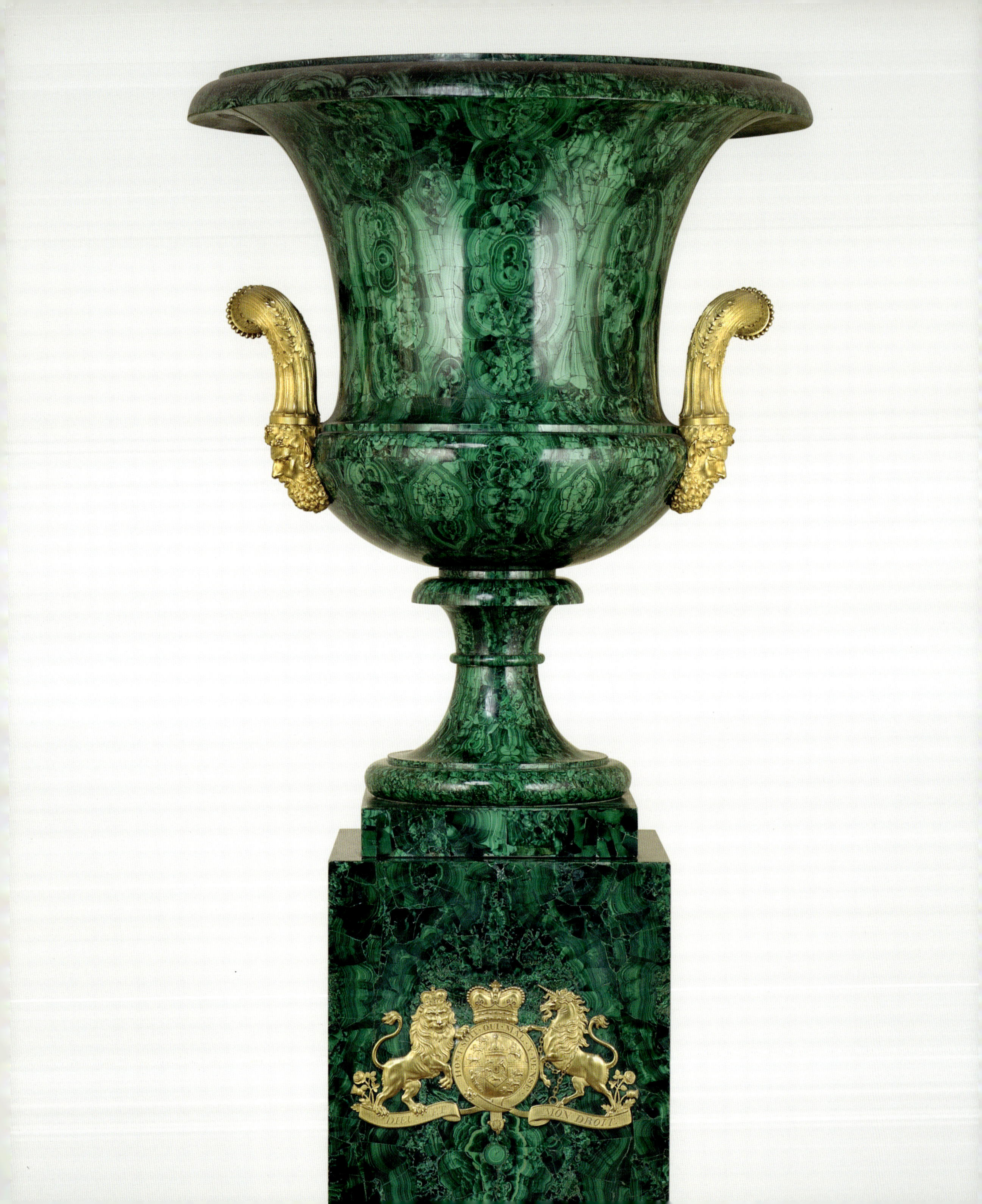
MON DROIT

Russia

Art, Royalty and the Romanovs

ROYAL COLLECTION TRUST

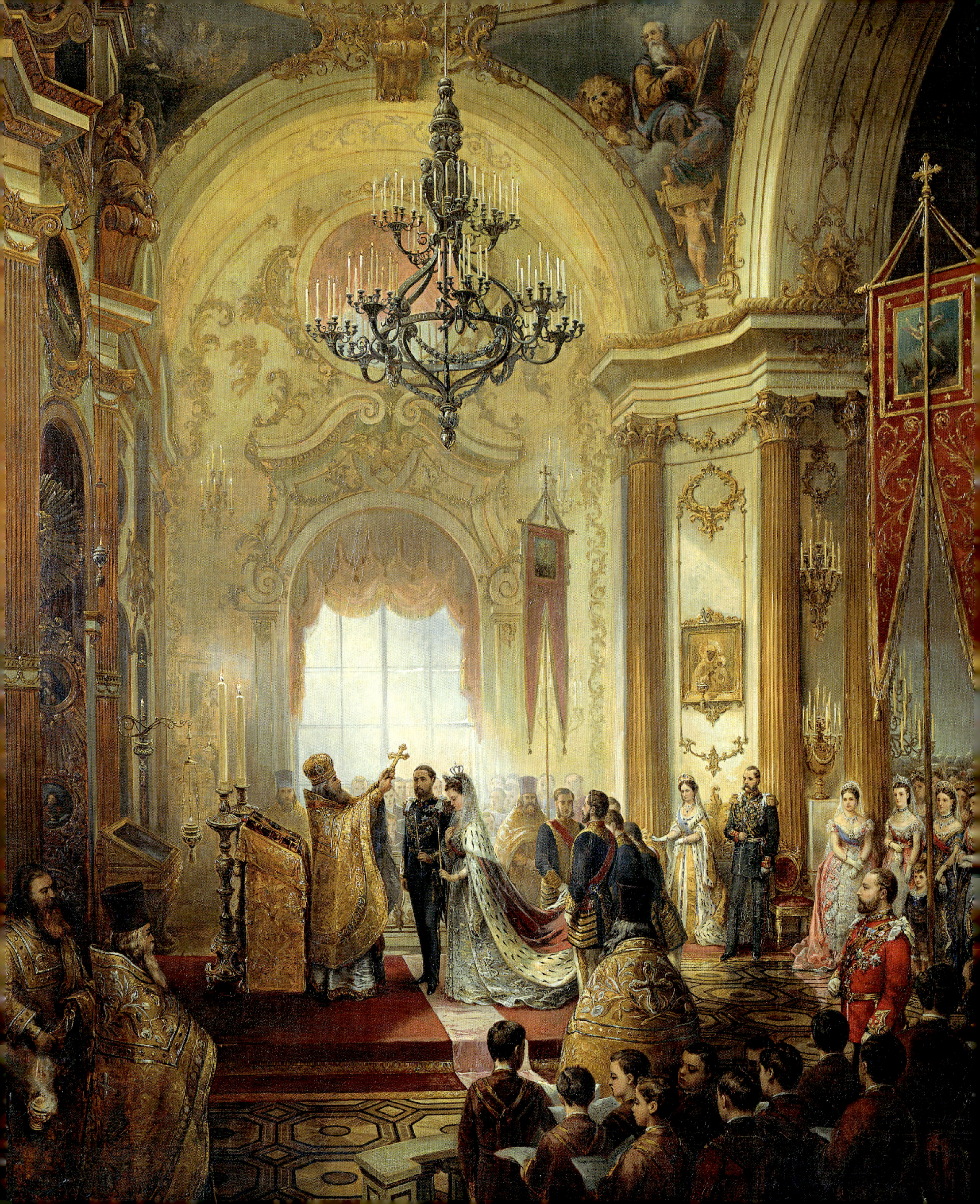

CONTENTS

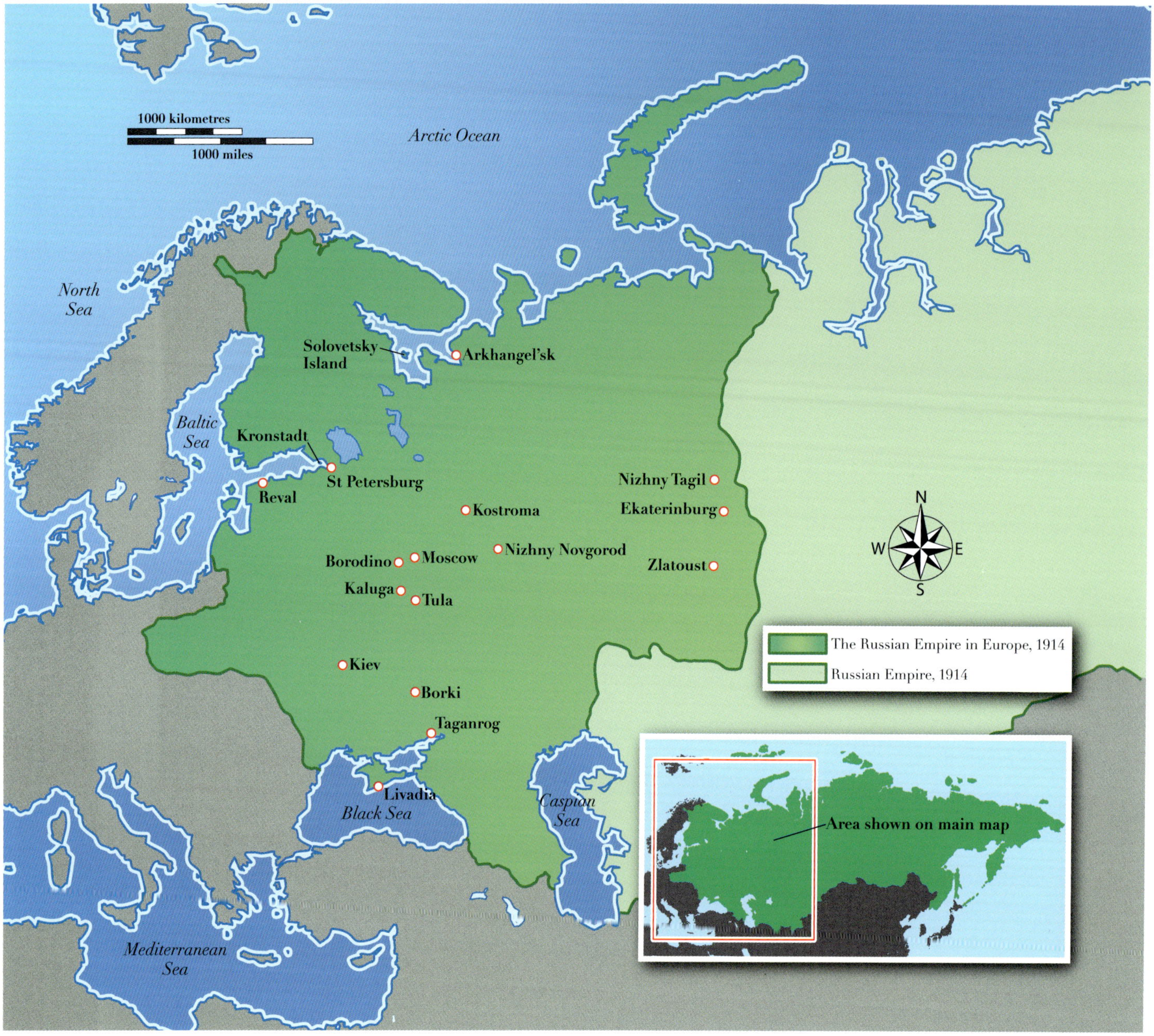

1000 kilometres
1000 miles
Arctic Ocean
North Sea
Baltic Sea
Solovetsky Island
Arkhangel'sk
Kronstadt
St Petersburg
Reval
Kostroma
Nizhny Tagil
Ekaterinburg
Borodino
Moscow
Nizhny Novgorod
Zlatoust
Kaluga
Tula
Kiev
Borki
Taganrog
Livadia
Black Sea
Caspian Sea
Mediterranean Sea
N
W
E
S
The Russian Empire in Europe, 1914
Russian Empire, 1914
Area shown on main map

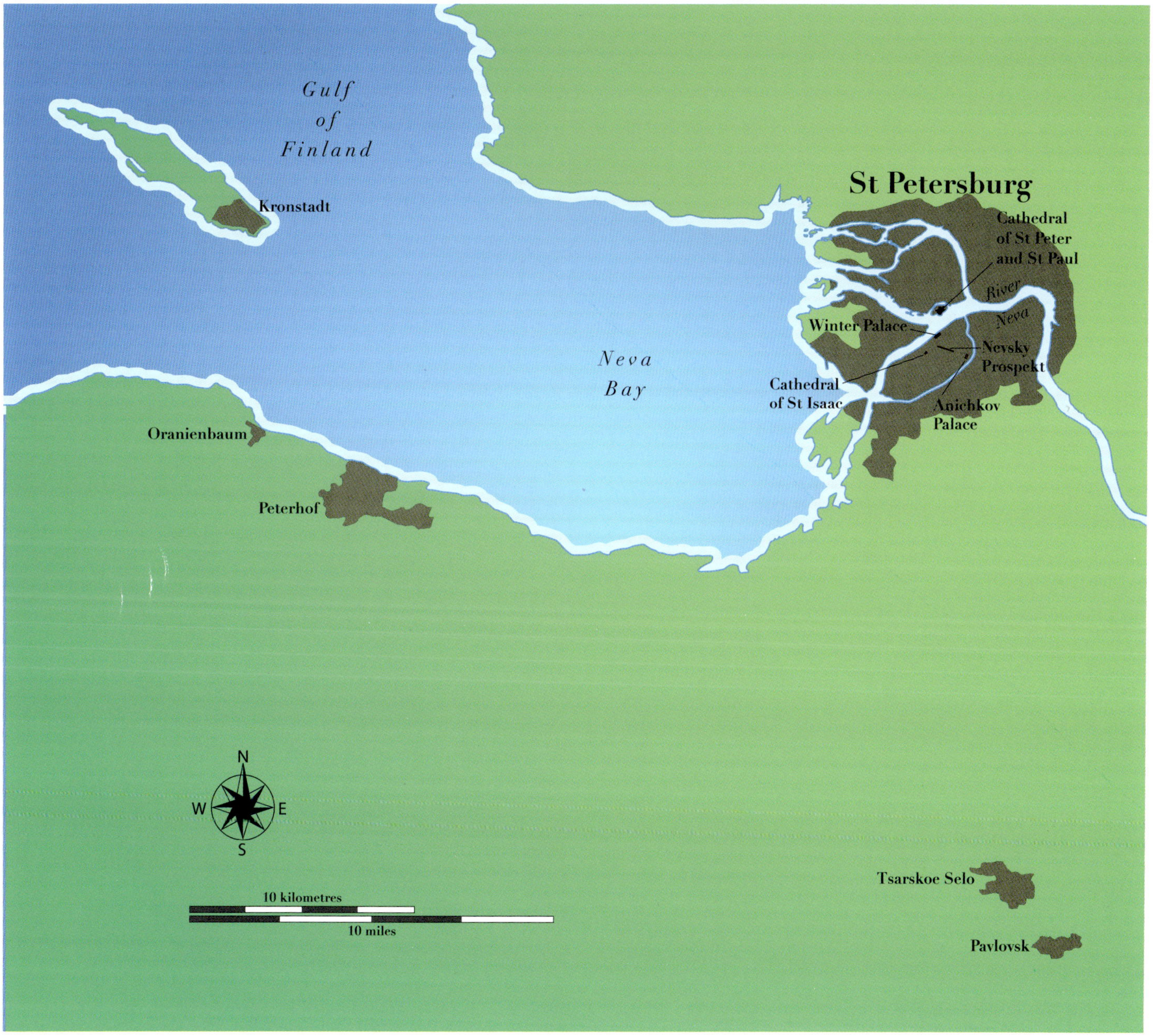
Gulf of Finland
Kronstadt
St Petersburg
Cathedral of St Peter and St Paul
River Neva
Winter Palace
Nevsky Prospekt
Cathedral of St Isaac
Anichkov Palace
Neva Bay
Oranienbaum
Peterhof
N
W
E
S
10 kilometres
10 miles
Tsarskoe Selo
Pavlovsk

Tsar Mikhail I
1596–1645; r. 1613–45

Maria Miloslavskaya
1624–69

m1

Tsar Alexei
1629–76; r. 1645–76

m2

Natalya Naryshkina
1651–94

Sof'ya Alekseevna (Regent)
1657–1704

Tsar Fedor III
1661–82; r. 1676–82

Tsar Ivan V
1666–96; r. 1682–96

m

Praskovia Saltykova
1664–1723

Ekaterina Ioannovna
1691–1733

Anna Leopoldovna
1718–46

Tsar Ivan VI
1740–64; r. 1740–1

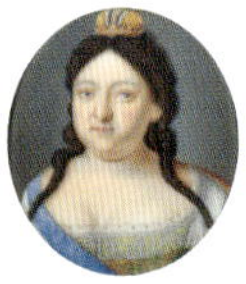

Empress Anna Ioannovna
1693–1740; r. 1730–40

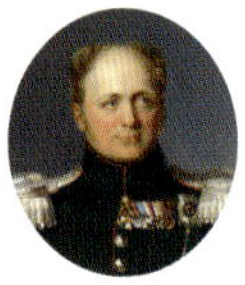

Emperor Alexander I
1777–1825, r. 1801–25

m

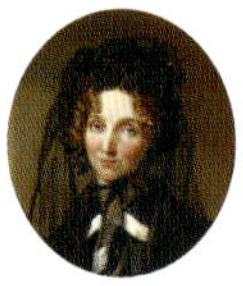

Empress Elizabeth
Alexeievna 1779–1826

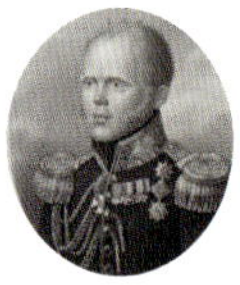

Grand Duke Constantine
Pavlovich 1779–1831

m

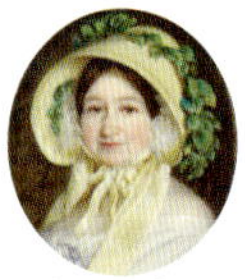

Princess Juliane of Saxe-Coburg-
Saalfeld, Grand Duchess Anna
Feodorovna 1781–1860

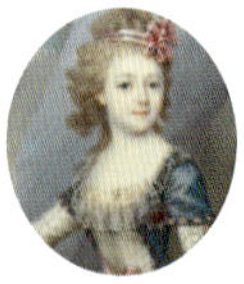

Grand Duchess Alexandra
Pavlovna 1783–1801

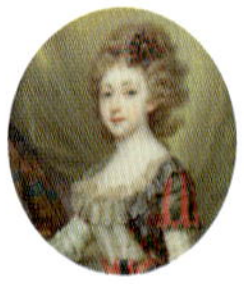

Grand Duchess Elena
Pavlovna 1784–1803

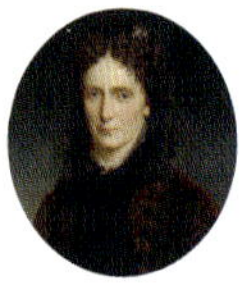

Empress Maria
Alexandrovna 1824–80

m

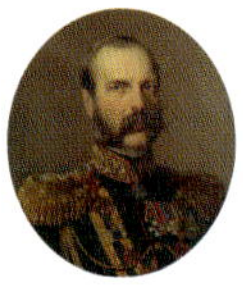

Emperor Alexander II
1818–81; r. 1855–81

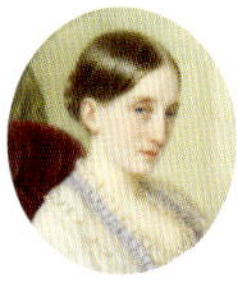

Grand Duchess Maria
Nikolaevna 1819–76

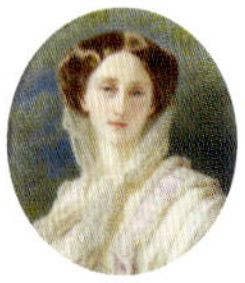

Grand Duchess Olga
Nikolaevna 1822–92

Grand Duchess Alexandra
Nikolaevna 1825–44

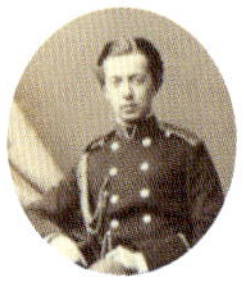

Tsesarevich Nicholas
Alexandrovich 1843–65

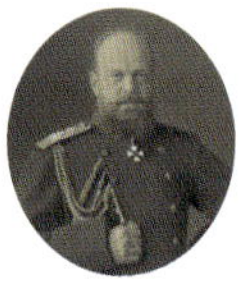

Emperor Alexander III
1845–94; r. 1881–94

m

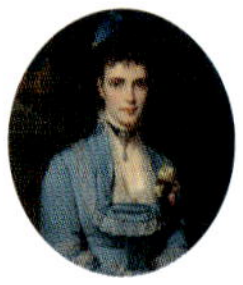

Empress Maria
Feodorovna 1847–1928

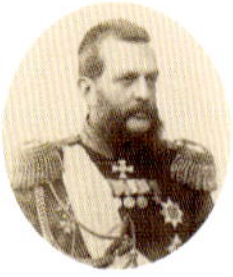

Grand Duke Vladimir
Alexandrovich 1847–1909

m

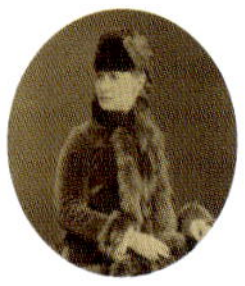

Grand Duchess Maria
Pavlovna 1854–1920

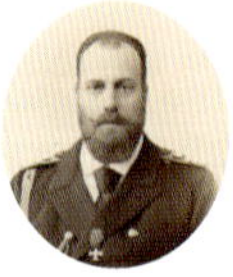

Grand Duke Alexei
Alexandrovich 1850–1908

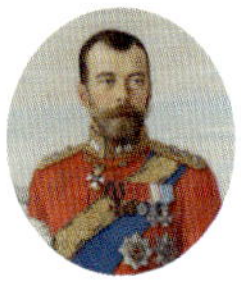

Emperor Nicholas II
1868–1918; r. 1894–1917

m

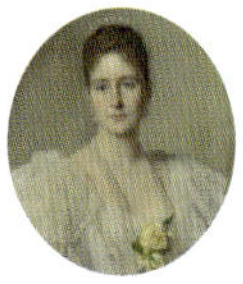

Empress Alexandra
Feodorovna 1872–1918

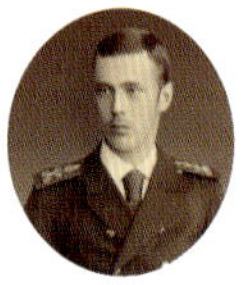

Grand Duke George
Alexandrovich 1871–99

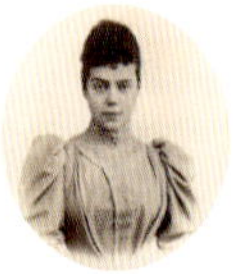

Grand Duchess Xenia
Alexandrovna 1875–1960

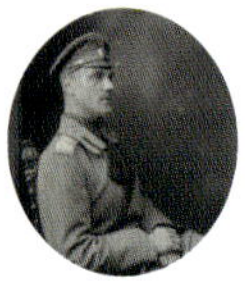

Grand Duke Michael
Alexandrovich 1878–1918

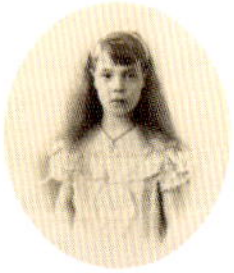

Grand Duchess Olga
Alexandrovna 1882–1960

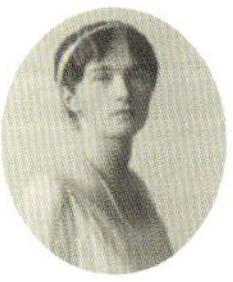

Grand Duchess Olga
Nikolaevna 1895–1918

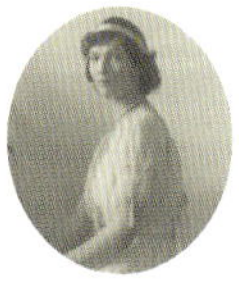

Grand Duchess Tatiana
Nikolaevna 1897–1918

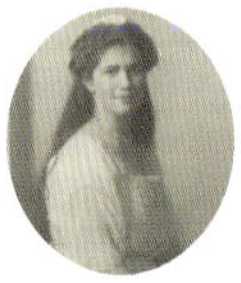

Grand Duchess Maria
Nikolaevna 1899–1918

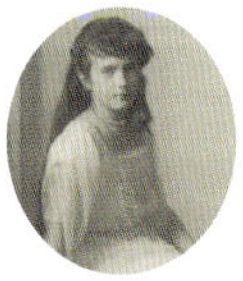

Grand Duchess Anastasia
Nikolaevna 1901–18

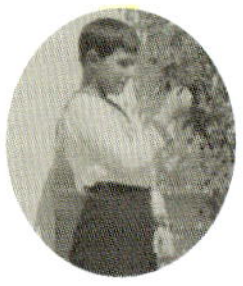

Tsesarevich Alexei
Nikolaevich 1904–18

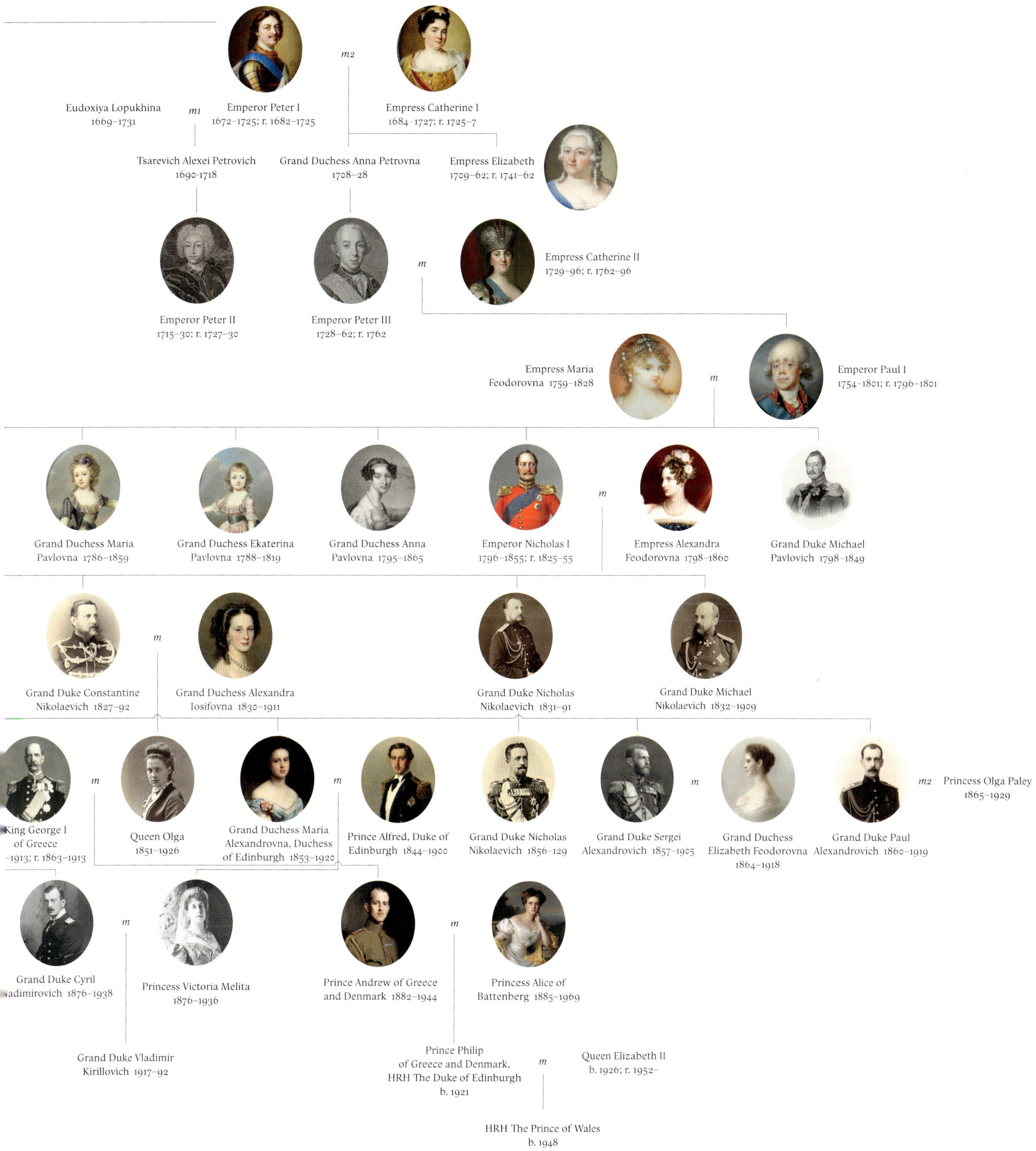
m2
Eudoxiya Lopukhina
1669–1731
m1
Emperor Peter I
1672–1725; r. 1682–1725
Empress Catherine I
1684–1727; r. 1725–7
Tsarevich Alexei Petrovich
1690–1718
Grand Duchess Anna Petrovna
1708–28
Empress Elizabeth
1709–62; r. 1741–62
m
Empress Catherine II
1729–96; r. 1762–96
Emperor Peter II
1715–30; r. 1727–30
Emperor Peter III
1728–62; r. 1762
Empress Maria
Feodorovna 1759–1828
m
Emperor Paul I
1754–1801; r. 1796–1801
Grand Duchess Maria
Pavlovna 1786–1859
Grand Duchess Ekaterina
Pavlovna 1788–1819
Grand Duchess Anna
Pavlovna 1795–1865
Emperor Nicholas I
1796–1855; r. 1825–55
m
Empress Alexandra
Feodorovna 1798–1860
Grand Duke Michael
Pavlovich 1798–1849
m
Grand Duke Constantine
Nikolaevich 1827–92
Grand Duchess Alexandra
Iosifovna 1830–1911
Grand Duke Nicholas
Nikolaevich 1831–91
Grand Duke Michael
Nikolaevich 1832–1909
m
King George I
of Greece
-1913; r. 1863–1913
Queen Olga
1851–1926
Grand Duchess Maria
Alexandrovna, Duchess
of Edinburgh 1853–1920
m
Prince Alfred, Duke of
Edinburgh 1844–1900
Grand Duke Nicholas
Nikolaevich 1856–129
Grand Duke Sergei
Alexandrovich 1857–1905
m
Grand Duchess
Elizabeth Feodorovna
1864–1918
Grand Duke Paul
Alexandrovich 1860–1919
m2
Princess Olga Paley
1865–1929
Grand Duke Cyril
adimirovich 1876–1938
m
Princess Victoria Melita
1876–1936
Prince Andrew of Greece
and Denmark 1882–1944
m
Princess Alice of
Battenberg 1885–1969
Grand Duke Vladimir
Kirillovich 1917–92
Prince Philip
of Greece and Denmark,
HRH The Duke of Edinburgh
b. 1921
m
Queen Elizabeth II
b. 1926; r. 1952–
HRH The Prince of Wales
b. 1948

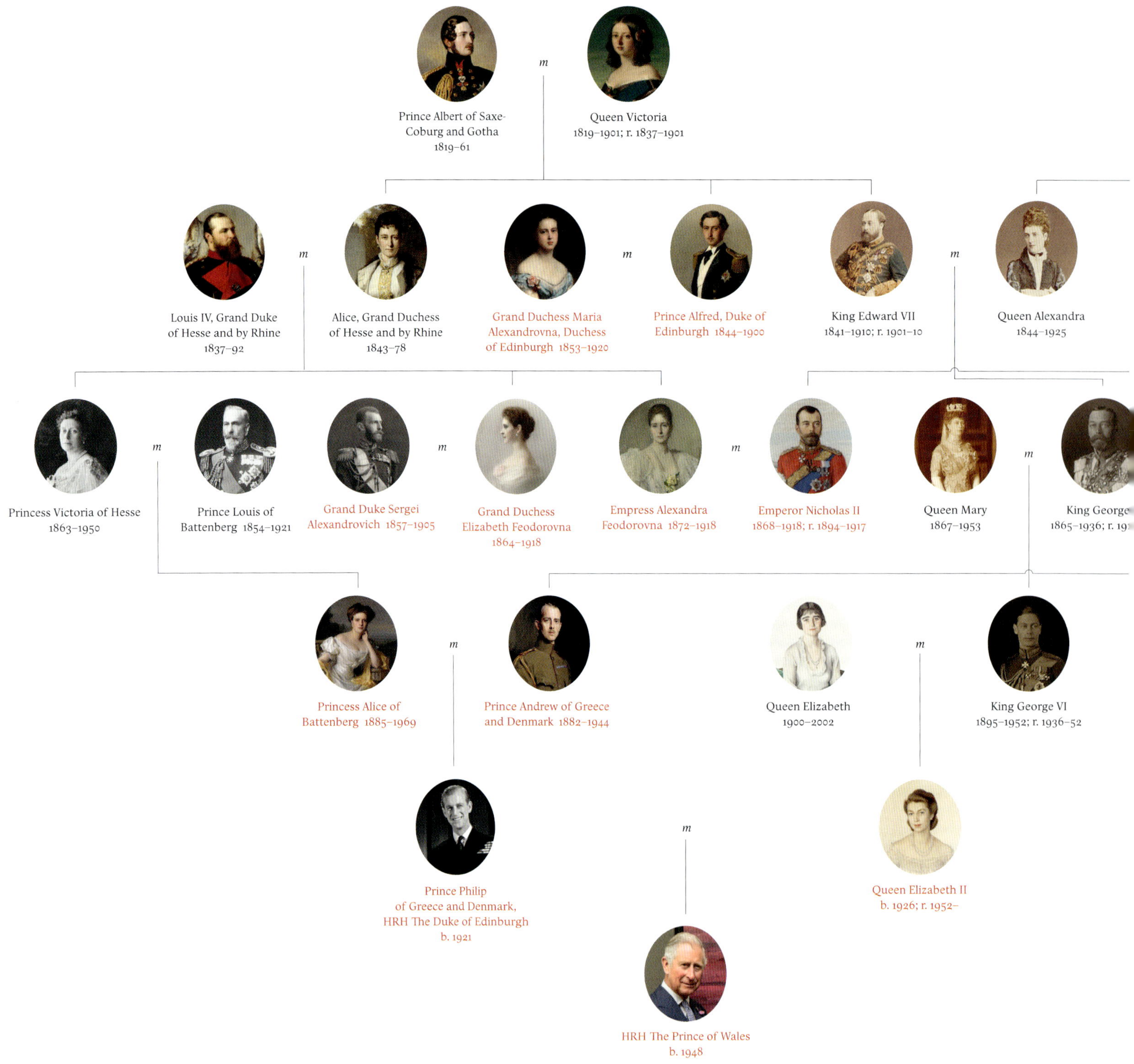
Prince Albert of Saxe-Coburg and Gotha 1819–61
m
Queen Victoria 1819–1901; r. 1837–1901
Louis IV, Grand Duke of Hesse and by Rhine 1837–92
m
Alice, Grand Duchess of Hesse and by Rhine 1843–78
Grand Duchess Maria Alexandrovna, Duchess of Edinburgh 1853–1920
m
Prince Alfred, Duke of Edinburgh 1844–1900
King Edward VII 1841–1910; r. 1901–10
m
Queen Alexandra 1844–1925
Princess Victoria of Hesse 1863–1950
m
Prince Louis of Battenberg 1854–1921
Grand Duke Sergei Alexandrovich 1857–1905
m
Grand Duchess Elizabeth Feodorovna 1864–1918
Empress Alexandra Feodorovna 1872–1918
m
Emperor Nicholas II 1868–1918; r. 1894–1917
Queen Mary 1867–1953
m
King George
1865–1936; r. 19
Princess Alice of Battenberg 1885–1969
m
Prince Andrew of Greece and Denmark 1882–1944
Queen Elizabeth 1900–2002
m
King George VI 1895–1952; r. 1936–52
Prince Philip of Greece and Denmark, HRH The Duke of Edinburgh b. 1921
m
Queen Elizabeth II b. 1926; r. 1952–
HRH The Prince of Wales b. 1948

The British, Danish and Greek connections of the Romanov dynasty

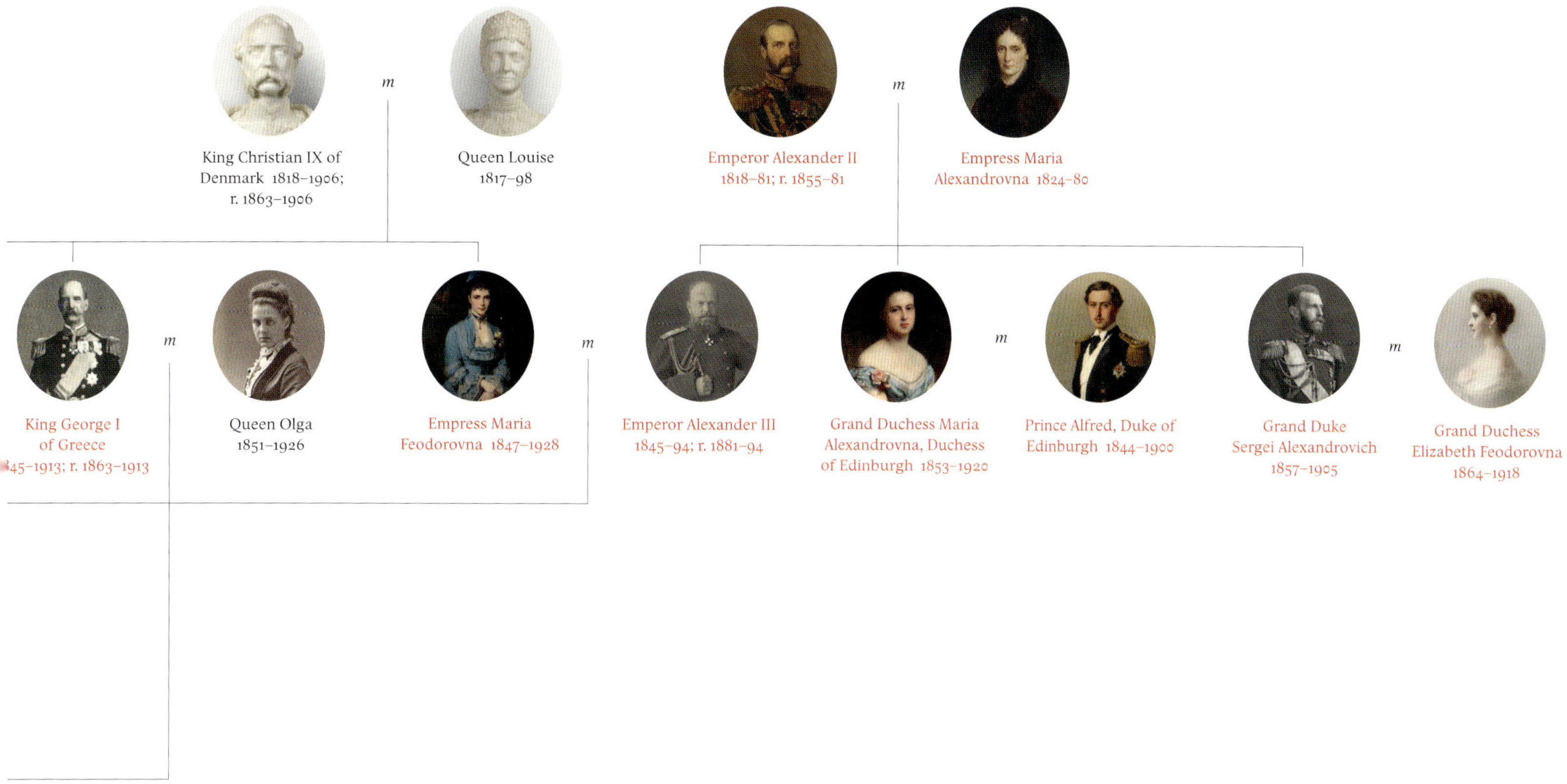

Names in red also appear on the Romanov family tree

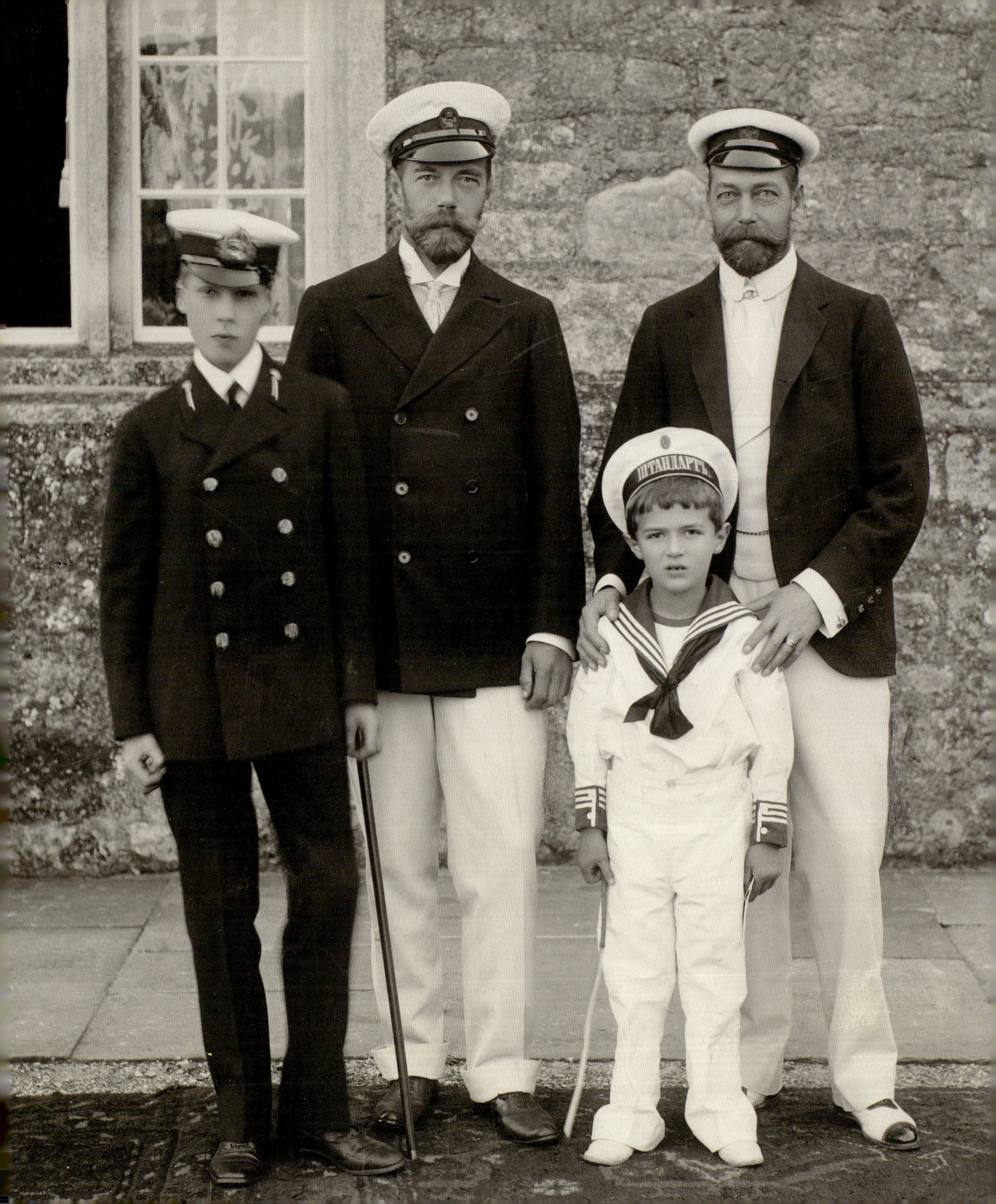
ШТАНДАРТЪ

CLARENCE HOUSE

It is now over three hundred years since the young Tsar, Peter I, arrived in London in 1698; his portrait by Kneller was a gift to King William III and remains in the Royal Collection. It was not until 1862 that a member of the British royal family, Prince Alfred, later Duke of Edinburgh, visited Russia. Soon afterwards, the two royal dynasties became linked through three marriages, all attended by Albert Edward, Prince of Wales and future King Edward VII. In 1866 the Prince's sister-in-law, Princess Dagmar of Denmark, married the Tsesarevich of Russia, later Emperor Alexander III. In 1874 The Prince of Wales's brother, Alfred, Duke of Edinburgh, married The Emperor of Russia's daughter, Grand Duchess Maria Alexandrovna. The Duke and Duchess of Edinburgh made their home in Clarence House where a Russian chapel was installed. In 1894 The Prince of Wales attended the marriage of his nephew and niece, the last Russian imperial couple, The Emperor Nicholas II and Princess Alix of Hesse. These diplomatic visits and dynastic ties have enriched the Royal Collection immeasurably with paintings, icons, books, sculpture, silver and photographs.

It was some time before royal visits resumed. But in 1973 my father, Prince Philip, The Duke of Edinburgh and a descendent of Empress Catherine the Great, initiated an era of modern relations when he visited the USSR. Previous to that, British and Soviet forces had fought alongside each other in the Second World War and had discovered through cultural exchange those profound affinities that transcend ideological difference. The Royal Collection played its part with contributions to exhibitions of Russian art through the twentieth century. Recently Kneller's portrait of Peter the Great was loaned to the Hermitage Museum, the former Winter Palace, to mark the tercentenary of the international city which Peter had founded shortly after his return from London.

This exhibition, therefore, provides another opportunity to celebrate the rich and complex relationships between the royal families and peoples of Russia and Great Britain.

Charles

EXHIBITING RUSSIA: THE HISTORICAL CONTEXT

On 11 June 1851 Queen Victoria, who had opened the Great Exhibition in Hyde Park some weeks previously on 1 May, noted in her Journal, 'we went first to look at the Russian exhibits, which have just arrived and are very fine: doors, chairs, a chimney piece, a piano as well as vases in malachite, specimens of plate and some beautifully tasteful and very lightly set jewelry'. The exhibition was essentially to highlight the achievements of technology and design, predominantly British, but Russia proved well able 'to illustrate the taste and skill displayed in the application of human industry to the raw material in the productions of sculpture, models and the fine arts', such as impressed the royal visitor. The Russian display or 'court', which had opened to the public only on 7 June, proved no less a revelation for many of the six million visitors to the exhibition and was enthusiastically received in the press. It was indeed the first instance of Russia on display in Great Britain.

Thirty years earlier, with the publication of Sir John Bowring's *Specimens of the Russian Poets* (1821), British reviewers had expressed their astonishment that Russians were capable of producing literary works that showed no signs of the barbarism and backwardness that the British had invariably associated with the Russians since their very first encounters of the Elizabethan era. Nevertheless, Russian barbarism remained a leitmotif of British reaction way into the twentieth century, defying all attempts to dispel myths and misconceptions, and each 'discovery' or 'revelation', whether occasioned by exhibitions such as in 1851, or by translations, or by personal encounters, was soon forgotten. However, in addition to the ever increasing number of translations from Russian literature, frequently undertaken, or interpreted, as pictures of Russian life and mores, that brought by the early twentieth century the names of Turgenev, Tolstoi, Dostoevsky and Chekhov comparatively wide recognition, there were also notable attempts to bring to the attention of the British public Russian works of art, primarily paintings, that had been understandably under-represented in the 1851 display.

It was in 1862 that the Russian section of the World Exhibition in London included examples of Russian painting from the reign of Catherine the Great (fig. 1) through to that of Alexander II and 78 canvases, including works by such as Dmitry Levitsky and Aleksei Venetsianov, Karl Bryullov and Ivan Aivazovsky, were on display. Another such exhibition in London in 1872 included a more contemporary selection of Russian art that was seen by a million visitors and received a generally warm reception from the critics, one of whom believed that 'for the first time, was England made acquainted with the recent movement in the direction of the literal study of nature. Landscapes, domestic scenes, and genre generally, were in the ascendant'. Towards the end of the century and during the years up the First World War there were Russian sections in several exhibitions, perhaps most notably in those of the Allied Artists' Association in 1908–11 and Roger Fry's 'Second Post-Impressionist Exhibition' of 1912, contributing to the 'Russian fever' associated with the London seasons of Diaghilev's Ballets Russes from 1911. It was during these years that Fabergé opened his first shop in Dover Street, later moving to more fashionable Bond Street, to offer Russian *objets de luxe* to aristocratic and wealthy customers eager to follow royal example. While contemporary Russian art was receiving most exposure, there was a slow but increasing interest in Russian folk art and aspects of national identity, to some degree shown in the Russian village created by Fedor Shekhtel for Glasgow's 1901 'International Exhibition' to house the Russian exhibits and another mock village at the 'Ideal Home Exhibition' in London in 1913. All these exhibitions and events were, however, in a sense a prelude to a major exhibition that opened at the Grafton Galleries on Bond Street on 1 May 1917.

'The Russian Exhibition' was an astonishing achievement at a time when Britain was locked in war and Russia was in the turmoil of revolution, but, according to *The Times*, 'in these days we all want to know more about our great Ally, the youngest of the Republics; and here is an opportunity of learning'. It was essentially a Russian festival, with performances of plays and music, lectures, a Russian restaurant and cooking demonstrations. Organised in support of the Anglo-Russian Hospital in Petrograd, of which Queen Alexandra, visiting the exhibition a few days after its opening, was the patron, it was much concerned with contemporary events, the Russian army, commercial links, and only three of its seven sections were devoted to paintings and *objets d'art*, all garnered from private collections in Britain, but many of great interest, as well as to so-called 'peasant industries' that included a large number of icons.

It was not until the end of 1929 that the icon's importance in Russian culture was given true emphasis in the 'Russian Ikon Exhibition' that opened at the Victoria and Albert Museum, London, and was a rare example of Anglo-Soviet artistic co-operation in the Stalin era, but the major event in the inter-war period was an 'Exhibition of Russian Art' that was ostensibly linked to the earlier exhibition by being held once more in aid of the Russian Red Cross, whose attention was now, however, focused not on Russia but on the sick and destitute Russians living in England. Its organisers noted the 'inadequate representation of Russian art' in 1917 and claimed that 'the present Exhibition, drawing, as it does, its contents from a large number of countries in Europe as well as from America, will, for the first time in history, present to the world outside Russia a picture of Russian Art in its various branches and phases, which does something like justice to its task'. Housed at 1 Belgrave Square with a setting by Mstislav Dobuzhinsky creating 'an atmosphere truly and fascinatingly suggestive of a Russian Palace', it filled 14 rooms with icons, paintings, engravings, stage designs, porcelain, silver, enamels, brocades, glass and jewellery. Russian painting was well represented from Levitsky and Vladimir Borovikovsky in the eighteenth century through to Bryullov and Ilia Repin in the nineteenth, but it was the stage designs by Ivan Bilibin, Leon Bakst, Natalia Goncharova and Aleksandr Benua (Benoit) that really took the eye. The overall richness, quality and coverage afforded by more than a thousand items in an exhibition about Russia has never been equalled in Britain. It had little to do with Soviet Russia and everything to do with old Russia, celebrated by the British who knew it then and by the Russians in emigration. Another three decades were to pass before Soviet institutions were involved in the mounting of a joint exhibition during the (very temporary) thaw in Anglo-Russian relations.

In 1965 the idea of a large exhibition to illustrate the historical relations between Great Britain and the USSR / Russia was first mooted, but it was brought to fruition in a great hurry when it was decided that it should coincide with the visit of the Soviet Premier, A.N. Kosygin to London in February 1967. For the first and last time during the Soviet period the British Foreign Office and the Soviet Ministry of Foreign Affairs worked closely with cultural organisations to produce an exhibition which the Soviet ambassador to Britain, M. Smirnovsky, called 'unique'. Unfortunately, the speed with which the exhibition had to be prepared meant that no substantial catalogue was ever published, merely a 31-page brochure, listing 223 exhibits which were arranged in seven chronological sections, but omitting all the numerous documents and books that were also on display.

Lavishly produced and illustrated catalogues have, however, been a feature of a steadily increasing number of exhibitions that have been mounted in the post-Soviet era, reaching a climax in 2017, a year marking not only the centenary of the February and October Revolutions but also, if unnoticed, of the 1917 Grafton Galleries exhibition. The twenty-first century began with the opening at Somerset House of the Hermitage Rooms, and although lasting but seven years, they were emblematic of the strong bonds forged by the State Hermitage's Director Mikhail Piotrovsky with Britain that have led to numerous treasures being loaned for exhibitions at, for instance, National Museums Scotland in Edinburgh, Norwich Castle and Houghton Hall. There have been exhibitions devoted to individual artists, movements and periods at numerous venues, such as the National Gallery, the Victoria and Albert Museum, the British Library, the Royal Academy, and Tate Modern, and outside London, at Edinburgh, Glasgow, and Norwich, for example. Local museums, city libraries and other institutions such as private art galleries and auction houses have taken the initiative to promote similar exhibitions, if on a smaller scale.

It is within this historical context of attempts to bring Russia to the British public that the exhibition which accompanies this publication occupies a distinctive place.

For the first time the curators and archivists of the Royal Collection have had the opportunity to search specifically for objects and documents that link the British royal family with the Romanovs over the centuries. Works of art from the Royal Collection have, of course, been on display on many previous occasions and in many places. Of particular renown is the extensive Fabergé collection initiated by King Edward VII and Queen Alexandra (cat. 264), continued with passion by Queen Mary (cats 282–284), and added to by subsequent generations of the royal family. Some 22 pieces (along with other items) were on public display for the first time in the Fabergé section of the 1935 exhibition, and many more at numerous further exhibitions held since 1949 and culminating fittingly with 'Royal Fabergé' at Buckingham Palace in 2011; most recently, the exhibition at the Sainsbury Centre in Norwich concentrated on the Sandringham animals created by Fabergé craftsmen for King Edward VII. The literally hundreds of Fabergé items in the Royal Collection are remarkable not only for their number but also as a relatively rare, but far from isolated, example of the active acquisition of Russian objects by members of the Royal Family.

Queen Victoria was impressed enough by the malachite vases she saw to purchase one to add to the fine – and huge – example that she already possessed, presented to her over a decade earlier by Nicholas I (p. 361) and brought from St Petersburg on a specially adapted steamer. Although the gift was in recognition of the gracious reception accorded to his son, Alexander Nikolaevich, in England, the Emperor himself was to pay a visit in 1844, bringing with him gifts of his own and adding thereby to Russian objects in the Royal Collection. Many other members of the Romanov dynasty visited Britain, beginning with the supposedly incognito arrival of Peter the Great in 1698. Such visits were, however, a particular feature of the nineteenth century, initiated by the Emperor Alexander I, arriving in London with the King of Prussia in June 1814, and followed at intervals by various tsesarevichs, and, early in the twentieth century, by Nicholas II and his family on informal visits to Balmoral and Cowes. During the Soviet period, following the thaw in Anglo-Russian cultural and political relations, there was the official visit in 1956 by First Secretary Nikita Khrushchev and Premier Nikolai Bulganin, who both met The Queen, as did Boris Yeltsin, the new President of Russia, in 1992. It was in 2003, however, that President Putin was to pay what was the first State Visit.

For the most part the British royal family were not obvious collectors of things Russian but recipients of gifts, if not from widespread family members, then from artists and craftsmen perhaps seeking royal patronage, or, most often, from visiting rulers and their families and other foreign dignitaries, who brought objects that were considered representative and distinctive of their culture. Although there are items dating from Peter the Great's visit and a number of objects, particularly books, testifying to George III's interest in travel and exploration (cats 12, 23, 42), the strength of the exhibition lies in the nineteenth and early twentieth centuries and is reflected in events that are climactic moments in Anglo-Russian relations or with particular resonance for the royal family, around which entries – be they documents and letters, coins and medals, jewellery and cameos, paintings and engravings – are grouped. Such are the Napoleonic Wars and the visit to England of Alexander I; the Crimean War, most notably registered in the Royal Collection by the great number of photographs by Roger Fenton, who sought and received royal patronage for their publication; the marriage of the Duke of Edinburgh to the Grand Duchess Maria Aleksandrovna in 1874 (cat. 174) that brought an unparalleled reaction in the press, popular literature, memorabilia, and paintings; the close family ties between the British and Russian royal families, demonstrated most eloquently in rarely seen paintings and photographs; the subsequent fall of the Romanov dynasty and the dilemma of the British royal family. The riches of the Royal Collection have been mined to provide an unusual, intriguing and, most probably, never-to-be-repeated view from above of contacts between two nations that are perceived to have been more often at odds than in harmony.

ANTHONY CROSS

NOTE TO THE READER

NAMES AND TRANSLITERATIONS

Russian names and words are transliterated using a modified version of the Library of Congress guidelines. For the names of members of the Imperial Family from the accession of Peter I, the common anglicised form is used. For all other Russian names, except in a few instances where an anglicised version of a name is well known, the Russian form is used.

DATES

Russia did not adopt the Gregorian calendar, which has been used by the majority of European countries from the mid-eighteenth century, but retained use of the Julian Calendar until after the Revolutions of 1917. As a result, until 1918, Russian dates were between 11 and 13 days behind the equivalent Gregorian date elsewhere. In correspondence, it was common practice in Russia at the time to write two dates, with the Julian date followed by the Gregorian. Where this applies to correspondence this convention has been followed in the catalogue. Unless indicated 'OS' (Old Style), dates follow the Gregorian Calendar.

TITLES

In October 1721, Peter I was declared Emperor of all the Russias and thereafter the title Emperor or Empress was used by all Russian monarchs until the end of the Romanov dynasty. Prior to 1721 the title Tsar was used. The term Emperor / Empress is the convention used in this catalogue to describe rulers and their consorts from 1721. Exceptions are made where the term Tsar / Czar / Tsarina or Tsaritsa is used in correspondence The official title borne by the designated heir of the Russian sovereign and therefore used in this catalogue is Tsesarevich.

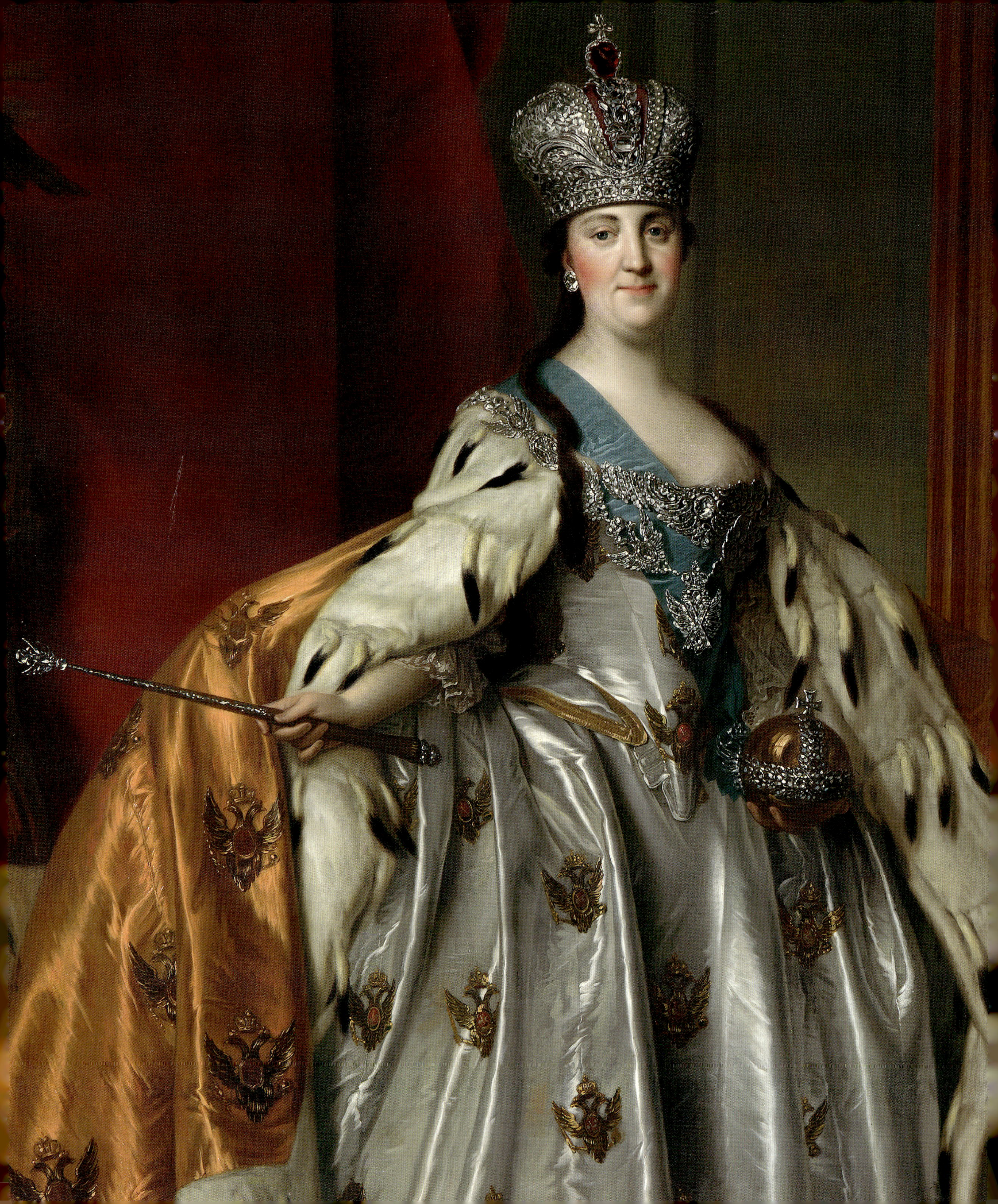

1

'A Country Little Known'[1]

STEPHEN PATTERSON

the feelings [...] might be taken as an additional pledge and security for the maintenance of peace and concord between two nations forced to love, esteem and admire each other, two nations which might be of the utmost encouragement, benefit and advantage to each other, two nations whose discord and dissention must convulse the civilised world to its centre but whose friendship, unity and concord must preserve peace, maintain order and promote with the utmost rapidity and to the greatest extent the general civilisation and general happiness of mankind.

(Lord Melbourne to the future Alexander II, Oxford, 22 May 1839)[2]

Over the past 450 years, since the first English traders braved the climate and challenges of uncharted territory to reach the lands of Rus', nearly 100 years before Blaeu's (1596–1673) maps were drawn, connections both positive and negative have been shared between Britain and Russia. These are reflected in the holdings of the Royal Collection, which has been enriched with portraiture of Russian rulers and family members; with icons and gifts large and small, both stately and intimate; with images of great cities, landscapes and peasants; with symbols of victory and tragedy; and with fine works of art fashioned by skilled craftsmen, using the riches of the Russian soil and the stone of the Urals. The country has been discovered through the pages of books describing the vastness of Russia and its peoples, as well as the correspondence of fellow rulers, family and friends. In the sixteenth and seventeenth centuries there were periods of exploration and discovery; in the eighteenth century, alliances and support; in the nineteenth century, the royal family shared the joys and sorrows of their imperial cousins on a personal level, while defending their own national interests; in the twentieth century, when revolution came, they tried to support them as far as was politically and logistically possible. These relations between Britain and Russia since the seventeenth century – specifically the British Crown and the Romanov family – demonstrate a complex interplay of emotions and events set against a constantly changing political landscape.

The relationship between the two nations has oscillated between alliance and adversary. This was particularly the case in the nineteenth century when, during the reign of Queen Victoria (r. 1837–1901), it was further complicated by the political and dynastic ties between the Houses of Saxe-Coburg and Gotha and Romanov, which, when revolution came in 1917, took a further twist. From the initial contacts of Muscovy and England in the sixteenth century, with trade and embassies exchanged between the two realms, through the Civil War and Bradshaw's failed embassy from Cromwell (1599–1658) to the court of Alexei Mikhailovich (1629–76), the arrival of Russian ambassadors to Charles II (1630–85), and the visit of Peter the Great (1672–1725) to William III (1650–1702) (to build knowledge of the West and skills for his navy), England's relations with Russia were complex. This was seen with the activities of Stuart agents in Moscow and St Petersburg following the 'Glorious Revolution' of

Catherine II, Empress of Russia (detail of cat. 25)

1688. Supporters of the deposed British dynasty hoped that Russian rulers would take the side of the exiled Jacobite claimants to the British throne. At the same time, representatives of the government in London were lobbying for Russian support. In 1725, letters of congratulation were written by the Stuarts to Catherine I (1684–1727)[3] on her accession. At this time, they sought the reversal of the agreement between Peter the Great and George I, 'the Elector of Hanover' (1660–1727), which had been signed shortly before the Emperor's death. Stuart–Romanov contact continued, with similar letters of congratulation being sent, on their accessions, to Peter II (1715–30)[4] in 1727, and to Empress Anna (1693–1740)[5] in 1730. Jacobite hopes of the possibility of Russian support for the 'legitimate rulers' of Britain were strengthened by the successful coup in Russia in 1741, engineered by the French ambassador, which saw the overthrow of Ivan VI (1740–64) and the regent Anna Leopoldovna (1718–46), and the succession of Empress Elizabeth (1709–62), Peter I's daughter.

The exiled 'Old Pretender', Prince James Edward Stuart ('James III', 1688–1766), wrote, 'I was glad to be informed of the particulars you mention of the late revolution in Muscovy it is a most extraordinary event and may have no doubt great consequences. I [...] shall consider what steps may be taken by me towards that court for some application must be made to it by me in this juncture.'[6] However, in Russia, as elsewhere, the Stuart cause was the victim – in part – of the web of alliances across Europe. These involved, in different configurations, France, Spain, Austria, Prussia, Russia, the northern realms and the Ottomans. In this, Britain was represented not just by its geographic location and naval power, but also by its Hanoverian links on the mainland of Europe. Although the Russian government might have been supportive of the legitimist Jacobite claims, they were more conscious of the key role held by British interests – both on the European mainland and at sea – in the maintenance of the balance of power. Encouraging an overthrow of the status quo in Britain from 1715 was never in Russia's interests.

Through the eighteenth century, the majority of contact was diplomatic or continued to be associated with trade. However, there was a distant dynastic connection which linked Catherine II (1729–96) and George III's mother, Augusta, Princess of Wales (1719–72), who were second cousins. The two women corresponded on the succession of the Princess of Wales's son as George III (1738–1820) in 1760[7] and on the succession of Catherine two years later (cat. 24). Catherine also wrote to George III seeking permission to appoint a Briton to her army.[8]

On many occasions throughout her reign, Catherine looked to Britain for ideas and skills, with Britons helping her to achieve her goal to modernise the country. Britons helped bring aspects of the Enlightenment to Russia, in the field of medicine; Thomas Dimsdale inoculated Catherine and her son, the future Emperor Paul, against smallpox, followed by thousands of others. Britons helped her expand the Russian navy, exemplified by Samuel Greig (1735–88) (who was born in Fife, entered Russian naval service as a lieutenant and ended his career an Admiral of the Imperial Navy). In the world of architecture, Charles Cameron (1745–1812), a Scot with Jacobite connections, worked for the Empress at Tsarskoe Selo and Pavlovsk to construct two of the finest architectural ensembles of eighteenth-century Russia. In the sphere of art, Britons helped with the dissemination of Catherine's imperial image, with James Walker (*c.*1758–1822) employed by the Empress to engrave the iconic images of her court and help promote her carefully controlled image around Europe, while many other Britons worked in Russia.

The growing position of Russia after the Great Northern Wars of the early eighteenth century, which saw her eclipse Sweden in the Baltic and push south against the

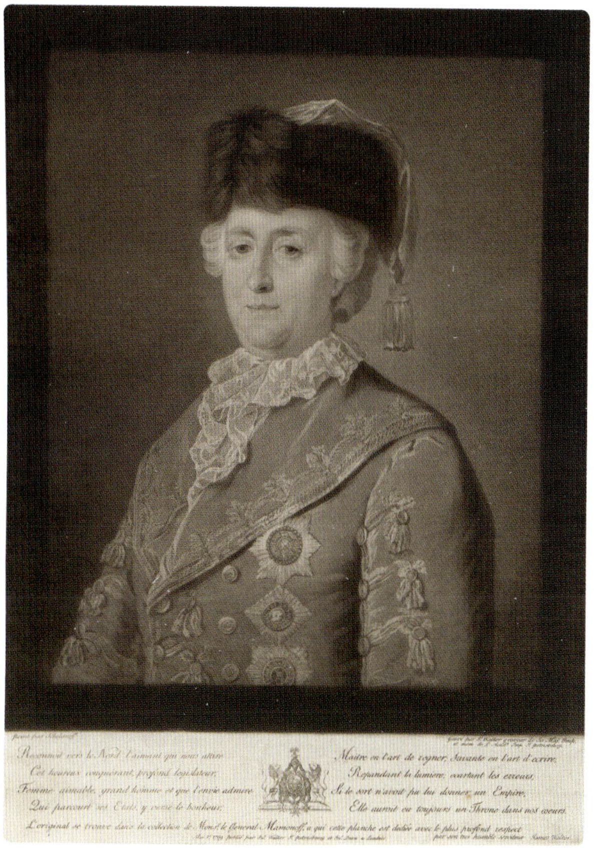

FIG. 1
James Walker
Catherine the Great, 1 May 1789
Engraving (with inscription),
39.8 × 29.1 cm
RCIN 614327

Ottoman Empire, increased her standing on the European stage. Russia's expansion and change in status resulted in alliances, which affected the British Crown in Britain and its monarch's Hanoverian holdings on the European mainland. The military activities of the Russian rulers in the eighteenth and early nineteenth centuries, from the battle of Poltava onwards, were recorded in the Royal Collection and appear in the collections of military maps gathered by William Augustus, Duke of Cumberland (1721–65), and George III. They include maps and details of the engagements of the wars of the Polish succession; the Russo-Turkish wars of 1735–9, 1768–74 and 1787–92 (including the battles of Chesma, Chocim and Ochakov depicting the successes of Aleksei Grigor'evich Orlov (1737–1808) and of Grigory Aleksandrovich Potemkin (1739–91)). There are also Russian plans of Cronstadt from 1782, and of Moscow at the time of Napoleon's (1769–1821) capture of the city in 1812 (cat. 57). These plans and maps are joined by the collection of prints of uniforms gathered by George IV (1762–1830) and the wide range of watercolours and prints of the Russian regiments throughout the period of the Napoleonic Wars (1803–15), depicting the variety of soldiers of the imperial army pitted against the French.

Prints were also collected of the events of the various wars of the French Revolution and Napoleonic age, where the British and Russians fought alongside each other. These alliances, and the prints they generated, spanned the wars of the Second Coalition until 1799 as well as the Third, Fourth, Sixth and Seventh Coalitions. They recorded the victory at Waterloo, Napoleon's defeat, and the regrouping of Europe at the Congress of Vienna. Russian rulers, particularly Catherine II and Alexander I (1777–1825), are well represented in the collection of Engraved Royal Portraits, a compendium of images of British and European rulers.

The important Russian contribution to the defeat of Napoleon was immortalised by Sir Thomas Lawrence (1769–1830) with the inclusion of portraits of key Russian contributors to the allied success in the series of portraits for the Waterloo Chamber at Windsor Castle. The portraits of Emperor Alexander I, Count Nesselrode (1780–1862) (cat. 69), Matvei Ivanovich Platov (1751–1818) (cat. 68), Alexander Ivanovich Chernishev (1785/6–1857) (cat. 71) and Feodor Petrovich Uvarov (1769–1824) (cat. 70) hang alongside the leaders of the other allies of the war.

The visit of Alexander I to England in 1814 (fig. 2) generated a great deal of enthusiasm and interest, although the Royal Collection appears not to have been enriched as a result of the visit by gifts from the Emperor himself. The visit of an allied ruler whose forces had helped defeat Napoleon did, however, cause poets to take up their pens and write odes (cat. 66). Alexander's visit, which saw him visit London, Oxford (cat. 67) and Portsmouth (much as Peter the Great (cat. 4) had done some 116 years earlier), also saw his involvement in the ceremonies of the Knights of the Order of the Garter, whose ranks he had joined the previous year (cat. 64). While there are varying views as to the success of the visit from the Prince Regent's perspective, the Emperor was polite in his letter (written in French) on departure: 'My visit to England leaves me with memories which will ever remain in my heart'.[9]

Visitors brought news of Russia, and a steady stream of Romanovs, emperors, empresses, grand dukes and grand duchesses were entertained in the years that followed. The future Emperor Nicholas I visited in 1816–17, a visit which included a gargantuan banquet of more than 100 courses, prepared by Marie-Antoine Carême (1784–1833), at Brighton Pavilion. The dinner was also attended by the Prince Regent, Frederick, Duke of York (1763–1827) and the Duke of Clarence, later William IV (1765–1837). By way of thanks for the Grand Duke's reception, the Prince Regent's daughter, Princess Charlotte (1796–1817), was sent the Order of St Catherine, which she is shown wearing with her 'Russian dress' (cat. 74) in her portrait after George Dawe (1781–1829) (cat. 75).

In 1839, Grand Duke Alexander (1818–81) – the future Alexander II – visited and was entertained by Queen Victoria. On 22 May 1839, at a dinner at Brasenose College, Oxford, the future Emperor proposed a toast to the 'long continued amity between Great Britain and Russia'. The prime minister, Lord Melbourne (1779–1848), replied in his speech, remembering the visit, 150 years before, of Peter the Great to William III. He continued that he could not 'but with gratitude remember other visitors [...] the Emperor Alexander – a man whose fineness, to whose energy, to whose enlightened politics and character this country, all Europe and the world still lay down a debt of immeasurable magnitude' and he believed the present Emperor (Nicholas I) was 'as much as any man in this world a man of honour, of truth and of justice.'[10]

These and other visits helped inform the Queen and the royal family about Russia. In October 1843, Grand Duke Michael Pavlovich (1798–1849) (who gave Prince Albert a set of drawings of Russian soldiers)[11] visited Queen Victoria: 'The Gd Duke led me in & sat next to me [...] He talked of when he was in the Army, — of Moscow, &c — All this interested me so much, particularly after reading in 1812.'[12]

Conveniently, the Queen and Prince Albert had just finished reading Ludwig Rellstab's novel, *1812: ein historischer Roman* (published that year), on their journey to and from Cambridge a few days earlier. The Queen had described the book thus: 'It was really fearfully interesting, & we got quite engrossed in it. The description of the breaking out of the fire in Moscow, is most vivid & thrilling.'[13] The following month she received reports from the French side of the campaign when she dined with General Colbert (1774–1853), a former colonel of the regiment of lancers of the imperial guard, who told her of 'the horrors of the Retreat from Russia' and described the burning of the city.[14] A year later, she came into direct contact with a wounded survivor of the campaign of 1812, Ernst Constantine, Landgrave of Hesse-Philippsthal (1771–1849), who dined with her and Prince Albert on 2 November 1844, and who had fought and lost a leg at the battle of Borodino, the horrors of which had been revealed in Rellstab's novel:

> *On our return I read in 1812, a most horrible, but very natural & forcible account of passing over the battlefield of Borodino, many days after the battle. Though the details are too terrible, it is however very useful & very necessary to read the accounts of the horrors of war particularly for those in whose hands are placed the decision of war & peace. It shows the frightful responsibility those take upon themselves who wantonly & unnecessarily begin a war!*[15]

Queen Victoria ruled through the reigns of four Russian emperors and met all of them at some point. The Queen's

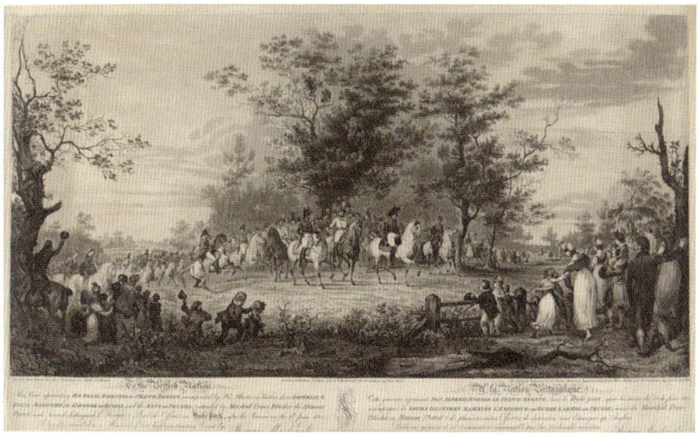

FIG. 2
After Alexander Ivanovitch Sauerweid
Review in Hyde Park attended by Allied Sovereigns. 20 June 1814, 12 June 1815
Etching and aquatint, 46.6 × 76.5 cm
RCIN 750689

views on Russia, over her reign of 60 years, see-sawed, as did her relationship with the Romanov rulers, who occupied what she described at the time of Nicholas II's accession in 1894, as 'this thorny throne'.[16]

Her reign also saw one of the lowest points of British–Russian relations – the Crimean (or Eastern) War in the mid-1850s. That war, which pitted Russia against the British, French, Turks and Sardinians, was in effect another Russo–Turkish war, one which the Russians felt was unduly weighted against them and their desire to control – if not destroy – the Ottoman Empire. What Nicholas I (1796–1855) did not realise was that Russian strength and influence in Central Europe and the Balkans, as well as its naval access to the Mediterranean through the Dardanelles, was seen as a greater threat than the oppression of the Christian minority in the Middle East whose maltreatment had – in part – precipitated the war. Queen Victoria's close interest in the campaigns and the welfare of her servicemen had a long-lasting impact on her approach to Russia, and her private observation to her journal on the death of the Emperor, whom she had hosted in London and Windsor in 1844, encapsulated her feelings for the leader with whose country her troops were engaged in war:

> *Poor emperor, he has alas! the blood of many thousands on his conscience, but he was once a great man, & he had his great qualities, as well as good ones.* […] *11 years ago, he was here, — all kindness, & certainly wonderfully fascinating & handsome. For some years afterwards, he was full of feelings of friendship for us!*[17]

Nicholas's approach to government and his perception of both his and Russia's position in Europe, which had been described to the Queen in 1850 – 'the Emperor Nicholas considered himself to have a mission on earth, which was to put a stop to all revolution, in which he included Constitutional Govt!'[18] – put him diametrically opposed to Queen Victoria constitutionally.

One of the long-term impacts of the Crimean War was a coldness between the two nations, which, as with Queen Victoria's reluctance to give Alexander II the Order of the Garter (cat. 115), and the arguments about Grand Duchess Maria's (1853–1920) title in the years following 1874, were on occasion personal. An example was in the observation by Queen Victoria in 1878, at the time of the Congress of Berlin, following the Russo-Turkish War of 1877–8:

> *I congratulated Ld Salisbury on their great success, & hoped I was satisfied.* [He said that] *The Russians (excepting Schouwaloff) were very sore, Gortschakoff & Jomini, especially.* […] *Speaking of the anti-English feeling in Russia, Ld Salisbury said he had observed to Ct Schouwaloff, that he 'should try & clear away the clouds between us', at which* [Schuvalov] *shook his head.*[19]

The challenges of Russo-British competition and mutual distrust in Afghanistan, India and the Far East, as well as the question of influence in the Balkans, Persia, the Ottoman Empire and the Mediterranean, added further complexity to the relationship.

In spite of closer family connections, for Queen Victoria (as indeed for the Romanovs), empire and country always came above family. This was tellingly seen at the time of the visit of Tsesarevich Nicholas Alexandrovich (the future Nicholas II (1868–1918) to India in 1891 when the Queen instructed that 'the Russian party will have to be carefully watched and not left alone'.[20]

SIMON VAN DER PASSE (*c.*1595–1647)

1 *Sir Thomas Smith (c.1558–1625)* 1617

Engraving, 16.5 × 9.8 cm (sheet of paper)
Inscribed: *VERA EFFIGIES PRÆCLARISSMI: VIRI DOMNI: THOMÆ SMITH EQVITIS AURATI ETC. // The honourable Sr Thomas Smith Knight, late Embas: / -ador from his Ma.stie to ye great Emperour / of Russie Gouernouz of ye Hon:ble and famous / Societyes of Marchents tradinge to ye East- / Indies, Muscovy, the French and Somez / Islands Company; Tresurer for Virginia etc. // Simon Passeus Sculp: Lond: A.o 1617; Compt: Holland excud*
RCIN 680630

Provenance Cassiano dal Pozzo; his brother, Carlo Antonio dal Pozzo; sold by his grandson to Clement XI, 1703; Cardinal Alessandro Albani by 1714; from whom bought by George III, 1762

Literature Franken 1881, no. 876; O'Donoghue 1908–25, IV, no. 1. II; Hollstein 1949–2010, XVI, no. 114. III; Hind 1952–64, II, p. 268, no. 51. III; McDonald 2017, III, no. 1504

The Dutch engraver Simon van der Passe worked in London from 1616 until 1621, before settling in Copenhagen from 1625, where he became engraver to the Danish king, Christian IV (1577–1648). During his time in London, he made this print[21] of the wealthy merchant, Sir Thomas Smith, published by Compton Holland (d.1622), for whom van der Passe was working as soon as he arrived in London.[22] Van der Passe has depicted Smith in a lettered oval, holding a map of Russia; he is surrounded by symbols of his merchant life, including anchors, a ship, a wooden barrel and other goods.

Sir Thomas Smith is known to have been governor of the Muscovy Company by 1600.[23] This English trading company was granted exclusive rights to trade with Russia in 1555. It is likely that Smith's position with the company led to his appointment by James I (1566–1625) in 1604 as special ambassador to the Tsar of Russia, Boris Godunov (*c.*1551–1605). Smith arrived at Archangel, the only Russian seaport at this time, on 22 July 1604, and made his way to Moscow, where he met with the Tsar. He returned to England the following May, having secured new privileges for the Muscovy Company. His travels, and an account of the upheavals being experienced in Russia after Godunov's sudden death in April 1605, were published the same year in the book, *Sir Thomas Smithes Voiage and Entertainment in Rushia* [*sic*].[24]

This engraving was originally part of the print collection of the Roman cardinal, Cassiano dal Pozzo (1588–1657). George III acquired much of Cassiano's collection in 1762 and the print is recorded in his collection in the album, *Heads of English Illustrious Personages*.[25] **RW**

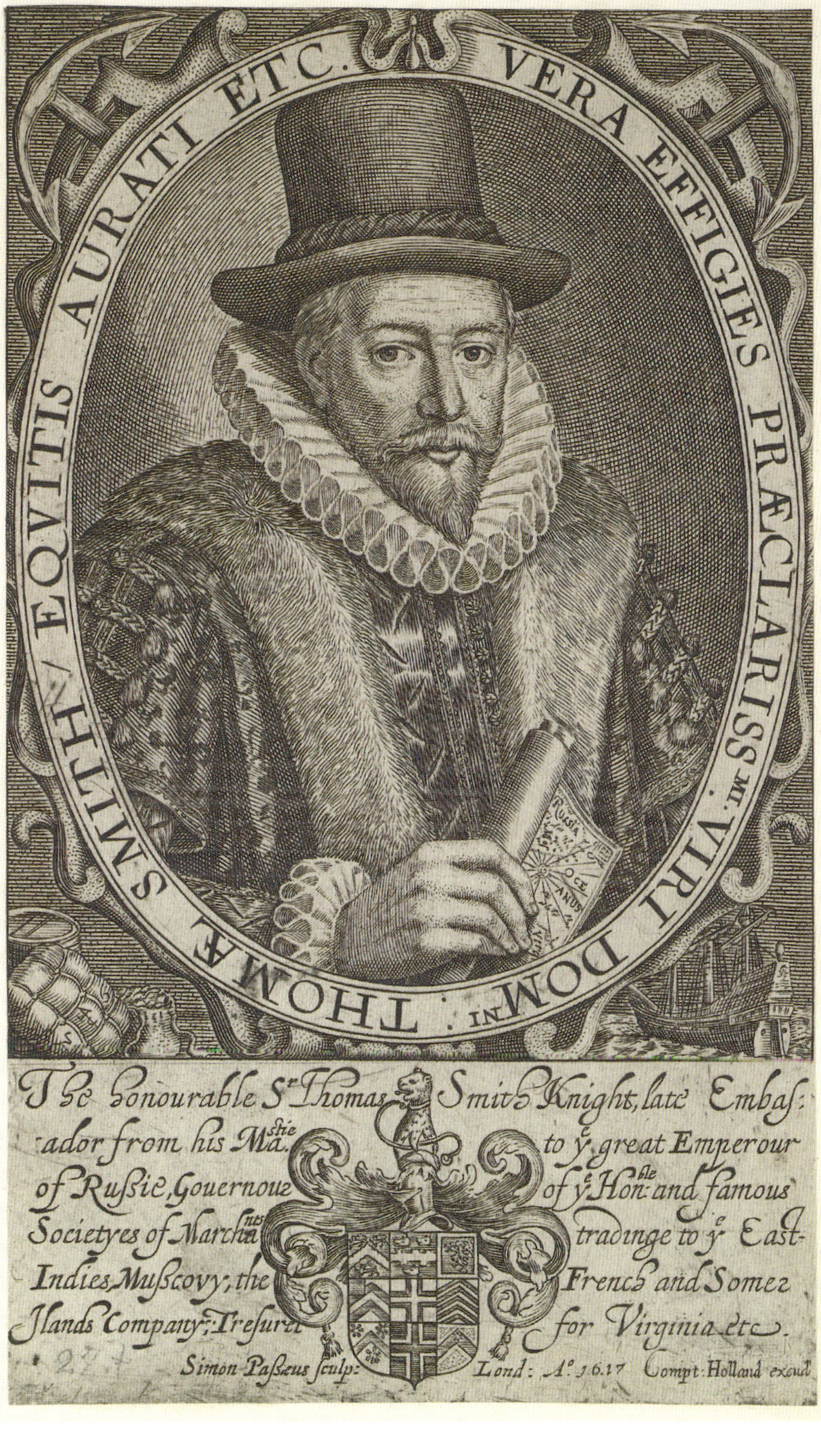
VERA EFFIGIES PRÆCLARISS.MI VIRI DOM.NI THOMÆ SMITH EQUITIS AURATI ETC.
The honourable Sr Thomas Smith Knight, late Embas:
:ador from his Ma.stie to ye great Emperour
of Russie, Gouernour of ye Hon:ble and famous
Societyes of Marchants tradinge to ye East-
Indies, Musscovy, the French and Somer
Ilands Company; Tresurer for Virginia etc.
Simon Passæus sculp: Lond: Ao. 1617 Compt: Holland excud

GUY MIÈGE (1644–*c*.1718)

2 *A Relation of three embassies from His Sacred Majestie Charles II to the Grand Duke of Muscovie, the King of Sweden, and the King of Denmark: performed by the Right Ho^ble^ the Earle of Carlisle in the years 1663 & 1664: written by an Attendant on the Embassies, and published with his L^ps^ Approbation* 1669

London: John Starkey
Bound in brown calf, 18.1 × 11.8 cm (closed)
RCIN 1072024

Provenance Acquired by George IV when Prince of Wales

Literature Dmitrieva and Abramova 2006, p. 272, no. 80; Cross 2014b, A9

Guy Miège was born in Switzerland, but came to England in 1661: 'Ever since I understood, that the World was not altogether shut up in my own Country, I have had a constant inclination to travail'.[26] He spent his first years in the household of Thomas Bruce, Earl of Elgin (1599–1663), and in 1663 was appointed under-secretary to Charles Howard, Earl of Carlisle (1629–85), for his embassy to Russia (Andrew Marvell (1621–78), the poet, was secretary). His passion for novelty and stimulation through travel encouraged him to pay particular attention to Russia, which he described as 'a country little known',[27] and after his return he sought permission from the Earl to publish his impressions of Russia, as well as to provide what he saw as an exact and accurate account of the embassy. The embassy's chief purpose was to renew exclusive, tariff-free trading rights that England had enjoyed with Russia up to the end of the reign of Charles I (1600–1649), but which had been withdrawn after 1649. Moreover, Tsar Alexei I (1629–76) had forbidden English traders access to inner Russia, confining their activities to the port of Archangel in the north. Russian traders had woken up to their own commercial interest, and to the fact that the exclusive English privileges were blocking home-grown activity; the execution of Charles I offered a perfect excuse for the cessation of diplomatic relations (which meant trade relations too) with England. Carlisle was keen to get these rights restored, and his entourage arrived in Archangel in September 1663, reaching the capital the following February. The embassy was not a success, firstly, because it was no longer in Russia's interest to restore rights to England that damaged its own merchants, and secondly, because Carlisle took offence at the way in which he was treated by several of the court officials. He refused the Tsar's personal gift to him at the end of the embassy, on the grounds that he had not been successful.[28]

For Miège, the embassy had the major compensation of allowing him to observe a little-known country in detail, which he was then permitted to publish. Written in a lively style, it describes the country of *Muscovie*, its climate and people, as well as the system of government and religion. He was much impressed by the country, which he proclaimed as 'incomparably pleasant and beautiful',[29] and 'exempt from Epidemical diseases'[30] (on account of the cold); but less so by the people, whom, he proclaimed, took after the Germans, 'being Corpulent and of strong Complexion',[31] and whose manners clearly did not find favour: 'Civility and Complacence amongst them is so rare, tis no wonder if they be very sparing of it before Strangers'.[32] **ES**

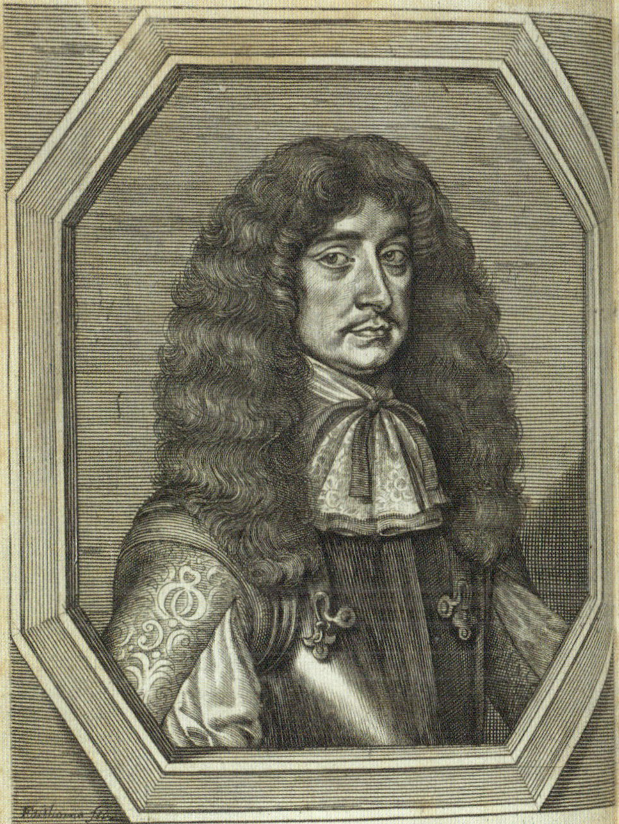

The Right Honble: Charles, Earle of Carlisle, vicount Howard of Morpeth, Baron Dacre of Gilsland, Lord Lieutenant in the Counties of Cumberland and Westmoreland, and one of the Lords of his Majesties most Honourable Privy Councell. etc.

A Relation
Of Three EMBASSIES
From his Sacred *MAJESTIE*

Charles II

TO THE
Great Duke of MUSCOVIE,
The King of SWEDEN, and
The King of DENMARK.

Performed by the Right Ho^ble the
EARLE of CARLISLE
in the Years 1663 & 1664.

Written by an Attendant on the Embassies,
and published with his L^ps Approbation.

LONDON,
Printed for *John Starkey* at the *Miter* in *Fleet-street* near *Temple-Barr*. 1669.

JOAN BLAEU (1596–1673)

3 *Nuevo Atlas del imperio de Russia* = *Atlas Maior* [*Spanish*] after 1662

Amsterdam: Joan Blaeu
Bound in brown calf, 53.7 × 37.5 cm (closed)
RCIN 1192818

Provenance Bookplate of Archibald Little (1838–1908). Acquired after 1908

Joan Blaeu's *Atlas Maior* ('Great Atlas') is an outstanding piece of work, demonstrating the cartographic and scholarly knowledge of seventeenth-century Amsterdam, as well as the craftsmanship of the city's papermakers, printers, engravers, colourists and binders. Blaeu, who had originally trained in law, went into partnership with his father Willem (1571–1638) by 1630. The Blaeu family did not exclusively print atlases – they were responsible for much more – but maps and atlases were amongst their staple work. (Willem succeeded Hessel Gerritsz (*c*.1581–1632), the engraver and cartographer, as official cartographer for the Dutch East Indian Company in 1633, and was then succeeded by Joan in 1638.) Nor were they the only family printing atlases in Amsterdam, competing with the Mercator / Hondius / Janssonius partnership through the 1630s to see who could produce the atlas with the most maps. In 1640 Blaeu published a third volume to his existing atlas, *Theatrum Orbis Terrarum*, first published in 1635, and aimed to bring this project to a glorious conclusion with the *Atlas Maior*, published from 1662. The atlas occupied at least nine volumes (the Dutch edition; the French and Latin editions took up more space) and contained nearly 600 maps. Blaeu started work on a Spanish edition,[33] but this was never completed, following a fire in 1672, which destroyed many of the printing plates. Existing copies, such as this one, are often made up from pages of Spanish text, with maps from the other language editions pasted onto the versos.[34]

Blaeu's view of the Kremlin, although published after 1662, is probably based on an original Russian map drawn *c*.1604, since it shows the Kremlin interior from that period. Most notable is the Tower of Ivan III ('the Great'; 1440–1505), which was raised in height in 1600 by Boris Gudunov.[35] Along with its companion map, the town plan of Moscow, the map of the Kremlin was probably originally engraved by Hessel Gerritsz, who is known to have possessed maps of Russia, and who designed the general map of Russia that appears in the atlas.[36] **ES**

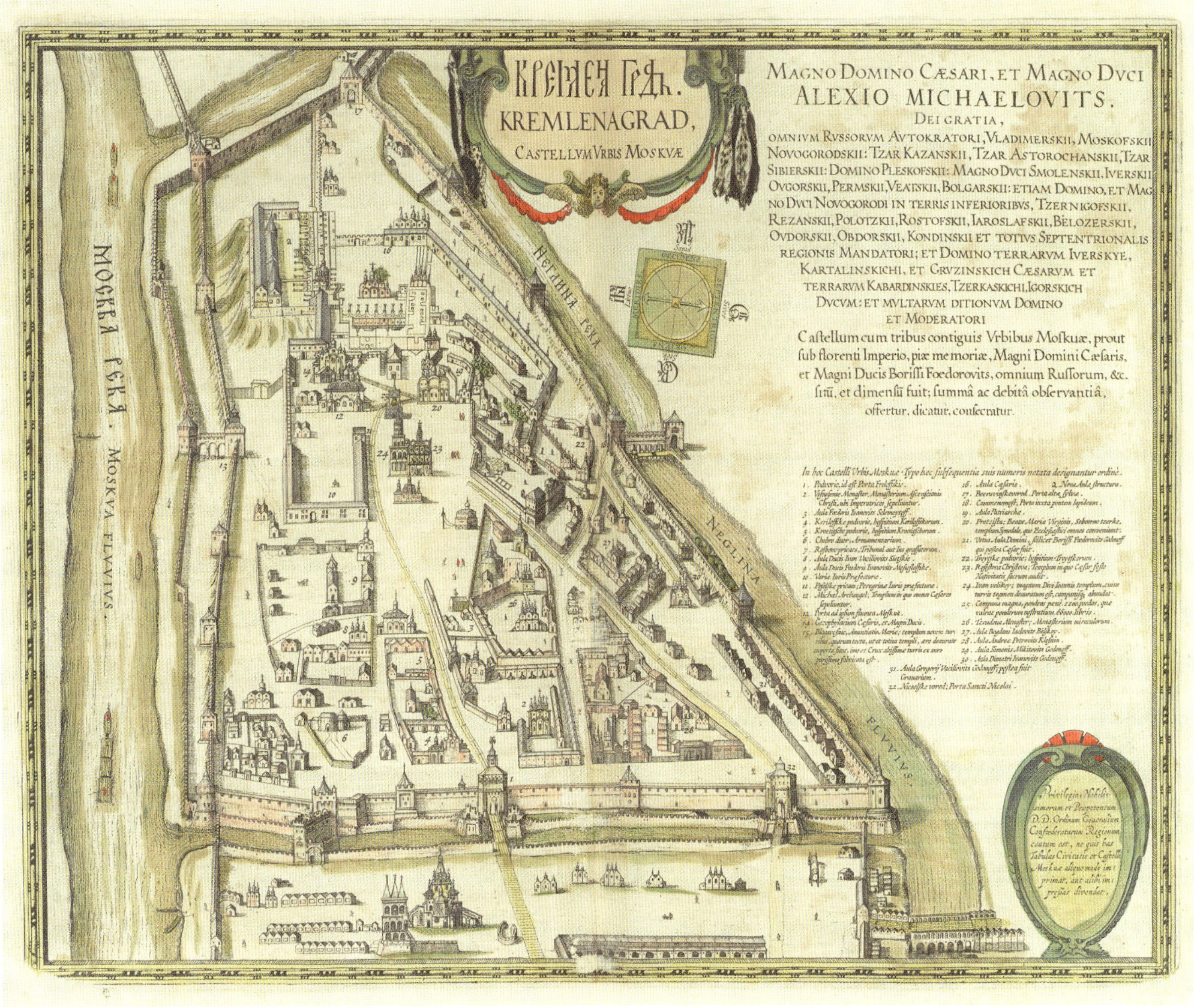

КРЕМЛЕН ГРАДЪ.
KREMLENAGRAD,
CASTELLVM VRBIS MOSKVÆ
MAGNO DOMINO CÆSARI, ET MAGNO DVCI
ALEXIO MICHAELOVITS,
DEI GRATIA,
OMNIVM RVSSORVM AVTOKRATORI, VLADIMERSKII, MOSKOFSKII
NOVOGORODSKII: TZAR KAZANSKII, TZAR ASTOROCHANSKII, TZAR
SIBIERSKII: DOMINO PLESKOFSKII: MAGNO DVCI SMOLENSKII, IVERSKII
OVGORSKII, PERMSKII, VEATSKII, BOLGARSKII: ETIAM DOMINO, ET MAG
NO DVCI NOVOGORODI IN TERRIS INFERIORIBVS, TZERNIGOFSKII,
REZANSKII, POLOTZKII, ROSTOFSKII, IAROSLAFSKII, BELOZERSKII,
OVDORSKII, OBDORSKII, KONDINSKII ET TOTIVS SEPTENTRIONALIS
REGIONIS MANDATORI; ET DOMINO TERRARVM IVERSKYE,
KARTALINSKICHI, ET GRVZINSKICH CÆSARVM ET
TERRARVM KABARDINSKIES, TZERKASKICHI, IGORSKICH
DVCVM; ET MVLTARVM DITIONVM DOMINO
ET MODERATORI
Castellum cum tribus contiguis Vrbibus Moskuæ, prout
sub florenti Imperio, piæ memoriæ, Magni Domini Cæsaris,
et Magni Ducis Borissi Foedorovits, omnium Russorum, &c.
sitū, et dimensū fuit; summâ ac debitâ observantiâ,
offertur, dicatur, consecratur.
In hoc Castelli Vrbis Moskuæ Typo hec subsequentia suis numeris notata designantur ordinè.
1. Podvorie, id est Porta Frolofskie.
2. Vosnesenie Monaster, Monasterium Ascensionis Christi, ubi Imperatrices sepeliuntur.
3. Aula Foedoris Ivanovits Schremeyteff.
4. Kerilofske podvorie, hospitium Kerilofskorum.
5. Kroetitske podvorie, hospitium Kroetitskorum.
6. Chobro dwor, Armamentarium.
7. Rosboene prickas, Tribunal aut Ius grassatorum.
8. Aula Ducis Ivan Vaciliovits Sietskie.
9. Aula Ducis Foedoris Ivanovits Mesieslofske.
10. Variæ Iuris Præfecturæ.
11. Posolske prickas; Peregrinæ Iuris præfecturæ.
12. Michael Archangel; Templum in quo omnes Cæsares sepeliuntur.
13. Porta ad ipsum fluvium Moskuæ.
14. Gazophylacium Cæsaris, et Magni Ducis.
15. Blagovesenie, Anuntiatio Mariæ; templum novem turribus, quarum tecta, ut et totius templi, ære deaurato coperta sunt, imo et Crux altissimæ turris ex auro purissimo fabricata est.
16. Aula Cæsaris. 2. Nova Aulæ structura.
17. Boerovitskovorod. Porta altæ sylvæ.
18. Cammenemost, Porta iuxta pontem lapideum.
19. Aula Patriarchæ.
20. Pretzista; Beatæ Mariæ Virginis, Soboerne tzerke, templum Synodale, quo Ecclesiastici omnes conveniunt.
21. Vetus Aula Domini, scilicet Borissi Foedorovits Godenoff qui postea Cæsar fuit.
22. Troytske podvorie; hospitium Troytskorum.
23. Rosestova Christova; Templum in quo Cæsar festo Nativitatis sacrum audit.
24. Ivan velikoy; magnum Divi Ioannis templum, cuius turris tegmen deauratum est, campanisque abundat.
25. Campana magna, pendens pené 2200 podas, quæ valent ponderum nostratium 66000 libris.
26. Tzeudova Monaster; Monasterium miraculorum.
27. Aula Bogdani Iacliovits Belskoy.
28. Aula Andreæ Petrovits Klesnin.
29. Aula Simonis Mikitovits Godenoff.
30. Aula Dimetri Ivanovits Godenoff.
31. Aula Gregorij Vacilovits Godenoff; postea fuit Granarium.
32. Nicoelske vorod; Porta Sancti Nicolai.
Privilegio Nobilissimorum et Praepotentum D.D. Ordinum Generalium Confoederatarum Regionum cautum est, ne quis has Tabulas Civitatis et Castelli Moskuæ aliquo modo imprimat, aut alibi impressas divendat.
МОСКВА РЕКА.
MOSKVA FLVVIVS.
НЕГЛИННА РЕКА
NEGLINA FLVVIVS.

SIR GODFREY KNELLER (1646–1723)

4 *Peter I, Tsar of Russia (1672–1725)* 1698

Oil on canvas, 241.7 × 145.6 cm
Signed and dated: *Petrus Alexeewitz. Magnus Dominus. / Tzar Et Magnus Dux Muscoviæ / Jussu Britanniæ Majestatis Godfridus Kneller Eques / ad vivum Pinxit, 1698*
RCIN 405645

Provenance Painted for William III; hung in the Drawing Room at Kensington Palace by 1700

Literature Millar 1963, no. 347; *Great Britain – USSR* 1967, no. 32; Stewart 1983, pp. 41, 46–7, 68 and no. 570; MacGregor 2004, p. 120

This portrait was painted as a gift to William III during Peter I's three-month stay in London from 11 January to 21 April 1698. The visit formed part of Peter's 'Grand Embassy', a part-diplomatic and part-fact-finding tour of the more advanced countries of Western Europe. His special interest lay in ship-building, having begun the construction of a Russian navy in 1685 and believing that the greatness of a country lay in its navy.

The Emperor sailed from Holland, incognito, as an officer called Peter Mikhailov, having spent three months boat-building with the Dutch East India Company. On his arrival, he first took lodgings at Norfolk Street, near the Strand, later moving to Deptford, where he resided at John Evelyn's (1620–1706) house, Sayes Court (the attraction being that it lay close to the shipyards and was more private). This episode of the Tsar's visit is well documented, as numerous reports and anecdotes chronicle the destruction wreaked on Evelyn's residence and garden: the house was reported to contain 'a trail of broken chairs dressers and beds [...] twenty five pictures very much tore and frames all broke' on his departure.[37]

Although there does not appear to be any documentary evidence, it is possible that Kneller first sketched the Tsar when the two monarchs met 'in secret' in Utrecht, on 1 September 1697 (OS). However, it appears that Peter had overcome his reluctance to be 'on display' or sit for any length of time, when it was reported on 22 February 1698 by the resident of the United Republics, L'Hermitage, that 'The Tsar was to be painted and the portrait was to be a gift for the king'.[38] Peter and the King are said to have had an easy relationship; they met at Norfolk Street and Kensington Palace, and dined together at Lambeth Palace.

Presented as a tall, virile, handsome warrior, the portrait forms part of a tradition of kings portrayed as military heroes. It was hailed as an excellent likeness, and was described by Russian diplomat Prince Boris Ivanovich Kurakin (1676–1727) as the 'famed portrait of His Czarish Majesty standing in all his imperial armour & so attractive that I have nowhere seen its equal'.[39] He is surrounded by the attributes of kingship: the crown set on a cushion to the left, and the ermine-lined cloak he is wearing, embroidered with the double-headed eagle. To the right is a vignette of ships on manoeuvres, an allusion, perhaps, to the mock sea battles organised by William III for Peter's entertainment at Portsmouth on 22 March, or to the *Royal Transport*, a yacht presented to the Tsar by the King.

This powerful image, engraved by John Smith in 1698 (fig. 3), was widely disseminated and became the prototype for the Tsar's image throughout his reign. **AB**

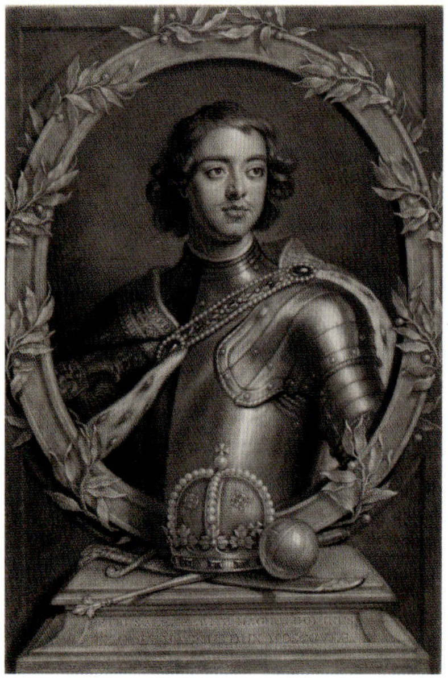

FIG. 3
John Smith, after Godfrey Kneller *Petrus I, Emperor of Russia, 1672–1725*
Mezzotint, 40.7 × 28.1 cm
RCIN 614206

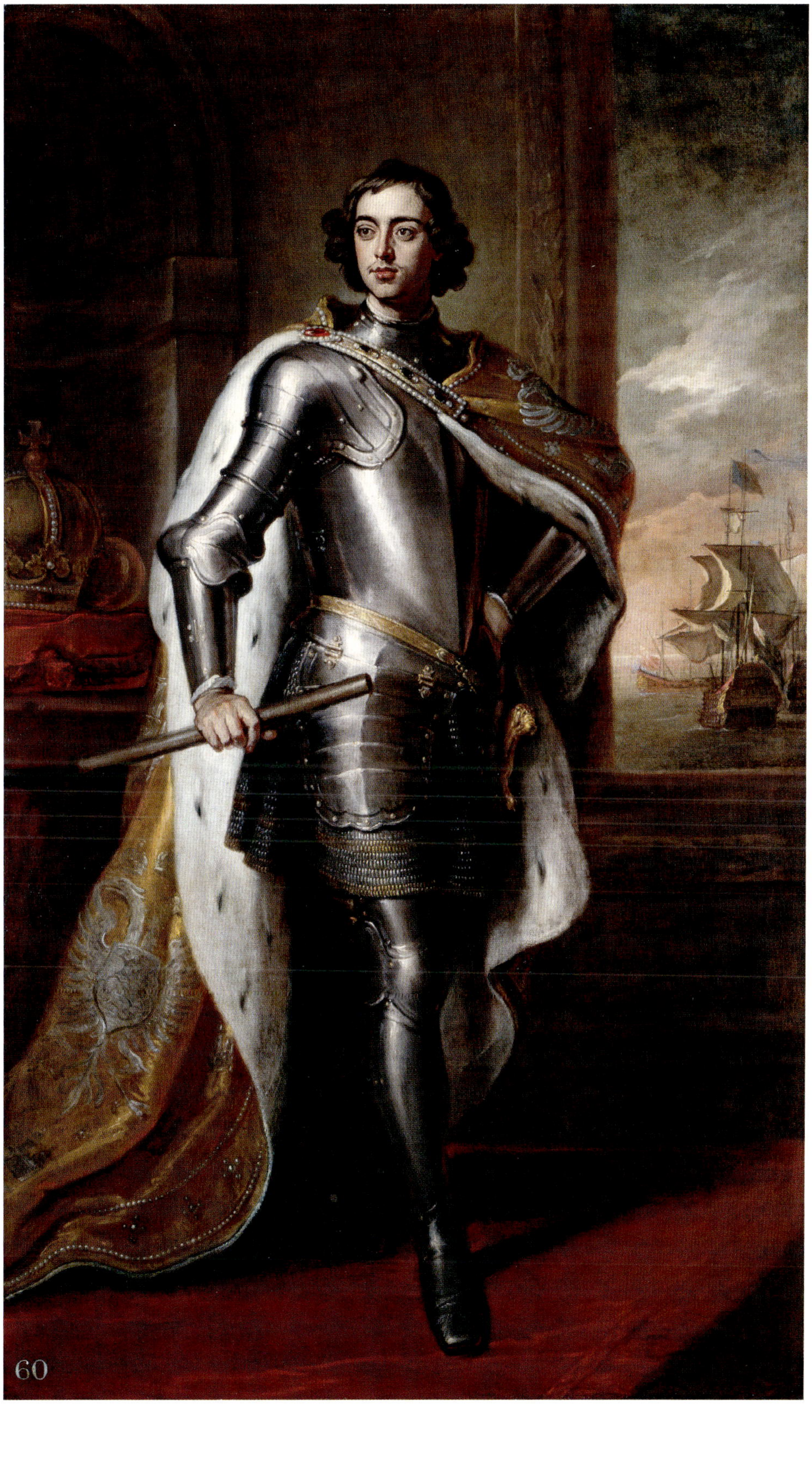
60

ATTRIBUTED TO JAN BLOMMENDAEL (*c*.1650–1699)

5 *Bust of William III (1650–1702)* *c*.1700

Marble, bust: 99.7 × 80.0 × 43.0 cm, pedestal: 50.7 × 89.0 × 53.0 cm
Marks: *DFA GUILELMO HENRICO D.G.P. ARAUSIO.BELG.GUB.M.BRIT.R.FIDEI.LIBERATIS Q VINDICI 1689*
RCIN 35857

Provenance First recorded in the collection of E.J. Coleman of 32 Grosvenor Square, London; sold Christie's, London, 30 July 1881, lot 105 (wrongly stated in the catalogue to have been at Newstead Abbey); B.W. Currie, Minley Manor, Hants; purchased by Queen Elizabeth, Christie's, London, 27 March 1937, lot 63 (with RCIN 35856)

This white marble bust of William III, wearing armour, a full-bottomed wig crowned by a laurel garland, a lace cravat and the collar and badge of the Order of the Garter, is supported on a later marble pedestal incorporating a tablet carved with the King's royal coat of arms and supporters.

The accuracy of the sculptured portrait to the King's likeness can be judged by comparison with Kneller's painted image of approximately the same date.

The bust relates closely to the example signed and dated 1699 by Jan Blommendael in the Mauritshuis at The Hague.[40] However, in the Royal Collection version, the details are far less well defined, with less undercutting. This bust and its companion, of Charles I (RCIN 35856), may both be copies, perhaps made for William III (fig. 4). Their condition has been affected by display in the open air during part of their history. The first meeting between Peter I and William III took place in Utrecht on 11 September 1697 and was marked by the striking of a medal.[41] Once in England, the Tsar dined with William at Kensington Palace on 23 January 1698 where he was shown the treasures of the Picture Gallery and he also visited St James's Palace.[42] **CDEG**

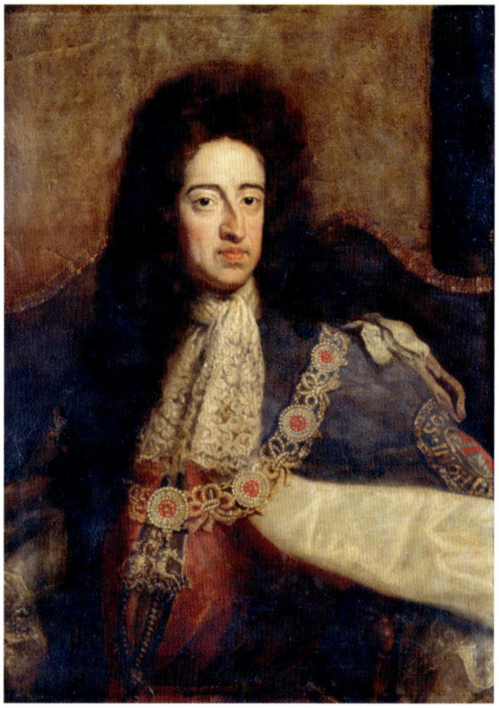

FIG. 4
Sir Godfrey Kneller
William III in Garter Robes, *c*.1695–1700
Oil on fresco, 91.4 × 66.0 cm
RCIN 404327

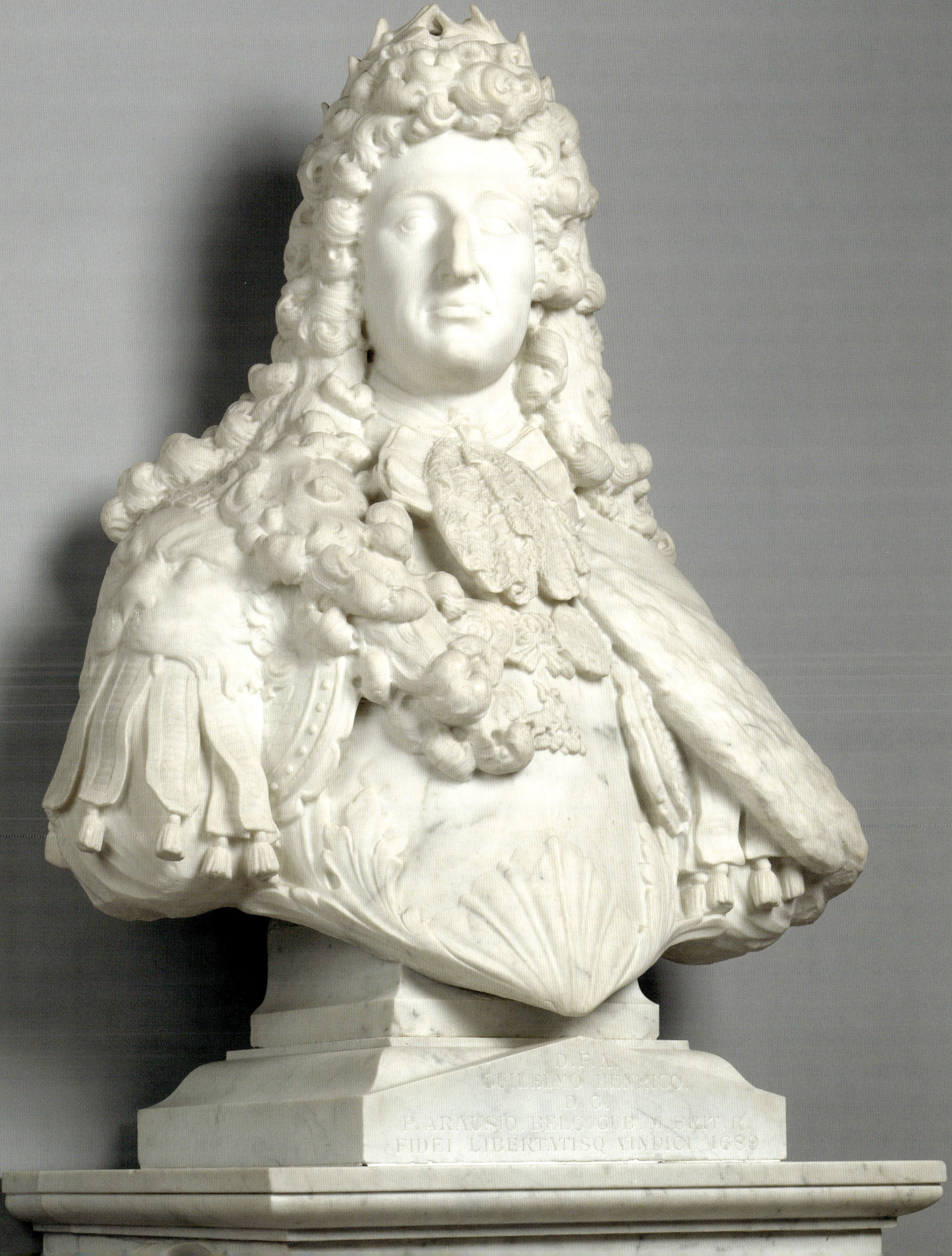
D. G.
FIDEI LIBERTATISQ VINDICI 1689

EMPEROR PETER I (1672–1725)

6 *Letter to the Agent of Prince James Edward Stuart (James III; 1688–1766), 'the Old Pretender', from St Petersburg* 5 January 1724

Manuscript, 20.1 × 15.5 cm
RA SP/MAIN/72/16

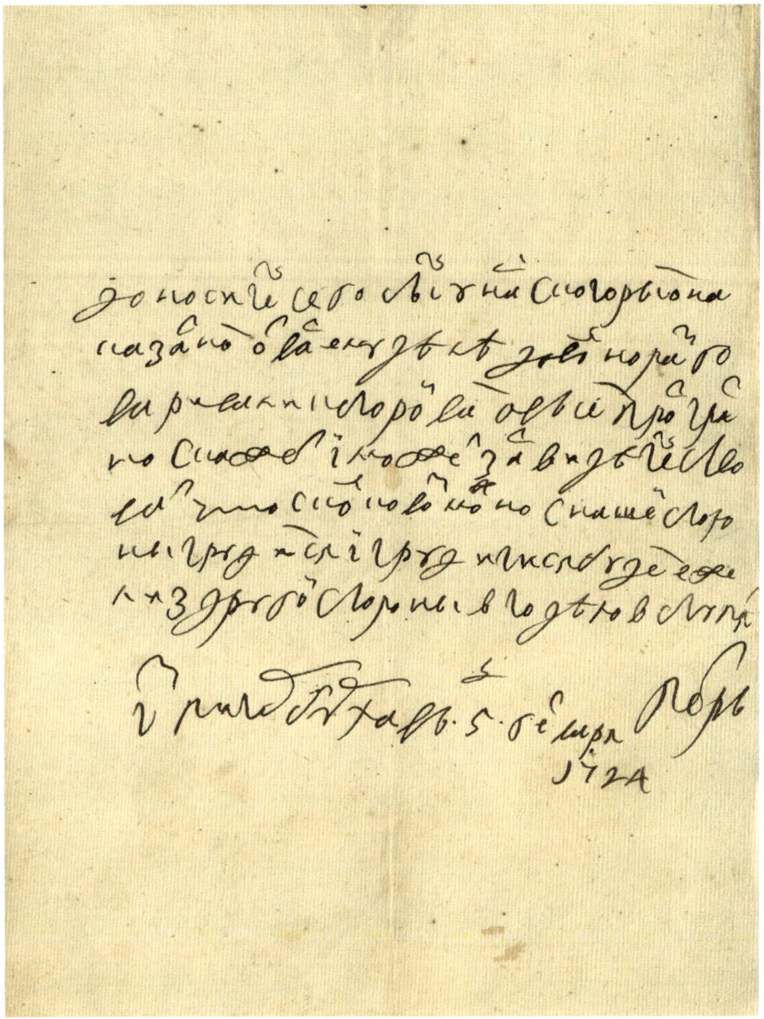

The bearer of this has been with us, and we have spoken to him a good deal about the affair with which he was commissioned. He will report to you at length about all points and will be in a position to testify that, so far as is possible, we from our side are at work and will continue our task, if from the other side they will enter this affair.
Peter
From Petersburg January 5 1724

This enigmatic letter, signed by Peter the Great, was one of the prizes in the archives of the Stuart court in relation to Russia. Written just over a year before the Emperor's death, it was sent at the time when the Stuarts were endeavouring to persuade him to side against the 'Elector of Hanover' in their attempts to isolate the Hanoverian succession of George I. This attempt came to naught – as Peter the Great allied himself with the Elector just before his death, an agreement which Jacobites attempted to persuade Catherine I to overturn – to no avail. The letter was to be reused in 1741, when the Empress Elizabeth's coup against Ivan VI and his mother, the regent Anna Leopoldovna, restored a legitimate ruler and dynasty. The intention was to show Elizabeth that her father had been favourable to the Stuart cause and thus be supportive in her turn. As such, the letter was specifically sought from the archive by the Pretender, and both James III and Charles Edward (the Young Pretender; 1720–88) wrote to the new Empress, congratulating her on her accession and the restoration of legitimate rule. James III's agents were buoyed by this turn of events in Russia and felt that it showed that legitimate rulers could be restored. SJP

RUSSIAN

7 *Snuffbox with portrait of Peter the Great (1672–1725)*
early eighteenth century

Tortoiseshell, gold, 4.1 × 13.8 cm
Inscribed on lid in Cyrillic: *ВЕЛИКИ.ИМПЕРАТОРЪ И САМОДЕРЖЕЦЪ ВСЕ РОСИСКИ*
RCIN 3903

Provenance Given by Queen Mary to King George V, 3 June 1932

Literature GV Boxes 1929–35, IV, no. 331

This large circular snuffbox of carved tortoiseshell is mounted with a gold hinge, and the lid has a finely carved portrait in tortoiseshell relief of Emperor Peter the Great in antique-style armour, the breastplate carved with the crowned, double-headed imperial eagle. The lid has been carved with an inscription to replicate a portrait medallion, but in tortoiseshell rather than bronze or precious metal. This box forms part of a group of works of art with portraits of Russian imperial rulers acquired by both King George V (1865–1936) and Queen Mary (1867–1953) after the Revolution. **CDEG**

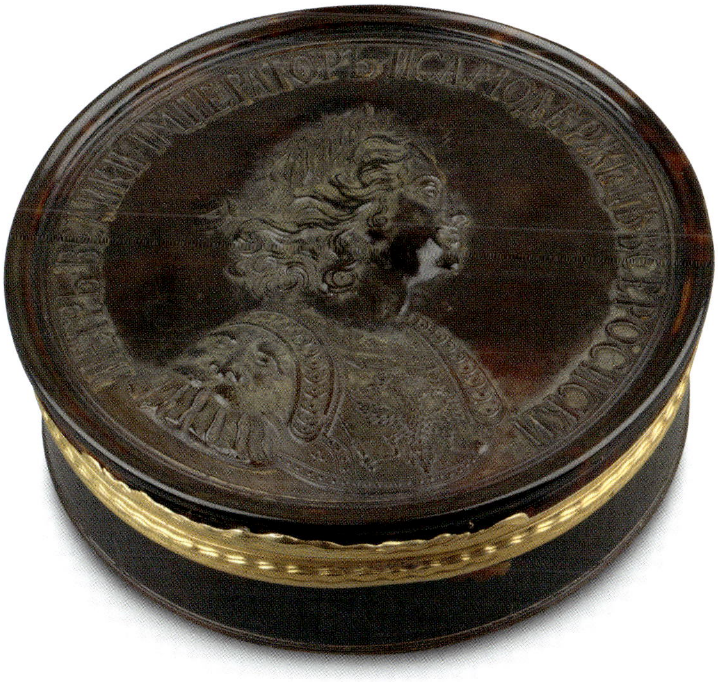

AFTER ÉTIENNE-MAURICE FALCONET (1716–1791)

8 *Statuette of the equestrian monument of Peter the Great (1672–1725)* early nineteenth century

Bronze, granite, gilt metal, 40.0 × 33.0 × 16.4 cm
Inscribed in gilt-metal letters on the side of the granite base: *Петру перьвому Екатерина вторая, лѣта 1782*
RCIN 8033

Provenance Probably acquired by King Edward VII and Queen Alexandra

The famous monumental statue created to honour Peter the Great, founder of St Petersburg, was commissioned by Catherine the Great and took 12 years to complete, finally being unveiled in 1782. The statue is known as 'The Bronze Horseman', after the celebrated poem by Alexander Pushkin (1799–1837) written in 1833. The French philosopher Denis Diderot (1713–84) suggested that Catherine commission the French sculptor Étienne-Maurice Falconet to execute the statue and he arrived in St Petersburg in 1766, accompanied by an apprentice, Marie-Anne Collot (1748–1821), who sculpted the Emperor's face, modelling it on his death mask and numerous painted portraits.

On 7 August 1782 the finished statue was unveiled in Senate Square in a ceremony attended by thousands, but Falconet himself was conspicuously absent due to a misunderstanding and later conflict with his patroness. The statue portrays Peter sitting heroically on his rearing horse, arm outstretched, pointing towards the river Neva, with his horse trampling a serpent, which represents the enemies of Russia and Imperial power.

The monument was widely reproduced in printed and painted works and numerous reductions of the statue were made. In this instance, the vast granite Thunder Stone on which the original bronze sits is made from a piece of polished red granite (fig. 5). The ruler's effigy was charged with meaning, not only due to its central placement in the city which he founded, but is reinforced by the inscription on the monument itself: 'To Peter I Catherine II'; an inscription which confirmed Catherine's legitimacy as Peter's successor. CDEG

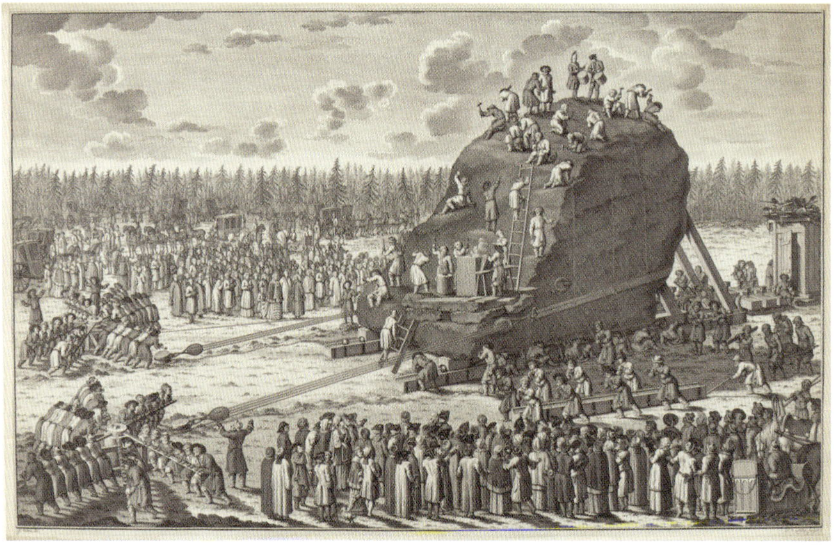

FIG. 5
After Yuri Matveevich Fel'ten
The Transport of the 'Thunder Stone'
Etching, 44.8 × 70.8 cm
RCIN 755731

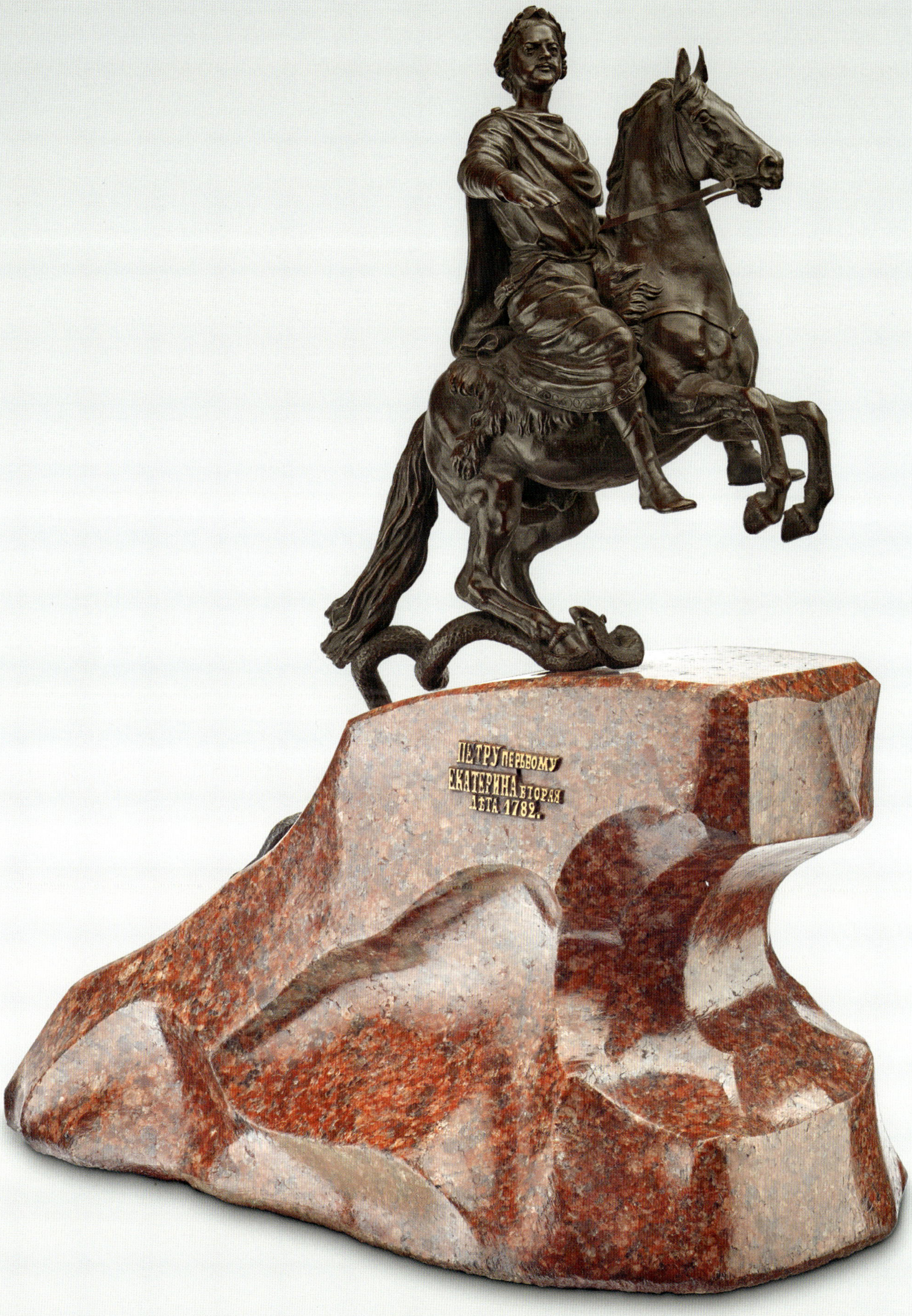
ПЕТРУ первому
ЕКАТЕРИНА вторая
лѣта 1782.

JOHANN GEORG KORB (1672–1741)

9 *Diarium itineris in Moscoviam perillustris ac magnifici Domini Ignatii Christophori* 1700

Vienna: Leopold Voigt
Bound in brown calf, with marbled edges, 30.3 × 20.8 cm (closed)
RCIN 1141851

Provenance Acquired by William IV

Literature Cross 2014b, B11

Johann Korb entered Moscow on 29 April 1699, as secretary to the embassy sent to Peter I by the Austrian Emperor Leopold I (1640–1705). Peter was still absent on his European tour, and the Austrian embassy did not meet him until 13 September. Korb's description of Peter gives two different sides to his character – the affable monarch, extending hospitality and favours to his diplomatic guests, greeting his loyal subjects as if private friends, versus the avenging dictator, who punished the Streltsy, who had rebelled against him, with the utmost savagery. Korb did not stint on his description of their torture and death, and it may be for this reason that copies of the original edition of this book are extremely rare. The German-Russian historian and bibliographer, Friedrich von Adelung (1768–1843), said of it in 1846: 'The scarceness of this work is commonly explained by the circumstance of Peter the Great's having had his displeasure at it expressed to the court of Vienna, especially on account of the circumstantial information about the tragic execution of the Streltsy, and that that Court allowed the unsold copies to be destroyed.'[43] The work was translated into English in 1863 by Count MacDonnell, who found a copy in the library of Henry, Cardinal York (1725–1807) in Frascati. He quotes an anonymous biographer of Peter in 1742, who says (in French): 'That work has become very rare, and I cannot tell what a help it has been to me for the early years of Peter the Great, being FULL OF ANECDOTES WHICH ARE NOT TO BE FOUND ANYWHERE ELSE'.[44]

The embassy remained in Moscow until July 1700, and thus witnessed the various ceremonies associated with Christmas in the Russian Orthodox calendar. One of these was the ceremony of the blessing of the rivers at Epiphany, celebrated in the Western calendar for the arrival of the Three Kings, but in the Orthodox calendar as the day of Christ's baptism in the River Jordan. Frozen rivers were broached on that day, the resulting hole in the ice being named Jordan, and the river waters blessed. It was then customary for people to bathe in the icy waters, to cleanse themselves of their sins. This image shows the Patriarch blessing the waters of the River Neglina (Neglinnaia), a tributary of the River Moskva in central Moscow. The Tsar's regiments led a procession out onto the ice, where an enclosure was erected; inside, a hole was cut in the ice for the Patriarch to bless the river water. After this, regimental banners were sprinkled with the river water, likewise the Tsar and soldiers, and some of the holy water was placed in vessels for the Tsar, Patriarch and nobles to take away.[45] In a larger hole in the ice on the left, Muscovites can be seen immersing themselves in the blessed river water. ES

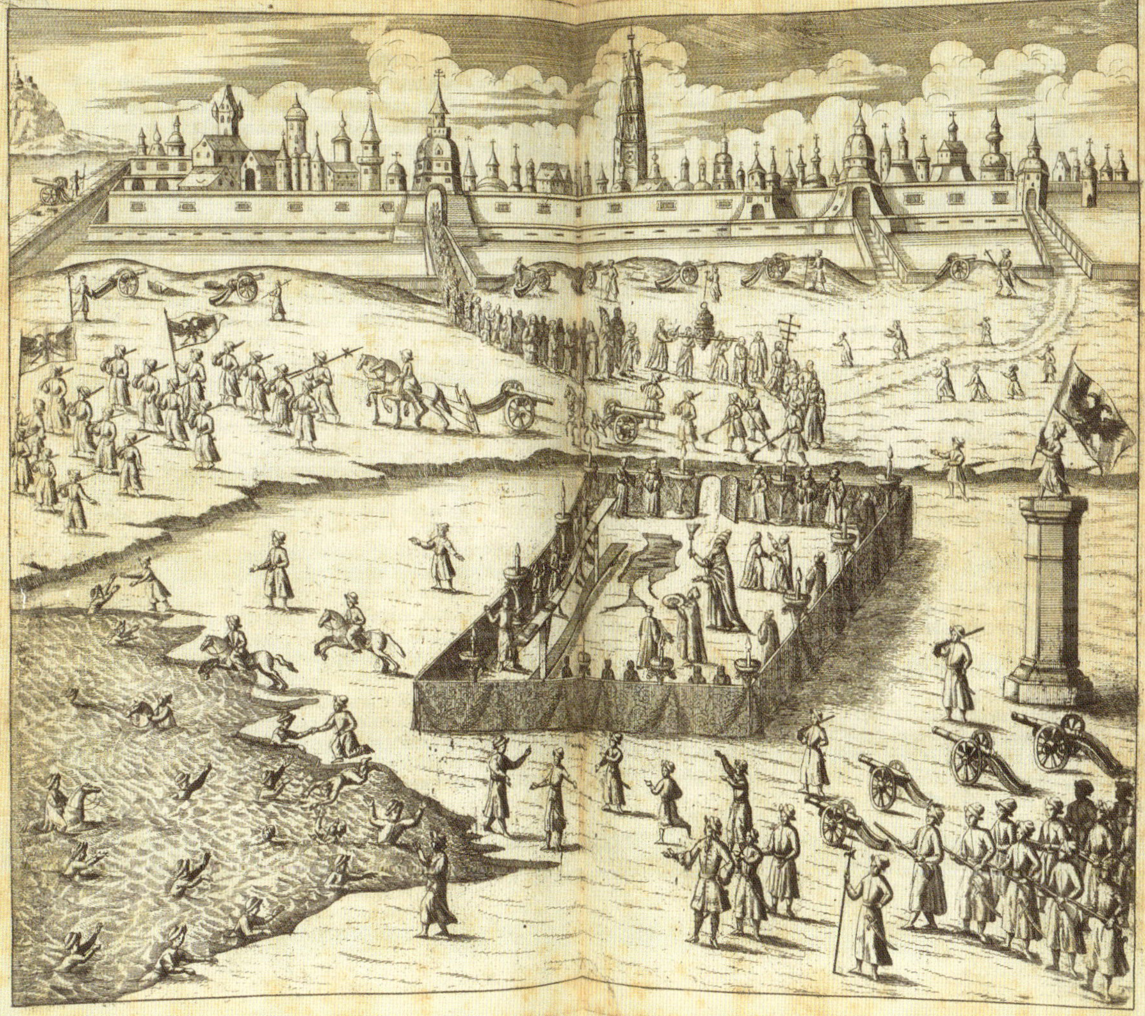

EVERT YSBRANTS IDES (1657–1708)

10 *Three years travels from Moscow over-land to China: thro Great Ustiga, Siriania, Permia, Sibiria, Daour, Great Tartary &c. to Peking* 1706

London: W. Freeman, J. Walthoe, T. Newborough, J. Nicholson & R. Parker
Half-bound in brown calf, 24.9 × 19.5 cm (closed)
RCIN 1140495

Provenance Acquired before 1860

Literature Cross 2014b, B6

In 1689 the first treaty between Russia and China, the Treaty of Nerchinsk, was signed. This gave Russia access to trade routes into Qing dynasty China in exchange for the Amur river, while the Chinese obtained a solid border and neutral neighbours. Evert Ysbrants Ides, an experienced Danish diplomat in the Tsar's service, headed a subsequent trade embassy dispatched by Peter the Great to China in March 1692, and they arrived at the Chinese border on 11 September 1693. On his return in January 1695 he wrote an account of the journey, first published in 1696, and dedicated to the Tsar; the book was intended to demonstrate to an ignorant world the size of Peter the Great's dominions, and attempt 'a short view of *Sibiria* and *Daour*' (an area near the border with China). As Ides says in his dedicatory letter: 'my ingagement is still inforc'd by this consideration, that your Imperial Majesty's Dominions out of *Europe*, are for the most part unknown, in regard that only *Russians*, and no *German* had hitherto travelled thro' great *Tartary* to *China*'.[46] Ides's book described the little-known eastern part of the Russian empire in detail, hence its later popularity; his book had appeared in both English and French by the early eighteenth century and was quoted in others' books about their own travels in Russia. ES

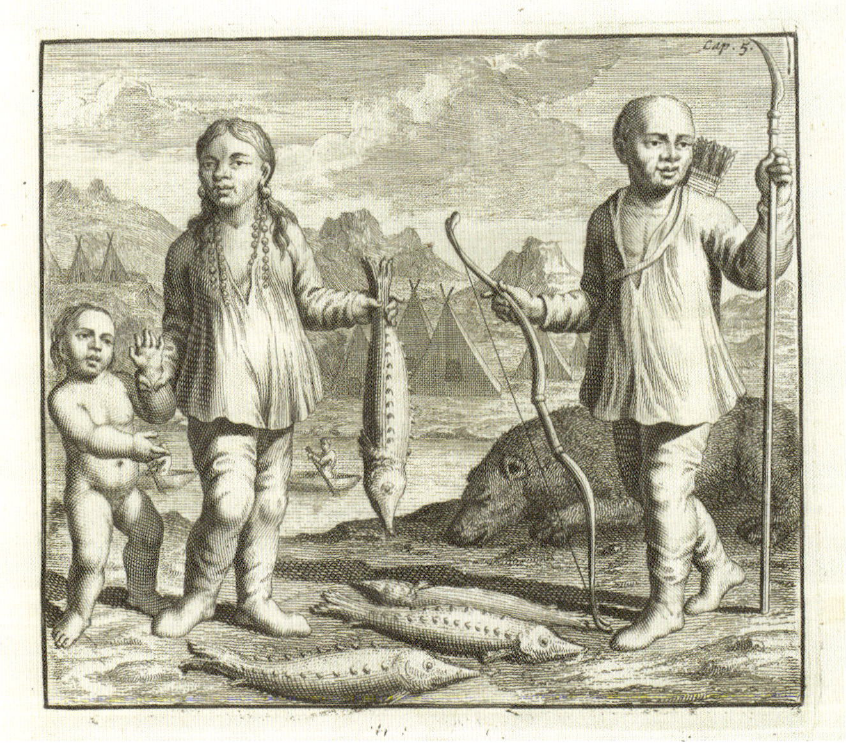

CAPTAIN JOHN PERRY (1670–1732)

11 *The state of Russia under the present czar* 1716

London: Benjamin Tooke
Bound in brown calf, with blind and gold tooling, 19.9 × 12.9 cm (closed)
RCIN 1026852

Provenance Acquired by George III for his Windsor Library (WL 55), and signed by him on title page

Literature Putnam 1952, pp. 3–66; Cross 2014b, B10

Peter the Great's visit to England in 1698 had many consequences: one of the best for Russia was the acquisition of the British naval skill set. The Emperor was eager to improve his own navy and recruited officers and men, shipwrights, gun makers, mathematicians (to teach navigation) and engineers. One of his chief finds was the hydraulic engineer John Perry, who already had two dry docks under his belt, at Portsmouth and Flushing, and whom the Emperor recruited for naval projects. Perry negotiated a salary of £300, expenses and bonuses for each completed project and set off for St Petersburg in April 1698. His first project was to build a canal between the rivers Volga and Don at Astrakhan (a project which ground to a halt in 1701 at the advent of war), followed by major improvements to the dry dockage at Voronezh (one of Russia's major southern towns, on the river of the same name, which is a tributary of the Don, and thus a route to the Black Sea) and to the capacity of the rivers to carry larger ships. He left in 1712, having failed to obtain any of his pay or benefits, blocked at every turn by old-fashioned bureaucracy.[47]

His poor treatment at the hands of 'the evil Offices […] who kept me out of my Pay',[48] did not cloud his judgment of Peter the Great himself, whom he clearly admired. His account of his travails was originally intended to put his side of the case for his ill treatment, but also ended up as a detailed and, above all, contemporary account of Peter's reign and his attempts to reform and Europeanise Russia. His protector, Charles Whitworth (1675–1725), the British ambassador of the time (cat. 80), would also write an account of Peter the Great's Russia and his own embassy, but this would not be published until 1758; thus Perry's account had no serious rival. Though it only went into one English edition, it was translated into several foreign languages, and became an essential source thereafter for those researching Peter the Great's Russia. **ES**

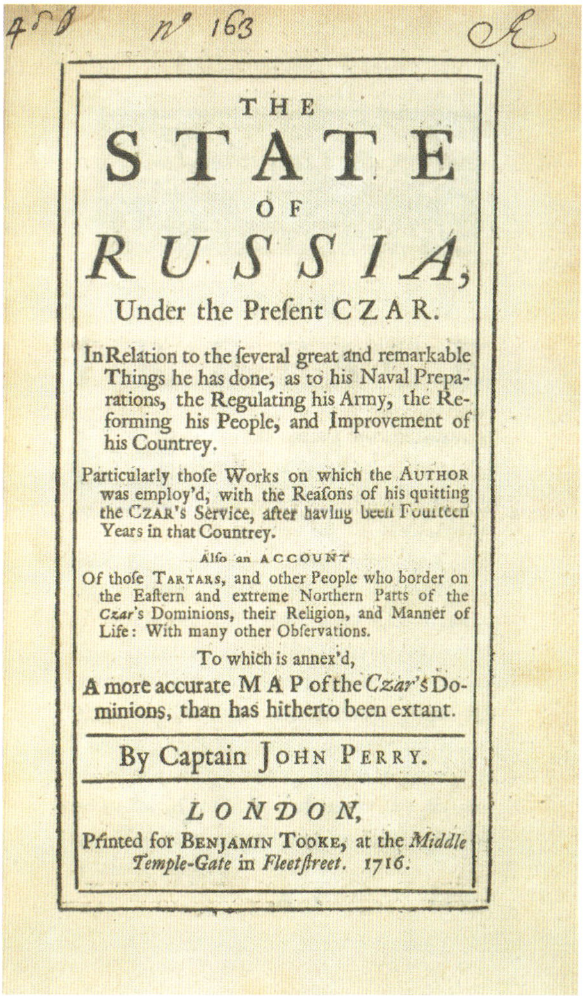
THE
STATE
OF
RUSSIA,
Under the Preſent CZAR.
In Relation to the ſeveral great and remarkable Things he has done, as to his Naval Preparations, the Regulating his Army, the Reforming his People, and Improvement of his Countrey.
Particularly thoſe Works on which the AUTHOR was employ'd, with the Reaſons of his quitting the CZAR's Service, after having been Fourteen Years in that Countrey.
Alſo an ACCOUNT
Of thoſe TARTARS, and other People who border on the Eaſtern and extreme Northern Parts of the Czar's Dominions, their Religion, and Manner of Life: With many other Obſervations.
To which is annex'd,
A more accurate MAP of the Czar's Dominions, than has hitherto been extant.
By Captain JOHN PERRY.
LONDON,
Printed for BENJAMIN TOOKE, at the Middle Temple-Gate in Fleetſtreet. 1716.

ADAM OLEARIUS (ÖLSCHLÄGER) (1603–1671)

12 *Voyages tres curieux & tres renommez, faits en Moscovie, Tartarie, et Perse, par le Sr. Adam Olearius, Bibliothecaire du Duc de Holstein, & Mathematicien de sa Cour ...* 1719

Leiden: Pierre Van der Aa
Bound in brown calf, rebacked, 32.4 × 20.9 cm (closed)
RCIN 1141229

Provenance Acquired by George III for his Windsor Library (WL 12)

Literature Cross 2014b, A4 (English edition)

In 1633, Frederick III, Duke of Holstein (1597–1659) sent an embassy to Russia and Persia, to establish trade links. Amongst those travelling was Adam Olearius, German secretary to the Duke, who was instructed by his master to keep records of the embassy and anything else of interest. In his preface, Olearius notes that he describes the customs and manners of the peoples they met, their religion and government, and the topography of the lands they travelled through, as well as much other valuable ethnographic information. Olearius had the advantage that many previous travellers had not, of being able to speak Russian, so he did not have to rely on interpreters. His work went into several different editions; the present one was preceded by at least 12 previous editions: four German, three French, two English, and three Flemish. The German editions, especially, were illustrated with maps and illustrations that were both beautiful and accurate ('cartes Géographiques & de Figures très-belles & très correctes'). Pierre van der Aa (1659–1733) improved the present edition by careful collation with and correction of previous editions, and added marginal notes to the text to aid navigation, extra articles, and an alphabetical index.[49]

Olearius, being interested in the religious customs of the Russians, recorded the various festivals that he and his colleagues attended, including the procession between the Kremlin and what is now known as St Basil's Cathedral, which recreated Christ's entry into Jerusalem on a donkey on Palm Sunday.[50] At the head of the procession was a willow tree mounted in a carriage, decorated with fruits, and accompanied by six boys singing Hosannas. Behind came church officials, and boyars, followed by the Tsar, Mikhail I (1596–1645), on foot, who led the Patriarch mounted on a white horse, symbolising Christ on the donkey. The Patriarch blessed the huge crowds attending the event (from his vantage point, Olearius could see more than 10,000 people). ES

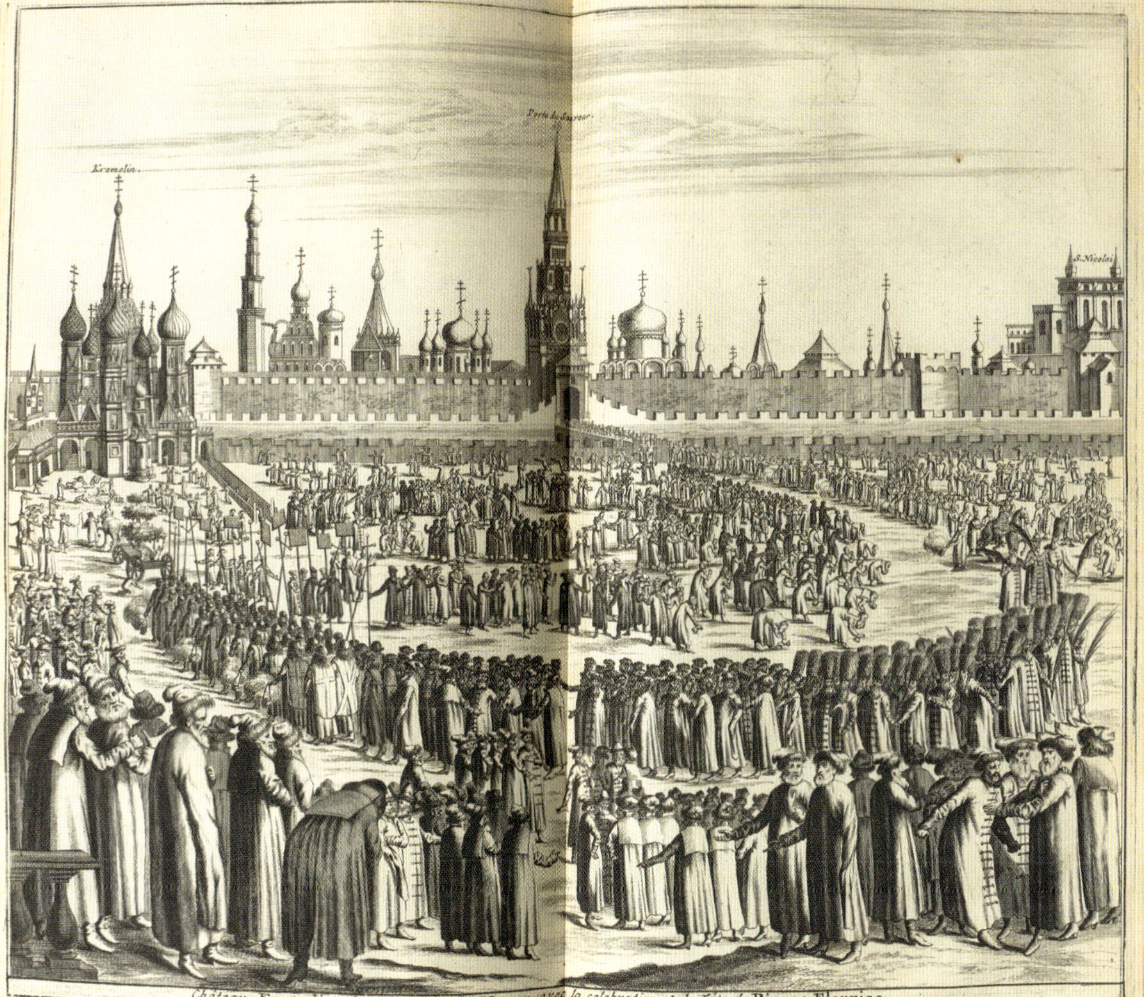

à Leide, chez Pierre vander Aa.

Château Kremelin, *dans la Ville de* Moscou, *avec la celebration de la Fête de* Pâques Fleuries.

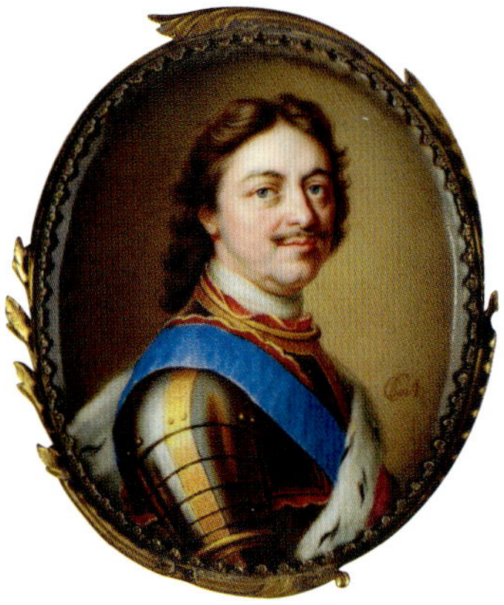 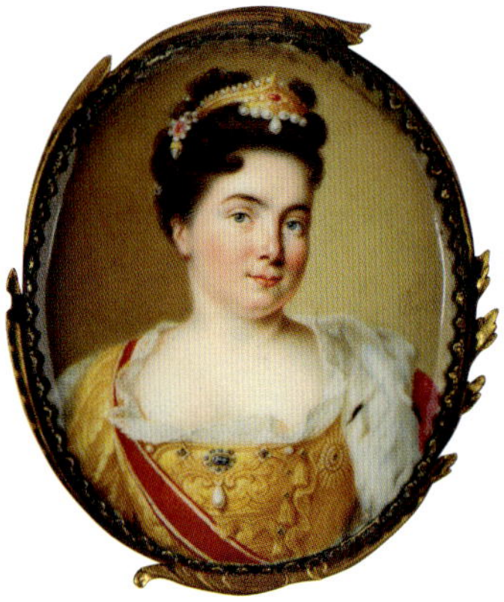

CHARLES BOIT (1662–1727)

13 & 14

Peter the Great (1672–1725) 1717

*Catherine I (1684–1727) c.*1717

Enamel, both 5.7 × 4.8 cm
Signed on the right: *C. Boit* (the 'CB' in monogram)
RCINS 421595 & 421596

Provenance Acquired for George IV when Prince Regent, August 1818, from Rundell, Bridge & Rundell; formerly in the collection of the Margravine of Ansbach

Literature *Great Britain – USSR* 1967, p. 16, nos 50, 51; Reynolds 1999, nos 401, 402

This pair of miniatures by Swedish artist Charles Boit depicts Peter the Great and his second wife, Catherine I. The portrait of Peter belongs to a series of 40 enamels, commissioned by the Tsar on the occasion of his visit to Paris in 1717. The miniature of Catherine commissioned at the same time from Boit, is derived from Jean-Marc Nattier's portrait of the Tsarina painted in Amsterdam in 1715.[51] Boit enjoyed the patronage of Queen Anne (1665–1714) until 1714, when his failure to produce a commissioned allegory of the battle of Blenheim to time led the artist to flee to the Continent or face imprisonment in Marshalsea debtors' prison.

Peter the Great, son of Tsar Alexei Mikhailovich and his second wife, Natalya Naryshkina (1651–94), became Tsar in 1682 after the death of his half-brother Feodor III (1661–82), assuming all powers in 1689 after the deposition of his half-sister, the Regent Sophia (1657–1704). Catherine I succeeded as Empress on her husband's death in 1725.

In this bust-length portrait, the Tsarina is depicted wearing an embroidered gold dress decorated with the red and silver sash of the Order of St Catherine. The Tsar is shown wearing armour, an Imperial Mantle and the sash of the Order of St Andrew. IM

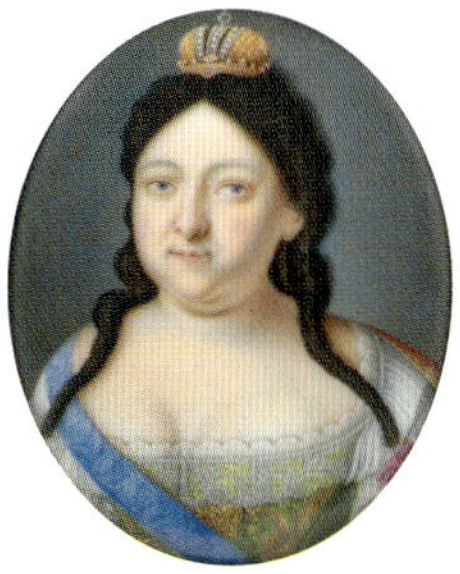

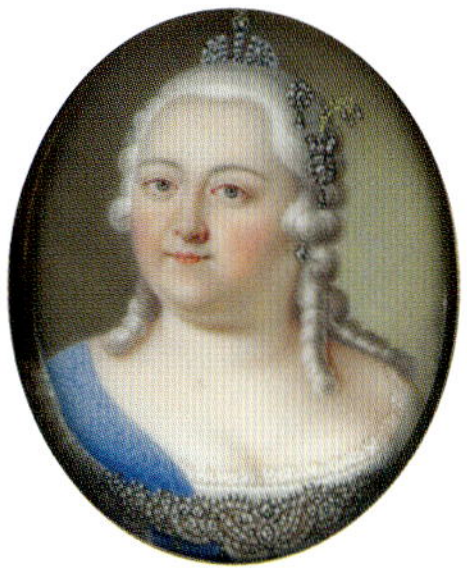

ANON., RUSSIAN SCHOOL, after LOUIS CARAVAQUE (1684–1754)

15 & 16 *Anna Ioannovna, Empress of Russia (1693–1740)* c.1800–1825

Elizabeth Petrovna, Empress of Russia (1709–1762) c.1800–1825

Enamel, 3.9 × 3.0 cm; 3.8 × 3.2 cm
RCINS 421598 & 421597

Provenance Presented to Queen Victoria by the Crown Princess of Prussia, 28 March 1863 (RL 1885, 198 & 197)

Literature Walker 1992, nos 1036, 1037

The image of Anna Ioannovna is after a portrait by Louis Caravaque, official portrait painter to the imperial court. The flat brushwork might indicate that the artist was trained in the icon tradition, rather than being a pupil of the emerging Russian Academy. The Empress is believed to have sat for Caravaque *c.*1730, on her succession to the throne after the death of her cousin, Peter II. She is depicted with the Imperial symbols of the crown and the sash of the Order of St Andrew.

Empress Anna was the daughter of Tsar Ivan V (1666–96), half brother of Peter I, and his wife, Praskovia Saltykova (1664–1723). She ruled as regent of Courland (a province in what is now Western Latvia) from 1711 to 1730, after the death of her husband, Frederick William, Duke of Courland (1692–1711), a mere two weeks after their marriage. She returned to St Petersburg in February 1730, as Peter II had recently succumbed to smallpox with no clear heir. A series of 'Conditions' were presented to the new Empress by Peter II's Privy Council, which she promptly dissolved. Some critics have named her reign 'the Age of Biron', in acknowledgement of her close personal relationship with her German advisor, Ernst Johann Biron (1690–1772), who is suspected of influencing her many 'Westernising' foreign and domestic policies.

The portrait miniature of Empress Elizabeth is also based on a portrait by Caravaque painted at the time of her accession in 1741. Prior to the establishment of the Academy of Arts as an adjunct to the Academy of Sciences in 1724, Caravaque ran an informal school of painting, based in the St Petersburg Post Office.[52] Peter the Great had contracted him 'to teach painting to such persons of the Russian nation as His Majesty shall send to him', this contract was upheld by both Empresses Anna and Elizabeth.[53] One such pupil was Ivan Vishniakov (1699–1761), who produced a very similar portrait of Elizabeth, now in the Tretyakov Gallery, Moscow. Another of Caravaque's pupils, M.A. Lopov (b.1723), produced a signed miniature of 1747, not dissimilar to this work, now in the State Russian Museum, St Petersburg.

Elizabeth Petrovna reigned as Empress of Russia from 1741 to 1762 after a *coup d'état*. Her reign was characterised by her advocacy of pro-Russian domestic policy, and her rejection of many of the German diplomats and artists who had enjoyed the patronage of Anna Ioannovna. **IM**

MOSCOW

17 & 18

Beaker 1733

Silver, gilt interior, 8.8 × 7.3 cm
Impressed with Moscow silver mark, 1733, and maker's mark, *EB*
RCIN 46498

Beaker 1773

Silver, gilt interior, 8.9 × 7.1 cm
Impressed with Moscow silver mark, 1773, and maker's mark, *I.C*
RCIN 46495

Provenance Given to King George V by Lord Rowton, 6 July 1893

Literature KGV 1904, fol. 1

A group of 12 Russian silver beakers was given to the Duke of York (later George V) on his wedding to Princess Mary of Teck in 1893 by Lord Rowton. Montagu William Lowry-Corry, 1st Baron Rowton (1838–1903), was secretary to Disraeli and was involved in the Congress of Berlin in 1878. He later became a member of the Privy Council and a knight of the Royal Victorian Order.

Russian silver beakers, or *stakany*, of this type were produced in huge quantities throughout the eighteenth century, for the nobility and merchants who followed court practice in using these table wares. Like these examples, they were more often than not made in Moscow, where there was a higher concentration of silversmiths and where labour was less expensive.

In spite of the vast numbers surviving today, they are nonetheless interesting for the variety of their decoration, with recurring symbols, emblems and allegorical references, largely derived from the volume, *Symbola et Emblemata*, published under Peter the Great's instruction in Amsterdam, with Russian translations, and compiled by Daniel de la Feuille in 1705. More than 800 engraved vignettes in the publication provided sources for artisans, including silversmiths, who often rendered the imagery inaccurately, thereby leaving out vital details which deprived their decoration of any real meaning.

The embossed decoration on RCIN 46498 features two ovals – one with a vine entwined around a stick with a church behind, the other with two cockerels in front of a trough. RCIN 46495, in the rococo taste, has embossed decoration of scrolls, leaves and cartouches on a matted ground with a gilt interior. **CDEG**

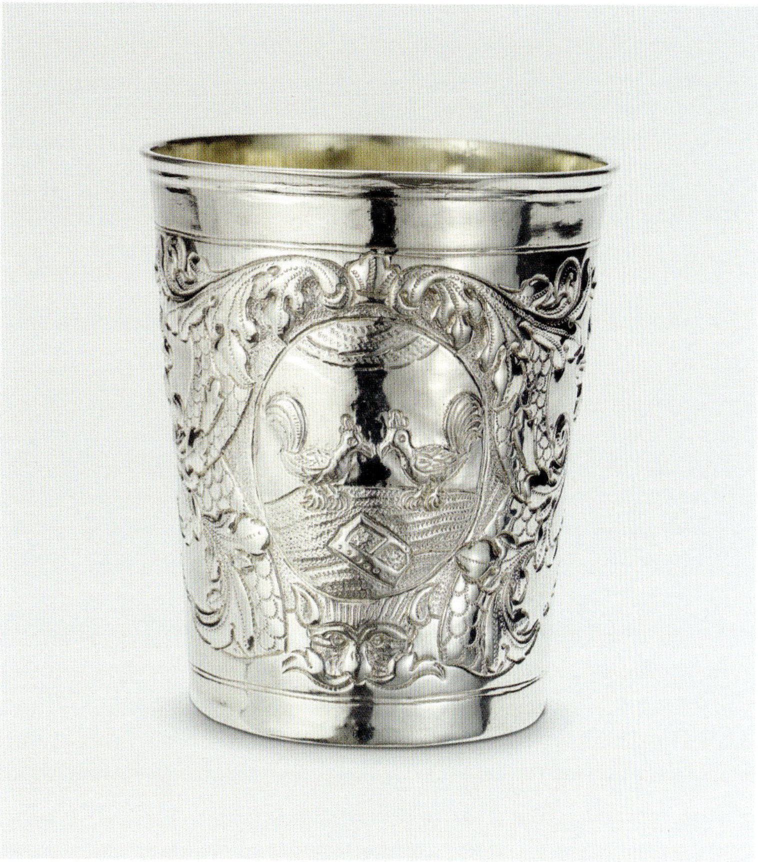

17

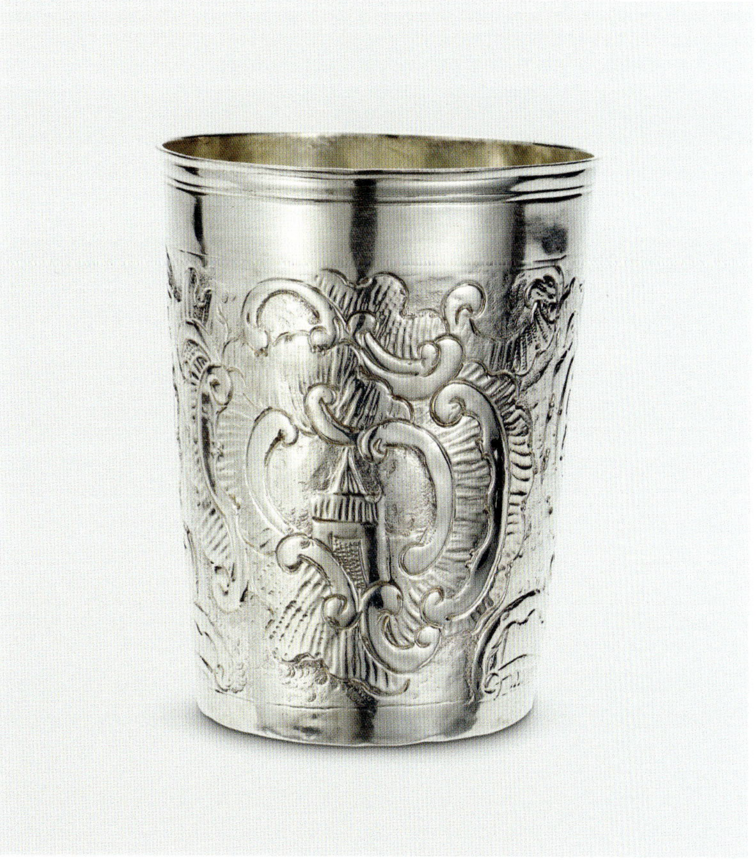

18

MOSCOW

19 *Kovsh* 1737

Silver, parcel gilt, 10.9 × 29.1 × 17.0 cm
Struck with city mark of Moscow, 1737, assay mark, *ЛА*, for Larion Artemiev (active 1734–43), and maker's mark, *G.B.*; inscribed: *БОЖЬЕЙ ВОЛЕЙ / АЛЕКСАНДЕР / ИМПЕРАТОР И / САМОДЕРЖЕЦ / ВСЕЙ РОССИИ / СИМ КОВШЕМ / ПОЖАЛОВАЛ / АТАМАНА / ПАВЛА / СЫНА КРАСНОЩЕКОВА / ЗИМОВОЙ СТАНИЦЫ / ЗА ЕГО ВЕРНЫЕ СЛУЖБЫ / 1805 ГОДА ИЮНЯ 25-ОГО ДНЯ* ('Alexander by the grace of God, Emperor and Autocrat of all Russia, granted this *kovsh* to Pavel, son of Krasnoshchekov, Ataman of the Cossacks' winter quarters, for his loyal services on 25th day of June 1805')
RCIN 46036

Provenance Presented to Pavel Krasnoshchekov, Ataman of the Cossacks, in June 1805, for his services in guarding the imperial residence during the winter of 1804–5; Royal Collection after 1914

According to its inscription, this presentation *kovsh* was given by Alexander I to Pavel Krasnoshchekov in 1804, for his work guarding the imperial residences during the winter of 1804. The *kovsh* was made almost 70 years earlier in Moscow, partly gilt, with the handle cast with a crown and a medallion of an imperial eagle. The bowl is likewise embossed with an imperial eagle, while the peak at the front of the bowl is mounted with a cast imperial eagle. The bowl is engraved with cartouches containing inscriptions with foliate surrounds. It was common practice for gifts to be presented to those in the service of the state of the appropriate rank in the form of objects – snuffboxes, watches, tiepins and brooches – bearing the emblems of the state. This *kovsh* fits into this category of official gift and was appropriate for its recipient according to the Table of Ranks, first instituted by Peter the Great in 1722. Don Cossacks were reputed for their military skill, contributing to the defense and expansion of the Russian Empire, particularly under Catherine II. CDEG

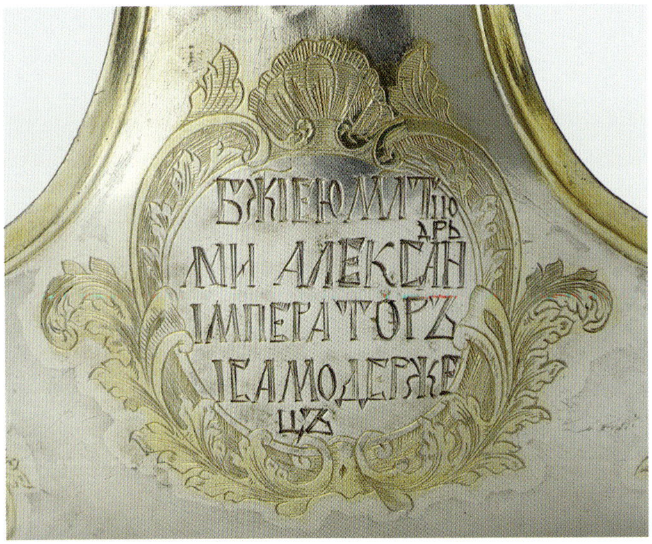

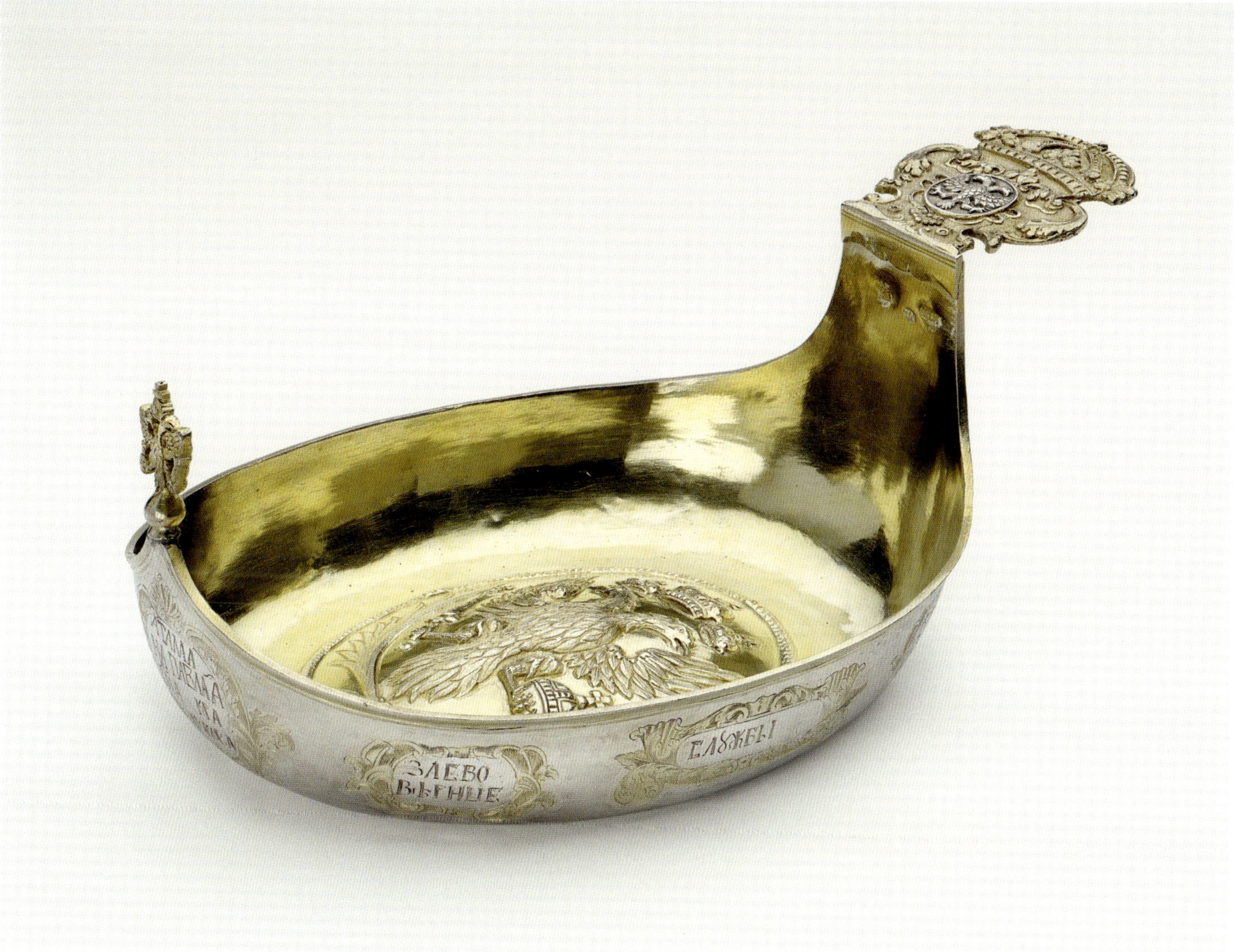
ЗЛЕВО
ВЪРНЦЕ
СЛУЖБЫ

VASILI KUNKIN

20 *Seal box* 1749

Silver, 5.6 × 12.6 × 13.2 cm
Struck with city mark of Moscow (1726–1761), 1749, *AS* (for Anders Zaitsev, 1735–49) and *BK* maker's mark of Vasili Kunkin, label: *Sandringham / Russian AD 1749*
RCIN 46041

Provenance Probably acquired by King Edward VII and / or Queen Alexandra

Literature Jones 2017, no. 252

Peter the Great began the process of granting titles in order to bring fresh blood to the nobility. New patents of nobility were presented in silk- or velvet-covered presentation folders to which were attached, by tasselled cords, boxes of this type in silver or silver gilt, which contained the official imperial wax seal.

This box was made in 1749 and so must relate to an award under Empress Elizabeth, although, like other imperial presentation items, boxes for this purpose were kept in stock and presented when required. The hinged lid is embossed, as all Russian seal boxes are, with the imperial coat of arms of a double-headed eagle holding the orb and sceptre in its talons, St George slaying the dragon portrayed on its breast, encircled by the collar of St Andrew, Russia's highest and oldest order of chivalry. The sides of the box are chased with alternating orbs and imperial crowns suspended from bows and linked by laurel swags. Various examples of seal boxes are known to have been sold after the revolution.[54] The box was kept at Sandringham House and is therefore most likely to be associated with either Edward VII or Queen Alexandra, but the circumstances of its acquisition are not known. CDEG

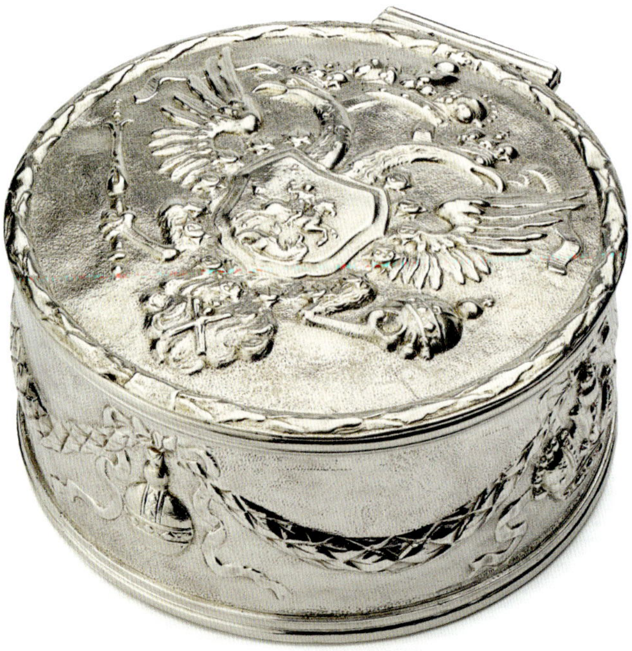

A.J. STRACHAN (*c.*1774–1850);
JACQUES ANTOINE DASSIER (1715–1759), medallist

21 *Snuffbox with portrait medallion of Empress Elizabeth of Russia (1709–1762)* (snuffbox) 1802–3, (medallion) 1754

Gold, 3.3 × 9.8 × 6.2 cm
Struck with the hallmarks for London, 1802–3, and maker's mark, *AJS* (for Alexander Strachan); inscribed on obverse of medallion: *D.G. ELISABETHA.I.IMP.AVTOCR.OMN.ROSS DASSIER*, and on reverse: *NOVA.SIBI.MONVMENTA.PARAVIT ACADEM.MOSQ.INSTIT MDCCLIV*
RCIN 4748

Provenance Purchased by Queen Mary, 1933, and given to King George V, 3 June 1933

Literature GV Boxes 1929–35, IV, no. 352

This richly chased gold box was made by Alexander James Strachan[55] and is designed in the classical style, with foliate scrolls and laurel swags on a chased sable ground. The box has canted corners, and the hinged lid is inset with a hinged laurel-wreath frame (allowing both sides of the medal to be seen) containing a portrait medallion of Empress Elizabeth of Russia by Jacques-Antoine Dassier marking the foundation of Moscow University in 1754. Son of the medallist Jean Dassier (1676–1763), Jacques Antoine was born in Geneva. After early instruction from his father, he went to Paris *c.*1732 to train under the goldsmith Thomas Germain (1673–1748). Following a period assisting his father, in 1740 he moved to London, where he was employed at the Royal Mint. It is notable that this early nineteenth century box should make such a feature of the image of a Russian ruler. **CDEG**

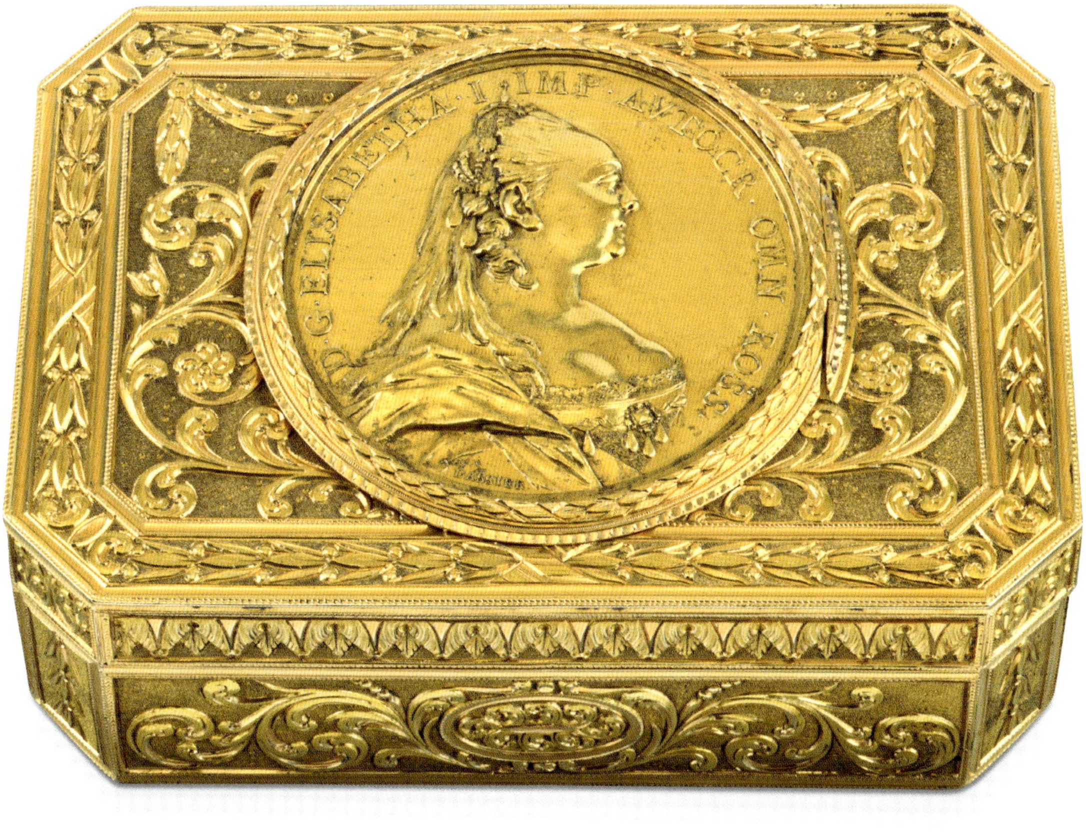

22 *Atlas Russicus mappa una generali et undeviginti specialibus vastissimum Imperium Russicum = Atlas Russien: contenant une carte générale et dixneuf cartes particulières ...* 1745

St Petersburg: Académie Imperiale des Sciences
Half-bound in brown calf, rebacked, 55.0 × 36.1 cm (closed)
RCIN 1046761

Provenance Possibly acquired during the reign of Queen Victoria

Atlas Russicus is the first full atlas of Russia, based on the first national survey of the whole country at a uniform scale for both European (13 maps) and Asiatic Russia (6 maps). It was based on work by Ivan Kirilovich Kirilov (1695–1737), first secretary of the Russian Senate, and Joseph Nicolas de l'Isle (1688–1768), French astronomer and cartographer to Louis XV (1710–74), who had been invited to Russia by Peter the Great to contribute to his grand mapping scheme. Peter's urge to Europeanise Russia also included reaping the benefits of being properly mapped according to European standards. From *c.*1700 he started creating home-grown geodesists (as he called surveyors / cartographers), founding the Moscow Mathematical and Navigational School in 1701, where students aged 12–17 (up to 20 after 1710), studied arithmetic, geometry and trigonometry. In 1715 he set up a geodesic institute within the St Petersburg Naval Academy, to which he invited skilled foreigners to train a new generation of Russians. He soon had his own geodesists ready to be packed off into the field to survey Russian territory and help compile a complete atlas of the Russian Empire. Part of Kirilov's atlas was published in 1734, but he died before he could publish the rest. The new atlas was eventually published in 1745, based on de l'Isle's survey, and maps produced by Peter the Great's geodesists. The atlas usually contains 20 maps, ending with a map of the whole Russian empire (missing from this copy).[56]

The map illustrated here shows the area of St Petersburg and the White Sea region, Russia's route to Europe before she established reliable warm-water routes, and Europe's first trade route to Russia in the sixteenth century. The White Sea was the route first used by English sailors in 1553, under the command of Richard Chancellor (d.1556), who landed in the area of Archangelsk (Archangel), before making contact with Moscow and journeying south to negotiate trading rights for the Muscovy Company. The White Sea had the disadvantage of freezing every winter, and the (slightly) warmer route through the Gulf of Finland (via St Petersburg) only became possible in the early eighteenth century, after Peter the Great's conquest of lands on the southern shores of the Gulf of Finland and the foundation of St Petersburg, which gave Russia better control over this more southern sea route. ES

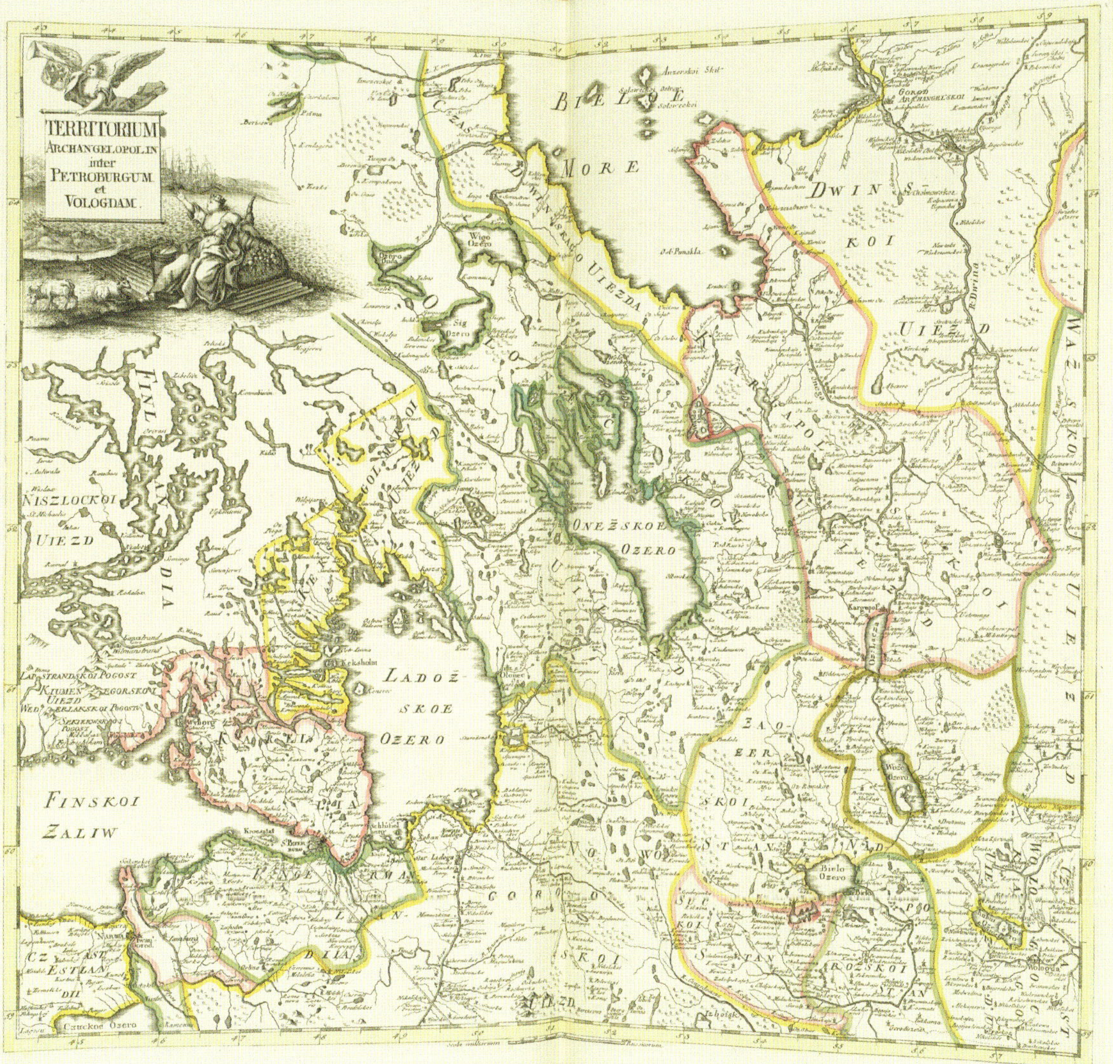
TERRITORIUM
ARCHANGELOPOLIN
inter
PETROBURGUM
et
VOLOGDAM.
BIELOE MORE
DWINSKOI UIEZD
ONEŽSKOE OZERO
LADOŽSKOE OZERO
FINSKOI ZALIW
NISZLOCKOI UIEZD
Bielo Ozero

N° 2

JEAN-BAPTISTE CHAPPE D'AUTEROCHE (1722–1769)

23 *Voyage en Siberie, fait par ordre du roi en 1761: contenant les moeurs, les usages des Russes …* 1768

Paris: Debure
Bound in brown calf, rebacked, 35.2 × 26.5 cm (closed)
Armorial bookstamp of George III on both boards
RCIN 1124459

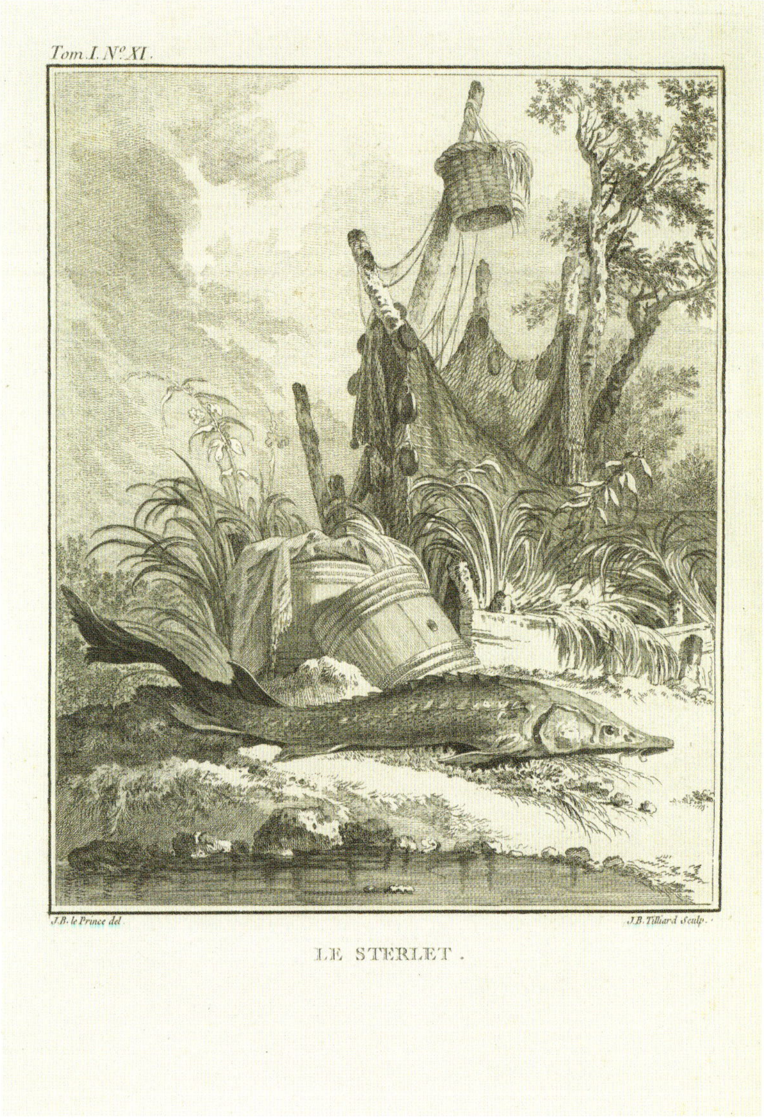

Provenance Acquired by George III for his Windsor Library (WL 56)

Literature Cross 2014b, C27 (English edition)

Chappe d'Auteroche was assistant astronomer at the Royal Observatory in Paris when he was asked to form part of the bevy of astronomers being dispatched to various parts of the globe to observe the transit of Venus in 1761. Recording and measuring the transit accurately was considered a crucial part of the ultimate goal to measure the solar system, and the previous transit had been in 1639. D'Auteroche reached Siberia on 18 May, in time to observe a lunar eclipse, and the transit on 6 June. The weather was fine, so that he was able to observe the entire cycle. He and his party had to be protected by Cossacks while they worked, since the superstitious natives blamed them for the unseasonally high floods, because they were disturbing the sun.

The results were published the following year from St Petersburg, not returning to France until 1763, after which he began working on *Voyage en Siberie*, published in 1768. His account was not complimentary towards the Russians, who, far from being a grand example of Enlightenment reform after Peter the Great's Europeanising work, he criticised as lazy, dishonest and corrupt. This enraged Catherine the Great, particularly as he had received sponsorship from Empress Elizabeth, and the Russian Academy of Sciences had published his results. A pamphlet entitled *Antidote ou Réfutation du mauvais libre superbement imprimé intitulé: Voyage en Siberie*, published in 1770, has been widely attributed to Catherine the Great's authorship. **ES**

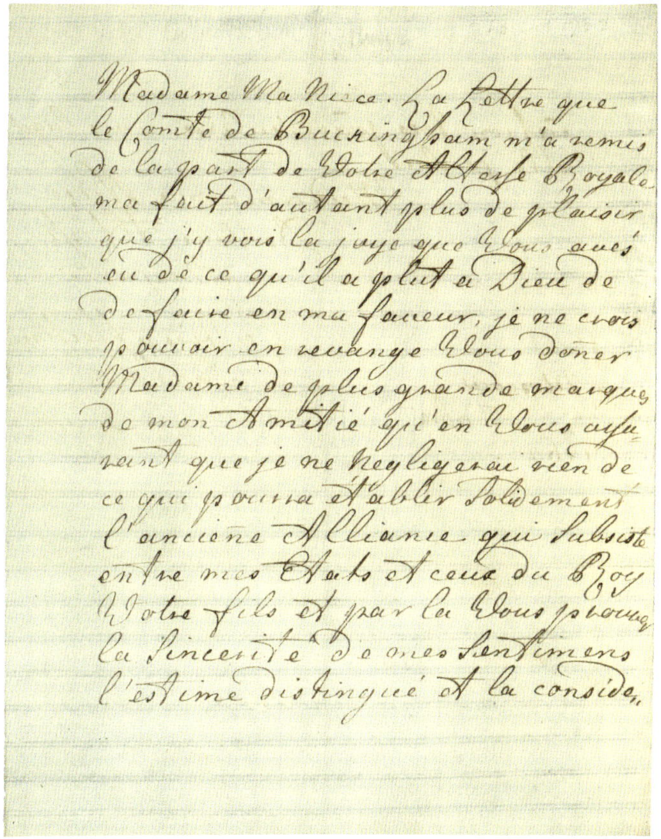

Madame Ma Niece. La Lettre que
le Comte de Buckingham m'a remis
de la part de Votre Altesse Royale
ma fait d'autant plus de plaisir
que j'y vois la joye que Vous avés
eu de ce qu'il a plut a Dieu de
de faire en ma faveur, je ne crois
pouvoir en revange Vous doner
Madame de plus grande marque
de mon Amitié qu'en Vous assu-
rant que je ne negligerai rien de
ce qui pourra établir Solidement
l'ancienne Alliance qui Subsiste
entre mes Etats et ceux du Roy
Votre fils et par la Vous prouver
la Sincerite de mes Sentimens
l'estime distinguée et la conside-

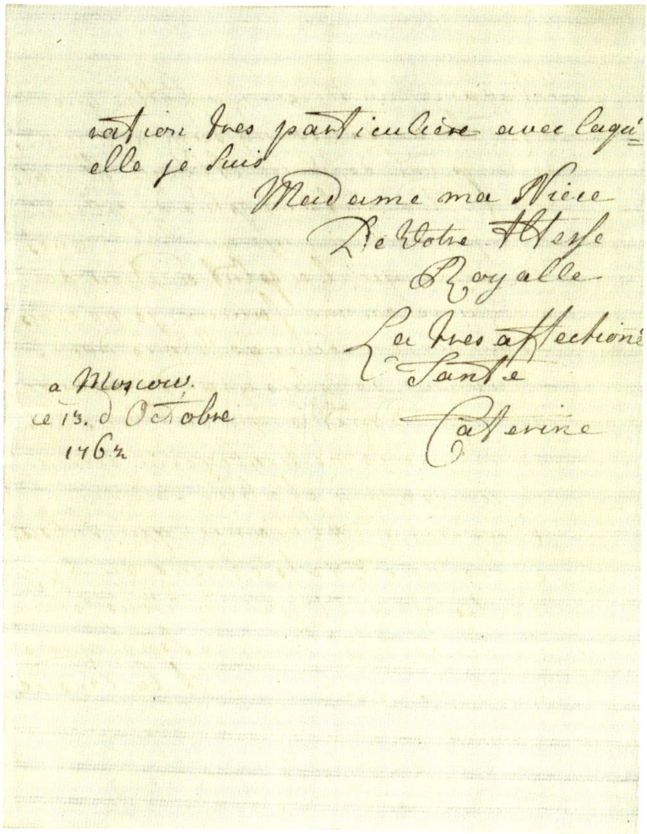

ration tres particuliere avec laque-
lle je suis

Madame ma Niece
De Votre Altesse
Royalle
La tres affectionée
Tante
Catherine

a Moscou
ce 13. d Octobre
1762

EMPRESS CATHERINE II (1729–1796)

24 *Letter to Augusta, Princess of Wales (1719–1792), from Moscow*
13 October 1762

Manuscript, 23.6 × 18.7 cm
RA GEO/MAIN/29

Written by the new Empress to her second cousin, George III's mother, some three weeks after her coronation on 22 September, the Empress, as sovereign, adopted the style of writing to her cousin as her 'niece' and signed the letter as if Augusta's aunt.

The Empress writes thanking the Princess for her letter, presumably one of congratulation on her coronation, which had been delivered by John Hobart, 2nd Earl of Buckinghamshire (1723–93), the British ambassador to Russia. In the letter she thanks God for the actions which have taken place in her favour and seeks to establish the ancient alliance between 'my states' (i.e. Russia) and 'those of your Royal son' (i.e. Great Britain).

Augusta and Catherine shared a great-great-grandfather, Johann VI of Anhalt-Zerbst (1621–67).

SJP

VIGILIUS ERIKSEN (1722–1782)

25 *Catherine II (1729–1796)* c.1765–9

Oil on canvas, 275.9 × 202.2 cm
RCIN 404774

Provenance ?Golitsyn family; presumably a gift to George III or George IV when Prince of Wales; first recorded in the Privy Chamber at Kensington, 1813; removed to Carlton House, 30 November 1813; returned to Kensington Palace by 1818 (Kensington Inventory 1818, no. 97, as by *Levitsky*, presumably Dmitry Levitsky (1735–1822))

Literature Andersen 1965, pp. 57–9; *Great Britain – USSR* 1967, p. 17, no. 55; Andersen 1970, no. 74; Rosenthal 2007, p. 318, no. 7

Painted during Eriksen's 15-year residency in Russia, this image displays all the elements of grand state portraiture. The Empress stands, resplendent, raised on a porphyry dais, commanding attention; this is not just a portrait, but a statement of magnificence and power. The orb and sceptre, symbols of rule, are clearly in her possession (not, as in Kneller's portrait of Peter the Great (cat. 4), part of the background). She wears a robe of silver brocade and imperial mantle emblazoned with the imperial double-headed eagle, and the imperial crown, made especially for the event by the court jeweller, Jérémie Pauzié (1716–79), decorated with over 5,000 diamonds and surmounted by a magnificent spinel of almost 400 carats (fig. 7). Eriksen would have looked to the near-contemporary state portraits by French artists Louis Caravaque and Louis Tocqué (1696–1772), but was probably equally cognizant of Hyacinthe Rigaud's (1659–1743) sumptuous portrait of Louis XIV (1638–1715).[57]

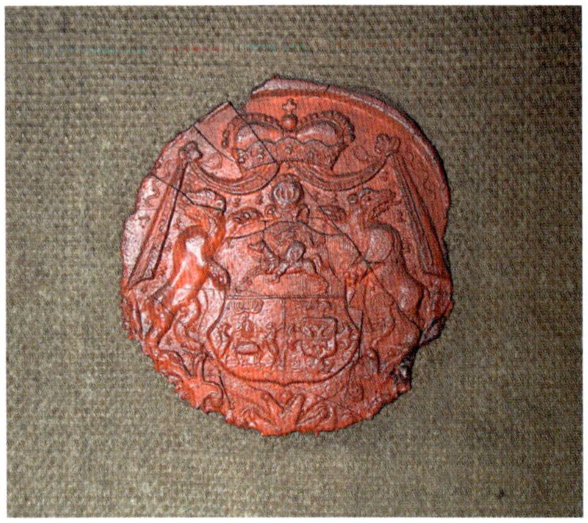

FIG. 6
Golitsyn seal on reverse of the painting

A wax seal on the back of the canvas, recently identified as the coat of arms of a member of the Golitsyn family (fig. 6), has called into question the long-held belief that the painting was a diplomatic gift to George III. The seal would suggest that the painting was at one stage owned by the Golitsyn family. The seal was identified by Richard Redgrave in the late nineteenth century as an imperial eagle, and thought at the time to indicate quality or the Empress's seal of approval. Catherine, ever concerned with her image, carefully monitored any copies of her likeness. Members of the Golitsyn family, one of the most aristocratic and noble houses in Russia, held senior positions at court as ambassadors and advisors, and were amongst Catherine's coterie during her reign.[58]

Answers to questions surrounding the arrival of the portrait have yet to be unearthed, but the painting is first mentioned in Benjamin Jutsham's receipts and deliveries books, which track the movement of paintings from royal residences.[59] Its delivery to the West Ante Room at Carlton House from Kensington Palace on 30 November 1813 suggests that it was relocated by the Prince of Wales to furnish the royal apartments in preparation for Alexander I and his entourage, who arrived on 6 June 1814.

The Danish artist Vigilius Eriksen made the arduous journey to Russia in 1757, disappointed by his prospects in his native land. Having recently been turned down in the first gold medal competition organised by the newly established Art Academy, he felt there were few prospects for him as a portrait painter. An example had been set by fellow artist Louis Tocqué, who had travelled to St Petersburg in 1756. Eriksen must have found favour with the court, as one of his

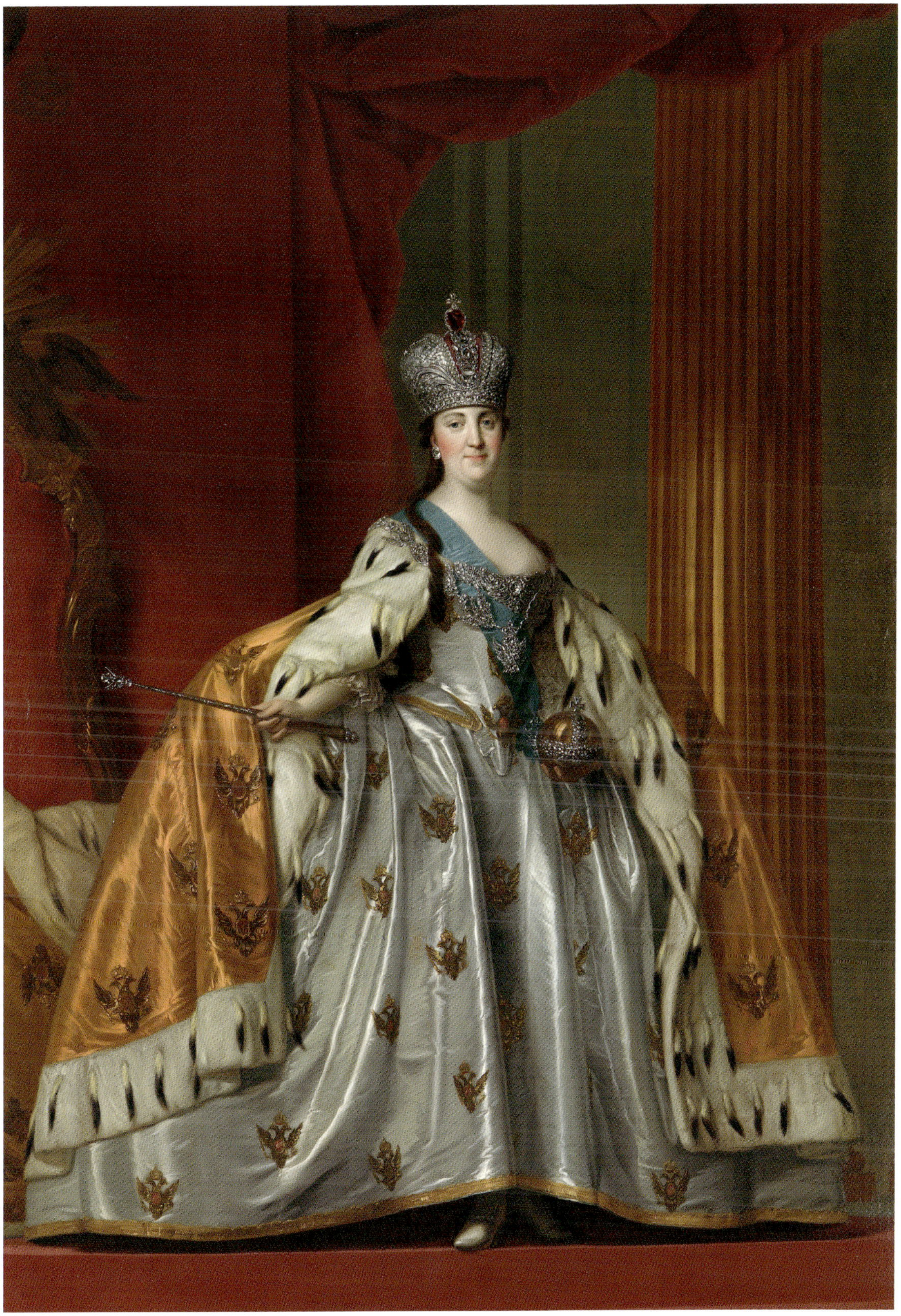

earliest known portraits is of Empress Elizabeth, daughter of Peter I.

This portrait of Catherine II forms part of a trio of 'iconic' images made by Eriksen of the Empress; statements of power and authority that illuminate her reign and her personality. These commissions gave him the opportunity to fulfil his aspiration and demonstrate that 'a portrait painter is just as important at Court as a painter of historical events'.[60] For Catherine, a minor German princess, seen by some as a usurper of the throne, it was critical to be seen as a dominant, powerful ruler. Eriksen travelled to Moscow in connection with this commission, and the coronation picture was delivered to the Academy of Fine Arts on 12 July 1765; a version was sent to Copenhagen two years later, and in 1769 another was sent to Berlin (Sanssouci, Potsdam). **AB**

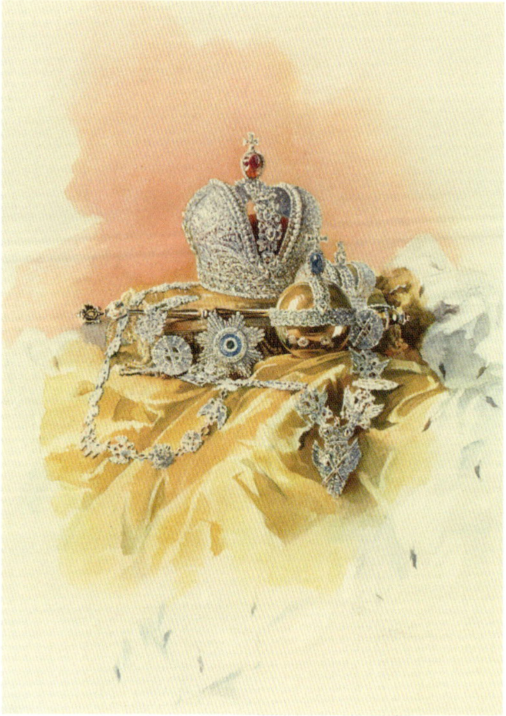

FIG. 7
V.S. Krivenko
Coronation regalia of Emperor Nicholas II, illustrated in *Les Solennités du Saint Couronnement* (1899) (see cat. 208)
44.8 × 34.2 cm
RCIN 1060000

DANIEL WOGE (1717–1797)

26 *Princess Christiana of Mecklenburg-Strelitz (1735–1794)* 1767

Oil on canvas, 215.4 × 175.4 cm
Signed and dated lower left: *D Woge pinxt 1767*
RCIN 402813

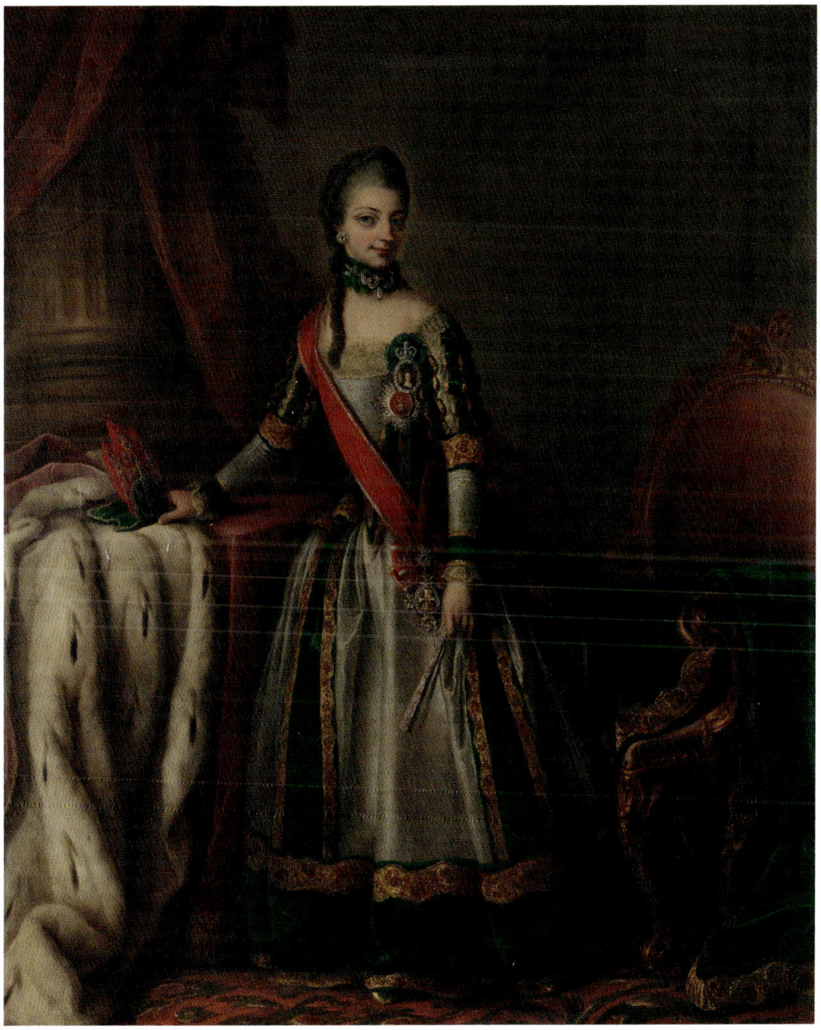

During conservation

Provenance Possibly acquired by Queen Charlotte, late 1760s; first recorded in the Dining Room at Frogmore House 1819

Christiana of Mecklenburg-Strelitz, younger sister of Queen Charlotte (1744–1818), was appointed to the First Class of the Order of St Catherine by Catherine II on 13 January 1766. The Order, founded by Peter the Great in 1714 in honour of his wife, the Empress Catherine (cat. 14), was only awarded to ladies of the highest distinction in Europe. Woge trained in Berlin under Antoine Pesne (1683–1757) and was later court painter to Adolphus Frederick IV of Mecklenburg-Strelitz (1738–94).

The sitter is depicted wearing the splendid green velvet and gold brocade costume of the Order, and the portrait may have been sent to her sister as a gift to mark her membership. She wears the sash over her right shoulder, with the badge, richly decorated with diamonds, attached at the base; the star of the order is pinned at her left breast, with a crowned portrait miniature of Queen Charlotte, in the style of a royal family order above.

The almond-shaped eyes of the sitter are a possible indication of a thyroid condition such as Graves' disease, which enlarges the eyeball. **AB**

IVAN PERMACK (PERMYAK) (active 1740–1750)

27 *Pair of flintlock pistols* mid-eighteenth century

Iron, steel, gold, silver, walnut, horn, length 48.9 cm, weight 1.03 kg, calibre 14 mm
Breech ends of barrels overlaid in gold, *St Petersbourg*, and stamped on underside with crowned or cusped *P*; locks signed: *Ivan Permack*; silver mounts unmarked
RCIN 37874.1–2

Provenance Probably acquired by King Edward VII, Sandringham House, late nineteenth century

Literature Purdon-Clarke 1910, nos 610, 614

This pair of flintlock pistols are richly decorated with walnut wood stocks, silver mounts and pattern-welded barrels. The stocks[61] are possibly Circassian walnut *juglans regia*, this area being renowned for finely coloured walnut.[62] The barrels are finely pattern-welded, fluted and faceted octagonal to hexadecagonal, demonstrating both high craftsmanship and technical skill. *Permack* (signed on the locks) may be an English version of Permyak or Permyakov. From 1757, Permyak was responsible for guns used by Empress Elizabeth, and held the position of gunmaker at the Hunting Department. In 1775 he became keeper of the Imperial Rustkammer.[63] Other firearms by Permyak, including a sporting rifle, are in the collection of the Kremlin Museums, Moscow.[64] **SDM**

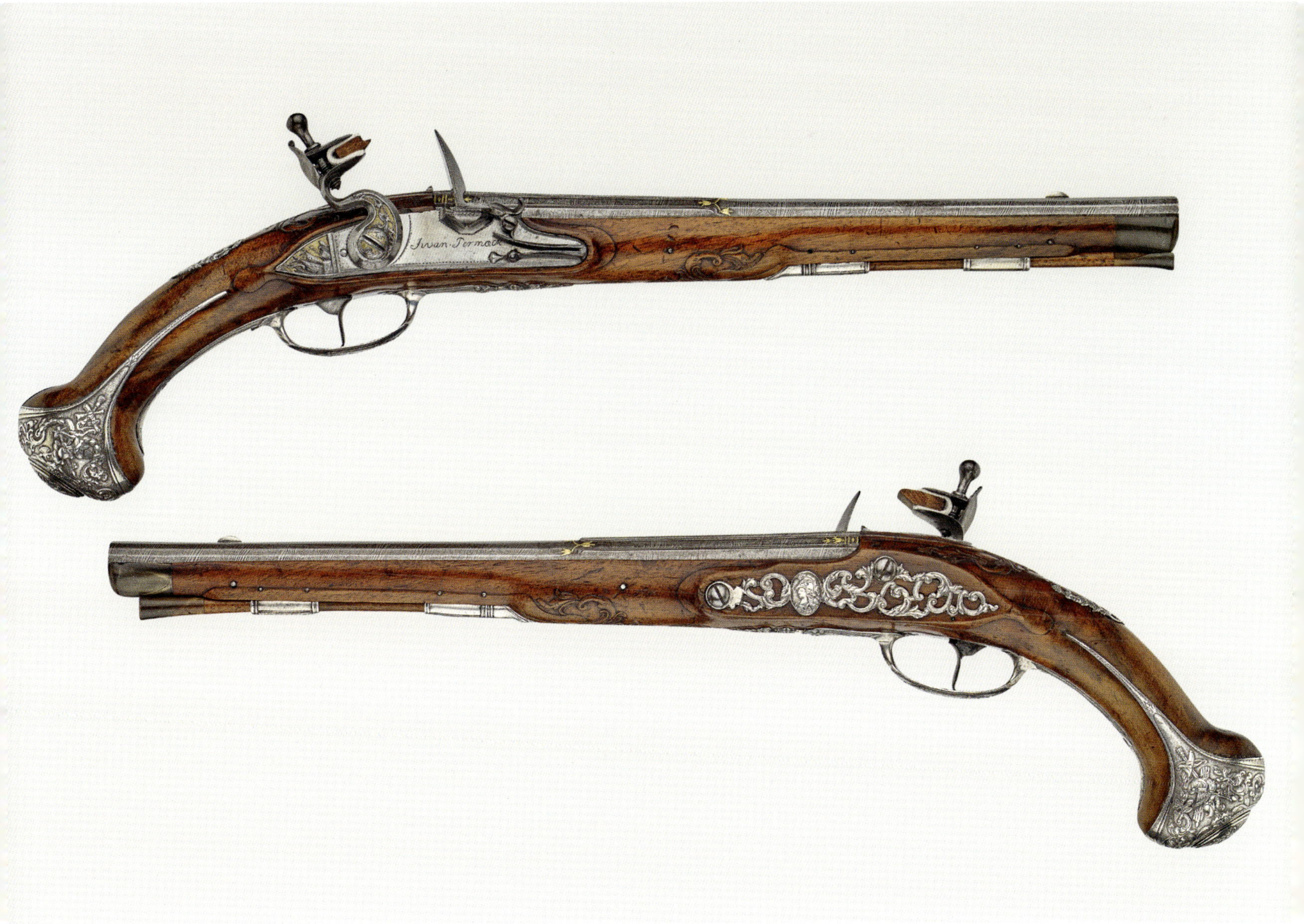

MIKHAIL SHIBANOV (active 1772–1789)

28 *Catherine II, Empress of Russia (1729–1796)* 1787–9

Oil on canvas, 72.3 × 56.8 cm
RCIN 400964

Provenance Sold by Thomas Agnew & Sons, London, 25 October 1901 (as Lampi / Drouais), where purchased by Grand Duke Paul Alexandrovich; hung firstly at his residence in Boulogne-sur-Seine, Paris, and later at Tsarskoe Selo;[65] purchased by Queen Mary, from the sale of the effects of the Grand Duke's second wife, Princess Olga Paley, Christie's, London, 21 June 1929, lot 46

Literature *Great Britain – USSR* 1967, p. 18, no. 60

From January to July 1787, Empress Catherine travelled by carriage to the Crimea to undertake an inspection of newly acquired lands as a result of wars against the Ottoman Empire. The visit was masterminded by her favourite, the military statesman Prince Grigory Potemkin (1739–91), and the portrait is said to have been painted in Kiev, by the serf artist Mikhail Shibanov, then in the service of Potemkin. The journey of about 750 miles would have been arduous and tiring, and this is reflected in the expression of resilience and fatigue in the sitter's eyes. It is a far more intimate and informal portrait than Vigilius Eriksen's staged, majestic state portrait of over 20 years earlier (cat. 25). The Empress's dress has always been described as her 'travelling costume'; indications of her status and military authority lie solely in the orders embroidered on her costume, the stars of the Orders of St Andrew, St George and St Vladimir, and in the cut and detailing of her jacket. Her fur-trimmed hat, seemingly anachronistic, appears to have been fashionable at the time.[66] Miniatures, after the painting by Petr Zharkov (1742–1803), were commissioned by the Empress to be distributed to each member of the Diplomatic Corps who accompanied her progress.[67] A near-contemporary engraving by James Walker, then resident in Russia, employed as engraver to the Empress, was published in St Petersburg and London in 1789 (see fig. 8). A version of the painting is in the State Russian Museum, and a number of copies exist of this enigmatic image.[68]

Acquired by Queen Mary in 1929 from the collection of the widow of Grand Duke Paul Alexandrovich (1860–1919), youngest child of Alexander II, the portrait hung in his residence in Paris, which he shared with his second wife, Princess Olga Paley (1865–1929) during their exile. Before that, its provenance is less certain. An inscription and label on the reverse of the painting suggest it once hung in the 'Gallery Mamonov', which may connect the painting to Catherine's then lover, 'red-coat' Count Alexander Matveyevich Dmitriev-Mamonov (1758–1803). Mamonov, a protégé of Potemkin, was asked by Catherine to accompany her to the Crimea, and was also immortalised by Shibanov, *c.*1786–8.[69] Within a catalogue of *British Mezzotint Portraits*, published in 1884, detailing all of Walker's Russian prints, is listed a print of Catherine after Shibanov, with the following description (in French): 'The original is to be found in the collection of Monsieur General Mamonoff to whom, with the greatest respect, this plate is dedicated'.[70] This dedication adds weight to the theory that the painting once belonged to Catherine's then lover.

Shibanov is said to have first belonged to Admiral Grigory Spiridov (1713–90), although he was later sold to Prince Potemkin. He studied in St Petersburg from 1772 to 1777, possibly under Levitsky. His modest oeuvre includes rural genre scenes as well as portraits of peasants, which were highly unusual at this time. Opinion seems divided as to whether the Empress actually sat to the artist: Blakesley states that the portrait was not painted 'from life', whilst Walker's recollections, published anonymously in London in 1821 as *Paramythia, or, Mental Pastimes* [...] state that Shibanov had to be locked 'up in a room to keep him from spirits, during the time her majesty was sitting', which, albeit a colourful anecdote, may be evidence of a meeting.[71] It is hard to believe that such a poignant and searching portrait of the ageing Empress could be produced without a sitting. **AB**

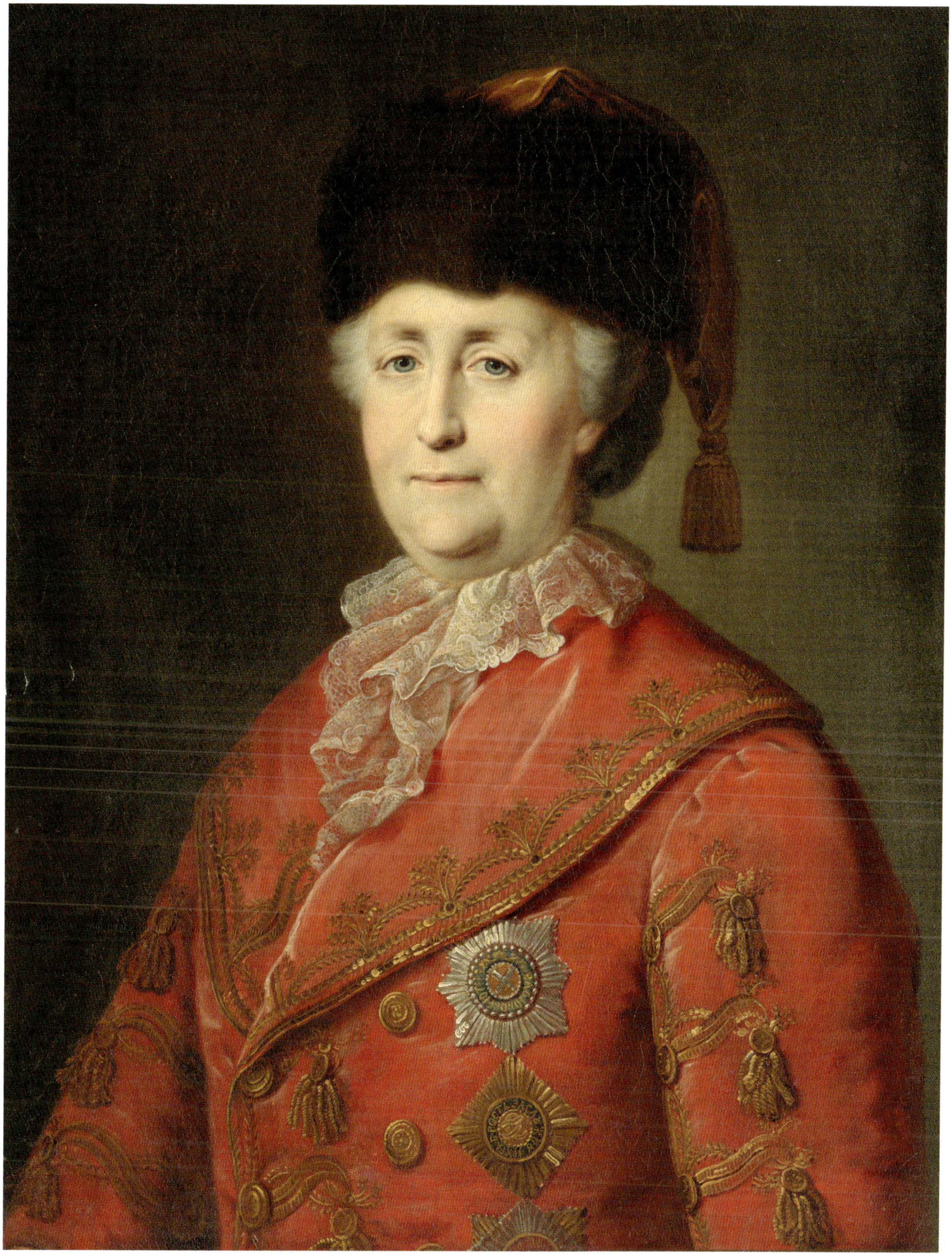

During conservation

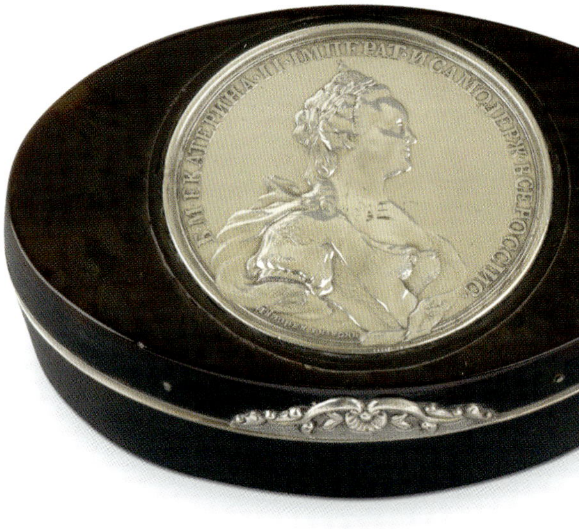

RUSSIAN

29 ***Snuffbox with portrait medal from the reign of Empress Catherine II (1729–1796)*** late eighteenth century

Tortoiseshell, silver, 4.0 × 11.7 × 7.8 cm
Medal inscribed: *Б.М.ЕКАТЕРИНА.II.IМРЕРАТ.И.САМОДЕРЖ.ВСЕ РОССIИС.* and *ТIМОѲЕИ IВАНОВЪ*
RCIN 3738

Provenance Acquired by King George V, 1929–35

Literature GV Boxes 1929–35, v, no. 380

The practice of mounting numismatics in European art dates back to ancient Rome. In the eighteenth and nineteenth centuries, a wider variety of works of art made in St Petersburg and Moscow were set with ancient and modern coins and medals, including jewellery, *kovshi*, cups, chalices, tankards and boxes. In this example the lid is set with a portrait of Empress Catherine by Timofey Ivanov (1729–1803).

The eighteenth-century vogue for taking snuff promoted the widespread production of small containers. The most practical ones were oval so that they were comfortable to hold and slipped easily into a pocket. **CDEG**

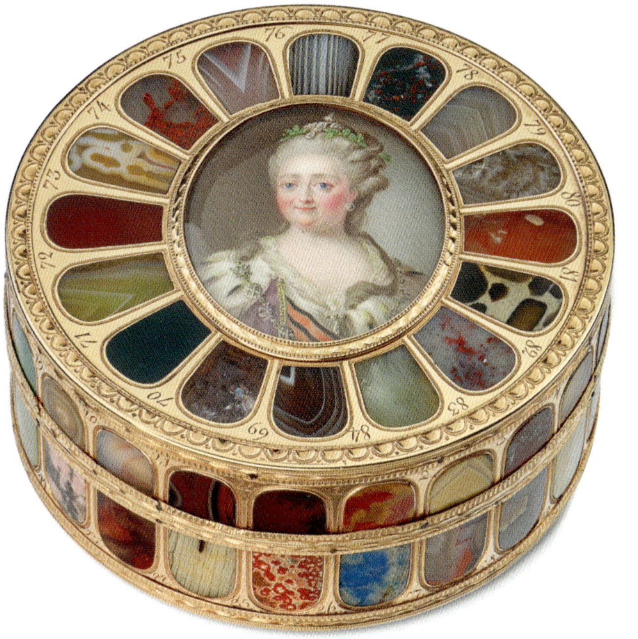

GERMAN

30 *Snuffbox with miniature of Empress Catherine II (1729–1796)* late eighteenth century

Gold, semi-precious stones, enamel, painted miniature on ivory, 3.3 × 7.2 cm
Label in Queen Mary's handwriting: *Catherine Mickaelovna / to her husband George Duke / of Mecklenburg Strelitz 1863*, and on the back: *To the King from the Queen Xmas 1931*; mount adjacent to each mineral specimen engraved with a number
RCIN 19122

Provenance Presented by Catherine Mikhailovna to her husband, George, Duke of Mecklenburg-Strelitz, 1863; given by Queen Mary to King George V, Christmas 1931

Literature GV Boxes 1929–35, III, no. 238; Walker 1992, no. 714; Kostyuk 2010, pp. 186–7

Collecting minerals became a fashionable pastime in the late eighteenth century and this was reflected in a new method of decorating snuffboxes, which were called 'cabinets of stones'. The first such boxes decorated with small samples of different minerals of various colours were made by Johann Christian Neuber (1736–1808) and came from Saxony. An example in the collection of the Hermitage by Neuber has a similar design to this box, with each sample of stone marked by a number engraved in the adjacent gold mount, as on this example.[72] It also contains a small booklet with a handwritten specification of each of the stones. No such document survives with this box and the maker is unknown. The miniature is a copy of one of the numerous portraits of Catherine II by Dmitry Levitsky, painted from 1783.

According to a note in Queen Mary's handwriting, this box was formerly in the ownership of George, Duke of Mecklenburg-Strelitz (1824–76) – husband of Grand Duchess Catherine Mikhailovna of Russia (1827–94), third daughter of Grand Duke Michael Pavlovich, youngest son of Emperor Paul I – who presented it to her husband in 1863. Queen Mary, in turn, gave it to King George V for Christmas in 1931.
CDEG

JAMES TASSIE (1735–1799)

31–33 *Three medallions with profile portraits of Emperor Paul I (1754–1801), Empress Catherine II (1729–1796) and Empress Maria Feodorovna (1759–1828)* c.1780

Porcelain, gilt metal, (RCIN 39436) 7.7 × 5.5 × 1.5 cm, (RCIN 39437) 7.7 × 5.2 × 1.3 cm, (RCIN 39441) 8.2 × 5.9 × 1.5 cm
(RCIN 39436) Impressed mark: *MAR. T*; printed label: *G.W. BOSWORTH BUXTON 48C*; (RCIN 39437) impressed mark: *MARIA.F.21 APR.1780*; printed label: *G.W. BOSWORTH BUXTON. A.* (RCIN 39441) impressed mark: *LERCI*; printed label: *G.W. BOSWORTH BUXTON 48B*
RCINS 39436, 39437, 39441

Provenance G.W. Bosworth, Buxton; purchased by Queen Mary, Sotheby's, London, 25 November 1947, lot 32

These three portraits of members of the Russian imperial family were purchased by Queen Mary as a framed group of six medallions. Of this group, the portraits of Catherine II and of Emperor Paul were modelled by Maria Feodorovna (Paul's wife) and are signed by her.

A talented amateur artist, Maria Feodorovna studied with Karl Leberecht (?1755–1827), a medallist and gem cutter whom Paul I appointed chief medallist at the court and director of the mint. Maria's subjects were generally members of the imperial family, including her ten children. A drawing of Maria's portrait of Catherine the Great as Minerva, the ancient Roman goddess of wisdom, served as a model for an engraving which was probably the guide for Tassie (fig. 8).[73] The same image of Catherine was struck as a medal at the time of her coronation in 1762. A further version of this image is in the Royal Collection, carved from ivory on a stone medallion.[74]

This connection between Catherine and Minerva stemmed from a carefully orchestrated series of allegories that not only alluded to the virtues and strengths of the ruler, but were also intended to legitimise her power after the political coup and assassination of her husband, Peter III (1728–62). The androgynous image of Minerva fused the belligerent aspects of Catherine's rule on which her authority rested with the classical virtues of reason and wisdom, whilst simultaneously bolstering her status as an enlightened ruler. CDEG

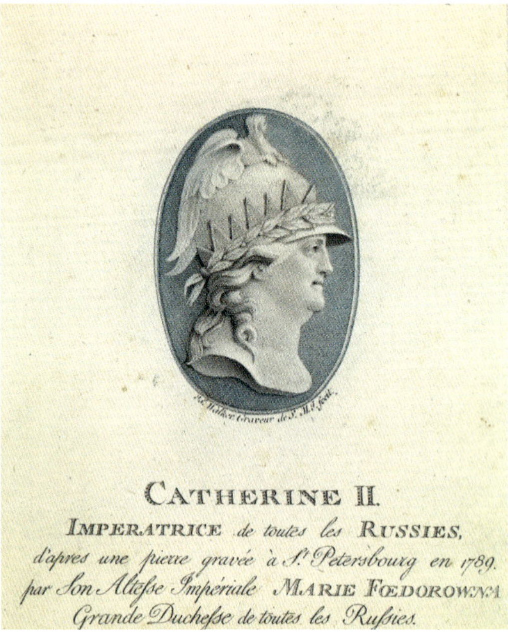

FIG. 8
After Empress Maria Feodorovna of Russia, engraver James Walker
Catherine II, Empress of Russia, c.1789
Print, 12.9 × 10.7 cm
RCIN 614351

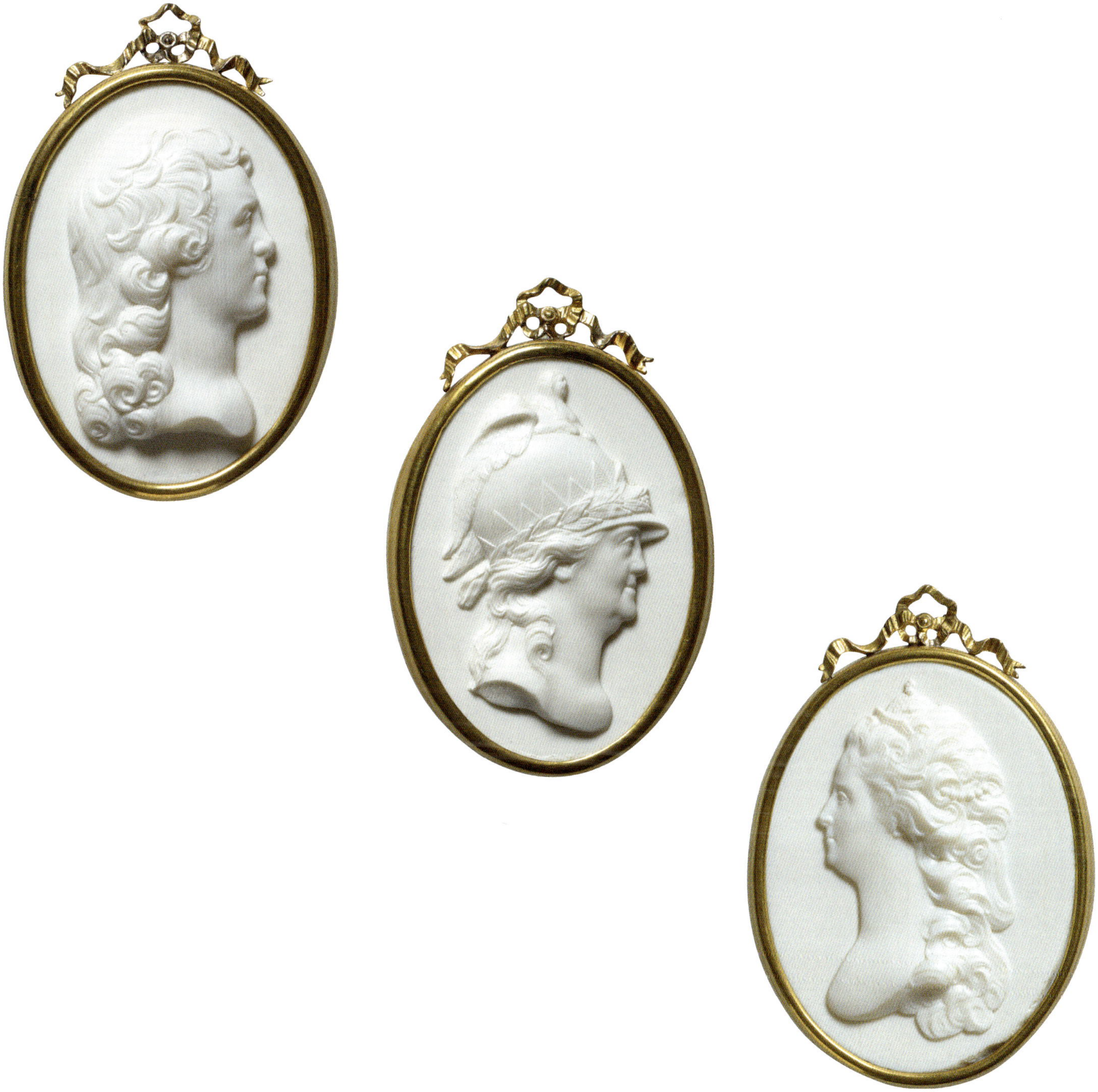

JOSIAH WEDGWOOD (& SONS), ETRURIA

34 *Medallion with profile portraits of Alexander I (1777–1825) and Grand Duke Constantine (1779–1831) as children* late eighteenth century

Jasperware, giltwood, 9.8 × 8.5 × 2.5 cm
RCIN 45774

Provenance Grand Duchess Xenia, 1929; by whom given to King George V, 1929

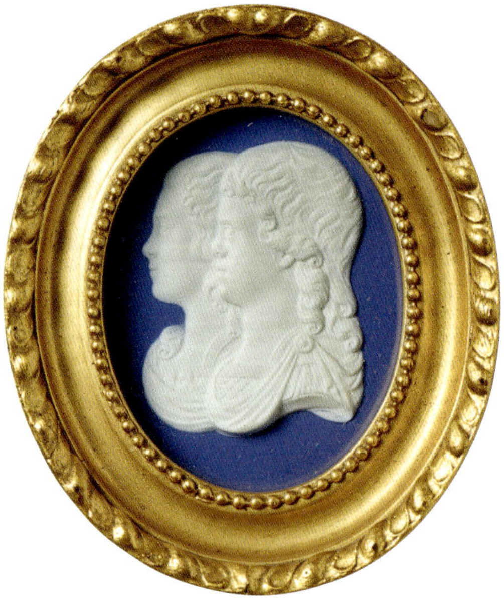

The exact provenance of this jasperware Wedgwood medallion is not known, but it was given to King George V for the Royal Collection by his cousin Grand Duchess Xenia (1875–1960), in 1929 and is likely to have been among a group of personal possessions formerly in the ownership of the imperial family, which were sent by her to George V. The invention of jasperware in 1774 by Josiah Wedgwood (1730–95) is recognised as one of his most important contributions to the development of ceramics. Jasper, a white stoneware that can be stained in a variety of colours, was well-suited to neoclassical ornament in the form of relief decoration, as seen in this medallion, which imitates antique and Renaissance cameos with the profile portraits of the two sons of Emperor Paul I. Later profile portraits of members of the Russian imperial family produced in jasperware by Wedgwood in the late nineteenth century include those of Nicholas II and Alexandra Feodorovna.[75]

Catherine II was the first Russian ruler to patronise the Wedgwood firm, and Charles Cameron used Wedgwood plaques in the bedroom and boudoir he designed for her at Tsarskoe Selo. In 1773 she commissioned from Wedgwood, via Alexander Baxter, British consul of Russia, an earthenware service decorated with views of Great Britain which became known as the Green Frog Service. CDEG

MALTSOV GLASS FACTORY

35 *Decanter* 1793

Glass, 17.3 × 11.7 × 9.8 cm
Engraved on front and back of decanter, and on lid, with crowned imperial eagle; engraved on front with *1793* and *ЄII* cipher
RCIN 3703

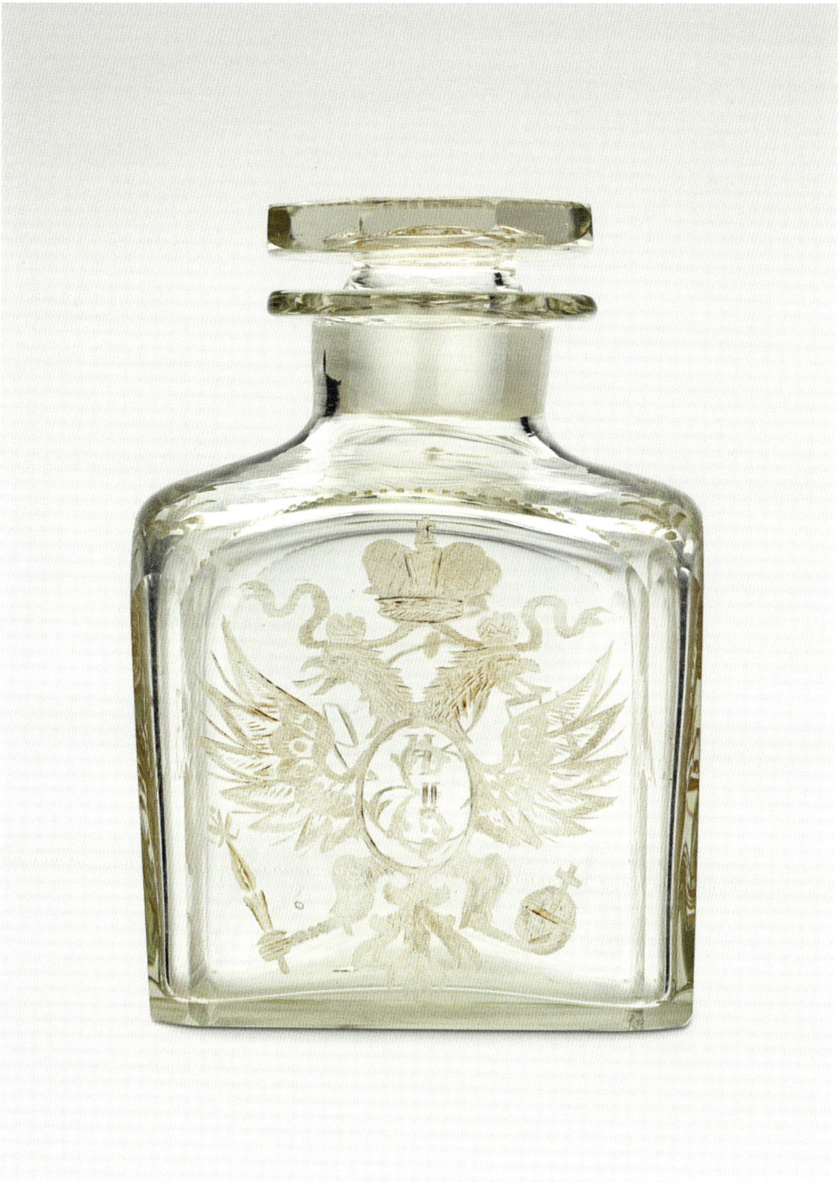

Provenance Probably acquired by Queen Mary; date of acquisition unknown

Literature Taylor 1988

The body of the decanter is engraved with the crowned double-headed eagle and on its breast the cipher of Catherine the Great, while on the reverse is the date 1793 and the repeated crowned cipher of the Empress. The style and embellishment of this decanter replicate earlier models produced during the reign of Empress Elizabeth (r. 1741–62). Many glassware services were produced for lavish court entertaining during the reigns of both Empress Elizabeth and Catherine the Great. These had originally been produced by state-owned glasshouses in Moscow, but these were closed by Peter the Great when he moved the Russian capital to St Petersburg in 1712. A new factory, administered by the Crown, was founded in St Petersburg in 1730 and became known as the Imperial Glass Manufactory. This government-owned factory was not the only source of glassware in the eighteenth century, however, and one of the best-known private factories was Maltsov, which was founded near Moscow and moved further east *c.*1756. Maltsov tended to cater for a more popular taste than the state-run factory by making cheaper vessels, such as this decanter, engraved with imperial motifs.
CDEG

ATTRIBUTED TO JOHAN FREDERICK KÖPPING (1718–1783)

36 *Coffee pot* 1780

Silver gilt, wood, 20.6 × 17.8 × 11.8 cm
Silver marks for St Petersburg, 1780, assayer's mark of Evgraf Borovshchikov, fineness mark 73, E.6;
Engraved: *No 2; obpa*; Label in Queen Mary's handwriting: *An 8½" silver-gilt jug St Petersburg AD 1780 Belonged to Empress Catherine Purchased 1933 Queen Mary's Book, Folio 40*
RCIN 49702

Provenance Possibly belonged to Empress Catherine II; purchased by Queen Mary, 1933

Literature QMB, I, fol. 40; Odom 2011, pp. 60–62

Queen Mary's interest in Russian decorative art, particularly pieces with provenance associated with past Russian rulers, no doubt encouraged her to purchase this silver-gilt coffee pot in 1933, which, according to a label inside the pot, belonged to Empress Catherine II of Russia. The design relates closely to an earlier example made for Empress Anna by Nikolai Dom (or Dohm; active 1714–48) in St Petersburg in 1735.[76] Dom was of French and German origin and is one of the first recorded foreign silversmiths in St Petersburg.

Dom's coffee pot was copied by Johan Frederick Köpping, the son of a Swedish goldsmith. Johan Frederick was apprenticed to his father, Claus Jacob Köpping, in 1718 and continued to work for him in St Petersburg until 1748. Köpping worked for the imperial court from 1750 until 1782, and from 1764 he was Court Keeper of Plate. Among other commissions, he created additional plate to supplement a service by Thomas Germain in Catherine II's collection. As Keeper, Köpping would certainly have had access to the coffee pot belonging to Empress Anna.

Köpping's coffee pot is slightly shorter than the Hillwood prototype and has a taller lid and more simply formed wooden handle, but the treatment of the metal, with a plain body chased with foliate and trellis patterns in cartouches beneath the lid and over the spout, together with the chased decoration of the lower body of alternating straps and acanthus leaves, is clearly derivative of the earlier example, and in both cases shows the direct influence of European silver of the same period. The body is engraved with an imperial eagle. CDEG

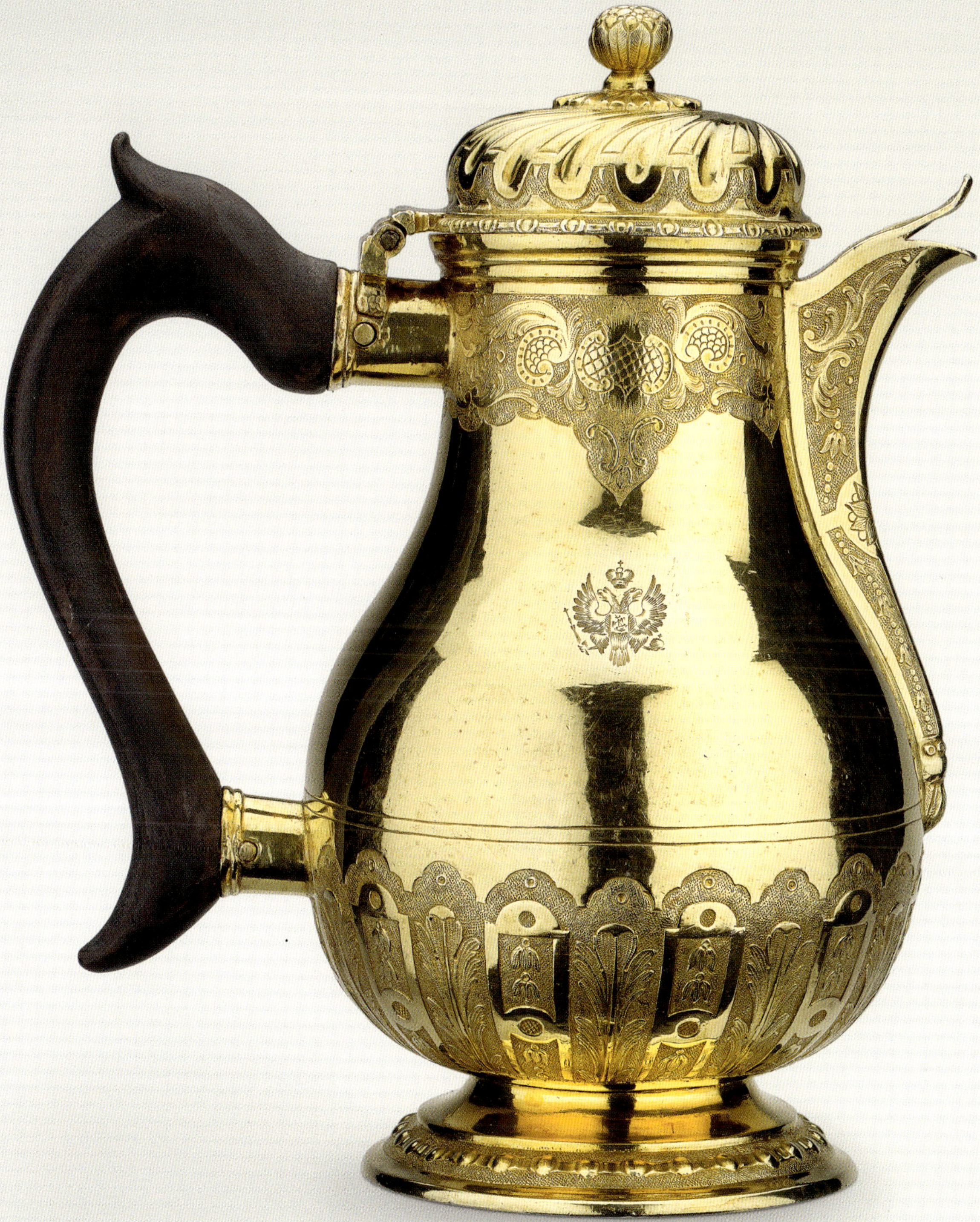

IMPERIAL PORCELAIN FACTORY

37 *The Cameo Service* 1855–82

Dinner plate and soup plate, hard-paste porcelain, gilt, (dinner plate) 3.3 × 27.0 cm, (soup plate) 4.5 × 26.8 cm
Underglaze stamp in blue: crowned *HI*; painted in gilt: *HC*
RCINS 58640, 58641

Provenance Given to King George V and Queen Mary on the occasion of their Silver Jubilee, 6 May 1935, by Sir Harold and Lady Zia Wernher

Literature Hermitage Amsterdam 2014

In 1776, Prince Ivan Sergeevich Baryatinsky (1740–1811), the Russian ambassador to Versailles, received instructions from Catherine II to oversee the commission of a service that was modelled with ancient cameos. This vast service of approximately 800 pieces was made at the Sèvres porcelain factory, with enormous technical difficulty – new moulds had to be made to create the requested shapes and each piece required up to eight firings. The Cameo Service was the most expensive created at the factory in the eighteenth century. It would have been used by Catherine for state functions and, when not in use, may have been displayed on a table.

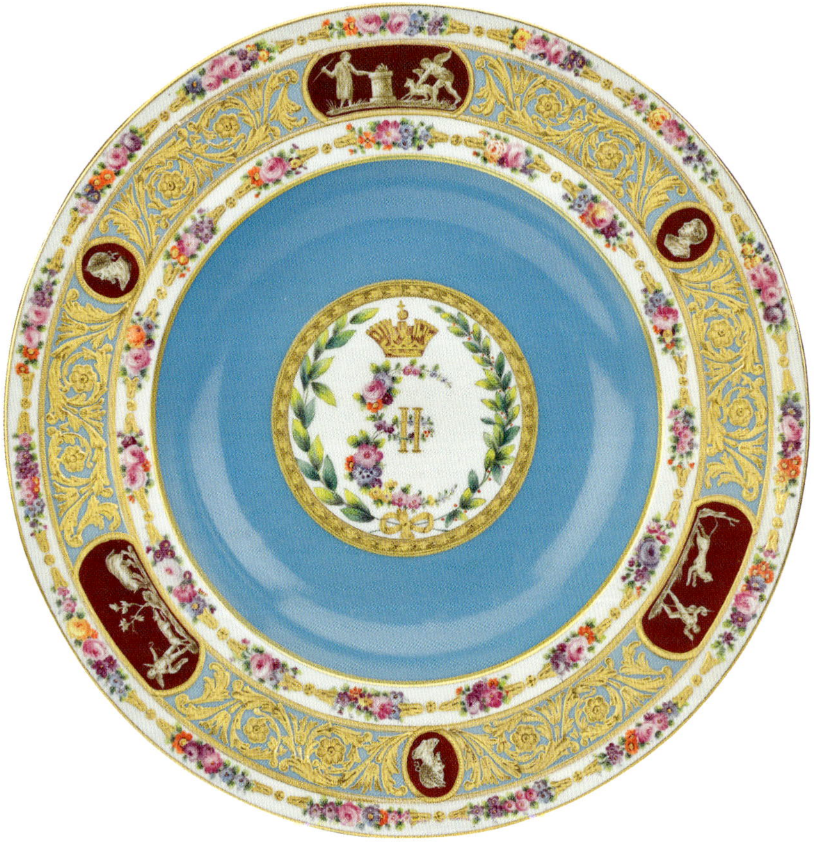

The service remained in the Winter Palace until December 1837, when several pieces were looted during a fire, later to appear in London, where, in 1840, the dealers Storr and Mortimer sold several pieces to the future 2nd Earl of Lonsdale (1787–1872). In 1856–7, the 4th Marquess of Hertford (1800–1870) bought many pieces of the service from Lonsdale and sold most of them back to Alexander II, but he kept six pieces for himself.[77] Some of the unsold Lonsdale pieces were offered in the Goode sale of 1895.[78]

Replacement pieces for the service were ordered from the Imperial Porcelain Factory by Nicholas I in 1840 and 1851, and by Alexander III (r.1881–94), including the 12 plates now in the Royal Collection, which were given to George V and Queen Mary in 1935. The replacement pieces have a central medallion with the cipher of Catherine II in flowers, a blue ground which attempts to recreate the *bleu céleste* of the original Sèvres pieces, and an arabesque in gold interrupted by three cameo-like heads and three oblong oval reserves with scenes in a Pompeian manner. The majority of the service, in all around 700 pieces, is in the State Hermitage Museum.

CDEG

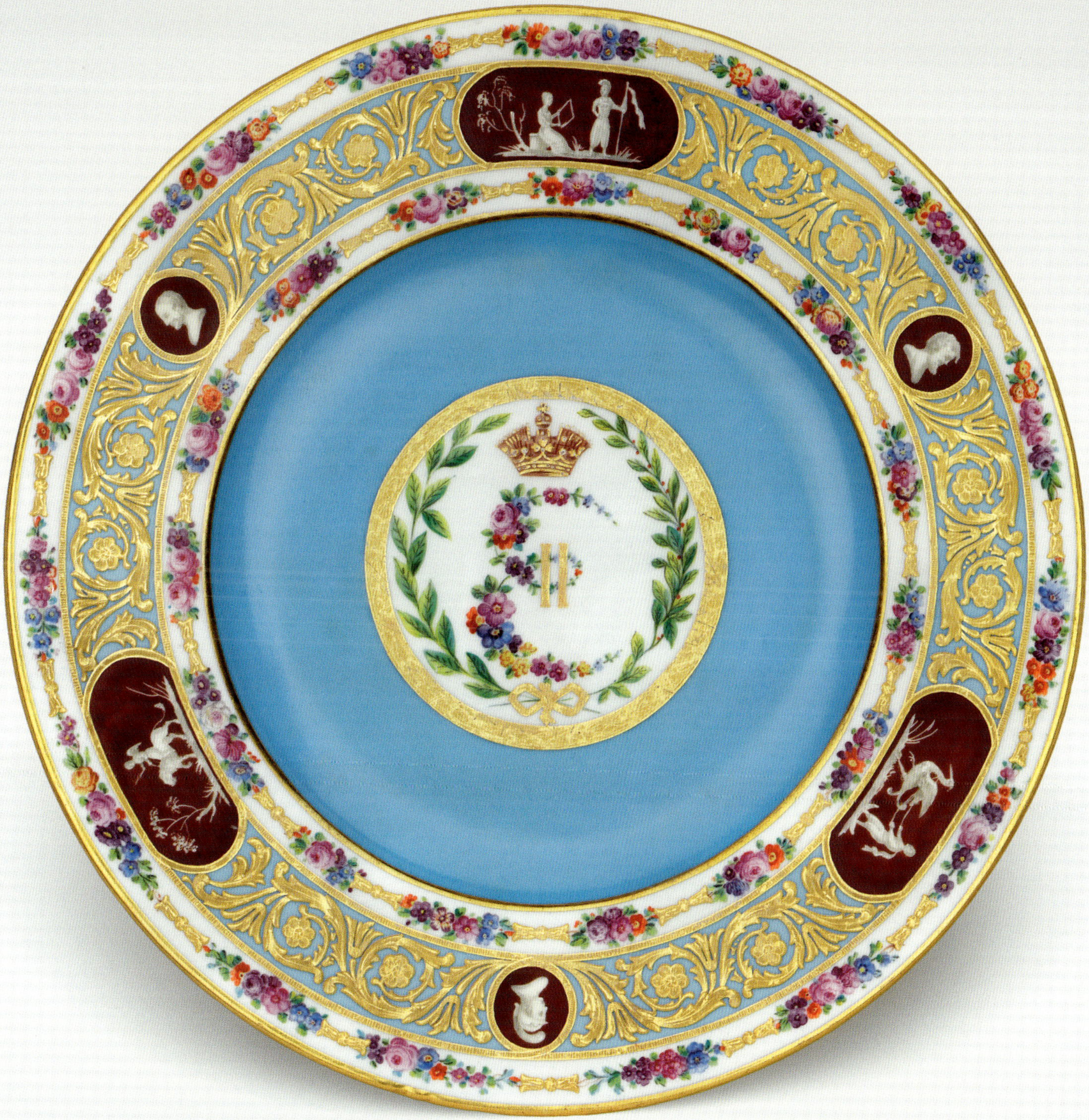

FRANCIS GARDNER FACTORY

38–40 *Plate from the Order of St Andrew Service* 1777

Dessert dish from the Order of St George Service 1777

Dessert dish from the Order of St Vladimir Service 1783

Hard-paste porcelain, respectively 3.0 × 24.8 cm; 6.5 × 29.8 × 23.5 cm; 6.8 × 29.7 × 23.4 cm
Marks: underglaze mark in blue 'G'
RCINS 59321, 59322, 59323

Provenance Presumably Queen Mary (1867–1953)

On 21 February 1766, the Department of Manufactures, founded under Peter the Great, granted the English businessman, Francis Gardner, the right to establish a factory for the making of porcelain wares. By 1770, Gardner's porcelain was highly praised, and with Catherine II's encouragement for all Russian industries, she gave Gardner an imperial commission to make services decorated with the ribbons, badges and stars of the most senior imperial orders. The services were to be used once a year at the Winter Palace in St Petersburg, where the knights of the orders dined on the feast day of their Order's saint.

As models for the new services, Catherine sent to Gardner examples from a service she had received from Frederick the Great of Prussia (1712–86), which included pierced baskets, cups and leaf-shaped dishes. In addition, Gardner took inspiration from a Meissen service with symbols of the Order of St Andrew, which Augustus III, Elector of Saxony (1696–1763), had presented to the Empress Elizabeth in 1743. The first order was placed in 1777 for the service of the Order of St George, which had 60 knights; the services for the Orders of St Andrew and St Alexander Nevskii, which had 30 knights each, were completed in 1780. Catherine was so pleased that she commissioned the service for the Order of St Vladimir in 1783 for 140 knights. The Royal Collection contains only these three examples and does not include a piece from the Order of St Alexander Nevskii Service. **CDEG**

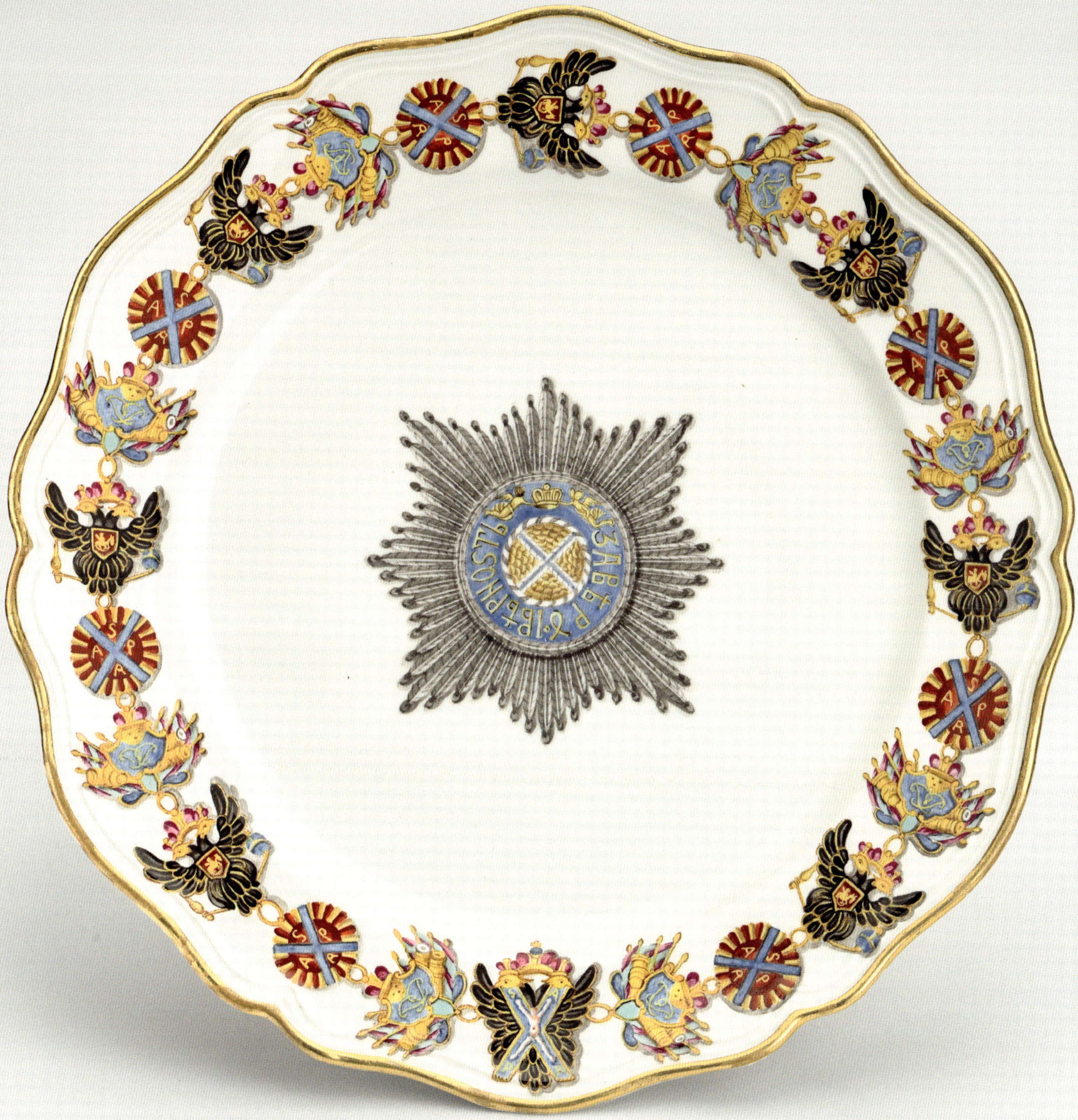

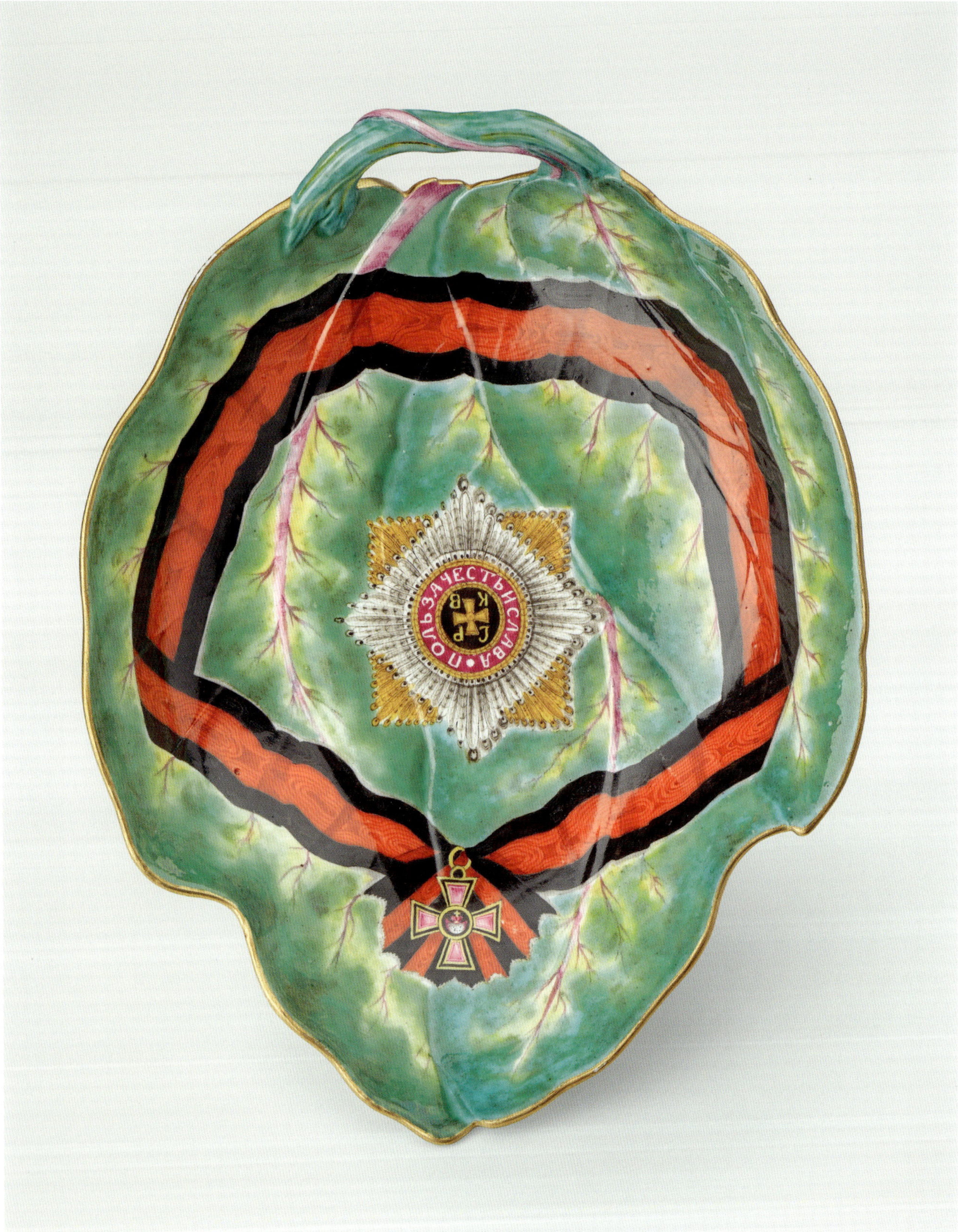
ПОЛЬЗАЧЕСТЬИСЛАВА

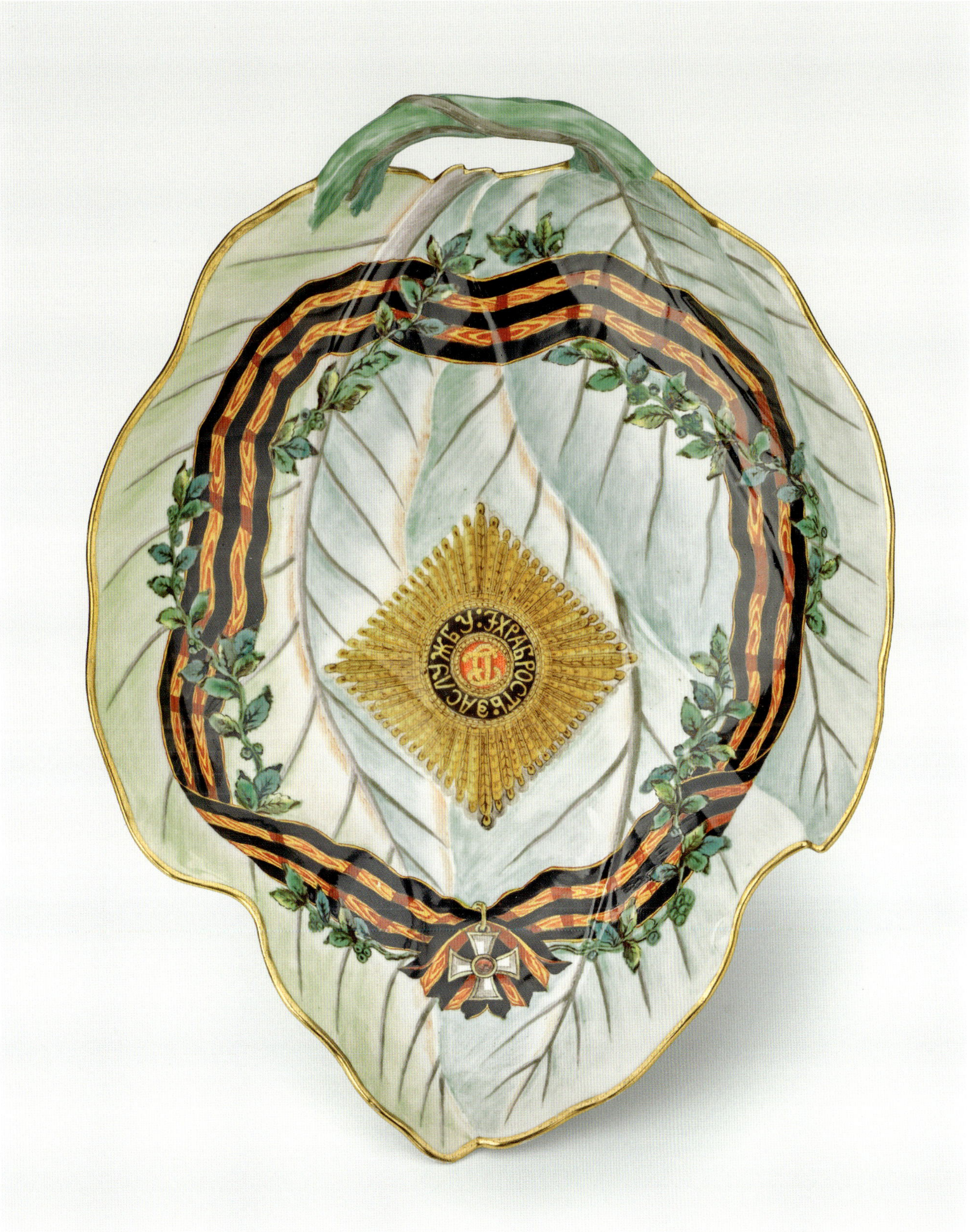

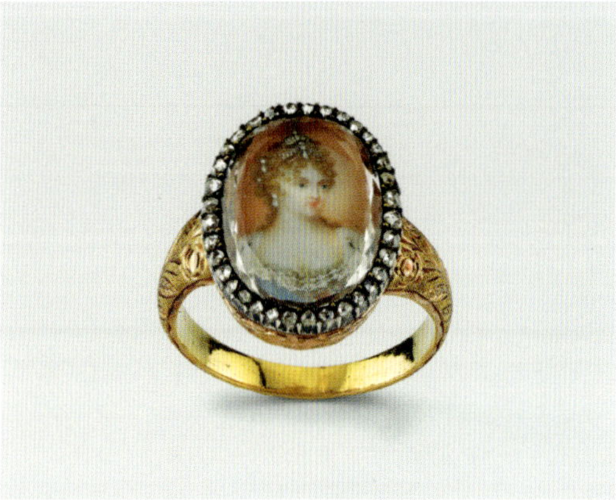

RUSSIAN

41 *Ring with a miniature of Maria Feodorovna (1759–1828), Empress of Russia* nineteenth century

Gold, diamonds, watercolour on ivory, 2.1 × 1.8 × 1.7 cm
RCIN 9017

Provenance First recorded in the Royal Collection during the current reign (1952–)

Literature Remington 2010, no. 1066

This gold ring, chased with incised foliage, is mounted with a diamond bezel containing a miniature of Maria Feodorovna, Empress of Russia. Princess Sophia Dorothea of Württemberg, eldest daughter of Frederick II, Duke of Württemberg (1732–97), married Grand Duke Paul of Russia (1754–1801) in 1776, only son of Empress Catherine the Great of Russia, and took the name Maria Feodorovna when she converted to Orthodoxy. Grand Duke Paul succeeded as Emperor Paul I in 1796, but was assassinated five years later. As Dowager Empress, Maria Feodorovna maintained considerable influence and lived in great state at the palace of Pavlovsk. Three of her four sons, Alexander I, Constantine I (for one day) and Nicholas I, reigned as emperors of Russia; she also gave birth to six daughters.

The low forehead and wide-set eyes of the sitter conform with the appearance of Maria Feodorovna as depicted in portraits by the court artist Gerhard von Kügelgen (1772–1820) *c.*1800. The sitter wears the ribbon and star of the Order of St Andrew, but of particular note is the large diamond tiara, possibly that worn by Russian grand duchesses on their wedding day, which contained the 13 carat Paul I pink diamond.[79]
CDEG

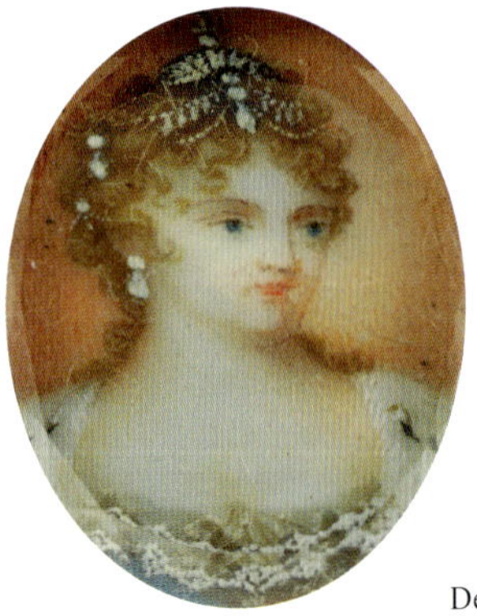

Detail of cat. 41

WILLIAM COXE (1747–1828)

42 *Travels into Poland, Russia, Sweden, and Denmark* 1784–90

London: J. Nichols for T. Cadell, 3 vols
Bound in brown calf, 29.4 × 24.2 cm (closed)
RCINS 1141280, 1141281, 1141282

Provenance Acquired by George III for his Windsor Library (WL 54)

Literature Putnam 1952, pp. 237–92; Cross 2014b, D28

William Coxe, onetime Fellow of King's College, Cambridge, became tutor to the sons of wealthy noblemen and accompanied Lord Herbert (1759–1827), later 11th Earl of Pembroke, on an extensive tour of Europe, 1775–9. They arrived in Russia on 20 August 1778, travelling first to Moscow, thence to St Petersburg via Novgorod, and finally leaving on 3 February 1779. Coxe's account of their travels, which was published by subscription in 1784 (George III headed the subscription list), was extremely detailed, not merely for their actual journey, the peoples they met and the places they visited, but also for its considerable descriptions of Russia's history. A third volume appeared in 1790, based on material gathered during Coxe's second visit to the country, 1784–5, while bear-leading Samuel Whitbread (1764–1815), son of the brewer. It became a very popular book, going through at least six editions in English alone (1784, 1785, 1787, 1792, 1802, 1803), with the fourth and fifth editions considerably rearranged and enlarged. Coxe's final edition was printed in a limited edition on large paper, a copy of which was presented to George III, now in the British Library. ES

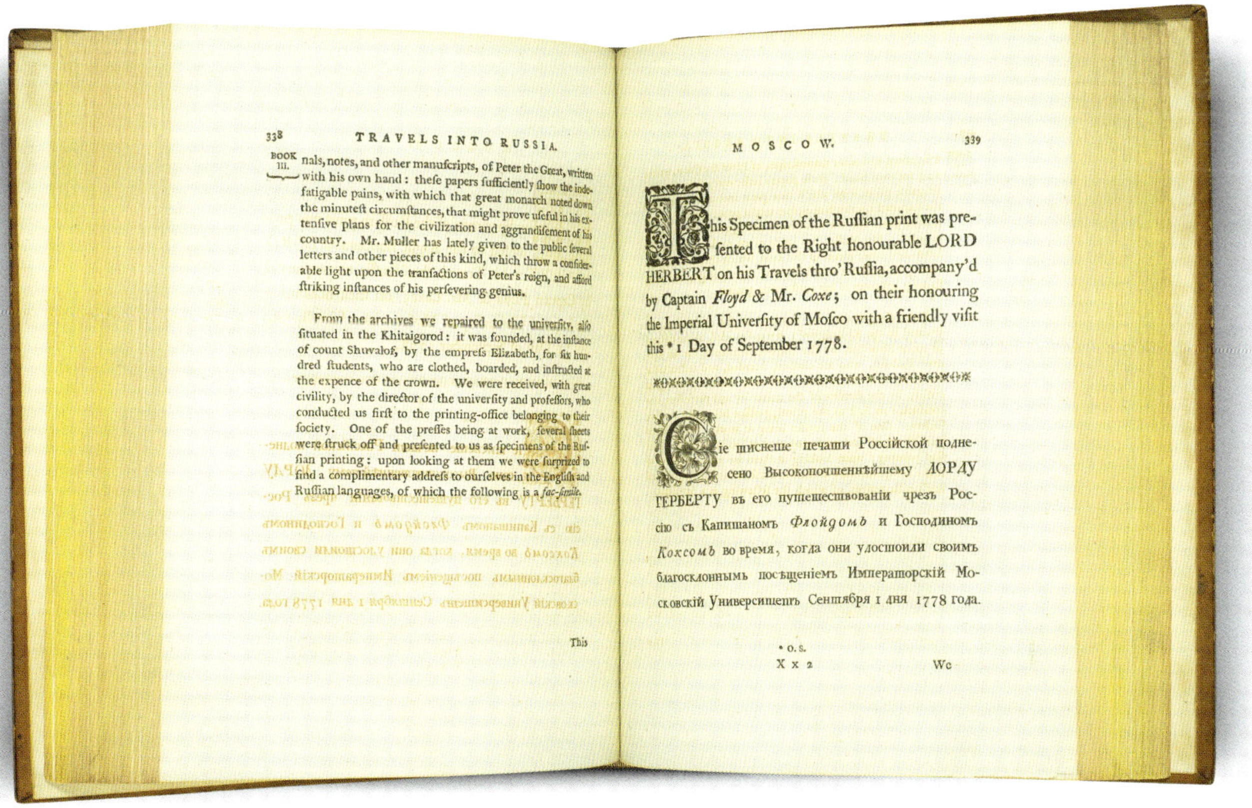

RUSSIAN SCHOOL, 18TH CENTURY, after JEAN-LOUIS VOILLE (1744–1804)

43 *Paul I, Emperor of Russia (1754–1801)* c.1797–1800

Oil on canvas, 74.9 × 58.1 cm
RCIN 404631

Provenance Stated to have been given by the Emperor to Lord Grenville, when Secretary of State for Foreign Affairs; bought at the Stowe sale, 12 September 1848,[80] lot 105, by Frederick Spencer, 4th Earl Spencer (1798–1857), who presented the painting to Queen Victoria, late 1848–9; first recorded in the Eighteenth Century Room, Buckingham Palace, 1860

This portrait, after a lost original by Jean-Louis Voille, painted in 1789, became the standard image of Emperor Paul I, the only son of Catherine the Great and Peter III.[81] It served as a model for artists both before and after his coronation in 1797, and numerous versions were produced. Paul is dressed in the dark green uniform of the Preobrazhensky Regiment, with the stars of the Orders of St Andrew and St Alexander Nevskii, and the neck badges of the Order of Malta and St Anne. The presence of the white enamelled Order of Malta, of which Paul became Grand Master in 1798, suggests the work was completed in the latter years of the eighteenth century. The portrait appears to be a fine copy, and the presence of a dark red ground suggests an artist who trained in France or who was close to Voille.

Raised for the first seven years of his life by his great-aunt, the Empress Elizabeth, Paul was a sensitive, intelligent child. The effect of his father's forced abdication and murder, coupled with his mother's rejection of him, may have led to an unstable personality, and elements of fragility can be perceived in this portrait. Paul was ridiculed after his death (he, too, was murdered), as evidenced by a caricature by John Kay (1742–1826) of 1804 (fig. 9).

Jean-Louis Voille was born in Paris and studied under the portrait painter François-Hubert Drouais (1727–75). From the early 1770s he worked in Russia, where, around 1780, he was appointed court painter to the heir to the throne. In the mid-1790s he returned to France.

A further contemporary copy of the painting, inscribed and dated *Kapal JEpke. / 1799*, is recorded hanging in Carlton House in 1816.[82] **AB**

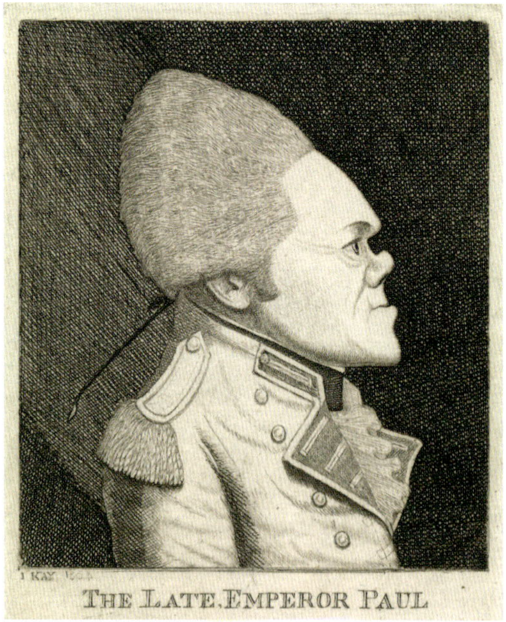

FIG. 9
John Kay
The Late Emperor Paul (of Russia), 1804 (with inscription)
Etching, 9.1 × 7.9 cm
RCIN 614401

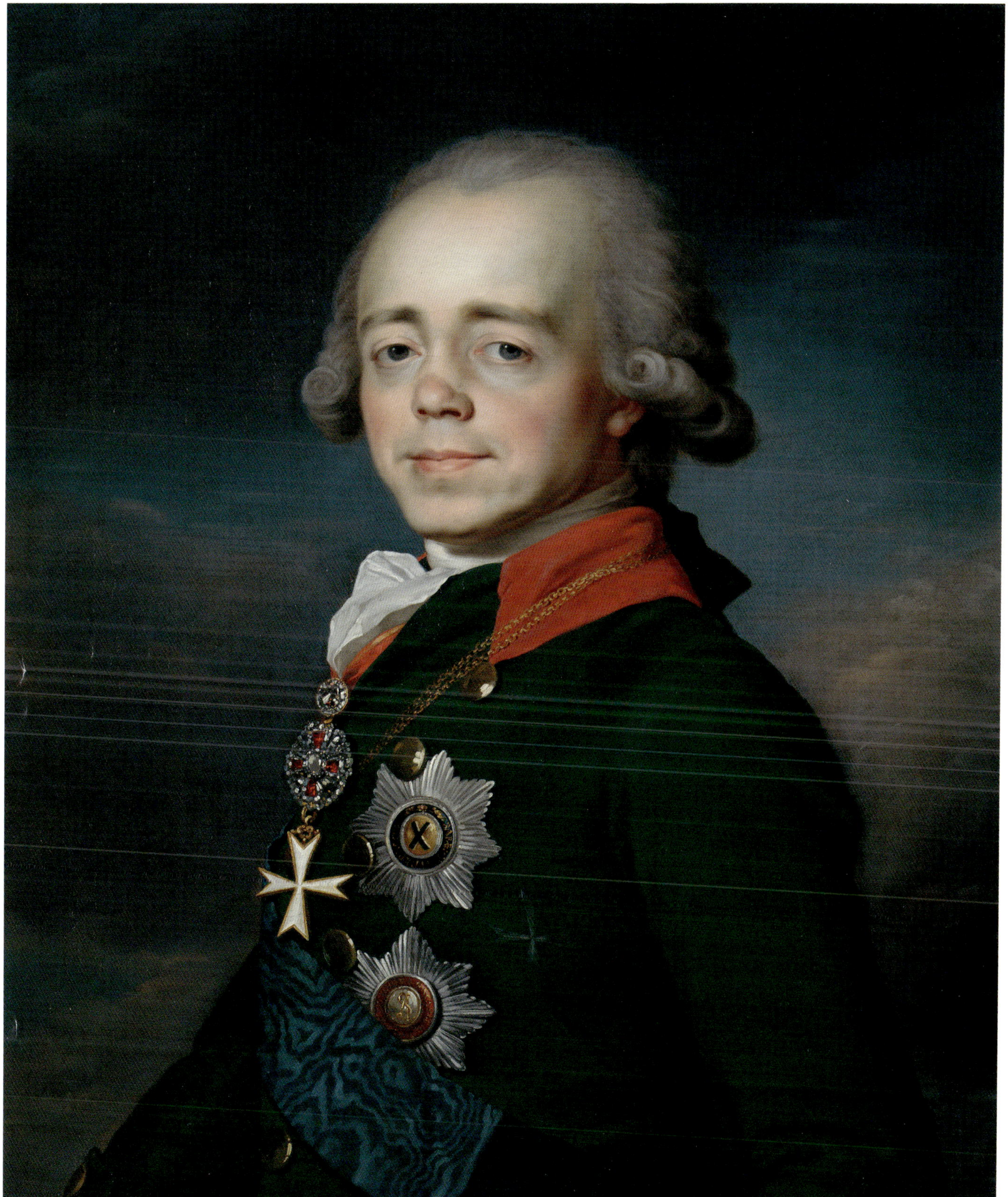

GRAND DUKE PAUL (FUTURE PAUL I) (1754–1801)

44 *Letter to King George III (1738–1820), St Petersburg* 15 October 1793

Manuscript, 31.6 × 44.0 cm
RA GEO/MAIN/7312

This state letter, written in Russian and German to 'His Majesty the King of England', announces the marriage of the future Emperor Alexander I to Princess Louise of Baden (1779–1826), who adopted the name Elizabeth Alexeievna on her marriage and adoption of the Orthodox faith. The marriage took place in St Petersburg on 28 September and this letter is one of a set dispatched to the courts of Europe announcing the nuptials, signed on the Russian original by the Grand Duke. The marriage was arranged by Empress Catherine between her 15-year-old, eldest grandson and the 14-year-old princess who was a niece of Grand Duke Paul's first wife. There were no surviving children of the marriage, with Elizabeth Alexeievna's two daughters dying in childhood. The relationship between the couple varied over time, with reconciliation just before the Emperor's unexpected death in 1825. His death was followed by that of Elizabeth Alexeievna on her return journey to St Petersburg five months later. SJP

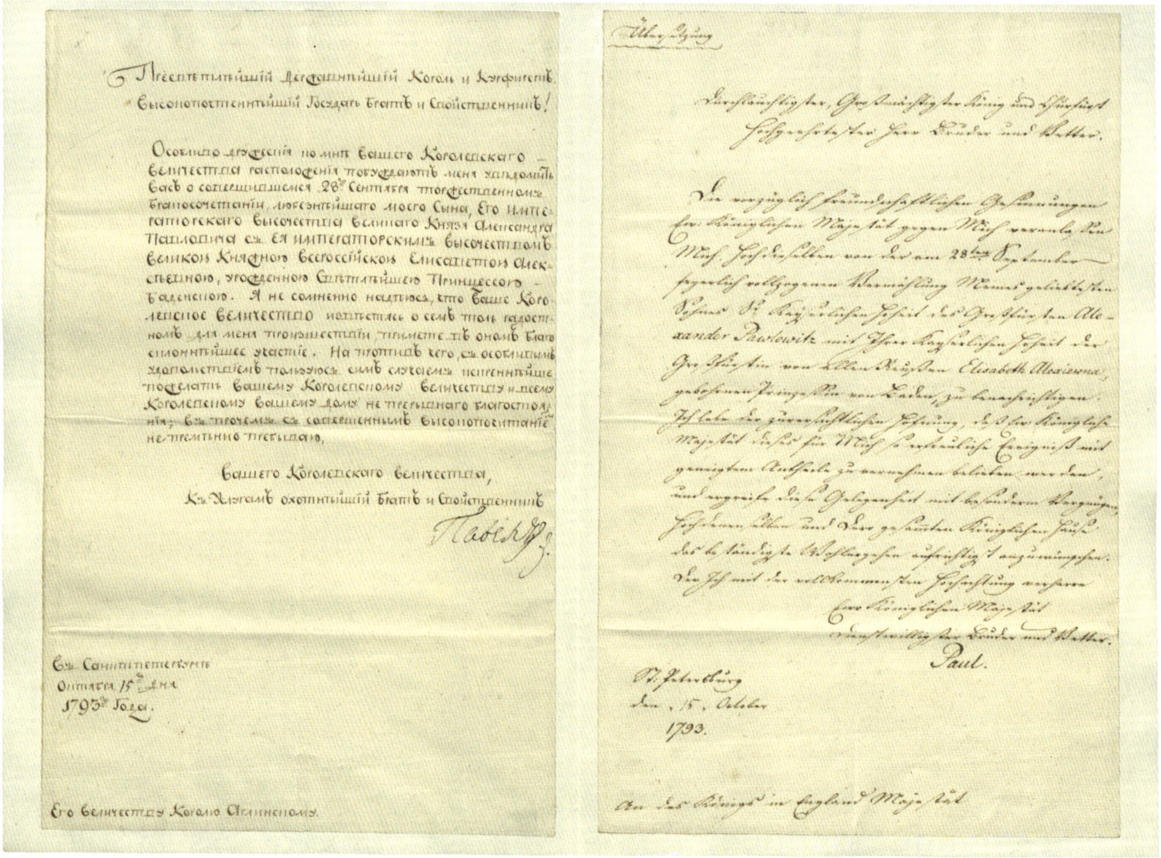

Durchlauchtigster, Großmächtigster König und Churfürst
Hochgeehrtester Herr Bruder und Vetter.

Paul.

St. Petersburg
den 15. October
1793.

An des Königs in England Majestät

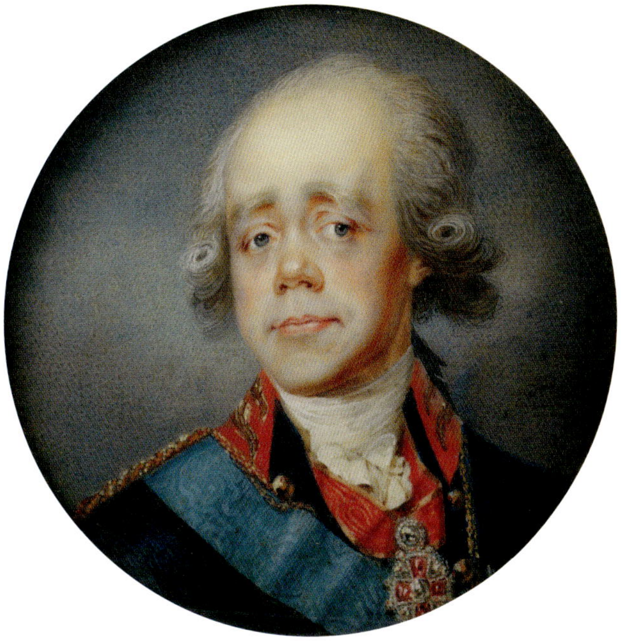

ATTRIBUTED TO GERIK (GERICKE), RUSSIAN SCHOOL

45 *Paul I, Emperor of Russia (1754–1801)* c.1796

Watercolour on ivory, diameter 8.2 cm
Signed at right over sitter's shoulder: *Gerik*
RCIN 420711

Provenance First recorded in the inventories in 1870 (RL 1870, 42.A.1)

Literature Cust 1910, nos. 51 / 2-41 / 2; Walker 1992, no. 712

Paul I, Emperor of Russia, is depicted wearing the uniform of the Preobrazhensky Regiment, a dark blue coat with a scarlet collar. Prominent is the Order of St Andrew and the badge of St Anne, hanging on a red and yellow ribbon. The visible badge of the Order of St Anne suggests that this miniature was painted after 1797, as the sitter incorporated the order into the Russian awarding system at the time of his coronation in 1797. The painting, signed on the right 'Gerik', perhaps by a descendant of the German engraver, Johann Ernst Gericke (active 1744–69), appears to derive from a number of earlier depictions of the sitter, notably those by French painter Jean-Louis Voille of 1789, and Stepan Shchukin (1762–1828), *c.*1796 / 7, now in the Hermitage.

The sitter is depicted frankly, his strabismus evident in the drooping of his left eye. An unhappy man, considered despotic by many, Paul I suffered a sudden death, murdered in his bedroom in St Michael's Castle in 1801. IM

ANON., RUSSIAN SCHOOL

46–49 *Grand Duchess Alexandra Pavlovna of Russia, Archduchess of Austria (1783–1801)* c.1796

Watercolour on ivory, 8.1 × 7.0 cm
Inscribed in ink on the backing card: *Madame la grande duchess Alexandre.*; in pencil: *now L...Austria*
RCIN 420710

Grand Duchess Elena Pavlovna of Russia, Princess of Mecklenburg-Schwerin (1784–1803) c.1796

Watercolour on ivory, 8.2 × 7.1 cm
Inscribed in ink on backing card: *Madame La Grande Duchesse Helene*
RCIN 420712

Grand Duchess Maria Pavlovna of Russia, Grand Duchess of Saxe-Weimar-Eisenbach (1786–1859) c.1796

Watercolour on ivory, 8.2 × 7.1 cm
Inscribed in ink on the backing card: *Madame La Grande Duchesse Marie*
RCIN 420713

Grand Duchess Ekaterina Pavlovna of Russia, Queen of Württemberg (1788–1819) c.1796

Watercolour on ivory, 8.2 × 7.0 cm
Inscribed in ink on card reverse: *Madame La Grande Duchesse Catherine*; possibly signed and dated along lower left edge (now illegible)
RCIN 420714

Provenance First recorded in the inventories in 1870 (RL 1870, 42.A.2, 23.C.8, 42.A.3, 42.A.4)

Literature Cust 1910, nos 51 / 1-41 / 1, 51 / 3-41 / 3, 51 / 4-41 / 4, 51 / 5-41 / 5; *Great Britain – USSR* 1967, pp. 23–4, nos 126, 127, 128, 129 (RCINS 420710, 420712, 420713, 420714); Walker 1992, nos 716, 717, 718, 719

These four miniatures of Paul's eldest daughters depict their sitters in a sentimental guise. The images are believed to be copies after bust length portraits by Dmitry Levitsky, Professor of Portrait Painting at the Academy of Arts. The miniatures may have been painted by one of the circle of Russian miniaturists Petr Zharkov, as several very similar autographed works depicting the eldest daughters can be seen at Pavlovsk Palace. The Grand Duchesses are all shown wearing the Order of St Catherine, bestowed on each daughter on the occasion of her christening. Unlike her elder sisters, Grand Duchess Ekaterina is depicted without a striped coat, her hair worn loose, demonstrating her immaturity. Grand Duchess Elena rests her elbow on a desk, a number of books visible at the left, perhaps illustrative of her grandmother Catherine the Great's keen supervision of the Grand Duchess's education.
IM

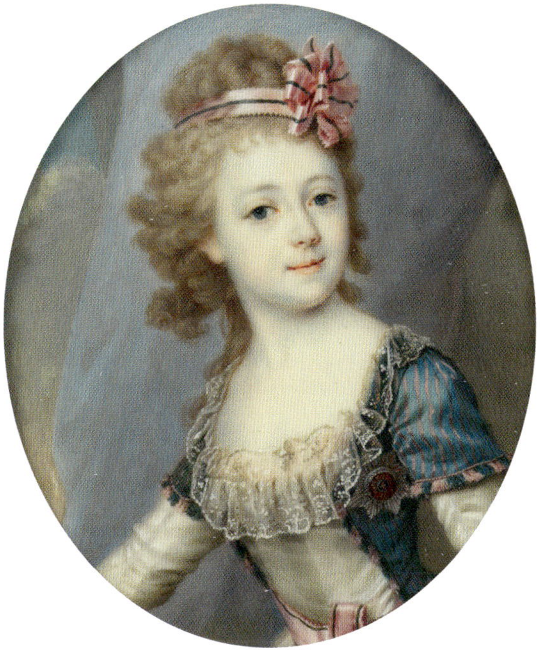

46

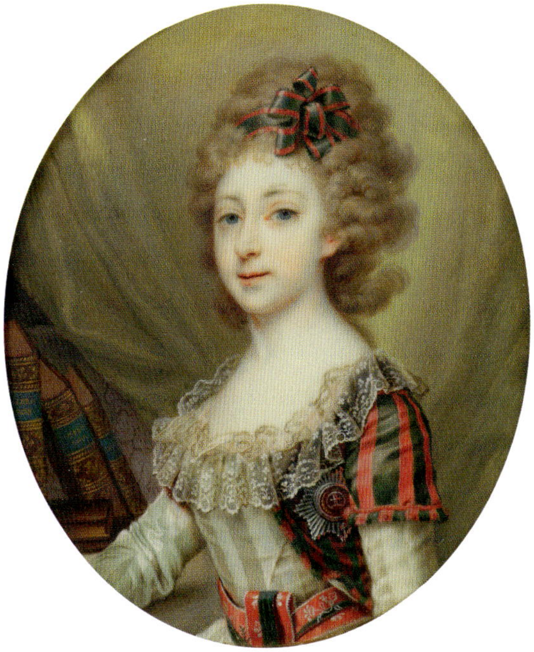

47

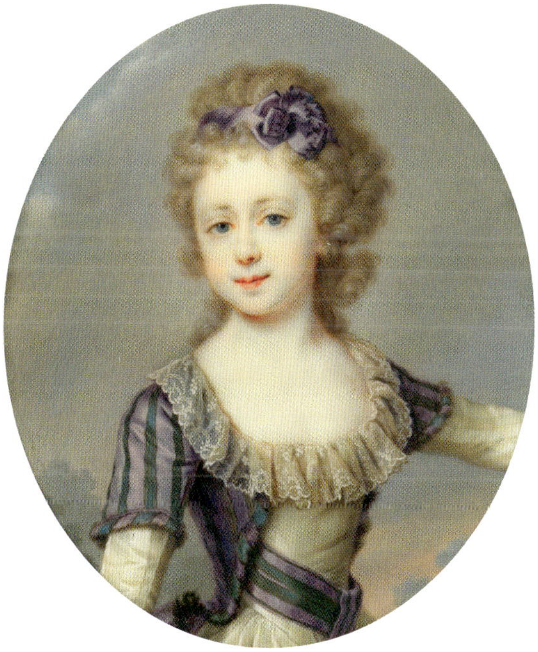

48

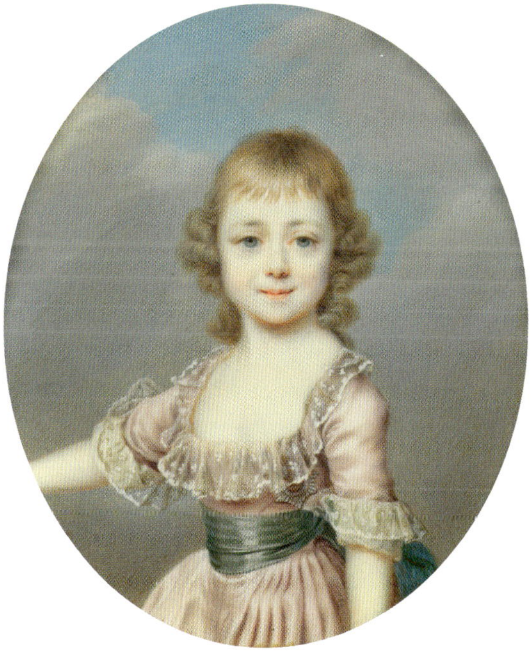

49

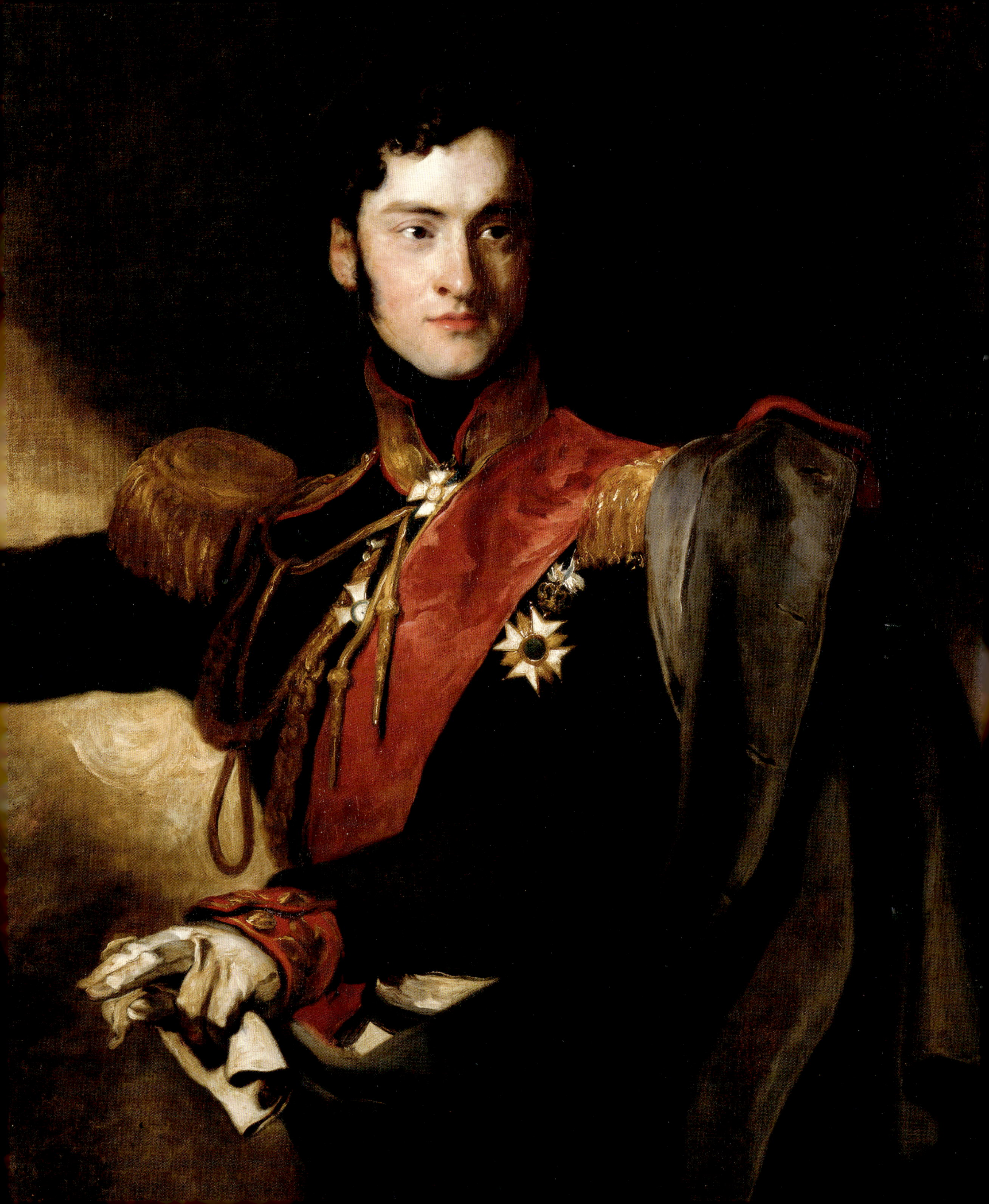

2

Ambassadors and Confused Relationships

STEPHEN PATTERSON

No country in Europe will furnish so fair a chance of success to socialism

(Lord Granville to Queen Victoria 1856)[1]

Throughout their reigns, British monarchs have been aware of other realms and states through reports from their ambassadors, a practice continuing to the present day, as well as from descriptions sent by friends, family and visitors to a nation. These descriptions were partly to engage interest and provide information about a country, but also to understand the approach of a country and its government or ruler towards Britain and its monarch. Key to a positive relationship with another nation was the relationship with that nation's representative – be they chargé d'affaires, minister or ambassador – the direct connection between the two countries. Over the period 1812–1917, Russian Emperors were served by 14 representatives, with Prince von Lieven (1774–1839) serving for 22 years and Baron de Brunnov (1797–1875) for 28 years.

Prince von Lieven, whose socialite wife Daria was as much a confidante of the British political establishment as her husband, was ambassador from 1812 to 1834. He represented Alexander I and Nicholas I, assisting with the arrangements for the visits of Alexander I in 1814 and of the future Emperor Nicholas to Britain in 1817. A frequent visitor to Brighton Pavilion, he reported to his imperial master, on among other matters, the pleasure of the Prince Regent on receiving the Order of St Andrew.[2] Lieven also passed on a message to St Petersburg that the Prince Regent thought 'the entirety of Europe, and Britain in particular, recognised in the Emperor the liberator of all, the head of the august coalition which had achieved the glorious aim of the liberty of Europe and the safety of its countries'.[3]

In 1835, Lieven, who was to be appointed tutor to the future Emperor Alexander II, was replaced as Nicholas I's representative to the Court of St James and William IV by Count Pozzo di Borgo (1764–1842). The count was to be the first imperial representative of Queen Victoria's reign and the future queen first met him at a Drawing Room in July that year;[4] they went on to meet at a number of court and social occasions before the Queen's accession.

Brunnov, who followed Pozzo di Borgo in 1840, was the Russian minister in London tasked with organising the visit of Nicholas I in June 1844 (cat. 101). This was a major event which brought a Russian Emperor to Britain for the first time in 30 years and was a visit which the Emperor himself saw as a watershed in relations between the two countries. Although often described as an unexpected visit, it had been planned since April of that year, with regular correspondence between the Emperor's representatives in London and their masters in St Petersburg. The Government, the Queen and Prince Albert were fully aware of the plan in London, and in April, the prime minister, Robert Peel (1788–1850), wrote to the Baron de Brunnov:

Alexander Ivanovich, Prince Chernyshev (detail of cat. 71)

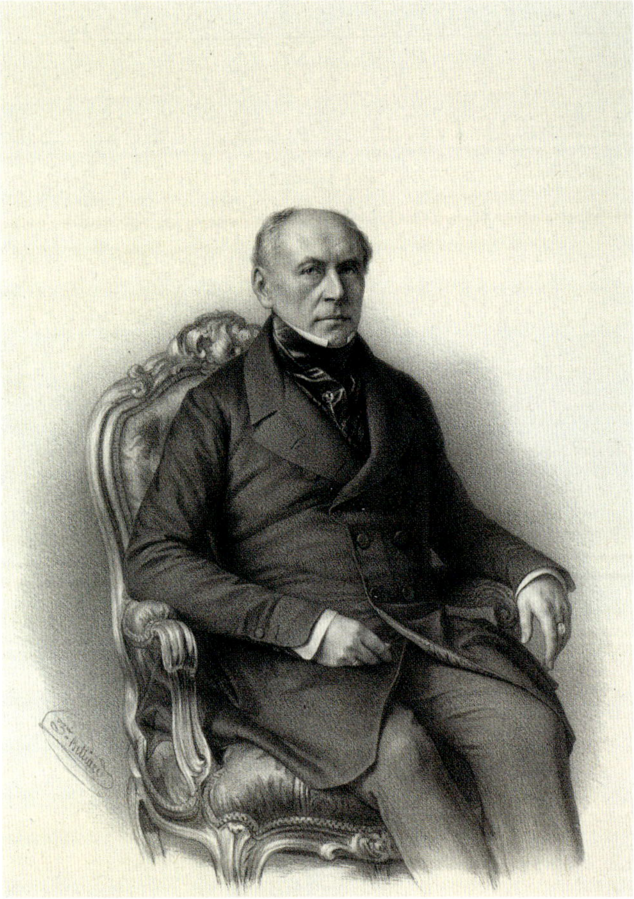

FIG. 10
Zéphirin Félix Jean Marius Belliard
Philipp, Baron de Brunnov (1797–1875), 1856
Lithograph, 21.3 × 15.8 cm
RCIN 2950743

'I spoke to the Queen and Prince Albert [...] they were greatly pleased at the prospect of a visit from the Emperor [...] The Queen and the Prince were really personally gratified at the thought of having the Emperor under their roof'.[5] The discussions at the time revolved around the differences between the two courts and constitutions, as well as foreign policy. The Emperor's generosity – £500 for Nelson's Column, given to the Duke of Wellington (1769–1852); £500 for the Wellington monument, given to the Duke of Rutland (1778–1857); £1,000 to the needs of Friends of Foreigners in distress; £200 to the vicar of the Parish of St George in London for the poor; and a subscription ball for Polish refugees – would not be remembered when policies in Moldavia and Wallachia, as well as toward the Ottomans, led to war in 1853 (fig. 10).

While meetings with some Russian representatives were, on many occasions, social, pleasant and easy, some were not. One such was when Baron de Brunnov presented the letter announcing Alexander II's accession on 3 May 1856, the first time that there had been an official meeting of the representative of the Russian monarch and the Queen since the outbreak of the Crimean War: 'He was so overcome, when he 1rst came in, that he could hardly speak, but seemed greatly relieved when I said, that I rejoiced to receive this letter & hoped that we should always be, on the best terms, & that "*les temps passés seront oubliés* [past times will be forgotten]'. I then added that much had happened since we had met, to which he replied: "*Mon Dieu! nous avons terriblement souffert* [My God! We have suffered terribly]"'.[6] This was the same baron who had delivered the insignia of the Order of St Andrew to Prince Albert and the Prince of Wales in the 1840s (cat. 116). It was also the Baron de Brunnov who attended a *bal costumé* in 1851 at Buckingham Palace dressed as a boyar, with a beard and wig, and was described by the Queen as: 'unrecognisable, & a typical Russian.'[7]

The post of minister (or envoy), was downgraded from the rank of ambassador in 1844, but was raised once more to that of ambassador in 1860 – not without resistance on the Queen's part. The argument for the raising of the role of minister to ambassador was that, in Lord John Russell's (1792–1878) view, 'The obvious advantage is that the British Ambassador will then see the sovereign as well as the French Representative.'[8] By extension, the Queen would have to receive the Russian ambassador. The Queen was not in favour, nor necessarily of Baron de Brunnov; however, she was advised by her minister that she should accept the appointment because 'Baron Brunnow [...] has so long resided here as minister, in the capacity of ambassador.'[9] The Queen wrote on 11 December 1860: 'There is nothing for it but to receive Baron Brunnow as ambassador'.[10]

Although he was an official representing a foreign monarch, the Baron also showed that the relationship between the monarch and an ambassador could be more personal, as when he expressed his appreciation of the kindness of the Queen at the time of his wife's death, which occurred at the same time as the state arrival of the Grand Duchess Maria Alexandrovna (cat. 190) in Britain in March 1874; duty came before family and the Baron ensured that his wife's death was kept private to ensure that the climax of the negotiations and celebrations following the Romanov marriage were not affected by his personal loss.

It was not just ambassadors and envoys who sent reports – their wives also contributed to the Queen's knowledge of the nation. In 1847, Queen Victoria received a detailed report of a meeting between the wife of her envoy, Lord Bloomfield (1802–79), and the Empress of Russia, Alexandra Feodorovna. During the audience, the Empress expressed an interest in reading the Queen's speech from the throne as she opened parliament, and her concerns about the famine in Ireland and the risk to the potato crop in Russia.[11]

In 1856, at the time of the coronation of Alexander II (cat. 105), the Queen learnt from her representative at the coronation, Lord Granville, of the state of the country: 'It is more than likely that popular revolts will take place and it is frightful to consider the immediate results of a revolution in a country organised as this is at present.' He went on to say that 'No country in Europe will furnish so fair a chance of success to socialism'.[12] With letters sent to her by both the ambassador and his wife, the Queen was fully informed of the situation in Russia, with an analysis of the military, political, social, transport and economic situation in the country. The letters provided information on a wide range of topics, from the size and splendours of the jewels of the Romanov court to the capability and morale of the military in both St Petersburg and Moscow. The Queen was informed about the state of the country, as well as the roads, railways, the condition of estates and the prospects of landowners, and the risks of taking a Russian maid (following an incident when one had been caught drinking castor oil from her mistress's dressing table), as well the superstitious comments circulating after the Empress's crown slipped from her head during the coronation ceremonies.

Of the coronation city, Granville reported on 30 August 1856: 'Moscow is one of the most striking towns in Europe. The position, the ancient and the semioriental architecture give it an imposing character, which is hardly equalled by any other capital'.[13] Some 20 years later, the Queen was receiving further reports, and at the time of the Duke and Duchess of Edinburgh's marriage in 1874 recorded: 'Received a most interesting letter from the Dean of Westminster from Moscow, which must indeed be a wonderful place.'[14]

Of course, any correspondence was bidirectional, and an opportunity for the views of the ambassador to be passed to St Petersburg as a report of conditions in London. Following the marriage of the Duke and Duchess of Edinburgh, and the challenges to the Grand Duchess because Queen Victoria appeared to act in a mode contrary to the long-negotiated marriage treaty, Baron de Brunnov wrote to the Tsesarevich, Alexander Alexandrovich, and (writing in French) pointed out, quite perceptively, that in the case of Queen Victoria: 'The Queen submits, with regret, to the discomfort imposed on her by the constitutional regime [....] by exercising on her family, a power which is more than absolute.'[15]

Similar insights into the life of a nation and the state of the imperial family arrived in London too. In one dispatch in February 1880, the Earl of Dufferin wrote about the health of the Empress. He also commented on his (and by extension Britain's) standing in Russian society at that time, noting that 'nothing can be more friendly than the attitude of Russian Society to your Majesty's Ambassador'.[16] Descriptions of weather, of public health and the security situation were also sent:

the weather is extraordinarily mild and St Petersburg is consequently in a very unhealthy condition. The mortality is stated to be double the usual rate, which is already double that of any other European capital, Diphtheria and typhus fever being the prevalent maladies. [...] The Emperor goes about with his carriage surrounded by a guard of Cossacks, but the police have been more successful in laying their hands upon various centres of Nihilistic propagandism.[17]

The time when ambassadors were recalled and replaced was often a moment when the relationship between states could be determined. On Shuvalov's (1827–89) recall to St Petersburg, and the delay in the arrival of his successor, Prince Lobanov-Rostovsky (1824–96), Disraeli (1804–81), then prime minister, wrote to Queen Victoria:

We have received no official information that Prince Labanoff is kept back with an unfriendly infection [...] As a matter of policy, we must represent to yr Majesty that it is wise to take no notice of the Czar's caprices. With regard to your receiving Ct Schouvaloff, [...] but yr Majesty may deign to recollect that one of the causes of Ct. Schouvaloff's unpopularity at his own court is the supposed friendship of His Excellency to England.[18]

It took another three months before Prince Lobanov-Rostovsky presented his credentials: 'At 4, received the new Russian Ambassador, Pce Labanoff [...] He is not distinguee in appearance, rather in Brunnow's style.'[19] Two years later, Queen Victoria wrote: '[saw] Ct Mohrenheim, the new Russian Ambassador, who has been long at Copenhagen';[20] but he only remained in place for two years.

First impressions of Baron de Staal, her last ambassador, were positive: 'Saw Madame de Staal, the new Russian Ambassadress, who is very agreeable & pleasing. She is the daughter of Gen: Pce Gortschakoff, who came to England for the funeral of the Duke of Wellington in 1852, & who afterwards commanded in the Crimea. [...] Baron & Baroness de Staal (he is also very agreeable, & prefers talking German) [...] dined'.[21]

On occasion, the ambassador would try to use the royal influence on their 'august master', as when Baron de Staal, reappointed by the new Emperor in late 1894, presented his recredentials to Queen Victoria, and she was formally told of the accession of Emperor Nicholas – as Baron de Brunnov had done for Alexander II's accession in 1856, and Prince Vorontsov (who took the opportunity to inform the Queen in detail of the horrors of Alexander II's assassination) had done for Alexander III's in 1881:

After tea went down with Beatrice to the Drawing room & received there M. de Staal with his recredentials, & the special Envoy Gen: Tchertkoff, sent to announce the Emperor's death & Nicky's accession [...] talked much of the poor Emperor's death, of Nicky [...] Both M. de Staal & Gen: Tchertkoff, were full of anxiety that Nicky should not overwork himself & begged me to write & urge this on him.[22]

Throughout the nineteenth century, the multiple (often contradictory) aspects of the relationship between Russia and Britain are clear from royal correspondence. The 'Great Game' and the role of Russia in Central Asia, with the perceived threat to India and Afghanistan; Russia's actions in relation to the Ottoman Empire and the Balkans would, in early 1878, elicit from Queen Victoria the statement: 'Russia - our worst enemy in her policy of ambitious aggression & duplicity.'[23] However this view of a nation and its policies were set to one side when there were concerns about the welfare of the Imperial family – and most especially the attempts on the life of the Emperor; especially after the two dynasties were joined by marriage. At the time of the assassination attempt on Alexander II in February 1880, when a bomb was placed underneath the dining room of the Winter Palace, the Queen was immediately telegraphed about the attempt by the ambassador, Lord Dufferin (1826–1902), who had rushed to the Winter Palace when the nature of the attack was known. He reported that the Emperor had said to him: 'Providence has again mercifully saved me', and observed that the Duchess of Edinburgh, whose rooms were close to the site of the blast, was unhurt and had exhibited great coolness and presence of mind.[24] The ambassador also commented that 'the imbecility of the police and of the officers responsible for the Emperor's safety is certainly superhuman.'[25] The Queen felt that the 'poor czar's life will be a dreadful one',[26] and wrote to the Emperor expressing sympathy and concern, at the same time as sending best wishes to him on the 25th anniversary of his reign; she expressed regard for Grand Duchess Maria (known as Marie by the British royal family), commenting on her sang-froid and courage, as well as speaking kindly of their joint grandchildren in their happy ignorance of the terrible events.[27] The Emperor responded, thanking her for her sympathy at the plot against his life.[28] Three months later, however, the Queen was advising the Foreign Secretary, Lord Granville (1815–91), that he should not trust too much Russia's promise and to be cautious,[29] and in June of the same year was strongly against any *rapprochement* with Russia, which she described as 'Our real enemy and rival'.[30] The irritation turned to horror with the assassination of Alexander II in March 1881; the Queen was kept fully informed of the details of the attack, even being sent a drawing of the device that had killed the Emperor.

The Queen's diary provided a blow-by-blow account of events as they unfolded and the flurry of telegrams (both personal and official) bearing updates:

> *This day* [...] *has been marked by a dreadful & never to be forgotten event. ... a telegram arrived, with the shocking news that the Emperor of Russia had been ... wounded!* [...] *After 6, came another ... announcing the poor Emperor's death, too dreadful! Soon after, got one from Ld Dufferin, saying the Emperor had been killed by the explosion of a bomb* [...] *Poor dear Marie, how terrible for her!* [...] *Feel quite shaken & stunned by this awful news. May God protect all dear ones! Poor, poor Emperor, in spite of his failings, he was a kind & amiable man, & had been good ruler, wishing to do the best for his country.*[31]

The letter to the Queen from her son, Alfred, Duke of Edinburgh (1844–1900), whose father-in-law had just been killed by the attack, reporting on their arrival in St Petersburg was poignant:

> *We then came up to the Winter Place where we are staying & went directly to the church in which the emperor's body is lying in state. What a different scene from the day on which we were married in the same church; Emperor & Empress gone & nothing but men old & young in tears & sobs. We went to the emperor's rooms where the broken hearted valets showed us the few tatters that remained of the uniform he had worn.*[32]

The royal sense of loss at the attack on a fellow monarch had the Queen (who was herself the target of eight assassination attempts) calling for bans on the sale of dynamite,[33] and the need for an extradition treaty to include assassins of 'poor maligned sovereigns' who were 'placed on a pinnacle to be aimed at'.[34] The support that the Queen gave to Russia and the new Emperor at his accession, in particular appointing him to the Order of the Garter (cat. 122), did not last however; in February 1883, her view was that 'Russia tries to thwart us in every direction'.[35]

The Queen's views on Russian foreign policy continued to be negative, in particular in relation to the Bulgarian monarchy and Prince Alexander of Battenberg (1857–93), whose treatment in 1886, at the time of his forced

FIG. 11
William Evans
Queen Victoria and Emperor Nicholas I, Windsor Castle, *c.*1844
Pencil, watercolour and bodycolour on card, 27.1 × 37.2 cm
RCIN 919784

abdication, she referred to as an 'outrage', with the observation that the 'Russian action against the Bulgarians has gone too far'.[36] The feelings could have been said to be mutual when the Emperor Alexander (the Prince of Wales's brother-in-law) was reported to have spoken of England with utter contempt in February 1887, saying that England had already quite withdrawn from European politics, was too weak to take any part in them and was not to be feared in any way.[37]

The dangers to the Romanovs continued, and in 1887 the Queen received news of reported conspiracies by 23-year-old students against the Emperor, and of bombs smeared with poison being found outside the Anichkov Palace.[38] Danger manifested itself not just in the guise of terrorist activity, when, the following year, the imperial family was involved in a railway accident near Borki, commemorated by a medal (cat. 196).[39] In the telegrams received after the event, the Queen was told of the accident which killed 21 people and came so close to killing the imperial family en masse – one of the victims was standing between the Emperor and Empress, and another was the Emperor's dog, sitting directly behind his master's chair; and she read of the panic as the Emperor and Empress hunted for the nine-year-old Grand Duke Michael (1878–1918), who had disappeared in the debris.

Reports of tragedies continued through to the next reign, in particular the catastrophe at Khodynka Fields in May 1896. On 30 May 1896 a 'Popular Festival' held to mark the coronation of Nicholas II turned to tragedy when more than 1,300 people were killed in a crush among the thousands gathered to receive food and gifts (cat. 206). The response was badly handled by the imperial authorities and the Emperor appeared to show an insensitivity to his people when he continued with planned celebrations including a ball at the French Embassy that evening. Papers in the National Archives record the Queen's concern at the events surrounding the tragedy, with a message, sent at her command by her ambassador, to the Russian foreign minister (and former ambassador to London), Prince Lobanov-Rostovsky 'expressing [...] Her Majesty's deep sympathy and concern [...] and how much Her Majesty felt for the wounded and suffering';[40] the Queen also made a personal contribution to the disaster relief fund.

Attempts, on occasion, were made to use the knowledge gained from personal experience of ambassadors, to sway Russian policy. At the death of Prince Lobanov-Rostovsky, the Queen was encouraged by the Prince of Wales to suggest Baron de Staal (1822–1907), the Russian ambassador in London, as a replacement foreign minister to the Emperor, the Queen being asked to encourage an appointment beneficial to her realm as 'it is absolutely necessary for maintenance of better relations between England and Russia'.[41] However, the Queen was against it, and her view was shared by the prime minister Lord Salisbury (1830–1903) that 'any interference would probably become known and would be resented by Russian statesmen'.[42] Although de Staal was not appointed, accusations of interference arose on any account, as the Austrian Emperor was reported to be concerned that the subsequent appointment of Count Muravyov (1845–1900) as foreign minister in St Petersburg was a direct effect of the Queen's influence on the new Emperor. The dual nature of this relationship was seen again with the imperial visit to Balmoral, where discussions between the Queen and Emperor ranged across France, Russia's desire to enter the Dardanelles, and the relationship between Britain and India – conversations carefully recorded in a memo by the Queen[43] which she sent to the prime minister. Lord Salisbury thanked the Queen for the memorandum of 'Your Majesty's most interesting and most valuable conversation with the Emperor Nicholas'[44] – which was echoed in the wide-ranging foreign policy discussions between the Emperor

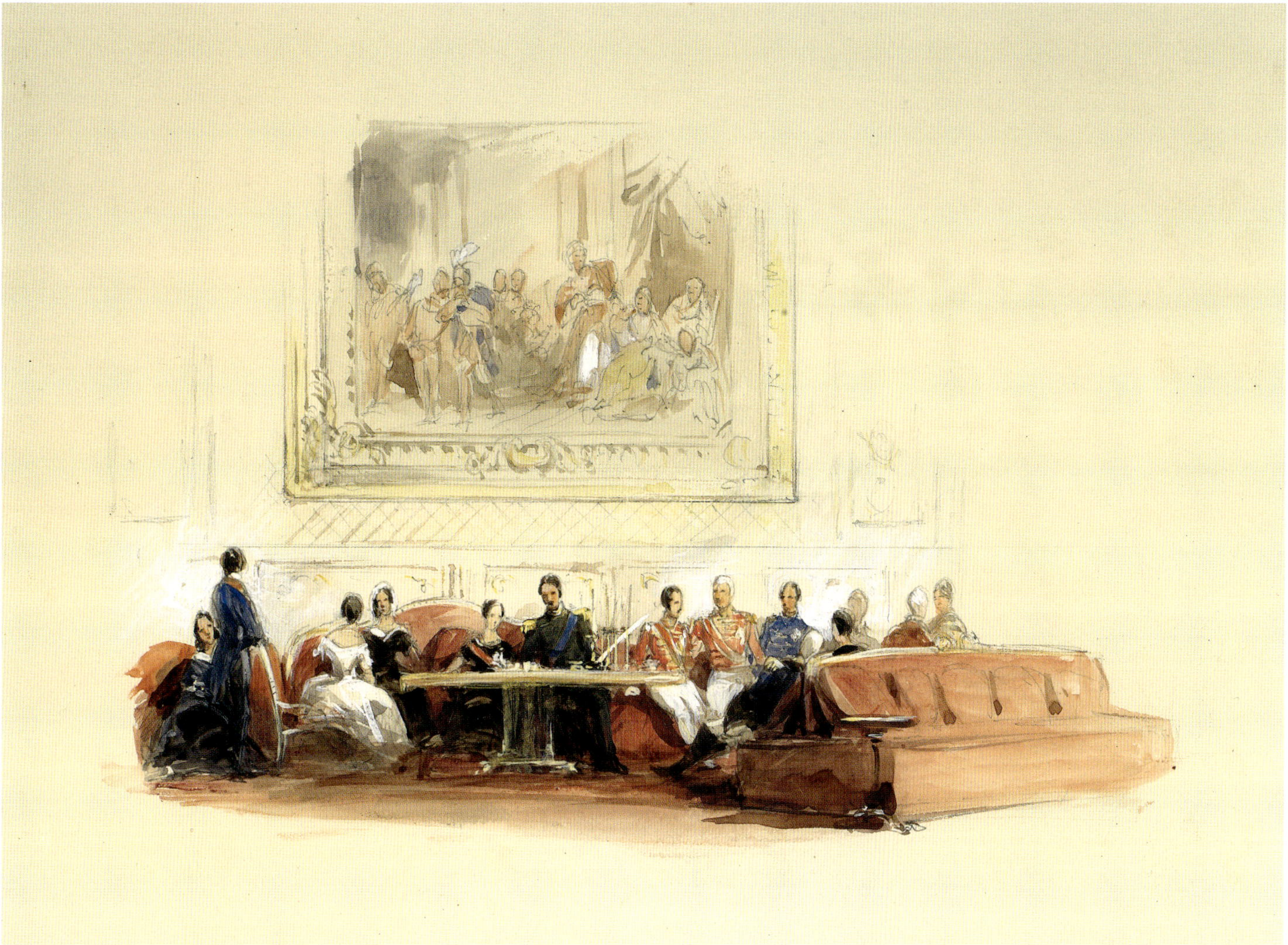

and King Edward VII (1841 1910) at Reval (now Tallinn) in 1908. The confused nature of the relationships was summed up by Lord Salisbury, who observed in September 1897 that 'the Russian administration especially in the foreign office clings to the "old traditions" despite the friendliness of the emperor'.[45]

By 1898, Queen Victoria, after 60 years of fluctuating relations with Russia observed that it was desirable to be on the best of terms with Russia, which was the only way to keep Germany in check.[46] She was informed that in both the court and society in Russia, there was a strong feeling in favour of an alliance with Britain,[47] an evolution of the relationship between the two countries which was a reflection of changing relations between Russia, Britain and Germany, influenced by the mutual dislike of the German and Russian Emperors. The following year, in August 1899, Lord Salisbury summed up the challenges of European diplomacy and the differing approaches of the authorities in St Petersburg, Berlin and Paris, describing the Russian government as 'Perfidious but pleasant in negotiation. On the whole the results to which it arrives are not worse than the results of the German Emperor's unreasoning caprice, or of the violent popular passions by which France is divided.'[48] This echoed Queen Victoria's last ambassador to St Petersburg, Sir Charles Stewart Scott (1838 –1924), who in June that year reported to her that 'things are going much better with us and Russia'.[49]

WILHELM ALEXANDER WOLFGANG VON KOBELL (1766–1853)

50 & 51

Bivouac of Cossacks 1802

Oil on panel, 31.8 × 43.2 cm
Signed and dated: *Wilhelm Kobel / 1802*
RCIN 400192

Bivouac of Cossacks 1802

Oil on panel, 31.9 × 43.3 cm
Signed and dated: *Wilhelm Kobell / 1802*
RCIN 400193

Provenance Purchased by George IV when Prince of Wales from Colnaghi, 27 December 1802; first recorded in Carlton House 1816 (nos 151, 152)

Literature *Great Britain – USSR* 1967, no. 155 (RCIN 400192)

Acquired by George IV when Prince of Wales in 1802, these contemporary scenes show Cossacks or 'Houlans' bivouacing, or resting in a temporary camp, as they journeyed across Europe to participate in the Napoleonic Wars, in their efforts to defeat Napoleon. Entitled 'Halt of the Houlans' and 'March of the Houlans' (Uhlans were a lancer regiment in the Russian, Prussian or Austrian armies) in an early nineteenth-century inventory, these small works suggest that the Prince of Wales was keenly aware of, and interested in the actions of his allies at this critical juncture in history. The paintings are recorded as hanging in the Middle Attic, situated next to the Prince Regent's Bedroom in Carlton House, amongst works by seventeenth-century Dutch Masters on a similar theme. They hung together with *A Hunting Party halting at a Wayside Inn* by Philips Wouwerman (1619–68) and *A Village Fair* by Isack van Ostade (1621–49), both recently purchased.[50] The soft, expansive skies, the interest in the surrounding landscape and the same absorption with everyday life on the road as a soldier are echoed in the works by Kobell. Attracted by the quality of the works, thinly painted on oak panels, and the subject matter – ordinary folk engrossed in everyday life – it appears that it was the visual similarity that attracted the Prince to these works, rather than the content.

Substantial Empire-style frames were commissioned for these scenes by the Prince of Wales to hang at Carlton House. AB

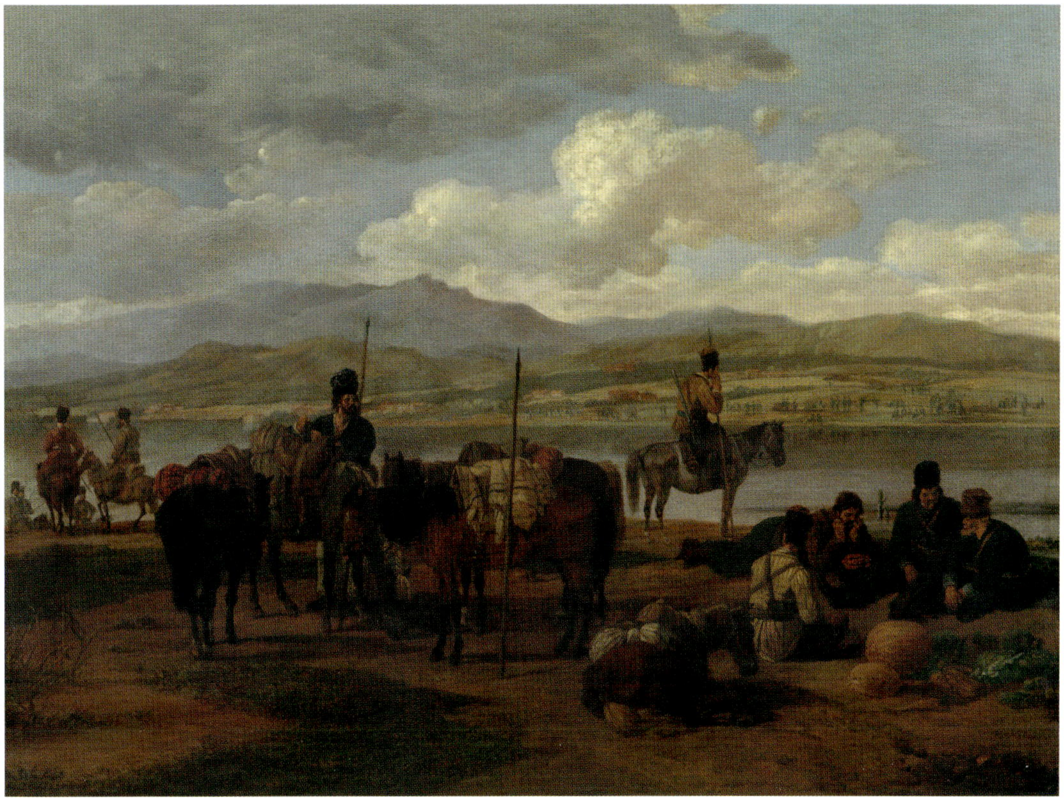

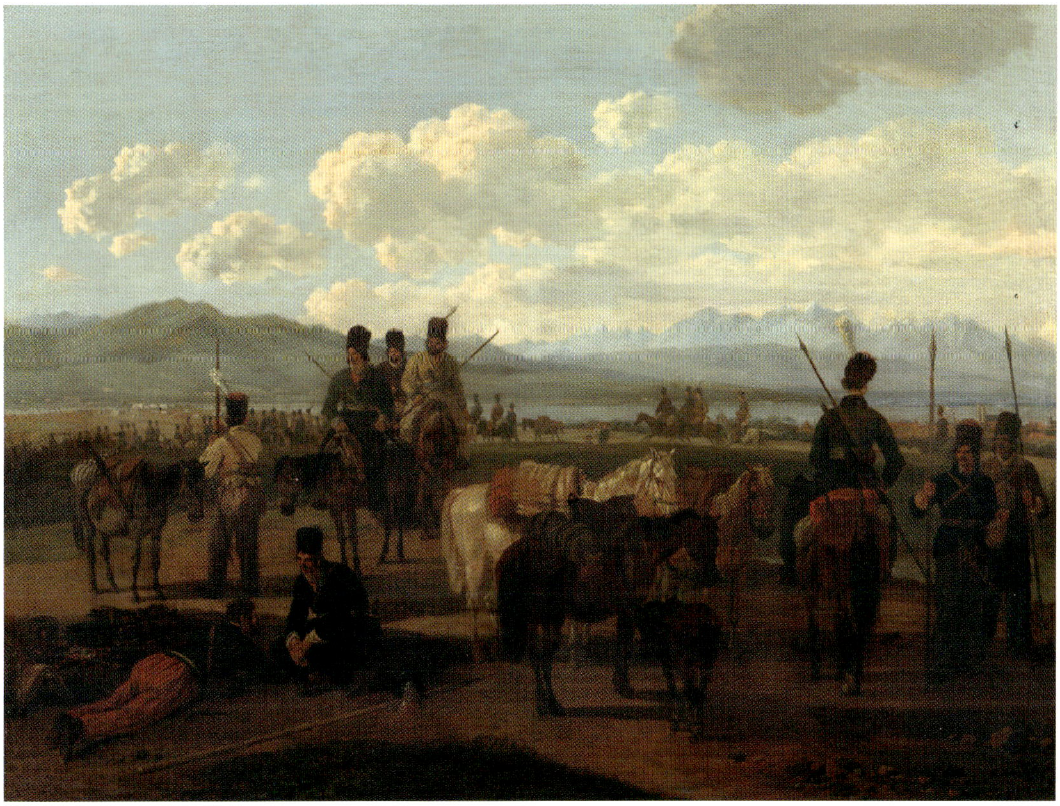

JEAN-PIERRE DROZ (1746–1823)

52–55 *Medal commemorating the Battle of Borodino* 1812

Silver, dia. 5.5 cm, weight 82.39 g
Inscribed on obverse: *NAPOLEON EMPEREUR ET ROI* ('Napoleon, Emperor and King'), and in the exergue: *BATAILLE DE LA MOSKOWA / 7 SEPTEMBRE 1812* ('Battle of the Moscova, 7 September 1812')
RCIN 444746

NICOLAS GUY ANTOINE BRENET (1773–1846)

Medal commemorating the French entry into Moscow (reverse) 1812

Silver restrike, dia. 4.1 cm, weight 37.21 g
Inscribed: *ENTRÉE Á MOSCOU* ('Entry into Moscow'), and in the exergue: *XIV.SEPTEMBRE/MDCCCXII* ('14 September 1812')
RCIN 444796

AUGUSTE FRANÇOIS MICHAUT (1786–1879)

Medal commemorating the French Army crossing the River Volga (reverse) 1812

Silver restrike, dia. 4.1 cm, weight 35.74 g
Inscribed in the exergue: *L'AIGLE FRANCAISE / SUR LE WOLGA. / M.DCCCXII* ('The French eagle on the Volga, 1812')
RCIN 444797

ROMAIN VINCENT JEUFFROY (1749–1826)

Medal commemorating the Battle of Borodino (reverse) 1812

Silver restrike, dia. 4.1 cm, weight 35.80 g
Inscribed: *BATAILLE DE LA MOSKOWA / VII SEPTEMBRE M.DCCCXII* ('Battle of the Moscova, 7 September 1812')
RCIN 444876

Provenance First recorded in the Royal Collection in the current reign (1952–)

Literature Bramsen 1904, nos 1164 (RCIN 444796), 1166 (RCIN 444797), 1162 (RCIN 444876); Forrer 1904–30, I, pp. 618–23 (RCIN 444746), 274–6 (RCIN 444796), 51–6, IV, pp. 60–64 (RCIN 444797), III, pp. 71–4 (RCIN 444876)

J.-P. Droz was a Swiss coin-engraver and medallist, and also an inventor of coin presses which, for the first time, could strike both sides of the medal at the same time. Feeling that his work was not receiving sufficient notice in France, in the 1780s he moved to the Soho Mint in Birmingham, where his work included designing new coins for George III. He returned to France in 1799, having been appointed Keeper of Coins and Medals by the Directory. The obverse of his medal to celebrate the battle of Borodino in 1812 is a laureate head of Napoleon, facing right. On the reverse, three warriors in lion-skins, like Hercules, one flourishing a club, strive together above two dead bodies. Overhead the French eagle soars. The battle of Borodino, also known as the battle of Moscova, took place on the Moscow-to-Smolensk road, near the confluence of tributaries of the Moskva river, as Kutusov tried to bar Napoleon's advance on Moscow. The Russian's 'great redoubt' in the centre of their line was eventually broken by a concentration of French artillery barrage, followed up by cavalry and infantry charges. The Russian forces withdrew from Moscow six days later, on 13 September.

The large number of medals minted in Paris to commemorate the achievements of Emperor Napoleon I were produced by several of the

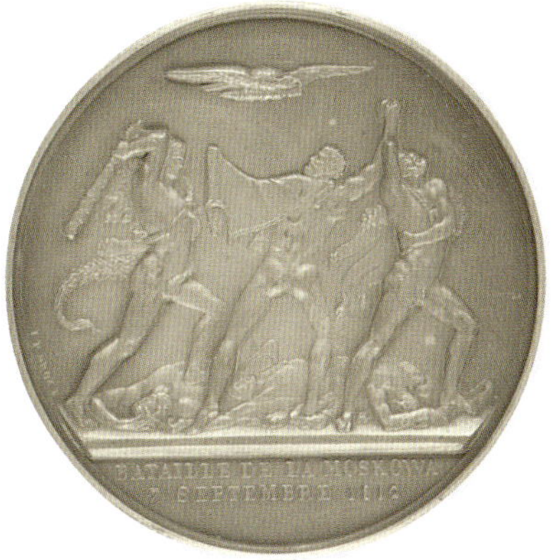

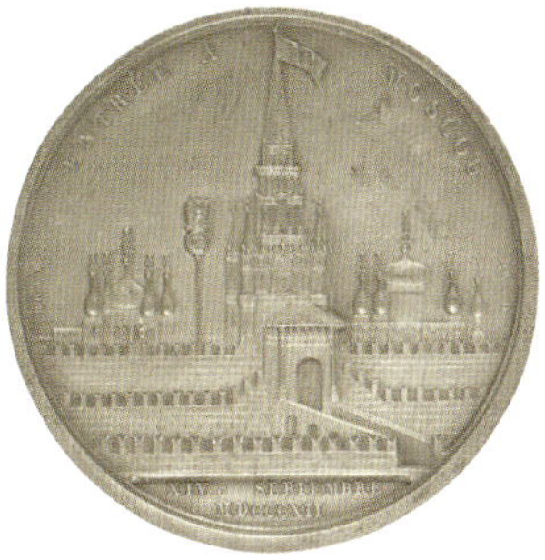

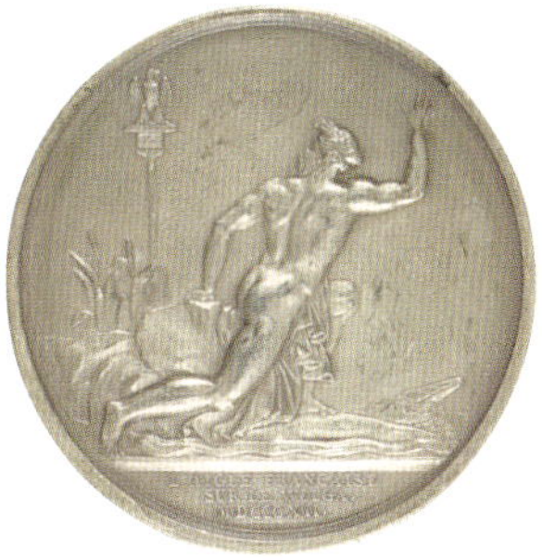

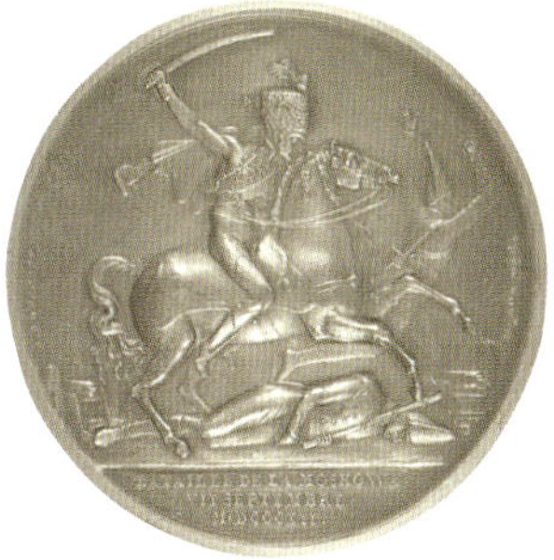

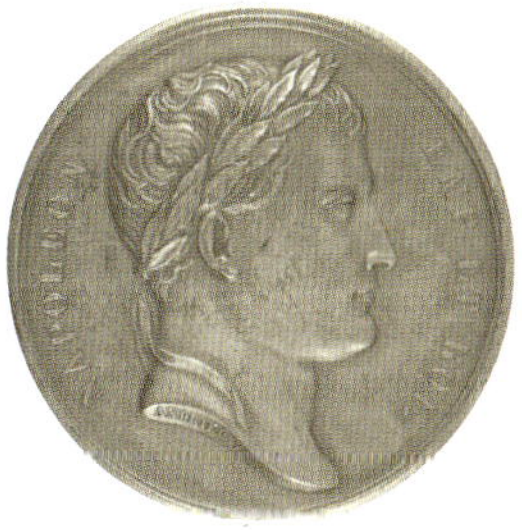

FIG. 12
Bertrand Andrieu (1761–1822)
Obverse
RCIN 444796

foremost medallists of the day, whose work also celebrated the kings of France who followed. The portraits of Napoleon and of Louis XVIII (1755–1824) by Andrieu were considered so beautiful that they were used for the obverses of many medals, with the reverses engraved by others. Michaut was also involved in designing coins. The reverse he designed shows the river god of the Volga staring at the French eagle standard set up in his rushes, symbolic of the French having crossed the river.

Jeuffroy was a gem-engraver as well as a medallist, and produced portrait medals of Louis XVI (1754–93) and his son before the French Revolution began, and at least one medal for the accession of Louis XVIII after Napoleon's defeat. His reverse in this group shows a French Hussar threatening a fleeing Russian soldier as his horse hurdles over a dead one.

Brenet's work included engraving the Emperor's head for use on the silver coinage and medals for the restored Bourbon kings. The reverse by him in this group shows the French tricolor flying from the Trinity Tower of the Kremlin, with the legend on either side.

All four of these French medals are restrikes by the Paris Mint. The Mint began reissuing medals for which they owned the dies in 1832, with a symbol called a *poinçon* on the rim and a note of the metal. These carry the conch as *poinçon*, which means that they date from 1880 or the decades after. **BW**

56 *Map case for Carte de la Russie Européenne* c.1812

Bound in red morocco, extensively gold-tooled with Napoleon's coat of arms on the box front, imperial laurel wreathes in the corners, 24.3 × 10.6 × 16.4 cm
RCIN 1146075

Provenance Originally owned by Napoleon I of France; later owned by Archduke Franz Salvator of Austria; purchased by John Jaffé of Nice, 1933, for presentation to King George V

This case once contained a large map of Russia (presumably in 11 sheets, now lost) used by Napoleon during his invasion of the country in 1812. It was acquired as part of a collection of Napoleon's books and maps at auction in Berlin, which were being sold by Archduke Franz Salvator (1866–1939). Napoleon was an avid book collector and reader, particularly the classics, and even had travelling libraries to take with him on campaign: 'The Emperor wants a portative library of a thousand volumes in 12mo., printed in good type, without margin, and composed as nearly as possible of 40 volumes on religion, 40 of epics, 40 of plays, 60 of poetry, 100 of novels, 60 of history, the remainder, to make up the 1,000, of historical memoirs'.[51]

The majority of the purchase was presented to the French people, to be displayed in the musée de Malmaison, but the Jaffés though it more appropriate to present the map case, and two cases of miniature copies of the English poets (which Napoleon had apparently bought to present to his son, Napoleon II, King of Rome, 1811–32), to King George V. European Russia is generally defined as being the western part of Russia situated on the European continent, bounded on the east by the Ural mountains. ES

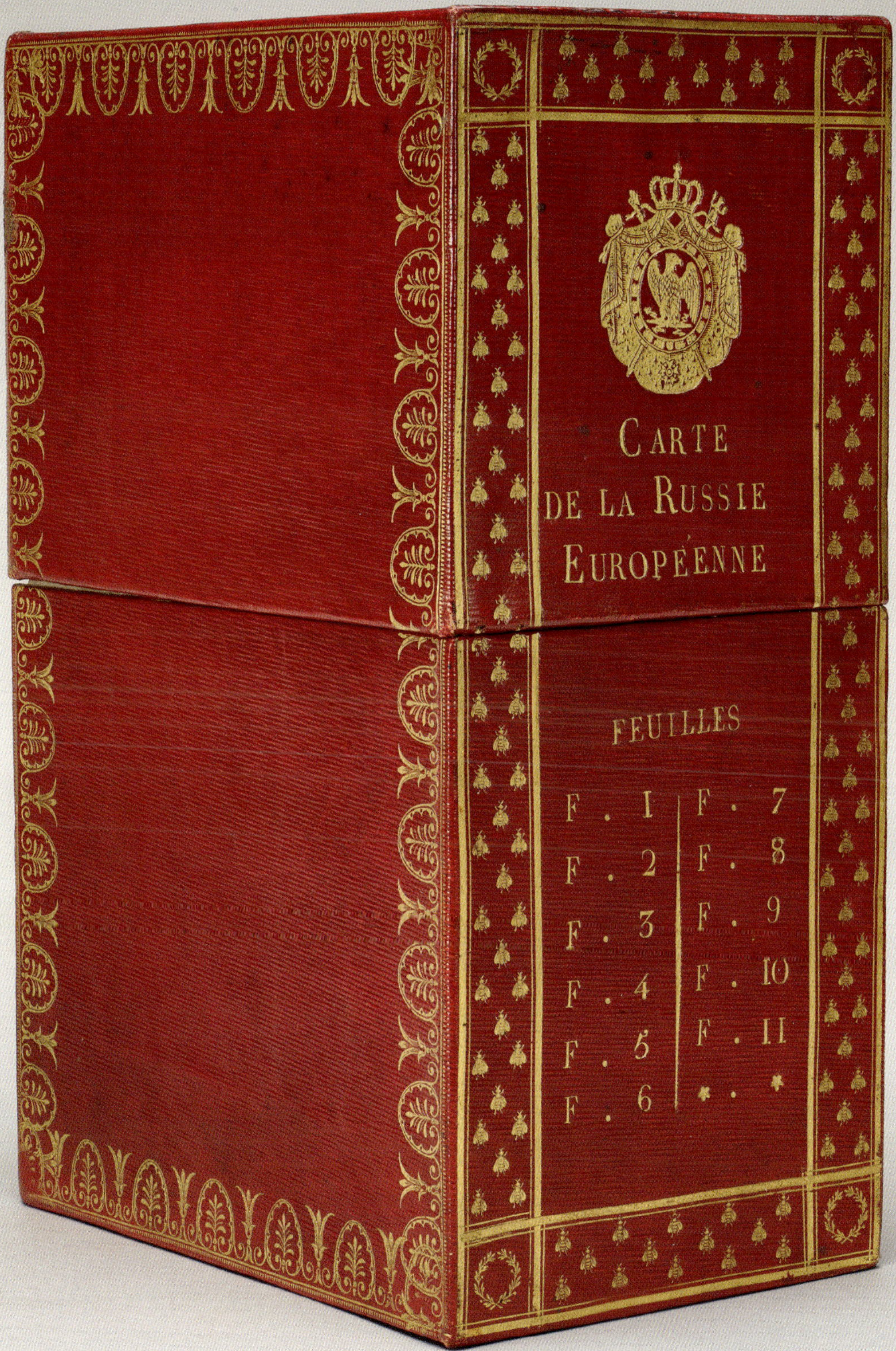
CARTE
DE LA RUSSIE
EUROPÉENNE
FEUILLES
F . 1 F . 7
F . 2 F . 8
F . 3 F . 9
F . 4 F . 10
F . 5 F . 11
F . 6 * . *

UNKNOWN CARTOGRAPHER, RUSSIAN SCHOOL

57 *Plan de la Capital Ville de Moscou …* c.1789–1812

Pen and ink with watercolour, 97.0 × 89.0 cm
Scale approx. 1:8,400
RCIN 710620

Provenance Presented by the First Master of Police in Moscow, de Caverine, to Prince William Frederick of Gloucester

This manuscript map of Moscow depicts the city's 20 quarters or districts, highlighted in different watercolour washes. The title, locations and key are in Russian Cyrillic script, with French translations written above, presumably added at a later date. The key lists the city's ramparts and the monasteries,[52] divided into their locations by quarter.

Moscow was built at the confluence of the rivers Moskva and Neglinnaia during the twelfth century, and the concentric development of the city from the walls of the *Kremlin* and *Kitai Gorod* (the area adjacent to the Kremlin), the *Belyi Gorod* or 'White City', and the *Zemlianoi Gorod* or 'Earthen City' to the outer wall known as the *Kamer College* can be clearly seen. From 1775, attempts were made by Empress Catherine II to improve the spatial planning and architecture of Moscow, in an effort to turn it into a more 'enlightened' city at the heart of her empire, following the example of classicism used in St Petersburg. It seems likely that the map derives from the 1789 plan by Ivan Marchenkov, itself a derivation of the plan created in 1775.[53] The tree-lined Boulevard Ring is clearly visible, replacing the fortified walls of the *Belyi Gorod*. In 1812, during the course of the Napoleonic Wars, much of Moscow was destroyed by fire when the Russians abandoned the city as Napoleon marched upon it. A plan to rebuild Moscow was finalised in 1817.[54]

There is a note under the title of the map, in French,[55] stating that the plan was presented by de Caverine, First Master of Police of Moscow, to Prince William Frederick of Gloucester (1776–1834), nephew of George III and, from 1805, 2nd Duke of Gloucester and Edinburgh (fig. 13).[56] Prince William Frederick had entered the army at the age of 13 and progressed rapidly, becoming a field marshal in 1816.[57] It is not clear why de Caverine presented him with this map; however, Prince William Frederick seems to have had an interest in Russia and owned a book describing the uniforms and military equipment of Catherine the Great's army.[58] **RW**

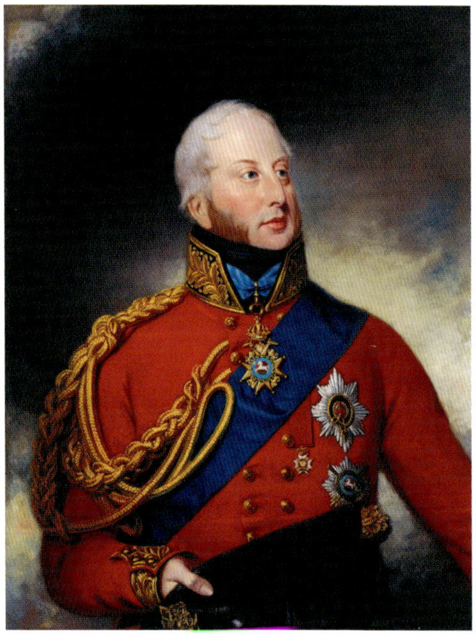

FIG. 13
British School, nineteenth century
William Frederick, 2nd Duke of Gloucester, c.1816
Oil on canvas, 92.5 × 76.3 cm
RCIN 407417

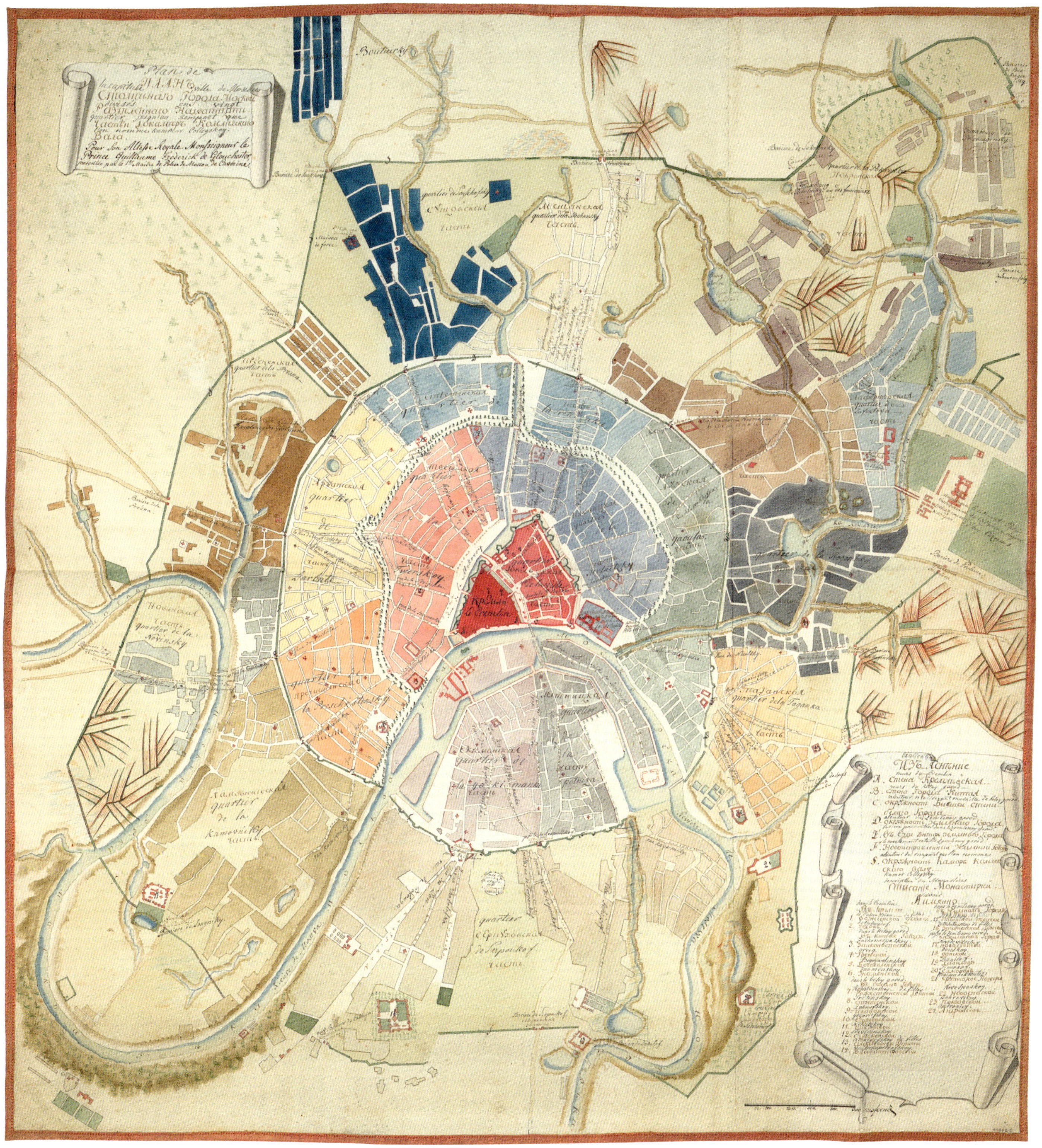
Plan de
ПЛАНЪ
Pour Son Altesse Royale Monseigneur le
Prince Guillaume Frederick de Glouchester
Boutirky
le Kremlin

GEORGE DAWE (1781–1829)

58 & 59

Alexander I, Emperor of Russia (1777–1825) c.1819–25

Oil on canvas, 240.2 × 155.0 cm
Signed lower right: *Geo. Dawe R.A. / Pinxt.*
RCIN 400098

Elizabeth, Empress of Russia (1779–1826) after 1 December 1825

Oil on canvas, 240.8 × 154.6 cm
RCIN 400076

Provenance Collection of Mrs Pitt; Duchess Marie of Saxe-Coburg and Gotha until 1860; Reverend Charles Whitworth Pitt; purchased by Queen Victoria for £190, 1861

Literature Millar 1969, nos 746, 747; Andreeva 2012, p. 141

These portraits were both painted in Russia during Dawe's ten-year tenure in the service of Alexander I. Originally they formed part of the collection of Mrs Pitt (née Frances Brompton), a close companion of Empress Elizabeth, passing to Duchess Marie of Saxe-Coburg and Gotha (1799–1860), until her death, when they returned to the collection of Mrs Pitt's son, the Reverend Charles Whitworth Pitt (b.1802), formerly Chaplain to the Duchess of Kent (1786–1861), Queen Victoria's mother. Reverend Pitt offered them to Queen Victoria in 1861, and on 26 July they arrived at Buckingham Palace 'in good order' in their 'massive gold frames'.[59] They are first recorded hanging on the Household Corridor in Buckingham Palace in 1876, and later, during the reign of King Edward VII, that of the Emperor in the Centre Room (fig. 14).

The figure of Alexander is a repetition of the versions in the State Hermitage Museum, one of which was painted in 1824. It is inscribed by the artist as having been completed after the 'first sitting given by the Emperor', on 28 May 1823. This and other repetitions are almost certainly based on the small image painted in 1818 (cat. 60).[60]

The tall, handsome Emperor stands amidst a barren landscape in the undress uniform of a Russian field marshal, with the Sword of Sweden, the star of St Andrew of Russia with

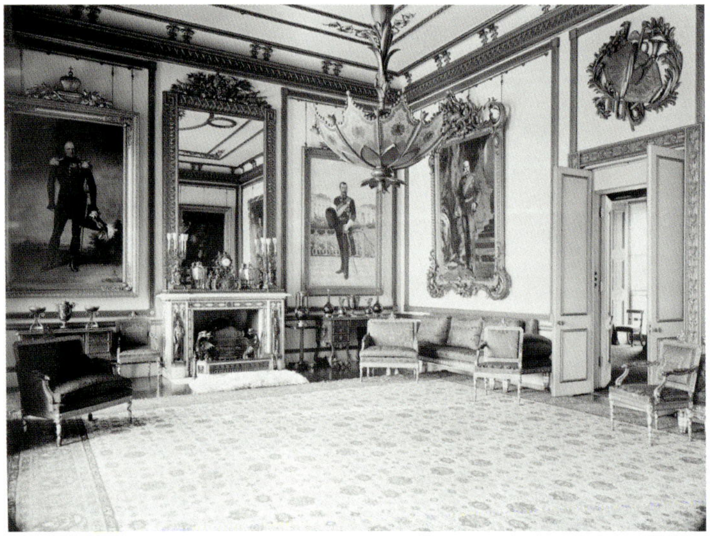

FIG. 14
Sir Alexander Nelson Hood
*Centre Room, Buckingham Palace, c.*1914
Gelatin silver print, 39.9 × 49.5 cm
RCIN 2101628

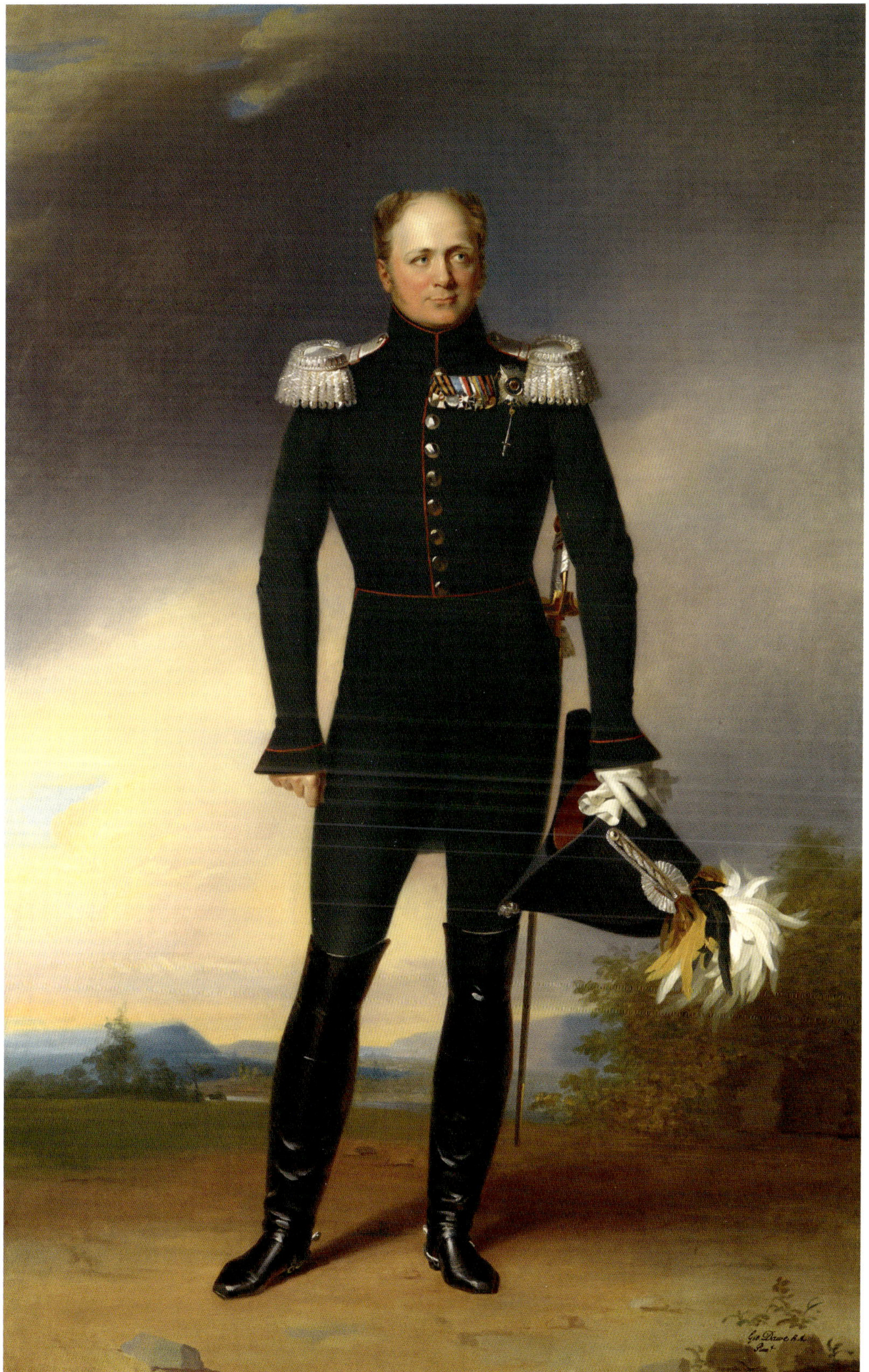

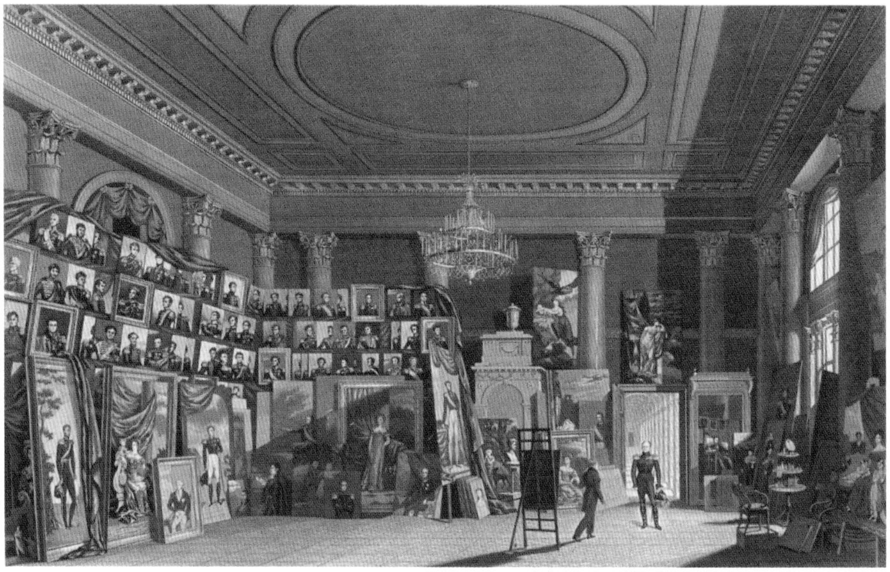

FIG. 15
After Andrey Efimovich Martynov
Mr Dawe's atelier in the Hermitage, St Petersburg, published 1 January 1826
Aquatint with engraving, 45.5 × 60.3 cm
RCIN 653427

the Order of the Garter, badges of St George of Russia and Maria Theresa of Austria, the Iron Cross of Prussia and the 1812 medal. A contemporary reviewer praised the monarch's 'majestic pose', the economic monochrome palette – which he compared to that of Van Dyck – and the dark cloud, introduced to 'better set off the head'.[61] A widely distributed engraving and aquatint by J. Bennet and Thomas Wright (1792–1849), published by Colnaghi & Co. in London on 1 January 1826, after a drawing by Andrey Efimovich Martynov (1768–1826), records a visit by the Emperor to Dawe's atelier, which was situated within the Winter Palace (fig. 15). The room is surrounded by recently completed portraits for the Emperor's Military Gallery, the stance of the Emperor echoing this pose.

The portrait of the Empress began as a three-quarter-length, but was presumably extended to create a companion portrait to that of her husband for Mrs Pitt. Dressed in mourning clothes, following her husband's death from typhus on 1 December 1825, the portrait must have been completed before the sitter's own death five months later. The grieving widow stands, hands clasped to her heart, as she contemplates a bust of her husband, in the guise of a classical god, dressed with a laurel wreath. In the distance, the sun sets over Taganrog, southern Russia, the place of Alexander's death and the couple's summer residence.[62] Despite an unhappy marriage, with both partners leading separate lives and having affairs, the couple were reconciled before their deaths and Elizabeth was inconsolable on his demise, recalling, 'I do not understand myself, I do not understand my destiny [...] what am I to do with my will, which was entirely subjected to him, with my life which I loved to devote to him.'[63] **AB**

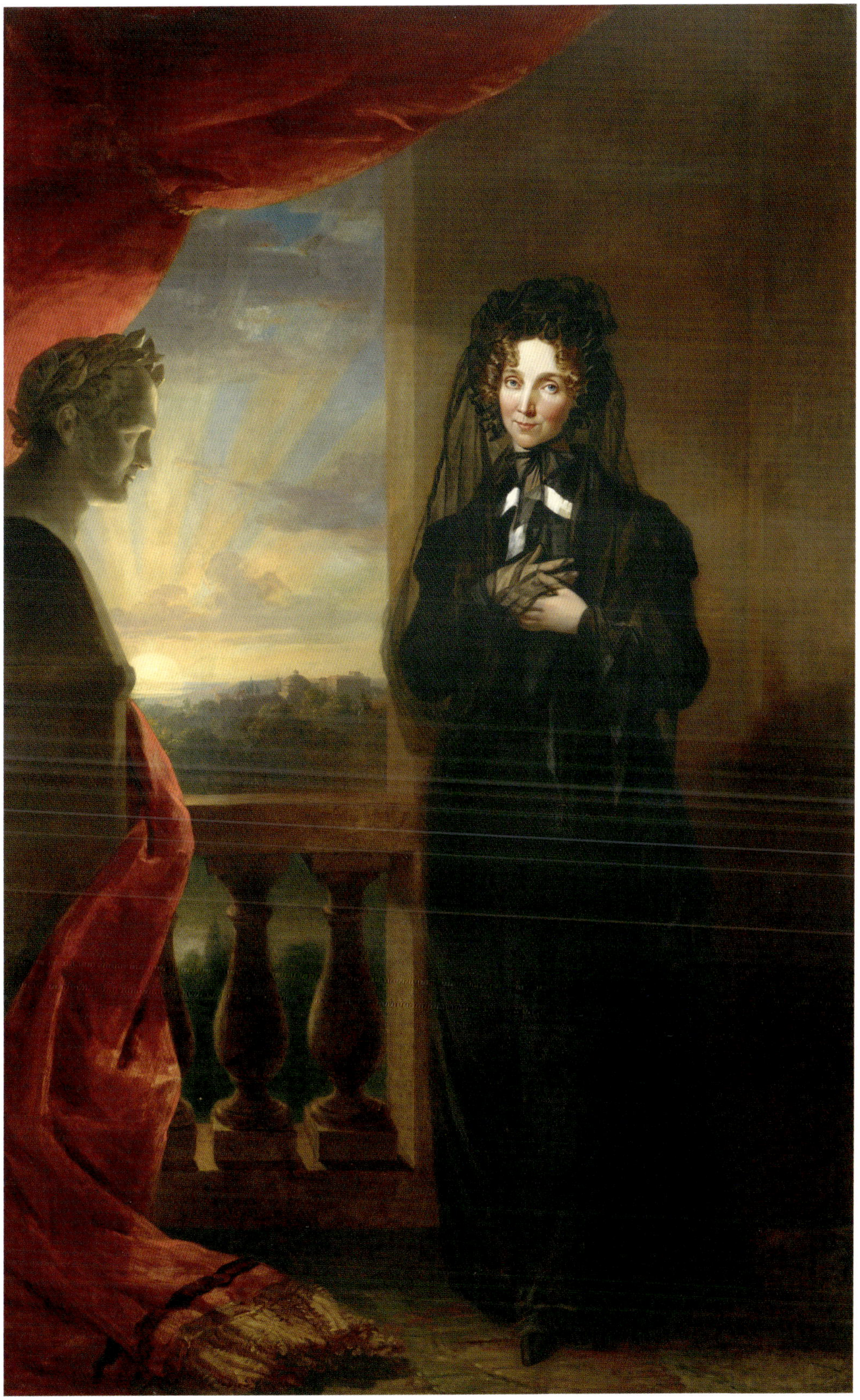

GEORGE DAWE (1781–1829)

60 *Alexander I, Emperor of Russia (1777–1825)* ?1818

Oil on canvas, 61.1 × 42.5 cm
Signed and dated: *Geo. Dawe. / 181[8]?*
RCIN 400570

Provenance Acquired by Prince Albert, September 1844

Literature Millar 1969, no. 745

This is the earliest of Dawe's portraits of Alexander I, who was to become his patron, and was used by him as a model for all subsequent large-scale portraits of the Emperor (cat. 58). The image also appears in many other forms – engravings, porcelain and miniatures. It was presumably painted in the autumn of 1818 at Aix-la-Chapelle (now Aachen), where the artist and Emperor first met, making it contemporary with the masterful full-length of Alexander by Sir Thomas Lawrence (fig. 16). Dawe was then in the retinue of Edward, Duke of Kent (1767–1820), travelling to Paris, Cambrai, Brussels and Aix-la-Chapelle, where ongoing negotiations of the congress of the Grand Alliance against France took place. He came to the attention of the Emperor whilst painting a portrait of Prince Volkonsky (1788–1865), and was invited to St Petersburg to paint over 300 portraits of Russian generals who had distinguished themselves in the war against Napoleon. The portraits were housed in the Military Gallery, specially created in the Winter Palace (the equivalent of the Waterloo Chamber at Windsor Castle). This would seem to contradict a label, on the reverse, written by Henry Dawe (1790–1848), a painter and engraver who also worked in Russia, stating that the portrait was 'painted by my brother Geo. Dawe R.A. during his stay in Russia. and was brought by him to England'.

Alexander wears the undress uniform of a Russian field marshal, with the Sword of Sweden, the star of St Andrew of Russia with the Order of the Garter, badges of St George of Russia, Maria Theresa of Austria, the Iron Cross of Prussia and the 1812 medal. AB

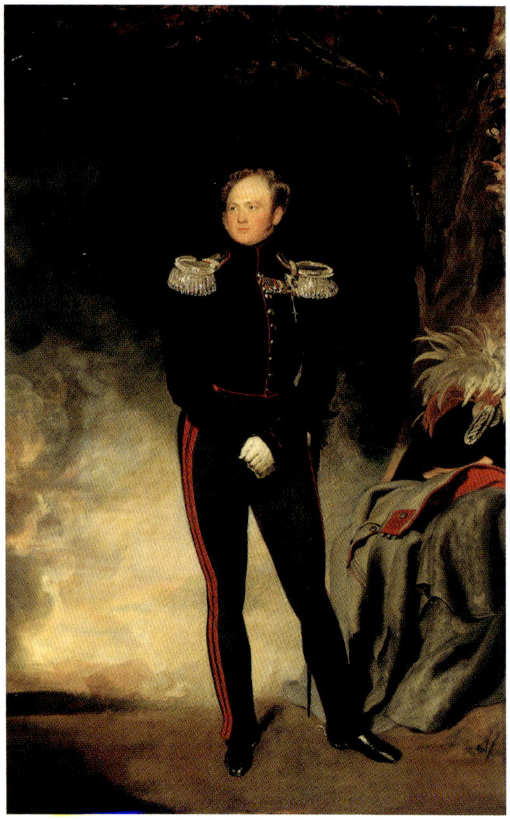

FIG. 16
Sir Thomas Lawrence
Alexander I, Emperor of Russia, 1814–18
Oil on canvas, 273.8 × 179.5 cm
RCIN 404942

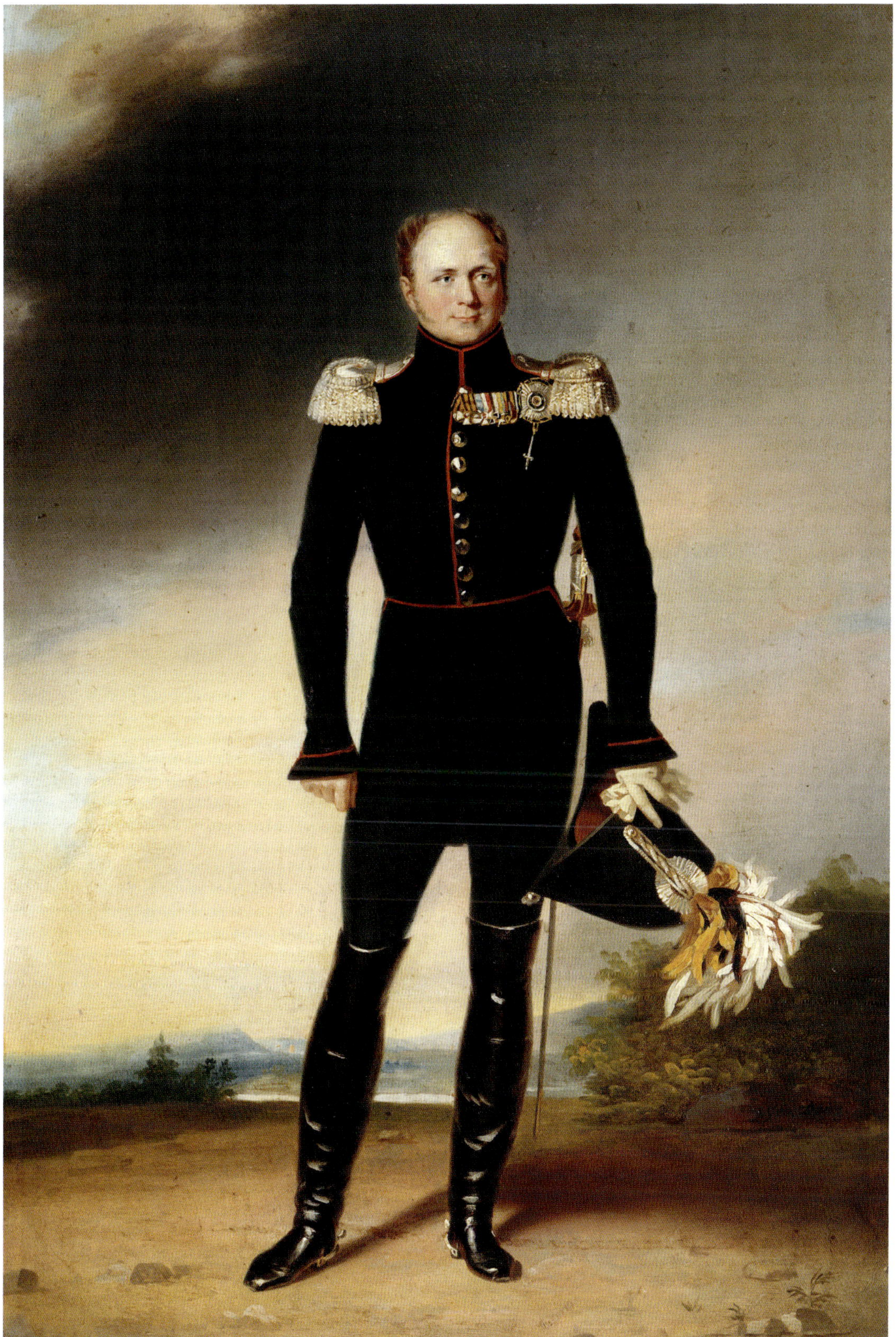

JOHN BOADEN (1792/3–1839)

61 *Alexander I, Emperor of Russia (1777–1825)* 1814

Oil on canvas, 75.3 × 62.8 cm
Inscribed on back with painter's name and date, 1814, on relining canvas
RCIN 406999

Provenance Acquired by George IV when Prince Regent; received at Carlton House from Colnaghi, 8 June 1814 (Carlton House 1816, no. 454, in the Armoury)

Literature Millar 1969, no. 686

This portrait of Alexander I was delivered to Carlton House only days after the Emperor's arrival in London on 6 June 1814, suggesting that it was not painted from life. Prints after a painting by Roman Maksimovich Volkov were circulating in London in 1814 and this is almost certainly the source from which the portrait was derived (fig. 17). The Emperor wears the dark blue uniform of a field marshal, with the ribbon and star of St Andrew of Russia and the badge of St George of Russia. In his comprehensive late nineteenth-century inventory, Richard Redgrave notes that the portrait was purchased by the Princess Royal, and therefore may have been a gift to her brother. The painting is recorded as hanging in the Armoury at Carlton House, surrounded by other portraits of European monarchs.[64]

The portrayal hints at the Emperor's genial personality; he appeared to have the common touch and seemed genuinely interested in people. His arrival in London was welcomed and he apparently spent one of his first evenings in London, bowing at the balcony of the Pulteney Hotel (seemingly having declined to stay at St James's Palace), to cheering crowds.[65] **AB**

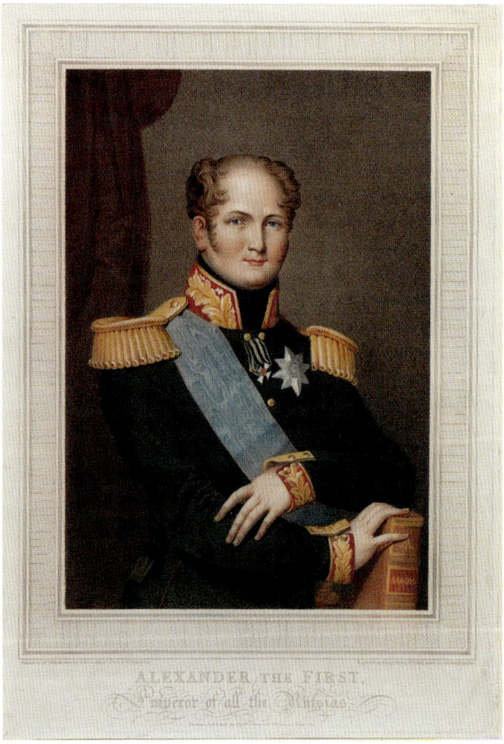

FIG. 17
Henry Meyer, after
Roman Maksimovich Volkov
Alexander the First (Emperor of Russia), 1814
Stipple engraving, printed in colours, with some hand colouring, 51.0 × 36.4 cm
RCIN 614509

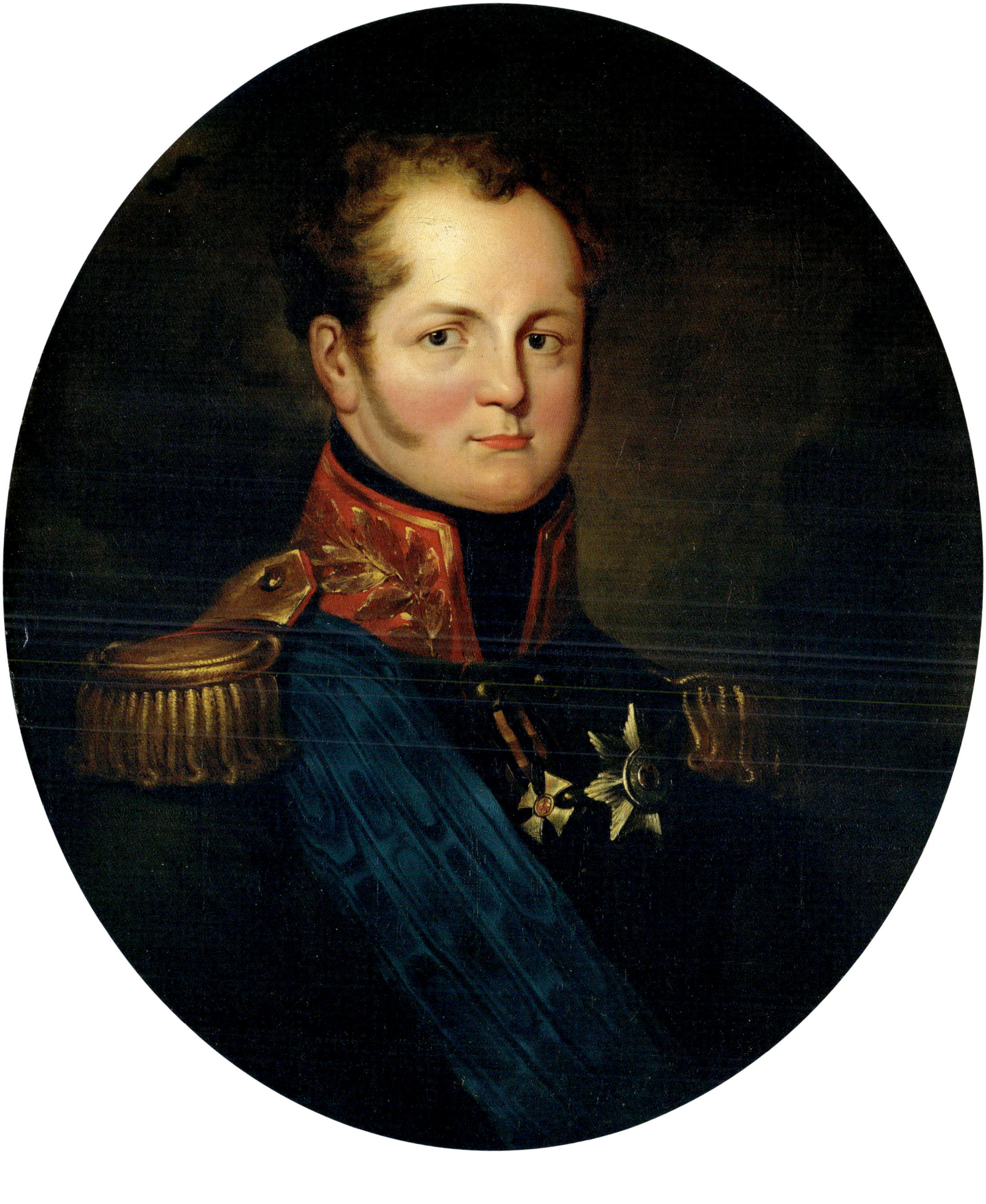

RUSSIAN

62 *Bust of Emperor Alexander I (1777–1825)* c.1812

Bronze, 16.6 × 12.5 × 7.5 cm
RCIN 2207

Provenance Acquired by George IV, 8 June 1812

Literature Jutsham Recs I, no. 199; 4 Mss Pte Prop. GIV, p. 23

This small portrait bust of the Emperor was probably produced in the early part of his reign (1801–25), when Alexander I succeeded his father, Paul I. The bust is recorded as being received from Lord Yarmouth (1777–1842) on 4 June 1812 by George IV's inventory clerk, Jutsham, and was then sent to Windsor Castle on 28 November 1828. The bust was originally more elaborately mounted, as recorded by Jutsham: 'on bronze & ormolu pedestal and plinth on a Marone [*sic*] coloured china column chased borders & square Ormolu plinth shade & stand. H: 25"'. Other versions of the same bust indicate how it might have appeared on its original column.[66] A further portrait bust in plaster was in the Collection until it was accidently destroyed in 1906; it was signed, *Paris le v mai par michalon* ('Paris 5 May by Michalon'), although this was life-size.[67]

A further contemporary portrait bust of Alexander I was made in Paris by Jean-Antoine Houdon (1741–1828) in 1814, and recorded in an engraving (fig. 18).

The present bust is recorded in Buckingham Palace by the early twentieth century, but the removal of the original pedestal is not recorded.

Lord Yarmouth became a member of the Privy Council and Vice Chamberlain of the Royal Household in 1812, and was made a Knight of the Order of the Garter in 1822. The bust depicts Alexander I in military uniform and wearing the sash and star of the Order of St Andrew. Following victories by the British and Russian allies in the Napoleonic Wars, images of Alexander I and the victorious Russian generals were popularised by numerous souvenirs produced in porcelain and glass, particularly following the Treaty of Vienna signed in 1815, and continued to be produced well into the 1820s.

CDEG

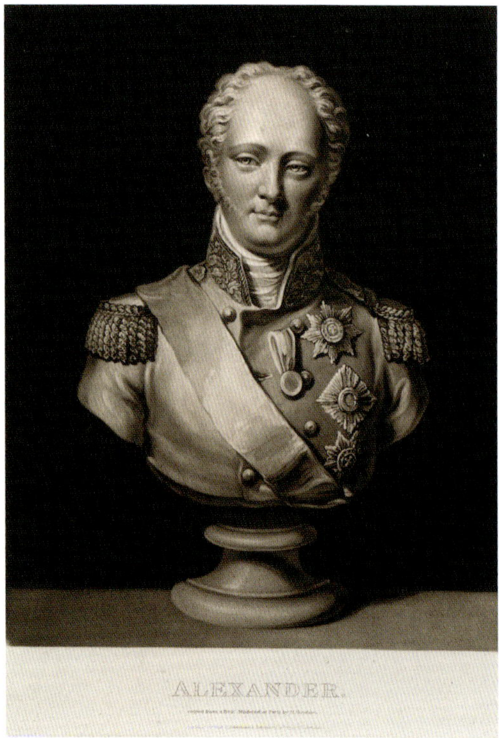

FIG. 18
After Jean-Antoine Houdon
Alexander I, Emperor of Russia, published 1 August 1814
Engraving
RCIN 614526

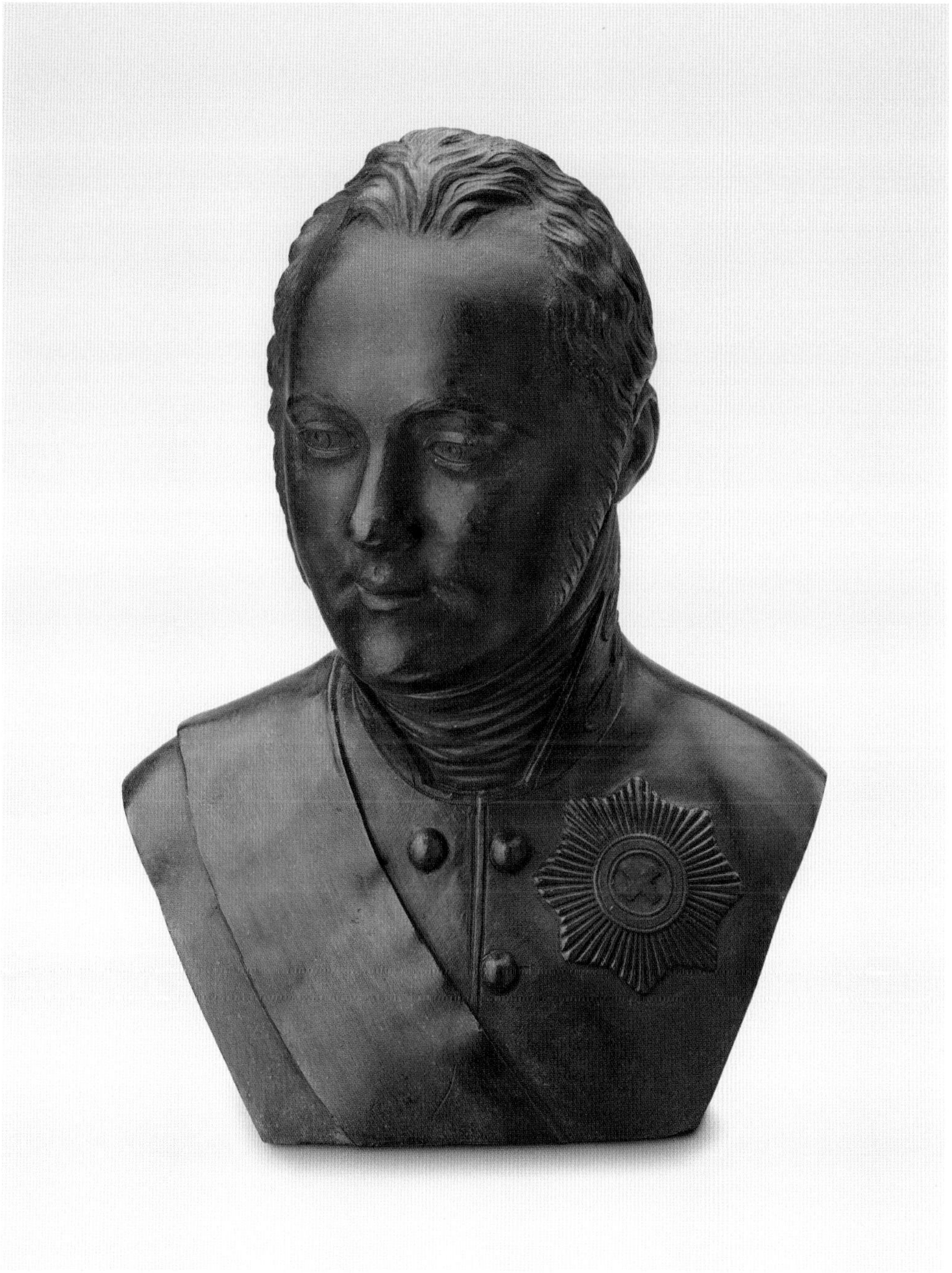

CONRAD HEINRICH KÜCHLER (active 1763–1821)

63 *Pattern ruble of Emperor Alexander I (1777–1825)* 1804

Bronze, dia. 4.09 cm, weight 26.58 g
RCIN 445440

Provenance First recorded in the Royal Collection in the current reign (1952–)

Literature Forrer 1904–30, iii, pp. 234–43; Pollard 1970

Küchler's initial place of work was Darmstadt, and he worked for various German mints before moving to the Soho Mint in Birmingham *c.*1790. There he produced dies for numerous coins, British, Danish, Portuguese and Russian. This last was the ruble of 1804, which was minted in gold, silver and bronze. He also produced a memorial medalet for Catherine the Great in 1796, and a medal for the Accession of Emperor Alexander I in 1801. The obverse of the ruble shows a uniformed bust of the Emperor facing right, with the legend: *ALEXANDER I. D:G. IMP.AVTOCR.RUSSOR* ('Alexander I, by the Grace of God, Emperor, and Autocrat of the Russians'). The reverse bears a cross of St George, with the date 1804. BW

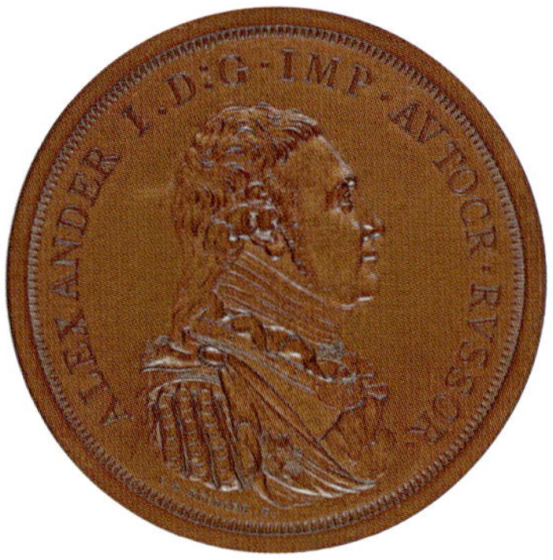

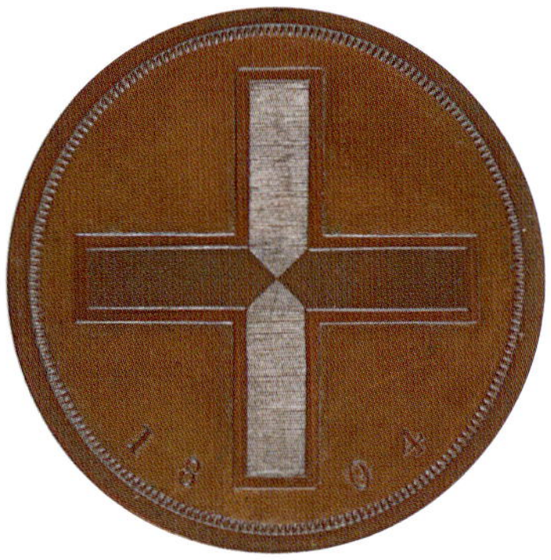

EMPEROR ALEXANDER I OF RUSSIA (1777–1825)

64 *Certificate of acceptance of the Order of the Garter* 1813

Vellum, 56.5 × 46.5 cm
RA GEO/MAIN/20913

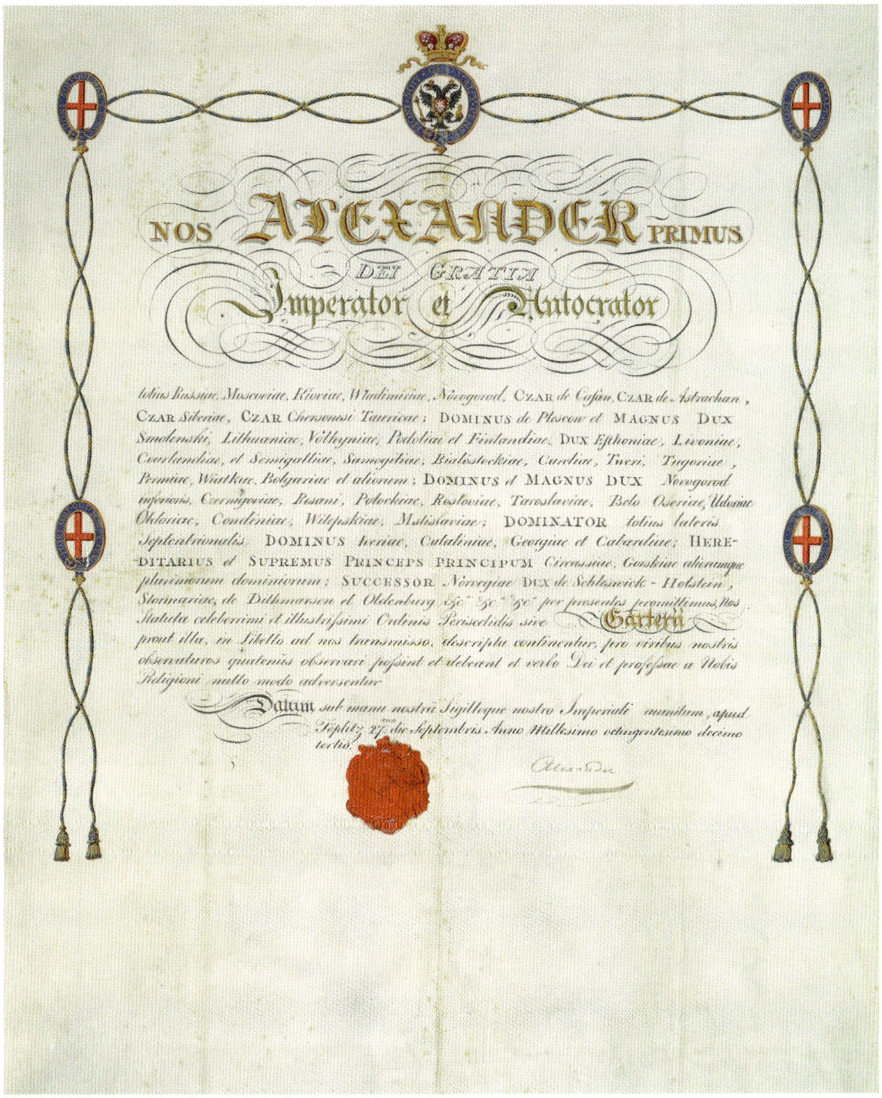
NOS ALEXANDER PRIMUS
DEI GRATIA
Imperator et Autocrator
totius Russiae, Moscoviae, Kioviae, Wladimiriae, Novogorod, CZAR de Casan, CZAR de Astrachan, CZAR Siberiae, CZAR Chersonesi Tauricae; DOMINUS de Plescow et MAGNUS DUX Smolenski, Lithuaniae, Volhyniae, Podoliae et Finlandiae, DUX Esthoniae, Livoniae, Courlandiae, et Semigalliae, Samogitiae, Bialostockiae, Careliae, Tweri, Tugoriae, Permiae, Wiatkiae, Bolgariae et aliorum; DOMINUS et MAGNUS DUX Novogorod inferioris, Czernigoviae, Resani, Polockiae, Rostoviae, Taroslaviae, Belo Oseriae, Udoriae Obdoriae, Condiniae, Witepskiae, Mstislaviae; DOMINATOR totius lateris Septentrionalis DOMINUS Iveriae, Cartaliniae, Georgiae et Cabardiae; HEREDITARIUS et SUPREMUS PRINCEPS PRINCIPUM Circassiae, Gorskiae aliorumque plurimorum dominiorum; SUCCESSOR Norvegiae DUX de Schleswick-Holstein, Stormariae, de Dithmarsen et Oldenburg &c. &c. &c. per presentes promittimus, Nos Statuta celeberrimi et illustrissimi Ordinis Periscelidis sive Garterii prout illa, in Libello ad nos transmisso, descripta continentur, pro viribus nostris observaturos quatenus observari possint et debeant et verbo Dei et professae a Nobis Religioni nullo modo adversentur.

Datum sub manu nostra Sigilloque nostro Imperiali munitum, apud Töplitz 27mo die Septembris Anno Millesimo octingentesimo decimo tertio.

Alexander

Alexander I was appointed a knight of the Garter by the Prince Regent, on behalf of his father, George III, in 1813. The investiture took place at Toplitz (now Teplice in the Czech Republic) on 27 September – the anniversary of the Emperor's coronation in 1802 – at the time of the signing of the Treaty of Toplitz during the Napoleonic War of the Sixth Coalition. The treaty between the Emperors of Austria and Russia and the King of Prussia in August 1813 resulted in the triple alliance against Napoleon that led to the coalition victory at the battle of Kulm.

The Emperor was invested with the Garter by Viscount Cathcart, British ambassador in St Petersburg, attended by the officers of the Order of the Garter and various senior Russian military officers and statesmen, including Count Nesselrode and General Uvarov, both of whom would be painted by Lawrence for the Waterloo Chamber (cats 69 and 70).

After the investiture with the insignia and habit of the Order, the Emperor was handed a copy of the statutes and returned a signed certificate of the acceptance of the Order – the current document.

Following a full rendition of the Emperor's titles, commencing with 'Emperor and sole ruler of the whole of Russia, of Moscow, Kiev, Vladimir, Novgorod …' Alexander committed to upholding the statutes of the Order, which he signed and sealed with the imperial seal.

Alexander attended the Garter service at Windsor in 1814; his Garter costume remains in the Hermitage collections in St Petersburg. SJP

PHILIP DODDRIDGE (1702–1751)

65 *Some remarkable passages in the life of the Honourable Colonel J. Gardiner, who was slain at the battle of Prestonpans, September 21, 1745 …* 1807

London: R. Mozley for J. Brambles, A. Meggitt & J. Waters
Bound in brown calf, 14.0 × 9.0 cm (closed)
Presentation inscription to Alexander I on first flyleaf: *Sire, / I beg your Majesty's acceptance of this small token of the respect which in common with the whole British nation, I entertain for your Majesty. May it serve your Majesty as a perpetual memento of your visit to our happy country. / A humble and obscure youth like me, would not have presumed upon a favourable reception, in daring in this manner to approach your Majesty, had I not been well assured that your Majesty knows not to refuse anything that comes from the hands of An Englishman.*
On rear flyleaf: *Det tibi Dominus Deus in omni opere bono perseverantiam* ('May the Lord God grant you perseverance in every good deed')
RCIN 1081550

Provenance Presented to Emperor Alexander I of Russia by Edmund Hepple, 12 June 1814; later acquired by Queen Victoria

At first sight a rather insignificant gift to the Hero of Europe, Philip Doddridge's life of James Gardiner was presented to Alexander I during his visit to England by one Edmund Hepple, on 12 June 1814. Gardiner had fought on the Hanoverian side against the Jacobites and had been killed at the battle of Prestonpans (21 September 1745). His bravery led to a certain popular notoriety at the time, augmented in print by his biography written by Philip Doddridge.

Doddridge was a nonconformist, independent minister, and a friend of Gardiner, whose life Doddridge saw as a classic account of the transition from sin to repentance and redemption, the ideal Christian hero. In the encomium he pronounced at Gardiner's funeral, he stated, 'I purpose publishing, in a distinct Tract, Some remarkable Passages of his Life, illustrated by Extracts from his own Letters, which speak in the most forcible Manner the genuine Sentiments of his Heart'.[68] The biography proved hugely popular, with a third edition produced by 1748, and at least 26 further editions before the end of the eighteenth century, as well as several translations and abridgements.

Walter Scott memorialised Gardiner in *Waverley*: 'In his early years he had been what is called, by manner of palliative, a very gay young man, and strange stories were circulated about his sudden conversion from doubt, if not infidelity, to a serious and even enthusiastic turn of mind.'[69] It is possible that these aspects of Colonel Gardiner's character led Mr Hepple to choose this book to give to the Emperor, whose own personal piety was known: 'Placing myself firmly in the hands of God I submit blindly to his will. […] My faith is sincere and warm with passion. Every day it grows firmer and I experience joys I never had known before'.[70] His sympathies may also have lain with Doddridge as an independent minister, given his interest in the Society of Friends (Quakers). This had public expression a week later, when Alexander attended a Quaker meeting on Sunday 19 June 1814 (the day after the lavish Guildhall banquet), and on the following Tuesday he met prominent Quakers, including William Allen (1770–1843), the scientist and philanthropist, at his hotel in London. He conversed with them for about an hour in perfect amity, and invited any Quakers who should come to St Petersburg to pay him a visit. A Quaker, Daniel Wheeler (1771–1840) and his family, would later be instrumental in helping to reclaim significant amounts of marshy land around St Petersburg.[71] **ES**

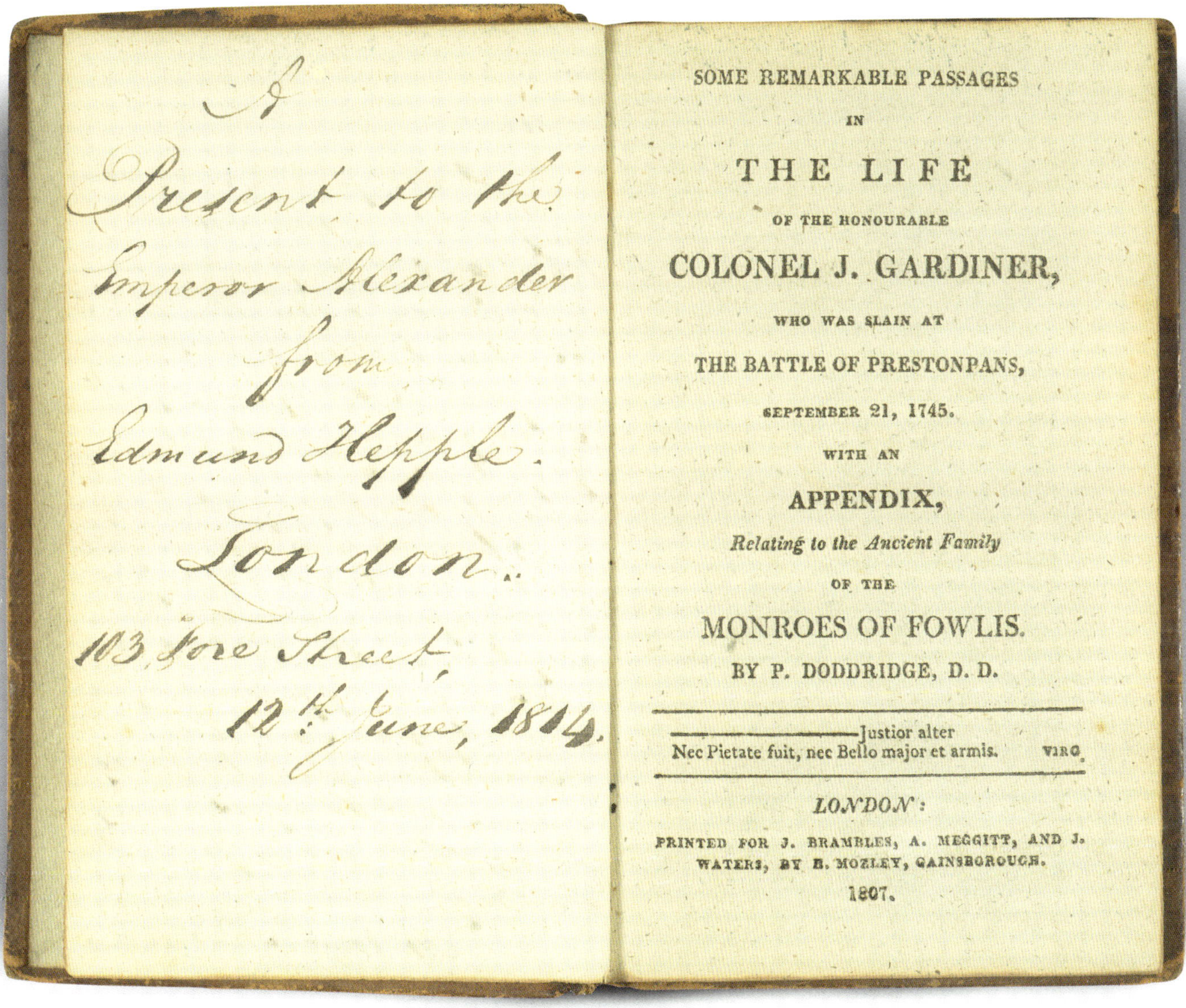

A
Present to the
Emperor Alexander
from
Edmund Hepple.
London.
103, Fore Street,
12th June, 1814.

SOME REMARKABLE PASSAGES
IN
THE LIFE
OF THE HONOURABLE
COLONEL J. GARDINER,
WHO WAS SLAIN AT
THE BATTLE OF PRESTONPANS,
SEPTEMBER 21, 1745.
WITH AN
APPENDIX,
Relating to the Ancient Family
OF THE
MONROES OF FOWLIS.
BY P. DODDRIDGE, D. D.

———Justior alter
Nec Pietate fuit, nec Bello major et armis. VIRG.

LONDON:
PRINTED FOR J. BRAMBLES, A. MEGGITT, AND J.
WATERS, BY H. MOZLEY, GAINSBOROUGH.
1807.

ROBERT SOUTHEY (1774–1843)

66 *Carmen Triumphale, for the commencement of the year 1814,* with *Odes to His Royal Highness The Prince Regent, His Imperial Majesty The Emperor of Russia, and His Majesty The King of Prussia* 1814

London: Longman, Hurst, Rees, Orme & Brown
Bound in red morocco, extensively gold tooled, with Prince of Wales's feathers badges prominent, blue watered silk doublures with gold tooling, gilt edges, 28.2 × 22.3 cm (closed)
RCIN 1081242

Provenance Probably presented to George IV when Prince Regent by Robert Southey, 1814

The visit to England in June 1814 by the allied monarchs, Emperor Alexander I of Russia and King Frederick William III of Prussia (1770–1840), was intended to mark the triumphant conclusion of the war with Napoleon, and to celebrate England's part in the conflict. Napoleon was exiled to Elba after the allies' entry into Paris in April 1814, and the allies were able to breathe a (relatively short, as it turned out) sigh of relief. Robert Southey, the new Poet Laureate, rose to the occasion with congratulatory odes: the traditional New Year ode, *Carmen Triumphale*, celebrating the Prince Regent's part in the conflict, followed by odes (later known by the title *Carmina Aulica*), which celebrated the royal allied leaders – the Prince Regent, the Emperor and the King of Prussia. The Emperor's ode looked back to the 1698 visit to London of Peter the Great, who toured Europe, soaking up European influences to take back to Russia and reform her 'uncultured strength',[72] and then looked forward to the saviour of Europe, sprung from that same country:

Little thought they that in that farthest North,
from PETER'S race should the Deliverer spring,
Destined by Heaven to save
Art, Learning, Industry [...]
As little did they [the French] *think,*
That from rude Muscovy the stone should come,
To smite their huge Colossus.[73]

Southey had only recently been appointed Poet Laureate, in November 1813, after Walter Scott had refused the role, and his laureateship was to be distinguished by the many poems that he wrote on national events. A more enduring and popular example of his work, however, was the first written version of *Goldilocks and the Three Bears*, published in 1837.

This volume was bound for the Prince Regent by Charles Hering, Sr, in a lavishly gold-tooled red goatskin, embellished with the Prince of Wales's feathers badge, and sumptuous, deep blue silk doublures. This binding style was also adopted for the presentation volume to the Prince Regent concerning the visit by the allied leaders to the Guildhall, hosted by the Corporation of London.
ES

ODE

TO

His Imperial Majesty, Alexander the First,

EMPEROR OF ALL THE RUSSIAS.

I.

CONQUEROR, Deliverer, Friend of human-kind,
The free, the happy Island welcomes thee!
Thee from thy wasted realms,
So signally revenged;
From Prussia's rescued plains;
From Dresden's field of slaughter, where the ball
Which struck Moreau's dear life,
Was turn'd from thy more precious head aside;
From Leipsic's dreadful day,
From Elbe, and Rhine, and Seine,

67 *An Account of the visit of His Royal Highness The Prince Regent and Their Imperial and Royal Majesties The Emperor of Russia and The King of Prussia to the University of Oxford in June MDCCCXIV* 1815

Oxford: Clarendon Press
Printed on vellum, fully bound in brown/maroon morocco, gold-tooled, gilt edges, 38.0 × 27.4 cm (closed)
Armorial bookstamp of the University of Oxford on both boards
RCIN 1080412

Provenance Presented to George IV when Prince Regent by the University of Oxford, 1815

Emperor Alexander I and King Frederick William III of Prussia arrived in England for their triumphal visit on 6 June 1814, and were almost immediately plunged into a round of banquets and grand events. On 14 June the Prince Regent escorted his guests and their suites to Oxford. They toured the Clarendon Press and witnessed the printing of the verse, *Thine, O Lord, is the greatness, and the power, and the glory, and the victory and the majesty*, in four different languages. At the Bodleian Library they were each given a large paper copy of Aristotle's *Poetics*. That evening they attended 'a sumptuous dinner to 200 persons' in the Radcliffe Camera, where Field Marshal Prince von Blücher (1742–1819) became wondrously drunk, owing to his predilection for strong ale washed down with cognac.[74]
The following day, the Emperor and King were awarded the honorary degree of Doctor of Civil Law at a ceremony in the Sheldonian Theatre (the Prince Regent had already received this honour for his patronage of the unrolling and deciphering of the Herculaneum papyri in 1810). After a tour of the Radcliffe Observatory and a trip to Blenheim and Stowe (after which the Emperor and the King returned to London), a further banquet was held in Christ Church Hall. In London, the Prince Regent had felt himself upstaged by his guests, and also by his estranged wife, Caroline, who was seen as the wounded party by the British populace, but in Oxford he had received a warm welcome, and showed the University to advantage to his illustrious guests. In the letter sent to Oxford to thank them for their reception, Lord Sidmouth (1757–1844) wrote, 'His Royal Highness's Visit to the University of Oxford has afforded His Royal Highness the highest gratification'.[75] ES

1 Chron. xxix. 11.

THINE, O LORD, IS THE GREATNESS, AND THE POWER, AND THE GLORY, AND THE VICTORY, AND THE MAJESTY.

לך יהוה הגדלה והגבורה והתפארת והנצח וההוד׃

Σοὶ Κύριε ἡ μεγαλωσύνη, καὶ ἡ δύναμις, καὶ τὸ καύχημα, καὶ ἡ νίκη, καὶ ἡ ἰσχύς.

Tua est, Domine, magnificentia, et potentia, et gloria, atque victoria: et tibi laus.

Luke ii. 14.

GLORY TO GOD IN THE HIGHEST, AND ON EARTH PEACE, GOOD WILL TOWARD MEN.

ΔΟΞΑ ΕΝ ʽΥΨΙΣΤΟΙΣ ΘΕΩΙ, ΚΑΙ ΕΠΙ ΓΗΣ ΕΙΡΗΝΗ, ΕΝ ΑΝΘΡΩΠΟΙΣ ΕΥΔΟΚΙΑ.

ܫܘܒܚܐ ܠܐܠܗܐ ܒܡܪ̈ܘܡܐ. ܘܥܠ ܐܪܥܐ ܫܠܡܐ. ܘܣܒܪܐ ܛܒܐ ܠܒܢܝ̈ܢܫܐ.

ٱلْمَجْدُ لِلّٰهِ فِي ٱلْأَعَالِي وَعَلَى ٱلْأَرْضِ ٱلسَّلَمُ وَفِي ٱلنَّاسِ ٱلْمَسَرَّةُ

مر خدايرا در بلندى ستايش وسلامت برزمين وخوش اميدوارى آدميانرا

Ϫⲉ ⲟⲩⲱⲟⲩ ϧⲉⲛ ⲛⲏⲉⲧϭⲟⲥⲓ ⲙ̀Ⲫϯ ⲛⲉⲙ ⲟⲩϩⲓⲣⲏⲛⲏ ϩⲓϫⲉⲛ ⲡⲓⲕⲁϩⲓ ⲛⲉⲙ ⲟⲩϯⲙⲁϯ ϧⲉⲛ ⲛⲓⲣⲱⲙⲓ·

Gloria in altissimis Deo, et in terra pax hominibus bonæ voluntatis.

𐍅𐌿𐌻𐌸𐌿𐍃 𐌹̈𐌽 𐌷𐌰𐌿𐌷𐌹𐍃𐍄𐌾𐌰𐌼 𐌲𐌿𐌸𐌰· 𐌾𐌰𐌷 𐌰𐌽𐌰 𐌰𐌹𐍂𐌸𐌰𐌹 𐌲𐌰𐍅𐌰𐌹𐍂𐌸𐌹 𐌹̈𐌽 𐌼𐌰𐌽𐌽𐌰𐌼 𐌲𐍉𐌳𐌹𐍃 𐍅𐌹𐌻𐌾𐌹𐌽𐍃:

Ehre ſey Gott in der höhe/ vnd friede auf erden/ vnd dem menſchen ein wohlgefallen.

Gode ſý ƿuldoꞃ on heahneſſe . ⁊ on eoꞃþan ſýbb, mannum godeſ ƿillan :-

Gogoniant yn y goruchaf i Dduw, ac ar y ddaear tangnefedd, i ddynion ewyllys da.

OXFORD,

AT THE CLARENDON PRESS,

JUNE 14. MDCCCXIV.

IN THE PRESENCE OF

HIS ROYAL HIGHNESS THE PRINCE REGENT,

HIS IMPERIAL MAJESTY THE EMPEROR OF ALL THE RUSSIAS,

AND

HIS MAJESTY THE KING OF PRUSSIA.

SIR THOMAS LAWRENCE (1769–1830)

68–71 *Matvei Ivanovich, Count Platov (1751–1818)* 1814

Oil on canvas, 270.4 × 179.6 cm
RCIN 405146

Karl Robert, Count Nesselrode (1780–1862) 1818

Oil on canvas, 143.0 × 112.4 cm
RCIN 404945

General Feodor Petrovich Uvarov (1769–1824) 1818

Oil on canvas, 127.1 × 102.2 cm
RCIN 404950

Alexander Ivanovich, Prince Chernyshev (1785/6–1857) 1818

Oil on canvas, 127.2 × 102.7 cm
RCIN 405150

Provenance Painted for George IV when Prince Regent, recorded in Carlton House 1819 (nos 664, 665, 655, 667), later in the Waterloo Chamber, Windsor Castle

Literature Garlick 1961, p. 2, no. 3 (RCIN 405146), p. 3, no. 4 (RCIN 405150); Millar 1969, nos 907, 915, 910, 892; Garlick 1989, nos 600, 782, 651, 188

These four portraits of distinguished Russian military leaders were commissioned from Sir Thomas Lawrence for George IV when Prince Regent, for his Waterloo Chamber – a great hall created by covering a courtyard with a huge sky-lit vault at Windsor Castle. The Waterloo Chamber was intended to honour all those who had played a part in overthrowing Napoleon. The concept grew from the suggestion of a triple portrait of the Prince Regent, Emperor Alexander I of Russia and Frederick William III of Prussia. However, Lawrence preferred single canvases, and embarked on full-length portraits of Platov and the Prussian Field Marshal Prince von Blücher, whilst they were in London in June 1814 following the Treaty of Paris. Lawrence travelled to Aix-la-Chapelle late in 1818, to complete the portrait of Count Nesselrode; portraits of Uvarov and Chernyshev were painted in Vienna in December 1818.

All four portraits were in Lawrence's studio at his death and were claimed by the King on 24 January 1830. William Seguier (1772–1843), Surveyor of the King's Pictures, was paid to clean and varnish the paintings and, in some cases, 'finish' the portraits; the costume and right hand of Uvarov, for example, do not seem good enough to be the work of Lawrence himself. The completion of the Waterloo Chamber took place during the reign of William IV, and the arrangement of canvases can be seen in Joseph Nash's (1809–78) watercolour of 1844 (fig. 19), with Platov visible to the upper left, Nesselrode to the bottom right.

The concept of a celebratory gallery was mirrored by Alexander I, who employed the English artist, George Dawe, to complete 332 portrait heads of Russian dignitaries, leaders and generals who had distinguished themselves in the wars against France. The Military Gallery, or War Gallery of 1812 within the Winter Palace was opened on 25 December 1826, the anniversary of Napoleon's expulsion from Russia (fig. 20).

The portrait of Platov, military commander, or 'Ataman' ('Hetman' in English), of the Cossacks was swiftly painted at Lawrence's house in Russell Square, which was guarded by mounted Cossacks.[76] The painting was highly praised when exhibited at the Royal Academy in 1815, and later described as 'a capital portrait, and represented

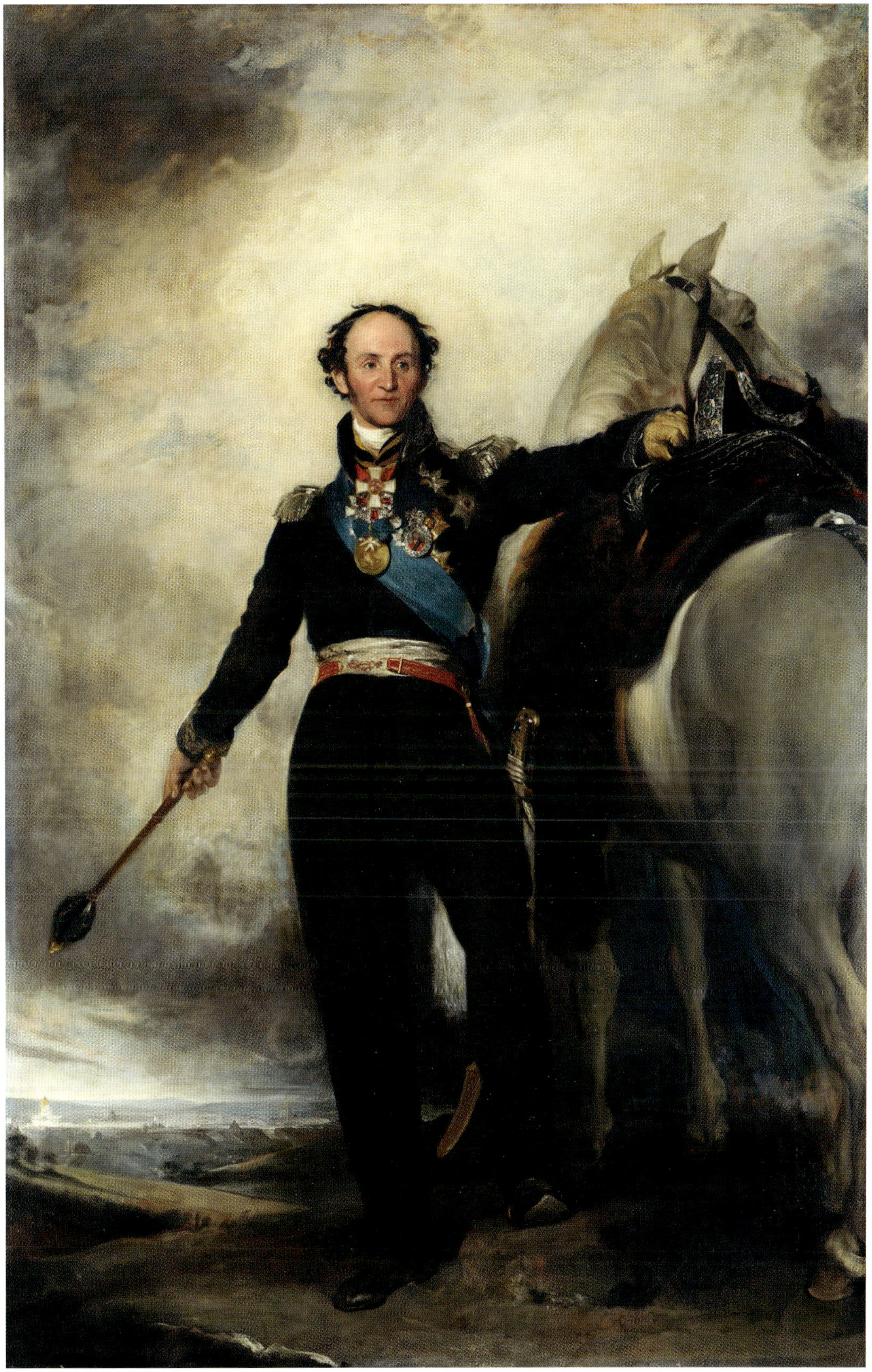

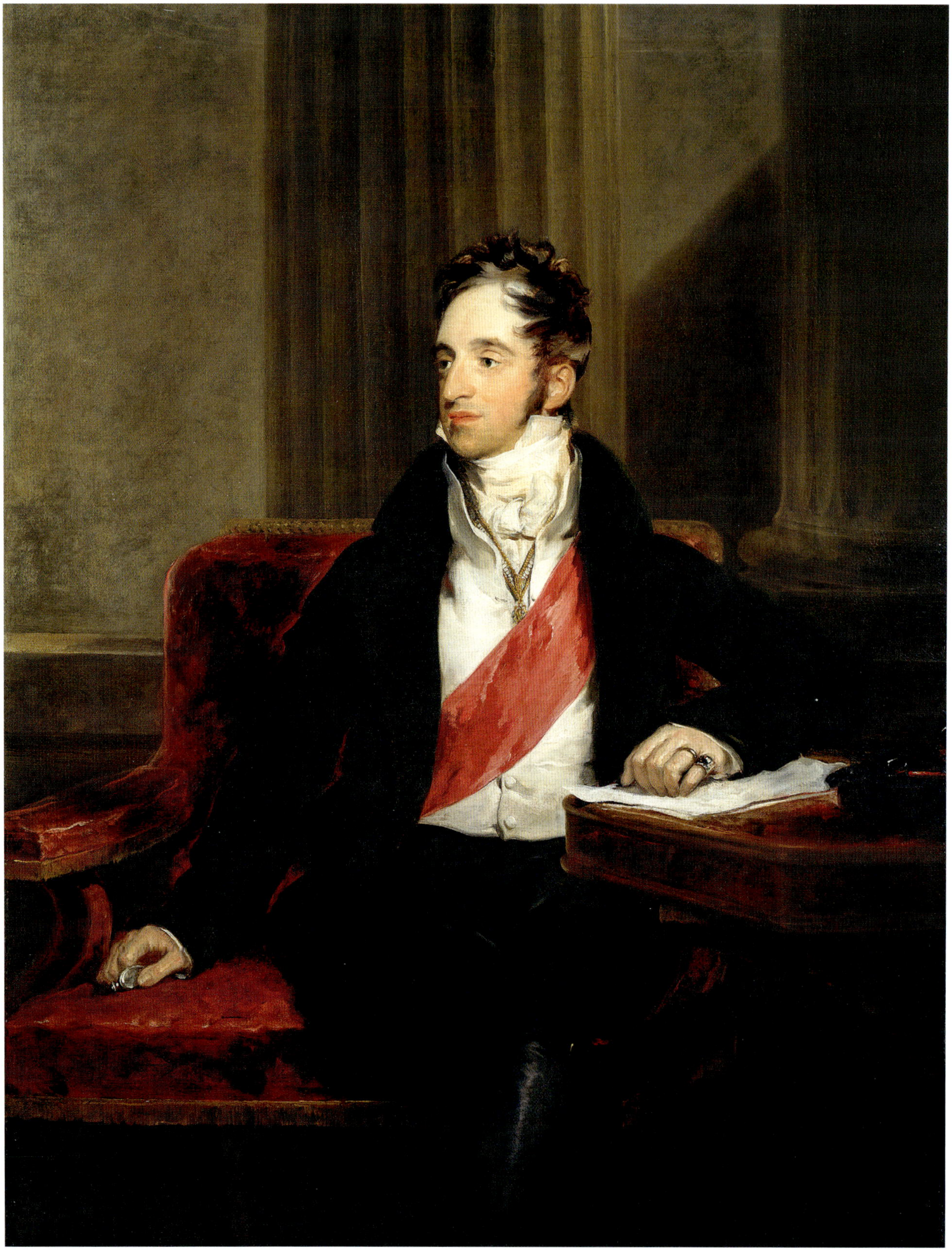

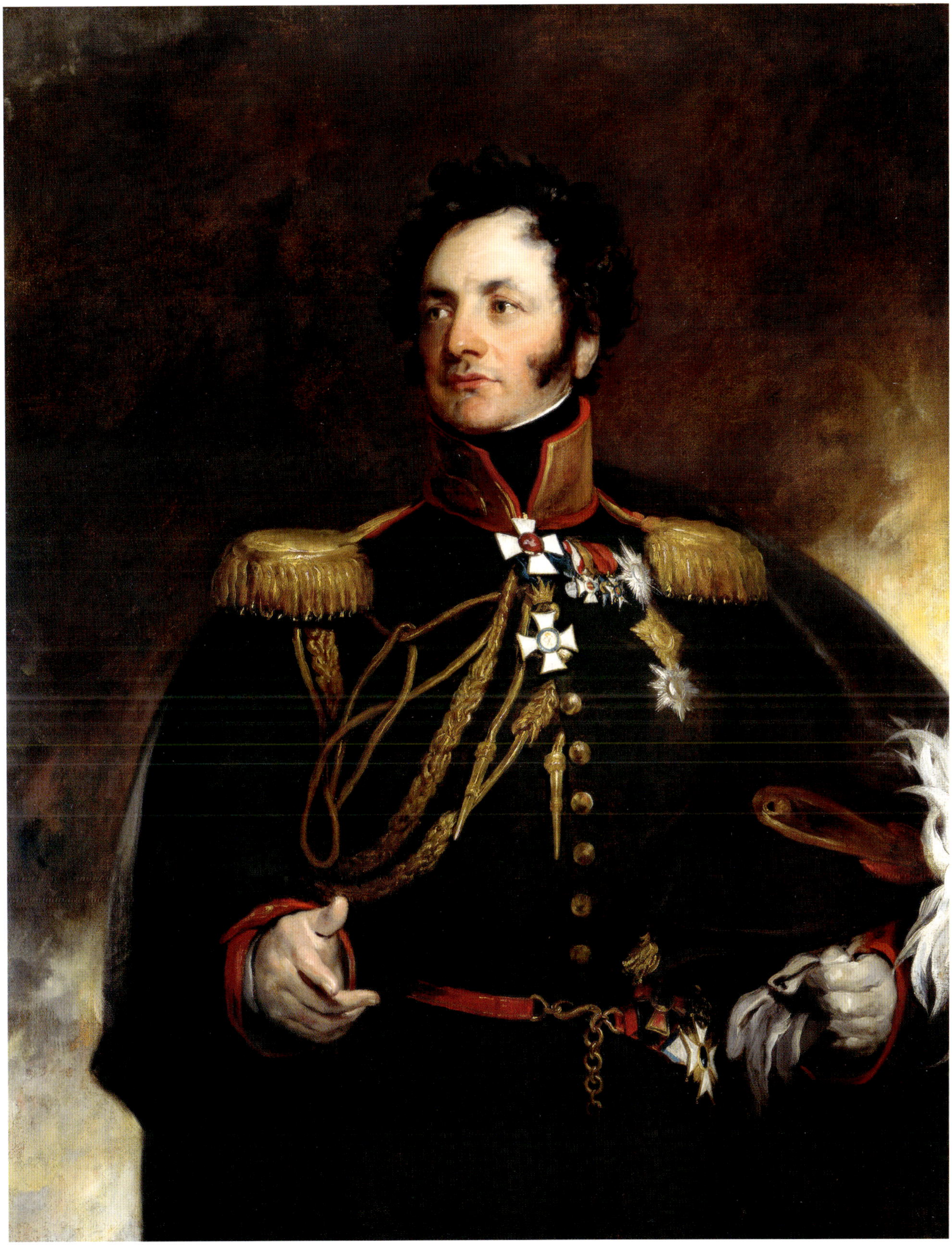

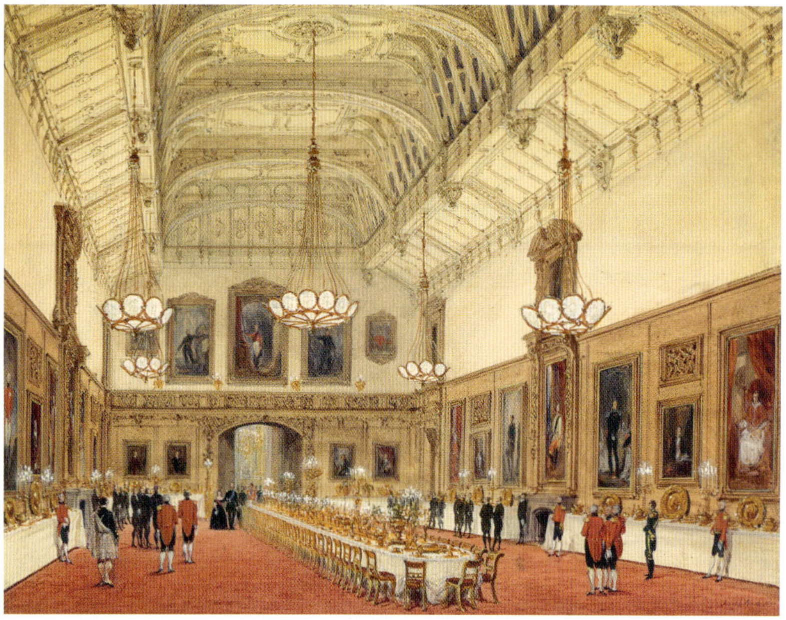

FIG. 19
Joseph Nash
Waterloo Chamber, 1844
Watercolour and bodycolour over pencil, 28.2 × 36.8 cm
RCIN 919785

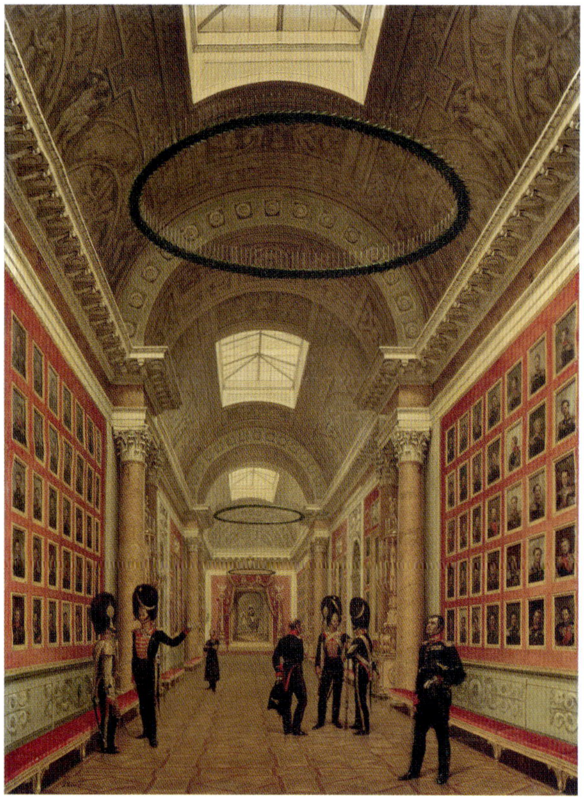

FIG. 20
Grigory Grigoryevich Chernetsov *The War Gallery of 1812 in the Winter Palace*, 1829
Oil on canvas, 121 × 92 cm
Hermitage, inv. no. ЭРЖ-2433

him with his long oval, Asiatic face, and with considerable expression of cunning, which was in fact his character'.[77] The composition is indebted to a portrait of the *Marquess of Granby* by Joshua Reynolds (1723–92), *c.*1766–70.[78] The expressive pose, his baton gesturing towards a city in the background (possibly Paris), the dynamic turn of his steed, surrounded by the whirling smoke of the battle, are all evidence of Lawrence's admiration of the Old Masters and of late Raphael, in particular.

The 'Russianness' of the sitters is not distinguishable by a facial type, as many of Lawrence's portraits share a Byronic presence – endowed with dark locks and an intense gaze. Uvarov and Chernyshev, however, are identifiable through their dark military uniforms: a high collar, gold epaulettes and the presence of military orders, most notably the Orders of St George and St Alexander Nevskii. Uvarov commanded a regiment of the Horse Guards and fought at Borodino in 1812, one of the most decisive engagements of the Napoleonic Wars. Two years later he led the cavalry in pursuit of the French in the retreat of Moscow, and in 1821 was promoted to Commander-in-Chief of the Corps of Guards. Prince Chernyshev, promoted to Colonel of the Cossacks in 1811, also fought at Austerlitz and later attended the Conferences at Aix-la-Chapelle and Vienna. Count Nesselrode, seated at a desk, amidst his papers, a watch or locket in his right hand, is honoured for his role as foreign minister to Alexander I and as Russian plenipotentiary at the Congress of Vienna. **AB**

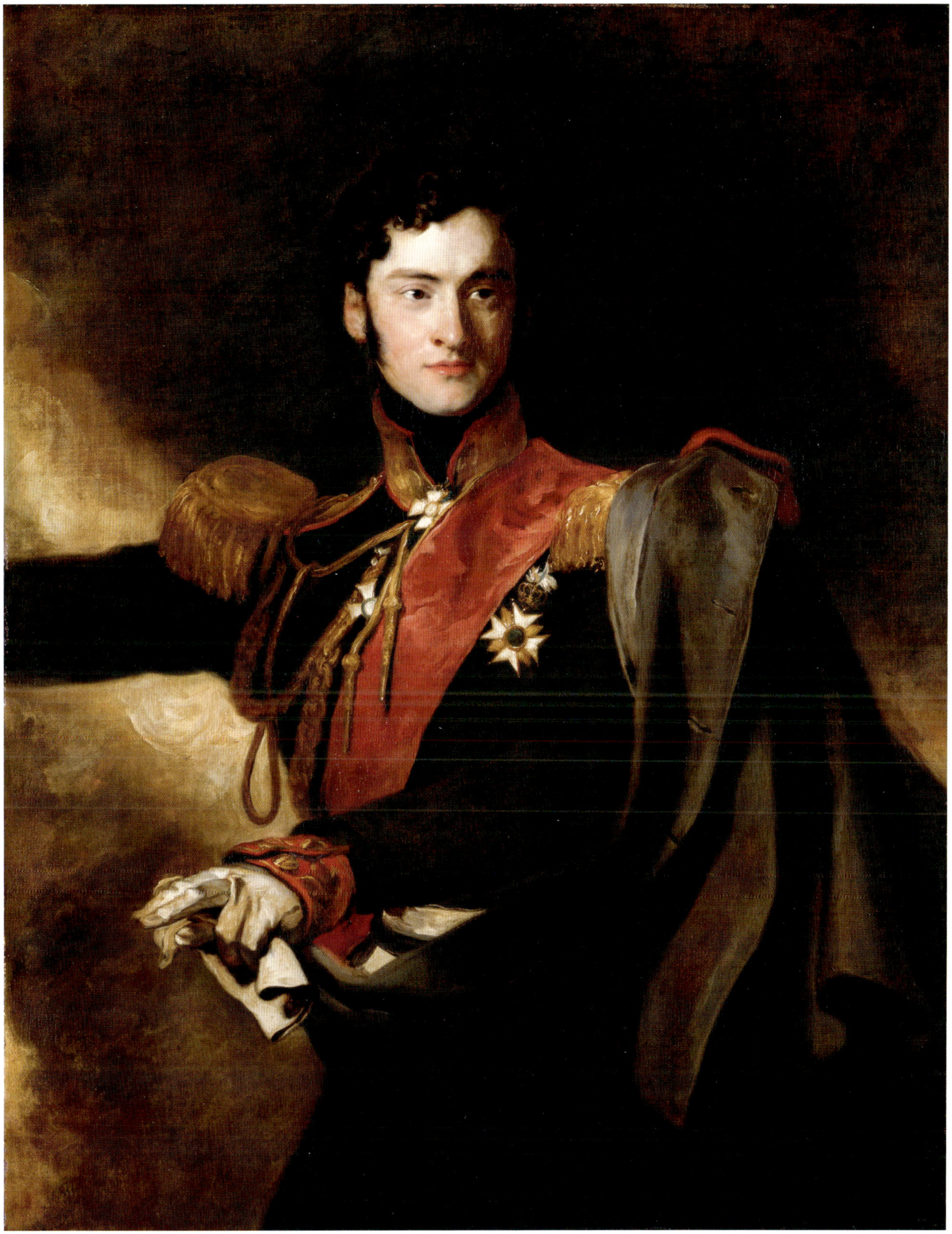

PETER TURNERELLI (1774–1839)

72 *Portrait bust of Matvei Ivanovich, Count Platov (1751–1818)* 1815

Marble, 69.0 × 50.0 × 30.0 cm
Signed and dated: *PLATOFF 1815 P. Turnerelli fecit. 1815.*
RCIN 35416

Provenance Purchased by George IV when Prince Regent, August 1815 (£157 10s.)

Literature De Bellaigue 1991, p. 50

Count Platov, a Russian general, commanded the 'Don Cossack' forces against the French during the Napoleonic Wars. He accompanied Emperor Alexander I to London in 1814 where he was presented with a sword by the Prince Regent and an honorary doctorate from Oxford University. In 1815, the Prince Regent, who had a passion for collecting busts of military heroes, commissioned Turnerelli to make a portrait bust of the general for the Second Room of the Armoury Attic Floor at Carlton House (fig. 21). A year earlier, the Prince Regent had already acquired for that room a portrait bust by Nollekens (1737–1823) of the British military hero, John Manners, Marquess of Granby (1721–70), who had previously defeated the French during the Seven Years War.

Count Platov is depicted with his head slightly tilted and turned to the left. He wears military uniform and orders including the Prussian Order of the Black Eagle, the Orders of Malta, St George and St Andrew of Russia. He also wears the miniature portrait of the Prince Regent set in diamonds. In contrast to Lawrence's heroic, youthful portrait image, Turnerelli depicts Platov as the battle-worn commander that he was, this bust having been sculpted just three years before Platov's death in 1818. For the same room in Carlton House, the Prince Regent also acquired two busts by Turnerelli, of the Duke of Wellington, and the German Field Marshal Prince von Blücher. CDEG

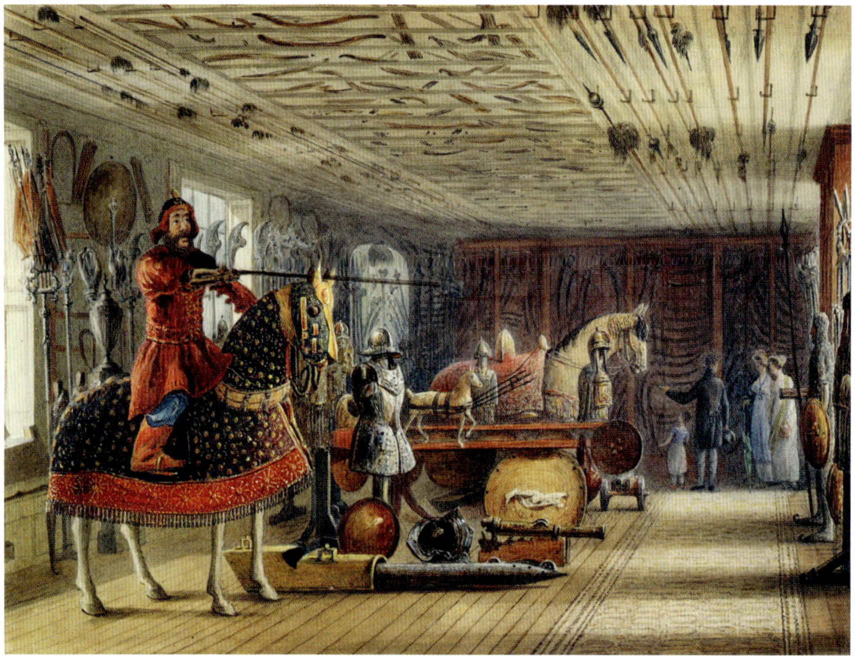

FIG. 21
Augustus Charles Pugin
Carlton House: The Armoury, 1814
Pencil, watercolour and bodycolour, 23.2 × 31.2 cm
RCIN 917092

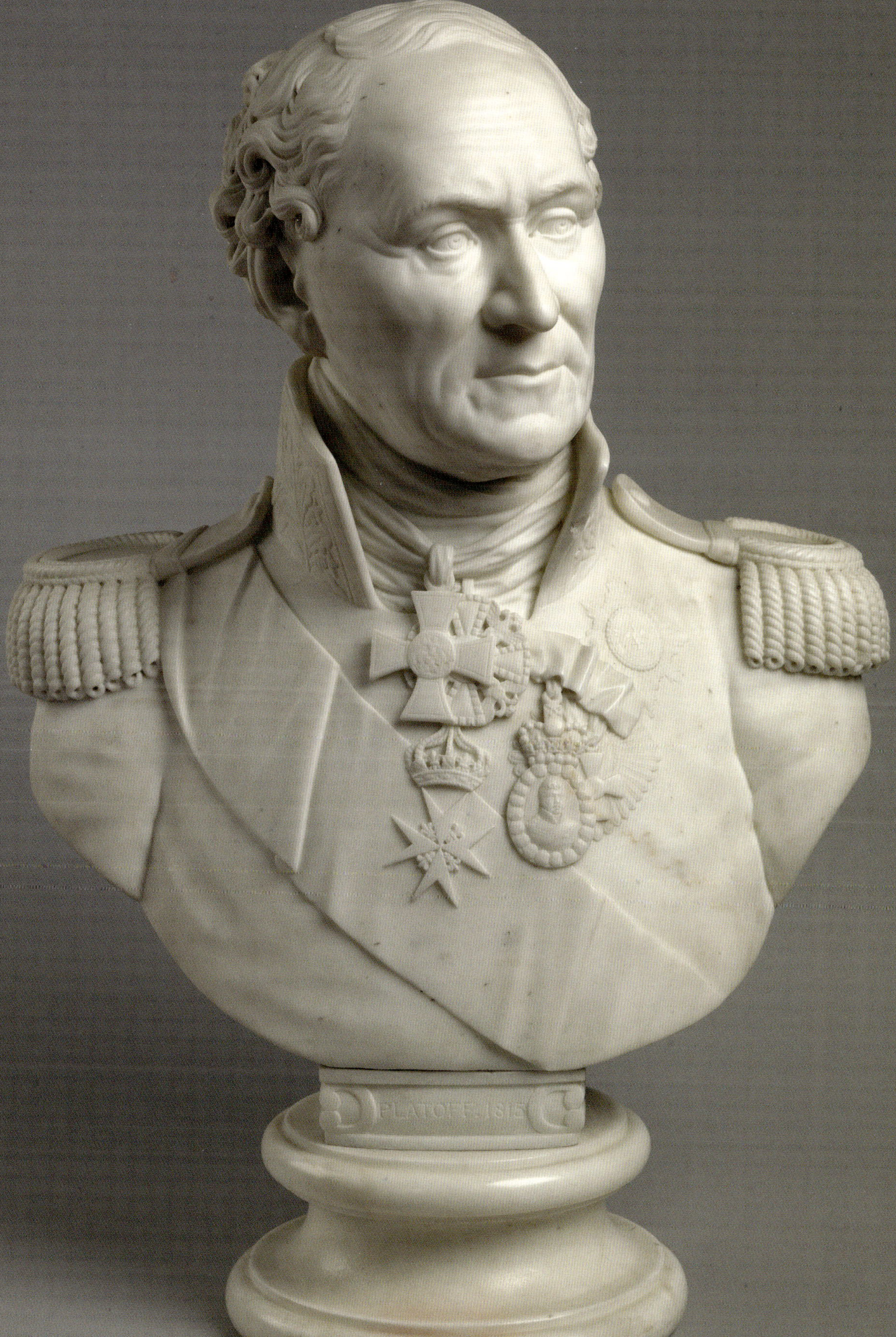
PLATOFF. 1815

PETER EDWARD STROEHLING (1768–*c*.1826)

73 ***Matvei Ivanovich, Count Platov, Ataman of the Cossacks (1751–1818)*** 1814

Oil on canvas, 92.7 × 111.8 cm
Signed and dated: *Stroehling/1814*; inscribed on a stone in foreground: *A/FONTAINEBLEAU/1814*
RCIN 407492

Provenance Probably painted for George IV when Prince Regent; received at Carlton House from Stroehling, July–November 1814; first recorded in Carlton House 1816 (no. 388, in Store)

Literature Millar 1969, no. 1107

In June 1814, Count Platov travelled to London as part of the suite of Alexander I of Russia. His reputation as a military hero and leader preceded him, and his arrival caused much excitement. Platov and his ally, the Prussian commander Field Marshal Prince von Blücher, were fêted and followed wherever they went; onlookers were even keen to acquire a hair from their horses as a souvenir. *The Times* reported a 'dress party' of the 'most magnificent and select that was ever assembled at Carlton House', and whilst the 'Royal Strangers of Russia and Prussia left at about half-past eleven von Blücher and Platoff, however, were not able to retire until half past one. The populace followed them to their residencies, huzzaing [cheering] "Long-live Blucher and Platoff."'[79]

The myth that surrounded Platov possibly rose from his command of the Don Cossacks, believed to be 'wild and ferocious' horsemen, whose arrival in London already in 1813 had provoked interest and suspicion. This was coupled with the legend that following the burning of Moscow, Platov is said to have offered his daughter's hand in marriage to anyone who captured the French Emperor, a challenge that spawned numerous satirical prints. A contemporary print by Edward Orme (1775–1848), published on 11 July 1814, after a painting by Alexander Orlovsky (1777–1832), bears some similarities to this equestrian portrait.[80]

Appointed as Ataman or Commander of the Don Cossacks in 1801, Platov became a Count in 1812, when he distinguished himself during the Napoleonic Wars; he continued to serve in the foreign campaigns of 1813–14. Here he is depicted as a conqueror, charging on a white horse, amidst the smoke and devastation of battle. He is dressed in the uniform of a Cossack General, wearing the badges of the Orders of Maria Theresa of Austria, St George of Russia, Malta and St Anne of Russia, and his silvered plume decorated with a crowned A. The ribbon and star of the Black Eagle of Prussia also adorn his uniform, together with a miniature of George IV when Prince Regent decorated with diamonds. The latter was presumably presented to Platov by the future king during his stay in London, 'as a mark of esteem, respect and amazement of those immortal feats effected for the good of his fatherland for the salvation of Europe'.[81]

The inscription, *A Fontainbleau*, on the stone in the foreground alludes to the military success of Platov and the Cossacks there; on 16 February 1814, his retinue had reduced the town of Fontainebleau, captured a general and some cannon, and taken prisoners.

The portrait, presumably commissioned (together with a companion portrait of von Blücher) by the Prince Regent, from Stroehling, then resident in London, was painted at the same time as Sir Thomas Lawrence was completing his full-length portrait of Platov for the Waterloo Chamber (cat. 68). **AB**

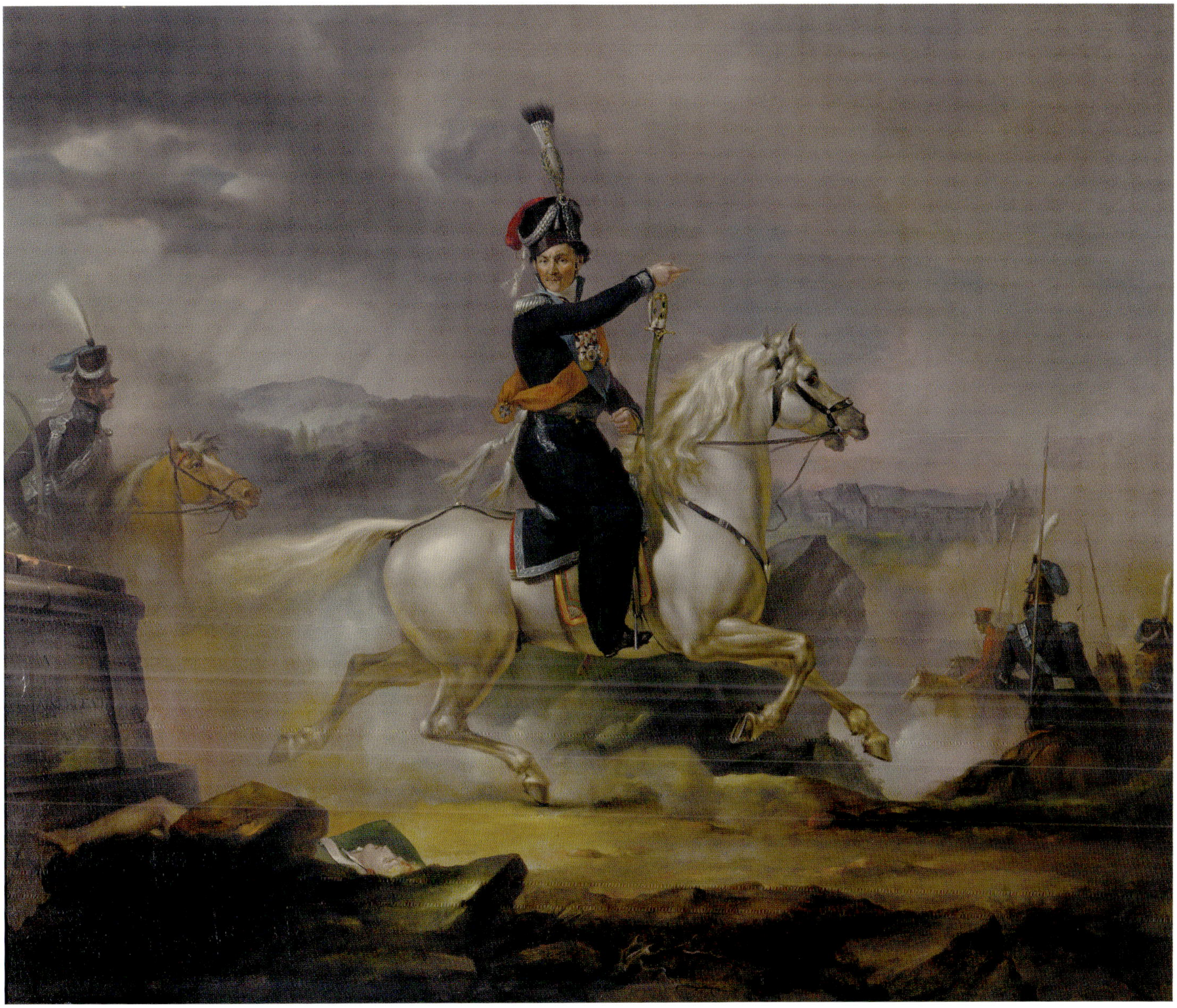

ENGLISH

74 *'Russian' dress belonging to Princess Charlotte (1796–1817)* c.1817

Silk, gold, metallic and silk lace, gold metallic fringe
RCIN 74709

Provenance Made for Princess Charlotte of Wales, *c.*1817

Literature Staniland 1997, pp. 72–5

One of a small number of surviving garments in the Royal Collection which belonged to Princess Charlotte, only daughter of George IV and Queen Caroline, and almost certainly one of the last made for her. It consists of a long straight skirt with a drawstring waist and separate bodice which are styled as a sarafan. The sarafan is a typical Russian woman's dress: tunic-like, sleeveless and front-fastening, they were initially high-necked with armholes, but later hung from breast-level shoulder straps. While the blue silk is probably of French manufacture, it is applied with rich gold lace embroidered in red silk, with gold tassels around the hem, which are all British, as is the dress itself. The exact date of production is likely to have been 1817, because the slightly flared skirt has a drawstring at the top which would have made it more comfortable for the Princess to wear during pregnancy. Princess Charlotte had married Leopold, Prince of Saxe-Coburg (1790–1865), later King of the Belgians, on 2 May 1816 and was pregnant when she chose to wear this dress for sittings for her portrait painted by George Dawe the following year.

The presence of Emperor Alexander I in Paris and London in 1814 may have influenced a small fashion trend for dress in the Russian style. In 1816 Princess Charlotte had worn a similar dress, which was described by Prince Leopold's private secretary, Baron Stockmar (1787–1863), in his memoirs: 'I thought her dress particularly becoming, dark roses in her hair, a short light blue dress without sleeves, with a low round collar, a white puffed-out Russian chemisette'.[82] Nonetheless, the Empire-line style of the bodice combined with the straight skirt also conformed to British Regency fashion of the time. The white lace chemise worn beneath the dress and depicted in Dawe's portrait (cat. 75) appears to have been made from diaphanous silk chiffon with a fine stripe, however this does not survive.
CDEG

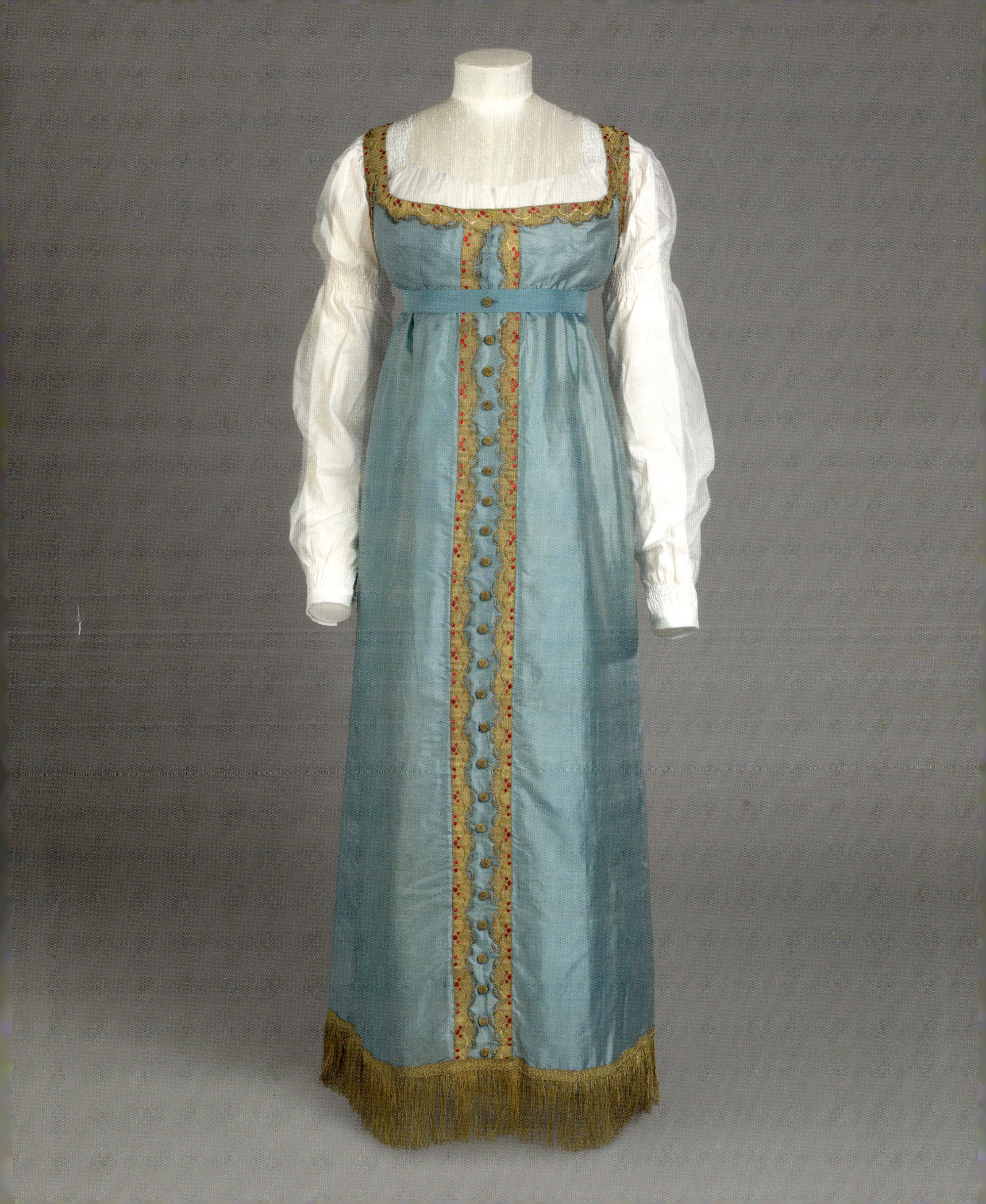

AFTER GEORGE DAWE (1781–1829)

75 *Princess Charlotte of Wales (1796–1817)* c.1817–22

Oil on canvas, 132.0 × 107.5 cm
RCIN 402491

Provenance Acquired by King Edward VII; first recorded in Buckingham Palace (Cust 1909, p. 185, as by Benjamin Robert Haydon)

Literature Millar 1969, no. 751

Princess Charlotte is seated elegantly on a *chaise longue*, dressed in her blue silk Russian-style dress, beneath which is a plain white undergarment. At her left breast she wears the star of the Order of St Catherine, which she received on 1 July 1817, from Maria Feodorovna, wife of Paul I, in gratitude for hospitality shown to her son Nicholas during his visit to London. (Princess Charlotte's husband, Prince Leopold of Saxe-Coburg, also served under the Russian Emperor during the Napoleonic Wars.) The portfolio beneath her arm may contain etchings and allude to her artistic endeavours.[83] In the numerous painted versions the gold scalloped braiding of the dress is reversed.

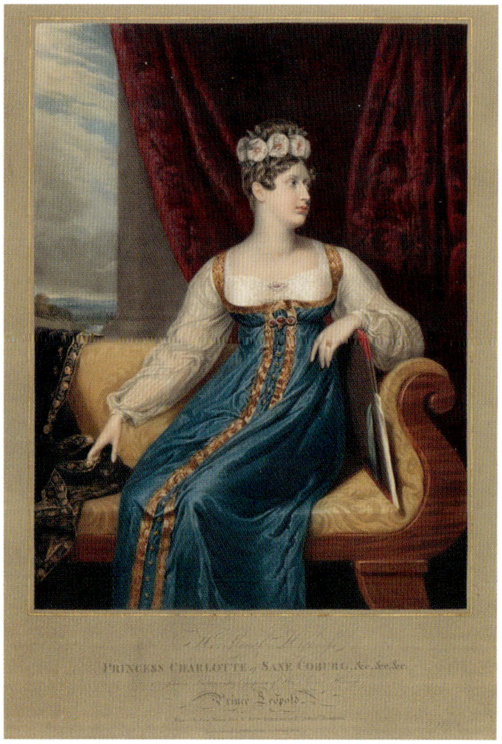

FIG. 22
Henry Edward Dawe
Her Royal Highness Princess Charlotte of Saxe Coburg, 1818
Mezzotint, printed in colour with hand-colouring, 56.4 × 39.1 cm
RCIN 605420

The portrait is a contemporary version of the full-length painting in the Belgian Royal Collection, dated 1817. The image was widely published, most notably by William Say (1768–1834) on 1 December 1817 and by Henry Dawe on 12 January 1818 (fig. 22). This variation differs in that the Princess wears the star of the Order of St Catherine, and her hair is dressed in a simpler manner.[84] Another autograph version of the painting, in reverse, with an elaborate lace blouse and without roses in her hair, is in the National Portrait Gallery.[85] Dawe exhibited two portraits of the Princess at the Royal Academy, in 1817 and 1818.[86] There is a further version in the Royal Collection.[87]

The painting was ascribed to Benjamin Robert Haydon (1786–1846) when it entered the Collection during the reign of Edward VII, although there is little evidence that the artist worked as a copyist, despite his financial difficulties. A version by Dawe was sold in the Duke of Cambridge's sale, in 1904, although the present painting is not believed to be that version.[88] **AB**

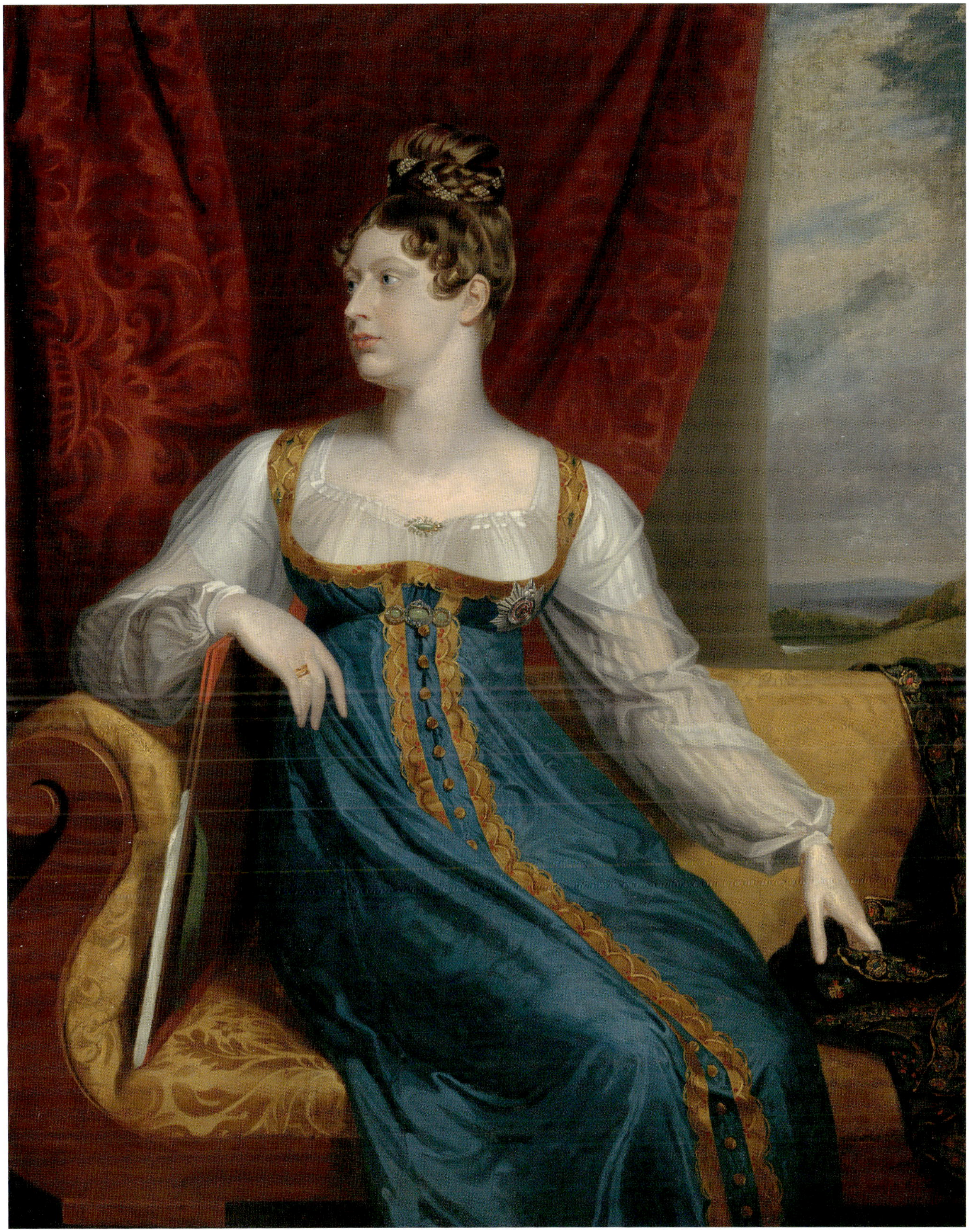

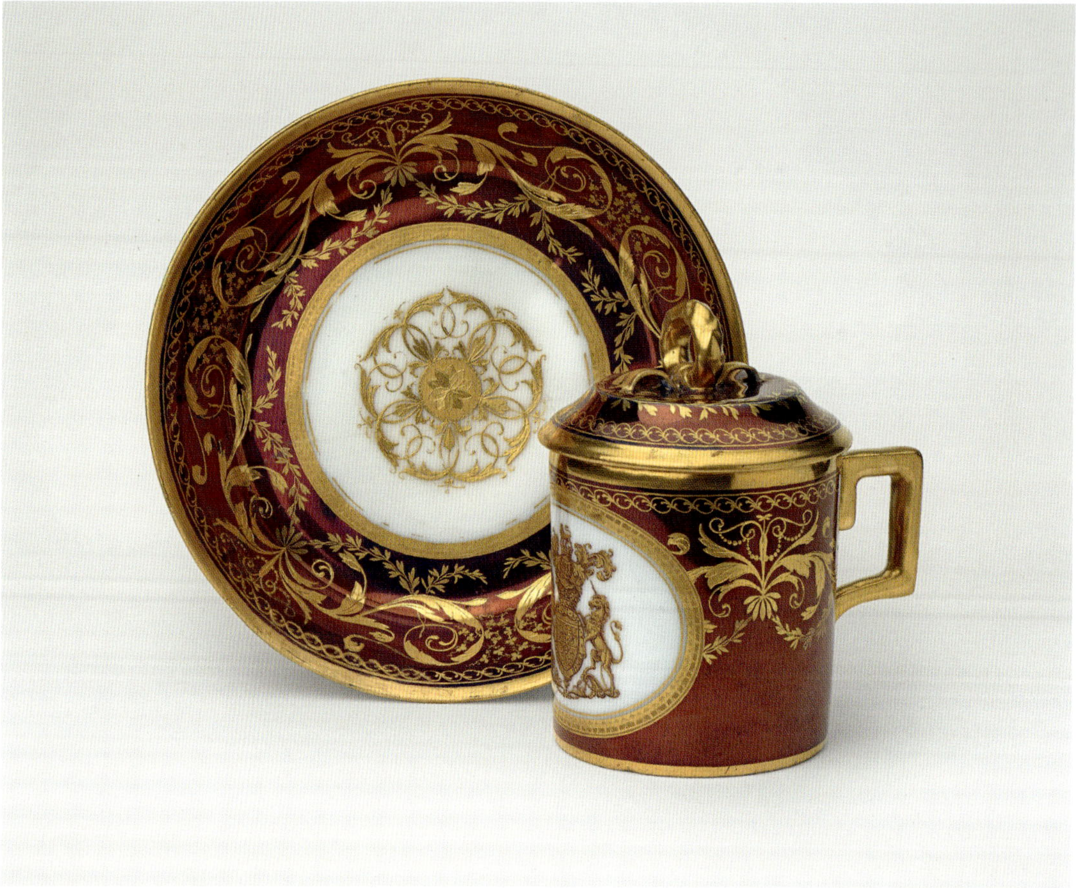

IMPERIAL PORCELAIN FACTORY

76 *Covered cup and saucer* 1796–1801

Hard-paste porcelain, cup and cover: 9.6 × 7.2 × 9.5 cm; saucer: 3 × 14.4 cm
Underglaze mark II
RCIN 39847

Provenance From the Collection of George, Duke of Cambridge, acquired by the Princess of Wales (later Queen Mary)

This aubergine lustre-ware covered custard cup, cover and saucer with gilt decoration has a flattened dome cover with gilt wreath finial flanked by applied gilt ribbons, a gilt border of foliage and interlaced ovals. This is a typical example of imperial porcelain of the period which largely copied French prototypes. The cylindrical cup has large reserves with the Royal Arms and supporters in gold on a white ground. Prince George, 2nd Duke of Cambridge (1819–1904), was the grandson of George III, cousin of Queen Victoria and maternal uncle of Queen Mary. The Duke was an army officer by profession and was Commander-in-Chief of the British Forces from 1856 to 1895. During the Crimean War he fought at the battles of Alma, Balaclava and Inkerman, and was at the siege of Sevastopol. He died in 1904, at which time his niece, the Princess of Wales (later Queen Mary), acquired this cup and saucer. CDEG

IVAN BUSHUYEV (1800–1833)

77 *Sabre and scabbard* 1824

Steel, gold, ivory, wood, silk velvet, length (overall) 99.6 cm, (blade) 83.7 cm, weight 2.022 kg
Etched on blade with ?*GFB* monogram and coat-of-arms
RCIN 61567

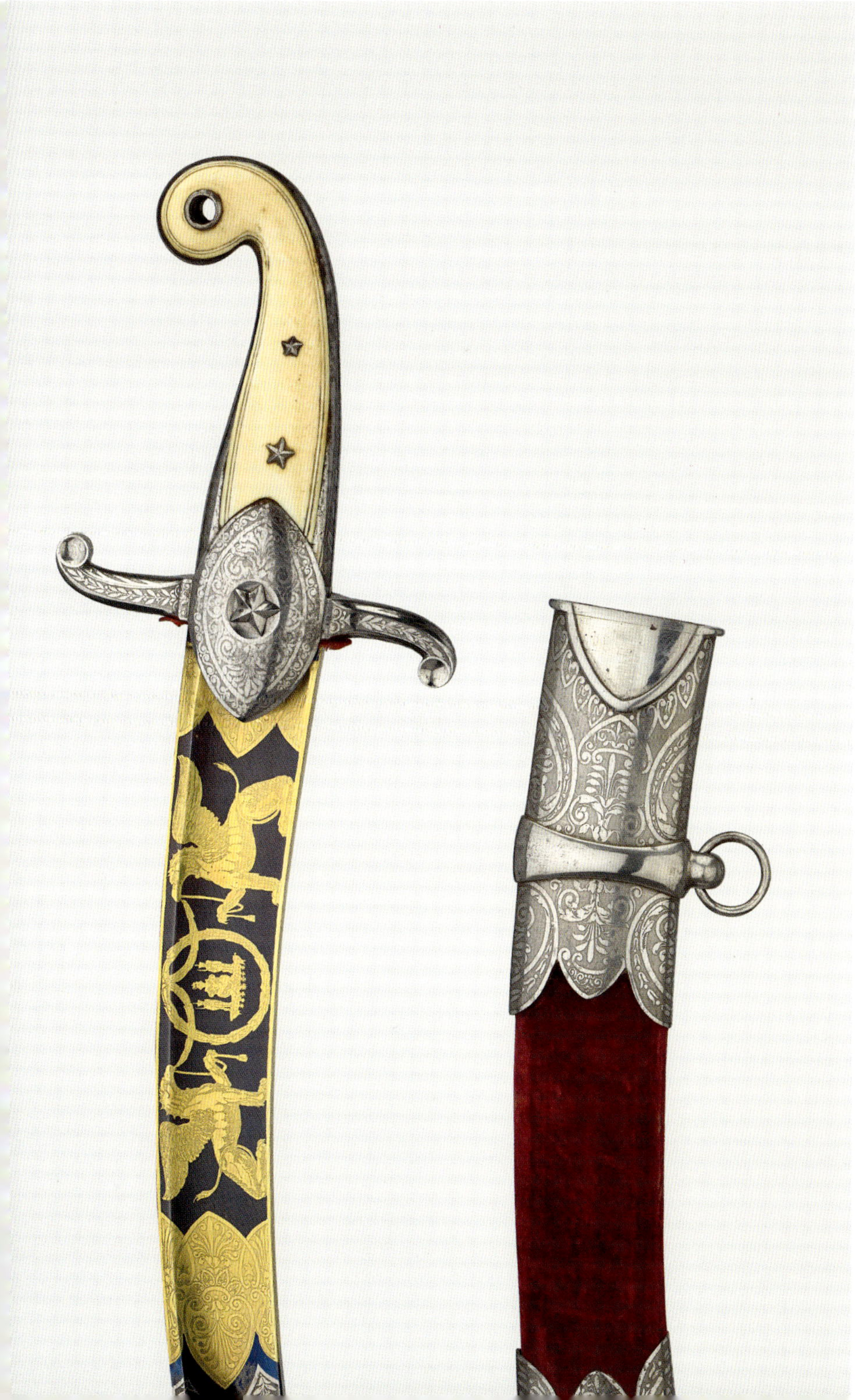

Provenance Recorded in George IV's Armoury at Carlton House, by 1825

Literature *Catalogue of arms* VI, no. 3253; *North Corridor*, no. 1619; Laking 1904, no. 831

The curved military sabre, with a pistol 'Mameluke'-style grip, was very popular throughout Europe for cavalry in the eighteenth and nineteenth centuries. This example is of high quality, for a noble officer. It has been decorated with acid-etched neoclassical designs, classical warriors representing victory, bluing, parcel gilding and burnishing. The monogram and coat-of-arms on the blade remain unidentified. The curved, wide, hollow ground blade remains extremely functional, being tough, flexible and light.

Ivan Bushuyev[89] was a sword cutler from Zlatoust in the Chelyabinsk region of the Urals, where arms, both fine and munition, were produced from about 1816. The son of a designer and draughtsman at the Zlatoust ironworks, he was first recorded as an ordinary workman in 1818–19, and became a master in 1822. A further weapon by Bushuyev (RCIN 61671) and another attributed to him (cat. 78) are in the Royal Collection and were possibly Russian gifts to George IV. **SDM**

ZLATOUST, RUSSIA

78 *Hunting knife and scabbard* 1823

Steel, gold, ivory, wood, silk velvet, length (overall) 37.0 cm, (blade) 23.1 cm, weight 0.290 kg
RCIN 61627

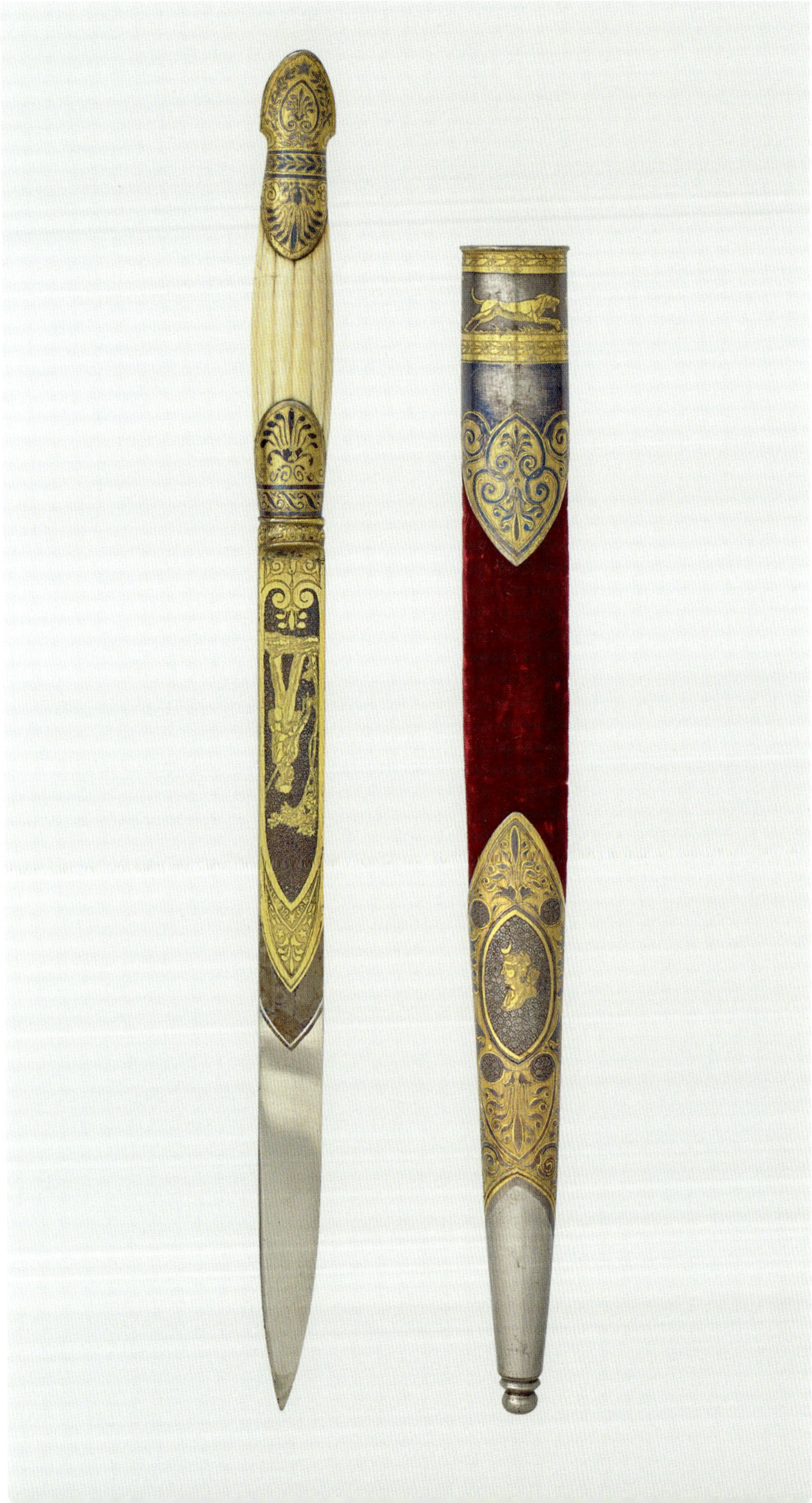

Provenance Recorded in George IV's Armoury at Carlton House

Literature *Catalogue of arms* VI, no. 3255; *North Corridor*, no. 525; Laking 1904, no. 826

This hunting knife, finely decorated in the late neoclassical style, is an example of the skill of craftsmen working in Zlatoust in the first quarter of the nineteenth century. Though unsigned it is probably the work of Ivan Busheyev (see cat. 77). The quality competes with the best work from Europe and was used as a gift by the Emperor to demonstrate Russian skill, taste and refinement. It was recorded in the Carlton House *Catalogue of arms* as received from the Royal Lodge, Windsor Park, on 1 November 1825, so must have been acquired by George IV soon after it was made.
SDM

IMPERIAL ARMS FACTORY, TULA, RUSSIA, BLADE POSSIBLY GERMAN

79 *Stirrup-hilted sabre* late eighteenth century

Pattern-welded steel, copper alloy, garnet, ebony, length (overall) 95.7 cm, (blade) 82.2 cm, weight 0.850 kg
RCIN 61683

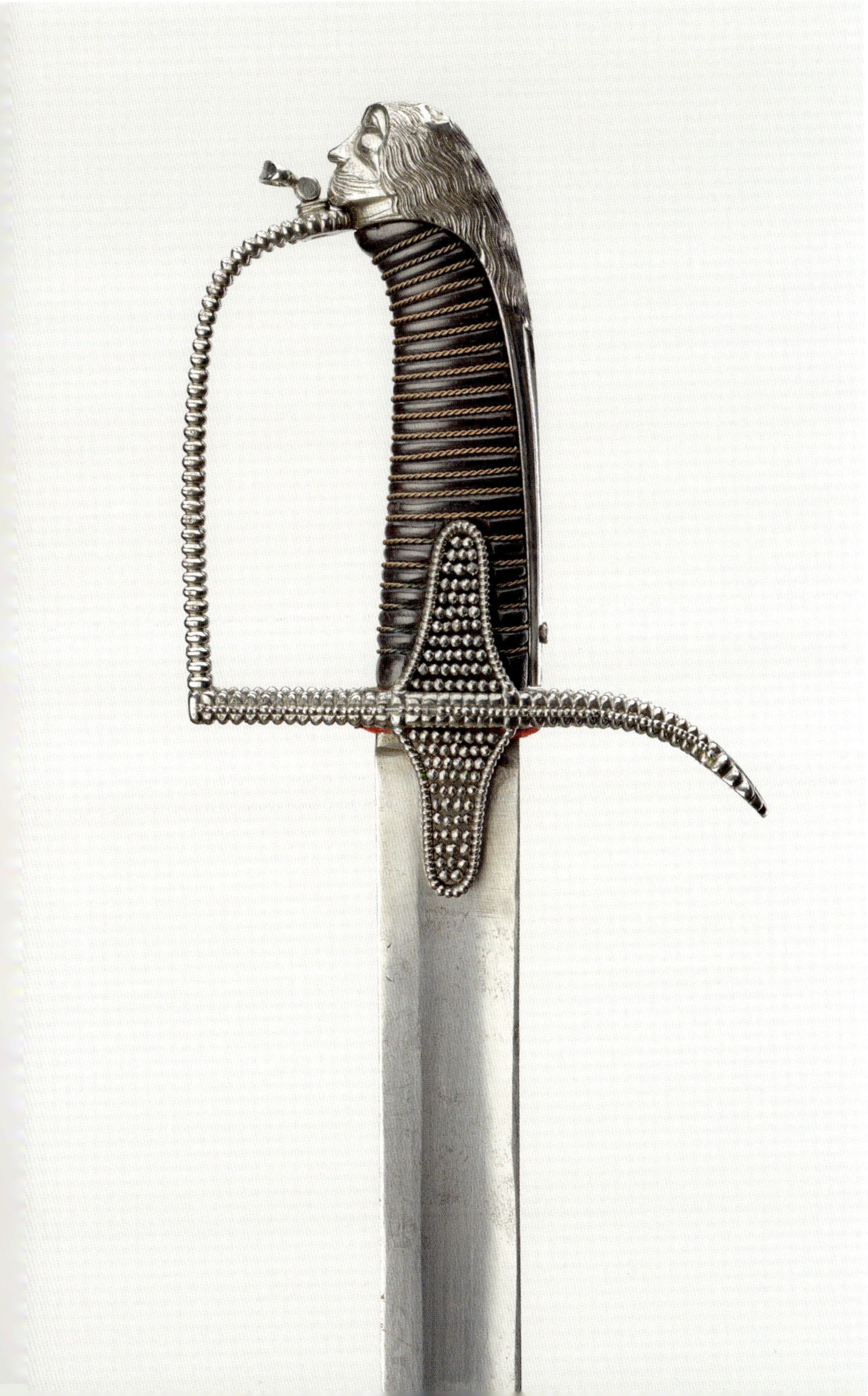

Provenance Recorded in George IV's Armoury at Carlton House

Literature *Catalogue of arms* I, no. 334; *North Corridor*, no. 1554; Laking 1904, no. 949; de Bellaigue 1991, no. 132

This light cavalry sabre was probably made at the Imperial Arms Factory in Tula, using an imported German blade. The pivot loop on the knuckle guard for a sword knot is in the Eastern European fashion,[90] while the use of cut steel suggests Tula workmanship. The hilt has an end cap of burnished, chiselled steel in the form of a lion's head, set with garnet eyes.[91] The guard is constructed of burnished, chiselled and faceted steel, set with faceted steel beads. The popular fashion for highly polished cut steel was very expensive in eighteenth-century Europe, with Tula rivalling the English centre of Woodstock, Oxfordshire,[92] for the finest-cut steel ware.

The blade is of pattern-welded construction, but unmarked. The sabre is recorded in the Carlton House *Catalogue of arms* as having a 'Brown fish skin scabbard, steel chape', now lost.
SDM

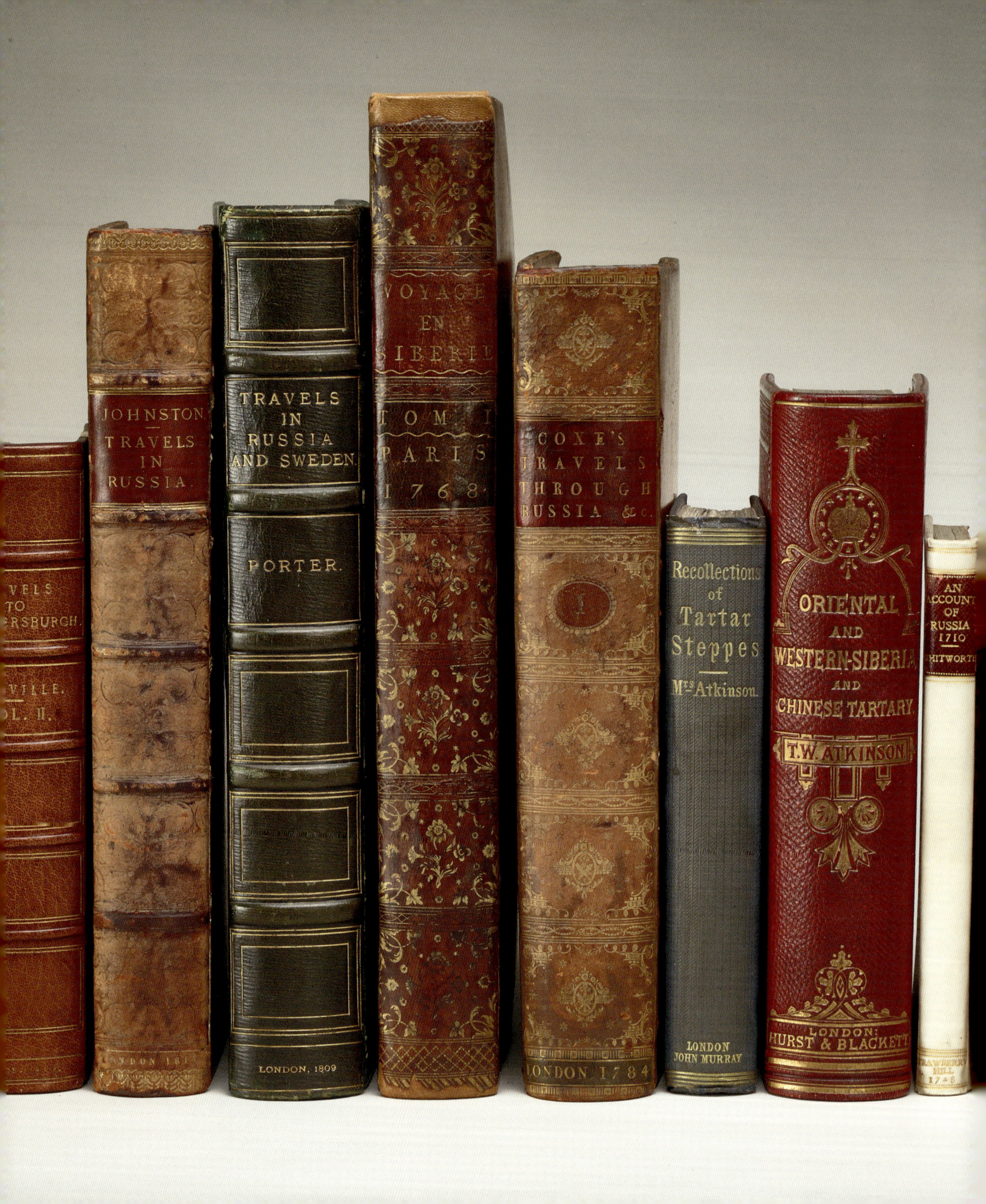
VELS
TO
ERSBURGH.
VILLE.
L. II.
JOHNSTON
TRAVELS
IN
RUSSIA.
TRAVELS
IN
RUSSIA
AND SWEDEN.
PORTER.
LONDON, 1809
VOYAGE
EN
SIBERIE
TOM. I
PARIS
1768
COXE'S
TRAVELS
THROUGH
RUSSIA &c.
I
LONDON 1784
Recollections
of
Tartar
Steppes
Mrs Atkinson.
LONDON
JOHN MURRAY
ORIENTAL
AND
WESTERN-SIBERIA
AND
CHINESE TARTARY.
T.W. ATKINSON
LONDON:
HURST & BLACKETT
AN
ACCOUNT
OF
RUSSIA
1710
WHITWORTH

3
Russian Books in the Royal Library

EMMA STUART

The earliest royal collections of books on Russia can be found in the British Library, which contains the Old Royal Library, books owned by monarchs *c.*1450–1757, and the King's Library, George III's scholars library, donated to the then British Museum by George IV in 1823. This is complemented by the present Royal Library, which contains other collections of George III, and books collected by his successors up to the present day. While this survey of such sources cannot be comprehensive, we can at least get a flavour of the books on Russia collected by our royal family over the centuries.

England's early relationship with Russia matured on the shop floor, through explorations by English merchants seeking a sea route into Russia as an alternative market for English goods. Before the penetration of the White Sea by Richard Chancellor in 1553 (cat. 22), Muscovy (as the principality of Moscow, the predecessor of the Tsardom of Russia, was known at the time) was considered a mysterious and exotic land to the east. By 1597, when Shakespeare composed his 'masque of the Muscovites' in *Love's Labour's Lost*, English perception of Muscovy had not really altered, despite the accounts of their Russian adventures by English merchants: Chancellor in 1553, Anthony Jenkinson (1529–1610/11) in 1557, George Turberville (1543/4–97), in 1568, and Giles Fletcher the Elder (*c.*1546–1611) in 1591, whose account was so unflattering that it was suppressed, probably at the request of the Russian Company (the English trading company). These early writings were anthologised in 1589 by Richard Hakluyt (*c.*1552–1616), in his *The Principall Navigations, Voiages and Discoveries of the English Nation*, and, later, in an enlarged edition of 1599–1600.

For any collector of English-language works on Russia, Hakluyt was an essential, and we find George III with a copy of the revised edition in his library. English merchants were not the first, nor only Europeans entering Russia during the sixteenth century, so we also find accounts in other languages in George III's collections: those of Sigismund von Herberstein (1486–1566), ambassador of the Holy Roman Empire in 1517 and 1526; of Paolo Giovio (1483/6–1552), who witnessed Dmitry Gerasimov's embassy to Pope Clement VII in 1525; of Martinus Broniovius, Polish ambassador in 1579; and of Antonio Possevino (*c.*1533–1611), papal nuncio to Muscovy in 1582. Von Herberstein's work was particularly influential, despite not being available in English, since it was the best eyewitness account of Russia available to Europeans at the time.

George III's acquisitions continued into seventeenth-century Russian history. Sir Thomas Smith's account of his trade embassy in 1603 appears in two first editions from 1605, and two copies of the first French account of Russia, by the mercenary soldier, Jacques Margeret (*c.*1565–1619), in 1607. George III also acquired a copy of Henry Brereton's *Newes of the present miseries of Rushia* [*sic*], first published in 1614, a near-contemporary account of the so-called 'Time of Troubles' after the death of Boris Gudunov in 1605, leading up to the election of the first Romanov Tsar, Mikhail, in 1613. George III also acquired several copies of the work of Adam Olearius (cat. 12), which was first published in German in 1647, followed by editions in French, Italian and

Selection of Russian travel books from the Royal Library, Windsor Castle

English. Anglo-Russian relations were broken off after the execution of Charles I in 1649, but after the Restoration of Charles II in 1660, a resumption of cordial relations was attempted, with a Russian embassy to London, chiefly in search of a loan (which they did not achieve). This did not augur well for the embassy to Russia by the Earl of Carlisle in 1664, to renegotiate England's old exclusive trading rights (cat. 2).

The reign of Peter the Great, and his visit to England in 1698, caused an upsurge in the acquisition of several accounts written during and immediately after his reign: the accounts of Johann Korb, who witnessed and recorded the revolt and punishment of the Streltsy (cat. 9), Ysbrants Ides (cat. 10), who described the little-known eastern part of Russia, Captain John Perry (cat. 11), who had been directly recruited by Peter I to build waterways in Russia, and Charles Whitworth (cat. 80), the first permanent British diplomatic representative in Russia.

Royal books on Russia ventured further into the interior; as Ides had described the eastern part of the country, so other travellers discussed the merits of Siberia, Ukraine, even as far afield as Kamchatka, and the perspective on Russia often turned eastwards, histories describing her in the same breath as China, Japan, India and Turkey. This expansion of geographical horizons is possibly partly due to the greater availability of better quality European maps of the whole empire, which had begun to appear in the seventeenth century (Blaeu's *Atlas Maior*, cat. 3), and atlases published in Russia under the aegis of Peter and his successors (*Atlas Russicus*, cat. 22). By the reign of Catherine the Great (1762–96), Russian territories had expanded to include the Crimea, the Caspian Sea, the Caucasus, Siberia, and the area known as Tartary, the eastern part of Russia stretching towards China. Royal collecting was also keeping abreast of scientific developments, such as Chappe d'Auteroche's 1768 publication on Siberia and the Transit of Venus in 1761 (cat. 23), and the work of Peter Simon Pallas (1741–1811) and Johann Gottlieb Georgi (1729–1802), who travelled over vast areas of Russia collecting natural history specimens for Catherine the Great. The unrest in Europe in the early nineteenth century did not prevent the expansion of Russia's geographical or imperial curiosity – George IV was presented with a copy of Yuri Lisianski's book of his 1803–6 circumnavigation of the globe (cat. 82), published in 1814.

As Napoleon's armies tightened their grip on Europe and Russia, British royal collecting continued to concentrate on accounts of travels, while also collecting more Russian dictionaries and other language tools. Considering the momentous events in Europe, very little was acquired specifically on the Russian wars, though George IV did buy a copy of Robert Wilson's (1777–1849) account of the Russian army from 1810 (Wilson later observed the French retreat from Moscow in 1812), as well as Eugène Labaume's (1783–1849) own account of the 1812 retreat, told from the French side. George IV's collection did reflect the 1814 visit to England by the victorious generals, including Emperor Alexander I, during which they visited Oxford (cat. 67) and were hosted in the Guildhall by the Corporation of London, while the Poet Laureate, Robert Southey, praised them all to the skies (cat. 66).

Russia has always been intriguing to English travellers, despite wars and diplomatic arguments. Thus far, we have encountered merchants (Chancellor and his colleagues), ambassadors (Carlisle and Whitworth) and naval engineers (Perry). Travellers also began to include tutors, such as William Coxe (cat. 42), or the governess, Lucy Finley (Atkinson) (1817–93; cat. 86), doctors, such as Granville (cat. 85), artists, such as Porter (cat. 81) and Thomas Witlam Atkinson (1799–1861; cat. 87), and missionaries, such as Henry Lansdell (1841–1919; cats 90–91), to name but a few. Napoleon's campaigns affected some of them – Porter was

FIG. 23
G.V. Vilinbakhov (*fl.* 2003), editor
Санкт-Петербург 1703–2003, 2003
Printed on paper, bound in dark blue goat with blue and silver tooling, the box embellished with the arms of St Petersburg
RCIN 1101571

obliged to leave Russia after the Franco-Russian Treaty of Tilsit, and Robert Johnston's (1783–1839) visit to war-torn Moscow (cat. 83) enabled him to describe the devastated scene for his readers.

St Petersburg, on the other hand, was seen as a tourist destination, described approvingly by Granville and Svinyin (cat. 84). The availability of English-language accounts of Russia enriched the collections in the Royal Library, particularly under Queen Victoria, who acquired or was presented with several travel titles which demonstrated the scale and range of her subjects' explorations into the vast Russian Empire. Unlike the Franco-Russian war of 1812,

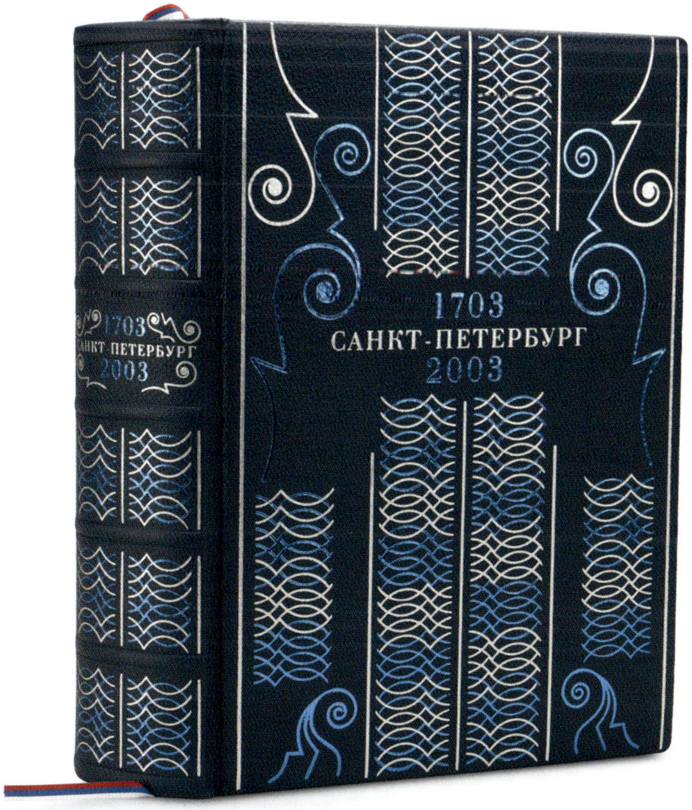

the Crimean War of 1853–6 was of immediate relevance to Britain, reflected in the range of books acquired, complemented by photographs of the campaign by Roger Fenton, described as the world's first war photographer. Well over 100 books were acquired on the Crimea, not just on the war itself, but describing the territory and the diplomatic background to the campaign. The other interesting feature of this period of royal collecting was the creation of a second Russian library collection, which was happy to copy what was in the main collection – that of Albert Edward, Prince of Wales (later Edward VII) at Sandringham. At no previous point had there been evident duplication in this subject (not even between George III and George IV – a similar situation of monarch and heir); this may be down to simple geography (Sandringham being at least 130 miles away from Windsor), and it must also be borne in mind that Edward was related by marriage to the Russian Emperor Alexander III (who had married Dagmar, sister to Edward's wife, Alexandra).

The last significant spike in royal collecting on Russia came about after tragedy – the death of Nicholas II and his family in 1918. This apparently galvanised King George V into a relative frenzy of book buying on Russia. Over the next two decades he collected such titles as *The Real Tsaritsa* (Dehn 1922), the memoirs of Maurice Paléologue (1859–1944), French ambassador to Russia up to 1917, books on the end of the Russian Empire, and the Soviet era (for example, *Secrets of the OGPU* by Essad-bey, 1933, and *The Red Terror in Russia* by S.P. Melgunov, 1925). Subsequent acquisitions during the reigns of King George VI and Her Majesty The Queen have largely concentrated on Nicholas and Alexandra, and on other points of contact, such as art and culture. The state visit of Vladimir Putin, the first state visit of a Russian ruler to Britain, was marked by the gift of a book commemorating the tercentenary of Peter the Great's founding of St Petersburg (fig. 23).

CHARLES, BARON WHITWORTH (1675–1725)

80 *An Account of Russia as it was in the year 1710* 1758

[Twickenham]: Strawberry Hill, 1st edn
Bound in vellum, top edge gilt, 19.8 × 12.5 cm (closed)
RCIN 1145671

Provenance Probably acquired by George III; in the Royal Library by King George V's reign

Literature Cross 2000, pp. 44–5; Cross 2014b, B16

Charles Whitworth's career in Russia began in 1704, when he was appointed British envoy to Russia to resolve certain trade disputes, the first permanent British diplomatic representative in Russia. His position was further strengthened in 1710 when he was promoted to the position of Ambassador Extraordinary, so that he could act as Queen Anne's official representative in apologising for the treatment of the Russian ambassador to London, A.A. Matveev (1666–1728), who had been beaten and imprisoned.

Whitworth returned to England in 1710, and produced this assessment of Peter's reign, probably as a government briefing document. It was not published until 1758, at Horace Walpole's Strawberry Hill Press, a manuscript copy having been purchased at an auction sale from the collection of M. Zolman, secretary to Stephen Poyntz (1685–1750), diplomat and courtier. Zolman's collection related purely to Russian history and affairs, and contained 'in many languages every thing that perhaps has been written on that country'.[1] The work was also serialised in the *Gentleman's Magazine*.[2] Whitworth's account is very deliberate and thorough, detailing all aspects of the country, particularly its ruler, for whom he gives a very considered character assessment and notes approvingly:

> *He is extremely curious and diligent, and has farther improved his Empire in ten years, than any other ever was, in ten times that space; and which is more surprizing, without any education, without any foreign help, contrary to the intention of his people, clergy, and chief ministers, but merely by the strength of his own genius, observation and example.*[3] **ES**

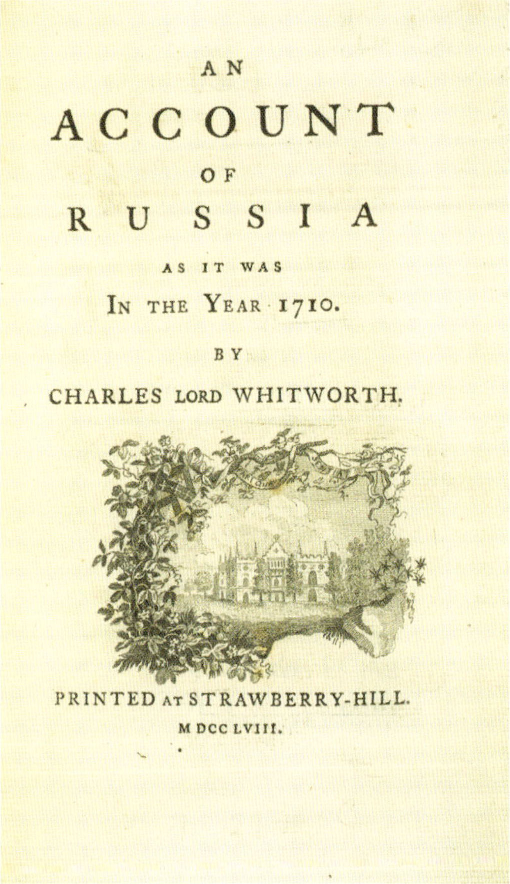
AN
ACCOUNT
OF
RUSSIA
AS IT WAS
IN THE YEAR 1710.
BY
CHARLES LORD WHITWORTH.
PRINTED AT STRAWBERRY-HILL.
MDCCLVIII.

ROBERT KER PORTER (1777–1842)

81 *Travelling sketches in Russia and Sweden, during the years 1805, 1806, 1807, 1808* 1809

London: Richard Phillips, 2 vols in 1
Half-bound in green morocco, by New, Eton, top edge gilt, 31.2 × 25.5 cm (closed)
RCIN 1141318

Provenance Acquired by George IV when Prince of Wales, 1809

Literature Putnam 1952, pp. 293–344; Turner 1996, pp. 263–4; Cross 2014b, F13

Porter was trained at the Royal Academy under the patronage of Benjamin West (1738–1820), having apparently been inspired to become a painter of battle scenes by one such belonging to Flora Macdonald (1722–90), the Jacobite heroine. In 1799 he became a founder member of the Brothers, a group of young artists wishing to establish history painting in England. After the enormous success of the equally huge history painting, *The Storming of Seringapatam*, Porter painted several more paintings depicting events in the Napoleonic Wars, of similar size, and thus secured a commission from Emperor Alexander I to go to St Petersburg and paint the walls of the Great Hall of the Admiralty. From 1805 to 1807, he lived in St Petersburg and made two trips to Moscow, before being obliged to leave the country after the Treaty of Tilsit, in which Russia allied herself with France. His experiences were documented in his *Travelling sketches*, published after his return, based on letters written to a friend, Henry Caulfield (1779–1808), and illustrated with his own pictures. He excused the rather unformed nature of his work by the fact that Caulfield was dying when he was endeavouring to put the book together, and confessed that it was:

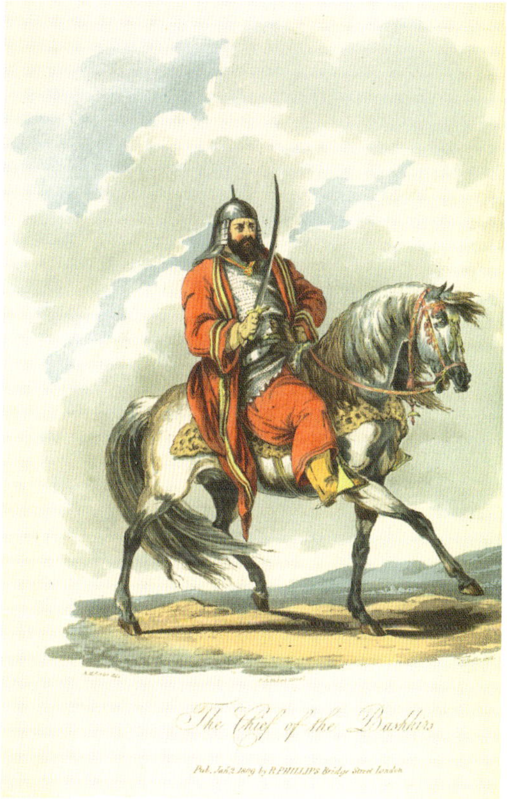

> *not the studied work of an Author bringing forward deep researches, valuable discoveries, and consequential observations,* [...], *but the familiar correspondence of a friend, noticing the manners of the people with whom he associates, their fashions, their amusements, the sentiments of the day; and mingling with these a few occurrences happening to himself, and the reflections to which they give rise.*[4]

ES

YURI LISIANSKI (1773–1837)

82 *A Voyage round the world, in the years 1803, 4, 5, & 6; performed, by order of His Imperial Majesty Alexander the First, Emperor of Russia, in the ship Neva* 1814

London: John Booth, and Longman, Hurst, Rees, Orme & Brown
Bound in red morocco with extensive gold-tooled decoration, watered silk doublures, gilt edges, dedicated to Alexander I, Emperor of Russia, 28.8 × 20.5 cm (closed)
RCIN 1141469

Provenance Acquired by George IV when Prince Regent

As Europe came to explore Russia, so Russia looked outwards beyond her borders. Her first circumnavigation of the globe was planned in 1802, sponsored by the Russian foreign minister, Count Nikolai Rumyantsev (1754–1826), and paid for by the Russian-American Company, originally set up in 1799 to fund the colonisation of Russian America (now Alaska) and to establish trading relations there. Alexander I appointed Adam Johann von Krusenstern (1770–1846) to lead the expedition, in two ships, *Hope* and *Neva*. His fellow captain was Yuri Lisianski, an officer from the imperial Russian navy.

The voyage had several objectives, mainly commercial and diplomatic – to establish trade with China and Japan, to establish a Russian ambassador in Japan, and to facilitate trade in Russian America. While friendly relations were established with China and Japan, attempts to gain trade advantages or install a Russian ambassador failed. The two ships had split after passing the Sandwich Isles, with von Krusenstern in the *Hope* sailing to Japan for the abortive effort to deliver an ambassador, while Lisianski continued to Alaska in the *Neva*. He and his crew took part in the battle of Sitka in 1804, against the Tinglit, the last armed conflict between Russia and Alaskan natives. On a more peaceful note, Lisianski was the first to describe the Hawaiian monk seal, a native of the Hawaiian Islands (one of which is now named after him). Other more material honours were presented to him on his return to Russia, including promotion to post-captain, a pension of 3,000 rubles, and the Order of St Vladimir (Third Class).

Various works were published on the expedition, including this one, first published in Russian in 1812 in St Petersburg, then in English in 1814. Von Krusenstern also published his account in St Petersburg, in both Russian and German, and later in English (1813). The naturalist Georg Heinrich Langsdorff (1774–1852), who accompanied the expedition but left at Kamchatka, published an account of the plants he observed on the voyage, in 1810. ES

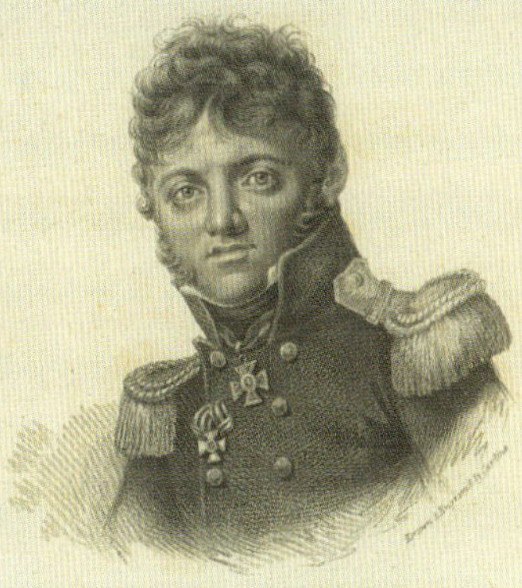

UREY LISIANSKY

K.G. & V.

A

VOYAGE ROUND THE WORLD,

IN

THE YEARS 1803, 4, 5, & 6;

PERFORMED,

BY ORDER OF HIS IMPERIAL MAJESTY

ALEXANDER THE FIRST, EMPEROR OF RUSSIA,

IN

THE SHIP NEVA,

BY

UREY LISIANSKY,

CAPTAIN IN THE RUSSIAN NAVY,

AND

KNIGHT OF THE ORDERS OF ST. GEORGE AND ST. VLADIMER.

LONDON:

PRINTED FOR JOHN BOOTH, DUKE STREET, PORTLAND PLACE; AND

LONGMAN, HURST, REES, ORME, & BROWN, PATERNOSTER ROW;

BY S. HAMILTON, WEYBRIDGE, SURREY.

1814.

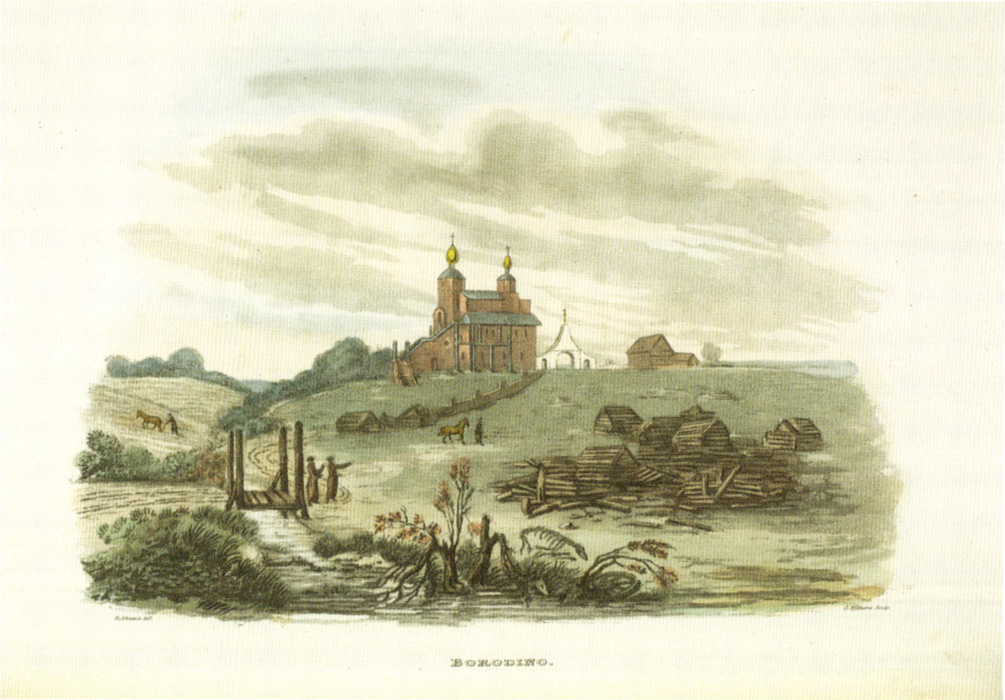

ROBERT JOHNSTON (1783–1839)

83 *Travels through parts of the Russian Empire and the country of Poland; along the southern shores of the Baltic* 1815

London: J.J. Stockdale
Bound in brown calf, marbled edges, garter cipher of William IV on both boards, dedicated to the Prince Regent, 30.5 × 25.0 cm (closed)
RCIN 1141298

Provenance Probably acquired by William IV

Literature Cross 2014b, F58

Johnston, an Oxford graduate, journeyed to Russia in 1814, reaching St Petersburg in July. His preface begins rather pompously on the political state of Europe and the liberating light of Russia: 'the flames of Moscow have burst a new light on man; the falling towers of the Kremlin have chimed the tyrant's parting knell, and proclaimed aloud, that Europe is free!'[5] His work derived from his own impressions, and he certainly offers detailed accounts of the towns and cities he travelled through. His arrival in Moscow not two years after Napoleon's siege led him to describe the devastation:

> *Here was to be seen every thing costly and magnificent; the grand mart of European and Asiatic splendour, the pride and envy of the northern world. / This is the spot we now gazed on; what a change! lowly and prostrate it now lies, its crumbling towers, falling into decay, its proud banners torn from their burning walls, and scattering their shivered fragments to the hollow winds – its temples torn – its gates demolished – its houses ransacked – its streets laid waste.*[6]

The site of the battle of Borodino similarly affected him: 'Nothing but the sad remnants of its desolation now remain; the whole is almost a desert'.[7] **ES**

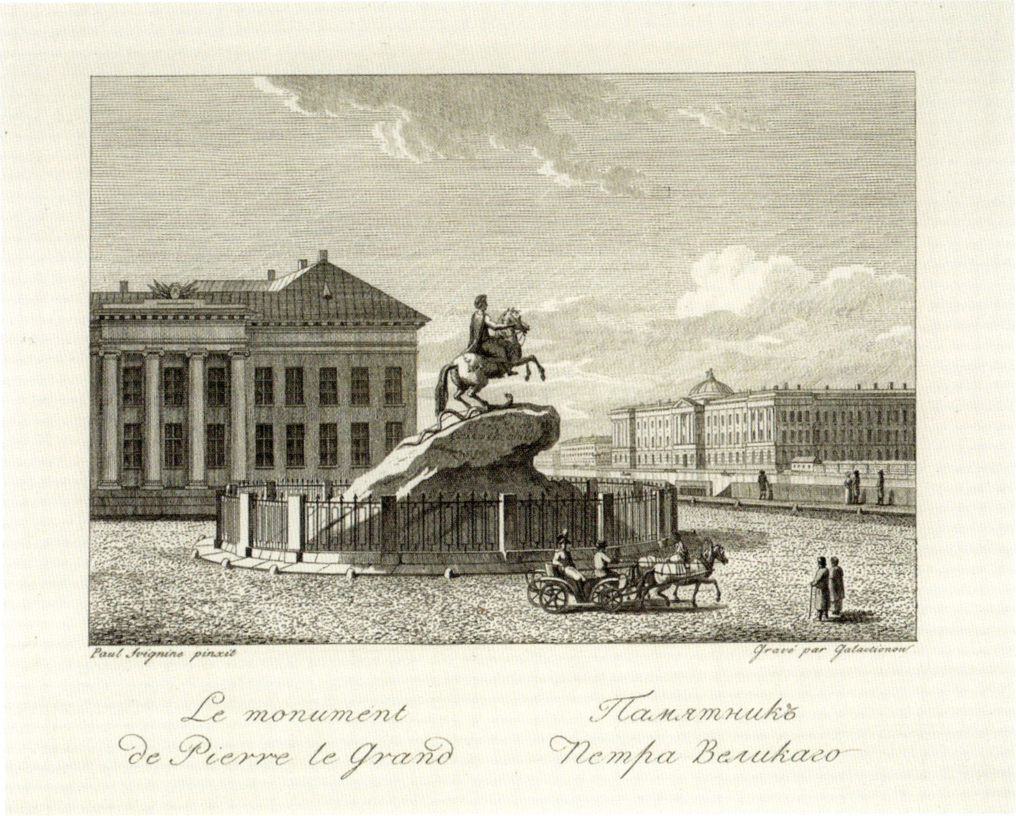

PAVEL SVINYIN (1787–1839)

84 *Достопамятности Санктпетербурга и его окрестностей = Description des objets les plus remarquables de St. Petersbourg et de ses environs 1816*

Saint Petersburg: V. Plaviltsikov
Bound in brown calf, marbled edges, *garter cipher of William IV on both boards,* 24.4 × 20.1 cm (closed)
RCIN 1141248

Provenance Acquired by George III for his Windsor Library (WL 56)

Before the work done by Granville, an Italian/Englishman visiting St Petersburg (cat. 85), the lack of a decent guidebook had been noticed, and restitution made, by a native Russian, Pavel (Paul) Svinyin. Svinyin had served at the Russian Consulate in Philadelphia 1811–13, and had already published works on Moscow and St Petersburg in English, but felt that St Petersburg – home of the Emperor Alexander, the pacifier of Europe – required more detail. Most works on Russia had been written by foreigners, he complained, and thus were lacking in accuracy; a Russian author should be able to do a better job. In order to render the book more palatable, he proposed adding an engraving to each section, to illustrate in pictures what was described in words. The text was printed in both Russian and French, in order to make the work useful to native readers as well as foreign visitors. **ES**

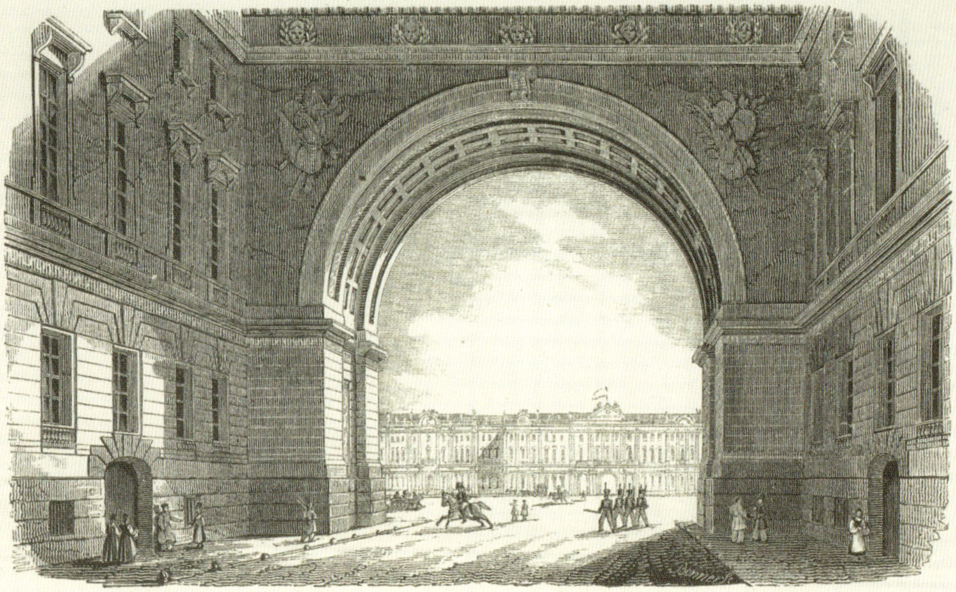

VIEW OF THE IMPERIAL OR WINTER PALACE AT ST. PETERSBURGH

ON THE SIDE OF THE SQUARE, SEEN THROUGH THE TROPHEAL ARCH OF THE ETAT MAJOR.

AUGUSTUS BOZZI GRANVILLE (1783–1872)

85 *St. Petersburgh: a journal of travels to and from that capital* 1828

London: Henry Colburn, 2 vols
Half-bound in brown morocco, top edge gilt, *Queen Victoria's bookplate, dedicated to George IV*, 22.7 × 15.6 cm (closed)
RCINS 1141203, 1141204

Provenance Unknown

Literature Cross 2014b, G5

Dr Granville, an Italian by birth who had settled in England, was a specialist in obstetrics and children's diseases. His private practice was both extensive and illustrious, owing partly to his excellent manners, and this was probably how he acquired the commission to accompany the Count and Countess Mikhail Vorontsov (1714–67 and 1722–76) on their return to St Petersburg from England. Granville nurtured their health on the sea voyage, even prescribing the Countess 45 drops of laudanum (a preparation of opium) to combat her seasickness.

Granville's brief stay in St Petersburg from October to December 1827 encouraged him to write his detailed account of the city in all its aspects. A modern description of the city was essential, not something 'lively, light and miscellaneous, though not always correct [... nor] short details [...] but a methodical account of the place and its establishments, which may be consulted by the stranger newly arrived in the capital of Russia anxious to become successively acquainted with the various objects of interest'.[8] The second and third editions of his book, published in 1829 and 1835, bore the rather more pointed title, *Guide to St Petersburgh: a journal of travels*. ES

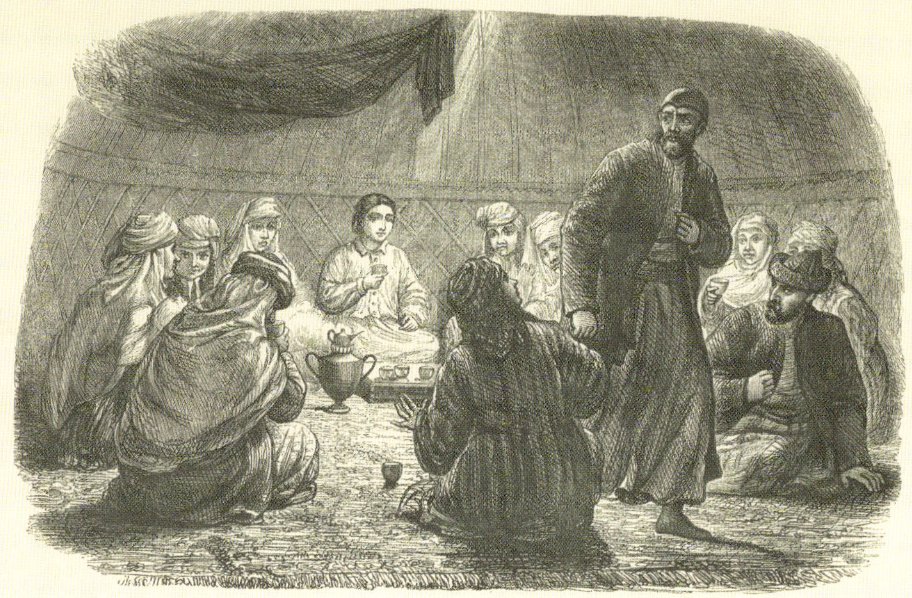
A TEA PARTY IN A KIRGHIS TENT.

LUCY ATKINSON (1817–1893)

86 *Recollections of Tartar steppes and their inhabitants* 1863

London: John Murray
20.5 × 13.7 cm (closed)
RCIN 1141872

Provenance Probably acquired by Queen Victoria after 1863

Literature Cross 2014b, G108

Lucy Finley, a governess in the household of General Muravyov (1796–1866) in St Petersburg, became acquainted with Thomas Atkinson in 1846, after his return from his first extensive trip to the interior of Russia. They were married in 1848, after which Lucy Atkinson accompanied her husband on his travels 'in countries where an English lady had never been seen before'.[9] She became an intrepid horsewoman and markswoman, skills for which she was much admired by the Russian peoples whom she met. Lucy Atkinson's account of their travels differs in emphasis from that of her husband; where he discussed scientific and artistic subjects, she addressed their adventures, and particularly those affecting herself, as a lonely English woman with a babe in arms. She also describes at various points meeting with exiles from the Decembrist uprisings of 1825, when various Russian army officers led a revolt against Emperor Nicholas I's assumption of the throne in place of his elder brother, who had renounced his claim to the throne in 1823. ES

THOMAS WITLAM ATKINSON (1799–1861)

87 *Oriental and Western Siberia: a narrative of seven years' explorations and adventures in Siberia, Mongolia, the Kirghis Steppes, Chinese Tartary, and part of central Asia* 1858

London: Hurst & Blackett
Bound in red morocco, gold-tooled with gilt edges, 25.0 × 17.2 cm (closed)
RCIN 1141995

Provenance Dedicated to Emperor Alexander II; presented to Queen Victoria and Prince Albert by the author, January 1858 (presentation letter tipped in at front flyleaf)

Literature Cross 2014b, G106

Thomas Atkinson was a flourishing architect when he read and was inspired by Alexander von Humboldt's (1769–1859) description of Siberia, and he determined to abandon architecture and turn explorer and artist. From March to November 1847 he travelled through the Urals, the Kirgiz Steppes and the Altai mountains, before returning to Moscow, where he met and married Lucy Finley, a governess. It was discovered after his death that he had married her bigamously, having a wife in England whom he had married in 1819. It is perhaps telling that he never mentions Lucy in his work, although she accompanied him on his subsequent travels to the Russian east in 1848–53, and wrote her own work on the journey (cat. 86).

During his extensive travels, made easier by the passport granted him by Emperor Nicholas I, Atkinson completed over 500 watercolours of people and landscapes, which were exhibited at the Colnaghi Gallery in London on his return in 1856. Queen Victoria noted in her Journal on 26 October: 'After luncheon we saw about 50 very interesting drawings & paintings done by a Mr Atkinson, who has for about 6 years been travelling in Siberia, & Mongolia, which must be most curious. He has seen all the Russian possessions there & all their unknown Forts.'[10]

Atkinson published two books on his travels, the present work and *Travels in the regions of the upper and lower Amoor* (1860), which was much praised at the time, but was later discovered to be plagiarised, in part, from a Russian publication of 1859 by Richard Maak on the same subject. ES

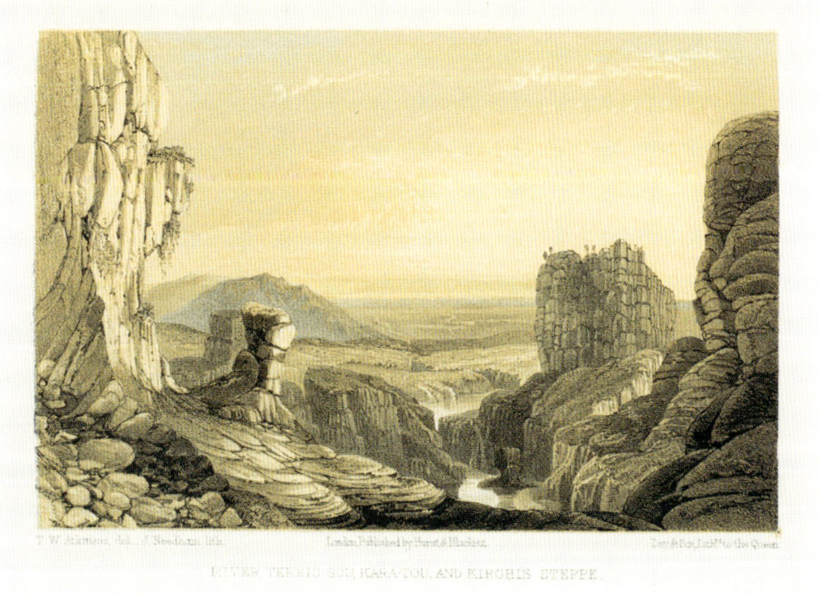

Oriental and Western Siberia: Plate 12, depicting the River Terric-sou, Kara-tou and Kirghis Steppe

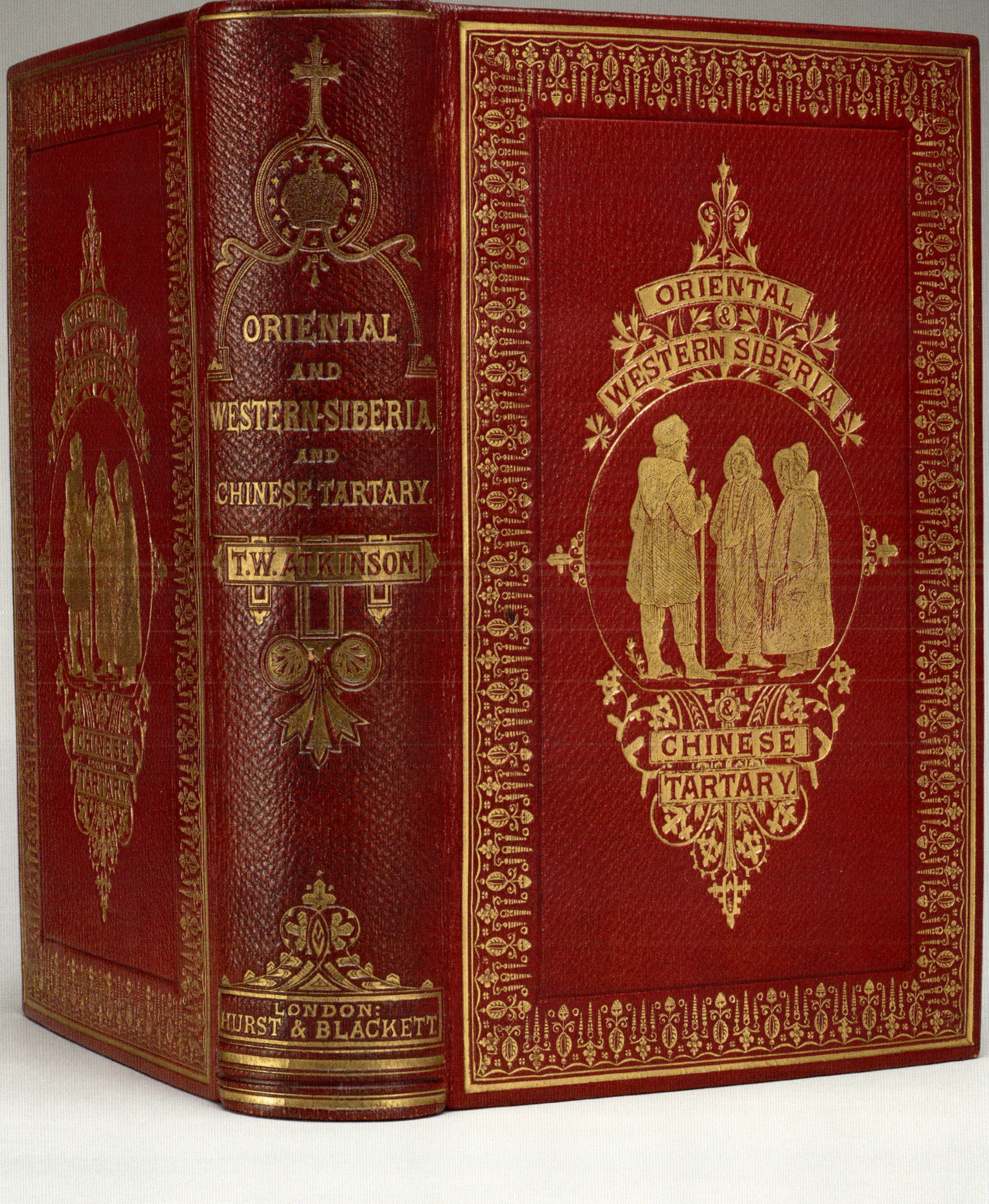
ORIENTAL
AND
WESTERN-SIBERIA,
AND
CHINESE TARTARY.
T.W. ATKINSON.
LONDON:
HURST & BLACKETT.
ORIENTAL
&
WESTERN SIBERIA
&
CHINESE
TARTARY.

THEODORE DE PAULY (1817–1867)

88 *Description ethnographique des peuples de la Russie: publiée a l'occasion du jubilé millénaire de l'empire de Russie* 1862

Saint Petersburg: F. Bellizard
Bound in green morocco, with gilt edges, 54.0 × 42.8 cm (closed)
RCIN 1070277

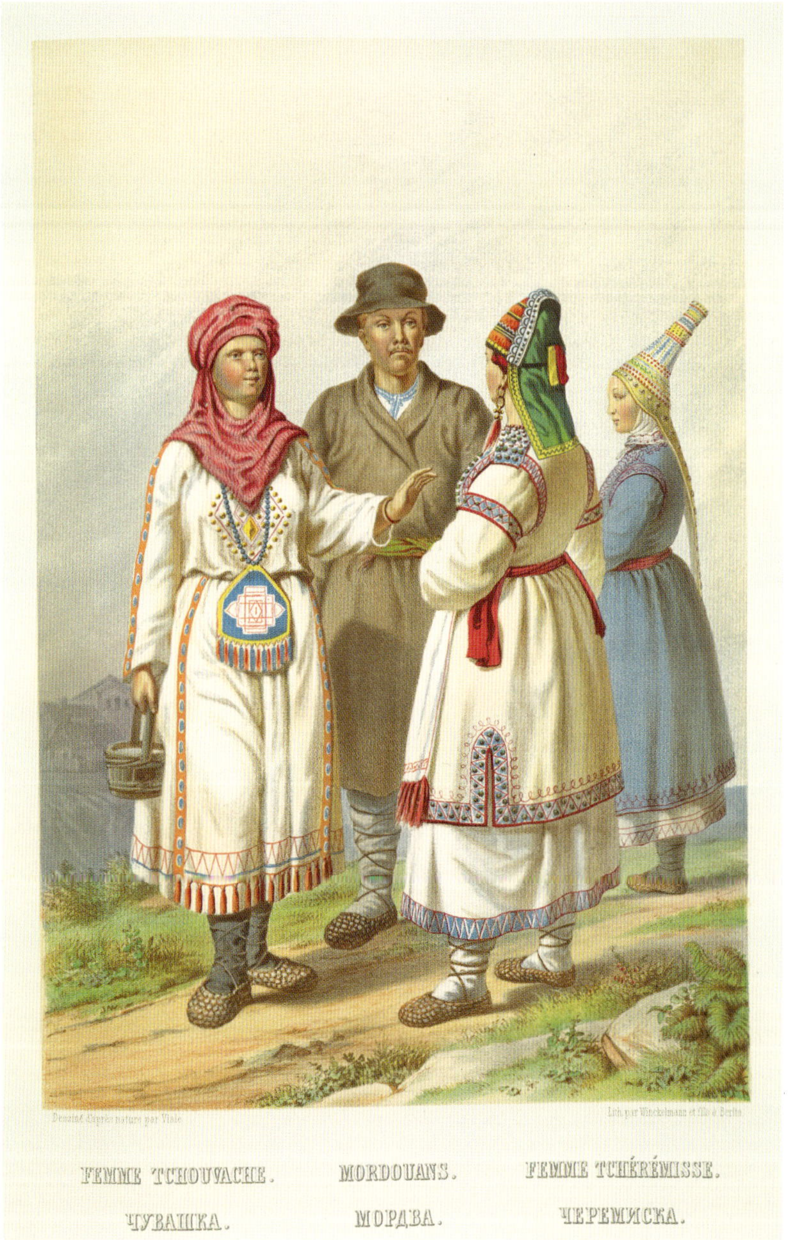

Provenance Presented to King Edward VII when Prince of Wales by the author, 31 July 1862

Theodore de Pauly, a member of the newly founded Imperial Russian Geographical Society (founded 1845), was the latest in a line of ethnographers, seeking to record the enormous range of peoples spread across both European and Asian Russia.

The work of Johann Gottlieb Georgi, published in 1776–80, had assembled for the first time a consolidated study of the peoples of Russia, after Georgi's own extensive travels into Siberia and several other parts of Asia. Published at the expense of Catherine the Great, it heralded state interest in and approval of ethnographic research, which continued on through the nineteenth century.

Pauly's work, compiled from many previous ethnographical studies, was illustrated with 62 chromo-lithographs, mainly executed from nature. The work was shown to Alexander II during production and the finished article dedicated to him. It was published to celebrate the 1000th anniversary of the Russian Empire. ES

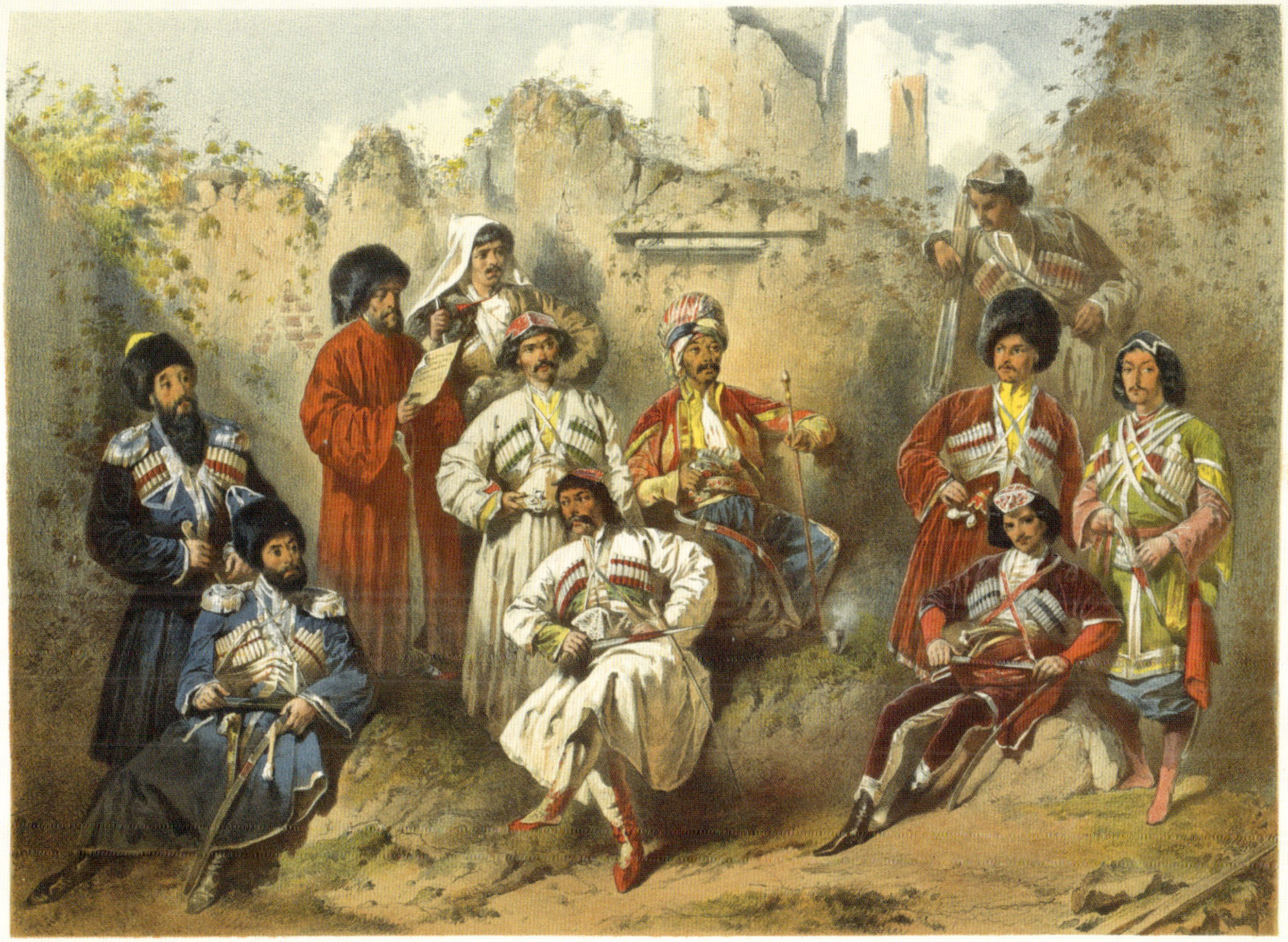

Dess. d'après la Photog. de Mr Zichy par N. Sauerweid — Imp. Lemercier Paris — Lith. par J. Laurens.

DÉPUTÉS DES PEUPLES DU CAUCASE

(présents au Couronnement de S. M. L'EMPEREUR à Moscou 1856)

ДЕПУТАТЫ КАВКАЗСКИХЪ ПЛЕМЕНЪ

(бывшие на коронации Государя ИМПЕРАТОРА въ Москвѣ 1856 г.)

THOMAS MICHELL (1836–1899)

89 *Handbook for travellers to Russia, Poland, and Finland: including the Crimea, Caucasus, Siberia, and Central Asia* 1888

London: John Murray, 4th edn, thoroughly revised
Bound in red morocco, gold-tooled with gilt edges, 18.7 × 13.0 cm (closed)
RCIN 1075918

Provenance Presented to Queen Victoria by the author, 7 November 1887 (presentation letter tipped in at flyleaf)

Literature Cross 2014b, I56

Murray's Red Handbooks were first introduced in 1836, packed with detailed and accurate information for the English traveller, taking advantage of the new railway and other travel networks across Europe. The series eventually covered all of Europe, England, Japan, New Zealand and India, its approval treasured, its criticism feared.

The first guide to Russia was written by Thomas Whatley in 1839, when it was included in the *Handbook for Northern Europe*; a second edition by William Jesse came out in 1848. The author of subsequent editions (1865–93) was Thomas Michell, whose diplomatic career as the British consul in St Petersburg, and his impeccable pedigree as guide and translator to the Prince of Wales during his visit to Russia in 1866, made him the ideal candidate to edit the guide to Russia. Michell's editions were thus based on personal experience and considerable knowledge. He thought it the best guide to Russia in any language, as he told Murray, 'for the Russians have nothing of the kind in their own language'.[11] **ES**

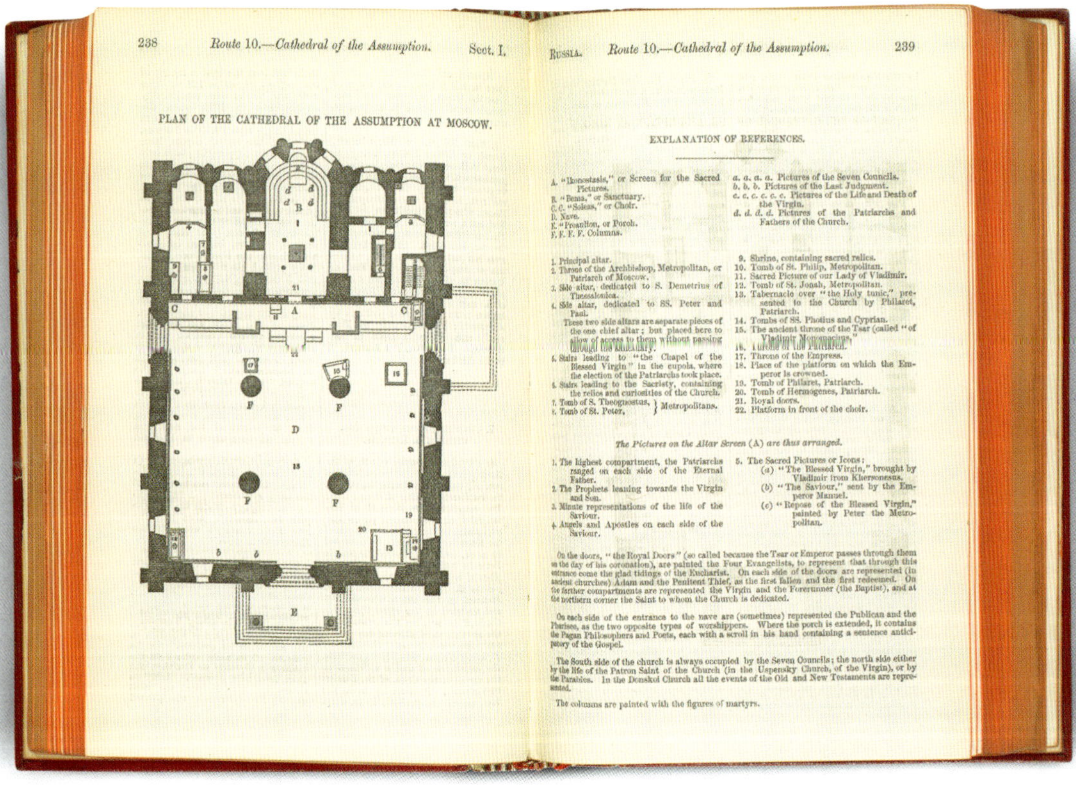

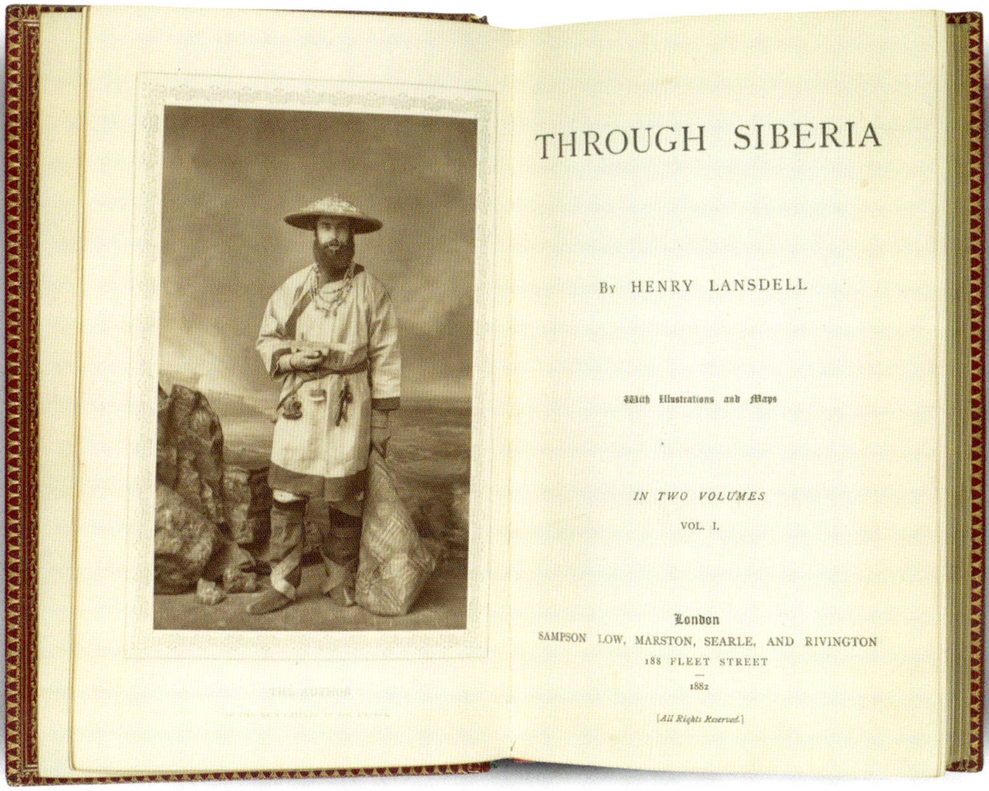

HENRY LANSDELL (1841–1919)

90 *Through Siberia* 1882

London: Sampson Low, Marston, Searle & Rivington, 2 vols
Bound in red morocco, gold-tooled, gilt edges, 21.6 × 15.1 cm (closed)
RCINS 1077444, 1077445

Provenance Presented to Queen Victoria by the author, 25 February 1882: 'To Her Most Gracious Majesty Queen Victoria These volumes are humbly presented, with unfeigned expression of loyalty and esteem, by Her Majesty's obedient subject, The Author'

Literature Cross 2014b, I171

Henry Lansdell, missionary, bold traveller, prison visitor, for whom no destination was too inaccessible, first started his journeys in the 1870s, first to the accessible parts of Europe, and then to far-flung parts of Asia, where his main focus was to distribute tracts and Bibles in several languages to the native population. *Through Siberia* was his first book, recounting his journey of May to September 1879, and it became very popular, going into five editions and published in German, Danish and Swedish.

In the preface he states that he has chosen to give a broader picture of Siberia than was warranted by his own (not inconsiderable) experiences, and has thus supplemented those from other sources. His chief object was to visit the prisons and other penal institutions with philanthropy rather than administration in mind, and to record a rather more accurate view of them than had hitherto been available. 'It has been comparatively easy [...] in England for writers to exaggerate on this subject [prisons] almost as they pleased, because scarcely any one could contradict them'.[12] The map of his travels shows the length of his journey from west to east, from Archangel to Vladivostok, amazingly accomplished entirely through interpreters, for 'I do not even speak Russ'.[13] ES

HENRY LANSDELL (1841–1919)

91 *Russian Central Asia: including Kuldja, Bokhara, Khiva and Merv* 1885

London: Sampson Low, Marston, Searle & Rivington, 2 vols
Half-bound in brown pigskin, with gilt edges, 22.1 × 15.5 cm (closed)
RCINS 1124069, 1124070

Provenance Presented to King Edward VII when Prince of Wales by the author, 7 July 1885

Literature Cross 2014b, J14

Lansdell's second journey through Russia after his Siberian adventures took him, from June to December 1882, far into Siberia to Omsk, before turning south to Russia in Asia, what are now Kazakhstan, Uzbekhistan, Turkmenistan and other countries bordering China, visiting Tashkent, Samarkand, Bokhara and, finally, Odessa. His book was intended for three different readerships: the general reader interested in the narrative; the armchair traveller who wanted to know somewhat of the country, geography, flora and fauna, and of the people, their language and religion; and finally those of a more scientific bent, for whom he wrote more detailed material on flora and fauna. The book was dedicated to Emperor Alexander III, in recognition of the kindness with which Lansdell was met throughout his travels in Russia. **ES**

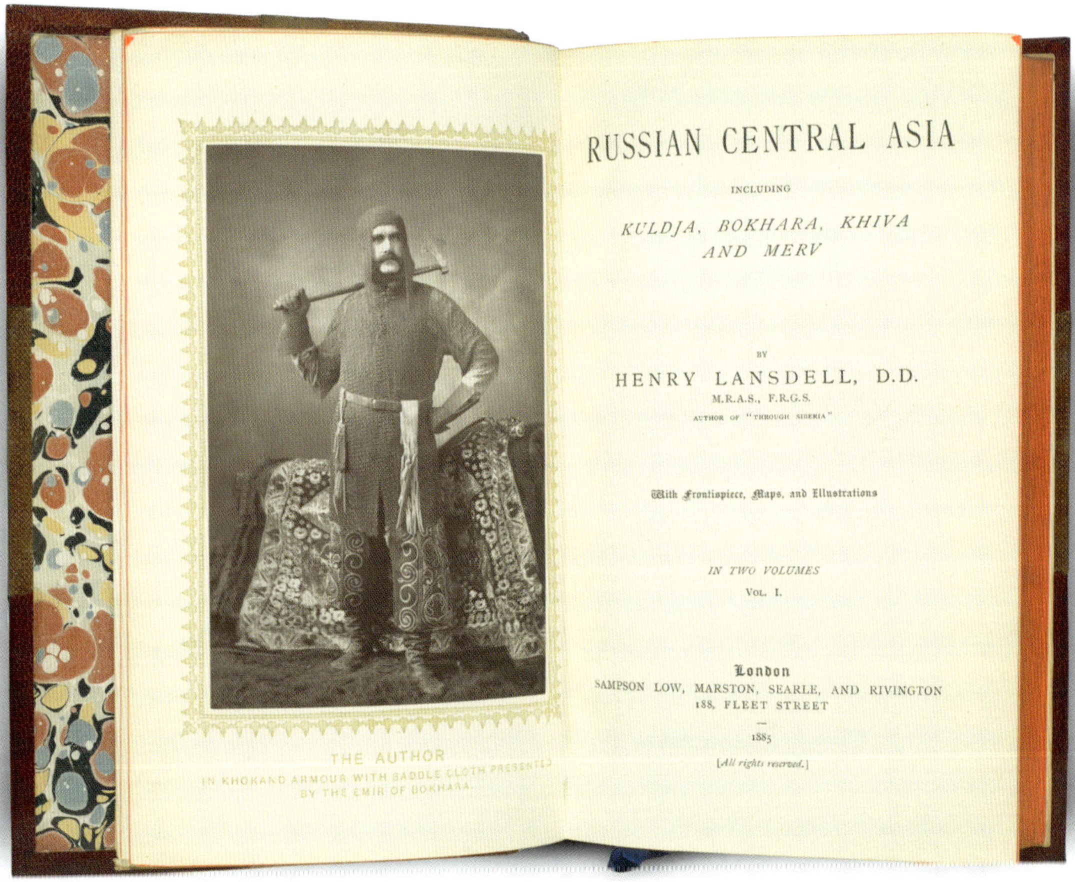

PRINCE ESPER ESPEROVICH UKHTOMSKY (1861–1921)

92 *Travels in the East of Nicholas II Emperor of Russia when Cesarewitch 1890–1891: written by order of His Imperial Majesty ... and translated from the Russian by Robert Goodlet; edited by Sir George Birdwood* 1896–1900

Westminster: Archibald Constable & Co., 2 vols
Yellow cloth binding, stamped with the imperial Russian coat of arms, bookplate of Queen Victoria, 39.5 × 30.5 cm (closed)
RCINS 1142852, 1142853

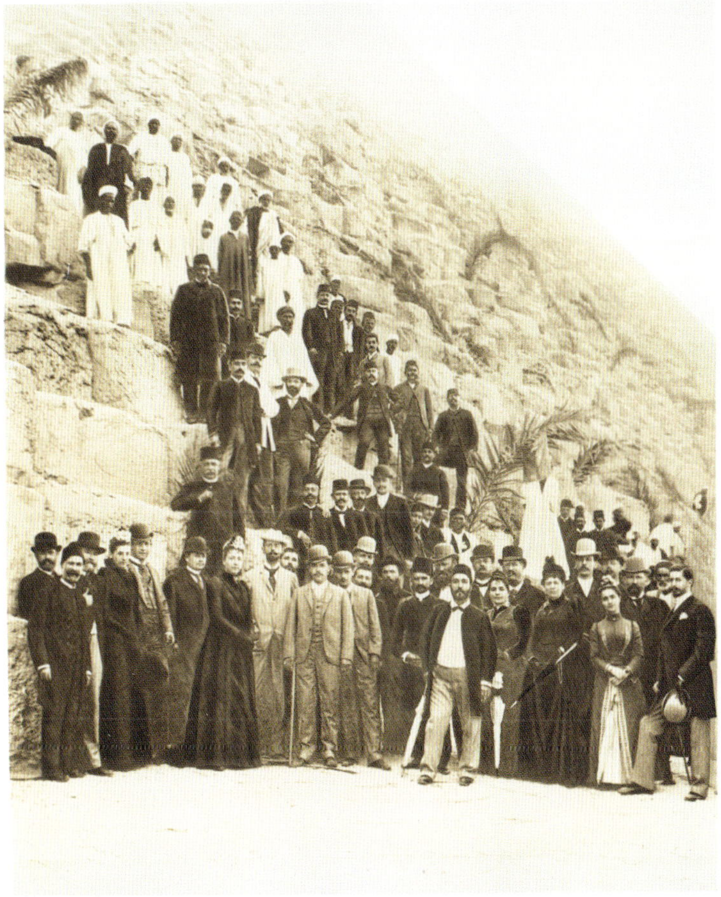

At the Pyramid of Cheops

Provenance Acquired by Queen Victoria

'Nothing gives so much breadth to the intellectual horizon, nothing has so much influence on the character, as immediate and living contact with the life of other lands'.[14] The tour to the East by Tsesarevich Nicholas in 1890–91 was an important part of the education of the future emperor, following on from Peter the Great's grand tour to Europe. The itinerary was devised by his tutor, General G.G. Danilovich, and took the Tsesarevich from Russia via Vienna to Greece, Egypt, India, Singapore, Java, Siam, China and, finally, Japan, from where he returned to St Petersburg via Vladivostok, travelling by land right across Russia. There had been the intention for Nicholas to journey to the United States after Japan, but an assassination attempt in April 1891 led to his trip being cut short.

Accompanying him on his journey was Prince Esper Ukhtomsky, poet and orientalist, a self-declared Buddhist and member of the Imperial Geographical Society. During the trip, Ukhtomsky collected significant amounts of information about the countries they travelled though, and on their return he began to write an account of the journey, with each chapter being approved by the Tsesarevich. It was published in Russian in 1893–7, in three volumes, followed by translations in English, French, German and Chinese. ES

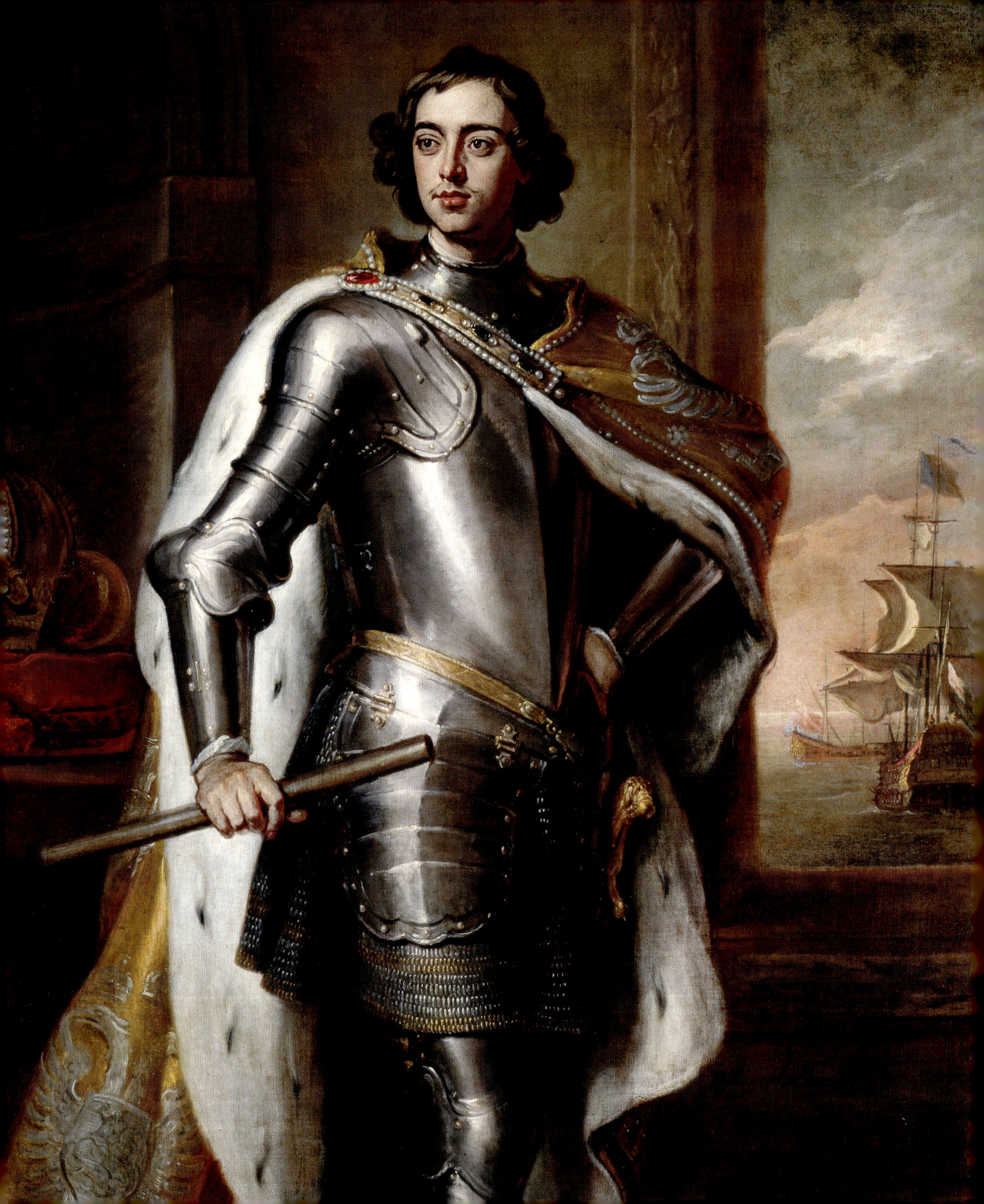

4

The Power and Purpose of Portraiture

ALEXANDRA BUCK

a portrait painter is just as important at Court as a painter of historical events

(Vigilius Eriksen to A.G. Moltke, January 1755)[1]

The state portrait is a powerful tool, a visual embodiment of all that monarchy entails, an assertion of authority and the divine right to rule, and for Emperor Peter I and Empress Catherine II this was no exception. Sir Godfrey Kneller's portrait of Peter I (a diplomatic gift from Peter to William III on his departure from London in 1698) (cat. 4) encapsulates a potent message of a young, energetic ruler, and reflects the ideals of a monarch, looking to the West, hoping to establish a new, 'open' Russia (epitomised by the new capital, St Petersburg, founded in 1703). The image was disseminated, not through copies of the original, but via printed sources, most notably the engraving by John Smith (1652–1743) of 1698, and spawned a host of painted copies, often of varying quality. The depiction by Kneller, who in 1690 had completed William III's state portrait, looks to European traditions of portraiture, to artists such as Peter Lely (1618–80) and Anthony van Dyck (1599–1641), and offered Peter something novel – a vitality and movement, evidence of psychological insight hitherto lacking in Russian traditions of portraiture. The native style, known as *Parsuna* painting, developed out of the conventions of icon painting; here the sitter is static, and the face mask-like.[2]

Similarly, the coronation portrait of Catherine the Great by the Danish artist Vigilius Eriksen, fulfilled the Empress's ambitions in promulgating the message that she was the legitimate ruler and an enlightened monarch. Throughout her reign, Catherine remained ever conscious of the message she was disseminating through portraiture. The Empress was hugely involved in the construction of her iconography, and, like Peter, remained heavily reliant on foreign artists to do this.[3] She is said to have maintained strict quality control of any copies and replicas sent out in order to give the right political message. It was documented, for example, that before sending a portrait as a gift to Frederick V of Denmark (1723–66) in 1766, it was dispatched to Moscow for approval by the Empress and its shipment was apparently delayed for months, presumably awaiting her approval.[4] Eriksen ran a small studio and it is assumed that he alone completed the small number of copies presented or dispatched, including cat. 25.

The intimate portrait of Catherine in travelling costume, by the serf-artist Shibanov, is unusual in the Empress's iconography, presenting her as an ageing ruler (cat. 28). In this depiction the sitter appears reflective, yet resilient, and her role as monarch is underplayed; however, the cut and colour of her jacket suggest military attire, and the embroidered insignia hint at her status. The references are subtle but this is a ruler on a military campaign. McBurney sees the attire as a wish to 'display her military readiness [...] she appears resolute and ready to engage without reference

Peter I, Tsar of Russia (detail of cat. 4)

FIG. 24
Petr Zharkov
Catherine the Great, 1788
Enamel
State Russian Museum,
St Petersburg

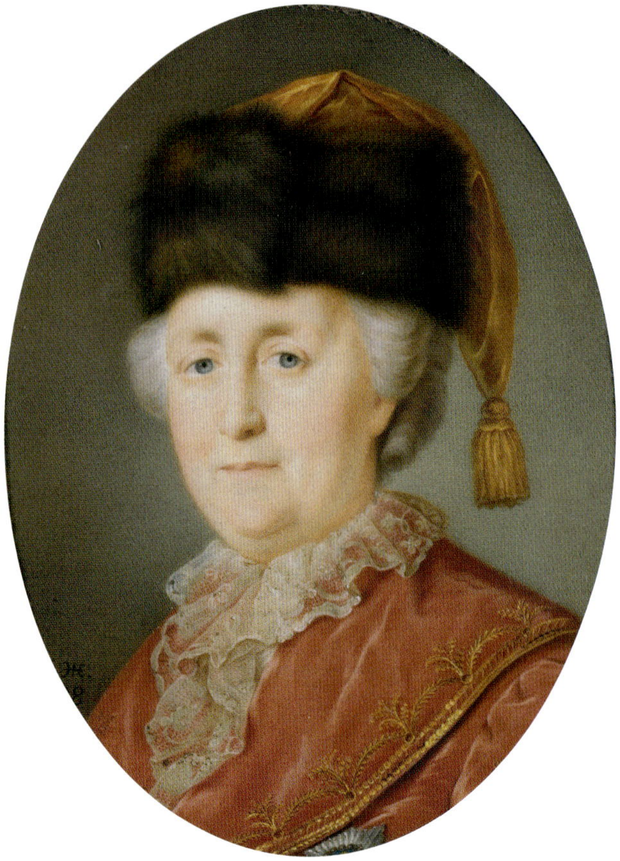

to or reliance on any divine or allegorical attributes'.[5] This is in sharp contrast to Eriksen's state portrait. The Empress must have approved of the image as it was engraved almost immediately by James Walker, employed as engraver to the Empress. The print was first published in St Petersburg on 1 November 1787, and in London on 1 May 1789 by James Dean (active 1777–98). Catherine also commissioned miniatures to be painted by Petr Zharkov, to be distributed amongst her soldiers (fig. 24) – an act which could only engender loyalty amongst her army.

In Britain, Queen Victoria was amassing and commissioning numerous copies of portraits of her extensive family, usually after her favourite court artists, notably Franz Xaver Winterhalter (1805–73) and Heinrich von Angeli (1840–1925). The Queen extensively patronised father and son, William Corden the Elder (1795–1867) and Younger (1819–1900), who produced copies to hang at her residences. In the duo she found proficient and adaptable artists, able to produce competent copies in oil (often varying the format to the original), original watercolour interior and exterior views, and copies in enamel. Corden the Elder trained as a porcelain painter at the Derby porcelain works before turning to oil painting. He secured royal patronage in 1829 with original oil portraits of Mr Batchelor, one of George IV's pages, and of Admiral Sir Edmund Nagle (1757–1830),[6] and by 1836 had moved to Windsor. By 1854 he had returned to the Staffordshire potteries.

Many works painted by father and son were commissioned for a particular location or setting, or as birthday gifts for Queen Victoria's mother, the Duchess of Kent. For example, in 1847, Corden the Elder was commissioned to paint half-length copies after Sir Thomas Lawrence of Charles X, King of France, and Louis-Antoine, Duke of Angoulême (hanging in the Waterloo Chamber at Windsor), to decorate a room in Buckingham Palace for the visit of the King and Queen of the Belgians. Similarly, Corden the Younger was commissioned to paint a reduced copy of the monumental portrait by Franz Krüger (1797–1857) of Nicholas I given to Queen Victoria (cat. 101), almost immediately after its arrival, to hang in the rooms occupied by the Emperor during his stay. In 1849, the Queen ordered a copy by Corden (RCIN 408909) to replace Winterhalter's portrait of the Duchess of Kent (RCIN 405129) which hung as an overdoor at Osborne, feeling that the original was 'in too much shadow' and could not be enjoyed. The Winterhalter was then transferred to a more prominent position at Buckingham Palace. These examples reflect both Queen Victoria's appreciation of her paintings and her involvement in particular hangs.

In 1844, Corden travelled to Coburg with his son, in connection with a commission to paint '7 pictures of the Duchesses, Princes and Princesses of Saxe-Coburg'. The paintings are currently attributed to the Younger Corden and are listed amongst Queen Victoria's acquisitions.[7]

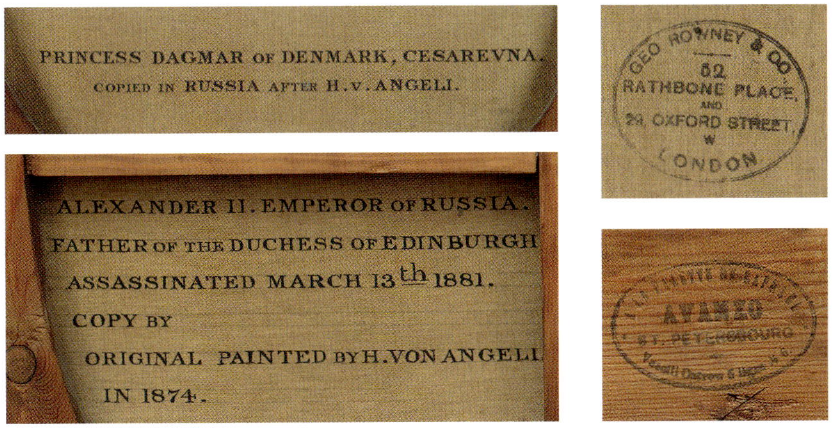

FIG. 25
Artists' suppliers stamps and inscriptions from Robert Antoine Müller, *Tsesarevna Marie Fedorovna*, and after Heinrich von Angeli *Alexander II, Emperor of Russia* (cats 161 and 113)

This included the lively portrait of Juliane, Princess of Saxe-Coburg-Saalfeld (1781–1860; later Grand Duchess Anna Feodorovna), after Vigée Le Brun (1755–1842; cat. 145), not because it was an exceptional portrait (which it is), but because it was an available image of the sitter. Two portraits in this group are after Vigée and two after the more obscure Carl Christian Vogel von Vogelstein (1788–1868). The five smaller pictures were intended as a family ensemble for Queen Victoria's bedroom in Windsor Castle, and by 1904 hung in the 'Coburg Rooms' at Windsor.

Robert Antoine Müller (active 1872–83) also painted portraits and copies for Queen Victoria. Little is known of the artist, who is recorded in London living in Notting Hill and (unusually for copyists) exhibited at the Royal Academy in 1872, 1876, 1877 and 1879. In 1881, Müller exhibited roundel portraits of the three children of the Duke and Duchess of Edinburgh, commissioned by the Queen and painted whilst the children were at Windsor in the care of their grandmother, whilst their mother tended to her dying mother in St Petersburg.[8]

In 1876, Müller travelled to Russia in order to copy a recently completed painting by Heinrich von Angeli of Princess Dagmar, later Maria Feodorovna of Russia (Princess Alexandra's sister) (fig. 58). It appears that the artist used a prepared canvas from a London supplier (which he either travelled with or found available in St Petersburg) and was to produce not an identical copy, but an over-half-length, on an oval format. This is recorded hanging in the Royal Visitors' Bedroom at Windsor by 1878, together with portraits of Prussian monarchs.[9] The request for the copy may simply be an example of Queen Victoria's admiration of von Angeli, and possibly reflects an intention to amass examples of his work. It appears that in Müller Queen Victoria found an artist skilfully able to mimic the liveliness of von Angeli's original (cat. 161).

Following the deaths of Empress Maria Alexandrovna (1824–80) and Emperor Alexander II in 1880 and 1881 respectively, Queen Victoria was keen to obtain copies of their portraits (cats 113 and 114), and the arrangement and payment for these works was entrusted to her son, Prince Alfred, then present in St Petersburg attending the funeral of the Emperor. As is the case with many copies, the author of these works, presumably a Russian artist, remains anonymous. The portraits, again after originals by von Angeli, appear to be derived from works of different sizes, a full-length portrait (see p. 182) and a comparable oval; they arrived in London in 1885 and are later recorded in the Royal Visitors Sitting Room at Windsor. Once again, this may be an example of the Queen amassing portraits after von Angeli, or may simply be a memory of her son's in-laws, whom she had last met in London in 1874.

Copies, or versions of state portraits in oil paint or print serve many purposes, from the transmission of a message of authority, power and enlightenment, to the sharing of a successful likeness, to more oblique references of military might – they are eminently suitable diplomatic gifts. In contrast, the examples of copies commissioned by Queen Victoria reflect her interest in her close and wider family, her involvement in specific arrangements of paintings, and admiration of her favoured artists.

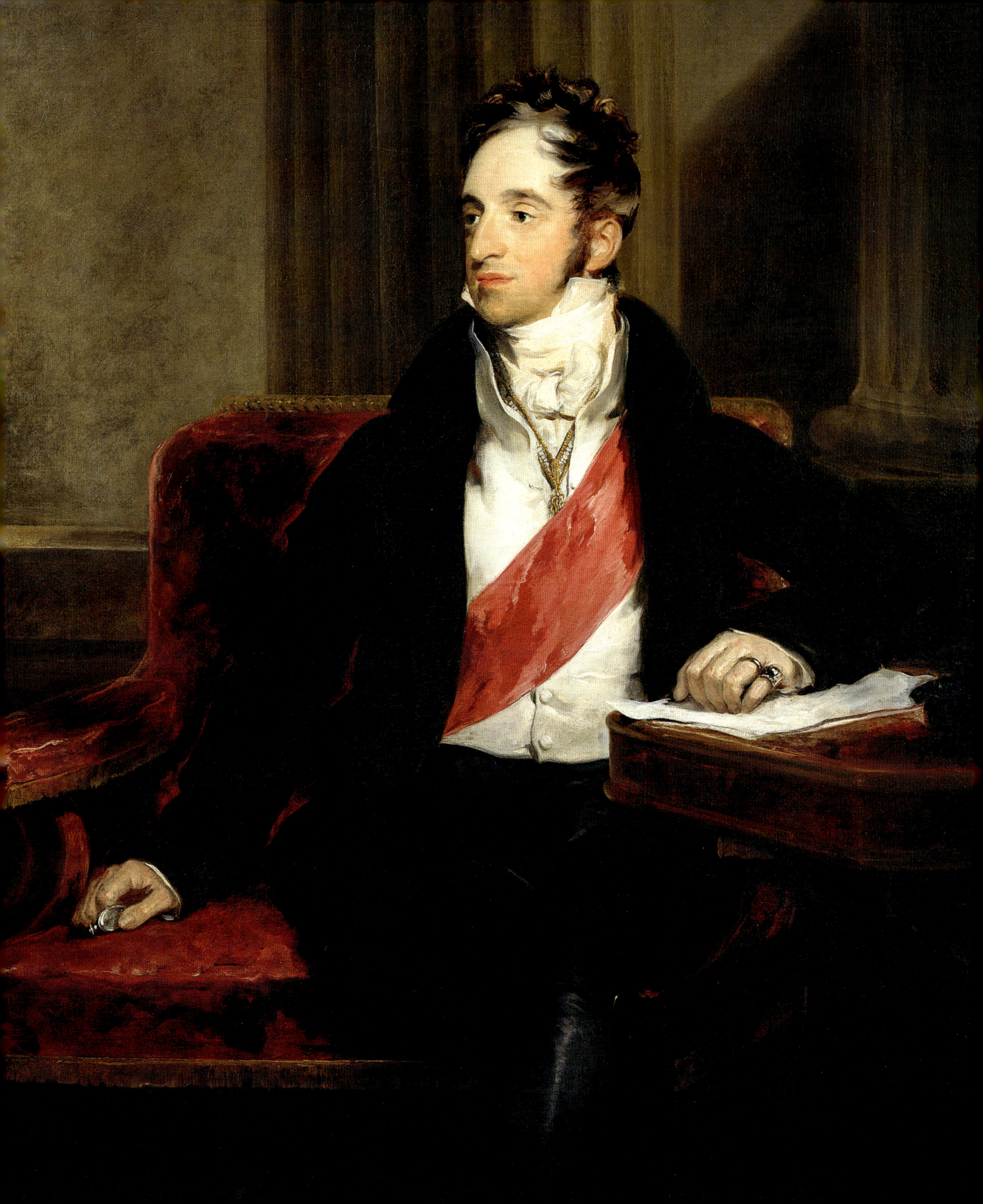

5
Revolution and New Relationships

STEPHEN PATTERSON

There have, of course, been many times in the past when Russia and Britain seemed to live in different worlds

(Her Majesty Queen Elizabeth II, Moscow, 18 October 1994)

Edward VII's succession to the throne in January 1901 saw a King who was uncle to both the Emperor Nicholas II (by marriage), and the Empress Alexandra Feodorovna; a King who had visited Russia some five times and was to visit Russian territorial waters once more in 1908.

Edward VII was well informed about the situation in Russia, not only from his ambassadors and ministers, but also from his contacts. In particular he was guided by the correspondence of Sir Donald Mackenzie Wallace, who was a confidant of both the King and the Russian Emperor. Wallace had accompanied Nicholas II on his visit to India in 1891, when he was assigned to the Grand Duke's suite because, in Queen Victoria's words, 'the Russian party will have to be carefully watched and not left alone.'[1] Wallace built up a close relationship with Nicholas II and was received by the Emperor on a number of occasions; reports of these meetings were passed to the King. This informal communication meant that the King had a good impression of the situation in Russia beyond that of the regular family correspondence.

Wallace's dispatches to the King's private secretary show that he was closely aware of the tensions in Russia, mentioning at one point in a memorandum of 1903: 'I have known personally some of them who took part in [revolutionary agitation] – those who escaped became more and more embittered and they determined on reprisals in the form of the assassination of high officials'.[2] He wrote that 'the country is at present passing through an agricultural and industrial crisis which has impoverished a large section of the peasantry and factory workers'. Wallace had travelled in the provinces of Smolensk, Vladimir, Moscow, Kharkov, Poltava, Voronezh and the country of the Don Cossacks, and then went to 'feel the pulse' of St Petersburg. A year earlier he considered that:

> *the autocratic power is still strong and the present emperor shows no sign of weakening it by voluntary concessions. [The revolutionary agitation] its strength in comparison with the autocratic power is insignificant.*
>
> *The emperor is becoming more and more conservative in his views and this tendency will soon become apparent in his foreign as well as his home policy.*[3]

While it can be assumed that any report to Lord Knollys (1837–1924), the King's private secretary, would have been seen by the monarch, that of 11 August 1906 was clearly read by the king, being annotated by Edward VII: 'Very interesting, ER'.[4] Among other snippets which the Emperor told Wallace were that he received the *Times* and *Daily Graphic* on a daily basis, but he was not prepared to talk about internal politics, although the discussions between the two did focus on the failure of the Duma. The King was

Charles Robert, Count Nesselrode (detail of cat. 69)

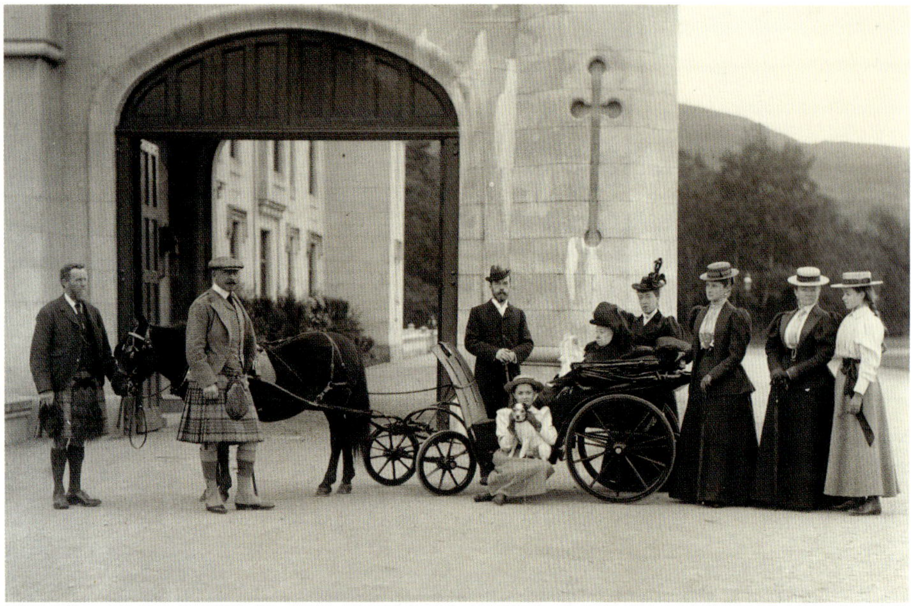

FIG. 26
W. & D. Downey
Queen Victoria with Nicholas II and Empress Alexandra, Balmoral Castle,
September 1896
Platinum print, 28.5 × 37.5 cm
RCIN 2160230

given Wallace's views on the subject, which he regarded as, 'A most interest[ing] account which [contains] most valuable information.'[5]

When Edward VII and Emperor Nicholas met at Reval in 1908, a meeting which the King was to stress was at the behest of the government and not of his own volition, topics of discussion included the Anglo-Russian treaty; the challenge of how to balance Russia, Germany and France; the issue of the Aland Islands; the 1857 Baltic treaties; the position of Germany in the Baltic; railways in Persia; and the Balkans, in particular the Danube–Adriatic railway, Crete, Afghanistan, Persia, Macedonia and Bosnia. The Bosnian issue had been openly raised in the press, with both monarchs asked to intervene against Austrian aggression in the area. The condition of the Jewish population of Russia was also to be raised with the Russian prime minister by the King. Gifts associated with the visit, an exchange of the rank of admiral to and from both the Emperor and King, a portrait (cat. 125) and a Fabergé bowl (cat. 126), were commensurate with the state nature of the occasion.

In a meeting of 10 December 1908, Wallace reported on a conversation with the Emperor who had asked for his thoughts on the Russian internal situation: Wallace replied that the country has quietened down since his last visit:

> *much to the satisfaction of the friends of order and very much to the disappointment of certain other people. On hearing this His Majesty smiled, half-closed one eye and nodded sympathetically*[6]

With informal conversations of this nature, albeit through an intermediary, Edward VII had some insight into his nephew's views and the state of his empire.

In the nineteenth and twentieth centuries the challenge of family versus national foreign policy dominated the relationship between the Russian rulers and the British Crown. The constitutional differences between the individuals, one an autocrat, the other a constitutional monarch, meant that in any correspondence there was also always a difference. For Nicholas II, a letter to the King could cover domestic affairs, foreign affairs, hunting, the family and the weather. The British Sovereign, particularly in the reign of Edward VII, often delivered a governmental message, but one written in the King's hand. In London, the King was acting in a correct constitutional capacity; however, in St Petersburg the autocratic emperor was speaking as one monarch to another, not to a government. In October 1908, the King was drawn into an attempt to keep Alexander Izvolsky (1856–1919) as foreign minister, penning a letter in his own hand which had been drawn up by his government. Edward VII wrote to Nicholas II in support of Izvol'sky: 'I am anxious to tell you how pleased I was to have the opportunity to meet Mr Izvol'sky again.'[7]

In his last letter to King George V, Emperor Nicholas II wrote, 'everything is being done to ameliorate this state of things which I hope will be overcome in April. But I never lose courage and egg on the ministers to make them and those under them work as hard as they can. But whatever the difficulties may be yet in store for us – we shall go on with this awful war to the end' (cat. 132).[8] Written four weeks before the Revolution, with the benefit of hindsight it is a poignant epistle that reflects the determination of the Emperor, whatever the situation, to pursue the (First World) War with Britain, Russia and France as allies against Germany, Austria and Turkey. Victory for the Allies and defeat of the enemy was at the heart of the concerns of both George V and Nicholas II, who congratulated each other on the success of the other's troops, and in which light the King decorated the Emperor, making him a British Field Marshal in January 1916[9] and appointing him a GCB in October of the same year.[10]

The February Revolution and the abdication of the Emperor on 15 March 1917, which caused King George V to confide to his diary, 'I am in despair',[11] presented a challenge to both the King and the British Government. On 19 March, the King telegraphed the former Emperor: 'Events of last week have greatly distressed me. My thoughts are constantly with you and I shall always remain your true and devoted friend as you know I have been in the past'. Unfortunately, the telegram was not delivered to the former emperor but instead fell into the hands of the new Russian government. What had been written as a private message by the King to his cousin then came to the attention of the Cabinet in London, who were concerned that a message had been sent without their knowledge.

'The king has been greatly perturbed about all the fuss with regard to what was intended as a private message from him to the Emperor'.[12] This message from Lord Stamfordham (1849–1931), the King's private secretary, to the prime minister encapsulated the challenge of the King in relation to his cousin Nicholas II and to the diplomatic dealings between Russia and Great Britain in the volatile days after the February Revolution; he supported his cousin in his heart, but had to separate the personal from the state. What role was King George V to take in 1917? Was he a cousin and friend of the Emperor, an ally, or the ruler of a constitutional democracy required to take the advice of his ministers, or (following Bagehot's maxim) there to advise the government? He had attempted to be a friend and relative when he had sent the telegram to the Emperor that had never been delivered. However, he was caught out when the government learnt about the private telegram which never reached the former Emperor, who was already under house arrest. His view reflected in his diary at the news of the Revolution – 'it is all Alicky's fault and Nicholas has been weak'[13] – shows a personal and private view of both the internal relationships of the imperial family and the relationship of the Emperor with his country.

Three days after the Emperor's abdication, Sir George Buchanan (1854–1924), the British ambassador in Petrograd, sent an assessment of the state of Russia to the government in London[14], reports which reached the King. Sir John Hanbury Williams (1859–1946), head of the British Military Mission to Russia, forwarded the Dowager Empress's personal views, which he had learnt in an audience with her, a day later.[15] By 21 March, the Russian government was keen for the former Emperor to leave the country, but on the same day, Sir Harry Verney (1872–1950), Groom-in-Waiting to King George V, urged that Nicholas should not leave Russia or travel to England, to avoid dangers to the British position in the new Russia.[16] On 22 March, Buchanan officially recognised the new Russian government on behalf of the British government, and the following day Lloyd George sent a message to Prince Lvov, its leader, in which he praised the Revolution, a message which brought concerns from the private secretary.[17]

Just as the Emperor and the King were focused on a successful outcome for the Allies, the major fear of the Allies after the Revolution was that Russia might withdraw from the war. Continued Russian involvement to maintain the Eastern Front was a key strategy. The suggestion (and agreement) by the British Government that the former Emperor and his family should be offered exile in Britain was never shared by the King, and throughout March and early April 1917, through his private secretary, he advised his ministers against giving asylum, not least because the King thought it would be as much the Empress's presence as the Emperor's which 'would raise all sorts of difficulties'.[18]

George V repeatedly made it clear to the Cabinet that any invitation for the imperial family to live in exile in Britain was from Downing Street, not the Palace. This was not for lack of charity or affection for his cousins, but a response to regular information being passed to him about the mood in Britain against Nicholas and Alexandra. The King faced challenges on a number of fronts: the year before there had been an uprising in Ireland, the press was against the Russian Emperor, whose strong support for the war effort had not dinted antipathy towards him, and the German name of the British royal family was publicly debated.[19]

Negotiations between the government and the Palace communicated by Lord Stamfordham, which led to the withdrawal of the government's invitation, were based on the realisation by Lloyd George that the situation was more difficult than had at first been perceived, and reached a conclusion on 10 April, when the King urged that Pavel Miliukov (1859–1943; Russian foreign minister) be told that the government must withdraw its consent to the ex-Emperor and Empress residing in England because of public opinion. It is possible that an article in *Justice* was the final point of persuasion for the King that the Emperor's residence in Britain was unwise;[20] the King had certainly been shown cuttings from the newspaper that were reportedly 'pro government', which were against the former Emperor travelling to Britain.[21]

Lloyd George agreed to ask Britain's French allies to give sanctuary to Nicholas and his family. The telegram finally withdrawing the invitation was sent to Buchanan in Petrograd, to pass to the Provisional Government on 13 April.[22] The withdrawal of an offer by the French government and the changing situation in Russia kept the former Emperor and his family in Russia. After this withdrawal of the British Government's offer of exile George V was kept abreast of developments in Russia: the attempted putsch by General Lavr Georgievich Kornilov in August 1917, which helped rebuild Bolshevik power, the looting of Tsarskoe Selo and the imperial family's move to Tobolsk in September 1917, and the arrest of the Grand Duke Michael for involvement in a monarchist plot.

Although the King eventually could not save his cousin and later spoke of his 'foul murder',[23] he received numerous reports on their fate, each more shocking than the last.[24] He and Queen Mary supported other members of the imperial family as actively as they could, most notably with the King's direct involvement in the rescue of his aunt, the Dowager Empress Maria Feodorovna, instructing the navy to bring her – and her suite – from the Crimea, paying for their expenses and for a special train for the Dowager Empress on arrival in Portsmouth.[25]

On the death of the Dowager Empress, the King paid the pensions of her surviving Russian staff for years to come. The King was asked by Admiral Amdrup (the Danish executor to Maria Feodorovna): 'His Majesty The King has

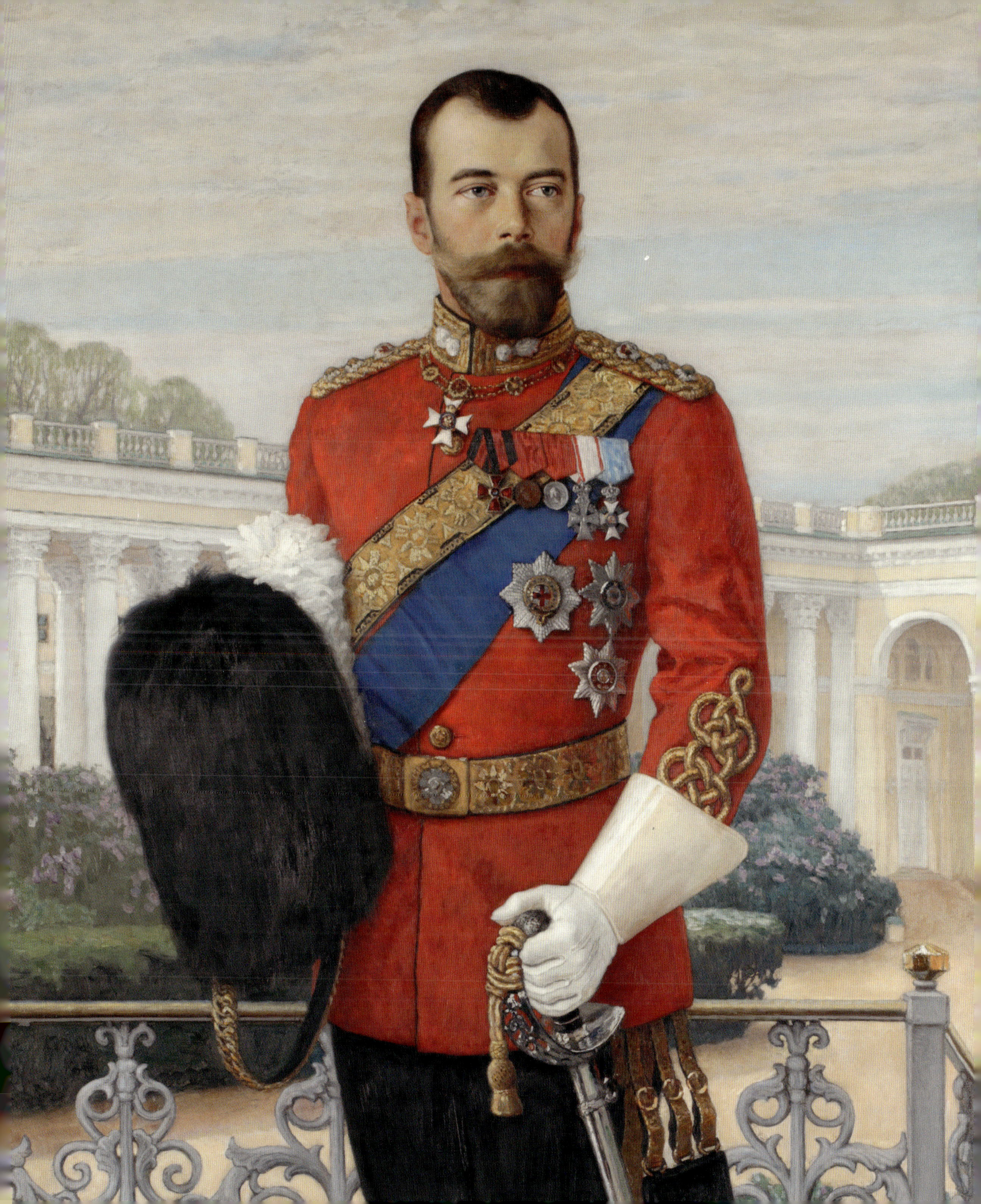

done very much for Her Majesty, The Empress who so often spoke to me of all what [*sic*] His Majesty had done for her. If His Majesty in memory of his lovely aunt could extend his great goodness to give a little pension to these persons I think Her Majesty in the heaven will be infinite grateful to His Majesty.'[26] Among the pensions paid were two to the Dowager Empress's Cossacks Polyakov (d.1934) and Yashchik (d.1946) (cat. 281).

As Queen Victoria had been reluctant to accept de Brunnov, the Russian minister in London raised to the level of ambassador in 1860 (see p. 70), so George V was concerned by the Soviet representative being raised to the level of ambassador some 84 years later, following the recognition of the USSR by the British Government in 1924. The King's predicament was his abhorrence at receiving any representative of the Soviet authorities, who had been involved (directly or indirectly) in the murder of Emperor Nicholas and his family: 'His Majesty referred to the strong protest which he had already made to the prime minister against any idea of being asked to receive with the usual friendly courtesies either an ambassador or minister from the Soviets who, if they did not actually plan, certainly approved of the brutal murder of the King's first cousins the late Emperor and Empress.'[27] When a treaty was signed with the Soviet Union in August 1924, it was signed in the name of the British Government, not that of the King.[28] The King was kept abreast of the expulsion from London in 1927 of the Soviet chargé d'affaires, Arkady Rosengolts (1889–1938), for supporting Soviet espionage in London. The maintenance of contacts with the former imperial family also raised concerns, and a possible visit in November 1927 by Grand Duke Nicholas Nicolaevich (1856–1929), Russian commander-in-chief in the First World War until 1915, was discouraged by the Foreign Secretary Sir Austen Chamberlain (1863–1937), for fear that it be seen as a conspiracy by the Soviet Government.[29]

In reply, the private secretary, Stamfordham, hoped that White Russians could come to Britain as the King had had to receive Soviet representatives who had probably connived at the murder of the Emperor.[30] This echoed the irritation of Alexander Kerensky (1881–1970) in October 1917, who threatened to send a telegram of congratulation to Sinn Fein because George V had received General Gurko (1864–1937), who had been exiled by the Provisional Government.[31] In 1929, the King still found it repugnant to shake the hand of an ambassador or minister of the Soviet Union,[32] and in August that year objected strongly to receiving a minister or ambassador and would accept nothing above a chargé d'affaires,[33] a message which was passed to the Foreign Office by the private secretary.[34] The ambassador appointed in 1929, after a two-year gap, and who had travelled with Lenin (1870–1924) in the sealed train to Petrograd in 1917, was Grigori Sokolnikov (1888–1939). The Foreign Office regretted that it was unpalatable to the King, but the appointment of an ambassador was, however, necessary.[35] The concerns about balance in response to both Romanov and Soviet sensitivities after the Revolution continued well into the 1930s. In 1936, the Romanov claimant, Grand Duke Cyril (1876–1938), wrote to King Edward VIII, informing the King of the death of his wife (Victoria Melita of Saxe-Coburg and Gotha (1876–1936), a daughter of the King's great uncle Alfred, Duke of Edinburgh and Grand Duchess Maria) and congratulating the King on his accession. As the Grand Duke wrote in a style that suggested that he was Emperor and addressed King Edward in his letter of condolence as 'Monseigneur mon frère', suggesting that they were equals, there was a concern in governmental circles that an inappropriate response would offend the Soviet government by suggesting recognition of the Grand Duke and thereby tacit acceptance of the continuation of the Romanov dynasty.[36] The situation was repeated in the letter to King George VI announcing

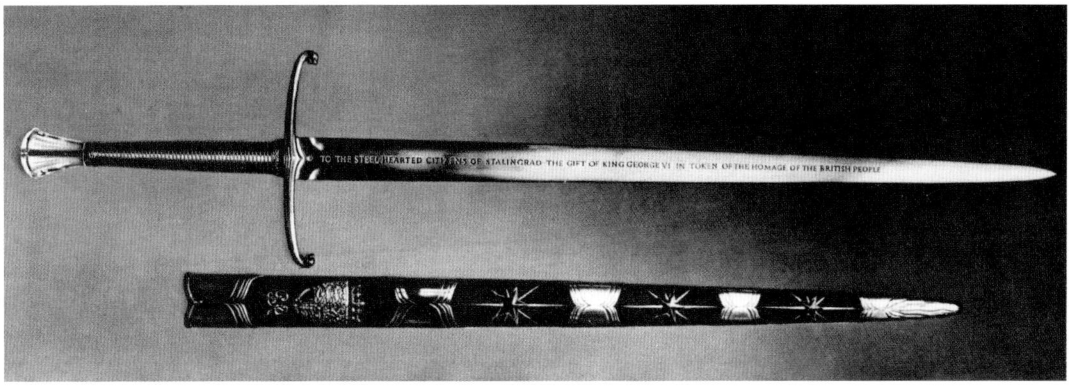

FIG. 27
The Sword of Stalingrad, 1943

Grand Duke Cyril's death, sent by his son, Grand Duke Vladimir (1917–92), in December 1938. The young Grand Duke asserted his position as the head of the Romanov family and, by extension, his assumption of the imperial title. In the response to both letters, the same formula was used, regretting the deaths of the Grand Dukes' relatives, but making no reference to the imperial title.[37] While use of titles and recognition was difficult, material help did come from King George VI when he assisted Grand Duke Vladimir secure training and employment at the Lister diesel engine factory in Stamford.

The positive side of the appointment of an ambassador was that the monarch received reports from their ambassador in Moscow – initially Sir Esmond Ovey (1879–1963) – who, with his successors, from January 1930 sent dispatches to the King, which addressed the state of affairs (as the ambassador saw it) in the Soviet Union. Topics covered included the availability of food, the attack on religion, propaganda against Britain, the currency and the position of the Communist Party. His dispatch of June 1930 included the observation that 'As far as anyone can make out Stalin is still master of the situation. He sits in the Kremlin and pulls the strings'.[38] The King was also informed by his ambassador about the new embassy building in Moscow (opposite the Kremlin), which the ambassador observed held a suitable room to hold portraits of the monarchs from the old embassy in Petrograd.[39] Updates on the situation in Russia were also to come from Lady Muriel Paget (1876–1938), who had met George V and Queen Mary in 1920 and worked to support distressed British subjects in Russia. She elicited £75 from the King and Queen for her charity in each of the years 1930, 1932 and 1933, donations that were advertised as a means of promoting her work. Her letters to the private secretary, apart from reporting on the state of affairs in Russia and events associated with her charity, included the raising of a crop of 300 lb of strawberries from the garden of the dacha that she established outside Leningrad.[40]

The ambassadors of the Soviet Union during King George VI's reign, Ivan Maisky (1884–1975), Fedor Gusev (1905–87), Georgiy Zarubin (1900–1958) and Andrei Gromyko (1909–89; who went on to become Soviet foreign minister), spanned the years of the Second World War, when, following the German invasion of Soviet territory in 1940, Britain and the Soviet Union were again allies, as they had been in 1812 and 1914. At Ivan Maisky's recall to Moscow in 1943, the King wrote to him expressing his sadness at the ambassador's departure, and it was mooted that he be offered an honorary GCB on his retirement, a suggestion that was made to the ambassador verbally, but which he asked not be made formally.[41]

Gusev was ambassador at the time of King George VI's decision to recognise the heroism of the people of Stalingrad (Volgograd) with a sword of honour (fig. 27), a project with which the King was closely and personally involved, in both idea and design. The 'Sword of Stalingrad' was presented by Churchill to Joseph Stalin (1879–1953) on behalf of the King for the people of the city at the Teheran Conference in 1943. It was Gusev who was instructed by the 'Supreme Commander-in-Chief of the Armed Forces of the Soviet Union' to visit the King on 15 December 1943, to express Stalin's 'gratitude for the magnificent gift which

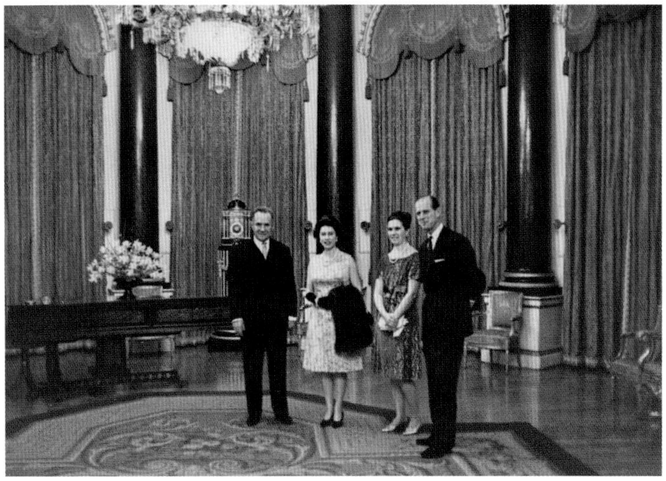

FIG. 28
HM The Queen, HRH The Duke of Edinburgh, Premier Andrei Kosygin and his daughter Liudmila Gvishiani in the Music Room, Buckingham Palace, 9 February 1967

Your Majesty presented to the citizens of Stalingrad as a sign of great appreciation of the heroic struggle of the Soviet People by the British People.'[42]

During the reign of King George VI, the thaw of communication with Soviet leaders began, with the addition of Kalinin (1875–1946) into the receipt of birthday and New Year messages sent by the King during the Second World War; however, the King also continued to wear the ribbon of the Order of St Vladimir, which he had received from his second cousin Nicholas II after seeing action at the Battle of Jutland.

The visit to Britain of First Secretary Nikita Khrushchev (1894–1971) and Chairman Nikolai Bulganin (1895–1975) in April 1956, while not a state visit, was the highest-level Soviet visit up to that point. Their stay, as guests of the British Government, included meetings at 10 Downing Street and at the Foreign Office, as well as visits to Birmingham, Oxford and Edinburgh. In the afternoon of 22 April, they had an audience of Her Majesty Queen Elizabeth II at Windsor Castle, where they were joined by HRH The Duke of Edinburgh (b.1921). The gifts of the Soviet visitors showcased a wide range of Soviet skills and products, including ceramics (cat. 137), hard stone carving and a painting (cat. 135). That there were gifts not only to The Queen, but also to The Duke of Edinburgh, Prince Charles (b.1948), Princess Anne (b.1950; a bear which lived at London Zoo), Queen Elizabeth The Queen Mother (1900–2002) (cat. 136) and Princess Margaret (1930–2002), was an indication of the cultural diplomacy surrounding the visit. As well as meeting The Queen, the visitors paid calls in London at Buckingham Palace and in Edinburgh at the Palace of Holyroodhouse, where visitors' books were signed. The visit to Windsor included a tour led by The Queen, and a display of works from the Royal Collection was prepared for the visitors.[43] The display in 1956 included an album of watercolours presented to Queen Victoria by Nicholas I. After the visit, it was decided to present the album to the Soviet President Kliment Voroshilov (1881–1969); it is now in the collection of the State Hermitage in St Petersburg.

The *Great Britain – USSR* exhibition, staged at the Victoria and Albert Museum to mark the 50th anniversary of the Russian Revolution, was opened in February 1967 by Premier Kosygin (1904–80), who dined with The Queen and The Duke of Edinburgh at Buckingham Palace (fig. 28). The Queen lent generously to the exhibition, which also included the Stalingrad (Volgograd) Sword, a return to the UK some 25 years after its gift to the citizens of the Hero City.

There were discussions at the time of a possible visit to the Soviet Union by a member of the Royal Family, but no visit was to be made until 1973, when Prince Philip, President of the International Equestrian Federation, visited Moscow, meeting President Nikolai Podgorny (1903–83), from whom he received a silver gilt and enamel coffee set.[44] The complicated relations between Britain and the Soviet Union in the 1970s and early 1980s meant that there were no high-level visits until President Mikhail Gorbachev (b.1931) visited The Queen for lunch at Windsor Castle in 1989. On that occasion, The Queen was given a carved walrus tusk,[45] and Prince Philip, a sword. Gorbachev, the last president of the Soviet Union, visited The Queen again in 1991, and the first president of the Russian Federation, Boris Yeltsin (1931–2007), met The Queen at Buckingham Palace in November 1992, on which occasion he extended a long-anticipated invitation for The Queen to visit Russia.

FIG. 29
HM The Queen and President Boris Yeltsin, Red Square, 18 October 1994

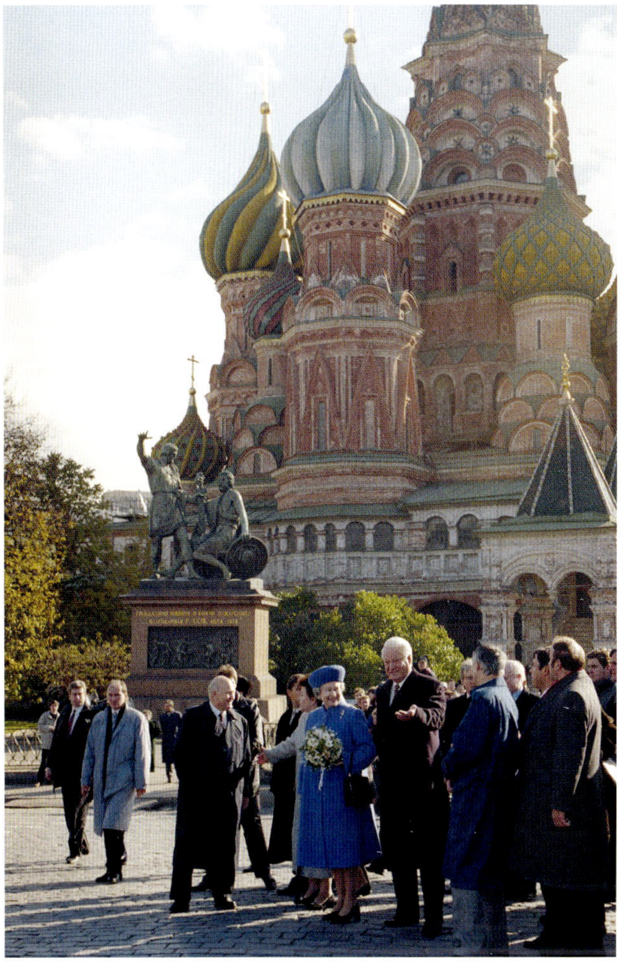

The Queen's State Visit to Russia took place in October 1994, and was the first time that a reigning British monarch had set foot on Russian soil. It included visits to Moscow and St Petersburg (fig. 29), a state banquet in the Faceted Palace of the Kremlin, where British ambassadors had been received by Russian tsars in the sixteenth and seventeenth centuries, and a return banquet on board the royal yacht *Britannia* in St Petersburg. The Queen received from President Yeltsin a portrait of herself painted by Sergey Prisekin (1958–2015),[46] as well as a samovar.[47] In turn, one of The Queen's gifts to the President was a box of seeds from the gardens at Buckingham Palace, an echo of the gifts of seeds and plants sent from Kew on the instructions of George III for Catherine II's gardens at Tsarskoe Selo and Pavlovsk in 1793. An additional gift was a dinner service, as Queen Victoria had sent a service to Nicholas I in 1844 (cat. 100).

In her speech at the Kremlin, The Queen began: 'Mr President, you and I have spent most of our lives believing this evening could never happen. I hope that you are as delighted as I am to be proved wrong.' She continued, 'There have, of course, been many times in the past when Russia and Britain seemed to live in different worlds'.[48] In her Christmas broadcast that year, The Queen commented: 'I never thought it would be possible in my lifetime to join with the Patriarch of Moscow and his congregation in a service in that wonderful cathedral in the heart of the Moscow Kremlin'.[49] Her Majesty received the patriarch's successor in London in 2016 (cat. 144).

Previous visits of Russian rulers from Peter the Great had been low-key events – due either to circumstances or the desire of the Russian visitor. The year 2003 saw the first State Visit of a Russian leader (Vladimir Putin, b.1952) to Britain, and it was perhaps fitting that his gift was a reference to the first Russian royal visitor, being a history of St Petersburg.[50]

Recent connections with Russia, visits formal and informal, have focused on common associations, most notably victory in 1945 as allies in the Second World War. Cultural connections have flourished with royal support, not least with HRH The Prince of Wales supporting the publication of the notebooks of the poet Alexander Pushkin. Another great Russian author was referenced by The Queen in her Kremlin speech in 1994. Some 130 years since her great-grandfather and Alexander II were painted by Nikolai Sverchkov (1817–98), travelling together across the snowy landscape of Russia in a troika (cat. 168), The Queen said, 'I have read that Gogol, in his famous metaphor comparing Russia to a galloping troika, asked in some trepidation: "Russia, where are you flying to?" There is now a reassuring answer to that question: "to a better future in partnership with our friends".'[51]

GEORGE DAWE (1781–1829)

93 *Charlotte (Alexandra Feodorovna), Empress of Russia (1798–1860), with her Eldest Children, Alexander (1818–1881) and Maria (1819–1876)* c.1821

Oil on canvas, 276.9 × 185.4 cm
RCIN 404608

Provenance Stated to have been in the possession of Adolphus Frederick, Duke of Cambridge (1774–1850), and to have hung at St James's until 1889, when bought by Grand Duke Paul Alexandrovich of Russia; purchased by Queen Mary from the sale of the effects of the Grand Duke's second wife, Princess Olga Paley, Christie's, London, 21 June 1929, lot 20

Literature Millar 1969, no. 748; Andreeva 2012, pp. 135–6

Born Princess Charlotte of Prussia, the future Empress Alexandra Feodorovna, nicknamed 'Mouffy', was the eldest surviving daughter of Frederick William III of Prussia. Her marriage to the future Emperor Nicholas I on 1 July 1817 was a political union, forging closer ties between their two countries; however, it appears the couple were ideally suited, and their relationship was described as a 'love-match'.[52] George Dawe chose to replicate his earlier portrait of Princess Charlotte of Wales (cat. 75), although here, the sitter's children, the future Emperor Alexander II and his sister, Maria, replace the portfolio and shawl of the earlier portrait.

The portrait was presumably painted in St Petersburg; although in 1820 the future Empress, suffering from depression following the birth of a stillborn daughter, returned to her family in Berlin until the following summer. Two versions of this portrait exist: one, dated 1821, in the Russian Museum, formerly in the Romanov Gallery of the Winter Palace; and the other, dated 1823, in the State Hermitage Museum, St Petersburg. In both these versions the Empress wears an elegant triple string of pearls.[53] The portrait, or a version of it, appears in the watercolour view of Dawe receiving Alexander I in his studio by Andrey Efimovich Martynov. An engraving of the painting by Thomas Wright was printed in London in 1826.[54]

It is not known when precisely the painting arrived in England, but it was stated to have hung at St James's Palace, in the apartments of Augusta, Duchess of Cambridge (1797–1889), a distant relation of the Empress, until her death. It was subsequently purchased by Grand Duke Paul Alexandrovich, grandson to the sitter, and hung in his residence in St Petersburg (fig. 30), and later at Tsarskoe Selo. Queen Mary purchased the painting (once owned by her maternal grandmother) in 1929, from the sale of the collection of the widow of Grand Duke Paul. **AB**

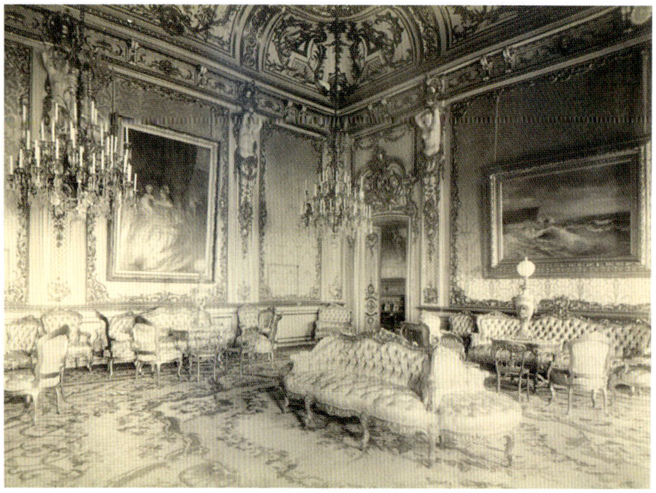

FIG. 30
Interior of Grand Duke's Palace in St Petersburg (the former Stieglitz palace), c.1900. Cat. 93 can be seen hanging on the left-hand wall
Collection of the Foundation of Russian History, Jordanville

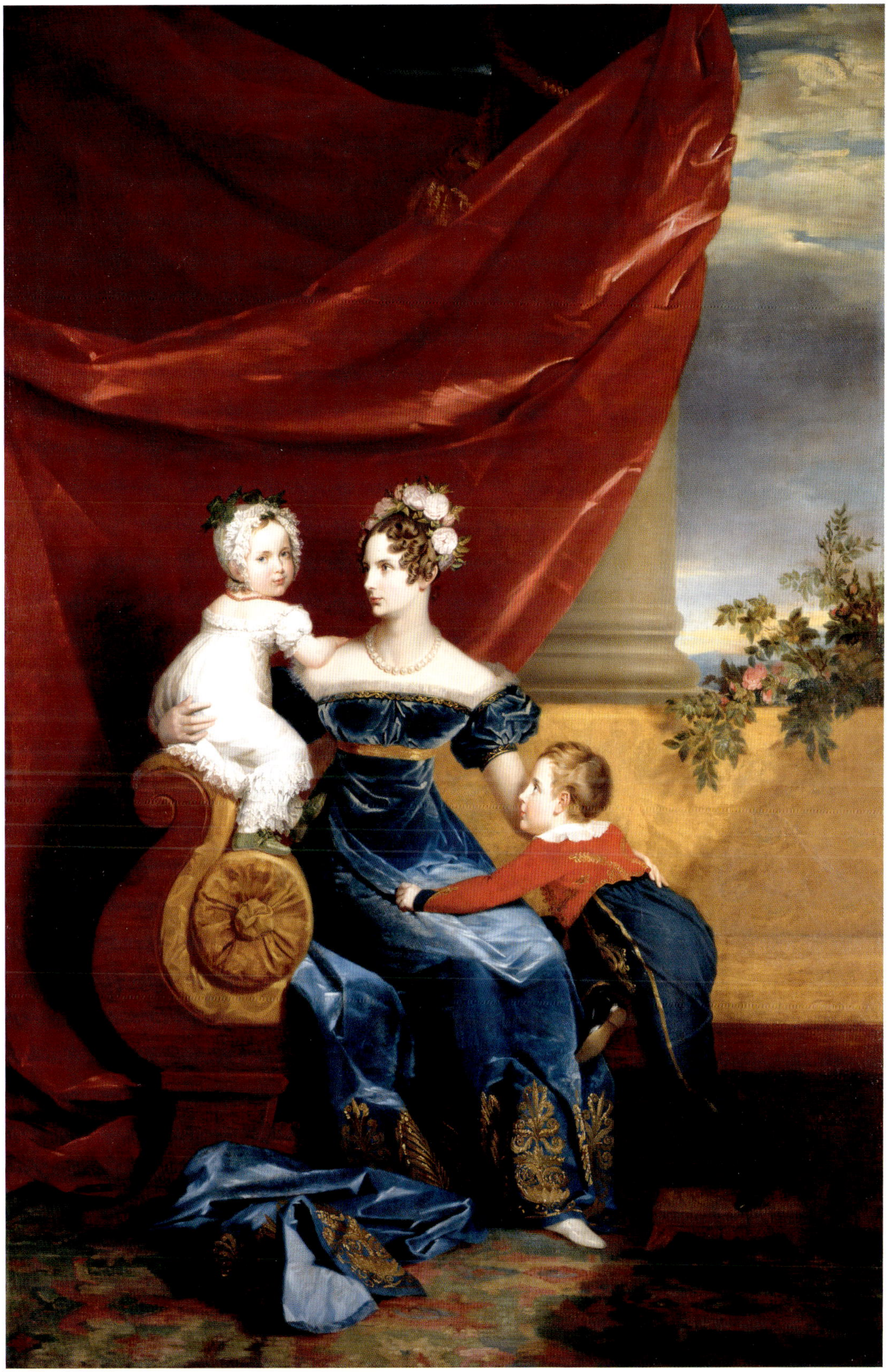

CARL TIMOLEON VON NEFF (1804–1877)

94 & 95

The Grand Duchesses Maria (1819–1876), afterwards Princess of Leuchtenberg, and Olga (1822–1892), afterwards Queen of Württemberg, daughters of Nicholas I, Emperor of Russia (1796–1855) 1840

Oil on canvas, 153.3 × 117.4 cm
RCIN 408911

Alexandra Feodorovna, Empress of Russia (1798–1860) 1840

Oil on canvas, 145.2 × 107.3 cm
RCIN 408912

Provenance Given to Queen Victoria by Nicholas I as a wedding present, 1840; first recorded on the Principal Corridor, Buckingham Palace, 1876

Literature Gudymenko 2016, pp. 86, 231

Since the late nineteenth century, these portraits were thought to be copies by the Scottish artist Christina Robertson (1796–1854), after Carl Timoleon von Neff (also known as Timofey Andreyevich Neff), and were believed to have been presented by Nicholas I at around the time of his visit to England in 1844. However, recent research reveals that they are the work of Neff himself, copies of earlier works, possibly commissioned by the Emperor as a wedding gift to Queen Victoria and Prince Albert.[55]

In 1838 the artist was commissioned to paint a portrait of two of the Emperor's daughters, Maria and Olga (State Russian Museum, St Petersburg); by this time the artist was a rising star at the Russian court, having succeeded Karl Bryullov (1799–1852) as painter to the imperial family. Neff's success was short-lived; having been eclipsed by the arrival in 1839 of Christina Robertson. Nonetheless, in 1840, Neff was commissioned to copy this portrait and paint the Empress (Pavlovsk State Museum), together with a repetition for Queen Victoria. On 15 October of the same year he received a payment of 2,857 rubles in silver for four paintings.[56] The first copy painted for the Emperor was hung in the

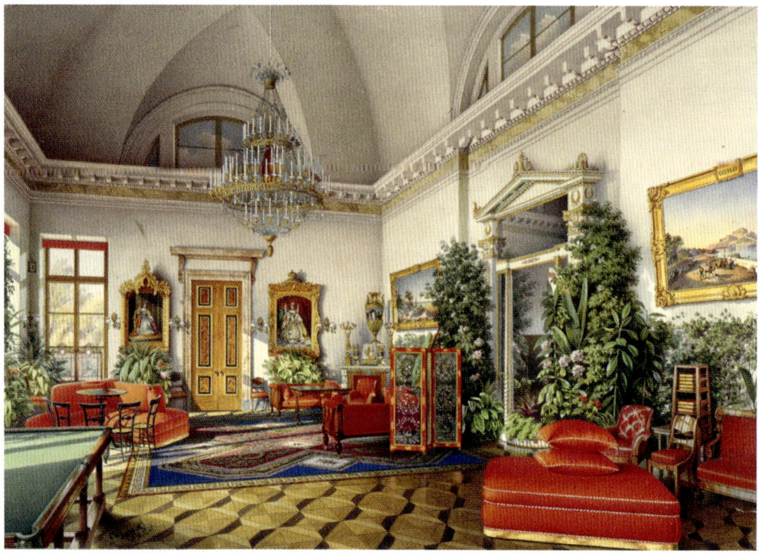

FIG. 31
?L. Premazzi
The Ceremonial Drawing-Room in the Alexander Palace, 1854
Watercolour and bodycolour, 29.0 × 41.8 cm
Tsarskoe Selo State Museum Reserve

Alexander Palace at Tsarskoe Selo (fig. 31). Neff later spent time in Europe and was commissioned to paint the decoration and iconostasis for the Russian chapel of Maria, Duchess of Edinburgh at Clarence House; he also worked in other churches in Europe, notably in Nice and Wiesbaden.

The Empress, wearing the ermine-lined coronation mantle and the diamond crown she had worn at her coronation, alongside her husband, Nicholas I, in September 1826, is depicted seated on an inlaid ivory throne, holding a feather fan. This static portrayal is in contrast to the earlier grand family portrait by George Dawe of the sitter, in which Maria, her eldest daughter, appears as a child (cat. 93). The pictures show evidence of pencil under-drawing, and squaring-up from the original; they are painted in a flat manner, with thin under-modelling rather crudely outlined. The portraits epitomise the briefly fashionable, stylised doll-like appearance of female sitters pioneered by Bryullov and his contemporaries.

The paintings must have arrived in their magnificent frames prior to the visit of Nicholas I, as Queen Victoria recorded her preparations on 1 June 1844 for the Emperor's imminent arrival: 'We [...] then walked over to the rooms which have been arranged for the Emperor [...] which we have brushed up & look as well as they possibly can; we have hung up some Russian Pictures including those of the 2 Grand duchesses & the Empress'.[57] **AB**

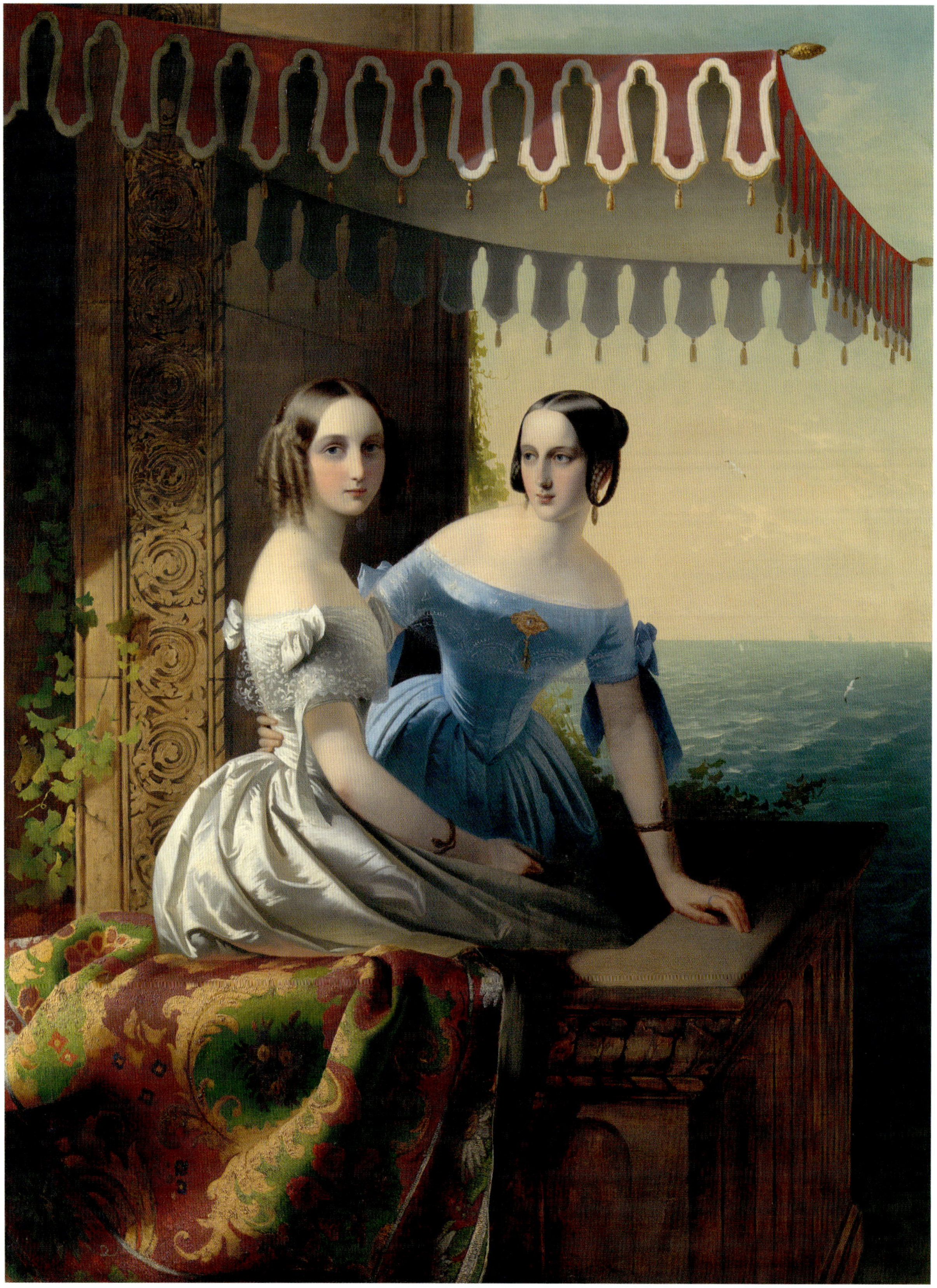

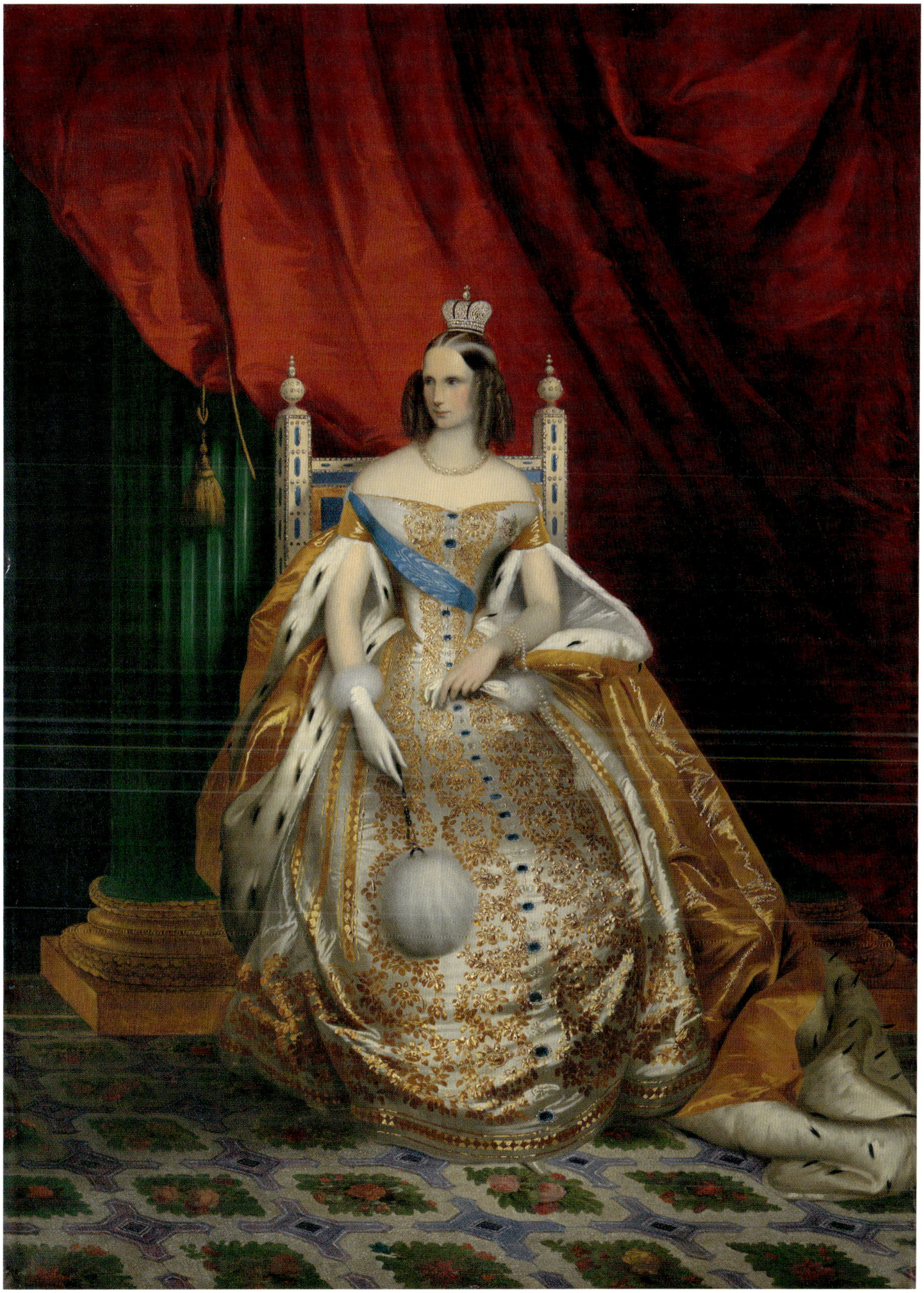

EMPEROR NICHOLAS I OF RUSSIA (1796–1855)

96 *Letter to Prince Albert (1819–1861), from London* 20 May/1 June 1844

Manuscript, 22.5 × 18.5 cm
RA VIC/MAIN/M/52/88

Emperor Nicholas I landed at Woolwich around 10 p.m. on 1 June 1844 and travelled to London, where he stayed at Ashburnham House, rather than at Buckingham Palace, as he wanted his visit to be low-key. In this letter he wrote to Prince Albert, announcing his arrival in England and expressing his desire to see Queen Victoria. Nesselrode had instructed the chargé d'affaires, Baron de Brunnov, in March that year that the emperor wanted the visit to be no longer than a fortnight, and that he wanted to travel incognito, with the simplicity that his brother, Grand Duke Michael, had experienced during his visit to England the previous year.[58] After two nights in London, he travelled with the Queen by train to Windsor, with another royal guest, the King of Saxony (1797–1854).

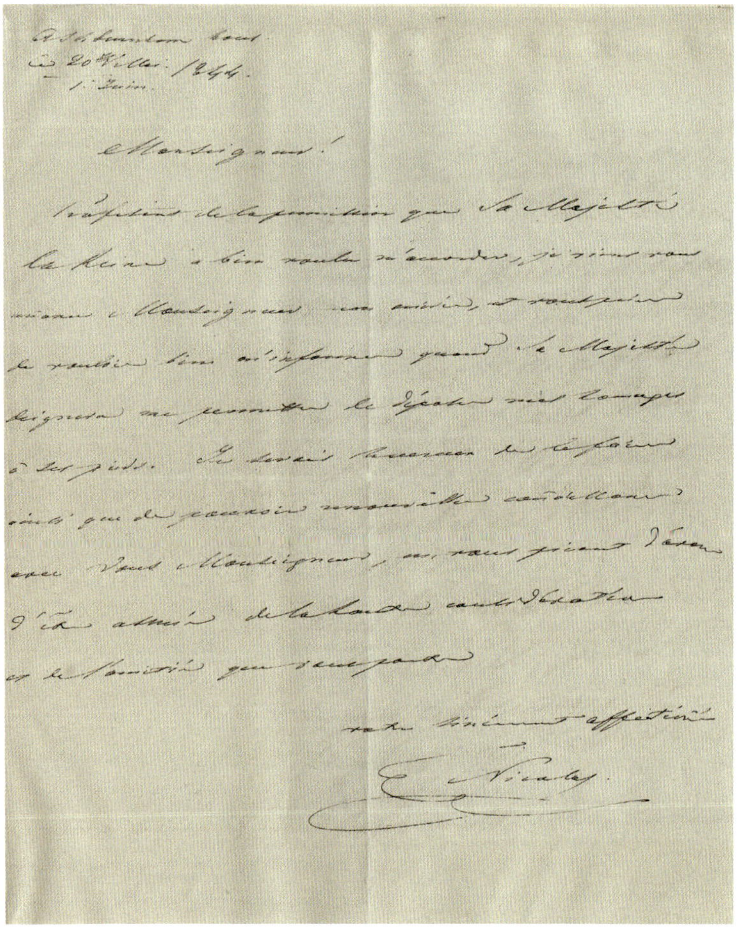
Ashburnham house
le 20 Mai 1844.
1 Juin.

Monseigneur!

Profitant de la permission que Sa Majesté la Reine a bien voulu m'accorder, je viens vous annoncer Monseigneur mon arrivée, et vous prier de vouloir bien m'informer quand Sa Majesté daignera me permettre de déposer mes hommages à ses pieds. Je serai heureux de le faire ainsi que de pouvoir renouveller connaissance avec Vous Monseigneur, en vous priant d'être assuré de la haute considération et de l'amitié que vous porte

votre bien affectionné
Nicolas.

On the evening of 2 June, the Queen recorded in her diary:

> *Albert stepped 1^{rst} out of the carriage, & then the Emperor, 'en grande tenue', in the red uniform of the Chevaliers Gardes, with high boots. He kissed my hand & I embraced him, [...] The Emperor's appearance is very striking; though 48, he is still very handsome, very tall, & with a very good figure. His features are quite classical, & regular. We took him to the rooms intended for him & there sat down.*[59]

The Emperor wore the uniform of the Chevalier Guard, which he would be depicted wearing in Krüger's painting (cat. 101), the Emperor's gift to the Queen in 1847.

While the Emperor met most of the royal family, including the Dowager Queen Adelaide (1792–1849), widow of William IV, as well as the Duchess of Cambridge and the Duchess of Gloucester, who had also met his brother, Alexander I, 30 years previously, one member of the royal party was absent: Queen Victoria's mother, the Duchess of Kent. The Duchess had left London at the end of April for a few months on the Continent, which would include visits to Paris and to Switzerland, where she would visit her sister, the Grand Duchess Anna Feodorovna, Nicholas's former sister-in-law.[60] **SJP**

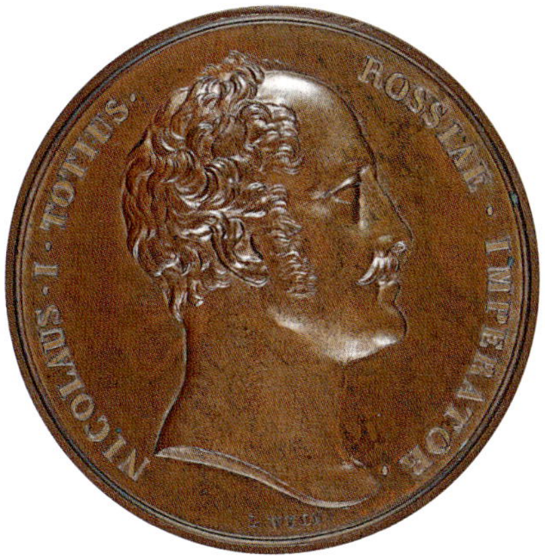

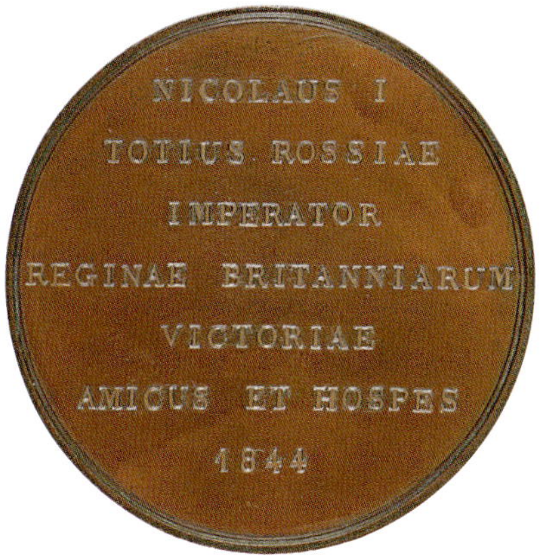

LEONARD CHARLES WYON (1826–1891)

97 *Medal commemorating the visit of Emperor Nicholas I to England* 1844

Copper, dia. 5.07 cm, weight 66.96 g
Inscribed on obverse: *NICOLAUS.I.TOTIUS.ROSSIAE.IMPERATOR* ('Nicolas I, Emperor of All Russia'), and on reverse: *NICOLAUS I/TOTIUS ROSSIAE/IMPERATOR/REGINAE BRITANNIARUM/VICTORIAE/AMICUS ET HOSPES/1844* ('Nicolas I, Emperor of All Russia, friend and guest of Victoria, Queen of the Britons, 1844')
RCIN 443524

Provenance Probably acquired by Queen Victoria *c.*1844; Royal Collection by 1990s

Literature Forrer 1904–30, VI, pp. 592–631; Brown 1987, no. 2151

The Emperor, having landed at Woolwich on 1 June 1844, was escorted by Prince Albert to Buckingham Palace the following day, and stayed in England until 9 June. The visit of the Emperor and the King of Saxony may well have put a strain on the Queen, since this was only two months before she gave birth to her fourth child, Prince Alfred (later Duke of Edinburgh).

The Emperor is shown on the obverse bare-headed, facing right. According to Royal Mint records, 15 of these medals were struck 'for the Emperor', with a further 14 struck that autumn.

Leonard Charles Wyon was the eldest son of William Wyon (1795–1851), chief engraver at the Mint from 1828 to 1851. He was appointed second engraver in 1843, aged 17, and this was one of his earliest pieces, 'in connexion with which he received a graceful letter of thanks from William Ewart Gladstone'.[61] Succeeding his father as chief engraver in 1851, he went on to engrave dies for numerous commemorative and service medals, as well as most of the coins of the British Empire during his 40 years in the post. **BW**

CARL JOHANN TEGELSTEN (1798–1852)

98 *Table* 1844

Hardstones, gilt bronze, glass, 78.6 × 73.5 cm
Stamped: *C. Tegelsten*
RCIN 1450

Provenance Presented to Queen Victoria by Emperor Nicholas I, 1844

Literature Marsden 2010, p. 241; Mavrodina 2007, p. 436

Following Emperor Nicholas I's visit in 1844, he sent Queen Victoria this elaborately decorated table, together with a very large St Petersburg porcelain vase (cat. 99). The Queen had originally been very much against the visit, which lasted from 1 to 9 June, and was therefore surprised to find herself succumbing to the attractions of 'this greatest of all potentates'.[62] The table was not necessarily a unique commission, as another similar example exists from the same period.[63] However, the Queen seemed impressed with the gifts when she viewed them for the first time in the State Apartments at Windsor on 2 December 1844: 'We went with Alexandrine & Ernest W. afterwards over the State Rooms & saw there a splendid & immense porcelain vase & "Pietra Dura" table, which the Emperor of Russia has sent me.'[64]

The table was placed in the White Drawing Room, where it is shown in Joseph Nash's view (fig. 32), prominently displayed in the window bay. Although not published until 1848, Nash's watercolours were specifically intended to record the way the Castle was used by the Queen and Prince Albert at the time of the visits of the Russian Emperor and King Louis-Philippe of France (1773–1850) in 1844.

In the list of the imperial gifts at the Peterhof Imperial Lapidary Workshops for the year 1844, the tabletop valued at 5,715 rubles is described as being decorated with a bouquet of flowers of different stones, and on a bronze base made in 'the English Shop'.[65] Unusually the tabletop is not inlaid in the traditional pietra dura technique, but carved in low and medium relief, necessitating the use of a glass protective cover, supported above the hardstone by the chased bronze rim. The Finnish-born silversmith and bronze-worker, Carl Johann Tegelsten, qualified as a master craftsman in St Petersburg in 1825. From around 1833, much of his work in bronze and silver was retailed by Nicholls and Plincke, one of the most fashionable shops in St Petersburg, founded in 1786 by Messrs Hoy and Bellis to trade in accessories, and taken over by Charles Nicholls (active 1829–52) and William Plincke (active 1829–52). The shop, known as the 'English Shop', or the *Magasin Anglais*, was located at 16 Nevskii Prospekt; it became one of the most fashionable in St Petersburg, supplying silver, bronze and furniture and receiving an imperial warrant in the 1840s. Amongst the most important imperial commissions were numerous pieces of furniture for Empress Maria Alexandrovna to furnish the Lyons Hall at Tsarskoe Selo,[66] and a chest for Alexander II's brother, Grand Duke Constantine (1827–92) and his wife, Alexandra Iosifovna (1830–1911).[67] **CDEG**

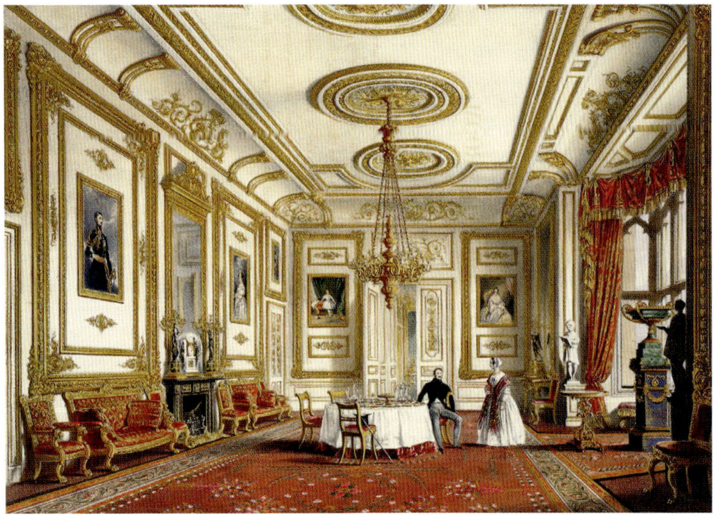

FIG. 32
After Joseph Nash
The White Drawing Room, 1848
Hand-coloured lithograph, 32.7 × 47.0 cm
RCIN 817132

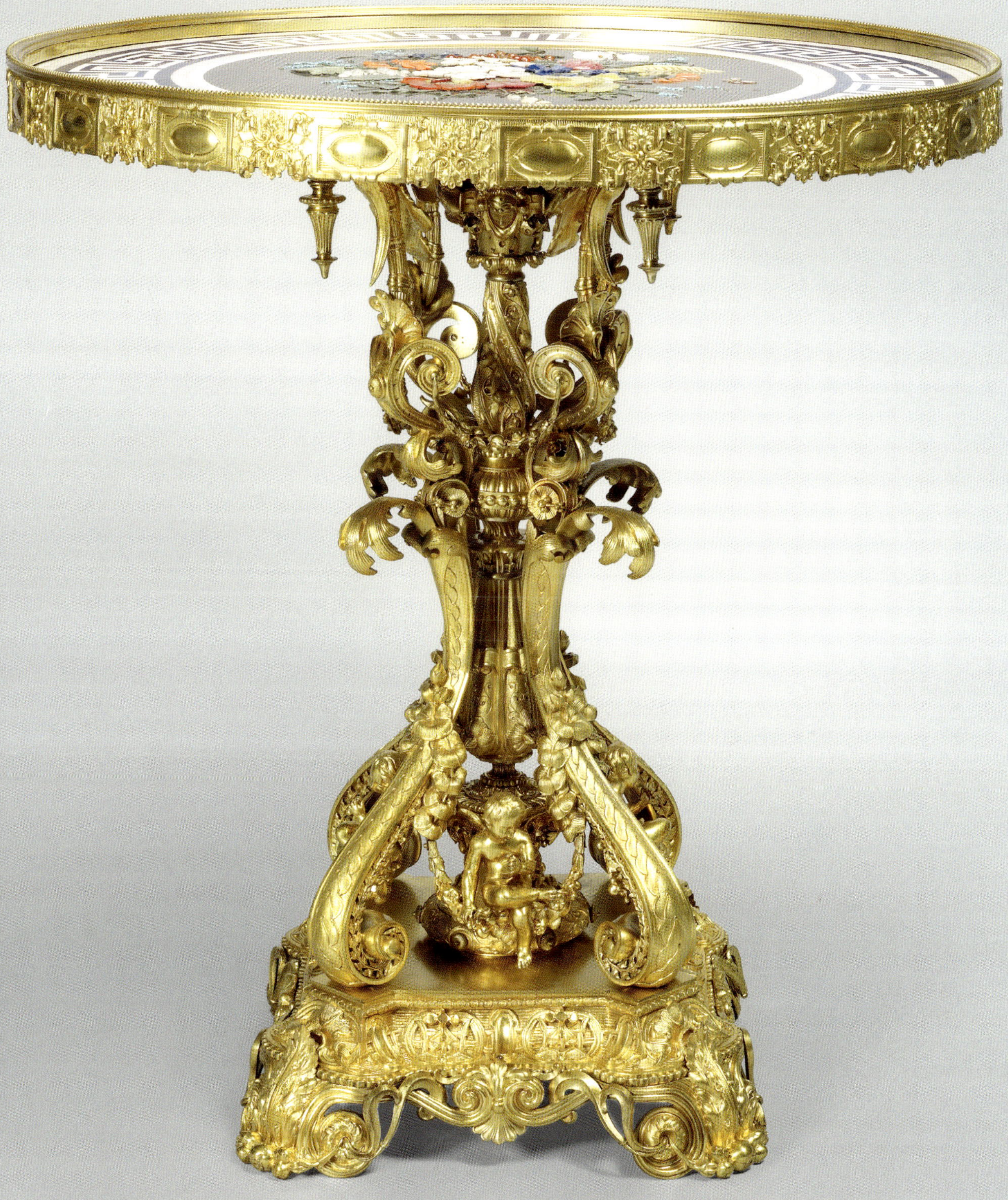

IMPERIAL PORCELAIN FACTORY

99 *Imperial presentation vase* 1844

Hard-paste porcelain, gilt bronze, 142.0 × 108.0 cm
Inscribed: *Czarhoe Selo / L'an 1844; Peterhoff / L'an 1844; N.Korniloff. / 1844* plus another signature
RCIN 41230

Provenance Given to Queen Victoria by Emperor Nicholas I, December 1844

Literature RA VIC/MAIN/Z/104/35, 23 October 1844; RA VIC/MAIN/QVJ (W), 2 December 1844

Following Nicholas I's return to Russia after his state visit to Britain in 1844, the Emperor dispatched this vase (together with its marble pedestal) and a mosaic table (cat. 98) to the Queen and Prince Albert. The gifts were transported in eight cases on the steamer *Mermaid* and arrived at Windsor in early December, with the Queen pronouncing the vase 'splendid & immense'.[68]

During the reign of Nicholas I, the production of large-scale vases supplied by the Imperial Porcelain Factory was enormous. Many were presentation gifts, but others were commissioned to furnish the palaces and dowries which the Emperor generously provided for his children.

The 'Medici' campana shape of the vase, named after the famous Medici Vase of the first century AD, which was placed in the Uffizi Gallery in 1780, served as a model for several vases of differing sizes made in the Imperial Porcelain Factory.

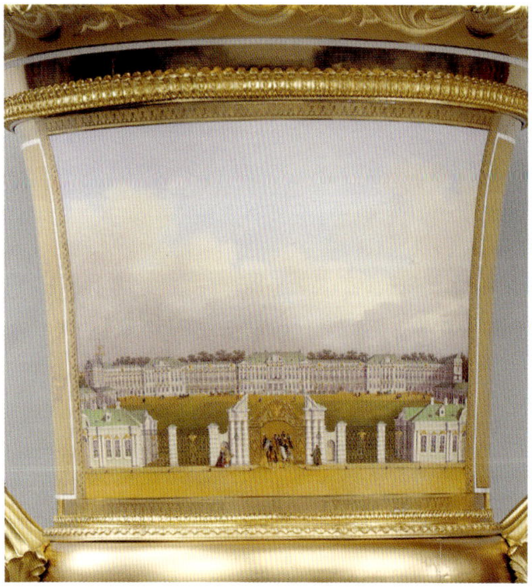

Detail of Tsarskoe Selo on the reverse of cat. 99

These included a vase of identical size to this one, with the same foliate mounts and fluted socle, and also painted with reserves, but depicting Emperor Nicholas I and dated 1836. Other examples are known and the model appeared in the work of the Imperial Porcelain Factory at least as early as 1830.

Decorated with matt and burnished gold, the vase is painted with large-scale views of the imperial palaces of Peterhof and Tsarskoe Selo on either side, carried out by Nikolai Kornilovich Kornilov (d.1852), one of the factory artists. The views by Kornilov are after those painted by Ivan Aivazovsky (1817–1900), an artist acclaimed for his seascapes. Aivazovsky's painting, *Peterhof Grand Palace*, which Kornilov copied for the vase, was one of six paintings commissioned by Emperor Nicholas I on 1 July 1844, through Prince Pyotr Volkonsky (1776–1852), minister of the imperial court.[69] The paintings were removed from Nicholas I's rooms in order to be copied for the vase. The view of Tsarskoe Selo is after the drawing by Mikhail Makhayev. The handles and the moulding around the rim of the vase are of gilt bronze. There was considerable debate about the decoration of the sides of the vase, which, in the end, were applied with the royal arms.[70]

Queen Victoria was evidently pleased with the gifts and wrote to Nicholas I on 23 October 1844 to tell him where she had had them placed: 'The vase which is superb, is placed in the drawing room where we spend our evenings [...] it is admired'.[71] The vase was placed in the window bay of the Green Drawing Room at Windsor Castle, where it stood until soon after Queen Victoria's death, when it was removed to Osborne House. It was returned to Windsor Castle in 1997.
CDEG

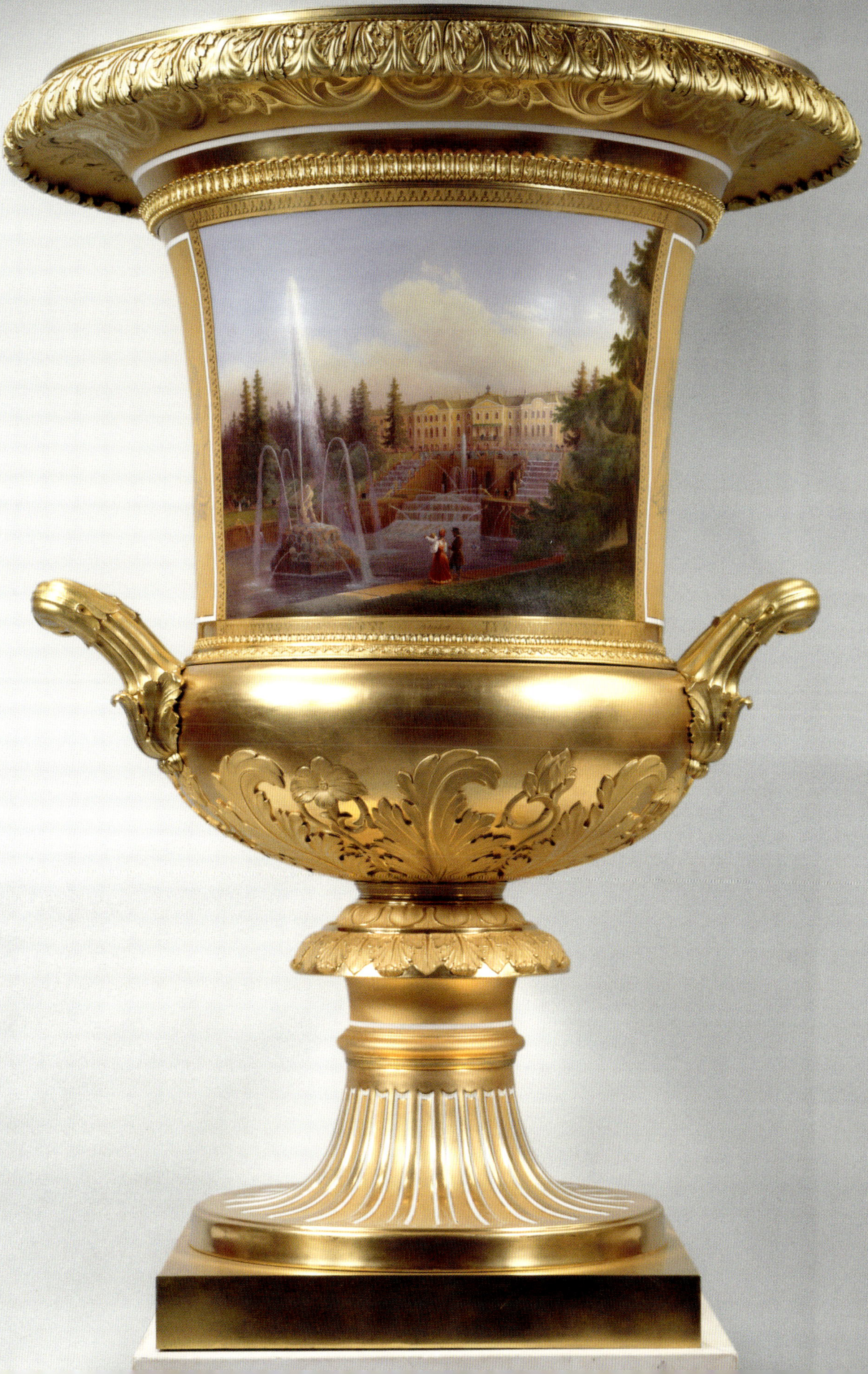

COALPORT

100 *Dessert service* 1845

Plate and dish, porcelain, polychrome painting, gilded, (plate) 2.7 × 25.5 cm, (dish) 11.0 × 37.0 × 32.3 cm
Gold transfer print on plate: *A.B. & R.P. Daniell To Her MAJESTY & THE ROYAL FAMILY Manufacturers London 129 NEW BOND ST & 18 WIGMORE ST*; gold transfer print on dish: *A.B.&R.P.DANIELL,* / To Her MAJESTY & THE ROYAL FAMILY* [enclosing] / [within ribbon] *MANUFACTURERS* / [Royal Arms] / [within ribbon] *LONDON* / [within ribbon] *129,NEW BOND ST. & 18,WIGMORE ST.*
RCINS 58710, 58711

Provenance Service ordered by Queen Victoria in 1845 for presentation to Emperor Nicholas I

Literature RA VIC/MAIN/Z/104/39, 1 July 1845

These specimens of a plate and dish are from a service ordered by Queen Victoria for presentation to Nicholas I following his visit to England in June 1844.[72] The design is based on the service made for William IV by the Worcester porcelain factory in 1831, heavily decorated in gilt and painted with the British orders of chivalry (see fig. 33). This service replaces the British orders with those of the highest Russian imperial orders. The pieces have the same royal blue ground and heavy gilt rim. In three large and three small cartouches with elaborate gold frames are the badges of the Orders of St George, St Alexander Nevskii, St Vladimir, St Stanislas, the White Eagle and St Anne, and in the centre of each piece, on a white ground, is the badge of the Order of St Andrew. Queen Victoria described the gifts she had sent to the Emperor in a letter of 1 July 1845: 'These objects are my portrait by Winterhalter [...] and porcelain service similar to that which you admired at Windsor'.[73]

The original service consisted of 62 pieces[74] and was sent to the Winter Palace, but the Emperor decided to use it for large banquets and a further 124 pieces were produced by the Imperial Porcelain Factory in St Petersburg. These reproduced the forms and decorative scheme of the Coalport pieces, but with minor variations in colour due to the different chemical composition of the paints used in the respective factories. The service was dispersed and sold after the Revolution, but the State Hermitage Museum retains 60 pieces in total, 30 by each of the two makers. CDEG

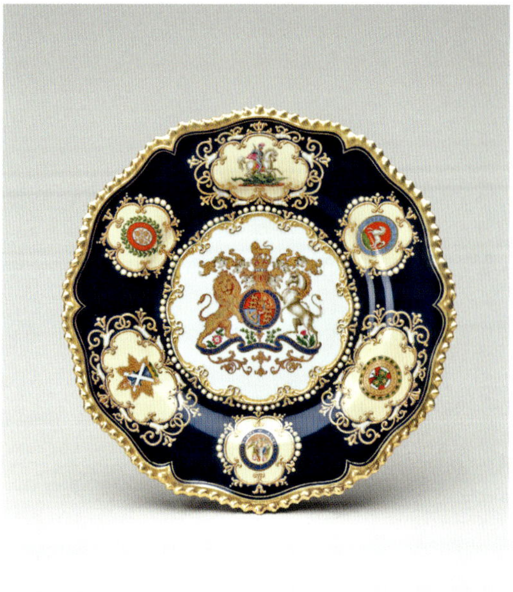

FIG. 33
Flight, Barr & Barr, Worcester
Dessert plate (part of the Coronation Service), 1830–33
Soft paste porcelain,
2.6 × 25.6 × 25.6 cm
RCIN 58393

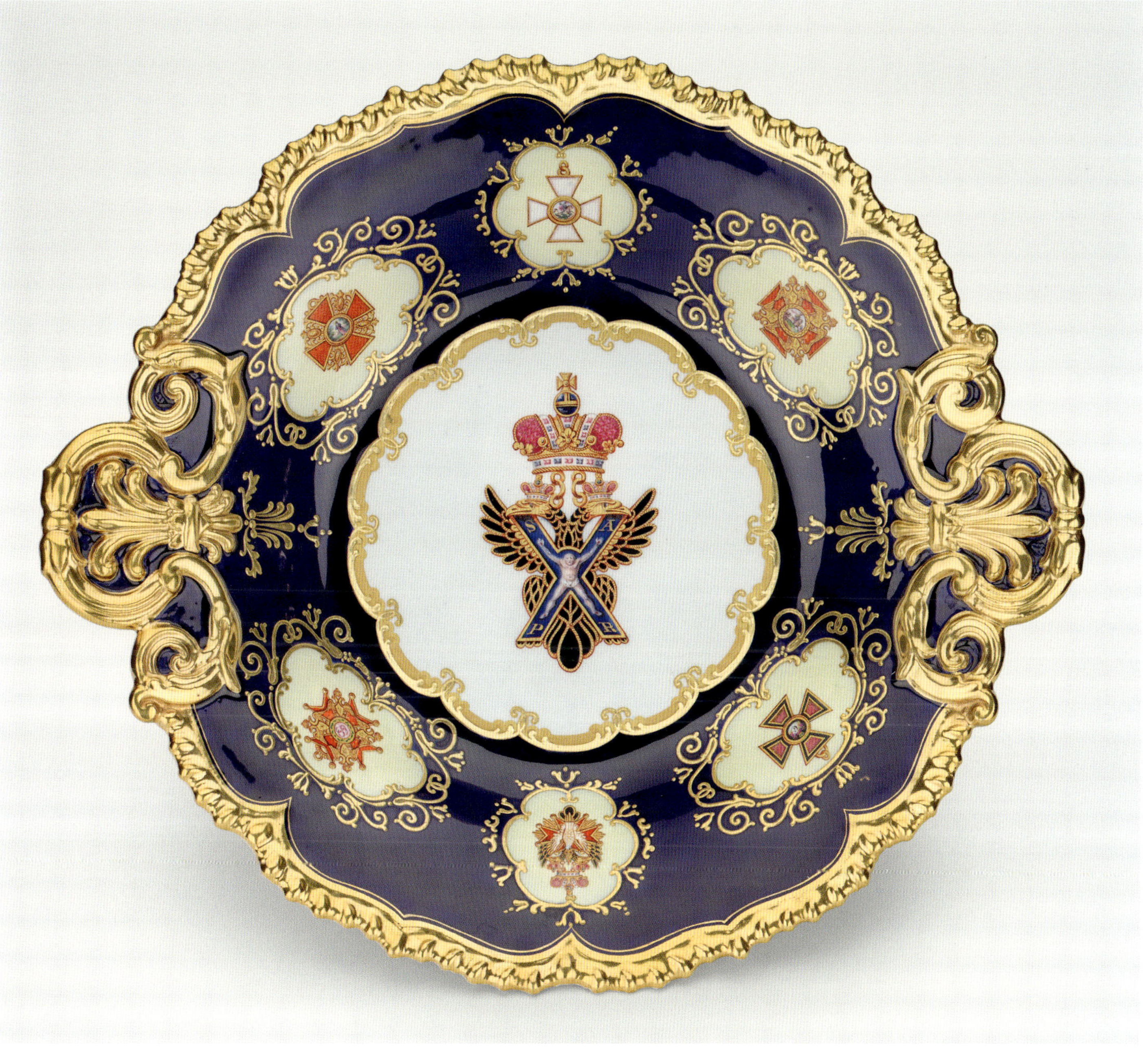

FRANZ KRÜGER (1797–1857)

101 *Nicholas I, Emperor of Russia (1796–1855)* 1847

Oil on canvas, 330.2 × 223.5 cm
Signed and dated: *F.Krüger.pinx. 1847*
RCIN 406814

Provenance Given to Queen Victoria by the sitter, November 1847; recorded hanging in the Principal Corridor, Buckingham Palace, 1876; sent to Windsor, 1922; recorded in the Guard Chamber at Windsor Castle, *c.*1925; recorded at Hampton Court, 1980 (rolled up)

Literature Osborn 1997, p. 58

The portrait was commissioned by Nicholas I as a gift for Queen Victoria, following his visit to England in 1844. On 10 November 1847, the Queen recalled in her Journal that 'Before dinner Baron Brunow presented a fine full length portrait of the Emperor of Russia which is an excellent likeness.'[75] The sitter was described by the Queen at the time of his stay as 'His appearance is *very striking* [...] he is still very handsome; very tall with a *very* fine figure [...] & *beautiful* Grecian profile.'[76]

The monumental scale rivals the spectacular equestrian portraits of allies Alexander I (1837) and Frederick William III of Prussia (1831), painted by the German artist for the Military Gallery of 1812 in the Winter Palace. Dressed in the striking red uniform of the Russian Cavalier Guard, with the white enamel badge of the Order of St George, and ribands and stars of the Order of the Garter and St Vladimir, the Emperor stands amidst a rough, stony terrain, a military engagement taking place in the background.

The magnificent Russian rococo revival frame is decorated with sprays of oak leaves and palm fronds, and flower heads between pierced rocaille centre ornaments; the imperial eagle adorns each corner.

Krüger, who studied with the artist Carl Wilhelm Kolbe the Elder (1759–1835), and later at the Berlin Academy, probably came to the attention of Nicholas through his father-in-law, Frederick William III of Prussia, and he became a favourite court painter. He first travelled to St Petersburg in 1836, and was subsequently there in 1844–5, 1847 and 1850–51. His interest in horses (his nickname was *Pferde Krüger*, 'Horsey Krüger') and his training with Kolbe, who was fascinated by nature, culminates in works that merge history, portrait and genre painting; the vignettes that flank the sitter add interest and a narrative to the portrait; similar scenes are often recycled in other works.

The portrait is said to have been painted in Berlin, but was sent to St Petersburg for corrections, prior to its dispatch to London in October 1847. From June to September that year, Krüger was engaged in painting a three-quarter-length variant for General Vladimir Baryatinsky (1817–75) (Pushkin Museum, Moscow) for his collection.[77] Studies for the portrait are in the Russian Museum, St Petersburg and the Staatliches Museum, Schwerin.[78] William

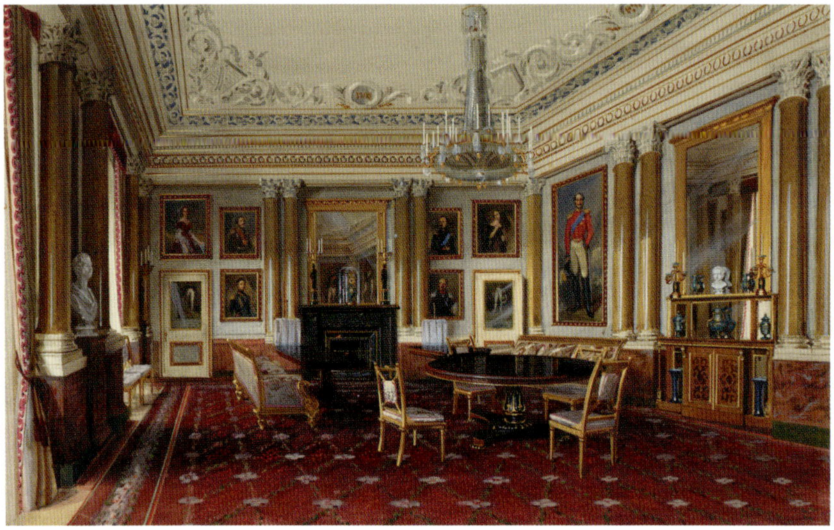

FIG. 34
James Roberts
Buckingham Palace: The 1844 Room, 1848–50
Watercolour, 24.0 × 39.3 cm
RCIN 919919

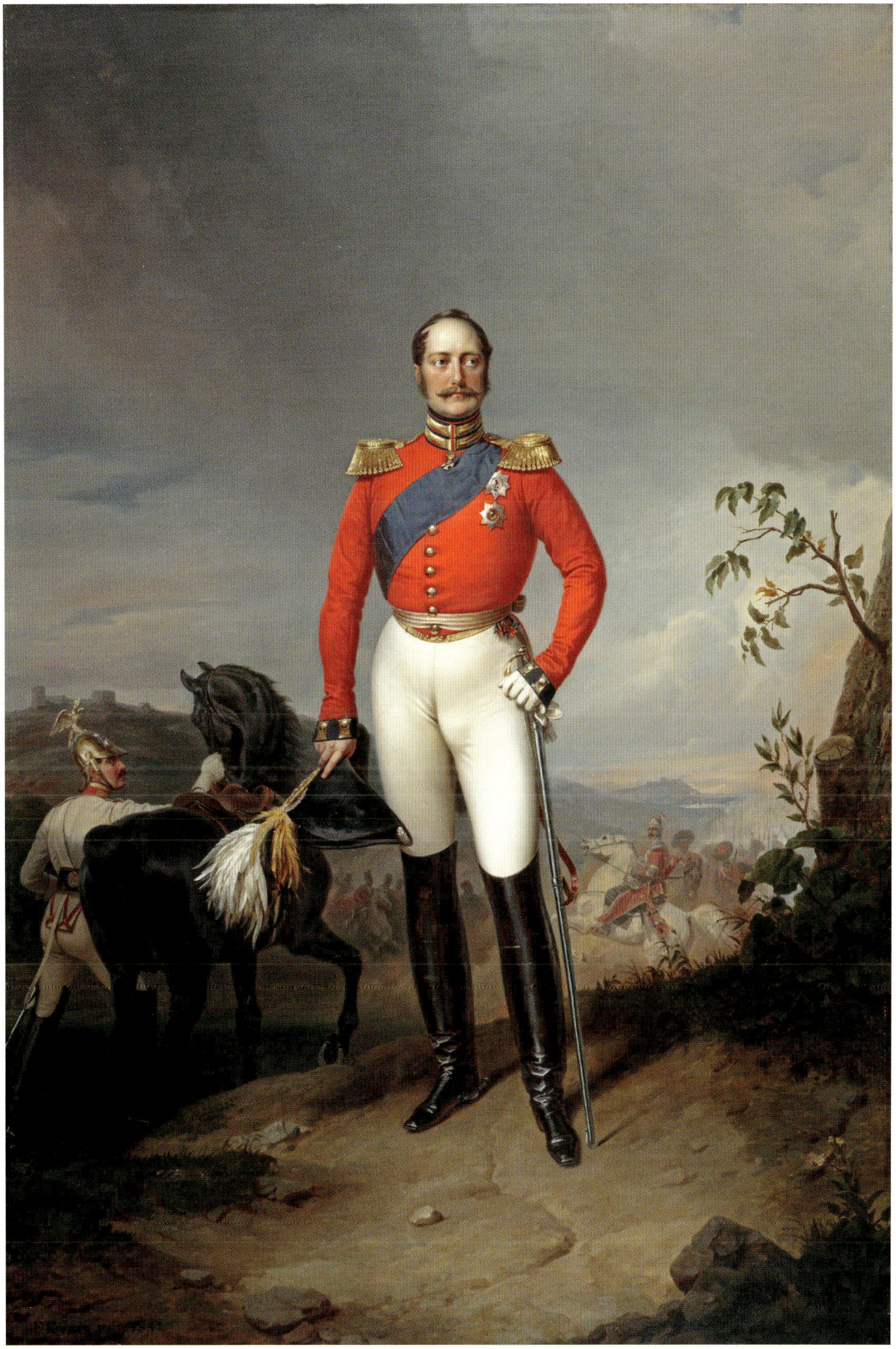

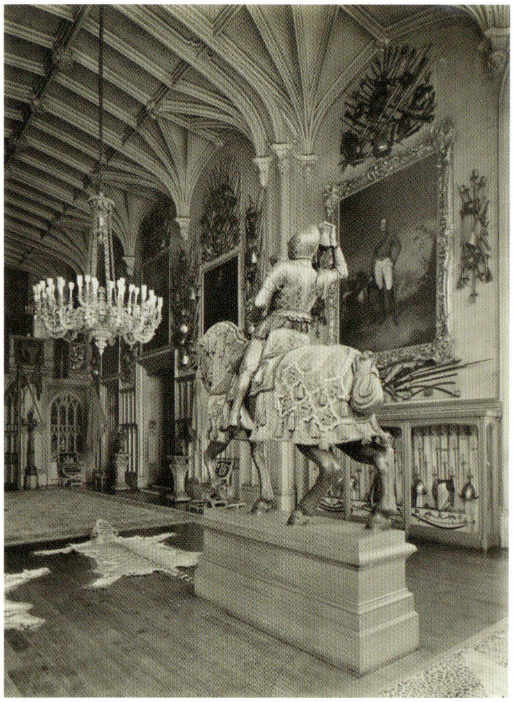

FIG. 35
Country Life
The Guard Room at Windsor Castle, 1931
Gelatin silver print, 20.8 × 15.7cm
RCIN 2100906

Corden the Younger was instructed to paint a reduced copy to hang in the rooms used by the Emperor during his stay.[79] The copy is recorded in a watercolour of the 1844 Room (named to commemorate the visit) by James Roberts (*c.*1800–1867), *c.*1848–50 (fig. 34). It appears that in 1863 the Queen wished to send the original portrait to Berlin for copying, which prompted some discussion; having inspected the painting in Buckingham Palace, Richard Redgrave (1804–88), Surveyor of the Queen's Pictures, concluded 'it would be a large case to send flat and I believe it does not fold and therefore on the whole it would be most advisable to roll it.'[80] It is unknown if the Queen's request was fulfilled.

Last recorded hanging in the Queen's Guard Chamber in Windsor Castle in a photograph taken for *Country Life* magazine (fig. 35), the portrait was taken down prior to the Second World War and rolled up for nearly 80 years. It has been recently conserved and shows little evidence of its chequered history. **AB**

FRANCIS GARDNER FACTORY

102 *Imperial Yacht Queen Victoria Service* c.1846

Plates, hard-paste porcelain, 3.0 × 26.7 cm (identical)
Фабрvкv Гарднерь v Москьv
RCIN 58174.1–2

Provenance Additions to the service commissioned by Queen Victoria and presented to Emperor Nicholas I

Literature Ross 1968, pp. 390–1

The Imperial Yacht *Queen Victoria* was built in 1844 on the Isle of Wight at the shipyard of Joseph White. The yacht was launched on 10 June 1846 at the Royal Yacht Squadron, in the presence of the Russian consul Temzensky. The yacht was luxuriously appointed, its main cabin decorated with rosewood and maple. It arrived in Kronstadt, with an English crew, in the autumn of 1846 and was incorporated into the Baltic Fleet. Nicholas I and his family regularly used the vessel for boat trips on the Gulf of Finland. From 1878 to 1880, the boat was used at the Maritime Training College, and was broken up in 1884.

Part of the furnishings for the yacht included a service commissioned by Queen Victoria from Minton. These identical plates were later additions to the service, made in Moscow in the Gardner factory, which was transferred to the yacht *Slavianka*. The service is of plain white porcelain; in the centre of the plates is the imperial double-headed eagle in black, the imperial crown in red and gold with St George and the dragon, and the sceptre and orb in gold. Below the eagle is a red banderole with 'The Queen Victoria' in Cyrillic on the original service gifted by Queen Victoria to Nicholas I. On the plates in the Royal Collection, which are later additions, the text is in Roman. CDEG

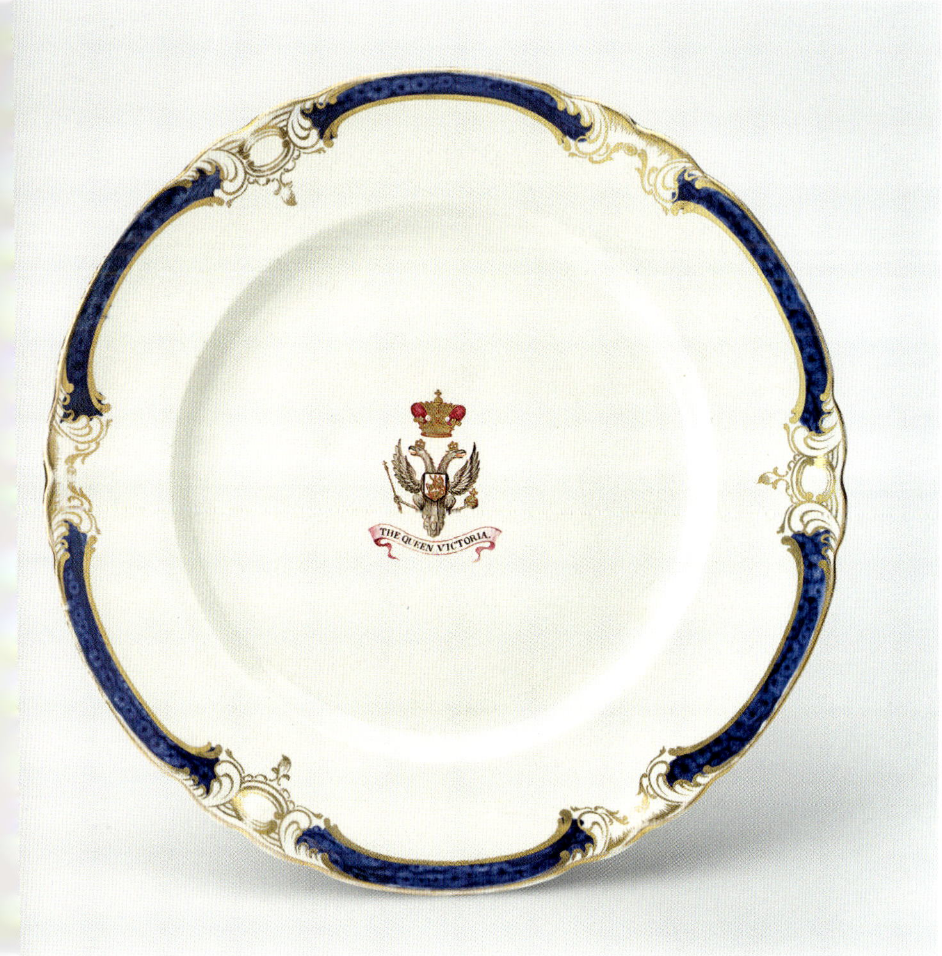

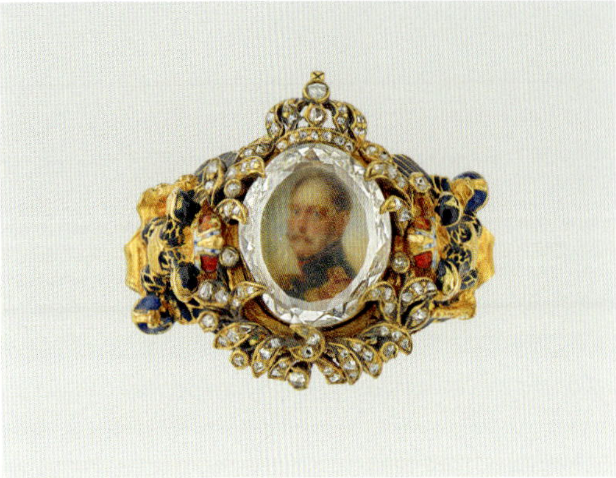

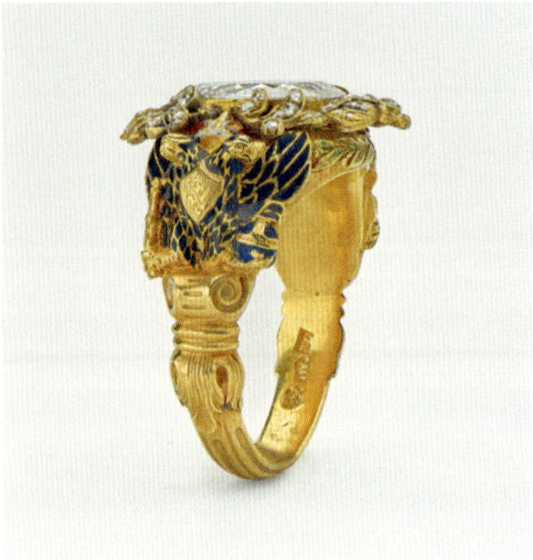

RUSSIAN; MINIATURE ATTRIBUTED TO IVAN WINBERG (d.1851)

103 *Presentation ring with a miniature of Emperor Nicholas I (1796–1855)*
c.1834

Gold, diamonds, enamel, watercolour on ivory, 1.3 × 1.2 cm
Inscribed on reverse of miniature: *Pour Prescrit - du - 29 Sept: 1834*
RCIN 9038

Provenance Acquired by Queen Mary (1867–1953)

In Russia from the reign of Peter I onwards, sovereigns presented gifts embellished with their image, like their counterparts in Europe. The gift was always to commemorate a special event, and when presented to Russian subjects it was a token of the monarch's appreciation and gratitude. Those given to foreigners were presented for diplomatic reasons. Russian sovereigns also presented members of their own family with jewellery set with miniature portraits, to commemorate occasions such as betrothals, weddings and anniversaries.

This large gold presentation ring contains a portrait of Emperor Nicholas I under a portrait diamond with faceted rim. The elaborate gold mount incorporates a pierced, diamond-set imperial crown surmounting the miniature, with gold, red and white enamel crowns flanking it, together with foliate mounts similarly set with diamonds and enamelled in blue. The miniature is attributed to Ivan Winberg (active 1825–46), an imperial court miniaturist, and is based on a portrait by Franz Krüger, court painter to Frederick William IV of Prussia, and subsequently to his brother-in-law, Emperor Nicholas I (cat. 101).

The inscription on the ring, *Pour Prescrit - du - 29 Sept: 1834*, presumably indicates the date of presentation, and literally translated means 'ascribed to'.

On 29 September 1834, Nicholas I arrived at Kaluga in central Russia, en route for Orel where a review of the 3rd Cavalry Corps was planned. He was received by the civil governor and by military authorities and was occupied with affairs of government for the rest of that day. In order to qualify for a portrait gift, such as this ring, Russian subjects had to hold one of the three highest service ranks, established by Peter the Great in 1722. Assuming that this ring was presented on the date with which it is inscribed, it would have had to be presented to an army officer with the rank of Field Marshal General (rank I), General of the Infantry (rank II) or Lieutenant General (rank III), but the identity of the exact recipient is not known. CDEG

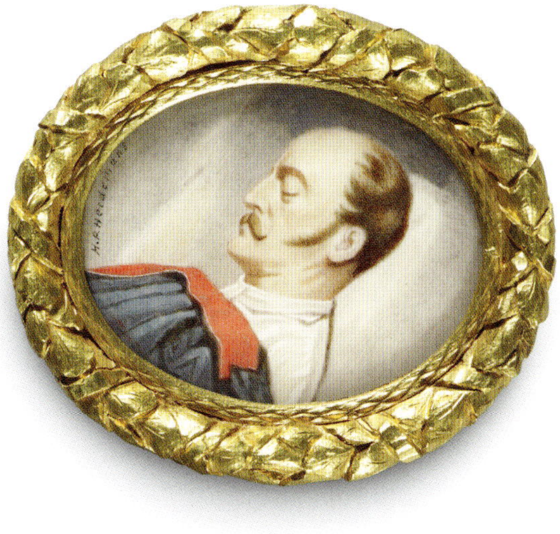

HENRI PHILIPPE HEIDEMANNS (1804–1864)

104 *Nicholas I, Emperor of Russia (1796–1855)* c.1855

Watercolour on ivory, oval, 3.3 × 4.1 cm
Signed in black paint *H.P. Heidemans* [sic]
RCIN 420777

Provenance First recorded in the Royal Collection during the reign of Queen Victoria

Literature Remington 2010, p. 292, no. 552

Emperor Nicholas I died on 2 March 1855, and a passage from one of his obituaries reads: 'Thus ended Emperor Nicholas, on a mattress of hay, with a soldier's cloak for cover, showing in his unexpected death a stoical resignation and an empire for which the violence of his character had not prepared us.'[81] This is exactly as the body of the Emperor is shown in this miniature: lying on a mattress of hay, with a soldier's cloak for cover. Both this miniature and another signed copy by the same artist in the Dutch Royal Collection are based on a daguerreotype by the Mouhot Frères.[82] While in The Hague in 1855, perhaps because of Henri Mouhot's (1826–61) earlier connections with Russia, the brothers were given the task of reproducing the original daguerreotype (possibly by Sergei Levitsky (1819–98)), which had been sent to the Queen Dowager of the Netherlands, Anna Pavlovna of Russia (1795–1865), sister of Nicholas I, in June 1855 by Count Vladimir Fedorovich Adlerberg (1791–1884), minister of the imperial court, so that copies could be distributed to 'people of high birth and dignity'.[83] The Royal Collection holds one of the copies produced by the Mouhot Frères (fig. 36).[84] **AN**

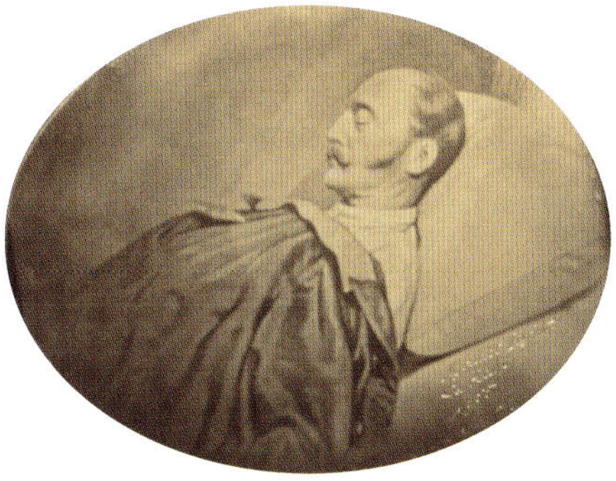

FIG. 36
Mouhot Frères
Nicholas I, 1855
After a daguerreotype, oval
6.1 × 7.5 cm
RCIN 614580

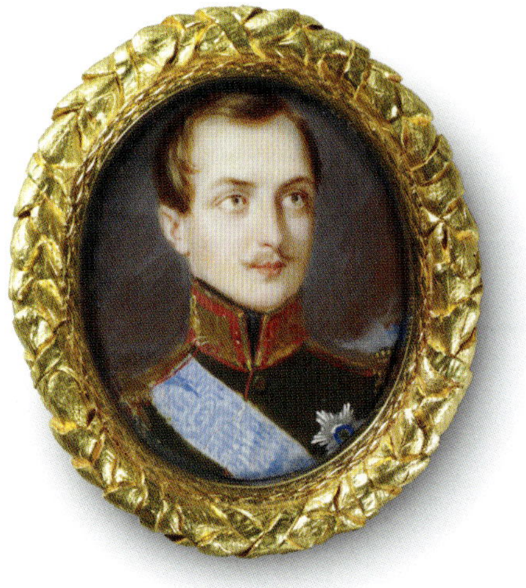

IVAN WINBERG (d.1851)

105 *Portrait miniature of Alexander II (1818–1881)* c.1838–48

Watercolour on ivory laid on card, 4.7 × 4.0 cm
RCIN 420719

Provenance First recorded in the Royal Collection, 1907

Literature Cust 1910, 51/10, *Great Britain – USSR* 1967, p. 24, no. 134; Walker 1992, no. 912

Ivan Winberg was the son of the Swedish goldsmith, Andreas Winberg (1756–after 1827), who had settled in St Petersburg in 1791. Ivan became professor of miniature painting at the Russian Academy in 1846. Though the composition of this portrait miniature is similar to a work by the Austrian miniaturist, Robert Theer (1808–63), painted in 1839, Winberg's portrait is painted in a loose, expressive manner. The star of the Order of St Andrew pinned to his breast and the sash are picked out in rapid white and blue gouache strokes. The miniature is presented in a later oval-format gilded Hatfield frame.

Alexander II, Emperor of Russia, was the eldest son of Emperor Nicholas I and Empress Alexandra Feodorovna. He married Marie, Princess of Hesse, in 1841, by whom he had eight children. In 1880, after the death of his first wife, he entered a morganatic marriage with his mistress, Catherine Dolgorukova, later Princess Yurevskaia (1847–1922). Perhaps the Emperor's greatest legacy was the reformism of his reign, which saw the emancipation of Russia's serf population in 1861. In 1881, after inspecting a roll call at the Mikhailovsky Manège (riding academy) in St Petersburg, the Emperor was assassinated by members of the People's Will movement. IM

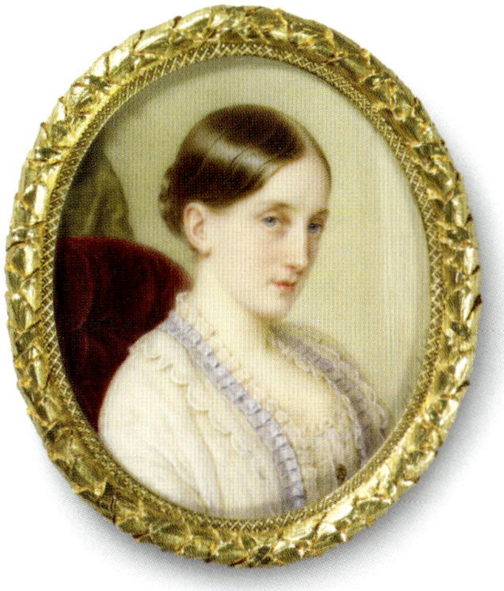

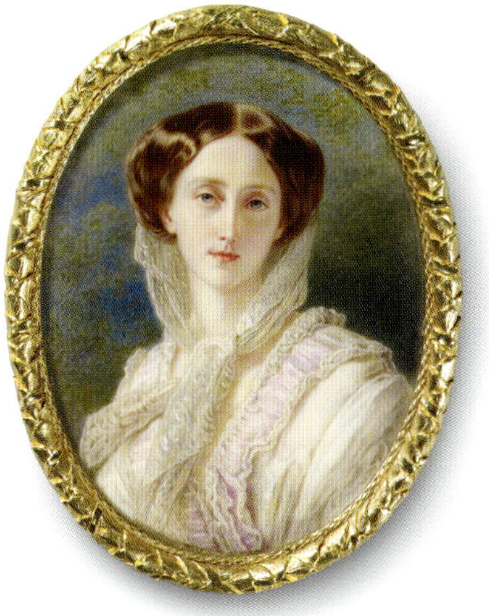

ANTON HÄHNISCH (1817–1897)

106 & 107

Marie, Grand Duchess of Russia, when Duchess of Leuchtenberg (1819–1876) 1853

Watercolour on ivory laid on card, 8.1 × 6.8 cm
Signed & dated: *Hähnisch 1853*
RCIN 420715

ANTON HÄHNISCH AFTER FRANZ XAVER WINTERHALTER (1805–1873)

Olga, Grand Duchess of Russia, when Crown Princess of Württemberg (1822–1892) 1857

Watercolour on ivory laid on card, 11.5 × 9.2 cm
RCIN 420716

Provenance Painted for Queen Victoria

Literature Remington 2010, nos 501, 502

These miniatures of two of Nicholas I's daughters, Marie and Olga, sisters to Emperor Alexander II, were painted for Queen Victoria by the Viennese miniaturist, Anton Hähnisch.

Both sisters travelled to England in the summer of 1853, and visited Queen Victoria at Osborne House in the August. Marie, who was in deep mourning following the death of her husband, Maximilian de Beauharnais, 3rd Duke of Leuchtenberg (1817–52), in November 1852, was described by the Queen as 'but little taller than me, a miniature as to features of her father [...] She is very lively, and has much frankness and abandon in her manner, & certainly is attractive. She seems very clever'.[85] The portrait was painted by Hähnisch, then resident in England, presumably in London or at Osborne, although the Duchess possibly appears more youthful than her years.

The miniature of Olga, Grand Duchess of Russia, is after a three-quarter-length portrait by Winterhalter, dated 1856, formerly in the possession of the Crown Princess of Württemberg herself.[86] Olga travelled to England in the summer of 1853, with her husband, Charles I of Württemberg (1823–91). The Queen reported to Leopold, King of the Belgians that 'Olga is still very handsome as to features, figure &c. but she is a wraith wh.is a sad thing for one who was so beautiful & is so young.'[87] **AB**

CRIMEAN PRISONER OF WAR

108 & 109

Box 1856

Carved wood, 8.5 × 22.0 × 13.0 cm
Label inscribed: *Carved by the Russian Prisoners of War at Lewes March 1856*
RCIN 84382

Box 1856

Wood, 27.0 cm
Label inscribed in Queen Victoria's hand: *Carved by the Russian prisoners 1856*
RCIN 84383

Provenance (RCIN 84282) Unknown; (RCIN 84383) Presumably acquired by Queen Victoria and Prince Albert

Following the final assault in the battle for the Aland Islands, in June to August 1854 (commemorated in a silver model of a cannon in the Royal Collection (RCIN 9224)), some 2,000 Russian prisoners of war were transported to England and France, 400 of them to Lewes in East Sussex, where they were housed in an empty naval prison. Although the officers were Russian, many of the ordinary soldiers were Finns conscripted into the Imperial army.

In the prison, a workshop was set up for the men to make wooden toys to sell, and the prison itself became a visitor attraction. These boxes are examples of their work, which was finely wrought in the tradition of Russian wood- and bone-carving. The prisoners' woodwork was popular and sales became lucrative, causing criticism that, as a result, they were too well-fed and some of them even owned gold watches. At the end of the Crimean War in 1856, the prisoners were released. These boxes evidently entered the collection of Queen Victoria and Prince Albert between 1854 and 1856, and were recorded in the museum at Osborne House, where they have remained on display.

A memorial stone was erected in Lewes to record the death of those prisoners who perished there. In 1877, the stone was replaced by a large obelisk, commissioned by Emperor Alexander II.
CDEG

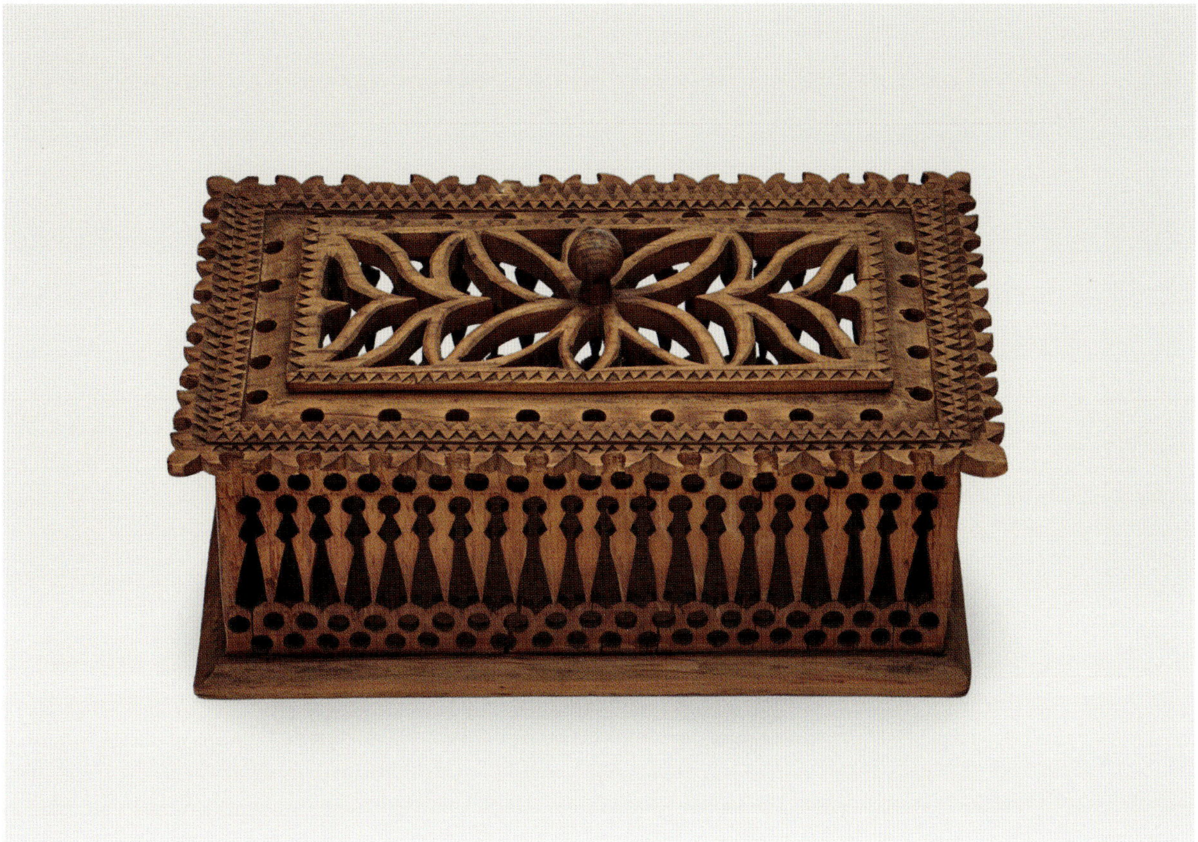

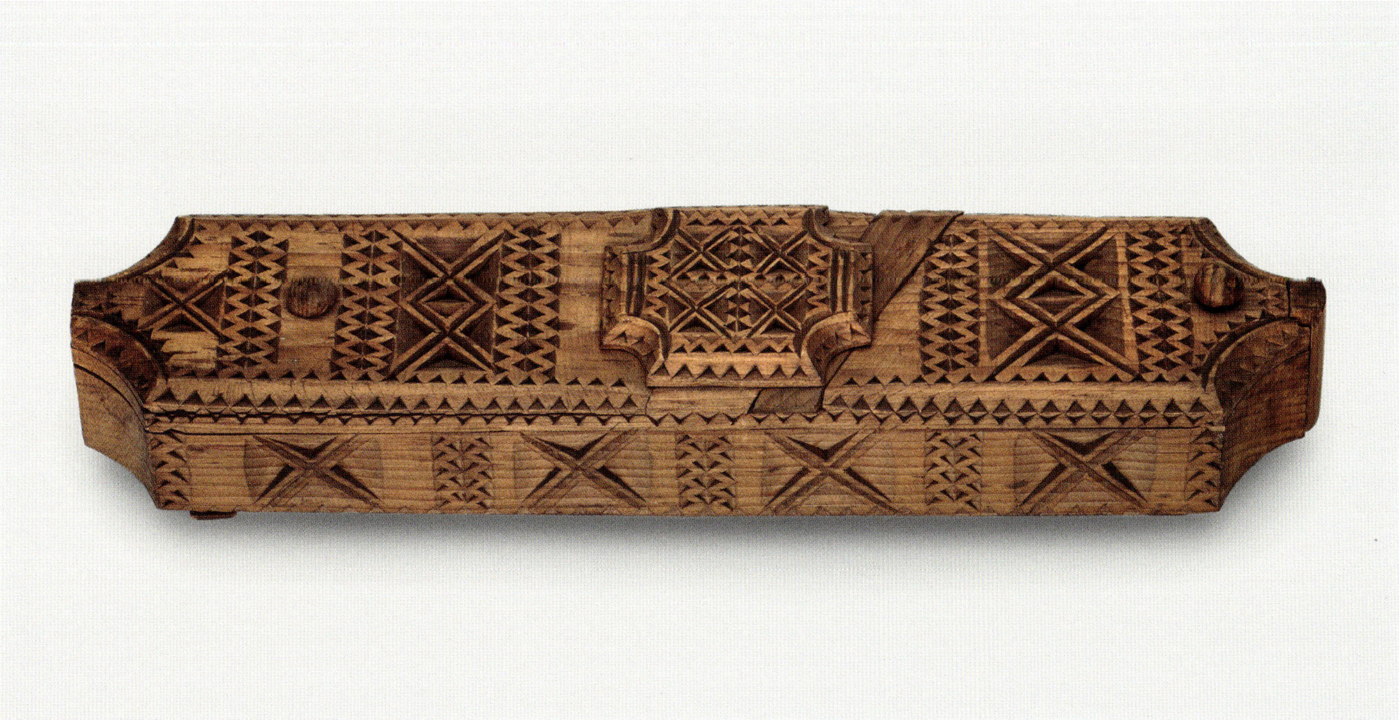

ELIZABETH SOUTHERDEN BUTLER, LADY BUTLER (1846–1933)

110 *The Roll Call: calling the roll after an engagement, Crimea* 1874

Oil on canvas, 93.3 × 183.5 cm
Signed and dated: *Eliz.th Thompson / 1874*, under a device composed of a cross within a capital ?C
RCIN 405915

Provenance Commissioned by the Manchester industrialist, Charles Galloway for £126; ceded to Queen Victoria, 1874

Literature Usherwood and Spencer Smith 1987, pp. 22–4, 27–39, 41–3; Butler 1922, pp. 101–4; Lloyd 1991, pp. 206–7, no. 77; Millar 1992, no. 185; Lloyd 1998, p. 114, no. 42

Painted nearly two decades after the end of the Crimean War (1853–6), this picture is assumed to represent a roll call following the battle of Inkerman of 5 November 1854. The painting captured the public's imagination when it was exhibited at the Royal Academy in 1874, causing such crowds that a policeman was stationed nearby to protect it and to move visitors on. It was equally celebrated as it toured England. The power of the painting lay in the fact that it was not a depiction of the action of war or the heroism of military commanders (or even a real event), but that it conveyed the reality of the suffering of the ordinary soldier in the aftermath of conflict, and the camaraderie between soldiers.

Amidst heavy snow, in the grey cold light of morning, the remnants of a battalion of Grenadier Guards gather, many exhausted and wounded, to answer a roll call given by a sergeant. The 3rd Battalion Grenadier Guards, who numbered 650, spent much of the battle defending a sandbag battery, and suffered heavy losses. Adjutant, Captain George Higginson (1826–1927), probably represented by the mounted soldier on the left, later recalled that barely 200 men answered the roll call.

Higginson later described the battle and how critical it was for the Guards to retain their colours (visible in the painting) – they were the only regiment to take them into battle:

> *Clustered round the colours* [...] *the men pressed slowly backwards, keeping their full front towards the enemy, their bayonets ready* [...] *As a comrade fell, wounded or dead, his fellow took his place and maintained the compactness of the gradually diminishing group that held on with unflinching stubbornness in protecting the flags.*[88]

The young military artist, Elizabeth Butler, recalled that she had 'long been turning "The Roll Call" in her mind', and she is quoted in her obituary as saying that she wished to portray the 'pathos and heroism' of war. She sought ex-soldiers as models and hunted for authentic uniforms and equipment to use in the painting. The artist described in her *Autobiography* how, at first, she drew the figure without the 'great coat', so as 'to get the figures well drawn first', adding 'how easily then could the thick less shapely great coat be painted on the well-secured foundation.' It is through the rendition of these heavy winter coats that the soldiers appear as a unified group, echoing their solidarity; however, a sense of their individuality is also evoked. The feeling of the coldness and exhaustion of the men is also palpable.[89]

The painting was commissioned by the wealthy Manchester industrialist, Charles Galloway (1833–1904), but it aroused the interest of both the Prince of Wales and Queen Victoria, who both wished to possess it. An offer to Galloway by the Prince of Wales was refused, and instead it was ceded to the Queen, who was delighted to have obtained it, even removing it from the Royal Academy so she could show it to Alexander II, who was visiting England in May that year. AB

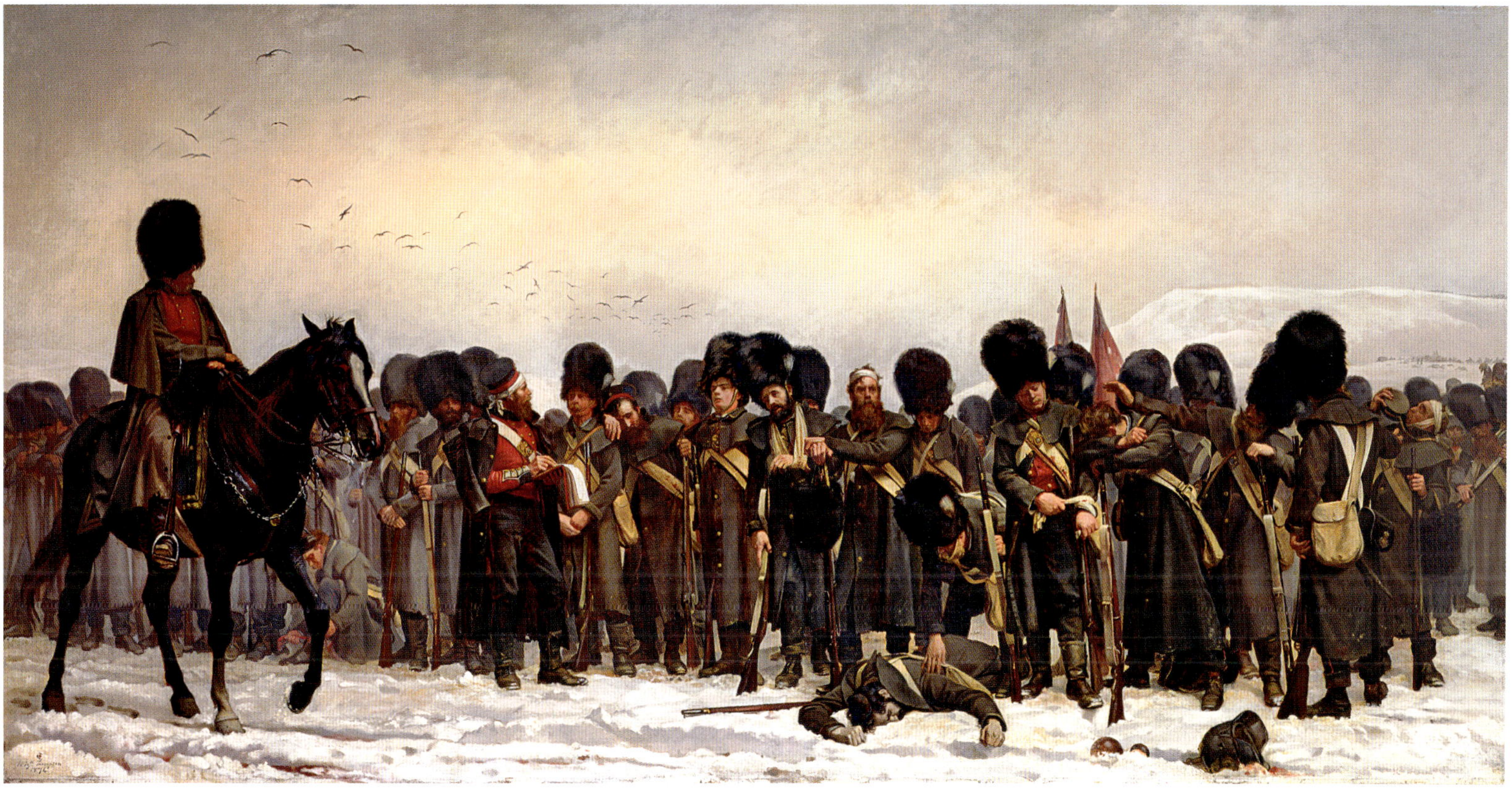

ANDREI DENIER (1820–1892)

111 & 112 *Shamil (1797–1871), St Petersburg* 1859

Albumen print with overpainting, oval, 38.0 × 28.4 cm, (sheet) 48.4 × 33.2 cm
Signed and dated along the right edge of the photograph: *H. Denier à St Petersbourg 1859*; sitter's signature on strip of paper pasted on mount below photograph: بن المنالي الفقير شهبيل; inscribed along bottom of mount: *Hommage du plus profond respect à Sa Majestè la Reine Victoria*
RCIN 2935078

Khazi Mahommed (1833–1902), son of Shamil, St Petersburg 1859

Albumen print with overpainting, oval, 38.0 × 28.5 cm
Signed along right edge of photograph: *H. Denier à St Petersbourg*
RCIN 2935079

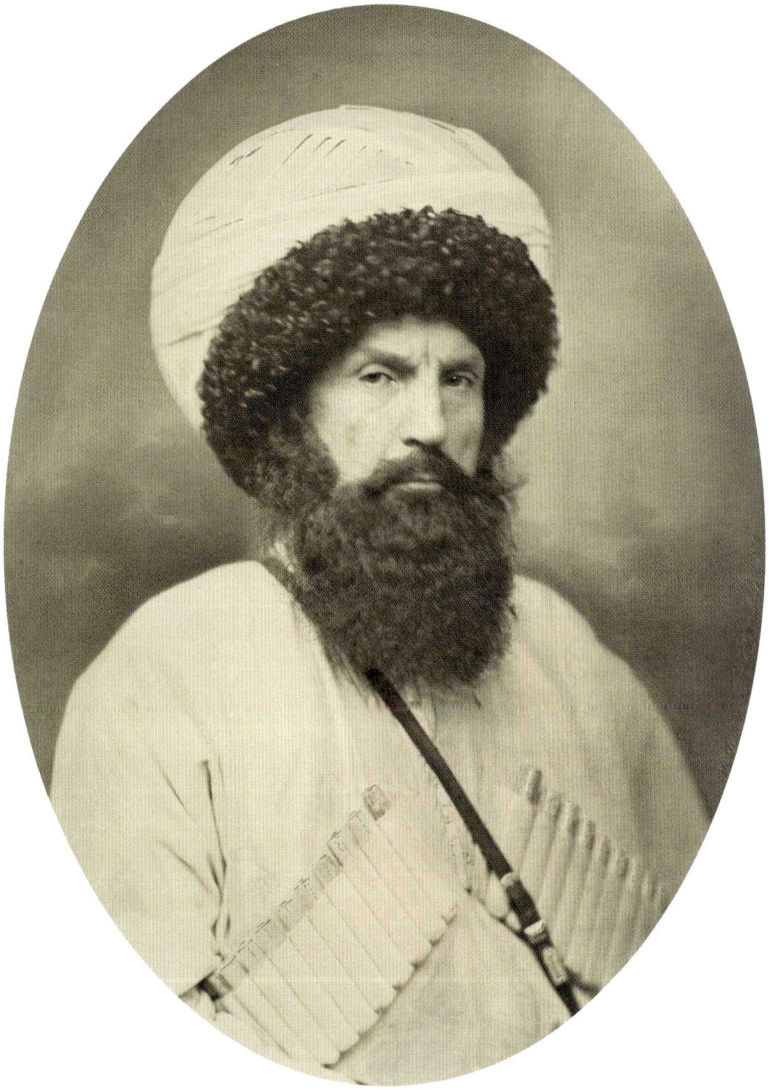

Provenance Presented to Queen Victoria by the photographer[90]

Literature Dimond 1995, nos 1–2

In 1834, Shamil, born in Gimry, became the third Imam of the so-called Caucasian Imamate, a military-theocratic state created in 1828 amongst the tribes of the north-eastern Caucasus to oppose Russian expansion into the region. Shamil's local knowledge of the mountainous territory, together with his military ability in conducting successful guerrilla-style operations, made him and his followers an incredibly difficult enemy for the cumbersome imperial army to fight. Under his leadership, the conflict lasted for 25 years, during which time his popularity in the West, as a romantic hero fighting for independence against the aggressive Russian power, grew to the point that almost 40 books on Shamil (nicknamed 'The Lion of Dagestan') had appeared in Europe and America between 1854 and 1859.[91] Such popularity explains the critical importance and remarkable exposure given to Shamil's capture, following his surrender on 25 August 1859: Russia, after the humiliating defeat suffered in the Crimea, could at this moment celebrate not only the conquest of that region of the Caucasus after a 30-year campaign, but also the submission to the Empire of a figure well-known and admired in the West. His capture

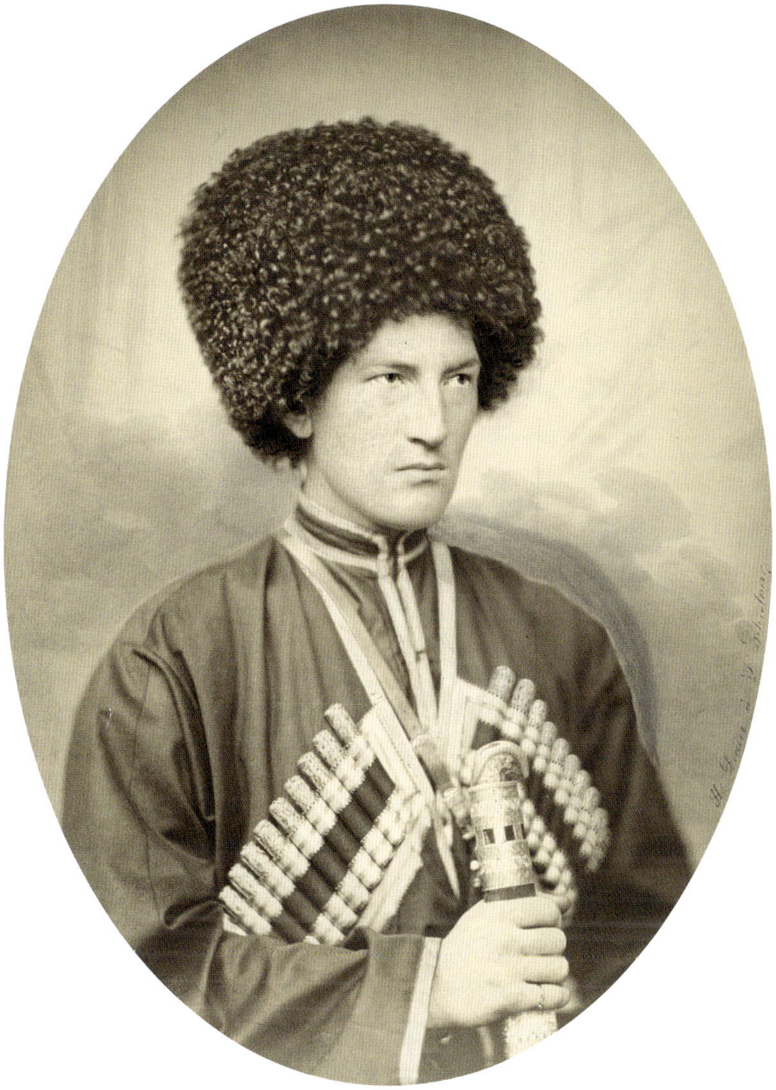

was so significant that Alexander II went to Chuguev to meet Shamil in person on 15 September 1859. There, the Emperor embraced and kissed him and invited him to review his troops, telling him that they would live together as friends.[92] On his arrival in St Petersburg, Shamil received a rapturous welcome; lodged in a hotel in Znamenskaya (today Vosstaniya) Square, with two of his sons and members of his suite, he was treated with every respect and regarded as a sort of (inter)national hero, praised by intellectuals, honoured by the Emperor and the aristocracy, painted by artists, as well as photographed by one of the city's leading portrait photographers, Andrei Denier.[93] Alexander II was undoubtedly aware of the importance of Shamil as an international symbol of his imperial magnanimity, and in 1866, following Shamil's pledge of allegiance to the Emperor, Alexander invited him to attend the marriage of his son, Tsesarevich Alexander, to Maria Feodorovna. The Prince of Wales, also present in St Petersburg for the celebrations, together with many other European diplomatic figures, received Shamil and his sons, who presented him with gifts.[94] Khazi Mahommed, seen here in a pendant portrait to that of his father, was one of the two sons of Shamil present at the moment of his surrender in 1859. Together with his brother, Mahommed Sheffi (1839–1904), he followed Shamil in his exile to Russia, which took them from St Petersburg, firstly to Kaluga, near Moscow, where a small mosque had been built for them, and then, from 1868, to Kiev. The young warrior was less keen than his father in accepting defeat, as might be perceived in his sullen gaze, captured in this photograph taken soon after their arrival in St Petersburg. Following his father's death in 1871, Khazi Mahommed moved his family to Constantinople, where he was eventually proclaimed 4th Imam in 1873.[95] During the Russo-Turkish war of 1877–8, he led a Dagestani regiment against Russia. Following Turkey's defeat, he was banished from Constantinople and exiled to Medina, where he died in 1902. **AN**

COPIES AFTER BARON HEINRICH VON ANGELI (1840–1925)

113 & 114 *Alexander II, Emperor of Russia (1818–1881)* c.1881–4

Oil on canvas, 90.3 × 71.8 cm
RCIN 404903

Maria Alexandrovna, Empress of Russia (1824–1880) c.1881–4

Oil on canvas, 90.0 × 72.0 cm
RCIN 404902

Provenance Painted for Queen Victoria; first recorded in the State Visitors, Sitting Room, Windsor Castle

Literature Windsor Castle Inventory of Paintings 1866, nos 2083, 2084; Millar 1992, nos 74, 75

Early in 1885, it was reported that two copies of the heads of the (late) Emperor and Empress, parents of Maria, Duchess of Edinburgh, had been painted for Queen Victoria in Russia. It appears that the commission, possibly initiated in March 1881, was managed by the Duke of Edinburgh, who was then in Russia to attend the funeral of Alexander II. Writing to the Queen on 28 March, Sir John Cowell (1832–94), having described the funeral, added: 'I mentioned to the latter [The Duke of Edinburgh] all that I was commissioned by Your Majesty to say to him respecting the paintings of the Emperor and Empress by Angeli. He understood all this & said he would give his careful attention to your wishes.'[96]

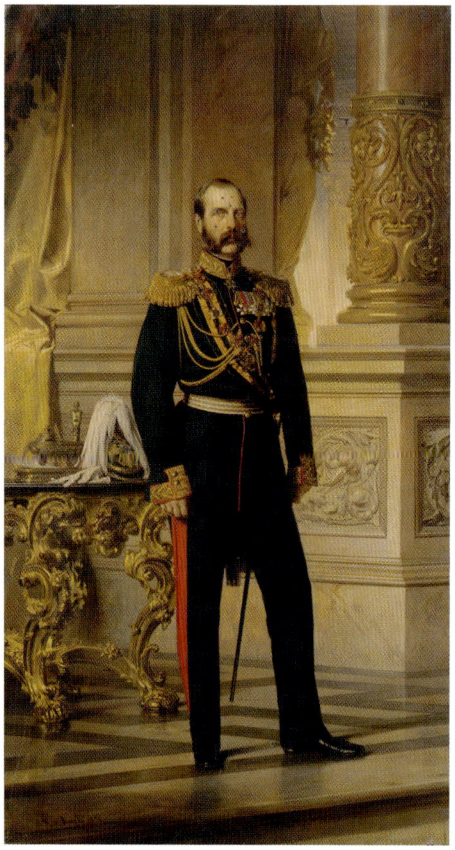

FIG. 37
Heinrich von Angeli
Alexander II, 1876
Oil on canvas, 271.0 × 150.0 cm
State Hermitage Museum, St Petersburg,
inv. no. ЭРЖ.II-693

The inference from labels on the reverse is that the portraits are after originals painted by Heinrich von Angeli in 1874; however, the portrait of Empress Maria is after an oval dated 1875 in the Hermitage, with the addition of a jewelled hairpin.[97] Queen Victoria described the sitter in 1874 as '*very* tall, *very* ladylike & amiable & *très-grand Dame*, with a sad expression & very delicate in appearance.'[98] The Empress had tolerated her husband's lengthy love affair and was of a fragile disposition, having suffered from tuberculosis for many years. The strain of ill-health is captured in this portrait.

The portrait of the Emperor is probably after the full-length portrait in the Hermitage – on which bayonet damage sustained during the Revolution is still visible around the face.[99] Attired in the uniform of a Russian general, he wears the collar of St Andrew and the ribbon and star of St George. On meeting the Emperor for the first time in over 30 years in 1874, the Queen was equally concerned with his appearance, describing him as 'so old, sad and worn'.[100]

They are both painted on Russian prepared canvases from a supplier in St Petersburg.[101] **AB**

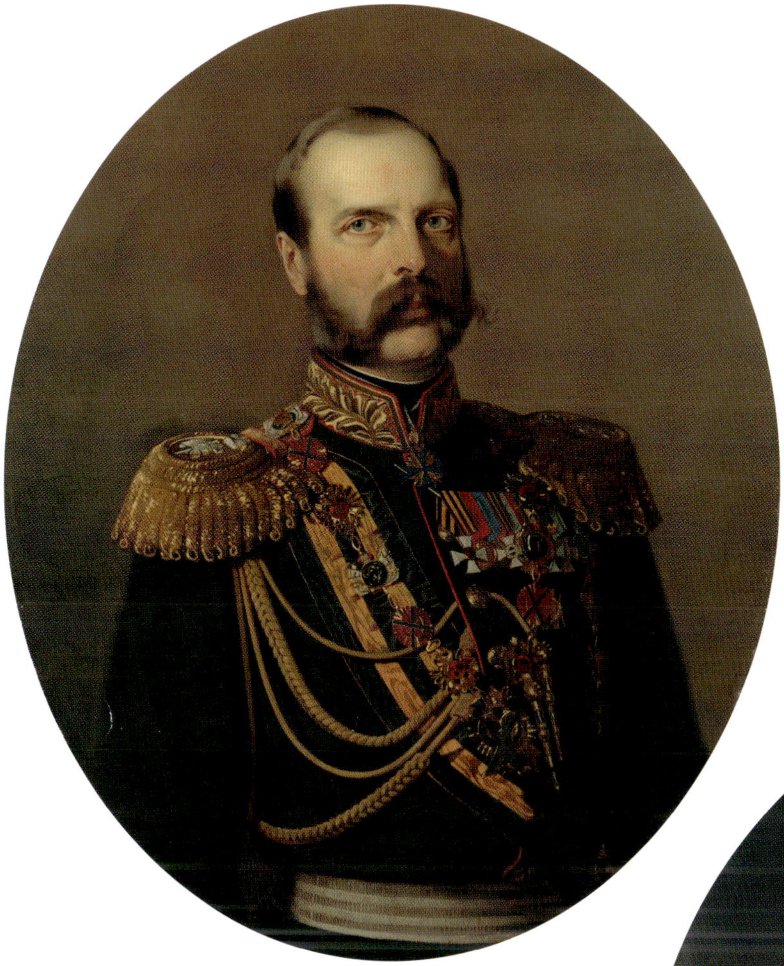

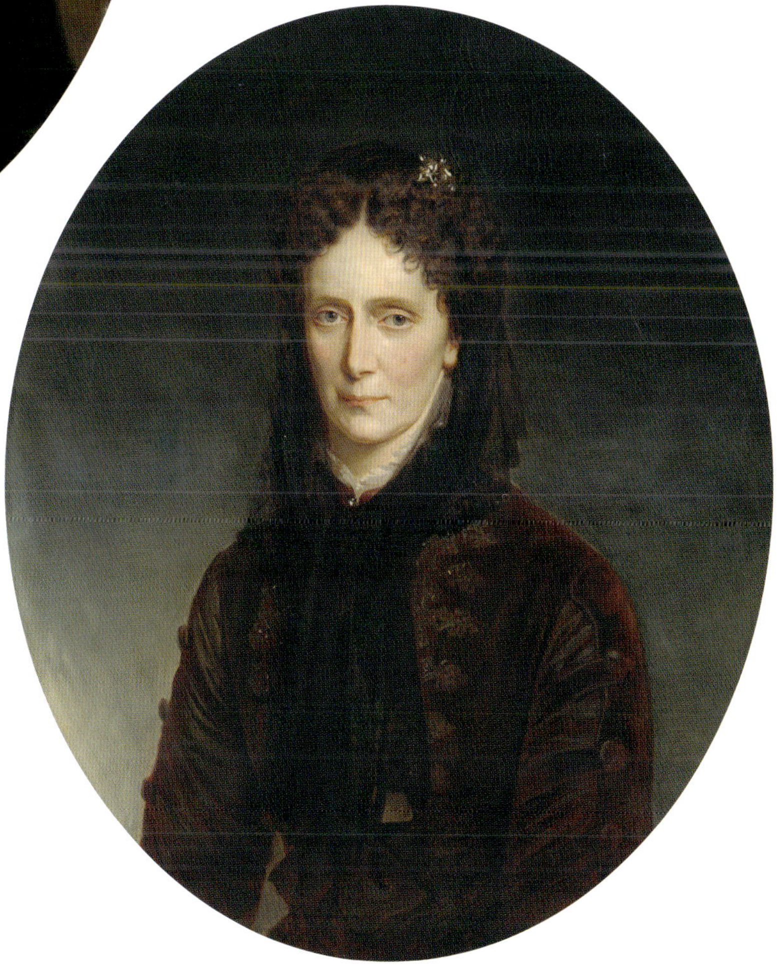

ROBERT GARRARD II (1793–1881) for R. & S. GARRARD & CO.

115 *Emperor Alexander II of Russia's collar and badge (Great George) of the Order of the Garter* 1867

Gold and enamel, (collar) 145.5 × 39.0 cm, (Great George) 5.4 × 4.2 × 2.1 cm
Hallmarked for London, 1867/8, in 22 carat gold
RCIN 440084.a–b

WILLIAM COMYNS (1885–1930) for R. & S. GARRARD & CO.

Emperor Alexander II of Russia's investiture badge (Lesser George) of the Order of the Garter 1867

Gold, 8.5 × 4.1 cm
Hallmarked for London, 1867/8, in 18 carat gold
RCIN 441392

Emperor Alexander II of Russia's star of the Order of the Garter 1867

Gold, silver and enamel, 9.2 × 8.3 cm
Engraved on reverse: *R & S Garrard & Co. / Goldsmiths and Jewellers / to the Crown / 25 Haymarket / London*;
stamped with maker's mark: *W.C*
RCIN 441399

ENGLISH

Emperor Alexander II of Russia's sash of the Order of the Garter ?c.1867

Moiré silk, 162.5 × 10.1 cm
RCIN 100030

Provenance Issued to Emperor Alexander II, 1867; returned to Queen Victoria, 1881

Literature Gavrilova 2015

In the years between 1813 and the end of the monarchy, all Russian emperors were appointed Knights of the Garter. This began with Emperor Alexander I, who was appointed in 1813, but only formally elected and installed as a Knight of the Garter during his visit to England in 1814, news of which was reported by Ambassador Lieven to the Russian foreign minister, Count Rumyantsev, on 19 July 1814.[102]

The bestowal of the Garter on Nicholas I by George IV in 1827 was followed by the appointments of Alexander II in 1867, Alexander III in 1881 and the future Nicholas II in 1893. The final appointment was to Michael Alexandrovich, brother of Nicholas II, and heir to the throne at the time of King Edward VII's coronation in 1902. Emperor Alexander II was invested 'with the Ensigns and Habit' of the Most Noble Order of the Garter in the Throne Room of Tsarskoe Selo on 28 July 1867.

The Emperor's appointment had long been in discussion – it was first suggested at the time of his visit to Britain in 1839 while he was Tsesarevich; however, at that time it was deemed inappropriate, and Queen Victoria felt that such an appointment would not be approved of by her Uncle Leopold, King of the Belgians. The Queen recorded in her diary a discussion of the topic with Lord Melbourne.[103] The topic was next discussed in October 1866, at the time of the visit

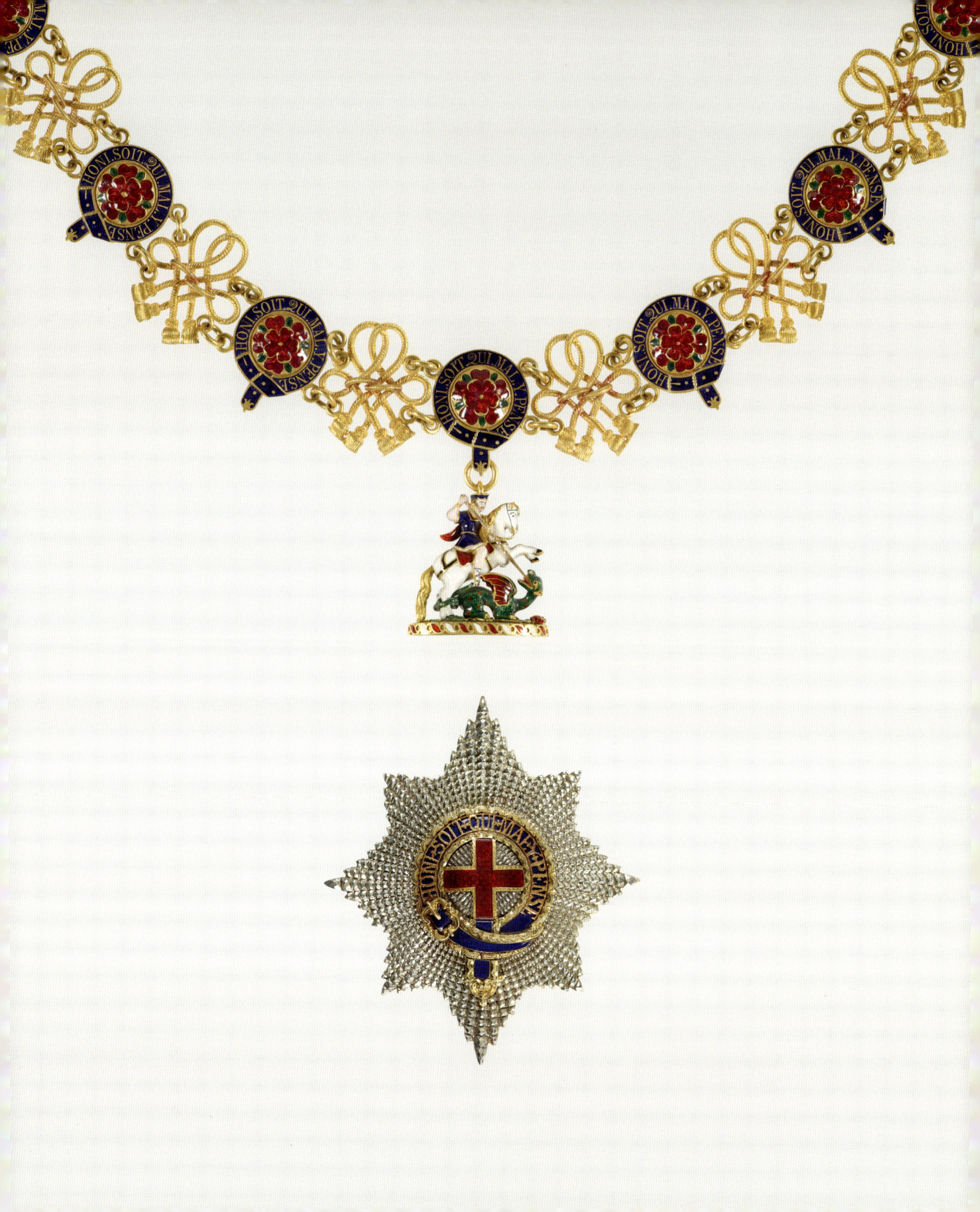
HONI SOIT QUI MAL Y PENSE

FIG. 38
W. & D. Downey
*Nicholas II, Emperor of Russia, when Tsesarevich, c.*1893
Platinum print, 32.5 × 18.8 cm
RCIN 2926952

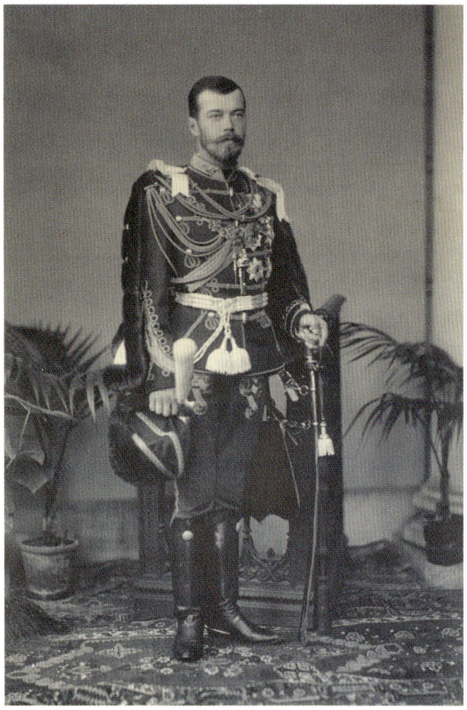

of Albert Edward, Prince of Wales, to Russia to attend the marriage of the future Alexander III to the Prince's sister-in-law, Princess Dagmar of Denmark. The visit also aimed to help rebuild relations between Russia and Britain.

An approach was made by Baron de Brunnov, Russian ambassador, for the Emperor to receive the Garter at this time. The Foreign Secretary, Lord Stanley (1826–93), reported the conversation to the Queen, suggesting that the Emperor would be 'greatly flattered and pleased if he were to receive the Garter from Your Majesty'. The Foreign Secretary went on to say that the Prime Minister, Lord Derby (1799–1869), agreed with the Foreign Secretary that 'such a compliment would not be unsuitable as showing a disposition, on the part of England, to renew with Russia those cordial relations which were interrupted by the Crimean war'.[104] Queen Victoria, however, was not in favour:

> *the most friendly relations sh^{d} exist between Engl^{d} & Russia, & it was in consequence of the representation made by Ld Derby, that the visit of the P. of W. w^{d} tend towards that object, that H.M. did not insist on the strong objection w^{h} she felt to that visit, at this time of year. To give the Garter to the Emp^{r} as well, seems to H.M. quite unnecessary*[105]

The matter rested until June the following year when the Prime Minister again raised it, this time at the behest of the Prince of Wales. There was a concern that the Emperor 'cannot but contrast this appearance of indifference very unfortunately with the [...] reception which He himself gave to the Prince of Wales. That which the Prince most desires is to have the Garter given to the Emperor; and although I am aware that it has been once refused, I have ventured to urge it on the Queen'.[106] The Queen was swayed by these arguments.[107]

In his response to Queen Victoria's agreement to the bestowal of the Garter on the Emperor, Lord Derby mentioned that 'from frequent conversations which he has had with Baron de Brunnow, that this is the Honor of which the Emperor is the most desirous, and by obtaining which He would be most flattered; and in a political point [...]; inasmuch as it will to a certain degree counteract the attractions which will be held out at Paris'.[108] The Emperor's desire might have been related to his father, Nicholas I's fondness for the Garter. Queen Victoria had been told in 1839 by Lord Melbourne – who, the Queen noted, had tears in his eyes – that Nicholas I 'never wore any other Foreign Order but that' (the Garter).[109]

News of the appointment was passed to the Prince of Wales, who wrote to the Queen: 'Let me now thank you [...] for having given the Emperor of Russia the Garter - & I hear that he is immensely pleased'.

The insignia was supplied by Garrard. The cost of the insignia and other items, three silver-gilt boxes, mantle, Garter shield, seven velvet cushions with tassels (for the investiture ceremony), the silver underhabit, plume, materials for the banner in St George's Chapel, trunks for transportation, Garter ribbon and binding of the statutes came to £538 2s.[110]

The Emperor wore his Garter insignia at the time of the marriage of his daughter, Grand Duchess Maria Alexandrovna, to Prince Alfred, Duke of Edinburgh, in January 1874, and during his subsequent visit to London in May that year. They were, in sadder times, to form part of the display of the Emperor's insignia at his funeral, after his assassination in 1881. Following the funeral, the insignia was returned to London and displayed, at Queen Victoria's command, at Windsor Castle.

While Queen Victoria prevaricated and delayed the appointment of Alexander II, she was generous and spontaneous with the appointment of Alexander III at the time of his sudden accession in 1881. The appointment was an overt act of support by the shocked Queen to the new Emperor, who had so unexpectedly succeeded to the throne after his father's murder. This act was recognised by the Emperor in his letter of thanks to the Queen (cat. 122), in which he expressed his personal appreciation for the Queen's concern and support, but also his political view of the relationship between Britain and Russia.[111] Nicholas II's appointment was similarly unexpected, but under happier circumstances; the young Tsesarevich receiving it from Queen Victoria at Windsor at the time of the marriage of George, Duke of York and Princess May of Teck in July 1893 (fig. 38). The Queen recorded in her Journal:

> *Just before 2, the young Césarewitch arrived, & I received him at the top of the staircase [...] He is charming, & wonderfully like Georgie. He always speaks English ... He is very simple & unaffected [...] Then [after luncheon] went into the Audience Room, where I invested Nicky with the Garter, after which he took leave.*[112] **SJP**

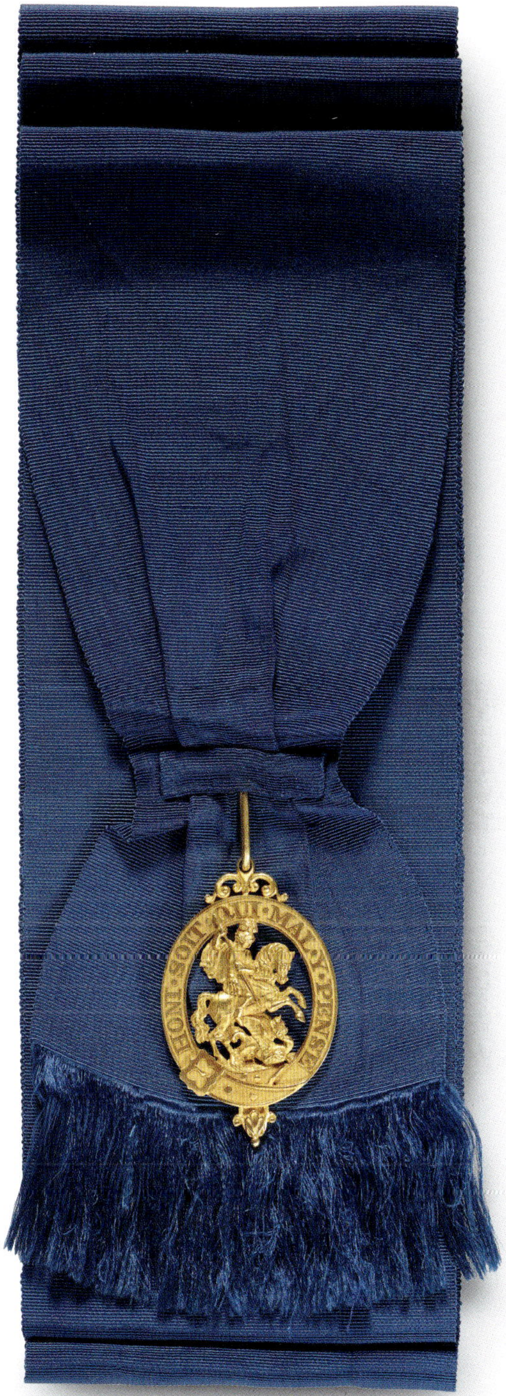

IVAN KEIBEL AND HEINRICH KAMMERER

116 *Collar and badge of the Order of St Andrew the First Called* 1842

Gold and enamel, (collar) 149.0 cm, (trophies) 4.5 × 4.6 cm, (eagles) 4.5 × 4.1 cm, (ciphers) 3.5 × 3.5 cm, (badge) 8.8 × 5.2 cm
St Petersburg city mark of a double-headed imperial eagle, and the date, 1842, with the maker's mark, *KK*, above
RCINS 441511 (collar), 441512 (badge)

MORTIMER & HUNT

Star of the Order of St Andrew the First Called with Garter c.1854

Silver, gold and enamel, 9.6 × 9.4 cm
Engraved: *Mortimer & Hunt / Jewellers to the Queen / London and Belonged to / A.E. /Prince of Wales*
RCIN 441513

Provenance (RCINS 441511–2) Presented to Albert Edward, Prince of Wales by Emperor Nicholas I, 1844; (RCIN 441513) Commissioned by Albert Edward, Prince of Wales

Literature Patterson 1996

The Order of St Andrew was founded in 1698 by Peter I, on his return from Europe. Peter's creation of the Order may have been influenced by the belief that the Scottish Order of the Thistle, refounded by James VII and II (1633–1701), dedicated to St Andrew, was in abeyance.

George IV was the first British monarch to receive the Order of St Andrew (along with the Orders of St Alexander Nevskii and St Anne), a reciprocal appointment to the Emperor Alexander I receiving the Order of the Garter. The Prince Regent was delighted with the appointment, and Lieven wrote to the state secretary, Count Nesselrode in St Petersburg, that in thanks for Lieven's part in the Prince Regent's investiture with the Orders of Russia, Lieven was invited to visit him at Brighton Pavilion; there he was presented with a portrait miniature, the imagery adapted to show the Prince Regent wearing his Russian Orders with a uniform matching that of a Russian general.[113] In the years until the fall of the monarchy in Russia, the Order of St Andrew was received by all British kings and a number of other members of the royal family.

The Order of St Andrew was awarded to William IV when Duke of Clarence, at the time of the imperial visit to London in 1814. While worn by Russian empresses, it was not bestowed on ladies, and thus Queen Victoria did not receive the decoration; however, Prince Albert did, receiving the insignia on 22 December 1843, as Queen Victoria reported in her Journal: 'Before dinner Baron Brunow brought Albert the Order of St. Andrew, the 1rst Russian order, which the Emperor has sent Albert calling him "Mon Frère et Cousin" which hitherto no one but the King of the French has done. This conferring of the order, is meant as a return for our civility to the Gd Duke Michael.'[114] The award, and the opportunity to address the Prince by the title 'Mon Frère et Cousin', was a way for the Emperor to express his recognition of Prince Albert's position and thus signal his regard for the Queen's consort.

Prince Albert, in his letter of thanks to the Emperor, wrote in similar terms:

> *Sir, my brother and cousin, the Baron Brunnow has delivered to me your Imperial Majesty's letter of the 23 of November together with the decorations of your Imperial Majesty's Order of St Andrew by which it was accompanied* [...]
>
> *And it affords me much pleasure to accept the order which your imperial majesty has had the goodness to transport and to which I will attach a particular value, both as a token of your Imperial Majesty's friendship and regard.*[115]

The insignia was brought to London by Prince Dimitry Nesselrode, son of the Russian foreign minister (cat. 69).[116]

Awards as a result of visits continued with Edward VII's appointment as a two-year-old,

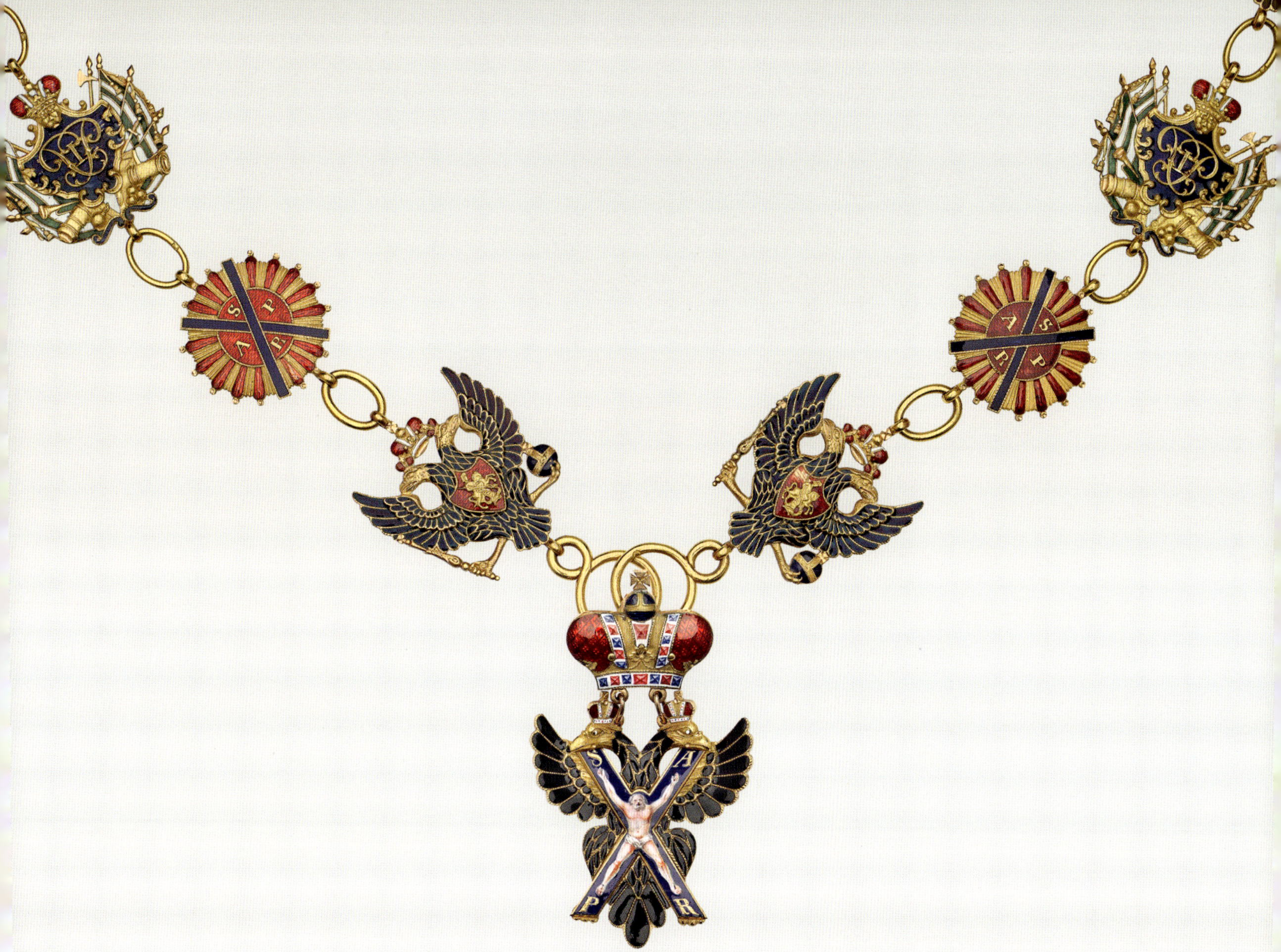
S A P R

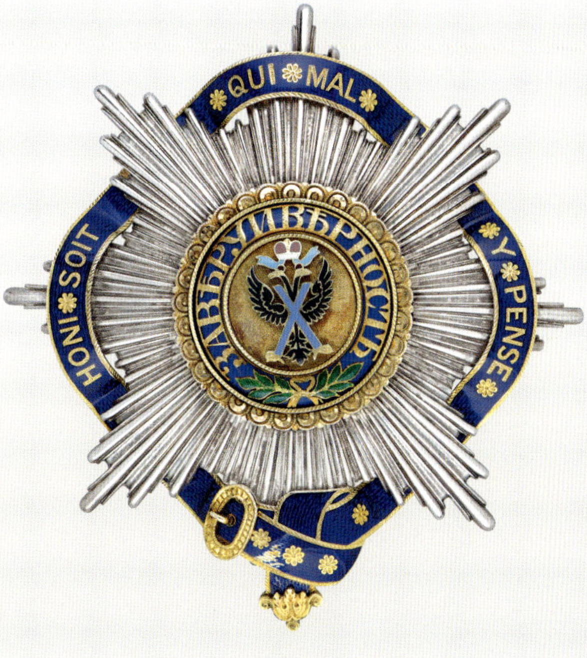
HONI SOIT
QUI MAL
Y PENSE
ЗАВѢРУИВѢРНОСТЬ

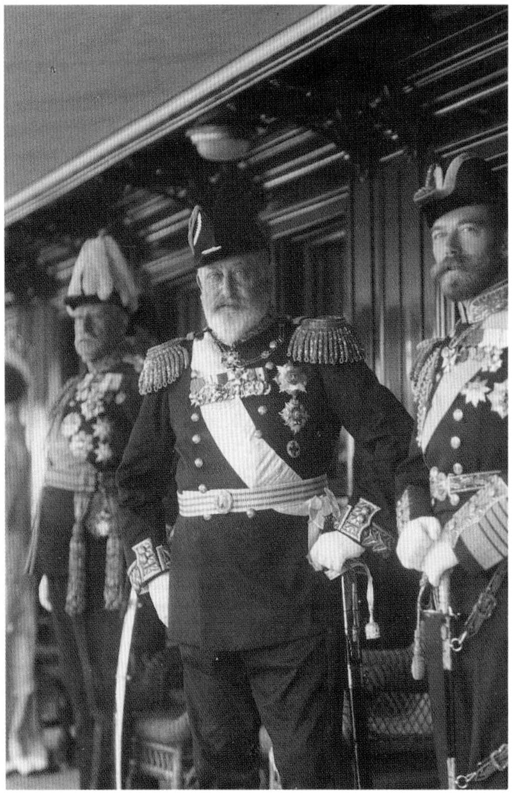

FIG. 39
C.E. von Hahn & Co.
King Edward VII and Nicholas II, Emperor of Russia on the deck of the Russian Imperial Yacht Standart *during the Cowes Regatta, 1909* (detail of King Edward VII), August 1909
Gelatin silver print,
16.4 × 22.0 cm
RCIN 2930293

which took place at the end of the visit of Nicholas I, as recorded in Queen Victoria's diary: 'After luncheon, [...] Baron Brunow brought the Gd Cross of St. Andrew to Bertie, which the Emperor has been kind enough to give him, & Albert brought him in to me, with the star & ribbon on.'[117]

The Queen recorded this cheerful sight in an impromptu sketch (fig. 51) – the young prince dressed in the 'Russian costume' that he was regularly depicted wearing at this time. The appointment was recorded in the Register of the Order on 28 May 1844.[118]

The future George V received the Order from his uncle, Alexander III, in August 1893, following his wedding and the bestowal of the Garter on his cousin (p. 187). The order was delivered to him by M. de Staal, Russian ambassador in London, and the Duke of York wrote his thanks to his uncle on 26 August that year:

> *My dearest Uncle Sacha,*
> *I must write you these lines to thank you for sending me the order of ST Andrew which I have just received from M.de Staal, I can assure you that I am very pleased & proud to have it, & I am much touched by your kindness in giving it me.*[119]

More widely bestowed than the Garter, it was held by all Grand Dukes in Russia and by close family members across the generations, which included Prince Albert's father, as brother-in-law of the Emperor Alexander. Later generations included Prince Andrew of Greece (father of HRH The Duke of Edinburgh), who received it at the time of his marriage to Princess Alice of Battenberg, he a cousin of Nicholas II, she a niece of the Empress.

Edward VII's collar was shortened in 1865 by Garrard, at a cost of £1 15s.,[120] in preparation for the wedding of the Prince's sister-in-law to the future Emperor Alexander III in St Petersburg. Based on portraiture, the Prince of Wales may well have worn two collars of the Order during his life, one in the form of 1842, and another after the second pattern which emerged following the heraldic reorganisations of Alexander II in 1856–7. He is depicted wearing a more modern collar in Tuxen's (1853–1927) painting of the marriage of Nicholas II in 1894 to that which he is seen wearing in Chevalier's (1828–1902) depiction of the 1874 wedding of the Duke and Duchess of Edinburgh (cat. 174).

The star entwined with the symbol of the Order of the Garter was commissioned by the Prince of Wales so that in Russia he could wear the Order of the Garter as well as the Order of St Andrew (cat. 116), this continued a tradition started by Emperor Alexander I.[121] **SJP**

ALBERT KEIBEL

117 *Badge and star of the Order of St Anne, First Class* c.1893

Silver, gold, enamel, (badge, including suspension loop) 7.5 × 4.9 cm, (star) 9.0 × 9.1 cm
Badge stamped on suspension ring with assay mark of St Petersburg, fineness mark 56 and maker's initials, *AK*, for Albert Keibel; star has silver marks for St Petersburg, an imperial eagle, fineness mark *84*, and maker's name, *Keibel*
RCINS 441518, 441519

Provenance Presented to King George V when Duke of York by Emperor Alexander III, 1893

Literature Patterson 1996

The Order of St Anne was founded by Karl Friedrich, Duke of Schleswig-Holstein (1700–1739) in 1735, in memory of his wife, Anna Petrovna (1708–28), eldest surviving daughter of Emperor Peter I. The Order was made a Russian Order by Emperor Paul I, grandson of Anna Petrovna and Karl Friedrich, on his coronation day, 5 April 1797; the Emperor can be seen wearing a badge of the Order in diamonds in his portrait after Voille (cat. 43).

The gold and red enamel badge, with gold filigree work between the arms, bears an image of St Anne, mother of the Virgin Mary, standing in a woodland. On the reverse are the entwined letters, *AJPF*, crowned, standing for *Anna, Imperatoris Petri Filia* ('Anna, daughter of Emperor Peter').

The silver star has at its centre a red enamel cross on gold background and is surrounded by the motto, *AMAN.*[tibus] *JUST.*[itiam] *PIET.*[atem] *FID.*[em] ('To the lovers of justice, piety and faith'), with two putti holding a crown above. SJP

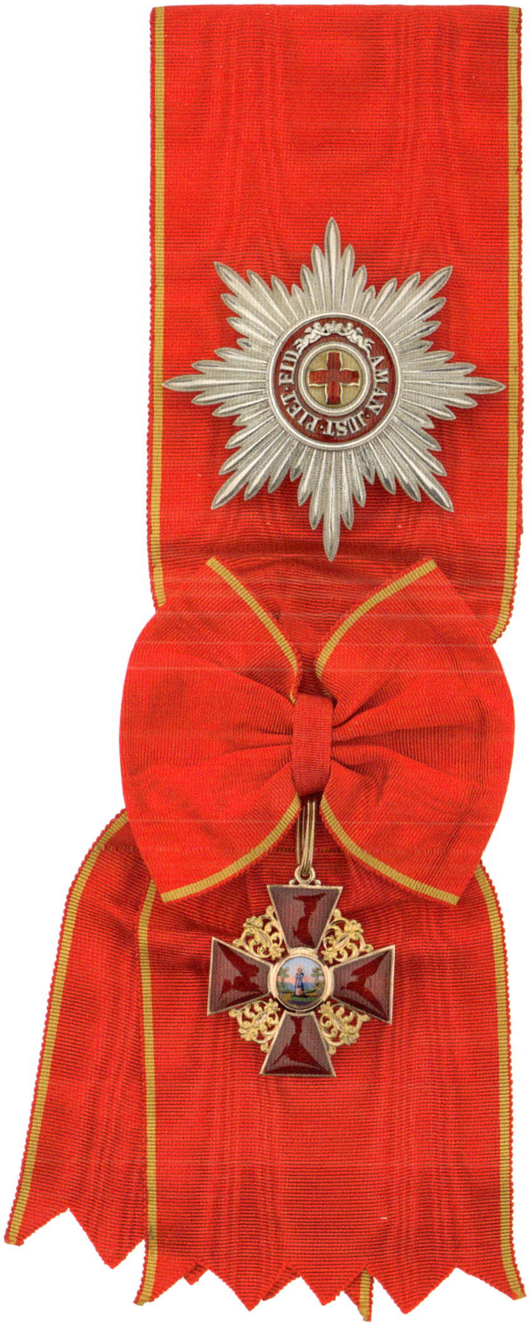

ATTRIBUTED TO KEIBEL

118 *Badge of the Order of St Alexander Nevskii* c.1842

Gold and enamel, 8.1 × 5.2 cm (inc. suspension loop)
Stamped on reverse with imperial eagle, below the enamel on the upper arm, with the assay mark of St Petersburg, and on the reverse of the loop: *184-*
RCIN 441514

WILLIAM CHAPMAN FOR R. & S. GARRARD

Star of the Order of St Alexander Nevskii c.1865

Silver, gold and enamel, 8.5 × 8.5 cm
Reverse engraved: *R. & S. Garrard & C°. / Goldsmiths to the Crown / Haymarket London*; also on reverse, stamp *W. C* of William Chapman, who entered his mark on 14 November 1859
RCIN 441515

Provenance (RCIN 441514) Presented to Albert Edward, Prince of Wales by Nicholas I, 1844; (RCIN 441515) Albert Edward, Prince of Wales

Literature Patterson 1996

The badge consists of a red enamel cross with, in the centre, an enamel scene depicting the saint on horseback, riding towards a city, while a hand from heaven holds a laurel wreath over his head. Between the arms of the cross are four imperial eagles, and on the reverse, the entwined and crowned cipher, *SA*. The star bears the saint's crowned cipher surrounded by the Order's motto: *ЗА ТРУДЫ И ОТЕЧЕСТВО* ('For labour and the fatherland'), above crossed crowned leaves. Founded by Empress Catherine I in 1725, the Order was dedicated to St Alexander Nevskii, Prince of Novgorod, Grand Prince of Kiev and Grand Prince of Vladimir (1221–63), who, according to chroniclers, defeated the Swedes on the banks of the Neva, and a combined German and Estonian army on Lake Peipus. The badge was part of the imperial appointment of 1844, while the star was made for Albert Edward, Prince of Wales, in preparation for his visit to St Petersburg for the marriage of his sister-in-law, Princess Dagmar of Denmark, to the Tsesarevich Alexander, later Emperor Alexander III. It was supplied by Garrard at a cost of £21.[122] SJP

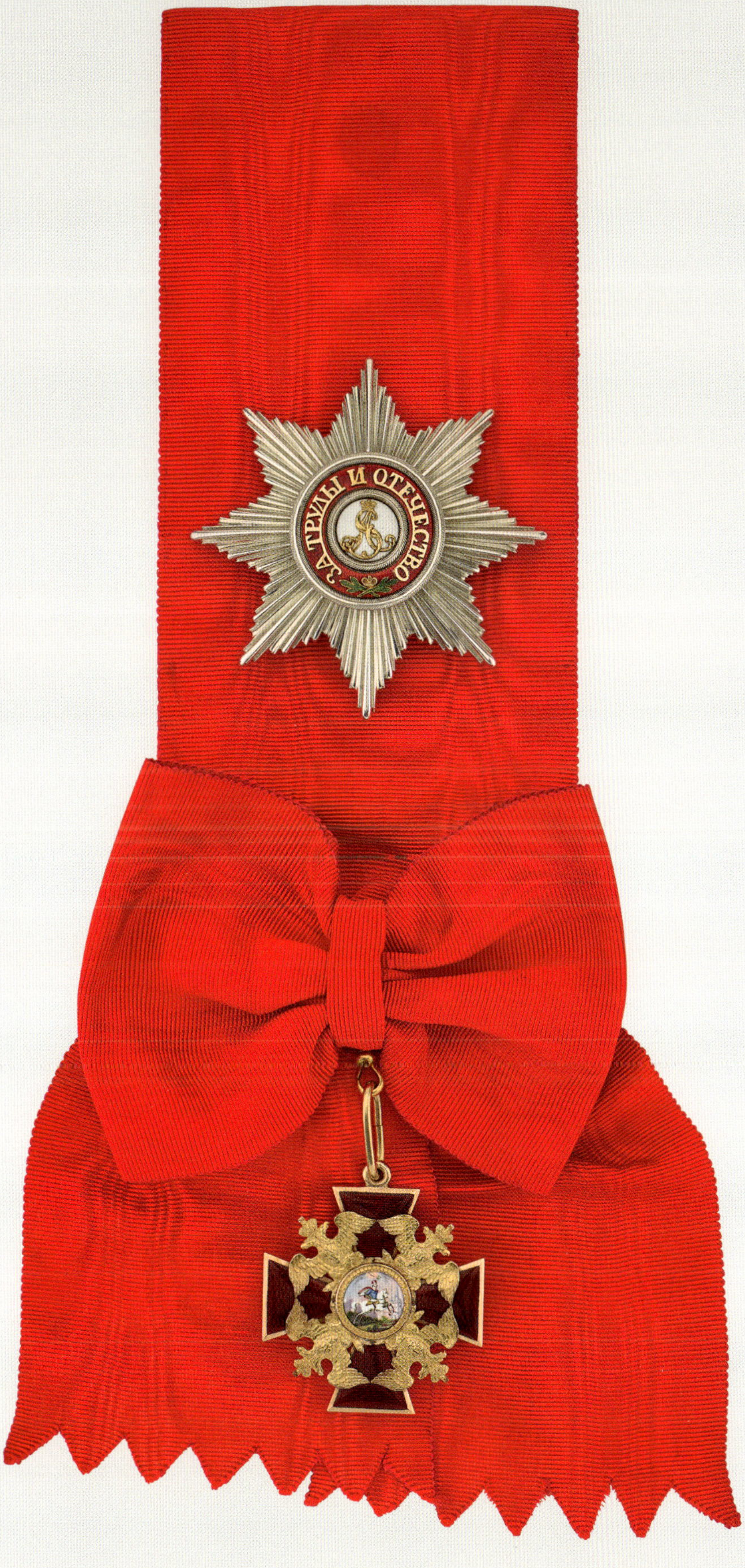
ЗА ТРУДЫ И ОТЕЧЕСТВО

KEIBEL & KAMMERER

119 *Badge of the Order of the White Eagle* 1842

Gold and enamel, 10.0 × 6.2 cm
Stamps of Keibel and Kammerer and assay mark of St Petersburg
RCIN 441517

KEIBEL

Star of the Order of the White Eagle c.1893

Silver gilt and enamel, 9.0 × 9.0 cm
Marked on star and pin with double-headed eagle, *KEIBEL* and assay mark of St Petersburg with fineness mark, 84
RCIN 441626

Provenance (RCIN 441517) Albert Edward, Prince of Wales or Prince Albert; (RCIN 441626) Part of the suite of insignia presented to King George V when Duke of York, 1893

The Order of the White Eagle was traditionally first founded by King Władysław of Poland (1260/61–1333) in 1325, and revived in 1705 by King Augustus II (1670–1733). It became a Russian Order in 1831, when it was integrated, along with the Order of St Stanislaus, with the Russian honours system.

The badge of gold and enamel bears a white eagle set on the badge of the Polish Order, superimposed on the Russian imperial (double-headed) eagle, surmounted by an imperial crown. On the reverse is the badge of the Polish Order of the White Eagle, on the Russian eagle's back, with the name of the Virgin Mary in the form of a stylised monogram. The suspension ring of an imperial crown is possibly (on stylistic grounds) not contemporary with the rest of the badge. The badge was presented to Albert Edward, Prince of Wales or to Prince Albert in 1843/44.

The silver-gilt star bears the motto of the Order, *PRO FIDE REGE ET LEGE* ('For faith, the king and the law'), on blue enamel surrounding a red and white enamel cross. SJP

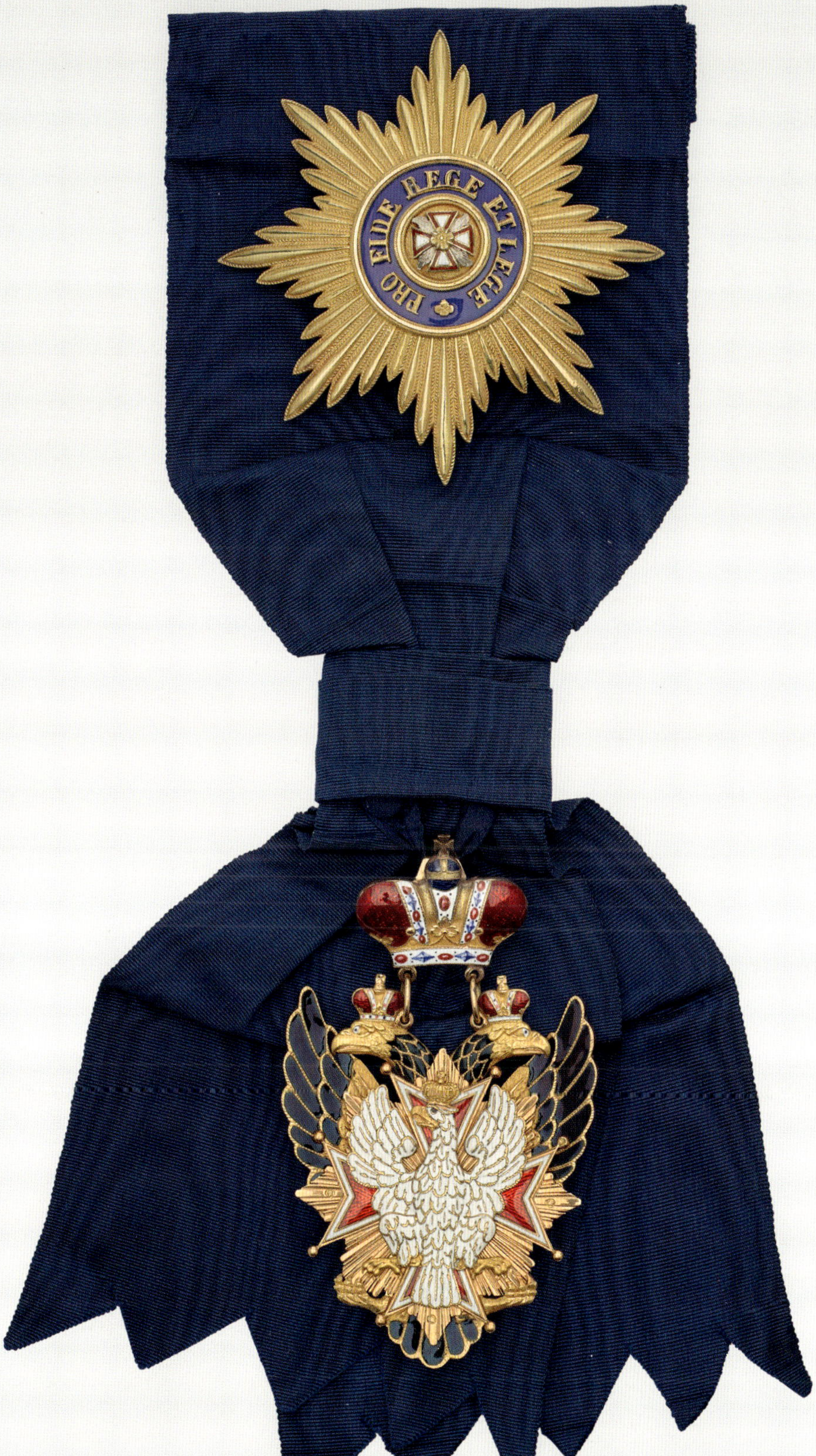
PRO FIDE REGE ET LEGE

ALBERT KEIBEL

120 *Badge and star of the Order of St Stanislaus, First Class* c.1893

Silver, gold, enamel, (badge, with suspension loop) 8.6 × 6.2 cm, (star) 9.1 × 9.0 cm
Badge marked on reverse with imperial eagle, assay mark of St Petersburg, fineness mark 56, and *AK*, for Albert Keibel; star marked, *Keibel*, with assay mark of St Petersburg and fineness mark 84
RCINS 441520, 441521

Provenance Presented to King George V, when Duke of York, by Alexander III, along with the Orders of St Andrew, St Alexander Nevskii, St Anne and the White Eagle, 1893

The Order was founded by King Stanislaus II Poniatowski of Poland (1732–98), in 1765, and was incorporated as a Russian Order by Emperor Nicholas I in 1831, at the same time as the Order of the White Eagle.

The red enamel badge of gold has four imperial eagles between the arms of the cross. In the centre, the monogram *SS* (*Sancte Stanislae*) is surrounded by a laurel wreath. The reverse is plain, without enamel, but with the repetition of the *SS* monogram. The silver star repeats the saint's monogram in red enamel, and the Order's motto, *PRAEMIANDO INCITAT* ('Encouraged by reward'). The motto is surrounded by four sets of oak leaves in gold, set on green enamel.

The silver smooth-rayed star has the saint's monogram in red enamel and the Order's motto, surrounded by four sets of oak leaves in gold. The reverse is gilt. SJP

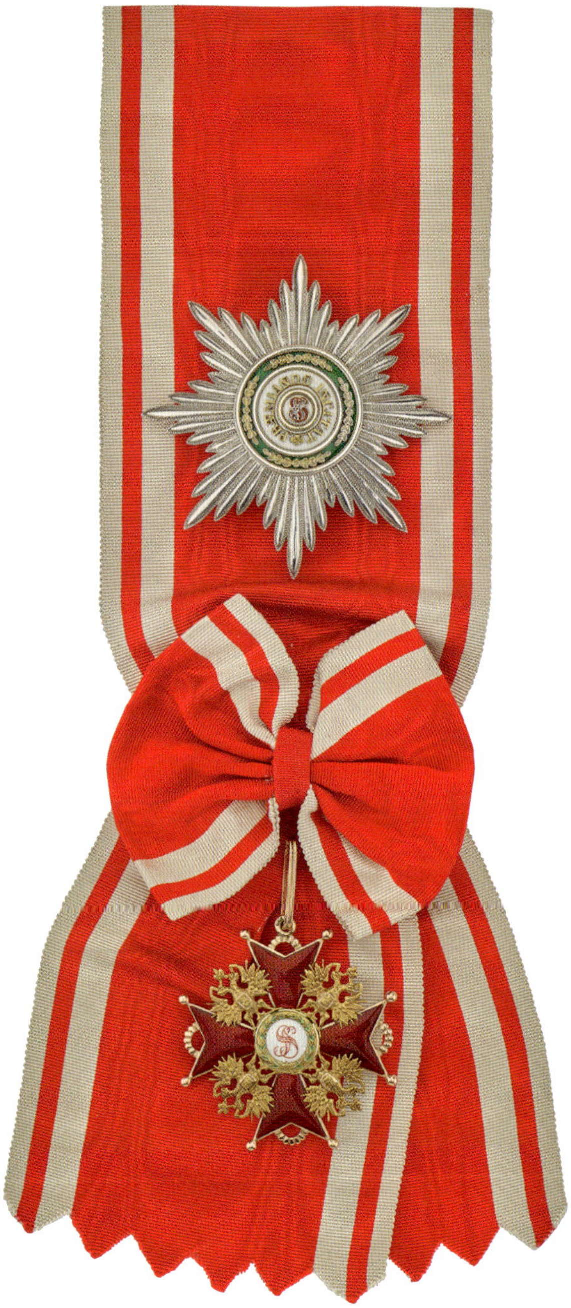

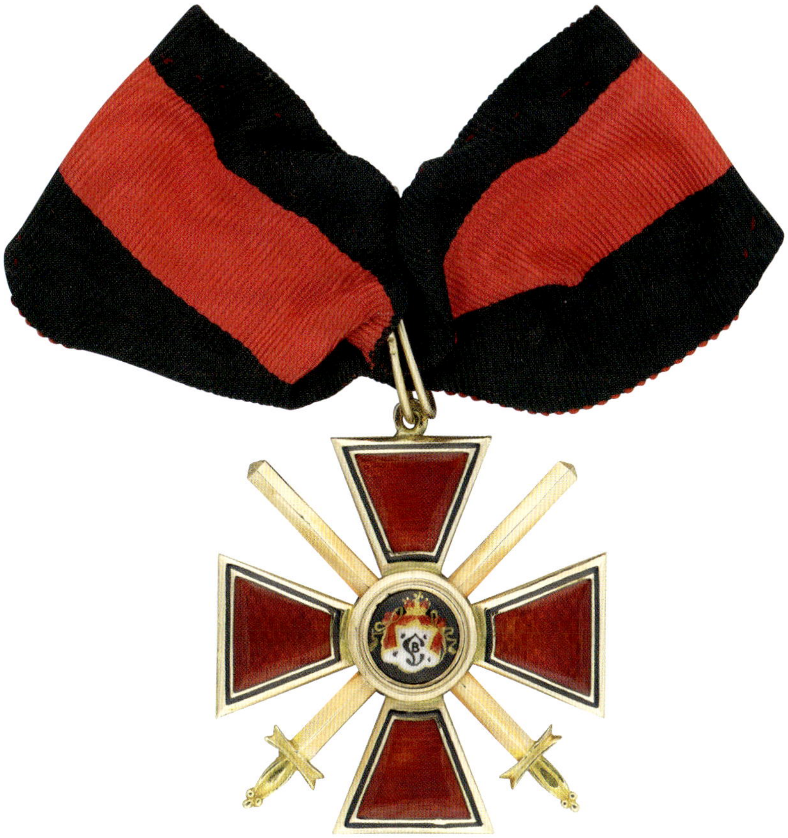

K. EDUARD

121 *Neck badge of the Order of St Vladimir, Third Class, with swords* c.1900

Gold and enamel, 4.9 × 4.3 cm, (loop) 1.7 cm
Beneath the enamel, on the reverse, marks of maker, K. Eduard, and workmaster, *ВД* (VD); below the enamel, fineness mark facing right on swords; on reverse of loop, fineness mark 56
RCIN 441516

Provenance Possibly Albert Edward, Prince of Wales

Literature Patterson 1996

The badge of gold and enamel has, in the centre of the cross, under a grand prince's crown on a royal mantle, the monogram of St Vladimir, Prince of Kiev (*c*.956–1015), who converted the Russian people to Christianity in 988. On the reverse appears the date of the Order's foundation by Catherine II: *22 СЕНТАБРА 1782* (22 September 1782, OS).

The ownership of this badge is unclear, as the future King George VI was appointed to the Fourth Class of the Order (with swords) for his service at the battle of Jutland, and all examples of the Order worn by Edward VII are shown without swords, indicating that he was appointed to the civil division, Third Class. The firm of Eduard, which made the badge, was, with Keibel, one of the two main suppliers of Orders and decorations to the imperial court at the turn of the twentieth century, and had exclusive rights from 1906. SJP

EMPEROR ALEXANDER III (1845–1894)

122 *Letter to Queen Victoria (1819–1901) from St Petersburg*

20 March/1 April 1881

Manuscript, 27.0 × 21.0 cm

RA VIC/MAIN/Z/106/4

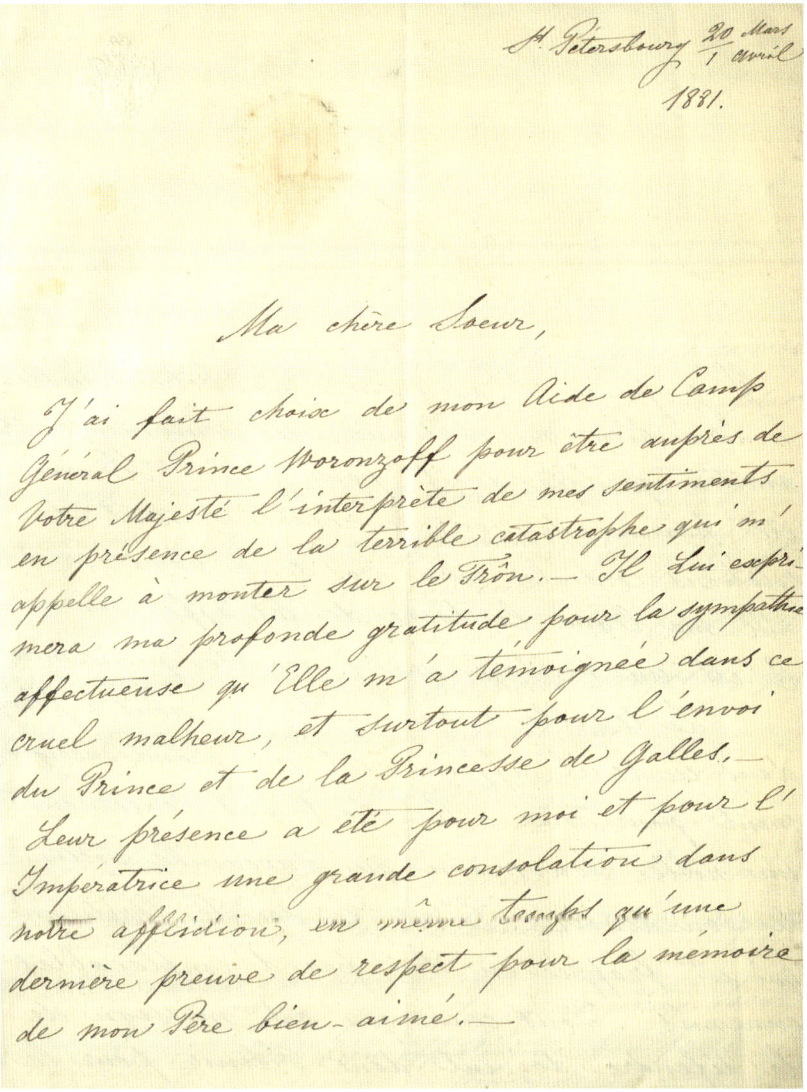

St Petersbourg 20 Mars / 1 Avril 1881.

Ma chère Soeur,

J'ai fait choix de mon Aide de Camp Général Prince Woronzoff pour être auprès de Votre Majesté l'interprète de mes sentiments en présence de la terrible catastrophe qui m'appelle à monter sur le Trône. — Il Lui exprimera ma profonde gratitude pour la sympathie affectueuse qu'Elle m'a témoignée dans ce cruel malheur, et surtout pour l'envoi du Prince et de la Princesse de Galles. — Leur présence a été pour moi et pour l'Impératrice une grande consolation dans notre affliction, en même temps qu'une dernière preuve de respect pour la mémoire de mon Père bien-aimé. —

Written in French (the European court language) by the new emperor of Russia, Alexander III, following his accession to the imperial throne after the assassination of his father on 1/13 March, this letter, formally announcing the Emperor's accession, was delivered to Queen Victoria by Prince Vorontsov when he saw the Queen on 8 April 1881 and regaled her with details of the assassination.

In the letter, the Emperor thanks the Queen for the presence of the Prince and Princess of Wales at the late Emperor's funeral; he comments that their presence had been a great consolation for him and the Empress. He speaks of his father dying a victim of his duty, of the threat to Christian society hit by its enemies, and continues that he hopes he could count on the Queen to be united with him in a common agreement to defend that society. As his father had done some eight years before, the Emperor asked for the Queen's affection for his sister, the Duchess of Edinburgh, and thanked the Queen for the Order of the Garter, which he appreciated as a mark of friendship. The Emperor also told the Queen how happy his father would have been at the re-establishment of cordial relations between the two countries, Britain and Russia. SJP

EMPEROR NICHOLAS II (1868–1918)

123 *Letter to King Edward VII (1841–1910), from St Petersburg*

16/29 January 1901

Manuscript, 20.2 × 12.6 cm

RA VIC/MAIN/F/23/27

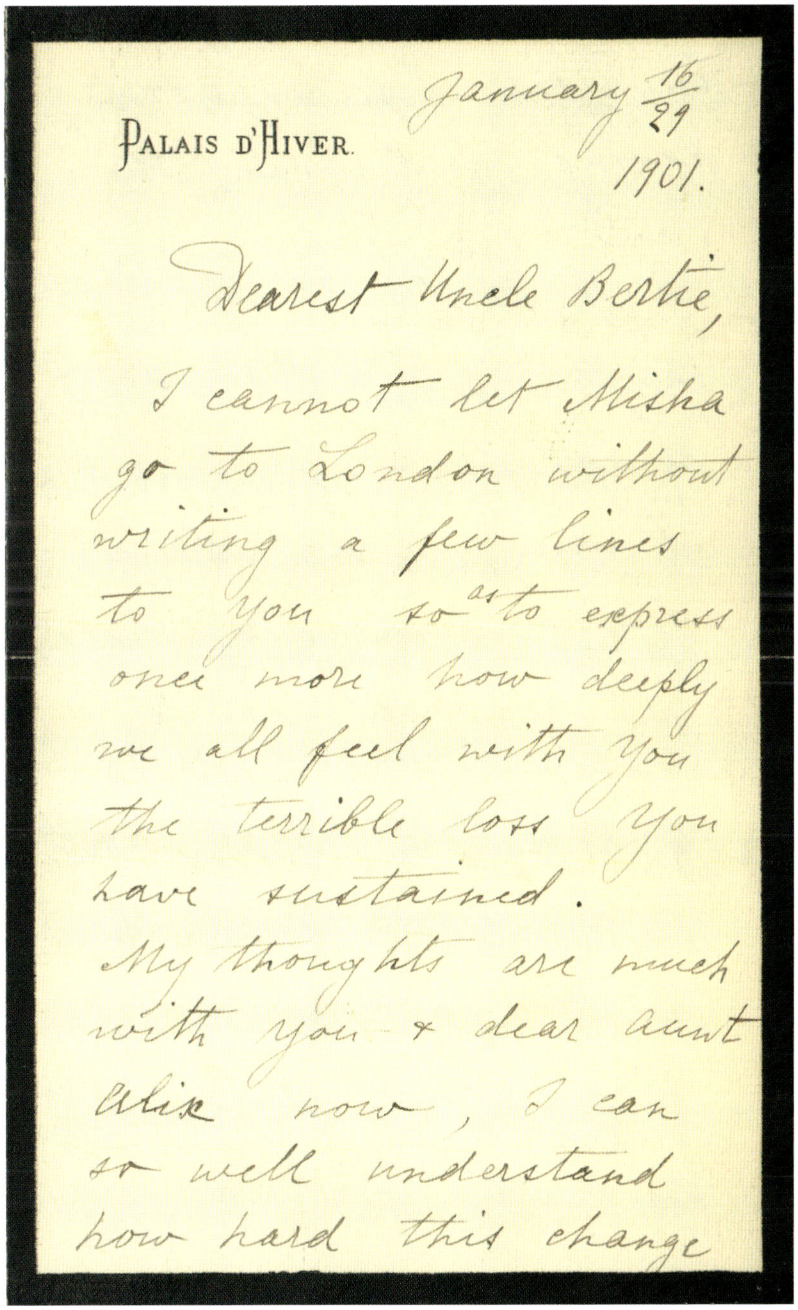

PALAIS D'HIVER.

January 16/29 1901.

Dearest Uncle Bertie,

I cannot let Misha go to London without writing a few lines to you so as to express once more how deeply we all feel with you the terrible loss you have sustained.

My thoughts are much with you & dear aunt Alix now, I can so well understand how hard this change

The letter was passed to the new King Edward VII, following his accession to the throne after the death of Queen Victoria on 22 January 1901. It was delivered by the Emperor's surviving brother (and the King's nephew), Grand Duke Michael Alexandrovich, who attended the Queen's funeral as the Emperor's representative.

The letter is written both by a relative passing his condolences to the new King and Queen (the Emperor's aunt), and as a fellow monarch with over six years' experience as a ruler. The Emperor remembers the kindness of the late Queen towards him in the past and the closeness that he felt towards her. He also hopes that 'the friendly relations between our two countries shall become still closer than in the past, notwithstanding occasional slight frictions in the Far East. May the new century bring England & Russia closer together for their mutual interests and for the general peace of the world'. The informal nature of the relationship can be identified in the language used by the Emperor at the end of the letter. While his father had written to Queen Victoria in 1881 as 'Votre bien affectionne bon frère', Nicholas signs this letter, 'Ever your devoted nephew and friend'. SJP

COLLINGWOOD & SONS, LONDON

124 *Royal Victorian Chain* 1902

Silver gilt, gold, enamel, (chain) 2.0 × 59.0 cm, (badge) 85.0 × 52.0 cm
Engraved on suspension loop, *24*, and on clasp, *xix*
RCIN 442785

Provenance Presented by King Edward VII to Emperor Nicholas II, 1904; sold by Gokhran, 1920s; collection of A. Khazin; presented to Her Majesty Queen Elizabeth II, 2016

Literature Gavrilova 2015

The Chain was intimately tied with the response of the British Royal Family to the news of the birth of a male heir to Nicholas II. The Princess of Wales wrote to her husband, the future King George V, on 14 August 1904:

> *My darling George, great was my delight yesterday to hear that dear Alicky has at last a son!* [...] *I am indeed glad for her, for them both, for Russia, that this heir has been born, what a comfort he will be to them in the midst of this horrid war and all their anxiety. I of course telegraphed Nicky.*[123]

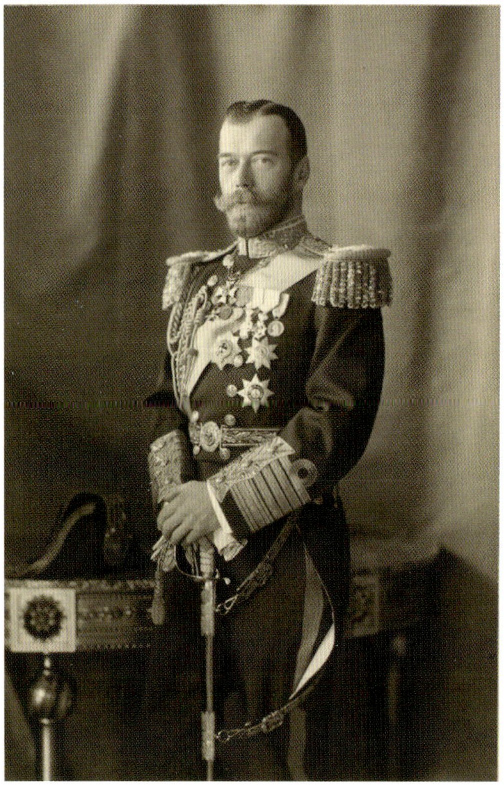

FIG. 40
Boissonnas & Eggler
Nicholas II, Emperor of Russia, c.1909
Gelatin silver print, 21.5 × 14.2 cm
RCIN 2926946

The Emperor wears the full dress uniform of a British Admiral of the Fleet, to which he was appointed at Reval in June 1908, along with the Royal Victorian Chain and the star and sash of the Order of the Garter.

On 21 August, the King wrote to the Emperor from Marienbad:

> *My dearest Nicky,*
> *I am sending these lines by Louis Battenberg whom I am so glad you have accepted as my representative at your own little boys christening on 24th. Nothing could have given me greater pleasure when the welcome news reached me and from the bottom of my heart do I congratulate you and dearest Alix on the birth of your son and heir* [...] *I beg your acceptance of the Victorian Chain on this occasion which I founded 2 years ago at my coronation and in remembrance of my beloved mother.*[124]

That the award and the messages were appreciated can be gleaned from the report of the British ambassador in St Petersburg, Sir Charles Hardinge (1858–1944), to the King, following the baptism ceremony at Peterhof. After describing the ceremonial, Sir Charles wrote to King Edward:

> *the Emperor and Empress Marie honoured the head of each mission with a few minutes conversation. In congratulating his majesty, I said that the birth of an heir to the throne had evoked much pleasure in England where the intimate relations existing between your Majesty's family and the Russian Imperial Family were well known and appreciated. His majesty replied that he had received a very warm and affectionate telegram and letter from your majesty and that he had been very much pleased at receiving the collar of the Victorian Order.*[125]

Along with the Royal Victorian Chain (fig. 40), which can be seen in Bogdanov-Belsky's (1868–1945) portrait of the Emperor (cat. 125), and which the Emperor wore during the meetings in

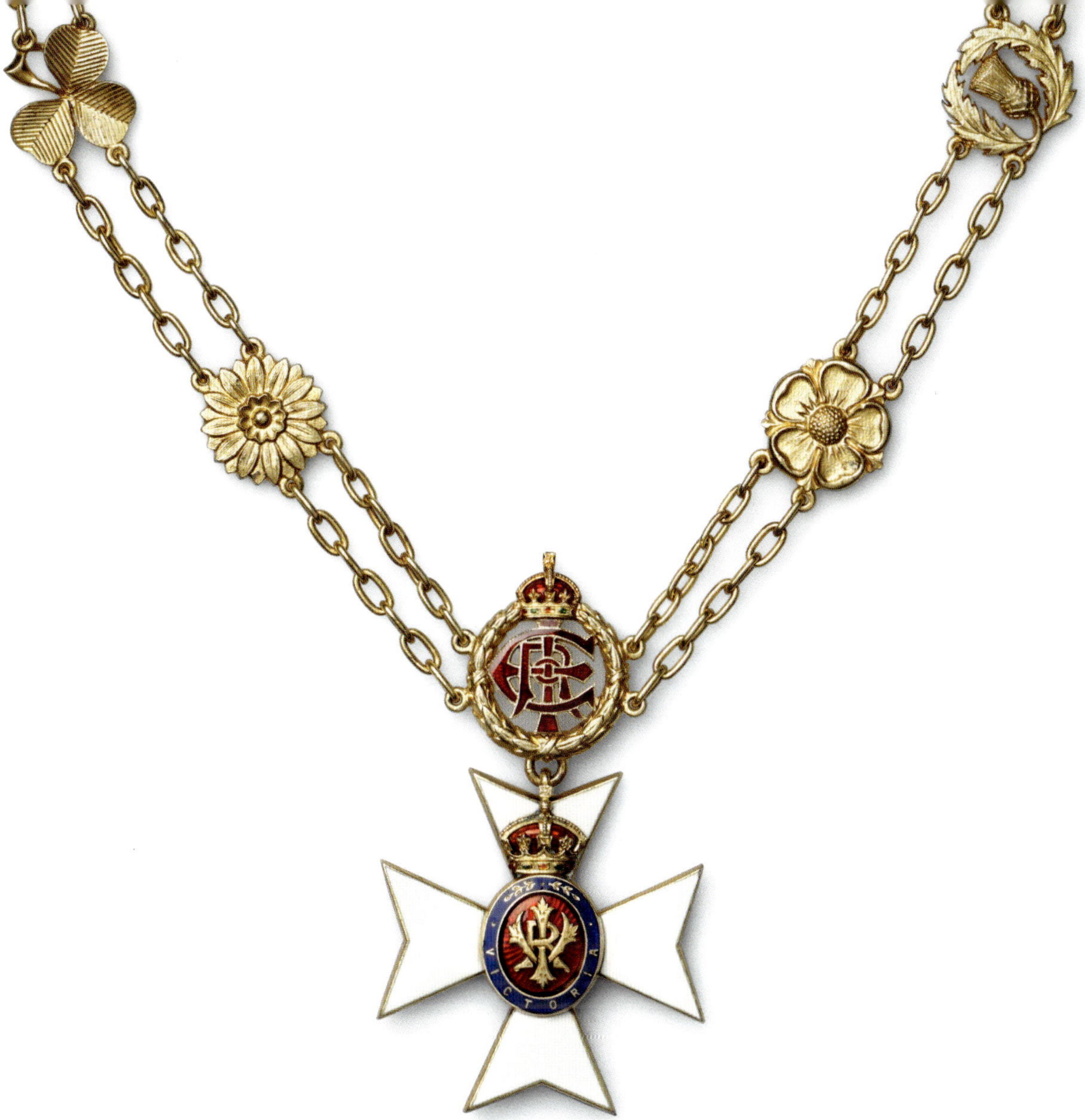

Reval and Cowes, the King sent the Tsesarevich a two-handled gold cup with commemorative inscription, supplied by Garrard; unusually, the British Royal Arms are surrounded not only with the Garter, but also the collar of the Order of St Andrew, which the King (as Prince of Wales) had received some 60 years before. The cup remains in the collection of the Moscow Kremlin Museums.

In 1914, the Chain was taken to Moscow from St Petersburg, along with the regalia and other treasures of the imperial collection and the Imperial Chancery, at the outbreak of the First World War. Confiscated after the February Revolution and nationalised following the October Revolution, it was sold by Gokhran at some point in the 1920s. Its provenance was confused because of a misunderstanding of the numbering on the chain, and it was only identified as the Emperor's in 2015. It was returned to Her Majesty Queen Elizabeth II for the Royal Collection in 2016, by its then owner.

SJP

NIKOLAI PETROVICH BOGDANOV-BELSKY (1868–1945)

125 *Nicholas II, Emperor of Russia (1868–1918)* 1908

Oil on canvas, 232.5 × 146.8 cm
Signed and dated: *Bogdanoff-Belsky 1908*
RCIN 406547

Provenance Presented to King Edward VII by the sitter, 1908; first recorded in the Centre Room, Buckingham Palace

Literature Cust 1909, p. 162

Painted by the Russian realist painter, Bogdanov-Belsky, this portrait of the Emperor was almost certainly presented to Edward VII after their meeting at Reval in June 1908, but before the imperial visit to Cowes in August 1909.[126] It was already recorded by Lionel Cust in the Centre Room at Buckingham Palace in his published catalogue of 1909. Nicholas II is dressed in the uniform of the 2nd Dragoons (Royal Scots Greys), to which he had been appointed colonel-in-chief in 1894. Photographs taken at Balmoral in 1896 record the sitter in the full uniform of the regiment (and may have been provided as a reference for the artist (fig. 41)). The Emperor wears the star and riband of the Garter and Royal Victorian Chain, the stars of the Orders of St Andrew and St Alexander Nevskii, and the badges of the Order of St Vladimir, the Danish Order of the Dannebrog and the Greek Order of the Redeemer.

By setting the portrait against the backdrop of the elegant northern façade and double colonnade of the Alexander Palace, the artist has created an entirely fictitious scene by amalgamating a terrace with its ornate iron balcony from the east wing of the palace building *c.*1896, by Silvio Dagnini (1867–1942), added as part of the remodelling of the palace in preparation for the residence of Nicholas II and his family. Access to the balcony was from the Empress's suite of rooms, it then wrapped round to the south side of the building, with steps down towards the Emperor's study. However, the structure adds a wonderful decorative quality to the painting and appears in numerous contemporary photographs.

Born into a peasant family in the Smolensk region, Bogdanov-Belsky trained under Ilya Repin (1844–1930), Russia's foremost realist painter, and later in Paris. In addition to portraits, he favoured genre and rural peasant scenes; this portrait exemplifies certain aspects of his style, notably the use of heightened colour and richly impastoed pigment. Passages of paint, for example the rendering of the lilac growing beyond the curlicues of the balcony, suggest an affinity with the symbolist painter, Victor Boris-Mustov (1870–1905). Indeed the presence of lilac in the painting may be an oblique reference to the Empress, whose favourite plant and hue this was.[127] Recent conservation has revealed the vibrancy of the original portrait, and also that the artist has used two different white pigments (lead white and zinc white) and has reworked certain areas, noticeably the sky, a number of times. **AB**

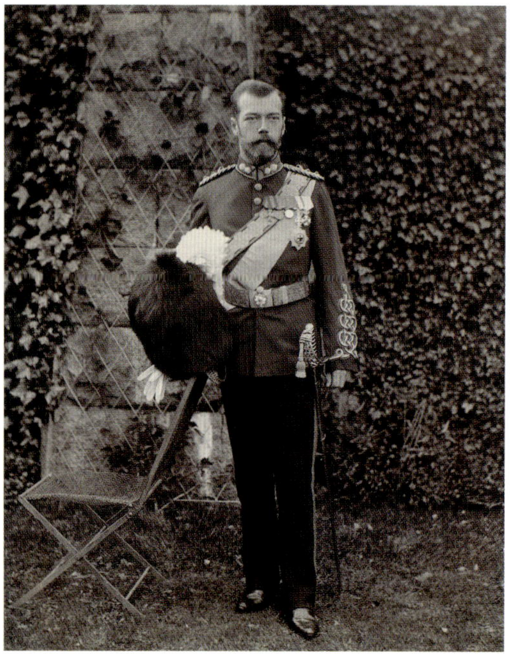

FIG. 41
Robert Milne
Czar in Scots Greys Uniform, September 1896
Gelatin silver print, 23.7 × 18.9 cm
RCIN 2160254

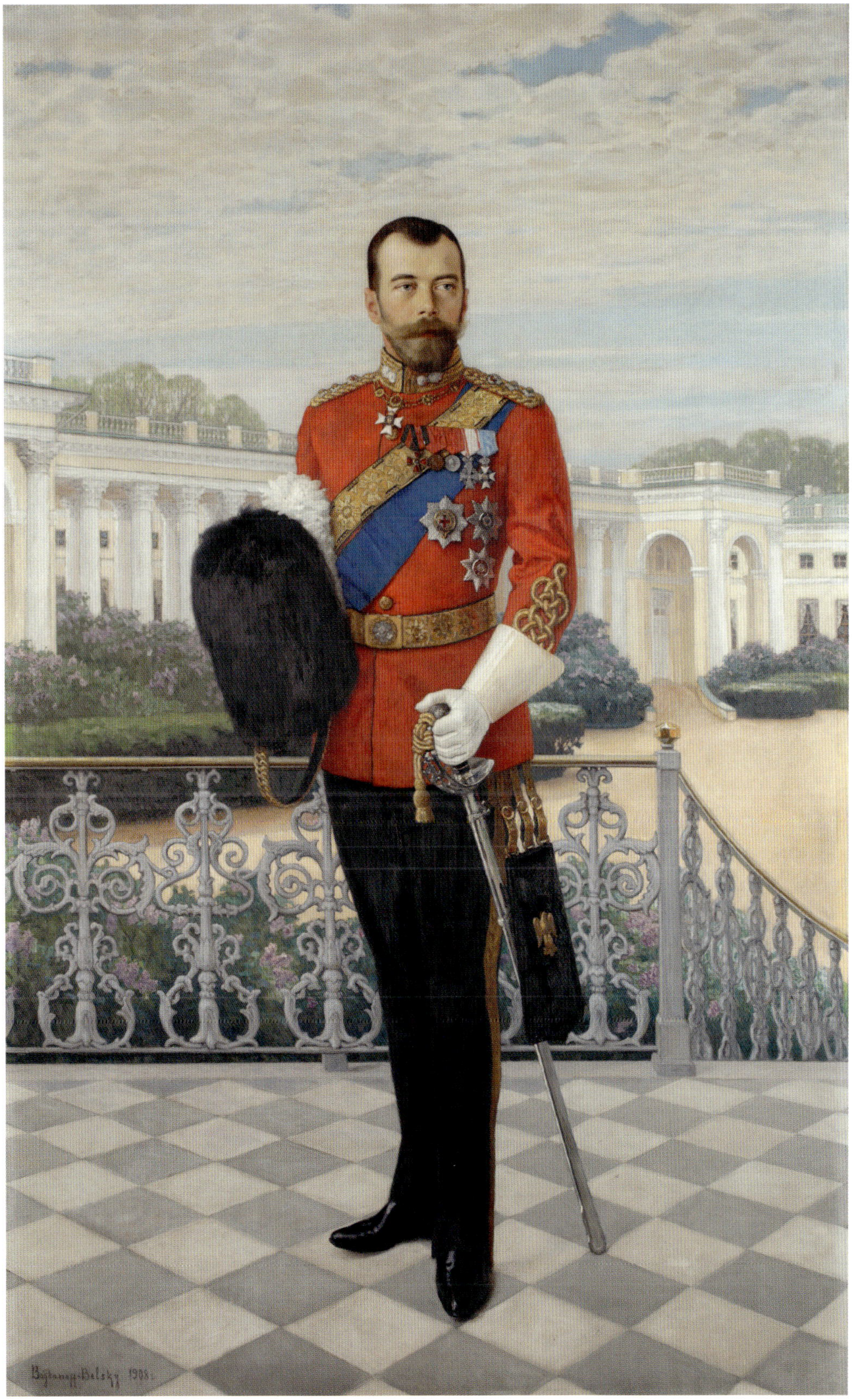

FABERGÉ; HENRIK EMANUEL WIGSTRÖM (1862–1923), workmaster

126 *Presentation bowl* 1908

Nephrite, silver gilt, enamel, moonstones, chalcedony, gold, 15.7 × 24.9 × 20.3 cm
Impressed with maker's mark of Henrik Wigström, 'FABERGE' in Cyrillic, assay mark of St Petersburg, and fineness mark, 88 zolotniks
RCIN 49821

Provenance Bought by Emperor Nicholas II; presented by him to King Edward VII and Queen Alexandra, to mark the meeting at Reval, 1908

Literature Bainbridge 1949, p. 92; de Guitaut 2003, p. 234; Tillander-Godenhielm 2005, p. 342

This vase was presented to King Edward VII by his nephew by marriage, Nicholas II, to mark their meeting at Reval in June 1908. The King was accompanied by Queen Alexandra and Princess Victoria, and they departed on the Royal Yacht *Victoria and Albert*, to be met by the Emperor and members of the imperial family on their yachts, *Standart* and *Polar Star*. The meeting involved diplomatic discussions, but was also a family reunion, with banquets and balls recorded in numerous photographs (cat. 128). The nephrite vase is mounted in silver gilt and gold, with white guilloché enamel, and is set with cabochon moonstones and chalcedony.

According to the accounts of the imperial cabinet, it was paid for on 23 May 1908 (2,500 rubles), but was not delivered to the King until November 1908. In return, King Edward VII presented his nephew with a naval sword made by Wilkinson, inscribed, *For His Imperial Majesty Emperor of All Russia Nicholas II from His Loving Uncle Edward Reval 1908*. The sword commemorated the King's appointment of the Emperor as an admiral of the fleet in the Royal Navy, a compliment which Nicholas II returned by according the King a similar honour in the Russian navy. The sword is now in the museum at Tsarskoe Selo. CDEG

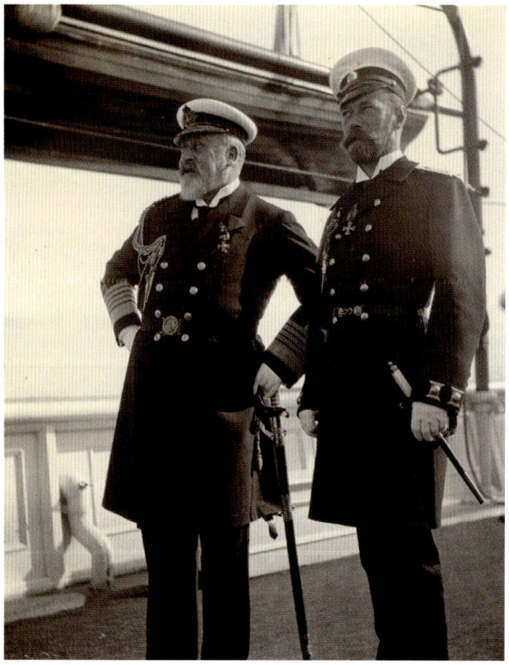

FIG. 42
Queen Alexandra
King Edward VII and Emperor Nicholas II at Reval, 1908
Silver gelatin print, 11.9 × 9.5 cm
RCIN 2916998

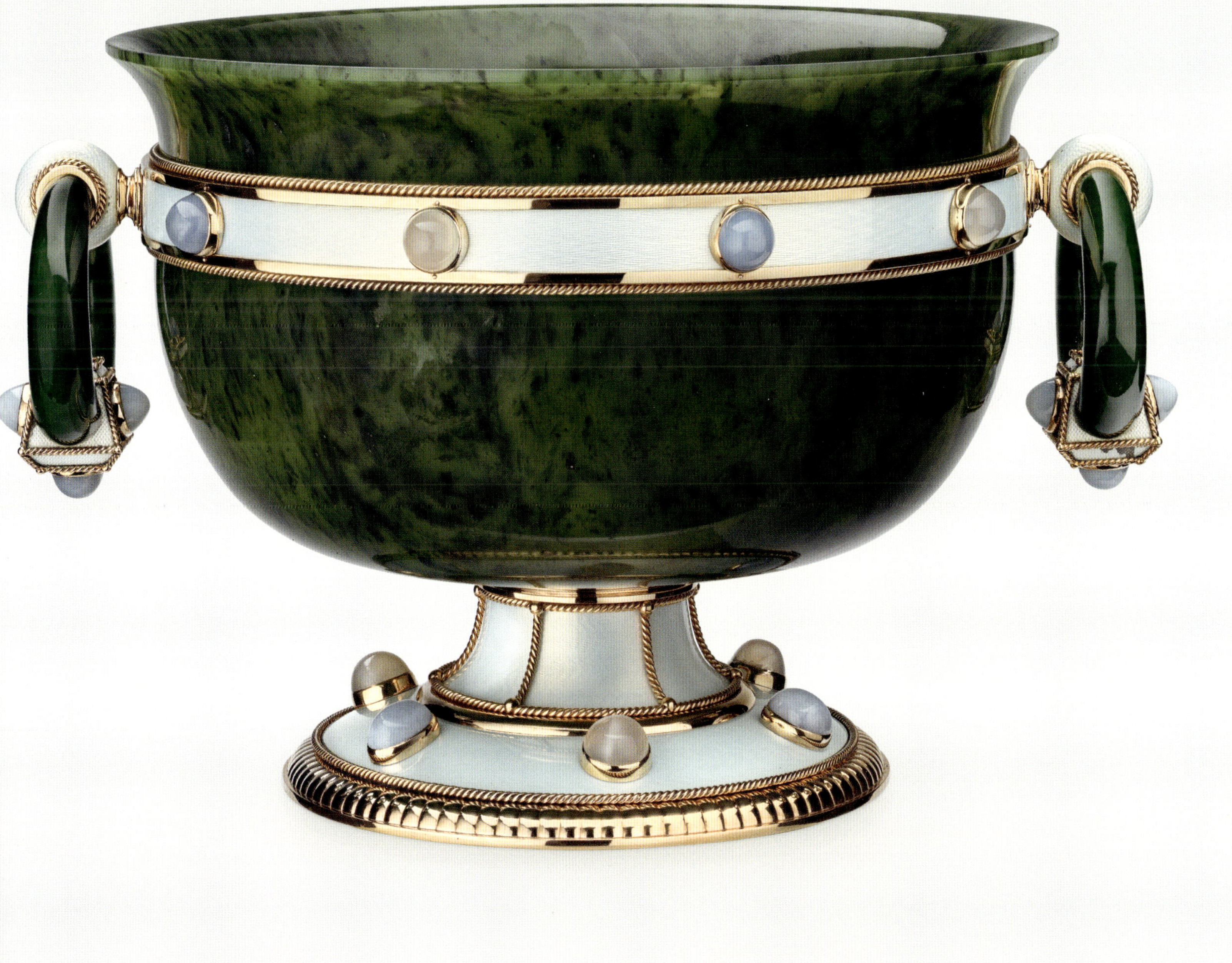

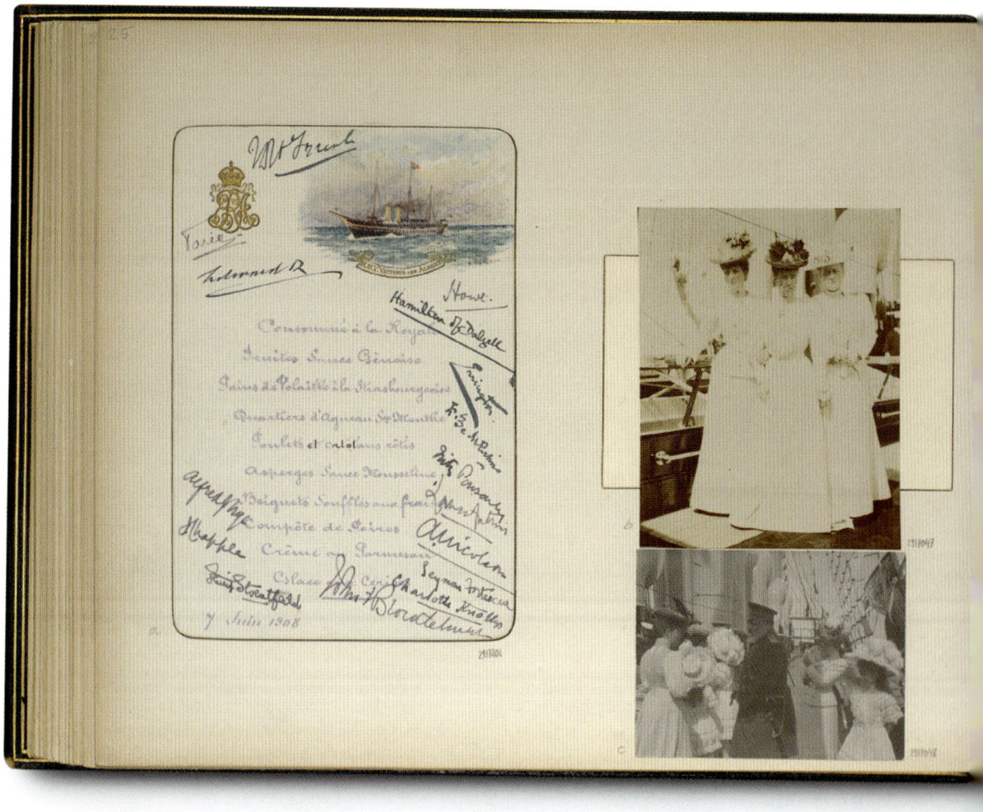

QUEEN ALEXANDRA (1844–1925)

127 ***State Visit to Russia, Reval*** 5–14 June 1908

Gelatin silver prints, (album page) 26.5 × 34.5 cm
RCINS (album) 2916968, (photographs) 2917047–2917048, (ephemera) 2917301–2917303

Provenance Compiled by Queen Alexandra

Literature Dimond 2004, pp. 123–5

This album, similar to others compiled by Queen Alexandra, contains photographs, menus, newspaper cuttings, postcards, music programmes and autographs, which she collected and later arranged as a memento of the state visit, which was also a family reunion. The opening shown here also includes the text of the speech delivered in English by Nicholas II, her nephew, on the occasion of a banquet given on board the Imperial Yacht *Standart* on 7 June.

A keen amateur photographer since the appearance on the market of the first box cameras in the late 1880s, Alexandra was one of the first members of the royal family to use photography to record moments connected with both public engagements and private occasions from her unique perspective.[128] Many of the photographs included in the album were taken by the Queen herself, others by her daughter, Victoria, as well as by members of the Russian imperial family, including Nicholas II and Alexandra Feodorovna (fig. 43), who had started taking snapshots from the mid-1890s, and the Dowager Empress, whose earlier interest in amateur photography probably stemmed from her sister, Alexandra. AN

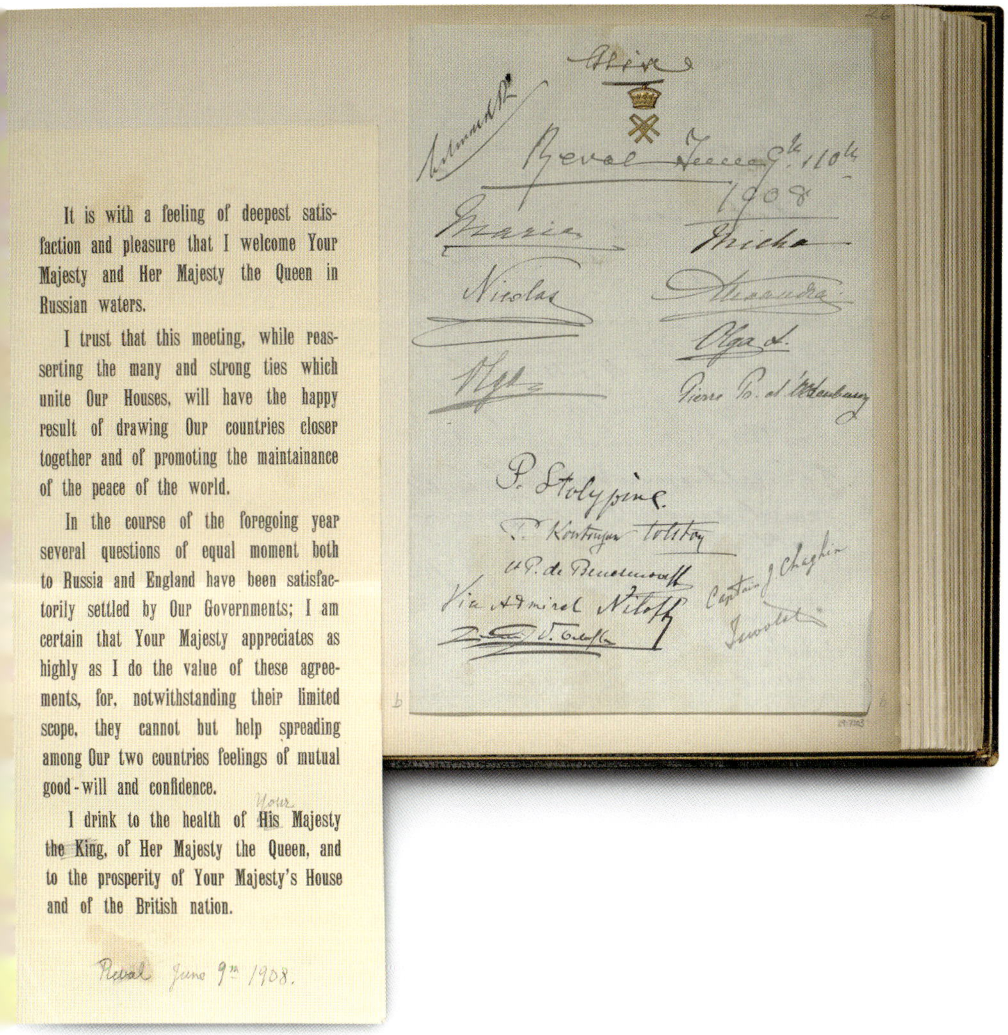

It is with a feeling of deepest satisfaction and pleasure that I welcome Your Majesty and Her Majesty the Queen in Russian waters.

I trust that this meeting, while reasserting the many and strong ties which unite Our Houses, will have the happy result of drawing Our countries closer together and of promoting the maintainance of the peace of the world.

In the course of the foregoing year several questions of equal moment both to Russia and England have been satisfactorily settled by Our Governments; I am certain that Your Majesty appreciates as highly as I do the value of these agreements, for, notwithstanding their limited scope, they cannot but help spreading among Our two countries feelings of mutual good-will and confidence.

I drink to the health of ~~His~~ Your Majesty the King, of Her Majesty the Queen, and to the prosperity of Your Majesty's House and of the British nation.

Reval June 9th 1908.

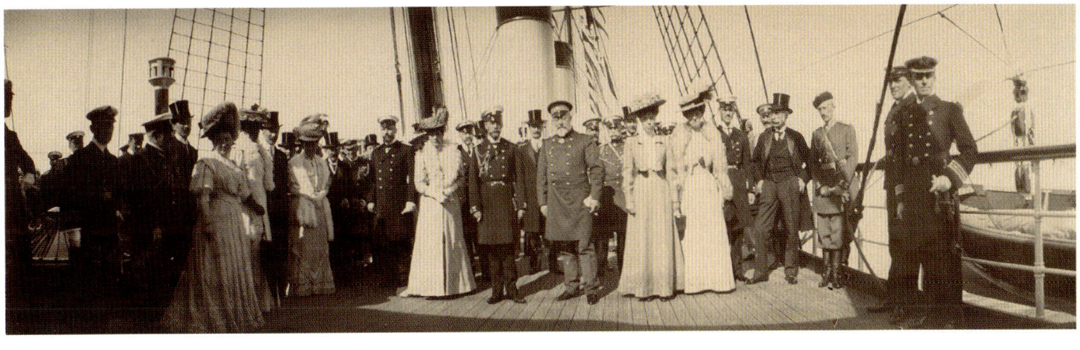

FIG. 43

Empress Alexandra Feodorovna

Group photograph on the yacht 'Standart', Reval, 1908

Gelatin silver print, 8.1 × 29.8 cm

RCIN 2917022

This photograph, from the same album, shows King Edward VII at the centre of the main group with Queen Alexandra and Emperor Nicholas II on his right and Grand Duchess Olga Alexandrovna and Princess Victoria on his left.

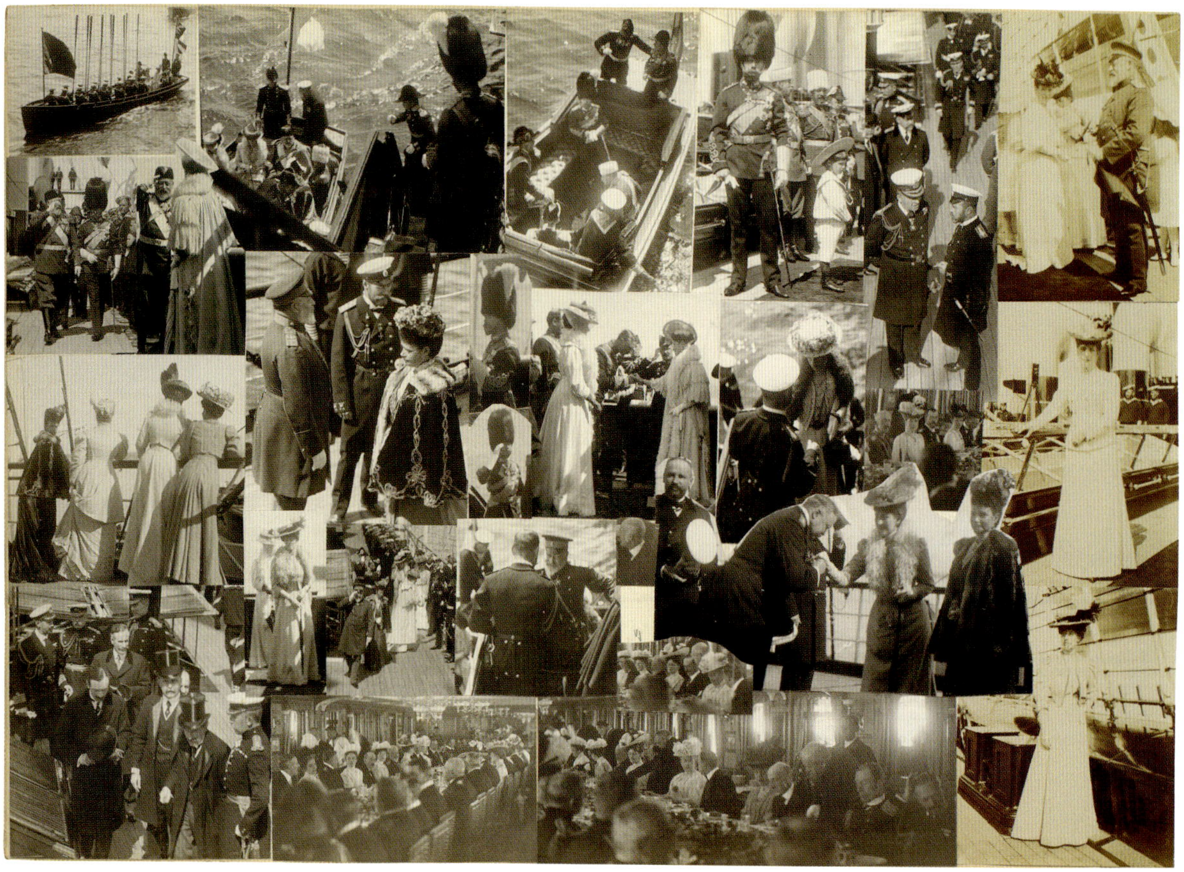

PRINCESS VICTORIA (1868–1935)

128 *Reval* June 1908

Gelatin silver prints, (album page) 36.0 × 51.5 cm
RCIN 2925747

Provenance Compiled by Princess Victoria

This is a page from an album compiled by Princess Victoria, second daughter of King Edward VII and Queen Alexandra. Known as 'Toria' by her family, she never married and remained a close companion to her mother until the latter's death in 1925. The two shared a keen interest in photography and this album page shows Princess Victoria's typical way of organising her photographs: trying to maximise the space offered by the page, in this case also cutting out some of the snapshots. Some of the photographs seen here, showing the party on board their yachts, are by Princess Victoria herself. Others were taken by her mother, by members of the imperial family and by Alexander Karlovich Yagelsky (d.1916), Russian court photographer and co-founder of C.E. de Hahn & Co. (active 1891–1916). **AN**

EMPEROR NICHOLAS II (1868–1918)

129 *Letter to King George V (1865–1936), from Tsarskoe Selo* 25 April/8 May 1910

Manuscript, 20.4 × 12.5 cm
RA GV/PRIV/AA43/129

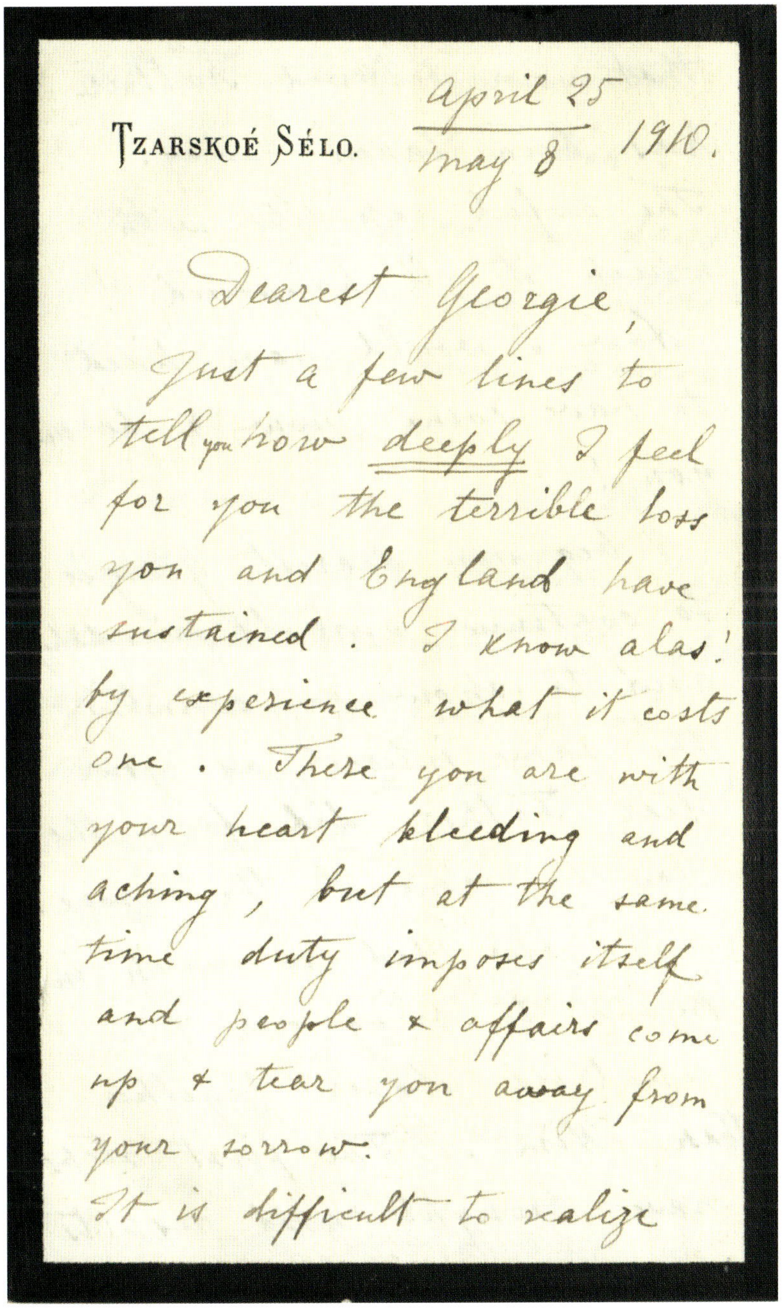

TZARSKOÉ SÉLO. April 25 / May 8 1910.

Dearest Georgie,

Just a few lines to tell you how deeply I feel for you the terrible loss you and England have sustained. I know alas! by experience what it costs one. There you are with your heart bleeding and aching, but at the same time duty imposes itself and people & affairs come up & tear you away from your sorrow.

It is difficult to realize

Nicholas II wrote to his first cousin, George V, following the death of the latter's father, King Edward VII, on 6 May 1910. This message of condolence eloquently sums up the dual nature both of their relations with their fathers as grieving sons and of their roles as sovereigns, with duties and responsibilities: 'a few lines to tell you how deeply I feel for you the terrible loss you and England have sustained. I know alas! by experience what it costs one'. As Nicholas continued: 'There you are with your heart bleeding and aching, but at the same time duty imposes itself and people & affairs come up and tear you away from your sorrow'. The Emperor wrote further, seeking the old friendship between the two cousins, as well as the good relations between Russia and Britain that had been fostered by King Edward. SJP

ATTRIBUTED TO NORDENSTRÖM

130 *King George V's (1865–1936) uniform of an admiral of the Russian fleet* 1909

Full dress tunic and trousers, cocked hat; wool, gilt metal and beaverskin
Hat stamped inside: СКОСИРЕВ
RCIN 33862

Provenance Gift from Emperor Nicholas II to King George V when Prince of Wales, 1909

Literature RA GV/PRIV/GVD/1909; GARF 601/1/1219/26

On 2 August 1909, the Prince of Wales (later George V) recorded in his diary that 'Nicky has most kindly made me an Admiral in the Russian Navy'.[129] The Emperor and his cousin and their families were at Cowes, Isle of Wight, for a family reunion. Nicholas II, Alexandra and their '5 delightful children' were present on board the Imperial Yachts *Standart* and *Polar Star* and stayed anchored off Cowes from 2 to 5 August, visiting Osborne House and hosting lunches and dinners for their English cousins. The Prince of Wales was particularly pleased to see his cousin Nicholas, as they had not met for 12 years, and his diary reveals his delight at the various meetings over the four-day visit: 'Papa proposed Nicky's health which he answered with very nice speeches. We then talked on deck. The fleet illuminated, fine sight, beautiful night but rather cold'.[130] It was during this visit that the two men were photographed together (cat. 278), an image which shows the striking family resemblance between them.

The full uniform has both winter and summer components, comprising in all a great coat, cape, jacket, tunic, two white tunics, trousers, waistcoat, shirt and two caps, frock coat, full dress trousers, cocked hat, sword belt and shoulder boards. The uniform is assumed to have been supplied by Lidval or Nordenström, as both firms made the uniforms of Nicholas II. The accessories were made in part by the firm of Skosirev in St Petersburg. CDEG

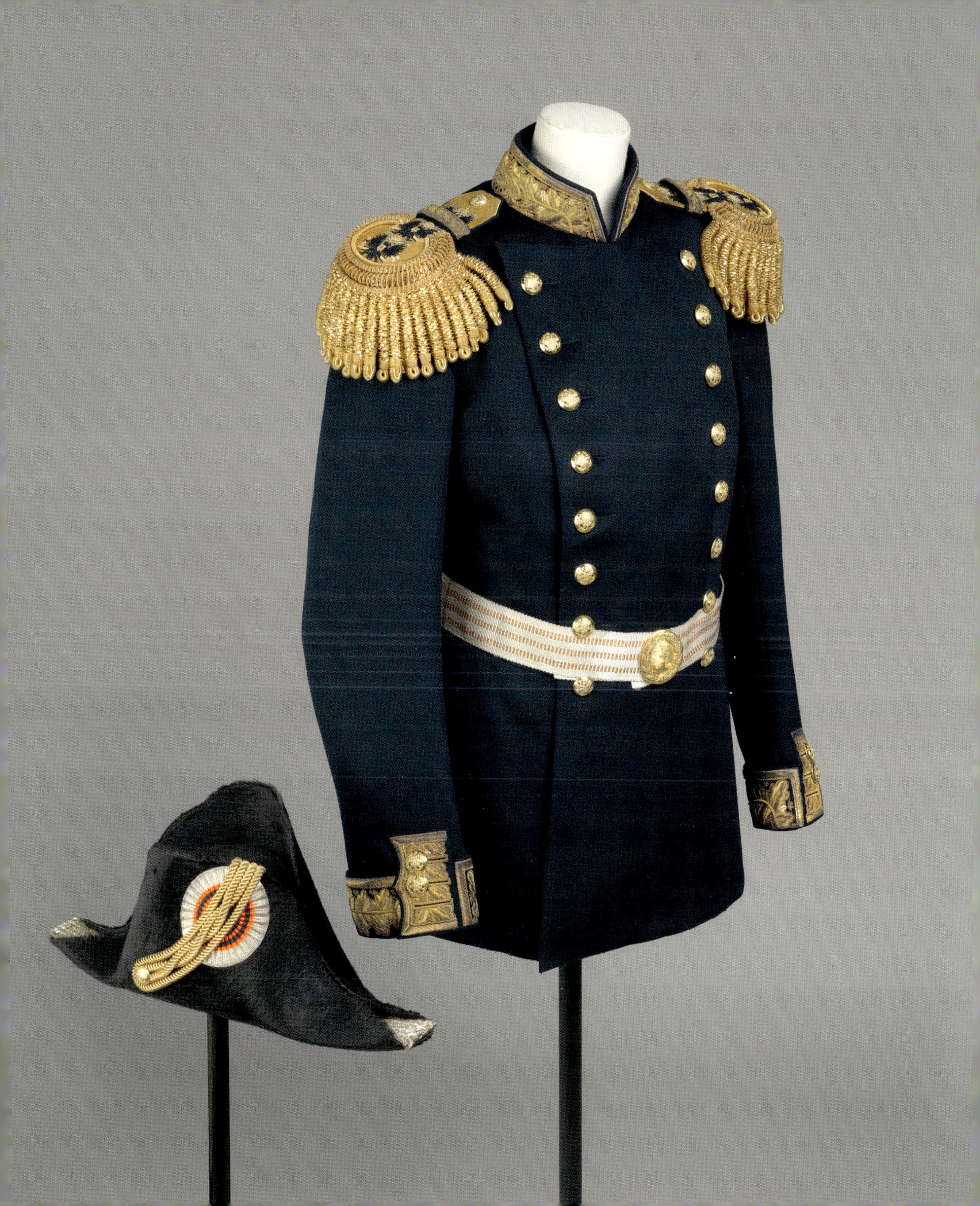

EMPEROR NICHOLAS II (1868–1918)

131 *Draft telegram text to King George V (1865–1936)*

1 August 1914.

Manuscript, 19.0 × 21.3 cm
RA PS/PSO/GV/C/Q/2551/2

Provenance Presented to King George V by Lieutenant Commander L.D. Jones, 20 October 1927

In this manuscript text of the telegram written by Nicholas II to his cousin, King George V, announcing that Russia and Germany were at war, the Emperor states that he would have accepted the King's proposal to mediate had it not been for Germany declaring war on Russia that afternoon. The Emperor commented that he had been avoiding war, but the desire of Austria to 'crush Servia' [*sic*] and make her a vassal of Austria, which would have upset the balance of power in the Balkans, was something that was unacceptable to Russia and 'to those powers who desire to maintain the balance of power in Europe'. Nicholas observed that his military advisers had urged a full rather than a partial mobilisation, 'owing to the quickness which Germany can mobilise in comparison with Russia', and that the justification for full mobilisation as a result of the bombardment of Belgrade had been proved by Germany's sudden declaration of war. Nicholas ends the telegram: 'In this solemn hour, I wish to assure you once more that I have done all in my power to avert war. Now that it has been forced upon me I trust that your country will not fail to support France and Russian fighting to maintain the balance of power in Europe. God bless and protect you. Nicky'.

The telegram contains the Emperor's drafting and alterations. This document was given to King George after the cessation of the war, a war which saw the greatest loss of both military and civilian lives that had been recorded up to that time; the Russian Revolutions; the deaths of his cousins and the end of imperial Russia – as such, it is a deeply poignant document. SJP

ПЛАТА	ТЕЛЕГРАММА	ПЕРЕДАНА
руб. коп. Передачу Отвѣтъ Нарочнаго Итого Принялъ	изъ №	го час. м. по пол. На станц. пров. № Передалъ
Разрядъ. Число словъ. т. сл. ш.	П О Д А Н А. „ „ го „ „ час. „ „ мин. по пол.	Служебныя отмѣтки. Via

His Majesty the King. London.

I would gladly have accepted your kind proposal had not german ambassador this afternoon presented a note to my government declaring war. Ever since the presentation of ultimatum at Belgrade Russia has devoted all her efforts to finding some pacific solution of the question raised by Austria's action. The object of that action was to crush Servia and make her a vassal of Austria. The effect of this would have been

EMPEROR NICHOLAS II (1868–1918)

132 *Letter to King George V (1865–1936), from Tsarskoe Selo*

4/17 February 1917

Manuscript, 18.1 × 11.3 cm
RA PS/PSO/GV/C/Q/2551/8

This, the last surviving letter of Nicholas II to King George V in the Royal Archives, was written in response to a letter sent by the King to the Emperor on 16 January 1917. That letter accompanied the mission sent to Russia by the Allied governments after the second conference at Chantilly, which was led by Lord Milner (1854–1925), with the aim of supporting Russia and its war effort.

In the letter now in the State Archives, Moscow, to which this is the response, King George wrote a short biography on each of the major members of the mission, Milner, Lord Revelstoke (1863–1929) and Sir Henry Wilson (1864–1922). He also wrote: 'I know full well that you will keep your promise to me to fight to the end, as we are prepared to do, whatever difficulties may confront us & whatever sacrifices it may entail.' He ended his letter: 'when the spring comes we must attack the enemy with all our strength at the same time & I am sure that he will not be able to resist us for long.'[131]

The departure of the mission was delayed, which gave King George the opportunity to write one more letter to the Emperor, dated 17 January, when he wrote of his sadness on the death of Count Benkendorff (1849–1917), who had been Russian ambassador in London since 1902 and had been instrumental in the success of the Reval and Cowes meetings between the Emperor and King Edward VII. The King went on to say that he wondered if Nicholas could appoint Count Sazonov (1860–1927) as ambassador, as it would give the King the greatest pleasure and he would know that 'we would have a real friend who would do everything to maintain & increase the friendliest relations which so happily exist now between Russia and England. I hope that you do not mind my having suggested him.' The King ended the last letter his cousin received from him: 'with best love to Alix from May and me. Ever dearest Nicky Yr most devoted cousin & true friend Georgie.'[132]

Sazonov had been ambassador between 1903 and 1907, working alongside Benkendorff. Circumstances in Russia prevented the Emperor appointing a new imperial ambassador; the next Russian ambassador, Konstantin Nabokov (1872–1927), represented the Provisional Government until the October Revolution.

This letter was delivered to the King by Lord Milner. The Emperor comments on the state of the Russian railways, the insufficiency of the rolling stock and the need for repairs to engines and carriages, which was blighted by the work of the factories being diverted to support the army. The Emperor comments similarly on the shortage of food and stores and the difficulties of transporting them when rivers and canals are frozen. After commenting on his regular encouragement of his ministers, the Emperor ends the letter with his best wishes for the King and for his family's welfare and happiness: 'Ever my dearest Georgie your most devoted cousin and friend Nicky'.

The Emperor makes no mention of the political and social situation which was to result in revolution. The February Revolution broke out on 23 February (OS), leading to the Emperor's abdication on 28 February (OS); three weeks after the letter was written. SJP

Tsarskoe Selo. February 4/17 1917.

My dearest Georgie,

I thank you very much for your kind long letter. I entrust mine to the care of Lord Milner, whose acquaintance I was very pleased to make. Twice I had the occasion of seeing all the members of your mission. I hope they will return safely to

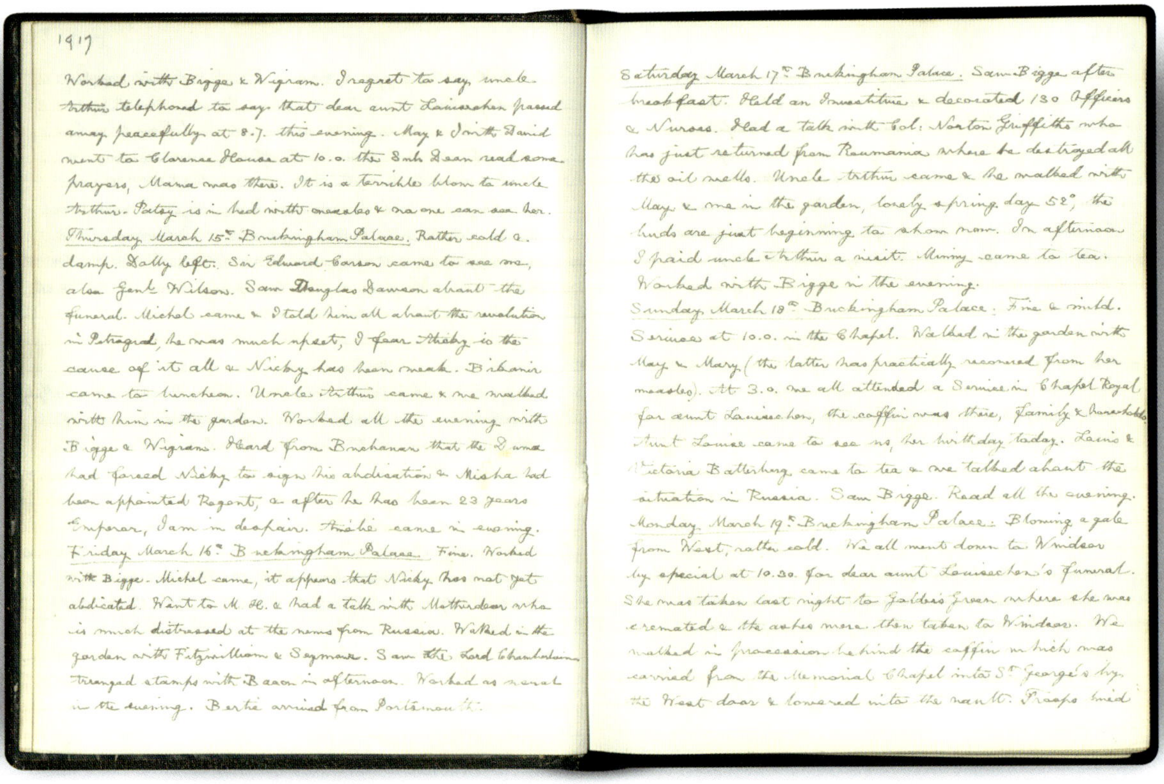
1917
Worked with Bigge & Wigram. I regret to say, uncle Arthur telephoned to say that dear aunt Louischen passed away peacefully at 8.7 this evening. May & I with David went to Clarence House at 10.0. the Sub Dean read some prayers, Mama was there. It is a terrible blow to uncle Arthur. Patsy is in bed with measles & no one can see her.
Thursday March 15th Buckingham Palace. Rather cold & damp. Dolly left. Sir Edward Carson came to see me, also Genl Wilson. Saw Douglas Dawson about the funeral. Michel came & I told him all about the revolution in Petrograd, he was much upset, I fear Alicky is the cause of it all & Nicky has been weak. [illegible] came to luncheon. Uncle Arthur came & we walked with him in the garden. Worked all the evening with Bigge & Wigram. Heard from Buchanan that the Duma had forced Nicky to sign his abdication & Misha had been appointed Regent, & after he has been 23 years Emperor, I am in despair. [illegible] came in evening.
Friday March 16th Buckingham Palace. Fine. Worked with Bigge. Michel came, it appears that Nicky has not yet abdicated. Went to M.H. & had a talk with Motherdear who is much distressed at the news from Russia. Walked in the garden with Fitzwilliam & Seymour. Saw the Lord Chamberlain. Arranged stamps with Bacon in afternoon. Worked as usual in the evening. Bertie arrived from Portsmouth.

Saturday March 17th Buckingham Palace. Saw Bigge after breakfast. Held an Investiture & decorated 130 Officers & Nurses. Had a talk with Col. Norton Griffiths who has just returned from Roumania where he destroyed all the oil wells. Uncle Arthur came & he walked with May & me in the garden, lovely spring day 52°, the buds are just beginning to show now. In afternoon I paid uncle Arthur a visit. Mimy came to tea. Worked with Bigge in the evening.
Sunday March 18th Buckingham Palace. Fine & mild. Service at 10.0. in the Chapel. Walked in the garden with May & Mary (the latter has practically recovered from her measles). At 3.0. we all attended a Service in Chapel Royal for aunt Louischen, the coffin was there, family & households. Aunt Louise came to see us, her birthday today. Louis & Victoria Battenberg came to tea & we talked about the situation in Russia. Saw Bigge. Read all the evening.
Monday March 19th Buckingham Palace. Blowing a gale from West, rather cold. We all went down to Windsor by special at 10.30. for dear aunt Louischen's funeral. She was taken last night to Golders Green where she was cremated & the ashes were then taken to Windsor. We walked in procession behind the coffin which was carried from the Memorial Chapel into St George's by the West door & lowered into the vault. Troops lined

KING GEORGE V (1865–1936)

133 *Diary, Buckingham Palace* 15 March 1917

14.3 × 20.0 × 5.0 cm
RA GV/PRIV/GVD/1917: 15 March

This entry in King George V's diary records the Russian Revolution and Nicholas II's abdication. The King is likely to have gathered the news of revolution a few days earlier – although it is not recorded in his diary. It is possible that the news was broken by General Wilson, recently back from the Allied mission to Russia. The King references the news by recording that he had met that morning with Grand Duke Michael Mikhailovich (Michel; 1861–1929) and had told him all about the revolution in Petrograd, observing that the Grand Duke was 'much upset'.

The King's observations are a chronology of the day, and give a sense of the turmoil at the time. With his comment, 'I fear Alicky is the cause of it all & Nicky has been weak', he was clearly aware of the problems in Russia and the influence of the Empress on the political situation. The news that evening from Ambassador Buchanan was also recorded: 'the Duma has forced Nicky to sign his abdication & Misha had been appointed Regent, & after he has been 23 years emperor, I am in despair'. The King's distress at his cousin's situation and the impact that this might have for the war was probably compounded by the fact that news of the Emperor's abdication came hours after the death of the King's aunt, the Duchess of Connaught (1860–1917), who, with Prince Arthur, the Duke of Connaught (1850–1942), had attended Nicholas and Alexandra's coronation in 1896 – a double blow for the royal family. SJP

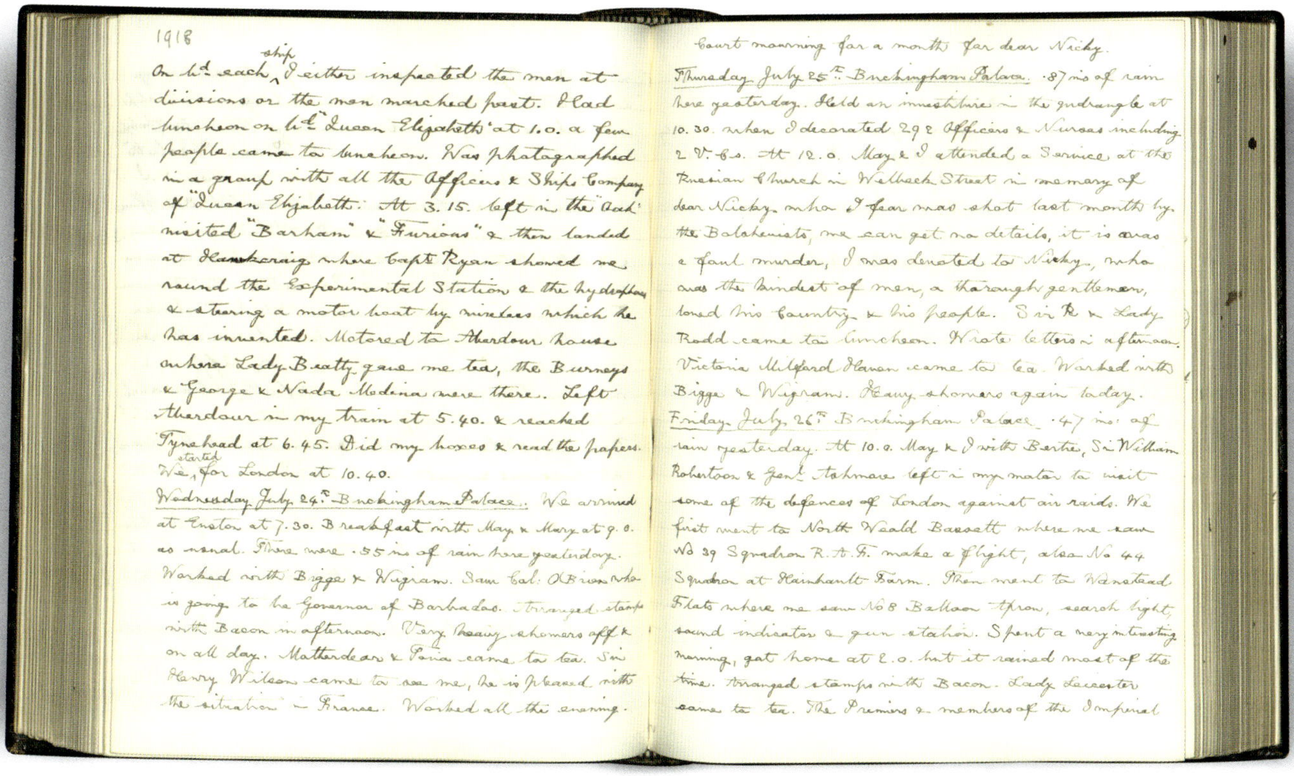

1918
On Bd. each ship I either inspected the men at
divisions or the men marched past. Had
luncheon on Bd. "Queen Elizabeth" at 1.0. a few
people came to luncheon. Was photographed
in a group with all the Officers & Ships Company
of "Queen Elizabeth". At 3.15. left in the "Oak"
visited "Barham" & "Furious" & then landed
at Hawkcraig where Capt. Ryan showed me
round the Experimental Station & the hydrophones
& steering a motor boat by wireless which he
has invented. Motored to Aberdour House
where Lady Beatty gave me tea, the Burneys
& George & Nada Medina were there. Left
Aberdour in my train at 5.40. & reached
Tynehead at 6.45. Did my boxes & read the papers.
We started for London at 10.40.
Wednesday July 24th. Buckingham Palace. We arrived
at Euston at 7.30. Breakfast with May & Mary at 9.0.
as usual. There were .55 ins of rain here yesterday.
Worked with Bigge & Wigram. Saw Col: O'Brien who
is going to be Governor of Barbados. Arranged stamps
with Bacon in afternoon. Very heavy showers off &
on all day. Mother dear & Toria came to tea. Sir
Henry Wilson came to see me, he is pleased with
the situation in France. Worked all the evening.

Court mourning for a month for dear Nicky.
Thursday July 25th. Buckingham Palace. .87 ins of rain
here yesterday. Held an investiture in the quadrangle at
10.30. when I decorated 292 Officers & Nurses including
2 V.Cs. At 12.0. May & I attended a Service at the
Russian Church in Welbeck Street in memory of
dear Nicky who I fear was shot last month by
the Bolshevists, we can get no details, it was
a foul murder, I was devoted to Nicky, who
was the kindest of men, a thorough gentleman,
loved his country & his people. Sir R & Lady
Rodd came to luncheon. Wrote letters in afternoon.
Victoria Milford Haven came to tea. Worked with
Bigge & Wigram. Heavy showers again today.
Friday July 26th. Buckingham Palace. .47 ins: of
rain yesterday. At 10.0. May & I with Bertie, Sir William
Robertson & Genl. Ashmore left in my motor to visit
some of the defences of London against air raids. We
first went to North Weald Bassett where we saw
No 39 Squadron R.A.F. make a flight, also No 44
Squadron at Hainhault Farm. Then went to Wanstead
Flats where we saw No 8 Balloon Apron, search light,
sound indicator & gun station. Spent a very interesting
morning, got home at 2.0. but it rained most of the
time. Arranged stamps with Bacon. Lady Leicester
came to tea. The Premiers & members of the Imperial

KING GEORGE V (1865–1936)

134 *Diary, Buckingham Palace* 25 July 1918

14.3 × 20.0 × 5.0 cm
RA GV/PRIV/GVD/1918: 25 July

In his diary, King George records attending a service at the Russian church in Welbeck Street, 'in memory of dear Nicky who I fear was shot last month by the Bolsheviks, we can get no details, it was a foul murder, I was devoted to Nicky, who was the kindest of men, a thorough gentleman, loved his family and his people.'

Earlier in the day he had decorated 292 officers, including two with the Victoria Cross, and nurses, at an open-air investiture in the quadrangle of Buckingham Palace. In many ways, the King was continuing that which he and the Emperor had both dedicated their lives to after the outbreak of war – supporting the troops and not allowing the enemy to defeat them. As Nicholas said in the last letter received by the King: 'But I never lose courage and egg on the ministers to make them and those under them work as hard as they can. But whatever the difficulties may be yet unsure for us – we shall go on with this awful war to the end.'[133]

After news broke of the deaths, first, of the former Emperor, and then of his family, the King was kept informed of the discoveries and investigations into the events in Ekaterinburg on the night of 16 July 1918. The King's distress at the events was summed up in July 1920 in a note commenting on a dossier sent to him, which the King was reported to have 'read – needless to say which much pain and horror'.[134] **SJP**

IGOR EMANUILOVICH GRABAR (1871–1960)

135 *A Winter's Day* February 1941

Oil on canvas, 78.7 × 95.0 cm
Signed and dated: *Игорь Грабарь 5/II 41* (Igor Grabar 5/II 41)
RCIN 403453

Provenance Presented to Her Majesty The Queen by Nikita Khrushchev and Nikolai Bulganin, April 1956

Presented to Her Majesty The Queen by Nikita Khrushchev and Nikolai Bulganin, during their visit to the United Kingdom, this painting by Igor Grabar, a prominent painter, publisher and art historian, displays the influence of French Impressionism transplanted to Russian soil, and celebrates a landscape that is uniquely Russian. Born in Budapest, Grabar initially studied law at St Petersburg University. In 1894 he enrolled in Ilya Repin's art class, but left just a year later to travel in Europe. He spent his formative years, 1896–9, at Anton Ažbe's (1862–1905) avant-garde art school in Munich, which numbered amongst its pupils Vasily Kandinsky (1866–1944) and Grabar's friend, Alexei von Yavlensky (1864–1941), plus a host of Russian impressionist painters. In 1929, Grabar was instrumental in organising a major touring exhibition of Russian icons, which was shown at the Victoria and Albert Museum in the autumn of that year.

It was in Munich that the artist possibly refined his technique, later superseded by a form of divisionism. According to Grabar, the summit of his career was the period 1903–7 (with February–April 1904 as the 'pinnacle'), and this painting, in a sense, can be seen as a reworking of those most fertile years and a return to the sublime snow scenes of that period. The painting echoes one of Grabar's masterpieces, *The Azure of February* (fig. 44), in terms of subject matter and, to a certain extent, technique: a thickly snow-covered landscape, looking up through a silhouette of spindly birch trees, the orange fanning out against an azure sky. The painting can be seen as a debt to both Monet's (1840–1926) series of poplars and his luminous snow scenes; however, the landscape also recalls the rich tradition of Russian realist landscape painting epitomised by artists such as Shishkin (1832–98) and Levitan (1860–1900), the waif-like birch (like Sverchkov's troika) synonymous with the Russian identity.

However, the painting lacks the energy and vitality of the earlier period – possibly in keeping with his changed role (after the Revolution, he was professor of art history at Moscow State University, until 1946, and director of the Scientific Central Restoration Studios, Moscow). The wild, frenetic brushstrokes and coloured highlights of *Azure* are replaced by a smoother, more restrained and conventional composition. The horizontal and more modest format of the landscape contrasts with the dynamic

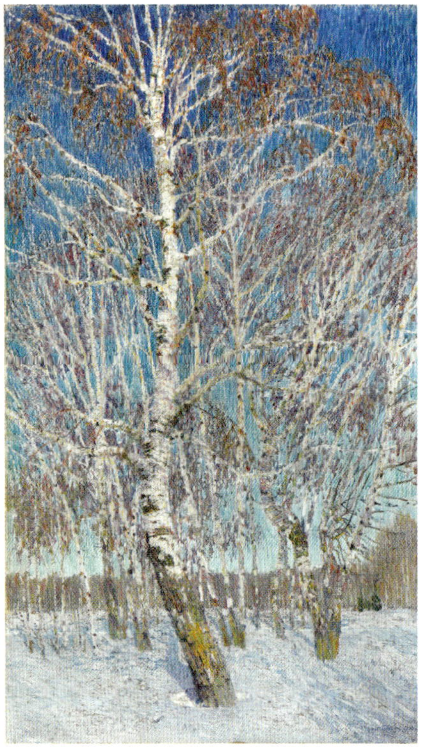

FIG. 44
Igor Grabar
The Azure of February, 1904
Oil on canvas, 141 × 83 cm
Moscow, Tretyakov Gallery

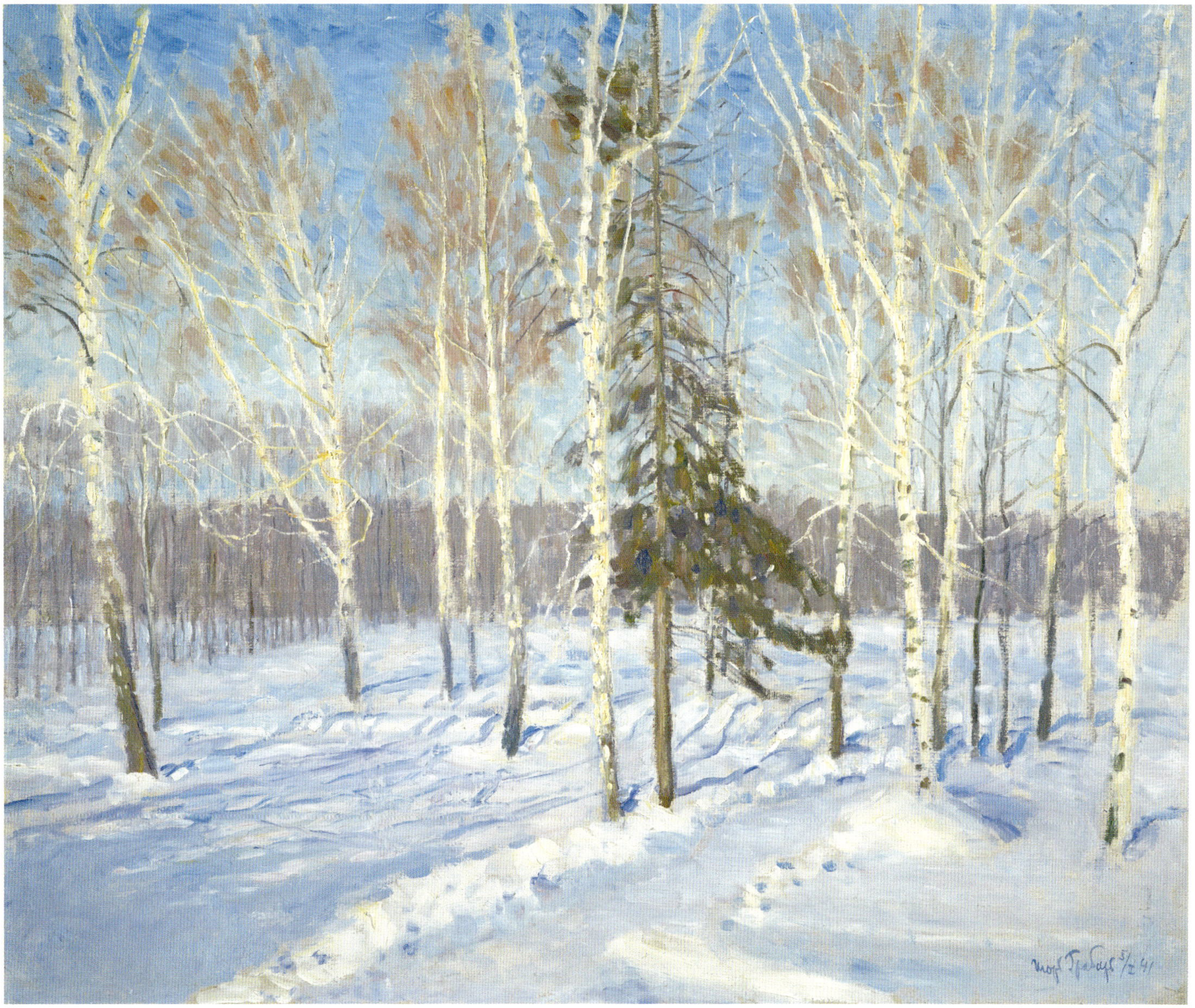

vertical format of 1904. Although the initial background sky and snow in both paintings is divided with the same warm purple line of trees, a much more economical palette is evident, and indeed less paint; Grabar has applied a dull pinkish white background to the canvas, which he leaves exposed in many areas beneath the loose brushwork. The paint is relatively smooth and fluid in application, with longer, flatter brushstrokes. Impasto is not used as a compositional element, but restricted, in a more academic manner, to the highlights on the trees. However, pinholes visible towards the corners of the composition, and the artist's retouching covering two of them, make it likely that the painting was executed *en plein air*, reinforcing its impressionist heritage. There is added poignancy to the scene, dated 5 February 1941 – it was painted just months before German tanks entered Russia, as part of Operation Barbarossa, destroying much of this cherished landscape.

Archival records reveal that Her Majesty The Queen was to be presented with a painting by Ivan Aivazovsky, one of Russia's foremost marine painters and now an increasingly sought-after artist. It is not known why the Grabar was considered a more appropriate gift.
AB & RDES

RUSSIAN

136 *Specimen box* *c.*1956

Agate, gilt metal, demantoid garnets, 13.8 × 26.2 × 18.3 cm
Label inscribed: *THIS BOX MADE FROM STONES FROM THE URAL MOUNTAINS WAS GIVEN TO HER MAJESTY QUEEN ELIZABETH THE QUEEN MOTHER BY MARSHAL BULGANIN AND MR KRUSCHEV APRIL 1956*
RCIN 100869

Provenance Given to Queen Elizabeth The Queen Mother, by Nikolai Bulganin and Nikita Khrushchev, April 1956

The Ural mountains in west central Russia contain some of the richest mineral deposits in the world; as a result, this source of precious and semi-precious stones has been used in Russian decorative art since the early eighteenth century. Large hardstone objects made in the eighteenth and nineteenth centuries, many produced in the specialist carving workshops in Ekaterinburg, in the southern Urals, usually vases based on classical forms, often mounted with elaborate gilt-bronze embellishments in the European style, eventually gave way to smaller pieces made at Kolyvan and in the workshops of Fabergé, Avenir Sumin (1858–1933) and Denisov-Uralsky (1864–1926). After the Revolution, the level of craftsmanship declined, as highly specialised skills were lost. This box, produced *c.*1956, is therefore a rare exception, presumably because of the unique circumstances of its presentation, but its exact place of manufacture is unknown. CDEG

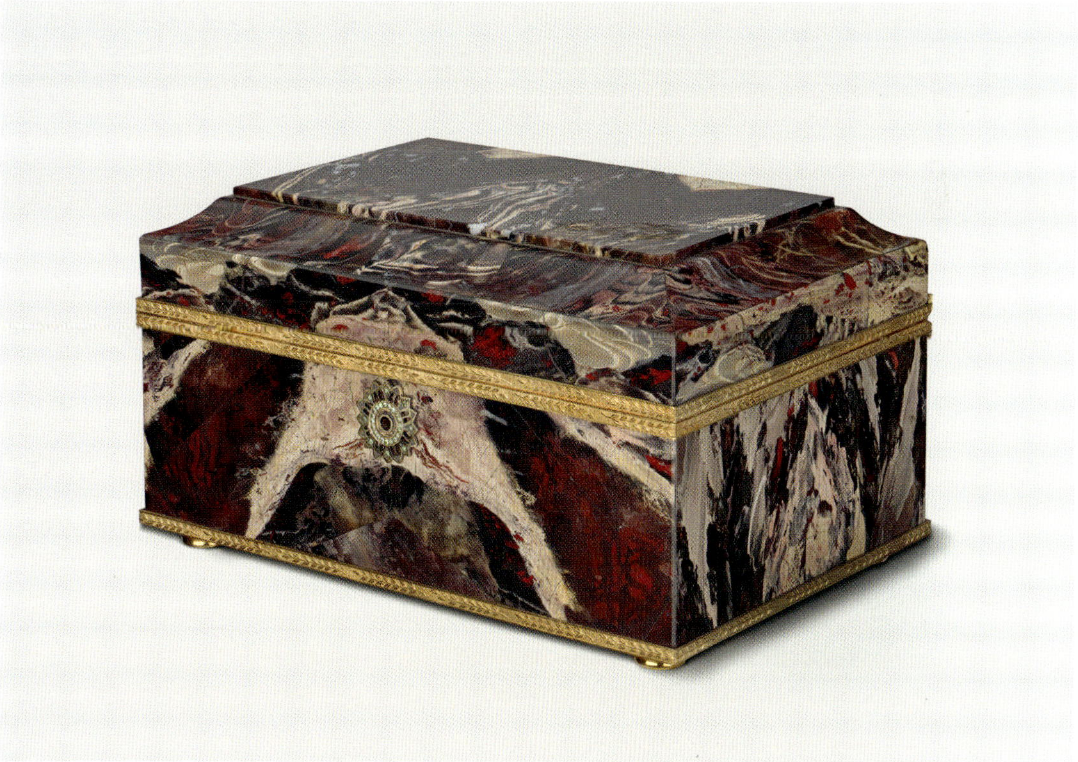

137 *Pair of vases* 1956

Hard-paste porcelain, 71.5 × 38.3 cm (identical)
Signed in blue underglaze in Cyrillic: 'G. ZIMIN'; dated *1956*; mark of the Imperial Porcelain Factory; one vase inscribed in blue underglaze: *ТЕПЛАЯ ЗИМА* and *ВЕТРЕННЫЙ ДЕНЪ*
RCIN 73045.1–2

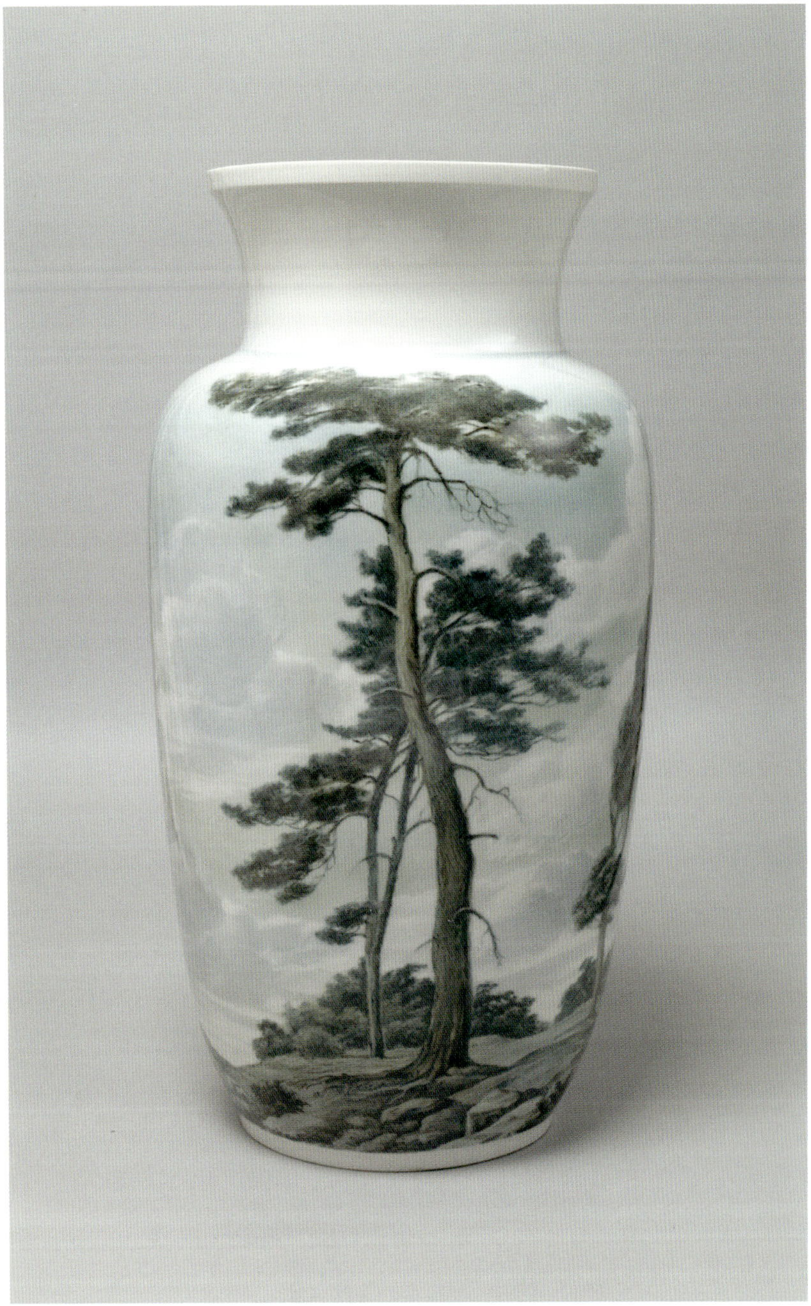

Provenance Presented to Her Majesty Queen Elizabeth II by Nikita Khrushchev and Nikolai Bulganin, April 1956

Presented as a diplomatic gift during the Soviet visit of 1956, this pair of vases is decorated with underglaze painting, a technique restored at the Imperial Porcelain Factory in the 1940s. The director of the factory worked with two veteran artists of this technique, Bolshakov and Grigory Zimin (1875–1958), the latter having painted the scenes on these vases. Their production included vases dedicated to the seasons of the year, such as this pair, one of which has a summer landscape entitled 'Stormy Day', and the other, 'Warm Winter'.

Zimin studied at the Baron Stieglitz Central School in St Petersburg from 1886 to 1888, and in the School of Drawing at the Society for the Promotion of the Arts from 1895 to 1901. In 1886 he was admitted as an apprentice to the painting studio of the Imperial Glass and Porcelain Factory, where in 1893 he was appointed painter. In 1903 he was sent to France, Germany, Sweden and Austria, to improve his skills in underglaze paintings. Zimin worked from his own sketches and became one of the leading masters of underglaze landscape painting. He continued to work at the Imperial Porcelain Factory in the periods 1917–24 and 1947–58. His work was exhibited at the Academy of Arts' annual spring exhibitions and retained its popularity beyond the imperial period. CDEG

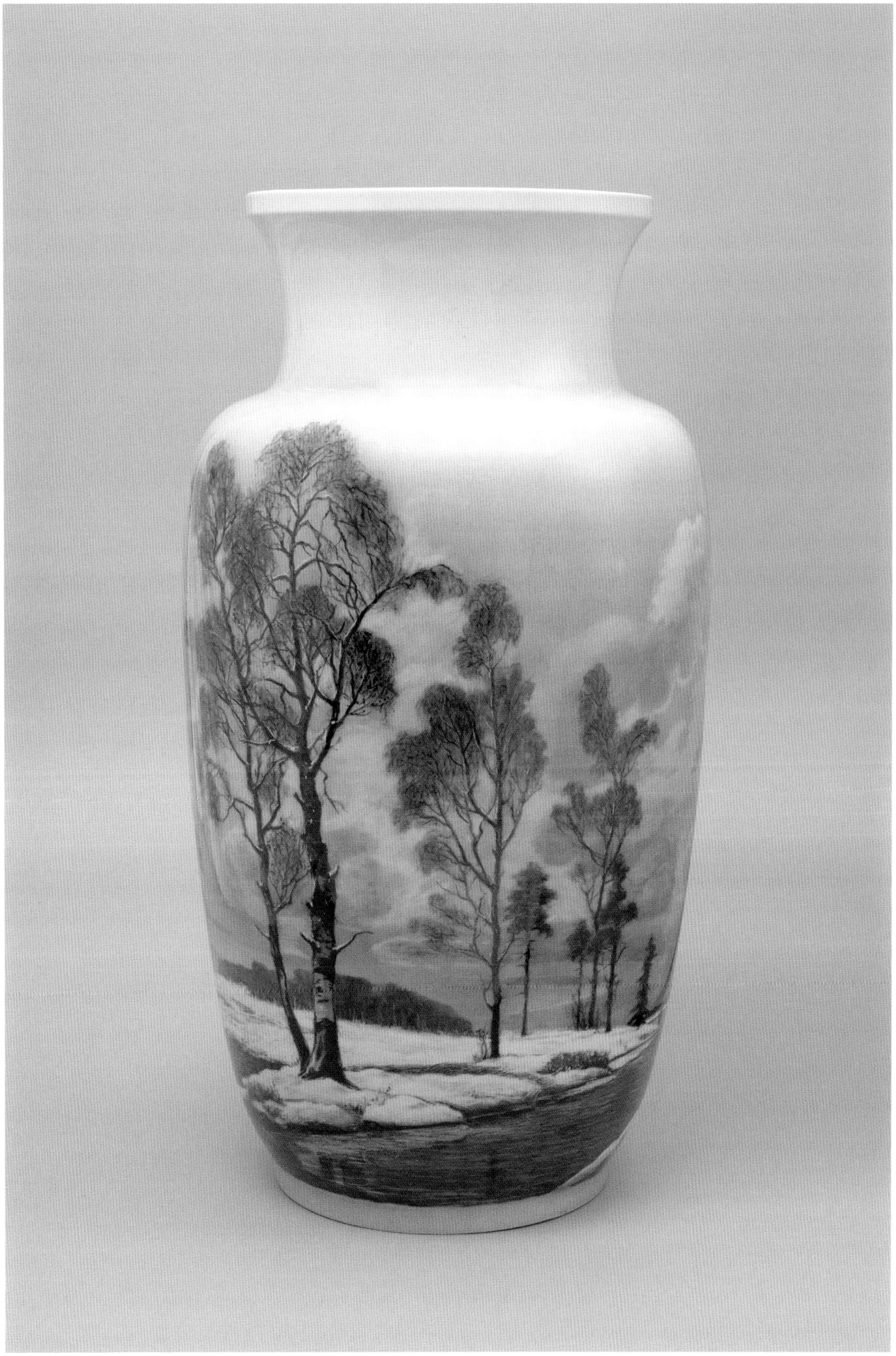

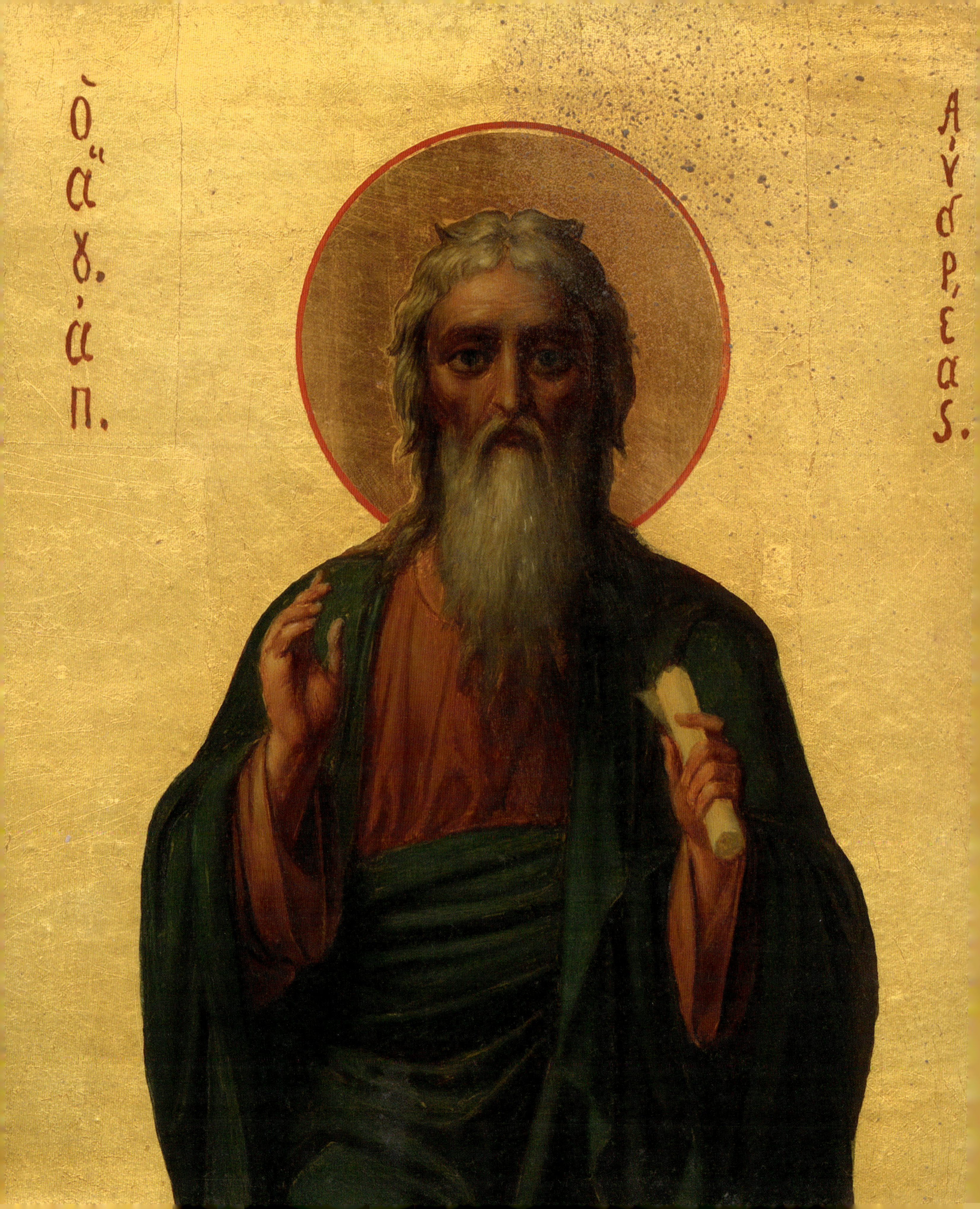
ὁ ἅγ. ἀπ.
Ἀνδρέας.

6

'Holy Russia' in the Royal Collection

STEPHEN PATTERSON

Although there was contact between the Orthodox churches and Britain from the late seventeenth century, there appears to have been little interaction between the British royal family and the Orthodox faith until the nineteenth century. The inclusion in George III's library of John Glen King's work on *The Rites and ceremonies of the Greek Church, in Russia; containing an account of its doctrine, worship, and discipline* (cat. 138), dedicated to the king was one opportunity to learn about the churches in the East. With its extensive illustrations, it provided a British audience with a greater understanding of the rites and practices of the Orthodox churches and was an attempt to correct some of the misunderstandings of travellers and commentators who had reported (often inaccurately) on the Russian church up to that time. From 1813, the main presence of the Orthodox church was the Russian Embassy chapel established in Welbeck Street which was frequented by Russian visitors to London, including Emperor Nicholas I in 1844.

The previous year, Queen Victoria had received a first-hand account of the Russian church from Grand Duke Michael Pavlovich, Nicholas's brother, who visited Windsor in 1843. The Queen recorded:

> *The Gd Duke spoke of their Church, which is a much severer one than the Roman Catholic. Their fasts are much more rigorous. On Wednesdays & Fridays in Lent, they are not allowed even to eat fish, & no butter or cream, & towards the end of Lent they are hardly allowed to drink at all. On great Feast Days, like Good Friday, Easter, & Xmas the service in the morning lasts 4 hours, & 2, in the evening. The music is very fine; all men's voices, unaccompanied, which must have a splendid effect.*[1]

Queen Victoria became more aware of the Russian Church and its liturgy from the Dean of Westminster, Arthur Stanley, who had studied in Russia in 1857 while writing his book, *Lectures on the History of the Eastern Church*, published in 1861; a copy of the second edition was presented to the Queen in 1862 (RCIN 1132101). It would be Arthur Stanley who would conduct the Anglican service at the wedding of Alfred, Duke of Edinburgh and Maria Alexandrovna in the Winter Palace (cat. 180) in 1874. While staying at Baden Baden in 1876, the Queen experienced an Orthodox service for herself when she visited a Greek chapel:

> *Service was going on & I remained for ½ an hour* [...] *The Priests move about a great deal & there was much swinging of incense.* [...]. *The long standing is very fatiguing, but I thought the service itself & the wonderfully beautiful chants most impressive.*[2]

As part of the negotiations on the marriage contract between the future Duke and Duchess of Edinburgh in 1874 the topic of religion was raised; one of the terms was that the Grand Duchess could continue to practise her Orthodox faith, although any children of the marriage would be raised as Anglicans. To make this possible, a chapel was installed for the Grand Duchess on the first floor of the refurbished Clarence House (fig. 45), with an

Detail of cat. 142

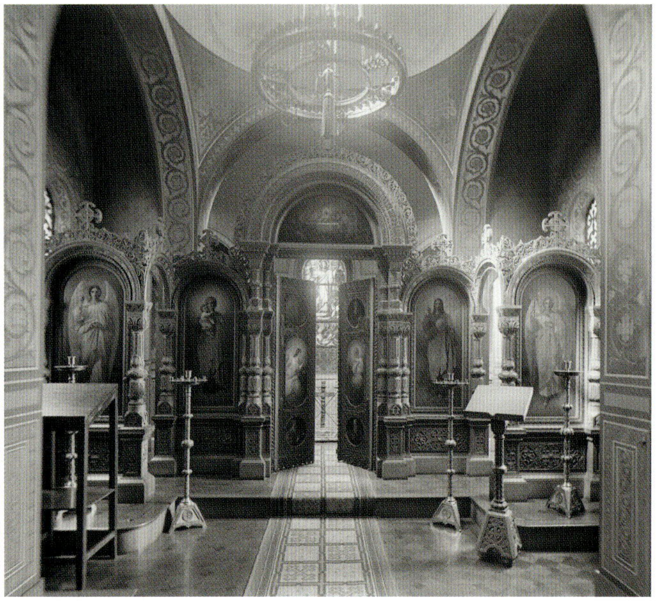

FIG. 45
Horatio Nelson King, Russian chapel, Clarence House
RCIN 2084496

FIG. 46
Christmas table at Osborne House, *c.*1873, including an icon of Christ
Albumen print, 17.5 × 23.5 cm
RCIN 2103819

iconostasis containing icons painted by Carl Timoleon von Neff. Queen Victoria's agreement to this was warmly welcomed in St Petersburg, with the Russian ambassador reporting to Alexander II the Queen's words at the opening of the Canterbury Convocation in July 1874 that year: 'I have confidence that the marriage of my son with the daughter of the Emperor of Russia serves to reaffirm the ties of friendship between two great Christian nations'.[3] After the Duke of Edinburgh's death in 1900, the house was taken up by his brother and sister-in-law, the Duke and Duchess of Connaught, and the chapel was disbanded, although the space, with some fragments of the original decoration, still survive. The chapel's iconostasis was moved to the Russian church in Darmstadt, founded by Nicholas II and Empress Alexandra in 1899, where it remains. It was in Darmstadt, in front of the iconostasis from Clarence House, that HRH The Duke of Edinburgh's parents, Prince Andrew of Greece (1882–1944) and Princess Alice of Battenberg (1885–1969), were married in 1903.

Initially the chapel at Clarence House had its own priest; however, it was served for most of its time by the priests of the Embassy church Welbeck Street. It was at that church that various members of the royal family attended memorial services for the imperial family throughout the nineteenth century, including King George V and Queen Mary who went to a service there on 25 July 1918, following the news of Nicholas II's death (cat. 134).

The marriage of her son and later the marriage of two granddaughters into the Russian imperial family increased Queen Victoria's awareness of the position and practices of the Church, and she was well-versed as to which members of the imperial family had converted to Orthodoxy on marriage, as shown in her response to news that Alexander III had issued a *ukase* (Imperial decree), enforcing the profession of the Orthodox faith on those marrying male members of the Romanov family.[4]

The most important icons in the Royal Collection came from the Oettingen-Wallerstein collection and include two with a clear Russian provenance: the Dormition icon (cat. 140) and the monastery of Solovetsky (cat. 139). Both were acquired by Prince Albert as part of the collection of a cousin, Prince Louis of Oettingen-Wallerstein (1791–1870),

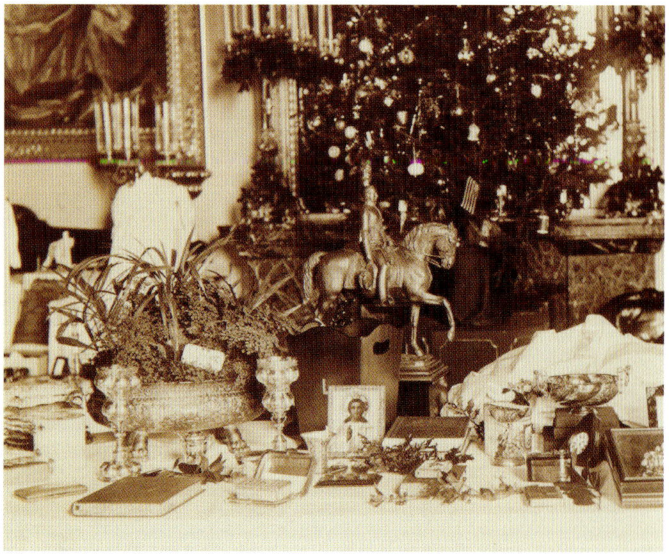

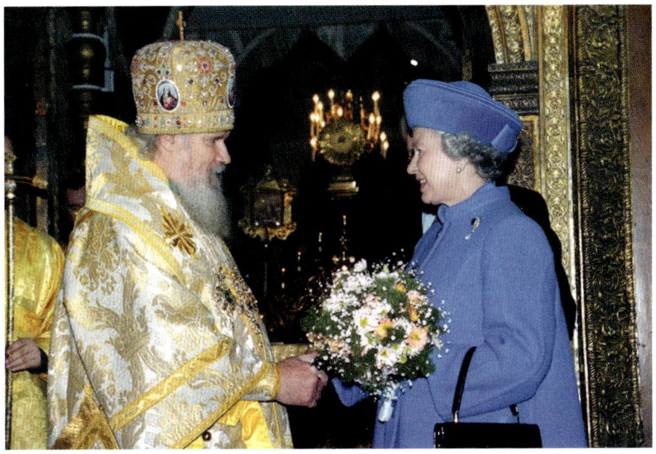

FIG. 47
Her Majesty The Queen with Patriarch Alexei II of Moscow and all Rus' in the Dormition Cathedral, Moscow, 18 October 1994

following an exhibition of the works at Kensington Palace. The 101 works were published in a catalogue of 1848, with the intention that they be sold to relieve Prince Louis's debts, and started with nine from the 'Byzantine school', gathered

> *to represent that style which was adopted by the Christian Artists in the East, after the time of Constantine the Great, and which, [...] exercised so marked an influence on the Fine Arts of the West.*[5]

Icons were presented to Queen Victoria; an example can be seen on her Christmas table of *c.*1873 (fig. 46). Icons were also sent to the Queen from the Crimea and displayed at the museum at Osborne House. They were also collected by Queen Alexandra and her daughter Princess Victoria. Gifts of icons to the sovereign have continued, most notably with those presented to Her Majesty The Queen by the Patriarch during her State Visit to Russia in 1994, and the visit of Patriarch Kirill to London in 2016 (cat. 144). The most poignant gift of an icon is perhaps that left by Queen Victoria's granddaughter, 'Ella' (Grand Duchess Elizabeth Feodorovna, 1864–1918), at her grandmother's grave at Frogmore mausoleum in 1913; the Grand Duchess, murdered during the Revolution, was herself to be depicted on icons following her canonisation as a martyr.

The Queen's meeting with Patriarch Alexei II during the 1994 State Visit (fig. 47) was not the first contact between the Russian Patriarchate and the British Crown. Other connections include a message sent in February 1918 by the first Patriarch of the twentieth century, Patriarch Tikhon (1865–1925), to King George V. In the message, the Patriarch reflected on the new political situation in Russia, stressing that, in his view, the Church 'Sobor' was the only legitimate legal assembly in Russia at that time, that it did not recognise the peace negotiated with the Germans by the 'Smolny' (the Bolshevik Party) and did not want the Allies to negotiate with the Germans.[6]

The conclusion of the Second World War, with Britain and the Soviet Union fighting as Allies, was the reason for the first meeting between a British monarch and representatives of the Patriarch, when, in June 1945, a delegation of the Russian Orthodox Church, on behalf of Patriarch Alexei I (1877–1970), led by Metropolitan Nikolai of Krutitsky (1892–1961), with the support of the Archbishop of Canterbury, Geoffrey Fisher (1887–1972), visited London. King George VI received the delegation at Buckingham Palace. During the audience, the King addressed the group: 'We recall with admiration the heroic sufferings and achievements of the Soviet peoples and armies which greatly contributed to the Allied Victory over the evil forces of Nazi tyranny. As our two countries have been comrades in the struggle and in the victory so we must stand together with all freedom-loving people to establish a righteous peace'.[7] The Patriarch responded, on 29 June: 'Pray accept my humble gratitude and prayerful wishes of prosperity and happiness to your Majesty and your great British people.'[8]

JOHN GLEN KING (1731/2–1787)

138 *The Rites and ceremonies of the Greek Church, in Russia; containing an account of its doctrine, worship, and discipline* 1772

London: W. Owen, J. Dodsley, J. Rivington, T. Becket and P.A. de Hondt
Half-bound in blue morocco, top edge gilt, 31.2 × 26.2 cm (closed)
RCIN 1051871

Provenance Dedicated to and acquired by George III

Literature Cross 2014b, D8

John Glen King came to St Petersburg some time after his ordination in 1756 as chaplain to the British Factory, the centre of the British mercantile community in the city. His post gave him the opportunity to research the history of the Russian Church. The notes he originally produced were only for himself and his friends, but further study led him deeper, and fired him to write a more accurate and scholarly account than those told by previous English travellers. They knew nothing of the language or the subject, 'but went into a church, stared about them, and then came home, and published an account of what they saw, according to their own imagination; [...] not seldom misunderstanding whatever they beheld'.[9] Apparently authoritative works would repeat these misunderstandings as plain fact (for example, he cites John Perry's account (cat. 11) of church ceremonies, much repeated by subsequent authors, as 'one continued series of blunders and absurdities'[10]).

The first version of this work was included as an appendix in Sir George Macartney's (1737–1806) *An Account of Russia, 1767* (1768), but King later published a fuller version in 1772, after receiving Fellowships of the Society of Antiquaries and of the Royal Society, and the degree of Doctor of Divinity from Oxford. His new academic reputation would have facilitated his publication, as would the patronage of George III, to whom the book is dedicated.

The work is well illustrated, giving plans of the layout of a Russian church, and the vestments and utensils used. This plate shows the iconostasis, the screen between the nave and the 'Holy of Holies' where the altar stood. The iconostasis was customarily adorned with icons, some set in specific places – for example, the scene of the Annunciation with the Virgin on the north side of the 'Royal doors' (in the centre of the screen), Christ on the south side, next to which would be placed an icon of the church's patron saint. Only the clergy were permitted behind the iconostasis; it is indicative of the religious significance of the Russian coronation, where the tsar entered into a holy marriage with Russia, that during his coronation he received communion behind the iconostasis, as if he were a cleric, for the first and only time, to signify his quasi-sacred status. ES

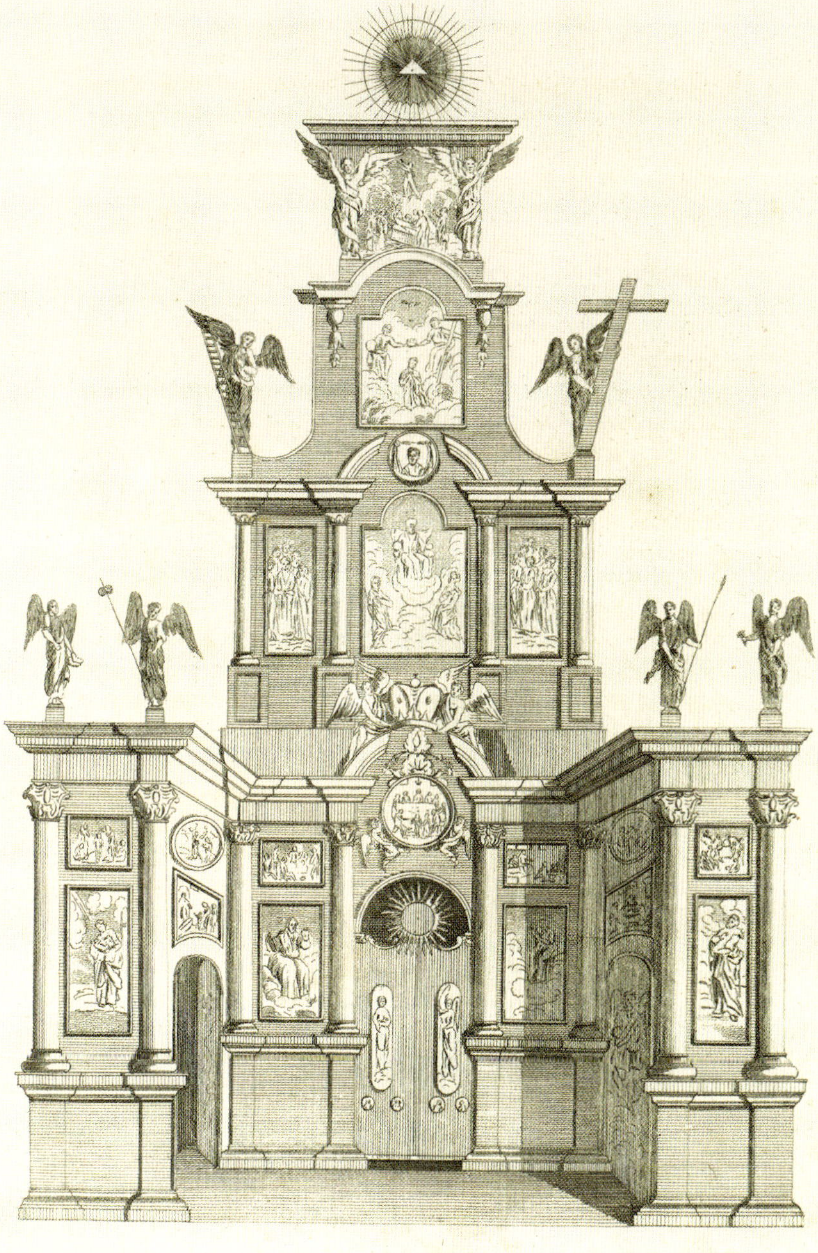

MOSCOW SCHOOL

139 *Icon of St Zosima and St Savvaty with the Monastery of Solovetsky*
?*c*.1600–1650

Oil on panel, 28.1 × 23.0 cm
Inscribed: *Ѡбитель сты(х) прп(до)бны(х) ω(т)Ђць Зосимы и СаватЂ(А) СОЛОВЄ(Ц)КИ(Х) ЧЮ(ДО)ТВО(Р)Ц(ωВ)*
('The Monastery of the holy and venerable fathers, Zosima and Savvaty, the performers of miracles at Solovetsky')
RCIN 403387

Provenance Purchased by Prince Albert as part of the Oettingen-Wallerstein collection, 1848

Literature Manchester 1857, no. 6

This icon (no. 8 in the Oettingen-Wallerstein listing) depicts the monastery founded by St Savvaty and St Zosima, monks of the so-called 'Northern Thebaid' (the tradition in Russia of monks living in the wilderness, as the early Christian monks and hermits had lived near Thebes in Egypt). Founded in 1436 on Solovetsky Island in the White Sea, it was a centre of spirituality and grew to be a major centre of prayer, icon painting and pilgrimage. It was also a centre of Old Believer activity, following the schism of the late seventeenth century after the alterations to the liturgy and church practices under Patriarch Nikon (1605–81). More than 20 of these icons are known; as a rule, they are of relatively small size and almost square in format. Depending on the date of painting, the monastery walls are constructed either of wood (an earlier version, built *c*.1578) or of stone.

The icon shows, in the centre, the two founding saints to right and left of an image of the Redeemer (made without hands), as if inside the centre of the Transfiguration (Preobrazhensky) Cathedral (1556–64), with the Dormition (Uspensky) Cathedral (1552–7) to the left with its icon of the Virgin, and the Nicholas (Nikolsky) Cathedral, with its icon of St Nicholas, to the right, all carefully detailed. To the left of the Dormition Cathedral, with the icon of the Virgin, is a shrine of St Zosima, showing the saint's relics in repose, and the shrine of St Savvaty next to the Transfiguration Cathedral. The presence of the icons and view of the saints' relics – giving the impression of a tour of the monastery's treasures, as well as its size – points to the icon as one for personal devotion, most likely for one of the monks of the monastery.

The geographical and physical isolation of the monastery is illustrated by its high walls with seven gates and eight towers (built in 1584–94 by an architect named Trifon) leading onto the White Sea (fig. 48). The riches of the sea around the monastery, with fish, ducks and geese in the waters, allude to the natural resources (along with salt, pearls, mica and wood) which supported the monastic community and a significant lay population. In a similar icon in the collection of Girton College, Cambridge,[11] whales and porpoises can be seen. While desolate and difficult to reach, the environs of the monastery and the island are clearly delineated by the icon painter; for example, the details of trees and foliage, and the island quality of the location is emphasised by the sweep of water around the monastery. The details of the buildings, and in particular the sense of activity and allusion to the sounds of monastery life, seen with the two bell-ringers pulling ropes, give animation to the image. The central cathedral of the monastery dedicated to the Transfiguration is presented as an image of Christ flanked by

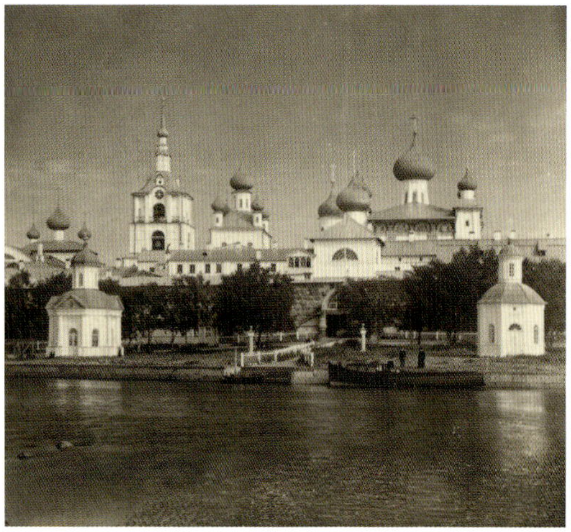

FIG. 48
Sergei Mikhailovich Prokudin-Gorskii
View of the Solovetsky monastery, 1915
Photographic print, 8.0 × 8.0 cm
Library of Congress, Washington, DC

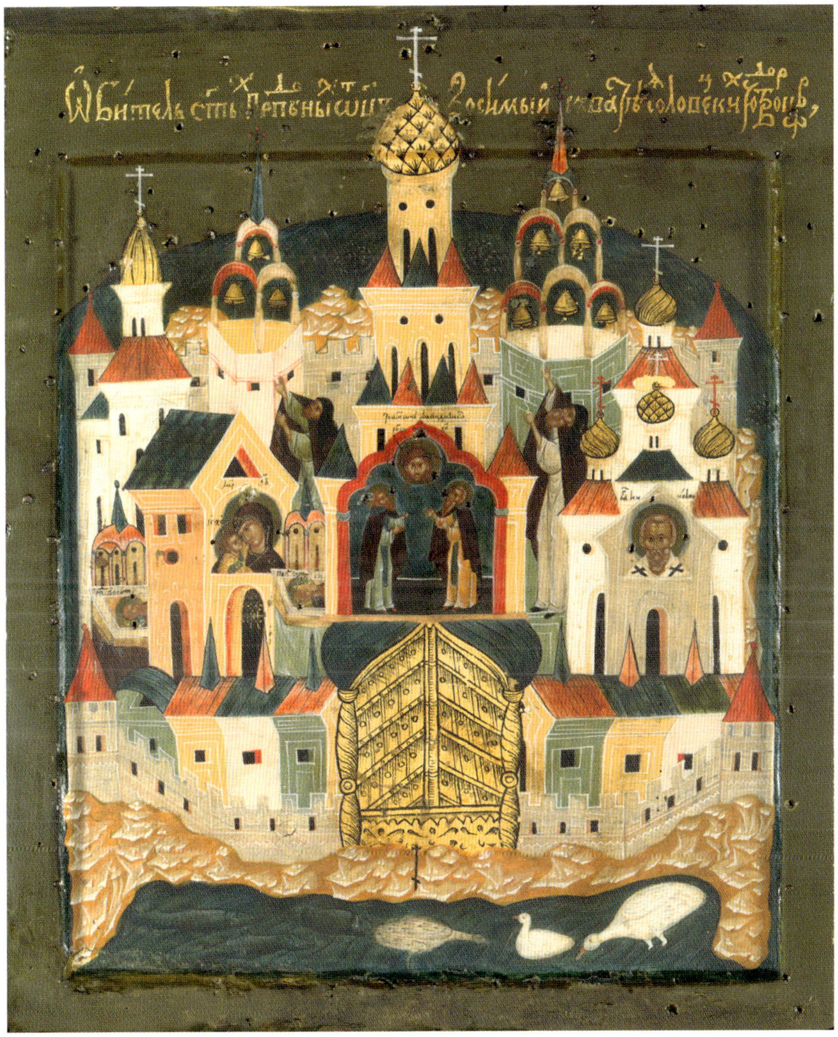

the two founding saints, rather than following the description of the events in the Gospel, where the prophets Elijah and Moses flanked the transfigured Christ, possibly suggesting that the founders of the monastery were echoing the patriarchs of the Old Testament. This can be compared with an icon in the Museum of Russian Icons, Moscow, showing the Transfiguration icon flanked by the two saints who were canonised in 1547.[12]

The icon is executed on a single piece of wood, probably lime, with two wooden battens fixed into the reverse of the panel. The build-up of the layers on the front of the panel follows a traditional technique; a canvas layer is applied over the panel, followed by the application of a white chalk ground, underdrawing, local gilding of the background, and finally the egg tempera paint layers. A particular feature of this icon is a thoroughly painted underdrawing layer in black paint, visible through the paint layers, particularly in the architecture.

Following its painting, the icon was covered with *basma*, sheets of embossed or engraved metal, which were pinned to the surface, surrounding and enhancing the key features of the painting, but obscuring other areas. At some point, this has been removed, but the holes, and in some cases the tacks, survive. Both this and the Dormition of the Virgin icon (cat. 140) bear the label, *II Zimmer*, on the reverse, which could refer to the hanging arrangements of these and other icons in the Oettingen-Wallerstein collection.

SJP & RDES

ATTRIBUTED TO MOSCOW SCHOOL

140 *Icon of the Dormition of the Virgin* c.1700

Oil on panel, 31.9 × 27.0 cm
RCIN 403491

Provenance Acquired by Prince Albert as part of the Oettingen-Wallerstein collection, 1848

Literature Manchester 1857, no. 5

The icon of the Dormition (no. 1 in the Oettingen-Wallerstein catalogue) was described as having being brought by a crusader, Count Helfenstein, from the East, and was preserved in the treasury of a sovereign German abbey until its secularisation. The Helfenstein and crusading connection can be discounted, but the possibility of the icon having been in a secularised Württemberg monastery is plausible (although which monastery is virtually impossible to identify).

The icon depicts the Dormition (death and resurrection) of the Virgin following the traditional Orthodox rendering of the narrative. The Virgin, following her death, is carried on a bier to her tomb by the Apostles, St Paul and St Joseph of Arimathea. The procession is accompanied by two of her three handmaids (Sepphora, Abigail and Jael), bishops, including James (Christ's brother) and Timothy, and other disciples. Under the gaze of the Holy Spirit, the Virgin's soul, wrapped as an infant (a reversal of the Nativity, when the Virgin carried the swaddled Christ child), is carried into Heaven in the arms of Christ, who is surrounded by a glory of light. At the head of the bier, the Apostle Peter censes the Virgin, while at the foot stands St Paul. Following the rendition of events by Dionysius the Areopagite (who is depicted top right), the bier was approached by Athonios, who wished to topple it over; he was prevented from doing so by the Archangel Michael, who cut off Athonios's hands when he touched the bier. The narrative continued that Athonios repented, converted and was healed. An interesting feature of this icon, in comparison to the painted underdrawing in the icon of Solovetsky, is that the outlines of the figures are incised into the ground layer – a technique usually used to identify areas to be gilded, rather than painted.

In the exhibition of *Art Treasures of the United Kingdom collected at Manchester*, this icon, that of the Solovetsky monastery (cat. 139) and another Oettingen-Wallerstein work, a Greek or Cretan icon of the Nativity (RCIN 403381), hung between an encaustic painting from Ancient Rome and a Cimabue triptych. **SJP & RDES**

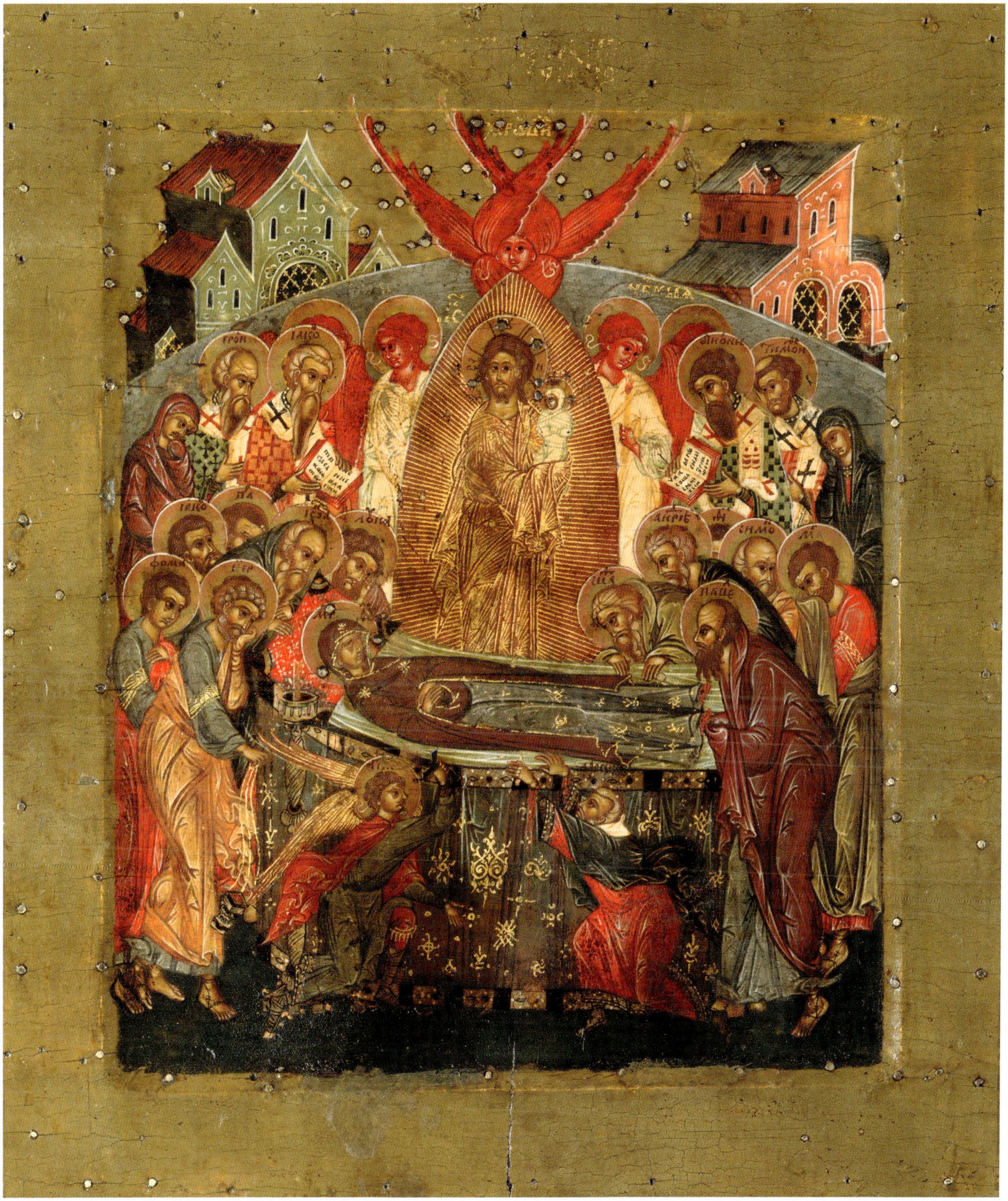

141 ***Напрестольное Евангелие*** (*Naprestol'noe Evangelie*, 'Altar Gospel') November 1789

Moscow: Synodalnaia Typografiia
Bound in wooden boards, with floral patterned metal overlay and clasps, enamels of Christ and the Four Evangelists on the front board, 31.2 × 26.2 cm (closed)
RCIN 1122471

Provenance Probably acquired by Queen Victoria, after 1856

The *Evangelie* (Gospel Book), in the Orthodox tradition, is revered in the same manner as the image of Christ – that is, as an icon, meaning an image, from the Greek εἰκών (*eikon*). It has a central place in the liturgy, which begins with the priest lifting the volume high and making the sign of the cross with it over the altar. When carried in procession, it is always accompanied by candles, particularly during the Divine Liturgy. On this occasion, it is carried at the head of the procession of the clergy, known as the Little Entrance, to the altar behind the iconostasis (cat. 138), before the readings take place. The faithful are then blessed with the Gospels after the readings.

The book traditionally lives on the altar, and is always bound in metal (usually gold or silver) or placed in a metal box; leather, being dead skin, is forbidden, since the Word of Christ is considered life-giving. This volume, believed to be from the Crimea, has a metal binding decorated with enamel roundels depicting the four Evangelists, with Christ at the centre. Unlike many other examples of this type of binding, this volume has no enamels on the back board, but has a cross surmounted by the sun as a centrepiece. The clasps have divine figures on them, possibly the Apostles Peter and Paul. The text was printed in red and black, with four Evangelist portraits at the beginning of each Gospel; the image of St John shows the most tangible evidence of use – marks from drops of candle wax. ES

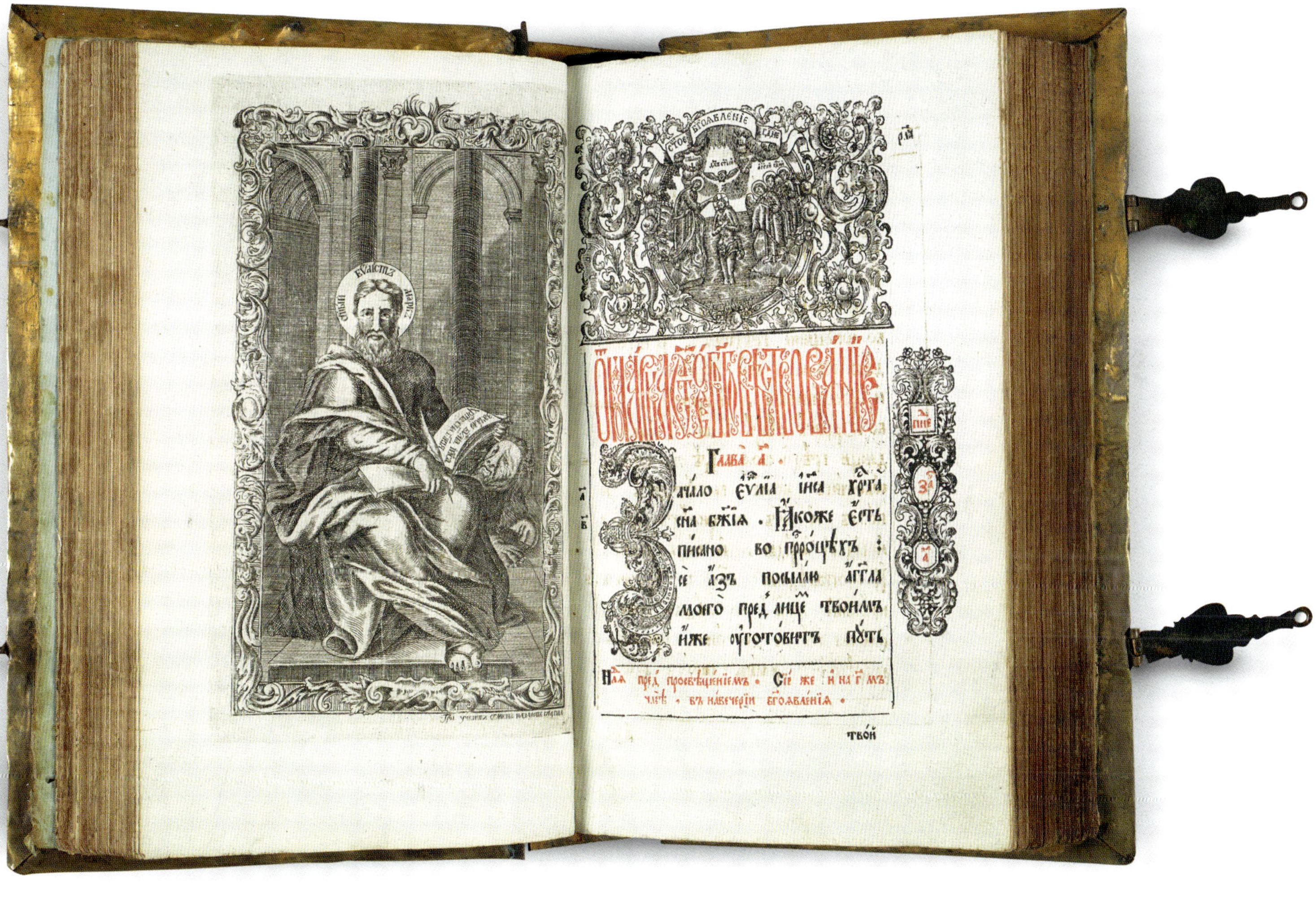
Глава а҃.
Зача́ло еѵⷢ҇лїа і҃са хрⷭ҇та
сн҃а бж҃їа. Ꙗ҆́коже є҆сть
пи́сано во прⷪ҇ро́цѣхъ:
се̑ а҆́зъ посыла́ю а҆́гг҃ла
моего̀ пред̾ лицеⷨ҇ твои́мъ
и҆́же оу҆гото́витъ пꙋ́ть
Нⷱ҇а пред̾ просвѣще́нїемъ. Сїе̑ же и҆ на г҃ мъ
чⷭ҇е. въ навечерїи бг҃оꙗвле́нїа.
твой

KHLEBNIKOV, SILVERSMITH; ICON PAINTER UNKNOWN

142 *Patronal icon of Prince Andrew of Greece* c.1889

Silver mount, wood, egg tempera, 21.9 × 32.1 × 2.0 cm (closed)
Struck with Moscow silver mark, 84 zolotniks, maker's mark in Cyrillic of Ivan Khlebnikov and 1889 assay mark with initials И.Е
RCIN 48599

Provenance Prince Andrew of Greece and Denmark; by descent, HRH The Duke of Edinburgh

Khlebnikov was a firm of silversmiths, established in Moscow by Ivan Khlebnikov (1819–81) in 1870. After his death, his sons Mikhail, Alexei, Nikolai and Vladimir, took over and rebranded the firm as Khlebnikov Sons and Partners. In the same year, the firm was awarded the title of supplier to the imperial court.

Here, Khlebnikov has mounted three panels to form a travelling icon, which was intended as a gift for Prince Andrew of Greece and Denmark, father of HRH The Duke of Edinburgh. In the centre panel of the triptych is St Andrew the Apostle, his patronal saint, flanked on the left with his parents' patronal saints, St George and St Olga (for his father, George I of Greece (1845–1913), and his mother, Queen Olga, formerly Grand Duchess Olga Constantinovna of Russia (1851–1926)). On the right wing are his maternal grandparents' patronal saints, St Constantine and St Alexandra (wife of the Emperor Diocletian), for Grand Duke Constantine Nikolaevich and Grand Duchess Alexandra Iosifovna (cat. 149). Above the image of the Apostle is depicted Saint Euthymius the Great, whose Orthodox feast day, 2 February, was the Prince's birthday. This triptych, therefore, brings together the Prince's most important saints. A travelling icon in a simple silver case with a securing hook, it would have been placed in the Prince's rooms; the small traces of candle wax on the surface suggest it had been used (as intended) for personal devotion. SJP

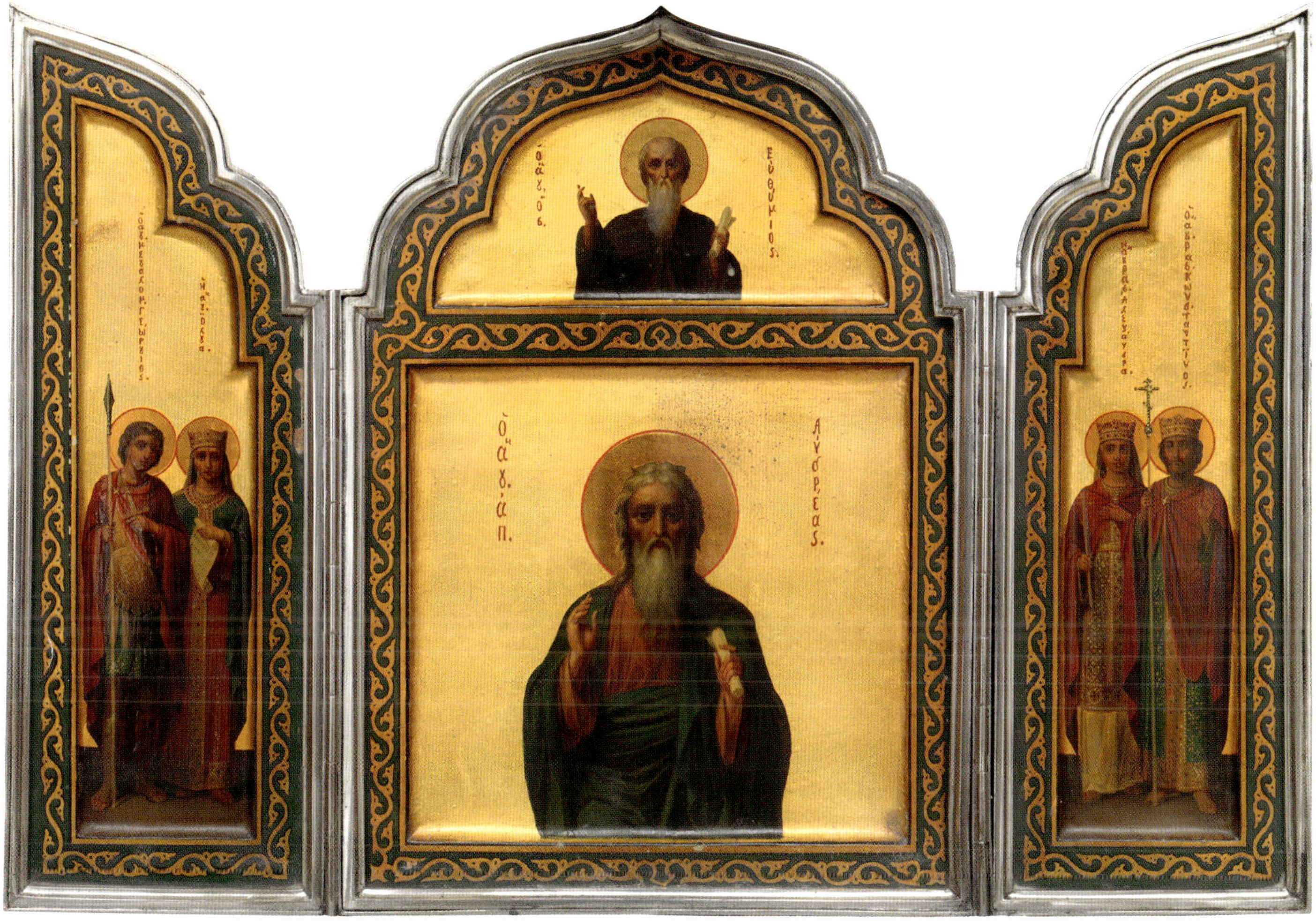

ATTRIBUTED TO VASILY PAVLOVICH GURIANOV (1867–1920)

143 *Icon of the Virgin of the Protecting Veil with Sts Martha and Mary*
*c.*1912–13

Oil on panel, frame 24.7 × 21.7 × 2.9 cm, icon 9.0 × 7.6 cm
Inscribed on reverse, in ink on silk: *Windsor 3 July 1913 / "The Lord is here & calleth thee" / St John Chapter 11 v. 28 / Martha Mary, House of Charity, Moscow / This little ikon of the Holy Virgin with Martha and Mary is a token of love from your ever grateful and devoted 'own child', your grandchild Ella. / THE ICON PLACED HERE BY H.I.H THE GRAND DUCHESS ELIZABETH FEODOROVNA. / 3RD JULY 1913. / THIS FRAME IS MADE FROM THE QUEEN ELIZABETH OAK.*
Engraved mark on metal icon mount: *8е Априля 1912г* (8th April 1912)
RCIN 407589

Provenance Placed at the Frogmore mausoleum by Grand Duchess Elizabeth Feodorovna, 1913

The icon depicts the Virgin with the protecting veil and the two saints to whom the convent of Martha and Mary was dedicated at its foundation, in 1908, by the widowed Grand Duchess Elizabeth Feodorovna. The dedication of the cathedral of the convent was to the Intercession of the Virgin (*Pokrov*), the same dedication as St Basil's Cathedral in Red Square, which commemorated a miraculous appearance of the Virgin at Blachernae in Constantinople in the tenth century, which, according to the chronicler, Nestor (*c.*1050/56–*c.*1114), saved the city from assault from pagan Rus'.

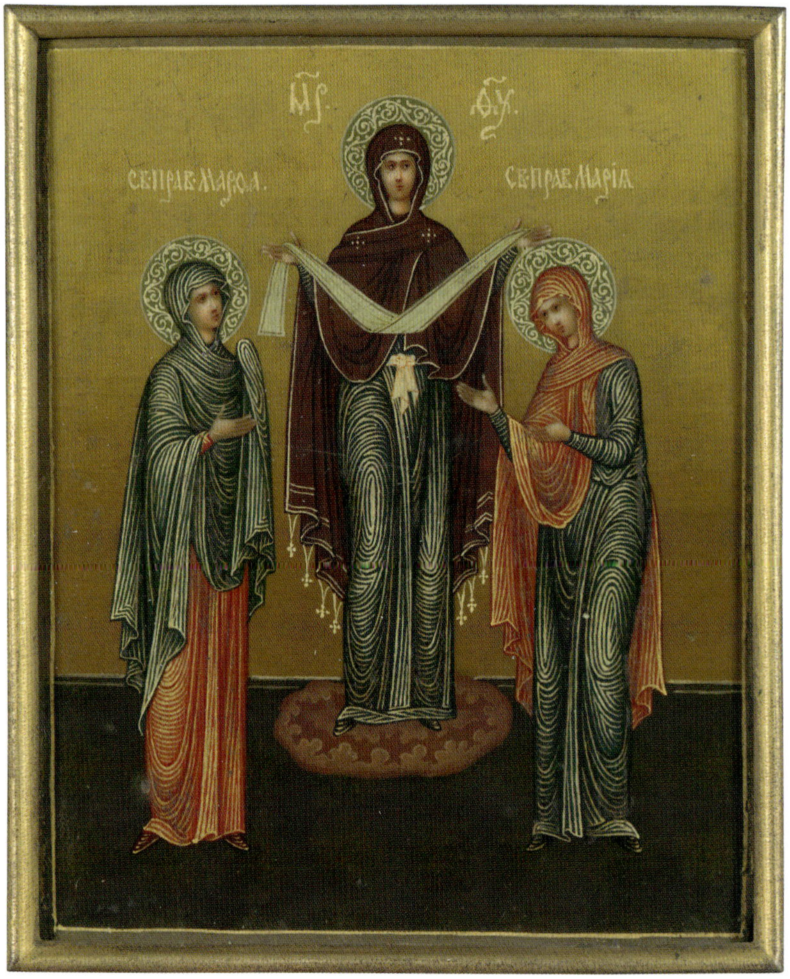

The Grand Duchess, elder sister of the Empress Alexandra Feodorovna, founded the monastery in the outskirts of Moscow after the assassination of her husband, Grand Duke Sergei (1857–1905), brother of Emperor Alexander III, in February 1905. She employed artists of renown, including the art nouveau architect, Alexey Shchusev (1873–1949), and the fresco painters and mosaicists, Nesterov (1862–1942) and Korin (1892–1967), to decorate the central church (*Katholicon*) of the monastery. Similarly, she employed icon painters of the highest standards of the time, and it is possible that this icon was painted by Vasily P. Gurianov, who was the chosen artist for icons for the imperial court. Other examples by the artist bear the same gold ground – for example, the icon of Sts Peter and Paul, St Pimen the Great and St Moses Murim in the Museum of Russian Icons, Moscow.[13]

The icon was placed by the Grand Duchess at the tomb of her maternal grandparents – Queen Victoria and Prince Albert – in the mausoleum at Frogmore, during her last visit to England in July 1913, when she visited the King and Queen at Buckingham Palace and lunched with the Dowager Empress Maria Feodorovna and Queen Alexandra at Marlborough House. SJP

RUSSIAN

144 *Icon of the Virgin of Tikhvin (icon of the Mother of God Tikhvin)* c.2016

Tempera on panel, patinated silver, silver gilt, enamel, cubic zirconia and synthetic pearls, 48.0 × 43.0 cm
Marks: 925, ΛΜΑΑΤ, HE
RCIN 408461

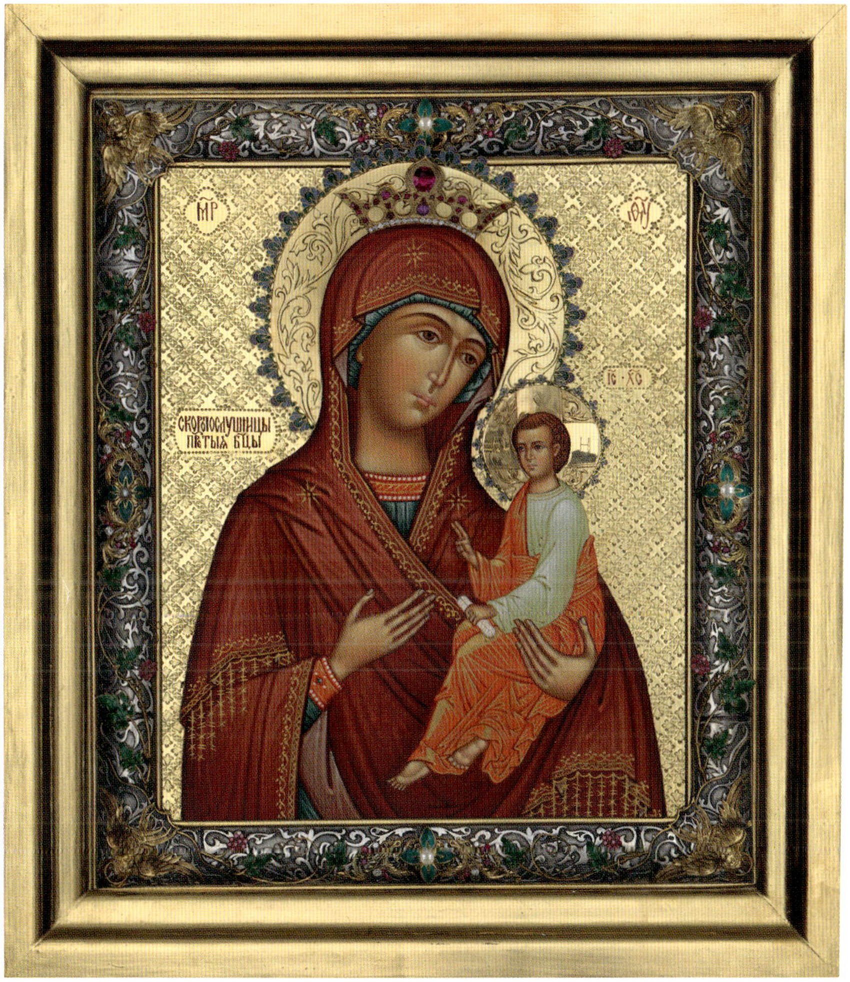

Provenance Presented to Her Majesty Queen Elizabeth II by Patriarch Kirill of Moscow, 18 October 2016

The visit by Kirill, Patriarch of Moscow and All Rus' in October 2016 was the first visit to the United Kingdom by a Russian Patriarch. It provided an opportunity for the Head of the Russian Orthodox Church to meet Her Majesty The Queen, Supreme Governor of the Church of England. The icon presented by the Patriarch is a modern rendition of the image of the 'Virgin Hodegetria', in which the Virgin holds the Christ child and gestures towards him as the source of salvation, 'the Way', thus prefiguring the words of Christ, 'I am the way, the truth and the life' (John 14:6). The form of the icon, which dates back to Byzantine times, was traditionally said to have been painted by St Luke; this example follows the tradition of icons of the Virgin of Tikhvin, an icon type venerated across Russia. SJP

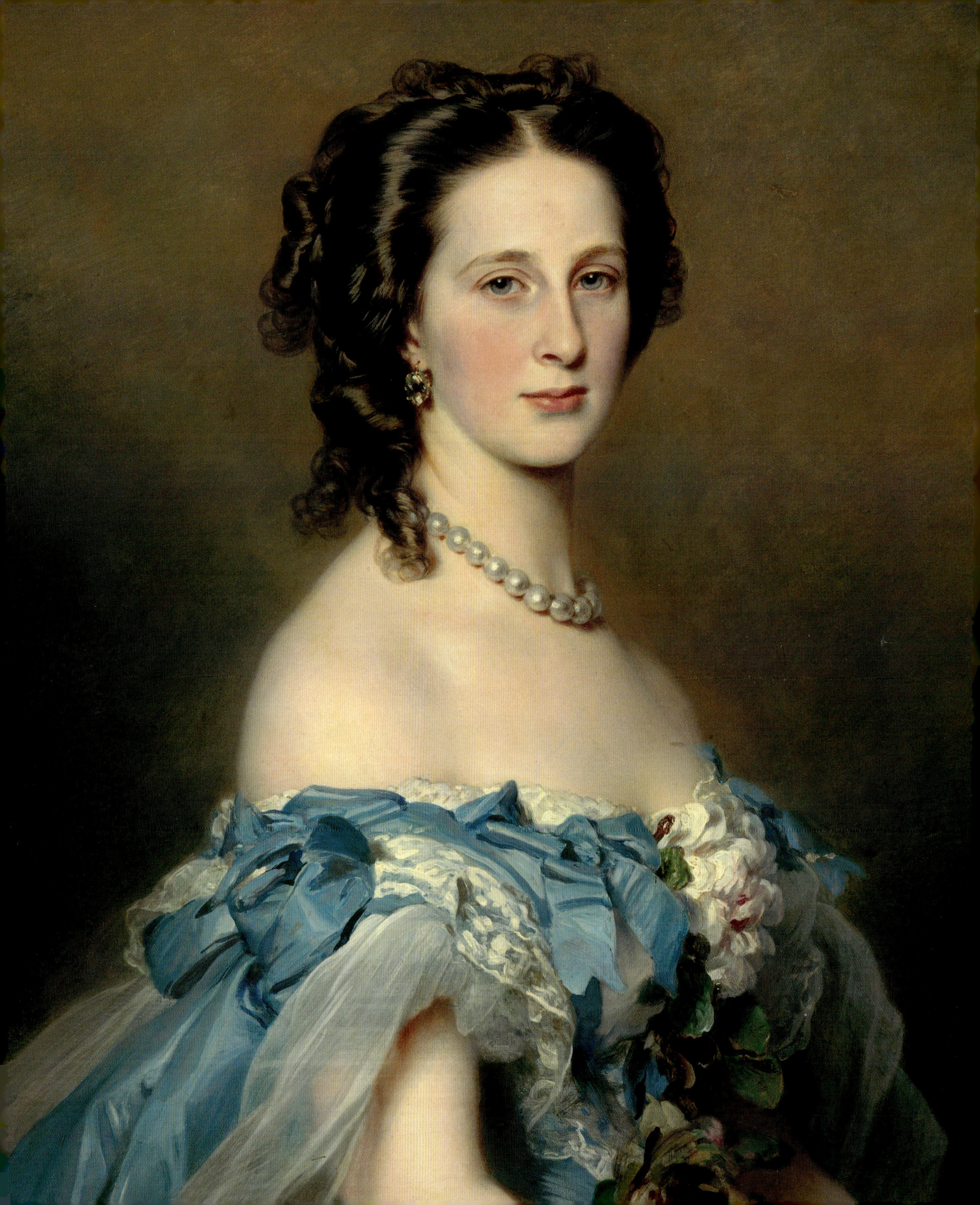

7
Dynastic Links

CAROLINE DE GUITAUT

it seemed to me like a dream when I reflected upon it, that we should be walking about with, and breakfasting with, the Emperor of Russia, the Gtest of all earthly monarchs

(Queen Victoria's Journal, 4 June 1844)[1]

Politics of both state and family were, as in any other period in British monarchical history, closely blended during the nineteenth century. But away from the business of nation and empire, the English and Russian royal families enjoyed a close relationship, and in spite of periods of political isolation, this continued until the tragic outcome of the Revolution in 1918. The relationship is documented through thousands of letters and telegrams, exchanged between cousins, aunts, uncles, parents, children, grandparents and family-in-law across Europe. Direct inter-dynastic marriage linked the English and Russian royal families in only a handful of instances, but the close family links between the crowned heads of Europe in the late nineteenth century – the result of power-play and matchmaking – resulted in a family network which stretched from England to Russia, from Denmark to Greece, across the continents of Europe, Asia, and beyond.

Many of the exchanges of correspondence are punctuated by significant events: betrothals, weddings, births, deaths and funerals, as well as family intrigues and scandals, which enable the reader to gain a deep insight into the dynamics of these relationships. Much of this correspondence has been published in volumes of letters and in the personal diaries of the protagonists, and has inevitably been the primary source for contemporary and retrospective biographies, books and catalogues. While this chapter references personal correspondence between the families held primarily in the Royal Archives at Windsor Castle and in the State Archive of the Russian Federation in Moscow, this is used only as background to the visual documentation of dynastic links, intimate family occasions and informal gatherings, seen through the paintings of Winterhalter, Tuxen and Chevalier (cats 148, 203, 174), or the photographs of Bergamasco (1830–96) and usually marked by the production of works of art, specially commissioned to commemorate these specific occasions.

The earliest links between the British and Russian royal families came via Germany and Prussia in the nineteenth century, and are illustrated through a number of portraits and miniatures. Queen Victoria's aunt, Juliane, Princess of Saxe-Coburg-Saalfeld became Grand Duchess Anna Feodorovna on her marriage to Grand Duke Constantine of Russia in 1796. Grand Duchess Anna was not only aunt to both Queen Victoria and Prince Albert, but her mother, Augusta, Duchess of Saxe-Coburg-Saalfeld, was Victoria and Albert's shared grandmother. Queen Victoria was particularly keen to document her family and ancestors through portraiture and, later, photography, engaging a number of artists whom she and Prince Albert favoured, including Franz Xaver Winterhalter, whom the Queen

Grand Duchess Alexandra Iosifovna of Russia (detail of cat. 149)

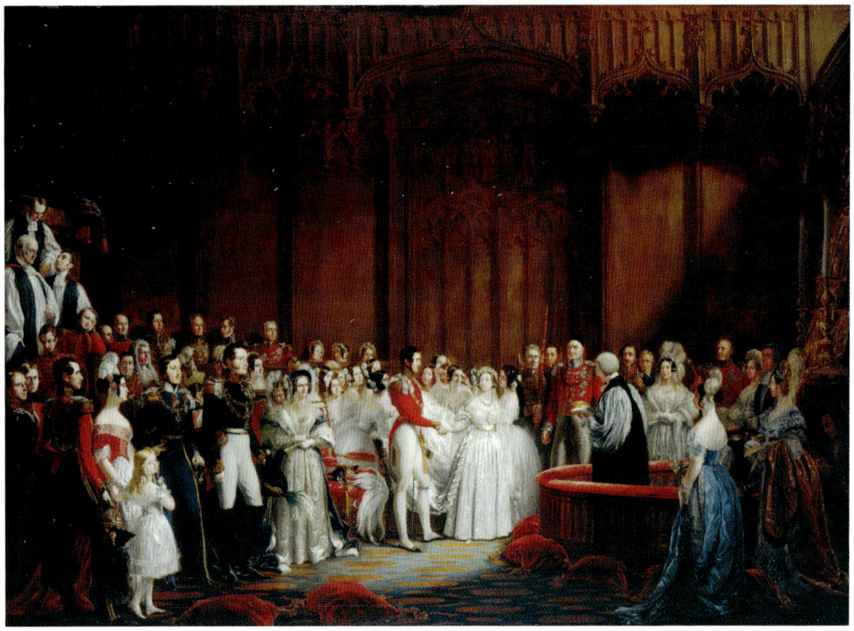

FIG. 49
Sir George Hayter
The Marriage of Queen Victoria, 10 February 1840, 1840–2
Oil on canvas, 195.8 × 273.5 cm
RCIN 407165

Facing
FIG. 50
Emile Marcovitch
The Family of Prince and Princess Andrew of Greece, 1929
Gelatin silver print, 17.7 x 23.5 cm
RCIN 2584778

commissioned to paint her aunt as a present for her own mother in 1848 (cat. 146) Sadly, Anna Feodorovna's marriage was not a happy one. Arranged by Constantine's grandmother, Catherine II, when he was 16 and Juliane was 14, they were to be separated only three years later, although it took 19 years for their marriage to be annulled. However, their union was to place the small Duchy of Saxe-Coburg at the dynastic heart of Europe, halfway between England and Russia. This was further emphasised by the marriage of Juliane's brother, Leopold, to the only child of George IV and Caroline of Brunswick in 1816, and, perhaps more significantly, by the marriage of Leopold's nephew, Prince Albert of Saxe-Coburg and Gotha, to Queen Victoria in 1840 (fig. 49).

An interesting dynastic portrait by Winterhalter, painted in 1846, depicts the young Queen with her future heir, Bertie (later King Edward VII), then aged five, dressed in a loosely fitted overshirt, described as his 'Russian dress'. The blouse is an adaptation of traditional boys' and men's shirts of the seventeenth century, which usually featured a cutaway collar with asymmetric placket applied with ribbon.[2] There are other instances of the young prince wearing a Russian-style tunic from 1843 onwards, and each one (as documented in cat. 116) seems to coincide with the presence of a member of the Russian imperial family in England. The blouse may have been a gift from Emperor Nicholas I, during his visit in 1844, but it would seem that, having documented the dress in her own Journal and sketchbook, Queen Victoria was acknowledging both her pleasure in her son's Russian-inspired costume and her own dynastic links to the Romanov dynasty.[3]

The 1844 visit of Nicholas I provided Queen Victoria with the opportunity of combining diplomatic discussions with an intimate insight into her happy domestic family life. 'I think our simple & unaffected reception of the Emperor in our home life [...] have made an impression on his mind.'[4] Such visits illustrate the dichotomy between political negotiation and personal friendship, which were ever present in the mutual relationship between the two ruling dynasties. Queen Victoria's comment could indicate that she was perhaps desirous of closer family union, considering the need to marry her nine children, and thus align both dynastic and political alliances. However, the Queen was deeply mindful of the potential political difficulties of such a direct union between her family and the Romanovs, and of the great differences between the two dynasties as she saw them: 'one has to keep in mind that he has been brought up with the greatest severity by an autocratic and unsociable mother, the father having been a madman & a perfect monster.'[5] The visit was marked by the usual

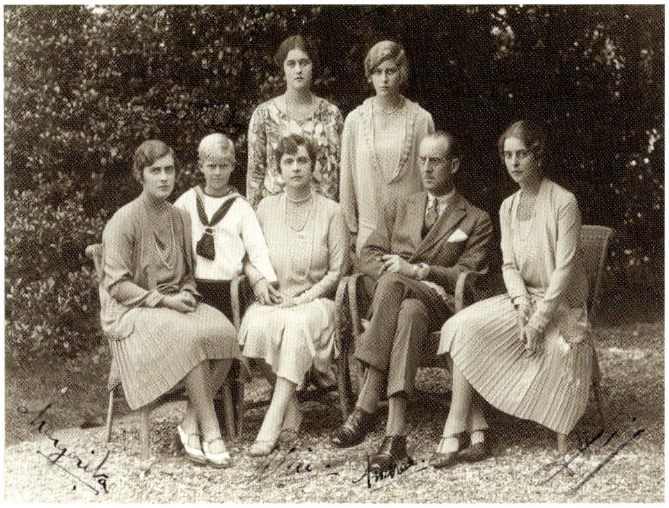

exchange of gifts, demonstrating examples of the best native products of both countries (cats 97–98). However, it is the personal gifts given by Queen Victoria, which are more intimate and carefully considered, which hint at a desire for closer familial allegiance. These gifts included a 'bracelet of enamel & diamonds containing my hair', which she begged 'the Emperor to place at his feet'; and a cup, 'similar to the one I had given at Ascot Races', which he had 'so much admired', and which she promised to send when it was completed.[6]

In 1847, Grand Duke Constantine, second son of Nicholas I and Alexandra Feodorovna, visited Queen Victoria. In a letter to the Queen, Lady Georgiana Bloomfield, Queen Victoria's maid of honour until her marriage to the diplomat and peer, 2nd Baron Bloomfield in 1845, who was secretary, and later envoy to St Petersburg, conveys on behalf of the Emperor and Empress, the 'warmest and most sincere thanks for the kind and flattering manner in which the Grand Duke Constantine has been received in England'.[7] Lady Bloomfield conveys an atmospheric and detailed description of all that she has seen and done, in both St Petersburg and Moscow: 'the situation and fine views of the sea between the trees' at Peterhof 'reminded me constantly of the Isle of Wight'. The success of Nicholas I's visit to London in 1844, and the mutual admiration between him and Queen Victoria, encouraged the Emperor to hope that one day the Queen would visit Russia, 'which he said would be the thing of all others which could afford him the greatest and most heartfelt pleasure'. It is evident that Queen Victoria wished to have the fullest possible visual record of the imperial family. Lady Bloomfield writes: 'I enquired only the other day whether there were any new engravings of the different members of the Imperial family, and was told there were none but should any be published Your Majesty may depend upon my sending them immediately'. In a later letter, dated 7 October, Lady Bloomfield describes the rebuilding of the Kremlin by the Emperor following the fire of 1812: 'it is in the same style as the old but so very large that it crushes all the churches and buildings near it which is to be lamented'.[8] She was particularly impressed by 'the ball room, St George's Hall as it is called is one of the finest I ever saw, 210 feet long and 70 wide, but nothing surprises me in this country than the number and enormous size of the Palaces and public buildings'. Eight years later, in 1855, Queen Victoria and Prince Albert were to make one of the most significant architectural additions to Buckingham Palace, with the building of the vast Ball and Concert Room by Thomas Cubitt (1788–1855), to the designs of Sir James Pennethorne (1801–71).

In 1848, Princess Alexandra of Saxe-Altenburg, daughter of Joseph, Duke of Saxe-Altenburg (1789–1868) and the Duchess of Württemberg (1799–1848), married Grand Duke Constantine Nikolaevich, second son of Nicholas I and Alexandra Feodorovna. Princess Alexandra took the name, Grand Duchess Alexandra Iosifovna, on her conversion to Russian Orthodoxy. As a wedding gift from the Emperor and Empress, the young couple received the Marble Palace in St Petersburg as their home, originally built for Count Grigory Orlov (1734–83), in 1768, to the design of Antonio Rinaldi (*c.*1710–94). The Grand Duchess's elegant portrait by Winterhalter (cat. 149) originally hung in their St Petersburg residence. The motivation for its commissioning may have been the success of the artist's masterful portrait of the Grand Duchess's sister-in-law, Empress Maria Alexandrovna.[9] In 1867, the couple's eldest daughter, Olga Constantinovna, married King George I of Greece, becoming Queen of the Hellenes. One of her eight children, Prince Andrew of Greece, was the father of HRH The Duke of Edinburgh (fig. 50). Following the wedding of Princess Elizabeth to Prince Philip of Greece and Denmark in 1947, the House of Windsor and the Romanov dynasty were linked once more.

WILLIAM CORDEN THE YOUNGER (1819–1900),
AFTER ELISABETH VIGÉE LE BRUN (1755–1842)

145 *Juliane, Princess of Saxe-Coburg-Saalfeld, Grand Duchess Anna Feodorovna (1781–1860)* 1844

Oil on canvas, 83.8 × 70.8 cm
RCIN 407174

Provenance Painted for Queen Victoria, 1844

This work is after a portrait of 1797 of Juliane, later Grand Duchess Anna Feodorovna, by Vigée Le Brun (Pushkin State Museum of Fine Arts, Moscow). Le Brun recorded that she painted two half-length portraits of the Princess during her sojourn in St Petersburg, and one of these was recorded in the Herzogliches Museum, Gotha before the Second World War.

The original portrait dates from around the time of the sitter's marriage to Grand Duke Constantine, brother to Alexander I and Nicholas I. However, her marriage was not a success; by 1813 she had settled in Switzerland, and the couple were divorced in 1820. The sitter was described by Vigée Le Brun in her *Memoirs* as 'not as outstandingly beautiful as her sister-in-law, but still very pretty. She must have been about sixteen and the most lively exuberance shone through her features'[10]. In 1844, William Corden accompanied his father, William Corden the Elder, to Coburg, in order to copy a number of family portraits. The visit was arranged by Prince Albert. In addition to this engaging portrait of Juliane, aunt to both Queen Victoria and Prince Albert, he painted her sisters, Antoinette (1779–1824) and Sophie (1778–1835), and their mother, Augusta, Duchess of Saxe-Coburg-Saalfeld (1757–1831), also grandmother to Queen Victoria and Prince Albert.[11] The portraits are recorded as hanging in Queen Victoria's bedroom at Windsor Castle in the nineteenth century.

Here, Corden, praised by Queen Victoria and Prince Albert for his skills in copying, captures some of the sitter's liveliness and youth; however, the arresting pose and striking contrast between her red shawl, white collar and mass of brown locks are thanks to the mastery of Vigée Le Brun's brush.

A further anonymous copy of this portrait is also in the Royal Collection.[12] AB

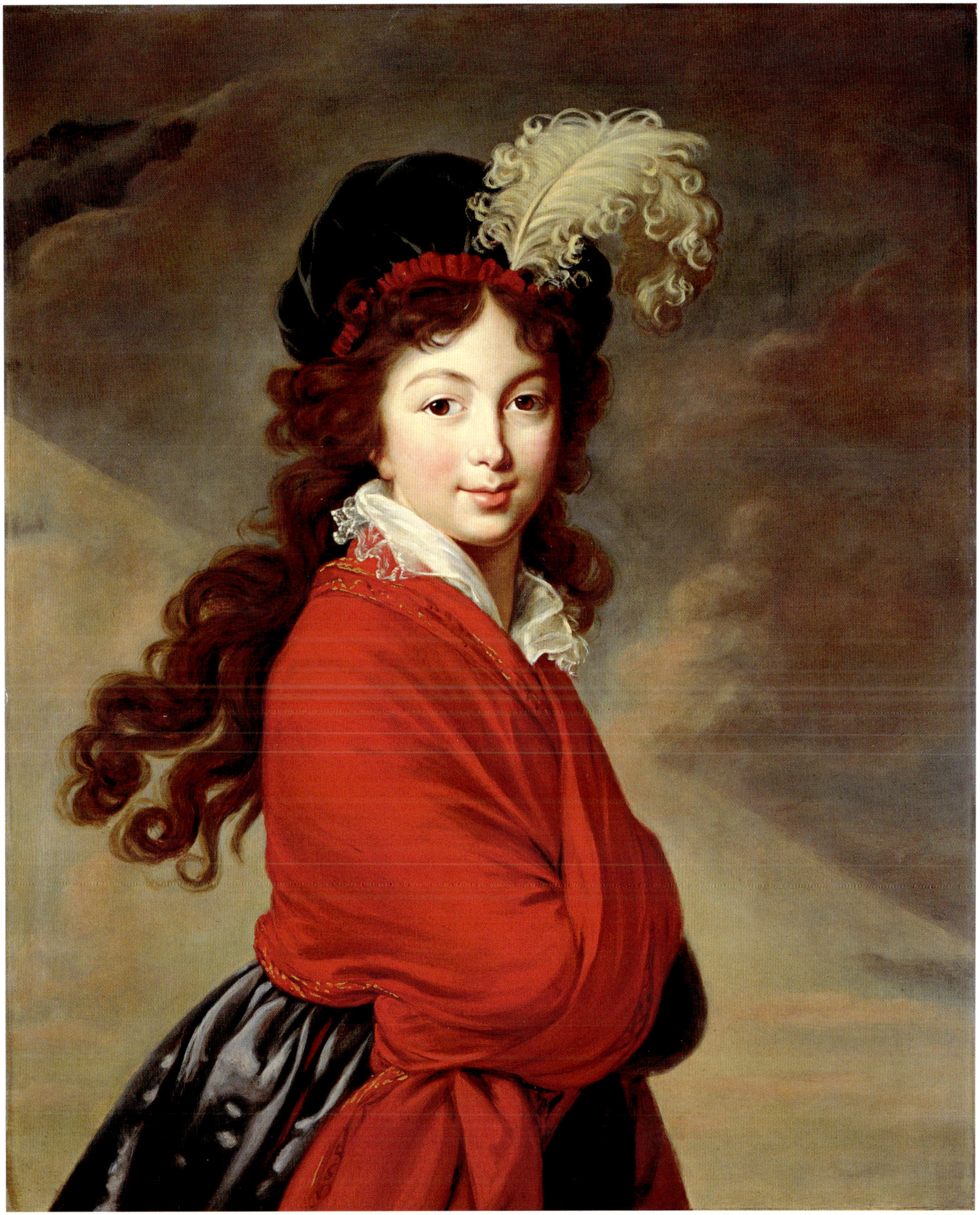

FRANZ XAVER WINTERHALTER (1805–1873)

146 *Juliane, Princess of Saxe-Coburg-Saalfeld, Grand Duchess Anna Feodorovna (1781–1860)* 1848

Oil on canvas, 140.9 × 97.7 cm
Signed and dated: *F Winterhalter / Boissière 1848*
RCIN 404524

Provenance Painted for Queen Victoria as a birthday present to the Duchess of Kent (the sitter's sister), 17 August 1848

Literature Millar 1992, no. 847

Here, Winterhalter depicts the sitter, over 50 years after Vigée Le Brun, with a wistful, almost world-weary expression following the failure of her marriage. Her niece, Feodora (1807–72), wrote of her 'life full of trials of all kind, her youth thrown away at that court, and now alone, amongst strangers here is indeed a bitter cup to the last [...] poor aunt, life must be a burthen to her; and her feelings are so young still'.[13]

The portrait was commissioned by Queen Victoria, the sitter's niece, as a birthday present for her mother, the Duchess of Kent, Juliane's sister, and is first recorded hanging at Frogmore House. In her Journal entry for 17 August 1848, the Queen described the portrait as 'an indescribably like and beautiful picture of Aunt Julia'.[14] The sitter's face is pleasingly framed by her straw hat, decorated with foliage, the delicate mauve of her dress subtly contrasting with the pale yellow ribbons. On her arm she wears a bracelet containing a miniature of Queen Victoria. A view of Boissière, near Geneva, where the Duchess was living, appears in the background. **AB**

GUGLIELMO FAIJA (1803–1873)

147 *Juliane, Princess of Saxe-Coburg-Saalfeld, Grand Duchess Anna Feodorovna (1781–1860)* 1848

Watercolour on ivory laid on card, 6.0 × 5.0 cm
RCIN 420722

Provenance Given by Queen Victoria to the Duchess of Kent, 17 August 1848; probably by descent to Queen Victoria, 1861

Literature Remington 2010, p. 237, no. 453

This is a bust-length copy by Guglielmo Faija, after the portrait by Winterhalter (cat. 146). and was also given as a birthday present to the Duchess of Kent by Queen Victoria. By 1841, her niece, Princess Feodora, reported to her half-sister, Queen Victoria: 'I went to see Mama and Aunt Julia, who I find very much changed, she looks now an old woman, such a pity, for she was so lovely once'.[15] **AB**

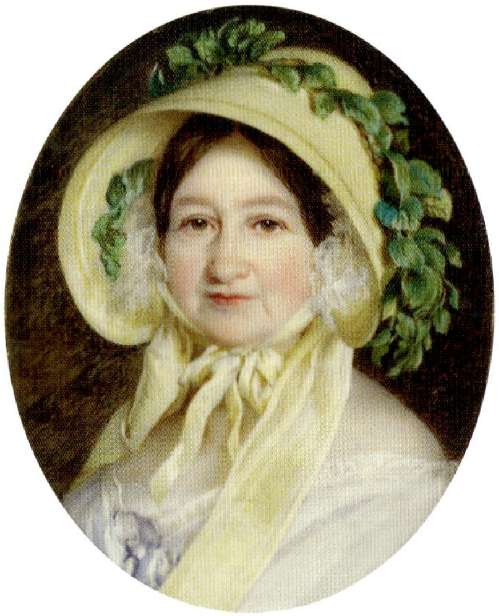

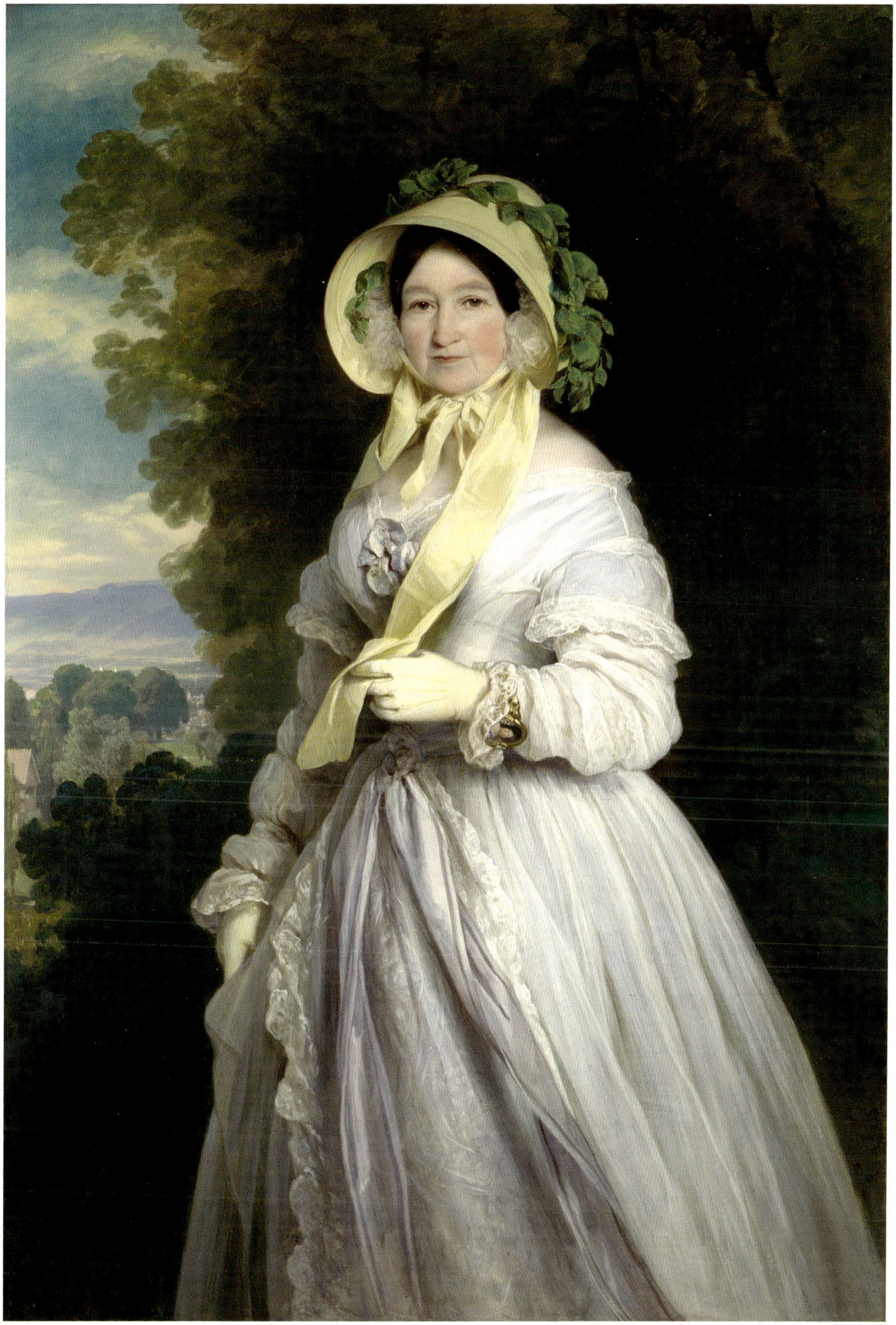

FRANZ XAVER WINTERHALTER (1805–1873)

148 *Queen Victoria (1819–1901) with the Prince of Wales (1841–1910)* 1846

Oil on canvas, 236.1 × 145.9 cm
Signed and dated, centre right: *f Winterhalter / 1846.*
RCIN 406945

Provenance Painted for Queen Victoria as a Christmas present for Sir Robert Peel; purchased by Queen Mary, Christie, Manson and Woods, London, 7 July 1939, lot 102

Literature Maas 1977, p. 25; Millar 1992, no. 822

As a young child, the Prince of Wales, or 'Bertie', was recorded on a number of occasions dressed in a Russian-style blouse, an adaptation of a traditional seventeenth-century Russian shirt, with broad sleeves, cut-away neck and braided decoration. On 8 October 1843, Queen Victoria recorded in her Journal that the Prince of Wales, aged nearly two, 'appeared at luncheon, in his new Blouse, which he is always to wear now [...] It is in fact a Russian dress.' The entry was accompanied by a small sketch.[16] The blouse may have been a gift from the Grand Duke Michael Pavlovich, brother to Emperor Nicholas I, who was then visiting the royal family.

Less than a year later, during Nicholas I's visit to England, Queen Victoria again sketched Bertie, on this occasion wearing a shirt decorated with the star and ribbon of the Grand Cross of St Andrew, presented to him by the Emperor (fig. 51). This double portrait, painted as a gift from Queen Victoria to her prime minister, Sir Robert Peel, records the Prince similarly attired. A striking red Russian-style shirt was also worn by the Prince in *The Royal Family in 1846*, which the artist was completing at the same time.[17] **AB**

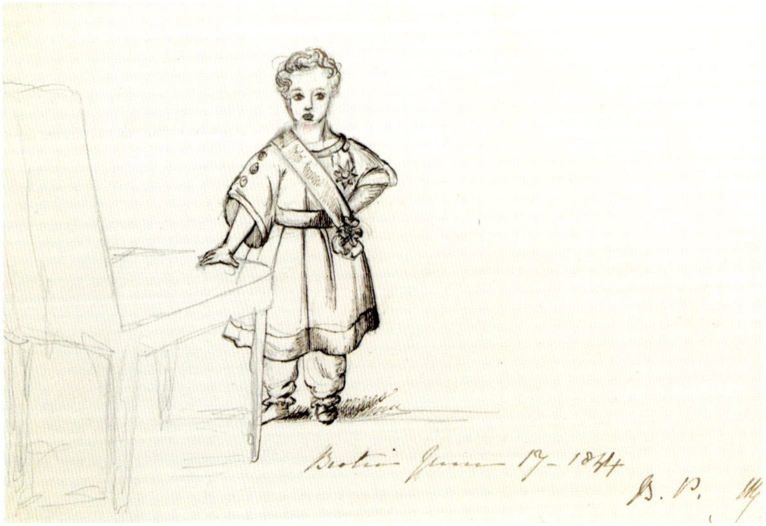

FIG. 51
Queen Victoria (1819–1901)
Bertie, 17 June 1844
Pencil and ink, 14.4 × 21.9 cm
RCIN 980024.ap

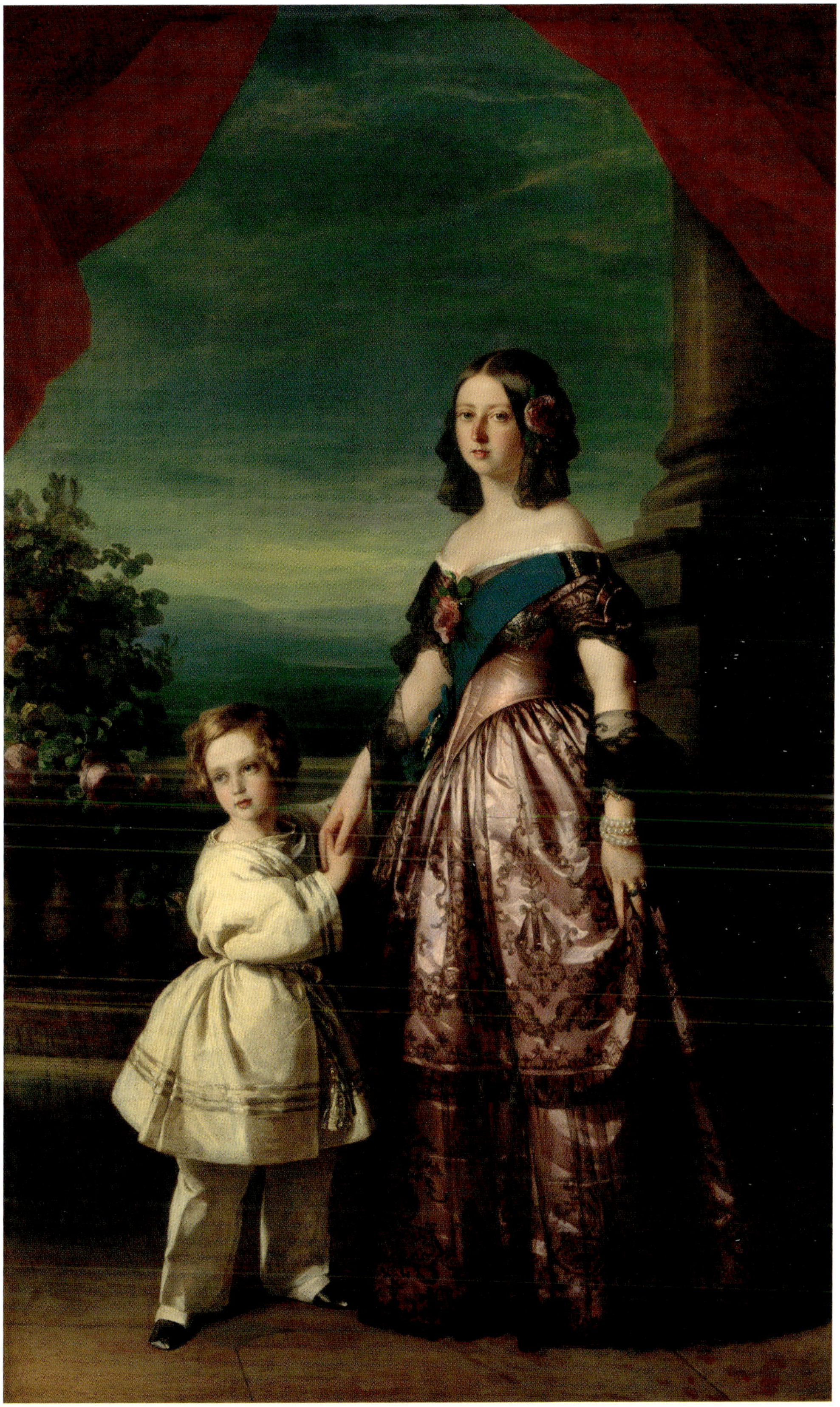

FRANZ XAVER WINTERHALTER (1805–1873)

149 *Grand Duchess Alexandra Iosifovna of Russia (1830–1911)* 1859

Oil on canvas, 147.5 × 109.0 cm
RCIN 408615

Provenance Collection of the sitter, Marble Palace, St Petersburg; by descent; exhibited at the Winter Palace during the Romanov tercentenary celebrations, 1912/13; presumably in the collection of Sir Robert Abdy by 1930s; later in a private collection; bequeathed to Her Majesty The Queen for the Royal Collection by Jane, Lady Abdy, 2016

Literature Ormond and Blackett-Ord 1987, pp. 226–38, no. 287A or 410; von Reisberg 2007, no. 661

Considered a great beauty in her youth, with a tall, graceful figure, the Grand Duchess Alexandra, or 'Sanny', was the fifth daughter of Joseph, Duke of Saxe-Altenburg and Amalie Therese Louise, Duchess of Württemberg. In September 1848 she married Grand Duke Constantine Nikolaevich, second son of Nicholas I, and younger brother to Alexander II; they had six children, including Olga Constantinovna, grandmother to HRH The Duke of Edinburgh. Their early years of marriage were happy and the couple shared a love of music; however, they gradually drifted apart.

Winterhalter never travelled to Russia, so the portrait was presumably painted in Germany (together with a lost portrait of her husband), possibly in Brückenau, a German spa town favoured by Russian aristocracy. It was here, in 1857, that the artist painted Maria Alexandrovna, Sanny's sister-in-law (Hermitage, St Petersburg).[18] Clearly painted to adorn a grand reception room, the sitter's face and shoulders are meticulously described, in contrast to the tulle and blue ribbon of her fashionable dress, which are thinly painted in a loose manner to skilfully imitate the textures and transparency of the fabrics. The artist returned to the painting once the underlayers were quite dry, to add highlights to the hair and floral corsage.

In the early twentieth century, the portrait hung in the Marble Palace, St Petersburg, one of the couple's residences, and in 1905 it was included in an exhibition of Historic Russian Portraits organised by the ballet impresario, Sergei Diaghilev (1872–1929), at the Tauride Palace. Its fate during the turbulent years of the Revolution is a little uncertain: on Sanny's death, it may have passed to the family of the sitter's brother-in-law, Grand Duke Michael Nikolaevich. The reverse is clearly inscribed with the abbreviation *A.I.M.K.*, possibly for the Academy for the History of Material Culture, which was located in the New Michael Palace, St Petersburg, during the post-revolution years.[19] It was later sold by the Bolsheviks, and in the mid-1930s is recorded in the collection of Sir Robert Abdy (1896–1976). **AB**

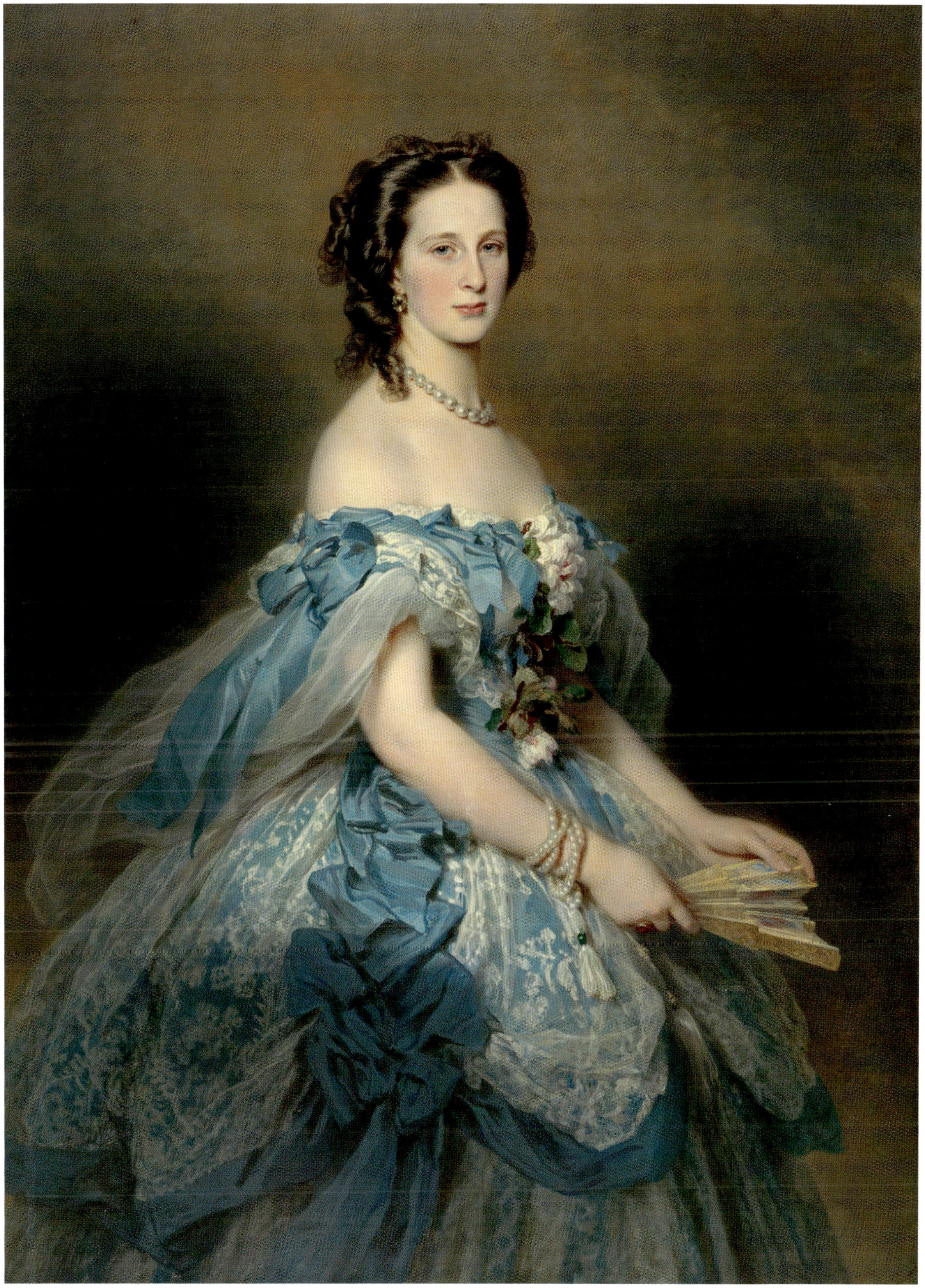

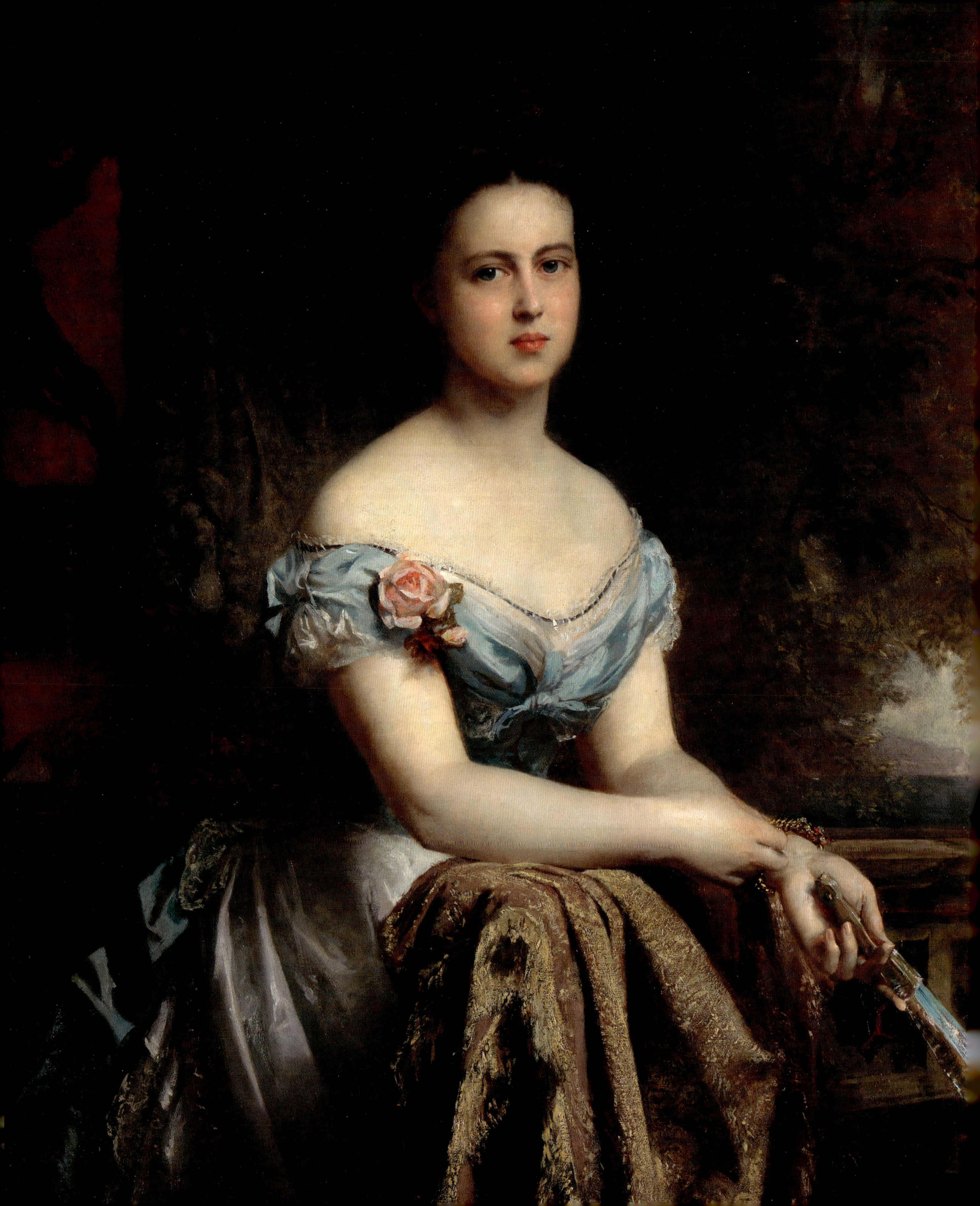

8

Dynastic Marriage

CAROLINE DE GUITAUT

my thoughts full of Russia & the coming day & longing for letters

(Queen Victoria's Journal, 23 January 1874)[1]

Before the 1860s, the diplomatic impasse caused by the Crimean War had subsided and Queen Victoria was once again receiving visits from members of the Russian family. Grand Duke Constantine visited in May 1857, Grand Duchess Maria in 1859, and Grand Duke Michael Nikolaevich (1832–1909) and Grand Duchess Olga (1839–91) stayed with the Queen at Windsor Castle in 1860. The Queen was clearly taken with the couple, describing them as 'very charming, distinguished and gentle'.[2]

Dynastic marriage had preoccupied rulers and royal families since the earliest times, and it was no less important in the mid-nineteenth century. Queen Victoria was focused not only on marrying her own children appropriately, but also her grandchildren, as far as she was able. Consideration of inter-dynastic marriage with the Romanov family, however, was fraught with complexity, given the Queen's wavering views on Russia and the anti-Russian feeling at home in the United Kingdom, following the Crimean War. One of the Queen's rivals in engineering diplomatic marriages for her children and grandchildren was Christian IX of Denmark, father of Princess Alexandra of Schleswig-Holstein-Sonderburg-Glücksburg and her sister, Princess Dagmar. While Queen Victoria has often been referred to as the 'grandmother' of Europe, the King of Denmark earned the nickname of its 'father-in-law'. Christian IX succeeded in marrying his three daughters into the royal houses of Russia, Hanover and England, the latter union appearing to be the result of much negotiation. Queen Victoria's determination to have her son and heir, Albert Edward, Prince of Wales married to Princess Alexandra appears to have been partly spurred on by the fact that other royal houses were interested in her as a bride, including the Russian court.[3] In spite of the complicated question over the Duchies of Schleswig and Holstein, the tragedy of Prince Albert's premature death in 1861, and the Prince of Wales's initial indifference to the idea of betrothal, the couple became engaged in September 1862 and were married on 10 March the following year. Three years later, after the death of Tsesarevich Nicholas Alexandrovich (1843–1865), Princess Dagmar, to whom he was betrothed, married his younger brother, Alexander Alexandrovich, thus directly linking the English, Russian and Danish royal houses for the first time.

The wedding of Tsesarevich Alexander and Maria Feodorovna, as she became known on her admittance into the Russian Orthodox Church, was attended by the Prince of Wales (the bride's sister, Alexandra, being pregnant and therefore unable to travel). A detailed journal of the Prince's visit, which lasted from 2 November until 7 December 1866, was written and illustrated by Arthur Ellis (1837–1907), one of his suite, and gives a vivid account of this first visit to Russia by the heir to the British throne (cat. 163;[4]

Maria, Duchess of Edinburgh, Grand Duchess of Russia (detail of cat. 173)

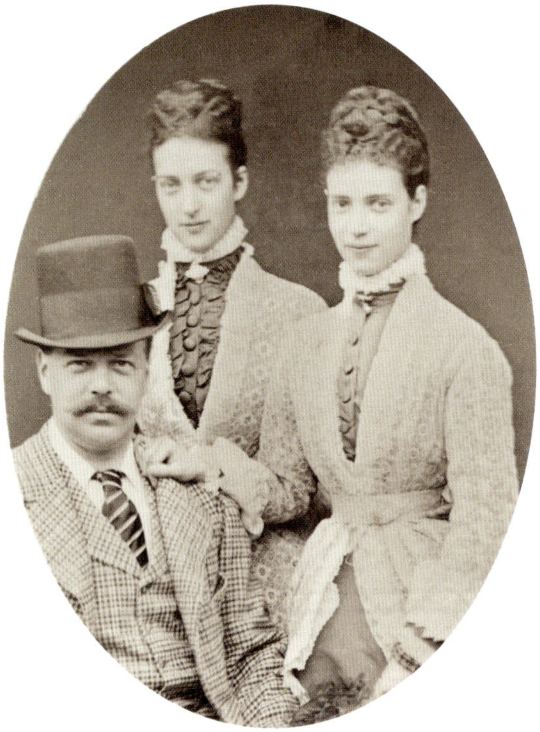

FIG. 52
Unknown photographer
Alexandra, Princess of Wales, Tsesarevich Alexander and Tsesarevna Maria Feodorovna of Russia, July 1873
Albumen photographic print pasted onto card, 5.2 × 4.0 cm
RCIN 2108897

fig. 53). The Prince of Wales was officially received at St Petersburg station by a guard of honour, to the sound of the British national anthem, after which he was received by the Russian and Danish royal families at the Winter Palace, where he stayed in a 'magnificent suite of 12 rooms, filled with pictures by the best masters and beautifully decorated and most comfortable'.[5] The wedding itself took place on 9 November in the Cathedral of the Winter Palace, and at '5pm the wedding banquet took place in the Nicholas Hall brilliantly lighted by thousands of wax candles only 550 sat down to dinner. The solid gold plate & old china very remarkable at the table where the imperial family and royal guests sat'.[6]

During his stay in Russia, the Prince made several shopping trips to Nevksii Prospekt, attended dinners, balls and illuminations, saw many productions of opera and ballet, and took part in a wolf hunt and a visit to Moscow. The Prince was also the recipient of numerous gifts: 'a Russian silver jar' on his birthday (9 November), '2 Russian Wolfhounds (white) beautiful creatures' from the Emperor, who also gave a 'v beautiful and valuable cloak lined throughout with sable with Siberian beaver collar black and very rare'.[7] In addition, he was given 'some beautiful specimens of caucases arms', and 'Schamyl's [*sic*] sons brought with them from their father for HRH's acceptance 2 pistols and a dagger of 18th century circassian ivory inlaid with gold very beautiful' (cat. 165).[8] The Prince of Wales was also photographed twice while in St Petersburg, once on 12 November by 'Levitzky', and a second time on 19 November: 'HRH with CP of Denmark went to the photographers Berga Masco' (fig. 56).[9] The same St Petersburg-based photographer was later to travel to England to photograph Queen Victoria (fig. 57).

Following the marriage of the Prince and Princess of Wales, Queen Victoria began to turn her attention to her second son, Prince Alfred, fondly known as 'Affie'. Prince Alfred had begun his training for the navy in 1856, aged just 12; he was passionate about his career and proved to be successful at it, but was dogged by ill health. Nonetheless, he was eventually to become Admiral of the Fleet in 1893.[10] Alfred visited Russia in August 1862, when he was on board HMS *St George*, significantly, this was the first British royal visit to the country. A watercolour records his visit to Oranienbaum (cat. 162), where he met the imperial family, and the good impression he made on them was ultimately to lay the ground for his marriage to the Emperor's only surviving daughter, Grand Duchess Maria Alexandrovna (1853–1920). Negotiations over the marriage were prolonged and complicated. There were strong views on both sides about the suitability of both Alfred and Maria, given the sensitivities of a direct union between England and Russia, with the Grand Duchess's rank and religion also a cause for concern in England. A letter from Queen Victoria's private secretary, on 15 June 1873, mentions 'some feeling in London about the Greek religion', the 'possible rivalry between Clarence and Marlborough Houses', and 'a great many little difficulties and trouble which considering she is the spoilt daughter of a semi Eastern despot may grow into

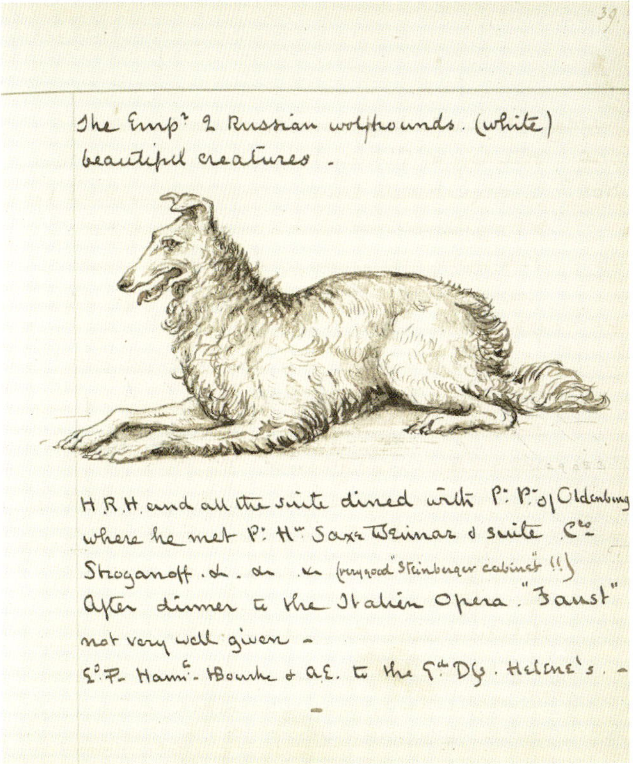

FIG. 53
Arthur Ellis
Journal of the Prince of Wales in Russia, 1866
Drawing of a wolfhound
RA VIC/ADDA 5/528, 19 November 1886

larger ones'.[11] The Prince of Wales acted as mediator and spoke to the Russian ambassador, at Affie's request, and he tried to encourage his mother to accept the union, in spite of certain conditions laid down by the Emperor, that his daughter should visit Russia during a portion of each year. Bertie wrote to the Queen to convince her: 'You are I know dearest Mama very anxious that Affie should marry - would it therefore not be a pity to thwart his wishes given that his mind is quite made up?'[12] In spite of the prolonged negotiations, the engagement was finally announced in Parliament in August 1873, and the couple married in St Petersburg on 23 January 1874: first, in the Cathedral of the Winter Palace, in an Orthodox service, and then in the Alexander Hall for the English ceremony, conducted, at the Queen's demand, by Arthur Stanley, Dean of Westminster (1815–81).

The lavish celebrations were recorded in numerous accounts by those members of the family who attended, including the Prince and Princess of Wales, and Prince Arthur, accompanied by Sir Howard Elphinstone (1829–90); the Crown Prince of Prussia (1831–88), the Crown Princess and Louis IV, Grand Duke of Hesse and by Rhine (1837–92) were also present. The Queen was anxious to receive news at Osborne House, where she was then in residence, and where she noted in her Journal, 'my mind entirely taken up with today's great event & I felt it trying to be absent!'[13] She had breakfast with her children, and placed at the table was a portrait of Maria, 'surrounded by a wreath of evergreens & some orange flowers, tied with bows of the Russian colours' (cat. 173).[14] The Queen received a long letter from the Dean of Westminster's wife, Lady Augusta (1822–76), a great confidante of Queen Victoria, who was charged to provide the most detailed account of the wedding; and also a telegram from the Empress, in which she wrote, 'we recommend our dear daughter to your maternal solicitude', to which Queen Victoria responded, 'it is with great emotion that I now receive the news of the accomplishment of the double ceremony'. The Queen continued, 'I look forward to the moment when I can kiss my dear daughter that will be the object of my most solicitude and tenderest affection'.[15] In spite of the distance, there were celebrations in England: on the Isle of Wight, the streets were decorated and there were illuminations in the evening. Two Royal navy ships, *Zealous* and the appropriately named *Royal Alfred*, had sailed over from Portsmouth and were moored and illuminated in Osborne Bay, from where a firework display was mounted. At dinner, the Queen wore her star and ribbon of the Order of St Catherine (cat. 272), and there were toasts to the health of the Duke and Duchess of Edinburgh and the Emperor and Empress of Russia.

The Grand Duchess was provided with a remarkable dowry by the Emperor.[16] Her trousseau consisted of sumptuous clothes by the finest couturiers. All in all, 'the complete collection filled the whole of the White Hall of the Winter Palace and was said to equal in quantity a season's stock-in-trade of any major Parisian emporium'.[17] More anxious than ever to document the wedding of one of

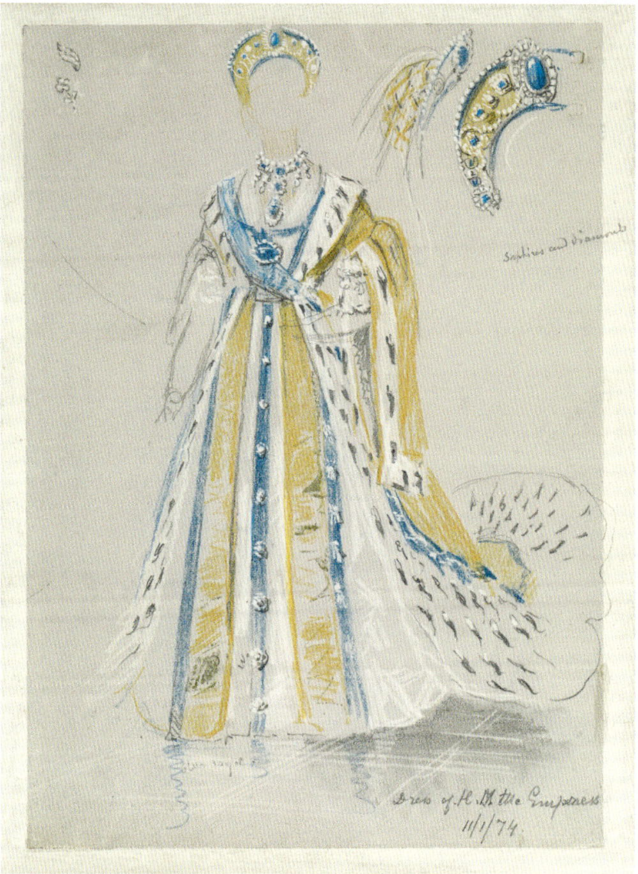

FIG. 54
Nicholas Chevalier
Full-length study of dress and jewelled headdress of the Empress of Russia,
11 January 1874
Pencil, watercolour, bodycolour, scraping out, 25.0 × 19.0 cm
RCIN 926239

her children due to her inability to attend, Queen Victoria commissioned the artist Nicholas Chevalier to paint the 'Greek' (Orthodox) ceremony (cat. 174). In preparation, Chevalier made several sketches which document the events in great detail, including the ensembles worn by the imperial family (fig. 54; cats 175–177). The marriage ceremonies were followed by lavish entertainments – two of the world's most renowned sopranos, Adelina Patti (1843–1919) and Emma Albani (1847–1930), performed to the sound of celebratory guns booming from the fortress of St Peter and St Paul. A banquet for 800 guests was held in the Nicholas Hall and this was followed by a ball, but the Duke and Duchess retired to Tsarskoe Selo, 'very tired but very happy',[18] before it had concluded. The festivities continued in St Petersburg for another week, after which a further week of celebrations was held in Moscow.

Having been thwarted in her attempt to meet her future daughter-in-law prior to the marriage,[19] Queen Victoria was most anxious to welcome the new Duchess of Edinburgh to England when the happy couple arrived at Windsor Castle on 7 March 1874. Once again, the occasion was documented by Chevalier (cat. 190), whose watercolour shows the town 'completely decked out with flags, flowers, festoons & inscriptions, some of which were in Russian'.[20] The Queen seemed delighted with her new daughter-in-law, who 'has a very friendly manner' and 'speaks English wonderfully well'. Maria seemed keen to aid the Queen in understanding her own native language; Maria 'came up to my room [...] & showed me the Russian alphabet'.[21] The two women appeared to delight in showing one another their jewels, which included Maria's 'splendid parure of sapphires and diamonds', which she wore for court on 13 March. At Buckingham Palace, following a processional carriage drive across London, which was decorated with 'some fancy inscriptions one was "Welcome fair Russ"',[22] the Queen, the Duke and Duchess, and other members of the royal family made an appearance on the balcony, to great cheering from the crowd below. A few days later, the Queen showed Maria some of the rooms at the Palace: 'after dinner we went into the 55 Room where hang all the pictures representing the events in connection with the Crimean War, portraits, scenes & c a strange coincidence with my Russian daughter there'.[23]

The couple moved into the Duke's London residence, Clarence House, which he had occupied since 1866, the same year in which he was created Duke of Edinburgh. Feeling that the house was unworthy of his wife, the Duke made alterations with the aid of a builder, Charles Waller, enlarging the house and bringing about a reorientation of its entrance to the south, to face St James's Park, and adding a Russian chapel for his wife.[24] The interiors were largely dominated by hunting trophies and souvenirs of the Duke's voyages abroad, to which the Duchess added some furniture from Russia (cats 187–189) and quantities of wedding gifts (cat. 185).

Difficulties soon arose over Maria's precedence and style, as the Emperor wished her to be called imperial, not royal, and Maria herself considered that she outranked her sister-in-law, the Princess of Wales. The matter was still under heated discussion when the Emperor visited England in 1874. The photographs of the visit (cat. 191) and the formal diplomacy of gift exchange (cat. 230) belie the difficulties caused by the conflicting wishes of the two families. On the death of his uncle, Ernest II, Duke of Saxe-Coburg and Gotha, on 22 August 1893, the Duchy passed to the Duke of Edinburgh, and the couple and their family moved to Coburg. Following Affie's death in 1900, Clarence House was given to the Duke of Connaught, and Maria was compelled to move her remaining possessions. Some of the Duke of Edinburgh's oriental works of art had been sold at auction in 1875, and in 1901 a further auction was arranged by King Edward VII.[25]

There were two further dynastic marriages during Queen Victoria's reign which united her grandchildren with the Romanov dynasty. Both brides were granddaughters of the Queen and were sisters, the daughters of the Grand Duke of Hesse (1837–92) and Princess Alice (1843–78), whose family were painted for Queen Victoria in 1879 by von Angeli (cat. 197). The first marriage took place in 1884, between Princess Elizabeth of Hesse and Grand Duke Sergei Alexandrovich, fifth son of Emperor Alexander II. Queen Victoria's granddaughter was a renowned beauty, who attracted the attention of several possible suitors from a number of royal houses. Her remarkable looks are seen in a watercolour portrait by Ekaterina Viskovatova (1838–1911) (cat. 204), which 'Ella', as she was known by her family, sent to the Queen in 1896. Even the Prince of Wales's private secretary, General Arthur Ellis, had cause to remark upon the elegance of Ella at her own sister's wedding in 1894, when he wrote to Queen Victoria that 'it was an open question whether the Gd Dsse Serge was more admired' than the bride herself.[26] The Queen, with customary confliction, was rather against Ella's choice of Sergei, but they had known one another since childhood, as the Grand Duke had paid many visits to Hesse, his mother's birth place, and after the death of his parents, the Emperor and Empress, they had become closer.

The wedding took place in the imperial chapel of the Winter Palace on 3 June 1884, and it was during the stay of the Hesse family in St Petersburg that Ella's younger sister, Alix, was to meet her future husband, the Tsesarevich Nicholas. The happy, though childless marriage of the Grand Duke and Grand Duchess Sergei was tragically cut short, when the Grand Duke was assassinated on 18 February 1905 in the Kremlin. Elizabeth, who was already deeply religious, turned away from her life of privilege and, having sold her personal possessions, became a nun, founding the Convent of Sts Martha and Mary in Moscow. In 1913, on her last visit to England, she placed an icon depicting the saints to whom her convent was dedicated on the tomb of her maternal grandparents, Queen Victoria and Prince Albert, at Frogmore Mausoleum (cat. 143).

The second of Queen Victoria's granddaughters to marry into the Russian imperial family was Ella's younger sister, Princess Alix of Hesse, who took the name Alexandra Feodorovna on her marriage to the future Nicholas II on 14 November 1894. The couple were related through several lines of European royalty (see family tree, pp. viii–xi). The Queen had wanted her favourite granddaughter to marry the Duke of Clarence, but Alix rejected his proposal. Alexander III and Maria Feodorovna were opposed to the marriage on the grounds of Alix's Lutheran faith and their anti-German stance. However, following Nicholas's second proposal, Alix accepted, and the engagement to the Tsesarevich Nicholas was announced on 21 April 1894, in Coburg. The Tsesarevich gave his fiancé a bracelet which his mother, Maria Feodorovna, had sent him, in the hope that 'Alix will look upon me as a loving mother who will receive her with open arms'.[27] Many relatives were present at the time, among them Queen Victoria, to attend the wedding of Alix's brother, Ernest, Duke of Hesse and by Rhine (1868–1937) to his first cousin, Princess Victoria Melita of Saxe Coburg and Gotha, known as 'Ducky', daughter of Affie and Maria. News of the engagement was received with great joy and was avidly reported in English newspapers. Queen Victoria received letters of congratulation, including one from the Archbishop of Canterbury, observing that the betrothal 'gives such satisfaction and such confidence to your majesty's subjects as to future peace and relations between such great nations'.[28] The couple were photographed with the ducal and imperial family in the garden at the New Palace, Coburg, on 23 April (fig. 55).

Alix returned to England with her grandmother, where, in June, the Tsesarevich joined her, to stay in England for

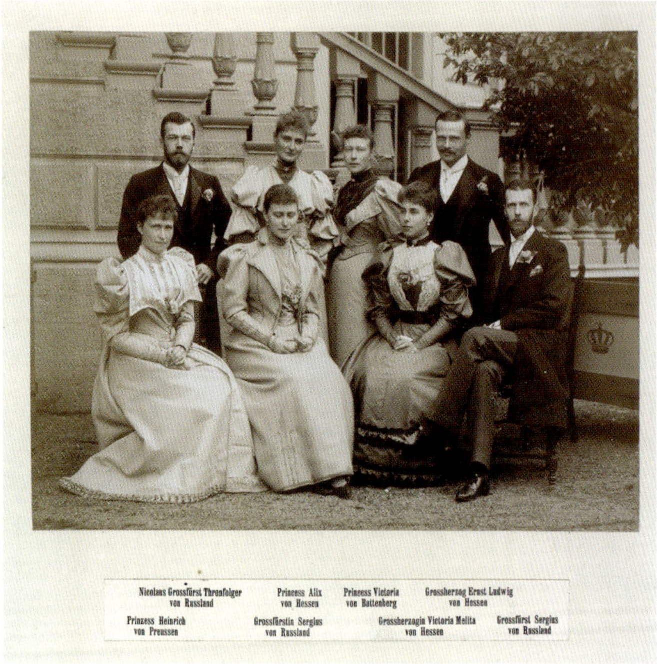

FIG. 55
Attributed to Carl Backofen (1853–1909)
Group photograph taken during the wedding celebrations of Ernest Louis, Grand Duke of Hesse and Princess Victoria Melita of Saxe-Coburg and Gotha, April 1894
Albumen print, 24.5 x 30.5 cm
RCIN 2929583

a month. On 14 June, he wrote from Windsor Castle to his mother, to say that he had spent three days with his fiancée at Walton-on-Thames, and was surprised that Queen Victoria had allowed him and Alix to go out for drives without a chaperone.[29] He was also given the privilege by the Queen of wearing a Windsor coat of dark-blue cloth, with red collar and cuffs, while in residence at the Castle, an honour usually reserved for members of the royal family and very senior ranking officials. The visit was completed by two days at Sandringham, where there was an auction at the stud, and two days at Marlborough House, before a final few days at Windsor. During the visit, the Duke and Duchess of York's eldest son, Prince Edward, later King Edward VIII, was christened, and both Nicholas and Alix were made godparents. The couple attended two operas in the Waterloo Chamber, and the Tsesarevich visited the barracks, where the Horse Guards invited him for dinner, but he was unable to 'give a definite answer because Granny loves me so and doesn't like me missing dinner - nor does Alix!'[30]

In the autumn of 1894, Alexander III's health began to deteriorate, and Alix was summoned, with Nicholas, to his deathbed, in order that he might give their betrothal his blessing. He died on 20 October and Nicholas succeeded as the new Emperor. Following the funeral, Nicholas and Alexandra were married, on 14 November, Maria Feodorovna's birthday. A medal was struck to mark the occasion (cat. 202), and Queen Victoria commissioned the Danish artist, Laurits Regner Tuxen, to record the scene in one of his most acclaimed works (cat. 203). On 5 November, Grand Duchess Sergei wrote to her grandmother to describe how the bride would be dressed on her wedding day: 'the dress is in embroidered silver cloth Russian court dress [...] I think it is heaven all in white and silver shining like rays of electric light and the red cloak relieves the whole'.[31] In spite of the beauty of the couple and the spectacle of the imperial chapel in candlelight, the sadness of the occasion, particularly for the Dowager Empress, weighed heavily on all attendees. 'All mourning put aside and an effort to appear cheerful - which was manifestly put on', reported Arthur Ellis.[32] Queen Victoria sent the bride various gifts for her wedding, for which Alix wrote to thank her, for the 'stuffs, shawls & a cape' for her trousseau, and 'the pendant with your dear portrait is so beautiful I shall prize it very much the lovely ring I wore for the wedding & ever since and when I look at it I have to think of the beloved giver'.[33] Alix went on to thank the Queen for making Nicholas colonel-in-chief of the Scots Greys, the uniform of which he later wore for a portrait by Bogdanov-Belsky, *c.*1908 (cat. 125). Queen Victoria celebrated the wedding at Windsor Castle, with a large dinner in honour of the imperial couple, during which she stood while the Russian anthem was played: 'how impossible it seemed that gentle little simple Alicky should be the great Empress of Russia'.[34]

NIELSINE CAROLINE PETERSEN (1853–1916)

150 & 151 *Bust of Queen Louise of Denmark (1817–1898)* 1908

Marble, 78.8 × 55.0 × 31.0 cm
Inscribed on front: *Louise / Dronning af Danmark 1898*; signed and dated on reverse: *Nielsine Petersen / 1908*
RCIN 2035

Bust of King Christian IX of Denmark (1818–1906) 1909

Marble, 78.8 × 57.0 × 35.0 cm
Inscribed on front: *Christian IX / Konge at Danmark 1906*; signed and dated on reverse: *Nielsine Petersen / 1909 / Kobernhavn*
RCIN 2036

Provenance Commissioned by Queen Alexandra, 1908

Literature Karčeva and Ėrmitaž 2016, nos H.ck.1902, H.ck.1903

Prince Christian of Schleswig-Holstein-Sonderburg-Beck was born on 8 April 1818 at Gottorf Castle in the Duchy of Schleswig; he was named after Christian of Denmark, later King Christian VIII (1786–1848), who was also his godfather. Prince Christian had hoped to secure the hand of Queen Victoria, his third cousin, but was unsuccessful, and on 26 May 1842, he married Princess Louise of Hesse-Kassel at the Amalienborg Palace, Copenhagen. There were several claimants to the Danish throne, but his marriage to Princess Louise, who herself was a claimant, secured Christian's position as heir presumptive to the childless Frederick VII (1808–63), and this was ratified in the London Protocol of 8 May 1852.

As King Christian IX of Denmark from 1863, he earned the sobriquet, 'father-in-law' of Europe, as four of his children, as monarchs or consorts, occupied the thrones of Denmark, Great Britain, Russia and Greece. His grandsons included Nicholas II, Constantine I of Greece (1868–1923), George V, Christian X of Denmark (1870–1947) and Haakon VII of Norway (1872–1957).

The pair of portrait busts by Nielsine Petersen in the Royal Collection is one of three known pairs, the other two being in the Danish Royal Collection and the Hermitage Museum collection.[35] Produced posthumously, in 1908–9, they are based on earlier portraits and depict the King in uniform and the Queen in evening dress, both wearing the Order of the Dannebrog and he the collar of the Order of the Elephant, Denmark's highest order of chivalry. The precise circumstances of their production is not known. The pair now in the Hermitage was recorded in the Winter Palace from 1910, and was confiscated from the Anichkov Palace in 1928, indicating that they were in the possession of the Dowager Empress Maria Feodorovna whose residence it was. The pair in the Royal Collection were commissioned by Queen Alexandra, according to a note from Colonel Rördam from Christiansborg Palace, Copenhagen, dated 14 January 1908. The note, written in French, states: 'Mlle N Petersen a statue in marble paid according to the order £1,065.'[36] CDEG

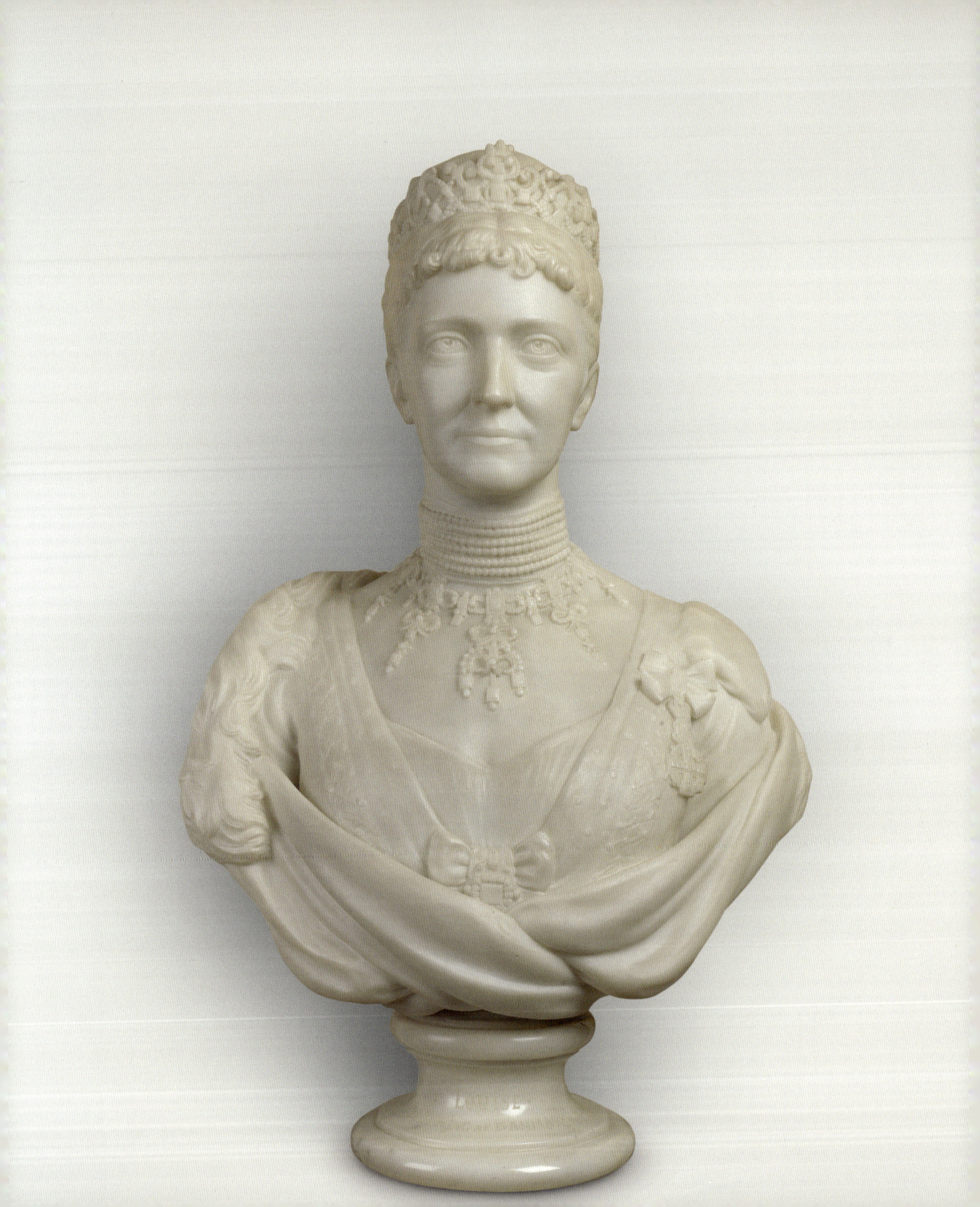

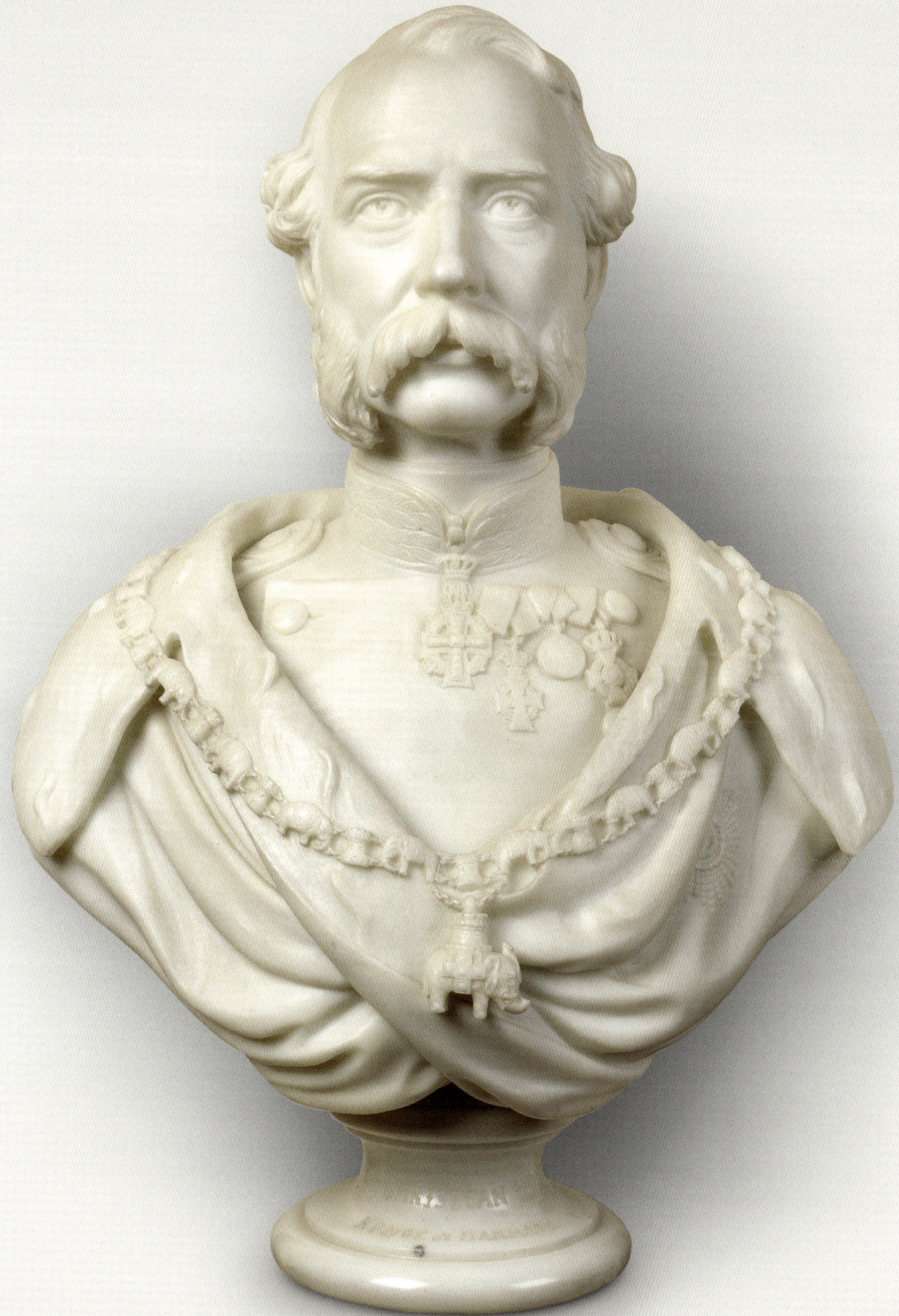

CHARLES BERGAMASCO (1830–1896)

152 & 153

Maria Feodorovna, Empress of Russia, when Tsesarevna (1847–1928) 1869

Albumen print laid on album page, (print) 13.2 × 9.5 cm
Blind stamp in lower right corner: *Bergamasco*
RCIN 2929463

Alexander III, Emperor of Russia, when Tsesarevich (1845–1894) c.1870

Albumen print laid on album page, (print) 13.3 × 9.4 cm
Blind stamp in lower right corner: *Bergamasco*
RCIN 2929465

Provenance Acquired by Queen Victoria

Charles Bergamasco was born in Turin in 1830, and moved to St Petersburg in 1848 to work as an actor, but soon decided to concentrate on photography, opening one of the first studios there in 1850. He became a highly successful portrait photographer and moved his studio to Nevskii Prospekt by 1860. His work was widely acclaimed and received many awards. Bergamasco attracted an affluent and cosmopolitan clientele, which included members of the Russian and European royal families, including Maria Feodorovna. Possibly at her suggestion, the Prince of Wales visited Bergamasco's studio in 1866 (fig. 56).[37] The Prince of Wales returned to the studio in 1874, when the Princess of Wales, Prince Alfred and Prince Arthur were also photographed. Queen Victoria's portrait was captured by Bergamasco a few years later, as recorded in her Journal: 'Was photographed in the orangery by Bergamasco, an Italian, established since 25 years at St. Petersburg, & came all the way, at his own request, to photograph me' (fig. 57).[38] In a letter to Queen Victoria, penned at Peterhof and dated 14 July 1877, Maria Alexandrovna wrote: 'At Zarskoe I had the children and myself photographed by Bergamasco and it succeeded so well, that I must send them to you by next messenger'.[39] **AN**

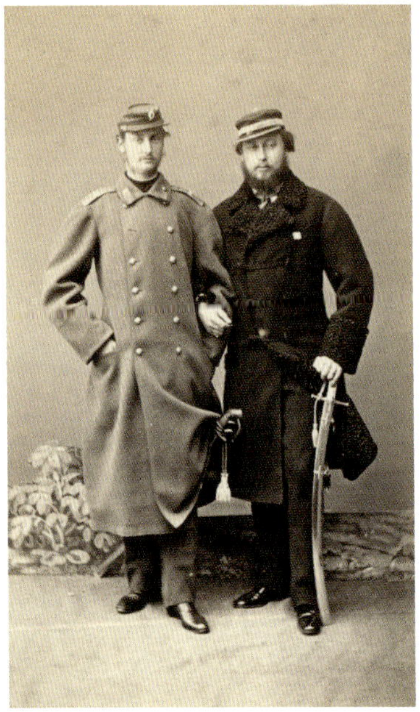

FIG. 56
Charles Bergamasco
Prince of Wales with the Crown Prince of Denmark (later King Frederick VIII),
19 November 1866
Albumen print, 8.4 × 5.1 cm
RCIN 2106811

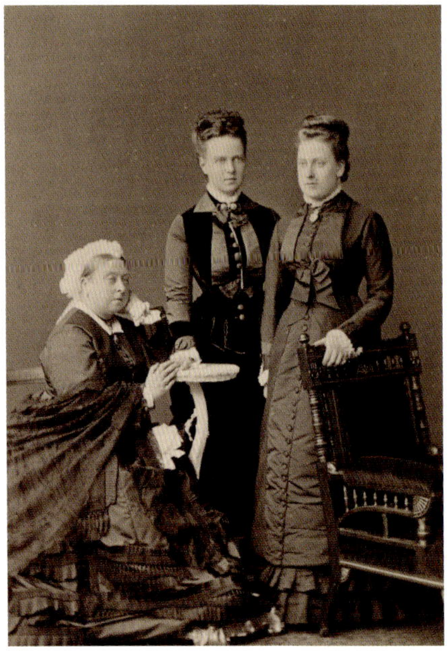

FIG. 57
Charles Bergamasco
Queen Victoria with Maria, Duchess of Edinburgh, and Princess Beatrice, 11 May 1877
Albumen print, 12.7 × 9.0 cm
RCIN 2105880

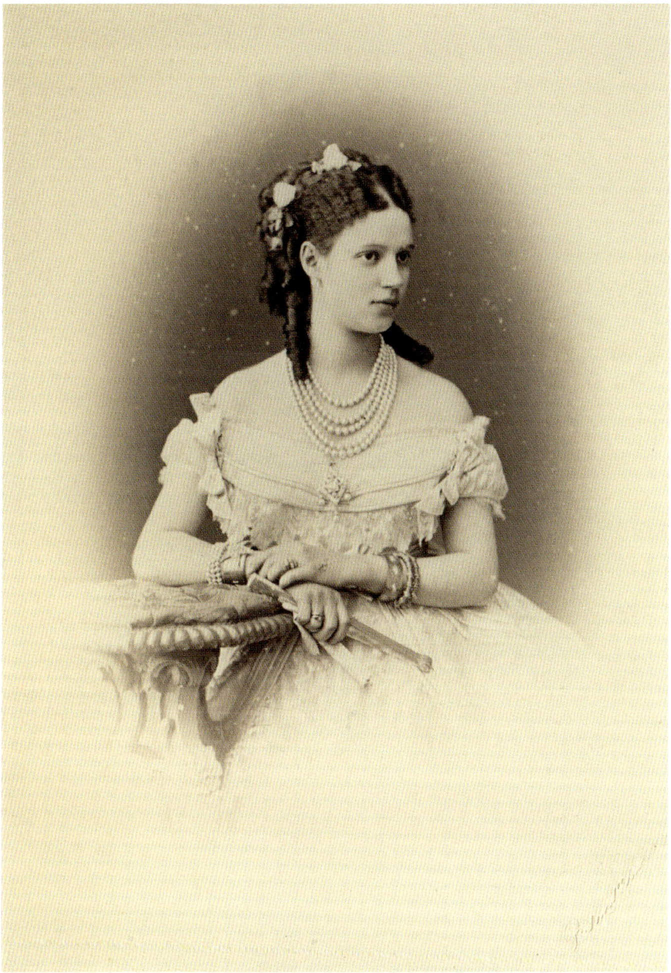

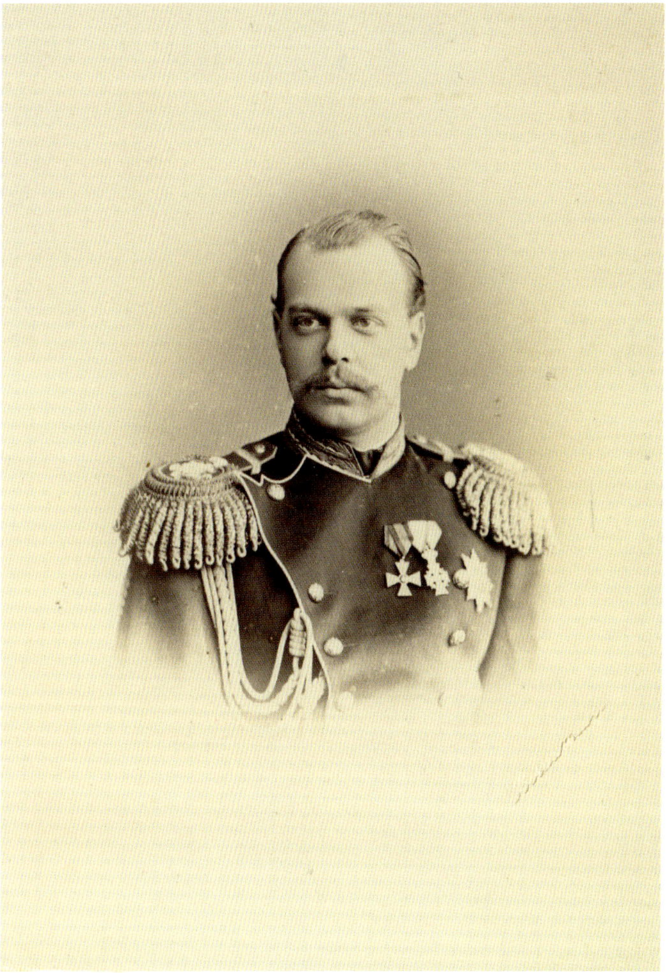

SERGEI LEVITSKY (1819–1898)

154 *Nicholas II, Emperor of Russia, when Grand Duke Nicholas Alexandrovich (1868–1918)* 1871

Albumen print laid on album page, (print) 8.4 × 5.5 cm
RCIN 2929464

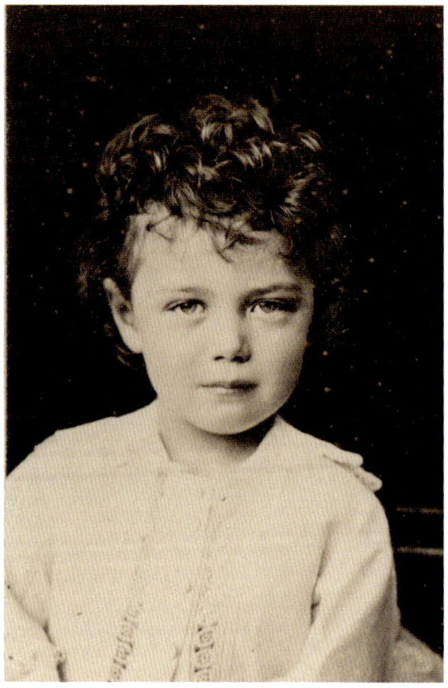

Provenance Acquired by Queen Victoria

This photograph of 'Nicky', as he was known in the family since childhood, was taken by Sergei Levitsky, one of the most important and influential Russian photographers of the nineteenth century. In his long and successful career, he portrayed the last four generations of Russian emperors. **AN**

JAMES RUSSELL & SONS (active 1860s – 1910s)

155 *Nicholas II, Emperor of Russia, when Grand Duke Nicholas Alexandrovich (1868–1918), and Grand Duke George Alexandrovich (1871–1899)* 1873

Albumen print laid on album page, (print) 8.7 × 5.7 cm
RCIN 2929466

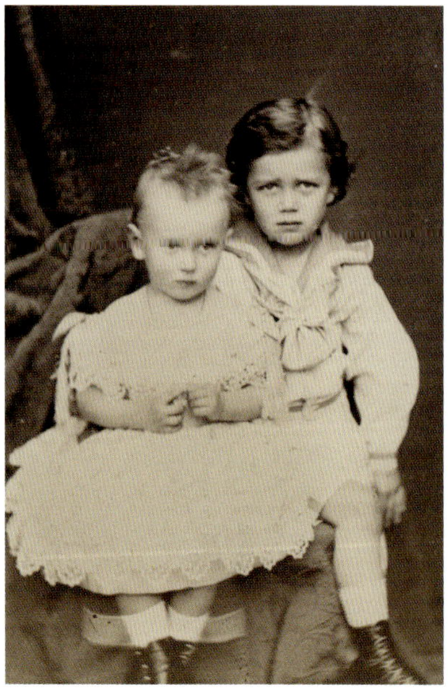

Provenance Acquired by Queen Victoria

In the summer of 1873, Maria Feodorovna came to Britain to visit her sister, Alexandra, Princess of Wales, accompanied, for the first time, by her husband, Tsesarevich Alexander of Russia, and their young children. They met Queen Victoria at Windsor Castle in June, and later at Osborne House, where they stayed between 29 July and 13 August, and where this photograph was probably taken. The Queen records the children's excitement at Osborne in her Journal: 'Breakfast in the tent, & Bertie's 5 children & little Nicky (Minny's eldest boy) came. They were in tremendous high spirits'.[40] **AN**

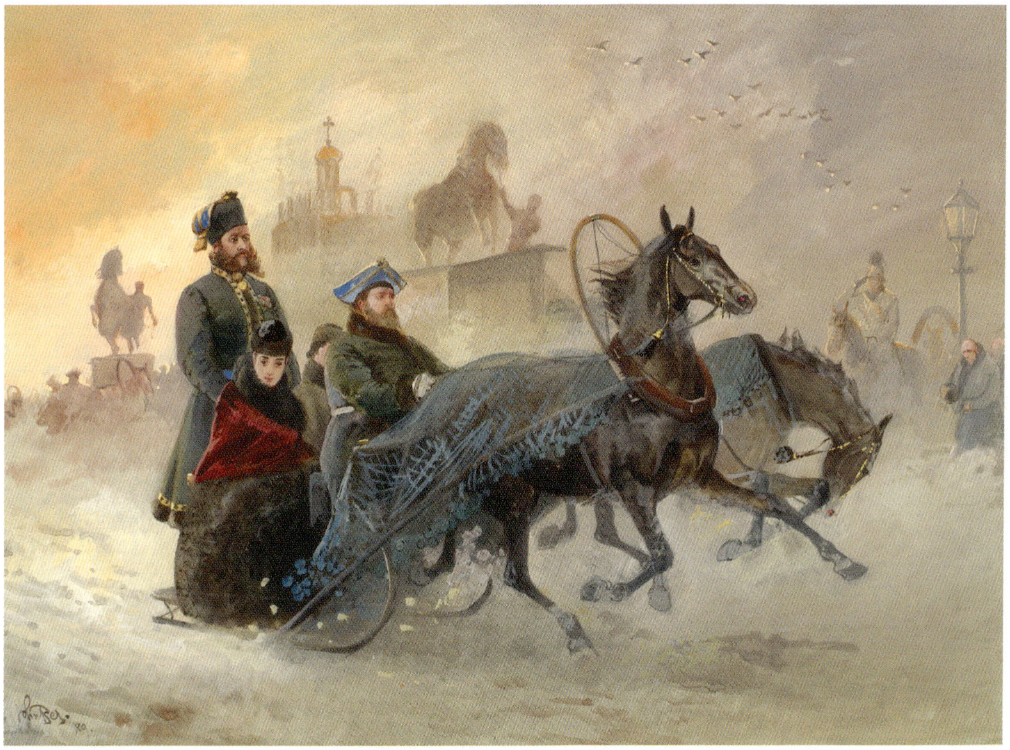

JOHN AXEL RICHARD BER (1853–1906)

156 *Maria Feodorovna, Empress of Russia (1847–1928), driving in a sleigh at St Petersburg in snow* 1889

Watercolour and bodycolour, 34.6 × 48.2 cm
Signed and dated bottom left: *John Ber. / 89*
RCIN 920950

Provenance Possibly Queen Alexandra when Princess of Wales

Literature Millar 1995, no. 233

John Ber[41] was a painter and illustrator who specialised in sporting subjects and animals. Born in Stockholm, he worked in America for five years from 1869, before travelling to the Russian court and on to London.[42] In London, in addition to his work for an English journal, he carried out watercolours for the Prince of Wales. Ber's atmospheric watercolour depicts the Empress in a traditional Russian sleigh, driven across the snow-covered Anichkov bridge in St Petersburg, in 1889. The Anichkov bridge crosses the Fontanka river, and is adorned with four equestrian statues by the sculptor Baron P.K. Klodt (1805–67), two of which are visible here. Sleigh scenes were a popular subject in Russian art of the nineteenth century.[43]

The Empress and her husband, Alexander III, had used the nearby Anichkov Palace as their St Petersburg residence since their wedding in 1866. From 1881, when Alexander became Emperor, the palace was used intermittently.[44] The vision of a carefree Empress, gazing directly at the viewer, contrasts with the reality of her situation. In 1881, her father-in-law, Alexander II, was assassinated when a bomb was thrown at him in St Petersburg. After this, Alexander III and his family lived in fear that they might be subjected to the same fate. It is likely that this watercolour entered the Collection through the Princess of Wales, perhaps a gift from the Empress herself. RW

FABERGÉ; JOHANNES ZEHNGRAF (1857–1908), miniaturist

157 *Frame with a portrait miniature of Maria Feodorovna (1847–1928)* c.1895

Four-colour gold, guilloché enamel, ivory, watercolour, 9.0 × 7.8 × 7.3 cm
Frame stamped with mark of Mikhail Perkhin, fineness mark of 56 zolotniks (before 1896) and 'FABERGE' in Cyrillic; miniature signed: *Zehngraf*
RCIN 40107

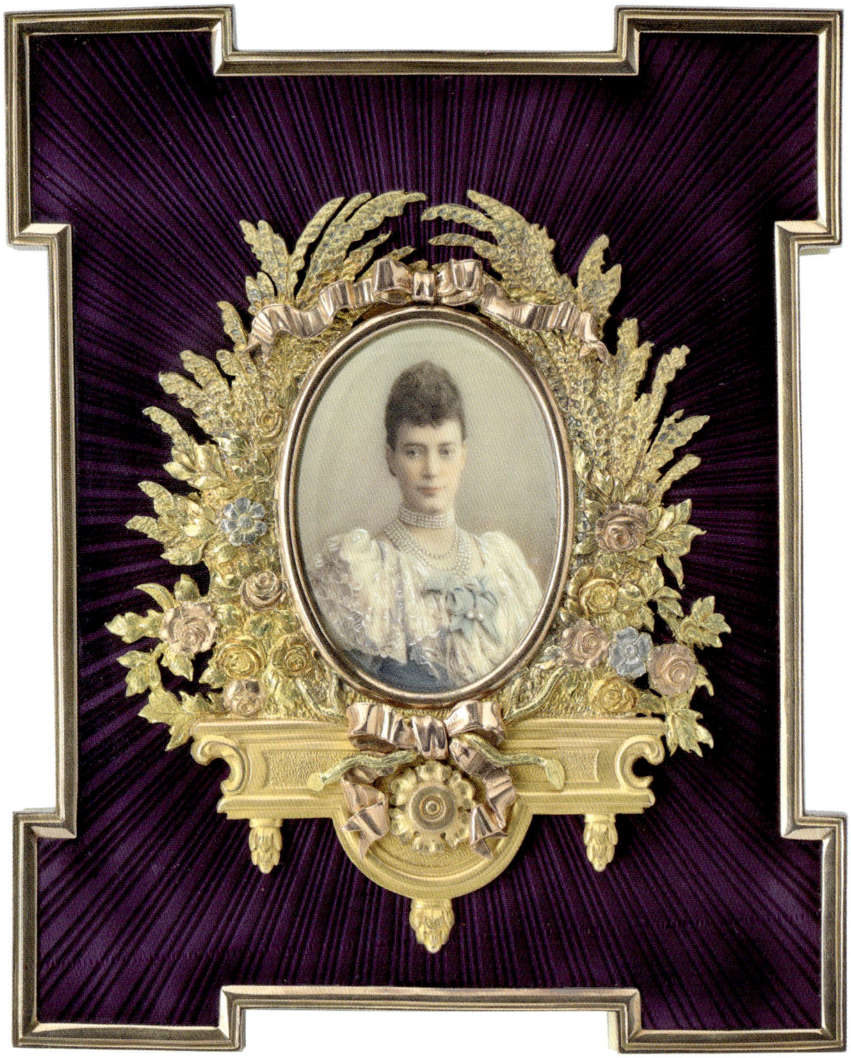

Provenance Acquired by Queen Alexandra

Literature De Guitaut 2003, p. 170

The portrait miniature of the Empress is painted by the Danish court miniaturist, Johannes Zehngraf, who worked at the Russian imperial court during the reign of Alexander III. The image is based on a photograph of Maria Feodorovna by Pasetti (1850–1912) of 1894.

The miniature has been mounted into an elaborately decorated frame of richly coloured magenta enamel, over a sunburst guillochage. The portrait is enhanced by the proliferation of coloured-gold bows, roses, foliage and ears of corn, and appears to be supported by a classical pediment. The Fabergé firm excelled at both techniques of guilloché enamelling and the use of quatre-couleur gold; decorative devices which were derived from French eighteenth century decorative art techniques.

The whole object seems to date from the period soon after the premature death of Alexander III in 1894 and the accession of Maria Feodorovna's son, Nicholas, as Emperor, and was almost certainly a gift from the Empress to her sister, Queen Alexandra. CDEG

FABERGÉ

158 *Bust of Emperor Alexander III (1845–1894) c.*1900

Smoky quartz, nephrite, two-colour gold, 17.6 × 7.5 × 5.3 cm
RCIN 40512

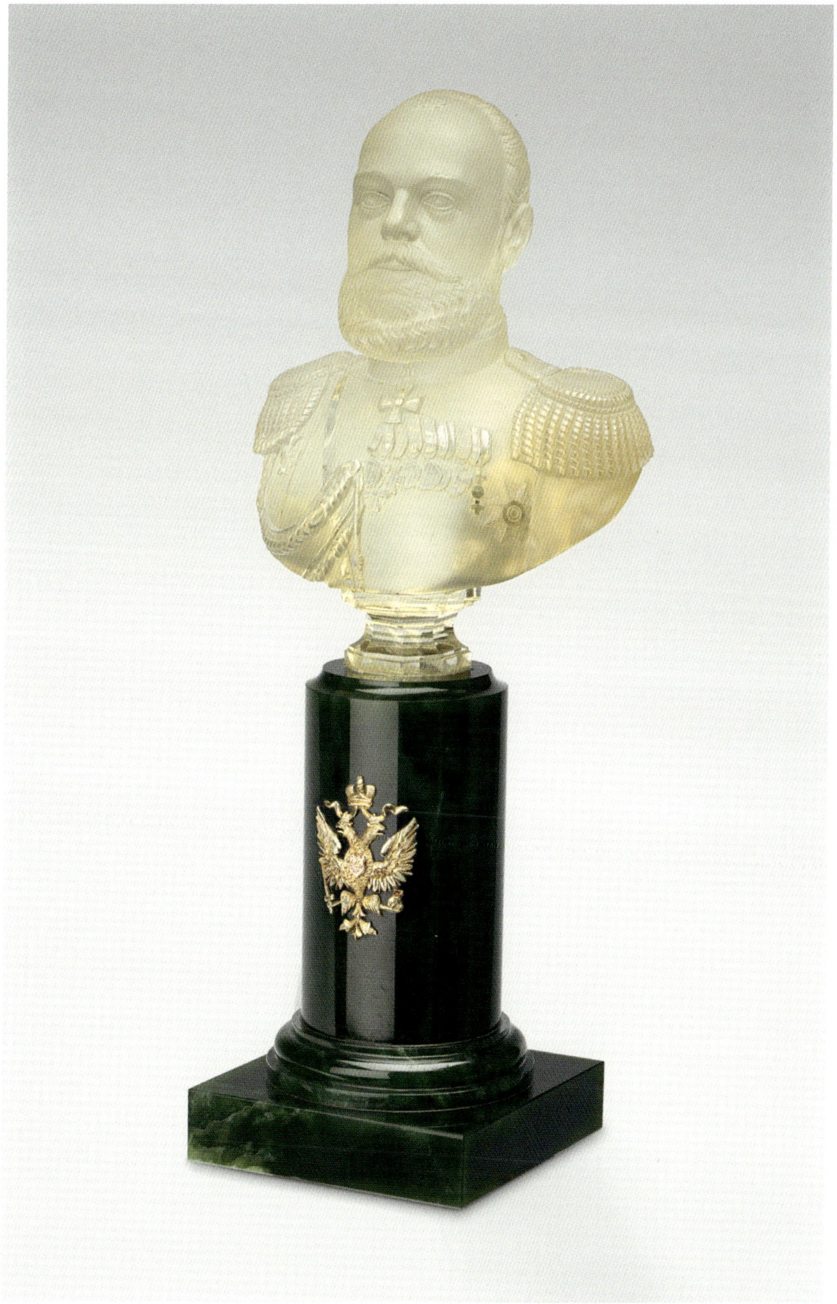

Provenance Acquired by Queen Alexandra; Princess Victoria's collection

Literature De Guitaut 2003, p. 186

The bust, carved from a single piece of translucent smoky quartz, depicts the Emperor in full dress uniform, with orders and medals, while the circular nephrite column is applied with the imperial eagle. The image is derived from numerous photographic, painted and sculpted images of the Emperor made *c.*1890. The exact date of this small portrait bust is not known and it could have been made posthumously as a commemorative piece. It was in the possession of the Emperor's sister-in-law, Queen Alexandra, and following her death in 1925 passed to her daughter Princess Victoria, also an avid collector of Fabergé's work. CDEG

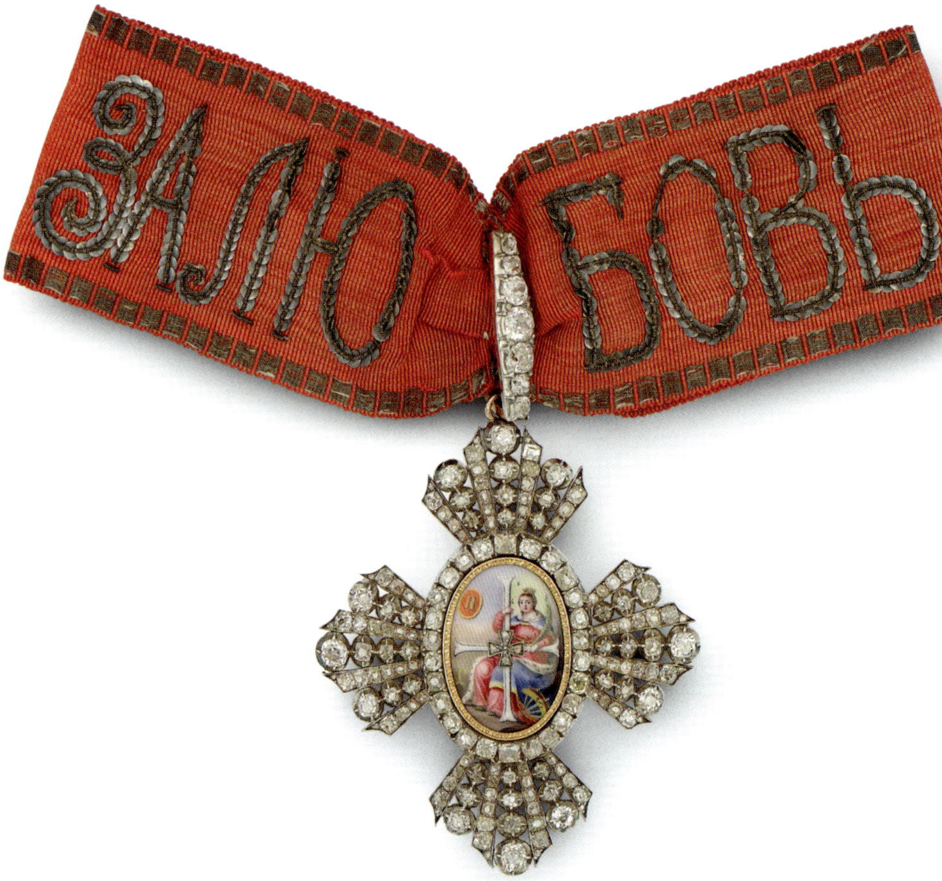

ATTRIBUTED TO WILHELM KEIBEL

159 *Badge and star of the Order of St Catherine the Martyr* c.1865

Gold, diamonds, enamel, silk, silver, (badge) 9.7 × 6.1 cm, (star) 8.5 × 8.2 cm
Scratch mark on star: *3561*; badge engraved: *KAM H77*
RCINS 441522, 441523

Provenance Presented to Queen Alexandra when Princess of Wales, whose appointment to the Order was registered on 25 May 1865[45]

The badge is formed of a cross set with brilliants, with, in the centre, an enamelled medallion of St Catherine, sitting next to her wheel of martyrdom, holding a white cross on which is placed a small diamond cross. Scattered around the composition are the letters *D*, *S* (on the wheel), *F* (by the saint's right foot) and *R* (on the sun), for *Dominum Salvator Fac Regem* (Psalm 19). Above the saint's head are the letters *CKЄ*, for the Holy Martyr Catherine. The whole is suspended from a rose- and silver-coloured ribbon, with the text embroidered in silver sequins, *ЗА ЛЮБОВЬ* ('For love'), the motto repeated from the star. On the reverse are two eagles feeding serpents to their brood in a nest on top of a mountain, surrounded by the motto, *AEQUAT MUHIA* [*sic*] *COMPARIS* ('She is equal to the duties of a consort').

In the centre of the diamond-set star with articulated arms is a diamond-set section of St Catherine's wheel, surrounded by the motto in rose-cut diamonds, *ЗА ЛЮБОВЬ И ОТЕЧЕСТВО* ('For love and the fatherland'), the whole surmounted by an imperial crown set with two large brilliants. The reverse has a gilt pin and supports for the arms of the star, and is fitted with eyelets for sewing onto a dress. SJP

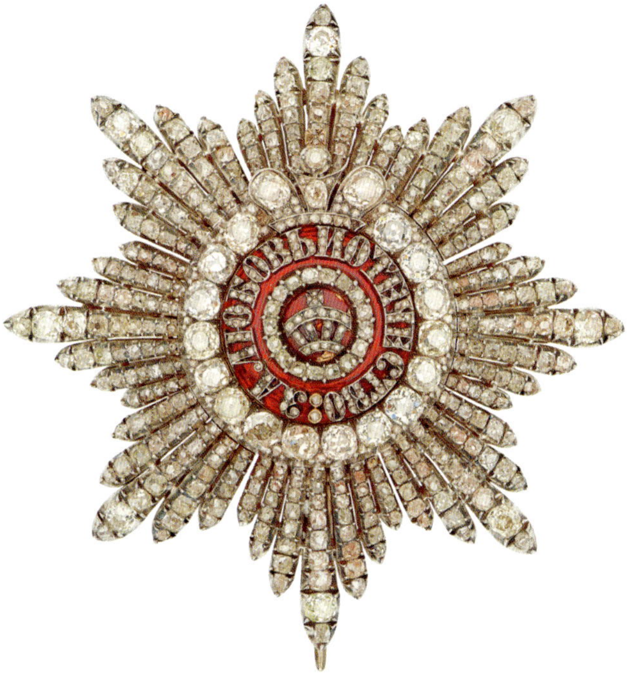

SERGEI LEVITSKY (1819–1898)

160 *Alexander III, Emperor of Russia (1845–1894)* c.1890

Watercolour over photograph on ivory laid on card, oval, 3.0 × 2.5 cm
RCIN 14818

Provenance Acquired by Queen Alexandra

Literature Remington 2010, p. 584, no. 1067

Disguised as a miniature, the portrait is in fact a hand-painted photograph by Sergei Levitsky. A larger copy of this portrait is also in the Royal Collection, with the addition of the ribbon of the Order of St Andrew covering the shoulder strap seen in the original photograph.[46] It is a known image that was also used as a source to create portraits of the Emperor by numerous Russian artists, including Nikolai Shilder (1828–98) and Alexander Fedorovich Pershakov (1843–1900).[47] **AN**

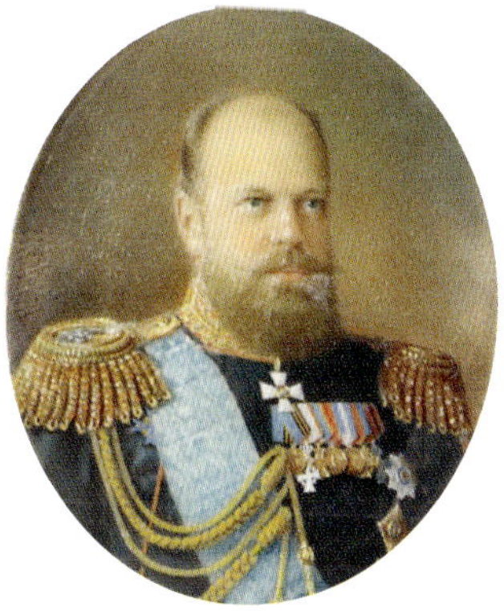

ROBERT ANTOINE MÜLLER (active 1872–1883), after BARON HEINRICH VON ANGELI (1840–1925)

161 *Tsesarevna Maria Feodorovna (Princess Dagmar of Denmark) (1847–1928)* 1876–7

Oil on canvas, 90.1 × 72.7 cm
RCIN 404018

Provenance Painted for Queen Victoria; first hung in the Royal Visitors' Bedroom, Windsor Castle

Literature Millar 1992, no. 76

This is a copy by Müller, after an enigmatic three-quarter-length portrait of Maria Feodorovna by Heinrich von Angeli in the Hermitage, dated 1874.[48] An inscription on the reverse records that it was painted in Russia, although it appears that the artist travelled with his own prepared canvases from George Rowney & Co.[49] Although a skilfully executed and accurate copy, the portrait lacks the softness and fluidity of the original. It is painted in a uniformly smooth and quite dense painting technique, over a light grey imprimatura layer (toned modelling layer). In the original portrait, von Angeli deliberately allows a lower, warm, transparent brown imprimatura layer to show through the looser, more fluid brushstrokes, giving greater depth and immediacy to the composition. Müller compensates for the lack of depth in the roses with coloured highlights.[50]

Contemporary writers described her as compelling, and she was said to love clothes and jewels, especially pearls. On first meeting the Princess in 1862, Queen Victoria, for whom this portrait was painted, described the sitter as 'quite different [to Alexandra], with fine brown eyes'.[51]

AB

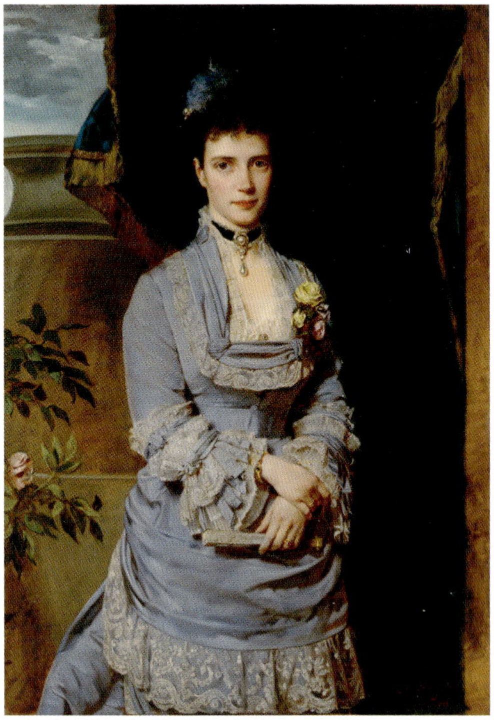

FIG. 58
Heinrich von Angeli
Princess Dagmar, Later Maria Feodorovna, Empress of Russia, 1874
Oil on canvas, 127.0 × 89.0 cm
State Hermitage Museum, St Petersburg, inv. no. ГЭ-6975
(originally at the Anichkov Palace, residence of Alexander III and Maria Feodorovna)

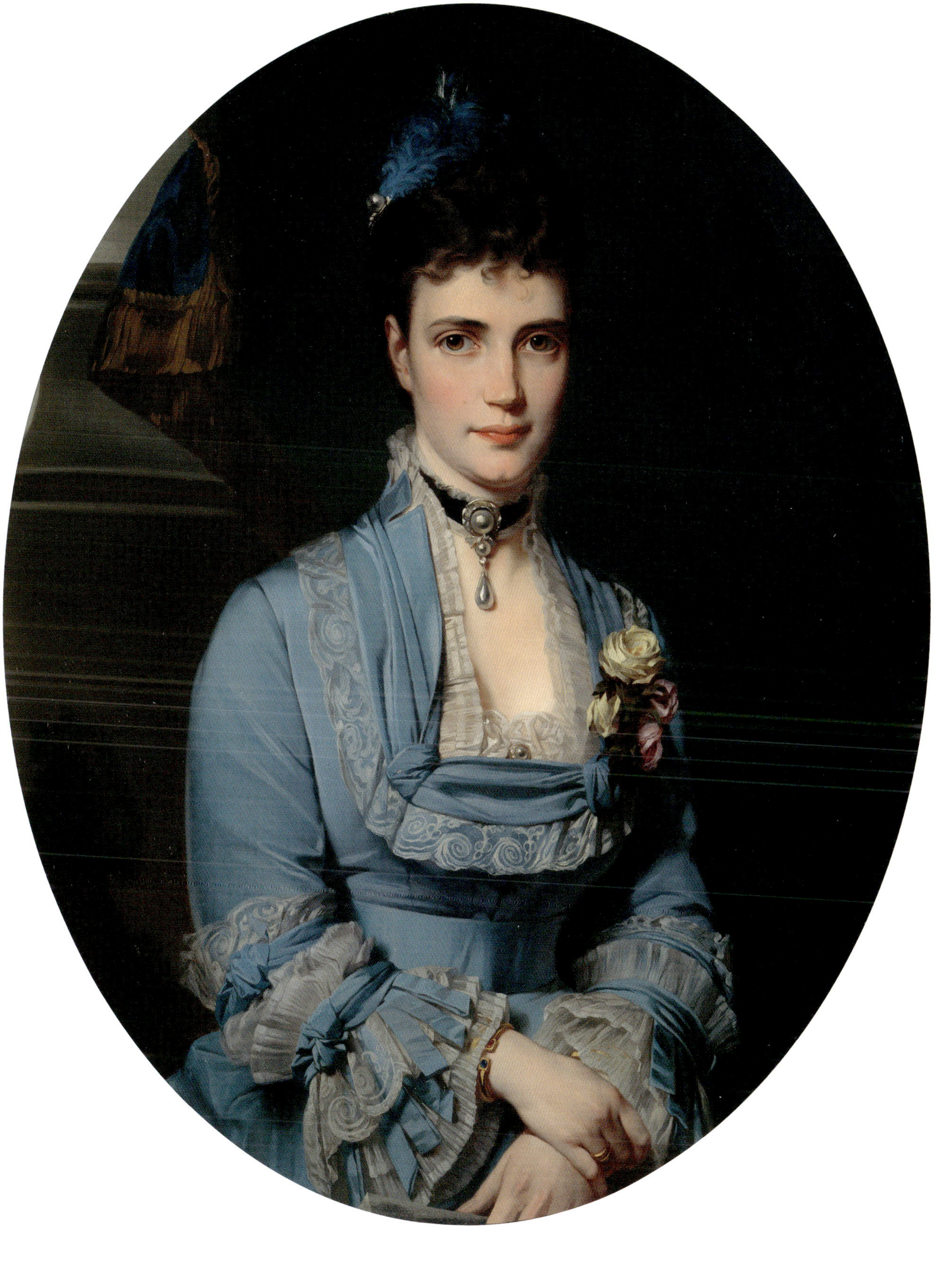

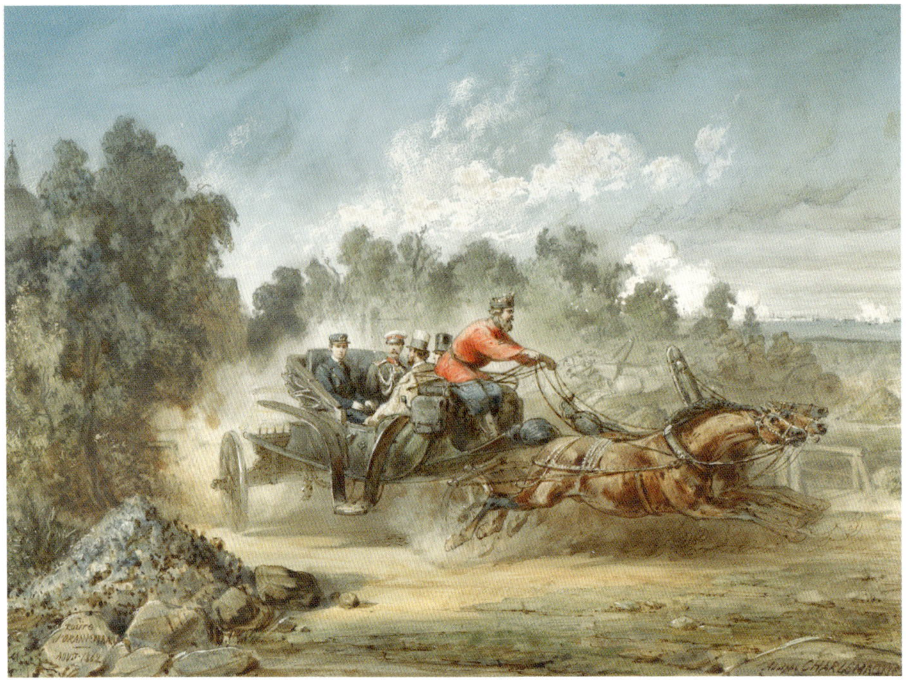

ADOLPHE CHARLEMAGNE (1826–1901)

162 *Prince Alfred (1844–1900) driving at Oranienbaum* 1862

Pencil, pen and ink, watercolour and bodycolour heightened with gum and with scraping out, 25.0 × 34.5 cm
Inscribed and dated bottom left: *ROUTE / d'ORANIENBAUM / AOUT. 1862*; signed bottom right: *Adolphe CHARLEMAGNE*
RCIN 914991

Provenance Probably Prince Alfred, Duke of Edinburgh; deposited in the Royal Library by Queen Mary, April 1947

Literature Possibly Clarence House Inventory 1909, 'Russian scene by Charlemagne'; Millar 1995, no. 860

Adolphe Charlemagne was a painter at the imperial court in St Petersburg. He studied at the Imperial Academy of Arts, before travelling to Munich and Paris, returning in 1861. In this watercolour, he portrays Prince Alfred and Alexander II driven at Oranienbaum, the imperial estate on the Gulf of Finland. His vigorous use of pen and ink to depict the horses in the foreground gives a strong sense of movement and he has scraped away the blue bodycolour of the sky to depict the clouds above the trees and along the horizon.

Prince Alfred arrived at Oranienbaum on 8 August 1862, two days after his eighteenth birthday. Alfred was serving with the Royal Navy on board HMS *St George*, which had arrived at the nearby sea port of Kronstadt.[52] He met and dined with Alexander II and his family on 10 August. Alexander, who can be seen here on the right, went with the Prince to Oranienbaum and to the Grand Menshikov Palace, which is just visible through the trees to the left. The two other gentlemen in the carriage are likely to be Major John Cowell, the prince's tutor, and John Lumley-Savile (1818–96), the chargé d'affaires.[53]

Queen Victoria had felt that it was 'advantageous for many reasons'[54] for the young prince to visit Russia during his service on the *St George*. Prince Alfred wrote of the kindness with which he was treated during his stay,[55] and Queen Victoria regarded the visit as 'very successful'.[56] **RW**

SIR ARTHUR ELLIS (1937–1907)

163 *Journal of the Prince of Wales (1841–1910) in Russia* 1866

Leather-bound notebook, 22.0 × 19.0 cm
Blind-stamped: *RUSSIA. / 1866, 87ff*
RA VIC/ADDA5/528

Provenance Presumably presented by the author and artist to Albert Edward, Prince of Wales (his bookplate)

Literature Millar 1995, no. 1674–92

Captain Arthur Ellis of the Grenadier Guards, who had fought in the Crimean War, at Kerch and in India, accompanied the Prince of Wales as Equerry during the Prince's visit to Russia in November 1866. The Prince travelled to Russia four years after his brother, Prince Alfred (later the Duke of Edinburgh) made the first British royal visit to the country in 1862.

The purpose of the Prince of Wales's journey was to attend the wedding of his sister-in-law, Princess Dagmar of Denmark, to the Tsesarevich Alexander Alexandrovich, second son of Emperor Alexander II and Empress Maria Alexandrovna. This first visit by the Prince of Wales to Russia was resisted by Queen Victoria, but the prince was enthusiastic: 'It would interest me beyond anything to see Russia', he wrote to the Queen in October, and he informed the Prime Minister, Lord Derby, that he would be 'only too happy to be the means in any way of promoting the *entente cordiale* between Russia and our own country'.[57] The Princess of Wales, Princess Dagmar's sister, was unable to travel as she was expecting the couple's third child, Princess Louise (1867–1931), and the Prince travelled with a suite including Ellis.

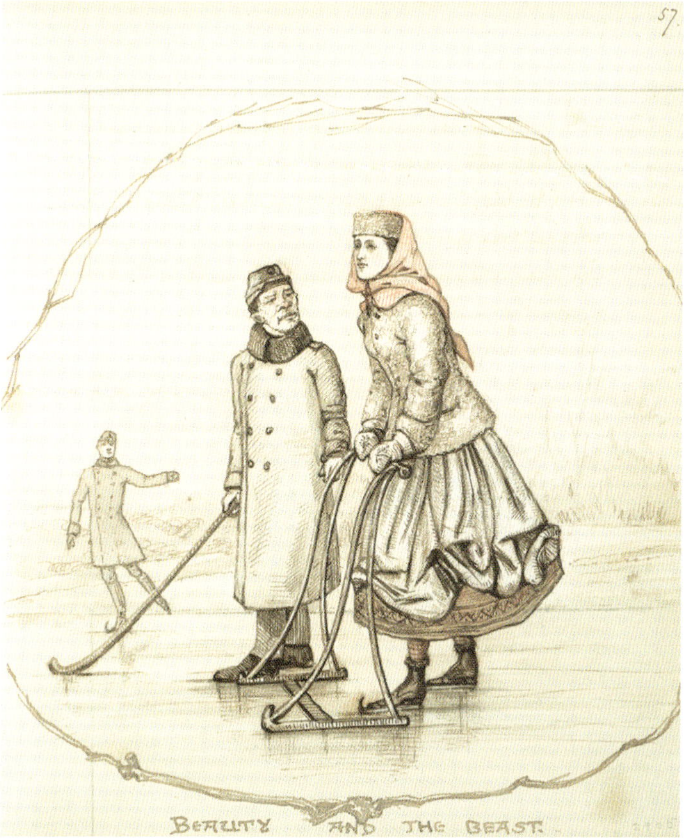

Ellis records each day of the trip and key events. Ellis also illustrated some of the protagonists and incidents of their stay, as well as the characters they met along the way, in a series of light-hearted sketches in sepia ink and wash, with some red and blue chalk. The 19 sketches start with the Russian General of Railways, who met the Prince at the border station between Prussia and Russia, where the prince was received with full honours. Other characters recorded are the guard standing outside the Emperor's rooms, a guard at Pavlovsk, dancers at the imperial ball following the wedding, Cossacks, the Emperor, the Grand Duchess Constantine learning to skate with her son's tutor (a sketch subtitled, 'Beauty and the Beast'), wolves, bears and wolf-hounds, two of which were presents from the Emperor to the Prince. SJP

CAUCASIAN CIRCASSIA

164 *Dagger (qama) and scabbard* mid-nineteenth century

Steel, gold, silver, niello, wood, leather, length (overall) 58.1 cm, (blade) 40.3 cm, weight 0.860 kg
Unidentified maker's mark of a five-pointed frond stamped on the blade
RCIN 37943

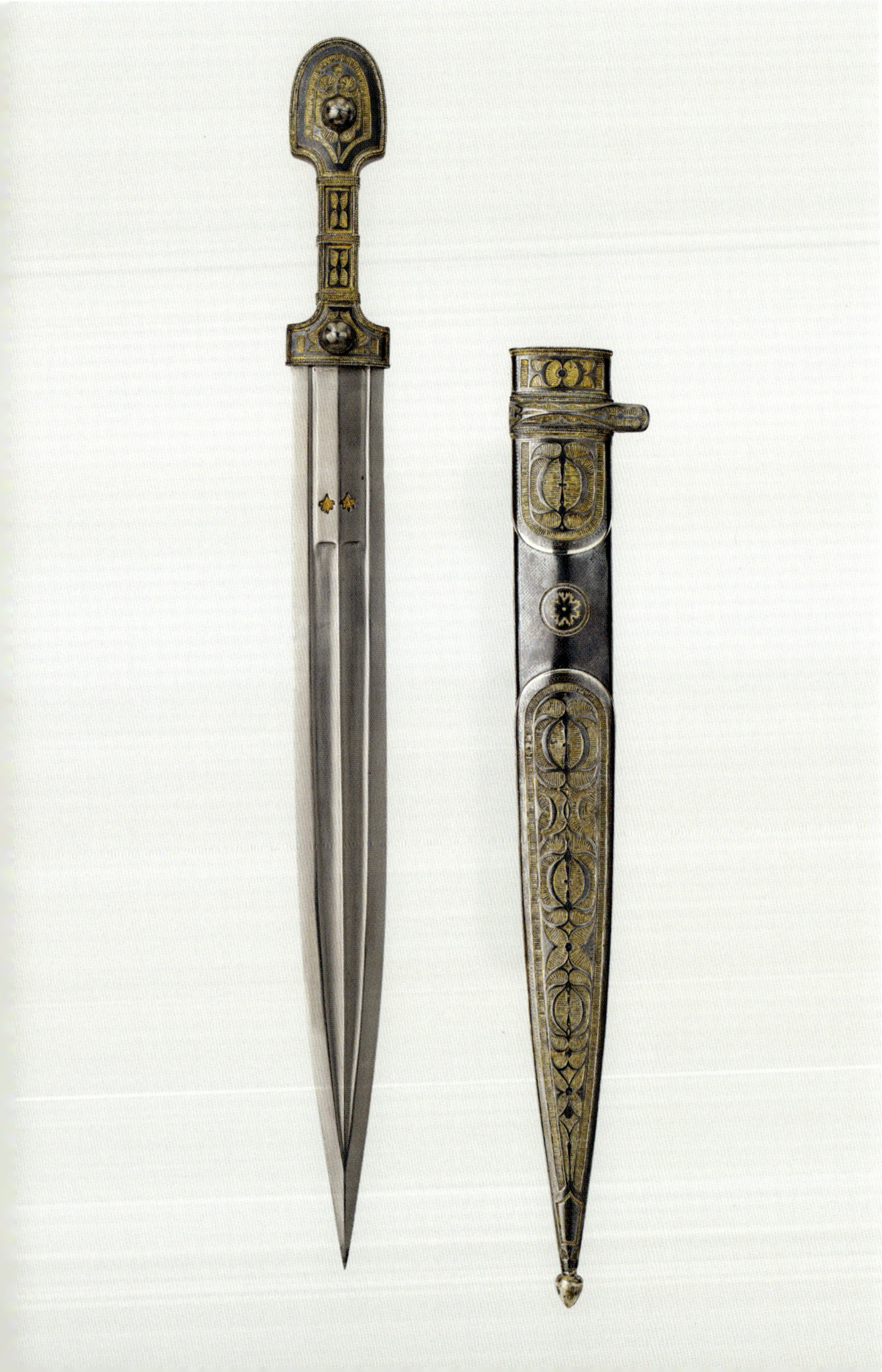

Provenance Part of the collection of arms and armour formed at Sandringham House by the Prince of Wales, later King Edward VII, late nineteenth century

Literature Purdon-Clarke 1910, no. 611

Silver and parcel-gilt metalwork with niello-filled engraving is an ancient, traditional form of decoration found on arms and armour in the Caucasus region and Russia, where it is called *chern*.[58] Tula, near Moscow, and Veliky Ustyug in the Vologada region, were well-known for such niello work.

Niello is a black metallic sulphide compound of sulphur, silver, copper and lead, applied using a similar fusion technique to that of enamel. The black, when used against bright silver, creates a striking contrast. Several gifts of arms were made to the Prince of Wales during his visit to Russia; on 22 November 1866, 'some beautiful specimens of Caucasus arms' were presented to the Prince by Circassian officers.[59] **SDM**

CAUCASIAN CIRCASSIA

165 *Dagger (qama), bi-knife and scabbard* mid-nineteenth century

Welded steel, gold, silver, niello, walrus ivory, wood, leather, textile, length (overall) 53.9 cm, (blade) 38.9 cm, weight 0.732 kg
Blade overlaid in gold with a cartouche in Persian (perhaps the maker?): *Bazli*; top of scabbard also dedicated in Persian to the owner: *Hamza*[60]
RCIN 37942

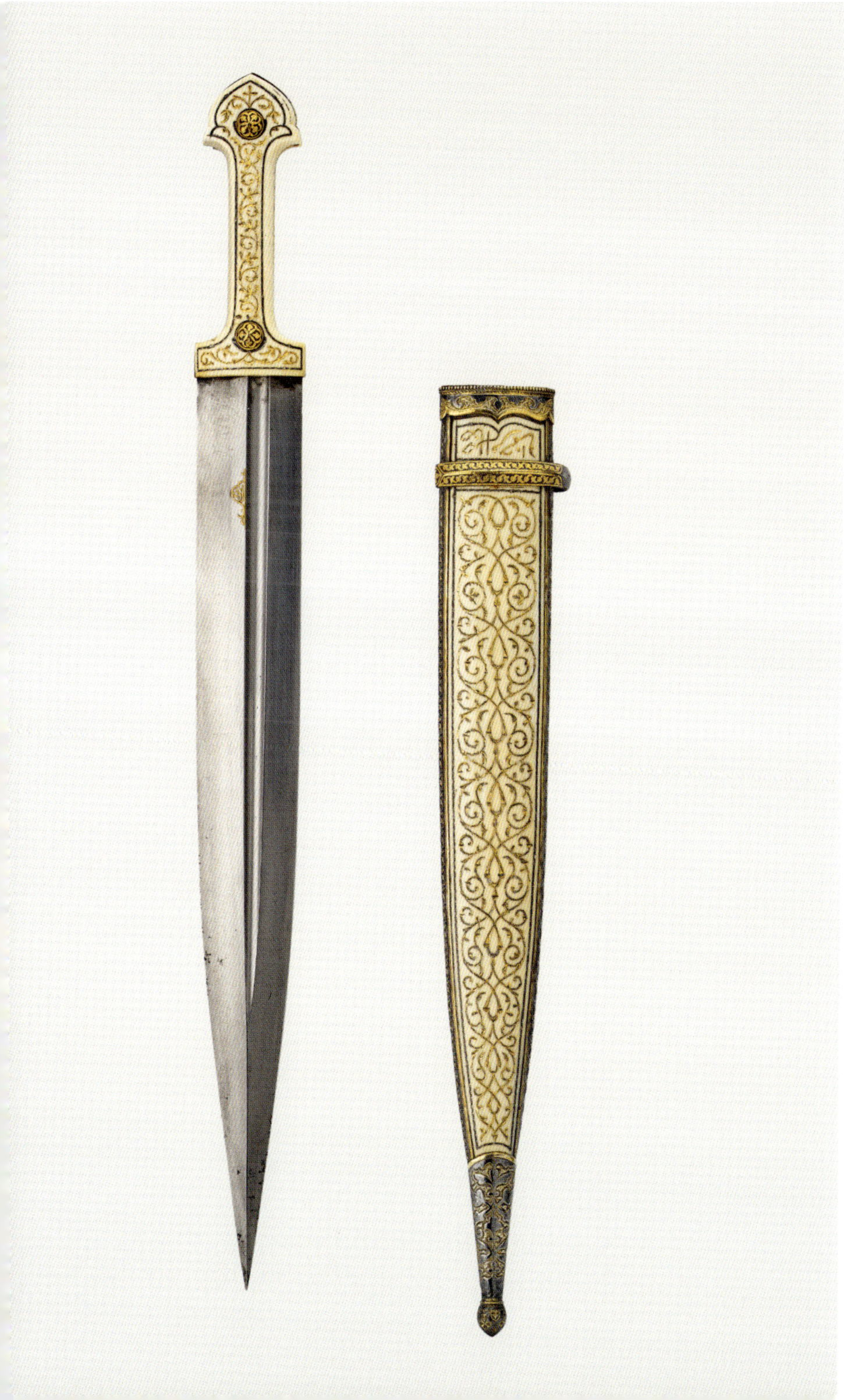

Provenance Part of the collection of arms and armour formed at Sandringham House by the Prince of Wales, later King Edward VII, in the late nineteenth century

Literature Purdon-Clarke 1910, no. 604

The blade of this *qama* is forged welded iron and steel, with a welded steel edge and a single offset central fuller on each side. The hilt is made of walrus ivory inlaid with gold and silver foil; the scabbard is heavily decorated with niello on a silver ground. The use of rich and exotic materials show the dagger is both a weapon and a status symbol. A similar *qama*, dated 1856, is in the Metropolitan Museum of Art, New York.[61] 'A dagger of 18th Century Circassian - ivory inlaid with gold - very beautiful' was presented to the Prince of Wales during his visit to Russia on 24 November 1866, by Imam Shamil's sons.[62] The Prince had met Shamil two days earlier. **SDM**

GEORGIA

166 *Dagger (qama) and scabbard c.* mid-nineteenth century

Steel, silver, glass, coral, wood, silk, length (overall) 60.0 cm, (blade) 38.7 cm, weight 0.746 kg
Stamped on the blade with an unidentified maker's mark
RCIN 37881

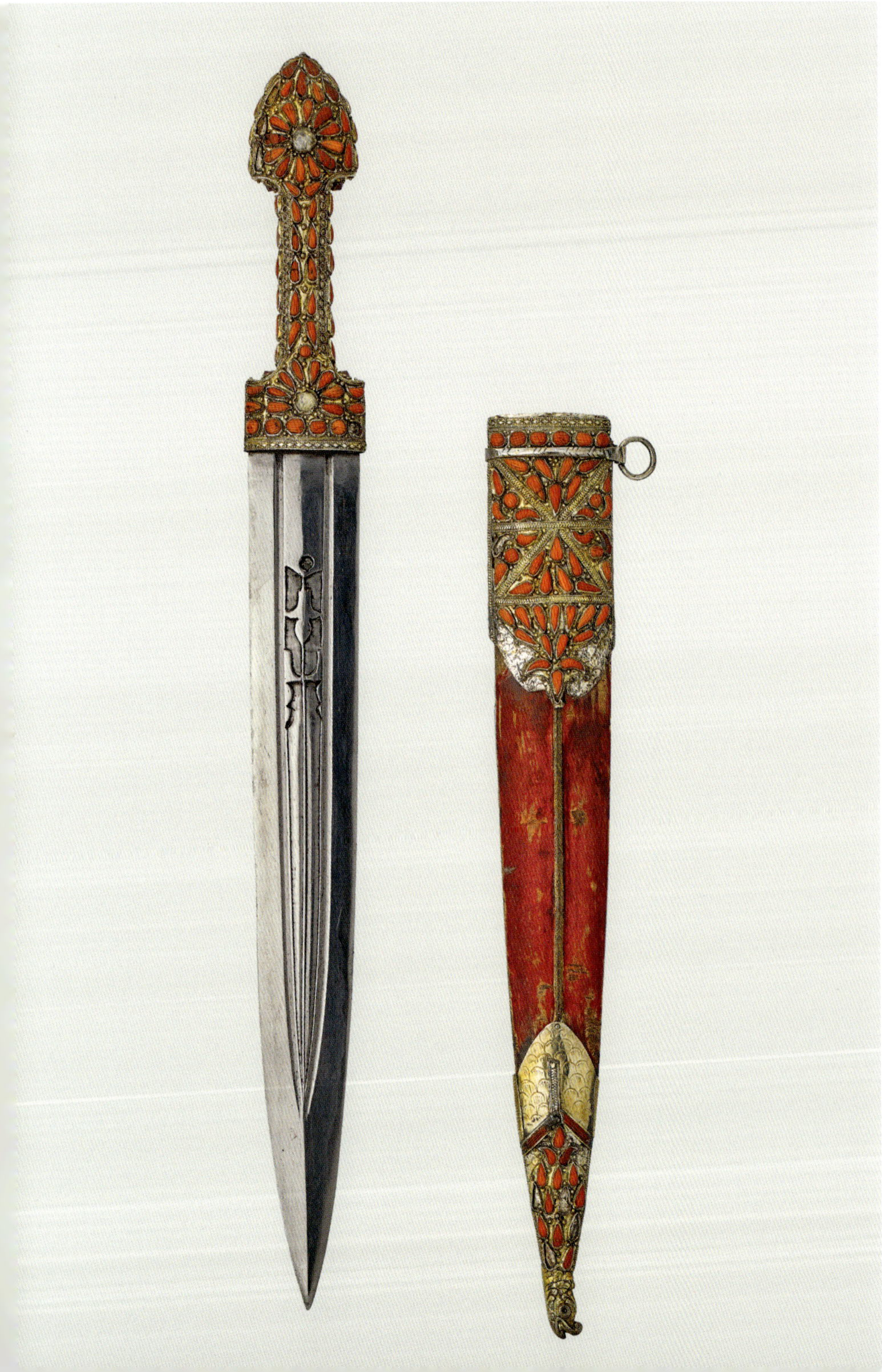

Provenance Part of the collection of arms and armour formed at Sandringham House by the Prince of Wales, later King Edward VII, late nineteenth century

Literature Purdon-Clarke 1910, no. 620

The *qama*, or *khama*, is the national weapon of Georgia;[63] as this example demonstrates, they are often heavily decorated with embossed and chased silver, encrusted with coral and stones.[64] As well as being a formidable weapon, the *qama* is used as jewellery, a symbol of the warrior and national pride. The *qama* is often argued to be the origin for the *kindjal* worn throughout the Caucasus. A very similar *qama*, with an almost identical blade and unidentified maker's mark, is in the Metropolitan Museum of Art, New York.[65]

SDM

FRANZ XAVER WINTERHALTER (1805–1873)

167 *Prince Alfred (1844–1900), later Duke of Edinburgh* 1865

Oil on canvas, 74.4 × 61.4 cm
Signed and dated: *fr. Winterhalter / 1865*
RCIN 404833

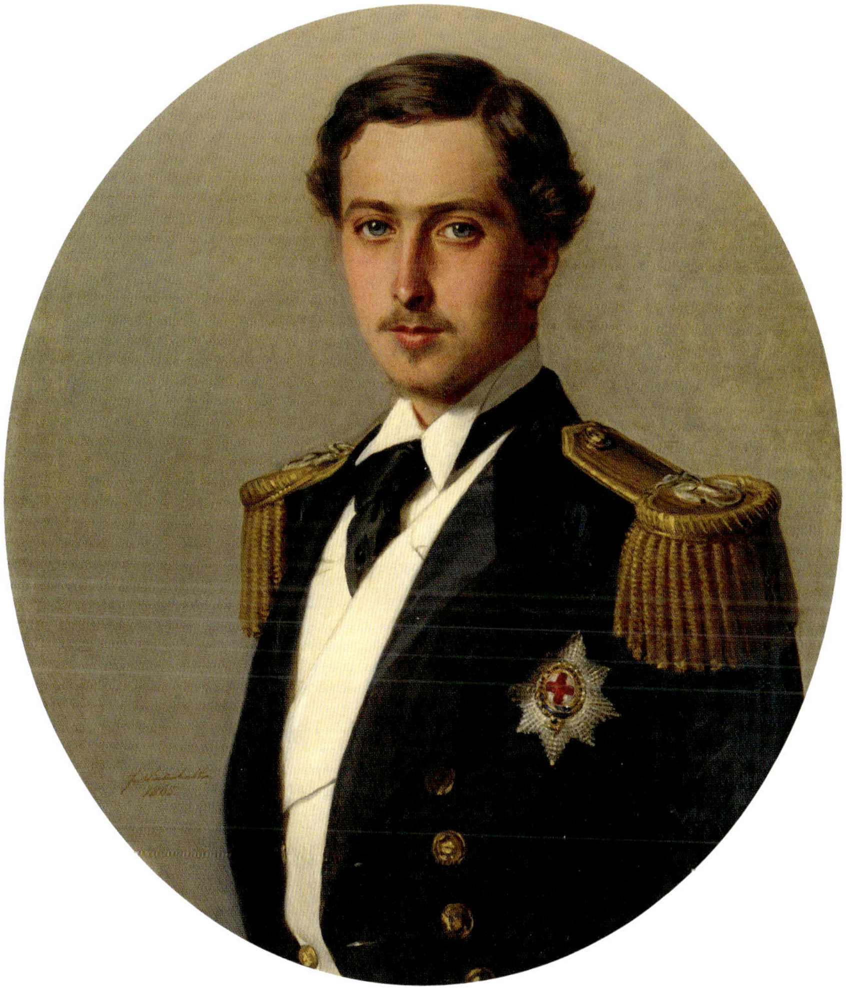

Provenance Painted for Queen Victoria; recorded in the Queen's Sitting Room, *c.*1872

Literature Millar 1992, no. 886

During the summer of 1865, Queen Victoria and her children travelled to the Rosenau, Germany, to spend time with her brother-in-law, Ernest II of Saxe Coburg and Gotha (1818–93). It was here that Winterhalter was invited to join the gathering and painted Princesses Helena (1846–1923) and Louise (1848–1939), and Prince Alfred.[66] On 23 August, the Queen recalled in her Journal that 'she went down to see Winterhalter's beautiful pictures which are progressing fast', and there are indications that the portrait was speedily done, yet the draughtsmanship appears effortless. The artist has captured the youthful gleam in the sitter's eyes, and the soft growth of hair on his chin.

Painted about eight years before his marriage to Maria Alexandrovna, Prince Alfred, or 'Affie', is depicted in naval uniform, with the star of the Garter. He had joined the Navy aged 14, and rose to the position of Admiral of the Fleet in 1893. In 1867, he undertook a world tour, visiting Australia, Japan and South Africa. **AB**

NIKOLAI EGOROVICH SVERCHKOV (1817–1898)

168 *Alexander II, Emperor of Russia (1818–1881) with Edward VII when Prince of Wales (1841–1910), in a troika at St Petersburg* c.1866

Oil on canvas, 72.0 × 113.0 cm
Signed: *N. de Swertchkow*; frame by Foord and Dickinson, 90 Wardour Street, London, painted on a thicker Russian canvas and stapled rather than tacked
RCIN 406576

Provenance Presumably a gift from Alexander II to King Edward VII, when Prince of Wales; first recorded at Sandringham, 1877

This atmospheric painting of the Prince of Wales and Emperor Alexander II in a troika, amidst a snow-covered landscape at dawn, was probably painted as a gift to commemorate the visit of the Prince of Wales to St Petersburg in 1866. The painting may recall a real occasion. It was included in a vast exhibition of paintings in Leeds in 1868, and later recorded at Sandringham.

Sverchkov had grown up amidst the imperial stables and studied horses from a young age, becoming a favoured artist of the Emperor and his wife, with his works adorning their private residences. He received his first commission from the Tsarevich Alexander, the future Emperor, in 1853, having recently been appointed an Academician at the Imperial Academy of Arts.[67] That the artist was allowed to build a house and studio at Tsarskoe Selo, *c.*1866, and lived there from 1870, is evidence of the esteem in which he was held by the Emperor and Empress.

A prolific artist, Sverchkov specialised in troika scenes – a powerful symbol of Russian identity – and this work is evidence of his proficiency.[68] The idea of movement is skilfully conveyed through the carefully observed horses and the rendering of the 'cloud' of snow, which contrasts with the thicker impasto of the heavier snow on the ground, and the dark scrubby plants pushing through. The carefully modelled heads of Alexander and his guest were probably added last, and are probably taken from contemporary photographs (figs 59, 60). The static figure to the right, part of Sverchkov's stock repertoire of peasant figures, bows to the passing royal guest; it also contributes to a sense of movement. The lively scene was presumably engraved and then the image adapted as a motif for smaller items of decorative art.

A second troika scene, painted on a fine French canvas, with a frame from a Parisian frame maker, was presented to the Prince of Wales, possibly *c.*1874 (at the time of the wedding of the Prince's brother, the Duke of Edinburgh, to Grand Duchess Maria). This was recorded at Buckingham Palace in 1909.[69] A further small sleigh scene was also recorded at Sandringham in 1877; this passed to Princess Victoria on the death of Queen Alexandra in 1925.[70] **AB**

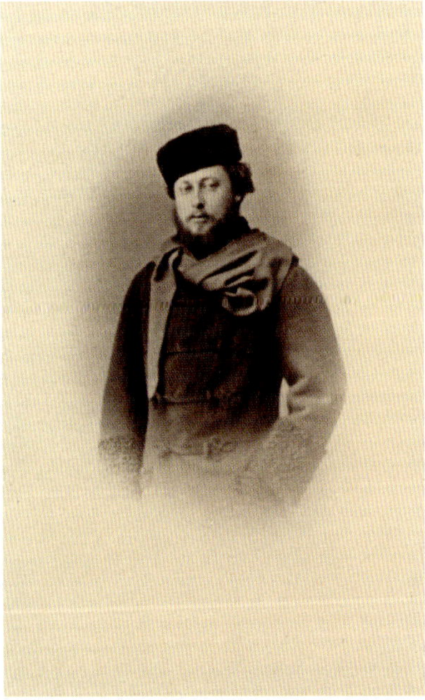

FIG. 59
After Charles Bergamasco
The Prince of Wales, November 1866
Carbon print, 8.5 × 5.4 cm
RCIN 2901543

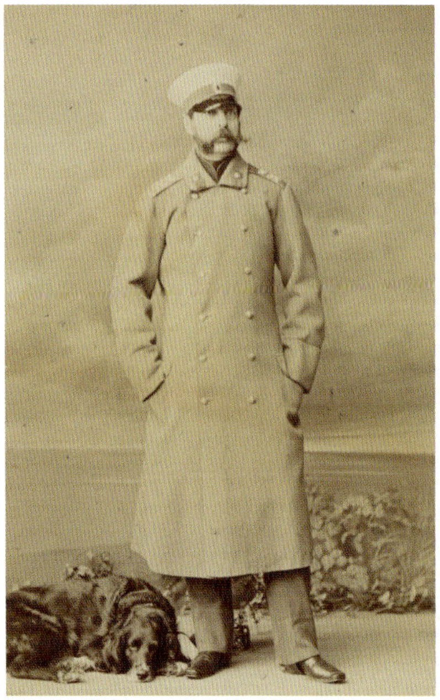

FIG. 60
Sergei Levitsky (1819–98)
Alexander II, Emperor of Russia, c.1870
Albumen print, 10.7 × 6.2 cm
RCIN 2927154

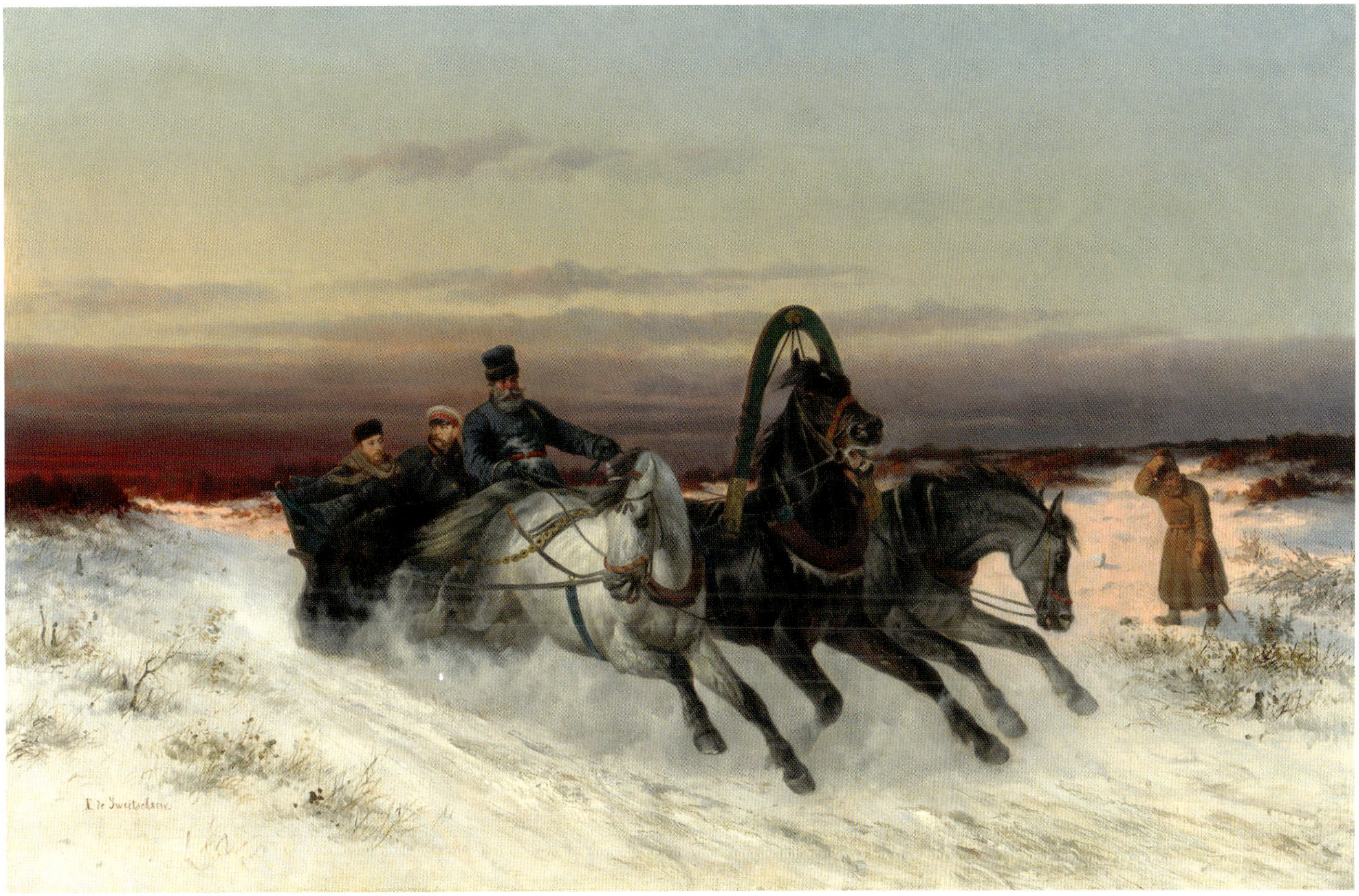

EKATERINBURG LAPIDARY WORKSHOPS

169 *Pair of tazzas on stands* 1866

Rhodonite, kalgan jasper, (overall) 17.5 × 10.3 cm (identical)
RCIN 7528

Provenance Presented to the Prince of Wales, 1866, by Emperor Alexander II

Literature *A Catalogue of the Works of Art at Marlborough House, London, and at Sandringham, Norfolk*, 1877, p. 43

This pair of tazzas, in carved and polished rhodonite, mounted on columnar porphyry stands, was produced in Ekaterinburg (Sverdlovsk), which became an important centre for stone carving from the end of the eighteenth century, due to its location in the Ural region, the primary Russian source of precious and semi-precious stones. A design for a similar tazza is held in the State Archive of Sverdlovsk, but it is dated February 1870. The design was, however, associated with the previous court order as this pair was presented to the Prince of Wales in 1866, presumably during the visit to Russia to attend the wedding of the Tsesarevich and Maria Feodorovna. **CDEG**

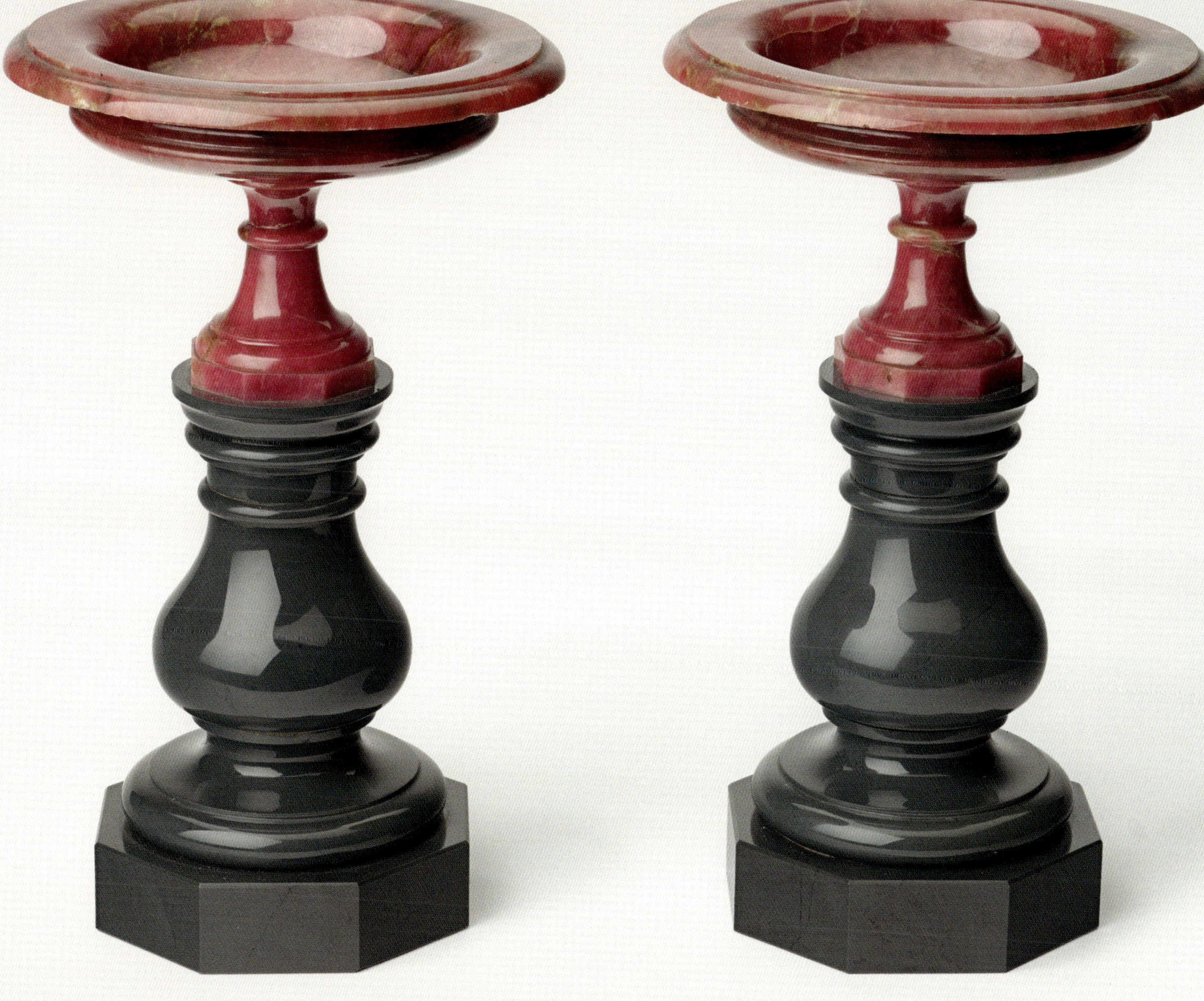

EKATERINBURG LAPIDARY WORKSHOPS

170 *Pair of tazzas on stands* 1856

Nephrite and rhodonite, (overall) 22.5 × 15.2 cm (identical)
RCIN 7546

Provenance Probably given to the Prince of Wales (later King Edward VII)

Literature State Archive of Sverdlovsk

This pair of tazzas, in carved and polished nephrite, mounted on columnar rhodonite stands, was produced in Ekaterinburg, like cat. 169. A design for the pedestal, with an indication of the vase, is held in the State Archive of Sverdlovsk. The pedestal in rhodonite was made to the design of August-Karl Andreyevich Beine (1816–58), who worked for the Imperial Cabinet from 1852 and participated in the organisation of the Russian stand at the Great Exhibition of 1851. In honour of his work, he received a letter of thanks from Prince Albert.[71] Although most likely to have been given earlier as gifts to Edward VII, when Prince of Wales, according to surviving accounts, Queen Alexandra was purchasing Russian hardstone pieces in the early twentieth century.[72] **CDEG**

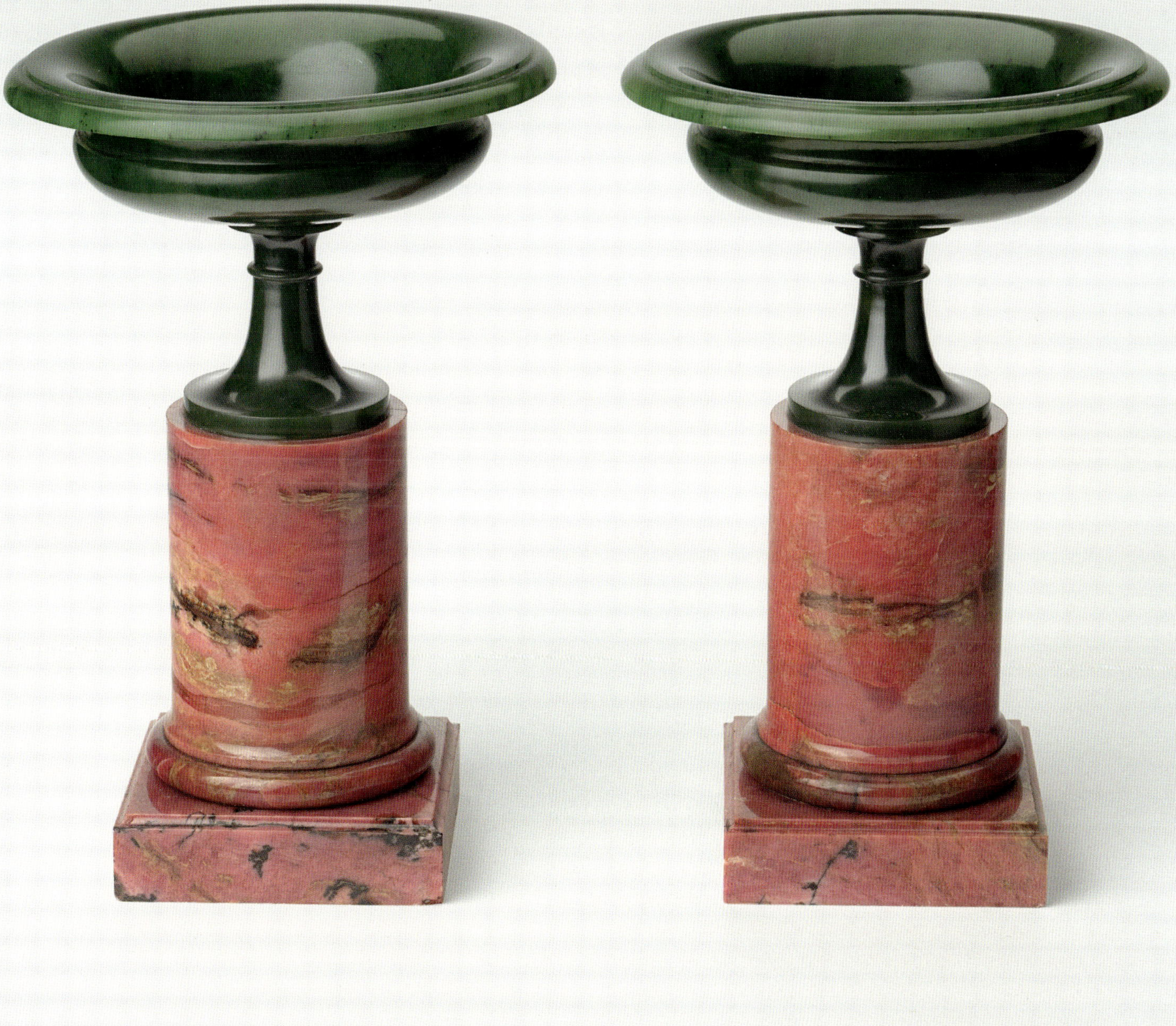

MARY THORNYCROFT (1809–1895)

171 & 172

Bust of Maria, Duchess of Edinburgh (1853–1920) (later Duchess of Saxe-Coburg and Gotha) 1876

Marble, 78.0 × 48.0 × 30.0 cm
Inscribed on front: *Marie*; and on back: *Mary Thornycroft, Sc. 1876*
RCIN 2092

SIR JOSEPH EDGAR BOEHM (1834–1890)

Bust of Alfred, Duke of Edinburgh (1844–1900) (later Duke of Saxe-Coburg and Gotha) 1879

Marble, 73.8 × 56.0 × 29.0 cm
Inscribed: *ALFRED 1879, H.R.H. ALFRED DUKE OF EDINBURGH, K.G. 1879, J.E. BOEHM*
RCIN 31620

Provenance (RCIN 2092): Probably commissioned by the Duke of Edinburgh, or possibly by Queen Victoria; (RCIN 31620): unknown

Grand Duchess Maria Alexandrovna was the only surviving daughter of Alexander II and Empress Maria Alexandrovna. She married Queen Victoria's second son, Alfred, Duke of Edinburgh (and from 1893, Duke of Saxe-Coburg and Gotha) on 23 January 1874, at the Winter Palace in St Petersburg, becoming the only Romanov to marry into the British Royal Family. The newly wed couple arrived at Windsor Castle on 7 March 1874, with the Duchess's substantial dowry and remarkable collection of jewellery by the leading suppliers to the imperial court, notably Bolin. Queen Victoria was delighted by her new daughter-in-law, often remarking on her sweet nature and elegant appearance.

Mary Thornycroft received numerous commissions from Queen Victoria and Prince Albert. In spite of the sitter's status – she had the distinction of being a Russian grand duchess (by birth), a British princess and royal duchess (by marriage), and the consort (and later widow) of a German sovereign duke – this portrait depicts the Duchess as a young woman of 23 years old, unencumbered by the trappings of her breeding, with simple drapery in a classical style.

The couple had five children: a son, Alfred, and four daughters, Marie, Victoria Melita, Alexandra and Beatrice. They lived at Clarence House in London, where a Russian Orthodox chapel was specially built so that Maria might continue to practise her faith. However, the marriage was not a happy one and Maria found it difficult to adapt to the British Court. In August 1893, Maria Alexandrovna became Duchess of Saxe-Coburg and Gotha, when her husband inherited the duchy on the death of his childless uncle, Ernest II, Duke of Saxe-Coburg and Gotha, the Duke of Edinburgh's eldest brother, later King Edward VII, having renounced the title when Prince of Wales. After the Duke's death in 1900, Maria continued to live in Coburg. At the outbreak of the First World War, she was divided in her sympathies, but sided with Germany against her native Russia. However, in the aftermath of the war in 1918, the duchy ceased to exist, and she died two years later, while living under reduced circumstances in exile in Switzerland.

The white marble bust of Alfred, Duke of Edinburgh, shows him bearded and wearing naval uniform and decorations, including the star of the Order of the Garter. The bust is dated four years after the marriage of Alfred and Maria Alexandrovna, while Alfred was still Duke of Edinburgh, before he acceded to the title of Duke of Saxe-Coburg and Gotha in 1893. The depiction in naval uniform makes reference to his distinguished naval career. He was promoted to Rear Admiral in 1878, eventually becoming Admiral of the Fleet on 3 June 1893.

The bust was probably commissioned by Queen Victoria and has been displayed in St George's Hall, Windsor Castle since 1929. **CDEG**

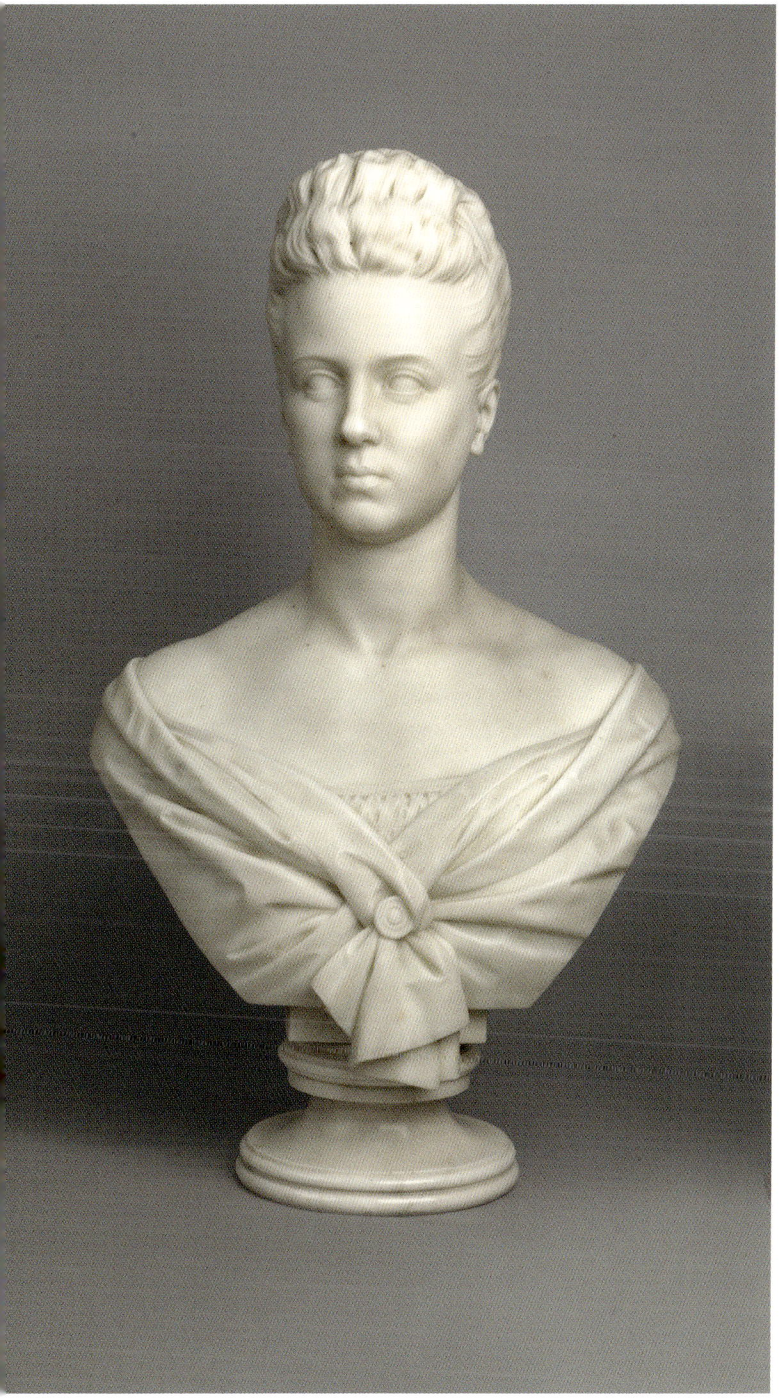
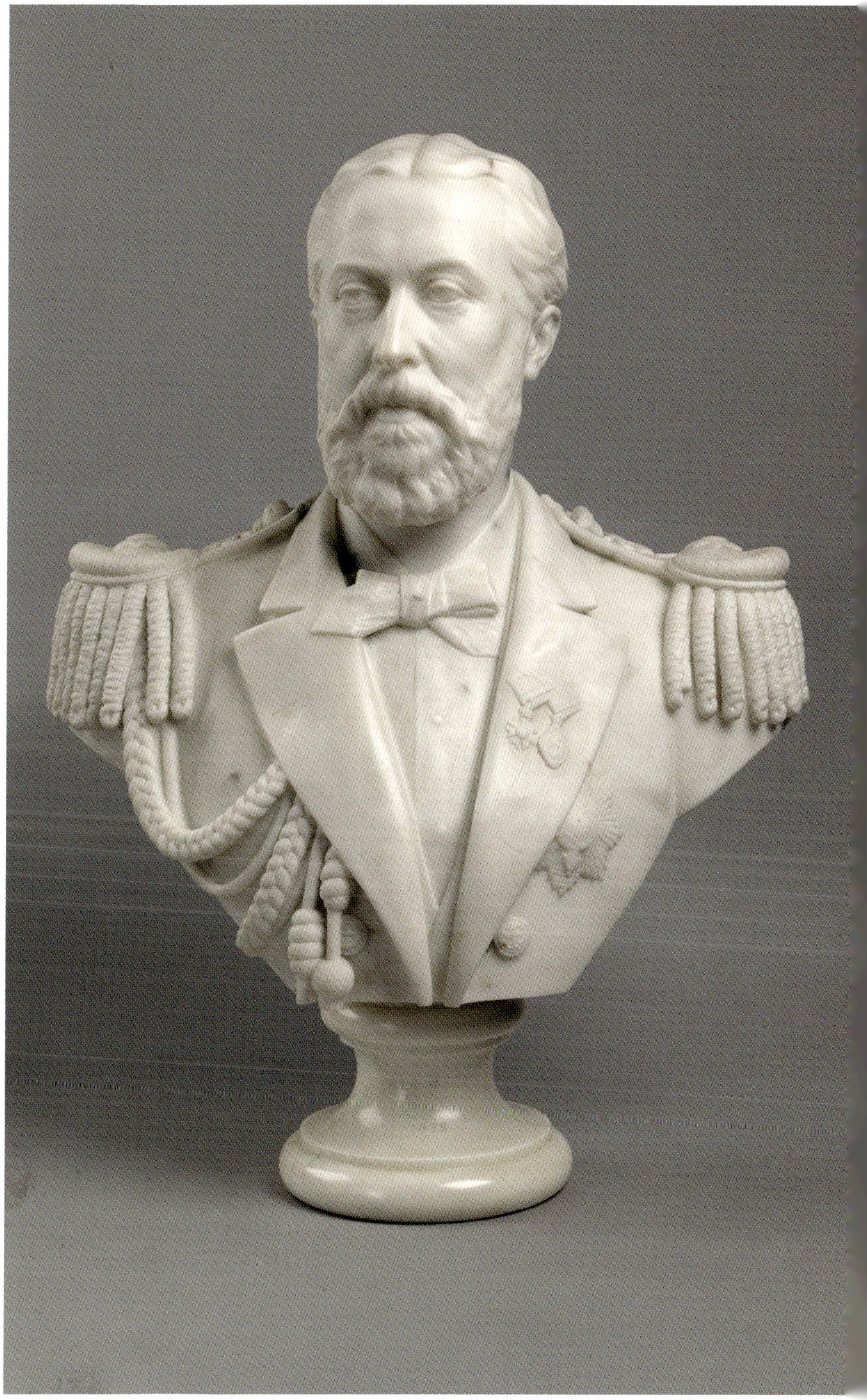

GUSTAV RICHTER (1823–1884)

173 *Maria, Duchess of Edinburgh, Grand Duchess of Russia (1853–1920)* 1873–4

Oil on canvas, 145.8 × 94.7 cm
Signed and dated: *Gustav Richter / Livadia / 1873*
RCIN 405024

Provenance Given to Queen Victoria by Emperor Alexander II

On 18 January 1874, Queen Victoria, writing from Osborne House, recorded that the 'Feldjäger' (the Queen's messenger) had arrived, bringing 'the long expected portrait of her [Maria], which is a gift from the Emperor. It is a lovely picture ½ length, and beautifully painted. She is standing on a balcony in a light blue evening dress, with a fan in her hand.' It appears that dispatch of the portrait was delayed because miniatures from the image were being painted as official presents from the couple. Days later, the Queen praised the likeness as 'beautiful & quite worthy of Winterhalter', and on the day of her son Alfred's wedding to the sitter in St Petersburg (cat. 174), the picture was 'surrounded by a wreath of evergreens & some orange flowers, tied with bows of the Russian colours', in honour of the occasion.[73] Up until this point, the Queen had only seen photographs of her future daughter-in-law, and when she arrived at the English court soon after the wedding, views of her personality were sometimes less than complimentary. However, assimilation into the British Court was challenging for Marie, as it differed significantly with the Court of St Petersburg, and this resulted in tensions and perceived snubs.

The German painter, Gustav Richter, who had studied in Berlin and was later a pupil of Léon Cogniet (1794–1880) in Paris, worked on the portrait during the late autumn of 1873 at Livadia Palace, near Yalta. The Grand Duchess was aged 20 at the time and later loathed having to sit for her portrait, conscious of her looks and figure. When painted by Carl Rudolph Sohn (1845–1908) in 1884 (cat. 194), she described the experience as a 'great bore', and an 'aggravation of sorrow'.[74]

The portrait was sent away to Georgina Koberwein Terrell (1853–1903) on three occasions between 20 December 1890 and 17 June 1891 for copying, and a copy was given by the Queen to the Duke of Edinburgh for his birthday.[75] The painting is recorded in a photograph of *c.*1890 hanging in the Oak Room, Windsor Castle, together with other portraits of Queen Victoria's daughters-in-law; their Gothic revival frames presumably commissioned for this ensemble (fig. 61). **AB**

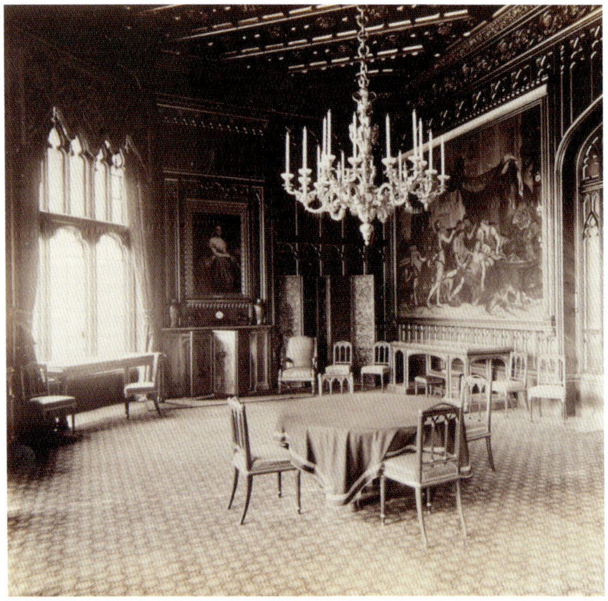

FIG. 61
Unknown
The Oak Room, Windsor, *c.*1890–5
Gelatin silver print, 22.4 × 27.7
RCIN 2935640

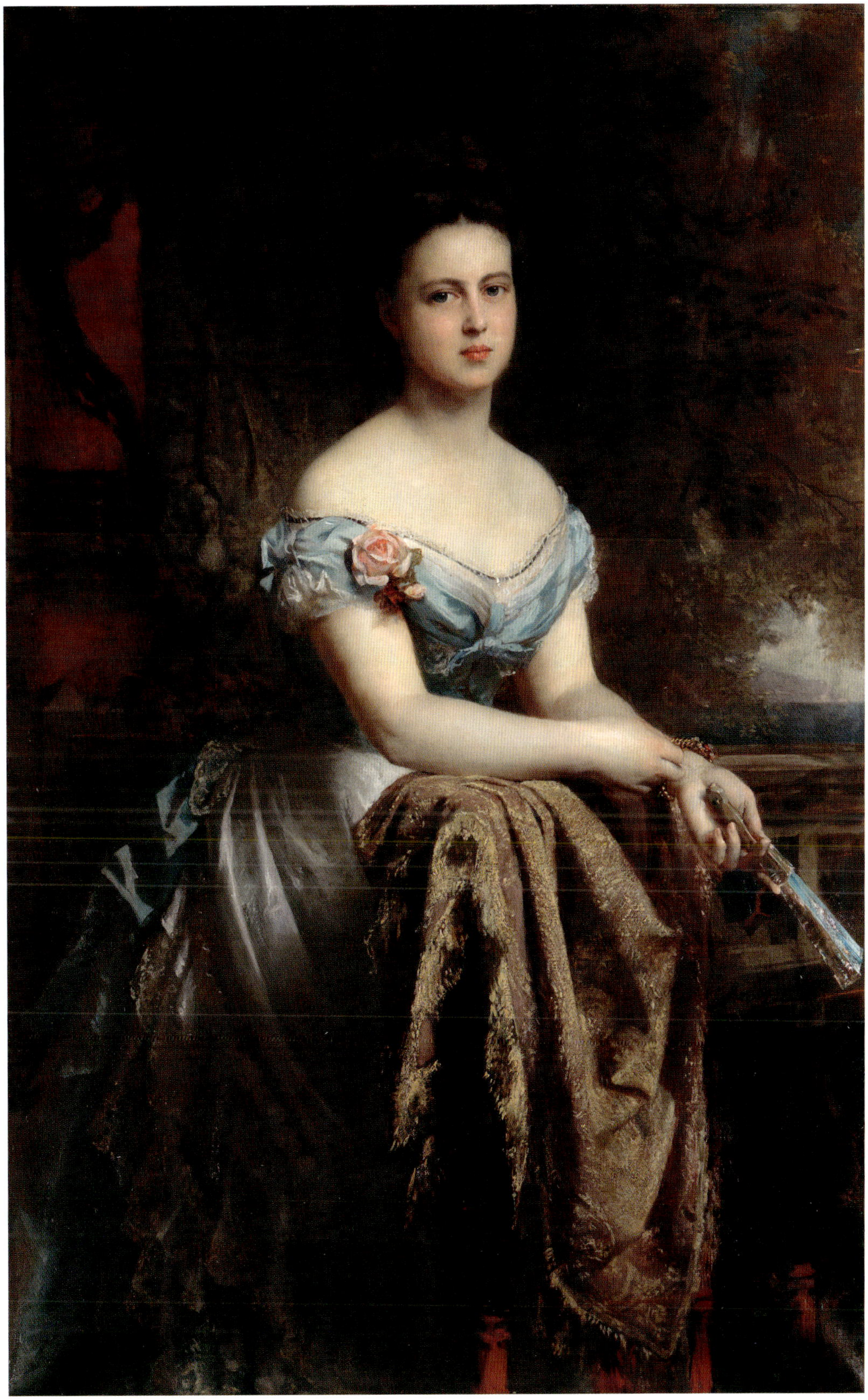

NICHOLAS CHEVALIER (1828–1902)

174 *The marriage of Prince Alfred, Duke of Edinburgh (1844–1900), 23 January 1874* 1874–5

Oil on canvas, 168.4 × 138.5 cm
RCIN 404476

Provenance Commissioned by Queen Victoria; first hung in the Grand Corridor, Windsor Castle, in late 1875; sent to Buckingham Palace, 1901, and first recorded in the King's Corridor, Buckingham Palace, 1909

Literature Millar 1992, no. 201

The marriage of Alfred, Duke of Edinburgh to Grand Duchess Maria, the only surviving daughter of Alexander II, took place in the Palace Cathedral on 23 January 1874. The bride and bridegroom stand holding lighted candles, whilst the Archbishop, resplendent in his official robes, holds a cross above them. Maria's parents, Alexander II and Maria Alexandrovna, stand to the right of the window, while the young Grand Duke Nicholas, later Nicholas II, can be glimpsed in front of his mother, Maria Feodorovna; to her right is her sister, the Princess of Wales, and the Crown Princess of Prussia (1840–1901). The Prince of Wales, clearly visible in profile, in a striking scarlet military jacket, was Queen Victoria's representative. The Orthodox ceremony was conducted by the Metropolitan Archbishop, and was followed by an English service, presided over by Dean Stanley, which took place in the Alexander Hall (cat. 180).

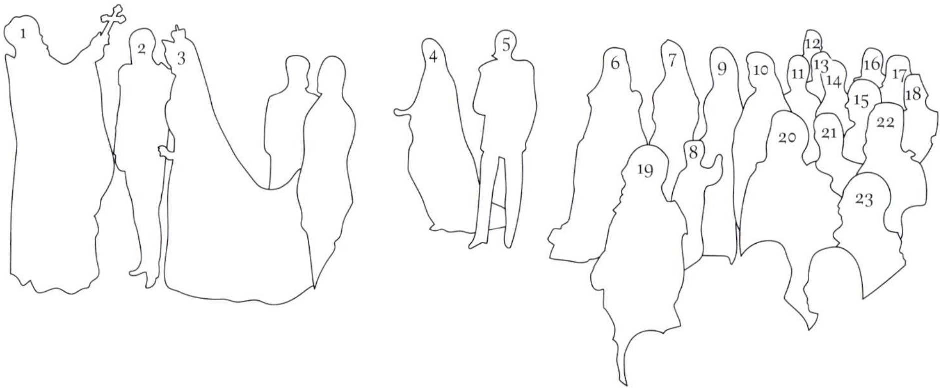

Key

1. Metropolitan Isidor of Novgorod, St Petersburg and Finland
2. Prince Alfred, Duke of Edinburgh
3. Grand Duchess Maria Alexandrovna, Duchess of Edinburgh
4. Maria Alexandrovna, Empress of Russia
5. Alexander II, Emperor of Russia
6. Crown Princess of Prussia, later Empress Victoria of Germany and Queen of Prussia
7. Alexandra, Princess of Wales, later Queen Alexandra
8. Grand Duke Nicholas Alexandrovich, later Nicholas II, Emperor of Russia
9. Tsesarevna Maria Feodorovna, later Maria Feodorovna, Empress of Russia
10. Grand Duchess Alexandra Iosifovna
11. Prince Arthur, Duke of Connaught
12. Grand Duke Serge Alexandrovich
13. Arthur Penrhyn Stanley, Dean of Westminster
14. Grand Duke Vladimir Alexandrovich
15. Grand Duke Nicholas Nikolaevich
16. Ernest II, Duke of Saxe-Coburg and Gotha
17. Grand Duke Alexei Alexandrovich
18. Grand Duke Constantine Nikolaevich
19. Albert Edward, Prince of Wales, later King Edward VII
20. Crown Prince of Prussia, later Emperor Frederick III of Germany and King of Prussia
21. Prince Alexander of Hesse and by Rhine
22. Prince Louis of Hesse by Rhine, later Louis IV, Grand Duke of Hesse and by Rhine
23. Crown Prince of Denmark, later King Frederick VIII

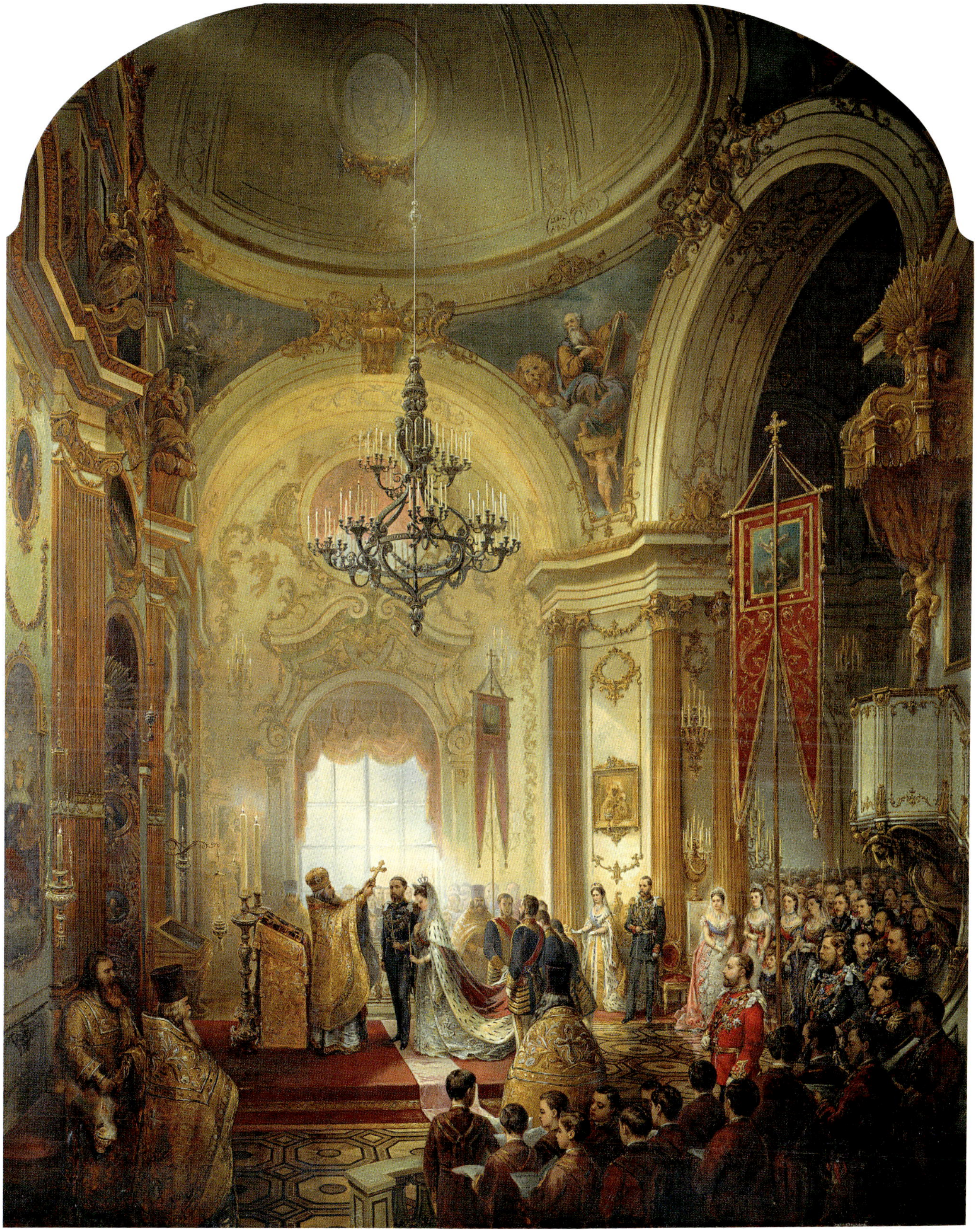

The commissioning of Chevalier to travel to St Petersburg to record the event was managed by Prince Alfred, who had first encountered Chevalier during his world tour of 1867, and had invited the artist to return with him to London. He subsequently travelled with Affie on his tour of the East on HMS *Galatea*. The artist, whose mother was Russian, had trained in Switzerland and worked in Australia and New Zealand.

Just days after the wedding, the Duke of Edinburgh sent his mother sketches by Chevalier of the two ceremonies (cats 179 and 180). The Queen chose to commission a painting of the Orthodox ceremony – the intimate setting, soft candlelight and abundance of fabric offering a richer and more cohesive composition than the vast open space of the Alexander Hall. By July 1875, Chevalier had forwarded a 'rough sketch in oil of the Ceremony of the marriage', requesting the Queen's permission to enlarge the 'future picture a triffle [*sic*] [...] so as to enable me to do full justice to so fine and important a subject'[76]. His request was accepted; however, he struggled to complete the painting in time for submission to the Royal Academy, and later to gain the Queen's approval. He was still working on it 'unremitingly [*sic*] and against time' on 24 March 1875, and after the exhibition had closed.[77] It was delivered to Windsor on 22 November 1875, and placed in the Corridor, but removed to Buckingham Palace in 1901. It was also agreed that the Queen, the Duke of Edinburgh and the Prince of Wales could buy 'whatever Pictures they might fancy',[78] based on studies of scenes the artist had witnessed.

Chevalier's oeuvre is diverse, encompassing illustration, cartoons and landscape painting; however, the success of this painting lies in its illustrative qualities and the artist's strong sense of design. The architectural interior, with its rich interplay of arches and domed ceiling, acts as a stage on which to present the bridal couple bathed in winter light. A wonderful interplay of gilt swags, the elegant chandelier and details like the snow settling on the window add liveliness and interest to the scene. However, it lacks the accomplishment and sophistication of the painting of the marriage of Nicholas II by Laurits Tuxen, set in the same chapel 20 years later (cat. 203). **AB**

NICHOLAS CHEVALIER (1828–1902)

175 *Full-length study of dress worn by the Tsesarevna (1847–1928)* 1874

Pencil, watercolour, bodycolour, gold paint and scraping out, 25.0 × 19.0 cm
Dated and inscribed in pencil: *Saraphan worn by H.I.H the Cesarewna on the 23/1/74*; with other notes
RCIN 926238

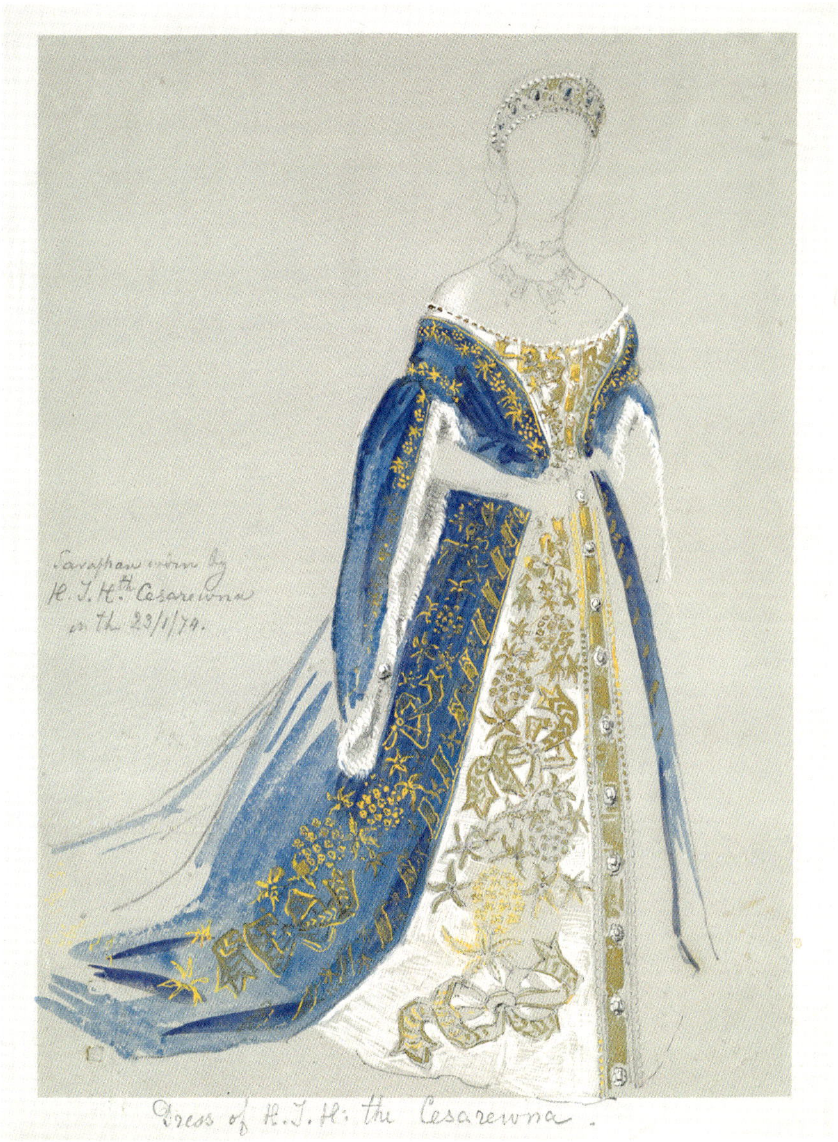

Provenance From an album of watercolours made at St Petersburg and Moscow, at the time of the marriage of Prince Alfred and the Grand Duchess Maria Alexandrovna of Russia, 1874, commissioned by Queen Victoria; purchased from The Winter Palace, Kensington High Street, London, 1986

Literature Stanley 1927, p. 215; Millar 1995, p. 204

Lady Augusta Stanley describes how both the Tsesarevich's wife, Maria Feodorovna, and her sister, the Princess of Wales, 'blazed with diamonds', and that the Tsesarevna's ensemble was 'a gown of gold-embroidered satin and train of sky-blue velvet emblazoned with imperial insigniae [*sic*]'.[79]

Chevalier represents the embroidery of the white satin of the dress and the bright blue silk velvet of the overdress with gold paint in star and ribbon motifs, while the touches of white down the central gold brocade seam of the dress indicate where diamonds were sewn on to fasten the gown and hold the ermine-lined sleeves together. The jewels are only faintly sketched, but are recognisable as Maria Feodorovna's sapphire parure including the so-called 'Wave Tiara', which has been attached to the gold fabric kokoshnik.

CDEG

NICHOLAS CHEVALIER (1828–1902)

176 *Full-length study of dress worn by the Princess of Wales (1844–1925), with details of jewellery and orders* 1874

Pencil, watercolour, bodycolour and silver paint with scraping out, 25.0 × 19.0 cm
Dated and inscribed in pencil: *Dress worn by H.R.H. the Princess of Wales 23 Jan. 1874*; with numerous other notes
RCIN 926235

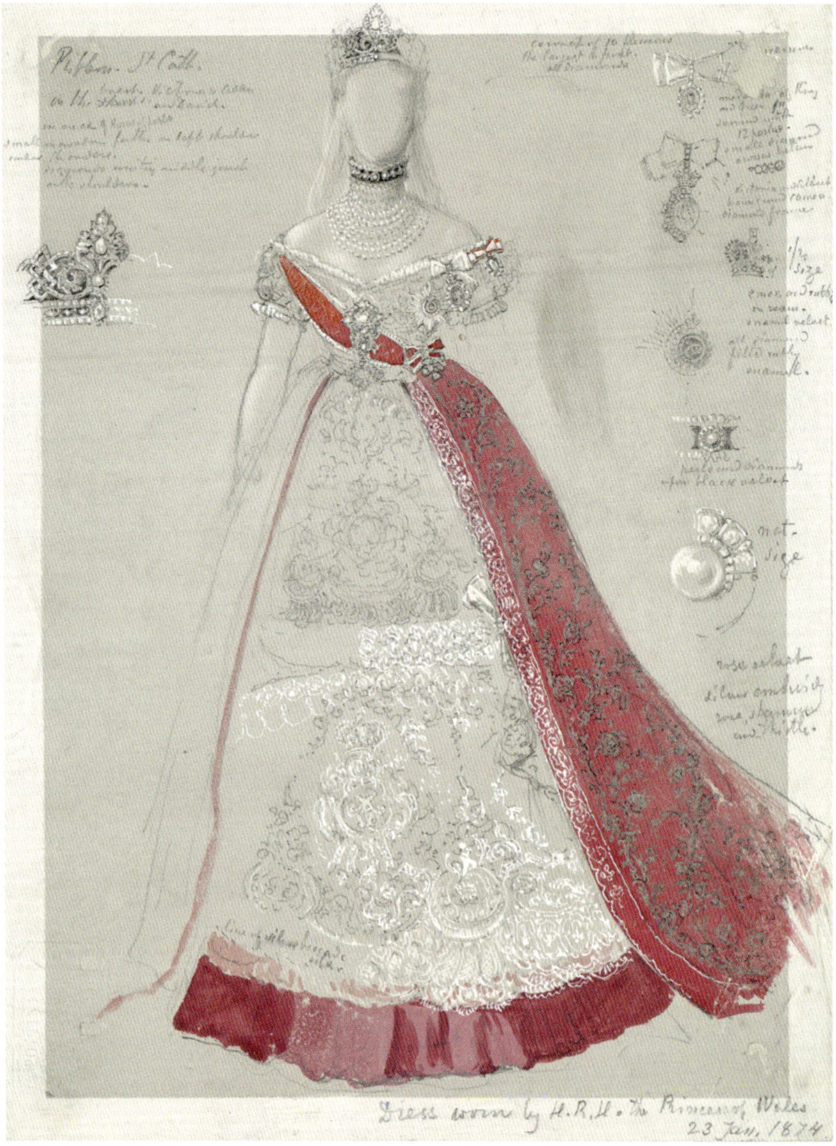

Provenance See cat. 175

Literature Stanley 1927, p. 217; Millar 1995, p. 203

In this evocative study, the sumptuous white brocaded silk of Princess Alexandra's court dress and the rich crimson velvet of her overskirt, woven with gold embroidery, are minutely described by Chevalier. In the finished work (cat. 174), for which this is one of several studies, the Princess of Wales stands next to her sister, Maria Feodorovna, but the accurate details of dress and jewels seen in this study and its two companions (cats 175 and 177) were not translated by the artist into the painting of the marriage of Prince Alfred and Grand Duchess Maria Alexandrovna.

Chevalier has taken delight in painting and noting the jewels worn by Princess Alexandra, which include a diamond tiara, a diamond collet necklace on a velvet band, several further diamond collet necklaces, a pearl and diamond necklace, a pearl and diamond brooch, the broad riband, star and badge of the Order of St Catherine, and family orders. The tiara, brooch and pearl and diamond necklace are from the parure of wedding jewellery made by R. & S. Garrard & Co., and given by Albert Edward, Prince of Wales to his bride on their marriage in 1863.[80]

While Queen Alexandra's jewels have largely remained in the ownership of the royal family, and many of them are worn by Her Majesty The Queen today, a large proportion of her wardrobe was dispersed and sold after the death of her unmarried daughter, Princess Victoria. This sketch, together with a large number of photographs in the Royal Collection, provides a valuable record of her uniquely fashionable taste.

CDEG

NICHOLAS CHEVALIER (1828–1902)

177 *Full-length study of dress worn by the Duchess of Edinburgh (1853–1920), with detail of agraffe and star* 1874

Pencil, coloured pencil, silver paint and scraping out, 25.0 × 19.0 cm
Dated and inscribed in pencil: *Silver Saraphan of H.I.H the Duchess of Edinburgh 23/1/74*; with other notes
RCIN 926237

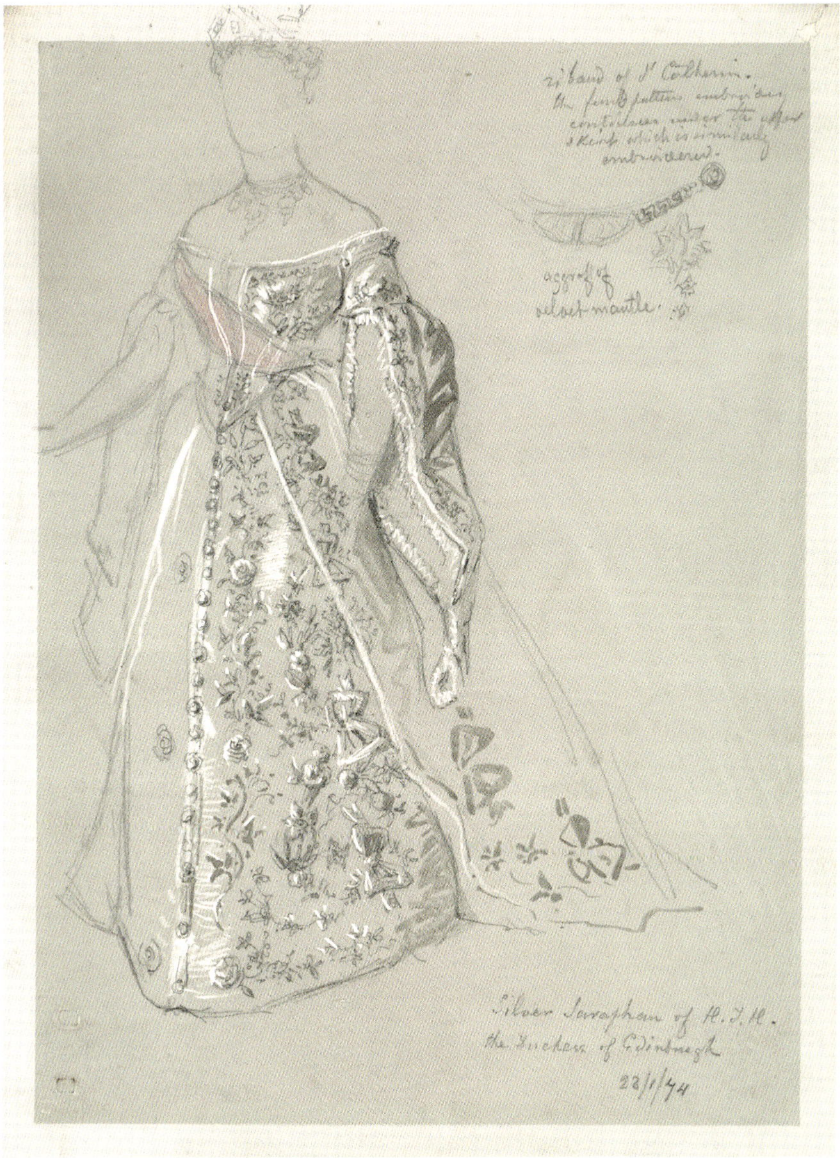

Provenance See cat. 175

Literature Stanley 1927, p. 215;
Millar 1995, p. 203

Chevalier's sketch accurately describes the silver and gem-set sarafan worn by all Russian imperial brides for their wedding, with its draped sleeves lined with ermine, together with the traditional kokoshnik headdress.

Lady Augusta Stanley's letters provide a vivid and detailed account of the wedding ceremony; she recalls how 'six gentlemen I think carried the long white cloth-of-silver train and the Mantel trimmed with ermine'.[81] Maria's remarkable jewels are indicated in Chevalier's sketch, both on the cloth of embroidered silver of the dress and mantle, and in the details that the artist has picked out at the top of the sheet, as reminders of the agaffe – the metal and gem-set fastening of the mantle – and the Order of St Catherine, the broad riband of which Chevalier has represented in pale pink, providing the only colour to an otherwise monochromatic sketch.

Lady Stanley recalls that 'the small graceful head so childlike, must have ached with the immense weight of jewels, the necklace of diamonds [...] the most beautiful I ever saw, and the gown was studded with them round the body and sleeves and down the front of the body and skirt'.[82] CDEG

NICHOLAS CHEVALIER (1828–1902)

178 *The Bal Polonaise at the Winter Palace, St Petersburg, 23 January 1874* 1876

Pencil, watercolour and bodycolour, 44.5 × 66.7 cm
Signed and dated: *N. Chevalier / 1876*
RCIN 451905

Provenance Commissioned by Prince Alfred, Duke of Edinburgh

Literature Millar 1995, no. 1018

Following the two wedding ceremonies for the Duke and Duchess of Edinburgh on 23 January 1874, the first, Orthodox, in the Palace Cathedral, and the second, an Anglican service in the Alexander Hall, the celebrations continued, with a banquet for 700 guests. Lord Augustus Loftus (1817–1904), British ambassador, wrote to Lord Granville, Secretary of State for Foreign Affairs in London:

> *Nothing can exceed the splendour of this Banquet. The display of magnificent jewels, the brilliancy of the uniforms, the mass of ornamental gold and silver plate the beauty of the varied Sevres china added to the vocal talents of the Patti, the Albani, Nicolini who executed the most lovely airs during dinner gave a charm and perfection to a scene which for its unrivalled beauty is almost indescribable. After the dinner a Bal Polonaise was given at the Palace at which I am told three thousand persons were present. No one but the Imperial Family and the foreign ambassadors danced the Polonaise and the only exception was that of Viscount Sydney [the Lord Chamberlain] who with myself was specially invited to dance the Polonaise with the Imperial Bride.*[83]

The ball took place in St George's Hall, or the throne room of the Winter Palace. The formal polonaise dance was led by the Emperor, with, as his partner, the bride, the Grand Duchess Maria Alexandrovna, and the Empress was led by the groom, the Duke of Edinburgh. Behind them, the Prince of Wales is seen leading his sister, the German Crown Princess, behind them, her husband, the German Crown Prince, leads the Princess of Wales. SJP

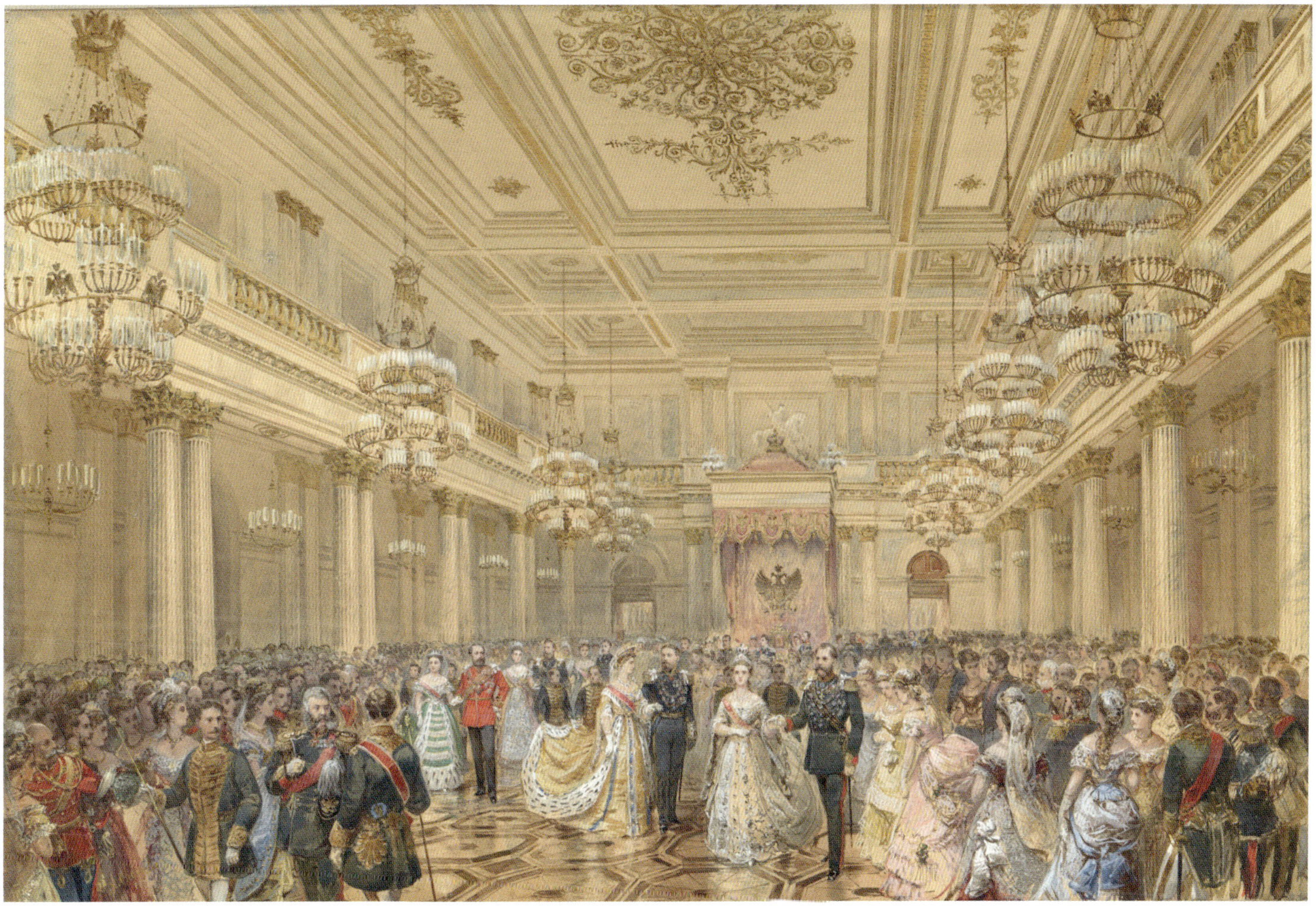

NICHOLAS CHEVALIER (1828–1902)

179 & 180

The Orthodox marriage service of Alfred, Duke of Edinburgh (1844–1900) and Maria Alexandrovna (1853–1920), 23 January 1874 1874

Pencil, pen and ink, watercolour and bodycolour with two flaps, 20.5 × 24.7 cm
Signed and dated: *N. Chevalier, 11/23 Janu. 1874*
RCIN 920784

The Anglican marriage service of Alfred, Duke of Edinburgh (1844–1900) and Maria Alexandrovna (1853–1920), 23 January 1874 1874

Pencil, pen and ink, coloured pencil and watercolour, 20.4 × 25.0 cm
Signed and dated: *N. Chevalier 11/1/74*
RCIN 920785

Provenance Commissioned by Prince Alfred, Duke of Edinburgh and sent to Queen Victoria

Literature Millar 1995, no. 1015

The sketch of the Orthodox Ceremony in the Palace Cathedral of the Winter Palace was sent by the Duke of Edinburgh to his mother, Queen Victoria, on 28 January 1874. 'I hope to be able to send with this by tomorrow's messenger two sketches by Chevalier & in one of the Greek ceremony, by using the little additional strips you will be able to follow the different parts of the service.'[84]

The three parts of the service that are captured followed the betrothal ceremony, with the entrance of the bride and groom, and the exchange of rings are explained with the addition of two flaps labelled '1st and 3rd part of ceremony': they were the 'crowning' (when nuptial crowns were held over the heads of the bride and groom by the groomsmen, Prince Arthur and Grand Dukes Alexei (1850–1908), Vladimir (1847–1909) and Sergei, brothers of the groom and bride); the procession around the Analogion (Gospel lectern); and the blessing at the end of the ceremony.

The Queen received the sketches on 2 February and recorded in her diary: 'Endless letters including another from Augusta S. & one from Affie, who sent me 2 very clever little sketches by Chevalier of the 2 marriages'.[85]

Part of the protracted negotiations for the marriage contract involved matters of faith, and the Grand Duchess being able to continue the practice of her Orthodox faith, the faith of any children and the marriage ceremonies. As a result, two services, one Orthodox and one Anglican, were performed. For the Anglican service, a temporary chapel was created in the Alexander Hall of the Winter Palace, and the service was conducted by the Dean of Westminster. In advance, he promoted the idea that, for the marriage to be legally valid under the terms of the Royal Marriages Act, the Anglican chapel in the Winter Palace had to be temporarily declared to be British sovereign territory. This view was rejected by Lord Selborne (1812–95), the Lord Chancellor, who reminded the Lord Chamberlain that a legal marriage contracted under foreign law was valid in the United Kingdom and, as such, as the marriage was legal in Russia, so it was in Britain.

The services were described by the ambassador:

> *The Greek service was performed with its impressive effect; the deep tone of the choir, the thrilling force of the chorus, the magnificent dress and jewelled ornaments of the priesthood [...] gave an imposing and solemn effect to the ceremony.*
>
> *After the termination of the Greek Service the procession moved to the Salle [...] for the performance of the Anglican Ritual.*[86] SJP

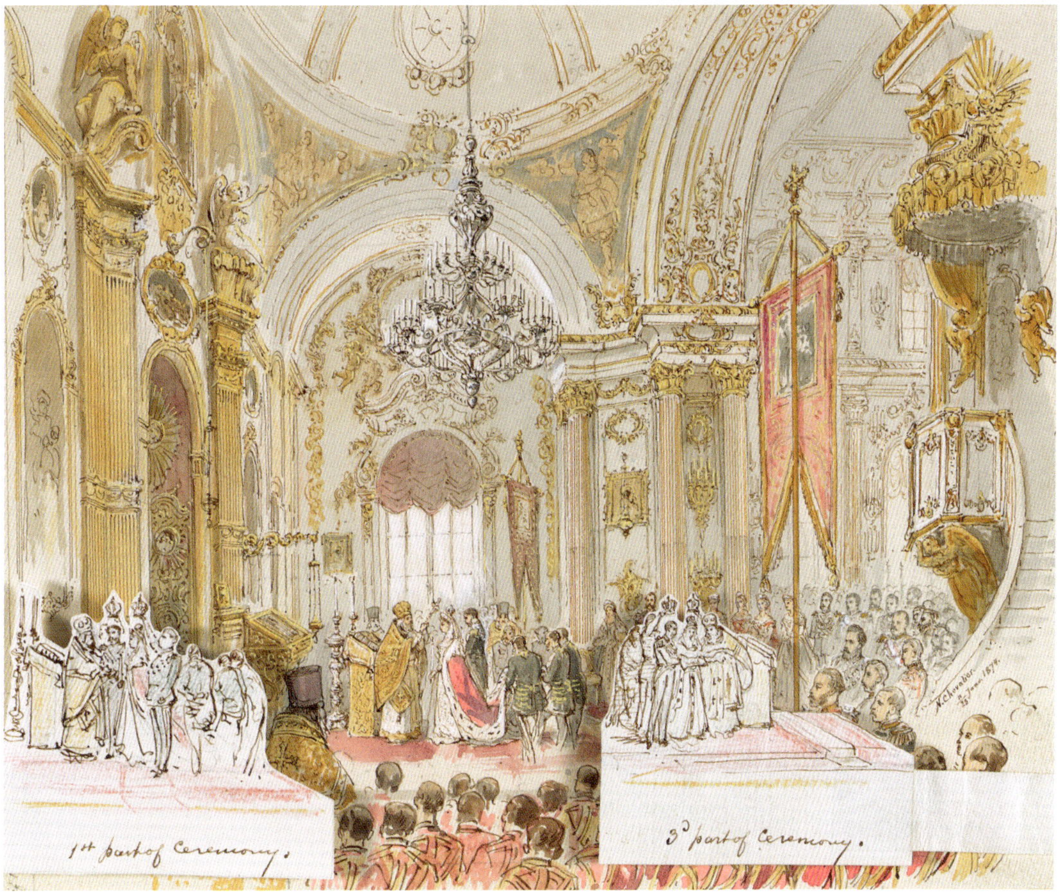
1st part of Ceremony.
3rd part of Ceremony.

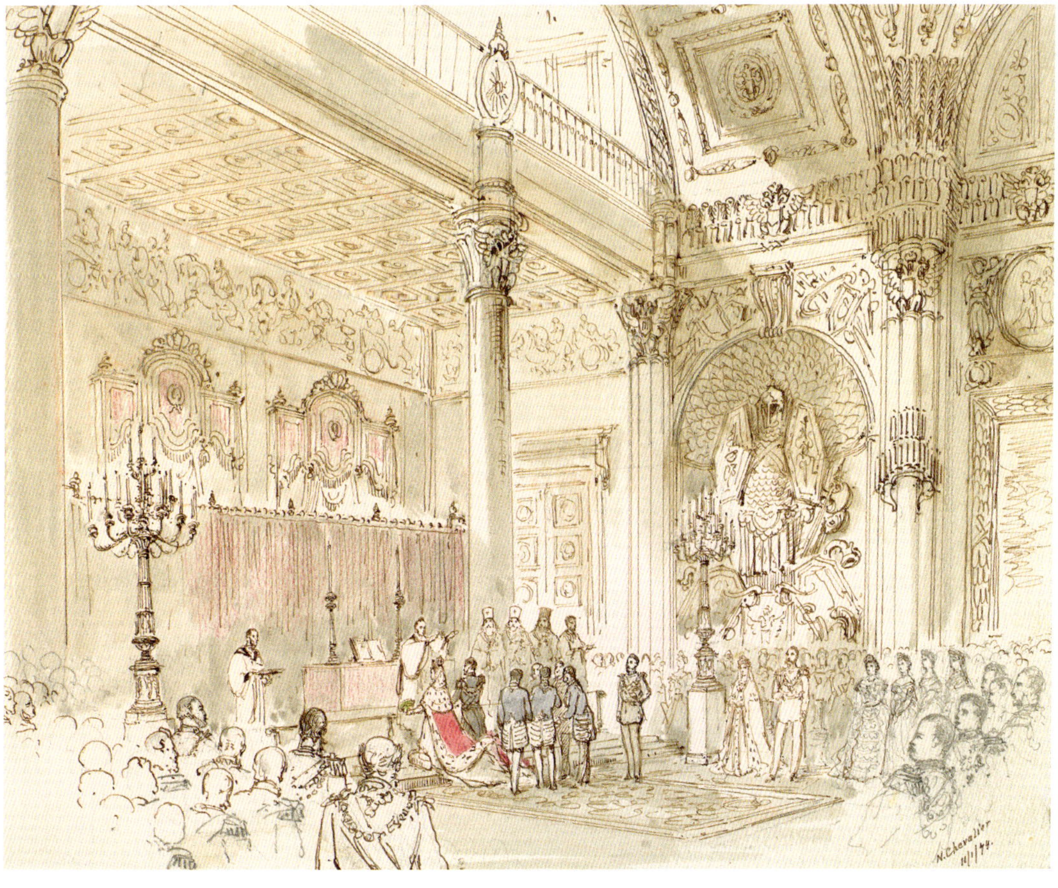
N. Chevalier

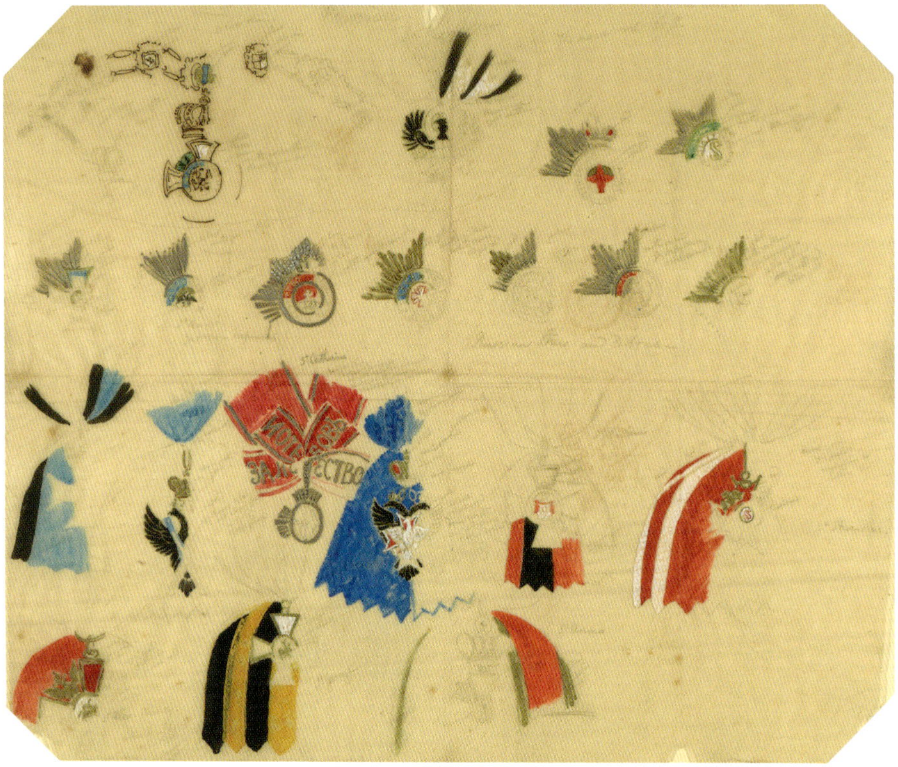

NICHOLAS CHEVALIER (1828–1902)

181 ***Tracings of orders and decorations*** 1874

Pencil, pen and ink, watercolour, bodycolour, gold and silver paint on tracing paper, 45.0 × 53.8 cm
RCIN 926298

Provenance From an album of watercolours made at St Petersburg and Moscow, at the time of the marriage of Prince Alfred and the Grand Duchess Maria Alexandrovna of Russia, 1874, commissioned by Queen Victoria; purchased from The Winter Palace, Kensington High Street, London, 1986

Literature Millar 1995, no. 1085; Patterson 1996

This sheet shows sketches of many of the orders and their colourful ribbons worn at the events surrounding the wedding of Maria Alexandrovna and Alfred, Duke of Edinburgh. The sketches capture the grandeur and colours of the Russian imperial court at a high point of Alexander II's reign, and would have been used by Chevalier as an aide-memoire for the painting of the marriage (cat. 174). The wide variety of orders from Russia and elsewhere are recorded in detail, with careful annotations regarding the colours and patterns in each design.

The orders depicted (from top left to bottom right) are the Hohenzollern House Order; the collar and eagle of Knights; the stars of the Orders of St Anne and St Stanislaus; the star and badge of the Order of Virtuti Militari; the stars and badges of the Orders of St Andrew the First Called, St Catherine the Martyr, the White Eagle and St Vladimir; the stars of St Alexander Nevskii and St George; the badge of St Stanislaus; and the badges and ribbons of St Alexander Nevskii, St George and St Anne. SJP

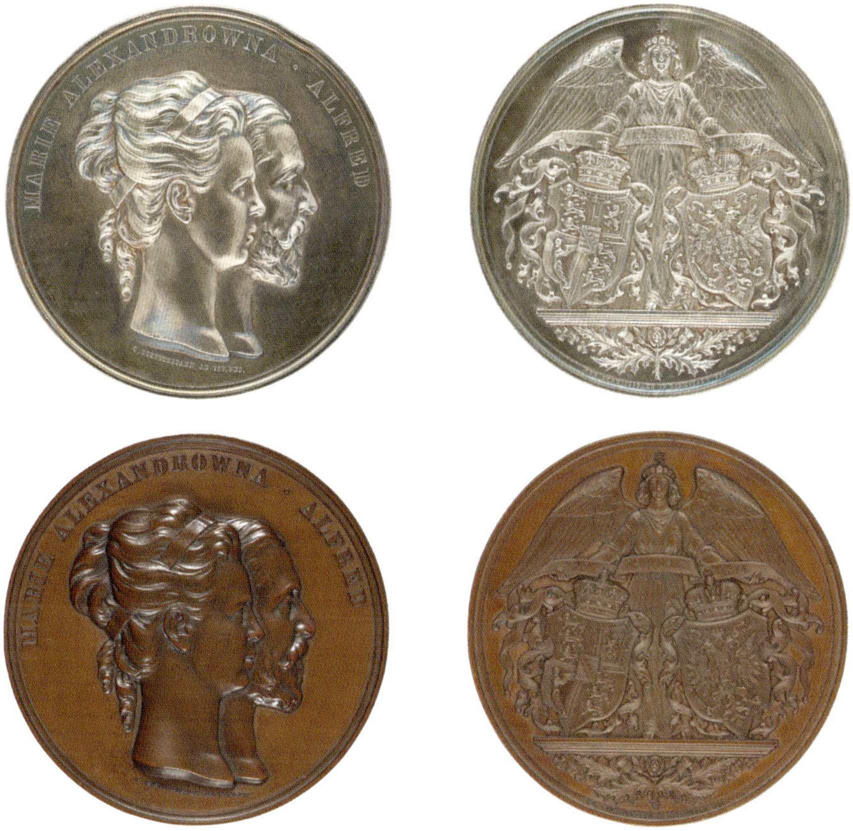

CHRISTIAN SCHNITZSPAHN (1829–1877)

182 & 183

Medals commemorating the marriage of Alfred, Duke of Edinburgh (1844–1900), to the Grand Duchess Maria Alexandrovna of Russia (1853–1920) 1874

Silver, dia. 6.33 cm, weight 105.47 g
RCIN 443392

Bronze, dia. 6.33 cm, weight 119.61 g
RCIN 443449

Provenance First recorded in the Royal Collection in the current reign (1952–)

Literature Forrer 1904–30, v, pp. 395–6

The two examples of this handsome medal show, on the obverse, the conjoint heads of the Grand Duchess and the Duke facing right, with the legend: *MARIE ALEXANDROWNA . ALFRED*. The reverse shows their arms accollés, with an angel behind, supporting a ribbon with *23 JANUARY 1874* on it. In the exergue is a joint emblem of rose, thistle and shamrock.

Schnitzspahn was the son of a court jeweller in Darmstadt, and after training in Berlin and London, he returned to Darmstadt, where he was appointed court and mint engraver in 1858. He produced medals for several German courts, including the Prussian one, and also for Russia. Probably commissioned by the bride's family, the medal gives precedence to the bride by placing her in front of the Duke; medals of the event minted in the United Kingdom reversed the couple. BW

IMPERIAL GLASS FACTORY;
SERGEI VERHOVTSEV (active 1867), silversmith

184 *Punch set* 1874

Glass, silver gilt, enamel, (tray) 7.0 × 74.0 × 64.3 cm, (jug) 36.0 × 26.5 × 25.5 cm, (8 glasses) 8.5 × 6.3 cm (diam.) (identical)
Imperial warrant mark of Sergei Verhovtsev, St Petersburg, 1874; glasses with the monogram mark of Alexander II and *1874*; Cyrillic inscription
RCIN 104208.a–k

Provenance Presented to the Prince of Wales, 1874

Literature RA/VIC/ADDA5/506, p. 92

This punch set was a gift to the Prince of Wales from Emperor Alexander II at the time of the marriage of Maria Alexandrovna to Alfred, Duke of Edinburgh on 23 January 1874.[87] The jug is applied with the monogram of the Emperor, Maria Alexandrovna and the Prince of Wales in enamels, together with an inscription surrounding the jug: *everyone can drink from the sky for the health of the spirited young as from this jug which can hold the Solovetskii Sea.* The glasses are similarly decorated with a Cyrillic inscription: 'Wine is not an obstacle but a daring consolation'.

Punch sets of this type with applied decoration in the old Russian style were popular in the 1870s and 1880s. Makers such as Ovchinnikov and Sazikov produced versions, often with similar inscriptions and elaborately decorated with enamels. The brightly coloured enamel decoration uses motifs directly inspired by the publication in 1870 of *Histoire de l'ornement russe du Xe au XVIe siècle d'après les manuscrits* by Victor Butovski, director of the Stroganov School for Technical Drawing.[88]

Sergei Fedorovich Verhovtsev worked with his father, Feodor Andreivich Verhovtsev, in the workshop founded by the latter in 1817; and after his father's death in 1867, he took over the business. He was a talented designer and silversmith and carried out various commissions for Alexander II, including the altar around Mother of God's footprints in Pochaev Lavra, from 1859 to 1861, and others at the St Andrew Cathedral in St Petersburg in 1867. The work of the Verhovtsevs focused mainly on religious objects for the Orthodox Church, but they produced a variety of domestic silver as well, and were one of the first firms to apply secular motifs to Orthodox plate. **CDEG**

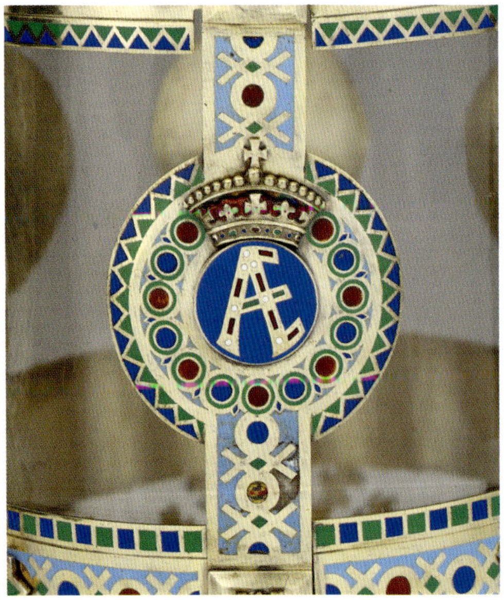

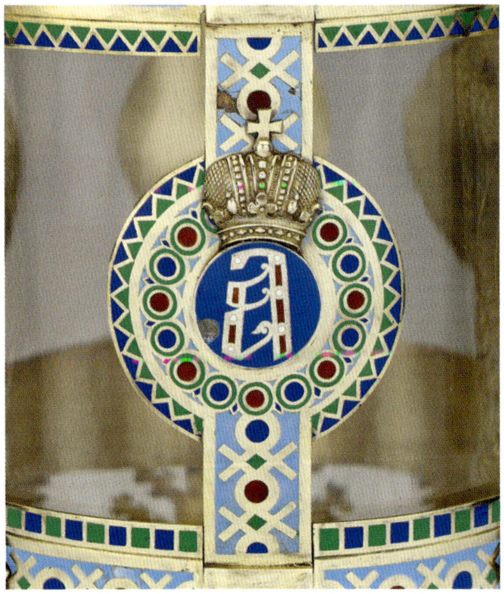

Details: Crowned monograms AE for Albert Edward, Prince of Wales, and A for Alexander II

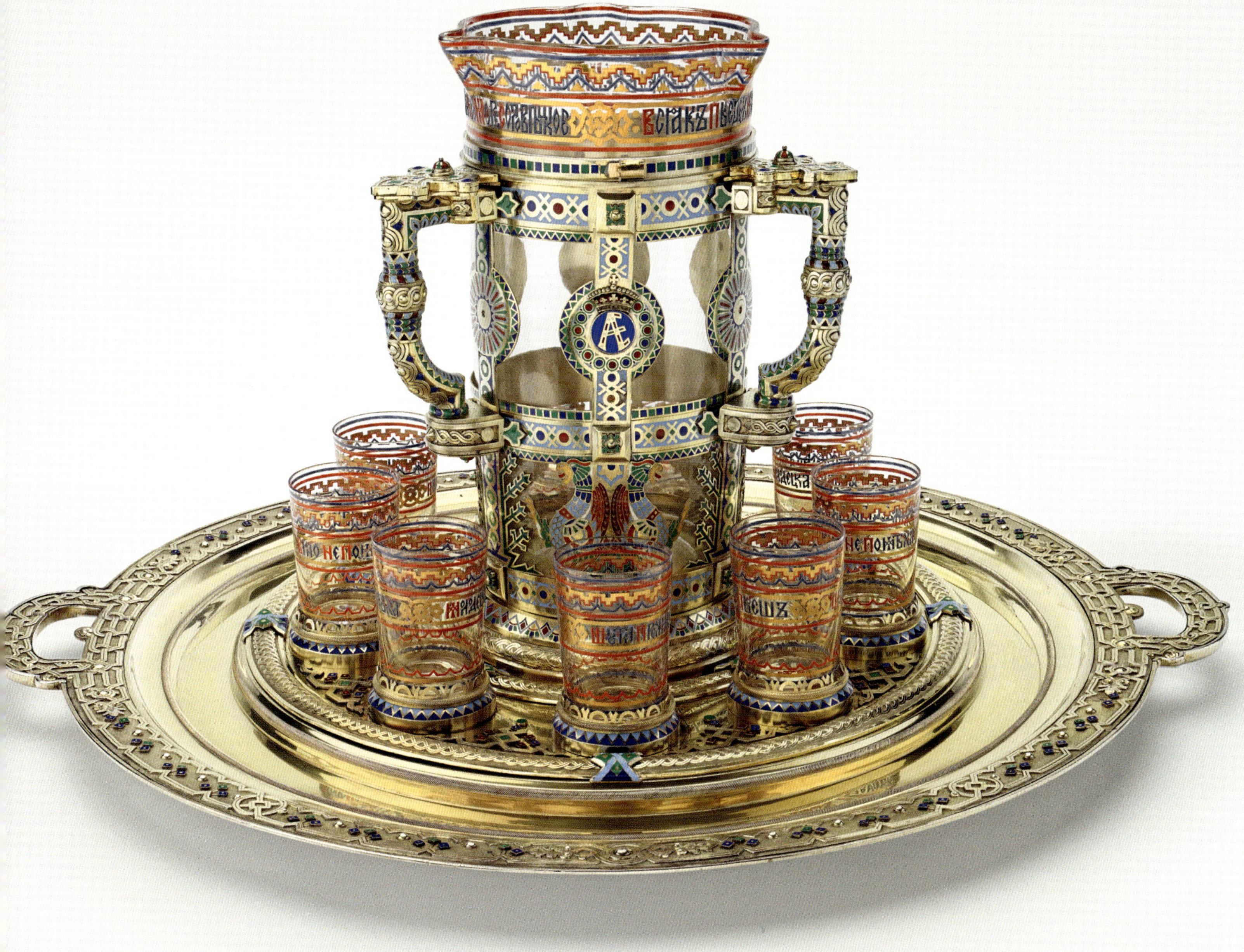

W.J. THOMAS, LONDON

185 *Casket* 1874

Gilt metal, 7.2 × 27.6 × 13.5 cm
Inscribed: *W.J. THOMAS 28 OLD BOND STREET LONDON & 7, KIRPITCHNAG PEREOULOK, ST PETERSBURG*
RCIN 3580

Provenance Wedding present to Prince Alfred, Duke of Edinburgh and Grand Duchess Maria Alexandrovna, 1874

Literature Kostyuk 2010, pp. 244–7

Made to commemorate the marriage of Alfred, Duke of Edinburgh and Grand Duchess Maria in 1874, this casket was produced by the firm of W.J. Thomas, who had retail premises in both London and St Petersburg.

The design of the casket is taken from Renaissance examples and is applied with gilt-metal strapwork in a geometric motif. The lid is centred by a reserve containing the cipher of Maria Alexandrovna in red and blue enamel, flanked by two reserves containing the Royal Arms in polychrome enamels. The sides are similarly applied with the cipher of Maria Alexandrovna and Alfred, Duke of Edinburgh.

The dynastic marriage between the house of Saxe-Coburg and Gotha and the Romanovs prompted not only the production of presents specially designed and made for the newly married couple, but also the exchange of official gifts at state and national level, such as the vase sent to Queen Victoria (cat. 230), and a richly ornamented gold and enamelled casket made by the goldsmith George Benson, and presented by the City of London on the occasion of Emperor Alexander II's visit to London in May 1874.[89] CDEG

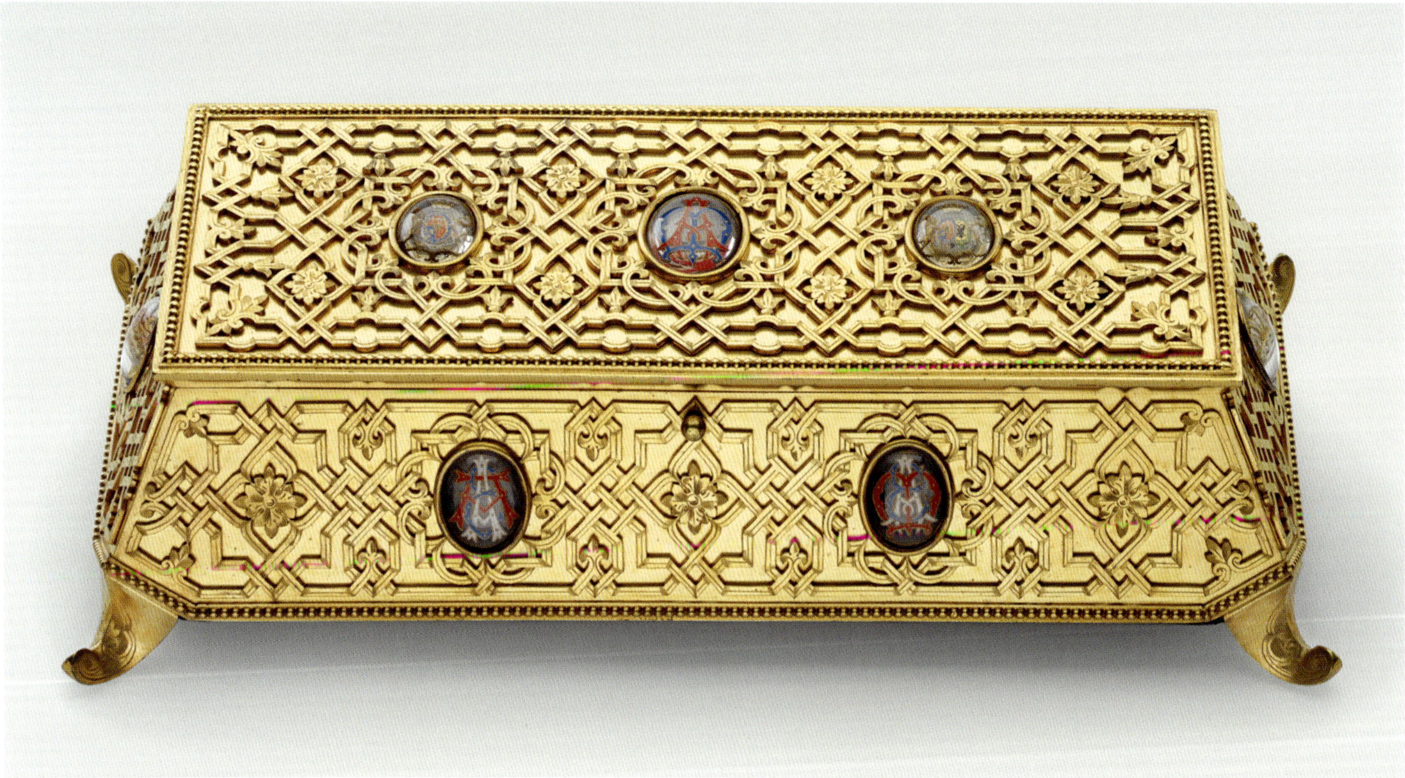

S.M. IKONNIKOV

186 *Salt cellar* 1873

Silver, 6.1 × 6.2 × 4.4 cm
Struck on backplate with fineness mark (84 zolotniks) and maker's mark of S.M. Ikonnikov; struck on base with city mark of Moscow; engraved: *Без соли, без хлеба – Половина обеда* ('A meal is incomplete without salt or bread'); inscribed on backplate: *Brought by Lady Augusta Stanley / from Russia and / given to V.R. March 7th 1874*
RCIN 16464

Provenance Presented to Queen Victoria, 7 March 1874, by Lady Augusta Stanley

Literature *Private Life* 1898, p. 254

The bread and salt ceremony, a traditional form of welcome in Slavic countries, particularly Russia, was practised in a domestic setting, but it also formed part of the ceremonial at the coronations of both Alexander III and Nicholas II, and at the weddings of all members of the Russian imperial family, including that of Maria Alexandrovna to Alfred, Duke of Edinburgh in St Petersburg on 23 January 1874.

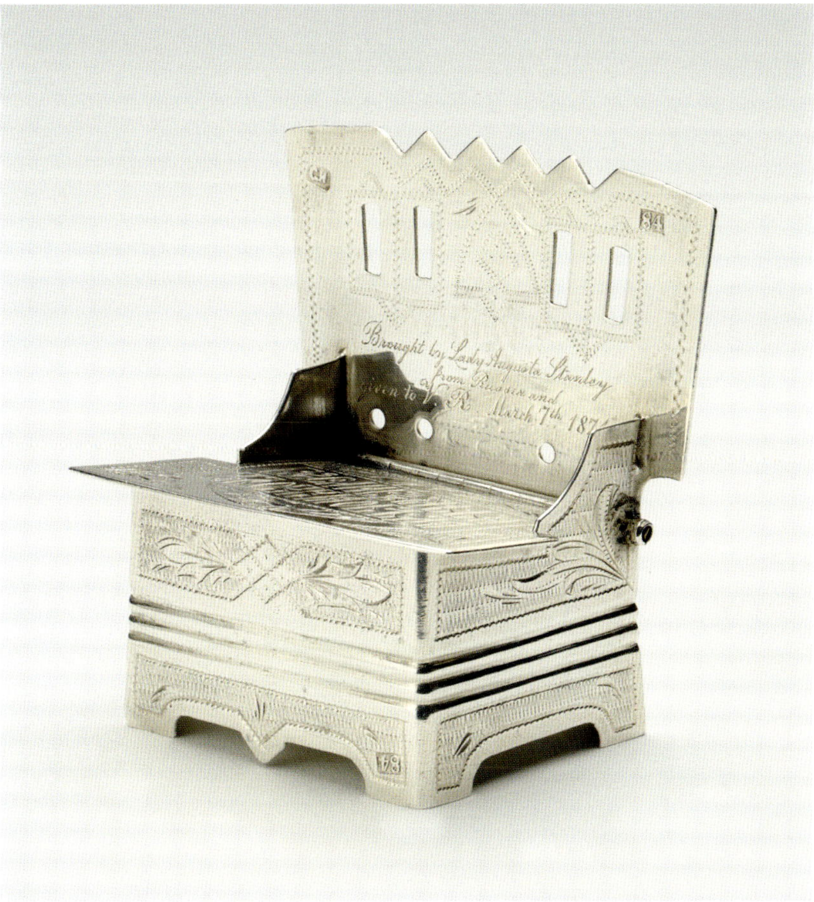

This salt cellar, in the form of a throne, is in a style typical of the 1870s and 1880s, when Russian silversmiths produced examples of such tableware on a vast scale, largely influenced by studies of Russian ornament derived from early manuscripts and folk motifs. This Russian style encouraged silversmiths to incorporate peasant motifs in their work, including objects which simulated wood, fabric, birch bark and embroidered folk textiles. These motifs are seen in this salt throne with the punched decoration and pierced back inspired by an *izba*, or peasant hut.

Presented to Queen Victoria on 7 March 1874, the day on which Maria Alexandrovna was introduced to her new mother-in-law, the salt was a gift from Lady Augusta Stanley, former Lady-in-Waiting to Victoria, Duchess of Kent and later to Queen Victoria. Lady Augusta's husband, Arthur Stanley, Dean of Westminster, had performed the English ceremony of marriage of Prince Alfred and the Grand Duchess Maria, at which Lady Augusta was one of the representatives of the Queen.

The salt appears in a description of the gold pantries at Windsor Castle, written in 1898. The anonymous writer, simply named as 'one of Her Majesty's servants', noted that the 'dainty little Russian salt-cellar of a square shape, presented by Lady Alice Stanley', was always used by the Queen, alongside a silver egg cup cast in the form of a chick.[90] CDEG

RUSSIAN

187–189

Suite of furniture c.1874

Wood, straw veneer, paint, (table) 78.2 x 124.5 × 79.5 cm, (chair) 83.0 x 47.0 × 46.8 cm, (mirror) 11.7 54.5 × 13.8 cm
Label: *ER/Clarence House/May*
RCINS 60761, 60762, 60765

Provenance Wedding present to Prince Alfred, Duke of Edinburgh and Grand Duchess Maria Alexandrovna, 1874

These three pieces form part of a suite of furniture made as a wedding present for the Duke and Duchess of Edinburgh in 1874. The suite comprises a mirror, two tables, four chairs and four stools, each made of a wooden carcase veneered in polychrome straw, with traditional Russian decorative motifs in red, yellow and green on a dark blue ground. The mirror and the larger of the two tables are applied with the conjoined British and Russian arms, which were added later.

This furniture is illustrative of the interest in peasant handicrafts which began in the late imperial period under Alexander III. The simple forms, particularly the shape of the chairs, are particularly reminiscent of peasant-style furniture, while the decorative motifs were no doubt influenced by those illustrated in rich colour in Victor Butovski's *Histoire de l'ornement russe du Xe au XVIe siècle d'après les manuscrits*, first published in 1870. This publication reproduced hundreds of medieval ornamental motifs, which galvanised a return to native motifs in the Russian decorative arts. The motifs here are almost pseudo-Russian and might indicate a provenance of Belarussian origin, possibly a maker who had exhibited at one of the international fairs from the 1850s until the end of the century.[91]

After the Revolution and the ravages of the Second World War, surviving examples in Russia of furniture of this type are very rare. CDEG

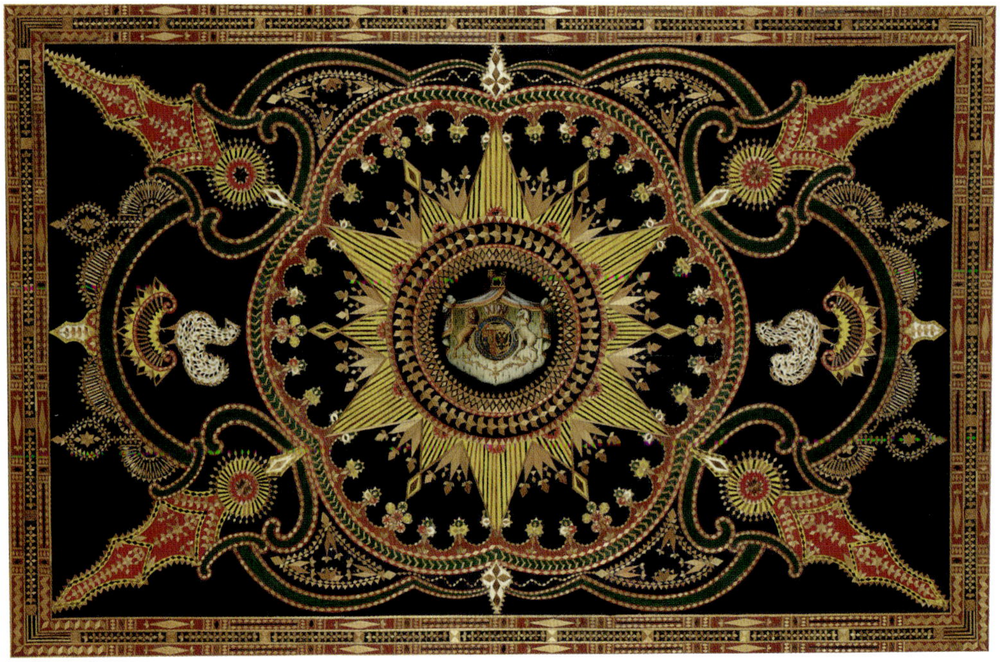

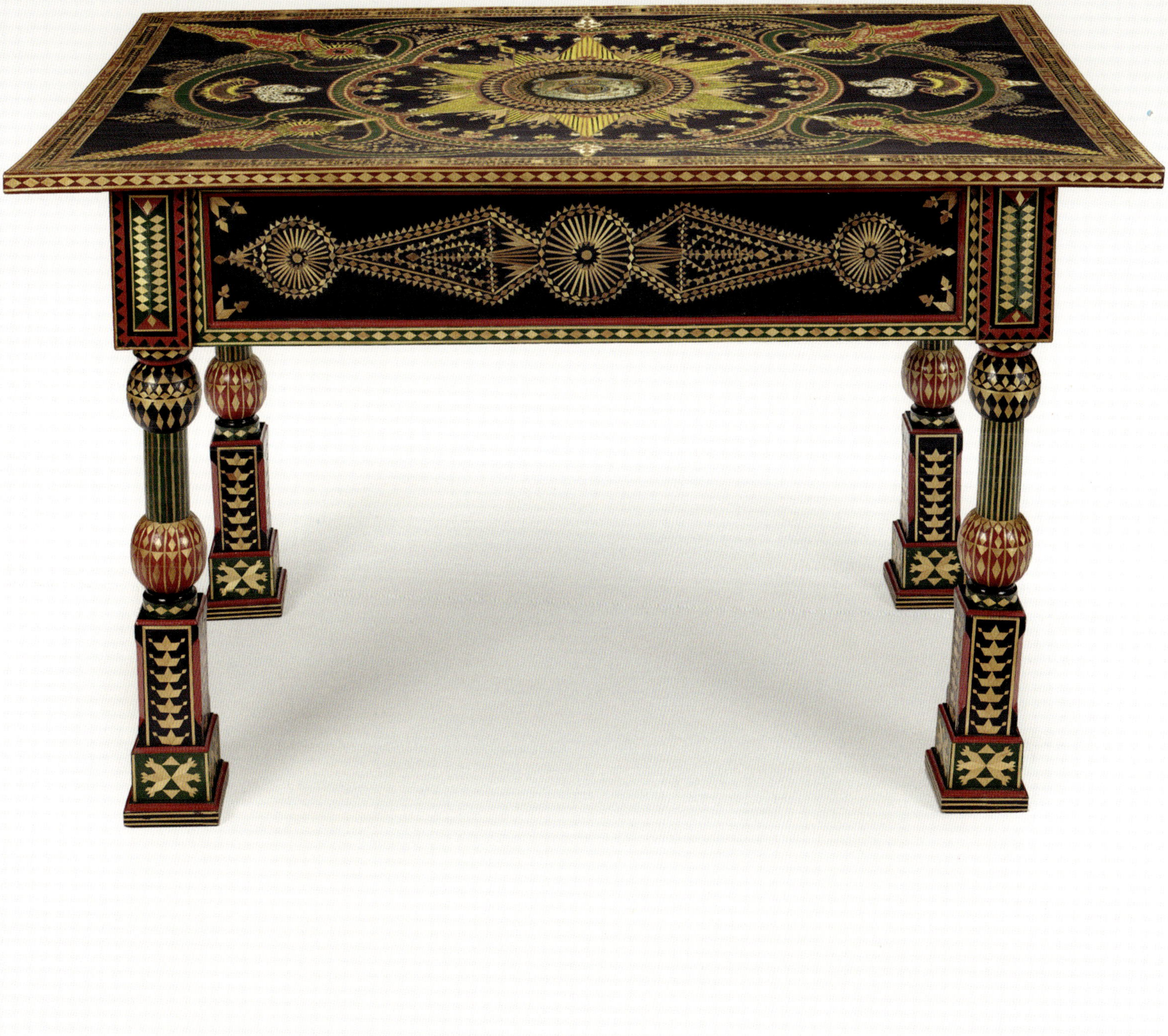

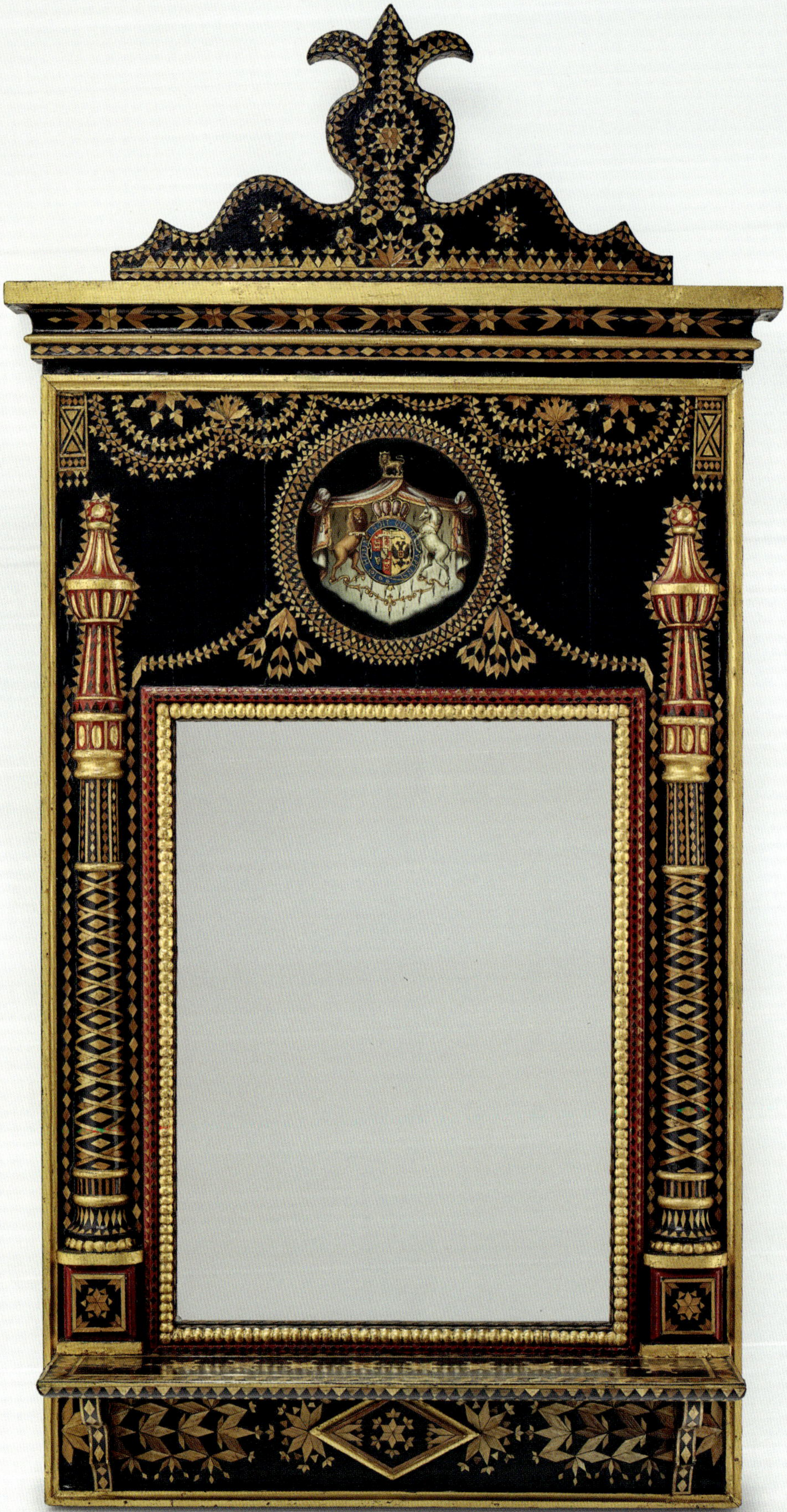

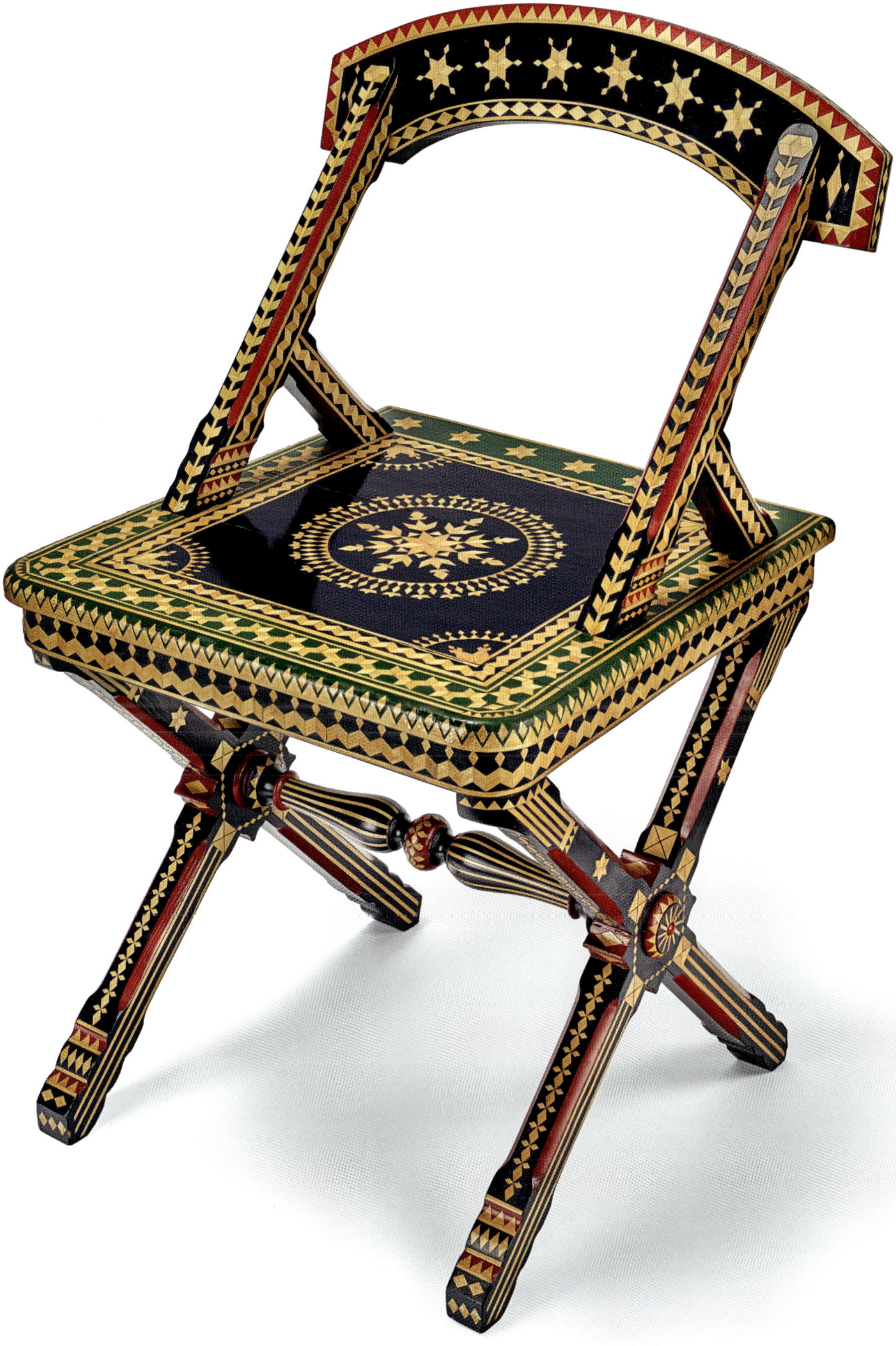

NICHOLAS CHEVALIER (1828–1902)

190 *The arrival of the Duke and Duchess of Edinburgh at Windsor, 7 March 1874* 1874

Pencil, pen and ink, watercolour and bodycolour, 24.4 × 29.4 cm
Signed: *N Chevalier 1874*
RCIN 920786

Provenance Commissioned by Queen Victoria for her Souvenir Album

Literature Millar 1995, no. 1086

Following their wedding in St Petersburg and a brief honeymoon at Tsarskoe Selo, the Duke and Duchess of Edinburgh travelled to Windsor, arriving on 7 March. They had left St Petersburg on 28 February, with a difficult parting from the Emperor and Empress; Queen Victoria observed: 'The distress of the poor Parents at parting with their daughter had been great & I do indeed think of & feel much for them'.[92]

This was to be Queen Victoria's first meeting with her new daughter-in-law, an anxious moment for both parties. The Queen was kept informed of their journey, via Berlin, Cologne (where they were met by the groom's sister, Princess Alice) and Brussels. At 9 a.m., on 7 March, they landed at Gravesend.

The meeting finally took place at the South Western Station at Windsor, and is depicted in the central lower vignette, flanked by roundels showing the presentation of a bouquet to the Duchess, and the bride and groom fêted by children. The composition shows the procession to the Castle – the design of an arch was possibly drawn from the triumphal arch erected in Windsor for the occasion – with views of Windsor Castle and the Guildhall bedecked by flags and coats of arms, both British and Russian, with celebrating putti, some on duty as Yeoman Guardsmen.

The Queen described the town as being 'lined with troops, was very full & completely decked out with flags, flowers, festoons & inscriptions, some of which were in Russian.'

The Queen's first impressions of her new daughter-in-law were positive: 'Dear Marie has a very friendly manner, a pleasant face, beautiful skin & fine bright eyes, & there is something very fresh & attractive about her. She speaks English wonderfully well'.[93] In the afternoon, the Duchess visited Queen Victoria in her rooms, where the Queen showed Maria her 'Russian album'. SJP

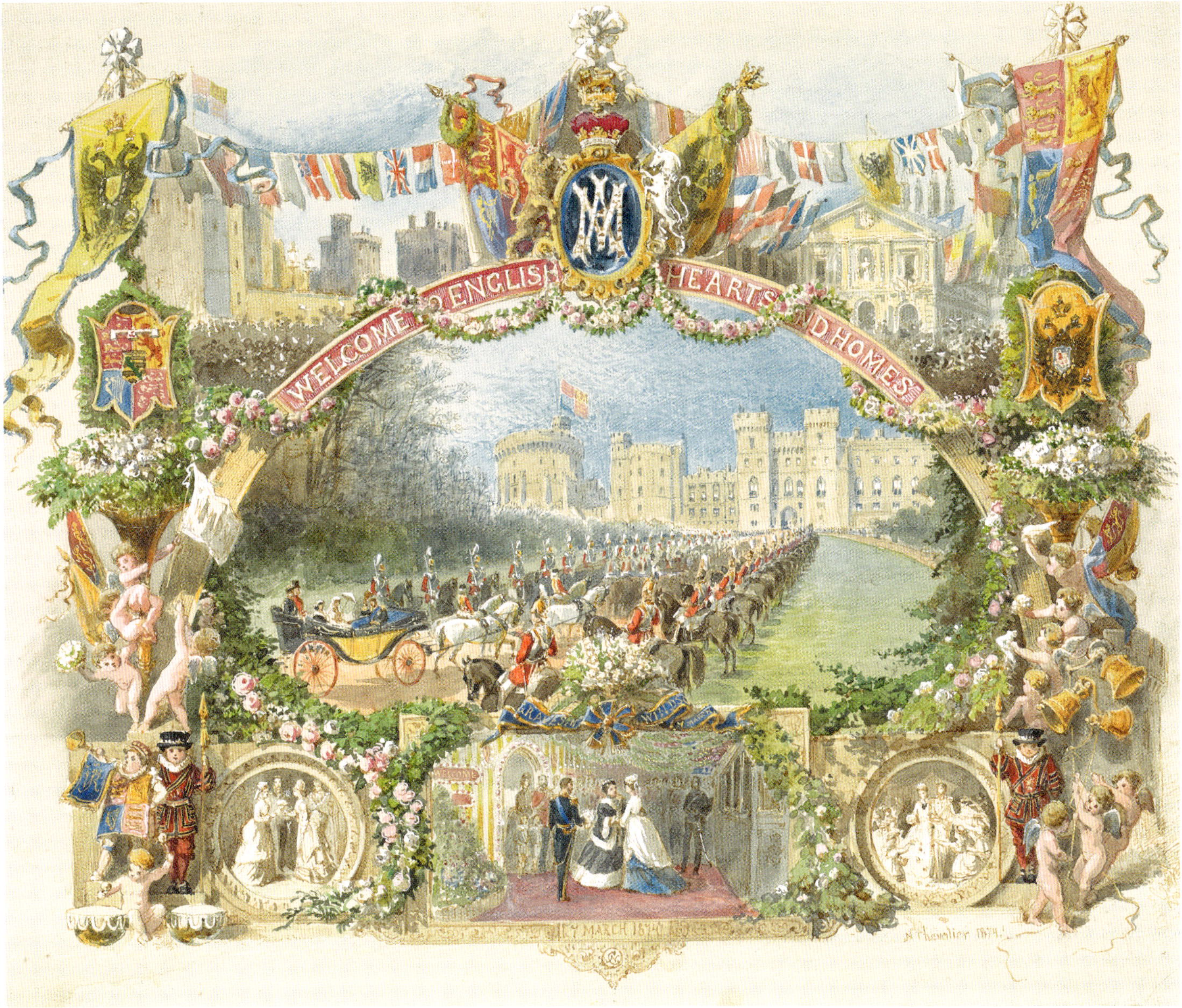
WELCOME
ENGLISH
HEARTS
HOMES
MARCH 1874
N Chevalier 1874

W. & D. DOWNEY (active 1855–1941)

191 *Alexander II, Emperor of Russia (1818–1881) with Prince Alfred, Duke of Edinburgh (1844–1900), Maria, Duchess of Edinburgh (1853–1920) and Grand Duke Alexei of Russia (1850–1908)* 18 May 1874

Albumen print, 14.1 × 9.6 cm, (cabinet card) 16.6 × 10.7 cm
Photographer's credentials printed on cabinet card
RCIN 2808970

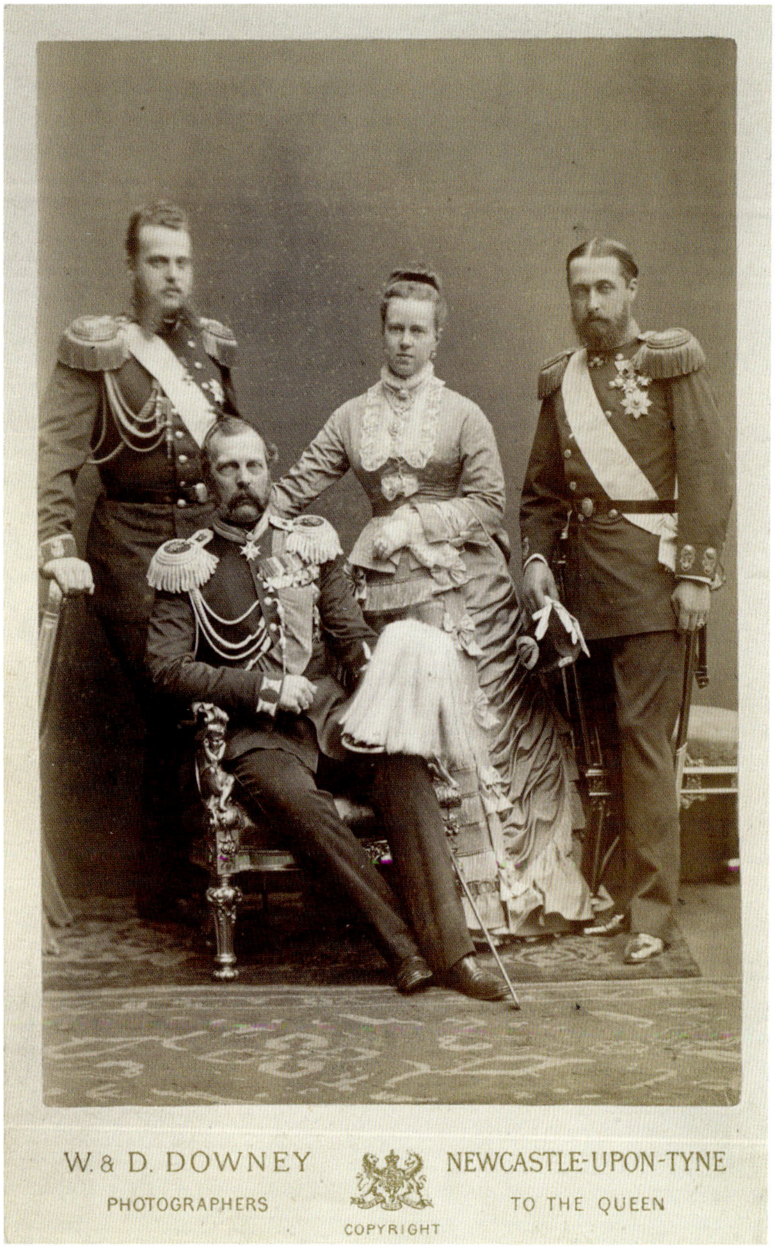

Provenance Commissioned by Queen Victoria

Emperor Alexander II visited Britain between 13 and 21 May 1874, following the marriage of his only surviving daughter to the Duke of Edinburgh earlier in the year.[94] He was received by Queen Victoria at Windsor Castle, where he spent the first two days of his stay. This was his second visit to the country, as the Queen recalled in her Journal: 'The Emperor looked terribly tired, & I own I was also. It is just 35 years that I took leave of him here, at Windsor, in June!'[95]

This photograph was taken at Buckingham Palace, where the Emperor spent the rest of his stay, which included a State Ball given in his honour on 19 May. It was reported in the *Court Circular* that 'Messieurs Downey, of Newcastle and London, attended at Buckingham Palace this morning by command, and had the honour of taking a photograph group of His Imperial Majesty the Emperor with the Grand Duke Alexis and the Duke and Duchess of Edinburgh'.[96] AN

EMPEROR ALEXANDER II (1818–1881)

192 *Letter to Queen Victoria (1819–1901), London* 9/21 May 1874

Manuscript, 24.1 × 19.3 cm
RA VIC/MAIN/Z/105/82

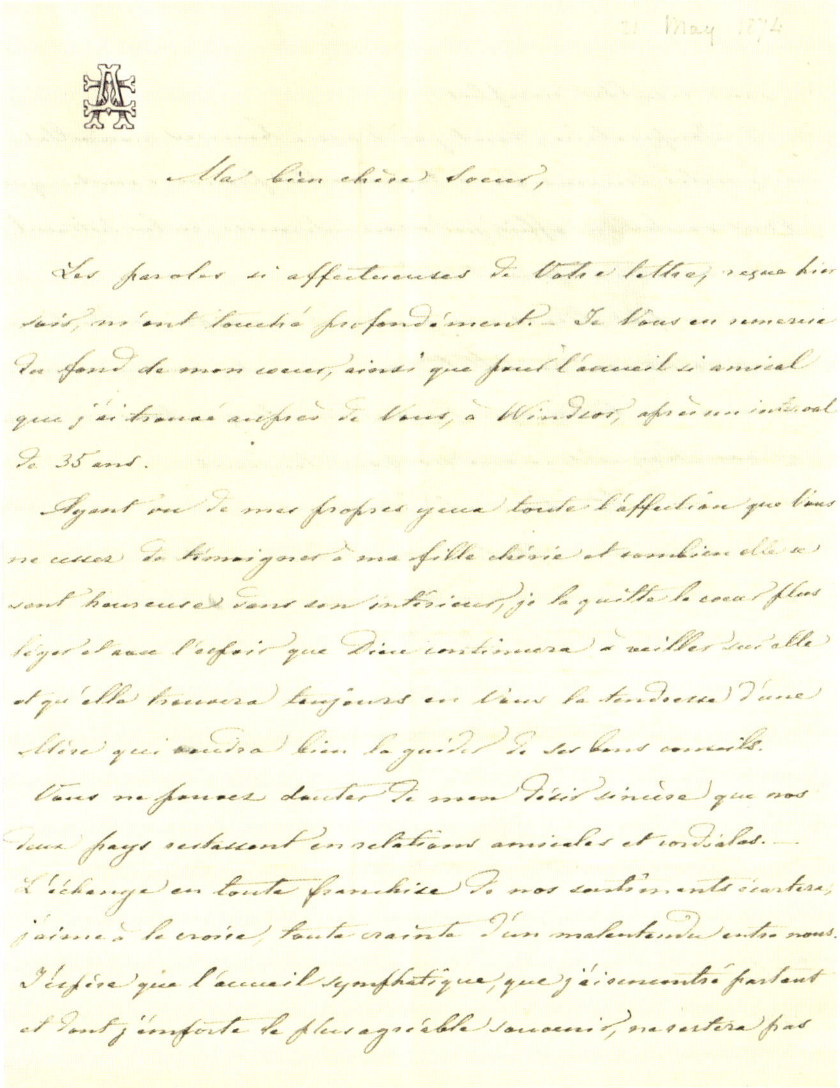
21 May 1874

Ma bien chère Sœur,

Les paroles si affectueuses de Votre lettre, reçue hier soir, m'ont touché profondément. — Je Vous en remercie du fond de mon cœur, ainsi que pour l'accueil si amical que j'ai trouvé auprès de Vous, à Windsor, après un interval de 35 ans.

Ayant vu de mes propres yeux toute l'affection que Vous ne cessez de témoigner à ma fille chérie et combien elle se sent heureuse dans son intérieur, je la quitte le cœur plus léger et avec l'espoir que Dieu continuera à veiller sur elle et qu'elle trouvera toujours en Vous la tendresse d'une Mère qui voudra bien la guider de ses bons conseils.

Vous ne pouvez douter de mon désir sincère que nos deux pays restassent en relations amicales et cordiales. — L'échange en toute franchise de nos sentiments écartera, j'aime à le croire, toute crainte d'un malentendu entre nous. J'espère que l'accueil sympathique, que j'ai rencontré partout et dont j'emporte le plus agréable souvenir, ne restera pas

Written at his departure from Britain, at the end of his visit in 1874, Emperor Alexander II thanks Queen Victoria for her hospitality and kindness, and remembers his visit to Windsor some 35 years previously. The Emperor also thanked the Queen, on behalf of his Empress, Maria Alexandrovna, for having bestowed on her the Order of Victoria and Albert, one of only a handful of appointments outside the circle of the Queen's immediate and extended family. He also passes on his son Alexei's thanks for the Queen's kindness to him. Alexei was to be a regular visitor to London to see his sister, the Duchess of Edinburgh.

The main thrust of the Emperor's letter is to ask the Queen to take care of his daughter, the Duchess; he expresses the hope that the Grand Duchess would always find in the Queen the tenderness of a mother. His other hope, echoed in letters from Russian rulers over many years, was for amicable and cordial relations between the two countries. SJP

BARON HEINRICH VON ANGELI (1840–1925)

193 *The Family of the Grand Duke of Hesse (1837–1892)* 1879

Oil on canvas, 168.0 × 149.6 cm
Signed and dated: *H. v. Angeli / 1879*
RCIN 408904

Provenance Painted for Queen Victoria; first recorded at Osborne, January 1879

Literature Millar 1992, no. 21; Rogasch and Ohm 1996–9, p. 265, no. V/7

Painted for Queen Victoria, this family group was to be a pendant to the ensemble of the Prince and Princess of Wales and their children completed by the artist in 1876; they were to hang together in the Dining Room at Osborne House.[97] It was to include the Queen's daughter, Princess Alice, her husband, Louis IV, Grand Duke of Hesse and by Rhine, and their children, Princesses Alix (Alicky) and Elizabeth (Ella), and Prince Ernest (Ernie). Princess Alice wrote to her mother, on 9 April 1878, that von Angeli had arrived at Darmstadt and was to start work immediately on preparatory studies for the heads. On 21 January 1879, the Queen noted that the Grand Duke had brought over the 'splendid picture' with him to Osborne. Tragically, Princess Alice had died of diphtheria on 14 December 1878 (the anniversary of Prince Albert's death), which undoubtedly added a sorrow and poignancy to the image of her daughter. However, the portrait later provided 'delight & comfort' to the Queen, which she described as 'splendidly grouped - so very like', noting that she thought 'Ella's expression is *just* hers & Ernie's an expression that he very often has'.[98]

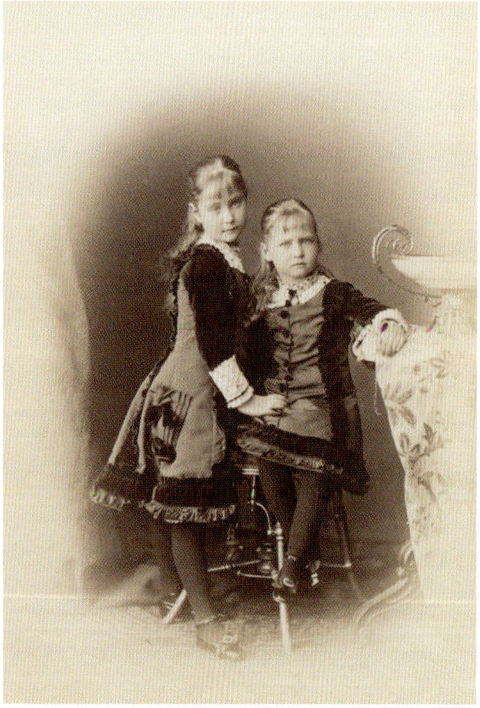

FIG. 62
Carl Backofen (1853–1909)
The Princesses Alix and Marie of Hesse, 1878
Albumen print, 14.0 × 9.7 cm
RCIN 2903220

Princess Alix, future wife of Nicholas II and Empress of Russia, aged between five and six, is depicted on the left, dressed in a velvet-trimmed dress. This attire was documented in a vignette photograph of Alix (together with her younger sister, May) by Carl Backofen (1853–1909) in May 1878 (fig. 62). Queen Victoria appeared ever charmed by her granddaughter, and her lively personality and looks were often noted. In the summer of 1878, she was described as 'a glorious child, handsomer than ever a great darling, with brilliant colouring, splendid eyes & a sweet smile', and the two enjoyed a unique relationship. Standing behind her father is Princess Elizabeth, who, on her marriage in 1884 to Grand Duke Sergei Alexandrovich, fifth son of Alexander II, also joined the Romanov dynasty. Sebag Montifiore describes Ella as 'a ravishing beauty', of 'rare intelligence, delightful sense of humour, infinite patience and generous heart'; her colouring of blonde hair with grey eyes and alabaster skin are equally noteworthy.[99] Their brother, Ernie, later Grand Duke of Hesse, stands to the right, whilst the couple's eldest daughter, Princess Victoria (1863–1950) was pronounced 'too big', and was not included. **AB**

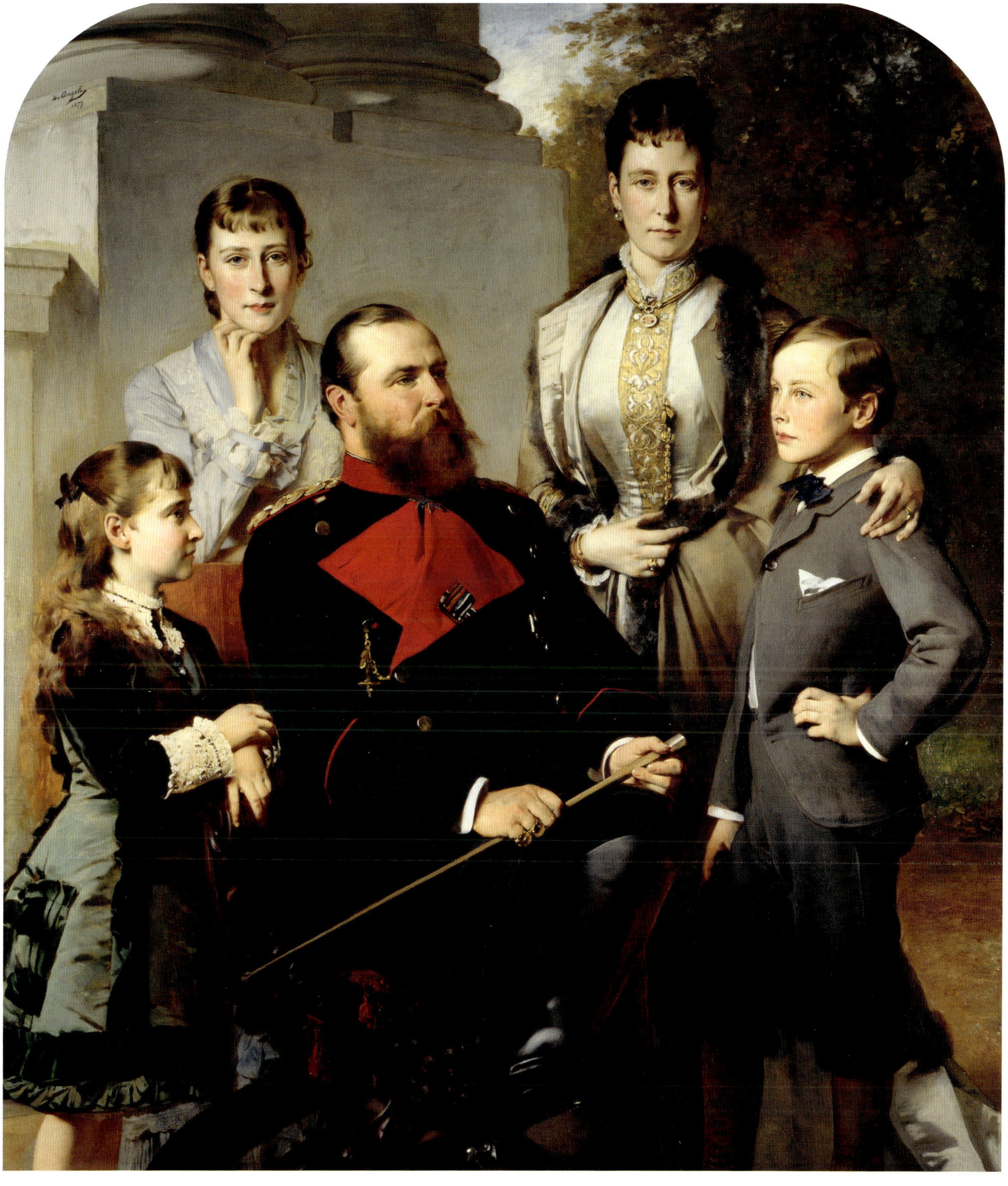

CARL RUDOLPH SOHN (1845–1908)

194 *Alfred, Duke of Edinburgh (1844–1900), with his family* 1884

Oil on canvas, 166.3 × 148.7 cm
Signed and dated: *Carl Sohn jr./ 1884*
RCIN 404784

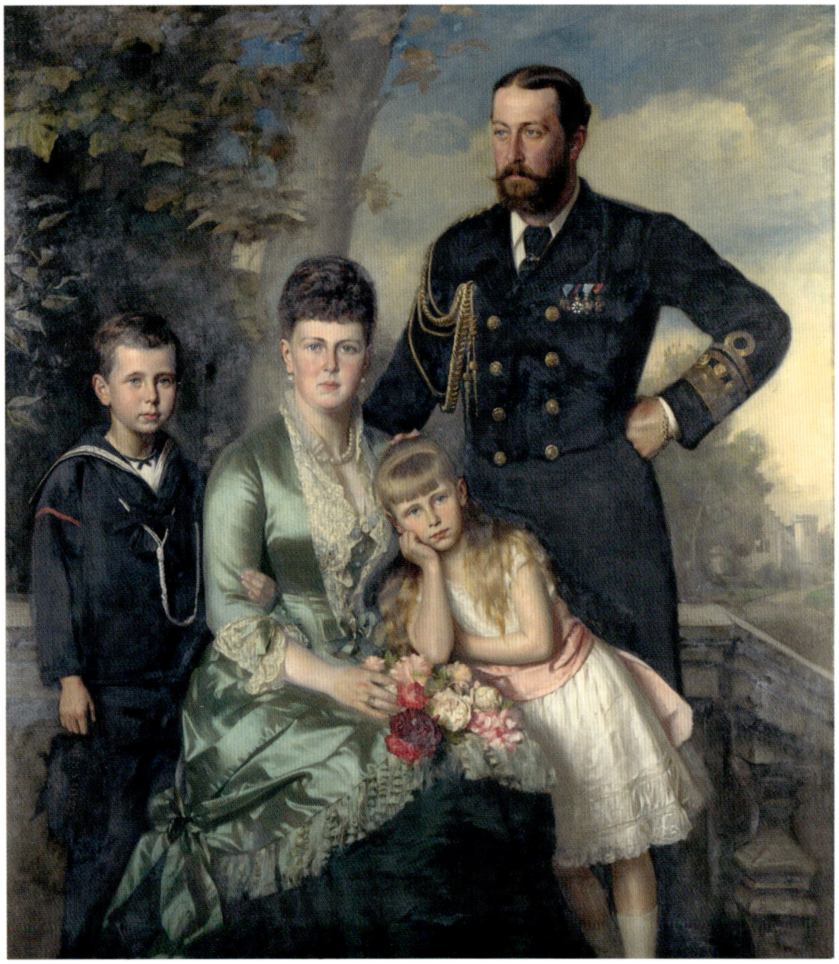

Provenance Painted for Queen Victoria; perhaps originally at Osborne; sent to Windsor, 1898

Literature Millar 1992, no. 638

In the autumn of 1883, Carl Sohn, court painter, was sent to Coburg to paint a family group, for Queen Victoria; it was to include the Duke and Duchess of Edinburgh, and their two eldest children, Prince Alfred (1874–99) and Princess Marie (1875–1938). The stepped façade of the Rosenau can be glimpsed in the background.

Maria, ever conscious of her looks, detested sitting to Sohn. 'I am simply furious', she wrote, 'besides hating the long sittings. I dislike still more having my pug-like face reproduced on canvas and handed over to posterity.'[100] A hint at her dissatisfaction can be perceived in her expression, and the awkward, stilted poses suggest that the artist may also have had to rely on photographs of the other sitters. An expression of boredom and endurance is equally visible in the pose and expression of the young princess.[101] On first seeing the group in an unfinished state, Queen Victoria commented that it was 'a fine picture, but Marie's likeness is not good'.[102] **AB**

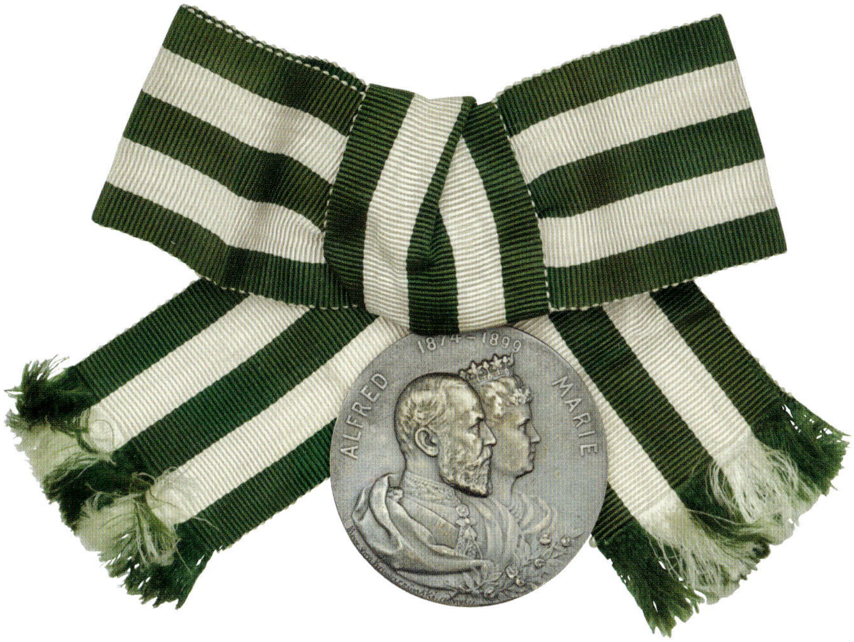

MAX VON KAWACZYNSKI (b.1860)

195 *Duke and Duchess of Saxe-Coburg and Gotha silver wedding medal* 1899

Silver, silk, dia. 3.5 cm
Maker's mark: *- Max - von - Kawaczynski - ad.- viv.- fec.-*
RCIN 441137

Provenance Presented by Prince Alfred, Duke of Edinburgh, Duke of Saxe-Coburg and Gotha, to Queen Victoria, with the accompanying note: 'For dearest Mama in remembrance of 23 January 1899. Alfred'

On the obverse are the profile heads of Duke Alfred and Duchess Maria of Saxe-Coburg, with the inscription, *ALFRED 1874 MARIE*. On the reverse is the motto of Saxe-Coburg, *TREU UND FEST* ('Faithful and strong'), above the Saxe-Coburg ducal crown, the conjoined coat of arms of Saxe-Coburg on the left with an inescutcheon of the British Royal Arms (in reverse), and, on the right, tied by a ribbon, the Russian imperial arms, above the wedding anniversary date, *23 JANUAR*. The medal is suspended from a ribbon of equal green and white stripes – the colours of Saxe-Coburg.

The silver wedding celebrations were celebrated in Gotha, and Queen Victoria sent her Lord-in-Waiting, Lord Clarendon (1846–1914), as her representative. On the actual anniversary, the Queen was at Osborne (as she had been 25 years previously) and recorded in her diary: 'Drank Affie & Marie's healths, this being their Silver Wedding day'.[103] Twenty-five years earlier, the toast was proposed by The Duke of Cambridge: 'At dessert George proposed the healths of the Duke & D^{ss} of Edinburgh, followed by Mine & those of the Emp^{r} & Empress of Russia'.[104] The Queen recorded in her diary on 24 January 1899:

> *Had a telegram from Ld Clarendon [...] that all had gone off well yesterday & that much enthusiasm had been shown by the inhabitants. Affie had had a very nice medal struck, to be worn on a green & white ribbon, which he has sent to all of us & to several of those who had been 20 years in his service, Ld Strafford is the only one of my gentlemen, alive, who attended his marriage.*[105] SJP

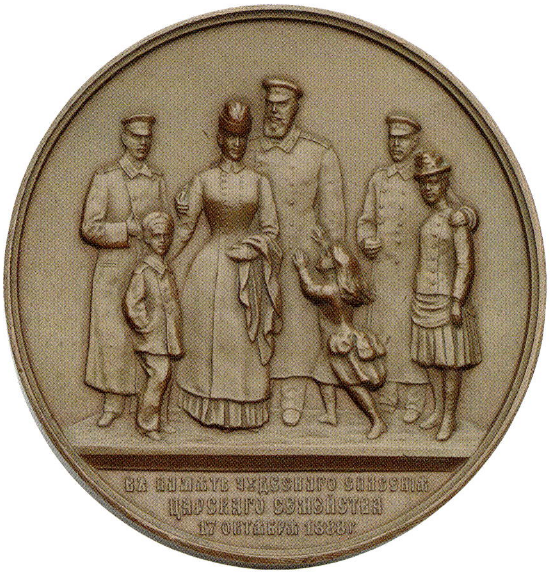

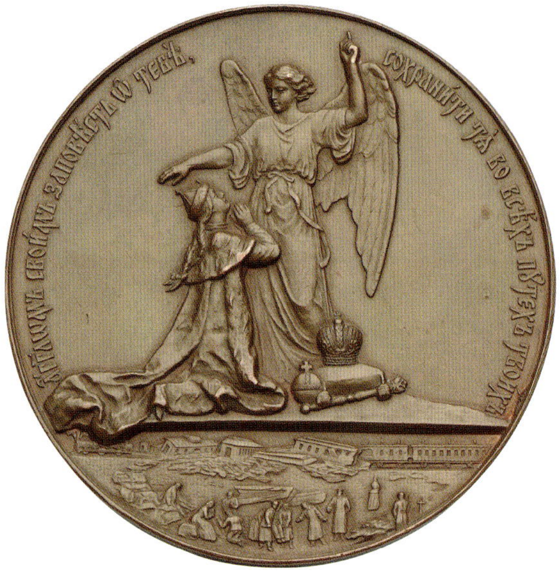

ABRAHAM GRILICHES (1849–1912)

196 *Medal commemorating the miraculous survival of the imperial family at the station of Borki near Kharkiv, 17 October 1888* 1888

Bronze, diameter 9.0 cm, weight 350.3 g
RCIN 60901

Provenance Given to HRH The Prince of Wales for the Royal Collection by Princess Bagration-Moukhransky, 2006

On the obverse Emperor Alexander III and Empress Marie Feodorovna stand flanked by their children Grand Dukes George and Michael, Grand Duchess Xenia (with arms outstretched towards her father), the Tsesarevich Nicholas and Grand Duchess Olga. The legend in the exergue reads 'В ПАМЯТЬ ЧУДЕСНОГО СПАСЕНИЯ / ЦАРСКОГО СЕМЕЙСТВА / 17 ОКТЯБРЯ 1888г. = In memory of the miraculous rescue of the Imperial Family 17 October 1888'.

On the reverse, an angel with arm raised pointing towards heaven appears before a kneeling bare-headed figure, the personification of Russia, who wears the Imperial Mantle with the regalia of crown, orb and sceptre lying to the right. Around the rim is the inscription 'АНГЕЛАМ СВОИМ ЗАПОВЕГАТЬ О ТЕВЕ СОХРАНИТИ ТЯ ВО ВСЕХ ПУТЯХЪ ТВОИХЪ' = 'He has give his angels orders to guard you wherever you go, a quote from Psalm 90 v:11.

Below in the exergue can be seen a depiction of the scene following the derailment of the Imperial train on 17/29 October 1888 as it travelled from the Crimea to St Petersburg. The derailment killed 21 and injured over 15; the Imperial family were all unhurt; their survival was deemed miraculous and attributed to Divine intervention. The emperor is reputed to have held up the roof of the Imperial carriage to help his family escape which may have resulted in the onset of the kidney disease which was to lead to his early death in 1894. The derailment which was thought to have been a failed assassination attempt was in fact a result of the speed of the imperial train, its configuration of axles and poor track maintenance. **BW**

ROYAL COPENHAGEN PORCELAIN MANUFACTORY;
ANTON MICHELSEN (1809–1877), silversmith

197 *Tankard commemorating the coronation of Emperor Alexander III (1845–1894) and Empress Maria Feodorovna (1847–1928)* 1883

Porcelain, silver, silver gilt, 20.0 × 15.0 × 10.6 cm
Impressed assay mark, *SG*, for S. Groth; marks of Anton Michelsen, *AM* surmounted by a crown, silver standard mark 925, town mark for Copenhagen, and underglaze porcelain mark for Royal Copenhagen Porcelain
RCIN 64538

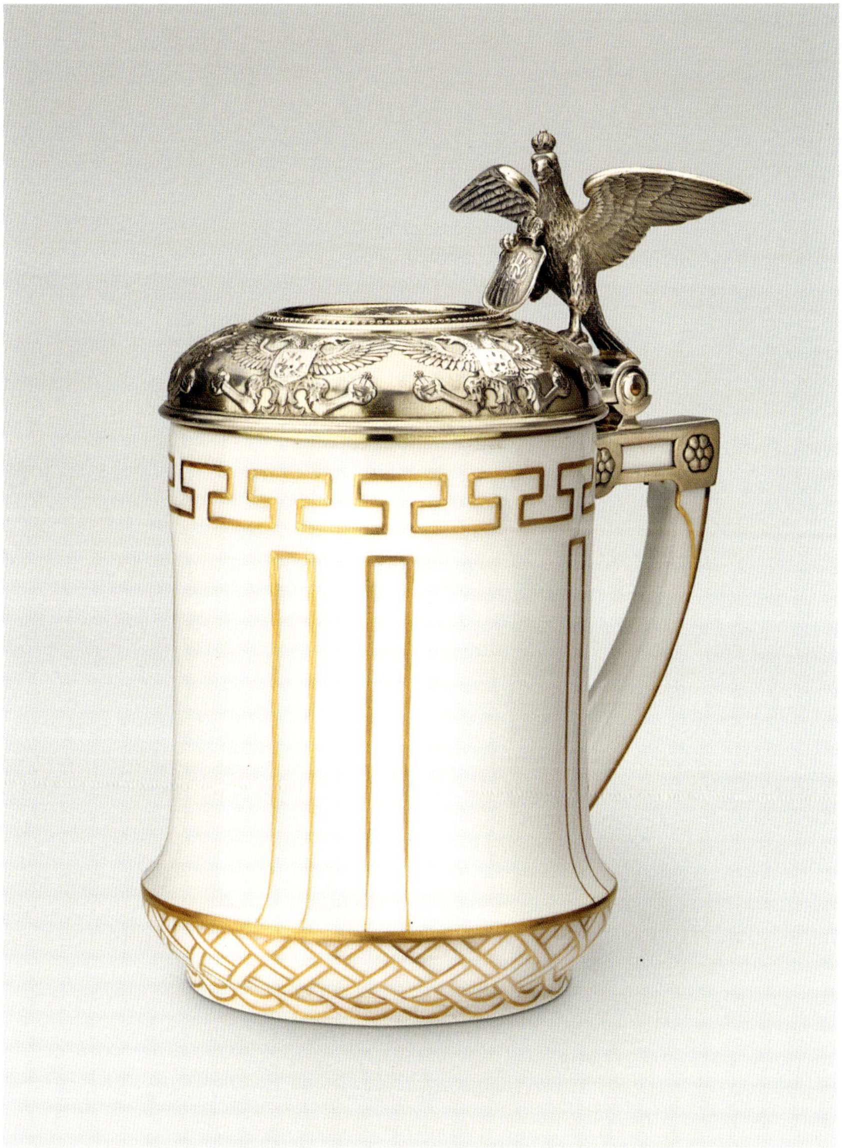

Provenance Probably acquired by Princess Alexandra, 1883

This tankard marries Danish porcelain with Russian silver, mirroring the dynastic links embodied in the imperial couple of Alexander III and Maria Feodorovna (formerly Princess Dagmar of Denmark). The white porcelain tankard is mounted in silver, with a hinged lid chased with a border of Russian imperial eagles, and set in the centre with a silver medallion commemorating the coronation of the Emperor and Empress, which took place on 27 May 1883, in Moscow. The silver mount and medal were made by the Danish court jeweller, Anton Michelsen, who had been appointed to the court in 1848. He made many objects commemorating royal occasions, and this coronation tankard was almost certainly acquired by the Empress's sister, Princess Alexandra. **CDEG**

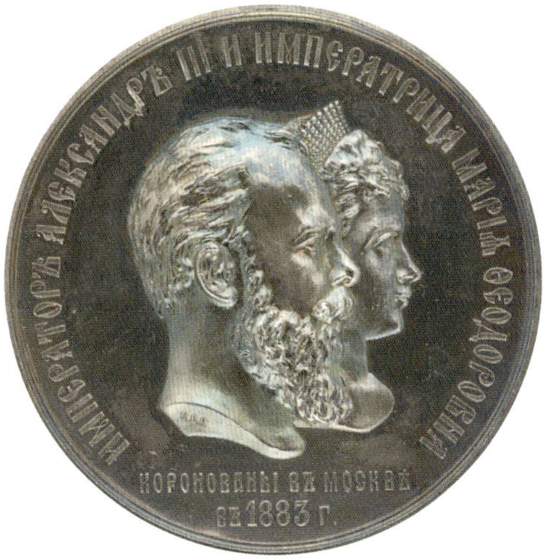

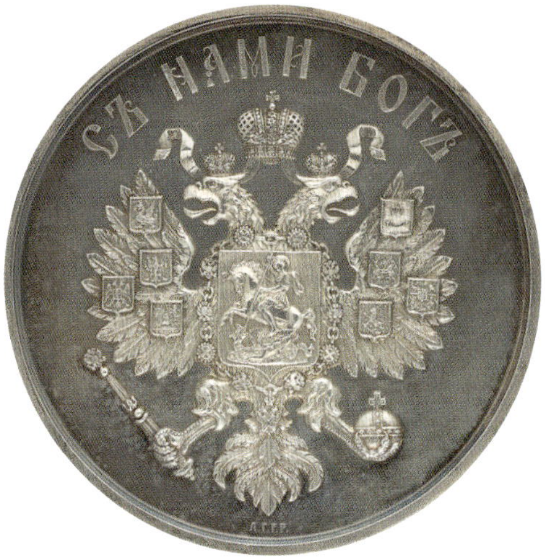

SERGEI VAZHENIN (1848–1923); AVENIR GRILICHES (1802–1905)

198 *Medal commemorating the coronation of Emperor Alexander III (1845–1894) and Maria Feodorovna (1847–1928)* 1883

Silver, dia. 6.51 cm, weight 137.20 g
Marked on the obverse: С.В.Р.; ИМПЕРАТОРЪ АЛЕКСАНДРЪ III И ИМПЕРАТРИЦА МАРІЯ ФЕОДОРОВНЯ and *КОРОНОВАНЫ ВЪ МОСКВА ВЪ 1883г* and on the reverse: А.Г.Г.Р; СЬ НАМИ БОГЪ
RCIN 445437

Provenance Acquired at the time of the coronation in 1883, presumably a gift to Queen Victoria

This handsome medal for the coronation on 27 May 1883 shows the heads of the imperial couple on the obverse, Alexander III bare-headed, but with his splendid beard, Maria Feodorovna wearing a tiara. The legend around the edge reads in Russian: 'Emperor Alexander III and Maria Feodorovna', and in the exergue: 'Coronation in Moscow in 1883'. The imperial double-headed eagle, holding sceptre and orb, and with the various shields displayed on its breast and wings, is shown on the reverse, with 'God is with us' above. **BW**

GRAND DUCHESS SERGEI OF RUSSIA (1864–1918)

199 *Letter to Queen Victoria (1819–1901), St Petersburg* 5/17 November 1894

Manuscript, 26.3 × 12.5 cm
RA VIC/MAIN/Z/274/25

The Grand Duchess writes informing the Queen that her sister, Alix of Hesse, and Nicholas II were to be married on 14/26 November, the birthday of the Dowager Empress. She gives news of the likely time of the service and, in particular, gives the Queen a sense of what the bride will wear, both in words and pictures: a white court dress with ermine mantle and white jewellery; diamonds – 'Alix being tall will look perfectly lovely'. The Grand Duchess paints a pen picture of the imperial family at this time of mourning: the Dowager Empress 'keeps up wonderfully in her fearful sorrow'; Alix 'looking well and not too tired'; 'poor Nicky', who 'has no rest and looks thin and pale'; and writes of how the Queen's letter of sympathy had 'deeply touched them'. Like many a family letter, it ends with apologies for not writing more often and thanks for birthday presents received to mark her 30th birthday, which fell on 1 November, the day of Alexander III's death. **SJP**

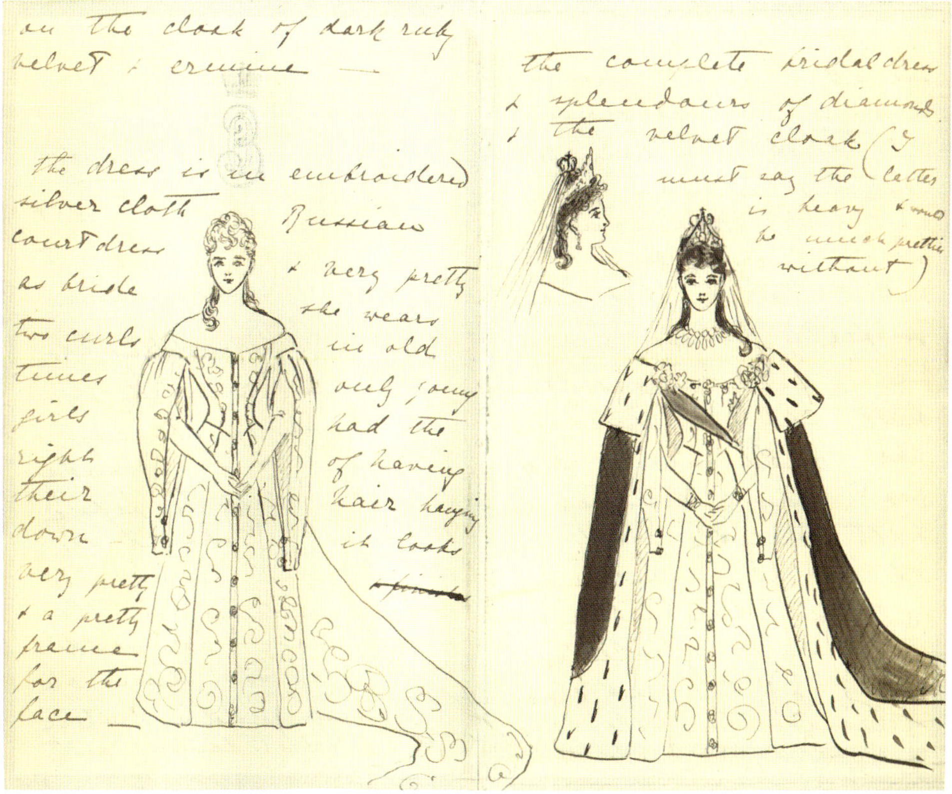

SERGEI LEVITSKY (1819–1898)

200 *Alexander III, Emperor of Russia (1845–1894)* 1894

Gelatin silver print with overpainting, 81.5 × 54.6 cm
Signed and dated on lower right corner: *Levitsky / 1894*
RCIN 2942112

Provenance Possibly acquired by or presented to the Prince of Wales during his visit to Russia, 1894

'Very tall & big, good natured & unaffected': these were the words used by Queen Victoria to describe the sitter, following their first meeting at Windsor Castle in 1873.[106] Alexander III was almost 2 metres tall, and both his towering stature and his imposing figure, as well as perhaps his unsophistication, are well conveyed by this enlarged photograph, possibly produced by Levitsky following the Emperor's death on 1 November 1894 (fig. 63). The Prince of Wales, who had visited him at the Livadia Palace in October, and heard of his death in Vienna, while travelling back to Britain, would return to Russia, accompanied by the Princess of Wales, to attend the Emperor's funeral (fig. 64).

At the first ever Russian exhibition exclusively dedicated to photography, organised at the Museum of Applied Knowledge in St Petersburg in February 1888, 'enlargement of photographs' was one of the seven categories for which awards would be presented.[107] Sergei Levitsky, one of the most authoritative figures of Russian photography, had been involved as one of the members of the committee. This, of course, would have prevented him from submitting, but not from displaying his own work at the exhibition, and indeed, a large, half-length portrait of Emperor Alexander III by Levitsky, probably very similar to this one, was placed at the entrance to the exhibition. Its visual impact, as well as the admirable technical skill and artistry involved in the accomplishment of such a large portrait, would certainly have impressed any visitor.[108] **AN**

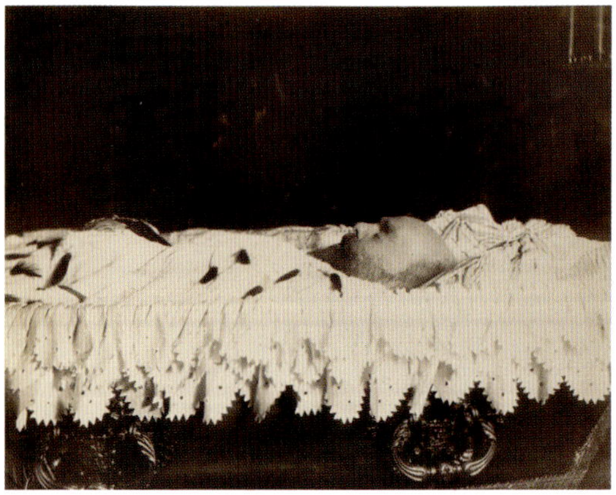

FIG. 63
Sergei Levitsky
Emperor Alexander III lying in state, November 1894
Albumen print, 17.9 × 23.5 cm
RCIN 2929594

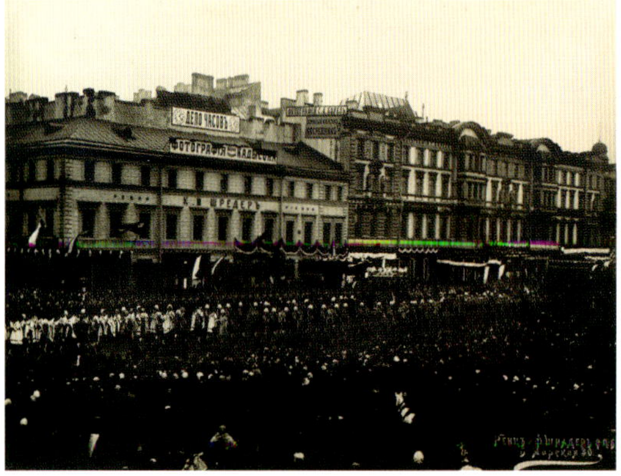

FIG. 64
Rentz & Schrader
Funeral Procession of Emperor Alexander III, November 1894
Gelatin silver print, 40.4 × 54.3 cm
RCIN 2929598

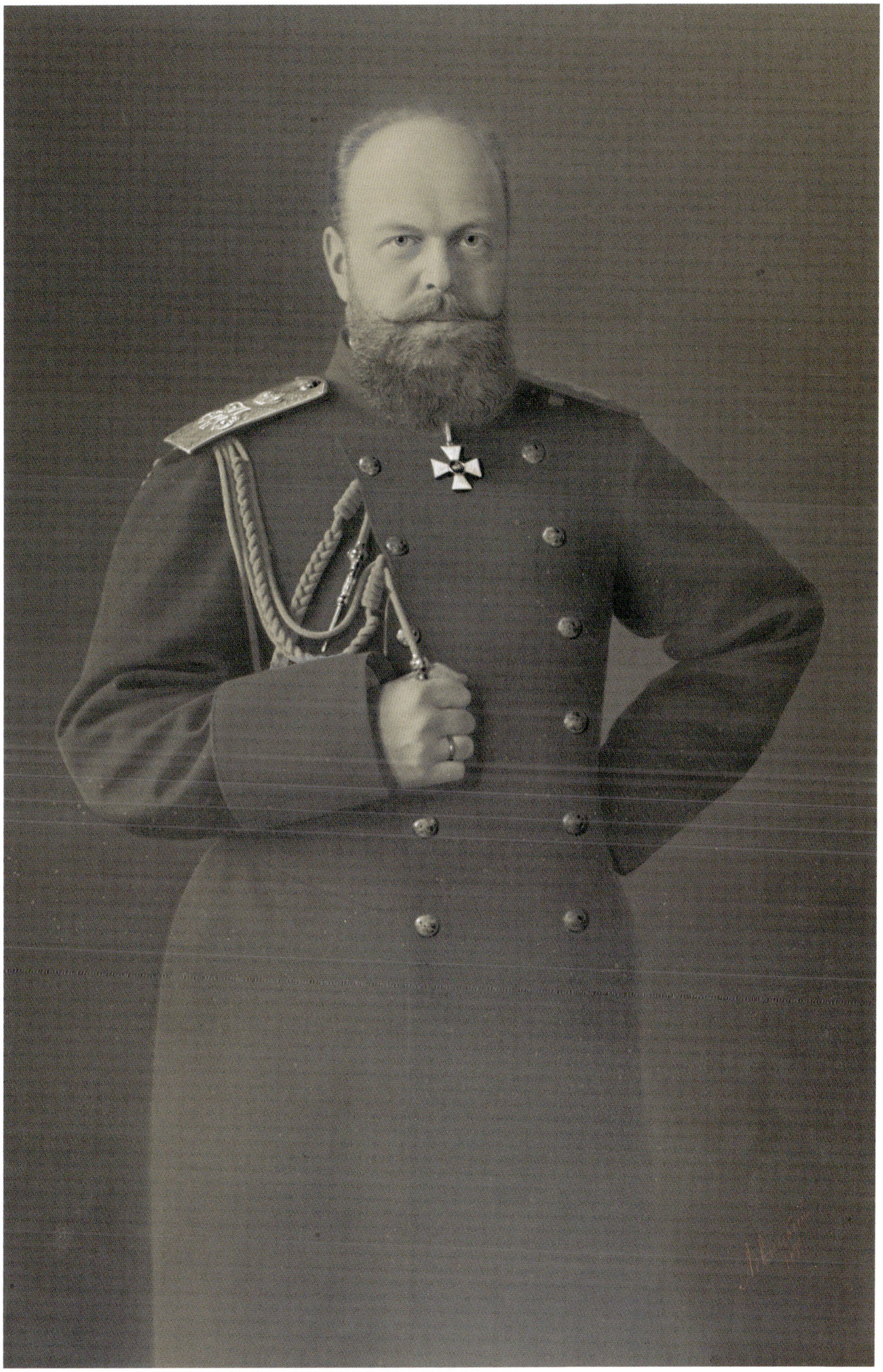

RUSSIAN

201 *Handkerchief commemorating the accession of Emperor Nicholas II (1868–1918)* 1894

Printed cotton, 69.5 × 69.0 × 69.0 cm
Printed in black: *COM DANILOF SHD: MANUF = MOSCOW*; printed with the following text in Cyrillic: Боже царя храни
RCIN 54101

Provenance Unknown

Many souvenirs were produced to mark the accession of Nicholas II in 1894, his wedding the same year, and his coronation in 1896 (cats 205–206). The long-established textile firm, Danilovskaya Manufactory, put out a series of printed kerchiefs bearing patriotic subjects, from images of monuments that recalled Russia's great history to portraits of the Emperor and Empress, accompanied by suitable texts. Permission to use the portraits of Nicholas and Alexandra had to be requested from the Chancellery of the Ministry of the Imperial Court. The handkerchief is printed with the Emperor's crowned cipher, the imperial arms and the inscription 'God Save the Tsar'.
CDEG

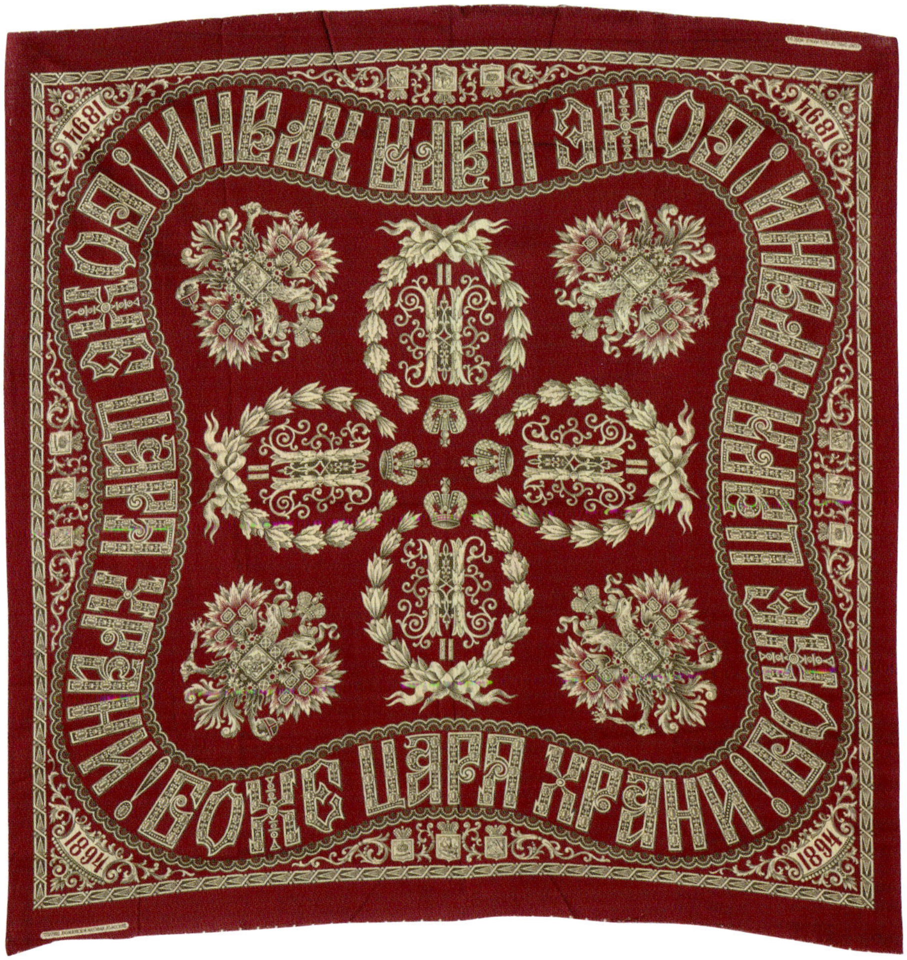

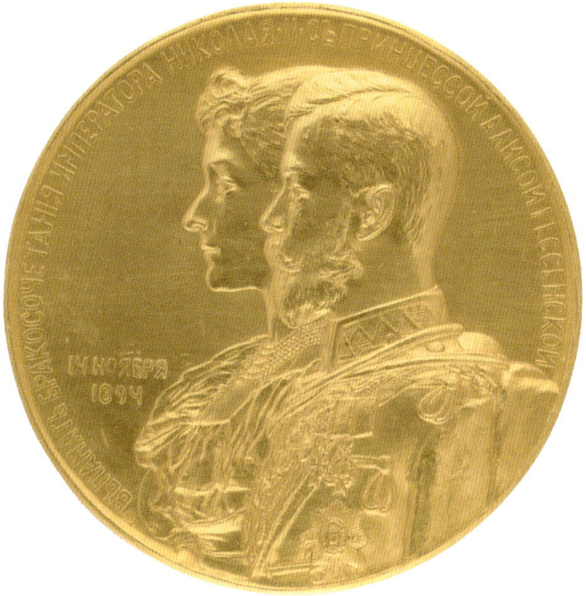

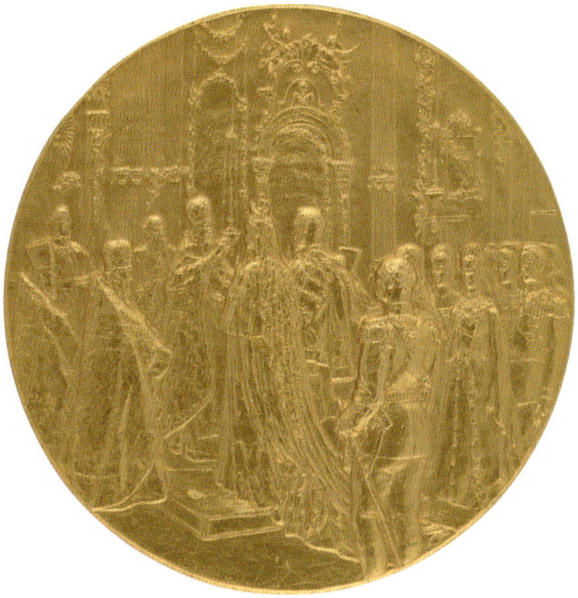

ANTON FEODOROVICH VASYUTINSKY (1858–1935)

202 *Medal commemorating the marriage of Emperor Nicholas II (1868–1918) and Princess Alix of Hesse and by Rhine (1872–1918)* 1894

Gold, dia. 7.1 cm, weight 275.56 g
Inscribed with maker's mark in Cyrillic: 'AB.'
RCIN 445438

Provenance First recorded in the Royal Collection in the current reign (1952–)

The obverse of this handsome medal shows conjoint head-and-shoulders portraits of the bridal pair, facing left. Nicholas II is in military uniform, with several Orders, including the collar of the Order of St Andrew. His bride wears a dress with a wide frill round the deep neckline, which leaves room on her neck to display five strands of pearls. Both are bare-headed. The legend round the edge reads: *ВЪ ПАМЯТЬ БРАКОСОЧЕТАНІЯ ИМПЕРАТОРА НИКОЛАЯ.II.СЪ ПРИНЦЕССОЙ АЛИСОЙ ГЕССЕНСКОЙ* ('In memory of the marriage between Emperor Nicholas II and Princess Alix of Hesse'), with the date, *14 НОЯБРЯ 1894* ('14 November 1894') to their left. This date is according to the Julian calendar, 12 days behind the rest of Europe (where the date was recorded as 26 November), since Russia did not adopt the Gregorian calendar until the twentieth century.

On the reverse, there is a detailed view of the marriage ceremony, which took place in the tragic circumstances of Nicholas's father, Alexander III, having died less than a month before. BW

LAURITS REGNER TUXEN (1853–1927)

203 *The marriage of Nicholas II, Emperor of Russia (1868–1918), 26th November 1894* 1895–6

Oil on canvas, 169.4 × 139.9 cm
Signed and dated: *L Tuxen. 1895-96*
Papier-mâché frame by Valdemar Kleis, Copenhagen
RCIN 404465

Provenance Commissioned by Queen Victoria (Tuxen was paid on 15 August 1896); sent to Osborne, 10 July 1897 (New Wing Corridor); Buckingham Palace, 1901; King's Corridor, Buckingham Palace, 1909

Literature Tuxen 1928, pp. 150–8; Noble 1990, pp. 20–3; Millar 1992, no. 790

The wedding between Nicholas II and Princess Alix of Hesse took place in the Palace Cathedral on 26 November 1894. The wedding was announced in April that year and was to take place on Empress Maria Feodorovna's birthday. Tragically, Emperor Alexander III died of kidney disease on 1 November, and the court was thrown into mourning, with the exception of the day of the marriage.

The royal couple stand, holding lighted candles, whilst the Metropolitan Archbishop of St Petersburg, Mgr Palladius (1827–98), makes the sign of the cross before them. Ella (Grand Duchess Elizabeth Feodorovna), writing to her grandmother, Queen Victoria, described her sister's dress as 'embroidered silver cloth Russian court dress & very pretty', helpfully including a sketch (cat. 199). She added that 'Alix being tall will look perfectly lovely'.[109] She wears the nuptial tiara, worn by all imperial brides, a small diamond crown and, beneath, a wreath of orange blossom; her imperial gold-embroidered mantle is lined with ermine. Nicholas II is dressed in the uniform of a hussar. In the background, George I of

Key

1. Metropolitan Palladius of St Petersburg and Ladoga
2. Member of the Holy Synod
3. King George I of Greece
4. King Christian IX of Denmark
5. Emperor Nicholas II
6. Alexandra Feodorovna, Empress of Russia
7. Dowager Empress Maria Feodorovna
8. Alexandra, Princess of Wales, later Queen Alexandra
9. Queen Olga of Greece
10. Grand Duchess Maria Alexandrovna, Duchess of Edinburgh
11. George, Duke of York, later King George V
12. Albert Edward, Prince of Wales, later King Edward VII
13. ?Count Illarion Ivanovich Vorontsov-Dashkov, Officer of the Imperial Court
14. Officer of the Imperial Court
15. ?Princess Louis of Battenberg, Princess Victoria of Hesse and by Rhine
16. Grand Duchess Elizabeth Feodorovna, Princess Elisabeth of Hesse and by Rhine
17. ?Princess Henry of Prussia, Princess Irene of Hesse and by Rhine
18. Ernest Louis, Grand Duke of Hesse and by Rhine
19. Grand Duke Vladimir Alexandrovich
20. Grand Duke Paul Alexandrovich
21. Grand Duke Serge Alexandrovich
22. Prince Henry of Prussia
23. Prince Alfred, Duke of Edinburgh, Duke of Saxe-Coburg and Gotha
24. Grand Duke Michael Nicholaevich
25. Grand Duke Alexei Alexandrovich

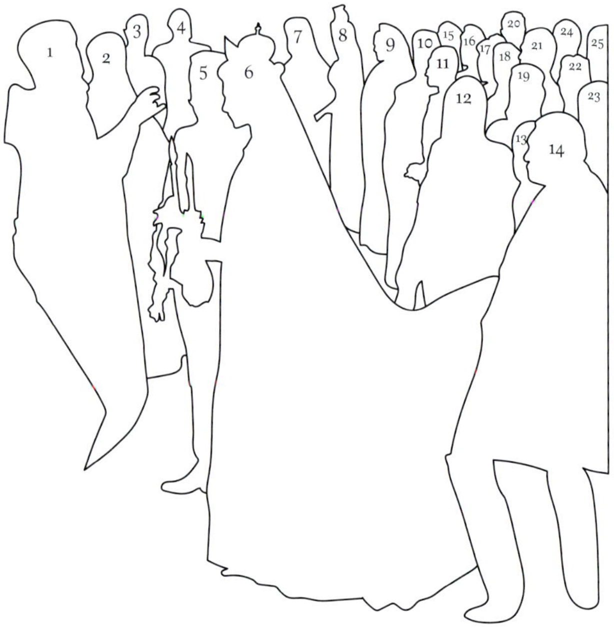

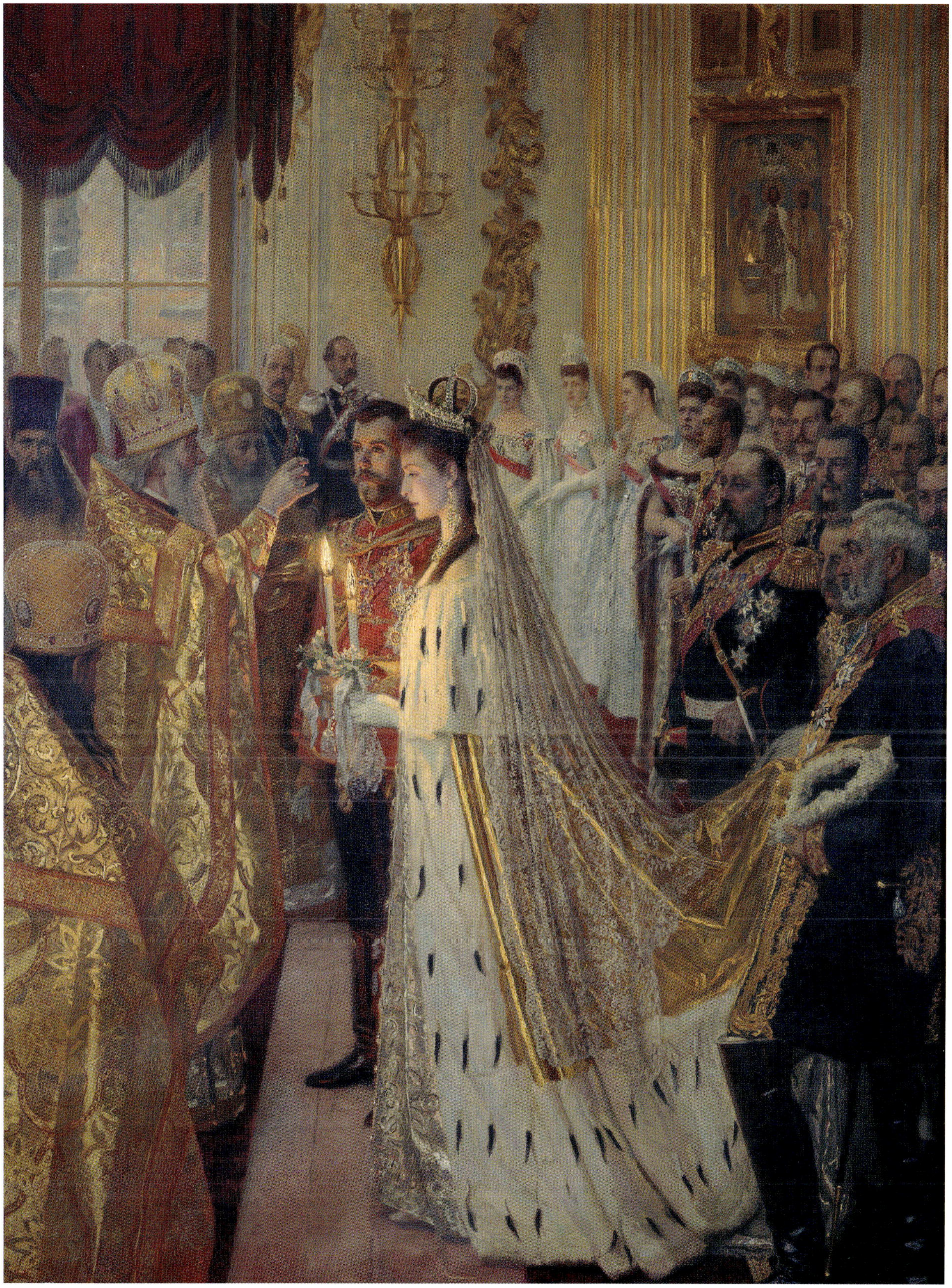

Greece stands to the left of Christian IX of Denmark, who looks towards his daughter, the Dowager Empress; the Princess of Wales and the Queen of Greece are also present. The Prince of Wales can be seen dressed in the uniform of the Russian Dragoons to the right of the portrait; his son, Prince George, is visible to his right.

Laurits Tuxen was commissioned to paint two pictures of the wedding: a smaller one for the Dowager Empress (ГЭ-6229, 1895, Hermitage), and a larger-scale version for Queen Victoria. He varied the combination and placing of figures according to the patron. The artist's autobiography, *En Malers Arbejde*, documents the genesis of both paintings, although it is sometimes difficult to discern which painting he is referring to.

Tuxen travelled to St Petersburg on 20 October 1894; he visited the Winter Palace on 24 November, and the following day, sketched in the chapel. On the day of the wedding, the artist found himself stationed with the choir, together with Ilya Repin and Mihály Zichy (1827–1906); here, he took advantage of the steps leading up to the pulpit, and from this vantage point he was 'intoxicated by the beauty of the scene, the singing, the richness of the colours, the light and the golden fabrics'. He likened the bride's head, softly illuminated from beneath to a 'Luini or a Leonardo'. The poignancy of the day was not lost on General Ellis, who, writing to Queen Victoria, described how, on this 'gloomy sunless day [...] a shadow of sadness seemed to hang over the whole ceremony, wh Yr Majesty can well realize'.[110] The following day, the court was to return to the deepest mourning.

On 30 November 1894, Tuxen showed a sketch to the Prince of Wales and it was agreed by 'everyone' that there was too little space. He also requested the inclusion of a number of figures. For the next 16 months, the artist was at work on the two pictures, travelling to Tsarskoe Selo in May 1895, to sketch and photograph the couple, whom he found 'easy and friendly', and to London in July. On 11 September, Tuxen noted that he had started to paint the Queen's version and both pictures were to occupy him until the end of the year. He worked on the bridal couple last, with his wife standing in for the Empress. A small, sketch-like study, dated 1895, is in the Schlossmuseum, Darmstadt. This was possibly painted for the Grand Duke of Hesse. **AB**

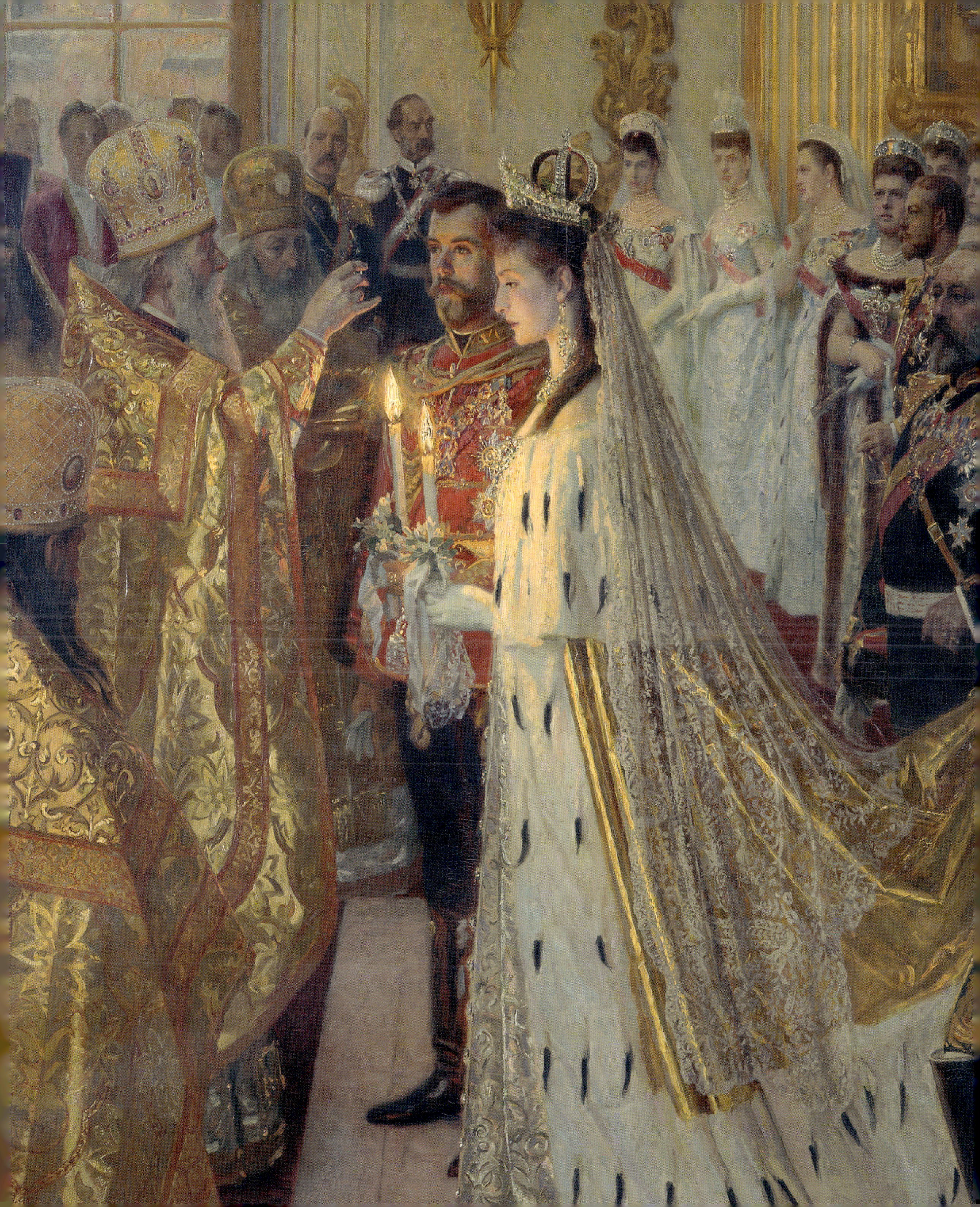

ATTRIBUTED TO EKATERINA IERONIMOVNA VISKOVATOVA (1838–1911)

204 *Grand Duchess Elizabeth Feodorovna (1864–1918)* 1896

Watercolour and pastel, 68.9 × 54.6 cm
Signed and dated: *C. Viskavatof 1896*
RCIN 452199

Provenance Sent as a birthday present by Grand Duchess Sergei to Queen Victoria, 1896

Literature Millar 1995, no. 5658

The Grand Duchess is shown in profile, wearing a white, low-cut, off-the-shoulder dress, with a pink rose at the front and jewellery of simple pearl earrings. The work was sent by the Grand Duchess as a birthday present to Queen Victoria in 1896, arriving in late May. It was described by Queen Victoria in a letter to her daughter, Princess Beatrice (1857–1944): 'Ella's present has arrived. It is a profile, very like and beautifully painted in pastel'.[111]

The artist, who received no formal training and specialised in portraits, lived in both St Petersburg and Moscow, and exhibited at the Academy of Arts and the Society of Russian Watercolourists. Examples of her work are held in the Vrubel Art Museum, Omsk. With her sister, Natalie, she was one of the first female students of St Petersburg University, studying at the Faculty of Law at a time when university statutes did not allow for female students, but did not prevent them either. She was a participant in the student revolutionary movement of the early 1860s; she was a close acquaintance of Polina Suslova (1839–1918), and also met and corresponded with Feodor Dostoevsky (1821–81), Suslova's lover.

Her father, Geronimo Corsini (1808–76), who was of Italian extraction, was an architect who designed – among other works – the railings of the Sheremetev Palace (the Fountain House) and the Apraksin Dvor market area, both in St Petersburg. Her husband, Pavel Alexandrovich Viskovatov (1842–1905), worked under General Field Marshal Prince Baryatinsky (1815–79). Baryatinsky had helped to subdue the Caucasus region and achieved the surrender of Shamil; he had met Queen Victoria in 1839, 1843, 1865 and 1874, and his death, in 1875, was recorded by the Queen in her Journal. Viskovatov was a professor of Russian literature at Tartu University, then director of the Gymnasium in St Petersburg, where he specialised in the works of Lermontov (1814–41), writing the author's biography. Ekaterina's sister, Natalie, married Nikolai Uchin, a close associate of the revolutionary Chernyshevsky (1828–89). In 1863, Nikolai and Natalie fled from Russia, and he was sentenced to death in his absence. Living in London and Geneva, he met many of the revolutionaries of the time, including Herzen (1812–70), Bakunin (1814–76) and Marx (1818–83). Pardoned in 1878, he and Natalie returned to Russia that year.

It is intriguing that an untrained artist, who had clear family connections to the revolutionary movement over a number of years, should be commissioned by the Grand Duchess at a time when her husband, Grand Duke Sergei, was actively controlling student activity and possible revolutionary ferment, as Governor of Moscow and commander of the Moscow Military District.
SJP

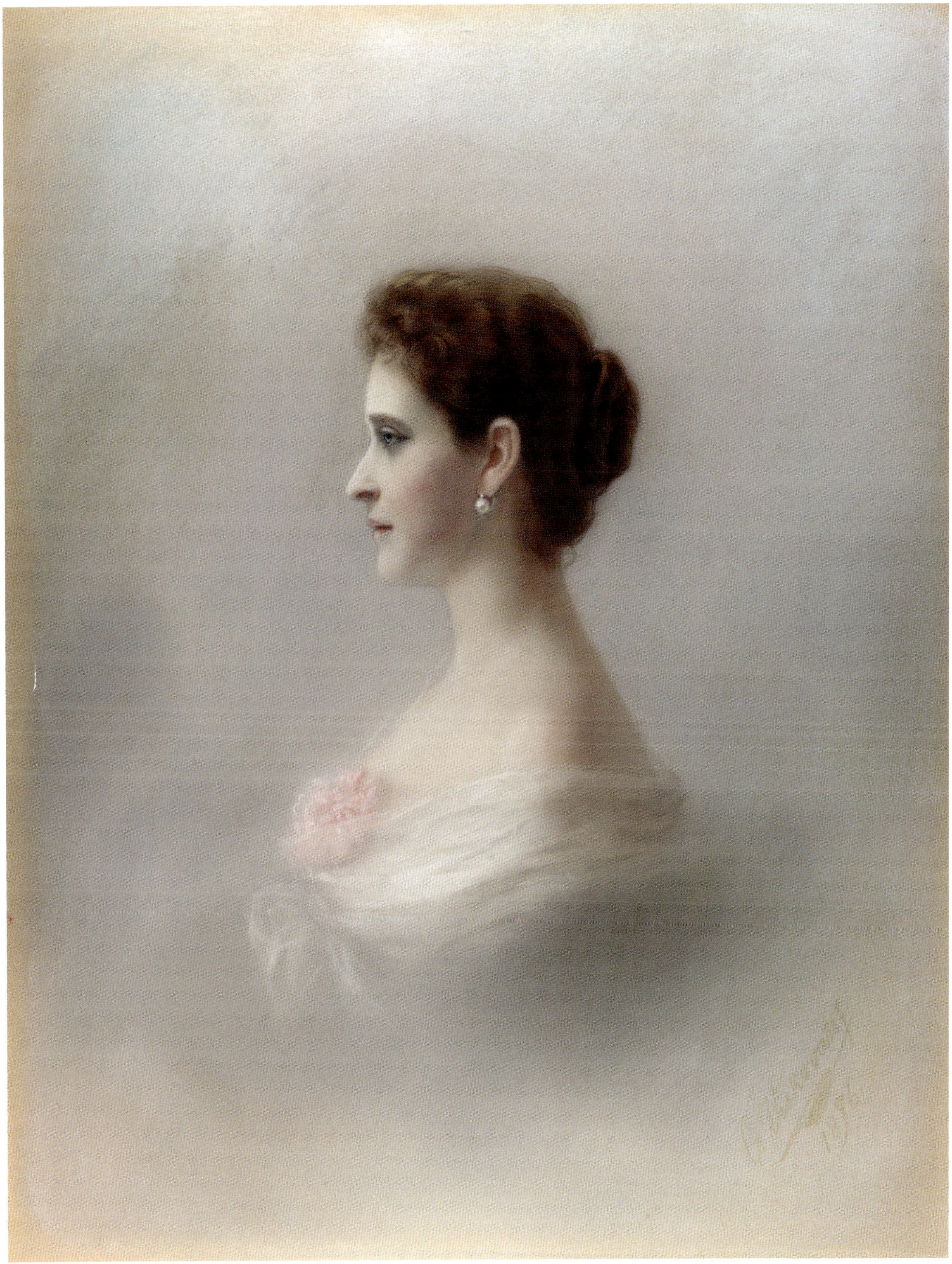

SARREGUEMINES

205 *Commemorative coronation cup* 1896

Earthenware, 13.5 × 8.5 × 8.5 cm
Painted in underglaze: *HA II 1896*; stamped: *SARREGUEMINES*
RCIN 32233.1–2

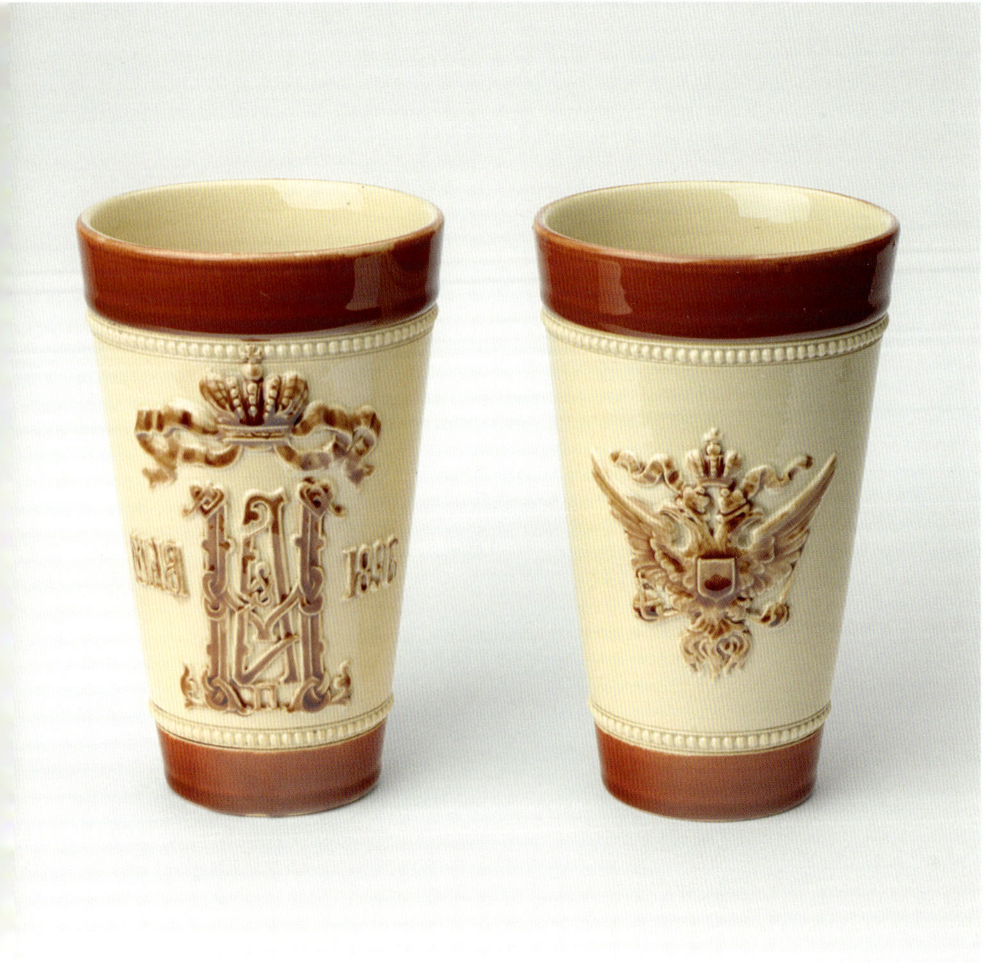

Provenance Probably acquired by King Edward VII and Queen Alexandra, 1896

Produced in France, at the Sarreguemines porcelain factory, established in 1709, the simple earthenware souvenir, marking the coronation of Nicholas II, is modelled in relief, with the cipher of Nicholas II (H II), the Imperial arms and date in a brown and cream glaze. The Sarreguemines firm was just one of those making a vast number of souvenirs to mark the Emperor's coronation. The cup was first recorded at Sandringham, indicating that it was originally in the collection of King Edward VII and Queen Alexandra. CDEG

RUSSIAN

206 *Commemorative coronation beaker* 1896

Metal, enamel, gilt decoration, 10.5 × 9.5 cm
Painted with crowned *HA II* monogram and *1896* on one side, and imperial eagle on the other
RCIN 54097.1–3

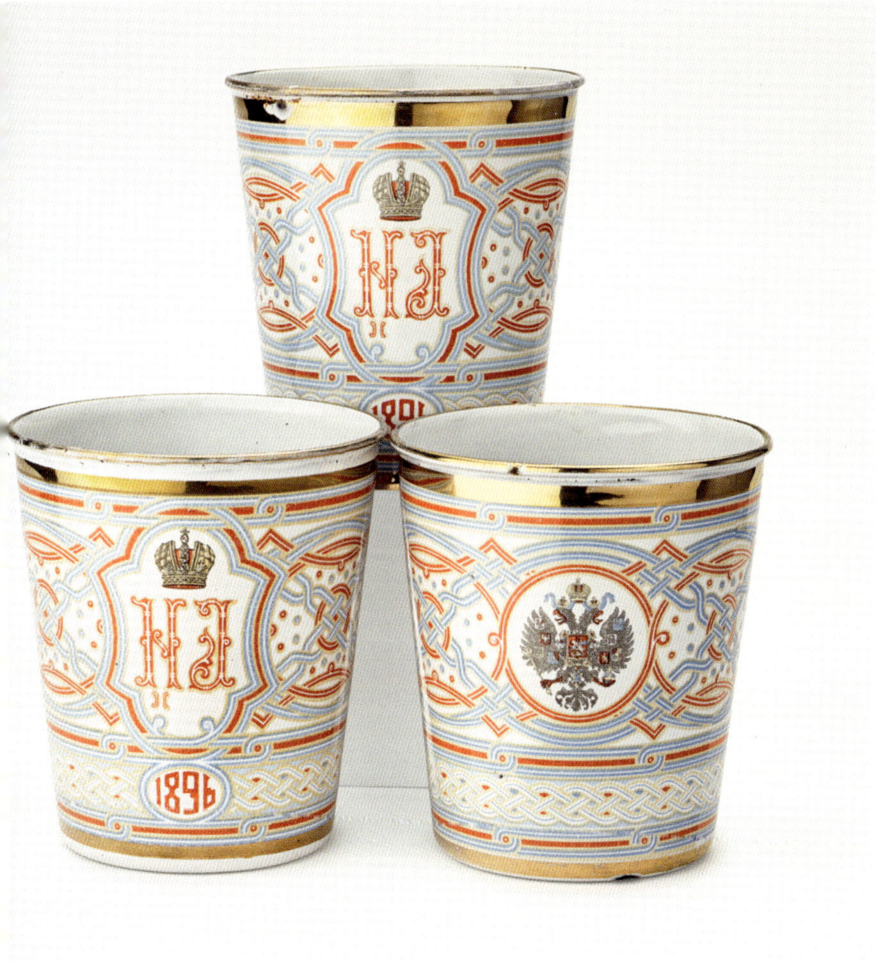

Provenance Acquired by Queen Mary

The planning for the coronation of Emperor Nicholas II on 26 May 1896 was handled by the Ministry of the Imperial Court and the specially appointed Coronation Commission. In addition, various temporary institutions were established, including a chancellery entrusted with the task of organising the open-air festivities for the people of Moscow. The festivities lasted for 21 days, from 6/18 May to 26 May/7 June.

On the morning of 18/30 May, thousands of enamelled metal coronation beakers, of which this is an example, were distributed to the people at Khodynka Fields, together with a sausage, nuts, raisins and figs, wrapped in a napkin decorated with a view of the Kremlin and the Imperial Arms. Rumours had spread throughout the city that the gifts were to include cattle, horses and even peasant houses, and, as a result, several hundred thousand people pressed towards the site, in anticipation of the food and gifts. This led to a great tragedy when, in the rush, more than a thousand people were trampled to death. The Emperor expressed his sorrow to the families of the dead, paid for the burial costs, and ordered that each family be given 1,000 rubles, but was also criticised for attending a ball that evening.

Queen Victoria was moved by the tragedy that took place at Khodynka Fields and was presented with an earthenware cup, bowl and plate, made for distribution to the people of Moscow, by her ambassador to Moscow, Sir Nicholas O'Conor (1843–1908), on 5 August 1896.[112] **CDEG**

BARON HEINRICH VON ANGELI (1840–1925)

207 *Alexandra Feodorovna, Empress of Russia (1872–1918)* 1897

Oil on canvas, 70.5 × 55.4 cm
Signed and dated: *HvAngeli 97*
RCIN 404572

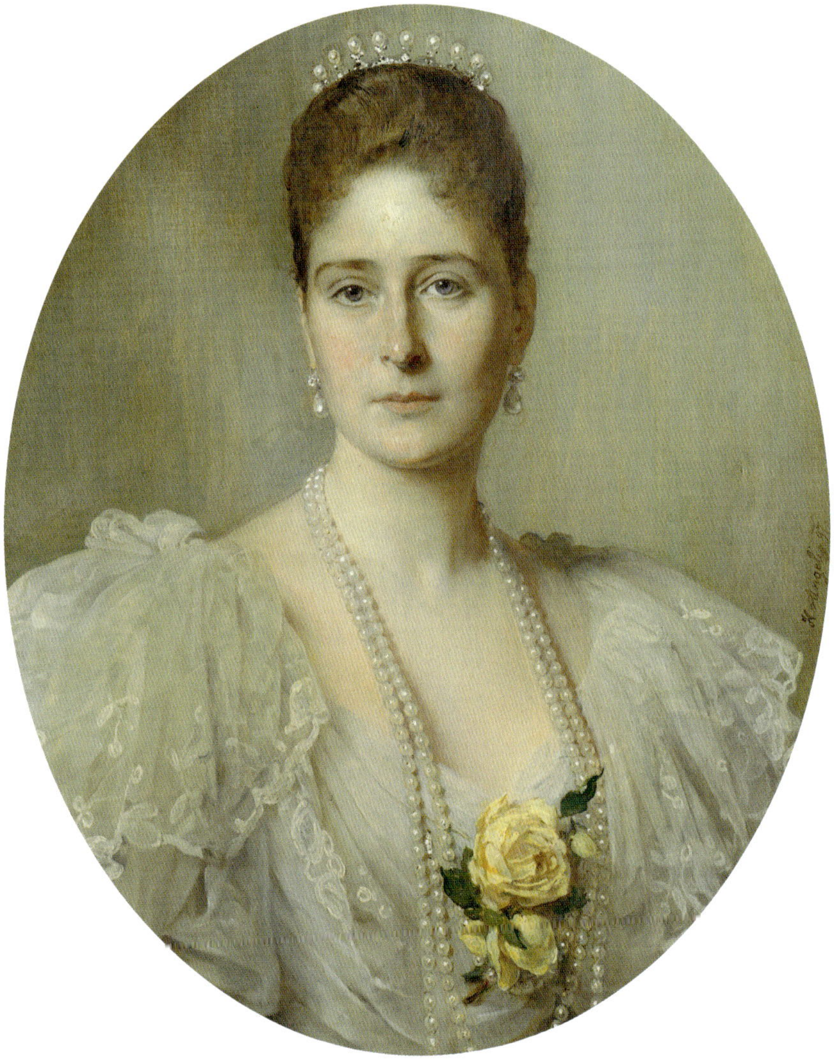

Provenance Painted for Queen Victoria

Literature Millar 1992, no. 23

This refined, cool portrait was presumably painted by Heinrich von Angeli when Alix and her husband, Nicholas II, stayed briefly at Balmoral from 22 September to 4 October 1896, with their daughter, Olga (1895–1918), who was just one. On 4 November 1896, Queen Victoria wrote to her daughter, the Empress Frederick, that the artist had been painting a head of 'Alicky', but that there had not been time to paint the Emperor.[113] The Queen recalled in her Journal when the couple arrived that she found her beloved granddaughter more beautiful than ever. There are slight pentimenti visible in the outline of the head and the shoulders. **AB**

VASILY SIL'VESTROVICH KRIVENKO (b.1854)

208 *Les Solennités du saint couronnement. Ouvrage publié avec l'autorisation de Sa Majesté L'Empereur par le Ministère de la Maison Impériale sous la direction de M.V.S. Krivenko [...] Traduction française de M.G. Korsow* 1899

St Petersburg: Expédition pour la confection des papiers de l'état
Pictorial binding with Russian double eagle, medallion profile portrait of Nicholas and Alexandra inset on front board, gilt edges, 44.8 × 34.2 cm (closed)
RCIN 1060000

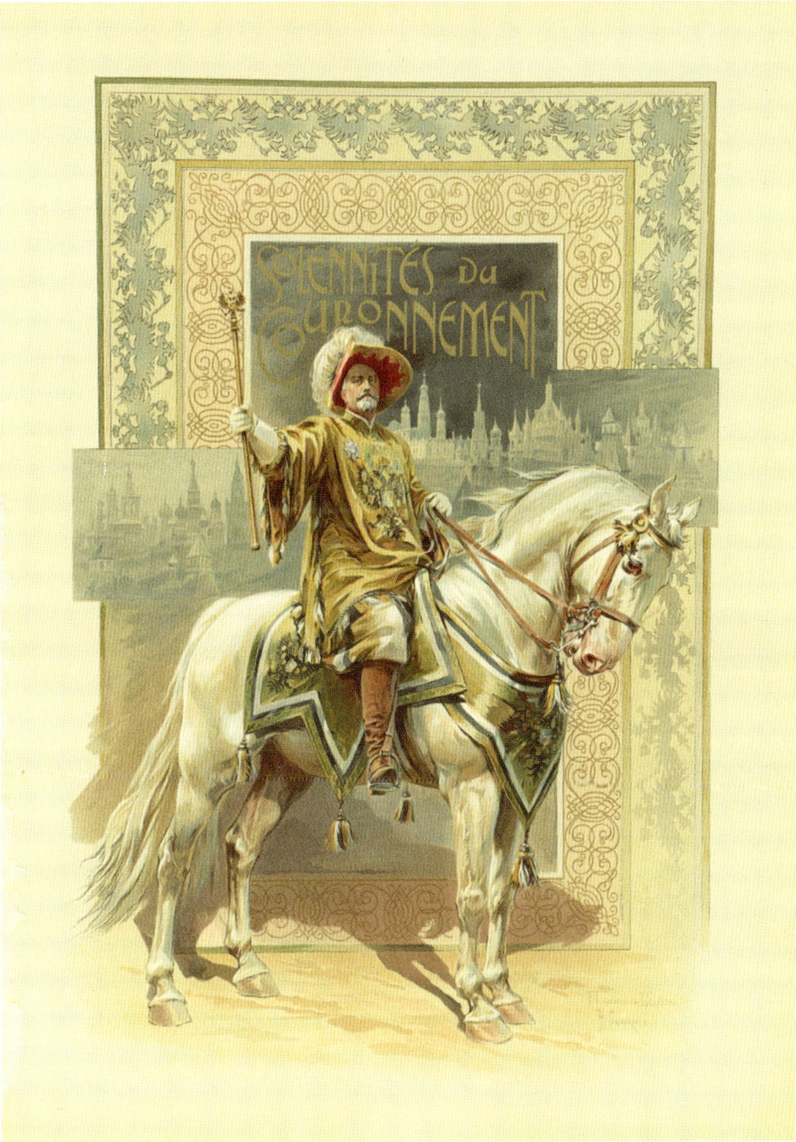

Provenance Presumably presented to Queen Victoria

This imposing book is the official publication, describing the coronation and accompanying festivities of Emperor Nicholas II and Alexandra Feodorovna on 26 May (14 May OS) 1896. Fully illustrated with colour images and rich chromolithographs, it sets the coronation in its historical context, with a history of Russian coronations from the early Byzantine emperors, all the way to Nicholas's father, Alexander III, before describing in detail the events of Nicholas's own coronation. The procedure was thus strictly grounded in history and tradition.

Nicholas and Alexandra stayed in the Petrovsky Palace outside Moscow for some days before their formal entrance into Moscow on 21 May, after which they went into formal retreat until the day of the coronation, which took place in the Uspensky Cathedral in the Kremlin. By tradition, Russian emperors crown themselves with the heavy Imperial Crown of Russia made for Catherine the Great in 1762. Nicholas had wished to crown himself with the crown said to have been used by the twelfth-century ruler, Vladimir Monomakh (1053–1125), which had the veneer of antiquity and also the solid advantage of being considerably lighter.[114] Arthur, Duke of Connaught, who was attending with his wife as representatives of Queen Victoria, sent an impressed telegram to his mother after the event: 'Coronation just over in splendid weather; most glorious and impressive ceremony; were four hours in church [...] both she [Alix] and Nicky were much moved with solemnity of the occasion'.[115] **ES**

KOLYVAN LAPIDARY MANUFACTORY

209 *Presentation dish* 1896

Beloretzky quartz, marble, 4.5 × 42.6 cm
Label with Cyrillic inscription: 'ORLITZ DISH / INSCRIPTION ROUND DISH: / "TO THEIR IMPERIAL MAJESTIES ON / THE DAY OF THE HOLY CORONATION" / FROM THE EMPLOYEES & WORKERS / OF THE LAPIDARIES of KOLYVAN 1896 / On top is the Imperial Double Eagle / In centre is monogram of Nicholas Alexandrovitch II, surmounted by the Imperial crown / At bottom are the Arms of the Lapidaries of Kolyvan; in black paint'
RCIN 49799

Provenance Presented to Emperor Nicholas II and Empress Alexandra Feodorovna, 1896; purchased by Queen Mary, 1938

Literature QMPP, IX, 131

This presentation dish was given to Nicholas II on the day of his coronation, 9 May 1896, by the employees of the lapidaries of Kolyvan. It takes the form of a bread and salt dish. Such dishes were usually produced in silver, niello or silver gilt, and were sometimes applied with enamel decoration. Other examples associated with commemorations of the imperial family in the nineteenth century were also made in finely carved wood.[116] They were used in the traditional Russian welcome ceremony, which also formed part of the coronation service of the Emperor. Many silver examples were presented to the imperial family throughout the nineteenth century, by makers such as Ovchinnikov and Sazikov; however, versions in hardstone appear to be less common. One other similar dish is known, which forms part of the collection of the Mining Museum, part of the Mining University, in St Petersburg (fig. 65). CDEG

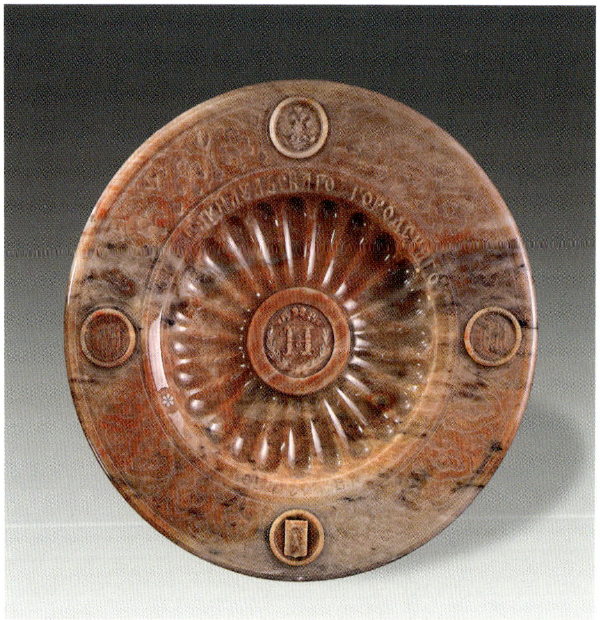

FIG. 65
Kolyvan, Barnaul
Presentation dish, 1891
Quartzite of Belorechensk, Altay, Russia, 40.0 cm
Mining Museum, St Petersburg

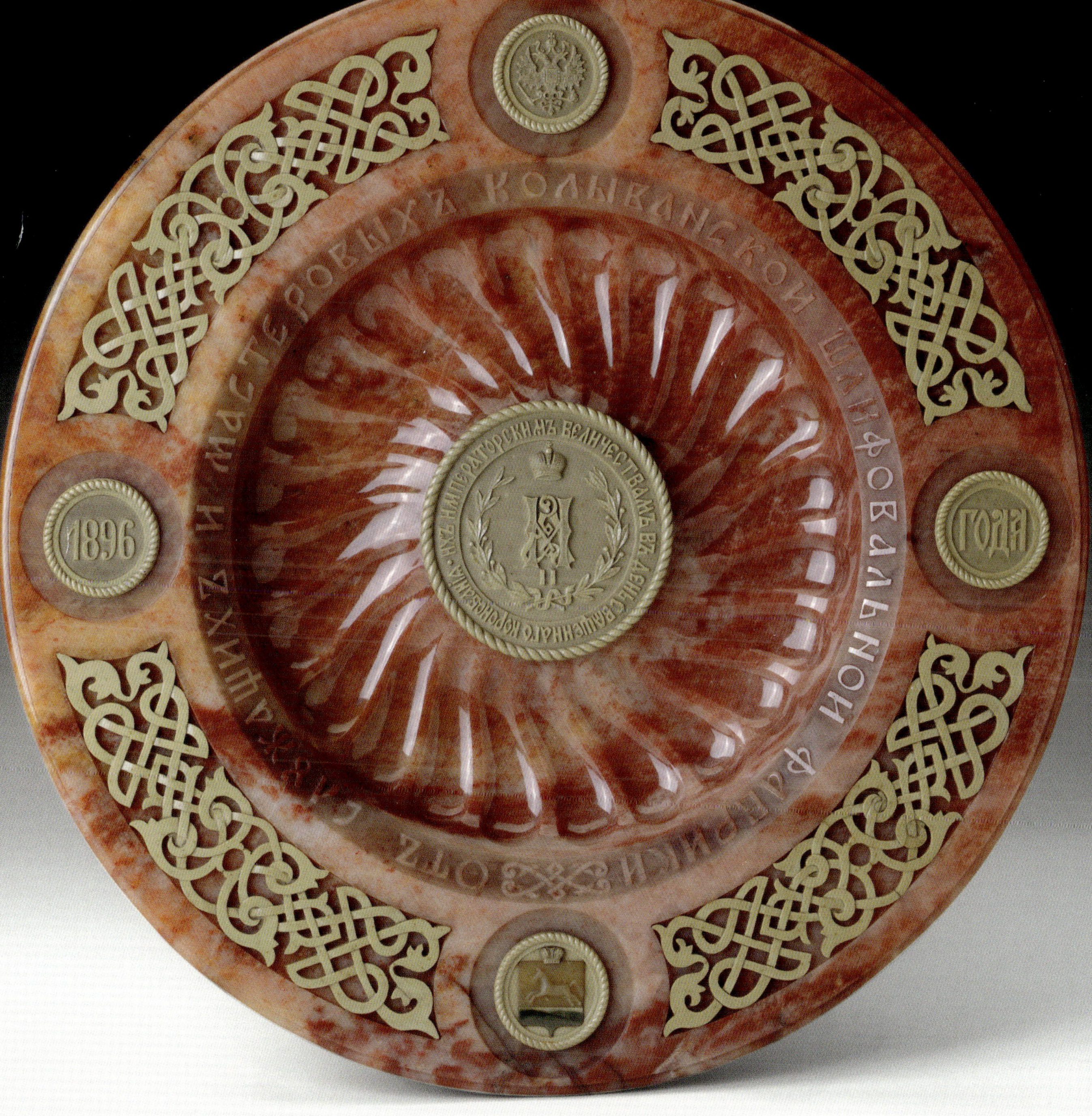
1896
ГОДА

A.A. LEVENSON, PRINTER

210 *Programme du spectacle de gala au Grand Théâtre Impérial de Moscou le 17 Mai 1896, donné a l'occasion du couronnement de sa Majesté L'Empereur Nicolas Alexandrovitsch et de sa Majesté L'Impératrice Alexandra Feodorowna* 1896

Moscow: A.A. Levenson
No. 49 of a limited edition, bound in brown calf, with the Russian coat of arms on the front, doublures of blue watered silk and blue gold-tooled leather, featuring the initials of Nicholas II and Alexandra, bound by A. Schnell, St Petersburg, 31.7 × 23.6 cm (closed)
RCIN 1047359

Provenance Possibly the copy given to HRH The Duke of Connaught, attending as Queen Victoria's representative

After the coronation of Nicholas and Alexandra on 26 May (14 May OS), the festivities continued throughout Moscow. On the evening of 29 May (17 May OS), a gala was staged at the Grand Imperial Theatre (now known as the Bolshoi Theatre), with a spectacular series of performances by the Imperial Opera of Moscow, the Imperial Ballet of St Petersburg and the Bolshoi Company of Moscow. The theatre was specially restored for the event; the official publication for the coronation festivities noted that it had completely changed, and that it was difficult to recall its sad foyers in the new parade of magnificent salons filled with subtle aromas.[117] The performances began with part of Glinka's (1804–57) opera, *Life for the Tsar*, a tale of heroism on behalf of the first Romanov Tsar Michael, followed by a new piece by Marius Ivanovich Petipa (1818–1910), Russia's premier ballet dancer and choreographer, creator of some of the cornerstones of the ballet repertoire. He composed for the event a one-act ballet, *La Perle*, to the music of Riccardo Drigo (1846–1930), in which the White Pearl, the most precious jewel in the world, is captured by the Genie of the Earth. A rich souvenir programme was created for the event, filled with sumptuous chromolithographic illustrations, copies of which were given to all of those who attended. They appear to have been printed in both Russian and French, with varying standards of binding (an 'ordinary' copy was bound in white board, with the Russian arms on the cover). This is a rather more lavish copy, one of the French ones, bound in brown leather. ES

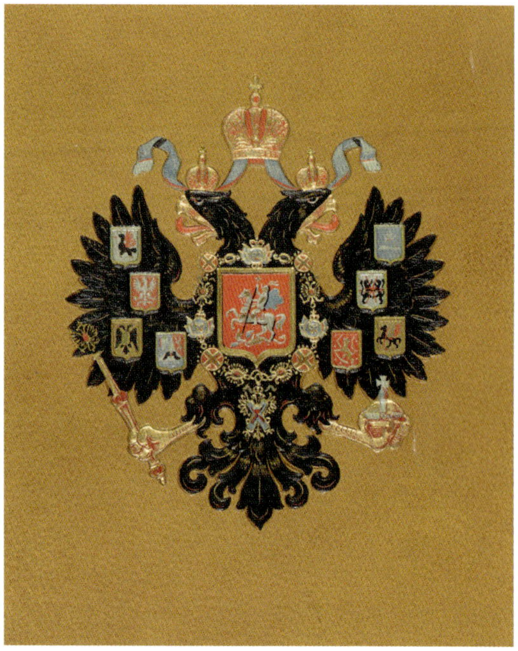

Detail of front board

renfermer dans sa prison nacrée. **Le Génie** l'implore de ne pas se soustraire à son admiration. Touchée par ses prières, elle consent à quitter sa conque. Cependant, les vagues ont averti le **Roi Corail**, gardien jaloux des trésors de la mer. Il arrive avec toute une armée. A sa vue les perles tremblent. **Le Génie**, malgré leurs prières, va être à jamais enfermé dans les abimes de la mer, sous la garde des monstres terribles. En vain les perles supplient— **le Roi Corail** est inexorable. **Le Génie** frappe le rocher de sa baguette. Le rocher s'entrouvre et il en sort une armée, appartenant au **Génie de la Terre:** soldats d'or, d'argent, d'airain et de fer. Un combat s'engage entre les coraux et les

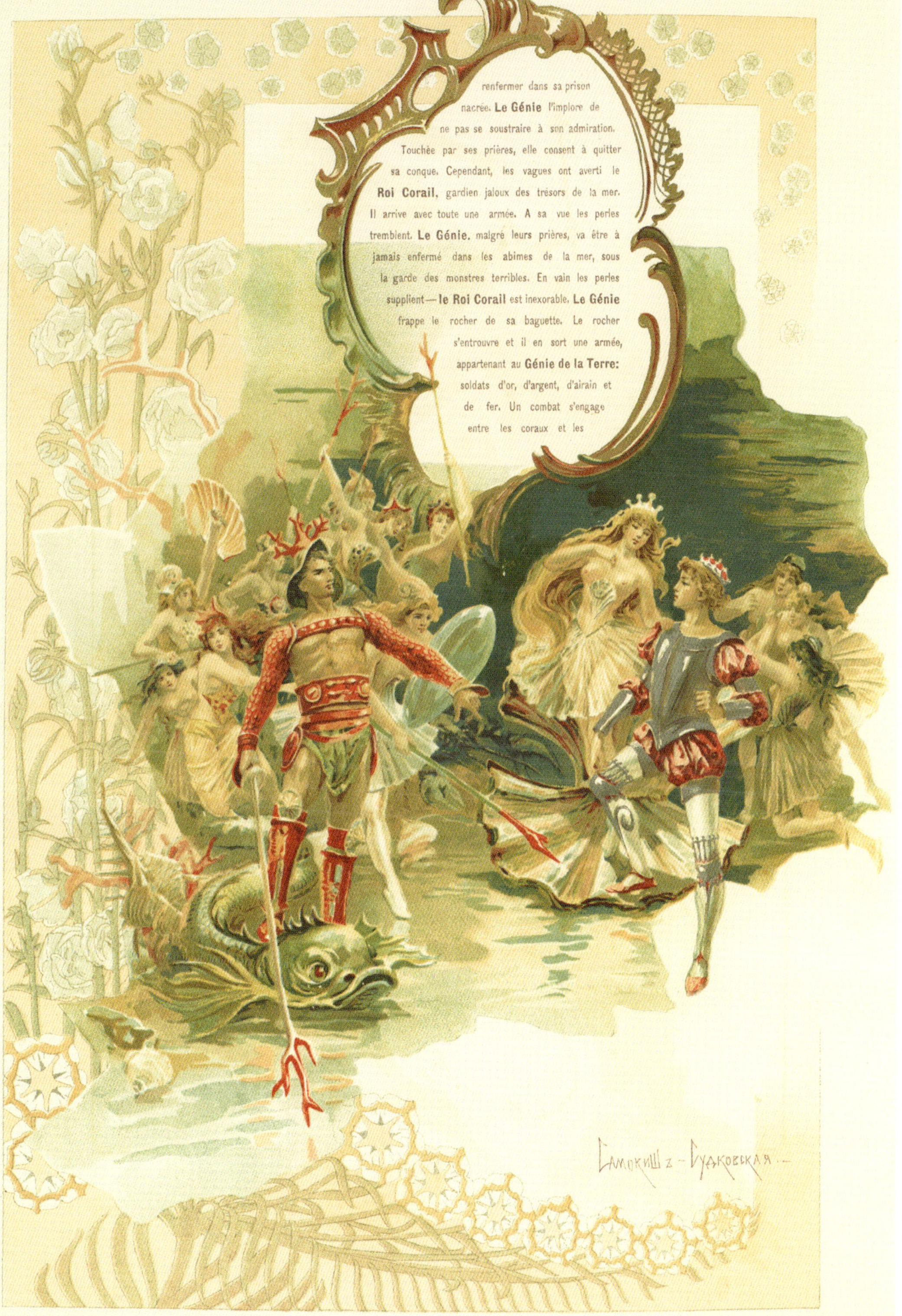

FABERGÉ

211 *Frame*, before 1896

Silver-gilt, guilloche enamel, four-colour gold, ivory, 11.0 × 6.8 × 1.5 cm
Mark of Johann Victor Aarne, silver mark of 88 zolotniks (before 1896); FABERGÉ in Cyrillic
RCIN 8560

Provenance Jointly purchased by Emperor Nicholas II and Empress Alexandra Feodorovna, 11 August 1898

Literature Pavlovsk catalogue, 2013, IX, p. 217, no. 3937

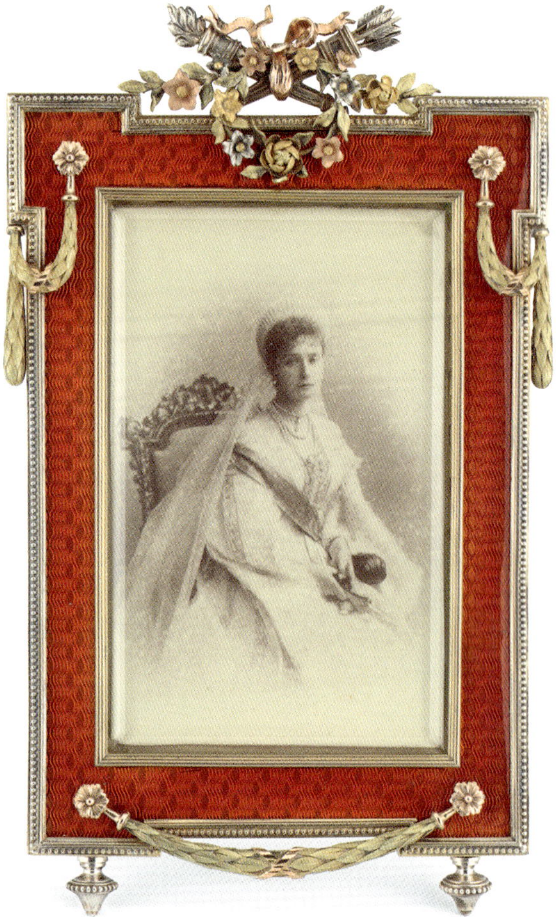

The workmaster Johann Victor Aarne (1863–1934) specialised particularly in the production of frames with vari-coloured gold decoration. These were extremely popular with Fabergé's clientele and with the increase in the popularity of photography the demand for frames rose immeasurably. Photographs of the interiors of the Imperial palaces including the private apartments of the Winter Palace and the Alexander Palace at Tsarskoe Selo show that both the Emperor and Empress's apartments were filled with frames containing photographs of their families. The same was true in England, where the private sitting rooms and studies of King Edward VII, Queen Alexandra and also the future King George V and Queen Mary were copiously arranged with frames and objets d'art.

This example is applied with red guilloché enamel with rich embellishments in red, yellow, green and white gold including laurel swags, flower trails and a cresting formed of a trophy of a flaming torch and a quiver of arrows signifying love. The account books of Nicholas II and Alexandra Feodorovna reveal that this frame was jointly purchased by the couple in August 1898, the year in which the photograph of the Empress which the frame contains was made. The Empress is shown in a widely disseminated studio portrait, wearing court dress and a diamond kokoshnik tiara.

The frame was obviously sent as a gift to the royal family in England although the exact recipient is not known. CDEG

ATTRIBUTED TO ST PETERSBURG IMPERIAL MINT;
ANTON FEODOROVICH VASYUTINSKII (1858–1935), designer

212 *Romanov tercentenary medal* 1913

Gilt bronze, silk, 3.2 × 2.8 cm
RCIN 441624

Provenance Possibly sent by Nicholas II to King George V

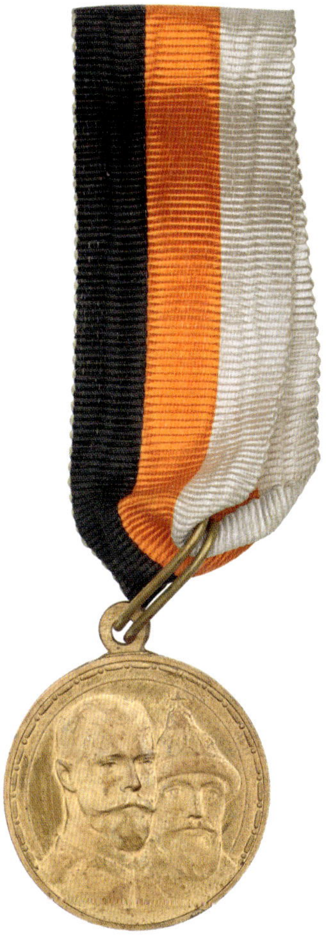

The design by Anton Vasyutinskii, senior medallist of the St Petersburg Imperial Mint, was approved by the Emperor on 19 January 1913, and over two million examples from a variety of mints, with over 200 variations, were produced by June 1914.[118]

The official tercentenary medal was issued to mark the 300th anniversary of the election of Mikhail Romanov to the Russian throne in 1613, and the ascendency of the Romanov dynasty. On the obverse are portraits of Mikhail I wearing seventeenth-century costume, with a wide, jewelled collar (*barma*) and the 'Cap of Monomakh', along with the current emperor, Nicholas II, in the uniform of the imperial family's Life-Guards 4th Rifle Regiment. On the reverse is the text, *ВЪ ПАМЯТЬ 300 - ЛѢТІЯ ЦАРСТВОВАНІЯ ДОМА РОМАНОВЫХЪ 1613-1913* ('In memory of the 300-year rule of the House of Romanov 1613–1913'). The ribbon of the medal used the Romanov dynastic colours of black, yellow and white, which had formed the colours of the national flag from 1858 to 1896. The medal was distributed widely and this example appears to have been sent to King George V, although it was never mounted.

The tercentenary celebrations across Russia, starting in St Petersburg in February 1913 and concluding in Moscow in May, included a tour by the imperial family down the Volga, taking in a visit to the Ipatiev Monastery, Kostroma, where Mikhail Romanov was offered the crown of Muscovy. The celebrations generated a broad market for commemorative materials, and, in particular, saw a return to early seventeenth-century designs, reflected in the medal design and a wide range of associated works. SJP

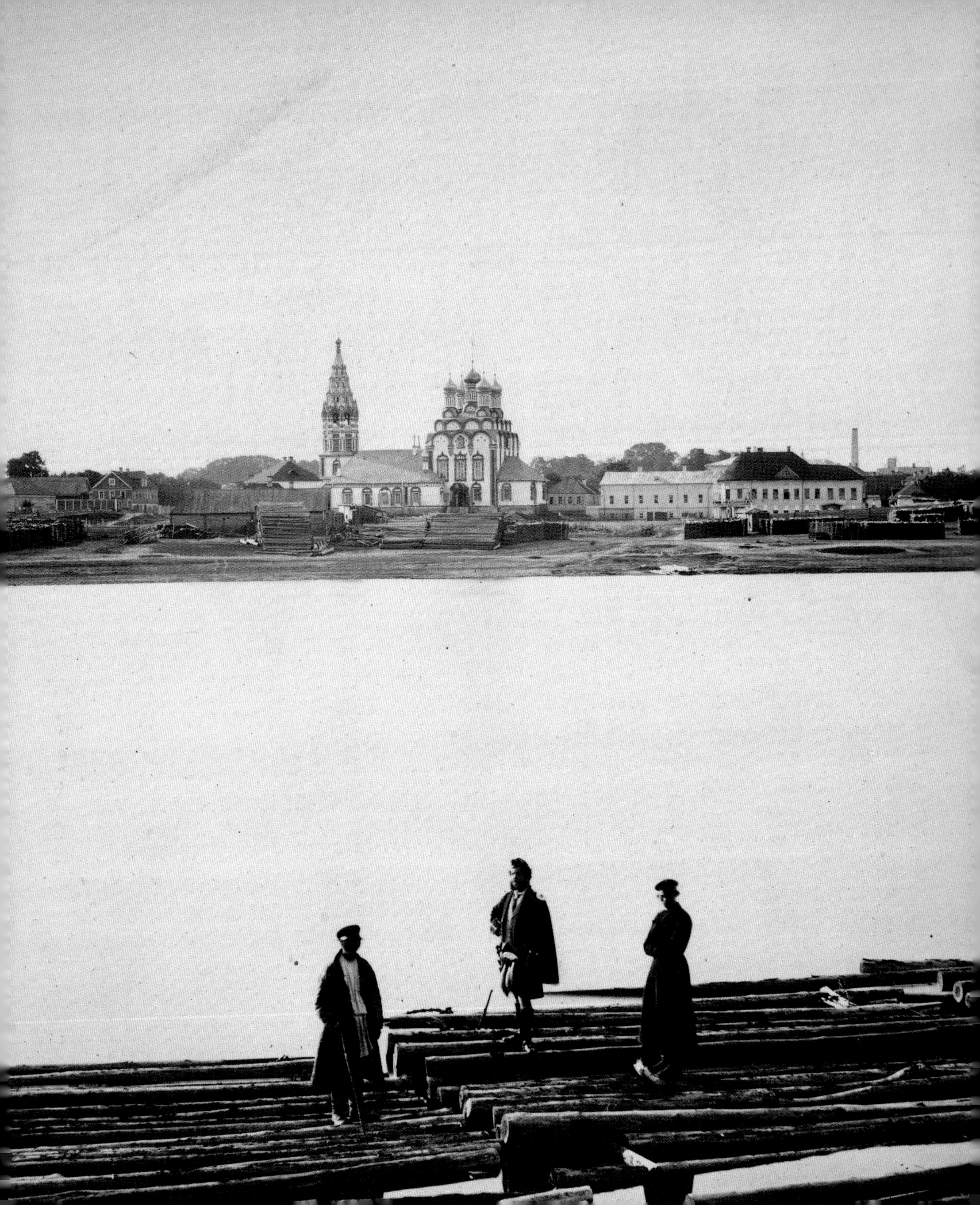

9

Russian Photography and Photographs of Russia in the Royal Collection

ALESSANDRO NASINI

In Russia, as in many other countries, scientists had been experimenting with photosensitive chemicals for decades prior to the announcement of Daguerre's invention at the Académie des Sciences in Paris on 7 January 1839. As soon as news of the daguerreotype process reached Russia, the Academy of Sciences of St Petersburg immediately asked one of its members, Josef Hamel (1788–1862), who was travelling in Europe at the time, to gather information about the new medium, and to send specimens, equipment and instructions to his colleagues at the Academy.[1] As in the rest of the world, the interest in photography grew quickly, soon progressing beyond the scientific community and entering the territory of commercial enterprise. As early as May 1840, the Moscow engraver and inventor, Alexei Grekov (1799–*c.*1855), started offering his services as daguerreotypist, as well as supplier of photographic equipment of his own manufacture.[2] One of Grekov's customers was Sergei Levitsky, who would later become one of the first and most important Russian photographers (cats 154, 160, 200). While Levitsky travelled to Europe in the 1840s to study chemistry and improve his photographic skills, fraternising with Daguerre, Niépce and Kilburn (1818–91), among others, many European photographers in the 1840s and 1850s chose to set up their studios in Russia, a market eager to explore this new sensational trend. Ivan Bianchi (1811–93) (cat. 214) and Charles Bergamasco (cats 152–153), for example, settled in St Petersburg, where, despite the astonishingly high concentration of professional studios, they succeeded in establishing thriving businesses.[3] International exhibitions, royal appointments or just simple word of mouth were invaluable ways to help their fame travel beyond Russian borders. In a letter to Theodore Martin (1816–1909), dated 29 December 1873, Queen Victoria wrote: 'The Queen has told P.ce Alfred what Mr Hills [possibly Robert Hills of the established photographic firm Hills & Saunders] says and has asked him to be photographed by Bergamasco at St. Petersburg'.[4] Prince Alfred would indeed be photographed by Bergamasco in 1874, and so would the Prince and Princess of Wales, and Prince Arthur. Bergamasco is probably the best-represented Russian portrait photographer in the Royal Collection, with over 300 photographs, followed by Levitsky (almost 200 photographs) and Pasetti (around 100 photographs).

Graduating from the prestigious Imperial Academy of Arts, St Petersburg was often a valuable first step in gaining a successful career as an artist or photographer, and such was the case for Andrei Denier (cats 111–112), Andrei Karelin (1837–1906) and the Edinburgh-born William Carrick (cats 223–224).[5] After a two-decades-long debate about the role of photography within the arts, similar in Russia to what had been discussed in Europe, at the end of the 1850s, the editor of *Svetopis*, the first journal exclusively dedicated to the new medium, stated that 'Photography combines in

Detail of cat. 220

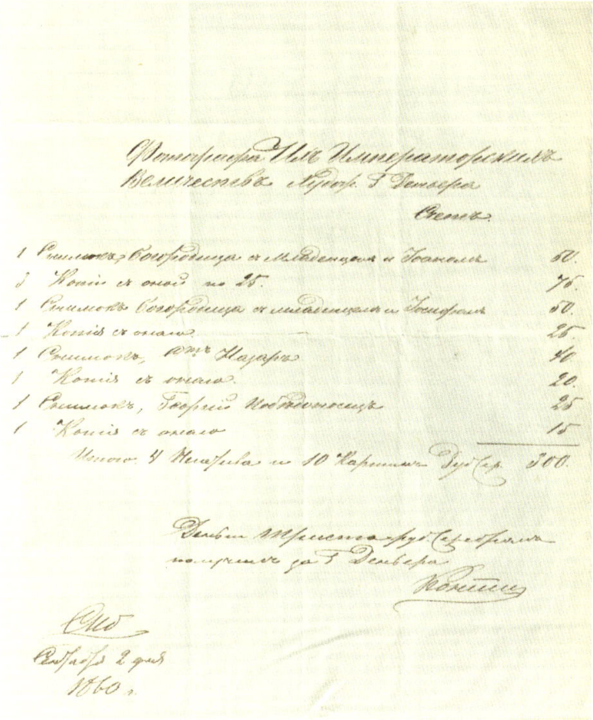

FIG. 66
Andrei Denier
Invoice, 2 July 1860
26.5 × 21.0 cm
RA VIC/ADDA10/85/558

its techniques and the objectives it seeks, the qualities of science, handicraft, and art'.[6]

As well as an art form in its own right, though, photography intrinsically also possesses the ability to record, reproduce and disseminate other forms of art. In 1854, Emperor Nicholas I instructed the director of the Hermitage, Fyodor Bruni (1799–1875), to have watercolours of the recently completed new museum building photographed.[7] Bianchi was entrusted by Bruni with the task and, between 1855 and 1857, he photographed at least 100 watercolours. A similar commission, eventually assigned to Denier in 1859, stemmed from the request of Prince Albert to obtain photographs of works in the Russian imperial collection, believed, at the time, to be by Raphael.[8] The Royal Archives hold the correspondence, initiated on 28 January 1857, between Prince Albert's Librarians, Dr Ernst Becker (1826–88) and Charles Ruland (1834–1907), and British representatives at St Petersburg, Sir John Crampton (1805–86) and the Hon. Edward Erskine (1817–83), relating to the commission of such photographs. This includes two invoices from Denier: the first listing four glass plate negatives and four corresponding prints, for a total of 300 rubles (fig. 66), and a second listing two further glass plate negatives and two corresponding prints, for a total of 100 rubles.[9] The total cost of 400 rubles (equivalent to around £6,600 today) was questioned at the time, and in a letter to Ruland, dated 5 September 1860, Erskine writes: 'I again remonstrated with M. Denier about his prices & he appeared to be most sincerely sorry that His Royal Highness should deem them exorbitant. But he assured me that he could not possibly undertake the job for less. He receives 100 Roubles for every Photographic likeness he makes & he declares that these copies of pictures are far more troublesome & take more time than portraits as he has to go out & take his Instruments with him. In short he says a day is lost every time he goes to the Gallery'.[10] By early October 1860, Prince Albert's librarian had received the six glass plate negatives and corresponding prints, and the considerable sum paid can be seen as a reflection of both the difficulty of the task and Denier's high reputation. In June 1861, as a sign of gratitude for the permission to reproduce the works, Prince Albert presented Alexander II with an album of photographs of drawings by Raphael in the Royal Collection.[11]

The relationship between photography and painting grew closer during the 1860s and 1870s, when a group of young artists, willing to break with the tradition of classicism and the formal education taught at the Academy, started painting everyday scenes in a realistic style, leaving the cities and wandering the vast land of 'Mother Russia' in search of subjects, hence acquiring the name *Peredvizhniki* ('Itinerants'). The work of photographers such as William Carrick (cats 223–224), Ivan Raoult (active 1870–84) and Maxim Dmitriev (1858–1948), as well as that of more ethnographically oriented Dmitry Nikitin (active 1870s–1900s), or the hand-painted photographs by Mikhail Bukar (active 1860s–70s), would be used as inspiration, and sometimes as a direct source, by realist artists and vice versa.[12] The Royal Collection holds two portfolios of photographs by Ivan Dyagovchenko (1835–87): one containing 21 views of the Moscow Kremlin (cat. 213), the other, 31 photographic reproductions of paintings shown at the Polytechnic Exhibition in Moscow in 1872.[13] Ivan Boldyrev (1850–after 1917) was another photographer admired by the artistic community, especially for his work in his native Don region. His remarkable talent as inventor and innovator included pioneering the use of lenses with exceptional depth of field able to produce results even under poor lighting conditions (cats 215–216) and flexible transparent film negative pre-dating any similar innovation.[14] Unfortunately he never found support from the formal Russian Technical Society, whose Fifth Section had been established in 1878 specifically to include photography and its applications. Often keen in praising new foreign technological innovations, the Fifth Section consistently ignored the insightful photographic inventions and pioneering ideas developed by Boldyrev, making him, perhaps, the most distinguished unsung hero in the history of photography in Russia. This attitude was supported by the fact that the vast majority of photographic materials had been imported to the country since the 1840s, reinforcing a trend which would continue up to the outbreak of the First World War.[15]

Due to its common perception as a 'truthful' medium, photography was considered by many a critical tool to record faraway places and events of major importance. Roger Fenton's photographs taken in the Crimea in 1855, despite being a commercial enterprise, represent one of the very first attempts to document a conflict (Fig. 68).[16] Events connected with the Russian-Turkish war of 1877–8 were recorded by various Russian photographers, including Alexander Dmitrievich Ivanov (active 1870s) and Dmitry Nikitin, and by the time war broke out between Russia and Japan in 1904, Viktor Bulla (1883–1938) was able to document the conflict in a recognisable photo-journalistic style.[17]

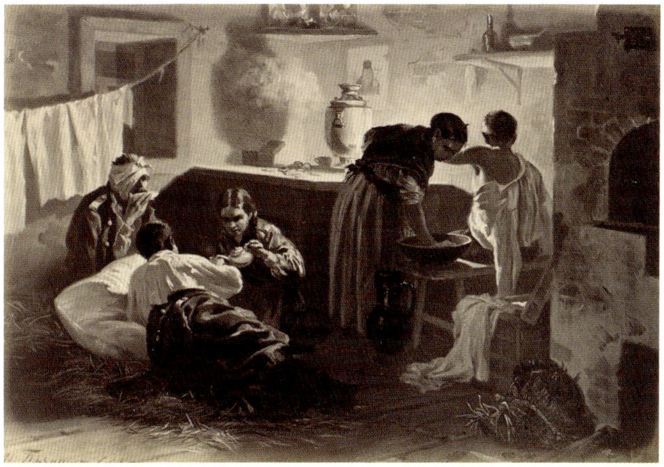

FIG. 67
Ivan Dyagovchenko
after I.M. Pryanishnikov
Episodes of Sevastopol Life, 1854–5: Care for the Wounded by Women in Sebastopol, 1872
Albumen print, 22.0 × 32.9 cm
RCIN 2500606

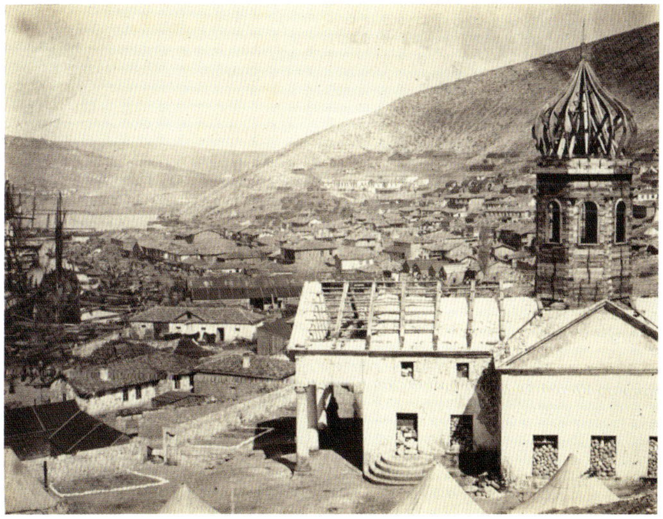

FIG. 68
Roger Fenton
Balaklava from above the Russian Church, March 1855
Salted paper print, 26.9 × 35.2 cm
RCIN 2500487

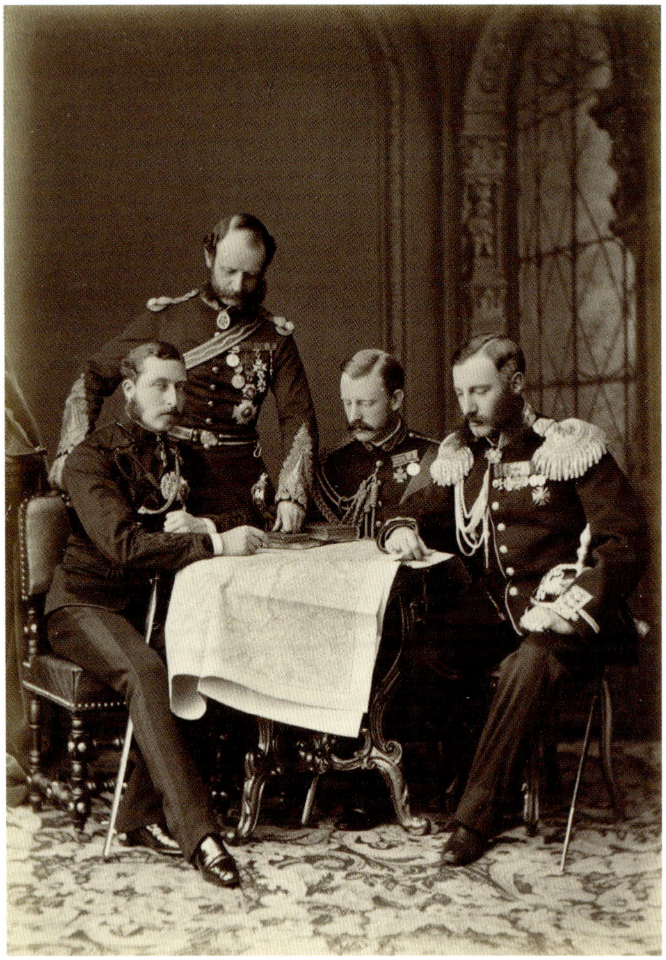

FIG. 69
Charles Bergamasco (1830–96)
Prince Arthur, Sir Howard Elphinstone, Major Piccard and Prince Orloff, 29 January 1874
Albumen print, 13.5 × 9.6 cm
RCIN 2902719

The desire to record and document distant places was behind the decision to include a photographer in the diplomatic mission representing Queen Victoria at the coronation of Alexander II in 1856. James Mack's (1827–64) photographs taken in Russia, presented to the Queen on the mission's return to Britain (cats 217–222), closed the geographical gap between the two countries and let Queen Victoria see, thanks to the 'truthful' eye of the camera, what the diplomatic mission had seen. Similarly, Queen Victoria was able to use photography to bring people virtually closer to her. Being an enthusiastic collector of photographic portraits, she would not miss opportunities to acquire items for her ever-expanding collection.[18] In a letter to the Queen from the Winter Palace, dated 28 January 1874, Sir Howard Elphinstone writes:

> *in accordance with the message received through Lady Ely, he [Elphinstone] sends herewith some photographs of the Imperial Family, and of other distinguished people here. He does not include any of the Czar or Czarevitch etc, in accordance with the message received. He will endeavour to obtain some others on the first opportunity. Prince Arthur was photographed today by Bergamasco, & the result has been satisfactory.*[19] (fig. 69)

Prince Arthur was in St Petersburg in 1874, together with other members of his family, to attend the marriage of his brother, Prince Alfred, Duke of Edinburgh, to Grand Duchess Maria Alexandrovna of Russia. Queen Victoria did not attend the ceremony, but received the wedded couple in Windsor on 7 March and recorded the event in her Journal: 'Marie [...] is very like her photographs'.[20]

By the end of the 1880s, with the advent of the first cameras aimed at the amateur market, photography started entering a new territory: the snapshot. These portable and easy-to-operate cameras soon became objects of interest to some members of the royal family, who started taking photographs and subsequently arranging them in albums. The Princess of Wales (cat. 127) had been one of the first in the family to acquire a box camera, closely followed by her brother-in-law, Prince Arthur (cats 254, 256) and her daughter, Princess Victoria (cat. 128). Their albums offer a glimpse of what had never been recorded before, and from a completely unique perspective. Members of the Russian imperial family would also start taking snapshots from 1896, arranging them in albums in a very similar manner. This soon became one of Nicholas II's favourite soothing activities: 'Fussed with some photographs, singling them out for gluing into the big album', he wrote in his diary on 29 October 1896, and, in the entry for 12 December 1913, 'After breakfast many people pestered me with intolerable questions which vexed and annoyed me! Had a good walk in between the showers. Glued photographs into the album'.[21]

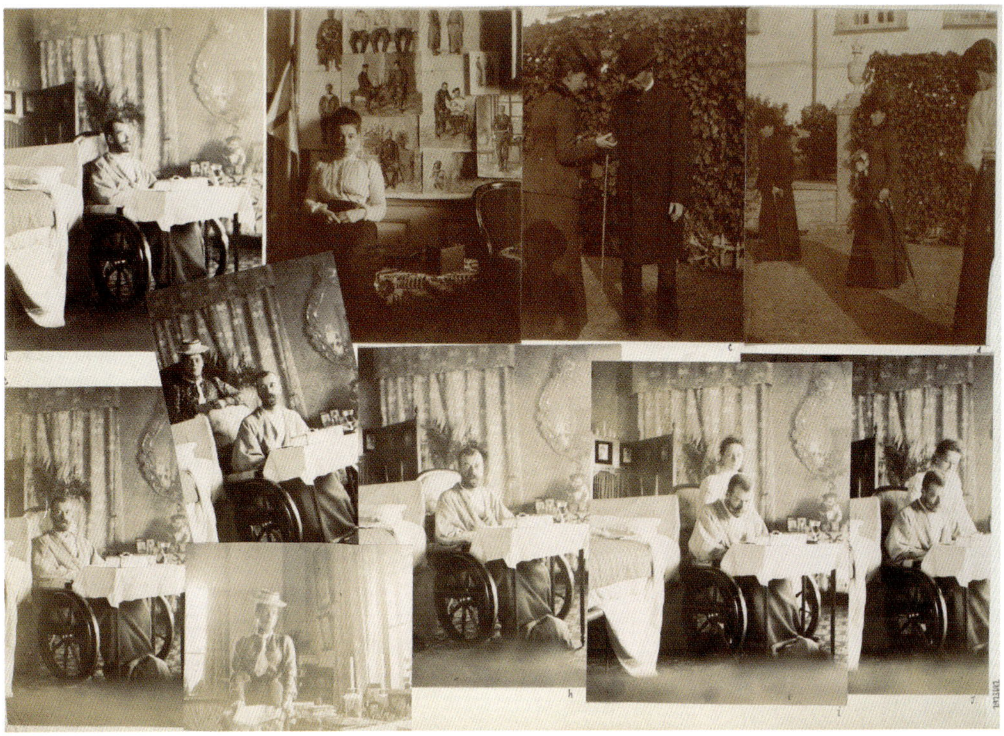

FIG. 70
Page from an album compiled by Princess Victoria 1900–1
Gelatin silver prints; album page 25.5 × 36.0 cm
RCIN 2923682

Members of the British and Russian royal families would also often exchange photographs, both snapshots and formal portraits, in correspondence (cat. 274). It is likely that Princess Victoria, for example, received from Empress Alexandra Feodorovna a series of intimate snapshots, showing the Emperor in a wheelchair while recovering from typhoid fever in Crimea in 1900 (fig. 70).

Informal snapshots, including those taken at Reval in 1908 by both families, and the hundreds taken by members of the Russian imperial family, would remain strictly private. What had survived the October Revolution and the Russian Civil War would not be seen by the people of Russia until relatively recent times, following the dissolution of the Soviet Union in 1991. The First World War and the series of events stemming from the October Revolution also inevitably affected the history of photography of the country. Pictorialism, which had become the prevalent aesthetic movement in photography between the 1890s and the first decades of the twentieth century, represented by figures such as Alexei Mazurin (1846–after 1915), Sergei Lobovikov (1870–1941) and Nikolai Svishchev-Paola (1874–1964), would eventually be superseded by the utterly modern and radical avant-garde movement. The works, for example, of Aleksandr Rodchenko (1891–1956), El Lissitsky (1890–1941) and Boris Ignatovich (1899–1976) represented a clear break with tradition and inaugurated a brand new and exciting chapter in the history of photography in Russia.[22]

IVAN DYAGOVCHENKO (1835–1887)

213 *St George's Hall, Grand Kremlin Palace, Moscow* 1873

Albumen print, 37.8 × 33.9 cm
Title and photographer's credentials printed on mount
RCIN 2103403

Provenance Possibly acquired by the Prince and Princess of Wales, during their visit to Russia on the occasion of the marriage of Prince Alfred, Duke of Edinburgh and Grand Duchess Maria Alexandrovna, 1874

Literature Dimond 2004, pp. 46–7

The Grand Kremlin Palace, replacing a previous baroque palace designed by Rastrelli (1700–1), was built between 1837 and 1849, under the supervision of Russian architect Konstantin Ton (1794–1881). It contains five large reception rooms named after the Orders of the Russian Empire, with St George's Hall being the largest. The palace played an important role during the celebrations connected with the coronation of Alexander II in 1856, as recorded in contemporary accounts. Lieutenant Colonel G.A. Maude (1817–94), a military attaché with the British diplomatic mission, described the Emperor's state ball on the evening of the coronation:

> *the candles in each chandelier are connected by a piece of cotton dipped in some composition, and the end of the cotton hangs down to about the height of a man [...] At the signal to light, the little hanging down ends are all touched with taper and away runs the flame from candle to candle in the prettiest manner possible [...] In this way the whole of St. George's Hall, which had 2,300 candles in it, was lit up in 7 minutes.*[23]

The exact same system is captured by Dyagovchenko in this photograph, which is part of a set of 21 views of the Kremlin Palace complex, presented in a lavish portfolio, with gold-embossed purple velvet covers and ivory moiré-silk inner flaps. Winner of the gold medal at the Polytechnic Exhibition in Moscow in 1872, for his 'photographic views', Dyagovchenko was soon after appointed photographer to the Tsesarevich Alexander Alexandrovich (as proudly shown on his credentials printed on the mount), and became one of the leading photographers in Moscow.[24] **AN**

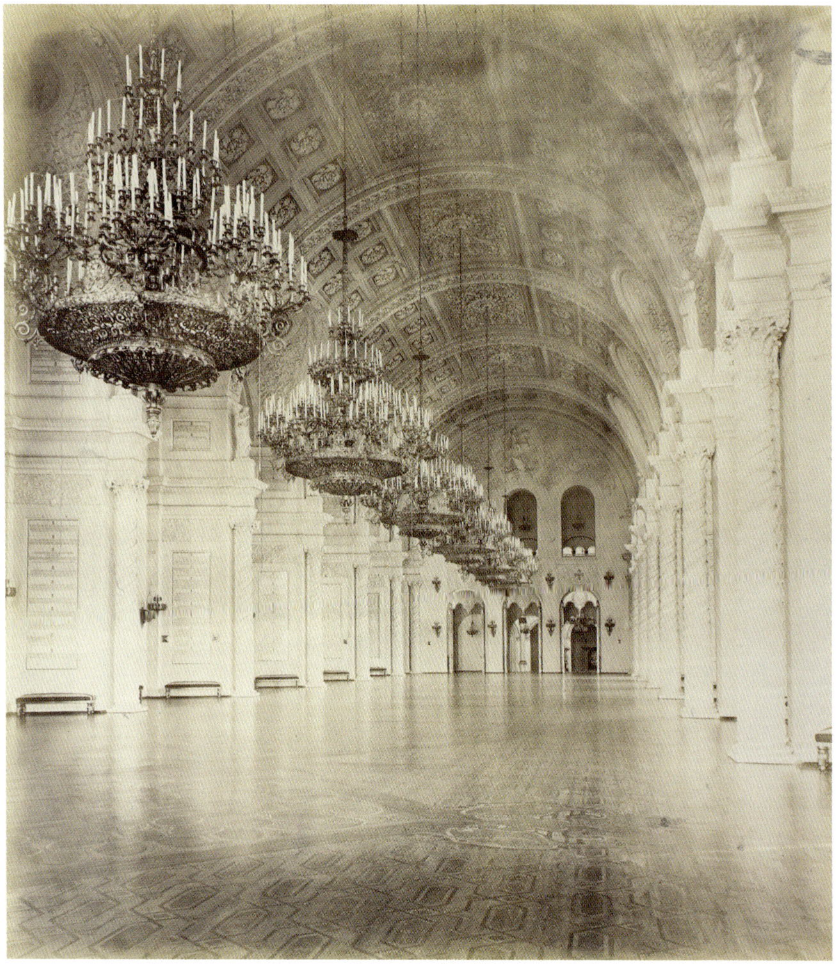

IVAN BIANCHI (1811–1893)

214 *Hermitage, St Petersburg* 1867

Albumen print laid on card, 35.2 × 28.7 cm, (sheet) 51.5 × 37.8 cm
Inscribed on mount: *Hermitage, St. Petersburg*
RCIN 2700763

Provenance Acquired by the Prince of Wales, following his visit to Russia on the occasion of the marriage of Tsesarevich Alexander Alexandrovich and Princess Dagmar of Denmark, 1866

The photograph is from a series of nine views, showing the suite of rooms provided to the Prince of Wales, later King Edward VII, during his visit to St Petersburg on the occasion of the marriage of his sister-in-law to the Tsesarevich, later Alexander III. This was the Prince of Wales's first visit to Russia, and a member of his suite, Arthur Ellis, an officer who had fought in the Crimean War, was given the task of keeping a journal. On the day of their arrival in St Petersburg, Ellis wrote: 'H.R.H. is lodged in the "Hermitage Palace", -a magnificent suite of 12 rooms,- filled with pictures by best masters, & beautifully decorated & most comfortable' (cat. 163).[25]

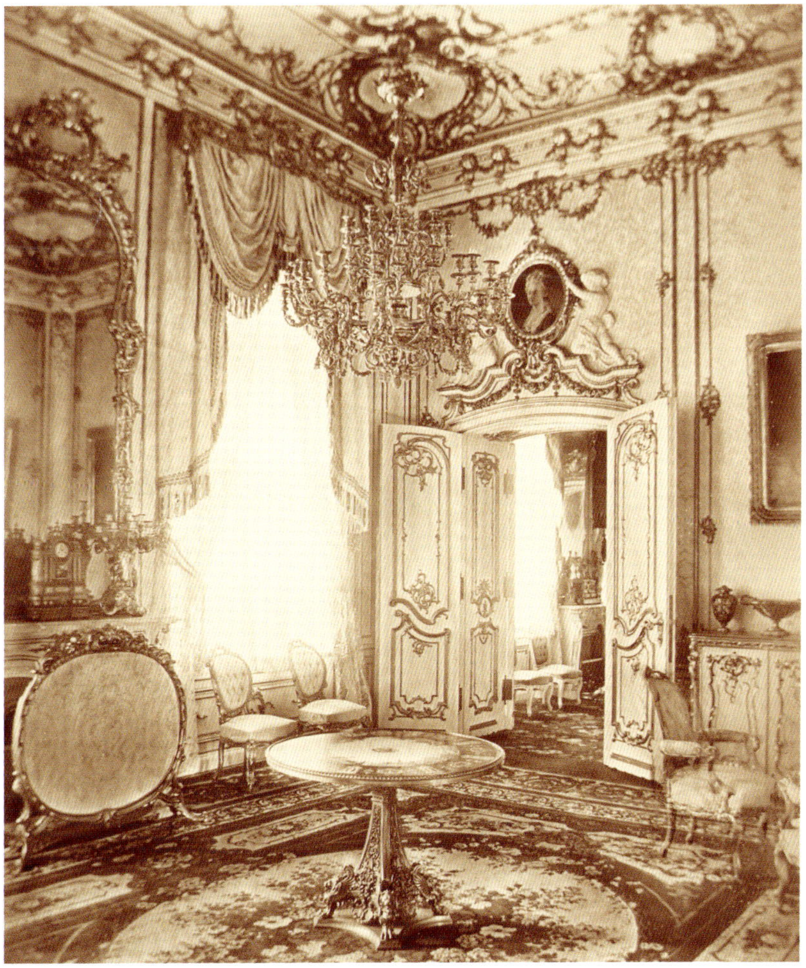

The rooms, perhaps at the Prince of Wales's request, were photographed by Ivan Bianchi the following year. In a letter dated 14 October 1867, to Count Vladimir Fedorovich Adlerberg, minister of the imperial court, the photographer writes (in French): 'I have completed the photographs of the apartments occupied by His Highness the Prince of Wales for the execution of which Your Excellency had been so kind to entrust me', and asks whether he could be accorded the title 'photographer of the Imperial Hermitage'.[26] The letter is signed, 'the very humble servant artist of the Imperial Academy and photographer Jean Bianchi. Resident, Nevskii Prospekt 54'. His request was not granted, despite the fact that, by this stage, Bianchi was one of the leading photographers in St Petersburg, whose studio occupied a prominent position on Ostrovsky Square, opposite the Imperial Public Library.[27] **AN**

IVAN VASILYEVICH BOLDYREV (1850–after 1917)

215 & 216

Fountains and the Grand Palace during night illuminations, Peterhof 1893

Gelatin silver print, 16.3 × 22.4 cm
RCIN 2103424

Cascade, illuminated fountains, triumphal arch and fireworks, Peterhof 1893

Gelatin silver print, 16.4 × 23.5 cm
RCIN 2103422

Provenance Presumably presented to Queen Alexandra, when Princess of Wales

Situated on the Gulf of Finland, almost equidistant between St Petersburg and Kronstadt (the city seaport on Kotlin Island), Peterhof consists of a collection of palaces, pavilions, chapels, fountains and formal gardens, spread across a vast parkland area originally established by Peter the Great, and subsequently developed by his successors. The site, however, especially its Lower Park, was occasionally decorated with spectacular illuminations, and was opened to the public to celebrate particular events and anniversaries, as shown in these photographs, which are part of a larger set capturing the celebrations of the tenth anniversary of the coronation of Alexander III, held at Peterhof.[28] The dates 1883–1893 can be seen on the decorations placed at the end of the Sea Channel, and bear testimony to the impressive technical skills of this pioneering Russian photographer. A self-taught amateur photographer from the Don region, in the early 1870s Boldyrev started modifying lenses to obtain a greater depth of field, and progressively developed a series of groundbreaking photographic innovations. Despite encouragement from figures such as Vladimir Stasov (1824–1906) for his artistic sensibility, and Dimitri Mendeleev (1834–1907) for his inventive talent, he unfortunately never received much appreciation or support from the Photographic Society.[29]

While many of the buildings at Peterhof were used by the Romanovs as private summer residences, the Grand Palace, seen here, has been connected with official celebrations and diplomatic relations since its grand opening on 13–14 August 1723. The occasion was recorded in a courtier's journal:

> *Immediately after our arrival we weighed anchor and sailed into the beautiful great canal which leads up to the centre of the residence* […] *As soon as we had disembarked, the Emperor showed T*[*heir*] *H*[*ighnesses*] *and all the other distinguished guests around both the garden and the houses. This place has grown immensely in the last two years; the fountains in particular are very beautiful, and have an abundant supply of water.*[30]

Peterhof, often called 'the Russian Versailles', continued to be used by the Romanovs making an impression on foreign visitors and diplomatic missions, as in 1856, when Lord Granville and his suite were invited to Peterhof to be presented to the new Emperor and Empress.[31]

These photographs by Boldyrev, therefore, record not only the anniversary of Alexander III's coronation, but also, incidentally, Peterhof's 170th anniversary. Moreover, it is possible that these photographs were among those displayed by Boldyrev at the fifth exhibition of the Photographic Society in 1898, when he was awarded an honourable mention for photographs made in artificial light and night photography of illuminations.[32] AN

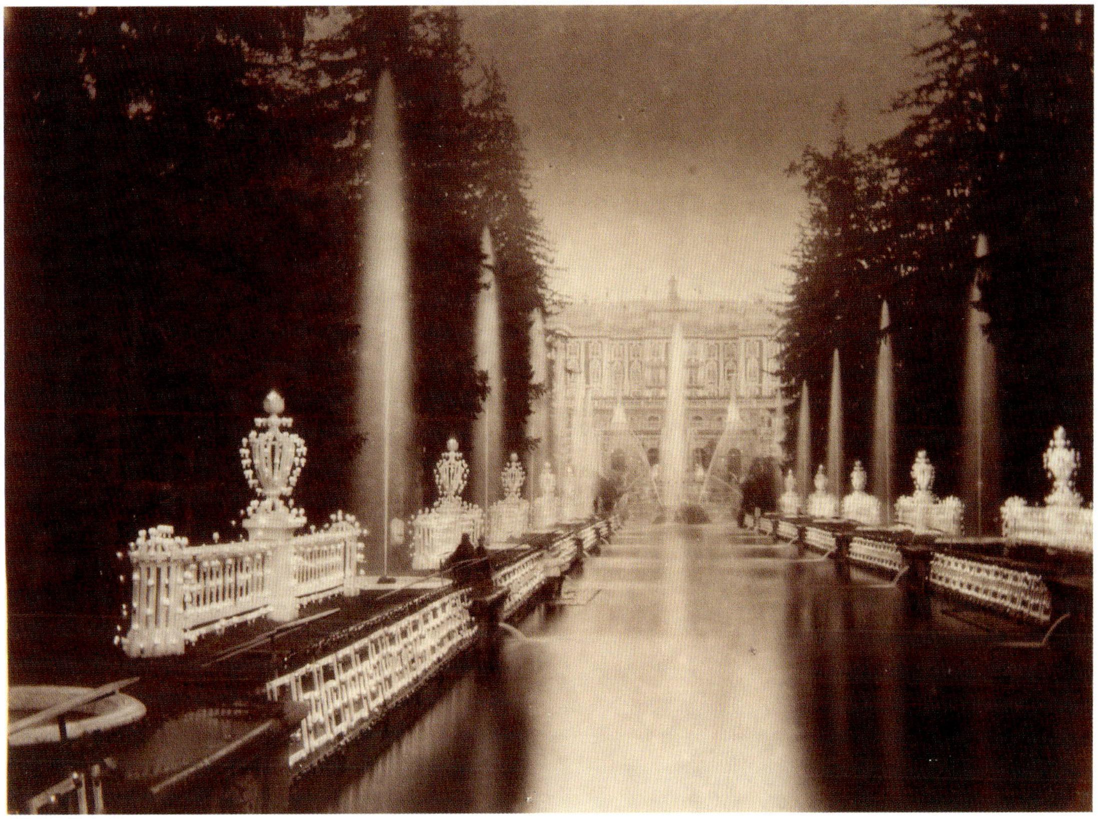

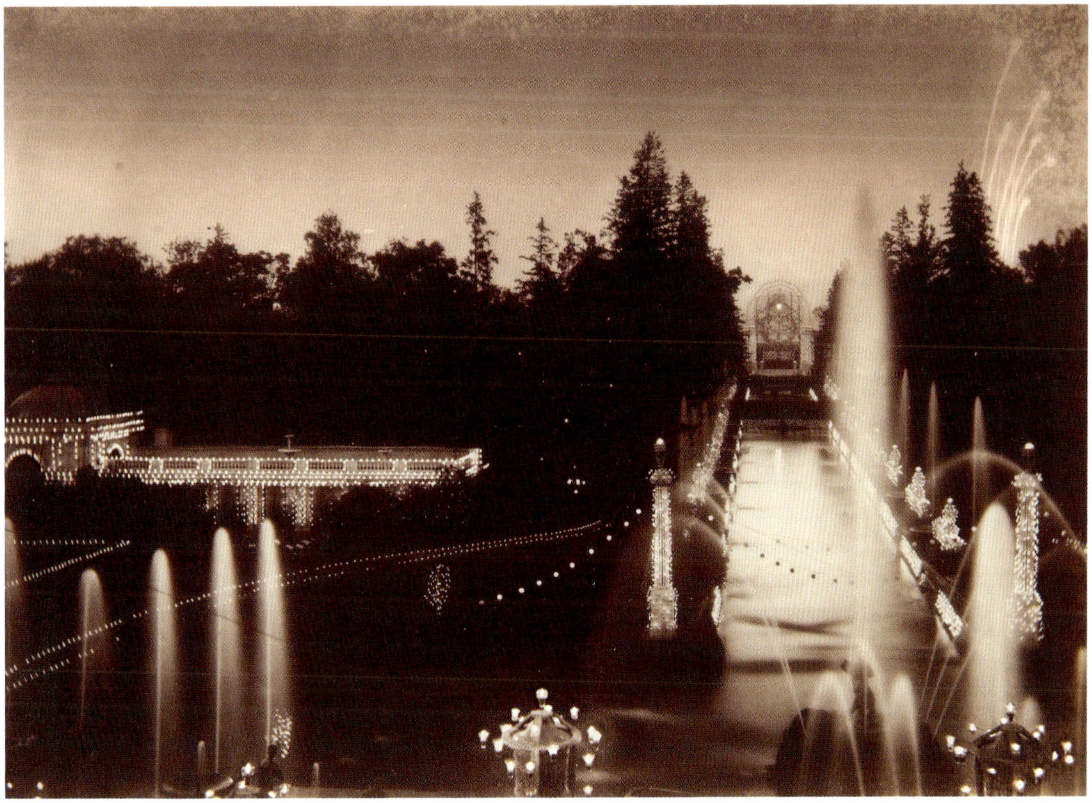

217–222

JAMES MACK (1827–1864)

Provenance Presented to Queen Victoria

As the Treaty of Paris, formally ending the Crimean War, had only been signed on 30 March 1856, the coronation of Alexander II, planned for September of the same year, was regarded as a diplomatic event of critical importance. It was therefore decided that, together with the appointment of Lord Wodehouse (1826–1902) as envoy-extraordinary to Russia, a special diplomatic mission, representing Queen Victoria, should also be sent to attend the ceremony, and Lord Granville was chosen as its head. 'Corporal Mack (photographer) accompanied us', records Granville in his journal.[33]

Born in Ireland, James Mack was serving as lance corporal in the Royal Sappers and Miners by 1851, when he was selected to be employed as surveyor and draughtsman at the Great Exhibition of the Industry of all Nations.[34] This also gave him the opportunity to meet Charles Thurston Thompson (1816–68), the man in charge of photographic arrangements at the exhibition.[35] In 1852, he was chosen to assist with arrangements for the display at Marlborough House of items acquired by the Royal Society of Arts.[36] In 1853, Henry Cole (1808–82) appointed Thompson de facto official photographer of the Department of Science and Art and, later, of the South Kensington Museum, a position confirmed in 1859.[37] Mack's involvement with photography, if not already at the Great Exhibition, is likely to have started at the South Kensington Museum, where Cole, its first Director, had been granted the presence of a detachment of sappers to help with various tasks, including assisting with photography.[38] Mack was also chosen to accompany Cole at the Exposition Universelle in Paris in 1855,[39] and, on their return to Britain in January 1856, 'the Board of Trade honoured the whole party with presents [...] Mack [received] an expensive photographic apparatus'.[40] Mack's role was to document the various places, monuments and anything of interest visited by the party during their stay in Russia.[41] In a letter dated 4 November 1856, Lord Panmure (1801–74), Secretary of State for War, writes to Queen Victoria, informing her that he 'has the honour to acquaint Your Majesty that the photographs taken by Corporal Mack of the Royal Engineers, while in attendance on Lord Granville, are now awaiting Your Majesty's pleasure, and Lord Panmure will despatch Corporal Mack to attend Your Majesty as soon as he learns the time which may be most convenient to Your Majesty. The photographs are intended as additions to Your Majesty's collection'.[42] The Queen, replying to Panmure three days later, writes: 'The photographs from Moscow will interest the Queen very much. She will be ready to receive them any day about two o'clock, if Lord Panmure will despatch the Corporal who made them with them'.[43] Mack eventually presented the photographs to the Queen on 11 November 1856, an event recorded in her Journal: 'We looked at some very pretty photographs, done during Ld Granville's stay at St. Petersburg, by a Corporal Mac [*sic*], of the Engineers, who brought the photographs & explained them. He is a remarkably intelligent, well educated young man'.[44] Both the rarity of the subjects and the excellent technical qualities of the photographs were perhaps behind Prince Albert's decision to display them, in December 1856, at the first exhibition organised in Edinburgh by the Photographic Society of Scotland.[45]

Following his return from Russia in October 1856, and the exhibition of his photographs by Prince Albert in Edinburgh, Mack was promoted to the rank of sergeant in February 1857. His association with the South Kensington Museum, however, where he eventually became sergeant superintendent of the photographic printing establishment, continued until his death in 1864.[46]

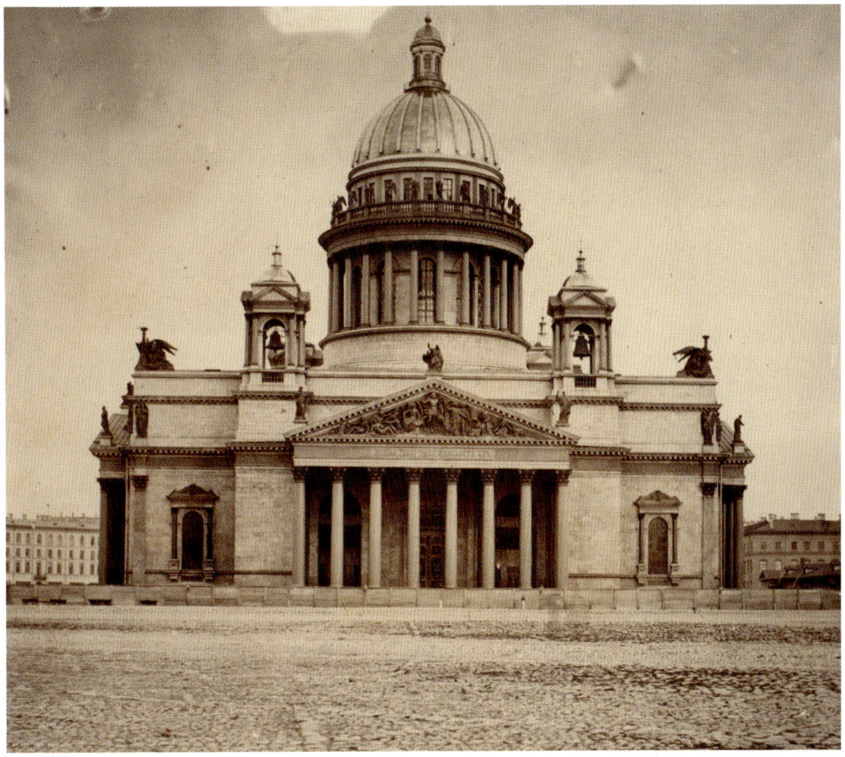

217 ***St Isaac's Cathedral, St Petersburg*** August 1856

Albumen print, 19.6 × 22.7 cm
Inscribed below photograph: *S.t Isaac's C.h S.t Petersburg. – Photographed by J. Mack. Corp.l R.E. Sept. 1856*
RCIN 2945144

St Isaac's Cathedral, originally commissioned by Alexander I in 1818, was only completed 40 years later, under Alexander II; it is seen here as a building site, with wooden fencing all around its perimeter. It is dedicated to Saint Isaac of Dalmatia, patron saint of Peter the Great, whose famous bronze equestrian sculpture, commissioned by Catherine the Great, is only a couple of hundred metres away, not too distant from where Mack placed his camera to take this photograph.

The cathedral was designed by French-born architect Auguste de Montferrand (1786–1858), and replaced an earlier structure, also dedicated to St Isaac. The exterior of this imposing, yet elegant, building is decorated by over 100 granite columns and numerous bronze statues by Ivan Vitali (1794–1855), including the four large angels on the corners of the main structure holding torches, which would be lit with gas to illuminate the city at Easter. The pediment on the north side of the cathedral, seen here, shows a depiction of the Resurrection of Christ, modelled by Philippe Lemaire (1798–1880) in 1842–4. Among de Montferrand's other works were the Alexander Column outside the Winter Palace and the monument of Nicholas I. The architect was also responsible for the completion and developments of the Kazan Cathedral, and the Nizhny Novgorod fair (visited, at the time of the coronation, by members of Granville's suite). **AN**

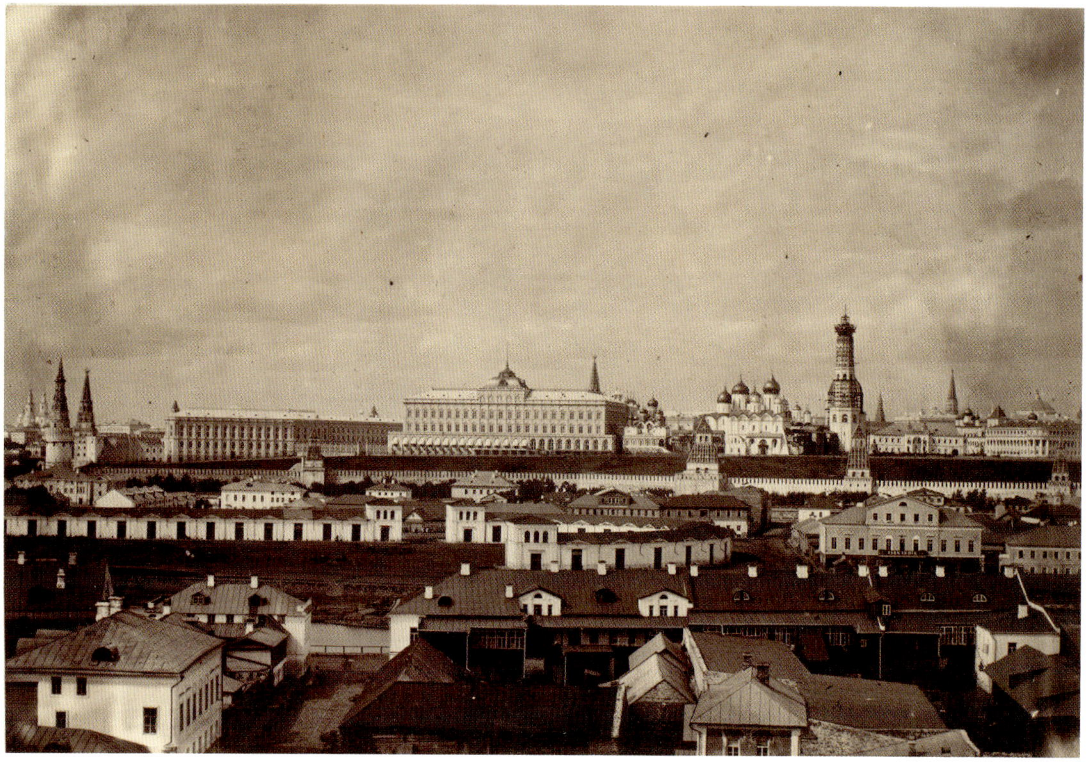

218 *The Kremlin, Moscow* September 1856

Albumen print, 19.2 × 28.4 cm
Inscribed below photograph: *The Kremlin, Moscow. – Photographed by J. Mack. Corp.l R.E. Sept 1856*
RCIN 2945147

It is likely that this photograph was taken from the bell tower of a church, possibly that of St Nicholas in Tolmachi, or the even taller one of the Church of the Resurrection of Christ in Kadashi, and it is testimony of Mack's advanced technical skills. Successful cityscapes of this kind, especially in Russia, are rare for the time.[47]

Looking from left to right, the photograph shows the Borovitsky Gate and the Armoury Palace, the Grand Palace and Cathedral Square, with the Cathedral of the Annunciation, the Dormition Cathedral, the Archangel Cathedral and the Ivan the Great bell tower; the domes of other Kremlin churches can also be seen. The Kremlin towers in the foreground and the Ivan Veliki tower are decorated with wooden structures that were to be used for the lighting up of the Kremlin as part of the evening celebrations of the coronation. To the right of the great tower, in the background, the Chudov Monastery (demolished in 1929) and the Nicholas Palace (birthplace of Alexander II) can also be seen.

The Grand Kremlin Palace was the work of Konstantin Ton, built between 1837 and 1849. The Russian architect visited Queen Victoria and Prince Albert at Windsor Castle on 31 December 1844, an event recorded by the Queen in her Journal: 'Later, I sat to Winterhalter & then we saw M. Thon, the Emperor of Russia's architect, who showed us some fine plans, for the Palace he is going to build for the Emperor at Moscow. He also showed us some plans of Churches.'[48] **AN**

219 *St Basil's Cathedral, Moscow* September 1856

Albumen print, 19.6 × 22.7 cm
Inscribed below photograph: *Cathedral of S.t Basil, Moscow. – Photographed by J. Mack. Corp.l R.E. Sept. 1856*
RCIN 2945148

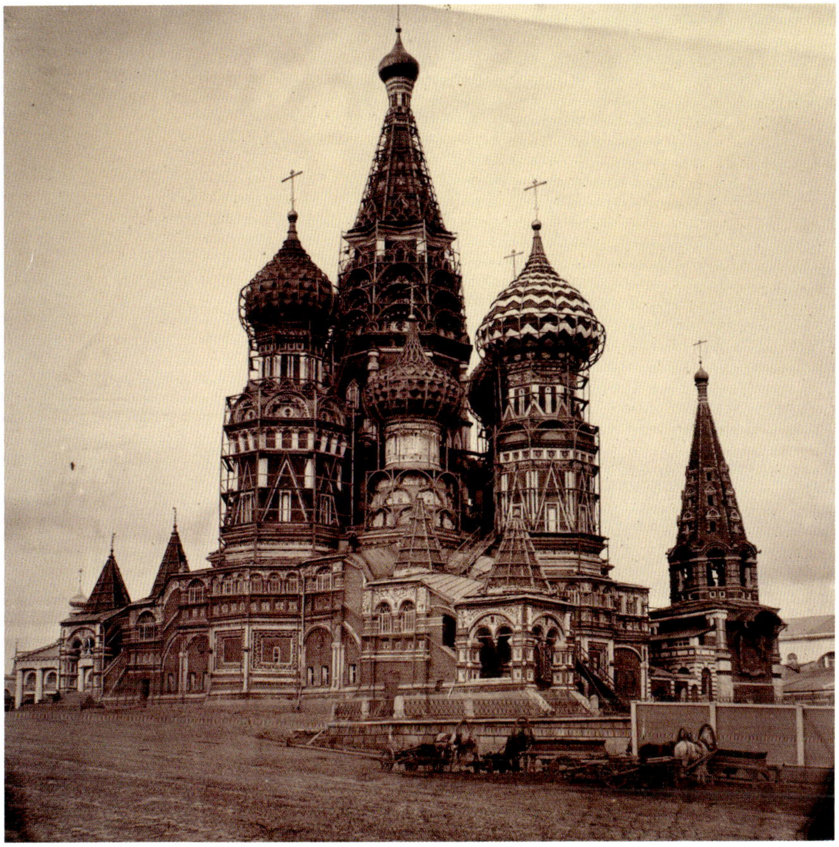

This photograph of St Basil's Cathedral clearly shows the complex and splendid system of illumination arranged for the coronation, as witnessed by visitors to the city, including Lieutenant Colonel Maude, who describes it in a letter:

> *we went out to see the illuminations, which they certainly manage to do much better in this country than we do. Every dome and every minaret was lighted up in the most beautiful manner and instead of putting a great patch of light, like we do, on one part of the house, they light up all the architecture, every door and window and pillar and column showing its outline in glittering lights. They have no gas, but glass pots full of tallow with a wick in them.*[49]

The original building, known as Trinity Church, was designed by Postnik Yakovlev (active 1550–62) and Ivan Barma (active 1554–61) for Ivan IV (the Terrible; 1530–84) in 1554, to commemorate the conquest of Kazan by Muscovite forces. Built between 1555 and 1561 at one end of Red Square, it consists of a series of chapels around a central church, encompassing a blend of oriental and traditional Russian styles. It became known as St Basil's Cathedral following the interment of the body of a venerated local saint, Vasily Blazhenny (Basil the Blessed; 1468–1557), on the site in 1557. The building saw a series of alterations and restorations across the centuries, including those following Napoleon's occupation of Moscow in 1812, completed in 1848. In this view of the cathedral from the south, the arcade of the Trade Rows, designed by Osip Ivanovich Bove (1784–1834) to replace the trading area built for Catherine II on a design by Quarenghi, can partially be seen in the background on the left. **AN**

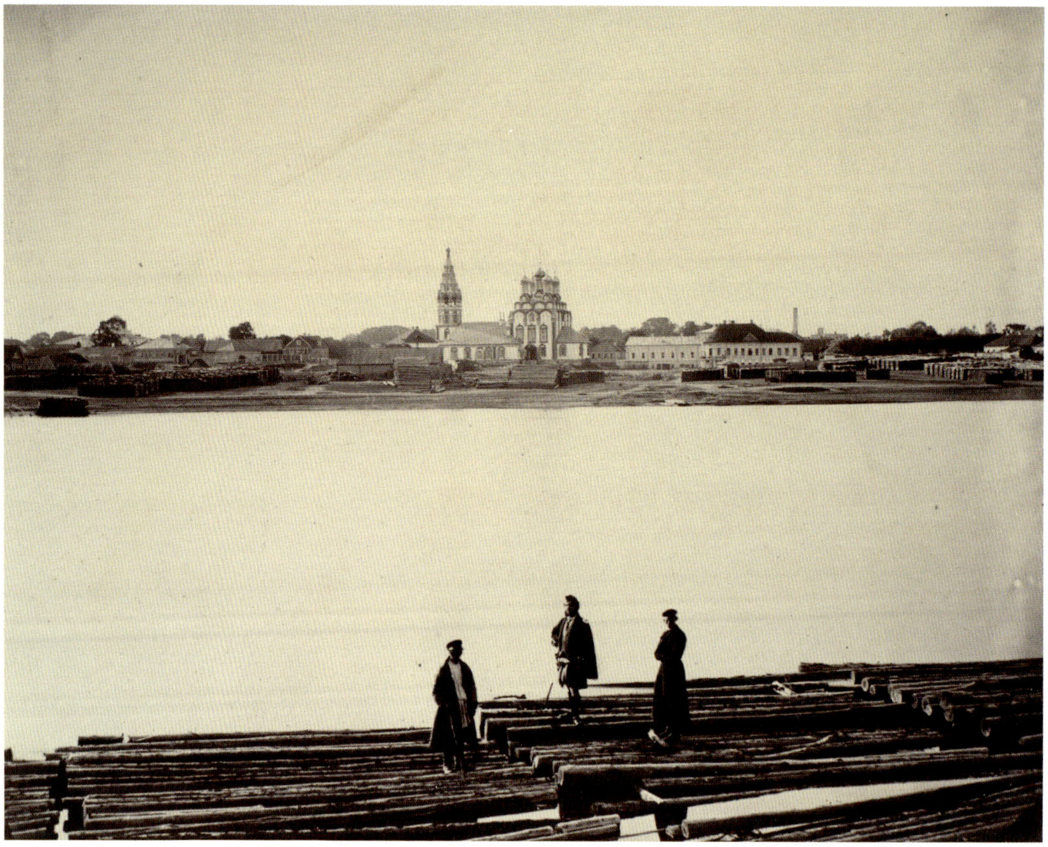

220 ***Church of St Nicholas, Moscow*** September 1856

Albumen print, 21.8 × 28.1 cm
Inscribed below photograph: *S.t Nicholas's Church. Moscow with Wood raft on the Moskwa. – Photographed by J. Mack. Corp.l R.E. Sept.r 1856*
RCIN 2945151

This beautifully composed photograph shows three figures balancing on floating tree trunks on the river Moskva in the foreground, the actual river in the middle ground, and the seventeenth-century church of St Nicholas the Wonderworker in the background. Intriguingly, the central figure, flanked by two serfs, is wearing full highland dress and is possibly a member of Lord Granville's diplomatic mission.

It is not known whether Mack saw Roger Fenton's photographs taken in Russia in 1852, and exhibited in London between 1853 and 1855, but there are some remarkable similarities in some of the views. This distant view of the church of St Nicholas in the Khamovniki region of Moscow, for example, closely resembles a distant view of Kiev taken by Fenton from the banks of the river Dnieper. **AN**

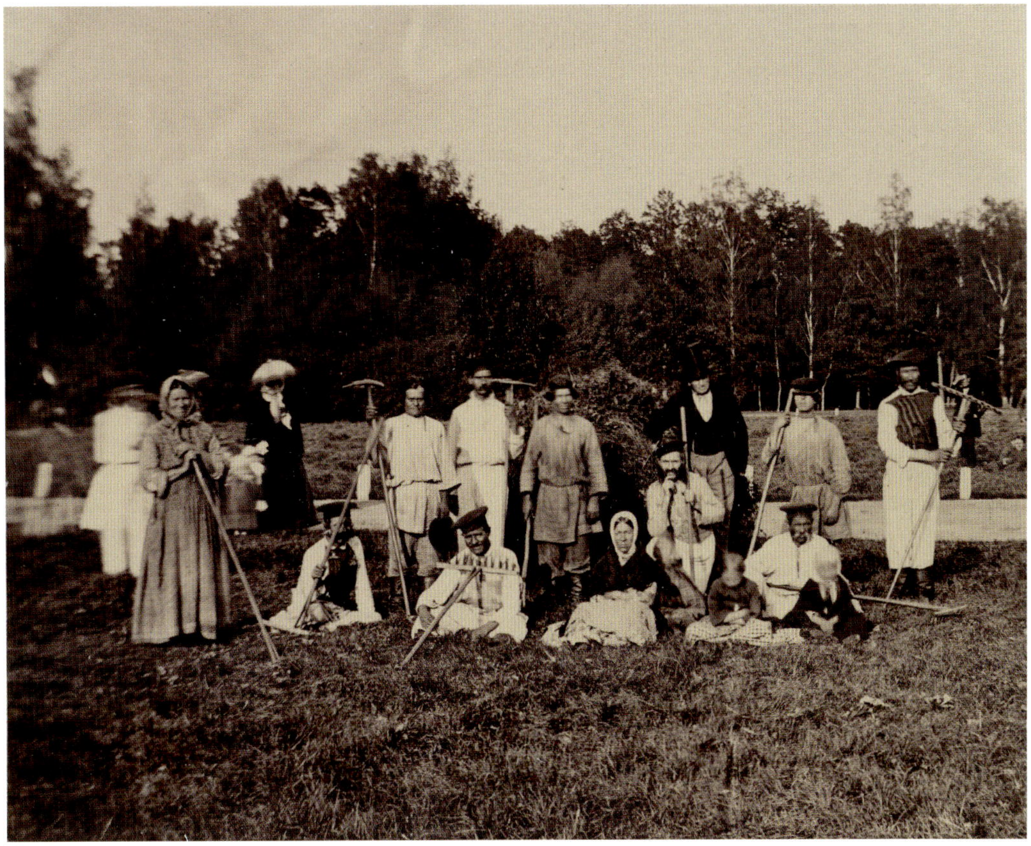

221 *Russian peasants hay making in Peterhof Park* 14 August 1856

Albumen print, 15.7 × 19.5 cm
Inscribed below photograph: *Russian Peasants Hay making in Peterhof Park. – Photographed by J. Mack. Corp.l R.E. Sept.r 1856*
RCIN 2945161

The diplomatic mission visited Peterhof on 14 August to be presented to the new Emperor and Empress, prior to their coronation. The photograph shows some members of the party amongst a group of agricultural labourers, who at the time were still bound to the land, according to the social and economic system known as serfdom. Such an antiquated feudalistic system might have attracted the curiosity of the visiting party, perhaps instilling in them the wish to be photographed among living relics of a medieval custom.

This is one of the surviving and perhaps only successful group photographs taken at Peterhof, as Lord Granville records a not-so-successful attempt earlier in the day:

> *At the Palais Anglais, Mack was again in requisition, as Prince Esterhazy wished to be presented in his costume. The day was dull; immobility was preached. As soon as the signal to be quiet was given, after a group had been most artistically arranged, with the Imperial carriages as background, Prince Paul with much gesticulation inquired whether it would be long before movement would be allowed. Everyone shook with laughter, and the result was perfectly un-make-out-able.*[50] **AN**

222 *Mujiks or serfs* September 1856

Albumen print, 15.5 × 14.2 cm
Inscribed below photograph: *Mujiks or Serfs. – Photographed by J. Mack. Corp.l R.E. Sept.r 1856*
RCIN 2945160

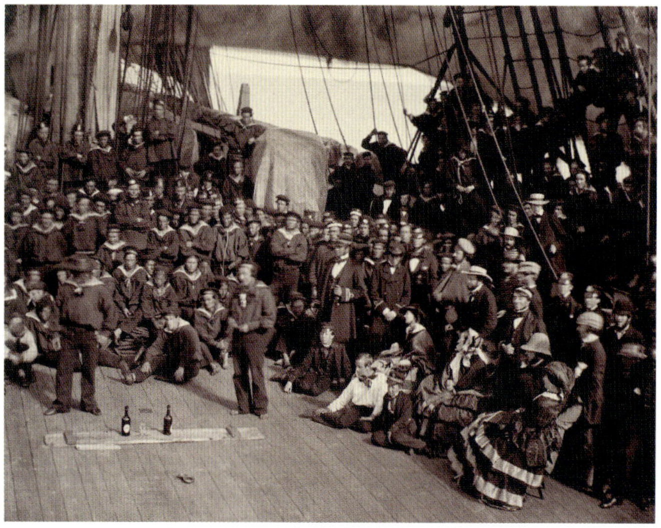

FIG. 71
James Mack
Sailors gathered on the deck of HMS St Jean d'Acre *to sing to Lord Granville and his suite*, September 1856
Albumen print, 21.1 × 27.4 cm
RCIN 2945156

This image of 1856 of three serfs (or mujiks) is remarkable as it was only after the abolition of serfdom by Alexander II in 1861 that peasants appeared as subjects in photographs.[51]

Most serfs were employed as agricultural labourers, but some would also work in the industrial sector, as described by Lieutenant Colonel Maude, following a visit to a factory on 27 September:

> *Lord G[ranville] and I had a ride together. We went to see a large cloth factory, where there were 1,500 people at work, all serfs. They look very comfortable, but work from 4 in the morning till 8 in the evening. They pay each £6 a year to their masters for leave to work off the estates. All sorts of cloth was made there but none of it goes into Europe; all eastwards and used in this country.*[52]

The fascination and curiosity this kind of social figure might have evoked in members of the visiting party (fig. 71) is probably one of the reasons behind Maude's decision to send a copy of this photograph to his wife.[53] **AN**

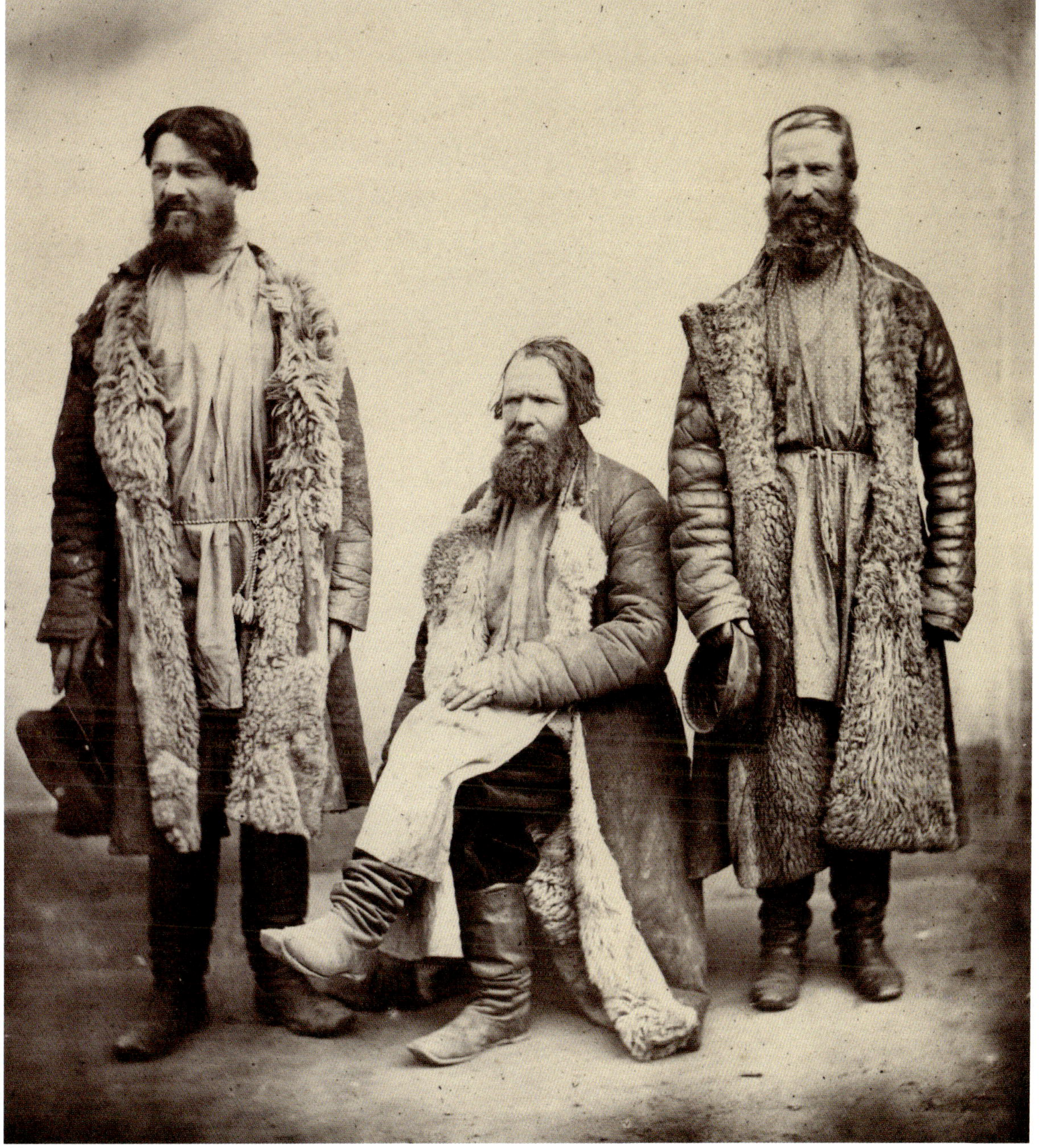

WILLIAM CARRICK (1827–1878)

223 & 224 *Itinerant musicians with bears, Finland* c.1863

Albumen print, 21.8 × 28.3 cm
RCIN 2935057

Military group, Karelia c.1863

Albumen print, 22.6 × 28.2 cm
RCIN 2935056

Provenance Possibly acquired by King Edward VII, when Prince of Wales

William Carrick, known in Russia as Vil'iam (Vasilii) Andreyevich Karrik, was a Scottish photographer who devoted much of his professional career to portraying members of Russia's lower classes and capturing folkloric rural scenes.[54] When he opened his studio on Malaya Morskaya Street in 1859, the market for portrait photography in St Petersburg was already close to saturation, mostly due to the lack of an established middle class. Carrick, perhaps inspired by the traditional depiction of 'Cries' (street vendors who announced their wares with calls and chants), soon had the idea of inviting to his studio all the *rasnoschiki* ('hawkers')

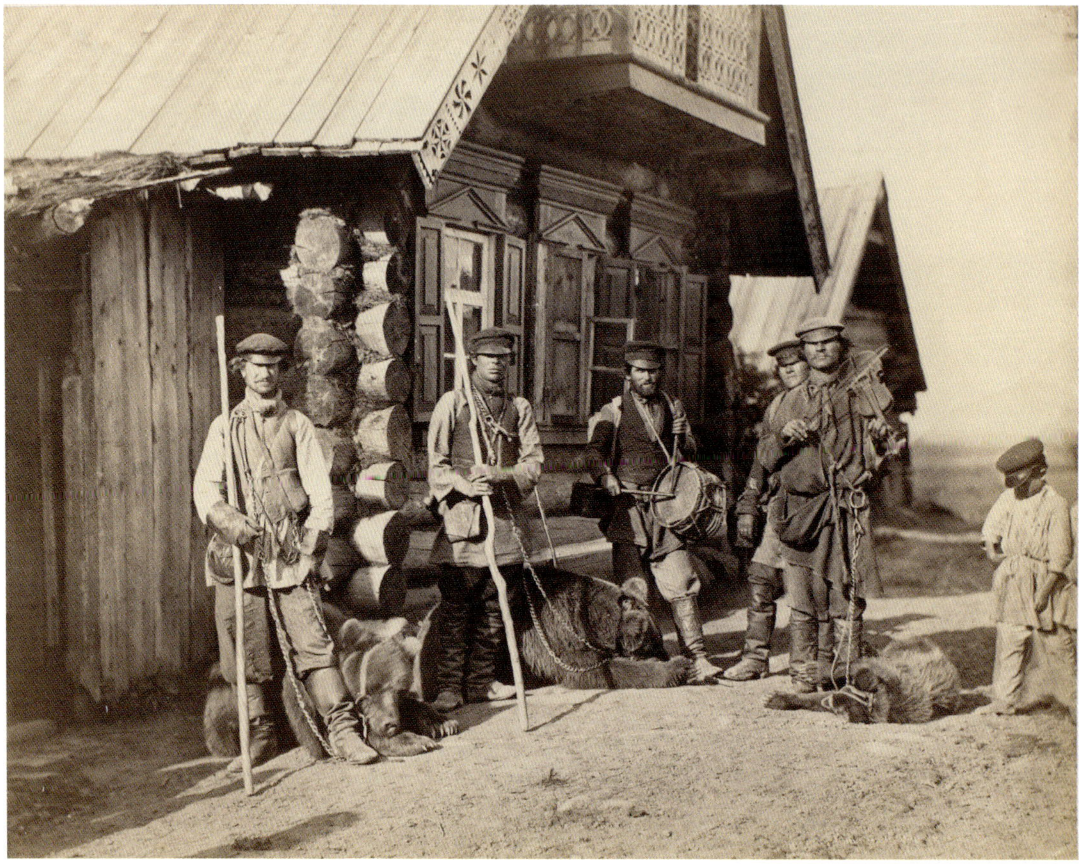

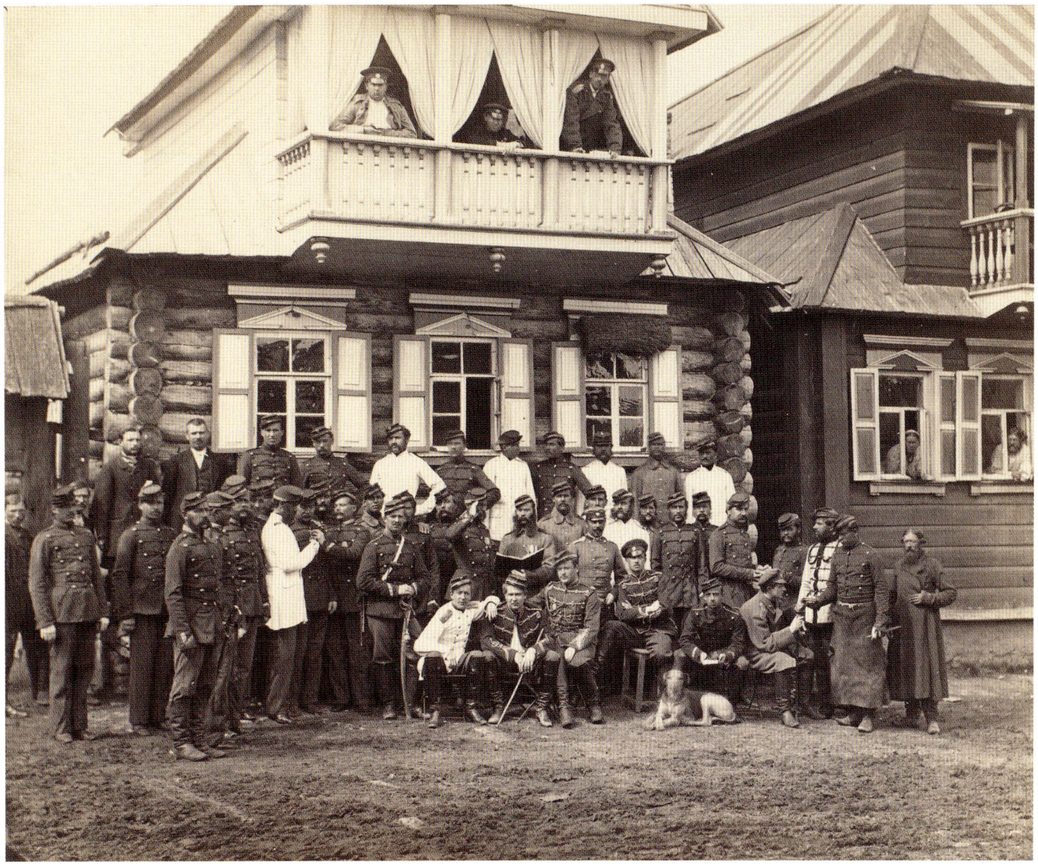

he could find on the streets of St Petersburg (most being former serfs recently emancipated by Alexander II's reform of 1861). In this way, he created an impressively large catalogue of 'Russian street types', in *carte-de-visite* format, which became popular with the tourist market, in particular, as well as with artists, who would use the photographs as a visual aid; but he did not fail to impress the ruling class either.[55]

As their success and technical confidence grew, Carrick and his lifelong associate, John MacGregor (d.1872), soon ventured outside the studio, leaving the city to explore and capture the countryside and its people, among the first photographers in Russia to do so. In the early 1860s, they travelled to Finland, where these photographs were taken, and in the 1870s, they explored territories along the 'Mother Volga' river, as far as the districts of Yaroslavl, Nizhny Novgorod, Kazan and Simbirsk (Ulyanovsk).[56]

Despite not always achieving commercial success, Carrick's work was highly regarded by the artistic community, in particular by the so-called *Peredvizhniki*, a group of Russian realist artists. Similarly, during his entire career as photographer, he supported artists by reproducing their work photographically, with Count Zichy being one of his most regular commissioners.[57] Carrick's artistic talent was recognised by various awards and, in 1876, by his prestigious appointment as Photographer of the Imperial Academy of Arts. **AN**

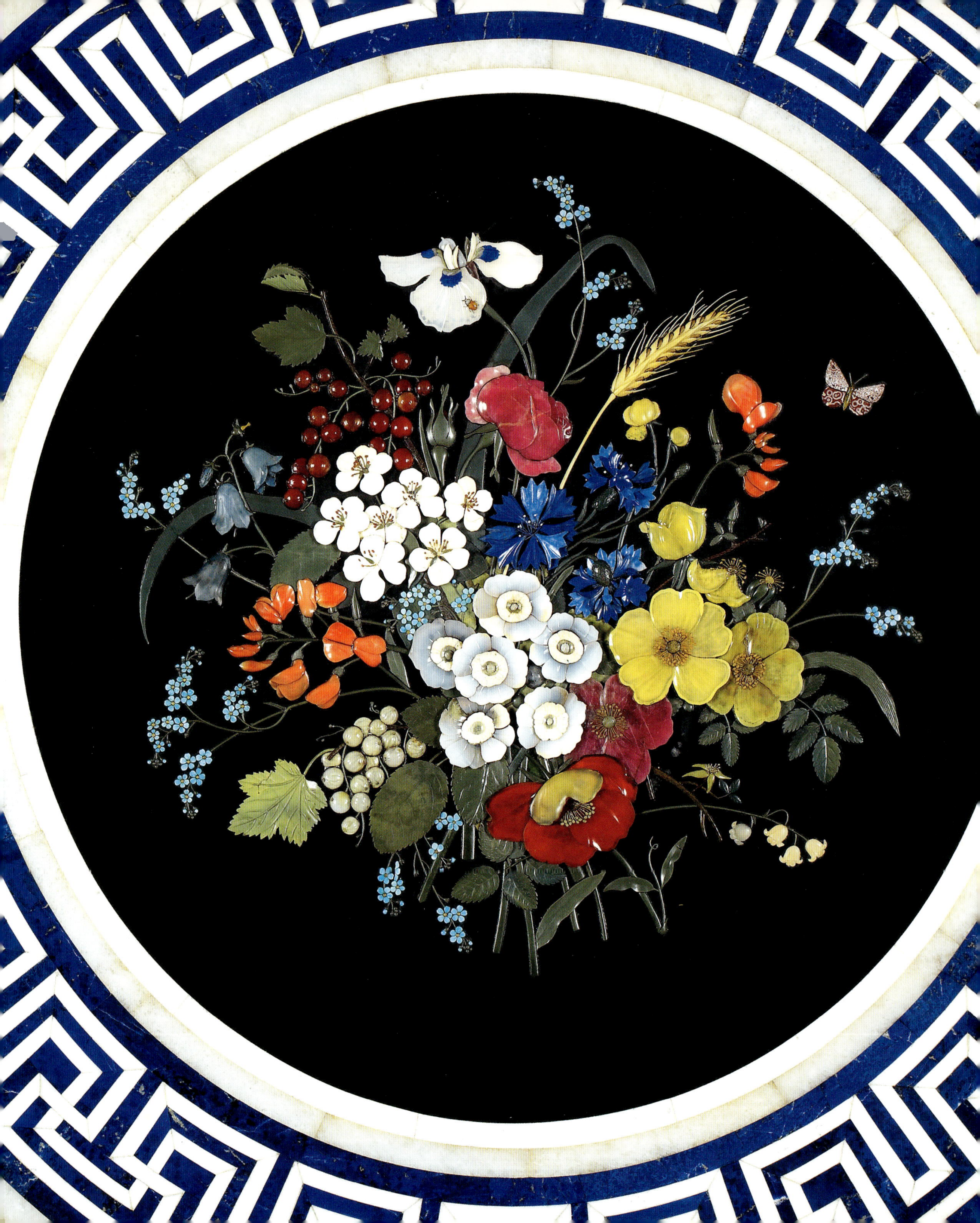

10

Russian Decorative Art in the Royal Collection: Exchanges in Patronage

CAROLINE DE GUITAUT

Russian decorative art in the Royal Collection is representative of a wide range of the country's native craftsmanship, including lapidary, metalwork, furniture, sculpture, porcelain, glass, textiles and jewellery. While of Russian manufacture and materials, these objects cannot be seen as a nationalist phenomenon, as Russia was not isolated during the imperial period. Indeed, Western European influence strongly determined the artistic endeavours of the nation, arguably until the late nineteenth century, when a truly indigenous style began to exert itself, part Russian revival and part *stil modern*, combining the influence of the Art Nouveau. What makes the examples of decorative art in the collection interesting is their diversity, and this is defined by the manner and circumstance of acquisition, as reflected in the themes of this catalogue and described in earlier chapters. Grand diplomatic gifts, occasionally monumental in scale (fig. 72), are showpieces of the best exponents in the national or regional tradition. Such gifts include lapidary from the Ekaterinburg Lapidary Workshops and Peterhof Imperial Lapidary Workshops (cats 225, 231), and fine metalwork, enamelling and porcelain from both Moscow and St Petersburg (cats 98, 99 and 126).

One of the most important and substantial gifts was the malachite vase, presented by Emperor Nicholas I to Queen Victoria following the visit of his son, the future Emperor Alexander II in 1839. The vase is monumental in scale, measuring almost 2 metres in height and is an exemplary piece produced by the Peterhof Imperial Lapidary Workshops. The vase had been made in 1836, a few years before the Emperor decided to give it as a gift to the queen and it had stood in the Hermitage. Nicholas I later had an identical vase made to replace it and specified that it should be situated in exactly the same place as the original that had been sent to England.[1]

Objects of decorative art received as personal gifts, or purchased by members of the Russian and British royal families to give to one another, largely in the nineteenth century, are no less important or finely crafted, yet are generally more modest. However, they still represent the work of the finest makers of the period, patronised by the imperial family, which by dint of this patronage became fashionable and successful, and were made official suppliers to the Russian imperial court. These include the Imperial Porcelain Factory, Demidov, Ovchinnikov, Kiebel, Sazikov, Hahn and Fabergé. After the Revolution, the royal family in England showed a continued interest in collecting works of Russian origin, particularly those associated with the Romanov dynasty, some of which had originally belonged to their Russian relations (cats 284, 209).

Like works in other media represented in this catalogue, the Russian decorative art reveals, in many instances, an aesthetic that was shared between the Russian and

Detail of cat. 98

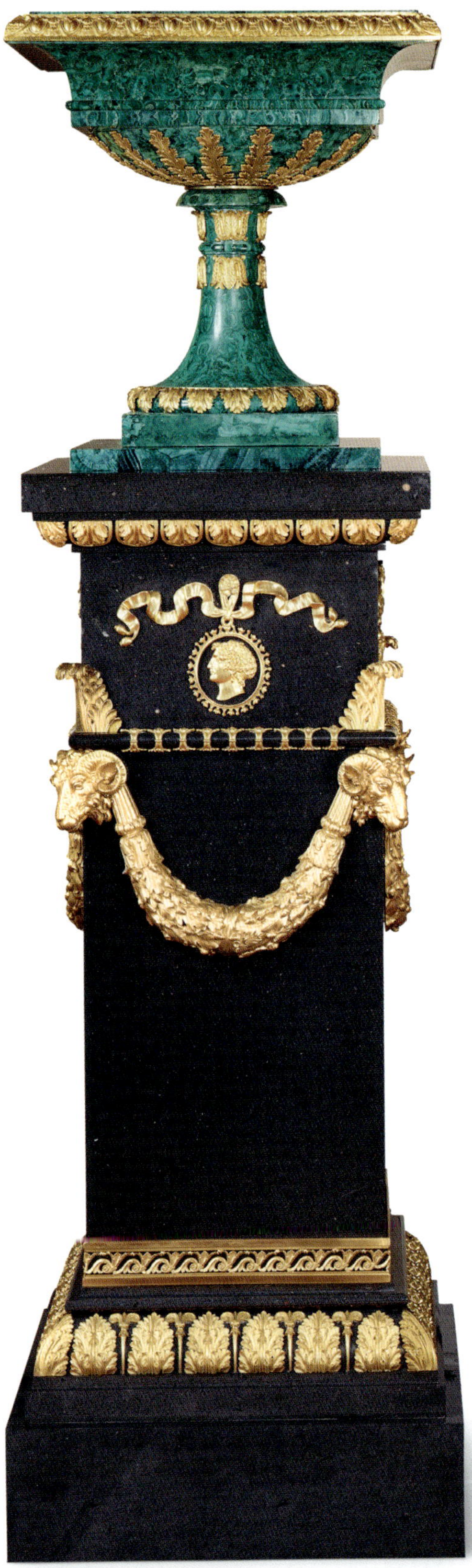

FIG. 72
Russian
Vase and pedestal, 1820–8
Malachite, porphyry, gilt metal, 176.0 × 51.0 × 51.0 cm
RCIN 53204

British royal courts. In the late nineteenth century and the beginning of the twentieth, both Nicholas II and Edward VII (and subsequently George V) lived in relatively simply furnished, often cluttered, Victorian domestic interiors, surrounded by objects designed in a broadly shared tradition, and with works made by firms who enjoyed the patronage of both families. These private rooms were in distinct contrast to the vast magnificence of the palatial reception rooms used for state occasions and official entertaining. This aesthetic had commenced with the increased Westernisation of the Russian capital St Petersburg, first established by Peter the Great in 1703, and populated by large numbers of British citizens from the eighteenth century onwards.[2] British expatriates included artists and craftsmen who sought to establish their firms in Russia, often encouraged by imperial patronage, including Francis Gardner, who created a porcelain manufactory in 1766 (cats 38–40); as well as numerous goldsmiths and silversmiths, many of whom were suppliers to the firm of Nicholls & Plincke, at 16 Nevskii Prospekt, otherwise known by its familiar name of 'the English Shop' (cats 235, 237, 239). Export of talent began to travel in the opposite direction in the early twentieth century, with the arrival of various Russian designers and craftsmen in London, supporting the burgeoning interest in the style, 'à la Russe'.[3] One of the most significant arrivals was the establishment of the only foreign outpost of the firm of Carl Fabergé in 1903.[4]

There are no pre-Petrine Russian works in the Royal Collection,[5] and very few from the eighteenth century which demonstrate the initial stylistic influences of the northern baroque of Germany and Scandinavia (fig. 73). Following Peter I's visit to France in 1717, the rococo style took hold in Russia. Examples of this influence in the Collection today include a coffee pot (cat. 36) and *kovsh* (cat. 19). Catherine the Great, depicted on several works in the Collection (cats

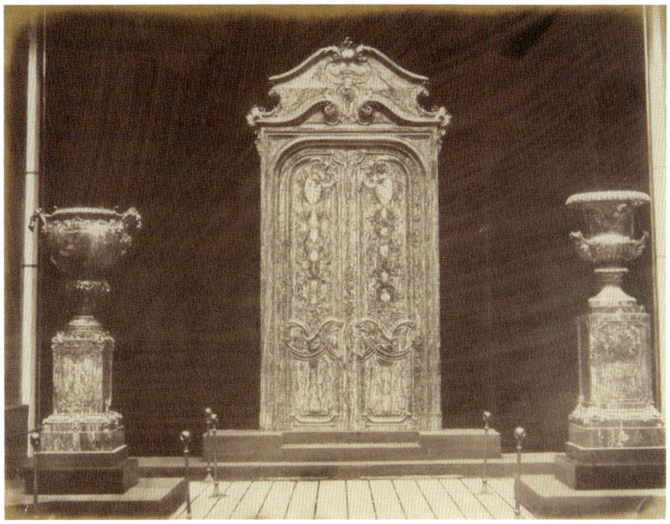

FIG. 73
Hugh Owen (1808–97)
Folding-doors veneered with malachite, 1851
Salted paper print, 16.0 × 21.0 cm
RCIN 2800089
The vase on the left of the image was acquired by Queen Victoria (cat. 229)

29–30), strengthened Russia's relationship with France by engaging in a sustained dialogue with French philosophers, and by buying extensively from French manufacturers, notably Sèvres, which produced the famous neoclassical Cameo Service in 1778, additional pieces for which were made later by the Imperial Factory (cat. 37). Among the many British architects, designers and craftsmen patronised by Catherine were the Scottish architect, Charles Cameron, and the firm of Wedgwood (cat. 34), from whom she ordered the famous Frog Service in 1773. Catherine's son, Paul I, and his consort, Maria Feodorovna, travelled to the West as the comte and comtesse du Nord, on their grand tour of Europe, collecting and ordering works to furnish their new summer palace at Pavolovsk. Maria was a talented amateur artist, who created various cameo portraits of the imperial family (cats 31–32). However, it was during the nineteenth century, and the reigns of Alexander I, Nicholas I and Alexander II, that the richest influx of works of decorative art into the Royal Collection took place, bolstered by the allegiances of the Napoleonic Wars and by dynastic marriage.

Alexander I's visit to England in 1814 prompted a shared stylistic output (cats 62, 72, 229); moreover, in addition to the King's celebratory Waterloo Chamber at Windsor Castle, there was even a short-lived adoption of Russian style in dress, demonstrated by the sarafan belonging to the King's daughter, Princess Charlotte (cat. 74). Russian works mainly in the Empire style were acquired by George IV, with the purchase, in the 1820s, of a magnificent pair of malachite candelabra (cat. 228), and the gift of a malachite vase and pedestal (cat. 226). Following Alexander I's death, George IV also received a malachite tazza with jasper pedestal in 1827, from the Dowager Empress Maria Feodorovna, which he incorporated into the decoration of his apartments at Windsor Castle (fig. 77).[6] The king had sent a sumptuously bound copy of Pyne's *Royal Residences* to the Empress in 1825.

After the French Revolution and the wars that followed Russian enthusiasm for all things French declined. Consequently, in the reign of Nicholas I, the Emperor's role as patron meant a reconnection with Russian artists and craftsmen, whom he avidly supported. He presented Queen Victoria with remarkable gifts following his state visit in 1844, in the form of a monumental porcelain presentation vase (cat. 99) and a hardstone and gilt-bronze table (cat. 98). In return, Queen Victoria sent a Coalport dessert service (cat. 100) and a Minton dinner and dessert service (cat. 102). Nicholas I was also responsible for starting the rage for the neo-Gothic style at Peterhof in 1825, when he commissioned the Scottish architect and landscape gardener, Adam Menelaws (*c.*1748/9–1831), to create an English-style estate with a cottage palace, the interior of which features neo-Gothic furnishings and *trompe l'oeil* wall paintings of Gothic tracery. The impact of international exhibitions of the mid- to late nineteenth century brought the work of Russian craftsmen to the attention of British audiences on a wide scale, with participation in the Great Exhibition of 1851 and the International Exhibition of 1862. For the first time, a truly 'Russian' style was discernible, many of the makers represented having trained at the Stroganov Institute[7] or the Stieglitz School,[8] where rigorous study of European and old Russian works of art and ornamentation was combined with a newfound confidence to create works of exceptional quality and original design.

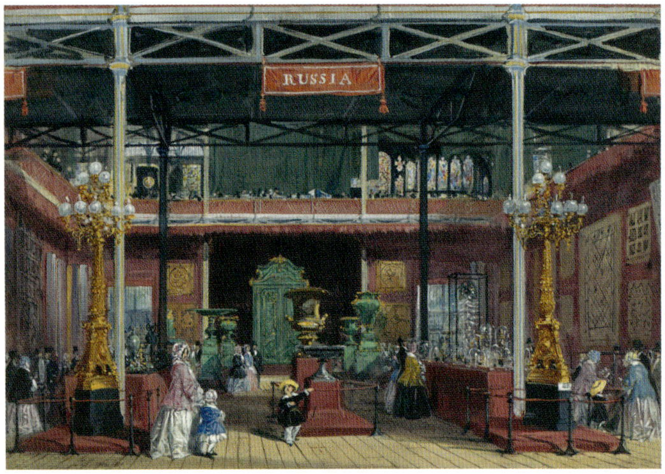

FIG. 74
Joseph Nash
The Great Exhibition: Russia, dated 1851
Pencil, watercolour and bodycolour,
33.0 × 48.3 cm
RCIN 919954

Opposite
Close up of cat. 184's polychrome enamel decoration in the old Russian style of the 1870s and 1880s

On one of her many visits to the 1851 exhibition, Queen Victoria was impressed by the plate, jewellery and malachite furniture. 'We went first to look at the Russian exhibits which have just arrived & are very fine: doors, chairs, a chimneypiece, a piano, as well as vases in malachite, specimens of plate & some beautifully tasteful & very lightly set jewellery'.[9] As a result, she purchased a monumental vase made by the Demidov workshops (cat. 227) and a paperweight.[10] Success at the international exhibitions also stimulated Russian confidence in home grown artistic talent. The artist and art historian Fedor Grigoryevitch Solntsev (1801–1892) was the main author of the seminal work *Drevnosti rossiiskago gosudarstva* (Antiquities of the Russian State) which in six volumes, produced between 1846 and 1853, recorded Russian armour, weapons, church plate and other medieval objects in the Kremlin Armoury and which, together with Victor Butovski's 1870 publication, was to have a profound influence on Russian silversmiths, porcelain manufacturers, glass-makers and woodworkers.

Other Russian works in the Royal Collection which are associated with national or international exhibitions include a rare set of straw-work veneered furniture, bearing the conjoined arms of Alfred, Duke of Edinburgh and Grand Duchess Maria Alexandrovna (cats 185–187). Stylistically, they make reference to the late nineteenth-century Russian Revival style, which became popular in Russian painting, architecture and the decorative arts in the late 1870s and 1880s, particularly in Moscow. This style was also seen in the interior of the Orthodox chapel created at Clarence House for the Duchess of Edinburgh (fig. 45), together with various *objets d'art* acquired by the couple.[11] The *fin-de-siècle* period saw a dual interest in the art nouveau style,[12] particularly associated with the taste of Empress Alexandra Feodorovna (cat. 285), and a neoclassical and neo-rococo style seen in the works of the Fabergé firm (see cats 245, 283, 260 and 270), which was patronised by both royal families until its demise in 1917. Meanwhile the *avant garde* artistic displays of the Ballets Russes caused a sensation in London, where, at the Royal Opera House in June 1911, Diaghilev's company made its British debut during the celebrations for the coronation of King George V and Queen Mary.

Following the Revolution, the King and Queen began to acquire examples of Russian decorative art which had strong associations with the Romanov dynasty. These included porcelain services made for the Imperial family (cat. 286) and even a Cossack uniform which had belonged to the Tsesarevich Alexei (1904–18). Continuing interest in Russian decorative arts was mainly demonstrated by the royal family through support of important early exhibitions in 1935, and even into the era of the cold war.[13] In 1989 Her Majesty Queen Elizabeth II made the first loans from the Royal Collection of Imperial works of art which had belonged personally to Nicholas II and Alexandra Feodorovna, when two Imperial Easter Eggs made by the Fabergé firm were lent to the Armoury Museum in the Moscow Kremlin.[14]

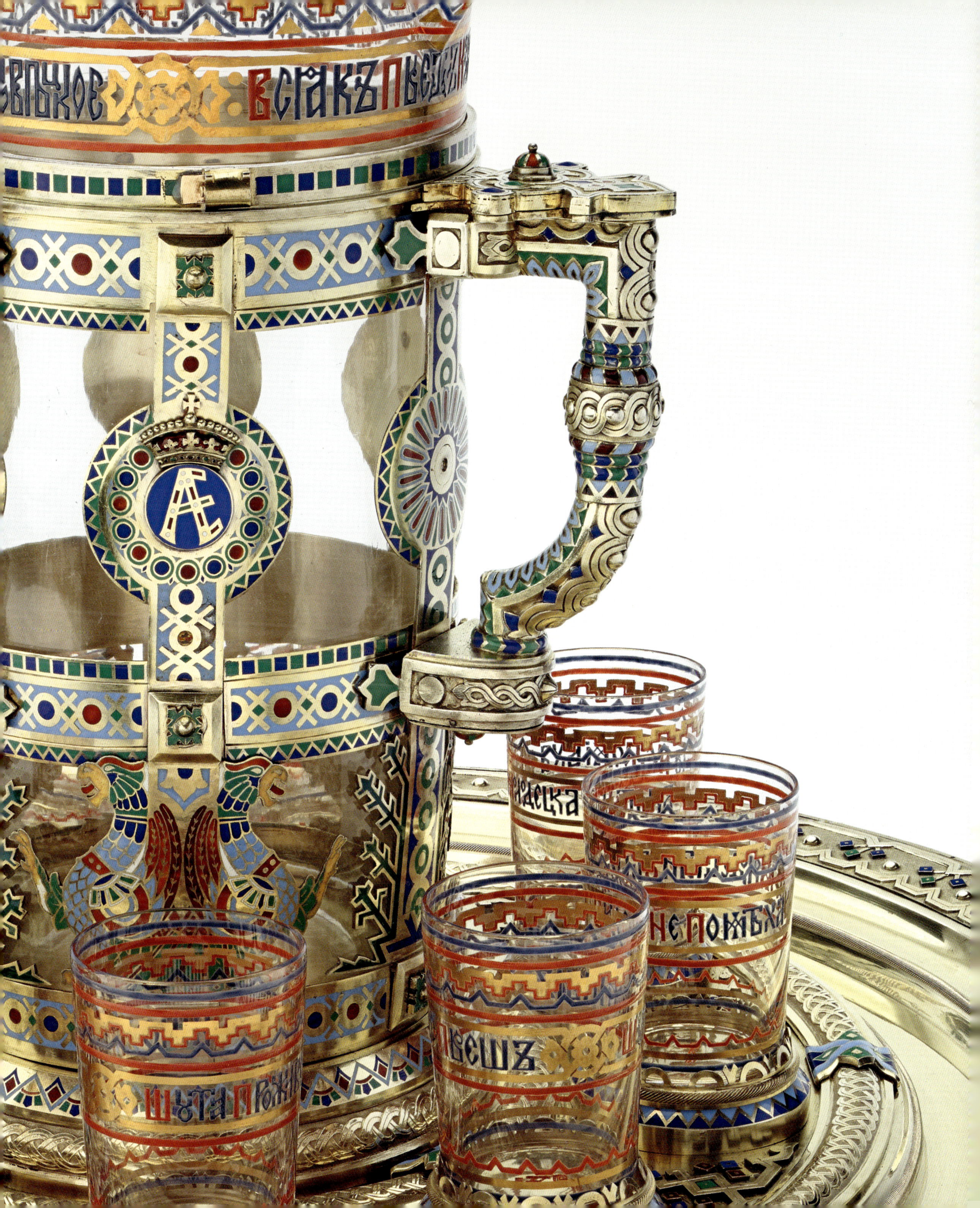

225 ***Baluster vase*** 1865

Carved and polished rhodonite, 111.5 × 35.0 cm
Vase incised on base in Cyrillic: '1865 Ekaterinburg Lapidary Workshops Director Polkovnik Miklashevsky'
RCIN 899

Provenance Supplied to Alexander II; probably presented to the Prince of Wales or Queen Victoria, 1865

This baluster-shaped vase and pedestal was produced in Ekaterinburg, which became an important centre for stone carving from the end of the eighteenth century. The vase is carved from three pieces of rhodonite, a dark pink hardstone veined with black and grey, deposits of which are found in the Ural mountains in Russia, and comprises a finial top section, ovoid body and a stepped pedestal, held together by an iron rod.

Colonel Petr Ivanovich Miklashevsky (1825–89), mentioned in the inscription, was director of the Ekaterinburg Lapidary Workshops during the period 1859–66. From 1853, works produced in the imperial lapidary factories were marked with the name of the factory, the date of production and the name of the director or main workmaster. A design for this vase is held in the state archive of the Sverdlovsk region. CDEG

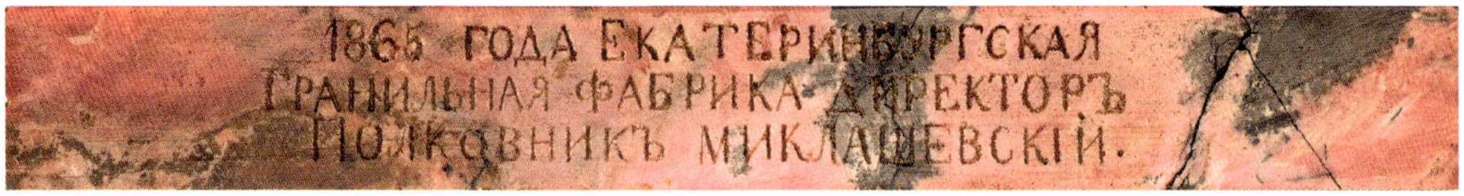

Detail of the inscription on the base of cat. 225

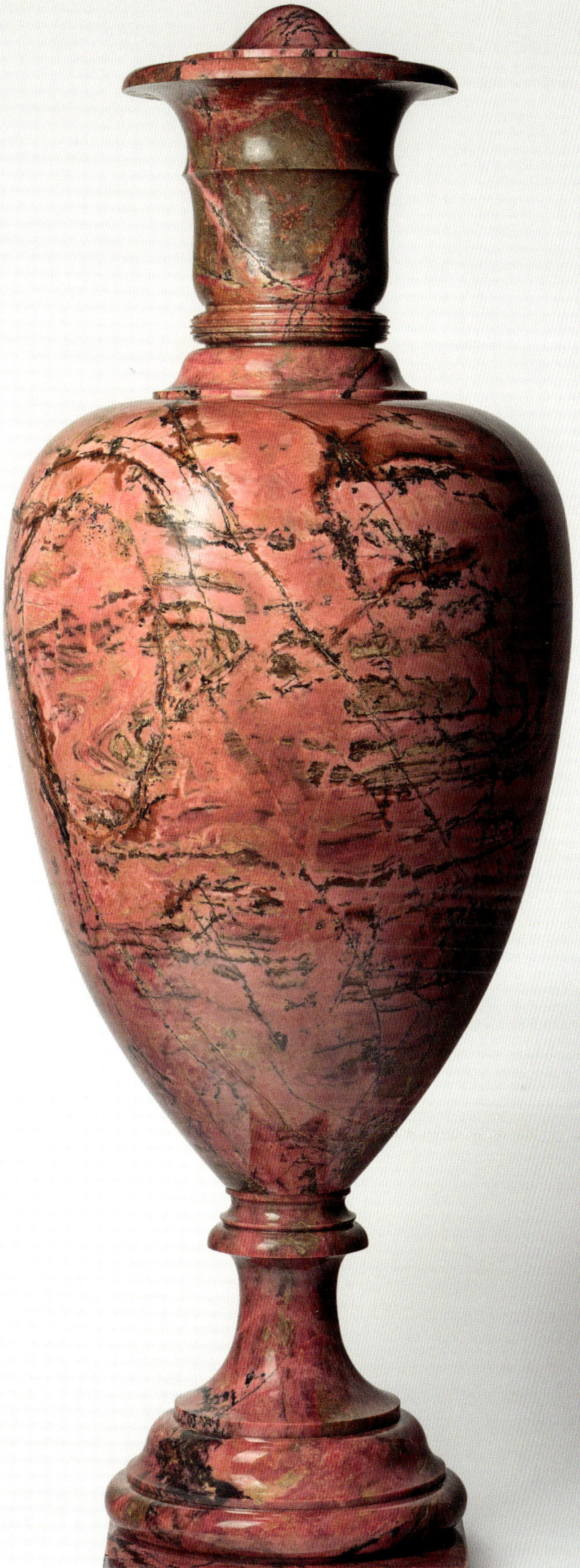

ST PETERSBURG

226 *Vase and pedestal* 1827

Malachite, gilt bronze, 224.0 × 71.0 × 64.0 cm
RCIN 1708

Provenance Sent by Empress Alexandra Feodorovna (consort of Nicholas I), via the Russian ambassador, Prince Lieven, to George IV; Benjamin Jutsham, the King's Inventory Clerk, records receipt of delivery in three cases, 21 November 1827

Literature Roberts 2001, p. 84

This large, malachite-veneered 'Medici', campana-shaped vase was made in St Petersburg, but the exact workshop is not known. A design for a similar vase was made by Ivan Galberg (1778–1863) in 1826 although this does not show the gilt-bronze mounts which were later applied to the front and back of the malachite pedestal.[15] Nicholas I had acceded to the Russian throne in December 1825, two years before the vase was sent by his consort Empress Alexandra Feodorovna via the Russian Ambassador Prince Lieven.[16] The exact reason for the gift is not known, however the application of the specially made gilt-bronze mounts of the British Royal Arms and the Russian Imperial Arms indicate that the vase was considered an important gift, perhaps with a diplomatic message.

George IV placed the vase in the central window bay of the new Large Drawing Room (now known as the Crimson Drawing Room) at Windsor Castle in 1828, supplanting a red marble and gilt-bronze font which had been presented to the king by Pius VII in 1816. The malachite vase was still situated in the Crimson Drawing Room in 1867, as seen in a photograph of the room by A. Disderi (1819–89). The vase is fitted with gilt-bronze handles, which are finely chased, terminating in Bacchic heads. The square-in-section malachite veneered pedestal sits on a stepped malachite base with gilt-bronze mounts in the form of acanthus leaves above a further gilt-bronze plinth applied with neoclassical scrolls and palmettes.
CDEG

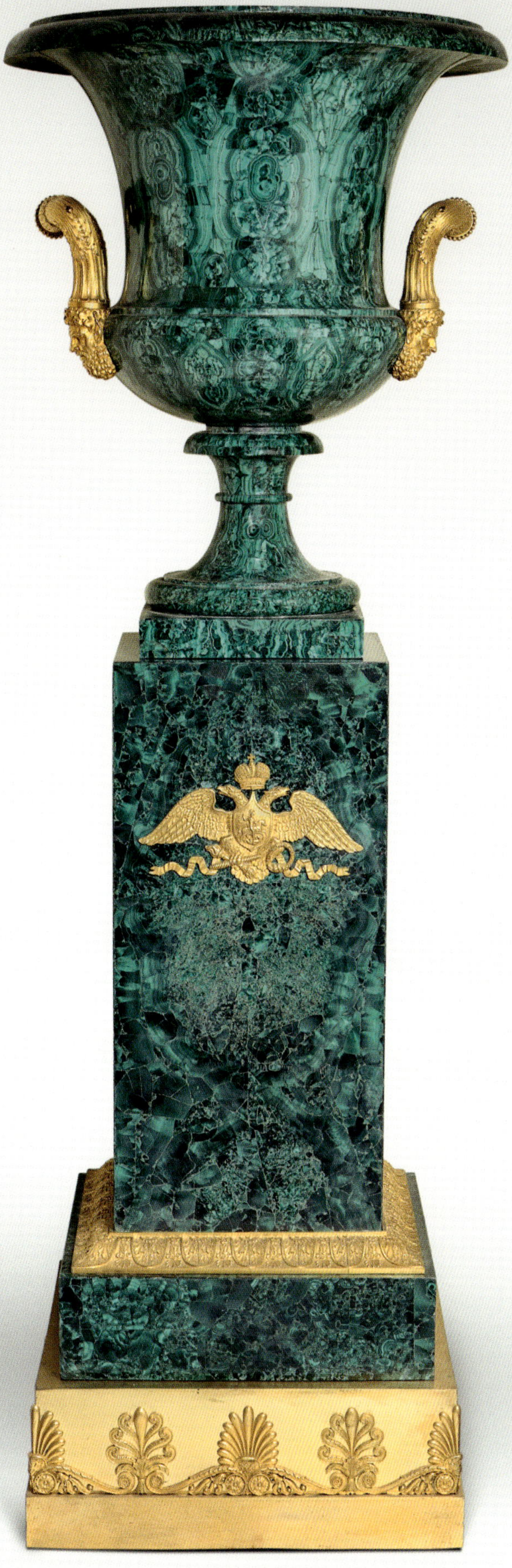

DEMIDOV LAPIDARY FACTORY

227 *Vase and pedestal* c.1850

Malachite, gilt bronze, 220.0 × 100.0 × 79.0 cm
RCIN 1709

Provenance Exhibited at the Great Exhibition, 1851; purchased by Queen Victoria and Prince Albert

Literature Odom and Paredes Arend 1998, p. 252

This large-scale, malachite, bulbous vase and pedestal, veneered with malachite mosaic, was made at the Demidov Lapidary Factory in St Petersburg, and was exhibited at the Great Exhibition in London in 1851, where displays also included a pair of double doors which had taken 30 men more than a year to produce, a chimneypiece in malachite mosaic, and some other large vases. This vase and pedestal are visible in a watercolour view of the Russian stand, commissioned by Prince Albert from Joseph Nash in 1851 (see fig. 74 and detail below). A number of the malachite pieces and some other objects did not go on display until over a month after the exhibition opened, as their shipment was delayed by ice in the Baltic Sea, a matter which did not escape Queen Victoria's notice on 19 May, on one of her numerous visits to the Great Exhibition: 'Next Russia whose department is almost entirely empty'.[17] Nearly a month later, on 11 June, the Queen remarked on the Demidov malachite pieces that she had seen: 'We went first to look at the Russian exhibits which have just arrived & are very fine: doors, chairs, a chimneypiece, a piano, as well as vases in malachite'.[18]

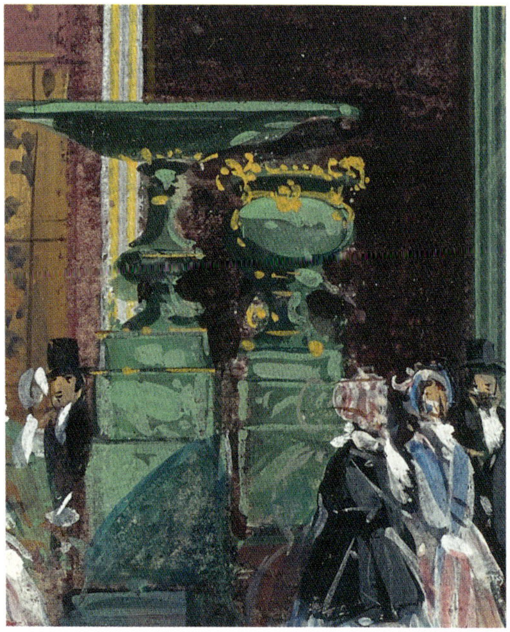

Joseph Nash
The Great Exhibition: Russia
dated 1851 (detail of fig. 74)

This vase is richly mounted in gilt bronze in neo-rococo style, in the form of foliage, flowers and tendrils that curve around the convex surface of the upper parts, and around the corners of the upper and lower parts of the pedestal. The malachite veneer is particularly notable for its evenly-matched mosaic and the treatment of the material together with its notably lighter colour contrasts markedly with cat. 226.

The Demidov Lapidary Factory was owned by the Demidov family, proprietors of numerous mines and foundries in the Urals, including the famous Nizhny Tagil malachite mine. In 1833, Prince Demidov (1812–70) presented Emperor Nicholas I with a monument of extraordinary opulence, of malachite and gilt bronze, in the shape of a Greek temple, supported by eight columns, now in the Hermitage Museum. It so impressed St Petersburg society that it single-handedly re-launched the vogue for malachite pieces. Leopold Joffriaud's perfection of the technique of cutting malachite, in 1840, with a machine fitted with a pair of rotary saws, meant that as soon as the lapidaries had mastered the new technique, they began to produce much larger pieces. According to correspondence in the Russian State Archive of Old Acts, the purchase of this vase by Queen Victoria is mentioned in a letter of Joffriaud, sent from London to St Petersburg on 13/25 June 1851.[19] CDEG

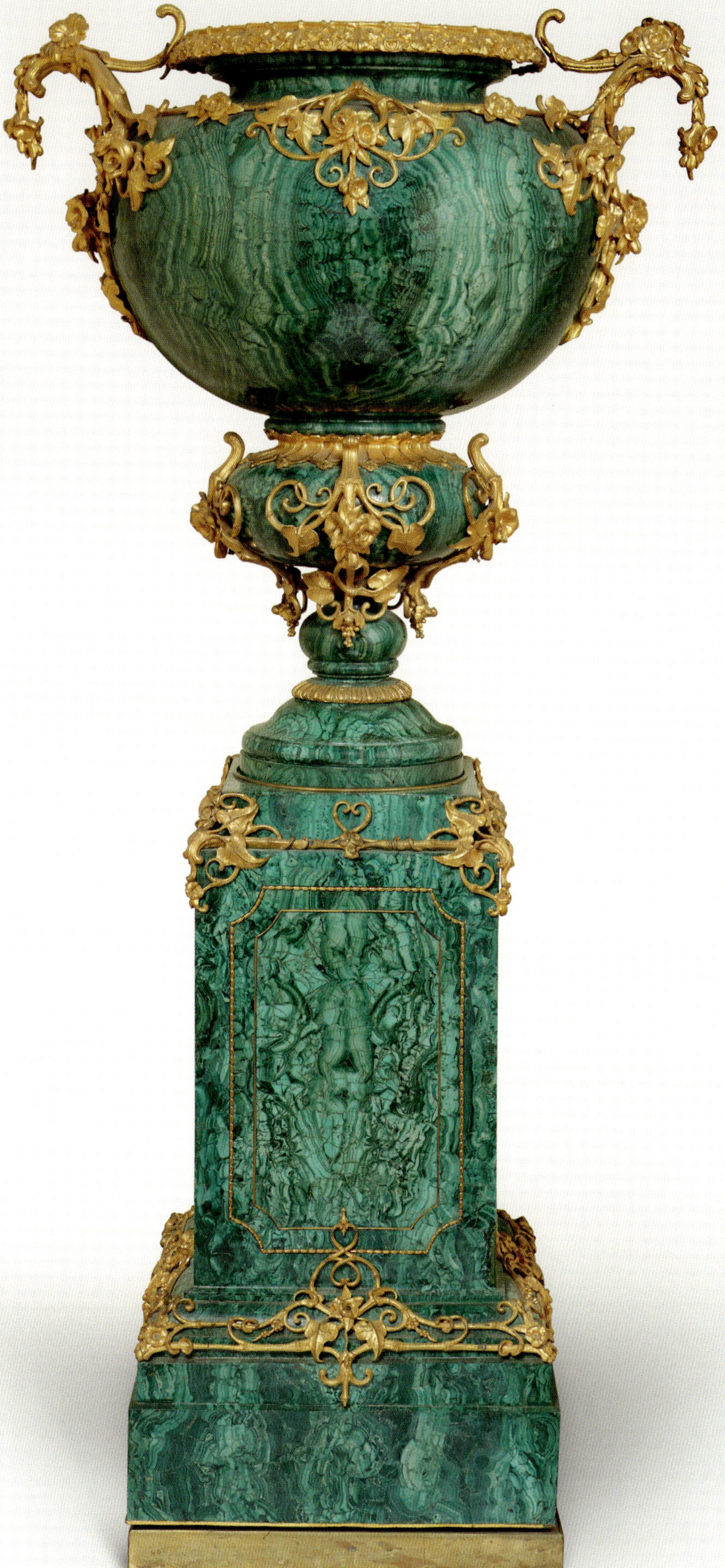

THOMIRE ET CIE

228 *Pair of candelabra* 1825–8

Gilded and chased bronze, malachite, 181.0 × 28.0 cm
RCIN 2731.1–2

Provenance Purchased for George IV, in Paris, by the King's confectioner, François Benois, together with a matching clock, for the equivalent of £500

Literature GIV Pictorial inventory; Mavrodina 2007, p. 122, no. II.134

This pair of eight-light candelabra are depicted in the Pictorial Inventory of 1827–33[20]. This three-volume record of the clocks, vases, candelabra and other items from Carlton House, George IV's London residence, with selected items from other royal palaces served as an aid to Nicholas Morel (active 1790–1830) in the creation of his furnishing schemes for the King at Windsor Castle. The candelabra were purchased by François Benois (active 1806–30), and can be seen in Douglas Morison's (1814–47) watercolour of the Music Room (Saloon) in 1843 (fig. 75). They were subsequently altered, the number of arms being reduced, and were later wired for electricity.

The candelabra were produced in the workshop of Pierre-Philippe Thomire (1751–1843), regarded as the most accomplished bronze-mounter and gilder of the early nineteenth century, supplying elaborate mounts in the Empire style to the leading Parisian cabinetmakers, for furniture, clocks, porcelain and hardstone objects. He was much patronised by Napoleon, who made him *ciseleur de l'Empereur* ('engraver to the Emperor'). One of his most famous commissions was to create the lavish malachite rotunda now in the Winter Palace, which was commissioned by Nikolai Nikitich Demidov (1773–1828) in 1827, and originally adorned the Villa San Donato near Florence, which he had built while serving as Russian ambassador in Italy. His son, Anatoly Nikolaevich Demidov, put the rotunda on display at the *Exposition des produits de l'industrie* in Paris in 1834, and presented it to Nicholas I in 1836. Two similar pairs of malachite and gilt-bronze candelabra are in the Hermitage Museum.[21] The column and base are the same shape, but instead of the winged figure, they have a laurel wreath mount on the sides of the pedestal. These are attributed to the Maderni Workshop. CDEG

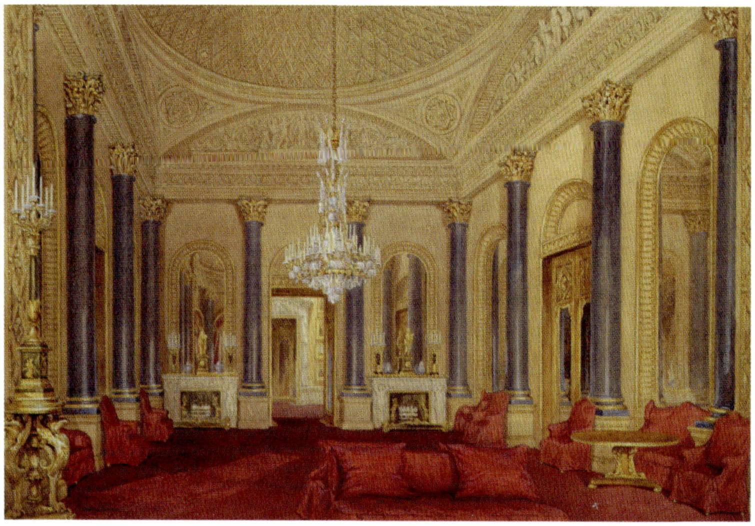

FIG. 75
Douglas Morison
Buckingham Palace: The Saloon, signed 1843
Watercolour and bodycolour, 27.0 × 40.2 cm
RCIN 919897

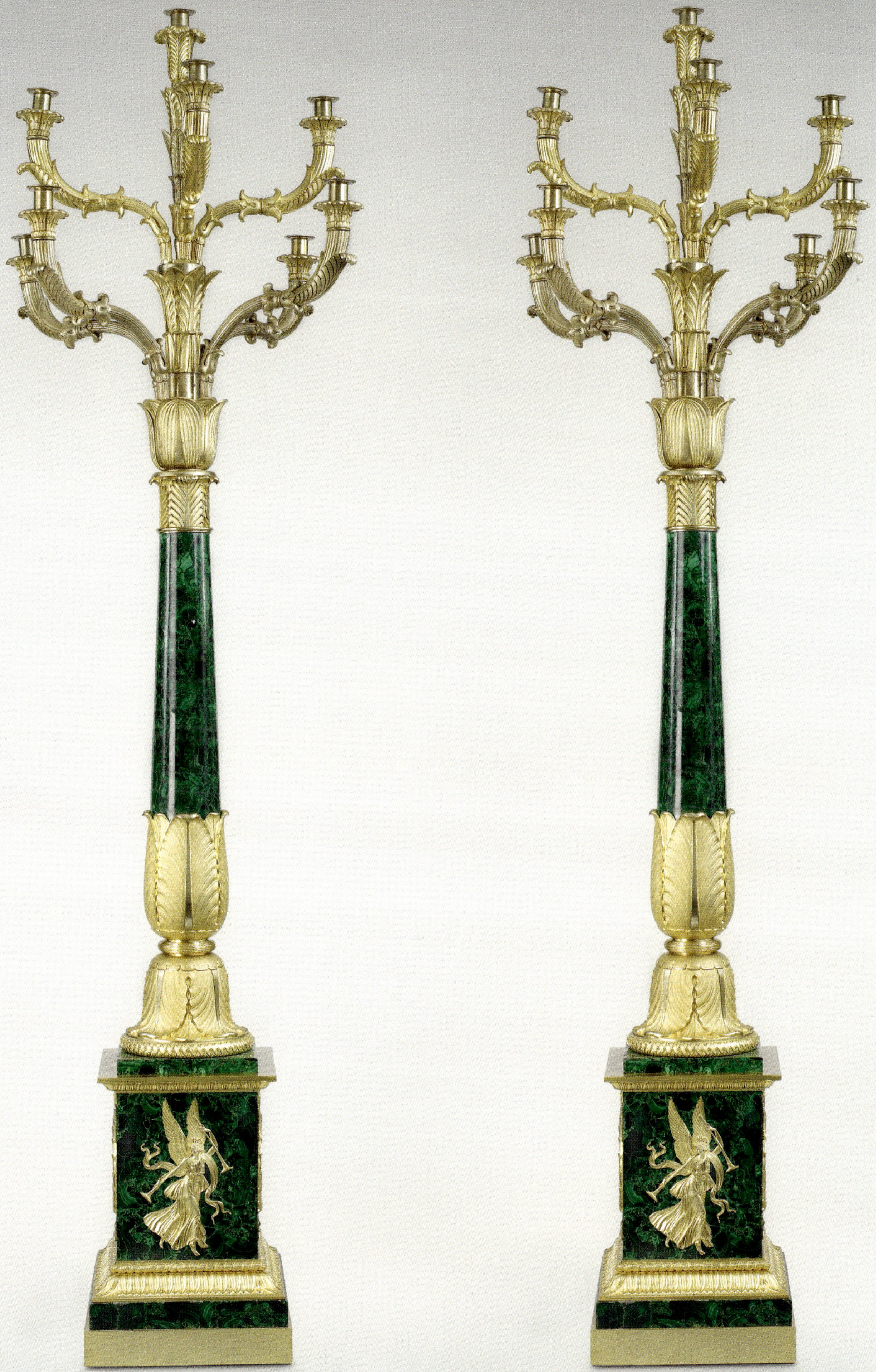

RUSSIAN; ATTRIBUTED TO NIKOLAI NIKITICH DEMIDOV (1773–1828)

229 *Pair of columns and vases* late eighteenth century

Malachite, granite, chased and gilded bronze, (vase) 35.0 × 17.0 × 15.5 cm (identical), (column) 177.0 × 32.0 × 24.0 cm (identical)
RCIN 35444.1–2

Provenance Acquired by George IV, *c.*1814

Literature M&S 518; Roberts 2001, p. 212

In 1824, George IV set about rebuilding and furnishing a lavish suite of private apartments at Windsor Castle, using the architect Jeffry Wyatville (1766–1840), and the decorators Morel & Seddon. Judging by various acquisitions made at this time, the King showed an appreciation of gilt-bronze mounted malachite. In 1827, Dowager Empress Maria Feodorovna wrote to the King to offer a malachite vase on a pedestal, and this, together with various other pieces, were incorporated into Morel and Seddon's decorative schemes at Windsor.

This pair of gilt-bronze mounted malachite vases and columns, with gilt-bronze laurel wreath bases and square plinths, furnished the bedroom of the King's closest companion, Lady Conyngham (1769–1861). Each vase has a waisted neck and ovoid body, mounted with satyr handles, dressed with vines, on turned socles, square bases and plinths with foliate borders. According to Jutsham, these vases were 'bought at the Princess of Wales' sale. If this provenance is correct, they probably came from the sale of furniture and other items at the Princess's house in Connaught Place, conducted by Robins prior to November 1814. They were restored at a cost of 4 guineas by Charles Brandt in July 1819, and sent to Morel & Seddon on 10 January 1828.

Columns of this type were very popular in the period 1800–1820. In 1816, Demidov encouraged Louis Carbonelle, a collaborator of Thomire, to propose gilt-bronze-mounted malachite objects to London society.[22] A pair were given by Alexander I to Napoleon I and are now in the Trianon at Versailles, transformed into candelabra.[23] A further pair are in the Malachite Room of the Winter Palace. Two further columns are mentioned in an exchange of correspondence between Demidov and the Thomire workshop in 1823. CDEG

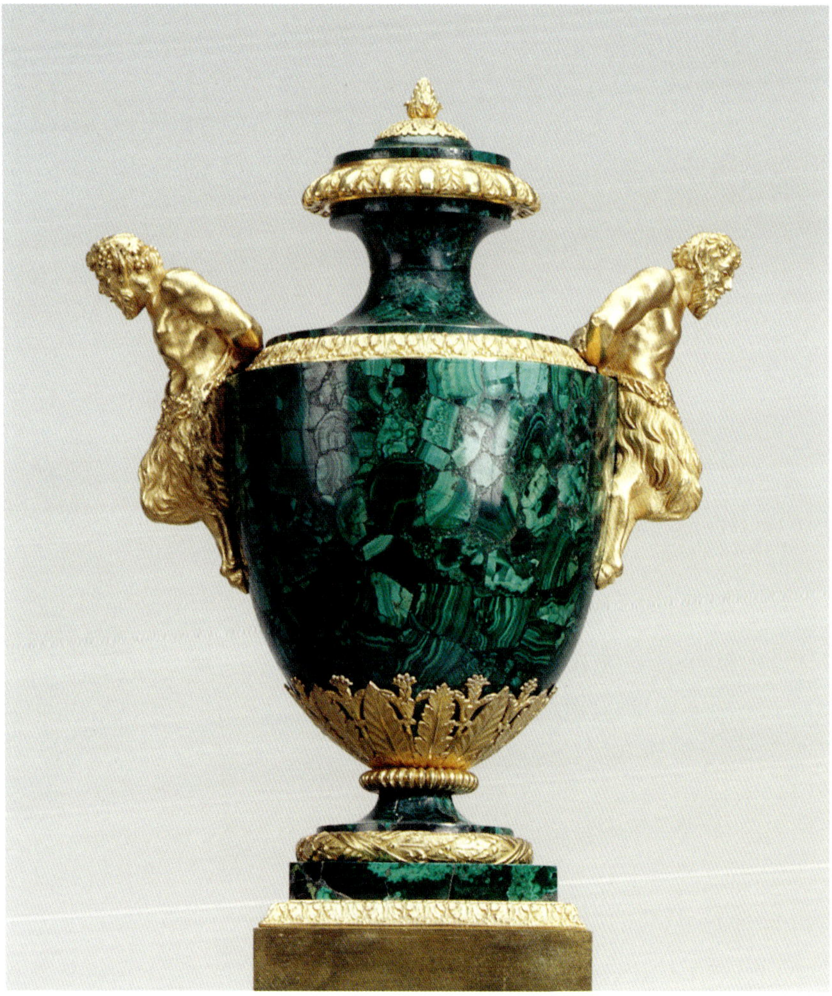

Detail of vase

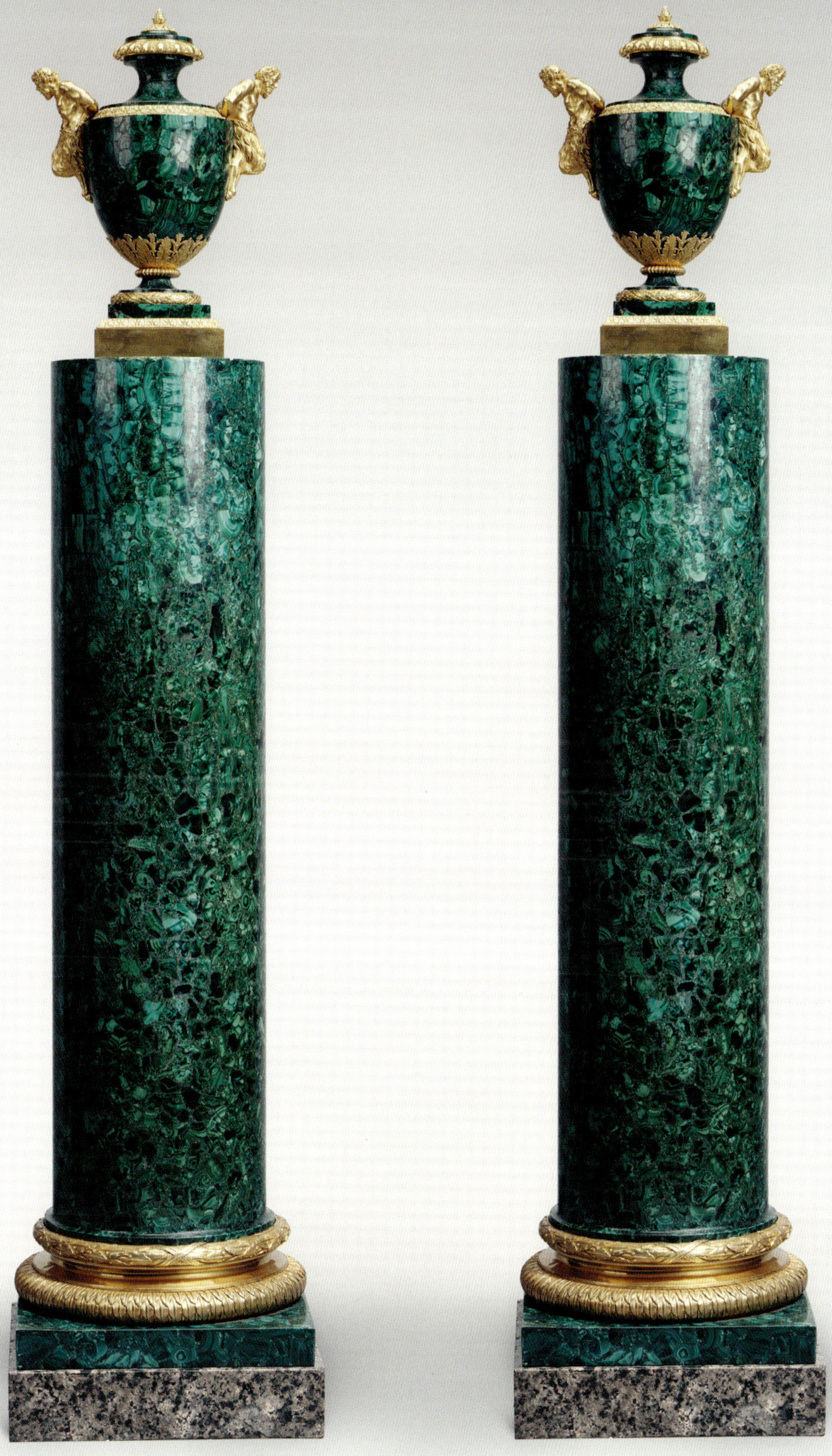

KOLYVAN FACTORY, EKATERINBURG

230 *Vase and pedestal* 1872

Korgon porphyry, (vase) 43.5 × 56.0 × 34.0 cm, green-grey porphyry (pedestal) 134.5 × 56.5 cm
Pedestal inscribed in Cyrillic: 'Column from Schlif factory, begun 22 June 1871, finished 30 November 1872'
RCIN 31653

Provenance Gift of Emperor Alexander II to Queen Victoria, 9 May 1874

Literature Decorative China *c.*1879, James Hollis and John W. Livingston, late 1870s, no. 394; Mavrodina 2007, p. 382, no. K.84

Carved from Korgon porphyry, much prized for its violet-grey hue and mounted via a cast iron rod onto the greenish-grey porphyry base, this vase was made at the Schlif / Kolyvan stone-carving factory and took 18 months to produce. The subtlety of the carving, which features both highly polished areas and areas which are left matt through the technique of fine chiselling, demonstrates the exceptional quality of the workmanship. The porphyry base is carved in high relief with four panels with pilasters between them. The tops of the pilasters are decorated with carved volutes and a rosette with a hanging foliate garland beneath.

A design for an identical vase and pedestal is held in the Russian State Historical Archives.[24] The drawing shows a pedestal with a vase, and is inscribed 'A vase made of greyish-violet jasper on a pedestal made of greenish grey porphyry, K. F. No 34. 25294 p. II Academy of Sciences'. The letters K. F. in this and other similar inscriptions in the Album stand for the Kolyvan factory. The number refers to the income-expenditure book of the Cabinet of His Imperial Majesty. The location of the vase was until now unknown until its identification in the Royal Collection and its inclusion in this exhibition.

The vase was given to Queen Victoria in May 1874, when Alexander II visited England. Correspondence in the Royal Archives records notification of the gift in April 1874, and the decision was made to have the 'two large vases' delivered to Buckingham Palace.[25] According to documents in the state archive of the Sverdlovsk region, the vase was presented to Queen Victoria in the presence of her daughter-in-law, the Duchess of Edinburgh, in Buckingham Palace, where it was assembled for the Queen to see by Ivan Sumin. Sumin was a member of the dynasty of stone carvers which included his son, Avenir Sumin, who became a rival of Fabergé in the production of small hardstone animals and other objects.

Described in the *Windsor Castle inventory of decorative china* as 'a very handsome Porphyry Vase, exquisitely sculptured, the handles of open work with beautifully finished foliage',[26] it was initially placed in the Sovereign's Entrance at Windsor Castle, before being moved to the Crimson Drawing Room, where it was placed prominently in the window bay overlooking the East Terrace (fig. 76), where it remained until 1908, when it was removed to the Orangery. It was then placed in store from 1934, and at some point suffered minor damage. An identical vase in the Fersman Mineralogical Museum was formerly in the Anichkov Palace, St Petersburg home of the Dowager Empress Maria Feodorovna and a later copy is in the Hermitage Museum.[27] CDEG

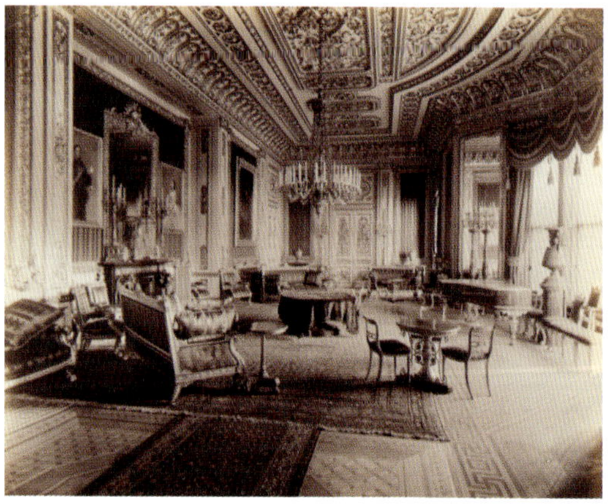

FIG. 76
*The Crimson Drawing Room, Windsor Castle, c.*1895
Gelatin silver print, 22.9 × 27.9 cm
RCIN 2935633

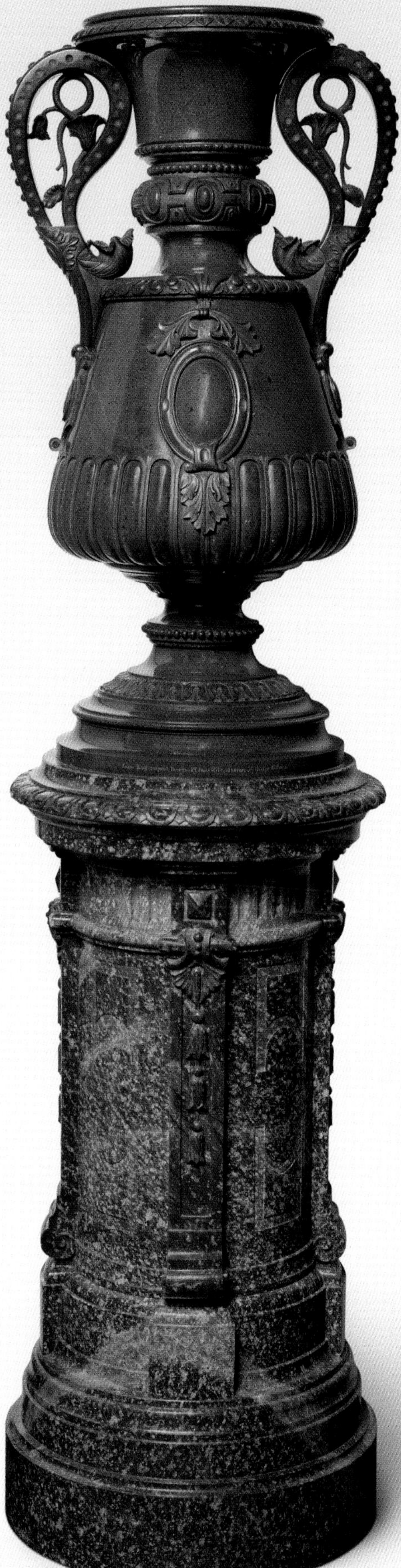

PETERHOF IMPERIAL LAPIDARY WORKSHOPS

231 *Paperweight* c.1830

Malachite, gilt metal, porcelain, 7.5 × 28.4 × 7.6 cm
RCIN 53554

Provenance Possibly given to Queen Victoria by Grand Duke Alexei Alexandrovich, 1880

Malachite was famously used to great effect in the late eighteenth and nineteenth centuries in Russia, for the veneering of monumental vases or large pieces of furniture. The skilled process of production was carried out in both Ekaterinburg and at the Imperial Lapidary Workshops at Peterhof. The majority of output was of large-scale pieces, which were intended for the furnishing of imperial palaces and residences, or for official gifts (cats 226–229). However, smaller objects, such as boxes, clocks and desk garnitures, made malachite accessible to the wider population, enabling them to purchase objects at affordable prices.

This finely produced paperweight is enhanced by chased gilt-bronze mounts, forming both the handle and the frames to the porcelain plaques, which show views of the Convent of St Alexander Nevskii (right) and L'hôpital impérial des pauvres malades (left), both in St Petersburg, published in Svin'yin (cat. 84). There are numerous surviving examples of similar paperweights and desk accessories, including an almost identical paperweight in the Hermitage, which was originally in the Marble Palace, residence of Grand Duke Constantine Nikolaevich, second son of Emperor Nicholas I.[28]

Queen Victoria was given a paperweight by Grand Duke Alexei in 1880, in memory of his mother, Maria Alexandrovna, consort of Alexander II.[29] Prince Albert purchased a malachite paperweight from the Great Exhibition, recorded as a 'malachite letter weight' in Queen Victoria's accounts, dated 14 November 1851. Given the early nineteenth-century style of this example, it is most likely to be that given as a gift to Queen Victoria by Grand Duke Alexei. CDEG

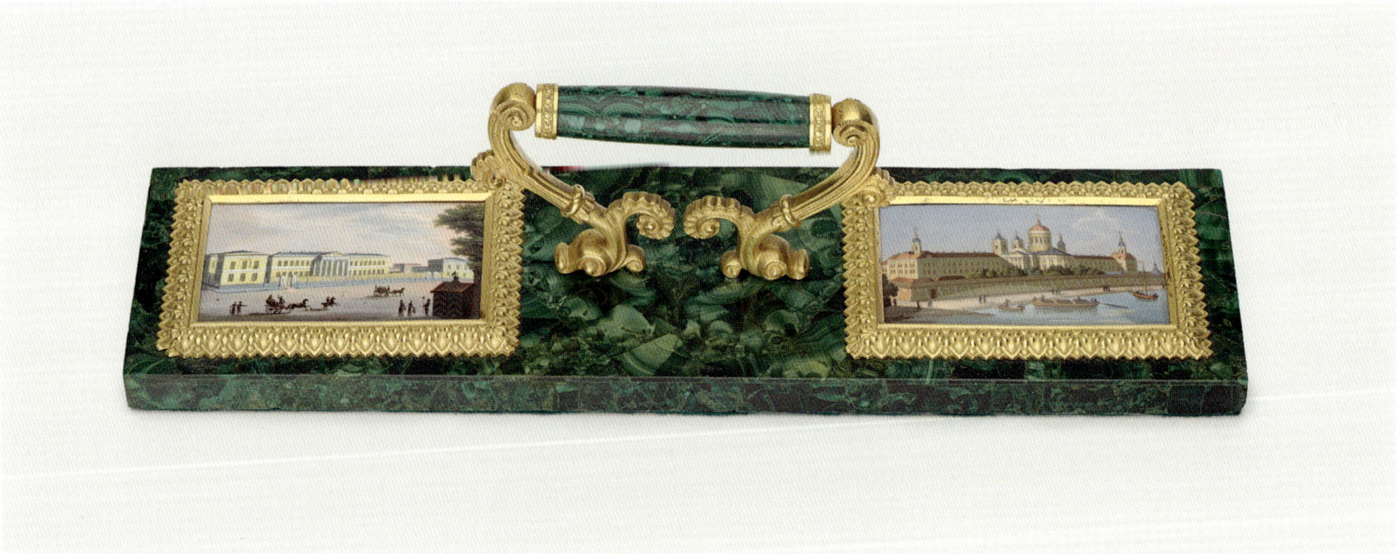

P.A. OVCHINNIKOV (1830–1888)

232 *Casket* c.1870

Nephrite, rubies, sapphires, enamel, pearls, silver gilt, 7.0 × 17.0 × 10.0 cm
Engraved in Cyrillic: падом. фад. П.А. Овшинникоба 'made by P.A. Ovchinnikov'
RCIN 40102

Provenance Possibly a gift to the Duke and Duchess of Edinburgh, 1874

The firm of Ovchinnikov was founded in Moscow by the serf, Pavel Akimovich Ovchinnikov, in 1851, and rose to become successful and famous, thanks to both imperial patronage, receiving the imperial warrant in 1865, and the high quality works in silver, gold, enamel and other materials that were produced. The firm constantly received gold medals at the various international exhibitions, and was in demand for its dishes, *kovshi*, and other objects, for souvenirs, presents and official and diplomatic gifts.

This casket, made from carved nephrite and mounted in gilt metal, is set with sapphires, rubies and pearls in a historicist style popular in Russia in the 1870s and 1880s and may have been exhibited at one of the international exhibitions given the unusual mark on the piece. In 1874, the Duke of Edinburgh was presented with a *bratina*, dish, eight *charkas* and a *kovsh*, all made in the seventeenth-century style. It is not possible to identify these with any certainty today in the Royal Collection, which contains 23 works by the firm but a group of pieces in the 'jewelled' enamelled historicist style may constitute parts of the service.[30] As part of Maria Alexandrovna's dowry, she was given a tea service produced by Pavel Ovchinnikov, designed by M.S. Kharlamov, each form taking its inspiration from ancient Russian ware, with the tea caddy taking the form of an ancient Russian trunk, or *skrynia*. CDEG

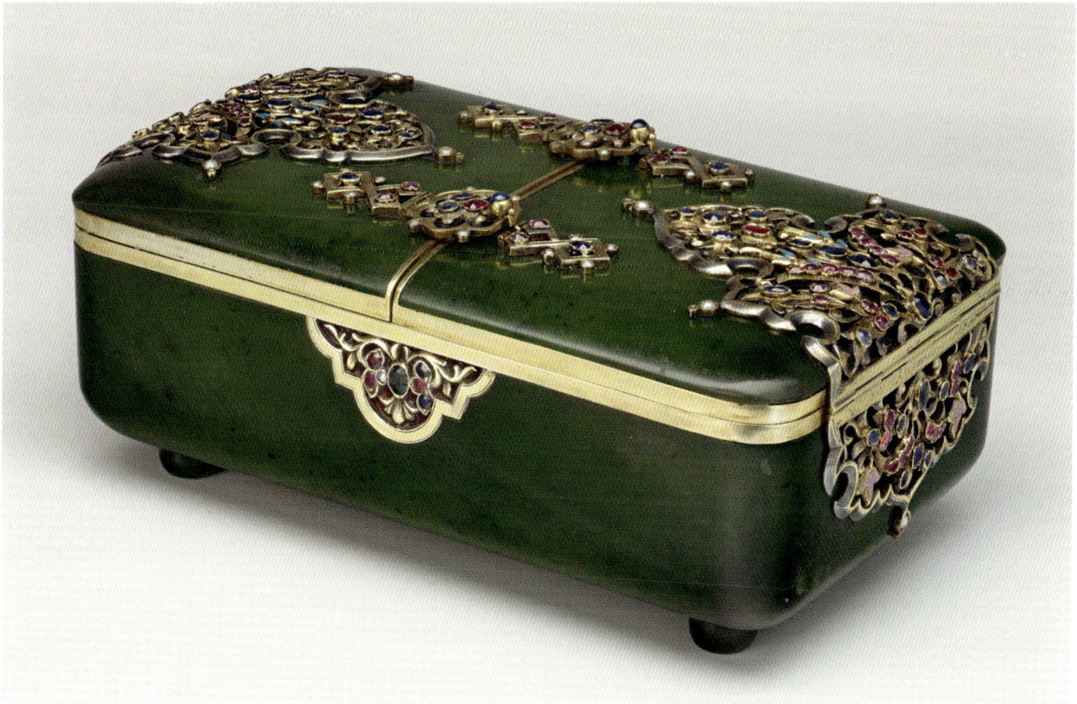

IMPERIAL PORCELAIN FACTORY

233 *Cup and saucer* *c.*1762–96

Porcelain, gilt decoration, 7.0 × 13.2 cm
Underglaze 'E' in Cyrillic
RCIN 3451.a–b

Provenance Possibly acquired by Queen Mary

This piece exemplifies the influence of Sèvres porcelain on the Russian Imperial Porcelain Factory from the mid-eighteenth century. The form of the straight-sided cup imitates the *gobelet litron* made at Sèvres, and numerous examples were made at the Imperial Porcelain Factory. The simple white and gold colour scheme incorporates urns, swags and vases in the neoclassical taste. The provenance of the cup and saucer is now known, but it is likely to have been acquired by Queen Mary in the 1920s or 1930s.
CDEG

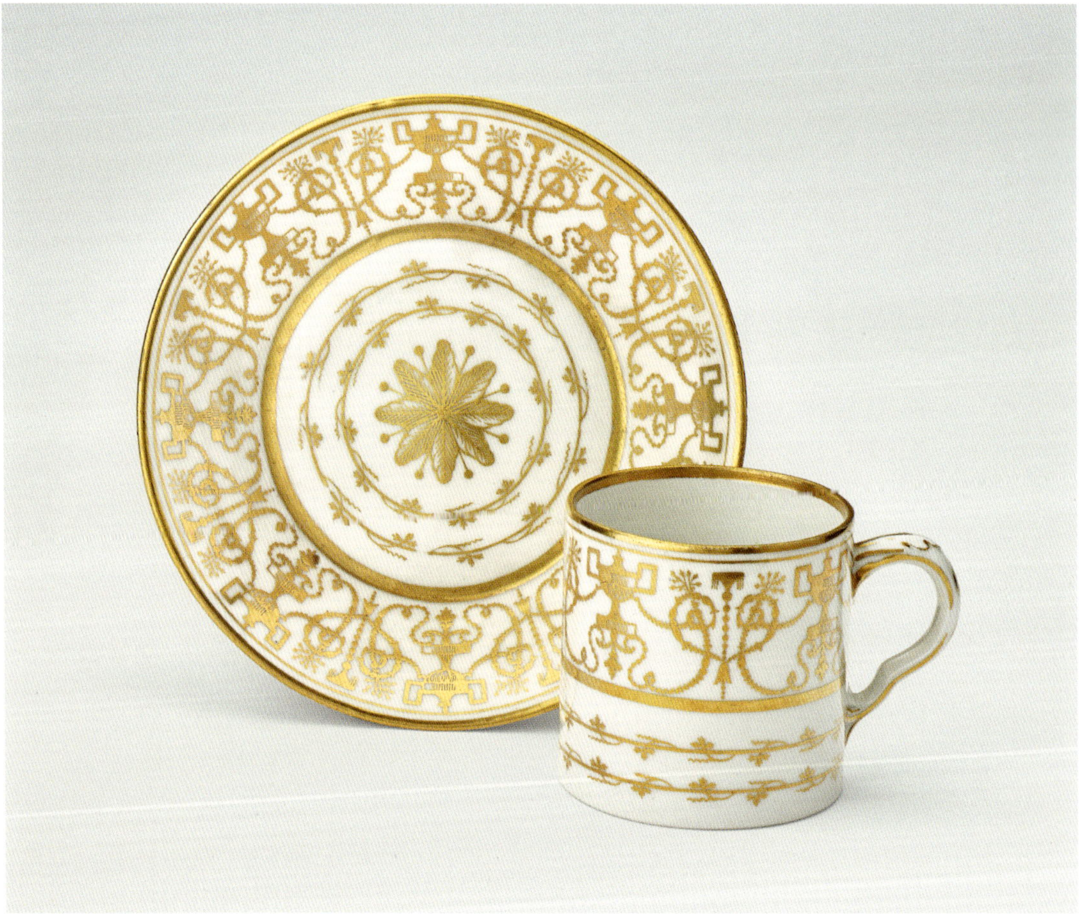

IMPERIAL PORCELAIN FACTORY

234 *Vase* 1907

Porcelain, 40.5 × 30.3 cm
Underglaze crowned *HII* monogram, above the date, *1907*
RCIN 28815

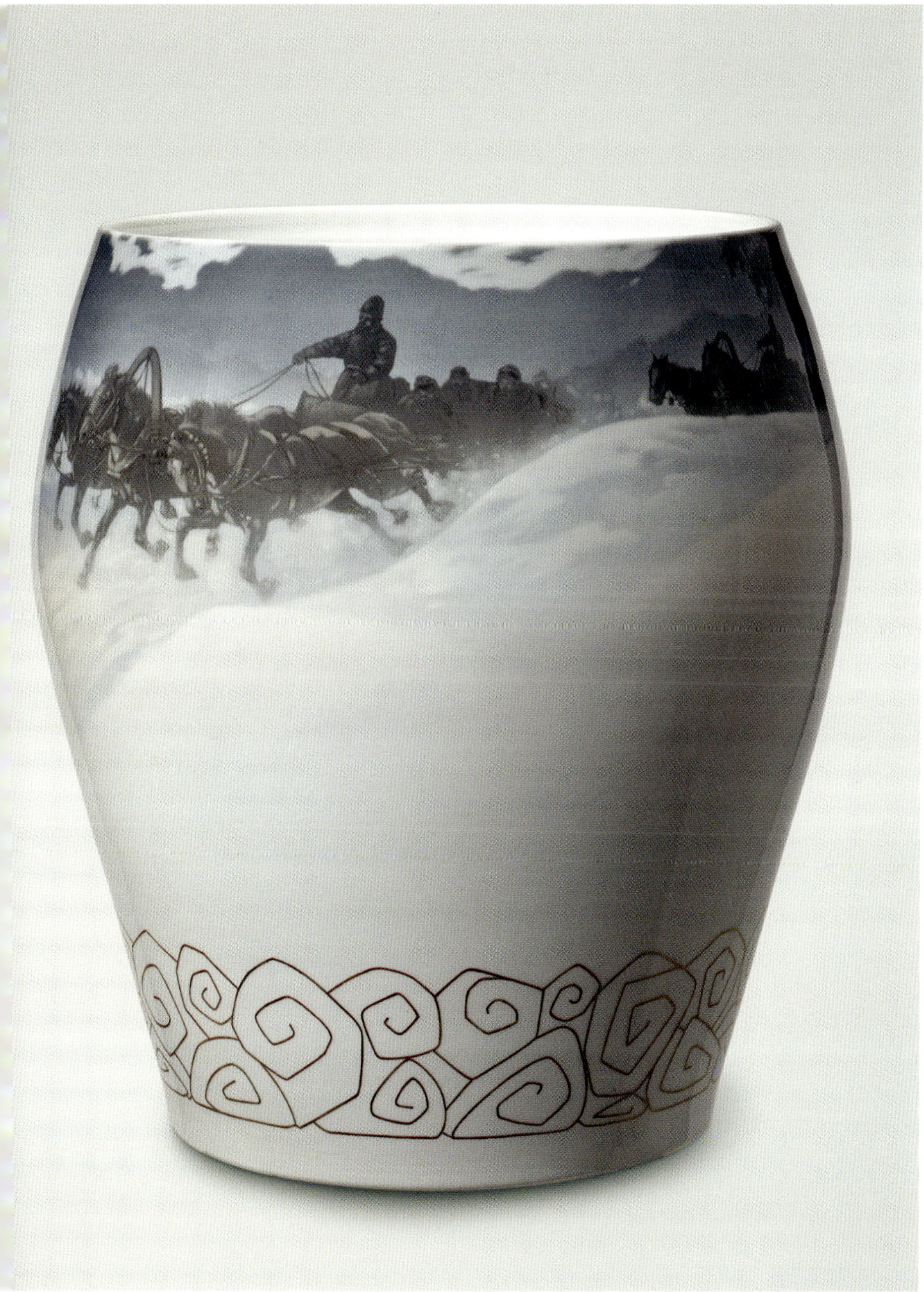

Provenance Probably acquired by Queen Alexandra

In 1889, the Royal Porcelain Factory at Copenhagen created a sensation in Paris at the international exhibition, with its display of porcelain decorated with underglaze painting. Only a small range of colours would withstand the heat of high fire, but the Danish factory had expanded the tones to include a variety of muted blues, greys and greens. Alexander III, being married to a Danish princess, collected this type of Danish studio porcelain, which he kept at Gatchina, his favourite palace. In 1892, he invited Karl Lisberg from the Royal Porcelain Factory, Copenhagen, to visit St Petersburg for six weeks, to teach this method to Russian artists, and the Imperial Porcelain Factory made the technical advance of introducing underglaze high-fire scenes.

This vase, in the Danish style, was made during Nicholas II's reign, and this style of production continued until the outbreak of the First World War. The scenes of Russian troikas and snowscapes are in muted tones of blue and grey, while the gold abstract border at the base references the neo-Russian style, mixing traditional Russian motifs with the '*stil modern*'. A second Imperial Porcelain Factory vase in the Danish style, but in ovoid form and painted with sprays of magnolias, exists in the Royal Collection.[31] Given Queen Alexandra and Maria Feodorovna's shared Danish heritage, these vases were almost certainly gifts from the imperial family to the Queen. CDEG

CARL TEGELSTEN (1798–1852)

235 *Model of the Tsar Bell* 1849

Silver, 15.2 × 10.7 cm
Assaymark of St Petersburg, 1849, and CT, maker's mark of Carl Tegelsten, inscribed inside the rim 1851 год; фев 26
RCIN 46101

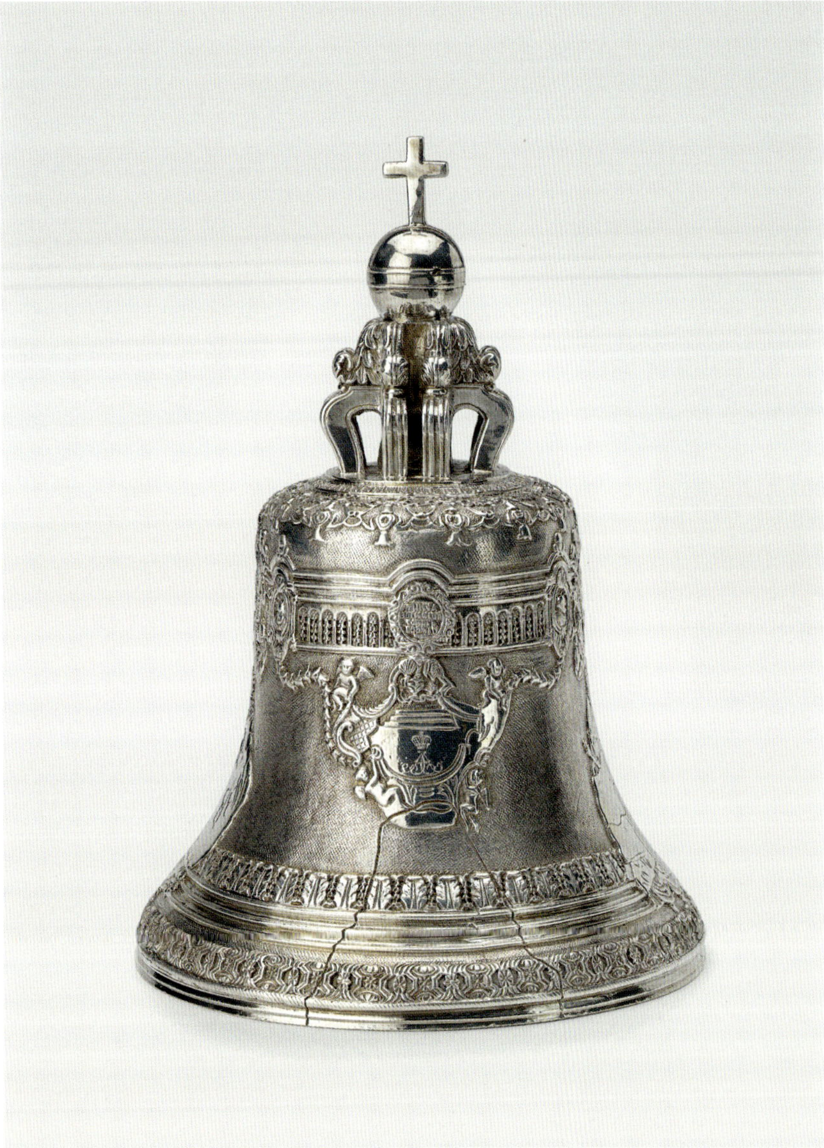

Provenance Possibly King Edward VII and Queen Alexandra

A silver model of the so-called Tsar Bell, or *Tsars-Kolokol*, it is decorated with portraits of Emperor Alexei and Empress Anna, angels and saints, and with the broken piece outlined.

The renowned Tsar Bell was the largest bell ever cast in bronze in Russia, and the third bell to be created for the Tower of the Kremlin. Each successive casting reused the bronze from its predecessor. The third bell, designed in 1733, was cast in Moscow, only a short distance from its current location, adjacent to Cathedral Square, but when it was being raised out of its casting pit, the wooden staves holding it in place were destroyed by fire; the bell fell back into its founding pit and a piece of the bell broke off.

The bell and its broken section remained in situ for a further century, until raised and placed on a stone plinth in 1836. This remarkable and famous work was repeatedly copied in miniature by a variety of silversmiths.

This model was made by Carl Tegelsten (cat. 98), who qualified as a master goldsmith in St Petersburg in 1825, and from around 1833 worked extensively for the firm of Nicholls & Plincke. There was another model of the bell in the Royal Collection, owned by King Edward VII, which is listed in the Garrard 1885 inventory and engraved with the Prince of Wales's feathers, although it cannot be traced in the Collection today. **CDEG**

RUSSIAN

236 *Salt cellar* 1859

Silver, niello, gilt, 8.0 × 6.5 × 5.5 cm
Struck with city mark of Moscow, assayer's mark (1859), and maker's mark, *BC*; seat engraved: *Без соли, без хлеба – Половина обеда* ('A meal is incomplete without salt or bread')
RCIN 46153

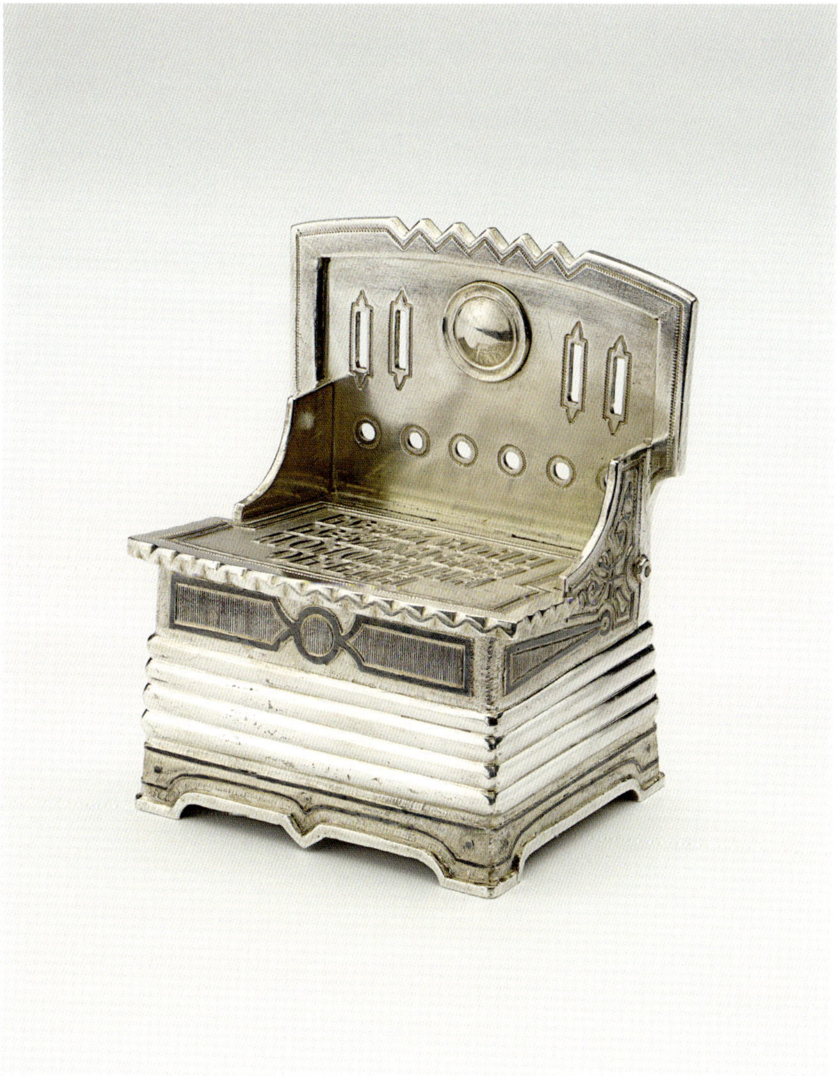

Provenance Possibly King Edward VII or Queen Alexandra, when Prince and Princess of Wales

The throne is pierced in the backplate with small circles and rectangles; the base is ridged to resemble planking, and it stands on bracket feet. The engraving on the seat is partly nielloed ('without salt, only half the meal'), and the interior is divided into two.

Traditionally, salt was associated in Russia with hospitality, and salt cellars were kept at the entrance to the home, guests being offered bread dipped in salt as a welcome. Bread and salt were also integral to the ceremonies of betrothal and marriage and to Imperial coronations. Salt cellars of this type became popular around 1845, when they were placed on the table before the guest, a piece of bread resting on the seat of the throne.

CDEG

ROBERT COLQUHON (1842–1879)

237 *Table ornament/paperweight* 1890–1910

Silver, rock crystal, 8.5 × 9.0 × 9.0 cm
Struck with maker's mark of Robert Colquhon, and partial St Petersburg silver mark; rock crystal painted in white: *M.1852*
RCIN 46157

Provenance Probably belonged to King Edward VII and Queen Alexandra

Table ornaments or paperweights depicting traditional Russian subjects were produced in large numbers by silversmiths such as Sazikov and Ovchinnikov. This particular example was made by Robert Colquhon, who established a workshop supplying the firm of Nicholls & Plincke, an English partnership operating between 1829 and 1898, otherwise known as the English Shop or Magasin Anglais. Situated on Nevskii Prospekt in St Petersburg, the firm capitalised on the Russian taste for English silver, and was the official supplier to the imperial family. The cast silver bear, an ancient Russian symbol, stands on an ice floe carved into a naturalistic shape from a piece of rock crystal, which has been polished to replicate the glassy surface of the ice. This object is an interesting statement on the interplay between Russian subject matter and English craftsmanship. CDEG

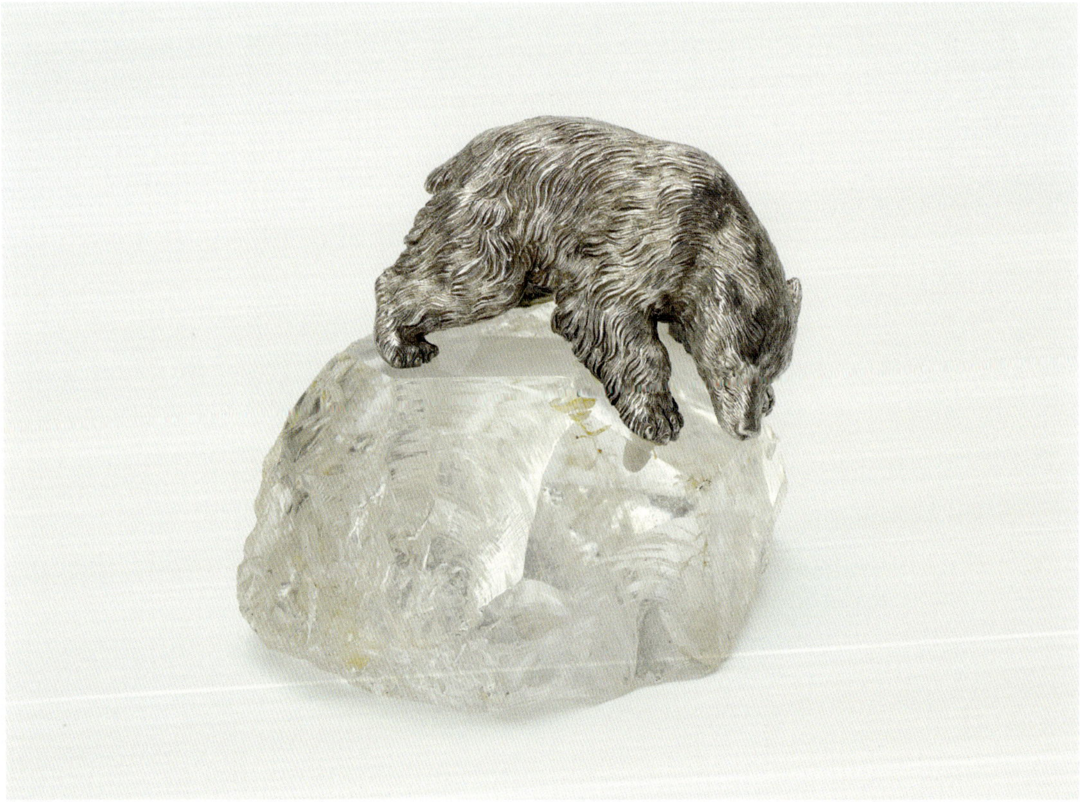

VASILI SEMENOV (active 1865–1890)

238 *Beaker* 1879

Silver, silver gilt, niello, 9.0 × 7.5 × 7.8 cm
Impressed with Moscow silver mark, 84 zolotniks, ?*18* (rubbed), and maker's mark for Vasili Semenov; inscribed on rim with motto in Cyrillic: 'Чара серебряная добрая пить из нея на здравіе'
'A fine silver cup with which to toast good health'
RCIN 46609

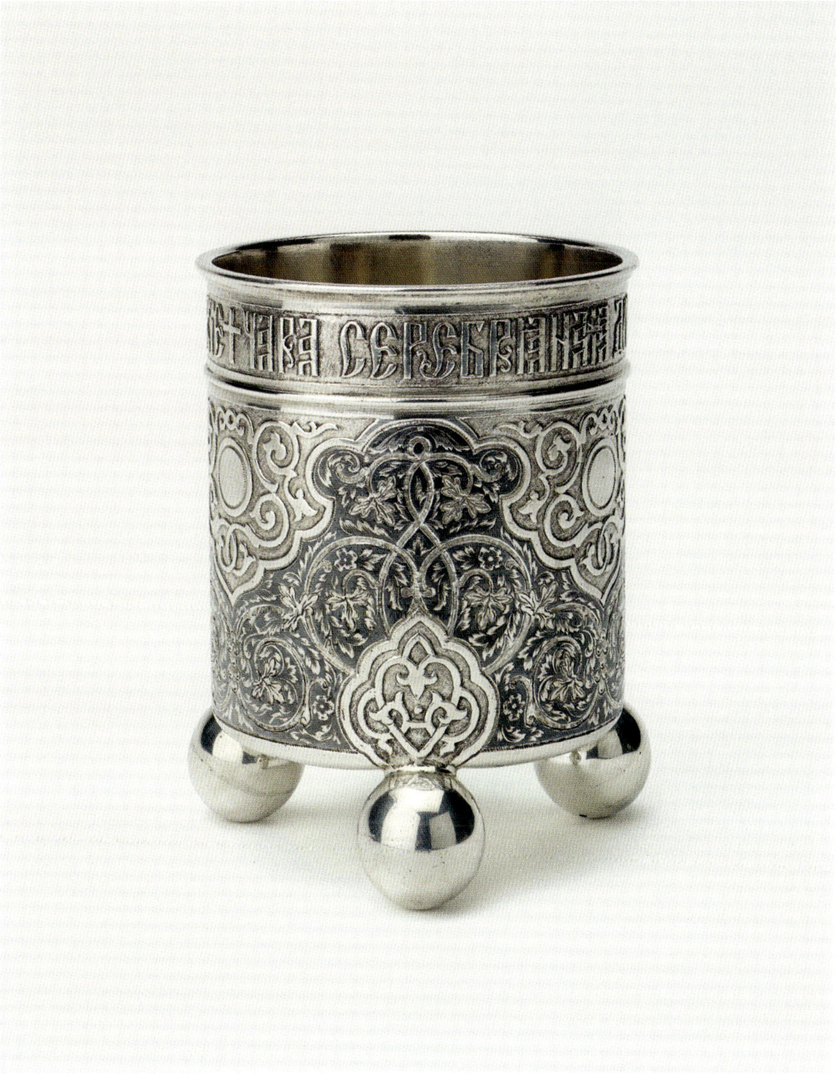

Provenance Possibly a gift to Queen Alexandra, as it is engraved with an *A* monogram on its base; listed in KGV 1904 as having 'belonged to King Edward VII'

The silver beaker is on three ball feet, with a nielloed body, with scrolls, foliage and flowers and reserves on a matted ground. The niello technique involves blackening an engraved pattern onto the metal through the application of an alloy, adhered through firing. The maker, Vasili Semenov, inherited the Moscow workshop of his father in 1865, and exhibited at the All-Russia Industrial and Art Exhibition of 1882. The form of this beaker copies almost exactly the beakers produced by the firm of Sazikov, goldsmith to the imperial court, with the Cyrillic inscription around the rim, the engraved cartouche plaques which descend from the rim towards the ball feet of the beaker, and the design of vine scrolls against a niello ground. Sazikov exhibited identical beakers, but in gilt, at the Universal Exhibition in Paris in 1867, and an example of just such a beaker is in the collection of the Hillwood Museum.[32] **CDEG**

KARL ALBRECHT (active 1874–1898),
NICHOLLS & PLINCKE, ST PETERSBURG, retailer

239 *Salt cellar* *c.*1876

Silver with gilt interior, 8.0 × 5.5 × 5.2 cm
Impressed with silver mark of St Petersburg (84 zolotniks), maker's mark of Karl Albrecht, and retailer's mark of Nicholls & Plincke; lid engraved inside: *EDDY / 8th Jany. 1876*
RCIN 46659

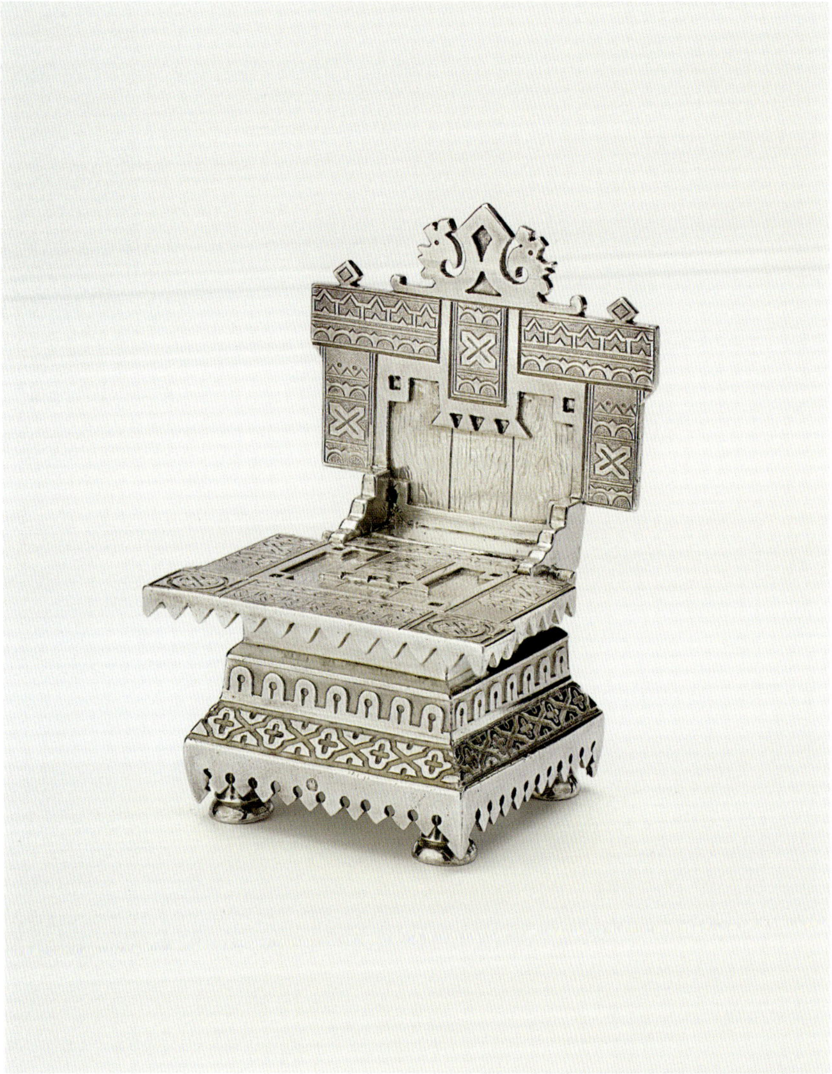

Provenance Birthday gift to Prince Albert Victor of Wales, 1876

The salt throne has a rectangular back, with an angular crest representing two cockerel heads; it is engraved with geometric patterns and a panelled central section, chased to resemble wooden graining. The stepped body is cast with bands of geometric designs, and it rests on four bun feet. This salt cellar is in the Russian style popular at the end of the nineteenth century (similar to cats 186, 236); carved wooden versions with similar motifs were also made from the mid-nineteenth century onwards.

This most Russian of objects was evidently purchased directly from the retailer, otherwise popularly known as 'the English shop' by the donor, possibly Prince Albert Victor's aunt Maria Feodorovna or another close member of the Russian family. It was a twelfth birthday present to Albert Victor of Wales (Duke of Clarence and Avondale), eldest son of King Edward VII and Queen Alexandra, who died at the age of 28 from pneumonia, caused by the influenza pandemic of 1889–92. CDEG

RUSSIAN

240 *Tankard* 1864

Silver, niello, 12.5 × 7.8 × 12.0 cm
Impressed with Moscow silver mark (84 zolotniks); engraved: *From / Mother dear*
RCIN 46911

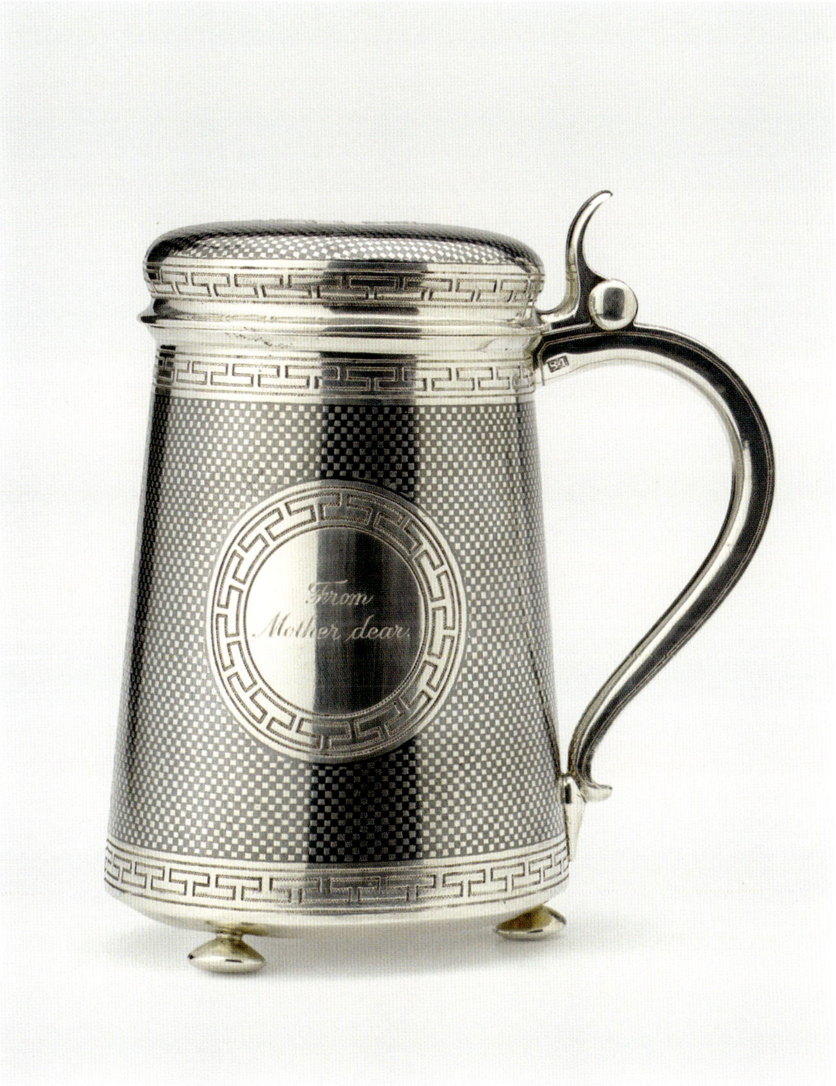

Provenance Given to King George V for his birthday, 3 June 1921, by Queen Alexandra

Literature KGV 1904, fol. xx

The tankard, which stands on three small bun feet, is decorated in a niello chequer pattern, with borders of angular Greek, key-like pattern and a domed lid. The body has a roundel on one side, with an inscription and a roundel on the lid.

The decorative vocabulary developed in the nineteenth century to include a fascination with creating *trompe l'oeil* surfaces in silver, also translated to niello, and wares resembling items created from tree bark or with the grain of sawn wood were also produced. Simple geometric patterns of the type found on this tankard were less common and were usually used for borders rather than overall decoration.

This tankard may be the work of the firm of Gustav Klingert, a workshop founded in Moscow in 1865. The business specialised in enamel wares, but also produced items in niello also. A number of their works of art have geometric or chequer-pattern borders, and items with Greek key motifs were also produced.

The tankard, a birthday gift to King George V from Queen Alexandra, is inscribed with the familiar name by which her son referred to her, 'Mother dear'. **CDEG**

RUSSIAN

241 *Tea set* 1880

Silver, parcel gilt, wood, (teapot) 14.0 × 21.5 × 10.5 cm, (milk jug) 9.5 × 11.0 × 7.5 cm, (sugar bowl and cover) 12.2 × 13.8 × 11.5 cm
Impressed with silver mark of St Petersburg and maker's mark ЛГ
RCINS 49573, 49574, 49577

Provenance Probably acquired by Queen Alexandra

These pieces form part of a tea and coffee service, which comprises, in addition, cream jug, slop bowl, coffee pot, tea kettle and cake basket. The pieces all bear the mark of the maker 'LG' (in Cyrillic), whose work is known, but who has not been definitively identified.

The surface of each piece of the service is chased to resemble woven strips of birch bark, fastened by small gilt staples and with plain borders. The oval basket has a hinged bail handle, and the kettle, teapot and coffee pot each has a leather-covered handle. The use of *trompe l'oeil* surfaces in ceramics and silverware was common in the late nineteenth century, as silversmiths adopted the Russian style, returning to traditional motifs seen in peasant craftsmanship on boxes, baskets and even shoes. There are many similar tea and coffee services from the same period which have survived in museum collections both in Russia and abroad, including an example in the Hillwood Museum,[33] also made in St Petersburg, but by Aleksandr Liubavin. CDEG

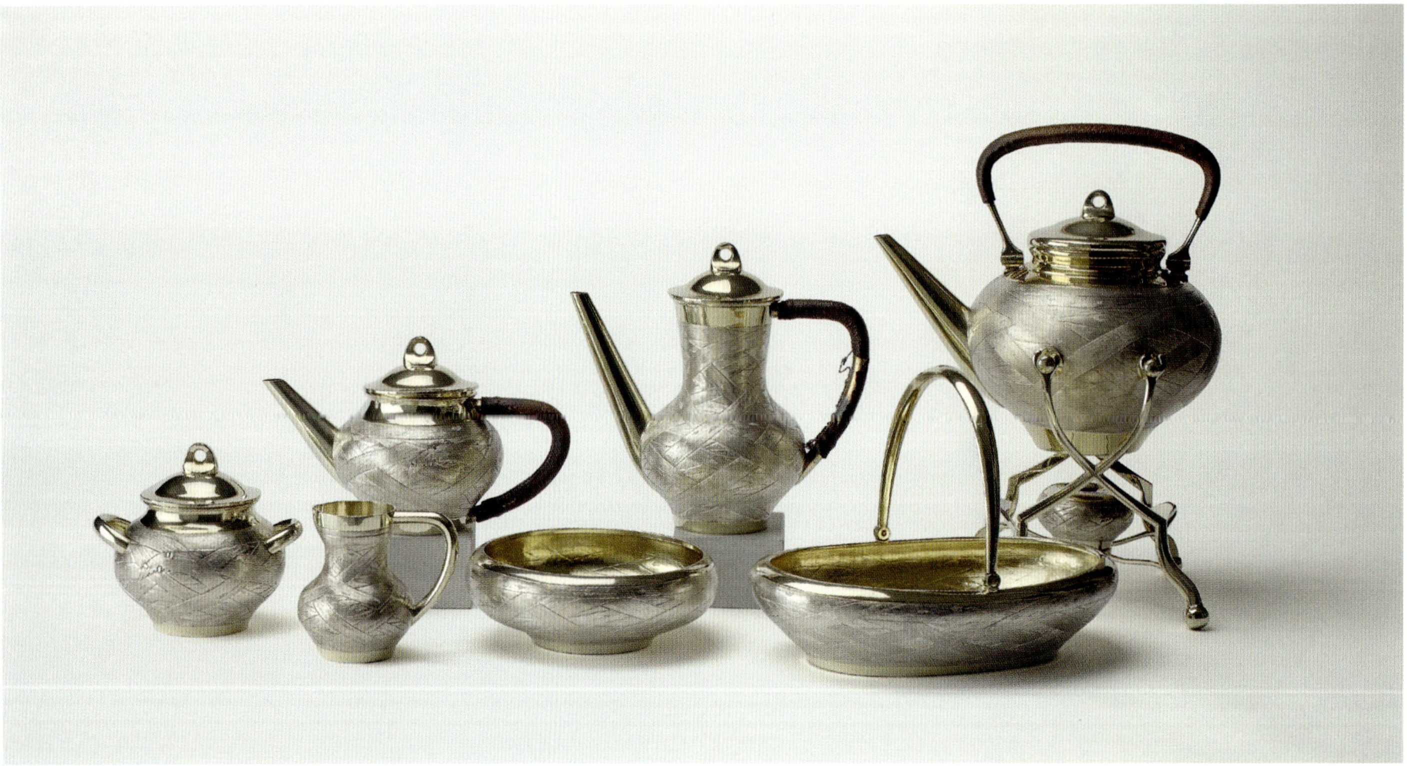

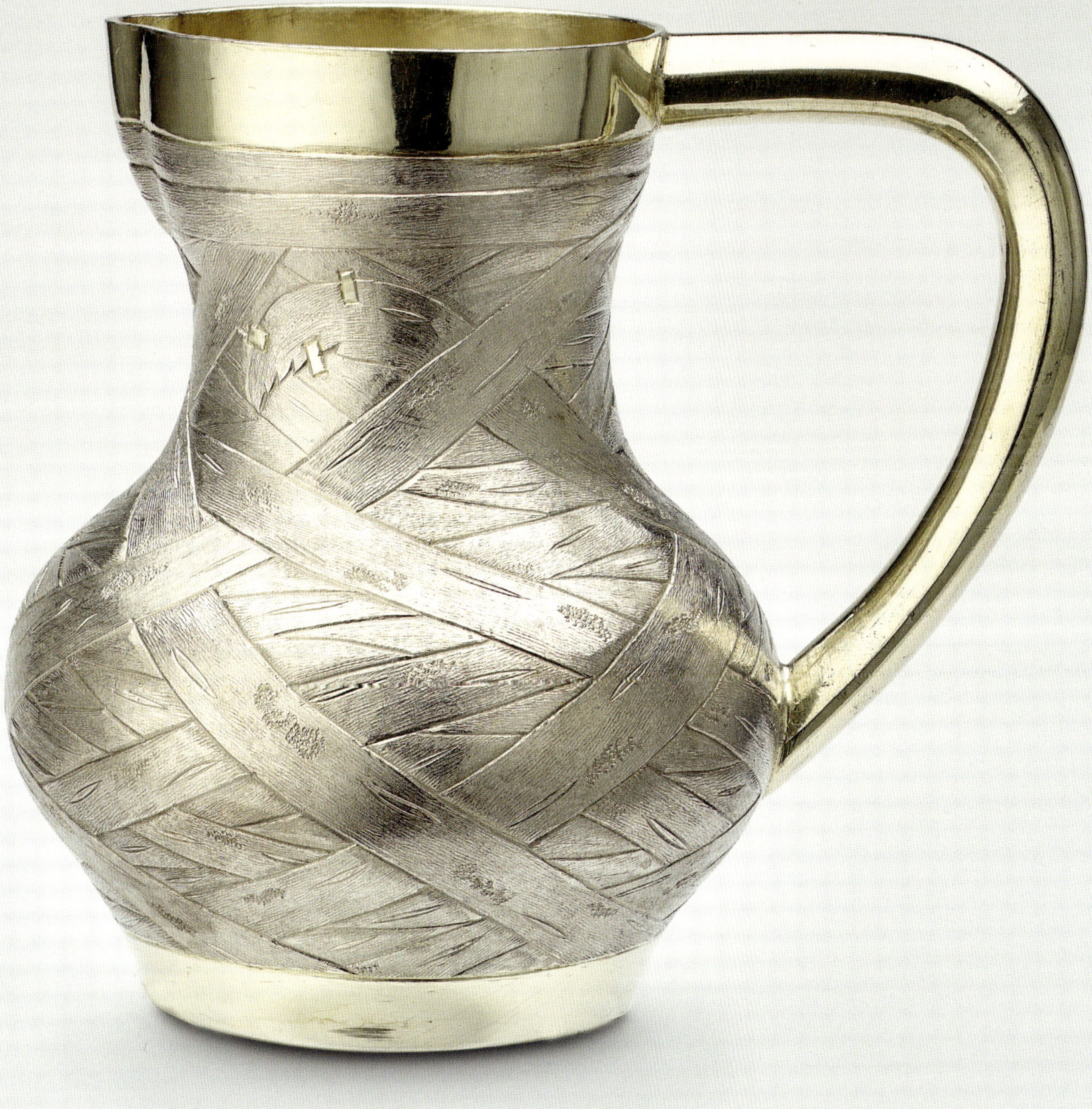

FABERGÉ

242 *Pair of decanters* before 1896

Crystal, silver, 15.8 × 10.0 × 12.0 cm
Struck with Moscow silver mark of 84 zolotniks (before 1896), 'C. FABERGE' and initials, 'CF', in Cyrillic
RCIN 100337.1–2

Provenance Purchased by Queen Elizabeth The Queen Mother, September 1973

Literature De Guitaut 2003, p. 241; Harrison *et al.* 2009, pp. 170–71

The Fabergé firm produced silver-mounted glass and porcelain objects in both Moscow and St Petersburg. However, as the centre of silversmithing, the production of such objects was more concentrated in the Moscow workshops of the firm. Glass and porcelain were supplied by a variety of Russian and foreign makers, the latter group including Gallé, Tiffany, Royal Doulton and the Rörstrand Manufactory.

These crimson crystal decanters are engraved with swirling foliate motifs and scrolls, enclosing a diaper pattern at the front of the body. This fluid, organic style is replicated in the silver mounts in the form of dolphins, their mouths forming the spouts, and their arched bodies, chased with scales, forming the handles. CDEG

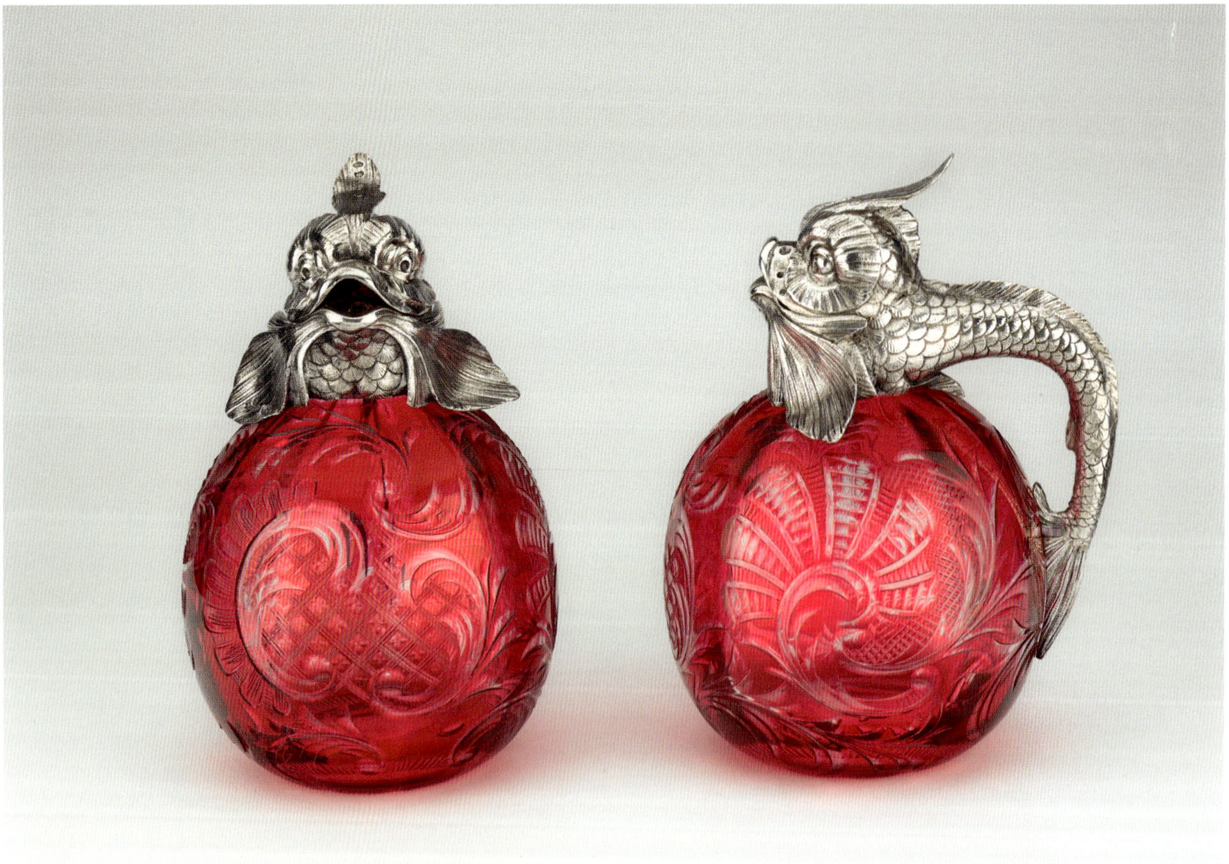

CARL BLANK

243 *Cigarette case* before 1896

Gold, guilloché enamel, diamonds, 1.5 × 8.9 × 8.3 cm
Impressed mark CB for Carl Blank; assay mark of 56 zolotniks for St Petersburg before 1896;
Engraved on interior of lid: *GIVEN TO TURKHAN PASHA / BY EMPEROR NICHOLAS II ACQUIRED BY QUEEN MARY / GIVEN TO KING GEORGE / in 1928*
RCIN 4058

Provenance Acquired by Queen Mary and given to King George V, 1928

Literature Tillander-Godenhielm 2005, pp. 174, 438

Carl Blank, a Finnish goldsmith, was head workmaster from 1882 to 1909 at the firm of Hahn, founded by Austrian-born Karl Hahn (active 1873–99) in 1873. Hahn was an important supplier to the Russian imperial court, receiving the title of purveyor to the court during the reign of Alexander III, for whom he made small items in silver and gold. Carl Blank also established his own workshop, making objects independently, which bear his own mark.

The sumptuous guilloché enamelling all over the surface of this cigarette case demonstrates the skill of Russia's goldsmiths and enamellers in the late nineteenth century. The lid is applied in one corner with the imperial double-headed eagle, indicating that this was an official presentation gift.

According to the inscription inside the lid, it was presented by Nicholas II to Turkhan Pasha (Turham Pasa; 1846–1927), although the exact date of presentation is not known, the inscription must have been a later addition. Turkhan Pasha was chargé d'affaires at the Turkish Embassy in St Petersburg in 1873, and after various other postings, returned to the city as ambassador between 1908 and 1913. It seems most likely that this box was presented to him during the earlier stages of his diplomatic career in Russia, given the hallmarked date. However, it was not unusual for such objects, destined to be official gifts, to be held in stock by the imperial court in readiness for presentation. Turkhan Pasha received two other distinguished honours from Nicholas II: he was made a knight of the Order of Alexander Nevskii in 1901, and received a snuffbox with the Emperor's portrait in 1913, the latter to mark the tercentenary of the Romanov dynasty.

Queen Mary purchased the box, in 1928, from the London dealers, Wartski, as a present for King George V.[34] CDEG

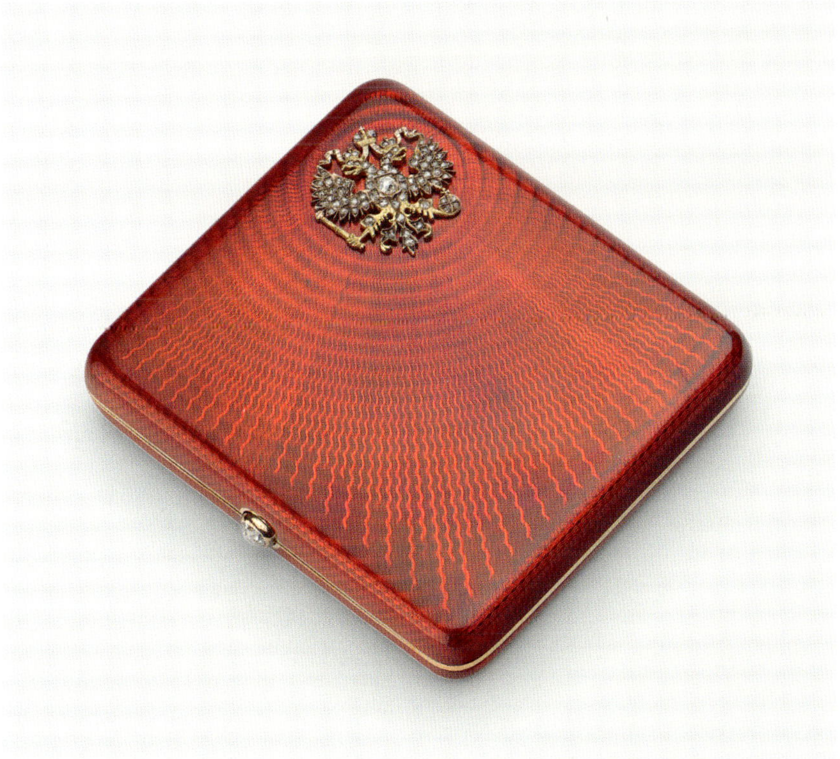

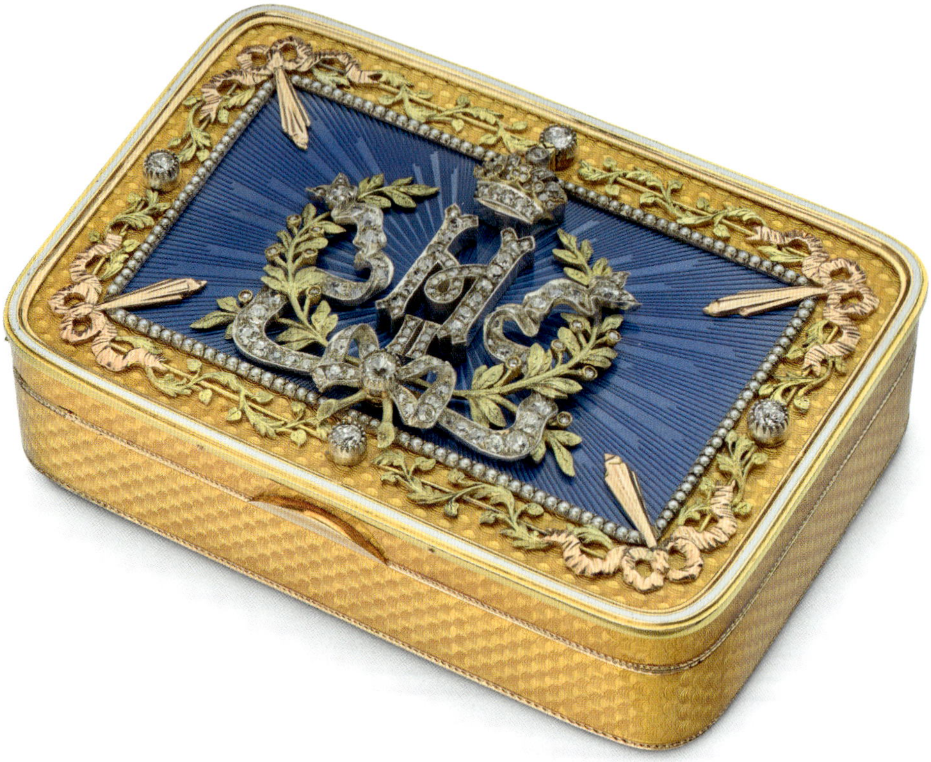

HAHN

244 *Presentation snuffbox with cipher of Nicholas II (1868–1918)* 1896–1908

Gold, enamel, diamonds, seed pearl, 9.2 × 6.5 × 3.0 cm
Impressed with mark of K. Hahn, mark of workmaster, Carl Blank, and assay mark of St Petersburg (1896–1908)
RCIN 19121

Provenance Given by Queen Mary to King George V, 3 June 1934

Literature GV Boxes 1929–35, IV, no. 358

Hahn was one of Fabergé's main competitors for imperial commissions, such as this presentation snuffbox. Many of the finest examples produced have the firm's overstamp with the mark of Carl Blank, head workmaster at the firm, who also made pieces in his own right such as cat. 243.

During the reign of Nicholas II, only 280 Russian subjects and 90 foreign dignitaries received imperial presentation snuffboxes with the Emperor's jewelled cipher, and of these, 59 were produced by the court supplier, Hahn. Boxes with the Emperor's cipher were presented to Russians in state service holding ranks three to five in the Table of Ranks,[35] to foreign dignitaries in connection with state visits, to ambassadors who had completed their mission, and also as a commemoration of a special event in Russia. The recipient of this box has not been traced.

Karl August Hahn established his jewellery firm in St Petersburg in 1874, and remained a competitor of Fabergé throughout the last quarter of the century. Hahn's presentation boxes were generally less sophisticated than those produced by Fabergé, both in their enamel colours and in the heaviness of the superimposed gold, silver and gemset mounts. Hahn is, however, perhaps best-known for creating the miniature imperial crown worn by Alexandra Feodorovna at the coronation in 1896, since the existing small crown was worn by the Dowager Empress Maria Feodorovna. **CDEG**

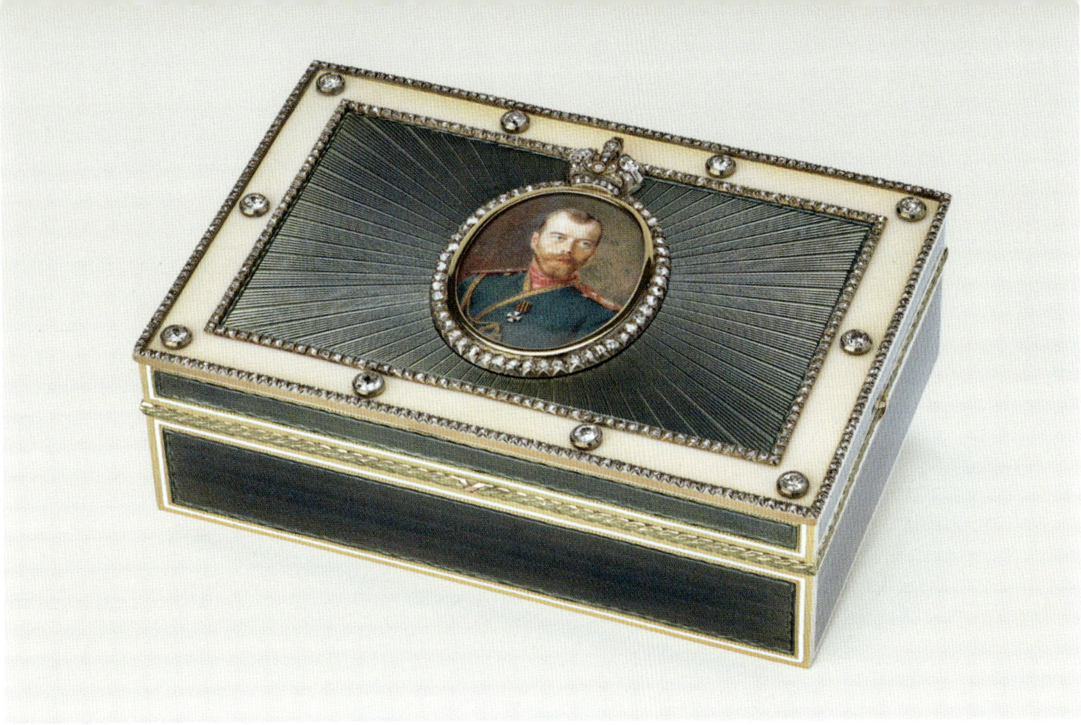

FABERGÉ

245 *Imperial presentation box* 1917

Gold, guilloché enamel, brilliant and rose-cut diamonds, watercolour on ivory, 3.2 × 9.5 × 6.4 cm
Impressed with maker's mark of Henrik Wigström, gold mark of 72 zolotniks (1908–17), and 'FABERGE' in Cyrillic
RCIN 19128

Provenance Presented on behalf of Nicholas II to Gabriel Hanotaux by the Grand Duke Nicholas of Russia, 1917; acquired by Queen Mary and given to King George V, 3 June 1934

Literature De Guitaut 2003, pp. 126–7

This imperial presentation box is an example of Wigström's finest craftsmanship in his favoured Louis XVI style, with sumptuous guilloché enamel in a sophisticated and unusual green hue – a demonstration of the unsurpassed range of enamel colours that the firm could produce. During the reign of Nicholas II, 54 jewelled gold boxes with the Emperor's portrait, were presented, 14 newly made and 40 from stock, these were made by a number of suppliers including Hahn and Fabergé. Snuffboxes with the portrait of the Emperor were presented in Russia to recipients of the highest ranks, including full generals, privy counsellors and knights of the Order of St Andrew. There were 34 foreign recipients, who were high-ranking foreign figures, including courtiers of foreign rulers and ambassadors.

This box, one of the last ever to be presented on behalf of Nicholas II, was given to the French academician and diplomat, Gabriel Hanotaux (1853–1944). Hanotaux had developed the rapprochement between France and Russia, had served as minister of foreign affairs in Russia from 1894 to 1898, and in honour of the 50th anniversary of the Russian Historical Society in 1916, was presented with this box. By the time of its presentation in May 1917, the Emperor had already abdicated. The miniature of Nicholas II was painted by Vassily Zuiev (1870–1941), and he is depicted wearing the uniform of the 4th Imperial Family Rifle Guards and the Order of St George, which he received on 25 October 1915. CDEG

FEODOR RÜCKERT (1851–1918), FOR FABERGÉ

246 *Kovsh* 1911

Silver gilt, cloisonné enamel, enamel *en plein*, 14.4 × 18.2 × 11.0 cm
Impressed with workmaster's mark of Feodor Rückert, Moscow silver mark of 91 zolotniks, 'C. FABERGE' in Cyrillic, initials of Carl Fabergé in Roman letters, and English import marks for 1911
RCIN 32475

Provenance Sold through the London branch of Fabergé, *c.*1911

Literature Muntian 2016, p. 131

This decorative *kovsh*, modelled on a traditional Russian drinking ladle, demonstrates the importance of the revivalist neo-Russian style in the late nineteenth century. Works in this style were particularly popular in Moscow, and one of the greatest exponents of it was the 'painter on enamel', Feodor Rückert, who established his silversmith and painting workshops in the city in 1886. Rückert produced his own pieces, as well as working in collaboration with Carl Fabergé's Moscow branch, which retailed his objects.

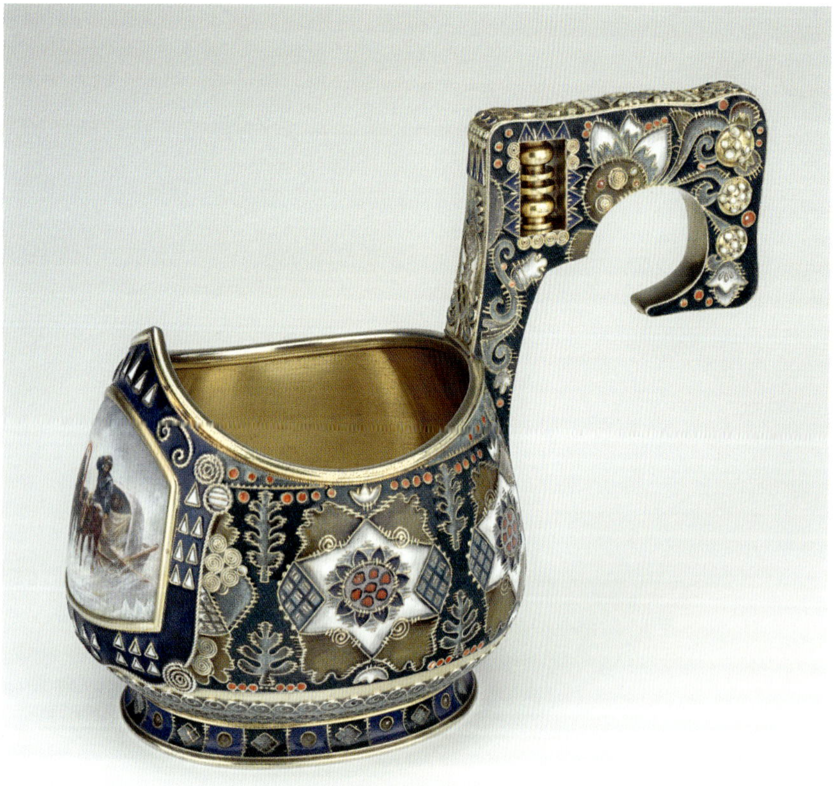

The form and decoration of this *kovsh* is typical of the work of Rückert, who used a palette of complementary muted colours of great sophistication and subtlety. These are applied using cloisonné enamelling in pan-Slavic motifs, which refer to the strong historicist ethic of Rückert's work. The silver-gilt wirework cloisons become a feature of the decoration in their own right, no longer necessarily separating the colours, which was their original function. The cloisons are inspired by other forms of contemporary applied art, from furniture to textiles, particularly those produced in the artists' colony at Abramtsevo, seen in the carved wood designs of Elena Polenova at the end of the nineteenth century which mix Art Nouveau and Russian motifs in the new neo-Russian style. The high arched and hooked handle is fitted with a silver-gilt turned device in a recess within the body of the handle. The front of the *kovsh* is painted in *en plein* enamels, creating a matt surface, with a view of horses pulling a troika.

The *kovsh* bears English import marks for 1911 together with Carl Fabergé's initials in Roman letters, which indicate that it was sold through the London branch of the firm; however, the purchaser is not known. It was recorded at Sandringham and is therefore assumed to have belonged to Queen Alexandra, who may well have purchased it or been presented with it as a gift.

CDEG

FEODOR RÜCKERT (1851–1918), FOR FABERGÉ

247

Kovsh 1913

Silver gilt, cloisonné enamel, *en plein* enamel, cabochon demantoid garnets, 15.3 × 18.7 × 11.4 cm
Impressed with maker's mark of Feodor Rückert, Moscow silver mark of 88 zolotniks (1908–17), 'C. FABERGE' in Cyrillic, and English import marks for 1913
RCIN 100327

Provenance Acquired by Queen Elizabeth The Queen Mother, date unknown

Literature Muntian 2016, p. 131

Rückert's mastery of cloisonné enamelling was often combined with enamels *en plein*, on a variety of objects, including snuffboxes, cigarette cases, caskets and vessels. In this example, the rich hues of the body of the *kovsh* are complemented by the brightly coloured image within the silver-gilt-rimmed reserve. The image depicts the *Reply of the Zaporozhian Cossacks*, after Ilya Repin's large painting of the same title, which he worked on between 1880 and 1891. The painting depicts an imagined historical tableau, set in 1676 and based on the legend of the Cossacks sending a reply to an ultimatum issued by the Sultan of the Ottoman Empire, Mehmed IV (1642–93). Repin's painting was purchased by Alexander III for 35,000 rubles in 1891, the highest price paid for a Russian painting at that time. The painting was hung in the Mikhailovsky Palace, St Petersburg, which was established as a museum by Nicholas II and is now known as the Russian Museum. To date, the identity of the miniature painter on the *kovsh* is not known as very few of the *en plein* enamel scenes on Rückert's work are signed. CDEG

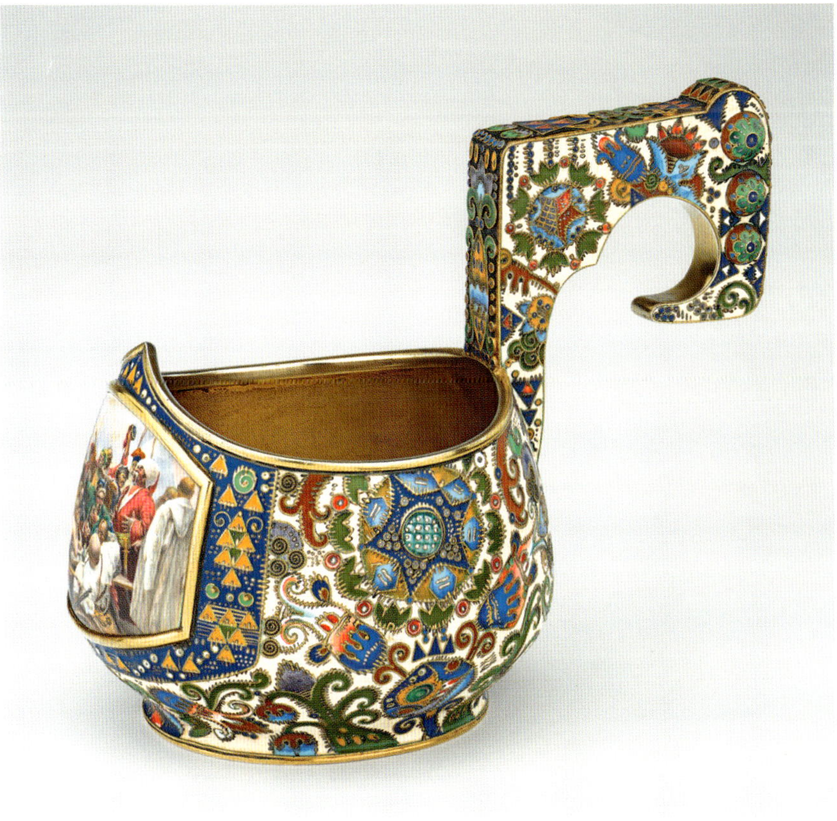

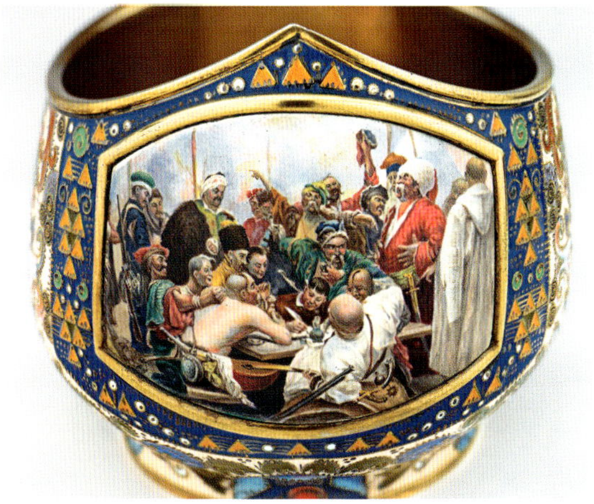

FABERGÉ

248 *Cigarette case* 1908

Gold, enamel, diamonds, 1.7 × 9.6 × 7.0 cm
Impressed with assay mark for Moscow (1896–1908), 56 zolotniks
RCIN 40113

Provenance Presented by the Hon. Mrs George Keppel to King Edward VII, 1908; returned by Queen Alexandra to Mrs Keppel, 1911; given by Mrs Keppel to Queen Mary, 1936

Literature Bainbridge 1949, p. 83; de Guitaut 2003, p. 153

This elegant cigarette case has a provenance unique in the history of Fabergé in the Royal Collection, having left the Collection in 1911, only to be returned over 20 years later. The case represents one of Fabergé's greatest expressions of the art nouveau style, with its sinuous diamond-set snake entwined around the front and back of the box. The moiré guilloché enamel is in one of Fabergé's most exceptional colours. However, the design is not purely decorative; the snake biting its tail is a symbol of unbroken and everlasting love, and thus it is not surprising to learn that the case was given to King Edward VII, in 1908, by his favourite mistress, Mrs George Keppel (1868–1947). Perhaps recognising the significance of the gift, Queen Alexandra returned it to Mrs Keppel as a memento, following the King's death in 1910. Twenty-five years later, in 1936, Mrs Keppel gave the case to Queen Mary, thereby ensuring that it would remain in royal ownership.[36] CDEG

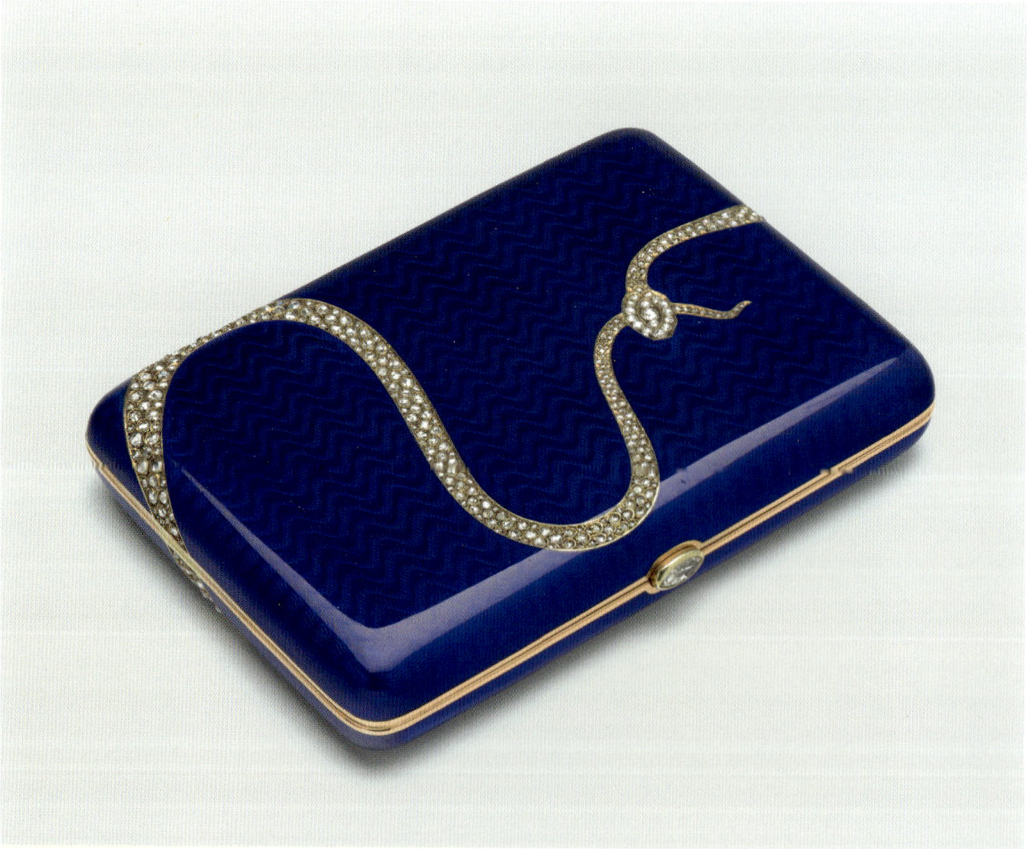

FABERGÉ

249–251

Philadelphus *c.*1900

Rock crystal, gold, nephrite, quartzite, demantoid garnets, 14.2 × 7.0 × 9.0 cm
Inscribed in Cyrillic: 'FABERGE'
RCIN 40252

Pansy, *c.*1900

Rock crystal, gold, nephrite, enamel, 10.7 × 5.5 × 4.0 cm
RCIN 40505

Chrysanthemum *c.*1908

Rock crystal, gold, nephrite, 24.6 × 11.3 × 7.0 cm
Inscribed with mark of Henrik Wigström, gold mark of 72 zolotniks (1908–17), and 'FABERGE' in Cyrillic
RCIN 40506

Provenance (RCIN 40252) Acquired by Queen Alexandra; (RCIN 40505) Probably acquired by Queen Alexandra; (RCIN 40506) Bought by Stanislas Poklewski-Koziell (1868–1939), councillor at the Russian Embassy in London during the reign of King Edward VII, from Fabergé's London branch, 27 December 1908, and given to Queen Alexandra

Literature (RCIN 40252) De Guitaut 2003, pp. 103–4

Queen Alexandra's collection of Fabergé flowers was rivalled only by those of her sister, her niece, Empress Alexandra Feodorovna, and the Grand Duchess Maria Pavlovna (1854–1920). The Queen acquired most of the examples in the Royal Collection, to which Queen Mary and Queen Elizabeth added a few more, to make a total of 26. The sources for Fabergé's flower studies lay in jewelled court bouquets made by Jérémie Pauzié, Catherine the Great's court jeweller, together with oriental examples also in the collection of the Hermitage Museum, where Fabergé helped with the repair of certain *objets d'art*.[37]

Fabergé's examples seem to have been driven by a desire to turn semi-precious stones into hyper-realistic flowers and plants, which at this period were known for their meaning as much as they were appreciated for their ability to offer a welcome reminder of the short spring and summer punctuating the long Russian winter. Philadelphus, or mock orange, is still a ubiquitous flower of the Russian spring. The pansy represents remembrance and became a favourite floral motif of the Art Nouveau period, while the chrysanthemum symbolised joy. **CDEG**

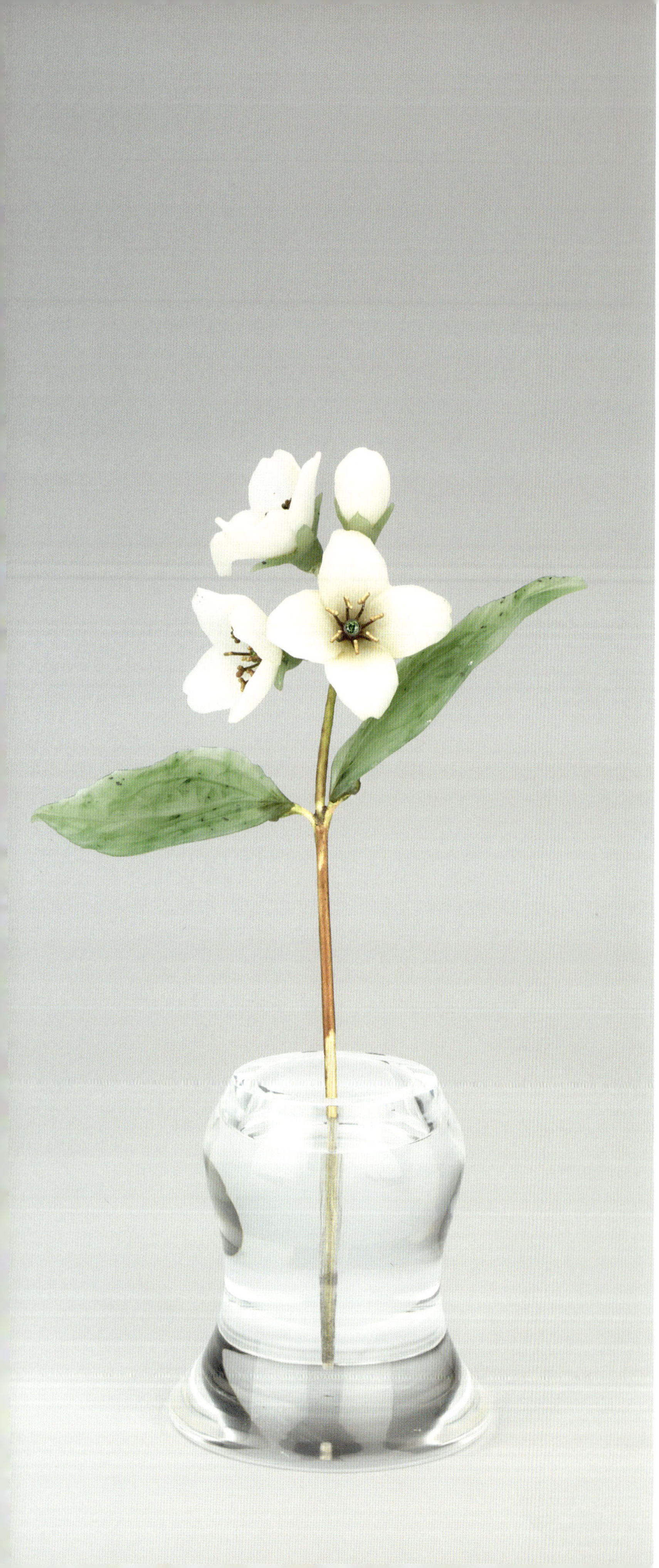

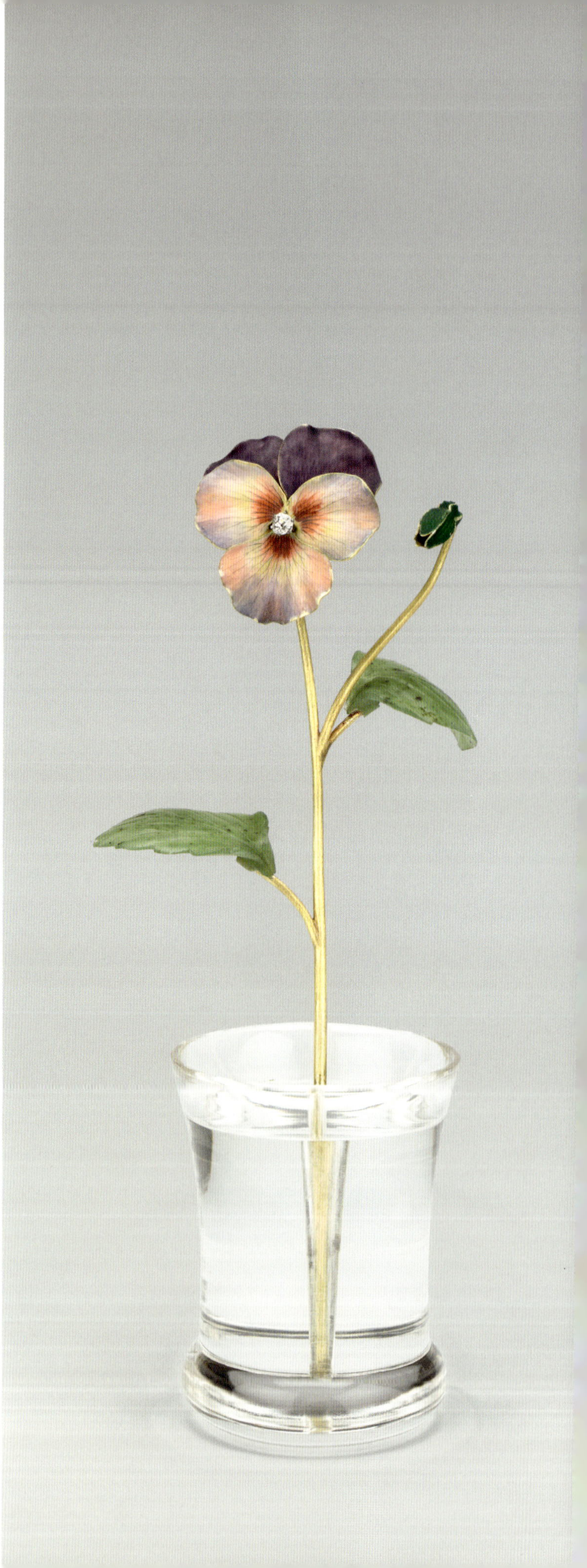

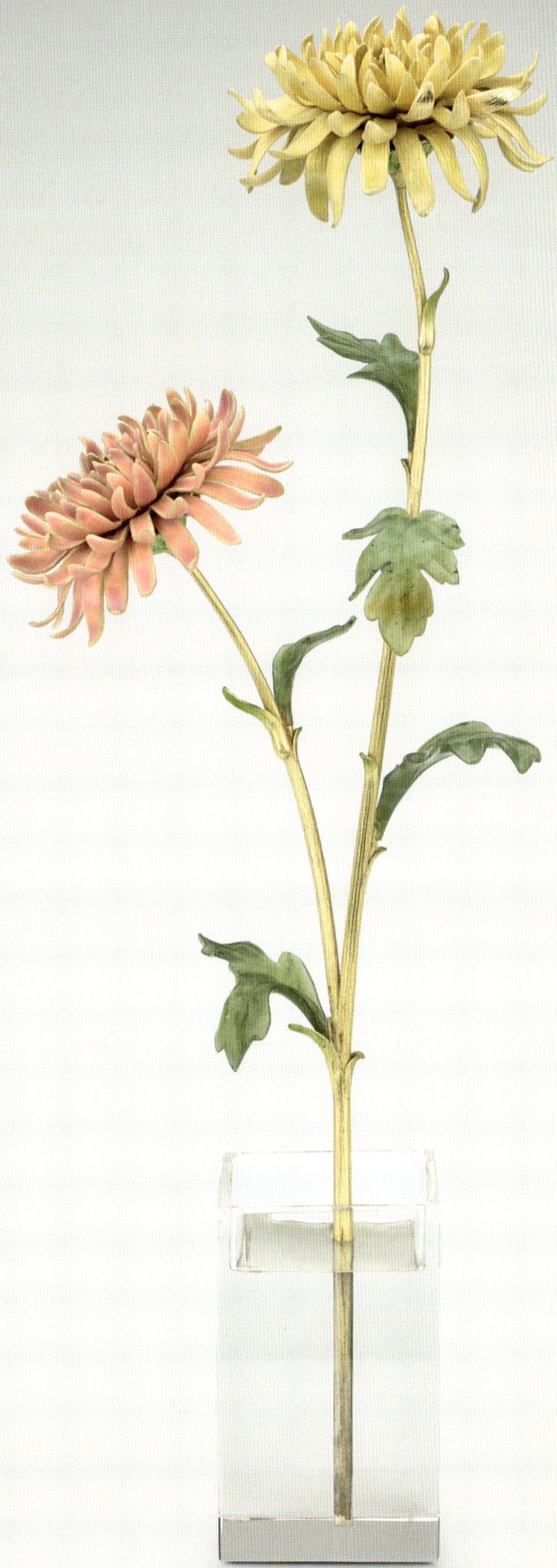

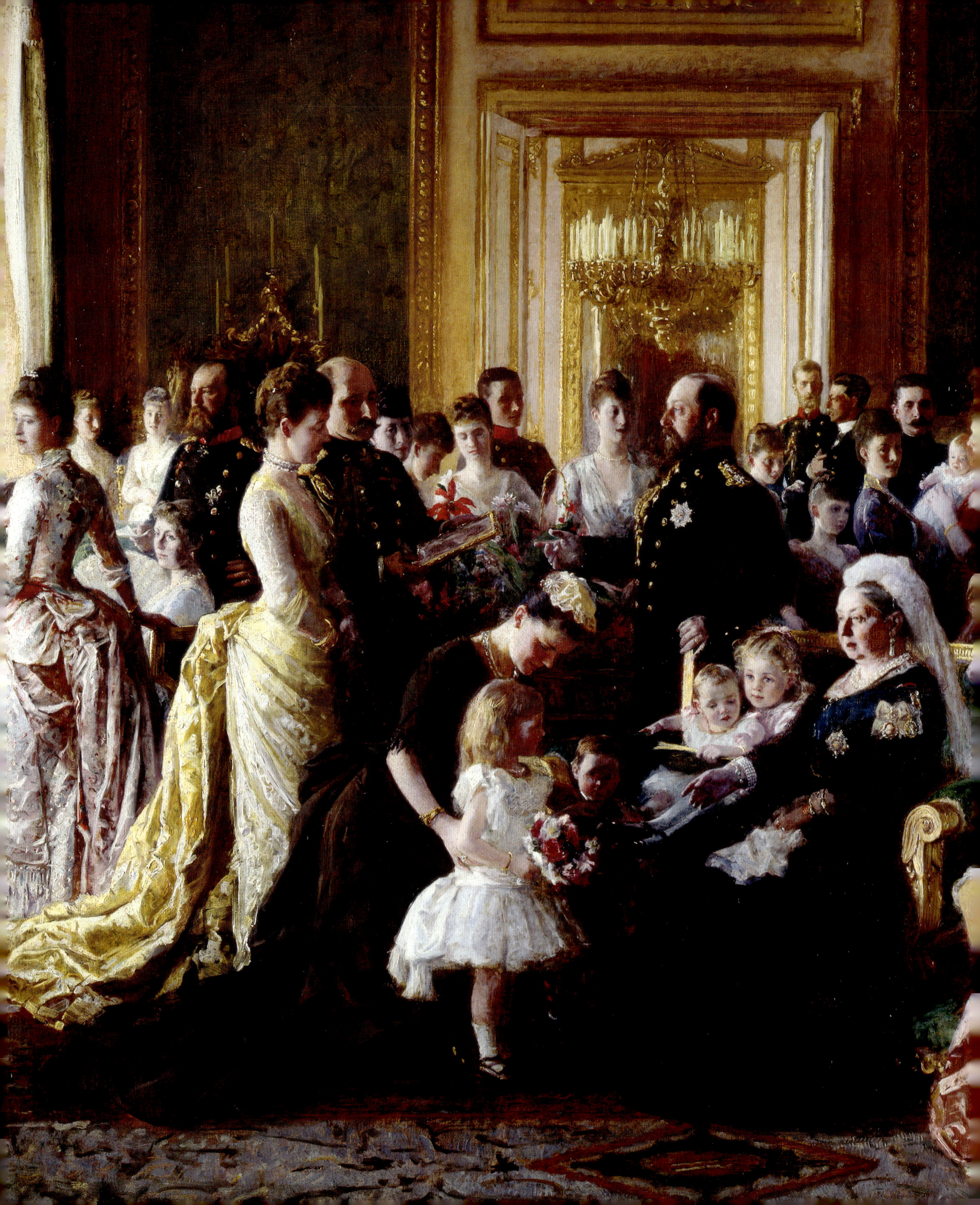

11

Family Gatherings

CAROLINE DE GUITAUT

It seems quite like a dream having dear Alicky and Nicky here

(Queen Victoria's Journal, October 1896)[1]

In the nineteenth century and the early part of the twentieth, the English, Russian and Danish ruling families spent considerable amounts of time visiting one another, holidaying together, recording the events through photography, through the giving and receiving of gifts, and even through the creation of film. The desire to record these family gatherings fostered the development of a renewed fashion for group family portraiture. One of the contemporary masters of this type of court painting was the Danish artist, Laurits Regner Tuxen, whose work first entered the Royal Collection following Queen Alexandra's commission to paint a study of the family of her parents at Fredensborg Palace, to record the gathering for Queen Louise's 65th birthday (cat. 252). Three further royal commissions were to follow, with group portraits painted to mark the Golden Jubilee of Queen Victoria in 1887 (cat. 253), the marriage of Nicholas II and Alexandra Feodorovna in 1894, and the marriage of the Duke and Duchess of York in 1893 (cat. 203; fig. 77). The reason for Tuxen's success was perhaps that not only did he seem remarkably adept at capturing, in detail, the individual personality of every protagonist in his composition and conveying it to the viewer, but that each painting is not merely a tableau, it truly embodies the emotion of the occasion. This is certainly true in his marriage portraits, as on both occasions the events were overshadowed by recent deaths in the immediate family. The Duke of York's wedding to Princess Mary of Teck took place 18 months after the death of the Duke of York's elder brother, the Duke of Clarence, to whom Princess Mary had been engaged. The Tsesarevich Nicholas, who represented the imperial family at the wedding, wrote to his mother, 'poor Aunt Alix looked rather sad in church – one can quite understand why! Georgie and his sisters also, but May was radiant.'[2] Included in the painting of Queen Victoria's family of 1887 were those from the Russian family who attended, including Grand Duke Sergei and Grand Duchess Elizabeth, Princess Alix of Hesse (who was to marry the Tsesarevich Nicholas), and Maria, Duchess of Edinburgh. Similarly, in the Tuxen painting of the marriage of Nicholas and Alexandra, the occasion was overshadowed by the recent death of the Emperor's father.

In the autumn of 1896, Nicholas II and Alexandra Feodorovna made their first trip to Britain since their coronation, to visit Queen Victoria. The visitors were received at Balmoral Castle, where the Queen was staying, and while political discussions did take place, the visit was overwhelmingly a family occasion, with many children and grandchildren of the Queen present to see the Russian family. The Duke of York (later George V) was pleased to see his cousin again, having been prevented from attending his coronation on 26 May. At the end of April, he had written to the Emperor to express his disappointment that it had been decided that the Duke and Duchess of Connaught should

The family of Queen Victoria in 1887 (detail of cat. 253)

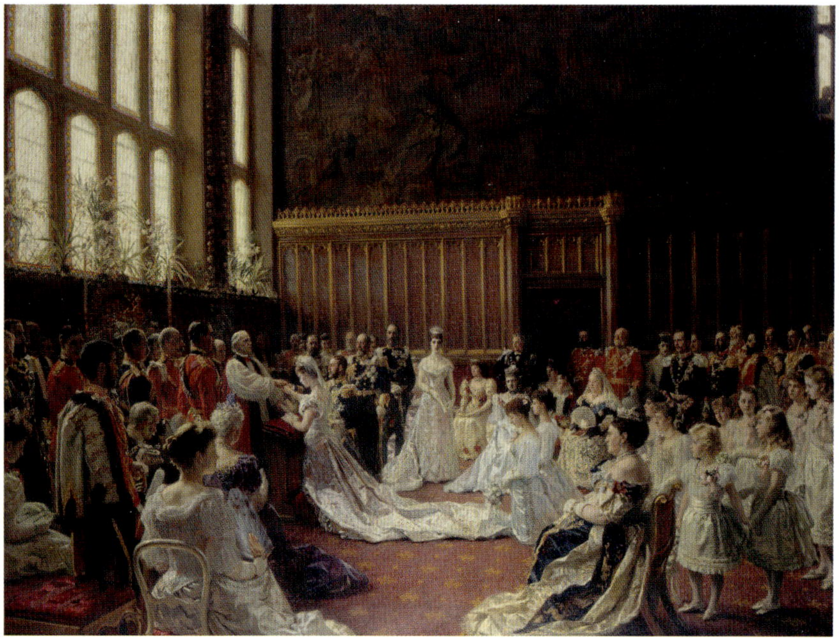

FIG. 77
Laurits Regner Tuxen (1853–1927)
The Marriage of George Duke of York with Princess Mary of Teck, 6 July 1893,
signed and dated 1894
Oil on canvas, 169.5 × 229.9 cm
RCIN 402437

attend as the Queen's official representatives: 'and when at last it was settled that the Connaughts were going I must say I was furious'.[3] Queen Victoria ensured that the visit was well-documented, purchasing watercolours of the torch-lit arrival and departure (cat. 255), and commissioning photographs by Robert Milne (1865–1952) (fig. 78). The Queen's Journal reveals her excitement at the arrival of her 'grandchildren':

> *Punctually at 8, the procession reached the door. The escort of Scots Greys came first, then the pipers & torch bearers, & finally the carriage containing Nicky, Alicky, Bertie & Arthur. I was standing at the door, & Nicky, got out first, whom I embraced, & then darling Alicky, all in white, looking so well, whom I likewise embraced most tenderly. She went round & shook hands with everybody who was standing in the Hall. A very smart Cossack had previously arrived & was at the door.*[4]

The visit was also recorded in an album of photographs compiled by the Duke of Connaught (cat. 256), and perhaps most interestingly of all, the first moving images of the royal family were captured. On 3 October, the family gathered on the Terrace near the Ballroom, and 'all were photographed by Downey by the new cinematograph process, which makes moving pictures by winding off a reel of films. We were walking up & down and the children jumping about'.[5] The Queen was sorry to see the Russian family leave, and this would be the last occasion on which they met. Nicholas and Alexandra's Christmas present to the Queen that year was a notebook case made by the Fabergé firm, which the Queen used the following year to record the names of all those who attended her Diamond Jubilee celebrations on 22 June 1897.[6] To mark the occasion, the Emperor and Empress sent a further Fabergé gift, a diamond and sapphire brooch which they had had specially designed (cat. 257).

Away from the pressures of ruling, at least temporarily, the family could relax, particularly in Denmark, where, due to the close relationship between Alexandra and Maria Feodorovna, they spent many happy annual holidays together. It was on these occasions that the personal expenditure of the Empress and her sister rose dramatically with their preferred suppliers of gifts,[7] and as a result, many Russian works of art entered the Collection. The majority of these were kept at Sandringham House, the country residence of Edward VII and Queen Alexandra, where visiting family from Russia often stayed with them. Both families frequently purchased works of art from the same makers, particularly Fabergé, and ultimately, Queen Alexandra was to form a collection that rivalled those

FIG. 78
Robert Milne (1865–1952)
Group portrait taken on the occasion of the visit of Emperor Nicholas II to Balmoral, September 1896
Gelatin silver print, 20.7 × 14.9 cm
RCIN 2160252

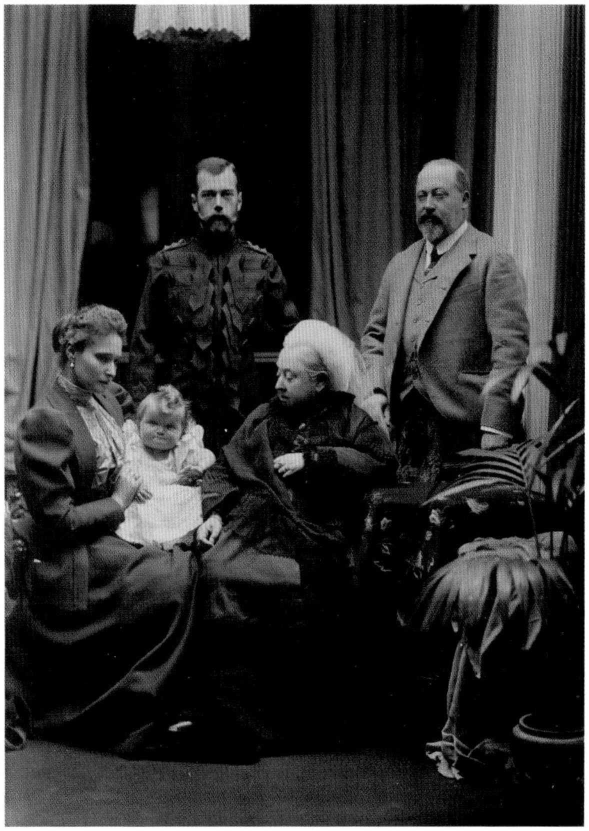

of both her sister and her niece, Alexandra Feodorovna (cats 249–251). In 1873, Maria Feodorovna, the Tsesarevich Alexander and their young children visited their family in England (cat. 155). They stayed at Windsor, but also visited the Isle of Wight, a visit that their son Nicholas would repeat more than 30 years later. From 1902 onwards, the Empress visited Queen Alexandra in England on several occasions, spending time at Buckingham Palace, Windsor Castle and Sandringham. While in London, she accompanied her sister on official visits, but also enjoyed visiting the National Gallery and the Wallace Collection, as well as several visits to the theatre.

After the official familial meeting at Reval of 1908, in August 1909, Nicholas II, Alexandra Feodorovna and their children made what would be their final visit to the royal family in England. The visit took place at Cowes on the Isle of Wight, where the families were present for the annual regatta, which had first been established by George IV in 1826. The royal family were staying on board HMY *Victoria and Albert*, and also at Osborne House. The Russian family arrived on 2 August on board the Imperial Yachts *Standart* and *Polar Star*. The Prince of Wales (later George V) recorded in his diary his delight at seeing his cousin, 'Dear Nicky looking so well & Alicky too, I had not seen him for 12 years'.[8] The families dined together on one another's yachts, visits were paid to Osborne House, and the occasion was marked by an exchange of gifts. The Prince of Wales was made an admiral of the Russian navy by the Emperor (cat. 130), and the Princess of Wales was given the Order of St Catherine (cat. 159), together with an amethyst brooch (cat. 275). Photographs were commissioned from the local photographer, A.W. Debenham (active *c.*1868–*c.*1925), including a double portrait of the Prince of Wales and his cousin, dressed virtually identically and showing the strong family resemblance (cat. 278). Film footage of the families on board their yachts was also taken.[9]

The final meeting of Nicholas II and George V would occur neither in England nor Russia, but in Germany, when the crowned heads of Europe attended the wedding of Princess Victoria Louise (1892–1980), daughter of Wilhelm II (1859–1941), in Berlin. Visits by other members of the imperial family continued into the second decade of the twentieth century. Nicholas II and George V would correspond regularly throughout the First World War, until January 1917, and according to their correspondence and to works now in the Royal Collection, they continued, remarkably, to send one another presents at Christmas (cat. 276). Following the Revolution and the murder of the Emperor, Empress, their children and many other members of the imperial family, some of those who managed to survive and escape, including the Dowager Empress Maria Feodorovna, came to England between 1918 and 1919. During this time and continuing into the 1920s and 1930s, George V and Queen Mary began to assemble a small but significant collection of works of art which had belonged to their Russian relations, as poignant reminders of happier times.

LAURITS REGNER TUXEN (1853–1927)

252 *The family of King Christian IX (1818–1906) and Queen Louise of Denmark (1817–1898)* 1885

Oil on canvas, 74.9 × 105.7 cm
Signed and dated: *L. Tuxen 1885*
Frame by Mogensens, Copenhagen
RCIN 402341

Provenance Painted for Alexandra, Princess of Wales, 1885; first hung in Queen Alexandra's Private Sitting Room, Marlborough House

Literature Tuxen 1928, pp. 100–11; Bligaard 1990, pp. 37–8, 68, no. 49; Noble 1990, pp. 4–9; Svanholm 1990, pp. 56–67, 243; Millar 1992, no. 785; Evans 1998, pp. 125–6, no. 122

United through marriage, the royal families of Britain, Russia and Denmark (and Greece) met annually at Fredensborg Palace during the early autumn. In 1882, an 'extra-large gathering' was assembled to mark the 65th birthday of Queen Louise of Denmark, mother to Princess Alexandra and the Empress Maria Feodorovna; and a year later, Laurits Tuxen was commissioned to record the occasion in a monumental painting now at Christiansborg.[10] This small-scale version (completed before the final work), was painted for Princess Alexandra and includes a number of additional characters, allowing it to be a more complete record of her family.

The artist was summoned to the palace in the autumn of 1883, and invited by Queen Louise to attend every 'grand dinner', allowing him to familiarise himself with the guests. After dinner, when the party retired to the Garden Room, he was able to make sketches of some of the sitters, later setting up a small canvas to establish the background and details of the composition.[11] Photographs were also taken by Clemens Weller (1838–1900), which Tuxen probably relied on to recall groupings and details of costume. The sitters are arranged in small, intimate groups – on the left, seated in an armchair, is the Prince of Wales, dressed in the uniform of the Danish Hussars, with Princess Alexandra and Prince Albert Victor; the King and Queen of Denmark are seated on a giltwood settee, and standing next to them are Alexander III and Maria Feodorovna, her arm around Grand Duke Michael; the young Tsesarevich Nicholas stands at the centre of the doorway, behind his mother.

Tuxen subsequently travelled to St Petersburg, Gmuden and London to make life-size studies of the figures and groups. He spent two months at Gatchina, where he managed a number of sittings with the Empress; however, the Emperor

FIG. 79
Unknown photographer
Group photograph in the Garden Room at Fredensborg, 1888
RCIN 2927303

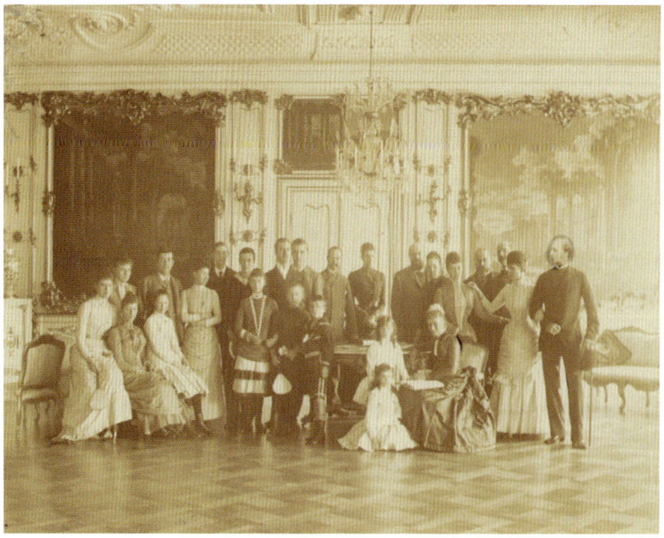

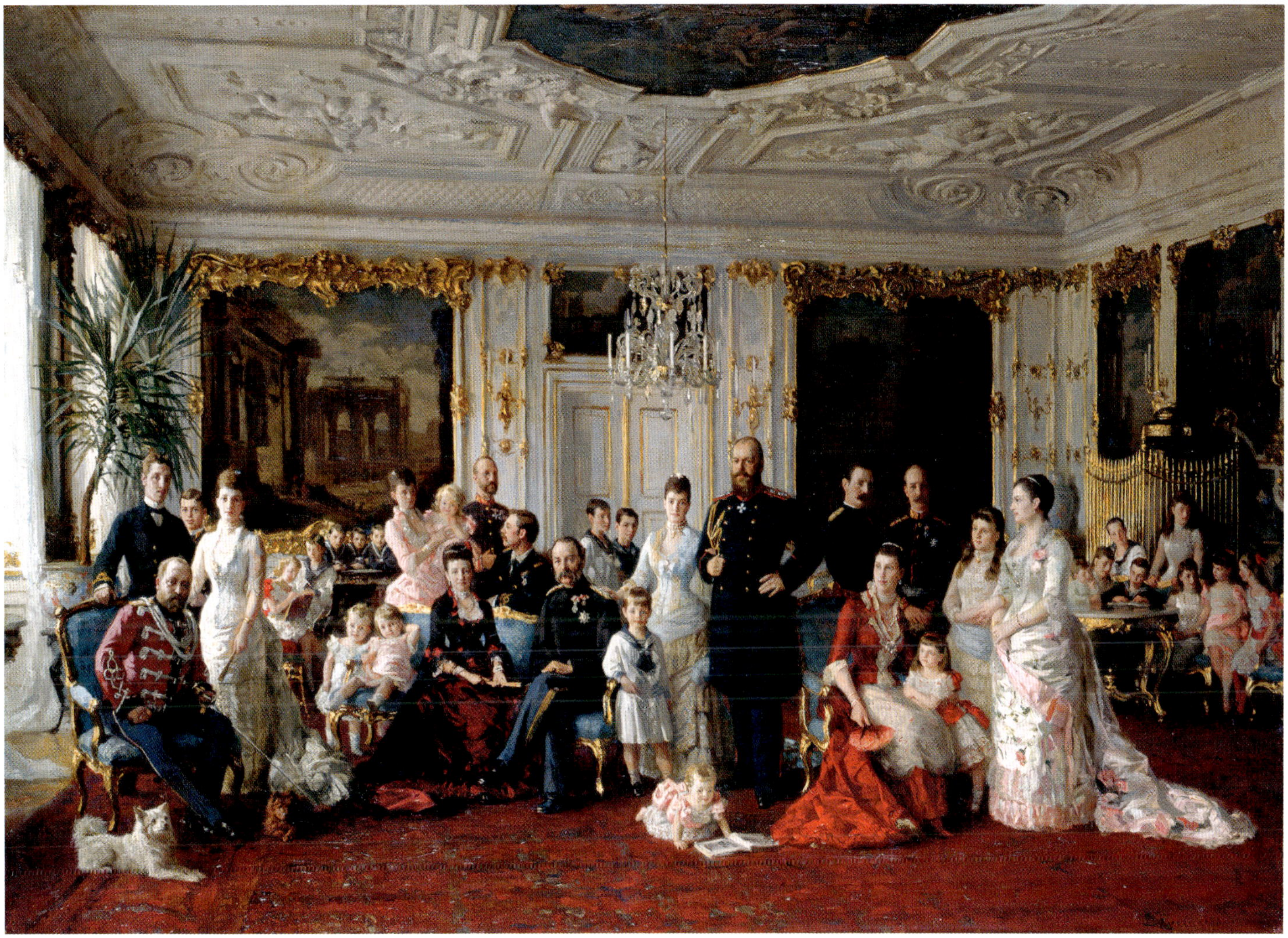

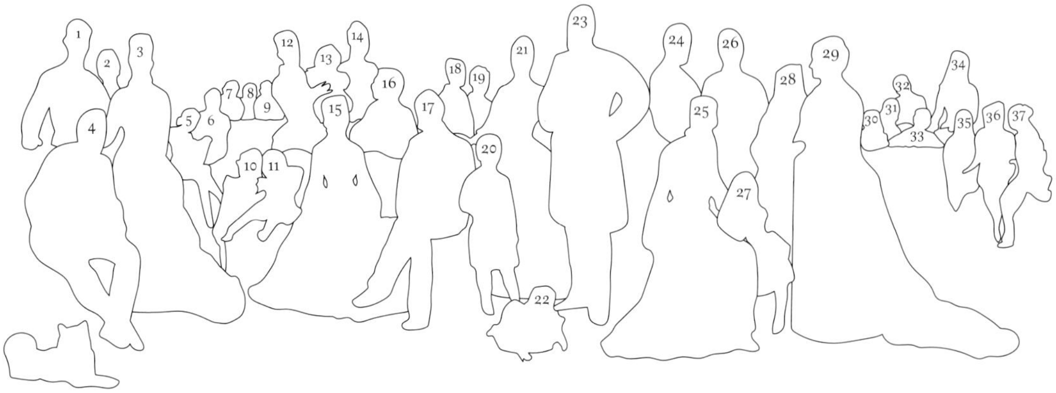

Key

1. Prince Albert Victor of Wales
2. Prince George of Wales, later King George V
3. Alexandra, Princess of Wales, later Queen Alexandra
4. Albert Edward, Prince of Wales, later King Edward VII
5. Princess Ingeborg of Denmark
6. Prince Harald of Denmark
7. Prince George of Greece
8. Prince Nicholas of Greece
9. Prince Constantine of Greece
10. Prince George William of Hanover and Cumberland
11. Princess Marie Louise of Hanover and Cumberland
12. Thyra, Crown Princess of Hanover, Duchess of Cumberland
13. Princess Alexandra of Hanover and Cumberland
14. Ernst Augustus, Crown Prince of Hanover, Duke of Cumberland
15. Queen Louise of Denmark
16. Prince Waldemar of Denmark
17. King Christian IX of Denmark
18. Prince Christian of Denmark, later King Christian X
19. Tsesarevich Nicholas Alexandrovich, later Nicholas II, Emperor of Russia
20. Grand Duke Michael Alexandrovich
21. Maria Feodorovna, Empress of Russia
22. Grand Duchess Olga Alexandrovna
23. Alexander III, Emperor of Russia
24. Crown Prince of Denmark, later King Frederick VIII
25. Crown Princess of Denmark, later Queen Louise of Denmark
26. King George I of Greece
27. Princess Thyra of Denmark
28. Princess Alexandra of Greece
29. Queen Olga of Greece
30. Princess Marie of Greece
31. Princess Louise of Wales
32. Prince Charles of Denmark, later King Haakon VII of Norway
33. Grand Duke George Alexandrovich
34. Princess Victoria of Wales
35. Princess Maud of Wales, later Queen of Norway
36. Grand Duchess Xenia Alexandrovna
37. Princess Louise of Denmark

gave only one sitting of three-quarters of an hour, subsequently allowing a servant dressed in his uniform to pose.[12] In London, the Prince and Princess of Wales and their son, Albert Victor, sat at Marlborough House, which probably resulted in the life-size sketch at Frederiksborg Castle.[13] Whilst in England, Tuxen was summoned to Windsor to see Queen Victoria, who records, on 17 March 1885, that she 'saw a charming, & very cleverly grouped sketch for a large picture of the King & Queen of Denmark & their whole family, by a young Danish artist of the name of Tuxen'.[14] Suitably impressed, the Queen was to commission the artist to paint numerous vast ceremonial paintings, including a gathering of her family to mark her Golden Jubilee (cat. 253), and the marriage of her grand-daughter, Alix, to Nicholas II in 1894 (cat. 203).

Away from court life, the atmosphere at Fredensborg was relaxed and informal; on arriving in August 1891, Oliver Montagu (1844–93), equerry to the Prince of Wales, recalled that he found Alexander III in the hall, 'running around after the children with a huge whip which he was cracking, dogs barking and children howling'.[15] The Prince of Wales, who initially enjoyed these convivial gatherings, wrote to a friend in September 1885: 'We are an immense family gathering – quite a Babel, as seven different languages are spoken.' Two years later, he noted that never less than 50 or 60 sat down to dinner.[16] The Princess of Wales, however, relished time spent with her sister (fig. 79). **AB**

LAURITS REGNER TUXEN (1853–1927)

253 *The family of Queen Victoria (1819–1901) in 1887* 1887

Oil on canvas, 165.7 × 226.1 cm
Signed and dated: *L Tuxen 1887*
RCIN 400500

Provenance Commissioned by Queen Victoria

Literature Tuxen 1928, pp. 114–22; Maas 1977, no. 29; Bligaard 1990, pp. 39–41, no. 53; Noble 1990, pp. 11–16; Svanholm 1990, pp. 68–72; Lloyd 1991, p. 208; Millar 1992, no. 786; Jensen and Ebbeson 2014, pp. 69–72

Queen Victoria had seen and admired the painting of *The family of King Christian IX and Queen Louise of Denmark* (cat. 252), and consequently wished for a comparable picture of her own family, gathered together to mark the Golden Jubilee. The setting was to be the Green Drawing Room at Windsor; the luxurious combination of green damask and gilding, lit with natural light, offered exciting possibilities for the artist. The heavy sofas were drawn into the centre of the room, and at the Queen's request, a bust of Prince Albert was to replace a clock on the mantelpiece. On 6 May 1887, the Queen wrote to the Duke of Connaught that she had seen a sketch which 'will be very pretty. It is not to be stiff & according to *Etiquette*, but prettily grouped'.[17] This may be the *modello* which hangs at the Royal Danish Embassy in London.[18] Tuxen himself envisaged the composition as a big family *conversazione*, and in this genre he surpasses both his British contemporaries and many artists of the early twentieth century (Sir John Lavery (1856–1941) might be the exception). He possessed the ability to achieve, almost effortlessly, a homogeneous composition, coupled with a liveliness and naturalness, as well as providing his patron with a powerful dynastic image.

However, the artist encountered certain difficulties with the portrait, with some guests refusing to be placed next to others. Other 'exalted guests' provided the artist with airbrushed photographs, hoping to avoid sittings and achieve a flattering representation of themselves. However, preferring to sketch from life, and having meticulously planned the composition, architectural background and orchestration of figures, Tuxen was able to work rapidly when sitters posed. He recalled how, one day, no fewer than eight sitters arrived, one after the other, 'so that I hardly had the time to wipe the brush between each new portrait'.[19]

In his autobiography, *En Malers Arbejde*, Tuxen recalled that, 'Among the young ladies one must note in particular the Princesses of Hessen-Darmstadt, the grandchildren of Queen Victoria. The eldest, the beautiful Princess Ella, was married to Grand Duke Sergius, and the youngest Princess Alix, at that time 16 years of age and the most graceful thing one could imagine'.[20] Ella is visible standing towards the left-hand side, dressed in a pale pink dress, with an ostrich feather fan, facing her uncle, the Duke of Edinburgh; her husband, Sergei, stands to the right of the door frame. Alix is to be glimpsed to the left of the door frame, looking out. Maria, Duchess of Edinburgh is seated to the extreme left.

The Queen was delighted with the painting, writing on 1 December 1887: 'The picture is beautiful, the Drawing room admirably painted & the likenesses very good ... the grouping & colouring, all, charming.'[21] On completion, a photogravure was published by I.P. Mendoza of King Street, St James's, to be given to all those present at the festivities. AB

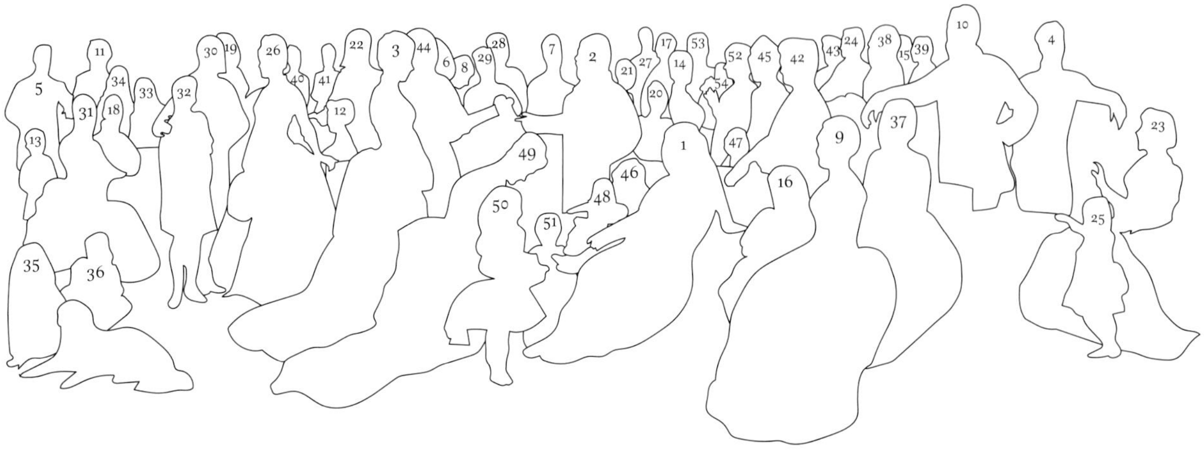

Key

1. Queen Victoria
2. Albert Edward, Prince of Wales, later King Edward VII
3. Alexandra, Princess of Wales, later Queen Alexandra
4. Prince Albert Victor of Wales
5. Prince George of Wales, later King George V
6. Princess Louise of Wales
7. Princess Victoria of Wales
8. Princess Maud of Wales, later Queen of Norway
9. Crown Princess of Prussia, later Empress Victoria of Germany, Queen of Prussia
10. Crown Prince of Prussia, later Emperor Frederick III of Germany, King of Prussia
11. Prince William of Prussia, later Emperor William II of Germany, King of Prussia
12. Princess William of Prussia, later Empress Augusta Victoria of Germany, Queen of Prussia
13. Prince Frederick William of Prussia
14. Hereditary Princess of Saxe-Meiningen
15. Hereditary Prince of Saxe-Meiningen
16. Princess Feodora of Saxe-Meiningen
17. Prince Henry of Prussia
18. Princess Irene of Hesse and by Rhine, later Princess Henry of Prussia
19. Princess Victoria of Prussia
20. Princess Sophia of Prussia, later Queen Sophia of Greece
21. Princess Margaret of Prussia
22. Louis IV, Grand Duke of Hesse and by Rhine
23. Princess Louis of Battenberg, Princess Victoria of Hesse and by Rhine
24. Prince Louis of Battenberg
25. Princess Alice of Battenberg, later Princess Andrew of Greece and Denmark
26. Grand Duchess Elizabeth Feodorovna, Princess Elisabeth of Hesse and by Rhine
27. Grand Duke Serge Alexandrovich
28. Prince Ernest Louis of Hesse and by Rhine, later Grand Duke of Hesse and by Rhine
29. Princess Alix of Hesse and by Rhine, later Alexandra Feodorovna, Empress of Russia
30. Prince Alfred, Duke of Edinburgh
31. Grand Duchess Marie Alexandrovna, Duchess of Edinburgh
32. Prince Alfred of Saxe-Coburg and Gotha
33. Princess Marie of Saxe-Coburg and Gotha
34. Princess Victoria Melita of Saxe-Coburg and Gotha, later Grand Duchess Victoria Feodorovna
35. Princess Alexandra of Saxe-Coburg and Gotha
36. Princess Beatrice of Saxe-Coburg and Gotha
37. Princess Helena, Princess Christian of Schleswig-Holstein
38. Prince Christian of Schleswig-Holstein
39. Prince Albert of Schleswig-Holstein
40. Princess Helena Victoria of Schleswig-Holstein
41. Princess Marie Louise of Schleswig-Holstein
42. Princess Louise, Marchioness of Lorne
43. Marquess of Lorne, later Duke of Argyll
44. Prince Arthur, Duke of Connaught
45. Princess Louise Margaret, Duchess of Connaught
46. Princess Margaret of Connaught
47. Prince Arthur of Connaught
48. Princess Patricia of Connaught
49. Princess Helena, Duchess of Albany
50. Princess Alice of Albany
51. Prince Charles Edward, Duke of Albany
52. Princess Beatrice, Princess Henry of Battenberg
53. Prince Henry of Battenberg
54. Prince Alexander of Battenberg

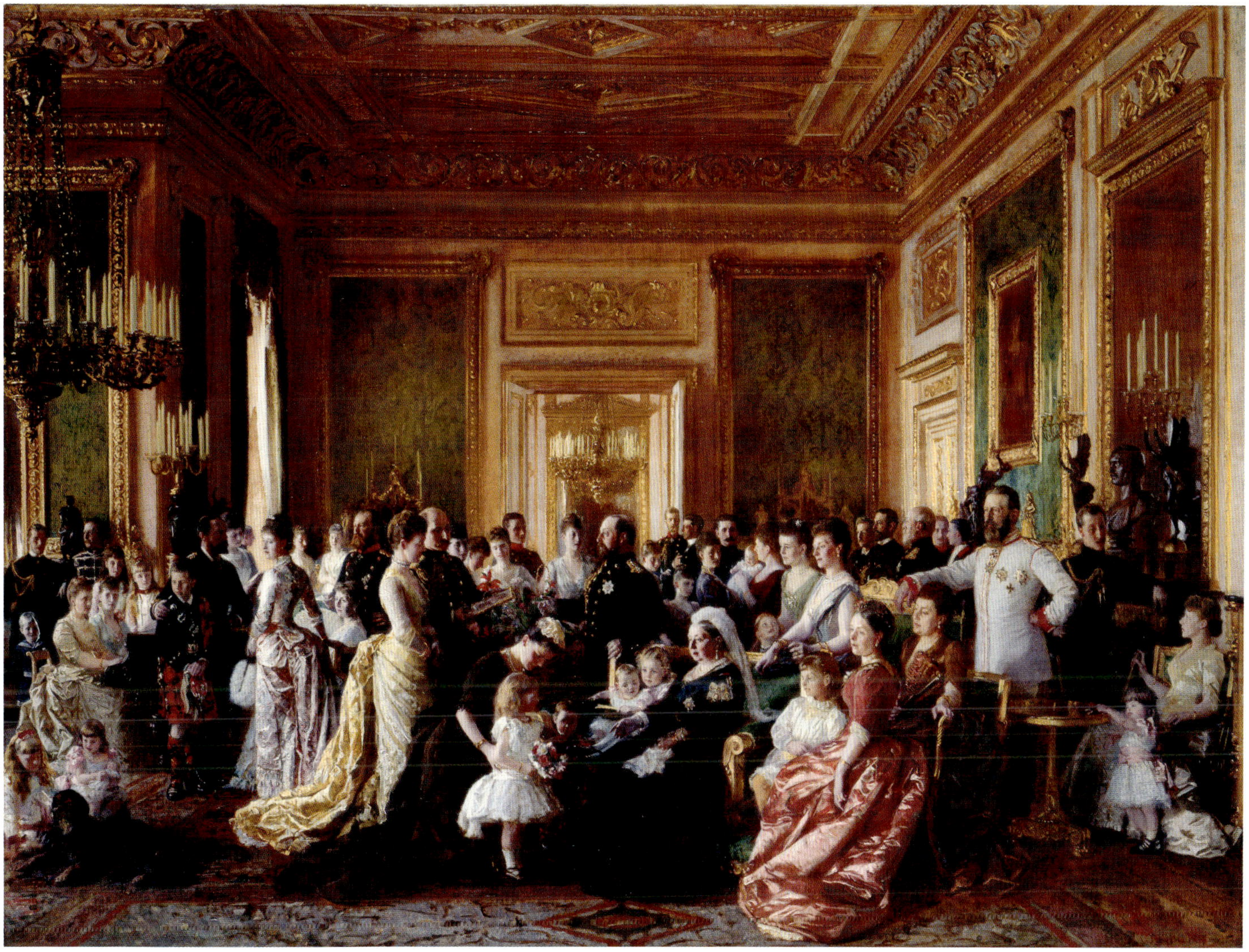

PRINCE ARTHUR, DUKE OF CONNAUGHT AND STRATHEARN (1850–1942)

254 *Connaught Album, vol. III* April 1895–June 1897

Gelatin silver prints, (album page) 30.3 × 41.5 cm
RCINS 2801836 (album), 2802083–2802095 (photographs)

Provenance Compiled by Prince Arthur, Duke of Connaught and Strathearn

The album, compiled by Prince Arthur, contains many photographs taken by the Prince himself, with one of the first Kodak cameras, which started appearing on the market from 1888 and produced the characteristic, round-format photographs seen here. The advent of such portable and easy-to-operate cameras, advertised with the well-known slogan, 'You press the button, we do the rest', made it possible to record events from an unusual perspective, such as various moments connected with Nicholas II's coronation in May 1896, as seen here, accessible only to a restricted number of privileged guests.

AN

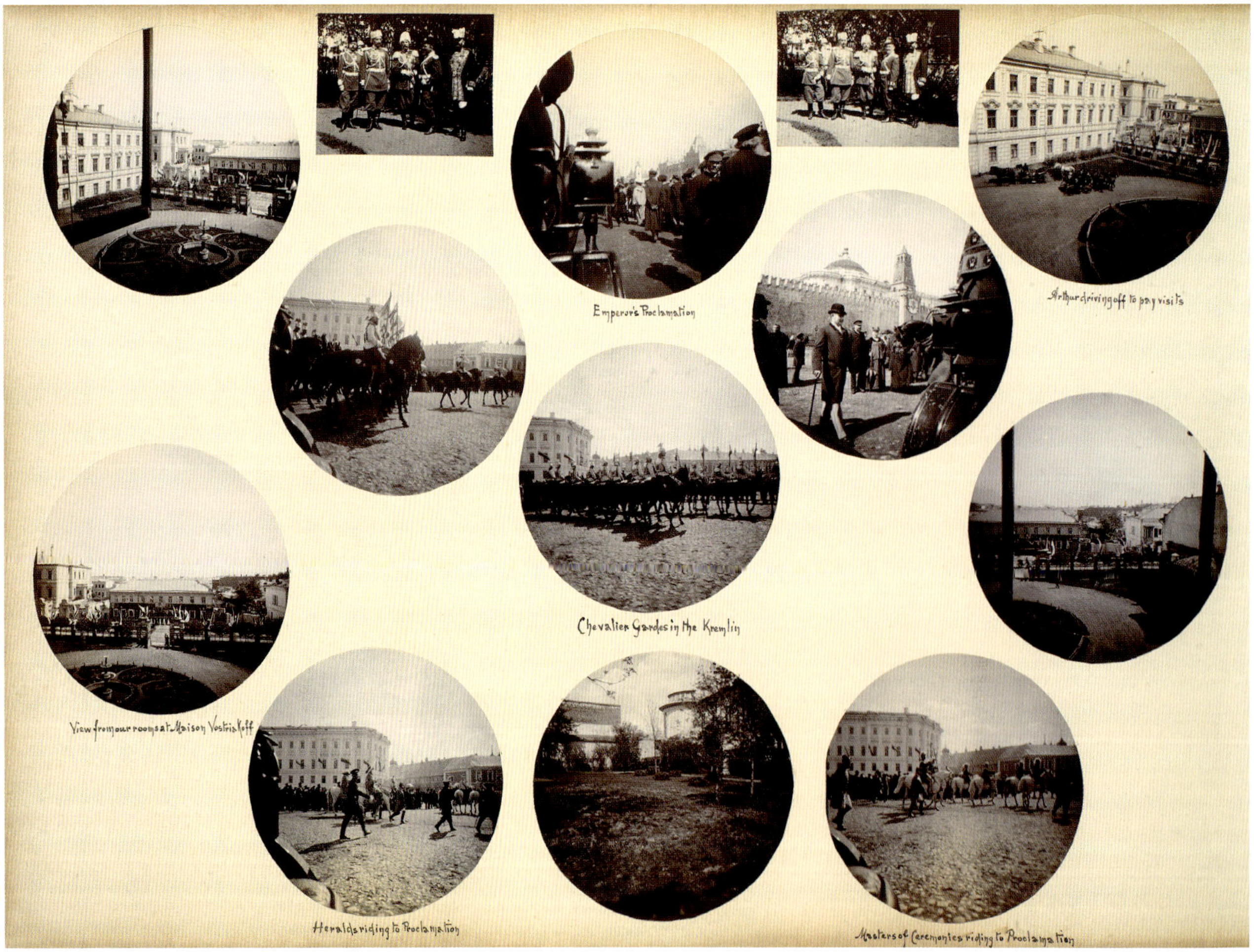

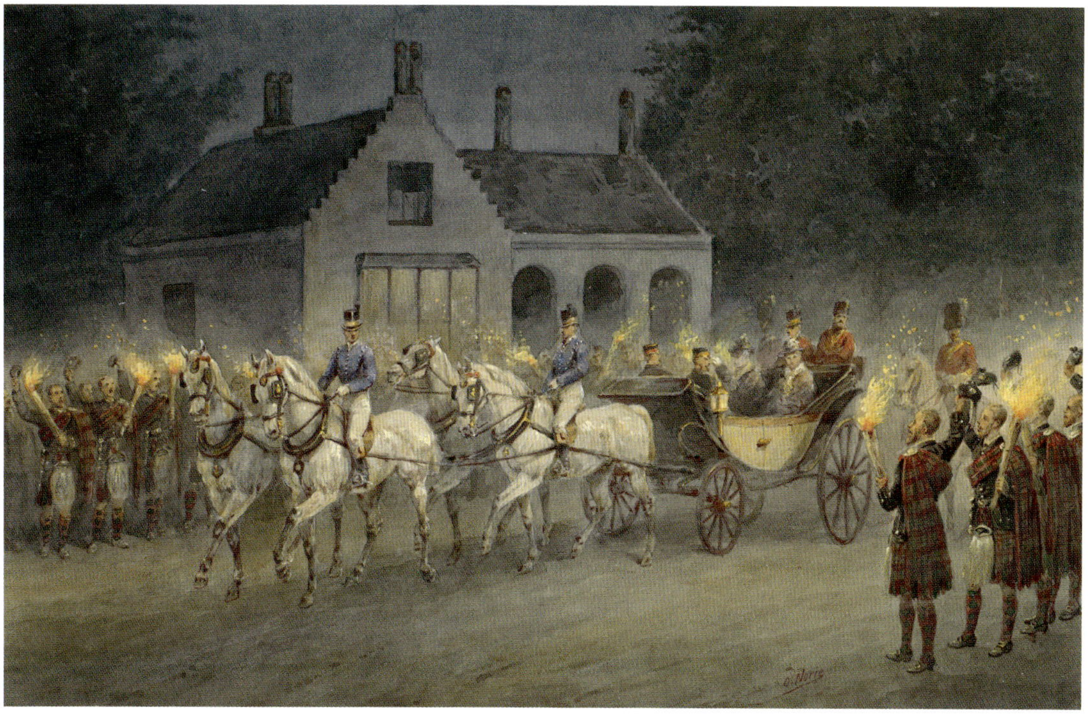

ORLANDO NORIE (1832–1901)

255 *Departure of the Emperor (1868–1918) and Empress of Russia (1872–1918) from Balmoral* 1896

Pencil, watercolour and bodycolour, 29.9 × 48.0 cm
Signed bottom right: *O. Norie*
RCIN 919538

Provenance Probably purchased by Queen Victoria from Ackermann & Co., Regent Street, 1896[22]

Literature Millar 1995, no. 4125

The last Emperor of Russia, Nicholas II, and his wife, Alexandra, visited Queen Victoria at Balmoral Castle, her Scottish home, in 1896. They arrived by imperial yacht at Leith on 22 September, and then travelled to Balmoral, where they stayed until 3 October. The young couple brought their 10-month-old daughter, Olga, with them to meet her great-grandmother.

The visit was principally a family reunion, with many of Queen Victoria's children and grandchildren travelling to Balmoral to greet the couple. The stay was also punctuated with discussions about international relations relating to Russia and Britain. Queen Victoria spoke to Nicholas regarding the Eastern Question, and the prime minister and Foreign Secretary, Lord Salisbury, gained assurances about Russia's intentions towards India.[23]

The watercolour by Orlando Norie shows the Emperor and Empress leaving Balmoral by carriage on the evening of 3 October, accompanied by Prince Arthur, Duke of Connaught and his wife, Louise. Highlanders are lined up outside the West Lodge, holding flaming torches. Queen Victoria recorded in her diary that, 'At 10 dear Nicky & Alicky left to my regret, as I am fond of them both [...] Went to the door to see our dear visitors leave. There were again the Highlanders bearing torches, but no pipes'.[24]
RW

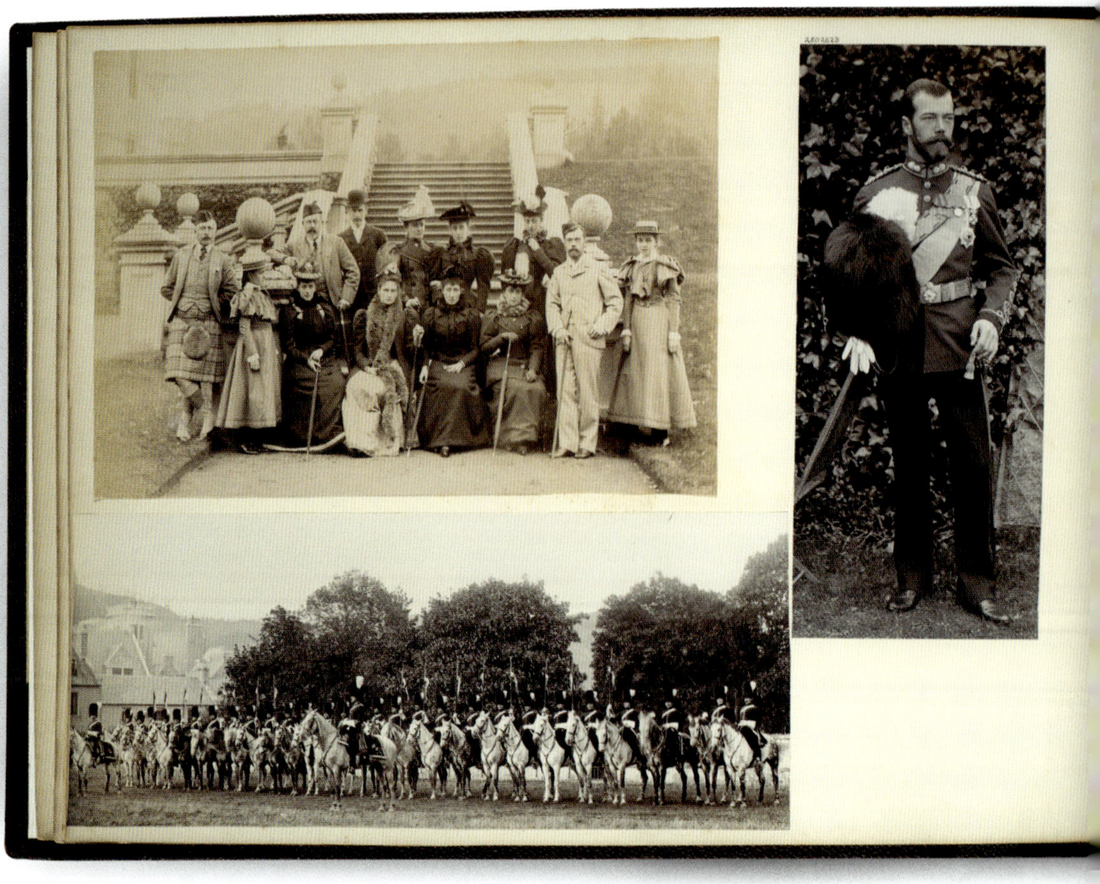

PRINCE ARTHUR, DUKE OF CONNAUGHT AND STRATHEARN (1850–1942)

256 *Connaught Album, vol. IV* September 1896–October 1898

Gelatin silver prints, (album page) 30.3 × 41.5 cm
RCINS 2802608 (album), 2802622–2802629 (photographs)

Provenance Compiled by Prince Arthur, Duke of Connaught and Strathearn

The newly crowned Emperor Nicholas II and Empress Alexandra Feodorovna stayed at Balmoral Castle between 22 September and 3 October 1896 (cat. 255). This opening of an album compiled by Prince Arthur shows the Royal Scots Greys in their role of imperial escort; Nicholas II wearing his uniform of colonel-in-chief of the regiment; the 'smart Cossack' mentioned by the Queen in her Journal (see p. 402); the Highlanders; and a group photograph taken in the grounds of the Castle.[25] The latter shows, standing (from left to right): Prince Arthur, his daughter, Princess Patricia of Connaught (1886–1974), the Prince of Wales, Prince Carl of Denmark, the Duchess of Connaught, Princess Helena Victoria of Schleswig-Holstein, Princess Victoria of Wales, Emperor Nicholas II and Princess Margaret of Connaught (1882–1920), and, sitting in front (from left to right): the Princess of Wales, Alexandra Feodorovna,

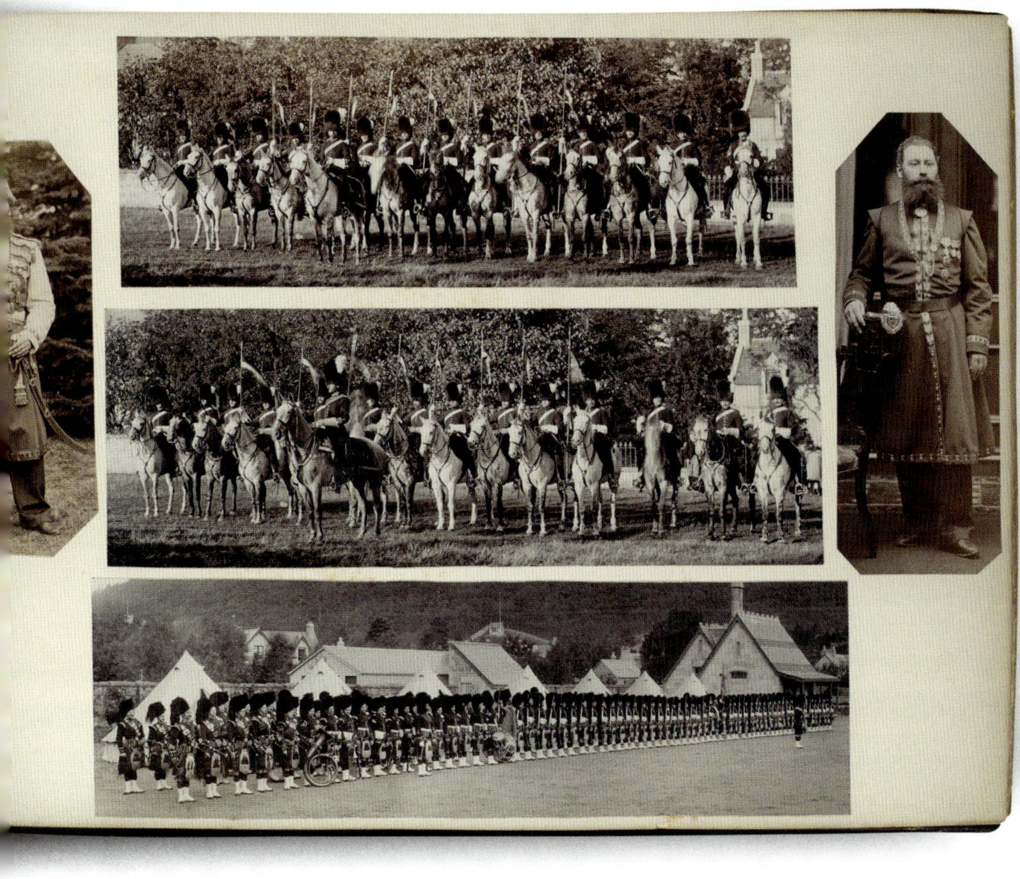

and Princesses Louise and Maud (1869–1938) of Wales.

During their stay, as well as various groups shot by professional photographers and numerous snapshots taken by family members, the first ever film footage recording the royal family was also produced. Downey's apparatus was captured in a snapshot by the Duke of Connaught (fig. 80). **AN**

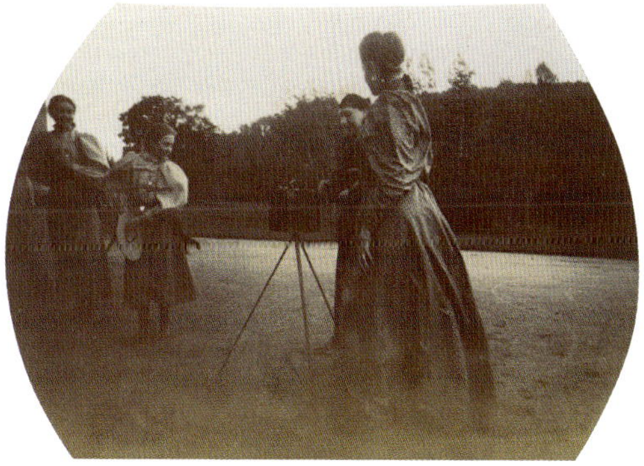

FIG. 80
Prince Arthur, Duke of Connaught
Empress Alexandra Feodorovna and Princess Beatrice inspecting Downey's cinematographic camera with Princesses Margaret and Patricia of Connaught, October 1896
Gelatin silver print, 5.9 × 8.5 cm
RCIN 2802387

FABERGÉ

257 *Diamond Jubilee brooch* 1897

Silver, gold, rose and brilliant diamonds, sapphires, 9.8 × 3.4 × 1.8 cm
RCIN 250482

Provenance Given to Queen Victoria by the Emperor and Empress of Russia, the Grand Duke and Duchess of Hesse (1868–1937 and 1876–1936), Grand Duke and Duchess Sergei of Russia, and Prince (1854–1921) and Princess Louis of Battenberg, 1897; bequeathed to Princess Christian

Literature RA VIC/ADDT/316/145; Pavlovsk 2013, p. 203

Among the many gifts received by Queen Victoria on the occasion of her Diamond Jubilee, this brooch was very much a personal family present from her grandchildren, acknowledging the achievements of her 60-year reign. It was described in Queen Victoria's *Inventory of Jewels* as follows: 'A Brooch diamond heart, with diamond date (Russian) in centre, cabochon sapphire on top & 2 sapphire drops. / Jubilee from T.I.M. The Emperor & Empress of Russia, Grand Duke & Duchess of Hesse, Grand Duke & Duchess Serge & Prince & Princess Louis of Battenberg. Jubilee 1897 / [Left] Princess Christian'.[26]

The brooch takes the form of a silver heart, mounted with diamonds, surmounted by a cabochon sapphire, and enclosing in Slavonic characters the number 60. Suspended from two diamond-set pampilles are two large cabochon sapphires. Fabergé's invoice is dated 29 May 1897 and amounts to 1,055 rubles, which was split between the Emperor and Empress.[27]

The Queen chose to wear the brooch during the official celebrations. In their telegram offering congratulations for her Jubilee on 23 June, Nicholas and Alexandra wrote, 'touched you wore our present'.[28] CDEG

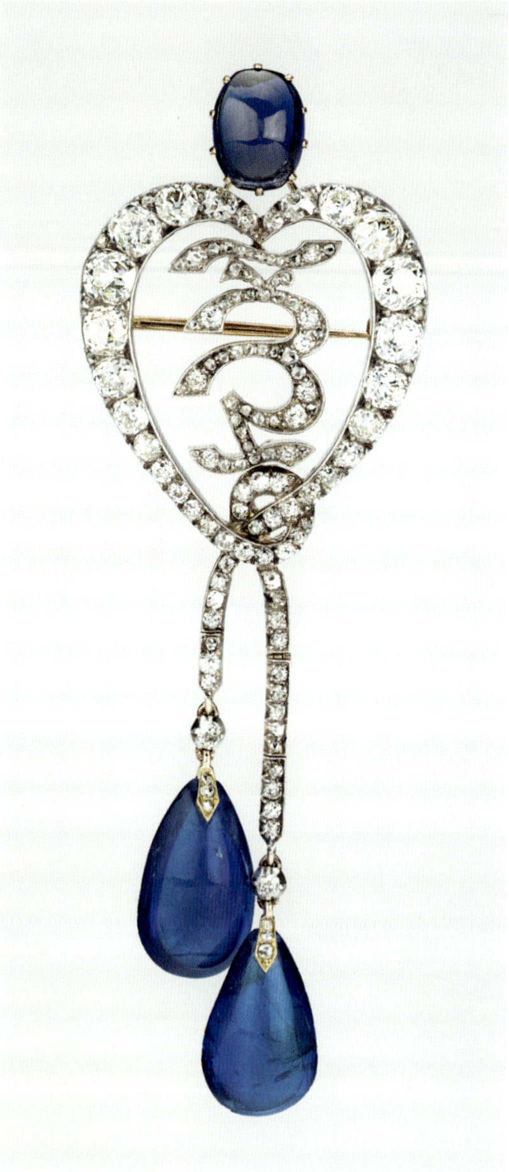

FABERGÉ

258 *Cigarette case*, 1903

Three-colour gold, rose diamonds, cabochon ruby. 1.4 × 9.4 × 6.8 cm
Moscow gold mark 56 zolotniks; C FABERGE (in Cyrillic)
RCIN 4344

Provenance Given to King Edward VII as a 40th wedding anniversary present by Empress Maria Feodorovna

Literature Bainbridge 1949, pl. 121; Inventory of George V, no. 43

Maria Feodorovna purchased presents for Easter, Christmas and family birthdays and anniversaries from the Fabergé firm from 1886 until 1916. These purchases included items, sometimes specially commissioned, to be sent to her sister and other members of the royal family in England.

This sumptuous cigarette case was specially made to mark the fortieth wedding anniversary of King Edward VII and Queen Alexandra and was sent to the king by his sister-in-law. This is indicated by the crowned EA cypher of gold set with rose diamonds on the front of the case and the date 10 March 1903 XL 1863–1903, indicating the anniversary and wedding dates of the couple, also in diamonds on the reverse. The body of the case is made in a radiating fluted design in alternate stripes of red and yellow gold, a combination often used by the firm's goldsmiths.
CDEG

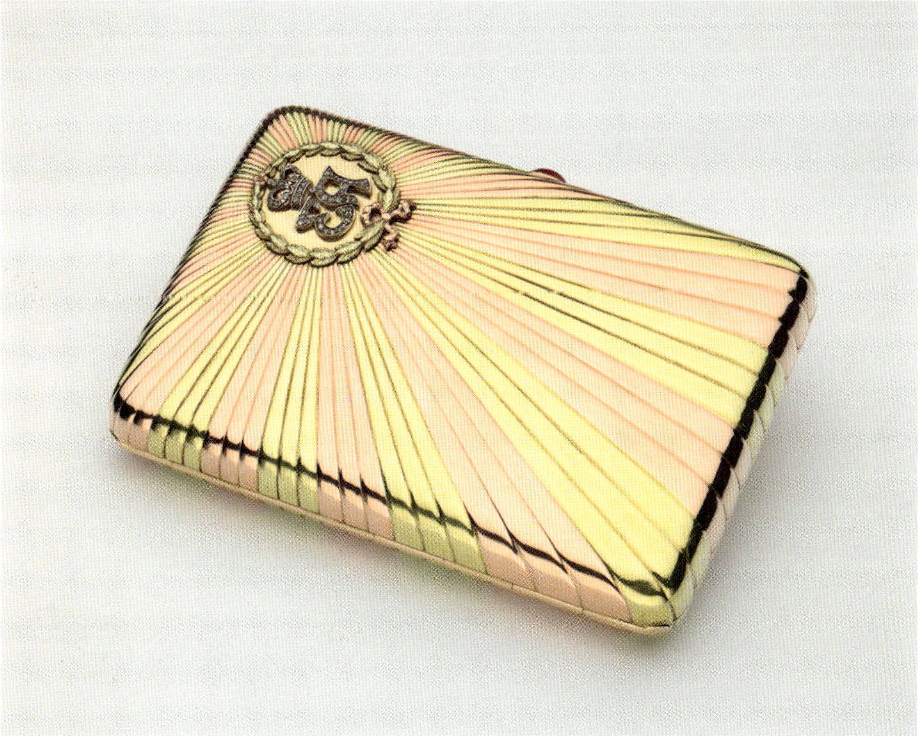

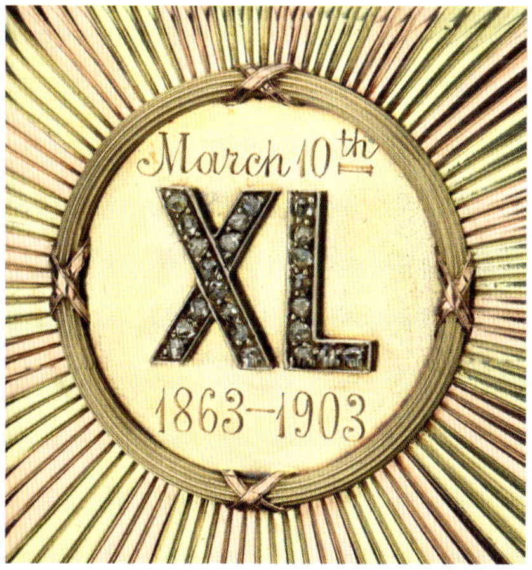

W. & D. DOWNEY

259 *Maria Feodorovna, Dowager Empress of Russia (1847–1928)* c.1910

Watercolour on ivory laid on card, oval, 5.5 × 4.3 cm
Signed along lower right-hand edge in black paint: *DOWNEY*
RCIN 421085

Provenance First recorded in the Royal Collection in the current reign (1952–)

Literature Remington 2010, p. 155, no. 268

The miniature is based on a photograph of Maria Feodorovna accompanied by her sister, Queen Alexandra, taken by Downey probably during her visit to Britain in 1907 (fig. 81). The two sisters shared a strong sibling bond that is often evident in the many photographs portraying them together across the decades, sometimes even dressed alike. At the time of the Bolshevik Revolution, the Dowager Empress was persuaded to reside in the Crimea, from where, as urged by her sister, she was eventually rescued and brought to England in 1919.[29] She would subsequently spend her last years at Hvidøre, a relatively small residence near Copenhagen, which the two sisters had acquired together in 1906, following the death of their father, Christian IX of Denmark.

Maria Feodorovna died in 1928 and was buried in Denmark. However, in accordance with her wishes, her body would eventually be interred next to that of her husband, Emperor Alexander III, in the Saints Peter and Paul Cathedral in St Petersburg, in 2006. **AN**

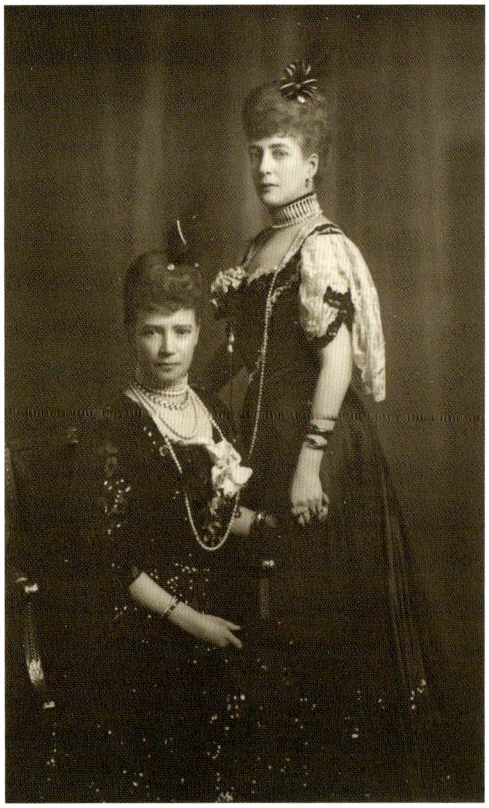

FIG. 81
W. & D. Downey
Queen Alexandra with Maria Feodorovna, Dowager Empress of Russia, c.1907
Platinum print, 28.4 × 17.7 cm
RCIN 2926685

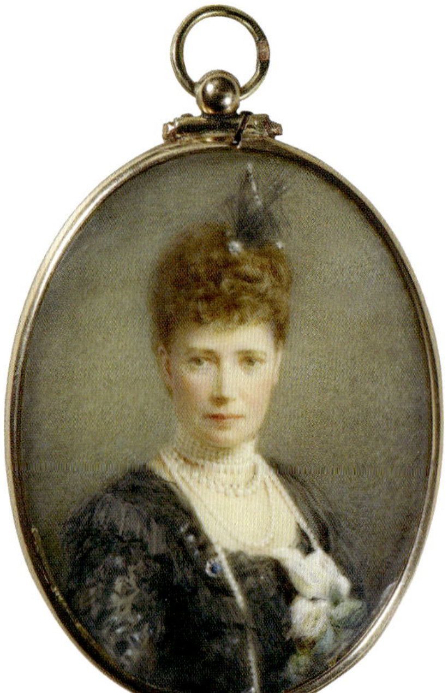

FABERGÉ

260

Fan c.1912

Gold, guilloché enamel, silk, mother-of-pearl, rubies, bone, 23.0 × 40.5 × 2.8 cm
Impressed with maker's mark of Henrik Emanuel Wigström, assay mark of 56 zolotniks, and 'FABERGE' in Cyrillic; paper label in Queen Mary's handwriting: 'From Queen Alexandra Xmas 1912'
RCIN 25136

Provenance Purchased by Queen Alexandra from Fabergé's London branch, 24 December 1912 (£26 10s.), as a Christmas gift for Queen Mary

Literature *Unfolding Pictures*, no. 75; de Guitaut 2003, no. 250

Queen Alexandra was introduced to the work of the Fabergé firm by her sister, Maria Feodorovna, in the late 1880s, and the two were to become, arguably, Carl Fabergé's most important clients. Part of the motivation for opening the only foreign branch of the firm in London was to maximise the opportunity presented by Fabergé's royal clientele, and Queen Alexandra, Edward VII, George V and Queen Mary, together with other members of the royal family, visited the branch and purchased goods regularly. Queen Alexandra's accounts reveal that she spent considerably more on the purchase of items destined as presents than on those to be kept by herself, and this fan is no exception.

The Queen purchased the fan for her daughter-in-law as a Christmas present in 1912, and Queen Mary recorded the gift on the original box for the fan, which still survives. The front guard is enamelled in blue and white, and the mother-of-pearl sticks are painted in gold, with leaf trails, flower heads and scrolls in a neoclassical design, in keeping with the work produced in Henrik Wigström's workshop. The silk leaf is painted with a central cartouche depicting a man and woman seated in a pastoral landscape, and two other cartouches with views of a river and a lake, within a gold painted rococo revival design of swags and trophies. CDEG

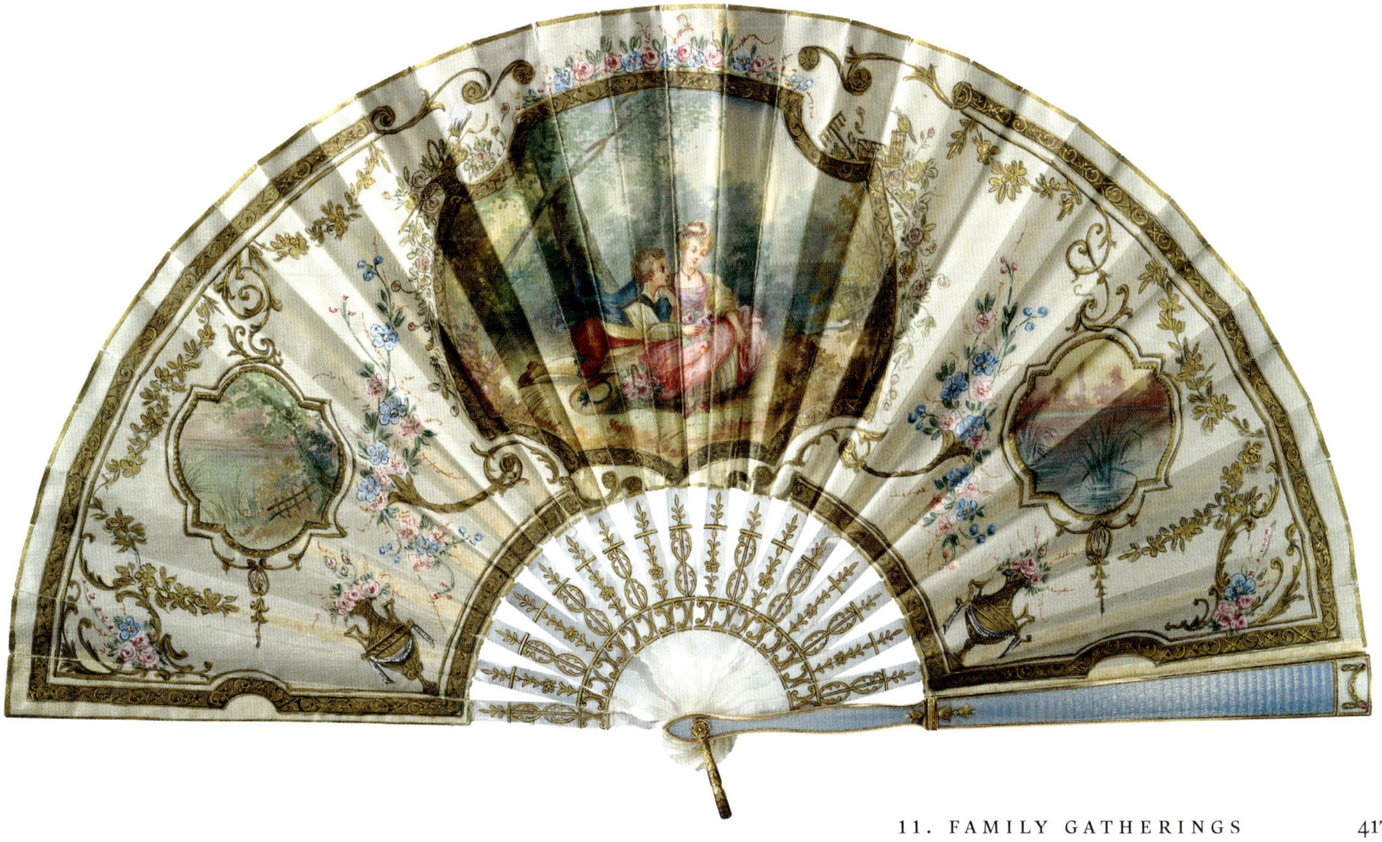

FABERGÉ

261 *Elephant automaton* 1892

Ivory, diamonds, enamel, gold, nickel, brass, 6.0 × 5.5 × 3.4 cm
Impressed with workmaster's mark of Mikhail Perkhin (1860–1903), 'FABERGE' in Cyrillic, and gold mark of 56 zolotniks (before 1896)
RCIN 9268

Provenance Made as the surprise for the Diamond Trellis Imperial Easter egg, 1892, given to Maria Feodorovna by Alexander III, 5 April 1892; confiscated, 1917, and transferred to the Sovnarkom; sold by the Soviet government in the 1920s; in the possession of Emanuel Snowman (1886–1970); purchased by King George V, 1935

Literature Fabergé, Proler, Skurlov, 1997, p. 253

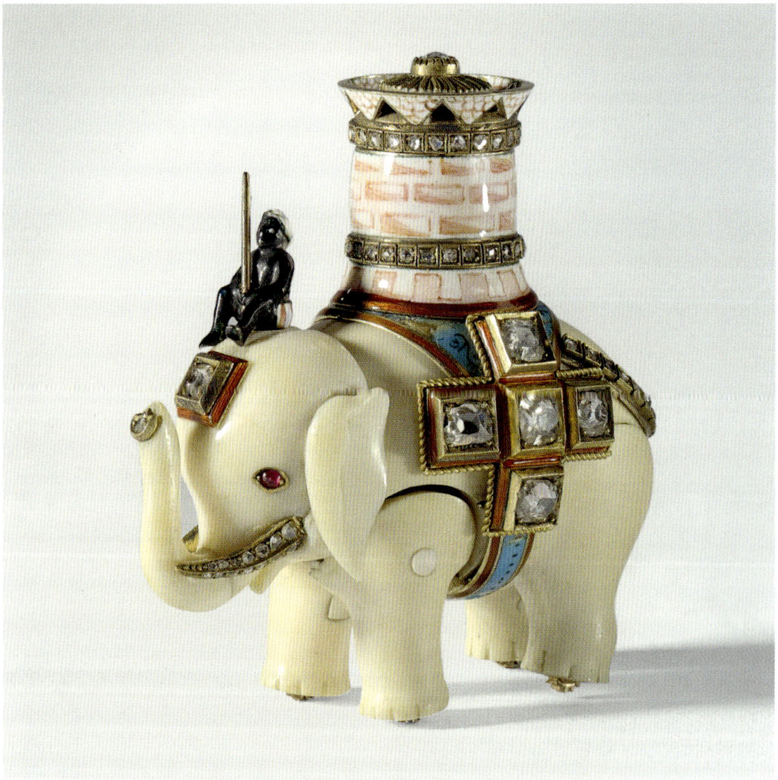

Fabergé's automata are extremely rare, and the few that the firm made usually feature as the 'surprise' inside imperial Easter eggs,[30] although in addition a few were made as individual *objets de fantasie*, including a silver elephant automaton in the Royal Collection.[31] It seems that King George V and Queen Mary were fascinated by automata made by the Fabergé firm. Queen Mary purchased the silver example in 1929, and the 'royal family' presented it to the King for Christmas that year, while George V himself went on to purchase this elephant automaton in 1935.

The automaton was not discovered to be the missing surprise from the 1892 diamond trellis egg[32] until the present author identified it in 2014. The elephant would have had a special significance for the original owner, Maria Feodorovna, given its embodiment in the insignia of the highest Danish order of chivalry, the Order of the Elephant and this might explain why this object went unrecognised as a work by Fabergé for so many years, given its similarity to the badge of that order. The materials used by Fabergé in the creation of this automaton differ, however, from those used in the badge of the Order, which is usually made of gold enamelled in white, whereas this automaton, unusually in Fabergé's *oeuvre*, is made of ivory with gold, enamel and diamond decoration. The mechanism may have been constructed by a Swiss maker, possibly Henry Moser & Cie (active from the mid-nineteenth century), who supplied Fabergé's clock movements. When wound by the ivory and gilt-metal key, the elephant walks along on ratcheted wheels, lifting its head up and down; it would originally have swung its tail, however, this was lost at some point in the lifetime of the surprise.

CDEG

FABERGÉ

262 & 263

Frame with an enamelled view of Sandringham House 1908

Nephrite, gold, half-seed pearls, sepia enamel, ivory, 9.0 × 15.2 × 7.1 cm
Impressed with mark of Henrik Wigström, gold mark of 56 zolotniks (1896–1908), and 'FABERGE' in Cyrillic
RCIN 40492

Box with a view of the Houses of Parliament 1908

Nephrite, two-colour gold, sepia enamel, 3.8 × 13.4 × 9.0 cm
Inscribed with mark of Henrik Wigström, gold mark of 56 zolotniks (1908–17), and 'FABERGE' in Cyrillic
RCIN 40498

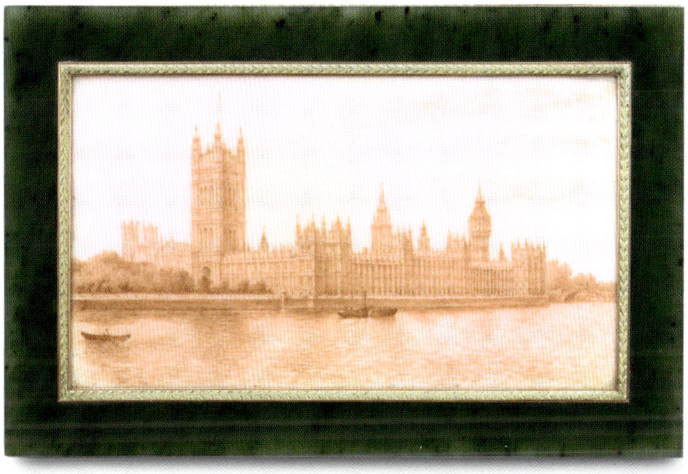

Provenance (RCIN 404912): Bought by King Edward VII from Fabergé's London branch, November/December 1908; (RCIN 40498): bought by Grand Duke Michael Alexandrovich from Fabergé's London branch, November 1908; by whom given to King Edward VII

The frame and box form part of a group of such objects with views of royal residences or famous sites in England. The majority were acquired by King Edward VII, Queen Alexandra and, later, by Queen Mary. Queen Alexandra purchased a box with views of Chatsworth House in Derbyshire which she gave to the Dowager Duchess of Devonshire (1832–1911) for Christmas 1908.[33]

Fabergé's craftsmen produced finely painted miniature views in enamels, usually from photographs, of buildings and monuments in Russia, and the idea was applied to the ever eager clientele of the London branch of the firm. CDEG

FABERGÉ

264 *Statuette of Persimmon* 1907

Silver, nephrite, 24.3 × 31.2 × 9.6 cm
Impressed with maker's mark of Henrik Wigström; silver mark of 91 zolotniks (1908–17), *FABERGE* in Roman letters, and English import marks for 1908; inscribed on a silver cartouche on front of base: *PERSIMMON 1908*
RCIN 32392

Provenance Commissioned by King Edward VII, 1907

King Edward VII and Queen Alexandra were Fabergé's most avid patrons in England, their enthusiasm for his work almost entirely influenced by the Queen's sister, Maria Feodorovna, and by the subsequent receipt of gifts from the Russian family. In 1907, the King decided to commission the firm to produce portrait models of his favourite horses and dogs, kept on the estate at Sandringham in Norfolk. The horses included this statuette of Persimmon, Edward VII's most successful racehorse, winner of the Derby and St Leger in 1896, and the Ascot Gold Cup and Eclipse Stakes in 1897. The Prince of Wales (later King George V) described the excitement surrounding Persimmon's Derby victory in his diary.

In order to fulfil this major commission, which was facilitated by the manager of the London branch, Henry Bainbridge (1874–1954), several sculptors were dispatched from Russia, including Boris Frödman-Cluzel (1878–1969), who stayed on the estate in Norfolk. He was a renowned sculptor, part of a movement of modern artists who produced – among other works – sculpted figures based on characters from Diaghilev's Ballets Russes.

In the memoirs of Swiss-born Franz Birbaum (1872–1947), one of Fabergé's designers, he recalls that due to the fine legs of the thoroughbred racehorse, it was impossible to sculpt this equine portrait from hardstone in the usual Russian tradition. As a result, the sculpture was cast in silver and fixed to a simple nephrite base. **CDEG**

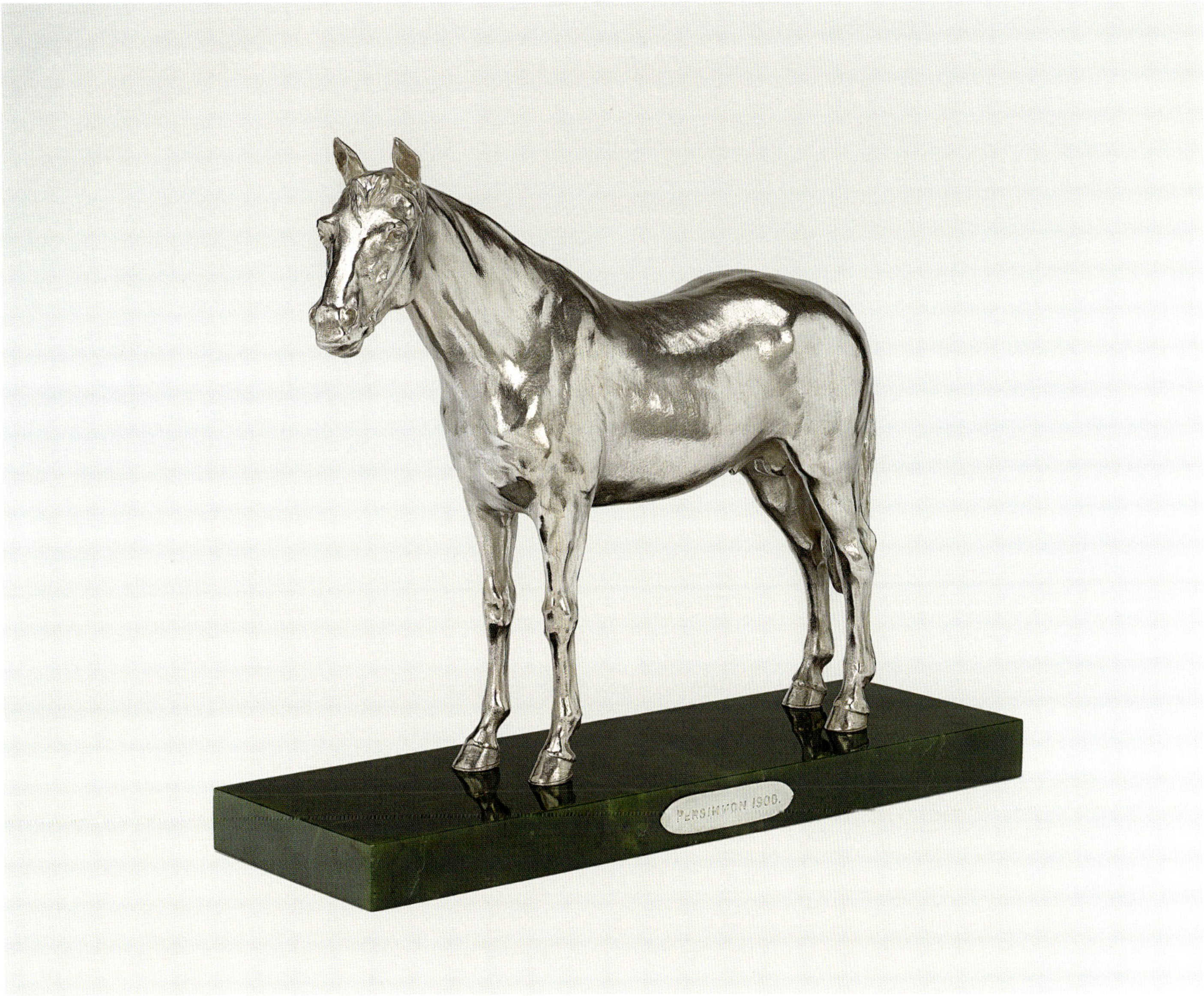
PERSIMMON 1908.

FABERGÉ

265 & 266

Caesar 1908

Chalcedony, ruby, gold, enamel, 5.1 × 6.5 × 2.2 cm
Inscribed on collar: *I Belong to the King*
RCIN 40339

Vassilka 1908

Silver, aventurine quartz, 13.4 × 21.1 × 9.0 cm
Impressed with silver mark of 91 zolotniks (1908–17), 'C. FABERGÉ' in Cyrillic, and English import marks for 1908
RCIN 40800

Provenance Commissioned by King Edward VII, 1907 (RCIN 40339 only): purchased from Fabergé's London branch by the Hon. Mrs Greville (1863–1942), 29 November 1910

Literature De Guitaut 2010, pp. 38–41

Whatever the original scope of Edward VII's so-called Sandringham commission, to have portrait models of the favourite dogs and horses kept on the Norfolk estate modelled from life as presents for Queen Alexandra, these two very different life studies are portraits of beloved royal dogs belonging to the King and Queen.

Caesar was the King's closest canine companion, whose final duty to his master was to follow the King's coffin at his funeral on 20 May 1910. Vassilka was one of a pair of Borzois, with Alex, given as a gift to the King and Queen by Alexander III and Maria Feodorovna. Vassilka was a champion dog, winning more than 75 prizes.

Both models show the skill of Fabergé's sculptors in capturing the personality of both animals. CDEG

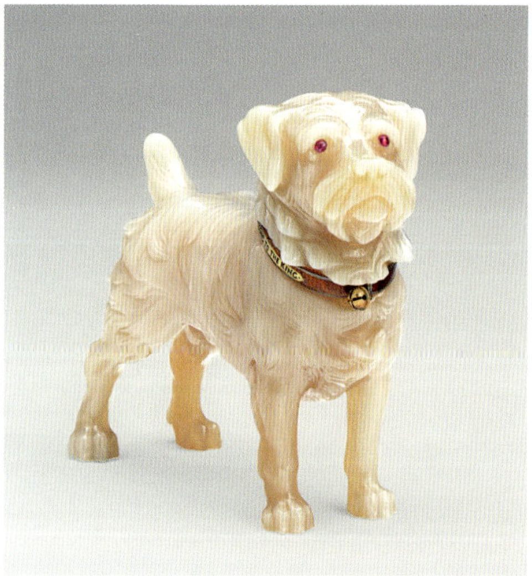

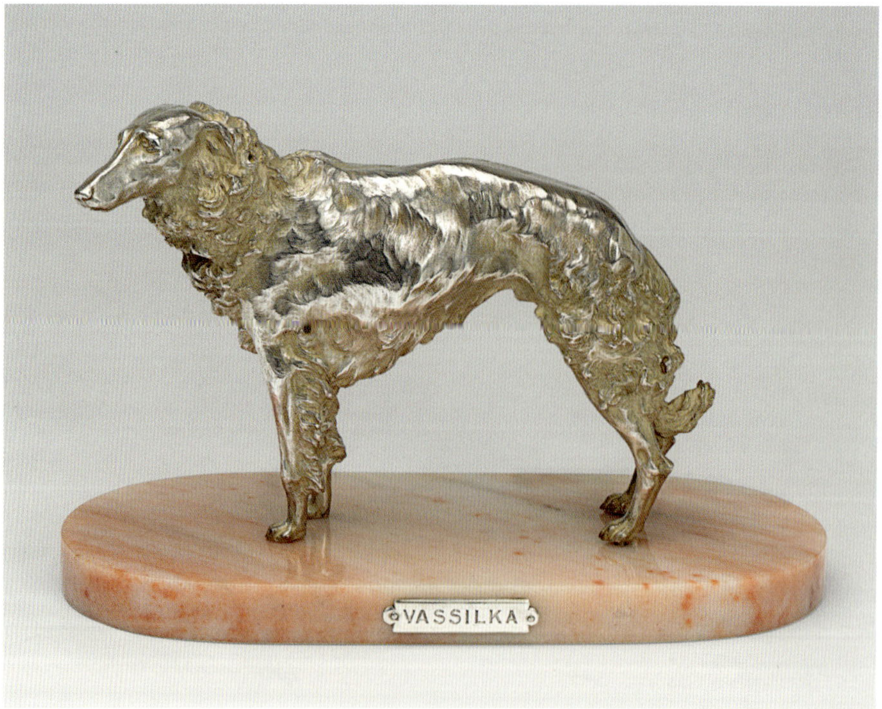

FABERGÉ

267–269

Water buffalo c.1913

Chalcedony, ivory, cabochon rubies, 5.9 × 8.4 × 3.3 cm
RCIN 40388

Koala bear c.1913

Agate, demantoid garnets, silver, 6.6 × 8.2 × 7.3 cm
Impressed with mark of Henrik Wigström, silver mark of 88 zolotniks (1908–17), and 'FABERGE' in Cyrillic
RCIN 40407

Lioness c.1900

Agate, diamonds, 3.7 × 9.4 × 3.6 cm
RCIN 40391

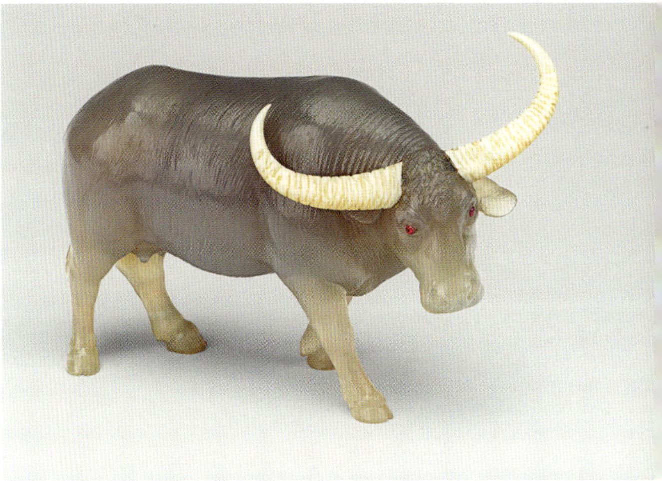

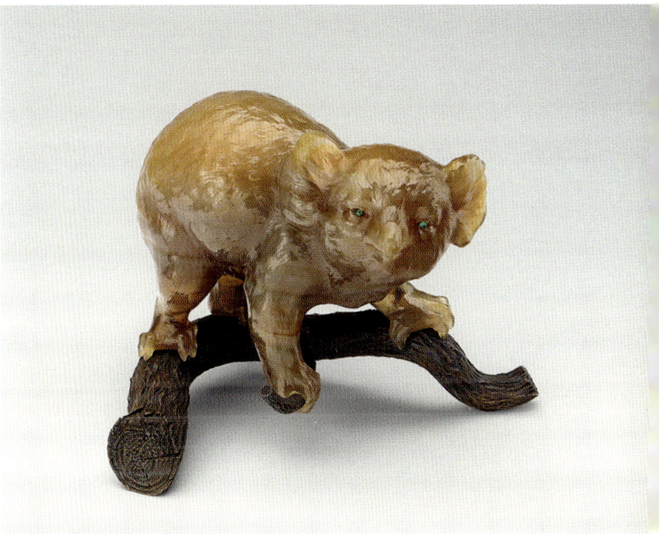

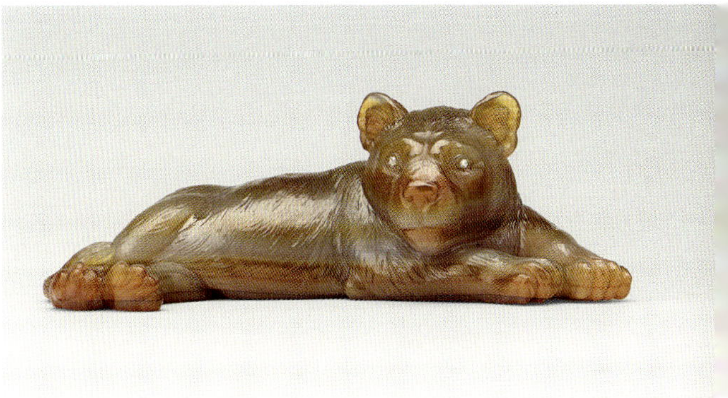

Provenance (RCINS 40388 and 40407): bought by King George V from Fabergé's London branch, 15 November 1913 (RCIN 40391); given to Queen Alexandra by her nephew, Emperor Nicholas II, Christmas 1901

Queen Alexandra rarely bought animals for herself, instead purchasing them to give away as presents. Her collection was largely formed through gifts, often suggested by Henry Bainbridge, manager of the London branch of Fabergé, as being in the ideal price bracket.[34] Other animals that arrived as gifts came directly from the family in Russia, such as this one from Nicholas II, of a recumbent lioness, with which she was 'perfectly delighted'.[35]

Alexandra's love of Fabergé's animal carvings was rivalled by both her husband and her son. Surviving invoices, together with the sales ledgers of the London branch, show that King George V purchased several animals for himself on 15 December 1913.[36] Of the seven items listed on the invoice from the London branch, four were animals, including this koala bear and an Indian cow, which is usually identified as a water buffalo.
CDEG

FABERGÉ

270

Patch box 1894

Four-colour gold, moss agate, diamonds, 4.6 × 4.1 × 2.5 cm
Impressed with maker's mark of Mikhail Perkhin, *MP*, gold mark of 56 zolotniks (before 1896), and 'FABERGE' in Cyrillic
RCIN 9133

Provenance Presented to Queen Mary when Duchess of York by Nicholas II and Alexandra Feodorovna, Christmas 1894

Literature QMB, I, no. 607; QMPP, I, no. 182

The lid of this exquisitely decorated gold box is centred by a panel of moss agate – an agate with deposits of ferrous and manganese oxides, forming dendritic and moss-like patterns, often used to mount small objects created by Fabergé. The agate is set in a border of diamonds and laurel swags, and the sides of the box are intricately applied with swags of roses in red, yellow and white gold, with scrolls in yellow gold above. Not only did the royal family purchase many pieces from the London branch of the Fabergé firm, but they were often sent pieces of Fabergé by the imperial family, for anniversaries, Easter and Christmas, and this box is just such an example. **CDEG**

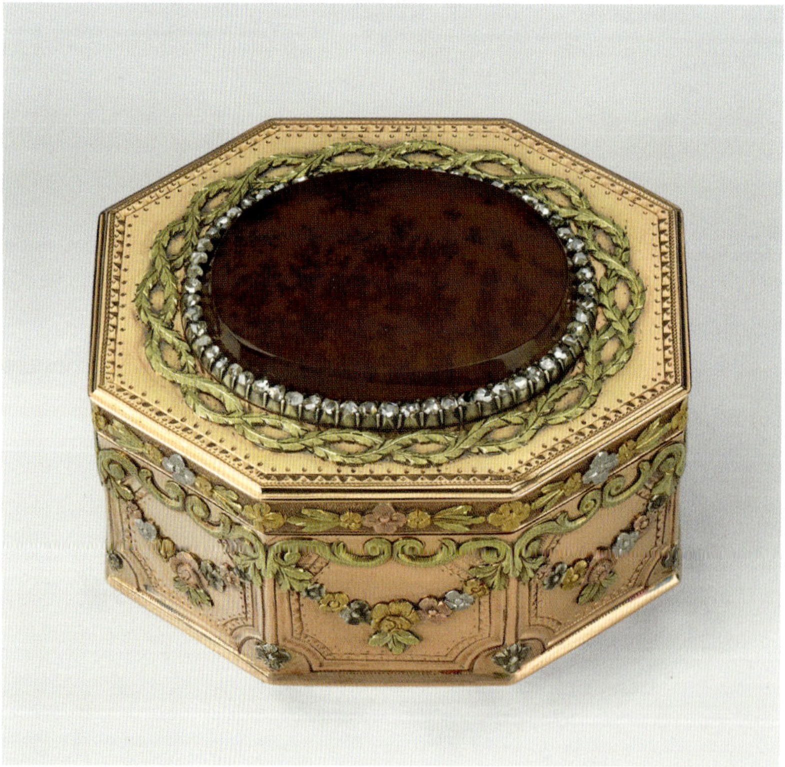

FABERGÉ

271 *Frame with a photograph of the Tsesarevich Alexei* c.1906

Silver gilt, four-colour gold, guilloché enamel, rubies, ivory, 10.2 × 8.4 × 5.0 cm
Impressed with mark of Victor Aarne (1863–1934) and 'FABERGE', both in Cyrillic, and silver mark of 88 zolotniks (1896–1908)
RCIN 40105

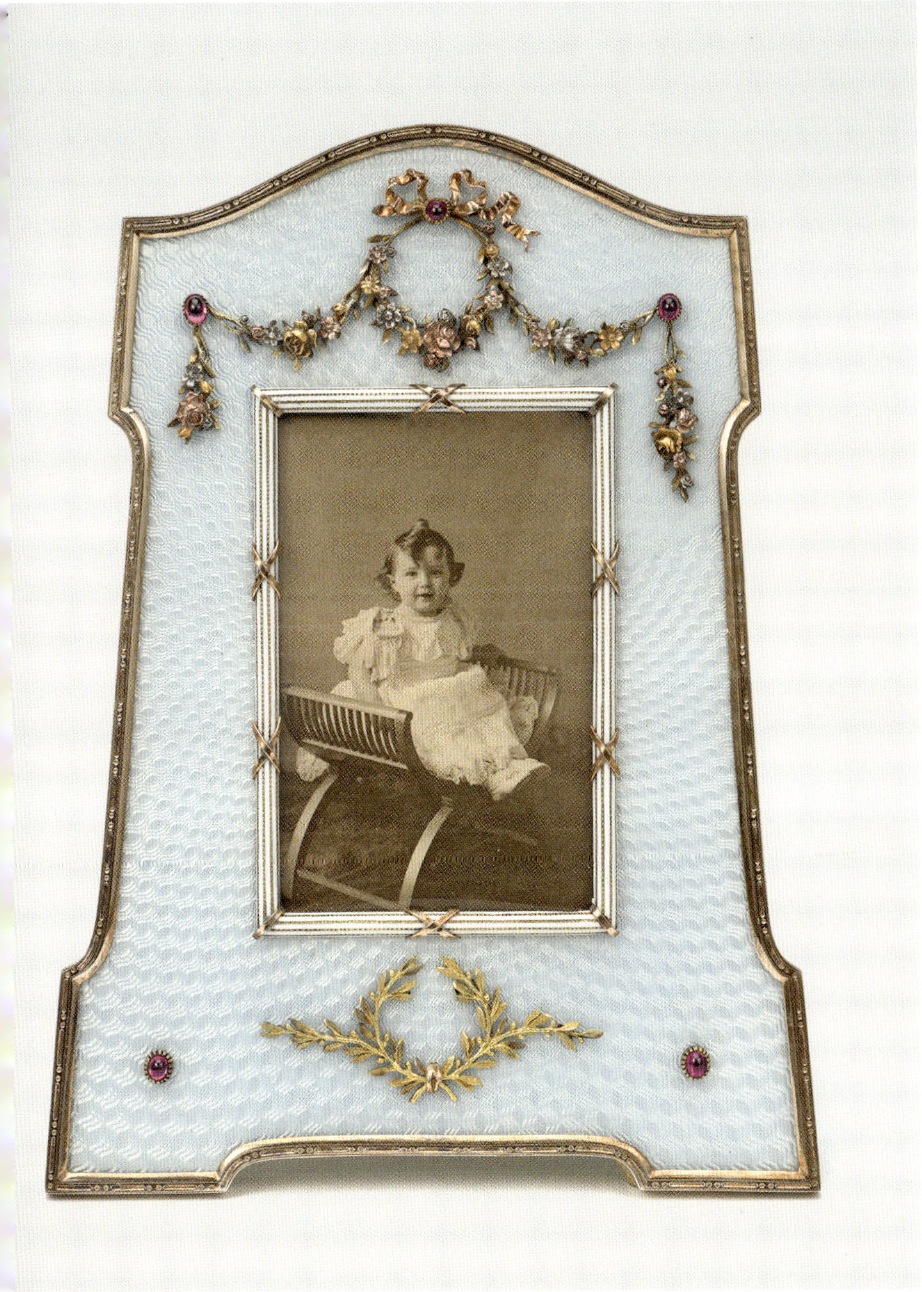

Provenance Bought by Alexandra Feodorovna, 21 July 1906 (165 rubles); possibly Queen Alexandra

Literature Pavlovsk 2013, p. 277

This frame is a typical example of Fabergé's work, combining fine, multicoloured, applied gold decoration and refined guilloché enamelling. It is also an example of how the Emperor and Empress purchased works by the Fabergé firm specifically to send to their English relations.

The frame is described in Fabergé's invoice as 'Alekceh 1906', implying that this photograph was taken specially to mark the Tsesarevich's second birthday and sent to close family members.[37] The exact recipient within the British royal family is not known, but is quite likely to have been Queen Alexandra, given her love of Fabergé's work, and that the photograph is of her great-nephew. CDEG

ATTRIBUTED TO K. HAHN

272 *Insignia of the Order of St Catherine the Martyr* c.1909

Gold, silver, diamonds, enamel, silk, leather, (badge) 9.1 × 5.6 cm, (star) 9.0 × 8.5 cm
Badge and star engraved: 25; fitted cream silk and velvet-lined red leather case, stamped with the imperial eagle
RCIN 441628

Provenance Presented to Queen Mary when Princess of Wales, by Nicholas II, 1909

Founded by Peter I in 1714, in honour of his wife, the future Empress Catherine I, the Order of St Catherine was the primary ladies' order of the Russian imperial honours system, with the Grand Mistress either the Empress, or the Dowager Empress if still alive during her son's lifetime. Appointments were made by the Grand Mistress, with the approval of the Emperor. The Order was only awarded to ladies of the highest distinction and there were two classes: the Grand Cross, which entitled the bearer to wear a star and badge with sash, and the Small Cross, which carried the right to wear the badge only.

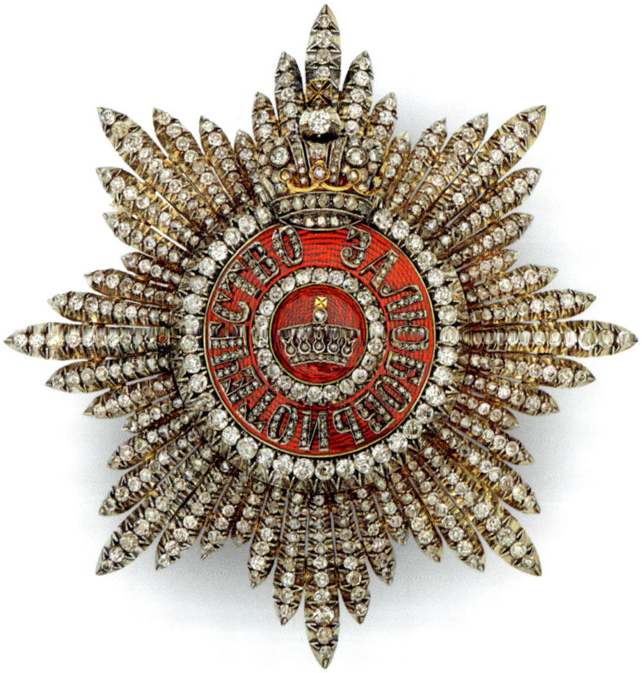

The first bestowal of the Order on a British princess was the appointment of Princess Charlotte, daughter of the future George IV, by Empress Maria Feodorovna in July 1817. The Dowager Empress wrote to the Prince Regent, offering the Order to his daughter as a mark of thanks for the kindness shown to Grand Duke Nicholas (the future Nicholas I) during his visit to Great Britain earlier that year.[38] The visit included a remarkable dinner at Brighton Pavilion on 18 January, with over 100 dishes, prepared by Antonin Carême. The Princess's great-aunt, Christiana of Mecklenburg-Strelitz, as the principal lady of the Mecklenburg court, had also received the Order (cat. 26).

The appointment followed receipt of a letter from the Prince Regent, praising the Grand Duke. The Prince Regent responded to the Empress in September,[39] and the Princess wrote to Maria Feodorovna on 6 September: 'I have just received from my father's hands the insignia of the Order of St Catherine which your majesty and the emperor your august son have had the grace to bestow upon me'.[40] Depicted in the portrait of the Princess after Dawe (cat. 75), the insignia is no longer in the Collection. Also not in the Collection – except for a miniature of the Order – are the badge and star bestowed on Queen Victoria some 20 years later, in July 1837, by Nicholas I and his wife, Alexandra Feodorovna. The Queen recorded in her Journal on 19 July 1837:

> *I gave audiences from various foreign Ambassadors, amongst which were Count Orloff, sent by the Emperor of Russia to compliment me. He presented me with a letter from the Empress of Russia accompanied by the Order of St. Catherine all set in diamonds […] Count Orloff […] dined here. I sat*

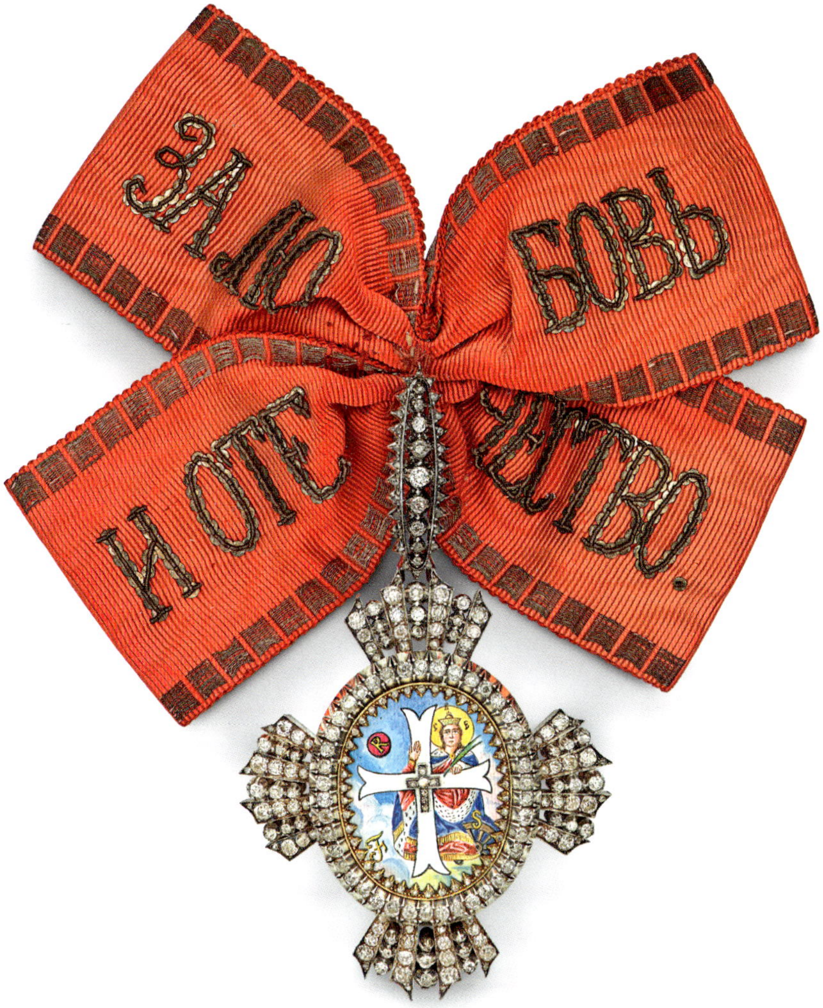

between Count Sebastiani and Count Orloff. I wore the Order of St. Catherine, which is a very handsome and a very distinguished Order; it was instituted by the Empress Catherine the 1st, Count Orloff told me, when she saved the Russian Army from the Turks.[41]

The insignia was worn by the Queen (who would normally wear the Order of the Garter) during the visit of Nicholas I in 1844, and she can be seen wearing the ribbon in the watercolour by Nash of her entering the Waterloo Chamber (fig. 19).[42] The star of this set of insignia was remodelled in 1892 by Garrard, who submitted a bill for 'unsetting 311 diamonds as rays of star of the Order of St Catherine of Russia and remounting 227 of the same as a new star of the same Order to the pattern of Her Imperial Highness the Grand Duchess Elizabeth Feodorovna's, employing the old centre',[43] and (with the badge) was bequeathed to the Queen's daughter, Princess Beatrice; they are no longer in the Collection.[44] The miniature badge worn by the Queen on her miniatures bar placed it senior to all the other orders she had received.

When Emperor Alexander II visited in May 1874, the Order was bestowed on Princesses Helena, Louise and Beatrice, who, with the Princess of Wales and Grand Duchess Maria Alexandrovna, the Duchess of Edinburgh, as well as the Queen herself, wore the Order at dinner on the evening of 16 May. Of Queen Victoria's and Edward VII's daughters, all received the Order, and the honour was repaid to the Empress Maria Alexandrovna when Queen Victoria appointed her to the equivalent British Order, the First Class of the Royal Order of Victoria and Albert, for which the Emperor thanked the Queen in his letter of 21 May 1874, when giving thanks for her hospitality during the visit (cat. 192).[45] This honour was also given to Alexandra Feodorovna in 1894.

Alexandra, Princess of Wales received the Order at the time of her sister's marriage to the Tsesarevich Alexander Alexandrovich in 1866, and it was worn by her regularly at state and family events, until she received the Order of the Garter in 1901. Queen Mary received the Order in 1909, during the imperial visit to Cowes.[46] Princess Victoria received it at the time of Nicholas II's accession and wedding in November 1894, as did Princess Maud (the future Queen of Norway), while Princess Louise, Duchess of Fife received it in 1909, alongside Princesses Patricia of Connaught and Beatrice of Saxe-Coburg and Gotha (1884–1966), both cousins of the Empress.

SJP

EMPRESS ALEXANDRA FEODOROVNA OF RUSSIA (1872–1918)

273 *Letter to Princess Louise, Duchess of Argyll (1848–1939), from Livadia Palace, Crimea* 17/30 May 1914

Manuscript, 17.0 × 12.7 cm
RA VIC/ADDA17/1186

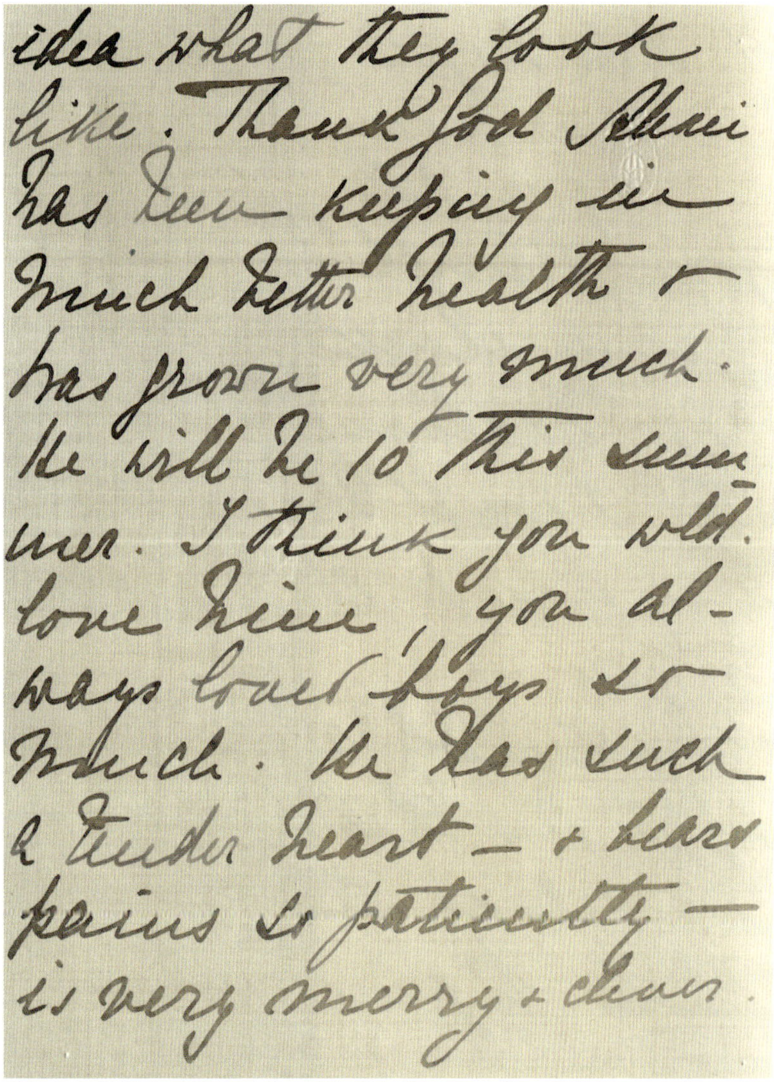
idea what they look like. Thank God Alexei has been keeping in much better health & has grown very much. He will be 10 this summer. I think you wld. love him, you always loved boys so much. He has such a tender heart – & bears pains so patiently – is very merry & dear.

This letter from Empress Alexandra Feodorovna to her aunt (Princess Louise was sister to the Empress's mother) was written shortly after the death of the 9th and 2nd Duke of Argyll, the Duchess's husband, on 2 May 1914. The Empress replies to a letter from the Duchess, who had been supported by the Empress's sister, Princess Victoria, following the Duke's death as a result of pneumonia. A letter of condolence and support, it also shows the Empress's deep faith: 'I too have ever found that in prayer alone one can gain strength to bear our crosses'. She continues that as an invalid for the past eight years, she had been strengthened by her faith and that the church services are 'most beautiful and consoling'.

With the letter were sent a number of photographs of the imperial children (cat. 274), 'to give you an idea what they look like'. Of the Tsesarevich Alexei (1904–18), she wrote, 'He has such a tender heart - & bears pains so patiently - is very merry and dear'. Perhaps remembering her aunt's artistic skills, Alexandra Feodorovna refers to the profusion of roses at Livadia, 'of every colour and sort', commenting, 'one longs to be an artist to paint from morn to night'. She ends by saying that the Tsesarevich ('Baby') is waiting to say his evening prayers with her.

The letter gives a very intimate view of the Empress, her faith and her children, and a specific provenance for the photographs which on so many other occasions have been pasted into albums or placed in frames for display. SJP

BOISSONNAS & EGGLER (active 1902–1916)

274 *Grand Duchesses Maria (1899–1918), Tatiana (1897–1918), Anastasia (1901–1918) and Olga (1895–1918) of Russia* 1914

Platinum print, 12.6 × 9.0 cm
RCIN 2119210; RA VIC/ADDA17/1187

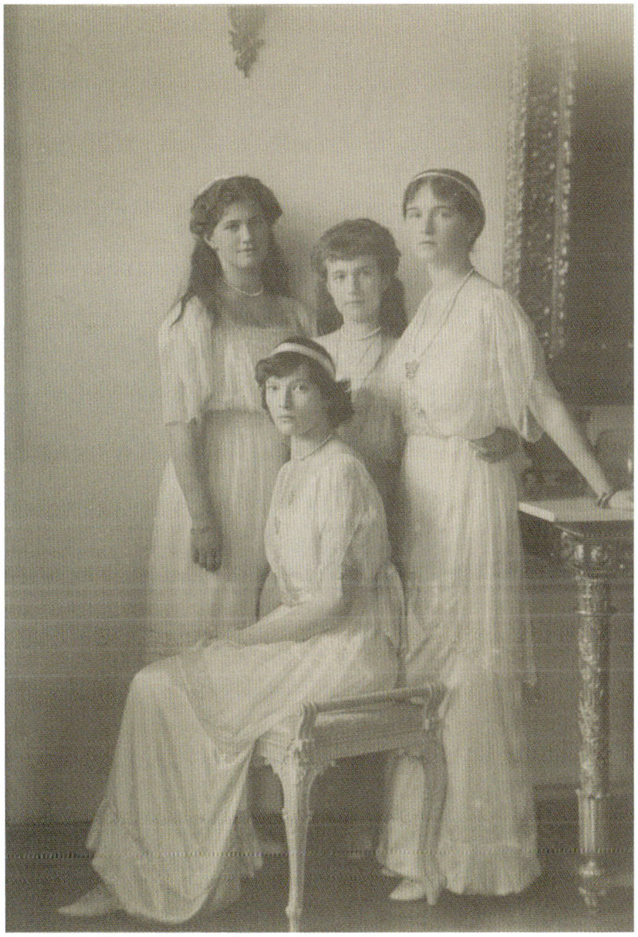

Provenance Presented to Princess Louise, Duchess of Argyll, by Empress Alexandra Feodorovna, 1914

This is one of the photographs enclosed with a letter (cat. 273) sent by Empress Alexandra to Princess Louise, sixth child and fourth daughter of Queen Victoria and Prince Albert, and maternal aunt to the Empress. Ten of the photographs are professional single and group portraits of the Empress's daughters, known collectively to the family in order of birth as OTMA, taken by the fashionable firm Boissonnas & Eggler,[47] and one is a snapshot of her son, Tsesarevich Alexei, possibly taken by the Empress herself (fig. 82). **AN**

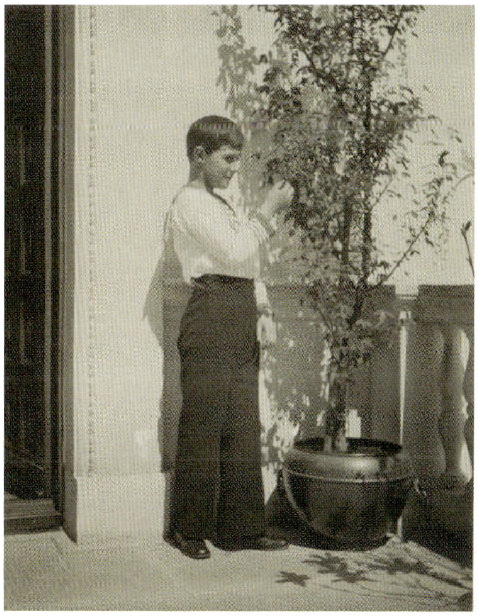

FIG. 82
Attr. to Empress Alexandra Feodorovna
Alexei Nikolaevich, Tsesarevich of Russia, 1914
Gelatin silver print, 11.7 × 9.2 cm
RCIN 2119220;
RA VIC/ADDA17/1192

ATTRIBUTED TO FABERGÉ

275 *Brooch* *c.*1909

Silver, amethyst, diamonds, 3.9 × 2.4 cm
RCIN 65654

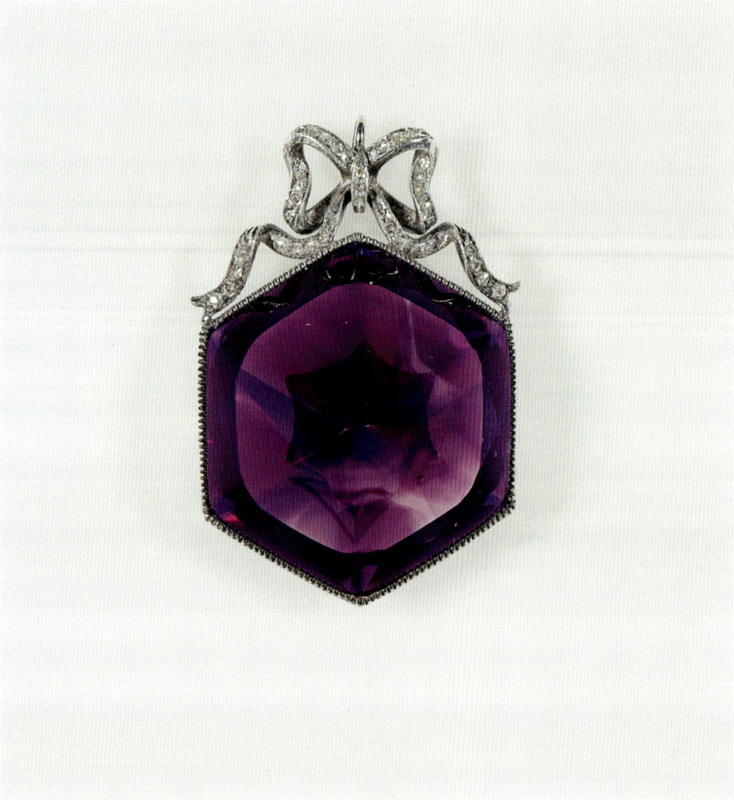

Provenance Given to Queen Mary when Princess of Wales, by Emperor Nicholas II and Empress Alexandra Feodorovna, August 1909

Siberian amethysts are famous for their intense purple body colour and fugitive highlights of red and blue. This hexagonal stone is mounted as a pendant, with a diamond-set silver bow, in a style reminiscent of jewellery produced in the workshop of Carl Fabergé's jewellery workmaster, Albert Holmström (1876–1925). The simple, delicate and unobtrusive mount allows the richly coloured stone to be the focus of the jewel. In keeping with the mounting of faceted Russian stones, the pointed side of the amethyst is mounted outermost, thereby ensuring it would sit flat against the chest of the wearer.

From 2 to 5 August 1909, Nicholas II, Alexandra Feodorovna and their children visited the Prince and Princess of Wales at Cowes, travelling on the Imperial Yachts *Standart* and *Polar Star*. Together they enjoyed luncheons and dinners, both on board the yachts and at Osborne House, during which this jewel was presented to the Princess of Wales. CDEG

PIETRO CANONICA (1869–1959)

276 *Bust of Emperor Nicholas II (1868–1918)* 1910

Bronze, 38.0 × 38.0 × 19.0 cm
Inscribed in Cyrillic on front plinth: 'NII'; signed on back: *P. Canonica*
RCIN 2239

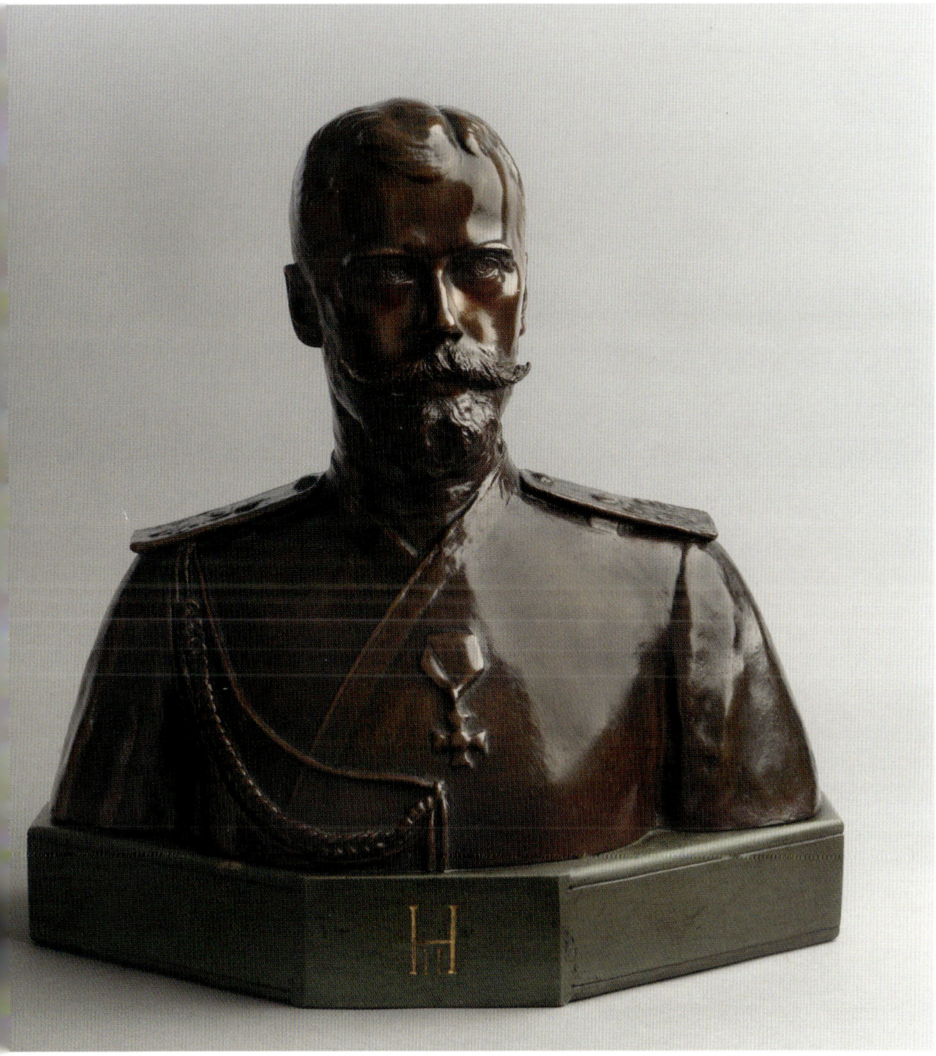

Provenance Sent as a gift to King George V by Nicholas II, Christmas 1912

Literature GARF 601/1/1219/45

The Italian sculptor, artist and composer, Pietro Canonica, received wide recognition for his sculpture through his participation in international exhibitions in Rome, London, Dresden, Brussels and St Petersburg. He received many commissions from European royalty, including from the British royal family, sculpting a marble bust of Princess Victoria of Wales and a bronze statuette of Queen Alexandra, both dated 1903, and a bust of King Edward VII, dated 1904, which the Queen paid for herself, at a cost of £680.[48] Although the latter is in marble, it incorporates the same shaped integral plinth as the bronze bust of Nicholas II, with canted front edges, inspired by classical prototypes.

Canonica undertook several commissions for the Russian court in 1910, when he made a bust of Alexandra Feodorovna in marble, now at Pavlovsk, and a bust of the Tsesarevich Alexei. This latter marble has been lost, but the plaster maquette survives in the Museo Pietro Canonica, Rome.

Canonica was commissioned to produce a monument to Nicholas II in 1913, having likewise been commissioned to make one for Emperor Alexander III, but the monument was destroyed in the Revolution in 1918.

This bronze was sent as a Christmas present to King George V in 1912. The King wrote to thank his cousin from York Cottage, Sandringham, on 29 December: 'It was dear of you and Alicky thinking of me again this Xmas and sending me that charming bust of yourself for which I thank you both a thousand times'.[49] **CDEG**

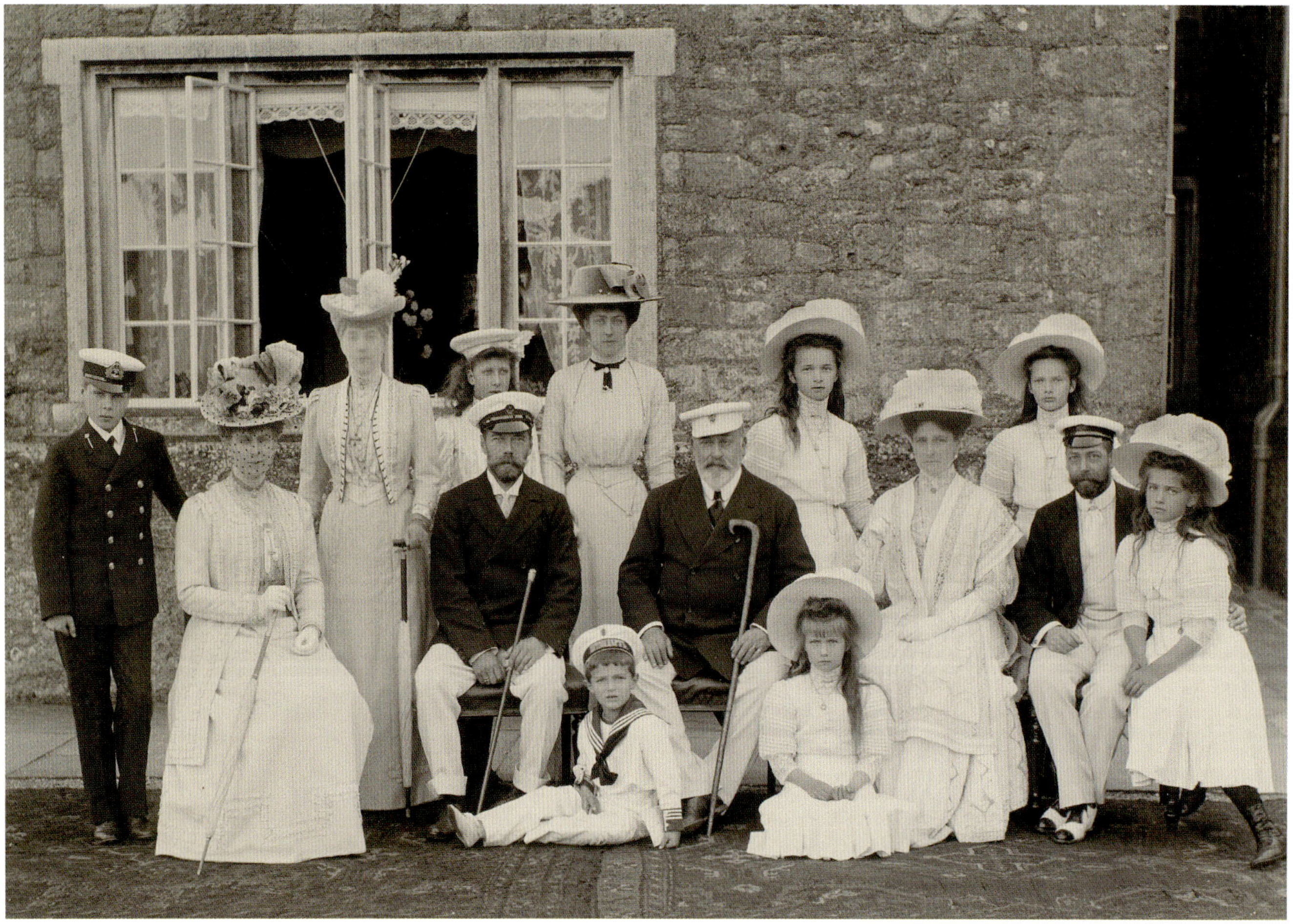

ARTHUR WILLIAM DEBENHAM (1875–1944)

277 *The British and Russian imperial families, Barton Manor, Isle of Wight* 4 August 1909

Gelatin silver print, 19.2 × 28.1 cm
Blind stamp on mount: *A.W. Debenham / COWES*
RCIN 2926731

Provenance Acquired by King George V

The photograph, taken in front of Barton Manor (adjacent to Osborne House), records what would be the last visit of the imperial Russian family to Britain. Standing at the back, from left to right, are: Prince Edward of Wales (later King Edward VIII and Duke of Windsor), Queen Alexandra, Princess Mary of Wales, Princess Victoria, and the Grand Duchesses Olga and Tatiana. Sitting, from left to right, are: the Princess of Wales (later Queen Mary), Nicholas II, Tsesarevich Alexei, King Edward VII, Grand Duchess Anastasia, Alexandra Feodorovna, and the Prince of Wales (later King George V), sharing a chair with the Grand Duchess Maria. **AN**

ARTHUR WILLIAM DEBENHAM (1875–1944)

278 & 279

Emperor Nicholas II of Russia (1868–1918) and George, Prince of Wales (1865–1936) 4 August 1909

Gelatin silver print, 23.9 × 17.2 cm
RCIN 2926729

Prince Edward of Wales (1894–1972), Emperor Nicholas II, Tsesarevich Alexei Nikolaevich (1904–1918) and the Prince of Wales 4 August 1909

Gelatin silver print, 24.8 × 19.0 cm
RCIN 2926730

Provenance Acquired by King George V

These photographs show the great familiarity between the two cousins, who also shared a remarkable resemblance. Lili Dehn (1888–1963), friend and confidante of Empress Alexandra Feodorovna, writes in her memoirs: 'He [Nicholas II] was always amused by the likeness between him and his cousin, King George. One day he showed me a photograph of the latter, saying, "Have you seen my last photograph, Lili? Doesn't it flatter me?"'[50] The Emperor and the Prince of Wales are seen here next to each other's first-born son and future heir. Looking at the photograph with today's eyes, though, the viewer may encounter a certain haunting aura, knowing that only one of the sitters would eventually be able fully to fulfil his duties as monarch. **AN**

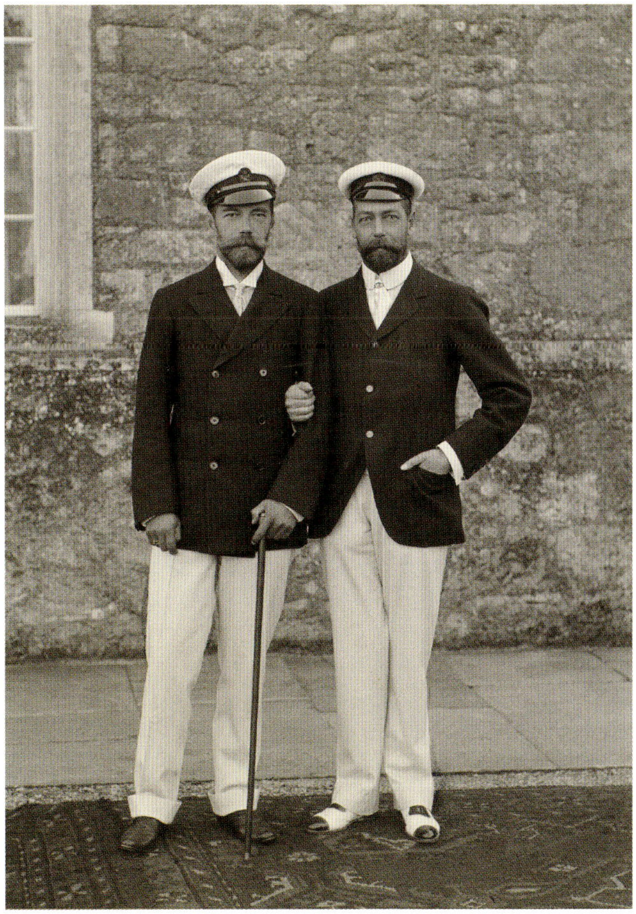

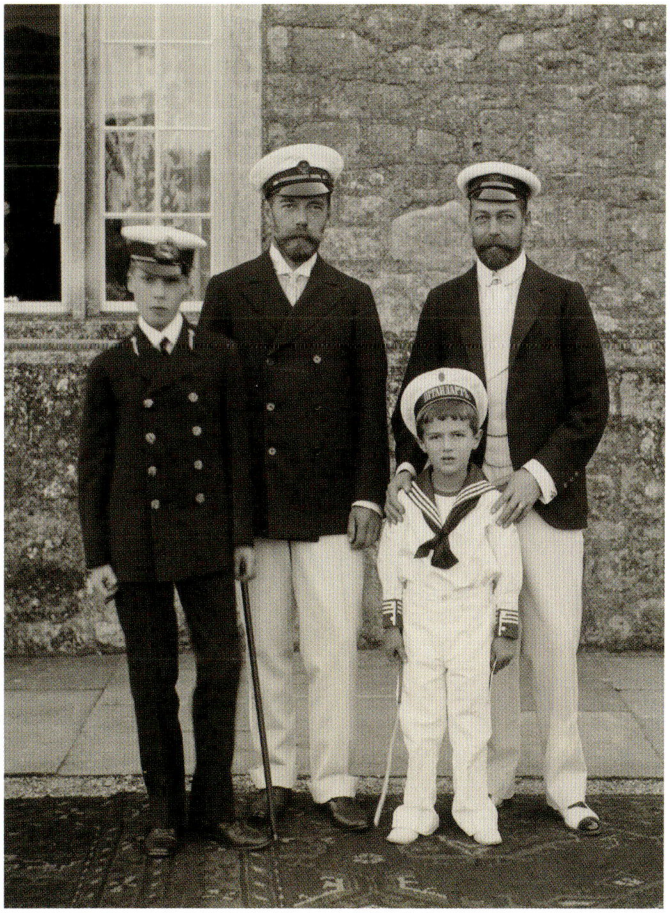

ERNST SANDAU (1880–1918)

280 *Nicholas II, Emperor of Russia (1868–1918), and King George V (1865–1936)* 24 May 1913

Gelatin silver print laid on card, 22.1 × 15.5 cm
Signed and dated by one of the sitters: *Georgie. / Berlin May 1913*; photographer's credentials printed on mount
RCIN 2926734

Provenance Acquired by King George V

Following Nicholas II's visit to the Isle of Wight with his family in 1909, the two cousins would meet again, and for the last time, in Berlin in 1913, on the occasion of the marriage of Prince Ernest Augustus of Hanover (1887–1953) and Princess Victoria Louise of Prussia, only daughter of Kaiser Wilhelm II, who was also a cousin of both Nicholas II and King George V. In his diary, the King wrote, 'At 4.0. we were dressed ready for the Wedding, I wore the 8th Cuirassier uniform, & were photographed, I was also done with Nicky.'[51] As a matter of courtesy, both sovereigns attended the celebrations wearing uniforms of regiments of the hosting country, which they served in honorary roles. Nicholas II is seen here as colonel-in-chief of the 8th (1st Westphalian) Hussar 'Emperor Nicholas II of Russia' Regiment; he is also wearing the collar of the Prussian Order of the Black Eagle and – among other stars and decorations – the star of the Order of the Garter. King George V is wearing his uniform of colonel-in-chief of the 8th (Rheinish) Cuirassiers 'Count Geßler' Regiment (fig. 83), an appointment he had received in 1902, which would become nulled in 1914, following Great Britain's declaration of war on Germany. Among his decorations worn for the occasion are the collars of the Orders of St Andrew and the Black Eagle, the Hohenzollern House Order, the Royal Victorian Chain, stars of the Orders of St Andrew, the Black Eagle and the Garter, as well as his medal bar, a sovereign's badge of the Order of the Bath, and the sash and badge of the Garter. **AN**

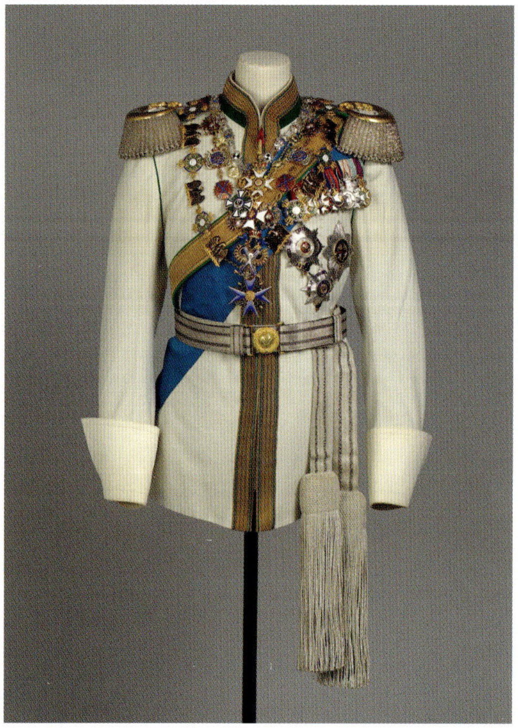

FIG. 83
Uniform of King George V as Colonel-in-Chief of the 8th (Rheinish) Cuirassiers 'Count Geßler' Regiment
RCIN 33886

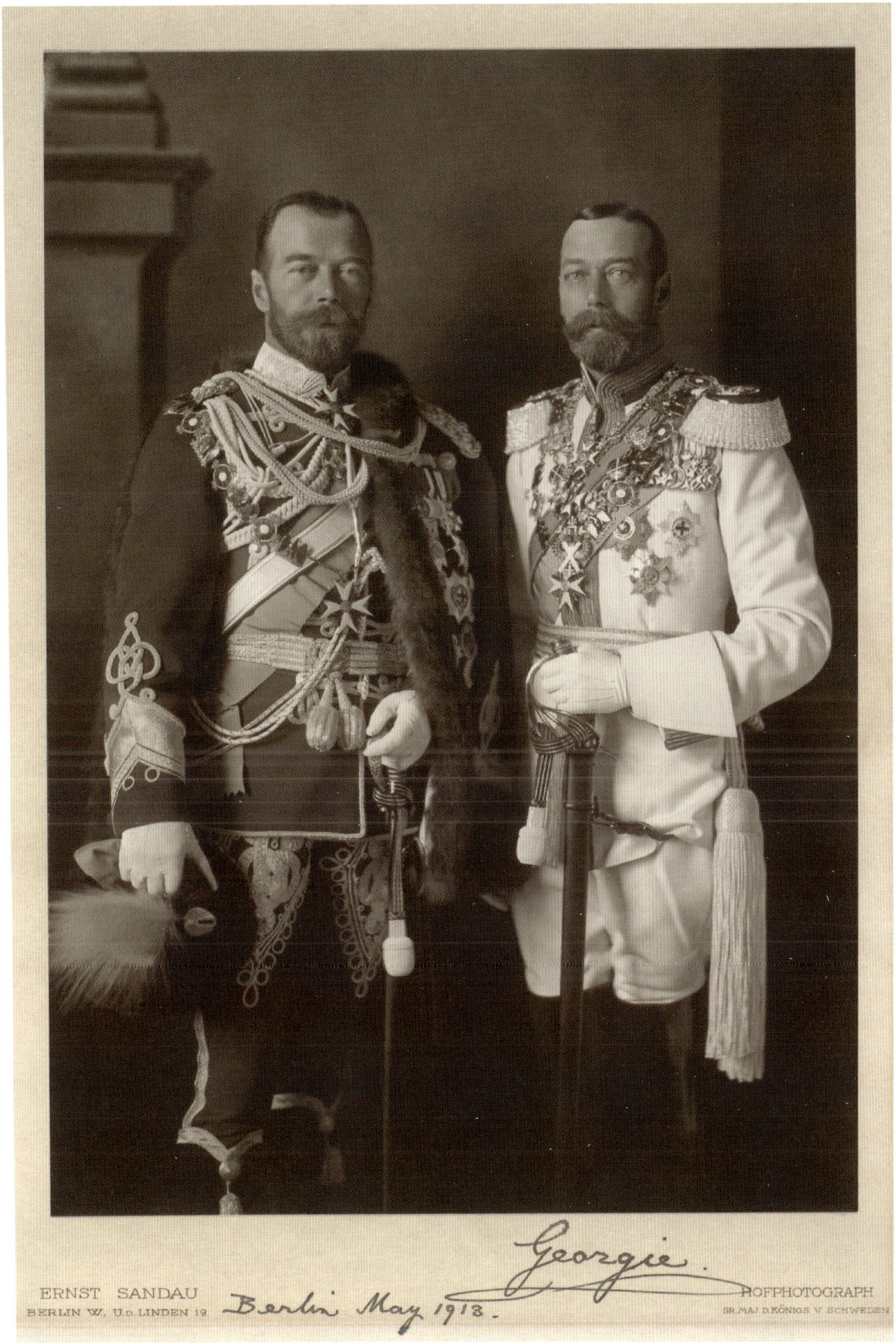
Georgie.
ERNST SANDAU
BERLIN W., U.D. LINDEN 19.
Berlin May 1913.
HOFPHOTOGRAPH
SR. MAJ. D. KÖNIGS V. SCHWEDEN

ALEXANDER GEFTER (1885–1956)

281 *Timofei Ksenofontovich Yashchik (1878–1946)* 1920

Pastel on buff paper, 90.0 × 69.5cm (sight); 124.0 × 104.0 cm (frame)
Signed top left: A Gefter
RCIN 402120

Provenance Commissioned by Empress Maria Feodorovna; purchased by Queen Alexandra, January 1921

This pastel portrait depicts the Russian Cossack Timofei Yashchik, one of the Cossack bodyguards of the Dowager Empress Maria Feodorovna, mother of Nicholas II and sister of Queen Alexandra. He is wearing the uniform of the Kuban Cossacks, the *cherkesska*, a coat in a deep blue with ornamental gun cartridges slotted across the chest, and a wool *papakha* hat. His imposing frame, with a clenched fist placed on his knee, is seen in a three-quarter view and fills the paper; the pastel embellishments on his uniform and white highlights on the weaponry have been mixed with a binder to give an impasto effect.

Yashchik commenced working for the Dowager Empress in 1916 (fig. 84), and after the Bolshevik uprising of 1917, travelled with her to one of the Imperial palaces in the Crimea, where she congregated with other family members. It became too dangerous to stay in Russia and in April 1919 the Dowager Empress set out for Britain on board the ship HMS *Marlborough*. Yashchik was amongst those accompanying her, and in May 1919, an identification card was issued for him in London, giving his residence as 'Marlborough House, Pall Mall'[52] where the Dowager Empress was staying with Queen Alexandra. By August, the Dowager Empress had decided to return to her native Denmark. Yashchik had been instrumental in providing safe passage to the Dowager Empress's daughter, Grand Duchess Olga, whom he took to his village, Nova Minskaia, where Olga gave birth to her second son, Guri. Olga finally reached Denmark in April 1920 and this portrait, commissioned by the Dowager Empress that year, probably reflects the high regard in which he would have been held for his loyalty. The completed pastel was sold to Queen Alexandra in January 1921.[53]

Alexander Gefter was a Russian naval officer and writer, who had taken lessons in painting while studying in the Legal Faculty at St Petersburg University. After the revolution he became involved in the anti-Bolshevik movement, and was in exile first in Finland, then Denmark, after which he moved to Paris where he painted portraits for a living. A preparatory study by Gefter survives for this work, dated 1920 and signed in Copenhagen.[54] The realism of this portrait is reminiscent of the Cossack portraits created by the Russian painters Vasily Surikov (1848–1916) and Ilya Repin (1844–1930) towards the end of the nineteenth century. **RW**

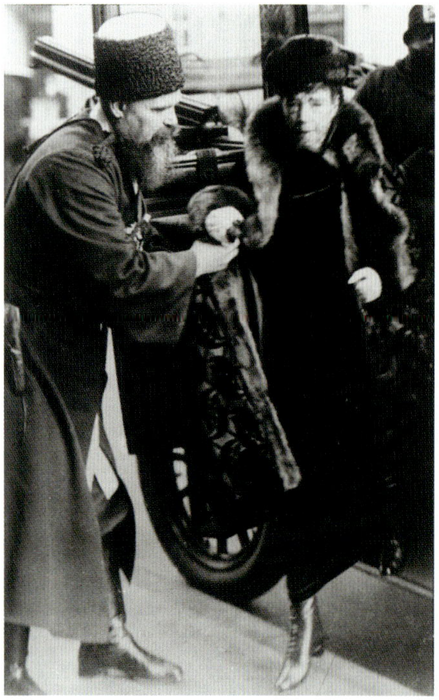

FIG. 84
Unknown photographer, *Timofei Yashchik helping the Dowager Empress Maria Feodorovna out of a car*, Royal Danish Library, Collection of Maps and Photographs

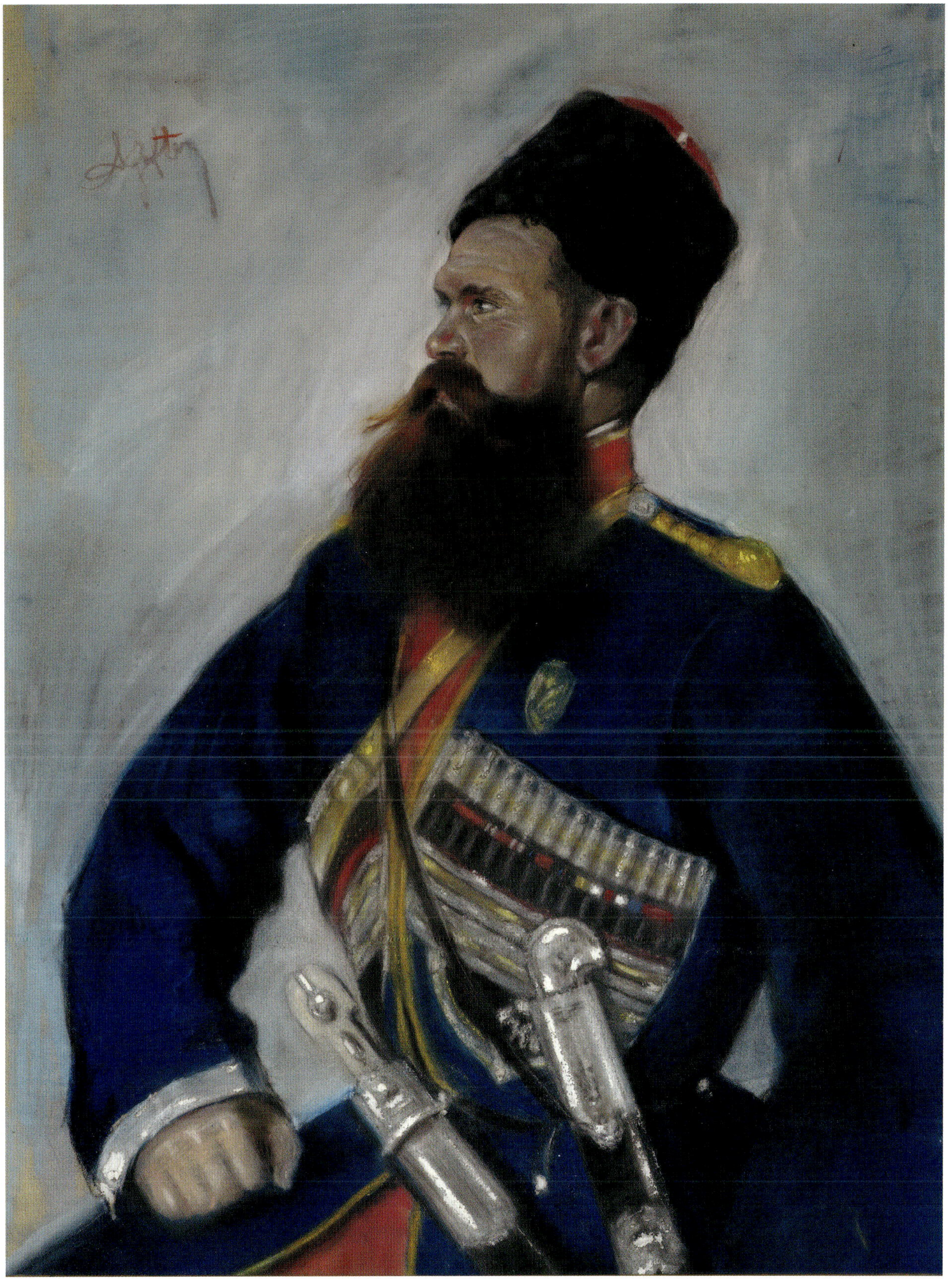

FABERGÉ

282 *Basket of Flowers Egg* 1901

Silver, parcel-gilt, gold, guilloché enamel, diamonds, 23.0 × 10.0 cm
RCIN 40098

Provenance Commissioned by Nicholas II for Alexandra Feodorovna, Easter 1901; confiscated by the Provisional Government, 1917; sold by the Antikvariat, 1933; purchased by Queen Mary, 1933

Literature QMB, III, no. 88; QMPP, VII, no. 187; de Guitaut 2003, p. 36

The identification of this work of art as an imperial Easter egg by the renowned jeweller and goldsmith, Carl Fabergé, was made comparatively recently, in the late 1990s, with the publication of Fabergé's original invoice, which identified it as the imperial egg for 1901. Prior to that, it was thought to be the work of the French jeweller and goldsmith, Boucheron, and was noted as such by Queen Mary when she acquired it.

The identification of the maker was hindered by the fact that the egg is completely unmarked. This is because the marks are presumed to have been lost when the base of the egg was repaired following damage sustained in the aftermath of the Revolution, which involved the re-enamelling of the base in blue, as opposed to the original oyster.[55]

The egg forms a basket with a diamond-set handle and geometric, diamond-set cagework over its body, into which are fitted strands of gold, in imitation of moss, and a profusion of gold, silver-gilt and enamel flowers, grasses and seeds, including husks of wheat, which are mounted *en tremblant*. **CDEG**

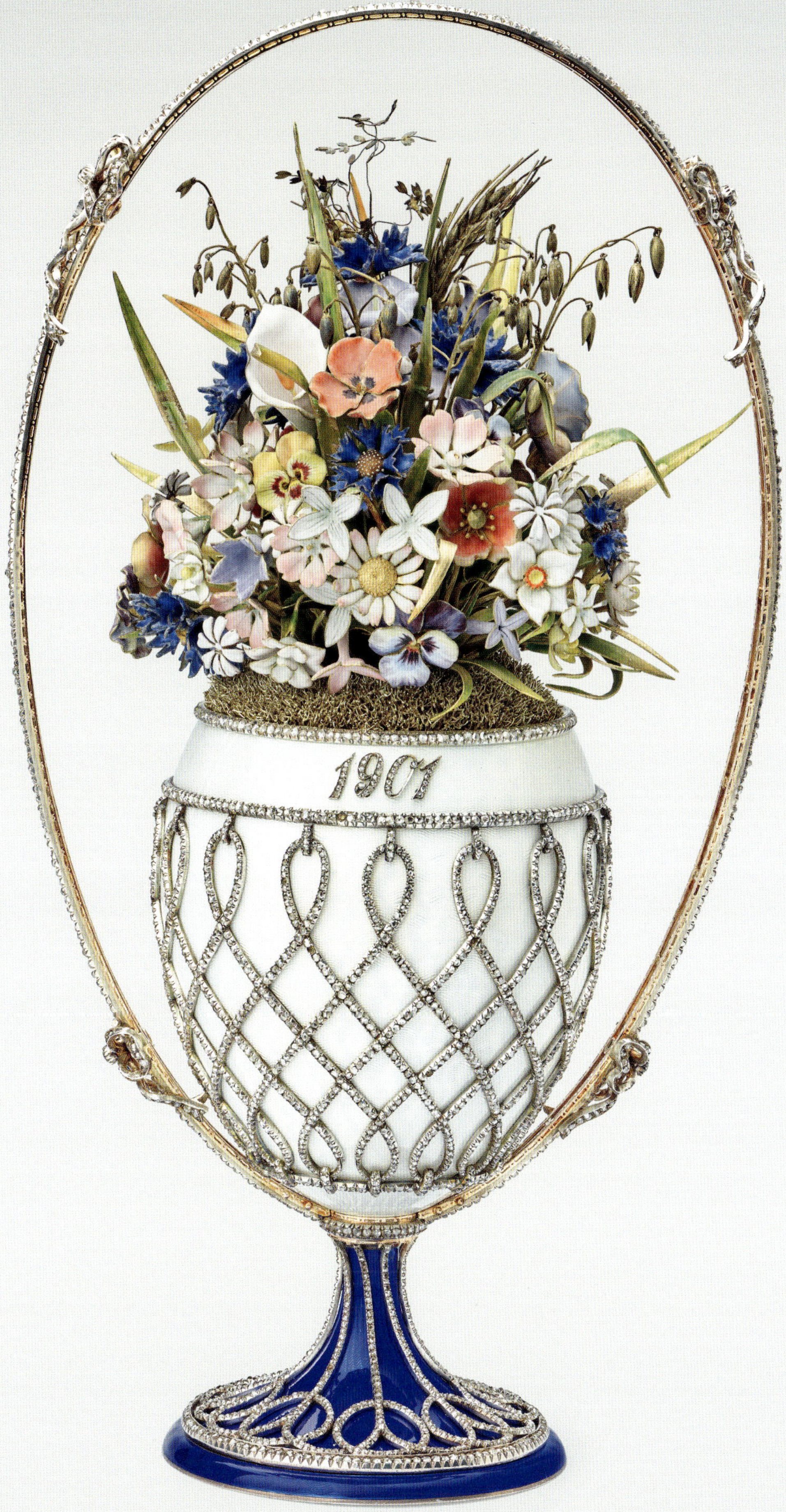
1901

FABERGÉ

283 *Colonnade Egg* 1910

Bowenite, four-colour gold, silver gilt, platinum, guilloché enamel, rose diamonds, 28.0 × 17.0 cm
Impressed with mark of Henrik Wigström, gold mark of 56 zolotniks (1908–17), and 'FABERGE' in Cyrillic
RCIN 40084

Provenance Commissioned by Emperor Nicholas II for Empress Alexandra Feodorovna, Easter 1910; confiscated by the Provisional Government, 1917; transferred to the Sovnarkom by 1922; ?Emanuel Snowman; acquired by Queen Mary and given to King George V, 1931

The Emperor's Easter present to his consort in 1910 was created by Fabergé as an allegory of the imperial family, specifically to commemorate the birth of their long-awaited son and heir, Alexei. Inside the classical temple, the pair of platinum doves represent the imperial couple, while the four seated female figures on the steps of the temple, each in a slightly different pose, represent their four children, Olga, Tatiana, Maria and Anastasia, collectively known as OTMA within the family, linked by multicoloured gold garlands of roses. Seated on the rotunda of the temple is a winged putto, representing the Tsesarevich Alexei. The rotunda is in fact formed of the top of the enamelled gold Easter egg, which is also a functioning rotary clock. The hour was originally indicated by a staff held in the putto's hand, but this was later lost.

The acquisition of the egg by Queen Mary is recorded in her manuscript annotation to her copy of *Twice Seven*, the autobiography of Henry Charles Bainbridge, manager of Fabergé's London branch. The annotation reads, 'above purchased by Queen Mary & given to King George V - 1931 -'.[56]
CDEG

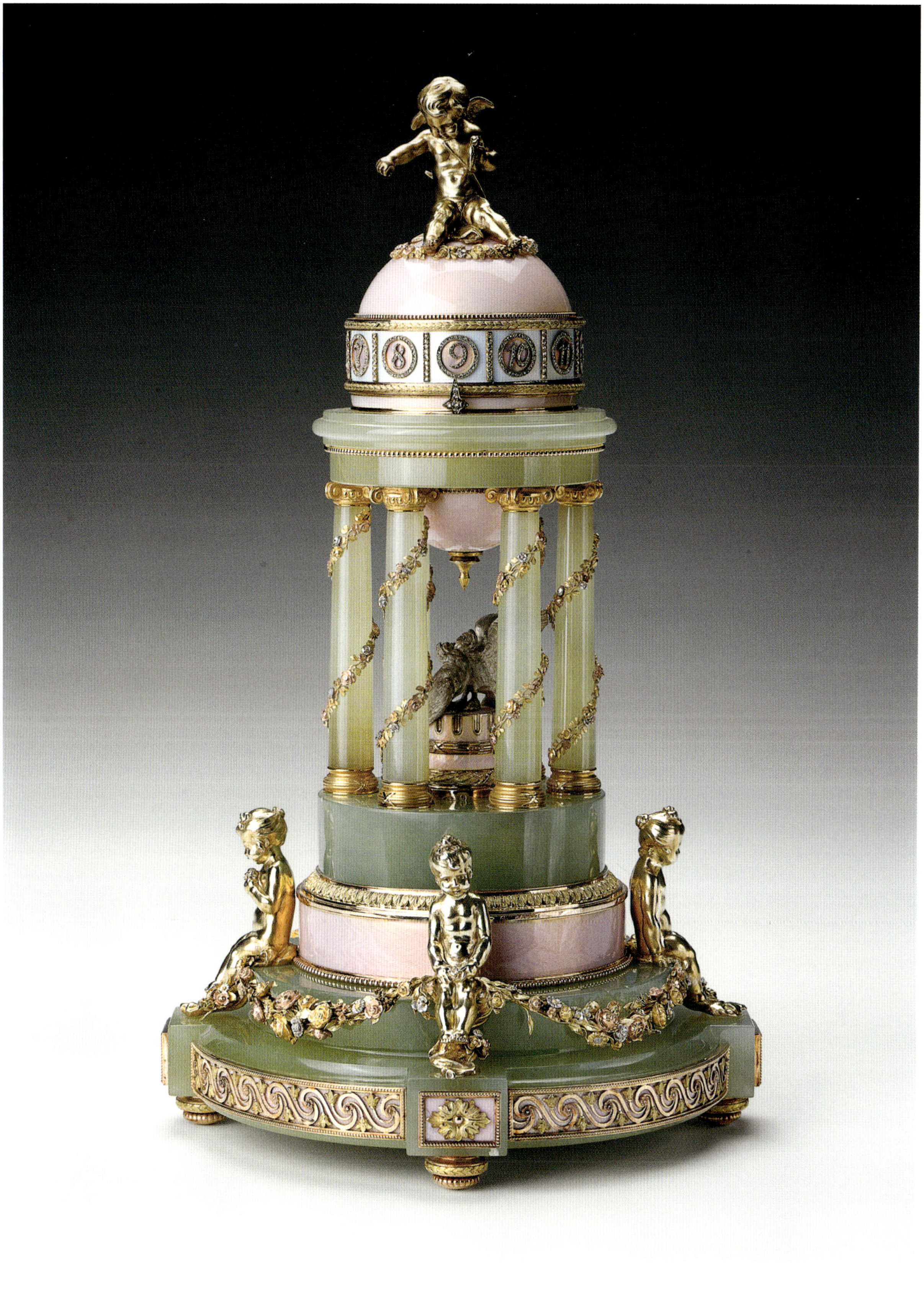

FABERGÉ

284 *Mosaic Egg and Surprise* 1914

Gold, platinum, enamel, rose and brilliant diamonds, rubies, demantoid garnets, topaz, quartz, sapphires, garnets, moonstone, (egg) 9.5 × 7.0 cm, (surprise) 7.9 × 5.5 × 2.9 cm
Impressed on egg: *C. Fabergé*, and on surprise: *G. Fabergé*
RCIN 9022.a–b

Provenance Commissioned by Nicholas II for Alexandra Feodorovna, Easter 1914; confiscated by the Provisional Government, 1917; sold by the Antikvariat, 1933, for 5,000 rubles; purchased by King George V from Cameo Corner, London, 22 May 1933, for £250 ('half cost'), probably for Queen Mary's birthday, 26 May

Literature QMB, III, p. 30; QMPP, VII, no. 164; Snowman 1987; Fabergé *et al.* 1997, pp. 219–21; de Guitaut 2003, pp. 40–1

King George V and Queen Mary were responsible for the three most significant additions to the royal Fabergé collection, through their purchase of the imperial Easter eggs presented to Alexandra Feodorovna in 1901, 1910 and 1914. These important acquisitions demonstrate not only their appreciation for Fabergé's work, but also their desire to acquire works which had once belonged to their Russian cousins.

This particular example is regarded as one of Fabergé's most technically accomplished works, and one of the most intricate imperial eggs made by the firm. This was certainly reflected in the price of 28,300 rubles, which made it the most expensive imperial egg supplied to the imperial family by Fabergé.

The egg was designed by Alma Pihl (1888–1976), granddaughter of August Holmström (1829–1903), Fabergé's principal jeweller. Pihl was apprenticed to her uncle Albert Holmström's workshop as a draughtsman in 1909, at the age of 20, and became an assistant designer. In 1913, she designed her first imperial egg, known as the winter egg, which was to be presented to the Dowager Empress Maria Feodorovna. Inspiration for the mosaic egg came from observing her mother-in-law working at her needlepoint by the fireside. Pihl translated the floral petit-point motif into a design of precious stones; a watercolour design for a brooch appears in Albert Holmström's stock book.[57] A second brooch was also made, but of a different shape.[58]

The mosaic egg is recognised for its technical ingenuity. The thousands of tiny precious stones are precisely cut, so that they slot into the hand-cut platinum cage which forms the body of the egg. The surprise, which fits into the egg by means of two gold clips inside, bears an enamelled portrait, replicating a cameo of the five children of Nicholas II and Alexandra; on the reverse is a basket of flowers, and each of their names inscribed in painted sepia enamel. **CDEG**

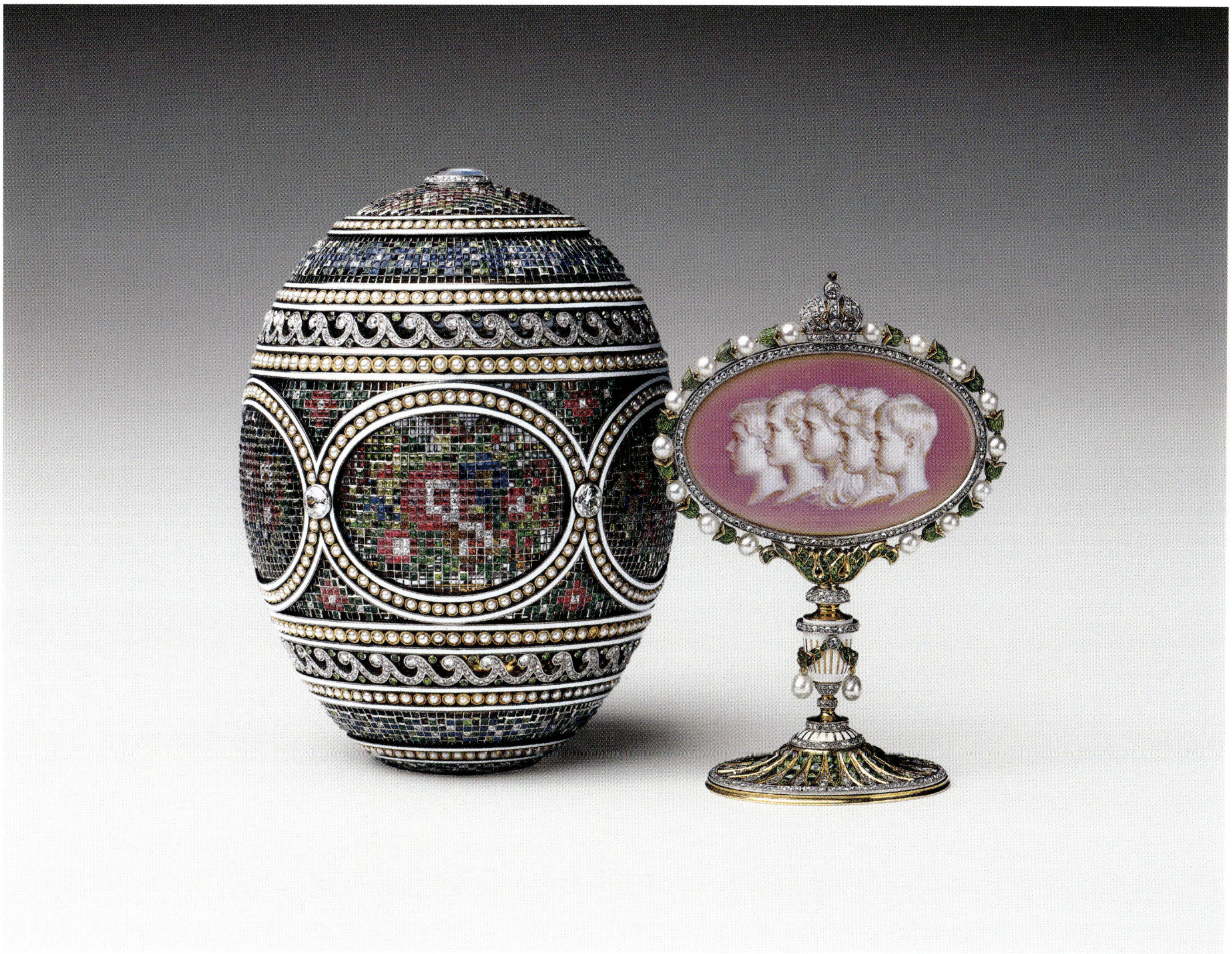

IMPERIAL GLASS MANUFACTORY

285

Vase 1916

Glass, 17.2 × 6.9 cm
Engraved with Imperial Glass Manufactory mark [crown] *N/ 11/ 1916*; label in Queen Mary's handwriting: *This vase had belonged / to the Empress of Russia / (killed 1918) + was sent to England to King George / V in 1919- with some / of the Emperor and Empress's posessions / clothes, toys & books, nothing / of value, these were / handed over to the / Emperor's sister the / Grand Duchess Xenia- / Mary R*
RCIN 54958

Provenance Alexandra Feodorovna; sent to King George V, 1918; given to Queen Mary by Grand Duchess Xenia

Literature Rappé *et al.* 2007, pp. 64–6

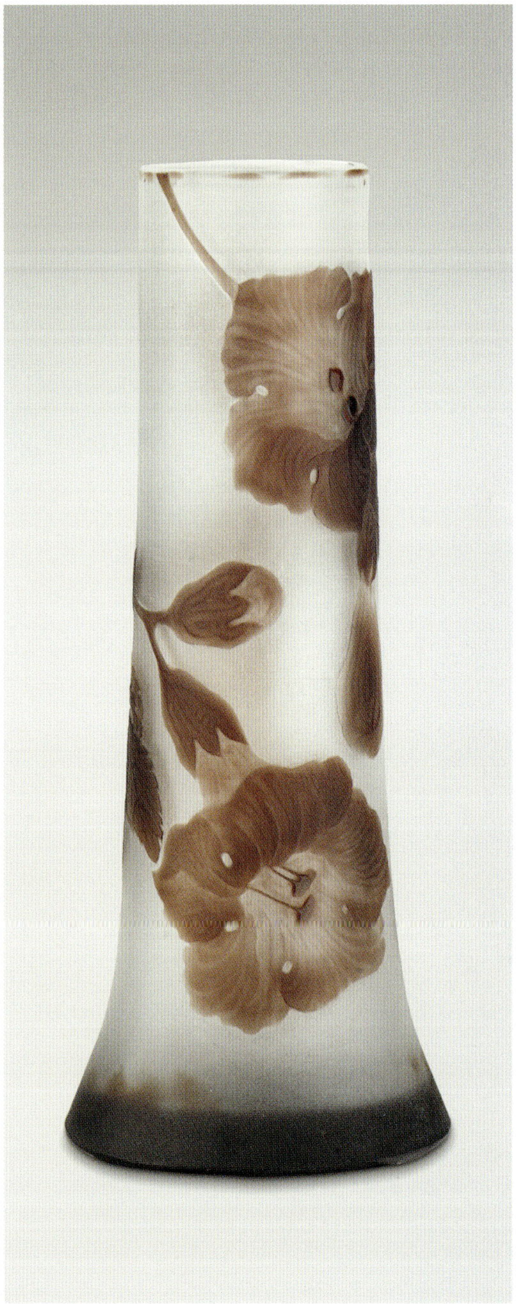

This vase imitates the work of the French master of glass in the art-nouveau style, Emile Gallé (1848–1904,) but was made in the Imperial Glass Manufactory. Several similar examples decorated the private apartments of Nicholas II and Alexandra Feodorovna in the Winter Palace, contrasting with the interiors that were in the Russian historical taste. These included vases made in the Imperial Glass Manufactory, alongside works by Gallé himself, some of which were mounted by Russian goldsmiths, including the Fabergé firm. Vases were also commissioned from the Imperial Glass Manufactory to match the furnishings of the Empress's boudoir or dressing room, where the walls were covered with lavender-striped silk. The Tsarina was particularly fond of the art-nouveau style in her choice of decorative objects and furnishings, and shared her enthusiasm for this aesthetic with her brother, the Grand Duke of Hesse (1868–1937). In Darmstadt, capital of the Grand Duchy of Hesse and by Rhine, an artists' colony was founded in 1899 under his patronage.

The first pieces in this style were made in St Petersburg in 1893, and mastery of the multi-layer glass technique was one the foremost achievements of the factory in the 1890s. At first, the designs were carved with etching being used in the early 1900s, the application of chemicals in several sittings allowing for the creation of smooth tonal transitions. This vase, of off-white opaque glass, has a design of flowers and foliage in tones of mauve-brown. Floral motifs constantly recurred in the drawings of the manufactory's artists, including Krasovsky, one of its most sought-after designers, whose surviving drawings include clematis, poppy capsule, nasturtiums, geranium, cherries, chamomile flowers and tulips.
CDEG

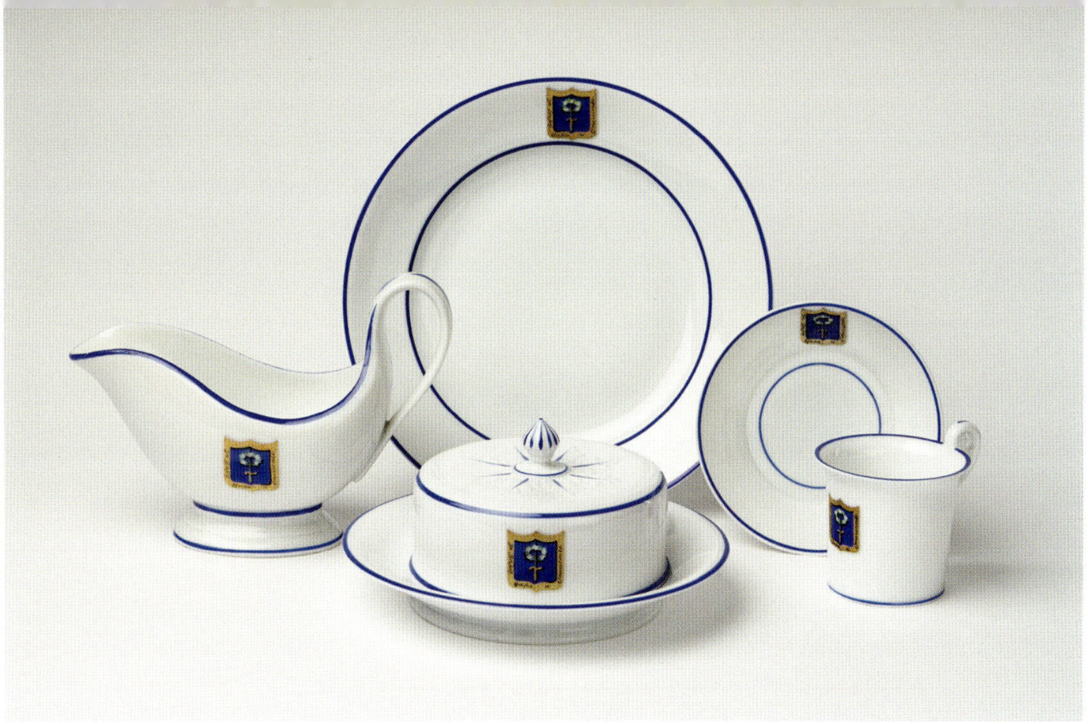

IMPERIAL PORCELAIN FACTORY;
VASILY ANDREEVICH ZHUKOVSKY (1783–1852)

286 *Alexandria Yacht Service* 1887–1911

Hard-paste porcelain, (cup) 8.4 × 8.5 × 10.4 cm, (saucer) 3.3 × 14.0 cm, (butter dish) 9.8 × 21.0 cm, (sauceboat) 15.0 × 10.6 × 21.5 cm, (dinner plate) 3.7 × 25.2 cm
Imperial porcelain mark of Alexander III and Nicholas II (1890–1911); each piece bears the motto, in Cyrillic: 'For Faith, Tsar and Fatherland'
RCINS 58621, 58625, 58629, 58631

Provenance Purchased by Lady Muriel Paget for King George V, August 1935 (£19 19s. 8d.)

Inspired by the so-called Cottage Service, which was commissioned for the Cottage Palace in Alexandria Park at Peterhof, built by Nicholas I and completed in 1829, the Alexandria Yacht Service was made for use on the Imperial Yacht *Alexandria* and is distinguished from the Cottage Service by a blue rather than gold band around the rim. The plain white service of imperial porcelain is decorated with the shield, symbol of the Cottage Palace, with a sword piercing a wreath of white roses, and the Cyrillic motto on the gold band forming the outer edge of the shield. The coat of arms was created by the poet, Vasilli Zhukovsky, tutor to Alexander Nikolaevich.

There were three imperial yachts called *Alexandria*, the first two commissioned by Nicholas I, in 1831 and 1851, and the third commissioned by Nicholas II in 1903. The components from the Alexandria Service in the Royal Collection comprise a breakfast and dinner service for 12 people. Additions were made to the original service to enlarge it, and probably also as replacements, as the pieces in the Royal Collection date from 1890 to 1911.

Lady Muriel Paget, who purchased the service on behalf of King George V, also found glasses from the Alexandria Service and bed linen belonging to Empress Alexandra, but the King declined to buy these. The service was sent to the King via a Soviet ship, wrapped in curtains from Alexei Nikolaevich's room, which were stamped with the imperial eagle. Lady Paget also offered these, but it is assumed she kept them when the King declined.[59] CDEG

RUSSIAN

287 *Tsesarevich Alexei's (1904–1918) colonel's uniform of a Kuban Cossack Ataman*, c.1910

Wool, glazed cotton, astrakhan, gilt metal, silk braid
Undershirt; tunic (cherkeska); hat; sword belt; sword; dagger; sash
Label applied to the cherkeska and undershirt: in ink in Cyrillic; 'The Alexander Palace, Quarters of the Heir, military wardrobe'; label applied to the weapons: in ink in Cyrillic, 'Field uniform of the Kuban Cossack Host'
RCIN 120486

Provenance Purchased by Lady Muriel Paget from a government shop in Leningrad, July 1935; given as a gift to King George V

The philanthropist and humanitarian, Lady Muriel Paget, began her philanthropic work in London, establishing an invalids' kitchen to provide meals for undernourished expectant mothers and the poor and invalided, under the patronage of Queen Mary. In 1915, she travelled to Petrograd, concerned by the dire situation on the Russia front, and set up the Anglo-Russian Hospital to treat wounded soldiers, which was partly funded by Empress Alexandra Feodorovna. To raise further funds, Lady Paget organised a Russian exhibition at the Grafton Galleries in London, in the spring of 1917, which was accompanied by concerts, lectures and dramatic performances. Given the Bolshevik *coup d'état* in October 1917, Lady Paget remained in Ukraine and was shortly afterwards evacuated from Russia; on her return to England, she was received by King George V and Queen Mary.

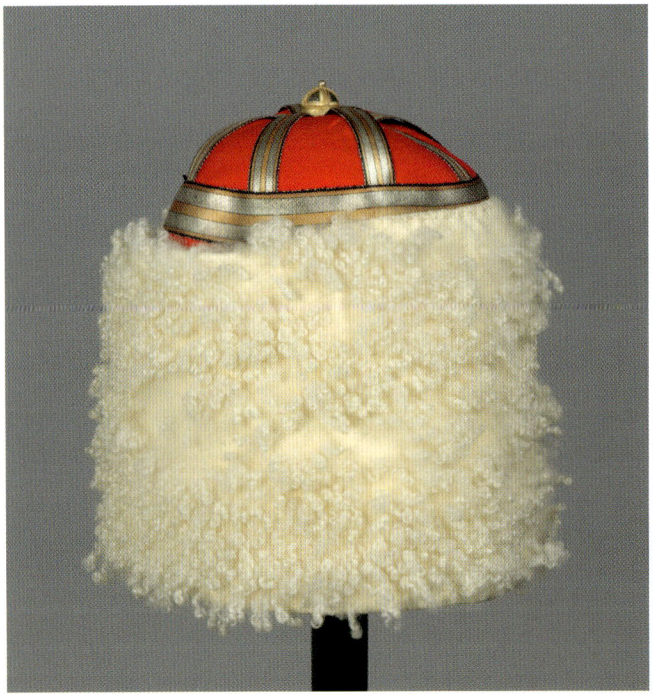

She returned to Russia in the 1920s, and in 1935 wrote to George V's Keeper of the Privy Purse (Lord Sysonby, 1867–1935), to tell him that she had found the Tsesarevich's uniform, purchased it and wanted to give it to the King as an unsolicited gift, which he duly accepted. In her letter she wrote, 'it is a very sad possession and everyone including myself has felt great emotions about it'.[60]

The uniform is of a type worn in the field and comprises a cherkeska, or woollen overshirt complete with fake ammunition held in woollen stitched slots on the chest, a glazed cotton undershirt with fine grey and white stripes, an astrakhan fur hat with a red felt crown surmounted by a gilt-metal crown, a sword belt with fine striped silk straps to hold the sword and dagger, braces for the breeches (now missing) and a passementerie sash or necktie. Lady Paget suggested to Sysonby that she try to trace the breeches and boots, which were part of the original uniform, an offer which was declined by the King.

This type of everyday as opposed to ceremonial dress probably dates from the First World War period when the Tsesarevich was in the headquarters at Mogilev with his father. From 1827 onwards, all heirs to the Russian throne were Atamans of all the Cossack troops, a position to which Alexei was appointed at his birth in 1904.[61]

CDEG

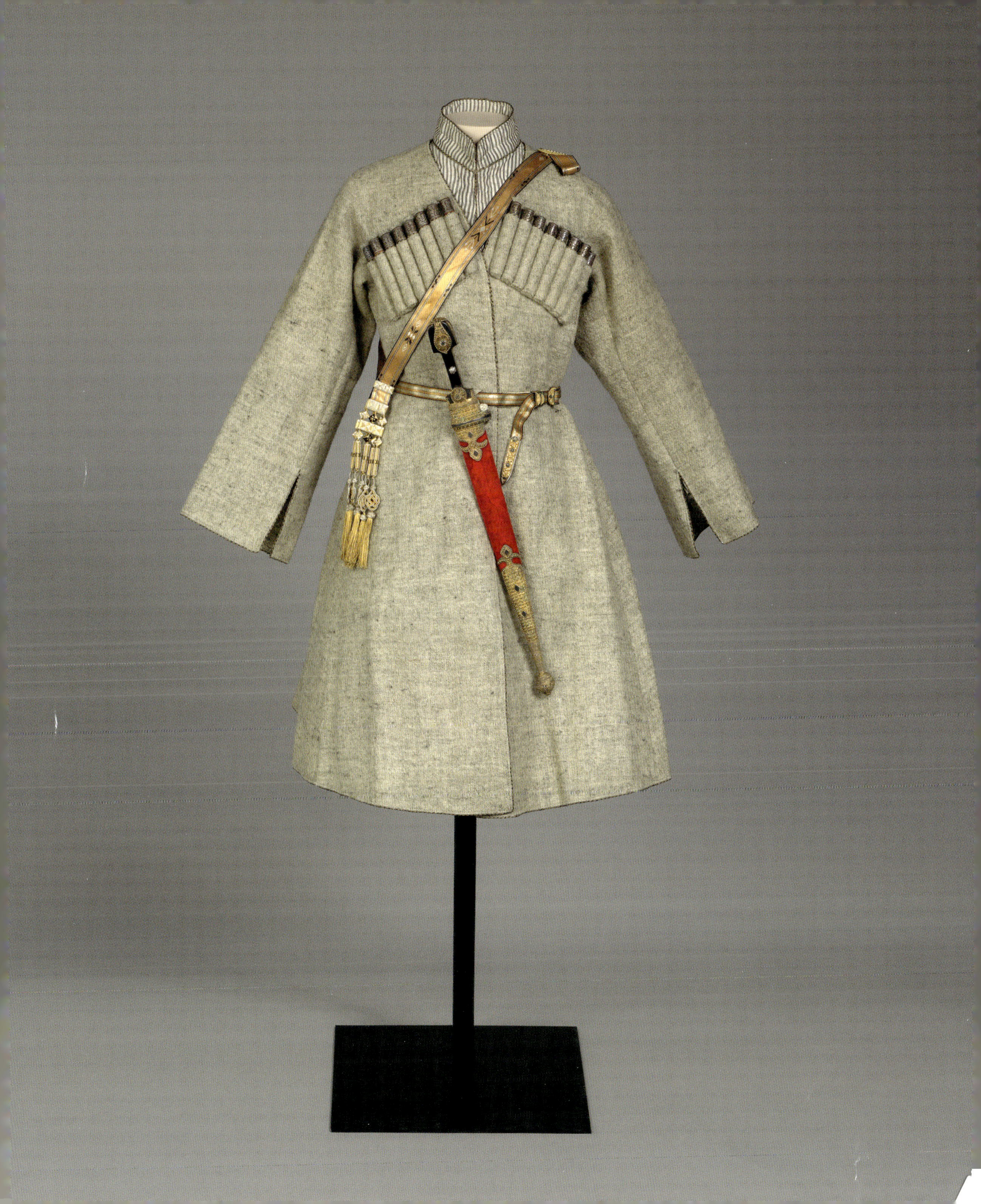

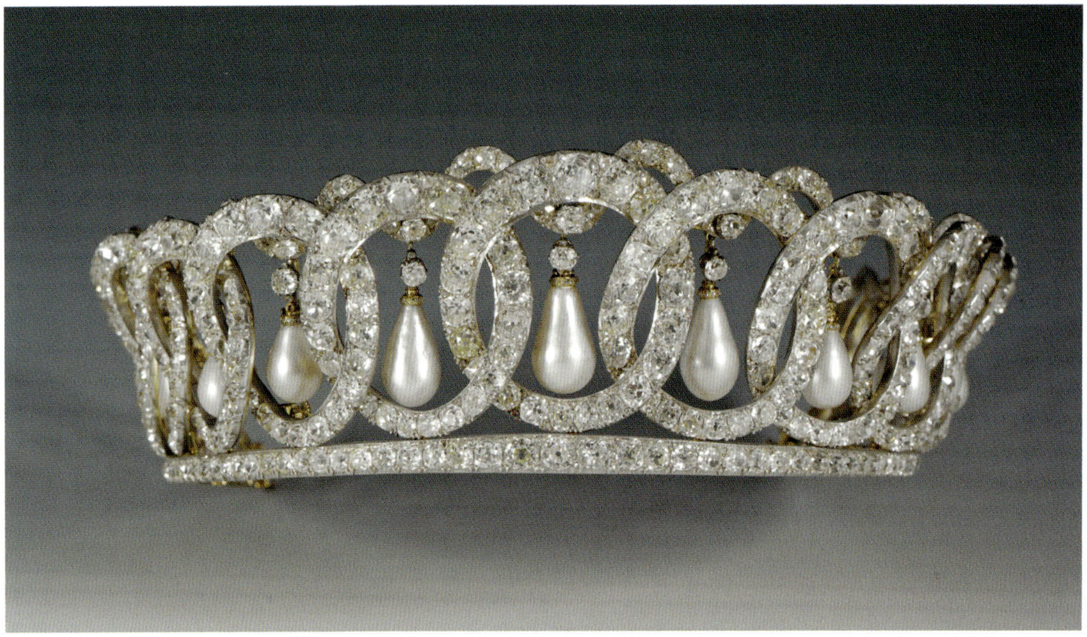

ATTRIBUTED TO C.E. BOLIN (active 1836–1917)

288 ***Vladimir tiara*** *c.*1874

Diamonds, silver, gold, pearls, 6.7 × 19.8 cm
RCIN 200145

Provenance Made for the Grand Duchess Maria Pavlovna, 1874; sold by her daughter, Princess Nicholas of Greece (1882–1957), to Queen Mary, 1921

Literature Papi 2010, pp. 94–5; Roberts 2012, p. 196

The Vladimir tiara is so-called because it was made for the Grand Duchess Maria Pavlovna, wife of Grand Duke Vladimir, probably at the time of her marriage to Alexander III's brother in 1874. The Grand Duchess owned a spectacular collection of jewels, which rivalled those of the two last empresses of Russia.

The tiara was almost certainly made by the jeweller to the imperial court, C.E. Bolin, a firm which held the distinction of having continuously served seven Russian sovereigns. By the early 1850s, the firm was employing up to 50 craftsmen, in several independent workshops in St Petersburg, and had a retail store at 71–73 Nevskii Prospekt. The firm took part in the Great Exhibition of 1851, and founded a branch in Moscow in 1852 with James Steuart Shanks (1826–1911), named Shanks & Bolin, soon renamed the Magasin Anglais by Muscovites (not to be confused with Nicholls & Plincke in St Petersburg, which was known by the same name).

During the Revolution, the Grand Duchess's jewels were smuggled out of Russia by her friend, Albert Henry Stopford (1860–1939). This tiara, together with other jewels, was bought by Queen Mary in 1921.

The tiara consists of intersecting brilliant-set circles, each hung with a claw-set pendant pearl. It was altered in 1924, to take 15 of the Cambridge emeralds as an alternative to the pearls. **CDEG**

SAVELY SORINE (1878–1953)

289 & 290

Portrait of HRH The Duchess of York (1900–2002) 1923

Pencil, watercolour and bodycolour, (frame) 133.0 × 111.0 cm
Signed lower left: *S.Sorine/1923*
RCIN 453400

Portrait of HRH Princess Elizabeth, Duchess of Edinburgh (1926–) 1948

Pencil, watercolour and bodycolour, (frame) 133.0 × 112.0 cm
Signed lower left: *S.Sorine/1948*
RCIN 453399

Provenance (RCIN 453400): Possibly commissioned by the Duchess of York (later Queen Elizabeth The Queen Mother) (RCIN 453399): Commissioned by Queen Elizabeth, 1948

Literature (RCIN 453400): Sorine 1929, pl. 1; Owens 2005, pp. 17–18; (RCIN 453399): Rogers 1986, pp. 13, 52

The Russian portraitist, Savely Sorine, studied painting at the Imperial Academy of Fine Arts in St Petersburg, where he trained with the renowned Russian artist, Ilya Repin (1844–1980). He won a travel scholarship and moved to Paris, exhibiting there in 1922 and 1923. He was a popular society portraitist in England and France in the 1920s and 1930s, and was influenced by the work of Ingres (1780–1867). His monographic exhibition at M. Knoedler & Co., London, in 1923, may have provided the impetus for the commission to paint the portrait of Queen Elizabeth The Queen Mother when Duchess of York, after her marriage to the future King George VI that same year.

The portrait of the Duchess of York is typical of those by Sorine. She is depicted in a white dress, seated against a white background. The simplicity of the composition and use of cool colours was especially appealing.[62] Drawn in pencil, with watercolour wash added afterwards, the only warmth in the portrait comes from the delicate flesh tones of the duchess's face, neck and hands. Sorine's use of green fabric draped over the brown chair, the green of the ribbons on the hat casually hanging from Elizabeth's arm, and the dark blue of her sapphire engagement ring punctuate the white of the dress with blocks of solid colour. The swathe of green fabric was evidently a studio prop, and is found again in Sorine's portrait of Madame Odile Bose (1878–1953).

In 1948, the newly married Princess Elizabeth, was given a signed, limited edition of the 1929 publication of Savely Sorine's *Portraits*, as a birthday present from the artist, who was commissioned to create a portrait of the Princess, 25 years after the portrait of her mother. The commission came from Queen Elizabeth,[63] and the portrait would serve as a pair. It uses the same effect of 'white on white', but here, the cool greys of the shadows are provided by watercolour wash, rather than the strong use of pencil found in the earlier portrait. The composition is similar, showing the princess seated, looking out to the viewer with a refined elegance, but here, a stroke of colour is provided by the blue of the bow around the dress, and the black cushion under her arm. A swathed curtain has been introduced into the background, and the light seems to emanate from behind it, providing a warm backlight to the princess's figure.

We know that in this year, the Duchess of York portrait was reframed, presumably to match the frame and slip of the new portrait of the Princess.[64] A further two portraits were proposed by Queen Elizabeth in 1948: one, a smaller, waist-length portrait of herself wearing a hat, and the other, a family group with Princesses Elizabeth and Margaret. It seems, however, that these portraits did not ever come to fruition.

Queen Elizabeth was a keen collector of modern British art. With the advice of Kenneth Clark (1903–83), she generally purchased existing works by contemporary artists. The commission of Sorine to portray Princess Elizabeth was a 'notable exception' to this practice.[65] **RW**

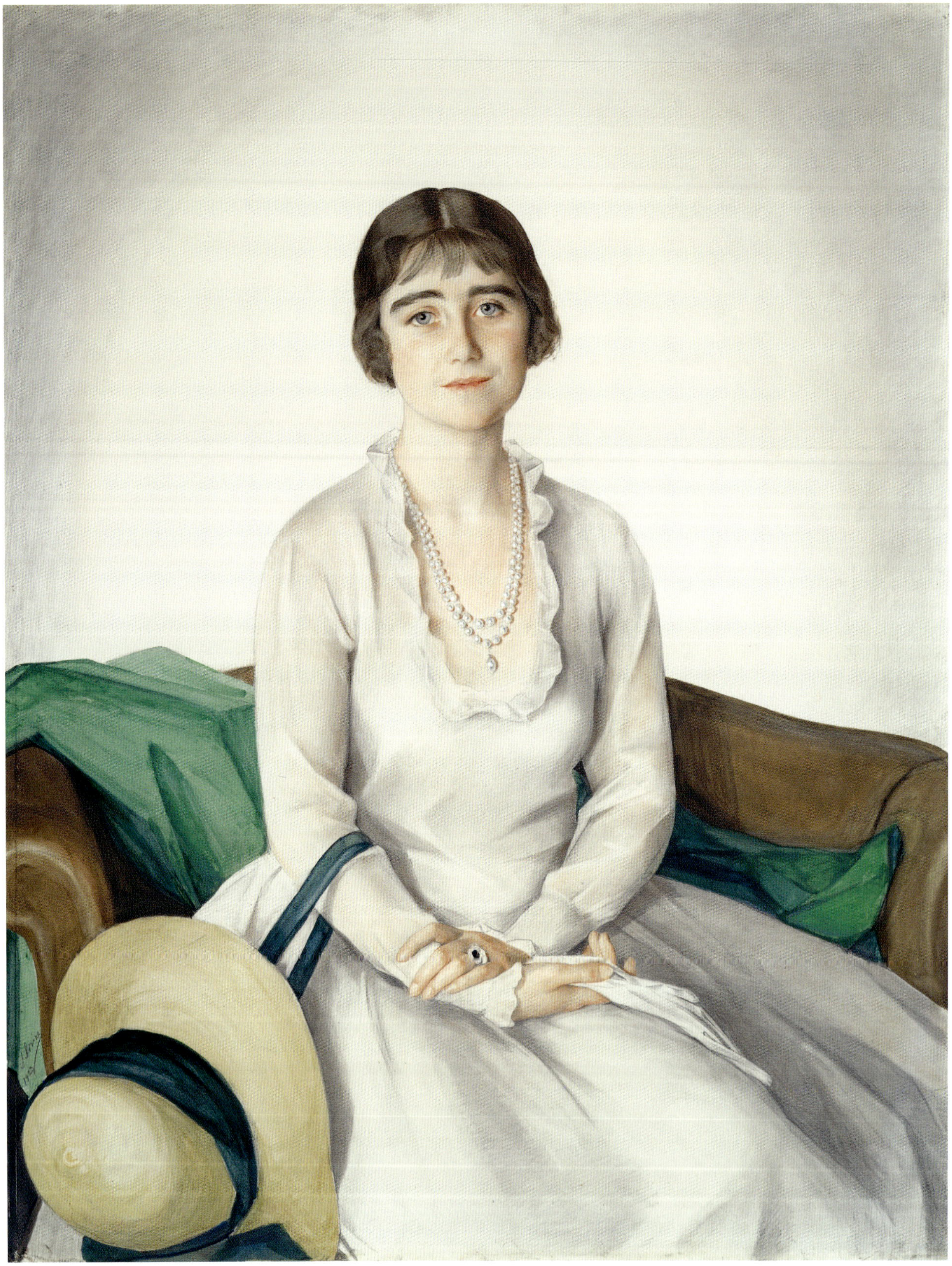

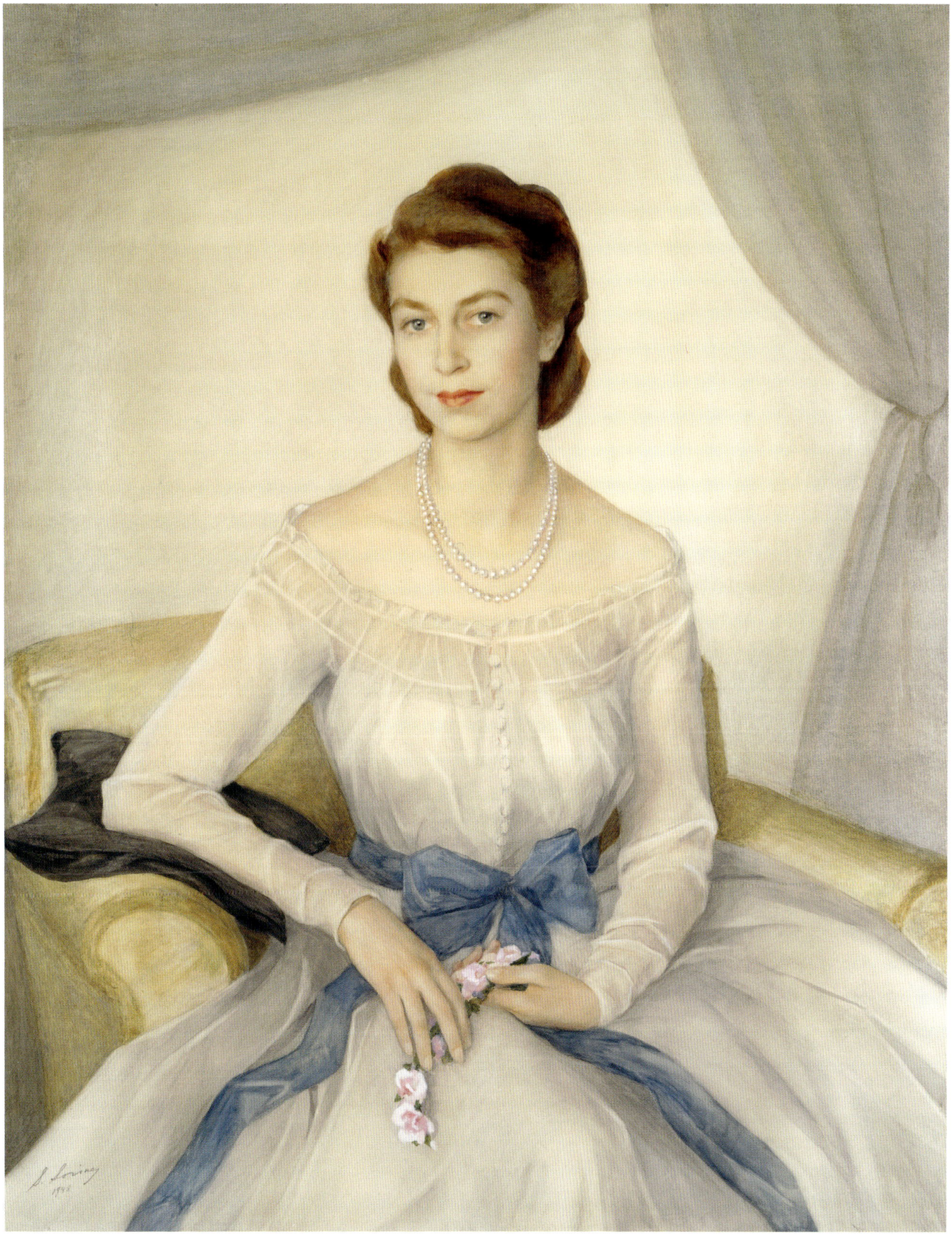

NOTES

CHAPTER 1

1 Miege, *A Relation of three embassies*, Preface, p. [2].
2 RA NEWS/CC/MAIN/1839: 22 May.
3 RA SP/MAIN/81/30.
4 RA SP/MAIN/116/57.
5 RA SP/MAIN/135/96.
6 RA SP/MAIN/239/94.
7 RA GEO/MAIN/242: 19 November 1760.
8 RA GEO/MAIN/1025: 13 November 1770.
9 RA GEO/MAIN/21494.
10 RA NEWS/CC/MAIN/1839: 22 May.
11 RA VIC/MAIN/M/52/92: 12/24 June 1844.
12 RA VIC/MAIN/QVJ (W): 30 October 1843.
13 RA VIC/MAIN/QVJ (W): 25 October 1843.
14 RA VIC/MAIN/QVJ (W): 23 November 1843.
15 RA VIC/MAIN/QVJ (W): 1 November 1843.
16 RA VIC/MAIN/QVJ (W): 1 November 1894.
17 RA VIC/MAIN/QVJ (W): 2 March 1855.
18 RA VIC/MAIN/QVJ (W): 29 November 1850.
19 RA VIC/MAIN/QVJ (W): 17 July 1878.
20 RA VIC/MAIN/N/46/81: 31 October 1890–91.
21 An earlier state was published in 1616 by J. Woodall; see RCIN 680629.
22 Griffiths 1998, p. 56.
23 He was also governor of a number of other merchant companies, including the East India Company. See *ODNB*, s.v. Smythe [Smithe], Sir Thomas.
24 Printed for Nathanyell Butter, London. A copy from George III's library can be found in the British Library, 150.a5.
25 See McDonald 2017, III, p. 805, which lists the prints as described in the album. For a discussion of the portrait prints acquired by George III, see Clayton 2017.
26 Miege, *A Relation of three embassies*, Preface, p. [1].
27 Ibid., Preface, p. [2].
28 Dmitrieva and Abramova 2006, pp. 116–17.
29 Miege, *A Relation of three embassies*, p. 27.
30 Ibid., p. 29.
31 Ibid., p. 39.
32 Ibid., pp. 47–8.
33 Koeman 1970, p. 50; van der Krogt 2005, p. 35.
34 Koeman 1970, pp. 7–32.
35 Koeman 1970, p. 60; van der Krogt 2005, p. 107.
36 Koeman 1970, p. 60.
37 Cross 2000, p. 25.
38 Cross 1998, p. 32.
39 V.N. Smol'ianinov (ed.), *Arkhiv kniazia F.A. Kurakina*, IV, Saratov 1893, p. 31: quoted and translated in Cross 2000, pp. 142–3.
40 Mauritshuis inv. no. 361.
41 MacGregor 2004, p. 117.
42 Ibid., p. 120.
43 Korb 1863, p. vii.
44 Ibid., p. iii.
45 Korb 1863, pp. 145–6; Bodin 2015, pp. 58–9.
46 Ides, *Three years travels*, p. [ii].
47 Putnam 1952, pp. 5–10; Cross 2000, pp. 46–8.
48 Perry, *The state of Russia*, p. 60.
49 Olearius, *Voyages tres curieux & tres renommez*, printer's preface, pp. [ii]–[iii].
50 Flier 1994, pp. 214–18.
51 Réau 1922.
52 Blakesley 2016b, p. 13.
53 Cracraft 2004, p. 207.
54 Three seal boxes are in the collection of the Hillwood Museum, Washington, DC, including one still attached to its presentation folder (inv. no. 57.1).
55 See Truman 2013, p. 346.
56 Postnikov 1996, pp. 9, 40–46.
57 1701, Louvre, Paris, inv. no. 7492.
58 The most likely candidates are: Alexander Mikhailovich (1718–83) diplomat, soldier, field marshal and governor of St Petersburg; Dmitry Mikhailovich (1721–93) Russian ambassador in Vienna during the reign of Catherine the Great, who opened the Golitsyn Hospital in Moscow; or Prince Dmitry Alekseyevich (1728–1803), Russian ambassador to the Netherlands and Fellow of the Royal Society, also Catherine's art adviser, who acquired many paintings from significant collections, including Diderot's library.
59 Jutsham Recs and Dels, 30 November 1813.
60 Eriksen to A.G. Moltke, January 1755, Danish National Archive, Copenhagen Record Office of the Academy of Fine Arts, Copenhagen, letters received 1753–7, quoted in Andersen 1965, p. 52.
61 The author is grateful to Alison Guppy, freelance conservator, for her comments on the wood stocks.
62 Edlin 1969, p. 157.
63 Rodionov 2012, pp. 109–10.
64 Inv. no. Op-412/1–2. The author is grateful to Fedor Panfilov of the Moscow Kremlin Museums for information about Permyak.
65 The author is grateful to Dr Wilfried Zeisler, chief curator at the Hillwood Museum, Washington, DC, for this information.
66 Pietro Rotari (1707–62), court painter to Empress Elizabeth, painted a large series of character heads of young women dressed in contemporary Russian costume, including a number wearing tasselled hats. The most famous group of these are displayed in the 'Cabinet of Muses', or Painted Hall, at Peterhof.
67 The State Russian Museum, St Petersburg, holds an example of the type of miniature by Zharkov, dated 1788, inv. no. Ж-3060 (reproduced as Fig. 24 in Chapter 4).
68 Shibanov, State Russian Museum, St Petersburg, inv. no. Ж-4963, is from the collection of Grand Duke Michael Pavlovich, youngest son of Paul I. There is also an 18th-century copy in the State Hermitage Museum, St Petersburg, inv. no. ЭРЖ-2702.
69 State Russian Museum, St Petersburg, inv. no. Ж-4963.
70 Chaloner Smith 1878–83, IV, p. 1435, no. 15a.
71 Blakesley 2016b, pp. 174–5; Cross 1993, p. 66.
72 State Hermitage Museum, St Petersburg, inv. no. Э-4184.
73 Prints of the engraving dated 1789, together with three others after Maria Feodorovna's models, are in the Royal Collection (RCINs 614351, 614380, 614435, 614436).
74 RCIN 45848.
75 In the collection at Tsarskoe Selo: ED-652-1, KP-3709, ED-653-1, KP-3710.
76 Hillwood Museum, Washington, DC, inv. no. 12.10.
77 Two wine-bottle coolers and four ice-cream coolers, Wallace Collection, London, inv. nos C474-5, C476-9.
78 Christie, Manson and Woods 1895, lot 295.
79 Papi 2010, p. 251.
80 Forster 1848.
81 Engraved by Ignaz Sebastian Klauber (1753–1817), 1797 (RCIN 614395); inscription states after an original of 1789.
82 RCIN 405730; Carlton House 1816, no. 545.

CHAPTER 2

1 RA VIC/MAIN/H/52/2: 30 August 1856.
2 AVPRI: 133/468/1814/6840/370/10: 6/18 January 1814.
3 AVPRI: 133/468/1814/6840/370/18: 14/26 January 1814.
4 RA VIC/MAIN/QVJ (W): 5 March 1835.
5 AVPRI: 133/468/1844/448–449: 16 April 1844.
6 RA VIC/MAIN/QVJ (W): 3 May 1856.
7 RA VIC/MAIN/QVJ (W): 13 June 1851.
8 RA VIC/MAIN/B/18/138: 19 October 1860.
9 RA VIC/MAIN/B/18/152: 10 December 1860.
10 RA VIC/MAIN/C/12/81: 11 December 1860.
11 RA VIC/MAIN/M/50/53: 23 June 1847.
12 RA VIC/MAIN/H/52/2: 30 August 1856.
13 RA VIC/MAIN/H/52/2: 30 August 1856.
14 RA VIC/MAIN/QVJ (W): 9 February 1874.
15 AVPRI: 133/468/1874/607: 19 April/1 May 1874.
16 RA VIC/MAIN/H/42/142: 11 February 1880.
17 RA VIC/MAIN/H/42/142: 11 February 1880.
18 RA VIC/MAIN/B/62/33: 19 November 1879.
19 RA VIC/MAIN/QVJ (W): 4 February 1880.
20 RA VIC/MAIN/QVJ (W): 12 December 1882. Artur Pavlovich Morengeim (1824–1907).
21 RA VIC/MAIN/QVJ (W): 2 December 1884.
22 RA VIC/MAIN/QVJ (W): 21 December 1894.
23 RA VIC/ADDA7/307: 4 January 1878.
24 RA VIC/MAIN/H/42/143: 17/18 February 1880.
25 RA VIC/MAIN/H/42/144: 18 February 1880.
26 RA VIC/MAIN/Y/172/30: February 1880.
27 RA VIC/MAIN/H/42/155: 24 February 1880.
28 RA VIC/MAIN/H/42/161: 6 March 1880 (23 Feb. 1880 OS).
29 RA VIC/MAIN/C/35/65A: 6 May 1880.
30 RA VIC/MAIN/A/52/35: 20 June 1880.
31 RA VIC/MAIN/QVJ (W): 13 March 1881.
32 RA VIC/MAIN/H/43/50: 17 March 1881.
33 RA VIC/MAIN/H/44/17: 8 April 1881.
34 RA VIC/MAIN/H/44/24: 11 April 1881.
35 RA VIC/MAIN/B/34/94: 8 February 1882.
36 RA VIC/MAIN/ADDU/127/3: 1 November 1886.
37 RA VIC/MAIN/H/45/97E: 7 February 1887.
38 RA VIC/MAIN/H/45/98–100: 16 March 1887.
39 RA VIC/MAIN/H/45/124–6: 31 October–2 November 1888.
40 TNA FO/65/1527/106: 6 June 1896.
41 RA VIC/MAIN/H/47/40: 1 September 1896.
42 RA VIC/MAIN/H/47/43–4: 2 September 1896.
43 RA VIC/MAIN/H/48/4: 2 October 1896.
44 RA VIC/MAIN/A/73/35: 8 October 1896.
45 RA VIC/MAIN/Q/2/200: 24 September 1897.
46 RA VIC/MAIN/A/74/59: 25 January 1898.
47 RA VIC/MAIN/H/48/59: 30 January 1898.
48 RA VIC/MAIN/A/75/77: 16 August 1899.
49 RA VIC/MAIN/QVJ (W): 30 June 1899.
50 RCINs 404848, 407234. Also listed are two other works by Kobell no longer in the Collection.
51 Bingham 1884, p. 400.
52 Reflecting the importance of religious life in the city: see Martin 2013, p. 12.
53 Schmidt 1989, p. 48.
54 For a full discussion of the restoration of Moscow after the fire, see Schmidt 1981.
55 *Pour Son Altesse Royale Monseigneur le Prince Guillaume Frederick de Glouchester, / presentée par le 1er Maitre de Police de Moscou, de Caverine* ('For His Royal Highness the Prince William Frederick of Gloucester, presented by the 1st Master of Police of Moscow, de Caverine').
56 When he inherited the title on his father's death. He was granted the style 'His Royal Highness' by the Prince Regent on his marriage to Princess Mary, daughter of George III, on 22 July 1816. However, the reference to 'His Royal Highness' in the inscription on this map cannot be used to help date its presentation, as other works created before 1816 also refer to him using this convention (e.g. RCIN 604228).
57 *ODNB*, s.v. Prince William Frederick, 2nd Duke of Gloucester and Edinburgh (1776–1834).
58 Anon., 'Description des uniformes et Equipage Militaires de Parade de L'armée Confirmée Par Sa Majesté Impériale' (RCIN 1082273).
59 RA PPTO/PP/MAIN/1861/8355: 26 July 1861, on receipt of the paintings at Buckingham Palace; RA PPTO/PP/MAIN/1861/8355: 9 July 1861, letter from Charles Whitworth Pitt to Queen Victoria.
60 Renne 2011a, nos 30, 31, 32.
61 Paul Swignine (Pavel Svin'yin), 'Noveyshie proizvedeniya G. Dova' ['The latest works by Mr Dawe'], Otechestvennyyezapiski ['Notes from the Fatherland'], St Petersburg 1823, translated in Renne 2011a, p. 74.
62 In the distance is what appears to be the domed roof of the Assumption Cathedral, not their residence, which was a single-storey building.
63 Troyat 1982, p. 292.
64 Carlton House 1816, nos 449–493, includes Christian IV, King of Denmark, Emperor Joseph II, Charles XII of Sweden and numerous equestrian portraits.
65 *Gentleman's Magazine* 1814, p. 613; Cross 2014a, p. 18.
66 Sold Christie's, London, 11 December 2003, lot 134.
67 Windsor Castle Inventory of Statuary, no. 276; the bust is recorded as being 2′ 6″ high and on a circular base.
68 Johnson 2014, p. 64.
69 Scott 1814, I, p. 93.
70 Palmer 1974, p. 260.
71 Ibid., p. 352.
72 Southey, *Carmen Triumphale*, p. 14.
73 Southey, *Carmen Triumphale*, p. 15 [2nd sequence].
74 Richardson 1966, p. 138.
75 *An Account of the visit*, p. 82.
76 See cat. 73 for further information on Platov and the visit.
77 Quote in Millar 1969, no. 910; see also Williams 1831, I, p. 345.
78 RCIN 405894; it hung in Carlton House with RCIN 405893, Frederick William Ernest, Count of Schaumburg-Lippe (1724–77), and is a similar honouring of German–English military comrades of the Seven Years War.
79 *The Times*, Friday, 10 June 1814.
80 British Museum no. 1868,0612.1056; painting said to be dated 1813, in the State Russian Museum.
81 Stroehling: E.I. Tarasov, *Donskoy ataman Platov* [Platov, Ataman of the Don Cossacks], St Petersburg 1903, quoted and translated in Renne 2011a, p. 164.
82 Von Stockmar 1872, p. 42.
83 Roberts 1987, p. 87.
84 The closest other version to this is GAC acc. no. 16182, also after Dawe, the only difference being the curtain tie.
85 NPG 51, 1817.
86 Portrait of the Princess exhibited at the Royal Academy in 1817 (No. 178) together with a portrait of her husband, Prince Leopold (No. 62). Royal Academy 1818 portrait of the late Princess (No. 42), and portrait of her husband (No. 78).
87 RCIN 406478 signed and dated 'G. Dawe. R.A. / 1817'.
88 Christie, Manson and Woods 1904, no. 83, 'her right arm against a portfolio', 55.0 × 43.0 in. (approx. 139.7 × 109.2 cm), annotated as sold for '50.8' to 'Blakesley'.
89 The author is grateful to the late A.V.B. Norman both for his unpublished research on the edged weapons in the Royal Collection (including RCIN 61567) and for information on Ivan Bushuyev and east European sabre fashions.
90 The author is grateful to the late A.V.B. Norman for his research on edged weapons (RCIN 61683).
91 The author is grateful to Alex Campbell-Ricketts, Inventory Clerk, Royal Collection Trust, for identification of the gemstones.
92 North 1998.

CHAPTER 3

1 *An Account of Russia*, p. xxiv.
2 *Gentleman's Magazine* 1758.
3 *An Account of Russia*, pp. 57–8.
4 *Travelling sketches*, p. v.
5 *Travels through parts of the Russian Empire*, p. vi.
6 Ibid., p. 243.
7 Ibid., p. 336.
8 *St Petersburgh*, I, pp. 422–3.
9 *Recollections of Tartar steppes*, p. vi.
10 RA VIC/MAIN/QVJ (W): 26 Oct. 1856.
11 Lister 1993, p. xix.
12 *Through Siberia*, I, p. vi.

13 Ibid., p. vii.
14 *Travels in the East of Nicholas II*, I, p. 1.

CHAPTER 4

1 Danish National Archive, quoted in Andersen 1965, p. 52.
2 Blakesley 2016a, p. 21.
3 McBurney 2014, p. 328.
4 Renne 2011b, p. 90.
5 McBurney 2014, p. 336.
6 RCIN 406492, painted for George IV for ten guineas.
7 Catalogue of Her Majesty's Private Pictures, Miniatures, Enamels &c &c, 1827 – Christmas 1856 (RCIN 1112580). The seven paintings are as follows: RCINs 406489–406491, 407130, 407174, 405424 and 406625, the largest and most expensive being RCIN 405424, Leopold, King of the Belgians, for the Grand Staircase at Buckingham Palace. It appears that in 1844, Herbert Luther Smith (1809–70) was also in Coburg, copying other family portraits, after Bergler (1753–1829), to hang at Osborne.
8 RCINs 400742, 400744, 400746.
9 RCINs 400647–400648, 404175.

CHAPTER 5

1 RA VIC/MAIN/H/46/81: 31 October 1890–91.
2 RA VIC/MAIN/W/43/149: 10 November 1903.
3 RA VIC/MAIN/W/43/149: 10 November 1903.
4 RA VIC/MAIN/W/49/89: 11 August 1906.
5 RA VIC/MAIN/W/49/89: 11 August 1906.
6 RA VIC/MAIN/W/54/138: 10 December 1908.
7 GARF N18 27 October 1908.
8 RA PS/PSO/GV/C/Q/2551/8: 4/17 February 1917.
9 RA PS/PSO/GV/C/Q/2551/5: 16/24 January 1916.
10 RA PS/PSO/GV/C/Q/1550/315: 20 October 1916.
11 RA GV/PRIV/GVD/1917: 15 March 1917.
12 RA PS/PSO/GV/C/M/1067/38: 29 March 1917.
13 RA GV/PRIV/GVD/1917: 15 March 1917.
14 RA PS/PSO/GV/C/M/1067/17: 18 March 1917.
15 RA PS/PSO/GV/C/M/1067/21: 19 March 1917.
16 RA PS/PSO/GV/C/M/1067/26: 21 March 1917.
17 RA PS/PSO/GV/C/M/1067/37, 29: 22 March 1917.
18 RA PS/PSO/GV/C/M/1067/51–2: 6 April 1917.
19 This discussion would result in the change from Saxe-Coburg and Gotha to Windsor for the name for the British royal dynasty on 17 July 1917.
20 RA PS/PSO/GV/C/M/1067/52: 6 April 1917.
21 RA PS/PSO/GV/C/M/1067/43: 1–2 April 1917.
22 RA PS/PSO/GV/C/M/1067/62: 13 April 1917.
23 RA GV/PRIV/GVD/1918: 25 July 1919.
24 RA PS/PSO/GV/C/Q/2521/159: 5 March 1919; RA PS/PSO/GV/C/M/1334A/136: 4 July 1919.
25 RA PPTO/PP/GV/MAIN2/9963. The King's Privy Purse paid £756 19s to cover the Empress's expenses.
26 RA PPTO/PP/GV/MAIN/21589: 21 October 1928.
27 RA PS/PSO/GV/C/M/2229/1: 22 January 1924.
28 RA PS/PSO/GV/C/M/1923/1: 8 August 1924.
29 RA PS/PSO/GV/C/M/2131/2: 25 October 1927.
30 RA PS/PSO/GV/C/M/2131/3: 26 October 1927.
31 RA PS/PSO/GV/C/P/284A/27: 30 October 1917.
32 RA PS/PSO/GV/C/K/2223/151: 26 June 1929.
33 RA PS/PSO/GV/C/M/2229/7: August 1929.
34 RA PS/PSO/GV/C/M/2229/9: 8 August 1929.
35 RA PS/PSO/GV/C/M/2229/19: 1 October 1929.
36 RA PS/PSO/GVI/PS/MAIN/633: 27 May 1936.
37 RA PS/PSO/GVI/PS/MAIN/3357: 26 December 1938.
38 RA PS/PSO/GV/C/P/284A/34: 26 June 1930.
39 Her Majesty The Queen was to lay the foundation stone of the new British Embassy in Moscow in 1994.
40 RA PPTO/PP/GV/MAIN2/23207: 11 July 1935 (letter from the Keeper of the Privy Purse to Lady Muriel Paget).
41 RA PS/PSO/GVI/PS/MAIN/6570: 6 September 1943, 9 September 1943.
42 RA PS/PSO/GVI/PS/MAIN/6484: 15 December 1943.
43 This was to be repeated during the visit of President Mikhail Gorbachev (b. 1931) to Windsor Castle in 1989.
44 RCIN 49891.
45 RCIN 36972.
46 RCIN 408371.
47 RCIN 40636.
48 Her Majesty The Queen's speech, State Banquet, Moscow, 18 October 1994.
49 Her Majesty The Queen's Christmas Day broadcast, 25 December 1994.
50 RCIN 1101571.
51 Her Majesty The Queen's speech, State Banquet, Moscow, 18 October 1994.
52 Cowles 1974, p. 163.
53 See Renne 2011a, no. 19.
54 RCINs 614582–614583.
55 The author is very grateful to Dr Elizaveta Renne, Curator of British and Scandinavian Painting, State Hermitage Museum, St Petersburg, for her knowledge and help in reattributing these portraits.
56 Gudymenko 2016, pp. 86, 231.
57 RA VIC/MAIN/QVJ (W): 1 June 1844; Queen Victoria's draft.
58 AVPRI: 133/468/1844/444–451: 16/28 March 1844.
59 RA VIC/MAIN/QVJ (W): 2 June 1844.
60 AVPRI: 133/468/1844/348–349: 14/26 April 1844.
61 Forrer 1904–30, VI, p. 625.
62 Letter to King Leopold, 4 and 11 June 1844; Benson and Esher 1908, II, pp. 12, 14.
63 For a similar table by the same maker, see Coleman Sparke 2014, p. 146.
64 RA VIC/MAIN/QVJ (W): 2 December 1844.
65 Mavrodina 2007, p. 436.
66 Ducamp 2012, p. 187.
67 Hillwood Museum, Washington, DC, inv. no. 32.22.
68 RA VIC/MAIN/QVJ (W): 2 December 1844.
69 RGIA Ф. 468. Оп. 10. Д. 4. Л. 267.
70 RGIA Ф. 468. Оп. 10. Д. 5. Л. 75.
71 RV VIC/MAIN/Z/104/35: 23 October 1844.
72 There are three specimen pieces in the Royal Collection which are presumed to have been acquired at the time of Queen Victoria's commission.
73 RA VIC/MAIN/Z/104/39: 1 July 1845.
74 RGIA, fond 469, inv. 9, part 4, 1845, file 1785.
75 RA VIC/MAIN/QVJ (W): 10 November 1847.
76 RA VIC/MAIN/QVJ (W): 2 June 1844; Queen Victoria's draft.
77 Savinskaya *et al.* 2009, no. 192.
78 Russian Museum, inv. no. Ж-7767, 31.5 × 22.5 cm; Staatliches Museum, inv. no. G862 (4676d, h, j). The author would like to thank Iraida Bott and Michael Asvarishch for information about other preparatory sketches of this work.
79 RCIN 406751.
80 RA PP/ADDL/1693: 14 February 1863; further letter dated 1 October 1863 (PPTO/PP/QV/ADD 1964), saying 'I have sent to ask Mr Redgrave if he thinks it will be safe to place it on a roller'.
81 Pichot 1855, p. 445. At the time of the Emperor's death, the Crimean War was still ongoing, but this was only the latest of a series of conflicts Russia had seen during the reign of Nicholas I, whose aggressive nature is clearly stated in the obituary.
82 The Mouhot brothers were Henri (1826–61), a French naturalist and explorer, and Charles (1828–95). Henri lived and worked as a teacher in St Petersburg between 1844 and 1854, the year in which he decided to travel around Europe with his brother, working together as daguerreotypists. For the miniature in the Dutch Royal Collection, see Schaffers-Bodenhausen and Tiethoff-Spliethoff 1993, p. 320, no. 397.
83 Wap 1855. The present location of the original daguerreotype is unknown.
84 The daguerreotype is first recorded in an 1870 inventory as 'Nicholas I - daguerreotype after death' (RL 1870 42.B.1). Post-mortem photography was a common practice in Victorian times, and often, especially for the less affluent, an after-death portrait would be the only photographic likeness of a family member, particularly of children. The Royal Collection holds several post-mortem portraits, including those of Emperors Alexander II (RCIN 2946793) and Alexander III (RCINs 2929594–2929595), all by Levitsky.
85 RA VIC/MAIN/Y/98/24: 10 August 1853.
86 Sold Christie's, London, 14 June 2006, lot 120.
87 RA VIC/MAIN/Y/98/24: 10 August 1853.

88 https://weaponsandwarfare.com/2015/08/04/the-guards-at-inkerman-1854 (accessed 8 June 2018).
89 For literature and bibliography, see Butler 1922, pp. 101–4, 111, 116, 118.
90 There is a mention of 'photography of Schamyl' being sent to Queen Victoria in a letter from The Hon. Edward Erskine (1817–83), British chargé d'affaires in St Petersburg, to Carl Ruland (1834–1907), Librarian at Windsor Castle, dated 16 July 1860 (RA VIC/ADDA10/85/554). However, it is clear in the text that the gift pre-dated the actual letter, meaning that it had been sent either earlier in 1860 or, more likely, in 1859. For such a gift, which may have included the photograph of Shamil's son, 'Sir John Crampton [British minister plenipotentiary to Russia] was authorised to make him [Denier] a present on the part of Her Majesty' (ibid.).
91 These were in addition to countless articles, poems and news accounts on Shamil and his struggle for liberty; see Barrett 1994, pp. 358–9. For an account of Shamil's life, see Blanch 1978.
92 Zaguliaev 1859; Chichagova 1889, p. 107. Chuguev (Chuhuiv) is now in Ukraine.
93 Andrei Denier, born in Mahilyow (Mogilev), Belarus, studied at the Imperial Academy of Arts, St Petersburg, between 1840 and 1851; soon after graduating, he opened a photographic studio in the Passage on Nevskii Prospekt. Together with Levitsky, Denier would soon be considered a great master of portrait photography, and was particularly known for the so-called 'Denier effect': the subject is seen in sharp detail, but with an overall soft-focus effect, achieved by printing from two negatives of different density.
94 RA VIC/ADDA5/528: 22 and 24 November 1866 (cat. 163); see also cats 164 and 165.
95 In 1869, Shamil was given permission by the Emperor to go on a pilgrimage to Mecca; he died in Medina, on 4 February 1871.
96 Cowell to Queen Victoria (RA VIC/MAIN/H/43/106: 28 March 1881).
97 State Hermitage Museum, St Petersburg, inv. no. 9526, signed and dated 1875, 68.0 × 55.0 cm.
98 The Queen and Empress had last met on 23 November 1874 when the Empress visited London at the time of the birth of her grandson, Prince Alfred of Edinburgh (1874–99): RA VIC/ADDA17/649. The Queen presented the Empress with 'a copy of Richter's picture of Marie': RA VIC/MAIN/QVJ (W): 23 November 1874.
99 State Hermitage Museum, St Petersburg, inv. no. ЭРЖ.II-693, dated 1876, 271.0 × 150.0 cm.
100 RA VIC/MAIN/QVJ (W): 17 May 1874.
101 Artists' materials supplier stamp on reverse: A LA PALETTE DE RAPHAEL / AVANZO / ST. PÉTERSBOURG / Vasaili Ostrow 6 Dgne No 6.
102 AVPRI: 133/468/1814/6840/370/297: 1/19 July 1814.
103 RA VIC/MAIN/QVJ (W): 23 February 1839.
104 RA VIC/MAIN/H/41/41: 22 October 1866.
105 RA VIC/MAIN/H/41/42: 22 October 1866.
106 RA VIC/MAIN/A/35/75: 3 June 1867.
107 RA VIC/MAIN/H/41/46: 5 June 1867.
108 RA VIC/MAIN/H/41/47: 6 June 1867.
109 RA VIC/MAIN/QVJ (W): 23 February 1839.
110 RA LC/LCO/AR/1867, p. 8.
111 RA VIC/MAIN/Z/106/4: 20 March/1 April 1881, cat. 122.
112 RA VIC/MAIN/QVJ (W): 1 July 1893.
113 AVPRI: 133/468/1814/6840/370/10: 6/18 January 1814.
114 RA VIC/MAIN/QVJ (W): 22 December 1843.
115 AVPRI: 133/468/1844/7523: 4 February 1844.
116 RA VIC/MAIN/M/52/34: 18 December 1843.
117 RA VIC/MAIN/QVJ (W): 17 June 1844.
118 RGIA 496/3/4-1780-1872.
119 GARF 677/1/753/4.
120 RA JEWEL/GARRARD/QV: 13 October 1865.
121 The star was engraved with the provenance 'Belonged to A.E. Prince of Wales' in 1928, RA JEWEL/GARRARD/GV: 1 March 1928.
122 RA JEWEL/GARRARD/QV: 13 October 1865.
123 RA QM/PRIV/CC7/112: 11 August 1904.
124 GARF 601/1/1388, pp. 27–8.
125 RA VIC/MAIN/W/44/196: 25 August 1904.
126 A note with a pencil inscription in English, dated 23 October 1908, was found on the rebate edge during conservation.
127 Her Mauve Room was said to have been decorated in the hue of a sprig of lilac given to her by her husband.
128 See Dimond 2004 for more information on Queen Alexandra's interest in photography.
129 RA GV/PRIV/GVD/1909: 2 August.
130 RA GV/PRIV/GVD/1909: 2 August.
131 RA PS/PSO/GV/C/Q/1550/317: 6 January 1917.
132 RA GV/ADD/COPY/182: 17 January 1917.
133 RA GEO/PSO/Q/2551/8: 4/17 February 1917.
134 RA PS/PSO/GV/C/M/1334A/153.

CHAPTER 6

1 RA VIC/MAIN/QVJ (W): 30 October 1843.
2 RA VIC/MAIN/QVJ (W): 6 April 1876.
3 AVPRI, Moscow, 133/468/1874/606: 21 June/3 July 1874.
4 RA VIC/MAIN/W/73/86: 31 August 1890.
5 Oettingen-Wallerstein 1848, p. 3.
6 RA PS/PSO/GV/C/Q1228/201: 11 February 1918.
7 RA PS/PSO/GVI/MAIN/7613: 20 June 1945.
8 RA PS/PSO/GVI/MAIN/7613: 29 June 1945.
9 King, *The Rites and ceremonies of the Greek Church*, p. xv.
10 Ibid.
11 Girton College, inv. no. 503.
12 Museum of Russian Icons, inv. no. ЧМ-7.
13 Collection of Russian icons with the support of the St Andrew's Fund, cat. no. 71.

CHAPTER 7

1 RA VIC/MAIN/QVJ (W): 3 June 1844.
2 Yefimova and Aleshina 2011, pp. 16–17.
3 RCIN 980024.ap; see fig. 51, p. 248.
4 RA VIC/MAIN/QVJ (W): 9 June 1844.
5 Ibid.
6 Ibid.
7 RA VIC/MAIN/M/50/53.
8 RA VIC/MAIN/M/50/54.
9 State Hermitage Museum, St Petersburg, inv. no. 7539.
10 Evans 1989, p. 171.
11 RCINs 406491, 406490, 406489; the portrait of Antoinette is after Vigée Le Brun, the others after Carl Vogel von Vogelstein.
12 RCIN 402496.
13 RA VIC/MAIN/Y/37/19.
14 RA VIC/MAIN/QVJ (W): 17 August 1848.
15 RA VIC/MAIN/Y 36/43.
16 RA VIC/MAIN/QVJ (W): 8 October 1843.
17 RCIN 405413.
18 In 1859, Winterhalter's passport records travelling from England to Germany (no date), Paris to Baden (May), and London to France (21 June).
19 The author is grateful to Dr Elizaveta Renne, Curator of British and Scandinavian Painting, State Hermitage Museum, St Petersburg, for this suggestion.

CHAPTER 8

1 RA VIC/MAIN/QVJ (W): 22 January 1874.
2 RA PP/QV/Y105/35: 23 October 1860.
3 Hibbert 2000, pp. 272–3.
4 RA VIC/ADDA5/528.
5 Ibid., 6 November 1866.
6 Ibid., 9 November 1866.
7 Ibid., 9 November; 19 November; 22 November 1866.
8 Ibid., 24 November.
9 Ibid., 19 November.
10 Van der Kiste and Jordaan 1984, p. 46.
11 RA VIC/ADDA/36/585.
12 RA VIC/MAIN/J/84/19.
13 RA VIC/MAIN/QVJ (W): 23 January 1874.
14 Ibid.
15 Ibid.
16 RGIA Фонд 468 оп. 6 д. 149.
17 Van der Kiste and Jordaan 1984, p. 94.
18 RA VIC/MAIN/QVJ (W): 24 January 1874.
19 Van der Kiste and Jordaan 1984, p. 94.
20 Ibid., 7 March 1874.
21 Ibid., 19 April 1874.

22 Ibid., 12 March 1874.
23 Ibid., 24 March 1874.
24 The chapel was demolished during alterations made in 1900.
25 *Catalogue of the Collection of … Specimens of Oriental Art formed by HRH The Duke of Edinburgh … Also the Collection of … Objects of Art and Vertu at Clarence House*, London, W. Clowes & Sons, 1875.
26 RA VIC/MAIN/Z/274/43.
27 King 1937, p. 74.
28 RA VIC/MAIN/Z/274.
29 Ibid., p. 82.
30 Ibid., p. 85.
31 RA VIC/MAIN/Z/274/25.
32 RA VIC/MAIN/Z/274/43.
33 RA VIC/MAIN/Z/274/49.
34 RA VIC/MAIN/QVJ (W): 26 November 1894.
35 State Hermitage Museum, St Petersburg, inv. nos H.ck.1902, H.ck.1903.
36 RA VIC/ADDA/21/218/11–15, no. 40.
37 Cat. 163; RA VIC/ADDA5/528: 19 November 1866.
38 RA VIC/MAIN/QVJ (W): 11 May 1877. The photographs from the sitting are in the Royal Collection.
39 RA VIC/MAIN/ADDA/A/20/1520. The photographs received by the Queen (RCINs 2903143–2903146) were pasted in one of her series of 44 albums, entitled *Portraits of Royal Children*.
40 RA VIC/MAIN/QVJ (W): 29 July 1873.
41 He also signed himself as 'John Beer'. Benezit 2006, s.v. Beer, John Axel Richard; Christie's, London, 12 June 2005, lot 260.
42 Millar 1995, no. 233.
43 See cat. 168 (RCIN 406576).
44 Hall 1999, p. 107.
45 TNA FO 372/44.
46 RCIN 2926786.
47 A copy of Shilder's portrait is at the Museum of Artillery, Engineers and Signal Corps, St Petersburg, inv. no. 25/166, while a slightly different version was sold at auction (Bukowski Auktioner, Stockholm, *Spring Classic Sale, F163*, Helsinki, 30–31 May 2012, lot 323). Pershakov's portrait is in Hillwood Museum, Washington, DC, inv. no. 51.78.
48 State Hermitage Museum, St Petersburg, inv. no. ГЭ-6975.
49 The author would like to thank Rosanna da Sancha, Senior Paintings Conservator, Royal Collection Trust.
50 Cowles 1974, p. 221.
51 RA VIC/MAIN/QVJ (W): 3 September 1862.
52 RA VIC/ADDA20/1214: letter from Prince Alfred to Queen Victoria, 11 August 1862.
53 Millar 1995, no. 860.
54 RA VIC/ADDA20/322: letter from Sir Charles Phipps (Keeper of the Privy Purse) to Sir Frederick Grey (Vice Admiral of the Royal Navy), 10 July 1862.
55 RA VIC/ADDA20/1215: letter from Prince Alfred to Queen Victoria, 14 August 1862.
56 RA VIC/MAIN/QVJ (W): 16 August 1862.
57 Lee 1925, pp. 268–9.
58 Untracht 1982, p. 382.
59 RA VIC/ADDA5/528, p. 47. The author is grateful to Stephen Patterson, Head of Collections Information Management, Royal Collection Trust, for the reference to arms in Ellis's account.
60 The author is grateful to Emily Hannam, Assistant Curator, Islamic and South East Asian manuscripts, Royal Collection Trust, for translation of the inscriptions.
61 Inv. no. 91.1.890a–c.
62 RA VIC/ADDA5/528: 24 November 1866.
63 Stone 1934, p. 519.
64 The author is grateful to Alex Campbell-Ricketts, Inventory Clerk, Royal Collection Trust, for assistance in identifying the stones.
65 Inv. no. 36.25 717a–b.
66 RCINs 405032, 404581. These are larger three-quarter-length portraits.
67 *Nicholas I in a sleigh*, 1853, State Russian Museum, St Petersburg, 73.0 × 92.0 cm, inv. no. Ж-2696; Chapochnikova and Gurevich 2001.
68 Blakesley 2016b, p. 228.
69 RCIN 406605. First recorded at Buckingham Palace in 1909: Cust 1909, p. 248.
70 *Sleighing across country in winter*: Marlborough House 1877, no. 1100, 10.0 × 12.0 in.; probably Cust 1909, p. 182; Marlborough House 1925, p. 149.
71 Budrina 2016.
72 RA VIC/ADDA/21/218/11–15.
73 RA VIC/MAIN/QVJ (W): 23 January 1874, from Osborne.
74 Millar 1992, no. 638.
75 Sent to Clarence House on 1 August 1891.
76 RA PPTO/PP/QV/MAIN/1874/17496: Chevalier to Sir Thomas Biddulph, 15 July 1874.
77 RA PPTO/PP/QV/MAIN/1875/18304: letter from Chevalier to Doyne C. Bell.
78 RA PPTO/PP/QV/MAIN/1874/17496: letter from Francis Knollys (the Prince of Wales's Private Secretary) to Sir Thomas Biddulph, 28 August 1874.
79 Stanley 1927, p. 215.
80 Roberts 2012, p. 82.
81 Stanley 1927, p. 217.
82 Ibid., p. 215.
83 TNA FO 83/834.
84 RA VIC/ADDA20/1367: 28 January 1874.
85 RA VIC/MAIN/QVJ (W): 2 February 1874.
86 TNA FO 83/834.
87 RA VIC/ADDA5/506, p. 92.
88 The Stroganov Institute was founded in Moscow in 1825, and renamed the Stroganov Institute for Technical Drawing in 1860; it became the Imperial Stroganov Institute in 1901, and is today the Stroganov Moscow State University for Arts and Industry.
89 State Hermitage Museum, St Petersburg, inv. no. Э-2.
90 *Private Life* 1898, p. 254.
91 The author is grateful to Dr Iraida Bott, Deputy Director, Tsarskoe Selo, for sharing her knowledge about furniture of this type.
92 RA VIC/MAIN/QVJ (W): 1 March 1874.
93 Ibid.
94 Alexander II's first daughter, Grand Duchess Alexandra (1842–9), had died of meningitis in infancy.
95 RA VIC/MAIN/QVJ (W): 13 May 1874.
96 'The Emperor of Russia', *The Times*, 19 May 1874, issue 28006, p. 11.
97 RCIN 402328.
98 Millar 1992, no. 21, letter to Princess Victoria of Hesse, 6 August 1879 (Hough 1975, p. 16).
99 Sebag Montefiore 2016, p. 472.
100 RA VIC/ADDA 20/1063.
101 RA VIC/ADDA 20/1063, quoted in full in Millar 1992, no. 638.
102 RA VIC/MAIN/QVJ (W): 3 December 1883.
103 RA VIC/MAIN/QVJ (W): 23 January 1899.
104 RA VIC/MAIN/QVJ (W): 23 January 1874.
105 RA VIC/MAIN/QVJ (W): 24 January 1899.
106 RA VIC/MAIN/QVJ (W): 21 June 1873.
107 For the other six categories see Barchatova *et al.* 1990, p. 18.
108 Born in Moscow, Levitsky graduated in law in 1839 but became captivated by the new medium of photography. His daguerreotype views taken in the Caucasus were awarded a prize at the Paris exhibition of 1843 and thereafter he travelled to France to study science at the Sorbonne and to improve his photographic skills. In October 1849 he returned to St Petersburg; establishing his own studio, he introduced the term 'svetopis' (light painting) to Russia. In 1877 he was awarded the title of Photographer to Their Imperial Majesties. Following his death in 1898 his son took over his studio, which remained active until 1914.
109 RA VIC/MAIN/Z/274/25.
110 RA VIC/MAIN/Z/274/43.
111 RA VIC/ADDA23/104.
112 RCINs 42897–42899.
113 RA VIC/ADDU/32.
114 Massie 1968, pp. 52–3.
115 Buckle 1932, pp. 45–6.
116 Fedoseyenko 1996, p. 168.
117 Krivenko, *Les Solennités du saint couronnement* (cat. 208), pp. 296–306.
118 http://antique-photos.com/en/component/content/article/166-awardsdatabase-en/russian-empire/539-sommemorative-medalfor-the-tercentenary-of-the-romanov-dynasty.html (accessed 24 January 2018).

CHAPTER 9

1 Hamel, a Russian scientist of German origin, spent much of his career travelling across Europe, in his role as correspondent for the Academy of Sciences, St Petersburg. Acquainted with figures such as Niépce (1765–1833), Daguerre (1787–1851) and Fox Talbot (1800–77), he was able to acquire, at an early stage, important details on the methods and processes they had developed. Hamel's correspondence on photography was eventually published in 1949 (Kravets 1949). The author is grateful to Roger Taylor for information on the existence of this publication.

2 Works by Alexei Grekov do not appear to survive, but his various newspaper advertisements and notices, and his booklet entitled *A Painter without Brush and Paint* (published anonymously, 1841), represent some of the earliest published material by a Russian professional photographer.

3 Charles Piazzi Smyth (1819–1900), Astronomer Royal for Scotland and amateur photographer, visited Russia in 1859 and remarked: 'some one had told us on ship-board that photography was miserable and hardly known in St. Petersburg; that was, nevertheless, a decided mistake for there is scarcely a more frequent sign to be met with along all the principal streets, than ФОТОГРАФІЯ ['Fotografija']; and all the specimens exhibited outside the *studios*, chiefly large-sized portraits, were among the finest things we have ever seen in that line': Smyth 1862, p. 308.

4 RA VIC/MAIN/Y/169/73.

5 Andrei Osipovich Karelin worked as both painter and photographer, as did Rafail Levitsky (1847–1940), Sergei's son. Karelin photographed Prince Alfred, Duke of Edinburgh, in 1875, but a copy of the photograph does not survive in the Royal Collection (Semenov and Khorev 1994, p. 237).

6 Ponomarev 1858, p. 81. *Svetopis* or 'light-painting' was also the name given by Sergei Levitsky to his studio in 1849.

7 GARF: F. 469, Op. 8, L. 1536: document dated 11 December 1854; see Redaelli *et al.* 2002, p. 34.

8 The request relates to the large-scale project begun by Prince Albert in 1853, known as 'The Prince Consort's Raphael Collection', which aimed to create a complete visual resource for the study of Raphael's work. The outcome of the project, completed in 1876, is preserved in the Print Room at Windsor Castle and comprises more than 4,000 prints and photographs. See Dimond 1987, pp. 46–9; Becker and Ruland 1863; Ruland 1876; and Montagu 1986.

9 RA VIC/ADDA10/85/558 and RA VIC/ADDA10/85/557 respectively.

10 RA VIC/ADDA10/85/555.

11 Copy of letter from Ruland to Count Shuvalov (1827–89), dated 4 June 1861 (RA VIC/ADDA10/85/560), and Shuvalov's reply, confirming receipt of the album, dated 30 June 1861 (RA VIC/ADDA10/85/561). The present whereabouts of the album is unknown. The photographs were taken by Charles Thurston Thompson (1816–68), who had established a studio at the South Kensington Museum: see p. 350.

12 Morozov 1953; see also Barkhatova 2005.

13 The latter, entitled *Episodes of Sevastopol Life of 1854–55* (RCIN 2500579), was commissioned by the renowned art collector and philanthropist P.M. Tretyakov (1832–98). The paintings were specially produced for the exhibition by realist artists such as V.Y. Makovsky (1846–1920) and I.M. Pryanishnikov (1840–94), both founding members of the *Peredvizhniki* group, and are today housed at the State Historical Museum in Moscow. The portfolio also contains four interior photographic views of the building hosting the exhibition (RCINs 2500611–2500614).

14 Boldyrev developed his flexible transparent film negative during the late 1870s and presented it at the Pan-Russian Industrial Exhibition of 1882 but it was ignored by the Commission (see Barkhatova 1989). George Eastman's patent for flexible gelatined-paper film was issued in 1884, while Hannibal Goodwin's process to produce celluloid film was patented in 1887.

15 The first factory to produce photographic materials (specifically gelatin dry plates) was established in Russia in 1881 by Albert Felisch (1837–1908) (Bower 1999, p. 11). By 1896, it was calculated that Russian photography was 85 per cent dependent on imports from abroad: Barchatova *et al.* 1990, p. 34.

16 The Royal Collection holds one of the largest and most complete sets of Fenton's Crimean photographs: Gordon 2017.

17 Viktor, the son of Karl Bulla (1853–1929), a photographer of German extraction, established a portrait studio in St Petersburg in 1875, but in 1886 shifted his interest to reportage. In 1896 Karl Bulla was appointed Photographer to the Ministry of the Imperial Court. The family firm remained active until the early 1930s.

18 See Dimond 1987; Marsden 2010, pp. 396–423; and Lyden 2014, pp. 107–27.

19 RA VIC/ADDA15/2139. Sir Howard Elphinstone became Prince Arthur's governor in 1859, and from 1871, comptroller of his household. Many photographs collected by Elphinstone are likely to have been pasted in the album (RCIN 2929453), which also contains cats 152–155.

20 RA VIC/MAIN/QVJ (W): 7 March 1874.

21 Shatsillo and Lukonin 1991, pp. 177, 437. See also Abrams 1998, pp. 230–38.

22 For pictorialism in Russia, see, e.g., Khoroshilov *et al.* 2002; Sviblova and Misalandi 2005. For Soviet photography, see, e.g. Morozov and Lloyd 1980; Goodman *et al.* 2015.

23 Maude 1996, p. 32, letter dated 16 September 1856.

24 Dyagovchenko opened his studio in Moscow in 1863; due to lack of business it closed six months later. He returned to his native Sergiyev Posad, where he began to improve his technical skills and practised at the Trinity Lavra of St Sergius, Russia's most important monastery; a photographic establishment had been set up here in 1858. In 1867 he returned to Moscow and established himself as a portrait photographer.

25 RA VIC/ADDA5/528: 6 November 1866.

26 GARF F. 472, Op. 31, D. 4, L. 68.

27 Born in Varese, Italy, Giovanni (also known as Ivan or Jean) Bianchi moved to Moscow, at the age of ten. He studied in Moscow and travelled across Europe between 1839 and 1846. Bianchi's earliest surviving photographs were taken in Paris in 1852. Bianchi became the first photographer in Russia to specialise in architectural and topographical views; in 1858 he received the title of Free Artist from the Imperial Academy of Arts. Despite his success in Russia, he retired to Switzerland in 1884 and died in 1893.

28 The album contains 10 photographs of the celebrations, including fireworks over the Gulf of Finland (RCINs 2103421–2103430) and 45 photographs with various views of Peterhof, including the Cottage Palace and the Dacha Alexandria (RCINs 2103431–2103475). The album was bound by the Russian firm, Alexander Petersen of St Petersburg.

29 The Photographic Society created on 10 March 1878 was formally known as the 'Fifth Section for Photography and its Applications of the Russian Technical Society'; the Technical Society with its original four sections had been founded in 1866.

30 Büsching 1787, p. 302.

31 The visit took place on 14 August 185: Fitzmaurice 1905, I, pp. 189–93; Maude 1996, pp. 7–8.

32 Barkhatova 2009, p. 361. Night photography, apart from a few early experiments, was first successfully seen in Britain in 1896 (in the photographs of Paul Martin (1864–1944) at the Royal Photographic Society) and in America in the photographs of Alfred Stieglitz (1864–1946) in 1898.

33 Fitzmaurice 1905, I, p. 189, St Petersburg,

14 August 1856. Mack's participation in the mission is also mentioned by a member of Granville's suite, Lieutenant Colonel Maude, in a letter to his wife, dated 7 August 1856: 'We have a Photographer with the Embassy, a sergeant of Sappers' (Maude 1996, p. 3).

34 Connolly 1855, II, pp. 140–59.

35 Royal Commission 1852, pp. 43–6.

36 Many of these would be photographed by Francis Bedford (1816–94) (RCINs 2800159–2800242).

37 Hamber 1996, pp. 393–454.

38 Physick 1975, p. 3.

39 Paris 1855, p. 4. Cole had been appointed commissioner for the British section.

40 Connolly 1857, II, pp. 151–4.

41 The party left Britain on board HMS *St Jean d'Acre* on 27 July, reached St Petersburg on 8 August and departed the city on 4 October 1856.

42 RA VIC/MAIN/E/8/81.

43 RA VIC/MAIN/E/8/83.

44 RA VIC/MAIN/QVJ (W): 11 November 1856.

45 Prince Albert, patron of the society, exhibited 15 photographs from the set of 19 presented to Queen Victoria (Taylor 2002, pp. 484–5). The first exhibition of the Photographic Society of Scotland in 1856 displayed more than 900 works by photographers such as Roger Fenton, Hill & Adamson, Oscar Rejlander, Antoine Claudet, Robert Macpherson, Bisson Freres, James Good Tunny, Ross & Thomson, James Valentine and George Washington Wilson. Mack also exhibited photographs from this set, together with a portrait of Sir John Burgoyne (1782–1871), at the 1858 exhibition of the Photographic Society of London, displayed at the South Kensington Museum: Taylor 2002, p. 485.

46 Physick 1975, p. 13; Hamber 1996, p. 418.

47 Apart from Roger Fenton's photographs, taken in 1852, the only other known photographic views of Russia from the early and mid-1850s are those by Ivan Bianchi.

48 RA VIC/MAIN/QVJ (W): 31 December 1844.

49 7 September 1856: Maude 1996, p. 26.

50 Fitzmaurice 1905, I, pp. 1[illegible]2–3

51 The only other known surviving early photographic portrait of members of the Russian working class is a daguerreotype in the State Historical Museum, Moscow, showing the Slakosov brothers, fireplace installers, taken between 1852 and 1856: Barchatova *et al.* 1990, p. 42; Rakhmanov and Barkhatova 1996, p. 38; Barkhatova 2009, p. 64; see also Stites 2005, p. 374 and fig. 64.

52 Maude 1996, p. 46.

53 This was one of three photographs sent by Maude, who wrote in the accompanying letter, dated 18 September 1856: 'I send you home the only photograph I have got that was done on board the "Acre" [...] I also send you a view of the Kremlin from the opposite side of the river [cat. 218] and three Russian peasants, or "moujiks", in their ordinary dress': Maude 1996, p. 39.

54 For more information on Carrick, see Ashbee 1976; Ashbee 1987; Ashbee and Lawson 1987; Balachenkova 2010.

55 In 1862, Carrick sent a set of 40 of his cards to Tsesarevich Nicholas Alexandrovich, who was so impressed by his work that he presented him with a diamond ring: Ashbee and Lawson 1987, p. 9. Carrick would receive a further diamond ring in the same year from Grand Duke Constantine Nikolaevich, in gratitude for his portrait: Balachenkova 2010, p. 46.

56 John MacGregor only participated in the 1860s expeditions and that of 1871. His premature death in 1872 had a profound effect on Carrick, who eventually returned to those river regions in 1875 and 1878. The two had met in Edinburgh in 1857 and MacGregor followed Carrick to St Petersburg once Carrick's studio was established in 1859. Carrick was the 'artist' and MacGregor 'the technician' and they worked together harmoniously until the death of MacGregor.

57 Count Mihaly Zichy was a court artist to the Russian imperial family. An exhibition of Carrick's photographs of paintings by Zichy was organised in St Petersburg in 1880: Balachenkova 2010, p. 165. Zichy met the Prince of Wales in Russia in 1866, and later visited him in Britain. The Royal Collection holds an album (RCIN 2861713) containing 46 photographic reproductions of Zichy's work, thought to be by Carrick.

CHAPTER 10

1 RGIA, Fund 515, register 15, file 380, sheet 65, 71.

2 See Cross 2003.

3 See Pritchard 2010.

4 For the history of the establishment of Fabergé's London branch, see McCarthy 2017.

5 For a history of the exchange of decorative arts between Russia and England in the sixteenth and seventeenth centuries, see Dmitrieva and Murdoch 2013.

6 RA GEO/MAIN/25002; restored between 1827 and 1829 by Morel and Seddon for the King's Writing Room. While some of this decoration is retained, particularly to the pedestal, the handles to the tazza were subsequently lost. However, they can be seen intact in Joseph Nash's view of the White Drawing Room at Windsor Castle, *c.*1846: RCIN 817132.t.

7 Kelly Trombly 2017, p. 195.

8 Ibid., pp. 24–5.

9 RA VIC/MAIN/QVJ (W): 11 June 1851.

10 RA/PPTO/PP/PAPC/PAP CACC/LED: 31 December 1851, £4 8s.

11 The iconostasis was painted by Carl Timoleon von Neff (see cats 94 and 95).

12 Known in Russia as 'stil modern'.

13 Major loans from the Royal Collection were made by Queen Mary to the *Exhibition of Russian Art* held in Belgrave Square in 1935, and by Her Majesty The Queen to the 1967 exhibition, *Great Britain – USSR*, held at the Victoria and Albert Museum.

14 De Guitaut 2003, pp. 39–40.

15 Document held in the State Archive of Sverdlovsk's Region.

16 Robinson 1902, p. 169.

17 RA VIC/MAIN/QVJ (W): 19 May 1951.

18 Ibid., 11 June 1851.

19 Russian State Archive of Old Acts, fond 1267 Demidoff, list 8, fol. 1480, p. 15.

20 RCIN 934874.

21 State Hermitage Museum, St Petersburg, inv. no. E3625.

22 Budrina 2016.

23 Versailles, Grand Trianon, inv. no. T 181 C.1.

24 RGIA, Fund 468, register 8, file 296, sheet 19.

25 RA/PPTO/PP/QV/MAIN/1874/16105.

26 RA PP/16105: 2 April 1874.

27 Hermitage Museum, inv. no. Э.7730.

28 Hermitage Museum, inv. no. ERKm-280.

29 RA/QV/QVJ/(W): 9 July 1880.

30 RCINs 14113 and 32527.

31 RCIN 2371.

32 Hillwood Museum, Washington, DC, inv. no. 12.113.1–7.

33 Hillwood Museum, Washington, DC, inv. no. 12.387.1–4.

34 Inventory of George V, no. 37.

35 Tillander-Godenhielm 2005, p. 179.

36 RA VIC/ADD/COPY/119.

37 Habsburg and Lopato 1993, pp. 457–8.

CHAPTER 11

1 RA VIC/MAIN/QVJ (W): 22 September 1896.

2 King 1937, p. 72.

3 RA GV/ADD/copy/152: 29 April 1896.

4 RA VIC/MAIN/QVJ (W): 22 September 1896.

5 Ibid., 3 October 1896.

6 De Guitaut 2003, p. 237.

7 RGIA, fond 544, Work 1.

8 RA GV/PRIV/GVD/1909: 2 August 1909.

9 Russian State Documentary Film and Photo Archive at Krasnogorsk: footage of the 1909 visit of Emperor Nicholas II to Cowes.

10 Christiansborg Palace, 440.0 × 670.0 cm; inv. no. CSB669A.

11 This sketch may be the one in the Nationalhistorike Museum, Frederiksborg, inv. no. A6818, 1883, 62.5 × 94.5 cm.

12 Frederiksborg Castle, signed and dated April 1884, inv. no. A2824.

13 Frederiksborg Castle, inv. no. A2823.
14 RA VIC/MAIN/QVJ (W): 17 March 1885.
15 Mapperton Papers, 287, Oliver Montagu to Aunt E (August 1891); quoted in Ridley 2013, p. 293.
16 Lee 1925, p. 573.
17 RA VIC/ADDA15/4849.
18 Owned by the Trust Fund of May 1956, Copenhagen, 74.5 × 93.5 cm, signed and dated: *L. T 87.*
19 Tuxen 1928, p. 118.
20 Ibid., p. 120.
21 RA VIC/MAIN/QVJ (W): 1 December 1887.
22 The payment of 6 gns on 2 December 1896, as recorded in the Royal Archives (RA PPTO/PP/QV/AVA CC/LED: 1865–1900), probably relates to this drawing. See Millar 1995, no. 4125.
23 RA VIC/MAIN/QVJ (W): 24 and 26 September 1896.
24 RA VIC/MAIN/QVJ (W): 3 October 1896.
25 Nicholas had been appointed by Queen Victoria as colonel-in-chief of the 2nd Dragoons (Royal Scots Greys) in 1894.
26 Garrard 1896.
27 RGIA, fond 525, 3, 85, 469, fond 525, 3, 9, 255.
28 RA VIC/MAIN/H/48/39.
29 Maria Feodorovna left Russia on board HMS *Marlborough* on 7 April 1919, together with other members of the deposed imperial family, including her daughter, Grand Duchess Xenia Alexandrovna. After a stop at Constantinople (12–18 April), the party reached Malta on 21 April, where they stayed until 28 April. Eventually they arrived in England in May 1919. The Dowager Empress spent the rest of the year there with her sister, between Marlborough House and Sandringham House, before moving to Denmark. An account of the little-known time spent in Malta can be found in Ingham 1949.
30 Examples of imperial Easter eggs with automata as the 'surprise' include the Swan Egg, 1906, the Peacock Egg, 1908, and the Orange Tree Egg, 1911.
31 RCIN 40486; see de Guitaut 2011, p. 114.
32 Now in the McFerrin Collection, Houston Museum of Natural Science, inv. no. 287.
33 Devonshire Collection, Chatsworth.
34 Bainbridge 1949, p. 97.
35 State Archive of the Russian Federation; letter from Queen Alexandra to Nicholas II, 29 December 1901, fond 640/1 file 1144/19.
36 RA/GV/PP3/3/588.
37 RGIA, fond 525, 3, 99, 210.
38 RA GEO/MAIN 22062.
39 RA GEO/MAIN 22082.
40 RA GEO/MAIN/50023–50024.
41 RA VIC/MAIN/QVJ (W): 19 July 1837.
42 RCIN 919785.
43 RA RG/RLED/V: 30 November 1892.
44 RA VIC/ADD/T/263.
45 RA VIC/MAIN/Z/105/82.
46 RA QM/PRIV/QMD/1909: 2 August.
47 The firm was founded in St Petersburg in 1902 by Swiss photographer Frédéric Boissonnas (1858–1946) and German photographer Fritz Eggler (1871–1923), taking over the studio of the Italian photographer Anacleto Pasetti (1850–1912), a favourite of the imperial family. During the First War World Eggler was exiled to Siberia but escaped to Switzerland, helped by Boissonnas. The latter eventually left Russia to focus his photographic career on his fascination for Greece and the southern Balkans.
48 RCINs 2002, 2218, 41406; RA GV/ADD/A21/218/11–15: 17–27 July 1905.
49 RA GV/ADD/COPY/170: 29 December 1912.
50 Dehn 1922, p. 199. Lili von Dehn (née Yulia Alexandrovna Smolskaia) was the wife of Captain Carl von Dehn (1877–1932), an officer on the Imperial Yacht *Standart*, and a member of the Emperor's personal guard.
51 RA GV/PRIV/GVD/1913: 24 May. GARF F. 601, Op. 1, D. 2172, L. 4: the Russian Emperor's copy of the photograph, unsigned.
52 Yashchik 2004, fig. 15.
53 RA VIC/ADDA21/220D, p. 62 (Queen Alexandra's Details of Payments 1918 to 1926) and RA VIC/ADDA21/219D, p. 127 (Queen Alexandra's Abstract Book), £62 10s.
54 The preparatory study is in the E.D. Feltsina Museum, Krasnodar, inv. no. KM 13251/1.
55 De Guitaut 2003, pp. 36–7.
56 Bainbridge 1933, p. 175.
57 Snowman 1993, p. 143.
58 Woolf family private collection; the brooch is octagonal and features the same motif.
59 RA GV/PP/23207: 2 August 1935, Lady Muriel Paget to Mr Colles from Leningrad: 'I have seen a breakfast and dinner service from the Tsar's yacht with his motto on it'; 7 August 1935, telegram to Lady Paget: 'Please buy breakfast and dinner service'.
60 RA GV/PRIV/PP/23207.
61 The author is grateful to Dr Victor Bezotosny of the Russian State Historial Museum for this information.
62 The American art magazine *Parnassus* described the use of 'white on white' by both Sorine and the artist de Monvel as 'very flattering to the subject, and harmonious to the pale tinted walls of many New York apartments'. See Sterne 1931, p. 5.
63 RA QEQM/PR10/PIC: letter from Savely Sorine to Arthur Penn, Treasurer to the Queen, 8 August 1948.
64 Ibid.
65 Owens 2005, p. 14.

BIBLIOGRAPHY

Abbreviations

AVPRI	Archive of Foreign Policy of the Russian Empire (Arkhiv vneshnei politiki Rossiiskoi Imperii), Moscow
BM	British Museum, London
GAC	Government Art Collection
GARF	State Archives of the Russian Federation (Gosudarstvennyi Arkhiv Rossyskoi Federatsy), Moscow
GEO	George IV
GVI	George VI
KGV	George V
NPG	National Portrait Gallery, London
QEQM	Queen Elizabeth The Queen Mother
QV	Queen Victoria
RA	Royal Archives, Windsor
RCIN	Royal Collection inventory number
RGIA	Russian State Historical Archives, St Petersburg
TNA	The National Archives, Kew

Manuscript Sources

BUCKINGHAM PALACE 1911
'Buckingham Palace: an inventory prepared for the Lord Chamberlain's Department by Messrs Trollope of London', RCIN 1112919

CARLTON HOUSE 1816
'A Catalogue of pictures forming the collection of His Royal Highness The Prince Regent in Carlton House, December 1816', RCIN 1112585

CARLTON HOUSE 1819
'Catalogue of His Majesty's Pictures in Carlton House, June 1819', RCIN 1112581

CATALOGUE OF ARMS I
'A Catalogue of arms: the property of His Royal Highness The Prince of Wales at Carlton House', I (6 vols), 1781–1800, RCIN 1113368

CATALOGUE OF ARMS VI
'A Catalogue of arms: the property of His Royal Highness The Prince of Wales at Carlton House', VI (6 vols), 1820–8, RCIN 1113364

CLARENCE HOUSE INVENTORY 1900
'Inventory of the collection of Alfred, Duke of Saxe-Coburg-Gotha, at Clarence House, made after his death', RA VIC/ADDQ/00/1440

INVENTORY OF GEORGE IV
'George IV Inventory of Clocks, etc.', *c.*1827–33, 3 vols, RCINS 933559–933561

INVENTORY OF GEORGE V
'Inventory of cigarette cases etc. in the collection of King George V', 1936, RCIN 1116308

JUTSHAM DELS
'An account of furniture &c. despatched from Carlton House, October 1820 – February 1830', RCIN 1112485

JUTSHAM RECS I
'An Account of furniture &c. received at Carlton House, 31 December 1816 – 21 June 1829', RCIN 1112775

JUTSHAM RECS AND DELS
'An Account of furniture &c. received and deliver'd by Benjamin Jutsham on account of His Royal Highness The Prince of Wales at Carlton House, 1806–1820', RCIN 1112484

KENSINGTON INVENTORY 1818
'Catalogue of the Pictures in the Palace at Kensington', RCIN 1115431

KGV 1904
R. Garrard and S. Garrard & Co., 'Inventory of plate the property of T.R.H. The Prince and Princess of Wales, 1904 now T.M. King George V and Queen Mary', RCIN 1115296

MARLBOROUGH HOUSE 1925
H.S. Middleton, 'Inventory of pictures at Marlborough House, November 1925', RCIN 1109468

MOREL AND SEDDON *c.*1830
Morel and Seddon Accounts, 'Accounts of Furniture Supplied for Windsor Castle By Order of the Lord Chamberlain's Office by Morel and Seddon', *c.*1830, RCIN 1114843

NORTH CORRIDOR
'Windsor Castle Inventory of Arms &c.', *c.*1850–66 (continuously updated until 1994), III (4 vols), RCIN 1122402

QMB
'Catalogue of Bibelots, Miniatures and other valuables, the property of HM Queen Mary', 1893–1945, 4 vols, RCINS 1114504–1114509

QMPP
'Catalogue of miniatures, jewels and other valuables, the property of Queen Mary', illustrated typescript, 11 vols, RCINS 1114193–1114199 and 1114500–1114503

RA VIC/ADDA5/506
Descriptive Inventory of Plate, *c.*1879

RA VIC/MAIN/QVJ (W)
Queen Victoria's Journal. The citations in this publication are drawn from the edited copy in the hand of Princess Beatrice, who destroyed the originals after her mother's death

REDGRAVE SHEETS
R. Redgrave and J.C. Robinson, 'Catalogue of the pictures in the collection of Queen Victoria', 1850–79, RCINS 1112488–1112499, 1112900 (Windsor Castle), 1112905 (Hampton Court), 1112913–1112921 (Buckingham Palace)

RL 1870
'Inventory of Miniatures in the Royal Library Windsor Castle March', RCIN 1112528

RL 1881
'Inventory of Miniatures in the Royal Library Windsor Castle', RCIN 112527

WINDSOR CASTLE INVENTORY OF PAINTINGS
'Windsor Castle Inventory of Paintings', 1869–2000, RCINS 1170001–1170015 and 1170021

WINDSOR CASTLE INVENTORY OF STATUARY
'Windsor Castle Inventory of Statuary, Busts &c.', *c.*1872, RCIN 1101202

Printed books and articles

ABRAMS 1998
H.N. Abrams, *Nicholas and Alexandra: The Last Imperial Family of Tsarist Russia*, Wilmington, DE

ANDERSEN 1965
T. Andersen, 'Vigilius Eriksen in Russia, 1757–1772', *Artes: Periodical of the Fine Arts*, I, pp. 45–93

ANDERSEN 1970
T. Andersen, 'Vigilius Eriksen: list of paintings 1757–1772', *Artes: Periodical of the Fine Arts*

ANDREEVA 2012
G.B. Andreeva (ed.), *Geniuses of War, Weal and Beauty: George Dawe, RA Pinx*, Moscow

ASHBEE 1976
F. Ashbee, 'Fotografs Maloy Morskoy', *Yunost*, 7, pp. 100–2

ASHBEE 1987
F. Ashbee, 'The Carricks of St Petersburg', in P. Dukes and A.G. Cross *et al.*, 1987, pp. 90–105

ASHBEE AND LAWSON 1987
F. Ashbee and J. Lawson, *William Carrick 1827–1878*, Edinburgh

ASTON 1929
G. Aston, *His Royal Highness The Duke of Connaught and Strathearn: A Life and Intimate Study*, London

BAEDEKER 1914
K. Baedeker, *Russia with Teheran, Port Arthur, and Peking*, London

BAINBRIDGE 1933
H.C. Bainbridge, *Twice Seven: The Autobiography of H.C. Bainbridge*, London

BAINBRIDGE 1949
H.C. Bainbridge, *Peter Carl Fabergé: His Life and Work, 1846–1920*, London

BALACHENKOVA 2010
A.P. Balachenkova, *Russian XIX Century Photographers: William Carrick, Scenes of Russian Life*, exh. cat., Rosfoto, St Petersburg

BALDWIN *et al.* 2004
G. Baldwin, M.R. Daniel and S. Greenough, *All the Mighty World: The Photographs of Roger Fenton, 1852–1860*, exh. cat., National Gallery of Art, Washington, DC, J. Paul Getty Museum, Los Angeles, Metropolitan Museum of Art, New York, and Tate Britain, London

BARKHATOVA 1989
E. Barkhatova, 'Donskie sjužety Ivana Boldyreva', *Nashje Nasledije*, IV (10), pp. 624–31

BARKHATOVA 2005
E.V. Barkhatova (ed.), *Au long de la Volga: Maîtres de la Photographie Russe au XIXe siècle*, exh. cat., Bibliothèque Royale de Belgique, Brussels

BARKHATOVA 2009
E. Barkhatova, *Russkaya Svetopis: Pervyj Vek Fotoiskusstva 1839–1914*, St Petersburg

BARCHATOVA *et al.* 1990
Y. Barchatova, T. Saburova and G. Mirolubova *et al.*, *A Portrait of Tsarist Russia: Unknown Photographs from the Soviet Archives*, London

BARRETT 1994
T.M. Barrett, 'The remaking of the Lion of Dagestan: Shamil in captivity', *The Russian Review*, 53 (3), pp. 353–66

BATTISCOMBE 1969
G. Battiscombe, *Queen Alexandra*, London

BECKER AND RULAND 1863
E. Becker and C. Ruland, 'The "Raphael Collection" of H.R.H. The Prince Consort', *Fine Arts Quarterly Review*, I, pp. 27–39

BELAVSKAIA AND GAFIFULLIN 2014
K.P. Belavskaia and R.R. Gafifullin *et al.*, *Gosudarstvennyi muzei-zapovednik Pavlovsk: Polnyi katalog kollektsii, t. XII, Miniatiura, vypusk I, Portretnaia miniatiura XVIII – pervoi treti XIX veka* ('Pavlovsk State Museum Preserve: Complete Catalogue of the Collections, XII, Miniature Painting, vypusk I, Portrait Miniatures of the Eighteenth and First Third of the Nineteenth Century'), St Petersburg

BÉNÉZIT 2006
E. Bénézit, *Dictionary of Artists*, Paris

BENSON AND ESHER 1908
C. Benson and Viscount Esher (eds), *The Letters of Queen Victoria: A Selection of Her Majesty's correspondence between the years 1837 and 1861*, 2 vols, London

BERRY AND CRUMMEY 1968
L.E. Berry and R.O. Crummey (eds), *Rude and Barbarous Kingdom: Russia in the Accounts of Sixteenth-century English Voyagers*, Madison, WI (repr. 2017)

BIJL 2017
Arnoud Bijl (ed.), *1917: Romanovs and Revolution: The End of Monarchy*, exh. cat., Hermitage Amsterdam

BINGHAM 1884
D.A. Bingham (ed.), *A Selection from the Letters and Despatches of the First Napoleon*, 2 vols, London

BLAKESLEY 2010
R. Blakesley, 'Pride and the politics of nationality in Russia's Imperial Academy of Fine Arts, 1757–1807', *Art History*, 33 (5), pp. 800–35

BLAKESLEY 2014
R. Blakesley, 'Ladies-in-waiting in waiting: picturing adolescence in Dmitri Levitsky's Smolny portraits, 1772–76', *Art History*, 37 (1), pp. 10–37

BLAKESLEY 2016a
R. Blakesley, *Russia and the Arts: The Age of Tolstoy and Tchaikovsky*, exh. cat., National Portrait Gallery, London

BLAKESLEY 2016b
R. Blakesley, *The Russian Canvas: Painting in Imperial Russia 1757–1881*, New Haven and London

BLANCH 1978
L. Blanch, *The Sabres of Paradise*, London

BLIGAARD 1990
M. Bligaard (ed.), *Laurits Tuxen: Portraetter og historiemalerier*, exh. cat., Museum of National History, Copenhagen

BLOCK
D. Block, 'Dating French medals by edge-markings', <www.historicalmedals.com/poincons.htm> (accessed 26 July 2018)

BODIN 2015
P.A. Bodin, 'Religious, cultural and political dimensions of winter-bathing in Russia', in G. Simons and D. Westurlund 2015, pp. 45–63

BOWER 1999
P. Bower, 'The nefarious career of Leon Warnerke', *Journal of the Association for Historical and Fine Art Photography*, 12, pp. 9–12

BOWRING 1821
J. Bowring, *Specimens of the Russian Poets*, London

BRAMSEN 1904
L. Bramsen, *Le Médaillier de Napoléon le Grand*, 3 vols, Copenhagen

BROOKS 2010
J. Brooks, 'The Russian nation imagined: the peoples of Russia as seen in popular imagery', *Journal of Social History*, 43 (3), pp. 535–57

BROWN 1987
L.A. Brown, *A Catalogue of British Historical Medals, 1760–1960. Vol. 2: 1837–1901*, London

BUCKLE 1932
G.E. Buckle (ed.), *Letters of Queen Victoria. Vol. 3: 1896–1901*, London

BUDRINA 2016
L. Budrina in N. Coquery, J. Ebeling, A.P. Khelissa and P. Sénéchal (eds), *Les progrès de l'industrie perfectionnée: Luxe, arts décoratifs et innovation de la Révolution française au Premier Empire*, Presses universitaires du Midi, pp. 136–45

BÜSCHING 1787
A.F. Büsching (ed.), 'Tagebuch, welches der großfürstliche Oberkammerherr Friedrich Wilhelm von Bergholz von 1721 bis 24 in Rußland geführet hat, drittes Stück von 1723', *Magazin für die neue Historie und Geographie, Halle 1787*, pp. 178–360

BUTLER 1922
E. Butler, *An Autobiography*, London, Bombay and Sydney

BUXHOEVEDEN 1928
S. Buxhoeveden, *The Life and Tragedy of Alexandra Feodorovna*, London

CHALONER SMITH 1878–83
J. Chaloner Smith, *British Mezzotint Portraits*, 5 vols, London

CHAPOCHNIKOVA AND GUREVICH 2001
N. Chapochnikova and D. Gurevich, *Svertchkov: Le peintre russe du Cheval 1817–1898*, Lausanne

CHICHAGOVA 1889
M.N. Chichagova, *Shamil' na Kavkaze i v Rossii*, St Petersburg

CHRISTIE, MANSON AND WOODS 1895
Christie, Manson and Woods, *Goode sale*, Christie's, London, sale cat., 17 July, London

CHRISTIE, MANSON AND WOODS 1904
Christie, Manson and Woods, *The Collection of Pictures of His Royal Highness The Duke of Cambridge Deceased*, Christie's, London, sale cat., 11 June 1904

CHRISTIE, MANSON AND WOODS 1929
Christie, Manson and Woods, *Catalogue of Ancient and Modern Pictures and Drawings Formed by Her Highness Princess Paley*, Christie's, London, sale cat., 21 June 1929

CHRISTIE, MANSON AND WOODS 1939
Christie, Manson and Woods, *Important Ancient and Modern Pictures and Drawings: The Property of the Late Sir Edmund Davis*, Christie's, London, sale cat., 7 July 1939

CLAYTON 2017
M. Clayton, 'The dal Pozzo albums of portrait prints in George III's library', in McDonald 2017, II, pp. 621–3

COLEMAN SPARKE 2014
C. Coleman Sparke, *Russian Decorative Arts*, Woodbridge

CONNOLLY 1855
T.W.J. Connolly, *The History of the Corps of Royal Sappers and Miners*, 2 vols, London

CONNOLLY 1857
T.W.J. Connolly, *History of the Royal Sappers and Miners, from the Formation of the Corps in March 1772, to the date when its Designation was Changed to that of Royal Engineers, in October 1856*, 2 vols, London

COWLES 1974
V. Cowles, *The Romanovs*, Harmondsworth

CRACRAFT 2004
J. Cracraft, *The Petrine Revolution in Russian Culture*, Cambridge, MA

CROSS 1980
A. Cross, *Russians in Eighteenth-century Britain*, Newtonville, MA

CROSS 1993
A. Cross (ed.), *Engraved in the Memory*, Oxford

CROSS 1998
A. Cross, 'Did Peter sit for Kneller at Utrecht in 1697?', *Study Group on Eighteenth-century Russia*, 26, pp. 32–42

CROSS 2000
A. Cross, *Peter the Great through British Eyes: Perceptions and Representations of the Tsar since 1698*, Cambridge

CROSS 2001
A. Cross, *Catherine the Great and the British*, London

CROSS 2003
A. Cross (ed.), *St Petersburg, 1703–1825*, New York

CROSS 2008
A. Cross, *St Petersburg and the British*, London

CROSS 2012
A. Cross (ed.), *A People Passing Rude: British Responses to Russian Culture*, Cambridge

CROSS 2014a
A. Cross, '"The enthusiasm that one has here for Russians": Alexander I visits England in 1814', *Russian Journal*, p. 18

CROSS 2014b
A. Cross, *In the Land of the Romanovs: An Annotated Bibliography of First-hand English-language Accounts of the Russian Empire (1613–1917)*, Cambridge

CUST 1909
L.H. Cust, *Catalogue of Paintings and Drawings in Buckingham Palace*, London

CUST 1910
L.H. Cust, *Windsor Castle: Portrait Miniatures*, London

DAFFORNE 1879
J. Dafforne, 'British painters: Nicolas Chevalier', *Art Journal*, 5, pp. 221–8

DANZIGER 2014
C. Danziger, 'The big junket', *Oxford Today*, Trinity Term <www.oxfordtoday.ox.ac.uk/features/big-junket#> (accessed 27 July 2018)

DE BELLAIGUE 1991
G. de Bellaigue (ed.), *Carlton House: The Past Glories of George IV's Palace*, exh. cat., The Queen's Gallery, London

DE GUITAUT 2003
C. de Guitaut, *Fabergé in the Royal Collection*, London

DE GUITAUT 2010
C. de Guitaut, *Fabergé's Animals: A Royal Farm in Miniature*, London

DE GUITAUT 2011
C. de Guitaut, *Royal Fabergé*, London

DE LA FEUILLE 1705
D. de la Feuille, *Symbola et Emblemata*, Amsterdam

DECORATIVE CHINA *c.*1879
J. Hollis and J.W. Livingston, *Windsor Castle Inventory of Decorative China*, 3 vols, London

DEHN 1922
L. Dehn, *The Real Tsaritsa*, Boston, MA

DEMIDENKO 2005
Iu. B. Demidenko, *Ivan Bianchi: Pervyj Svetopisec Peterburga*, exh. cat., State Museum of the History of St Petersburg, St Petersburg

DIMOND 1987
F. Dimond (ed.), *Crown and Camera: The Royal Family and Photography 1842–1900*, exh. cat., The Queen's Gallery, London, National Museum of Film and Photography, Bradford, Alinari Museum, Florence

DIMOND 1995
F. Dimond (ed.), *Presenting an Image: Photographs from the Royal Photographic Collection, Windsor Castle*, exh. cat., Drawings Gallery, Windsor Castle

DIMOND 2004
F. Dimond, *Developing the Picture: Queen Alexandra and the Art of Photography*, London

DMITRIEVA AND ABRAMOVA 2006
O. Dmitrieva and N. Abramova, *Britannia and Muscovy: English Silver at the Court of the Tsars*, New Haven

DMITRIEVA AND MURDOCH 2013
O. Dmitrieva and T. Murdoch (eds), *Treasures of the Royal Courts: Tudors, Stuarts and the Russian Tsars*, London

DUCAMP 2012
E. Ducamp (ed.), *The Summer Palaces of the Romanovs: Treasures from Tsarskoye Selo*, London

DUKES AND CROSS *et al.* 1987
P. Dukes and A.G. Cross *et al.*, *The Caledonian Phalanx: Scots in Russia*, Edinburgh

EDLIN 1969
H. Edlin, *What Wood Is That? A Manual of Wood Identification*, London

ELLIOT 1992
D. Elliott (ed.), *Photography in Russia 1840–1940*, exh. cat., Museum of Modern Art, Oxford

EVANS 1989
S. Evans (trans.), *The Memoirs of Elisabeth Vigée-Le Brun*, London

EVANS 1998
M. Evans (ed.), *Princes as Patrons: The Art Collections of the Princes of Wales from the Renaissance to the Present Day*, exh. cat., National Museum of Wales, Cardiff

FABERGÉ *et al.* 1997
T. Fabergé, L.G. Proler and V.V. Skurlov, *The Fabergé Imperial Easter Eggs*, London

FEDOSEYENKO 1996
O. Fedoseyenko, *Historicism in Russia: Style and Epoch in the Decorative Arts 1820s–1890s*, exh. cat., State Hermitage Museum, St Petersburg

FITZMAURICE 1905
E. Fitzmaurice, *The Life of Granville George Leveson Gower, Second Earl Granville, K.G., 1815–1891*, 2 vols, London

FLIER 1994
M.S. Flier, 'Breaking the code: the image of the Tsar in the Muscovite Palm Sunday ritual', in M.S. Flier and D.B. Rowland 1994, pp. 213–42

FLIER AND ROWLAND 1994
M.S. Flier and D.B. Rowland, *Medieval Russian Culture*, II, Berkeley

FORRER 1904–30
L. Forrer (comp.), *Biographical Dictionary of Medallists ... 500 BC–AD 1900*, 6 vols, London

FORSTER 1848
H.R. Forster, *The Stowe Catalogue: Priced and Annotated*, Stowe, sale cat., 15 August 1848

FRANKEN 1881
D. Franken, *L'oeuvre gravé des Van de Passe*, Amsterdam and Paris

FRANKLAND 1993
N. Frankland, *Witness of a Century: The Life and Times of Prince Arthur Duke of Connaught, 1850–1942*, London

FRANKLIN AND WIDDIS 2010
S. Franklin and E. Widdis, *National Identity in Russian Culture: An Introduction*, Cambridge

GARLICK 1961
K. Garlick, *Sir Thomas Lawrence, PRA 1769–1830*, exh. cat., Royal Academy, London

GARLICK 1989
K. Garlick, *Sir Thomas Lawrence: A Complete Catalogue of the Oil Paintings*, Oxford

GARRARD 1885
R. Garrard and S. Garrard & Co., *Descriptive inventory of Plate &c. at Marlborough House. The Property of HRH the Prince of Wales. 1885. Now Edward the VII*, London

GARRARD 1896
Inventory of Jewels &c. the Property of Her Majesty The Queen, London

GAVRILOVA 2010
L.M. Gavrilova, *Sovereign Knights: Foreign Orders of Russian Emperors*, Moscow

GAVRILOVA 2015
L.M. Gavrilova, *РЫЦАРСКИЕ ОРДЕНА ЕВРОПЫ*, Moscow

GENTLEMAN'S MAGAZINE 1758
Gentleman's Magazine, XXVIII, October–November 1758, pp. 457–61, 527–30

GENTLEMAN'S MAGAZINE 1814
'Diary of the Proceedings of the Allied Sovereigns', *Gentleman's Magazine*, LXXXIV (1), pp. 612–19

GOODMAN *et al.* 2015
S.T. Goodman, J. Hoffmann and A. Lavrentiev (eds), *The Power of Pictures: Early Soviet Photography, Early Soviet Film*, exh. cat., Jewish Museum, New York

GORDON 2017
S. Gordon (ed.), *Shadows of War: Roger Fenton's Photographs of the Crimea, 1855*, The Queen's Gallery, Edinburgh and London

GREAT BRITAIN – USSR 1967
Great Britain – USSR, exh. cat., Victoria and Albert Museum, London

GRIFFITHS 1998
A. Griffiths, *The Print in Stuart Britain, 1603–1689*, London

GUDYMENKO 2016
J.J. Gudymenko, *Pridvornyj živopisec Timoleon Neff*, St Petersburg

HABSBURG AND LOPATO 1993
G. von Habsburg and M. Lopato, *Fabergé: Imperial Jeweller*, London

HAKLUYT 1589
R. Hakluyt, *The Principall Navigations, Voiages and Discoveries of the English Nation*, London

HALL 1999
C. Hall, *Little Mother of Russia: A Biography of the Empress Marie Feodorovna*, London

HAMBER 1996
A.J. Hamber, *'A Higher Branch of the Art': Photographing the Fine Arts in England, 1839–1880*, Amsterdam

HARRISON *et al.* 2009
S. Harrison, E. Ducamp and J. Falino, *Artistic Luxury: Fabergé, Tiffany, Lalique*, exh. cat., Cleveland Museum of Art, OH

HERMITAGE AMSTERDAM 2014
Hermitage Amsterdam, *Dining with the Tsars: Fragile Beauty from the Hermitage*, Amsterdam

HERMITAGE AMSTERDAM 2017
Hermitage Amsterdam, *1917: Romanovs and Revolution: The End of Monarchy*, Amsterdam

HIBBERT 2000
C. Hibbert, *Queen Victoria: A Personal History*, London

HIND 1952–64
A.M. Hind, *Engraving in England in the Sixteenth and Seventeenth Centuries*, 3 vols (III: comp. M. Corbett and M. Norton), Cambridge

HOLLSTEIN 1949–2010
F.W.H. Hollstein, *Dutch and Flemish Etchings, Engravings and Woodcuts, c.1450–1700*, 72 vols

HOSKING 2012
G. Hosking. *Russia and the Russians: From Earliest Times to the Present*, London

HOUGH 1975
R. Hough (ed.), *Advice to a Grand-daughter: Letters from Queen Victoria to Princess Victoria of Hesse*, London

HUGHES AND BARTLETT 2004
L. Hughes and R. Bartlett (eds), *Russian Society and Culture in the Long Eighteenth Century*, Münster

HUTCHINGS 2004
S. Hutchings, *Russian Literary Culture in the Camera Age: The Word as Image*, London and New York

INGHAM 1949
R. Ingham, *What Happened to the Empress*, Hamrun

IVANOV 2011
Музей русской иконы, Moscow

JENSEN AND EBBESON 2014
M.B. Jensen and L.V. Ebbeson (eds.), *Tuxen: Colour, Countryside and Crown*, exh. cat., Skagens Museum, Skagen

JOHNSON 2014
C.D. Johnson, 'Artful instruction: Philip Doddridge's Life of Colonel James Gardiner', in P. Thompson 2014, pp. 63–77

JONES 2017
K. Jones, *European Silver in the Collection of Her Majesty The Queen*, London

KARČEVA AND ĖRMITAŽ 2016
E.I. Karčeva and G. Ėrmitaž, *Zapadnoevropejskaja skul'ptura XIX–XX vekov: katalog kollekcii* ('Western European Sculpture, 19th and 20th Centuries: Catalogue of the Collection'), St Petersburg

KELLY TROMBLY 2017
M. Kelly Trombly, *Fabergé and the Russian Crafts Tradition: An Empire's Legacy*, London

KHOROSHILOV AND LOGINOV 2003
P. Khoroshilov and A. Loginov, *Shedevry Fotografii iz Chastnykh Sobranii: Russkaia Fotografiia 1849–1918*, Moscow

KHOROSHILO V *et al.* 2002
P. Khoroshilov, A. Loginov, T. Saburov and I. Semakova, пикториальная фотография в россии, *1890–1920-е годы / Pictorial Photography in Russia: 1890s–1920s*, exh. cat., State Russian Museum, St Petersburg

KING 1937
E.J. King (ed.), *The Letters of Tsar Nicholas and Empress Marie*, London

KITAEV 2015
A. Kitaev, *Peterburg Ivana Bianki. Poste Restante*, St Petersburg

KIVELSON 2006
V. Kivelson, *Cartographies of Tsardom: The Land and its Meaning in Seventeenth-century Russia*, Ithaca, NY, and London

KOEMAN 1970
I.C. Koeman, *Joan Blaeu and his Grand Atlas: Introduction to the Facsimile Edition of the Grand Atlas, 1663*, Amsterdam

KORB 1863
J.G. Korb, *Diary of an Austrian Secretary of Legation at the court of Czar Peter the Great; translated from the original Latin by and edited by the Count MacDonnell*, London

KORDIK 2001
E. Kordik, 'The photographic collection in the Russian Museum of Ethnography', in A. Mäkelä and N. Sederholm 2001, pp. 52–63

KOSTYUK 2010
O. Kostyuk, *Masterpieces of European Jewellery from the Sixteenth to Nineteenth Centuries in the Hermitage Collection*, St Petersburg

KOTILAINE AND POE 2003
J. Kotilaine and M. Poe (eds), *Modernizing Muscovy: Reform and Social Change in Seventeenth-century Russia*, London

KRAVETS 1949
T.P. Kravets (ed.), *Dokumenty po istorii izobretenija fotografii: Perepiska Ž.N. Niepsa, Ž.M. Daggera i drugih lic*, Moscow

LAKING 1904
G. Laking, *Windsor Castle Armoury*, London

LEE 1925
S. Lee, *King Edward VII: A Biography. Vol. I: From Birth to Accession 9th November 1841 to 22nd January 1901*, London

LEVIN 2013
C.C. Levin, *Zhenckie nagrady pocciyckoy imperii*, Moscow

LEVITT 1998
M.C. Levitt, 'An antidote to nervous juice: Catherine the Great's debate with Chappe d'Auteroche over Russian Culture', *Eighteenth-century Studies*, 32 (1), pp. 49–63

LEVYKIN 2004
A.K. Levykin (ed.), *Benefit, Honour, Glory: Russian Decorations*, Moscow

LIEVEN 1993
D. Lieven, *Nicholas II: Emperor of all the Russias*, London

LISTER 1993
W.B.C. Lister (ed.) (intro. J.R. Gretton), *A Guide to the Microfiche Edition of Murray's Handbook for Travellers*, Bethesda, MD

LLOYD 1991
C. Lloyd (ed.), *The Queen's Pictures: Royal Collectors Through the Centuries*, exh. cat., National Gallery, London

LLOYD 1998
C. Lloyd (ed.), *The Quest for Albion: Monarchy and the Patronage of British Painting*, exh. cat., The Queen's Gallery, London

LYDEN 2014
A.M. Lyden, *A Royal Passion: Queen Victoria and Photography*, exh. cat., J. Paul Getty Museum, Los Angeles

MAAS 1977
J. Maas, *'This Brilliant Year': Queen Victoria's Jubilee 1887*, exh. cat., Royal Academy, London

MACGREGOR 2004
A. MacGregor, 'The Tsar in England: Peter the Great's visit to London in 1698', *The Seventeenth Century*, 19

MÄKELÄ AND SEDERHOLM 2001
A. Mäkelä and N. Sederholm (eds), *The Memory of the Photograph: Cataloguing and Classification Practices in the Nordic Countries, the Baltic States and Russia*, Copenhagen

MAKSIMOVA 2013
A.V. Maksimova (ed.), *Sbornik dokladov meždunarodnoj konferencii 'Fotografija v muzee', 21–23 maja 2013*, St Petersburg

MANCHESTER 1857
Art Treasures of the United Kingdom, exh. cat., Trafford Park, Manchester

MANDACHE 2011
D. Mandache, *Dearest Missy: The Correspondence between Marie, Grand Duchess of Russia, Duchess of Edinburgh and Saxe-Coburg and Gotha and her daughter, Marie, Crown Princess of Romania*, London

MARLBOROUGH HOUSE 1877
A.S. Cole, *A Catalogue of the Works of Art at Marlborough House, London, and at Sandringham, Norfolk, belonging to Their Royal Highnesses the Prince and Princess of Wales*, London

MARSDEN 2010
J. Marsden (ed.), *Victoria and Albert: Art and Love*, exh. cat., The Queen's Gallery, London

MARTIN 2013
A.M. Martin, *Enlightened Metropolis: Constructing Imperial Moscow, 1762–1855*, Oxford

MASSIE 1968
R.K. Massie, *Nicholas and Alexandra*, London

MAUDE 1996
G.A. Maude (ed. J.A. Maude), *Letters from Russia 1856 (Detailed Personal Observations of the Coronation of Tsar Alexander II)*, Moss Vale, NSW

MAVRODINA 2007
N. Mavrodina, *The Art of Russian Stone Carvers 18th–19th Centuries: The Catalogue of the Collection*, St Petersburg

MCBURNEY 2014
E. McBurney, 'Art and power in the reign of Catherine the Great: the state portraits', PhD thesis, Columbia University

MCCARTHY 2017
K. McCarthy, *Fabergé in London: The British Branch of the Imperial Russian Goldsmith*, London

MCDONALD 2017
M. McDonald, *Ceremonies, Costumes, Portraits and Genre*, 3 vols (The Paper Museum of Cassiano dal Pozzo, Series C: Prints, Part 1), London

MERRIDALE 2014
C. Merridale, *Red Fortress: The Secret Heart of Russia's History*, London

MILLAR 1995
D. Millar, *The Victorian Watercolours and Drawings of Her Majesty The Queen*, 2 vols, London

MILLAR 1963
O. Millar, *The Tudor, Stuart and Early Georgian Pictures in the Collection of Her Majesty The Queen*, 2 vols, London

MILLAR 1969
O. Millar, *The Later Georgian Pictures in the Collection of Her Majesty The Queen*, 2 vols, London

MILLAR 1992
O. Millar, *The Victorian Pictures in the Collection of Her Majesty The Queen*, 2 vols, London

MONTAGU 1986
J. Montagu, 'The "Ruland/Raphael Collection"', *Visual Resources*, 3 (3), pp. 167–83

MOROZOV 1953
S. Morozov, *Russkie Putešestvenniki Fotografij*, Moscow

MOROZOV 1955
S. Morozov, *Russkaya Khudoshestvennaya Fotografiya: Ocherki po Istorii Fotografii 1839–1917*, Moscow

MOROZOV 1977
S. Morozov, 'Early photography in Eastern Europe: Russia', *History of Photography*, 1 (4), pp. 327–47

MOROZOV AND LLOYD 1980
S. Morozov and V. Lloyd (eds), *Soviet Photography 1917–1940: The New Photojournalism*, London

MUNTIAN 2016
T. Muntian, *Feodor Rückert and Carl Fabergé*, Moscos

NOBLE 1990
C. Noble, 'Laurits Tuxen: portrait and history painter' (unpublished, later ed. and trans. into Danish), in Bligaard 1990, pp. 37–48

NORTH 1998
A. North, 'Polished steel wares of Woodstock', *Journal of the Antique Metalware Society*, 6, pp. 1–6

NOVIKOV 2015
P.V. Novikov, 'Portret Kubanskogo Kazaka-Konvoytsa T.K. Yashchika', *Kulturnaya zhizn' Yuga Rossii*, no. 3 (58), pp. 140–1

ODNB 2004
Oxford Dictionary of National Biography, Oxford, online edn, May 2009, <http://www.oxforddnb.com> (accessed 27 July 2018)

ODOM 2011
A. Odom, *Russian Silver in America: Surviving the Melting Pot*, Washington, DC

ODOM AND PAREDES AREND 1998
A. Odom and L. Paredes Arend, *Russian and Imperial and European Treasures from the Hillwood Museum*, Washington, DC

O'DONOGHUE 1908–25
F. O'Donoghue, *Catalogue of Engraved British Portraits preserved in the Department of Prints and Drawings in the British Museum*, 5 vols

OETTINGEN-WALLERSTEIN 1848
L.K.E. von Oettingen-Wallerstein, *Descriptive Catalogue of a collection of ancient Greek, Italian, German, Flemish, and Dutch pictures (belonging to Prince L. d'Oettingen-Wallerstein) now at Kensington Palace*, London

ORMOND AND BLACKETT-ORD 1987
C. Blackett-Ord, S. Foister and R. Ormond, 'Appendix: The portraits of Franz Xaver Winterhalter: an annotated edition of Franz Wild's list of 1894', in R. Ormond and C. Blackett-Ord 1987, pp. 226–38

ORMOND AND BLACKETT-ORD 1987
R. Ormond and C. Blackett-Ord (eds), *Franz Xaver Winterhalter and the Courts of Europe 1830–70*, exh. cat., National Portrait Gallery, London

OSBORN 1997
M. Osborn, *Franz Krüger*, Berlin (first published 1910)

OSBORNE 1876
Catalogue of the Paintings, Sculpture and other Works of Art at Osborne, London

OWENS 2005
S. Owens (ed.), *Watercolours and Drawings from the Collection of Queen Elizabeth The Queen Mother*, The Queen's Gallery, Edinburgh and London

PALMER 1974
A. Palmer, *Alexander I: Tsar of War and Peace*, London

PAPI 2010
S. Papi, *The Jewels of the Romanovs: Family and Court*, London

PARIS 1855
Great Britain Imperial Commission, *Paris Universal Exhibition, 1855: Catalogue of the Works Exhibited in the British Section of the Exhibition, in French and English; Together with Exhibitors' Prospectuses, Prices Current, &c.*, London

PATTERSON 1996
S. Patterson, *Royal Insignia: British and Foreign Orders of Chivalry from the Royal Collection*, London

PAVLOVSK 2013
The State Culture Preserve Pavlovsk: Full Catalogue of the Collections, IX, St Petersburg

PHYSICK 1975
J. Physick, *Photography and the South Kensington Museum*, London

PICHOT 1855
A. Pichot (ed.), 'L'Empereur Nicolas', *Revue Britannique*, XXVI, pp. 429–46

POLLARD 1970
J.G. Pollard, 'Matthew Boulton and Conrad Heinrich Küchler', *The Numismatic Chronicle and Journal of the Royal Numismatic Society*, 10 (7th ser.), p. 299

PONOMAREV 1858
F. Ponomarev, 'Istoriia fotografii', *Svetopis*, 3, pp. 72–81

POPOV 2013
A.P. Popov, *Rossijskie Fotografy (1839–1930): Slovar'-Spravočnik*, Kolomna

POSTNIKOV 1996
A. Postnikov, *Russia in Maps: A History of the Geographical Study and Cartography of the Country*, Moscow

PRIESTLEY 1969
J.B. Priestley, *The Prince of Pleasure and his Regency 1811–20*, London

PRITCHARD 2010
J. Pritchard (ed.), *Diaghilev and the Golden Age of the Ballets Russe*, London

PRIVATE LIFE 1898
The Private Life of the Queen, by one of Her Majesty's Servants, London

PURDON-CLARKE 1910
C. Purdon-Clarke, *Arms & Armour at Sandringham: the Indian collection presented by the Princes & nobles of India to HM King Edward VII when Prince of Wales on the occasion of his visit to India 1875–76. Also some Asiatic African and European weapons & war relics*, London

PUTNAM 1952
P. Putnam, *Seven Britons in Imperial Russia 1698–1812*, Princeton

PYNE 1819
W.H. Pyne, *The History of Royal Residences*, London

RAEBURN 1991
M. Raeburn (ed.), *The Twilight of the Tsars: Russian Art at the Turn of the Century*, exh. cat., South Bank Centre, London

RAKHMANOV AND BARKHATOVA 1996
N. Rakhmanov and E. Barkhatova, *Russkaia Fotografiia: Seredina XIX–Nachalo XX Veka*, Moscow

RAPPE *et al.* 2007
T. Rappé, E. Anisimova, N. Guseva, M. Lopato and F. Leidelmeijer, *Art Nouveau during the reign of the last Tsars*, exh. cat., Amsterdam

RÉAU 1922
L. Réau, 'Portraits français de Pierre le Grand', *Gazette des Beaux-Arts*, 5 (11), pp. 304–5

REDAELLI 2005
M. Redaelli and P. Todorovic Redaelli, *Squarci di storia pietroburghese e moscovita nelle immagini del fotografo Ivan Bianchi*, Losone

REDAELLI *et al.* 2002
M. Redaelli, P. Todorovic Strähl and E. Anisimova, *Ivan Bianchi: Un ticinese pioniere della fotografia a San Pietroburgo*, Lugano

REMINGTON 2010
V. Remington, *Victorian Miniatures in the Collection of Her Majesty The Queen*, London

RENNE 2011a
E. Renne, *Sixteenth- to Nineteenth-century British Painting: State Hermitage Museum Catalogue*, New Haven and London

RENNE 2011b
E. Renne, '"The Court also needs a Portraitist, as much as a Historical Painter ...": Vigilius Eriksen in the service of the Empress', in S. Mentz and M. Skougaard (eds.), *Danish–Russian Cultural Relations 1700–1900*, Fredriksborg, pp. 87–94

REYNOLDS 1999
G. Reynolds, *The Sixteenth- and Seventeenth-century Miniatures in the Collection of Her Majesty The Queen*, London

RICHARDSON 1966
J. Richardson, *George the Magnificent: A Portrait of King George IV*, London

RIDLEY 2013
J. Ridley, *Bertie: A Life of Edward VII*, London

ROBERTS 2001
H. Roberts, *For The King's Pleasure: The Furnishing and Decoration of George IV's Apartments at Windsor Castle*, London

ROBERTS 2012
H. Roberts, *The Queen's Diamonds*, London

ROBERTS 1987
J. Roberts, *Royal Artists: From Mary, Queen of Scots to the Present Day*, London

ROBERTS, SUTCLIFFE AND MAYOR 2005
J. Roberts, P. Sutcliffe and S. Mayor, *Fans in the Royal Collection: Unfolding Pictures*, London

ROBINSON 1902
L.G. Robinson (ed.), *Letters of Dorothea, princess Lieven, during her residence in London, 1812–1834*, London and New York

RODIONOV 2012
E. Rodionov, 'ПЕТЕРБУРГСКИЕ ОРУЖЕЙНИКИ ПЕРМЯКОВЫ И ГАТЧИНСКИЙ АРСЕНАЛ', in *Война и оружие. Новые исследования и материалы.* Труды Третьей международной научно практической конференции 16–18 мая 2012 года Часть III, St Petersburg, pp. 109–10

ROGASCH AND OHM 1997
W. Rogasch and B. Ohm (eds), *Victoria & Albert: Vicky & the Kaiser*, exh. cat., Deutsches Historisches Museum, Berlin

ROGERS 1986
M. Rogers (ed.), *Elizabeth II: Portraits of Sixty Years*, National Portrait Gallery, London

ROSE 1983
K. Rose, *King George V*, London

ROSE AND PODMOSHENSKY 2004
Fr. S. Rose and Fr. H. Podmoshensky (comp. and trans.), *The Northern Thebaid: Monastic Saints of the Russian North*, Platina, CA

ROSENTHAL 2007
N. Rosenthal (ed.), *Citizens and Kings: Portraits in the Age of Revolution*, exh. cat., Galeries nationales du Grand Palais, Paris, and Royal Academy, London

ROSS 1968
M.C. Ross, *Russian Porcelains*, Norman, OK

ROYAL COMMISSION 1852
Royal Commission, *First Report of the Commissioners for the Exhibition of 1851*, London

RULAND 1876
C. Ruland, *The works of Raphael Santi da Urbino as Represented in the Raphael Collection in the Royal Library at Windsor Castle, formed by H.R.H. The Prince Consort, 1853–1861, and Completed by Her Majesty Queen Victoria*, privately published, Weimar

SAVINSKAYA *et al.* 2009
L. Savinskaya, V. Sadkov and A. Poznanskaya, *Germanija, Avstrija, Švejcarija XV–XX veka – Danija, Islandija, Norvegija, Finlandija, Švecija XVIII–XX veka: sobranie živopisi; Gosudarstvennyj Muzej Izobrazitel'nych Iskusstv Imeni A.S. Puškina* ('The Pushkin Museum of Fine Arts: Germany, Austria, Switzerland XV–XX centuries; Denmark, Iceland, Norway, Finland, Sweden XVIII–XX centuries. Collection of paintings'), Moscow

SCHAFFERS-BODENHAUSEN AND TIETHOFF-SPLIETHOFF 1993
K. Schaffers-Bodenhausen and M. Tiethoff-Spliethoff, *The Portrait Miniatures in the Collections of the House of Orange-Nassau*, Zwolle

SCHMIDT 1981
A.J. Schmidt, 'The restoration of Moscow after 1812', *Slavic Review*, 40 (1) (Spring), pp. 37–48

SCHMIDT 1989
A.J. Schmidt, *The Architecture and Planning of Classical Moscow: A Cultural History*, Philadelphia

SCOTT 1814
W. Scott, *Waverley, or 'Tis sixty years since*, Edinburgh

SEBAG MONTEFIORE 2016
S. Sebag Montefiore, *The Romanovs 1613–1918*, New York

SEEGEL 2012
S. Seegel, *Mapping Europe's Borderlands: Russian Cartography in the Age of Empire*, Chicago

SEMENOV AND KHOREV 1994
A.A. Semenov and M.M. Khorev (eds), *Andreĭ Osipovich Karelin: Tvorcheskoe nasledie nizhegorodskogo hudozhnika i fotografa / Andrey Osipovich Karelin: Creative Heritage of the Nizhny Novgorod, Artist and Photographer*, Nizhny Novgorod

SHATSILLO AND LUKONIN 1991
K.S. Shatsillo and S.M. Lukonin (eds), *Dnevniki Imperatora Nikolaya II*, Moscow

SHIPOVA 2006
T.N. Shipova, *Fotografy Moskvy (1839–1930): Biograficheskij Slovar-Ppravochnik*, Moscow

SIMONS AND WESTERLUND 2015
G. Simons and D. Westurlund, *Religion, Politics and Nation-Building in Post-Communist Countries*, London

SMITH 1999
E.A. Smith, *George IV*, New Haven and London

SMITH 2013
L. Smith, 'Shopping in St Petersburg: Lewis Carroll's photographs and icons', *Art History*, 36 (5), pp. 968–93

SMYTH 1862
C. Piazzi Smyth, *Three Cities in Russia*, London

SNOWMAN 1987
A.K. Snowman, 'Two books of revelations: the Fabergé stock books', *Apollo*, 126, p. 150

SNOWMAN 1993
A.K. Snowman, *Fabergé Lost and Found*, London

SORINE 1929
S. Sorine (Foreword by A. Salmon), *Portraits*, Berlin

STANILAND 1997
K. Staniland, *In Royal Fashion: The Clothes of Princess Charlotte of Wales and Queen Victoria, 1796–1901*, London

STANLEY 1927
A. Stanley, *Letters of Lady Augusta Stanley: a young lady at court, 1849–1863*, London

STERNE 1931
K.G. Sterne, 'On view in the New York Galleries', *Parnassus*, 3 (4) (April), pp. 3–9

STEWART 1983
J.D. Stewart, *Sir Godfrey Kneller and the English Baroque Portrait*, Oxford

STIEGLITZ 1898
A. Stieglitz, 'Night photography with the introduction of life', *American Annual of Photography and Photographic Times Almanac*, pp. 204–7

STITES 2005
R. Stites, *Serfdom, Society, and the Arts in Imperial Russia: The Pleasure and the Power*, New Haven and London

STONE 1934
G.C. Stone, *A Glossary of Construction Decoration and Use of Arms and Armor*, New York

SVANHOLM 1990
L. Svanholm, *Laurits Tuxen: Europas sidste fyrstemaler*, Copenhagen

SVIBLOVA AND MISALANDI 2005
O. Sviblova and E. Misalandi (eds), *Тихое сопротивление : русский пикториализм 1900–1930-х / Quiet Resistance: Russian Pictorialism. 1900–1930s*, exh. cat., Fondazione Querini Stampalia, Venice, and Somerset House, London

TAYLOR 1998
K.V.H. Taylor, *Russian Art at Hillwood*, Washington, DC

TAYLOR 2002
R. Taylor, *Photographs Exhibited in Britain 1839–1865*, Ottawa

THOMPSON 2014
P. Thompson (ed.), *Beyond Sense and Sensibility: Moral Formation and the Literary Imagination*, Bucknell

TILLANDER-GODENHIELM 2005
U. Tillander-Godenhielm, *The Russian Imperial Award System 1894–1917*, Helsinki

TISDALL 1957
E. Tisdall, *The Dowager Empress*, London

TOMÁŠKOVÁ 2013
S. Tomášková, *Wayward Shamans: The Prehistory of an Idea*, Oakland, CA

TROYAT 1982
H. Troyat (trans. E.P. Dutton), *Alexander of Russia: Napoleon's Conqueror*, New York

TRUMAN 2013
C. Truman, *The Wallace Collection Catalogue of Gold Boxes*, London

TURNER 1996
J. Turner (ed.), *The Dictionary of Art*, xxv, London

TUXEN 1928
L. Tuxen, *En Malers Arbejde gennem tredsindstyve Aar fortalt af ham selv*, Copenhagen

UNTRACHT 1982
O. Untracht, *Jewelry Concepts and Technology*, London

USHERWOOD AND SPENCER SMITH 1987
P. Usherwood and J. Spencer Smith, *Lady Butler: Battle Artist 1846–1933*, exh. cat., Gloucester

VAN DER KISTE AND JORDAAN 1984
J. van der Kiste and B. Jordaan, *Dearest Affie ... Alfred, Duke of Edinburgh, Queen Victoria's Second Son 1844–1900*, Gloucester

VAN DER KROGT 2005
P. van der Krogt, *Joan Blaeu, Atlas Maior of 1665: 'the greatest and finest atlas ever published'*, Cologne

VILMUSEN 1997
K. Vilmusen (ed.), *Marie Feodorovna, Empress of Russia*, exh. cat., Christiansborg Palace, Copenhagen

VON REISBERG 2007
B. von Reisberg, *Franz Xaver Winterhalter*, Melbourne

VON STOCKMAR 1872
E. von Stockmar, *Memoirs of Baron Stockmar*, London

WALKER 1992
R. Walker, *The Eighteenth- and Early Nineteenth-century Miniatures in the Collection of Her Majesty The Queen*, London

WAP 1855
Dr Wap (ed.), 'Het photografisch etablissement der heeren Gebr. Mouhot, te 's-Gravenhage', *Astrea: Maandschrift voor Schone Kunst, Wetenschap en Letteren*, 5, p. 119

WATCHEL 2002
A. Watchel, 'Dostoevsky's *The Idiot*: the novel as a photograph', *History of Photography*, 26 (3), pp. 205–15

WHITTAKER 2003
C.H. Whittaker, *Russia Engages the World, 1453–1825*, Cambridge, MA

WILLIAMS 1831
D.E. Williams, *The Life and Correspondence of Sir Thomas Lawrence*, London

WOODWARD 2007
D. Woodward (ed.), *The History of Cartography. Vol. III: Cartography in the European Renaissance*, pt 2, Chicago and London

YASHCHIK 2004
T.K. Yashchik, *Riadom s imperatritsei: vospominaniis leib-kazaka*, St Petersburg

YEFIMOVA AND ALESHINA 2011
L. Yefimova and T. Aleshina, *Russian Elegance: Country and City Elegance from the 15th to the early 20th Century*, London

ZAGULIAEV 1859
M.A. Zagulaiev, 'Obshchestvennyi listok', *Syn Otechestva*, 4 October, p. 1089

INDEX

Numbers in **bold** refer to main entries; numbers in *italics* refer to figures

ACKNOWLEDGEMENTS

Like its many predecessors, this catalogue has been written entirely by members of the Royal Collection's curatorial staff, for whose hard work and many valuable insights much gratitude is owed.

Many colleagues have provided invaluable assistance in the preparation of this catalogue, none more so than Professor Anthony Cross, Emeritus Professor of Slavonic Studies at the University of Cambridge, whose guidance, knowledge, expertise and encouragement has proved invaluable to the editors and authors. The assistance of Professor Mikhail Piotrovsky, Director of the State Hermitage Museum, St Petersburg, and Dr Elena Gagarina, Director of the Moscow Kremlin Museums, in facilitating both access to their collections for research and the assistance of their curatorial staff during and after visits in 2017 is gratefully acknowledged. At the Hermitage grateful thanks are due to Mariam Dandamaeva, Dr Ekaterina Khmelnitskaya, Dr Elizaveta Renne, Dr Nina Tarasova, Dr Lyubov Vikhrova and Dr Georgy Vilinbakhov, and at the Kremlin, Maria Bogoslovskaya, Liudmila Gavrilova, Ekaterina Karavaeva, Victoria Menyaylo, Fedor Panfilov and Anastasia Parshina.

Elsewhere in Russia the generous assistance and scholarship of Boris Asvarishch, Michael Asvarishch, Elena Barkhatova, Alexander Belousov, Dr Viktor Bezotosny, Dr Iraida Bott, Dr Liudmila Budrina, Tatiana Cheboksarova, Alex Dmitriev, Ekaterina Fedorova, Galina Korneva, Sergei Levin and Pavel Novikov is gratefully acknowledged.

Many other scholars have freely shared their knowledge and expertise and the authors would particularly like to thank Tom Bergroth, Dr Polly (Rosalind) Blakesley, Susanna Brown, Thea Burns, Jeremy Cheek, John Goldfinch, Yolande Hodson, Wladyslaw Maximowicz, Alice Milica Ilich, the late A.V.B. Norman, Louise Pearson, Sven Philip Jørgensen, Ella Ravilious, Katya Rogatchevskaia, Leila Sauvage, Danielle Sellers, Roger Taylor, Tony Wolstenholme and Dr Wilfried Ziesler.

The authors have depended on the patience and expertise of colleagues in the Royal Archives at Windsor Castle, led by Allison Derrett, Laura Hobbs, Bill Stockting and Oliver Urquhart Irvine. The assistance of Melanie Wilson was invaluable in gathering and checking sources. In Russia, the assistance of the Director, Larisa Kruchkova and colleagues of the State Archive of the Russian Federation, the Director and staff of the Russian State Historical Archives and the Director and staff of the Archive of Foreign Policy of the Russian Empire is gratefully acknowledged.

The presentation of new research in the catalogue would be of little value without the remarkable efforts of Royal Collection photographers Stephen Chapman, Tung Tsin Lam and Eva Zielinska-Millar and with additional help from Nick Moss and Richard Shellabear of Todd-White Art Photography. The photographic programme was managed with patience and efficiency by Karen Lawson and Daniel Partridge under the guidance of Shruti Patel. A huge debt of gratitude is due to the Royal Collection's conservators who have worked for many months in the preparation of objects for photography and display. The knowledge and expertise of Karen Ashworth, Claire Chorley, Nicola Christie, Carly Collier, Michael Field, Megan Gent, Martin Gray, Adelaide Izat, Sonja Leggewie, Simon Metcalf, Clara de la Peña Mc Tigue, Rosanna de Sancha, Puneeta Sharma, Kate Stone, Emma Turner, Shaun Turner, Jane Wallis, David Wheeler and Sophy Wills has also provided many valuable insights which have enriched the catalogue entries.

The production of this book has been expertly overseen by Elizabeth Silverton under the direction of Kate Owen and with the assistance of Polly Atkinson, Rosie Bick, Nina Chang, Sam Harris, Tom Love and Georgina Seage. The in-house production team has been ably supported by Nick Finegold, colour reproduction, Laura Parker, designer, Katherine Bogden Bayard, typesetting assistant, and Debbie Wayment, production manager.

Finally, many current and past curatorial colleagues in the Royal Collection have readily offered their help, including Rufus Bird, Alexandra Campbell-Ricketts, Sophie Gordon, Emily Hannam, Alice Houghton, Kathryn Jones, Isabella Manning, Sir Jonathan Marsden, Rosie Razzall, Vanessa Remington, Desmond Shawe-Taylor and Nicola Turner Inman.

LIST OF CONTRIBUTORS

AB	Alex Buck
CDEG	Caroline de Guitaut
SDM	Simon Metcalf
IM	Isobel Muir
AN	Alessandro Nasini
SJP	Stephen Patterson
RDES	Rosanna de Sancha
ES	Emma Stuart
RW	Rhian Wong
BW	Bridget Wright

First published 2018 by

Royal Collection Trust
York House
St James's Palace
London SW1A 1BQ

Reprinted 2019

ISBN 978 1 909741 55 3
101598

British Library Cataloguing in Publication data:
A catalogue record of this book is available from the British Library

Edited by Alison Tickner
Designer: Laura Parker
Maps drawn by Stefan Chabluk
Project Manager: Elizabeth Silverton
Production Manager: Debbie Wayment
Colour reproduction: Zebra, London
Typeset in Trivia Humanist
Printed on 150 gsm GardaMatt
Printed and bound in Italy by Printer Trento

MIX
Paper from responsible sources
FSC® C015829

Half-title: cat. 159 (star)
Facing title page: cat. 226 (detail)
Facing contents page: cat. 174 (detail)
Page vi: The extent of the Russian Empire in 1914
Page vii: Map of St Petersburg showing places mentioned in the text
Facing Foreword: cat. 279
Endpapers: cat. 135 (detail)

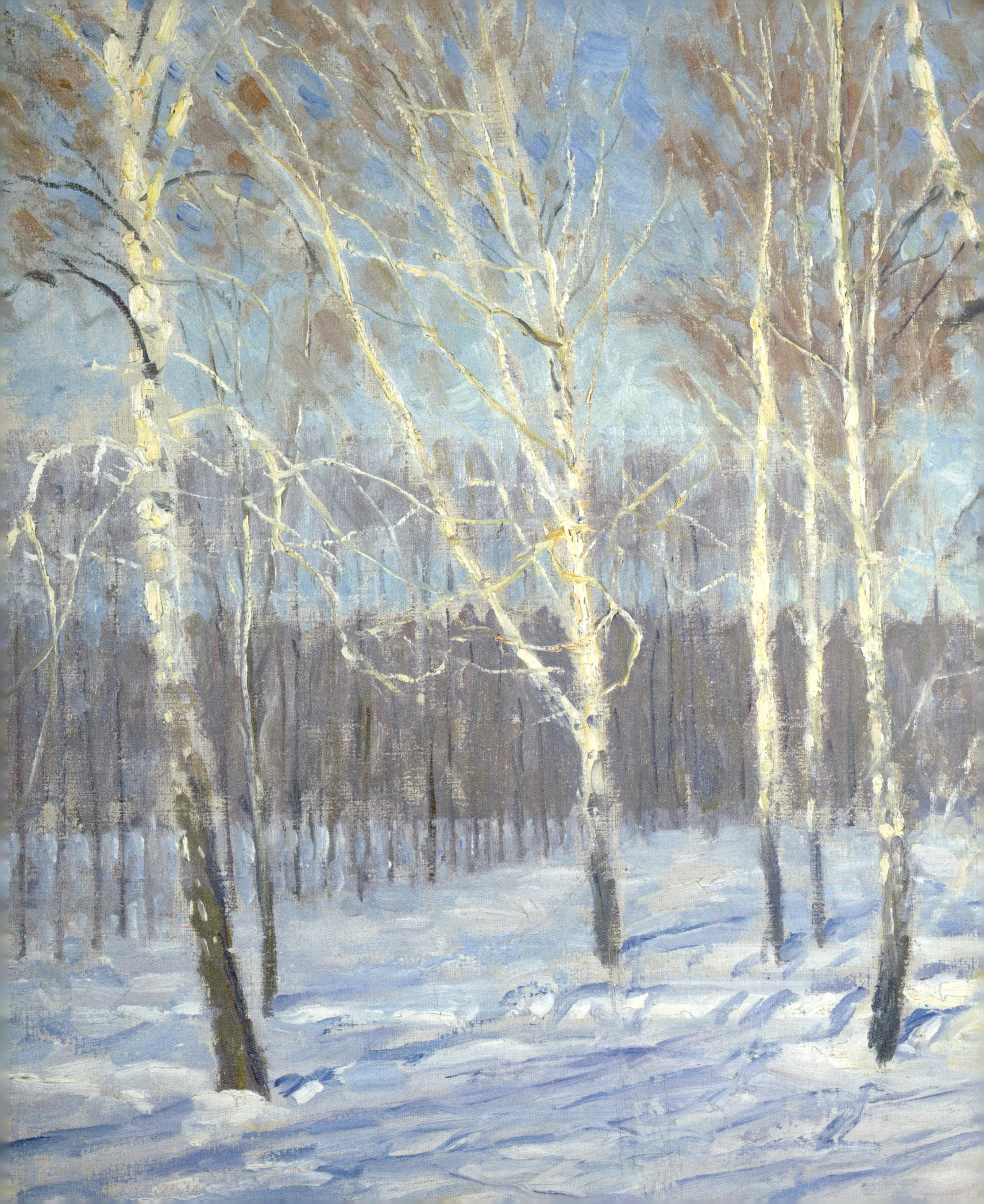